Ian Longfield

  *NEW CENTURY* WORLD • WIDE

D1446980

.RENCH
DICTIONARY

FRENCH-ENGLISH/ENGLISH-FRENCH

(American English)

Compiled by
RICHARD SWITZER, Ph.D.
Associate Professor of French, University of Wisconsin

and
HERBERT S. GOCHBERG, Ph.D.
Associate Professor of French, University of Wisconsin

with a

TRAVELER'S CONVERSATION GUIDE
Containing hundreds of expressions and items of information
useful to tourists, students, and business people

NEW CENTURY PUBLISHERS, INC.

Printing Code
18   19   20   21

Library of Congress Catalog Card Number: 82-81060

ISBN 0-8329-9682-3 Paper
ISBN 0-8329-9681-5 Thumb Indexed, Cloth

Printed in the United States of America

A PRACTICAL TOOL OF COMMUNICATION

For many years the French language has been a favorite subject of study in high school and college throughout the English-speaking world. Today it is more than a subject of study; it is a practical tool of communication in almost every corner of the globe. It is second only to English itself as a universal tongue.

Whether one travels abroad as a tourist, an exchange student, a business agent or an employee of the government, a good speaking acquaintance with the French language is an asset of great personal value. Even for the stay-at-home whose travels are purely literary, the ability to read French may become an unfailing source of profit and enjoyment.

For a thorough, up-to-date mastery of the language, nothing can be more useful than a thoroughly up-to-date French-English, English-French Dictionary. That is exactly what is provided here. Within the covers of this book are all the translated words and phrases needed to understand, read, and speak both languages. Many of the new words have never before appeared in any French-English dictionary.

Features of special value to every user of this dictionary are a complete guide to French pronunciation and a brief but comprehensive guide to French grammar.

Also included is another extra feature, a **Traveler's Conversation Guide,** which lists in English and translates into good idiomatic French hundreds of the most commonly used questions, phrases, expressions, and road signs of practical value to tourists. With the help of this Guide, one can travel with greater convenience and enjoyment wherever the French language is spoken.

CONTENTS

Pronunciation Guides 5
  Vowels 5
  Consonants; Silent Letters 6
  Elision; Linking; Stress; Intonation 7

Useful French Grammar Guides 7
  Articles; Partitive Construction 7
  Gender (nouns and adjectives); Plurals 8
  Unstressed Pronouns; Adverbs 9
  Interrogation; Negation 10
  Regular Verbs: **-er** 10
    -ir; -re 11
  Irregular Verb Forms 11

Abbreviations 14

FRENCH-ENGLISH 15

ENGLISH-FRENCH 253

Traveler's Conversation Guide 501
  Taxi; Hotel 501
  Restaurant 502
  Money; Post Office; Railroad 503
  Automobile; Photography 504
  Shopping; Stores 505
  General Expressions 506
  Divisions of Time 507
  Conversions 508

French Road Signs 509
  Road Signs 509
  Road Symbols 510

PRONUNCIATION GUIDES

1. **Ordinary Vowels.** French vowels are pronounced much more precisely and cleanly than English vowels. This is due, in part, to the fact that in English the muscles involved in speech are usually very relaxed. In French these muscles are markedly tense during articulation. While it is impossible to give faithful comparisons between the sounds of English and French, the following examples provide useful approximations of French sound patterns.

French Spelling	Examples	English Sound
a, a + s, à, â	pas, là, âme	father, bah
è, ê, ai, ei, -ais, e followed by two consonants	père, bête, peine, laid, selle, parlais	send
é, final er, -et, -ez, -ai	été, aller, palet, donnez, parlai	pay
e	le, petit	per
i, y	mine, y	machine
i (as semi-vowel)	rien	year
o, ô, -ot, au, eau	rose, vôtre, complot, gauche, beau	open
o, au	donner, auto	love
œ, œu, eu, ue	œil, bœuf, heure, orgueil	hurt
oi	loi	swat
ou	vous	soon
u	vu, puis	*No example

2. **Nasal Vowels.** Nasalization occurs during speech when sound is accompanied by air being expelled through the mouth *and* nose. In general, vowels followed by *n* or *m* are nasalized, except when followed by a vowel or another *n* or *m*. In French the words pin and pain are nasalized, but not peine and penne.

French Spelling	Examples	English Sound
an, am, en, em	pan, champ, enfant, emploi	tong
in, im, ain, aim, ein, yn, ym, en	pin, impie, pain, faim, ceinture, syndicat, sympathie, bien	tang
on, om	bon, pompier	only
un, um	un, parfum	lung

* Vowel may be reproduced by uttering the sound of *ee*, as in *seen*, with the lips rounded.

5

3. Consonants. Listed below are French consonants which differ from English in one or more respects.

French Spelling	Examples	English Sound
c (before a, o, u)	canne, corps, cube	can
c (before e, i, y)	cent, cire, cygne	ceiling
ç	français	ceiling
ch	chien	share
g (before a, o, u)	garçon, gober, légume	gone
g (before e, i, y)	gens, gifler, gyroscope	azure
gn	cogner	onion
gu (before e, i)	guerre, gui	gone
h	halte	Always silent

Although all **h**'s are silent in French, a distinction is made between the *mute* **h** and the *aspirate* **h**. The latter is indicated by an asterisk (*h) in this dictionary. *Aspirate* **h** prevents linking and elision. *Mute* **h: l'heure;** aspirate **h: le haut monde.**

il (final), ill (between vowels)	travail, travailler	player
j	juger	azure
q (final)	coq	cock
qu	quel	kill
r	raison, carotte	*No example
s (between vowels)	raison	pose
s (other cases)	seigneur, masseur, censure, pasteur	sing, missile
th	théâtre	test
ti (before vowels)	patience, nation	missile
w	wagon, watt	very, watt
y	fuyant	yes

SILENT LETTERS

e is sient when its elimination does not form a group of three consonants; **-ent** is silent when it is final in a third person plural verb. Final consonants are usually silent.

---

* The trilled *r*, formed in the front of the mouth with the tip of tongue, is heard in some parts of France. The Parisian French *r*, in contrast, comes from well back in the mouth. The sound is caused by friction between the back of the tongue and the soft palate, accompanied by vibration of the vocal chords.

6

ELISION

Monosyllables ending in **e** and the word **la** elide to **l'** before a word beginning with a vowel or a silent *h*. **si** contracts before **il.**

si plus **il** = **s'il**   **le** plus **homme** = **l'homme**

LINKING

An otherwise silent final consonant is pronounced in careful speech when the following word begins with a vowel and is closely linked grammatically.

STRESS

The syllables in French words are pronounced with almost equal force, with a very light stress on the last pronounced vowel.

INTONATION

The voice tends to rise on the accentuated syllable in a given word group, and on the next-to-last syllable of a sentence. It then falls on the last syllable.

USEFUL FRENCH GRAMMAR GUIDES

ARTICLES

1. **Definite Article**

Masc. **le** (**l'** before vowel)
le garçon the boy
l'arbre the tree

Fem. **la** (**l'** before vowel)
la dame the lady
l'école the school

Pl. **les**
les pommes (the) apples

2. **Indefinite Article**

Masc. **un**
un homme a man

Fem. **une**
une fête a holiday

Pl. **des**
des amis (some) friends

3. **Partitive Construction.** In French the definite article is often used with the preposition **de** to express the partitive. In some cases, **de** alone signifies a partitive construction. The definite article used by itself may refer to specific objects or to a whole category of objects. The following examples will be helpful:

Avez-vous du pain?	Have you any bread?
Je n'ai pas de pain.	I haven't any bread.
Il a des amis.	He has (some) friends.
L'homme est riche.	The man is rich.
Le lait est blanc.	Milk is white.
Les hommes sont des animaux.	Men are animals.

7

4. **Contractions with Articles**

à plus *le* = **au**   *à* plus *les* = **aux**   *de* plus *le* = **du**   *de* plus *les* = **des**

GENDER OF NOUNS AND ADJECTIVES

Nouns in French are masculine or feminine. The gender of a noun is predetermined by history and usage. Modifying words will be of the same gender and number as the noun.

Un bon ami (*m.*)	A good friend
La main droite (*f.*)	The right hand

Some nouns, because of the nature of the reference, may be either masculine or feminine.

Un élève, une élève a pupil   **Un enfant** a child, a boy
Une enfant a child, a girl

The feminine of most adjectives and nouns is indicated by adding **-e** to the masculine form.

grand, grande   **ami, amie**

Most adjectives ending in **-e** in the masculine remain invariable in the feminine.

Un champ fertile   **Une terre fertile**

Other regular patterns of gender are as follows:

Masculine	Feminine	Masculine	Feminine
beau	belle	lion	lionne
chameau	chamelle	ancien	ancienne
heureux	heureuse	pieux	pieuse
sec	sèche	blanc	blanche
danseur	danseuse	reveur	reveuse
acteur	actrice	moteur	motrice
neuf	neuve	veuf	veuve

PLURALS

Most words add **-s** to indicate the plural.

Singular **le grand garçon**	*Plural* **les grands garçons**
la petite fille	**les petites filles**

Masculine words ending in **-s** or **-x** remain unchanged in the plural.

Singular **le chapeau gris**	*Plural* **les chapeaux gris**
le moment heureux	**les moments heureux**

Most words ending in **-al, -au, -eu,** and **-eau** form the plural ending in **-x.**

Singular	Plural	Singular	Plural
cheval	chevaux	beau	beaux
feu	feux	château	châteaux

UNSTRESSED PRONOUNS

1. Direct Object Pronouns

me	me; myself	**la**	her; it
te	you; yourself	**nous**	us; ourselves
se	himself; herself; themselves	**vous**	you; yourself; yourselves
le	him; it	**les**	them

2. Indirect Object Pronouns

me	to me; to myself	**lui**	to him, her
te	to you; to yourself	**nous**	to us; to ourselves
se	to himself, herself; to themselves; to each other	**vous**	to you; to yourself; to yourselves
		leur	to them

3. The unstressed words **y** (to it, to them, there) and **en** (of it, of them, from it, some, any) appear in the same part of the sentence as the unstressed pronouns.

The position of pronouns in normal French word order is at times similar to English usage. In many instances, however, the position varies, particularly in the use of the unstressed pronouns. In declarative, interrogative and all negative sentences, these pronouns appear *before* the verb. The examples below will be helpful:

Je vous parle.	I am speaking to you.
Il le voit.	He sees him.
Y êtes-vous allé?	Did you go there?
Je n'en vois pas.	I don't see any.
Nous nous habillons.	We are dressing (ourselves).
Elles se sont parlé.	They spoke to each other.
Je lui ai donné le livre.	I gave him the book. (her)
Je le lui ai donné.	I gave it to him. (to her.)
Les avez-vous?	Do you have them?
Je leur en parlerai.	I'll speak to them about it.
Elle me l'a vendu.	She sold it to me.
Nous les y verrons.	We'll see them there.

ADVERBS

Most adverbs are derived from corresponding adjective forms by adding the suffix **-ment** to the feminine form of the adjective.

Adjective	*Adverb*
heureux	**heureusement**
cruel	**cruellement**
final	**finalement**

Some adverbs follow a variant of the above pattern.

Adjective	*Adverb*
négligent	**négligemment**
évident	**évidemment**
constant	**constamment**

9

INTERROGATION

Interrogation is indicated in French in several ways, just as in English. The use of the interrogative pronouns, adjectives, and adverbs; the inversion of verb and subject; the addition of a questioning phrase at the beginning or end of the sentence; a simple change in the inflection of the voice—all are signs of interrogation.

Qui êtes-vous?	Who are you?
Quel est son nom?	What is his name?
Qu'a-t-elle fait?	What has she done?
Comment le sait-il?	How does he know (it)?
Qu'est-ce qui est tombé?	What fell?
Pourquoi ne me parlez-vous pas?	Why don't you speak to me?
Est-ce que c'est vrai?	Is it true?

NEGATION

Verbs are made negative in French by the use of **ne** before the verb and one of several negative words after the verb. In some cases, **ne** may appear without an accompanying sign of negation, but for the most part both signs are found.

Je ne sais pas.	I don't know.
Je ne sais danser.	I don't know how to dance.
Il ne lui écrit jamais.	He never writes to her.
Il n'a rien vu.	He saw nothing.
Je ne la verrai plus.	I won't see her any more.
Elle n'aime personne.	She loves no one.

When negative signs such as **personne** and **rien** are used as subjects of the sentence, the following order is found:

Personne ne le sait.   No one knows it.

The use of **ne . . . que** (only) follows the same pattern as the above.

Je ne vois que deux choses.   I only see two things.

REGULAR VERBS

In each of these conjugations, the endings refer to 1st, 2nd, and 3rd person, singular and plural.

1. -er Verbs. Example: **donner**

Present participle, donnant; *Past participle,* donné
Present donne, -es, -e, -ons, -ez, -ent
Future donnerai, -as, -a, -ons, -ez, -ont
Conditional donnerais, -ais, -ait, -ions, -iez, -aient
Present subjunctive donne, -es, -e, -ions, -iez, -ent
Imperfect donnais, -ais, -ait, -ions, -iez, -aient
Past definite donnais, -as, a, -âmes, -âtes, -èrent

2. -ir Verbs. Example: finir

Present participle finissant; *Past participle* fini
Present finis, -is, -it, -issons, -issez, -issent
Future finirai, -as, -a, -ons, -ez, -ont
Conditional finirais, -ais, -ait, -ions, -iez, -aient
Present subjunctive finisse, -es, -e, -ions, -iez, -ent
Imperfect finnissais, -ais, -ait, -ions, -iez, -aient
Past definite finis, -is, -it, -îmes, -îtes, -irent

3. -re Verbs. Example: rendre

Present participle rendant; *Past participle* rendu
Present rends, -ds, -d, -dons, -dez, -dent
Future rendrai, -as, -a, -ons, -ez, -ont
Conditional rendrais, -ais, -ait, -ions, -iez, -aient
Present subjunctive rende, -es, -e, -ions, -iez, -ent
Imperfect rendais, -ais, -ait, -ions, -iez, -aient
Past definite rendis, -is, -it, -îmes, -îtes, -irent

4. Examples of Compound Verb Tenses

Present Perfect	J'ai donné	I gave, have given
(Past Indefinite)	Il a fini	He finished, has finished
	Il est allé	He went, has gone
Past Perfect	Nous avions vendu	We had sold
(Pluperfect)	Ils avaient parlé	They had spoken
	Elle etait arrivée	She had arrived
Future Perfect	Vous aurez obéi	You will have obeyed
	Je serai venu	I will have come
Past Conditional	Tu auras rendu	You will have given back
	Elles auraient pleuré	They would have cried
	Vous auriez beni	You would have blessed
	Elle serait devenue	She would have become
Past Anterior	Il eut fendu	He had split
	Vous eûtes étudié	You had studied
	Je fus tombé	I had fallen
Perfect Subjunctive	Elle ait bondi	She jumped, has jumped
	Nous ayons tordu	We twisted, have twisted
	Vous soyez resté	You remained, have remained

IRREGULAR VERB FORMS

The following list deals with the frequently used irregular verbs. Only the basic pattern of irregularity is given. Where forms and tenses do not deviate from regular patterns, they are not listed; it may be assumed that they are like regular forms.

absoudre like **résoudre;** *p.p.* **absous**
accueillir like **cueillir**
acquérir *p.p.* **acquis;** *pres.* **acquiers -s, -t, acquérons, -ez, acquièrent** *fut.* **acquerrais;** *pres. subj.* **acquières, -es, -e, acquérions, -iez, acquièrent**
admettre like **mettre**
aller *pres.* **vais, vas, va, allons, -ez, vont;** *fut.* **irai;** *pres. subj.* **aille, -es,**
-e, allions, -iez, aillent
apercevoir like **recevoir**
apparaître like **connaître**
appartenir like **tenir**
apprendre like **prendre**
asseoir *p.p.* **assis;** *pres.* **assieds, -ds, -d, asseyons, -ez, -ent;** *fut.* **assiérai**
assortir like **sortir**
atteindre like **craindre**

11

avoir *pres. p.* ayant; *p.p.* eu; *pres.* ai, as, a, avons, -ez, ont; *fut.* aurai; *pres. subj.* aie, -es, -e, aient
battre *pres.* bats, -ts, -t, -ttons, -ttez, -ttent
boire *p.p.* bu; *pres.* bois, -s, -t, buvons, -ez, boivent; *pres. subj.* boive, -es, -e, buvions, -iez, boivent
bouillir *pres. p.* bouillant; *pres.* bous, -s, -t, -illons, -illez, -illent
commettre like **mettre**
comprendre like **prendre**
concevoir like **recevoir**
conclure *p.p.* conclu; *pres.* conclus, -s, -t, -ons, -ez, -ent
concourir like **courir**
conduire *p.p.* conduit; *pres.* conduis, -s, -t, -sons, -sez, -sent; *past def.* conduisis
confire like **suffire**
connaître *p.p.* connu; *pres.* connais, -aît, -aissons, -aissez, -aissent
conquérir like **acquérir**
consentir like **mentir**
construire like **conduire**
contenir like **tenir**
contredire like **dire**
convaincre like **vaincre**
convenir like **venir**
coudre *pres. p.* cousant; *p.p.* cousu; *pres.* couds, -ds, -d, -sons, -sez, -sent
courir *p.p.* couru; *pres.* cours, -s, -t, -ons, -ez, -ent; *fut.* courrai
couvrir like **ouvrir**
craindre *p.p.* craint; *pres.* crains, -s, -t, craignons, -ez, -ent
croire *p.p.* cru; *pres.* crois, -s, -t, croyons, -ez, croient; *pres. subj.* croie, -es, -e, croyions, -iez, croient
croître *p.p.* crû; *pres.* croîs, -s, -t, croissons, -ez, -ent, *past def.* crûs; *imp. subj.* crusse
cueillir *pres.* cueille, -es, -e, ons, -ez, -ent; *fut.* cueillerai
cuire like **conduire**
decévoir like **recevoir**
découvrir like **ouvrir**
décrire like **écrire**
dédire like **dire**
déduire like **conduire**
défaire like **faire**
dépeindre like **craindre**
détruire like **conduire**

devoir *p.p.* dû; *pres.* dois, -s, -t, devons, -ez, doivent; *fut.* devrais *pres. subj.* doive, -es, e, devions, diez, doivent; *past def.* dus
dire *p.p.* dit; *pres.* dis, -s, -t, -sons, -tes, -sent
discourir like **courir**
disparaître like **connaître**
dissoudre like **résoudre**; *p.p.* dissous
dormir *pres.* dors, -s, -t, -mons, -mez, -ment
ecrire *p.p.* écrit; *pres.* écris, -s, -t, -vons, -vez, -vent; *past def.* écrivis
élire like **lire**
endormir like **dormir**
entreprendre like **prendre**
envoyer *pres.* envoie, -es, -e, envoyons, -ez, envoient; *fut.* enverrai; *pres. subj.* envoie, -es, -e, envoyions, -iez, envoient
être *pres. p.* étant; *p.p.* été; *pres.* suis, es, est, sommes, êtes, sont; *fut.* serai; *pres. subj.* sois, -s, -t, soyons, ez, soient
étreindre like **craindre**
exclure like **conclure**
faire *p.p.* fait; *pres.* fais, -s, -t, -sons, -tes, font; *fut.* ferai; *pres. subj.* fasse; *past def.* fis
falloir *p.p.* fallu; *pres.* (3rd per. sing. only) faut; *fut.* faudra; *pres. subj.* faille
feindre like **craindre**
frire *p.p.* frit; *pres.* fris, -s, -t, -ons, -ez, -ent
fuir *pres.* fuis, -s, -t, fuyons, -ez, fuient; *pres. subj.* fuie, -es, -e, fuyions, -iez, fuient
geindre like **craindre**
haïr *p.p.* haï; *pres.* hais, -s, -t, haïssons, -ez, -ent
inscrire like **écrire**
instruire like **conduire**
joindre like **craindre**
lire *p.p.* lu; *pres.* lis, -s, -t, -sons, -sez, -sent
maintenir like **tenir**
mentir *pres.* mens, -s, -t, -tons, -tez, -tent
mettre *p.p.* mis; *pres.* mets, -ts, -t, -ttons, -ttez, -ttent
moudre *pres. p.* moulant, *p.p.* moulu; *pres.* mouds, -ds, -d, -lons, -les, -lent

mourir *p.p.* **mort;** *pres.* **meurs, -s, -t, mourons, -ez, meurent;** *fut.* **mourrai;** *pres. subj.* **meure, -es, -e, mourions; -iez, meurent;** *past def.* **mourus**

mouvoir *p.p.* **mû;** *pres.* **meus, -s, -t, mouvons, -ez, meuvent;** *fut.* **mouvrais;** *pres. subj.* **meuve;** *past def.* **mus**

naître *p.p.* **né;** *pres.* **nais, naît, naissons, -ez, -ent;** *past def.* **naquis**

nuire like **conduire**

obtenir like **tenir**

offrir like **ouvrir**

ouvrir *p.p.* **ouvert;** *pres.* **ouvre, -es, -e, -ons, -ez, -ent;** *past def.* **ouvris**

paître like **connaître**

paraître like **connaître**

parcourir like **courir**

partir *pres.* **pars, -s, -t, -tons, -tez, -tent**

parvenir like **venir**

peindre like **craindre**

permettre like **mettre**

plaindre like **craindre**

plaire *p.p.* **plu;** *pres.* **plais, -ais, -aît, -aisons, -aisez, -aisent**

pleuvoir *pres. p.* **pleuvant;** *p.p.* **plu;** *pres.* (3rd. per. sing. only) **pleut;** *fut.* **pleuvra**

poursuivre like **suivre**

pouvoir *p.p.* **pu;** *pres..* **peux, -x, -t, pouvons, -ez, peuvent;** *fut.* **pourrai;** *pres. subj.* **puisse**

prédire like **dire**

prendre *p.p.* **pris;** *pres.* **prends, -ds, -d, prenons, -ez, -nent;** *pres. subj.* **prenne, -es, prenions, -iez, prennent**

prescrire like **écrire**

produire like **conduire**

promettre like **mettre**

recevoir *p.p.* **reçu;** *pres.* **reçois, -s, -t, recevons, -ez, reçoivent;** *fut.* **recevrai;** *pres. subj.* **reçoive, -es, -e, recevions, -iez, reçoivent**

reconnaître like **connaître**

réduire like **conduire**

repentir like **mentir**

résoudre *pres. p.* **résolvant;** *p.p.* **résolu, résous;** *pres.* **résous, -s, -t, résolvons, -ez, -ent;** *pres. subj.* **résolve**

rire *p.p.* **ri;** *pres.* **ris, -s, -t, -ons, -ez, -ent**

rompre *pres.* **romps, -s, -t, -ons, -ez, -ent**

satisfaire like **faire**

savoir *p.p.* **su;** *pres.* **sais, -s, -t, savons, -ez, -ent;** *fut.* **saurai;** *pres. subj.* **sache**

secourir like **courir**

séduire like **conduire**

sentir like **mentir**

servir *pres.* **sers, -s, -t, -vons, -vez, -vent**

sortir *pres.* **sors, -s, -t, -tons, -tez, -tent**

souffrir like **ouvrir**

soumettre like **mettre**

sourire like **rire**

soutenir like **tenir**

suffire *pres.* **suffis, -s, -t, -sons, -sez, -sent**

suivre *pres.* **suis, -s, -t, -vons, -vez, -vent**

surprendre like **prendre**

taire like **plaire** (without circumflex)

teindre like **craindre**

tenir *p.p.* **tenu;** *pres.* **tiens, -s, -t, tenons, -ez, tiennent;** *fut.* **tiendrai;** *pres. subj.* **tienne, -es, -e, tenions, -iez, tiennent**

traduire like **conduire**

tressaillir like **cueillir**

vaincre *p.p.* **vaincu;** *pres.* **vaincs, -cs, -c, vainquons, -ez, -ent;** *past def.* **vainquis**

valoir *p.p.* **valu;** *pres.* **vaux, -x, -t, valons, -ez, -ent;** *fut.* **vaudrai;** *pres. subj.* **vaille, -es, -e, valions, -iez, vaillent**

venir like **tenir** (compound tenses conjugated with être as auxiliary verb)

vêtir *p.p.* **vêtu;** *pres.* **vêts, -ts, -t, -tons, -tez, -tent;** *past def.* **vêtis**

vivre *p.p.* **vécu;** *pres.* **vis, -s, -t, -vons, -vez, -vent**

voir *p.p.* **vu;** *pres.* **vois, -s, -t, voyons, -ez, voient;** *fut.* **verrai;** *pres. subj.* **voie, -es, -e, voyions, -iez, voient;** *past def.* **vis**

vouloir *p.p.* **voulu;** *pres.* **veux, -x, -t, voulons, -ez, veulent;** *fut.* **voudrais;** *pres. subj.* **veuille, -es, -e, voulions, -iez, veuillent**

ABBREVIATIONS

a.	adjective	math.	mathematics
adv.	adverb	mech.	mechanics
agr.	agriculture	med.	medicine
anat.	anatomy	mil.	military art
arch.	architecture	min.	mining
art.	article	mus.	music
ast.	astronomy	*n.*	noun
auto.	automobile	naut.	nautical
avi.	aviation	*past def.*	past definite
biol.	biology	phot.	photography
bot.	botany	phy.	physics
chem.	chemistry	*pl.*	plural
coll.	colloquial	poet.	poetry
com.	commerce	pol.	politics
cond.	conditional	*p.p.*	past participle
conj.	conjunction	*prep.*	preposition
dent.	dentistry	*pres.*	present
eccl.	ecclesiastic	*pres. p.*	present participle
elec.	electricity	print.	printing
ent.	entomology	*pron.*	pronoun
f.	feminine	rad.	radio
fig.	figuratively	rail.	railway
fut.	future	rhet.	rhetoric
geol.	geology	*sing.*	singular
gram.	grammar	*subj.*	subjunctive
imp.	impersonal	theat.	theatre
imper.	imperfect	*v.*	verb
infin.	infinitive	vet.	veterinary
interj.	interjection	*vi.*	verb intransitive
interr.	interrogative	*vt.*	verb transitive
m.	masculine	zool.	zoology

FRENCH-ENGLISH

A

à *prep.* to, at, in, with
abaisse-langue *m.* tongue depressor
abaissement *m.* lowering, falling; drop; abasement
abaisser *vt.* to lower; abase; **s'—** to humble oneself; resort, stoop, cringe
abandon *m.* abandonment, neglect; abandon; **à l'—** uncared for, at random
abandonner *vt.* to abandon, give up; **s'—** to resign oneself; give way, yield
abasourdi *a.* astounded, amazed; **–ssement** *m.* bewilderment, consternation
abasourdir *vt.* astound, stupefy, amaze
abat *m.* sudden shower; **pluie d'—** drenching rain
abâtardir *vt.* corrupt, debase, bastardize
abat-jour *m.* lamp shade; shutter, blind, skylight
abattage *m.* slaughter; (coll.) reprimand; felling (trees)
abattant *m.* flap; **— a.** depressing
abattement *m.* prostration; dejection
abattis *m.* giblets, feet; slaughtered animals; felling
abattoir *m.* stockyard; slaughterhouse
abattre *vt.* to fell; demolish; slaughter; depress; **s'—** to alight; (avi.) crash; calm down, abate; become depressed
abattu *a.* depressed, humbled
abbaye *f.* abbey
abbé *m.* abbot; priest, superior; ecclesiastic
abbesse *f.* abbess
abcéder *vi.* to abscess
abcès *m.* abscess
abdication *f.* abdication
abdiquer *vt.* to abdicate; resign
abdomen *n.* abdomen

abdominal *a.* abdominal
abécédaire *m.* child's first speller, reader or primer
abeille *f.* bee
aberration *f.* aberration, alienation
abêtir *vt.* to stupefy, blunt
abhorrer *vt.* to abhor, detest, loathe
abime *m.* abyss, chasm
abimer *vt.* to damage, ruin, spoil; **s'— to** spoil; be engulfed
abject *a.* abject
abjuration *f.* abjuration, renunciation
abjurer *vi.* to abjure, renounce
ablatif *m.* ablative
ablution *f.* ablution, purification
abnégation *f.* abnegation, sacrifice
aboiement *m.* barking, baying
abois *m. pl.*, **aux — at** bay; **mettre aux —** to make desperate
abolir *vt.* to abolish, repeal, suppress
abolition *f.* abolition; **–iste** abolitionist
abomination *f.* abomination
abominer *vt.* to abominate, detest
abondamment *adv.* abundantly
abondance *f.* abundance, wealth; **parler d'—** to speak extemporaneously
abondant *a.* plentiful, abundant, abounding
abonder *vi.* to abound, be plentiful
abonné *m.* subscriber
abonnement *m.* subscription; (rail.) commuter ticket; season ticket
abonner *vt.* to enter a subscription (for someone); **s'— a** to subscribe to
abonnir *vt.* to improve, correct
abonnissement *m.* improvement
abord *m.* approach; **–s** *pl.* outskirts; **d'— at** first

abordable *a.* accessible, receptive, approachable

aborder *vt.* to approach, accost; undertake; — *vi.* (naut.) to land

aborigène *a. & m.* aboriginal, native

abortif *a.* abortive

abot *m.* hobble; fetter for horse

aboucher *vt.* **s'—** confer; bring together

about *m.* end of wood piece (to be added to another), butt end

aboutement *m.* abutment; placing end to end

abouter *vt.* to place end to end

aboutissement *m.* result, outcome; (med.) heading of an abcess

aboyer *vi.* to bark, yelp

abrasion *f.* abrasion

abrégé *m.* resumé, digest, abridgment; **en — briefly**

abrégement *m.* abridgment; abridging

abreger *vt.* to shorten; abbreviate

abreuer *vt.* to water; soak; flood

abreuvoir *m.* trough for water

abri *m.* shelter; protection; **à l'— de** under cover of, sheltered from; **sans — homeless**

abricot *m.* apricot; **–ier** *m.* apricot tree

abriter *vt.* to shelter, protect

abri-voûte *m.* bomb shelter

abroger *vt.* to abrogate

abruti *m.* stupid person, fool; — *a.* stupid

abrutir *vt.* to stupefy

abrutissement *m.* stupefaction, degradation

absent *a.* absent; absent-minded

absentéisme *m.* absenteeism

absenter *v.,* **s'—** to be away, step out

abside *f.* apse

absinthe *f.* (liqueur) absinthe; wormwood

absolu *a.* absolute, unlimited

absolument *adv.* absolutely; completely

absolution *f.* absolution

absolutisme *m.* absolutism

absorbant *a.* absorbing; absorbent

absorber *vt.* to absorb; **s'—** to be absorbed

absorption *f.* absorption

absoudre *vt.* to absolve; forgive; remit

abstenir *v.,* **s'—** to abstain

abstention *f.* abstention

abstinence *f.* abstinence; abstention

abstinent *a.* abstinent, abstemious

abstraction *f.* abstraction

abstractionnisme *m.* (art) abstractionism

abstraire *vt.* to abstract, consider separately

abstrait *a.* abstract; engrossed; inattentive

absurde *a.* absurd; silly; preposterous

absurdité *f.* absurdity; nonsense

abus *m.* abuse, misuse; mistake; breach

abuser *vi.* to take advantage, impose; misuse; — *vt.* to deceive; **s'—** to be mistaken

abusif *a.* abusive; contrary to rule or law; improper

Abyssinie *f.* Abyssinia

abyssinien *a.* Abyssinian

acacia *m.* acacia

académicien *m.* academician

académie *f.* academy; school; university; learned society

académique *a.* academic

acajou *m.* mahogany

acariâtre *a.* quarrelsome; nagging

accablant *a.* overwhelming; annoying

accablement *m.* dejection, discouragement

accablé *a.* worn out; overwhelmed; (fig.) weighed down

accabler *vt.* to discourage; wear out; crush, overwhelm

accalmie *f.* (naut.) calm, lull, respite

accaparer *vt.* to corner (the market); monopolize

accéder *vi.* to agree; accede; to have access to

accélérateur *m.* accelerator; — *a.* accelerative

accélération *f.* acceleration

accélérer *vi.* to accelerate

accent *m.* accent; tone; emphasis, stress

accentuer *vt.* to accent, accentuate, stress

acceptabilité *f.* acceptability

acceptable *a.* acceptable

acceptation *f.* acceptance

accepter *vt.* to accept, agree

acception *f.* meaning, acceptation

accès *m.* approach; access; attack, fit; **par — by fits and starts**

accessible *a.* accessible

accession *f.* accession, adhesion, union

accessoire *m. & a.* accessory

accident *m.* accident; **— de terrain** unevenness of ground

accidenté *a.* rough, uneven; varied

accidentel *a.* accidental, unexpected

accidenter *vt.* (coll.) to involve in an accident; to make uneven

accise *f.* excise tax

acclamation *f.* acclamation

acclamer *vt.* to acclaim, hail

acclimatation *f.* acclimation

acclimater *vt.* to acclimate

accointance *f.* acquaintance; familiarity

accointer *vt.* to make acquainted; **s'—** to become friendly

accolade *f.* embrace; accolade; knighting; (print.) bracket, brace

accoler *vt.* to fasten; join, link

accommodage *m.* preparation *or* dressing; hairdressing

accommodant *a.* accommodating, easygoing, obliging; courteous

accommodement *m.* agreement, compromise, settlement; reconciliation

accommoder *vt.* to adjust; fix up; fix over; arrange; **s'**— to adjust, adapt; make oneself comfortable; compromise; come to terms with

accompagnateur *m.* accompanist

accompagnement *m.* accompaniment; **tir d'**— *m.* (mil.) covering-fire

accompagner *vt.* to accompany, be with, come with, go with

accompli *a.* accomplished; fulfilled; perfect

accomplir *vt.* to accomplish, do; complete

accomplissement *m.* accomplishment, achievement; completion

accord *m.* accord; agreement; (mus.) chord; harmony, tune; **d'**— in agreement; agreed, all right; **être d'**— to agree; **tomber d'**— to come to an agreement, agree

accordé *m.* bridegroom, fiancé

accordéon *m.* accordion

accorder *vt.* to reconcile; accord; tune; **s'**— agree, be in agreement; be in tune, harmonize

accore *a.* abrupt, sheer; vertical (coast); — *m.* (naut.) prop used during boat construction

accort *a.* gracious, compliant

accoster *vt.* to approach; accost

accoter *v.,* **s'**— **à** to lean against

accotoir *m.* support; prop; stanchion

accouchement *m.* delivery (birth); lying-in

accoucher *vi.* to give birth; — *vt.* to attend someone giving birth; deliver (baby)

accoucheur *m.* obstetrician

accoucheuse *f.* midwife

accoudoir *m.* armrest, sill; (arch.) rail

accouplement *m.* coupling; joining; pairing

accoupler *vt.* to couple, join, pair

accourcie *f.* shortcut

accourcir *vt.* to shorten; hasten

accourir *vi.* to rush up to, flock together

accoutrement *m.* bizarre attire; garb

accoutrer *vt.* to dress up ridiculously, to rig out

accoutumance *f.* habit, custom

accoutumé *a.* accustomed; customary, usual

accoutumer *vt.* to accustom; **s'**— get used to, become accustomed to

accréditer *vt.* to accredit; give credence to

accroc *m.* tear, rip; difficulty; hindrance, hitch

accrocher *vt.* to hang up; bump; catch (by hook), hook; embarrass; **s'**— hold on, cling, grab; clinch (in boxing)

accroire (faire) *vt.* to believe; **enfaire** — impose on; **s'en faire** — be self-conceited

accroissement *m.* growth, increase

accroître *vi.* to grow; — *vt.* to increase, enhance

accroupir *v.,* **s'**— to crouch, squat

accroupissement *m.* crouching, cowering

accueil *m.* reception; welcome

accueillant *a.* cordial, hospitable, gracious

accueillir *vt.* to receive, welcome, greet

accul *m.* blind alley

acculer *vt.* to drive back, corner

accumulateur *m.* battery, cell

accumulation *f.* accumulation

accumuler *vt.* to accumulate

accusateur *a.* accusing; — *m.* **accuser;** — **public** *m.* attorney-general

accusatif *a. & m.* accusative

accusation *f.* accusation, indictment

accusé *m.* accused; defendant; notice; — **de réception** receipt; — *a.* accentuated, marked

accuser *vt.* to accuse; reveal; announce; accentuate, heighten

acerbe *a.* bitter, sour, sharp, astringent

acerbité *f.* acerbity; bitterness, sharpness

acéré *a.* sharp, keen

acescent *a.* becoming acid

acétique *a.* acetic

acétone *f.* acetone

acétylène *m.* acetylene

achalander *vt.* to supply *or* **attract** customers; to stock, supply

acharné *a.* stubborn, tenacious, persistant; desperate

acharnement *m.* tenacity, obstinacy, rancor

acharner *v.,* **s'**— to be tenacious; persist

achat *m.* purchase; — *vt.* **faire des —s** to buy

achée *f.* worms used for bait

acheminement *m.* progress; direction

acheminer *vt.* to send, forward; **s'**— **to** go ahead, move

acheter *vt.* to buy, purchase

acheteur *m.* purchaser, buyer

achevé *a.* finished; perfect; accomplished

achèvement *m.* finish(ing), completion; finished quality

achever *vt.* to finish, complete; finish **off,** dispatch

achoppement *m.* obstacle; **pierre d'**— *f.* stumbling block

achopper *v.,* **s'**— to stumble

acide *n. & a.* acid

acidité *f.* acidity

acidulé *a.* acid, acidulated; **bonbon —** *m.* drop; fruit-flavored hard candy

acier *m.* steel; **— fondu** cast steel; **— trempé** tempered steel; **cœur d'—** hard heart; **fil d'—** steel wire

aciérer *vt.* to convert to steel

aciérie *f.* steel mill

acmé *f.* acme

acné *f.* acne

acompte *m.* part payment, payment on account, installment

à-coup *m.* jerk, jolt

acoustique *a.* acoustic(al); **cornet —** *m.* ear trumpet; **— f.** acoustics; **— m.** speaking-tube

acquéreur *m.* purchaser

acquérir *vt.* to acquire, win

acquiescement *m.* acquiescence, consent

acquiescer *vi.* to acquiesce, consent, agree

acquis *a.* acquired; **— m.** acquired knowledge *or* experience

acquisition *f.* acquisition

acquit *m.* receipt; release; **par — de conscience** to ease one's conscience; **pour — paid**

acquittement *m.* (com.) payment in full; legal acquittal

acquitter *vt.* to acquit, discharge; (com.) receipt; **s'—** discharge, fulfill

acre *m.* acre

âcre *a.* acrid, sharp, bitter

âcreté *f.* bitterness, sharpness

acrimonie *f.* acrimony

acrimonieux *a.* acrimonious

acrobate *m. & f.* acrobat; rope-dancer

acrobatie *f.* acrobatics; stunt

acrobatique *a.* acrobatic

acropole *f.* acropolis

acrostiche *m.* acrostic

acrylique *a.* acrylic

acte *m.* act, action; title; deed; certificate; **— de naissance** birth certificate; **—s** *pl.* proceedings

acteur *m.* actor

actif *a.* active; **— m.** credit side of a ledger; asset; (gram.) active voice

actinique *a.* actinic

actinium *m.* actin

action *f.* action; act; lawsuit; (mil.) engagement; (com.) share of stock

actionnaire *m. & f.* stockholder

actionné *a.* active, busy

actionner *vt.* to put in motion; begin a court action, sue

activer *vt.* to activate; make active

activeur *m.* activator

activité *f.* activity; **en — active**

actrice *f.* actress

actuaire *m.* actuary; Roman scribe

actualité *f.* something real; present, thing of the moment; **—s** *pl.* newsreel; news items

actuel *a.* present, current

actuellement *adv.* at present, now, today, really

acuité *f.* acuteness, keenness

adaptateur *m.* adaptor

adapter *vt.* to adapt, adjust; **s'—** adapt oneself

addenda *m.* addition(s)

additif *m. & a.* additive

addition *f.* addition; (restaurant) check

additionnel *a.* additional

additionner *vt.* to add up; adulterate, cut (with water)

adénoïde *a.* adenoids; **végétations —s** *f. pl.* adenoids

adent *m.* notch, groove; dovetail, mortise

adepte *n.* partisan; expert; adept

adéquat *a.* equivalent; adequate

adhérence *f.* adherence

adhérent *a.* adherent; adhesive; **— m.** supporter; adherent; subscriber to a belief

adhérer *vi.* to adhere, stick, cling; subscribe, belong

adhésif *a. & m.* adhesive

adhésion *f.* adhesion; adherence

adieu *m.* farewell

adipeux *a.* adipose

adjacent *a.* adjacent, adjoining

adjectif *a.* adjectival, adjective; **— n.** adjective

adjectivement *adv.* adjectively

adjoindre *vt.* to adjoin, join on, add

adjoint *a. & m.* assistant, deputy, adjunct

adjonction *f.* addition, annex

adjudant-chef *m.* master sergeant, sergeant-major

adjudicataire *m. & f.* highest bidder; beneficiary of adjudication

adjudication *f.* adjudication; knocking down (at auction sale); contract; **mettre en —** contract for

adjuger *vt.* to adjudicate, award, knock down at auction

adjurer *vt.* to adjure; entreat; bind *or* command under oath

admettre *vt.* to admit, allow

administrateur *m.* administrator; director

administratif *a.* administrative

administration *f.* administration; management; direction

administrer *vt.* to administer, manage, direct

admirateur *a.* admiring; **— n.** admirer

admiratif *a.* admiring

admiration *f.* admiration

admirer *vt.* to admire; wonder
admissibilité *f.* admissibility
admissible *a.* admissible
admission *f.* admission
admonestation *f.* admonition
admonester *vt.* to admonish
adolescence *f.* adolescence
adolescent *a. & m.* adolescent
adonner *v.* **s'— à** to devote oneself to
adopter *vt.* to adopt
adoption *f.* adoption
adorateur *m.* adorer
adoration *f.* adoration, worship
adorer *vt.* to adore, worship
adosser *vt.* to place back to back, lean back against; **s'—** to lean (back)
adoucir *vt.* to soften, moderate; relieve, ease; **s'—** to become mild, soften
adoucisseur *m.* water softener
adrénaline *f.* adrenalin
adresse *f.* address; skill; adroitness
adresser *vt.* to address; **s'— (à)** to address oneself to; apply to; speak to
adroit *a.* skillful, clever, adroit
aduler *vt.* to adulate
adulte *m. & a.* adult
adultération *f.* adulteration
adultère *m.* adultery; **— a.** adulterous
adultérer *vt.* to adulterate
advenir *v.* to happen, come about; become
adverbe *m.* adverb
adverbial *a.* adverbial
adversaire *m.* adversary, opponent
adverse *a.* contrary; adverse
adversité *f.* adversity, affliction
aération *f.* aeration, renewal of air
aéré *a.* airy, well-aired
aérer *vt.* to air, ventilate; aerate
aérien *a.* aerial; **ligne –ne** *f.* airline
aérodrome *m.* airport
aérodynamique *f.* aerodynamics; **— a.** aerodynamic
aérofrein *m.* airbrake
aérogare *f.* airline terminal
aérogramme *m.* airletter
aérographe *m.* airbrush
aéronaute *m.* aeronaut
aéronautique *f.* aeronautics; **— a.** aeronautic
aéronef *n.* airship, aircraft
aéroplane *m.* airplane
aéroport *m.* airport
aéroporté *a.* airborne
aéropostal *a.* relating to airmail
aérostat *m.* balloon
aérothermodynamique *f.* aerothermodynamics
aérotransporté *a.* airborne
affabilité *f.* affability, kindness
affable *a.* affable, courteous

affadir *vt.* to dull; make insipid
affadissement *m.* state of becoming faded; dulling, loss of taste
affaiblir *vt.* to weaken; **s'—** to grow weak; droop
affaiblissement *m.* weakening
affaire *f.* business, lawsuit; matter, deal; **–s** belongings; business; **chiffre d'—s** *m.* receipts (total business); **homme d'–s** *m.* business man; **avoir — à** to have to deal with
affairé *a.* busy
affairement *m.* activity, bustle
affairer *v.* **s'—** to be busy, hustle and bustle
affaissement *m.* collapse, depression, weakness
affaisser *v.* **s'—** to collapse, sink
affâiter *vt.* to train falcons
affamé *a.* starved, famished; greedy
affamer *vt.* to starve
affectation *f.* affectation; pretense; designation
affecter *vt.* to affect; feign; assume; (mil.) draft; designate; **s'—** to be moved
affectif *a.* affective; emotional
affection *f.* affection; mental state; (med.) ailment; **–né** *a.* affectionate
affectionner *vt.* to be fond of; take an interest in
affecteux *a.* affectionate
affermer *vt.* to rent by lease
affermir *vt.* to strengthen; harden; **s'—** to become firmer
affété *a.* affected
affichage *m.* posting on billboards
affiche *f.* poster, bill; **–r** *vt.* to post, advertise; make a show of
afficheur *m.* bill poster
affidavit *m.* affidavit
affidé *a.* trustworthy; **— m.** confederate; spy
affier *vt.* give one's word
affilé *a.* sharp; **avoir la langue bien –e** to have a sharp tongue, gossip; **d'—e** *adv.*
affiler *vt.* to sharpen
affilier *vt.* to affiliate, associate closely
affiloir *m.* hone; steel; knife sharpener
affiner *vt.* to refine; improve
affinité *f.* affinity; tendency to combine
affiquets *m. pl.* gew-gaws; knickknacks
affirmatif *a.* affirmative, positive
affirmation *f.* affirmation; assertion
affirmer *vt.* to affirm, assert; **s'—** assert oneself
affleurer *vt.* to make even; be even with
affliction *f.* affliction
affligé *a.* afflicted; sad; vexed
affligeant *a.* sad, distressing, bad (news)

affliger *vt.* to afflict; grieve, sadden, trouble

affluence *f.* affluence; abundance; crowd; heures d'— *f. pl.* rush hours

affluent *m. & a.* tributary

affluer *vi.* to flow; abound

afflux *m.* influx

affolement *m.* panic, distress; infatuation

affolé *a.* maddened, panic-stricken; infatuated

affoler *vt.* to madden, panic; infatuate; s'— to be panic-stricken; be madly in love with

affouiller *vt.* to undermine; wash away

affranchir *vt.* to emancipate, free; to stamp (letter)

affranchissement *m.* postage; liberation, emancipation

affres *f. pl.* anguish; dread

affrètement *m.* chartering, freighting

affréter *vt.* to charter, freight

affreux *a.* frightful; horrible

affriander *vt.* to make appetizing; lure; entice

affrioler *vt.* to attract; allure

affront *m.* insult; disgrace; reproach

affronter *vt.* to face; brave; s'— be in opposition

affubler *vt.* to fit out bizarrely; muffle

affût *m.* gun carriage; hunting post; être à l'— be on watch; lie in wait

affûter *vt.* to sharpen tools

affûtiau *m.* trifle; knickknack

Afghan *m. & a.* Afghan

afin, — que *conj.* so that, in order that; — de *prep.* in order to

Africain *m. & a.* African

Afrique *f.* Africa

afro-asiatique *a.* Afro-Asian

agaçant *a.* irritating, annoying

agacement *m.* annoyance, irritation

agacer *vt.* to irritate, annoy; egg on

âge *m.* age; period, epoch; — viril manhood; d'un certain — middle-aged; bas — infancy; eutre deux —s of middle age; fleur de l'— prime of life; moyen — Middle Ages; quel — avez-vous? how old are you?

âgé *a.* old, aged; of age

agence *f.* agency; bureau

agencement *m.* arrangement; -s *pl.* fixtures

agencer *vt.* to adjust, arrange; equip

agenda *m.* memorandum book; appointment book

agenouillé *a.* kneeling

agenouiller *v.,* s'— to kneel

agenouilloir *m.* kneeling stool, kneeler

agent *m.* agent; — de change stockbroker; — de police policeman

agglomération *f.* agglomeration; settlement (of people)

aggloméré *m.* briquette, compressed fuel

aggluntiner *vt.* to unite; s'— agglutinate, to cake

aggraver *vt.* to aggravate, worsen

agile *a.* agile, nimble

agilité *f.* agility

agioteur *m.* (com.) speculator

agir *vi.* to act; operate; (com.) manage; prosecute; il s'agit de it is a question of

agitateur *m.* agitator; stirrer, stirring-rod

agitation *f.* agitation

agité *a.* agitated; upset; restless

agiter *vt.* to agitate, shake, stir; disturb; debate

agneau *m.* lamb

agneler *vi.* to lamb

agnelin *m.* lamb's skin (with wool)

agnès *f.* innocent girl, ingénue

agnostique *m. & a.* agnostic

agonie *f.* agony, death throes

agonir *vt.* abuse; (coll.) insult highly

agonisant *a. & m.* dying; dying person

agoniser *vi.* to lie dying; be at death's door

agrafe *f.* clasp, hook, clip, clamp; — et porte hook and eye

agrafer *vt.* to clasp, hook, fasten

agrafeuse *f.* stapler

agraire *a.* agrarian

agrandir *vt.* to enlarge; s'— to grow, expand

agrandissement *m.* enlargement; aggrandizement

agrandisseur *m.* (phot.) enlarger

agrarien *m. & a.* agrarian

agréable *a.* pleasant, agreeable

agréer *vt.* to accept; approve; allow; — *vi.* to suit, be acceptable

agrégation *f.* degree required for teaching in a lycée; aggregation, aggregate

agrégé *m.* holder of the agrégation

agréger *vt.* to admit (to a society); accept; incorporate

agrément *m.* charm; ornamentation; pleasure; note d'— *f.* (mus.) grace-note

agrémenter *vt.* to embellish, adorn; trim

agrès *m. pl.* gymnasium equipment; (naut.) gear; rigging

agresser *vt.* to attack, commit aggression on

agresseur *m.* aggressor

agressif *a.* aggressive

agression *f.* aggression

agressivité *f.* aggressiveness

agreste *a.* rustic; rural

agricole *a.* agricultural; comices -s *m. pl.* county fairs

agriculteur *m.* farmer

agriculture *f.* agriculture
agriffer *v.*, **s'**— to hang, grip by claws
agripper *vt.* to snatch, grab; **s'**— to clutch at; come to grips
agronomie *f.* agronomy
agrouper *vt.* to group
aguerrir *vt.* to train in war, season, inure
aguet *m.* watch, watching; **–s** *pl.*, **être aux –s** to be on the lookout
ahaner *vi.* to groan, pant; sigh
aheurtement *m.* stubbornness, obstinacy
ahuri *a.* astounded
ahurir *vt.* to astound, amaze
ahurissement *m.* stupefaction
aiche, éche *f.* bait
aide *f.* help, aid; — *m. & f.* helper, aide, assistant; **à l'**—! *interj.* help!; **à l'**— **de** by means of
aide-mémoire *m.* reminder; memory aid
aider *vt.* to aid, help, assist
aïeul *m.* grandfather; **–e** *f.* grandmother; **–s** *m. pl.* grandfathers, grandparents
aïeux *m. pl.* ancestors
aigle *m.* eagle
aiglefin *m.* haddock
aiglon *m.* eaglet
aigre *a.* sour; sharp; harsh; — *m.* sourness, mustiness
aigre-doux *a.* bittersweet; sweet and sour
aigrefin *m.* adventurer, swindler; haddock
aigrelet *a.* somewhat bitter
aigrette *f.* aigrette; crest; cluster of feathers, diamonds, etc.
aigreur *f.* bitterness; (med.) heartburn
aigrir *vt.* to embitter; turn sour; make ill-humored
aigu *a.* acute, sharp; bitter, intense; piercing, shrill
aiguillage *m.* (rail.) switch; switching
aiguille *f.* needle; (clock) hand; pointer, indicator; (rail.) switch; magnetic needle
aiguiller *vt.* (rail.) to switch; direct
aiguilleur *m.* switchman
aiguillon *m.* goad; stinger; thorn; stimulus
aiguiser *vt.* to sharpen, stimulate
ail *m.* garlic
aile *f.* wing; blade; (auto.) fender
ailé *a.* winged
aileron *m.* wing tip; (avi.) aileron; fin
ailette *f.* wing; fin; blade
ailleurs *adv.* elsewhere; **d'**— besides, furthermore; **par** — besides; otherwise
aimable *a.* pleasant, kind, amiable
aimant *m.* magnet
aimanter *vt.* to magnetize
aimer *vt.* to love, like; — **bien** to like, be fond of
aine *f.* groin
aîné *a.* elder, eldest

aînesse *f.* seniority; primogeniture
ainsi *adv. & conj.* so, thus; — **que** just as; **et** — **de suite** and so forth
air *m.* air; tune, melody, appearance; manner; **avoir l'**— to seem; **au grand** —, **en plein** — outdoors, open air
airain *m.* bronze, brass
aire *f.* area; floor; surface; eyrie; wind direction
airelle *f.* cranberry
aisance *f.* ease; **lieu d'** — *m.* toilet
ais *m.* stave, board
aise *f.* comfort, ease; **à l'**— comfortable; **mal à l'**— uncomfortable; indisposed; — *a.* happy, content
aisé *a.* easy; well-off
aisselle *f.* armpit
aisément *adv.* easily
ajour *m.* opening; openwork
ajournement *m.* (mil.) deferment; postponement; legal summons
ajourner *vt.* to adjourn, postpone, defer
ajouter *vt.* to add; supply; interpolate
ajuster *vt.* to adjust; fix; ornament, dress
alambic *m.* (chem.) still
alambiquer *vt.* to distill; (fig.) make overly subtle
alanguir *vt.* to make languid, feeble
alarme *f.* alarm
alarmer *v.*, **s'**— **de** to become alarmed at
alarmiste *m. & a.* alarmist
Albanais *n. & a.* Albanian
Albanie *f.* Albania
albâtre *m.* alabaster
albatros *m.* albatros
album *m.* album, scrapbook; coloring book
albumen *m.* albumen
albumine *f.* albumen, egg white
alcaloïde *m.* alkaloid
alchimie *f.* alchemy
alchimiste *m.* alchemist
alcool *m.* alcohol; **–ique** *m. & a.* alcoholic
alcoolisme *m.* alcoholism
alcôve *f.* alcove
aléa *m.* chance, hazard
aléatoire *a.* risky; contingent (law); **–ment** *adv.* by chance
alène *f.* awl
à l'entour *adv.* in the vicinity; around
alentours *m. pl.* vicinity, neighborhood
alerte *f.* alarm, warning; — **d'avions** (avi. mil.) scramble; — *a.* alert, brisk, watchful
alerter *vt.* to alert, warn
aléser *vt.* to bore (tube, gun, etc.), grind
alevin *m.* fish fry; young fish
aleviner *vt.* to stock with young fish
algarade *f.* unmotivated attack; insult
algèbre *f.* algebra

algébrique *a.* algebraic
Alger *m.* Algiers
Algérie *f.* Algeria; **–n** *m. & a.* Algerian
algue *f.* seaweed; alga
aliboron *m.* jackass
aliéné *m.* deranged person, lunatic; **—** *a.* mad
aliéner *vt.* to give over, transfer; alienate
alignée *f.* line, row
alignement *m.* alignment
aligner *vt.* to align; (com.) balance an account
aliment *m.* food, nourishment
alimentaire *a.* alimentary; subsistance; **pension —** *f.* alimony; **régime —** *m.* diet
alimentation *f.* feeding; nourishment; provisionment
alimenter *vt.* to feed; maintain
alinéa *m.* indentation, paragraph
alité *a.* bedridden, confined to bed
allaitement *m.* nursing, nourishing on milk
allaiter *vt.* to suckle, nurse
allant *a.* active; **—** *m. pl.* activities, comings and goings
allécher *vt.* to entice; attract
allée *f.* walk, alley, path; going
allégation *f.* allegation; statement
alléger *vt.* to lighten; relieve
allègre *a.* gay, lively
alléguer *vt.* to allege
alléluia *m.* hallelujah
Allemagne *f.* Germany
Allemand *n. & a.* German
aller *vi.* to go, ride; **— à** to fit, suit; **— bien** to be well; **— mal** to be ill; **billet d'— et retour** *m.* round-trip ticket; **s'en —** to go away, go off
allergène *m.* (med.) allergen
allergie *f.* allergy
allergique *a.* allergic
alliage *m.* alloy; mixture
alliance *f.* alliance; union; wedding ring
allié *a.* allied; **—** *m.* ally; in-law, relative by marriage
allier *vt.* to alloy; ally; join; mix
alligator *m.* alligator
allitération *f.* alliteration
allocation *f.* allowance, subsidy; item
allocution *f.* address, speech
allonge *f.* extension; elongating piece; hook for hanging meat; boxing reach
allonger *vt.* to lengthen; extend; **s'—** to lie down; grow longer
allongement *m.* lengthening
allouer *vt.* to allocate, allow
allumage *m.* lighting; ignition, spark
allume-gaz *m.* gas stove lighter
allumer *vt.* to light; fire; ignite; turn on;

s'— catch fire
allumette *f.* match
allure *f.* gait; bearing; speed
allusif *a.* allusive, containing an allusion
allusion *f.* allusion
alluvial *a.* alluvial
almanach *m.* almanac, calendar
aloès *m.* aloes
aloi *m.* purity, quality
alors *adv.* then; **— que** *conj.* while, whereas; **— même que** even though, even when
alose *f.* shad
alouette *f.* lark
alourdir *vt.* to make heavy; **s'—** to become heavy
alourdissant *a.* oppressive
alourdissement *m.* heaviness; dullness
aloyau *m.* sirloin of beef
alpaga *m.* alpaca
alpage *m.* mountain pasture
Alpes *f. pl.* Alps
alpestre *a.* Alpine
alphabet *m.* alphabet
alphabétique *a.* alphabetical
alpin *a.* Alpine
alpinisme *m.* mountain climbing
alpiniste *m.* mountain climber
Alsace *f.* Alsace
Alsacien *n. & a.* Alsatian
altérable *a.* alterable
altération *f.* alteration, falsification
altercation *f.* altercation; dispute
altérer *vt.* to spoil; tamper with, distort; make thirsty
altéré *a.* altered; avid
alternance *f.* alternation
alternatif *a.* alternating
alternation *f.* alternation; succession
alternative *f.* alternative
alterner *vi.* to alternate
altesse *f.* (titre) highness
altier *a.* haughty
altièrement *adv.* haughtily, proudly
altimètre *m.* altimeter
altitude *f.* altitude; **— absolue** (avi.) absolute altitude
alto *m.* alto; viola; alto horn
altruisme *m.* altruism
altruiste *n.* altruist; **—** *a.* altruistic
alumelle *f.* plane (tool)
aluminium *m.* aluminum
alun *m.* alum
alvéole *m.* cell of honeycomb; socket of tooth; compartment, pigeonhole
alvéolé *a.* honey-combed
alvin *a.* abdominal; **flux —** *m.* diarrhea
amabilité *f.* amiability; kindness
amadou *m.* tinder
amadouer *vt.* to wheedle, coax

amaigrir vt. to make thin; — vi. to become thin
amaigrissant a., **régime** — m. weight-reducing diet
amaigrissement m. reducing, dieting; emaciation
amalgamation f. amalgamation
amalgame m. amalgam, mixture
amalgamer vt. to amalgamate; blend
amande f. almond
amandier m. almond tree
amant m. lover
amarrage m. (naut.) mooring
amarre f. (naut.) hawser, painter, cable
amarrer vt. to moor; make fast
amaryllis f. amaryllis
amas m. heap, pile, accumulation
amasser vt. to heap up, pile up, amass
amateur m. amateur, fan; devotee; connoisseur
Amazone f. Amazon; horsewoman; riding habit; **monter en** — ride side-saddle
ambages f. pl., **parler sans** — to stop beating around the bush
ambassade f. embassy
ambassadeur m. ambassador
ambassadrice f. ambassador's wife
ambiance f. atmosphere, environment
ambiant a. surrounding
ambidextre a. ambidextrous
ambigu a. ambiguous; — m. cold buffet; — **comique** comic play
ambiguïté f. ambiguity
ambitieux a. ambitious
ambitionner vt. to have ambitions to
ambivalence f. ambivalence
amble m. trot, amble
ambre m. amber; — **gris** ambergris
ambré a. amber-colored
ambulance f. ambulance
ambulancier m. ambulance attendant
ambulant a. itinerant; traveling; **marchand** — peddler; — m. railway post office
ambulatoire a. ambulatory; movable
âme f. soul, spirit, life
amélioration f. improvement, amelioration
améliorer vt. to improve, ameliorate
aménagement m. arrangement; preparation; furnishings
aménager vt. to prepare; fix up; arrange; outfit
amende f. fine, penalty; **faire** — **honorable** apologize courteously
amendement m. amendment; improvement; fertilizer
amender vt. to improve; amend; **s'**— reform
amène a. affable

amener vt. to bring; introduce, bring in; lead to
aménité f. amenity, pleasantness
amenuiser vt. to thin, make thin
amer a. bitter; — m. landmark
américain a. & m. American
américaine f. bicycle relay race; surrey
américaniser vt. Americanize
américanisme m. Americanism; American studies
Amérindien m. & a. Indian (of America)
Amérique f. America
amerrir vi. to land on the water
amertume f. bitterness
améthyste f. amethyst
ameublement m. furniture
ameuter vt. to gather hunting hounds; stir up
ami m. friend; sweetheart; — a. friendly
amiable a. amicable; **à l'**— adv. amicably
amiante m. asbestos
amibe f. amoeba
amibiase f. amoebic dysentery
amibien a. amoebic
amical a. friendly
amicale f. club, group
amict m. amice
amidon m. starch
amidonnage m. starching
amidonner vt. to starch
amincir vt. to make thin
aminé a. amino
amiral m. admiral
amirauté f. admiralty
amitié f. friendship; liking; **–s** pl. regards
ammoniaque f. ammonia
amnésie f. amnesia
amnésique m. & f. amnesia victim
amnistie f. amnesty, pardon
amnistier vt. to amnesty, pardon
amoindrir vt. to lessen, reduce, diminish
amollir vt. to soften; weaken; **s'**— to grow softer
amollissement m. softening
amonceler vt. to heap up, pile up
amoncellement m. heap, pile
amont m. upper portion of a river; **en** — upstream
amorce f. fuse, detonator; bait; beginning
amorcer vt. to prime a gun; bait; start
amorphe a. amorphous
amortir vt. to deaden, muffle, dull; amortize, redeem
amortissable a. redeemable
amortissement m. amortization; deadening, damping; depreciation; (arch.) finial, crowning ornament; **caisse d'**—f. sinking fund
amortisseur m. shock absorber
amour m. love; passion

amouracher *v.*, **s'— (de)** to become infatuated (with)

amourette *f.* love affair

amoureux *a.* in love; amorous; **—** *m.* lover; suitor

amour-propre *m.* self-esteem, pride, vanity

amovible *a.* movable; removable

ampère *m.* ampere; **–mètre** *m.* ammeter

amphibie *a.* amphibious; **—** *m.* amphibian

amphibologique *a.* ambiguous, equivocal

amphigouri *m.* hodge-podge; nonsense

amphithéâtre *m.* amphitheater; lecture hall

amphore *f.* amphora

ample *a.* wide, vast; ample, full; roomy, spacious; **—ur** *f.* fullness

ampliation *f.* amplification, expansion; duplicate

amplificateur *m.* amplifier; (phot.) enlarger; **—** *a.* enlarging, amplifying

amplification *f.* amplification; enlarging

amplifier *vt.* to amplify; enlarge; magnify

amplitude *f.* amplitude, extent

ampoule *f.* blister; sealed phial; ampule; (elec.) light bulb

ampoulé *a.* pompous, high-flown; blistered

amputé *m.* amputee

amputer *vt.* to amputate

amulette *f.* amulet, charm

amusement *m.* amusement, fun, entertainment

amuser *vt.* to entertain; amuse; **s'—** to have a good time

amusette *f.* plaything; toy; small amusement

amygdale *f.* tonsil

amygdalite *f.* tonsilitis

an *m.* year; **jour de l'—** New Year's day; **par —** yearly

ana *m.* collection of ancedotes and sayings

anachorète *m.* hermit

anachronique *a.* anachronistic

anachronisme *m.* anachronism

anagramme *f.* anagram

anal *a.* anal

analogie. *f* analogy

analogique *a.* analogical

analogue *a.* analogous; **—** *m.* analogue

analphabète *n.* & *a.* illiterate

analphabétisme *m.* illiteracy

analysable *a.* analysable

analyse *f.* analysis; résumé, summary

analyser *vt.* to analyse

analytique *a.* analytical

ananas *m.* pineapple

anarchie *f.* anarchy

anarchique *a.* anarchical

anarchiste *m.* & *f.* anarchist

anathématiser *vt.* to curse, anathematize

anathème *m.* anathema

anatomie *f.* anatomy

anatomique *a.* anatomical

anatoxine *f.* antitoxin

ancêtre *m.* ancestor

anche *f.* (mus.) reed

anchois *m.* anchovy

ancien *a.* old; former; ancient; **—** **élève** *m.* alumnus; **–nement** *adv.* formerly

ancienneté *f.* seniority; age, antiquity

ancrage *m.* anchorage

ancre *f.* anchor; **–r** *vt.* to anchor

Andalou *m.* & *a.* Andalusian

Andalousie *f.* Andalusia

Andes *f. pl.* Andes

Andorre *f.* Andorra

andouille *f.* pork, tripe sausage; (coll.) idiot, fool

andouiller *m.* antler

andouillette *f.* small pork or tripe sausage

androgène *m.* (biol.) androgen

âne *m.* ass, donkey; fool

anéantir *vt.* to destroy, annihilate

anéantissement *m.* destruction, annihilation

anémie *f.* anemia

anémié *a.* anemic

anémique *a.* anemic

anémomètre *m.* anemometer

anémone *f.* anemone

ânerie *f.* huge blunder; gross ignorance

anesthésie *f.* anesthesia

anesthésier *vt.* anesthetize

anesthésique *a.* & *m.* anesthetic

anesthésiste *m.* anesthetist

ange *m.* angle; **être aux —s** to be delighted

angélique *a.* angelic; **—** *f.* angelica

angélus *m.* angelus

angine *f.* quinsy, tonsillitis; angina

anglais *m.* the English language; **— basique** basic English; **-es** *f. pl.* long curls; **—** *a.* English; **filer à l'-e** to take French leave; **pommes à l'-e** boiled potatoes

Anglais *m.* Englishmen

angle *m.* corner; angle

Angleterre *f.* England

anglican *a.* Anglican

angliciser *vt.* Anglicize

anglophile *m.* & *a.* Anglophile

Anglo-Saxon *m.* & *a.* Anglo-Saxon

angoisse *f.* anguish, agony

angoisser *vt.* to anguish; afflict

anguille *f.* eel; **nœud d'—** *m.* slipknot

angulaire *a.* angular; **pierre —** *f.* cornerstone

anguleux *a.* angular

anicroche *f.* small obstacle, snag

ânier *m.* mule driver, muleteer
animadversion *f.* reproof, blame
animal *m.* animal, beast; — *a.* animal
animateur *m.* animator; organizer
animation *f.* animation; movement, life
animé *a.* animated; lively; **dessin** — *m.* cartoon (movies)
animer *vt.* to animate, enliven; move, encourage
animosité *f.* animosity
anion *m.* anion
anis *m.* anise; **—ette** *f.* (liqueur) anisette
ankylose *f.* stiffness of the joints
ankylosé *a.* stiff
ankyloser *vt.* to stiffen; **s'—** to stiffen; rust
annales *f. pl.* annals
anneau *m.* ring; link
année *f.* year
annelé *a.* ringed, annulated
annexe *f.* annex; supplement
annexer *vt.* to annex; append
annexion *f.* annexation
annihilation *f.* annihilation
annihiler *vt.* to annihilate
anniversaire *m.* birthday; anniversary
annonce *f.* advertisement; announcement
annoncer *vt.* to announce; predict; **s'—** to give promise of being
annonceur *m.* advertizer, sponsor
Annonciation *f.* Annunciation
annotateur *m.* annotator
annotation *f.* annotation
annoter *vt.* to annotate
annuaire *m.* directory (phone); yearbook; annual
annuel *a.* yearly, annual
annuité *f.* annuity; yearly payment
annulaire *a.* annular
annulation *f.* annulment
annuler *vt.* to annul, cancel
anoblir *vt.* to ennoble
anodin *a.* soothing; harmless; — *m.* anodyne
anomal *a.* irregular, abnormal
anomalie *f.* anomaly, irregularity
ânonner *vi.* to speak haltingly; stutter
anonymat *m.* anonymity
anonyme *a.* anonymous; — *n.* anonymity
anophèle *m.* anopheles, mosquito
anorak *m.* hooded jacket; rainproof sport jacket
anormal *a.* abnormal
anse *f.* handle; inlet, bay
antagonisme *m.* antagonism
antagoniste *n.* antagonist; — *a.* antagonistic; opposite
antan *m.* yore, yesteryear
antarctique *a.* antarctic
antécédent *a.* previous, prior, antecedent; — *m.* antecedent; **—s** *pl.* past history

Antéchrist *m.* Antichrist
antédéluvien *a.* antediluvian
antenne *f.* antenna; aerial
antérieur *a.* anterior; front; previous, earlier
anthologie *f.* anthology
anthracite *f.* anthracite, hard coal
anthropoïde *n. & a.* anthropoid
anthropologie *f.* anthropology
anthropologue *m.* anthropologist
anthropophage *m.* cannibal; — *a.* cannibalistic
anthropophagie *f.* cannibalism
antiaérien *a.* antiaircraft
antibiotique *m.* antibiotic
antibrouillard *a.* anti-fog; **phare** — *m.* fog light
antichambre *f.* antichamber, waiting room
antichar *a.* (mil.) antitank
anticipation *f.* anticipation
anticiper *vt.* to anticipate, forestall
anticlérical *a.* anticlerical
anticorps *m.* antibody
antidater *vt.* to antedate
antienne *f.* anthem
antigel *m.* antifreeze
antihistaminique *m.* antihistamine
Antilles *f. pl.* West Indies
antilope *f.* antelope
antimite *m.* moth repellant
antimoine *m.* antimony
antimoral *a.* immoral
antinomie *f.* antinomy, contradiction
antinomique *a.* contradictory
antiparticule *f.* (phys.) antiparticle
antipathie *f.* antipathy, repugnance
antipathique *a.* antipathetic
antiproton *m.* antiproton
antiquaille *f.* rubbish, junk
antiquaire *m.* antiquary; antique dealer
antique *a.* antique, ancient
antiquité *f.* antiquity; antique
antirabique *a.* antirabies
antiradar *a.* anti-radar
antirouille *m.* rust preventative
antisémite *m. & f.* antisemite
antisémitisme *m.* antisemitism
antiseptique *m. & a.* antiseptic
antisocial *a.* antisocial
antithèse *f.* antithesis
antitoxine *f.* antitoxin
antivol *m.* antitheft device, burglar alarm
antonyme *m.* antonym
antre *m.* cavern, lair, den
anus *m.* anus
Anvers *m.* Antwerp
anxiété *f.* anxiety
anxieux *a.* anxious, concerned, uneasy

aorte *f.* aorta
août *m.* August
apaiser *vt.* to appease; calm; **s'—** to abate, calm down
apanage *m.* lot, portion
aparté *m.* (theat.) aside
apathie *f.* apathy
apathique *a.* apathetic
apatride *a.* stateless
apercevoir *vt.* to perceive, see; **s'—** de to discover, realize
aperçu *m.* brief account; first glimpse; **par —** rough guess
apéritif *m.* apéritif, appetizer, small, before-dinner drink
apeuré *a.* frightened
aphasie *f.* aphasia
aphone *a.* soundless, voiceless
aphonie *f.* aphony, loss of speech
aphorisme *m.* aphorism
aphte *m.* mouth canker; cold sore
aphteux *a.* cankerous; **fièvre aphteuse** *f.* hoof and mouth disease
apiculteur *m.* beekeeper
apitoiement *m.* pity, compassion
apitoyer *vt.* to cause pity, move to pity; **s'—** sur to sympathize with
aplanir *vt.* to level, smoothe; plane
aplatir *vt.* to flatten; **s'—** to become flat; lie flat, fall flat
aplomb *m.* balance, poise; plumb; assurance; **d'—** level, even, plumb
apocalypse *f.* Apocalypse, Revelations; (fig.) obscure text *or* allegory
apocalyptic *a.* obscure; allegorical; apocalyptic
apocope *f.* (gram.) apocope, elision; (med.) amputation
apocryphe *a.* apocryphal
apode *a.* apodal, footless
apogée *m.* apogee, zenith
apologétique *a.* apologetic
apologie *f.* justification, defense, apology
apologue *m.* apologue, fable
apoplectique *a.* apoplectic
apoplexie *f.* stroke; apoplexy
apostasie *f.* apostasy; back sliding
apostat *m. & a.* apostate
aposter *vt.* to station; place in ambush
apostille *f.* annotation, postscript, endorsement
apostiller *vt.* to annotate, endorse; add postscript
apostolique *a.* apostolic
apostrophe *f.* apostrophe
apothéose *f.* apotheosis
apothicaire *m.* apothicary, pharmacist
apôtre *m.* apostle
apparaître *vi.* to appear; become apparent
apparat *m.* pomp, show

apparaux *m. pl.* fittings (of a ship)
appareil *m.* appliance, machine; apparatus; telephone; **—** photographique camera; **—** plâtré (med.) cast
appareiller *vi.* to set sail; prepare to leave; **—** *vt.* to equip; match (with); cut
apparemment *adv.* apparently
apparence *f.* appearance, semblance
apparent *a.* apparent; **–é** *a.* related
apparenter *v.*, **s'—** to be related
apparier *vt.* to match, pair (off)
apparition *f.* apparition; appearance
appartement *m.* apartment
appartenance *f.* appurtenance
appartenant *a.* belonging, pertaining to
appartenir *vi.* to belong; appertain
appas *m. pl.* charms
appât *m.* bait, lure, attraction
appâter *vt.* to lure; fatten; feed (baby or invalid)
appauvrir *vt.* to impoverish; **s'—** to become poor
appauvrissement *m.* impoverishment
appeau *m.* bird call; lure, decoy
appel *m.* appeal; call; roll call; telephone buzzer
appelant *m.* decoy; appellant (law)
appelé *m.* draftee
appeler *vt.* to call; call up; invoke, summon; **—** *vi.* appeal (law); **s'—** to be named; je m'appelle my name is
appellation *f.* appellation; brand name; **—** contrôlée registered trademark
appendice *m.* appendix
appendicite *f.* appendicitis
appentis *m.* lean-to
appesantir *vt.* to make heavy; **s'—** to insist
appétissant *a.* appetizing
appétit *m.* appetite; desire
applaudir *vt.* to applaud; approve
applaudissements *m. pl.* applause
application *f.* application; diligence
applique *f.* ornamentation; wall candlestick, wall bracket
appliqué *a.* diligent, studious
appliquer *vt.* to apply; adapt; **s'—** to apply; apply oneself
appoint *m.* (com.) balance
appointements *m. pl.* salary
appointer *vt.* to pay a salary; sharpen; settle a case at law
appontage *m.* landing (on the deck of an aircraft carrier)
appontement *m.* crane; dock
apponter *vi.* to land on the deck of an aircraft carrier
apport *m.* contribution, share
apporter *vt.* to bring; procure, use

apposer *vt.* to apply, affix, put
appréciable *a.* appreciable
appréciation *f.* appreciation; appraising, estimate, evaluation
apprécier *vt.* to appreciate; appraise, value, evaluate, estimate
appréhender *vt.* to apprehend; dread, fear
appréhension *f.* apprehension
apprendre *vt.* to learn; find out, hear; teach, show
apprenti *m.* apprentice
apprentissage *m.* apprenticeship
apprêt *m.* preparing, cooking and seasoning; affectation; —s *pl.* preparation
apprêter *vt.* to prepare; s'— prepare oneself
appris *a.*, **mal** — ill-bred
apprivoiser *vt.* to tame; make sociable
approbateur *a.* approving
approbation *f.* approval, approbation
approchable *a.* accessible
approchant *a.* somewhat like, approximately
approche *f.* approach; —s *pl.* access
approché *a.* approximate
approcher *vt.* to bring near; — *vi.* to come close; s'— to approach
approfondi *a.* thorough, deep
approfondir *vt.* to deepen; examine thoroughly; s'— to deepen
appropriation *f.* appropriation
approprier *vt.* to make appropriate, conform; s'— to appropriate
approuver *vt.* to approve (of); agree to
approvisionnement *m.* supply, provisions; provisioning
approvisionner *vt.* to provision; s'— to buy provisions; take in supplies
approximatif *a.* approximate
approximation *f.* approximation
appui *m.* support; prop; ledge, sill
appui-bras *m.* armrest
appui-livres *m.* bookends
appui-tête *m.* headrest
appuyer *vt. & vi.* to press; lean; support; s'— to lean, depend; insist
âpre *a.* rough, harsh; bitter, sharp; eager
après *prep.* after; next to; d'— according to; from, after; — *adv.* afterward, later, et —? so?, so what?; then what?
après-demain *m.* day after tomorrow
après-dîner *m.* period after dinner, evening
après-guerre *f.* postwar period
après-midi *m. or f.* afternoon
âpreté *f.* bitterness; harshness, roughness
à-propos *m.* opportuneness; aptness
apte *a.* apt, proper, suited, suitable
aptitude *f.* aptitude, capacity, qualification

apurement *m.* audit, verification
apurer *vt.* to verify, audit
apyre *a.* fireproof
aquafortiste *m.* etcher
aquaplane *m.* aquaplane, surfboard
aquapoumon *m.* aqualung
aquarelle *f.* watercolor
aquarelliste *n.* water-color artist
aquatique *a.* aquatic
aqueduc *m.* aqueduct
aqueux *a.* aqueous, watery
aquifère *a.* water-bearing
aquilin *a.* aquiline
aquilon *m.* north wind; cold blast
ara *m.* macaw
Arabe *m.* Arabian; — *a.* Arabian, Arabic
Arabie *f.* Arabia; — **Soudite**, — **Saoudite**, — Séoudite Saudi Arabia
arable *a.* arable
arachide *f.* peanut
araignée *f.* spider; **toile d'**—*f.* spider web
araser *vt.* to level
aratoire *a.* agricultural
arbalète *f.* crossbow
arbalétier *m.* crossbowman; rafters
arbitrage *m.* arbitration
arbitraire *a.* arbitrary
arbitre *m.* arbiter; umpire, referee; **libre** — free will (philosophy)
arbitrer *vt.* to arbitrate; referee
arborer *vt.* show off; — **un drapeau** hoist a flag
arbousier *m.* arbutus
arbre *m.* tree; (mech.) shaft; — **moteur** driveshaft; — **à cames** camshaft
arbrisseau *m.* shrub
arbuste *m.* shrub, bush
arc *m.* bow; arch; arc
arcade *f.* archway; **série d'—s** *f.* arcade
arcane *m.* mystery
arcature *f.* blind arcade; row of arcades
arc-boutant *m.* flying buttress
arceau *m.* arched opening; small arch
arc-en-ciel *m.* rainbow
archaïque *a.* archaic
archange *m.* archangel
arche *f.* arch; ark
archéologie *f.* archeology
archéologue *m.* archeologist
archer *m.* bowman, archer
archet *m.* (mus.) bow
archevêché *m.* archdiocese; archbishop's palace
archevêque *m.* archbishop
archi- *prefix* arch-
archipel *m.* archipelago
architecte *m.* architect
architectural *a.* architectural
architecture *f.* architecture
archives *f. pl.* archives

archiviste *m. & f.* archivist
arçon *m.* saddle bow; saddle; wool carder
arctique *a.* arctic
ardemment *adv.* ardently
ardent *a.* ardent; burning; fiery
ardeur *f.* ardor; heat; fire; zeal
ardillon *m.* tongue of a belt buckle
ardoise *f.* slate; score
ardu *a.* arduous; steep; difficult
are *m.* 100 square meters (about 120 square yards)
arène, –s *f. s. or pl.* arena, bull ring
aréner *vi.* to sink, settle
aréneux *a.* sandy
arête *f.* fishbone; ridge; edge; angle; — **du nez** bridge of the nose
argent *m.* silver; money
argenté *a.* silver; silver-plated; silvery
argenter *vt.* to plate with silver
argenterie *f.* silver plate, silverware
argentifère *a.* silver-bearing
argentin *a.* silvery; tinkling
argenture *f.* silvering; **l'— des glaces** silvering on mirrors
argile *f.* clay
argileux *a.* of clay, clayey
argonaute *m.* argonaut; nautilus
argot *m.* slang; **–ique** *a.* slangy
argousin *m.* prison guard
arguer *vt.* to infer; — *vi.* to argue
argument *m.* argument, summary, reasoning
argumentation *f.* argumentation; arguing
argumenter *vt.* to argue
argus *m.* spy; argus
argutie *f.* subtlety; quibbling
aride *a.* arid, dry, barren
aridité *f.* aridity
ariette *f.* air, song
aristocrate *m. & f.* aristocrat; — *a.* aristocratic
aristocratie *f.* aristocracy
aristocratique *a.* aristocratic
aristolélicien *a.* Aristotelian
arithméticien *m.* arithmetician
arithmétique *f.* arithmetic; — *a.* arithmetical
arlequin *m.* Harlequin
arlésien *a.* from Arles
armagnac *m.* brandy of Armagnac
armateur *m.* ship outfitter, shipowner
armature *f.* armature; (arch.) steel framework, iron braces; (mus.) signature
arme *f.* arm, weapon; **–s portatives** small arms; **maître d'–s** *m.* fencing master; **place d'–s** *f.* parade ground; **salle d'–s** *f.* fencing school
armé *a.* armed; **béton —** reinforced concrete
armée *f.* army

armement *m.* armament; arming; weaponry; equipment; loading; cocking
Arménie *f.* Armenia; **–n** *m. & a.* Armenian
armer *vt.* to arm; (naut.) to fit out; commission; reinforce; equip, outfit; load; cock; — *vi.* arm oneself
armistice *m.* armistice
armoire *f.* wardrobe; cupboard
armoiries *f. pl.* arms (heraldic), **coat of arms**
Armor *m.* (Celtic) Brittany
armorial *m.* armorial, book of heraldry
Armoricain *m. & a.* Breton
armure *f.* armor; (mus.) signature
armurier *m.* armorer, gunsmith
aromate *m.* aromatic substance
aromatique *a.* aromatic
aromatiser *vt.* to perfume; flavor
arôme *m.* aroma, flavor
aronde *f.* swallow; **queue d'—** *f.* dovetail
arpège *m.* arpeggio
arpent *m.* acre (= approximately 1½ American acres); **–er** *vt.* to survey, measure
arpenteur *m.* surveyor
arqué *a.* arched; bowed
arquebuse *f.* musket
arquer *vt.* to arch, bend, bow; curve; — *vi.* bend, sag
arrache-clou *m.* claw hammer
arrache-pied, d'— *adv.* uninterruptedly
arracher *vt.* to tear out; uproot, pull a tooth
arracheuse *f.* digger (potatoes, sugar beets)
arrangement *m.* arrangement; settlement; **–s** *m.* terms
arranger *vt.* to arrange, fix, settle; **s'—** to manage; agree, come to an agreement
arrangeur *m.* arranger
arrérages *m. pl.* arrears; money due
arrestation *f.* arrest, custody
arrêt *m.* stop; decree; verdict (law), sentence; arrest; **mandat d'—** *m.* arrest warrant; **chien d'—** *m.* hunting dog, pointer
arrêté *m.* decree, order; police decision
arrêter *vt.* to arrest; stop; settle; close (an account); determine, fix; engage; point (dog); **s'—** to stop
arrêtoir *m.* stop, catch
arrhes *f. pl.* deposit, security
arrière *m.* back; stern; rear; **vent — ** *m.* tail wind; **en —** *adv.* back, backwards; behind; **en — de** *prep.* behind
arrière- *prefix* rear-; after-; great- (relationship by blood)
arriéré *m.* arrears; — *a.* backward; overdue
arriéré *m.* arrearage; — *a.* deferred; be-

hind
arriere-ban *m.* reserve
arrière-bouche *f.* pharynx
arrière-boutique *f.* back room of a shop
arrière-garde *f.* rear guard
arrière-goût *m.* aftertaste
arrière-pays *m.* hinterland, back country
arrière-pensée *f.* ulterior motive
arrière-plan *m.* background
arrièrer *vt.* to delay; **s'—** stay behind
arrière-saison *f.* end of autumn
arrière-train *m.* rear; hindquarters
arrimer *vt.* to stow away
arrimeur *m.* stevedore
arrivage *m.* arrival of goods *or* ships
arrivée *f.* arrival, coming, approach
arriver *vi.* to arrive; happen; succeed; — à to reach, attain; manage to
arrivisme *m.* social climbing
arrogamment *adv.* arrogantly
arrogant *a.* arrogant
arroger *v.*, **s'—** to claim, assume with presumption
arrondir *vt.* to round off, make round; enlarge
arrondissement *m.* administrative district; ward
arrosage *m.* sprinkling; watering; basting; **tuyau d'—** *m.* garden hose
arroser *vt.* to water; baste; drain an area
arroseur *m.* sprinkler
arrosoir *m.* watering can; shower head
arrondir *vt.* to make round; increase; double
arsenic *m.* arsenic
art *m.* art; cunning; **beaux —s** fine arts
artère *f.* artery
artérial *a.* arterial
artériosclérose *f.* hardening of the arteries
artésian *a.* artesian; from Artois
arthrite *f.* arthritis
arthritique *a. & n.* arthritic
artichaut *m.* artichoke
article *m.* article; item; **— de fond** editorial
articulation *f.* articulation; joint; enumerated legal facts
articulé *a.* articulated; articulate
articuler *vt.* to affirm, declare; articulate
artifice *m.* artifice, trick; **feu d'—** *m.* fireworks
artificiel *a.* artificial
artificier *m.* maker of fireworks
artificieux *a.* sly, artful, full of artifice
artillerie *f.* artillery; ordnance
artilleur *m.* artilleryman
artisan *m.* craftsman, artisan
artiste *m. & f.* artist; **— a.** artistic
artistique *a.* artistic
arum *m.* calla lily; arum

aryen *a.* Aryan
as *m.* ace; expert
ascendant *m.* influence; **—s** *pl.* ancestry, lineage; **— a.** ascending
ascenseur *m.* elevator
ascension *f.* ascent; Assumption
ascète *m. & f.* ascetic
ascétique *a.* ascetic
ascétisme *m.* asceticism
asdic *m.* sonar, submarine detector
aseptique *a.* aseptic
Asiatique *m. & f. & a.* Asiatic
Asie *f.* Asie: — Mineure Asia Minor
asile *m.* asylum, refuge, shelter
aspect *m.* aspect, appearance, sight; look
asperge *f.* asparagus
aspergès *m.* sprinkler for holy water; time of sprinkling with such water
asperger *vt.* to sprinkle
aspérité *f.* asperity, roughness
asphalte *m.* asphalt
asphalter *vt.* to asphalt
asphyxie *f.* asphyxia
asphyxier *vt.* to asphyxiate
aspirant *m.* officer candidate; candidate
aspirateur *m.* vacuum cleaner; aspirator; **— de buée** *f.* ventilator
aspiration *f.* aspiration; intake
aspiré *m.* aspirate; **— a.** aspirated
aspirer *vi.* to aspire; — *vt.* to aspirate: take in; inhale
aspirine *f.* aspirin
assaillant *m.* assailant; aggressor
assaillir *vt.* to assail, attack
assainir *vt.* to make healthy, purify
assaisonnement *m.* seasoning, condiment; dressing
assaisonner *vt.* to season, flavor
assassin *m.* murderer; **— a.** murderous
assassinat *m.* assassination, murder
assassiner *vt.* to assassinate, murder
assaut *m.* assault, attack; bout
assécher *vt.* to drain, dry up
assemblage *m.* collection; assembly, assemblage; joining, joint (in carpentry)
assemblée *f.* assembly; meeting
assembler *vt.* to assemble; join; gather; **s'—** to meet, assemble
asséner *vt.* to strike a blow
assentiment *m.* assent, agreement, approval
asseoir *vt.* to seat; place, lay; **s'—** to sit down, be seated
assermenté *a.* sworn
assertion *f.* assertion
asservir *vt.* to enslave; **s'—** à to obey
asservissement *m.* slavery
assez *adv.* enough; rather; sufficiently
assidu *a.* assiduous; **—ité** *f.* assiduity
assidûment *adv.* assiduously; punctually

assiéger *vt.* to besiege
assiette *f.* plate; dish; position
assignation *f.* assignation; (com.) assignment; summons
assigner *vt.* to summon; assign; subpoena
assimiler *vt.* to assimilate; compare
assis *a.* seated, sitting; **place —e** *f.* seat
assise *f.* layer, stratum; **—s** *pl.* criminal court sessions
assistance *f.* audience; spectators; aid, assistance; **— judiciare** public defender's office; **— sociale** social work, welfare work
assistant *m.* assistant; bystander; **—s** *pl.* audience; **—e sociale** *f.* social worker
assister *vt.* to help; **— à** *vi.* to attend, be present at
association *f.* association; partnership
associé *m.* associate, partner
associer *vt.* to associate; **s'—** to enter into partnership; join in; be associated with
assoiffé *a.* thirsting, greedy
assolement *m.* crop rotation
assoler *vt.* to rotate crops
assombrir *vt.* to darken; **s'—** to get gloomy
assommant *a.* boring; crushing, telling
assommer *vt.* to knock down; kill; bore
assommoir *m.* blunt instrument, bludgeon; (coll.) bar, dive
Assomption *f.* Assumption
assorti *a.* matching
assortiment *m.* assortment; set; matching
assortir *vt.* to match
assoupir *vt.* to make sleepy; lull; **s'—** to doze off, fall asleep
assouplir *vt.* to make supple
assouplissement *m.* suppleness, docility
assourdir *vt.* to deafen; muffle
assourdissant *a.* deafening
assouvir *vt.* to gratify, satiate, surfeit
asujettir *vt.* subdue, subjugate; oblige; **s'—** to submit
asujettissement *m.* submission; subduing, subjugation
assumer *vt.* to assume, take on oneself
assurance *f.* assurance; insurance; **— par groupe** group insurance; **—s sociales** *pl.* social security
assuré *a.* assured; confident; secure; firm, steady; insured
assurément *adv.* certainly, assuredly; confidently
assurer *vt.* to assure; secure; insure; **s'—** to make sure
Assyrie *f.* Assyria; **—n** *m. & a.* Assyrian
astérie *f.* starfish
astérisque *m.* asterisk
astéroïde *m.* asteroid
asthmatique *m. & a.* asthmatic

asthme *m.* asthma
asticot *m.* maggot, worm
astigmatisme *m.* astigmatism
astiquer *vt.* to polish; clean up
astrakan *m.* Persian lamb
astre *m.* star
astreindre *vt.* to oblige, force, compel; **s'— (à)** to force oneself
astringent *a. & m.* astringent
astrologie *f.* astrology
astrologue *m.* astrologer
astronaute *m.* astronaut
astronautique *f.* space travel, astronautics
astronef *f.* space ship; space capsule
astronome *m.* astronomer
astronomie *f.* astronomy
astronomique *a.* astronomical
astrophysigne *f.* astrophysics
astuce *f.* astuteness, guile, wile
astucieux *a.* astute, crafty
asymétrique *a.* asymetrical
atavique *a.* atavistic
atelier *m.* workshop; studio
atermoyer *vi.* to stall, delay
athée *m.* atheist; **— a.** atheistic
athéisme *m.* atheism
athénée *m.* secondary school
athlète *m.* athlete
athlétique *a.* athletic
athlétisme *m.* track, athletics (sports)
Atlantide *f.* Atlantis
atlantique *a.* Atlantic
atmosphère *f.* atmosphere
atmosphérique *a.* atmospheric
atome *m.* atom; iota, speck
atomique *a.* atomic
atomiser *vt.* to atomize; subject to radiation; destroy with an atomic bomb
atomiseur *m.* atomizer
atomiste *m. & f.* atom scientist
atonal *a.* atonal
atonalité *f.* atonality
atone *a.* atonic, unaccented; atonal; dull
atours *m. pl.* women's finery
atout *m.* trump; **sans —** no trump
âtre *m.* hearth, fireplace
atroce *a.* atrocious
atrocité *f.* atrocity
atrophie *f.* atrophy
atrophier *vt.* to atrophy, waste away
attabler *v.*, **s'—** to sit down at the table
attache *f.* fastener, tie, clip; leash; tether
attaché *m.* attaché
attacher *vt.* to attach, fasten, join, tie; **s'— (à)** to grow fond (of); apply oneself (to)
attaquant *m.* attacker; aggressor
attaque *f.* attack; fit; **—r** *vt.* to attack
attardé *a.* late; behind; delayed
attarder *vt.* to delay; **s'—** to linger

atteindre *vt.* to reach, attain; strike, hit; wound
atteinte *f.* attack; blow; reach; injury
attelage *m.* team; pair; harnessing; coupling
atteler *vt.* to harness, yoke; hitch; couple
attelle *f.* splint
attenant *a.* adjoining, next
attendant *adv.*, **en** — meanwhile; for the moment; **en** — **que** *conj.* until
attendre *vt.* to wait for, expect; **s'** — (à) to expect
attendrir *vt.* to make tender; move, affect; touch; **s'** — to be moved
attendu *prep.* in view of; — **que** *conj.* since, whereas.
attentat *m.* criminal attack *or* attempt; outrage
attente *f.* expectation; waiting; hope
attenter *vi.* to make an attempt
attentif *a.* attentive; careful
attention *f.* attention, care; —! *interj.* watch out!; **faire** — to pay attention, be careful
atténuant *a.* extenuating; attenuating
atténuer *vt.* to attenuate; diminish, reduce
atterrage *m.* (naut.) landfall; landing
atterrer *vt.* to crush, overwhelm; demolish
atterrir *vi.* (avi.) to land
atterrissage *m.* (avi.) landing
atterrissement *m.* alluvion; descent (balloon)
attestation *f.* attestation, testimony
attester *vt.* to attest (to); witness
attiédir *vt.* to make lukewarm; **s'** — to become lukewarm
attifer *vt.* to deck out, ornament
attirail *m.* paraphernalia, gear
attirance *f.* attraction, temptation
attirant *a.* attracting, attractive
attirer *vt.* to attract, lure; **s'** — to bring upon oneself
attiser *vt.* to stir up; excite
attitré *a.* official
attitude *f.* posture, attitude, position
attractif *a.* attractive
attraction *f.* attraction; **-s** *pl.* shows, entertainment
attrait *m.* charm, attraction
attrape *f.* snare; trick
attrape-mouches *m.* flypaper; flycatcher (bird)
attrape-nigaud *m.* booby trap
attraper *vt.* to catch; take in; trick
attrayant *a.* attractive
attribuer *vt.* to attribute, ascribe
attribut *m.* attribute
attribution *f.* attribution; sphere, power
attrister *vt.* to sadden; **s'** — to become sad
attrouper *vt.* to assemble

aubaine *f.* windfall
aube *f.* dawn; board; paddle; (eccl.) alb; **roue à —s** *f.* paddlewheel
aubépine *f.* hawthorn
auberge *f.* inn; — **de la jeunesse** youth hostel
aubergine *f.* eggplant
aubergiste *m. & f.* innkeeper
aucun *pron. & a.* no one, none; no; any
aucunement *adv.* not at all, by no means, in no way
audace *f.* boldness, audacity
audacieux *a.* audacious, bold; impudent
au-dehors *adv.* outside
au-delà *adv.* beyond; — **de** *prep.* beyond
au-dessous *adv.* below, under; — **de** *prep.* below, under
au-dessus *adv.* above, over; — **de above,** over
au-devant *adv.*, **aller** — to go, meet; anticipate
audience *f.* hearing, audience
audiologie *f.* audiology
audio-visuel *a.* audio-visual
auditeur *m.* listener, hearer; **-s** *pl.* audience
auditif *a.* audial, auditory, auditive
audition *f.* hearing; audition
auditionner *vt.* to listen to; audition
auditoire *m.* audience
auge *f.* trough; hod
augmentation *f.* increase; salary raise
augmenter *vt.* to augment; increase; raise; enlarge; — *vi.* increase; rise
augure *m.* omen; **de bon** — auspicious
augurer *vt.* to augur; foresee
auguste *a.* august
aujourd'hui *adv.* today, nowadays; **d'** — **en huit** in a week, a week from today
aumône *f.* alms, charity
aumônier *m.* chaplain
aune *f.* ell (= 45 inches); measure, standard; — *m.* alder
auparavant *adv.* before, previously
auprès *prep.*, — **de** near, close to; next to, with; compared with; — *adv.* nearby
auquel *pron.* to whom, to which
auréole *f.* halo; glory, aureola
auréomycine *f.* aureomycin
auriculaire *a.* aural, auricular; **doigt** — *m.* little finger
auricule *f.* auricle; outer ear
aurifier *vt.* to fill a tooth with gold
aurore *f.* dawn; — **boréale** aurora borealis
ausculter *vt.* (med.) to auscultate
aussi *adv.* also, too; — . . . **que as . . .** as; — *conj.* therefore, so
aussitôt *adv.* immediately; — **que as** soon as
austère *a.* austere, stern, severe

austérité *f.* austerity
austral *a.* southern
Australie *f.* Australia; **–n** *m. & a.* Australian
autan *m.* south wind; storm
autant *adv.* as much, as many; **d'—** as much as; **d'— plus, (moins)** all the more (less); **d'— plus que** all the more because
autel *m.* altar
auteur *m.* author; creator; cause
authenticité *f.* authenticity
authentifier *vt.* to authenticate
authentique *a.* authentic; sincere
auto *f.* automobile, auto, car
autobiographie *f.* autobiography
autobus *m.* bus
autocar *m.* intercity bus, sightseeing bus
autochenille *f.* caterpillar-tread vehicle
autochtone *a.* native
autoclave *m.* pressure cooker; sterilizer
autocopier *vt.* to duplicate, ditto
autocrate *m.* autocrat
autocratie *f.* autocracy
autocratique *a.* autocratic
autocritique *f.* self-criticism
autocuiseur *m.* pressure cooker
autodestruction *f.* self-destruction
autodétermination self-determination
autodidacte *a.* self-taught
autodrome *m.* race track (auto.)
auto-école *f.* driving school
autogène *a.* welded
autogire *m.* autogiro
autographe *m. & a.* autograph
autographier *vt.* to autograph
automate *m.* automaton
automatique *a.* automatic; **—** *f.* automation
automatiser *vt.* to introduce automation in
automatisme *m.* automation
automnal *a.* autumnal
automne *m. or f.* autumn
automobilisme *m.* driving, motoring
automobiliste *m.* motorist
automoteur *a.* self-propelling; **train —** *m.* diesel-powered train
autonome *a.* autonomous
autonomie *f.* autonomy
autoplastie *f.* skin grafting
autoportrait *m.* self-portrait
autopropulsion *f.* self-propulsion
autopsie *f.* autopsy
autopsier *vt.* to perform an autopsy on
autorail *m.* railway diesel car
autorisation *f.* authorisation
autoriser *vt.* to authorize, empower
autoritaire *a. & m.* authoritarian
autoroute *f.* highway; expressway

autorité *f.* authority; **–s** *pl.* officials, authorities
auto-stop *m.* hitchhiking; **faire l'—** to hitchhike
autostrade *f.* superhighway, expressway
autour *adv.* about, around; **— de** *prep.* about, around
autre *a.* other, another; different; **—part** elsewhere; **d'— part** on the other hand; **de temps à —** from time to time, occasionally; **l'un et l'—** both; **l'un ou l'—** either; **ni l'un ni l'—** neither
autrefois *adv.* formerly, once
autrement *adv.* otherwise; differently
Autriche *f.* Austria
autrichien *a. & m.* Austrian
autruche *f.* ostrich
autrui *pron.* others
auvent *m.* shed; cover, roof; penthouse
auvergnat *a.* from Auvergne
auxiliaire *a. & n.* auxiliary
avachir *v.,* **s'—** to become deformed; become flabby
aval *m.* guarantee; downstream portion of a river; **en —** downstream
avaler *vt.* to swallow
avaliser *vt.* to guarantee, co-sign
avaliseur *m.* co-signer
à-valoir *m.* part-payment
avance *f.* head start, lead; advance; loan; **d'—** in advance; **en —** early
avancé *a.* advanced; **heure –e** *f.* late hour
avancement *m.* advancement, advancing; furthering; progress; projection
avancer *vt.* to advance; hasten; further; promote; extend, put out; **—** *vi.* advance, move forward, progress; to be fast (clock)
avanie *f.* public insult; affront
avant *prep. & adv.* before; **— (de)** before; **en —** forward; **— que** *conj.* before; **—** *m.* front portion; (naut.) bow
avantage *m.* advantage; profit
avantager *vt.* to favor; give an advantage
avantageux *a.* profitable, advantageous; vain
avant-bras *m.* forearm
avant-coureur *m.* forerunner
avant-dernier *f.* next-to-last
avant-garde *f.* vanguard
avant-goût *m.* foretaste
avant-guerre *f.* prewar period; **d'—** *a.* prewar
avant-hier *adv.* day before yesterday
avant-port *m.* outer port
avant-poste *m.* outpost
avant-projet *m.* preliminary consideration (of a plan or project)
avant-propos *m.* foreward

avant-scène *f.* proscenium; stagebox
avant-veille *f.* second day previous, two days before
avare *a.* miserly, stingy
avaricieux *a.* avaricious, stingy, miserly
avarie *f.* damage; loss; deterioration
avarié *a.* spoiled, damaged
avec *prep.* with; **d'—** from
aveline *f.* filbert
avenant *a.* coming; becoming; in keeping
avènement *m.* succession; coming; advent
avenir *m.* future; **à l'—** henceforth
avent *m.* (eccl.) Advent
aventure *f.* adventure, intrigue; **bonne —** fortune telling; **à l'—** *adv.* at random
aventurer *vt.* to venture, risk; **s'—** to venture
aventureux *a.* adventurous; risky
aventurier *m.* adventurer
avérage *m.* average
avéré *a.* verified, established
avérer *v.*, **s'—** to appear, prove
averse *f.* shower, downpour
averti *a.* informed; on guard; experienced
avertir *vt.* to warn; inform, notify
avertissement *m.* warning; notice; preface
avertisseur *a.* warning; **— *m.*** warning device; horn; alarm
aveu *m.* confession, avowal, admission
aveugle *a.* blind; **— *m. & f.*** blind person
aveuglement *m.* blinding; (fig.) blindness
aveuglément *adv.* blindly
aveugler *vt.* to blind
aveuglette, à l'— *adv.* blindly, gropingly; at random
aveulir *vt.* to weaken; enervate
aviateur *m.* aviator
aviation *f.* aviation; air force
avide *a.* greedy; eager, avid
avidité *f.* avidity, eagerness
avilir *vt.* to vilify; lower in value; **s'—** to lower oneself, stoop to; become lower in value
avilissement *m.* vilification
aviné *a.* drunk (from wine)
avion *m.* airplane; **par —** by air mail
aviron *m.* oar; rowing; **donner un coup d'—** lend a helping hand
avis *m.* advice; opinion; notice; **à mon —** in my opinion; **changer d'—** to change one's mind
avisé *a.* prudent; shrewd, wary
aviser *vt.* to notify; warn; notice; **— à** *vi.* to take care of, see to; **s'— (de)** to take into one's head (to)
avivage *m.* polishing, brightening; revival
aviver *vt.* to sharpen; irritate; make brighter
avocat *m.* lawyer; advocate; **poire d'—** *f.* avocado

avocatier *m.* avocado tree
avoine *f.* oats
avoir *vt.* to have; get; **— chaud (froid, raison, tort)** to be hot (cold, right, wrong); **qu'avez-vous?** what's the matter?; **y — *v.*, il y a** there is, there are, it is; ago; **— *m.*** property, possessions; credit (ledger)
avoisiner *vt.* to neighbor, be near, border on
avorter *vi.* to miscarry; go wrong, fail
avorton *m.* miscarriage; abortion; abortive offspring
avoué *m.* attorney, lawyer
avouer *vt.* to avow, confess, admit
avril *m.* April
axe *m.* axis; axle; Axis
axillaire *a.* axillary
axiomatique *a.* axiomatic
axiome *m.* axiom
axonge *f.* lard
azalée *f.* azalea
azotate *m.* nitrate
azote *m.* nitrogen; **–ux** *a.* nitrous
azotique *a.* nitric
aztèque *a.* Aztec
azur *m.* azure
azuré *a.* azure, bluish
azyme *a.* unleavened

B

baba *m.* rumcake
babeurre *m.* buttermilk
babil *m.* babble, babbling; baby talk
babillard *a.* babbling; talkative; **— *m.*** chatterbox; tattler
babiller *vi.* to babble, chatter about nothing
babine *f.* heavy lip; chop; **se lécher les –s** to lick one's chops
babiole *f.* bauble, toy, trinket
bâbord *m.* (naut.) port side
babouche *f.* heelless slipper
babouin *m.* baboon
Babylone *n.* Babylon
Babylonien *m. & a.* Babylonian
baby-parc *m.* playpen
bac *m.* ferry; vat, tank; box, bin; (coll.) bachelor's degree
baccalauréat *m.* bachelor's degree
baccara *m.* baccarat
bâche *f.* tarpaulin; tank; hotbed frame
bachelier *m.* lycée graduate
bachot *m.* small boat; (coll.) bachelor's degree
bacillaire *a.* caused by a bacillus
bacille *m.* bacillus
bâcle *f.* bolt, bar of a door
bâcler *vt.* to botch, patch together; bolt,

bar; block, obstruct
bactérie *f.* microbe, bacterium
bactériologie *f.* bacteriology
bactériologue *m.* bacteriologist
badaud *m.* loafer; stroller
badigeon *m.* whitewash
badigeonner *vt.* to whitewash; fill with plaster; (med.) paint the throat
badin *a.* playful, joking, fooling
badinage *m.* banter, fooling, playfulness
badine *f.* switch, wand, rod
badiner *vi.* to joke, play, be playful; trifle, fool; — *vt.* tease
badminton *m.* badminton
bafouer *vt.* to make fun of; scoff at; ridicule without pity
bafouiller *vi. & vt.* (coll.) to stammer; (fig.) speak disconnectedly
bâfrer *vt. & vi.* (coll.) to devour, guzzle
bagage *m.* baggage; **plier** — to pack up and go; –**s** *m. pl.* baggage, luggage
bagarre *f.* riot, brawl, fight
bagatelle *f.* trifle; (fig.) something frivolous
bagnard *m.* prisoner, convict
bagne *m.* penitentiary; penal servitude
baguage *m.* banding (tree)
bague *f.* ring; **jeu de** –**s** merry-go-round
baguenauder *vi.* to trifle, waste time
baguer *vt.* to ring, band (tree); baste (cloth)
baguette *f.* switch, rod; drum stick; wand; long thin loaf of bread
baguier *m.* jewel box
bahut *m.* trunk, chest; (coll.) school
bai *a.* bay horse
baie *f.* berry; bay, gulf; (arch.) bay
baignade *f.* swimming; swimming place
baigner *vt.* to soak, bathe
baignoire *f.* bathtub; (theat.) orchestra box
bail *m.* (*pl.* **baux**) lease
bâillant *a.* yawning; open, ajar
bâillement *m.* yawn; opening; gap
bâilleur *m.* bondsman
bâiller *vi.* to yawn, gape; be ajar
bailli *m.* bailliff
bâillon *m.* gag
bâillonner *vt.* to gag; muzzle; (fig.) silence
bain *m.* bath; **costume de** — bathing suit, swim suit; –**s** *pl.* baths; spa, hot springs, resort
bain-marie *m.* water bath; double boiler
baïonnette *f.* bayonet
baisemain *m.* hand-kissing
baiser *m.* kiss; — *vt.* to kiss (hand, brow); (fig.) compliment
baissant *a.* setting (sun); falling; failing
baisse *f.* fall, decline, drop
baisser *vt.* to lower; — *vi.* to fall, drop,

go down; sink; **se** — to stoop; bow down; — *m.* fall, falling; setting (of sun)
bajoue *f.* jowl
Bakélite *f.* Bakelite (trademark)
bal *m.* ball, dance
balader *v.*, **se** — to wander, stroll
baladeuse *f.* cart; trailer, portable light, trouble light
baladin *m.* buffoon; actor
balafre *f.* gash; slash; scar; –**r** *vt.* to gash; scar
balai *m.* broom; (elec.) brush; carpet sweeper; **manche à** — *m.* (avi.) control stick; — **à laver** mop
balance *f.* scales; balance; balance sheet
balancement *m.* rocking; hesitation; poising
balancer *vt.* to balance; swing, rock; weigh for and against — *vi.* to hesitate; fluctuate, waver; swing
balancier *m.* pendulum; beam; balance wheel; coin-press lever
balançoire *f.* seesaw, teeter-totter; swing
balayer *vt.* to sweep
balayette *f.* whisk broom
balayeur *m.* street cleaner, street sweeper
balayeuse *f.* carpet sweeper; street-cleaning truck
balayures *f. pl.* sweepings
balbutier *vi.* to stutter, stammer, mumble
balbuzard *m.* buzzard
balcon *m.* balcony
baldaquin *m.* canopy, tester
baleine *f.* whale; whalebone, stay
baleinier *m.* whaling ship
baleinière *f.* whaleboat
balise *f.* buoy, marker, beacon
baliser *vt.* to mark with buoys or lights
balistique *a.* ballistic; — *f.* ballistics
baliverne *f.* nonsense, stupidity, humbug
balkanique *a.* Balkan
Balkans *m. pl.* Balkans
ballant *a.* swinging, slack (rope), dangling
ballast *m.* ballast
balle *f.* ball; bullet; husk; — **traçante** tracer bullet
ballerine *f.* ballerina
ballet *m.* ballet
ballon *m.* balloon; ball; — **d'essai** trial balloon
ballonner *vi.* to swell, puff up
ballot *m.* bundle; bale; package of merchandise
ballottage *m.* balloting; indecisive first ballot
ballotter *vt.* to agitate; — *vi.* to move about; to be shaken
ballottine *f.* chicken loaf
balnéaire *a.* bathing; **station** — *f.* resort
balourd *a.* dull, heavy; stupid,

balsa *m.* balsa wood
Balte, Baltique *n. & a.* Baltic
balustrade *f.* balustrade, railing
balustre *m.* baluster
bambin *m.* little child
bambou *m.* bamboo
ban *m.* proclamation; cheer; **–s** *pl.* (eccl.) banns
banal *a.* banal, trite, commonplace
banalité *f.* triviality, triteness; overused expression
banane *f.* banana
bananier *m.* banana tree
banc *m.* bench; seat; pew; shoal
bancal *a.* bow-legged, bandy-legged
bandage *m.* bandage, truss; winding
bande *f.* band; strip; group; cushion (billiards)
bandeau *m.* headband; blindfold; **en –x** hair parted in the middle
bandelette *f.* band, headband, fillet
bander *vt.* to bandage; bind; blindfold; wind; **se —** to band together, join together
banderole *f.* streamer, pennant
bandit *m.* bandit
bandoulière *f.* sling; bandoleer; **en —** *a.* over the shoulder
banian *m.* banyan tree
banlieue *f.* suburbs; **de —** *a.* suburban
banlieusard *m.* suburbanite
banne *f.* basket, hamper; tarpaulin; awning
bannière *f.* banner, flag
bannir *vt.* to banish, exile
bannissement *m.* banishment, exile
banque *f.* bank; **— du sang** blood bank
banqueroute *f.* bankruptcy
banqueroutier *m.* bankrupt person
banqueter *vi.* to banquet, feast
banquette *f.* seat (train, bus); bank (earth or sand)
banquier *m.* banker
banquise *f.* ice pack, floe
banquiste *m.* charlatan
baptême *m.* christening, baptism; **nom de — christian name
baptiser *vt.* to christen, baptize
baptismal *a.* baptismal
baptiste *m. & f.* Baptist
baptistère *m.* baptistry
baquet *m.* tub, washtub
bar *m.* bar; bass, perch
baragouiner *vt. & vi.* (coll.) to jabber; pronounce badly
baraque *f.* hut, shack; hovel
baratte *f.* churn; **–r** *vt.* to churn
Barbade *f.* Barbados
barbare *a.* barbarous, cruel; barbaric; — *m.* barbarian

barbarie *f.* barbarity; **orgue de — m.** barrel organ, organ-grinder's organ
barbarisme *m.* barbarism
barbe *f.* beard; **se faire la — to shave; rire dans sa — laugh up one's sleeve
barbelé *a.* barbed; **fil de fer — m.** barbed wire
barbet *m.* water spaniel
barbiche *f.* goatee
barbier *m.* barber
barbillon *m.* barb
barbiturique *m. & a.* barbiturate
barbon *m.* old man; greybeard; (coll.) old fogy
barbouiller *vt.* to daub, smear, dirty; mess up, bungle
barbu *a.* bearded
barbue *f.* brill
barde *m.* bard; — *f.* fat used for larding
bardeau *m.* shingle; lath
barder *vt.* to lard; armor
bardot *m.* mule; laughing stock
barème *m.* tables of figures
barguette *f.* flat boat used as a ferry
barguigner *vi.* to hesitate
baricant *m.* small barrel
baril *m.* barrel, small cask
barillet *m.* small barrel; revolver cylinder; spring case
bariolage *m.* medley of colors
bariolé *a.* speckled ; multicolored
barman *m.* bartender
baromètre *m.* barometer
barométrique *a.* barometric
baron *m.* baron; **–ne** *f.* baronness
baroque *a.* irregular; baroque
barque *f.* bark (small boat)
barrage *n.* (mil.) barrage; dam; barrier; (sports) play-off
barre *f.* bar; helm; stroke; dividing line
barreau *m.* bar; rung
barrer *vt.* to bar; cross out
barrette *f.* biretta; bar; barrette, slide; pin
barricade *f.* barricade; **–r** *vt.* to barricade
barrière *f.* barrier; starting gate; fence; **— du son** sound barrier
barrique *f.* cask; barrel
barrir *vi.* to trumpet (elephant)
baryton *m.* baritone; baritone horn
baryum *m.* barium
bas (basse) *a.* low; vulgar, cheap; **— m.** stocking, hose; lower part, bottom; foot; **— adv.** softly; down, low; **en —** downstairs, below
basalte *m.* basalt
basane *f.* sheep skin
basané *a.* tanned, sunburned, swarthy
bas-côté *m.* church side aisle; highway shoulder
bascule *f.* scale; balance; seesaw

basculer *vi.* to swing, rock, seesaw; dim (headlights)

base *f.* base, basis, foundation

baser *vt.* to base, found

bas-fond *m.* hole; hollow; shoal; **–s** *pl.* dregs

basilic *m.* sweet basil

basilique *f.* basilica

basique *a.* basic

Basque *m. & f. & a.* Basque

bas-relief *m.* bas-relief

basse *f.* (mus.) bass; tuba

basse-cour *f.* poultry yard; backyard

basse-fosse *f.* dungeon

bassesse *f.* baseness, lowness, meanness

bassin *m.* basin; dock; (anat.) pelvis

bassine *f.* pan (round and shallow)

bassiner *vt.* to sprinkle, water; warm; (coll.) bore, weary

bassinet *m.* small basin

bassinoire *f.* bedwarmer; (coll.) bore

basson *m.* bassoon, bassoonist

bastille *f.* fort, fortress

bastion *m.* bastion

bastonnade *f.* beating

bas-ventre *m.* abdomen

bat *m.* bat

bât *m.* pack saddle

bataclan *m.* paraphernalia

bataille *f.* battle, fight

batailler *vi.* to battle

batailleur *a.* quarrelsome, fighting

bataillon *m.* battalion

bâtard *m.* bastard; medium-sized loaf of bread — *a.* not pure bred; inferior

bâtarde *f.* cursive writing

bâtardeau *m.* temporary dam

bateau *m.* boat

bateau-maison *m.* houseboat

bateau-mouche *m.* Parisian excursion boat

batelée *f.* boatload

bateler *vt.* to transport by boat; — *vi.* to perform tricks, juggle

bateleur *m.* trickster, juggler, tumbler

batelier *m.* boatman

bâter *vt.* to saddle (a pack animal)

bâti *m.* frame; basted garment; basting thread

bâtiment *m.* building; ship

bâtir *vt.* to build; baste (clothing)

bâtisse *f.* masonry; building

bâtisseur *m.* builder

batiste *f.* batiste

bâton *m.* stick, cudgel; baton

bâtonner *vt.* to beat; cross out

bâtonnier *m.* dean of lawyers (in France)

battage *m.* beating, threshing; churning

battant *m.* bell clapper; part of door or furniture that swings on a hinge; **porte**

à deux –s double door; — *a.* pelting, driving; **porte —** swinging door

batte *f.* bat; mallet

battement *m.* beating; throbbing, pulsing, pulsation; shuffling (cards)

batterie *f.* battery; (mus.) percussion; — **de cuisine** kitchen utensils

batteuse *f.* threshing machine

battoir *m.* paddle

battre *vt.* to beat, strike; mint; defeat; clap; shuffle cards; **se —** to fight

baudet *m.* donkey, ass; sawhorse; (fig.) idiot

baudrier *m.* shoulder belt, sword belt

bauge *f.* lair, den

baume *m.* balm, balsam

bauxite *f.* bauxite

bavard *a.* talkative, gossipy

bavarder *vi.* to chatter, gossip

Bavarois *m. & a.* Bavarian

bave *f.* slobber, drool; drivel

baver *vi.* to drool, slobber

bavette *f.* bib; **tailler une —** to chat

Bavière *f.* Bavaria

bavocher *vi.* to be smeared, poorly printed

bavoir *m.* bib

bavure *f.* seam (of a mold)

bayer *vi.* to gape, stare

bazar *m.* bazaar; variety store

béant *a.* agape, gaping, yawning

béat *a.* smug, complacent, sanctimonious

béatification *f.* beatification

béatifier *vt.* to beatify

béatitude *f.* beatitude

beau, bel (belle) *a.* fine, fair, beautiful, handsome; **vous avez — faire** no matter what you do

beaucoup *adv.* much, many; **de — by far**

beau-fils *m.* son-in-law; stepson

beau-frère *m.* brother-in-law

beau-père *m.* father-in-law; stepfather

beauté *f.* beauty

beaux-arts *m. pl.* fine arts

beaux-parents *m. pl.* father-in-law and mother-in-law; (coll.) in-laws

bébé *m.* baby

bec *m.* beak, bill; spout; point

bécane *f.* old locomotive, switch engine

bécarre *m.* (mus.) natural

bécasse *f.* woodcock

bécassine *f.* snipe

bec-de-cane *m.* door handle; door bolt (like a beak)

bec-de-corbeau *m.* wire cutters

bec-de-lièvre *m.* harelip

bêche *f.* spade; **–r** *vt. & vi.* to dig, spade

bêchoir *m.* hoe

becqueter *vt.* to peck (at)

bedeau *m.* beadle

Bédouin *m. & a.* Bedouin

bée *a.* open; **bouche — agape;** flabbergasted; **— *f.*** large opening
beffroi *m.* belfry
bégayer *vi.* to stutter; stammer
bégaiement *m.* stammering
bégonia *m.* begonia
begue *a.* stuttering, stammering
bégueter *vi.* to bleat
béguin *m.* hood, cap; infatuation
beige *a.* beige; unbleached
beignet *m.* fritter; doughnut
béjaune *m.* novice, beginner; one having no knowledge of a matter at hand
bêler *vi.* to bleat
belette *f.* weasel
Belge *n. & a.* Belgian
Belgique *f.* Belgium
bélier *m.* ram
bélitre *m.* scoundrel
belladone *f.* belladonna
belinogramme *m.* wire photo
belinographe *m.* wire photo transmitter
belle *adv.* **l'échapper —** to have a narrow escape
belle-de-jour *f.* morning glory
belle-fille *f.* daughter-in-law; stepdaughter
belle-mère *f.* mother-in-law; stepmother
belle-sœur *f.* sister-in-law
belliciste *m.* warmonger
belligérance *f.* belligerance
belligérant *m. & a.* belligerant
belligueux *a.* warlike
bémol *m.* (mus.)
bémoliser *vt.* (mus.) to flat
bénédicité *m.* grace before meals
bénedictin *m.* (liquer) benedictine; **–e *f.*** benedictine nun
bénédiction *f.* benediction
bénéfice *m.* benefice; profit; advantage
bénéficiaire *a.* beneficiary
bénéficier *vi.* to benefit, profit
benêt *a.* stupid; **— *m.*** simpleton
bénévole *a.* kind; well-intentioned
Bengale *m.* Bengal
Bengali *n. & a.* Bengal
bénignité *f.* benignness; kindness; mildness
bénin (bénigne) *a.* benign; benignant; mild, gentle; kind
bénir *vt.* to bless, consecrate
bénitier *m.* holy-water font
benjamin *m.* youngest child, favorite child
benne *f.* hamper; hopper; body (dump truck); mine elevator
benôit *a.* indulgent
benzine *f.* benzine
benzoate *m.* benzoate
béquille *f.* crutch; **–r *vi.*** to walk with crutches

béquillon *m.* cane, crutch
bercail *m.* (eccl.) fold
berceau *m.* cradle; arbor; (arch.) tunnel vault; (mech.) motor support
bercelonnette *f.* cradle, bassinet
bercer *vt.* to rock; soothe; (fig.) lull to sleep
berceuse *f.* lullaby; rocking chair; rocking cradle
béret *m.* beret
berge *f.* steep bank, edge
berger *m.* shepherd
bergère *f.* shepherdess; armchair
bergerie *f.* fold, sheepfold; pastoral poetry
béribéri *m.* beri-beri
berlingot *m.* hard candy (caramel)
berkélium *m.* berkelium
berline *f.* carriage; sedan; mine truck
berne *f.* banter; **en — at half mast**
berner *vt.* to toss in a blanket; fool; haze
bernacle, bernache *f.* barnacle
berrichon *a.* from Berry
béryl *m.* beryl
béryllium *m.* beryllium
besace *f.* beggar's bag; wallet
besicles *f. pl.* spectacles
besogne *f.* work, task; **–r *vi.*** to work
besogneux *a.* needy
besoin *m.* need, want; necessity; misery; **avoir — de** have need of; **au — if necessary**
bessemer *m.* Bessemer converter
bestialité *f.* bestiality
bestiaux *m. pl.* cattle, livestock
bestiole *f.* little animal
bétail *m.* cattle, livestock
bêtatron *m.* betatron
bête *f.* animal; beast; **— *a.*** stupid, foolish
bêtifier *vt.* to make stupid
bêtise *f.* stupidity; nonsense
béton *m.* concrete; **— armé** reinforced concrete
bétonner *vt.* to make of concrete
bétonnière *f.* cement mixer
bette *f.* beet
betterave *f.* beet; **— sucrière** sugar beet
betting *m.* odds (racing)
beuglement *m.* bellow, bellowing; lowing
beugler *vi.* to low, bellow
beurre *m.* butter; **–r *vt.*** to butter
beurrée *f.* slice of bread and butter
beurrier *m.* butter dish
beuverie *f.* drinking party
bévatron *m.* bevatron
bévue *f.* blunder, big mistake, gaff
biais *m.* bias, slant; **— *a.*** oblique; **en — at an angle, askew**
biaiser *vi.* to go at an angle; hedge
bibelot *m.* knicknack, trinket

biberon *m.* nursing bottle; drinker
Bible *f.* Bible
bibliobus *m.* mobile library
bibliographe *m.* bibliographer
bibliographie *f.* bibliography
bibliographique *a.* bibliographical
bibliophile *m.* bibliophile
bibliothécaire *m. & f.* librarian
bibliothèque *f.* library; book shelves, bookcase
biblique *a.* Biblical
bicamérisme *m.* (pol.) two-house system
bicéphale *a.* two-headed
biceps *m.* biceps
biche *f.* hind, darling
bichlamar *m.* pidgin English
bichon *m.* lapdog
bichonner *vt.* to curl; (fig.) caress
bicoque *f.* shack, hut
bicorne *a.* two-cornered
bicyclette *f.* bicycle
bidet *m.* nag, horse; sawhorse; sitz-bath
bidon *m.* can (for liquids); canteen
bief *m.* millrace; section of a canal (between two locks)
bielle *f.* (mach.) connecting rod, tie rod
bien *adv.* well; rightly; indeed; properly; quite; much, many; — **que** although; **si — que** so that; **tant — que mal** indifferently, so-so; — *m.* good; fortune; estate; welfare
bien-aimé *m.* beloved
bein-être *m.* well-being
bienfaisance *f.* charity, beneficence
bienfaisant *a.* charitable; beneficial
bienfait *m.* benefit, favor
bienfaiteur *m.* benefactor
bien-fonds *m.* real property, real estate
bienheureux *a.* very happy; blessed
biennal *a.* biennial
bienséance *f.* propriety, convention
bienséant *a.* proper, appropriate, fitting
bientôt *adv.* soon; shortly; **à —** goodbye, see you soon
bienveillance *f.* kindness, benevolence
bienveillant *a.* kind, benevolent
bienvenu *a.* welcome; **-e** *f.* welcome
bière *f.* coffin; bier
biffer *vt.* to cross out; cancel
bifteck *m.* beefsteak
bifurcation *f.* fork in a road; (rail.) junction; turnoff
bifurquer *vt. & vi.* to fork; bifurcate
bigame *a.* bigamous; — *m.* bigamist
bigamie *f.* bigamy
bigarreau *m.* white-heart cherry
bigarrer *vt.* to speckle
bigarrure *f.* mixture of colors or designs
bigle *f.* beagle hound; — *a.* squint-eyed
bigler *vi.* to squint

bigot *a.* bigotted, excessively devout; hypocritical; — *m.* bigot; hypocrite
bigoterie *f.* bigotry
bigoudi *m.* small hair curler
bijou *m.* jewel, gem, stone
bijouterie *f.* jewelry; jeweler's shop
bijoutier *m.* jeweler
bilan *m.* balance sheet
bilatéral *a.* bilateral
bile *m.* bile, gall; (fig.) anger
biliaire *a.* biliary, bilious
bilieux *a.* bilious; choleric
bilingue *a.* bilingual
billard *m.* billiards; billiard table; billiard parlor
bille *f.* billiard ball; child's marble; log; block of wood; rolling pin; (mech.) ball; **stylo à —** *m.* ballpoint pen
billet *m.* note; bill; ticket; card; — **d'aller et retour** round-trip ticket; — **simple** one-way ticket; — **de correspondance** transfer
billevesée *f.* nonsense; fantasy
billon *m.* copper coin
billot *m.* block; chopping block
bimensuel *a.* semi-monthly
bimestriel *a.* bimonthly
bimoteur *a.* bimotor, two-engine
binaire *a.* binary
bine, binette *f.* hoe
binocle *m.* pince-nez, eye glasses (nose)
biochimie *f.* biochemistry
biogenèse *f.* biogenesis
biogénétique *f.* biogenetics
biographe *m.* biographer
biographique *a.* biographical
biologie *f.* biology; — **moléculaire** molecular biology
biologique *a.* biological
biologiste *m.* biologist
biophysique *a.* biophysical
biopsie *f.* biopsy
bipède *a.* two-footed; — *n.* biped
biplace *m. & f. & a.* two-seater
biplan *m.* biplane
Birman *m. & a.* Burmese; **-ie** *f.* Burma
bis *adv.* encore; (mus.) repeat, twice; house numbers(A, ½)
bis aïeul *m.* great-grandfather; **-e** *f.* great-grandmother
bisannuel *a.* biennial
biscornu *a.* two-horned; odd; (fig.) bizarre
biscotte *f.* rusk
biscuit *m.* cooky, wafer, cracker; unglazed porcelain
bise *f.* cold wind; north wind
biseau *m.* beveled edge; bevelling tool
biseauter *vt.* to bevel; mark cards (to cheat)
biser *vt.* redye; — *vi.* spoil, degenerate;

get brown (cereals)
bismuth *m.* bismuth
bisque *f.* rich, creamy soup
bissac *m.* bag, wallet
bisser *vt.* to give or ask for an encore
bissextile *a.*, **année —** *f.* leap year
bistouri *m.* scalpel
bistre *a.* bistre, black-brown; **-r** *vt.* to brown
bisulfite *m.* bisulfate
bisut(h) *m.* freshman
bitume *m.* asphalt; bitumen; **—** *vt.* to asphalt
bitumineux *a.* bituminous
bivouac *m.* bivouac, bivouac area
bizarre *a.* odd; strange, bizarre
bizarrerie *f.* oddness, whim; oddity
blackbouler *vt.* to blackball
blafard *a.* pale, pasty
blague *f.* tobacco pouch; joke; **sans —**? really?
blaguer *vi.* to joke; hoax
blagueur *m.* jokester, joker
blaireau *m.* badger; shaving brush
blâmable *a.* censurable, blameworthy
blâme *m.* blame; disapproval
blâmer *vt.* to find fault with; blame
blanc (blanche) *a.* white; blank; innocent; clean; (print.) space free of type; **fer —** *m.* tin; **—** *m.* white, whiteness (linen); **— de chaux** whitewash
blanchâtre *a.* whitish
blanche *f.* (mus.) half note
blancheur *f.* whiteness
blanchir *vt. & vi.* to whiten, bleach; wash; scald (raw food)
blanchissage *m.* laundering, washing
blanchisserie *f.* laundry
blanchisseuse *f.* laundress
blanc-manger *m.* blancmange pudding
blanquette *f.*, **— de veau** veal in white sauce
blasé *a.* bored
blason *m.* coat of arms; heraldry
blasphématoire *a.* blasphemous
blasphème *m.* blasphemy
blasphémer *vi.* to blaspheme
blatte *f.* cockroach
blé *m.* wheat; grain; **— noir** buckwheat
blême *a.* wan, livid, pale
blêmir *vi.* to turn pale
blèse *a.* lisping
bléser *vi.* to lisp
blessant *a.* offensive, mortifying; injurious
blesser *vt.* to wound, hurt, offend; injure
blessure *f.* wound; injury
blet *a.* overripe
blettir *vi.* to overripen
bleu *a.* blue: **—** *m.* blue; bruise; coveralls;

(coll.) draftee; bluing; **petit —** letter sent by pneumatic tube
bleuâtre *a.* bluish
bleuet *m.* cornflower
bleuir *vt.* to make blue; **—** *vi.* to become blue
bleuté *a.* bluish
blindage *m.* armor plate
blindé *a.* armor-plated, armored
bloc *m.* block; lump; tablet, pad of paper; **bloc; en —** in a lump, in large quantities
blocaille *f.* rubble
blockhaus *m.* blockhouse
bloc-notes *m.* writing pad, note pad
blocus *m.* blockade
blond *a.* blond; fair
bloquer *vt.* to blockade; block, obstruct
blottir *v.*, **se —** to nestle; crouch; huddle
blouse *f.* blouse; smock; jacket
blouson *m.* jacket (sport or military)
bluette *f.* spark, flash
bluffer *vt. & vi.* to bluff
blutage *m.* act of bluing
bluter *vt.* to sift flour
blutoir *m.* sifter
boa *m.* boa
bobine *f.* bobbin; spool; reel; coil; roll
bobiner *vt.* to roll, spool, wind
bocage *m.* grove, small woods
bocager *a.* wooded
bocal *m.* bottle (druggist's), jar; fishbowl
bock *m.* beer, glass of beer
bœuf *m.* ox; beef; steer; **— bourguignon** beef in wine sauce
boggie *m.* (rail.) truck, bogie
Bohême *m.* Bohemia
bohème *f.* (fig.) Bohemia; **— a. & n.** bohemian, person living from day to day; beatnik; gypsy
bohémien *a.* Bohemian; **—** *m.*; gypsy; vagabond; unconventional person
Bohémien *m.* Bohemian
boire *vt.* to drink; swallow an insult; absorb; **— un coup** to have a drink; **—** *m.* drink, drinking
bois *m.* wood; forest; antlers; **— de lit** bedstead; **— contreplaqué** plywood; **— fondu** plastic wood
boisé *a.* wooded; panelled
boiserie *f.* woodwork; panelling, wainscoting
boisseau *m.* bushel
boisson *f.* beverage, drink
boite *f.* box; can, tin; **— de nuit** night club
boiter *vi.* to limp
boiteux *a.* lame
boîter *m.* watch case
boitte *f.* fish bait
bol *m.* bowl; bolus, large pill
bolchevisme *m.* Bolshevism

boléro *m.* bolero; bolero jacket
bolide *m.* meteorite; (fig.) racing car
Bolivie *f.* Bolivia; **—n** *m. & a.* Bolivian
bombance *f.* feasting
bombarde *f.* mortar; ancestor of oboe
bombarder *vt.* to bombard, bomb
bombardier *m.* bomber (plane); bombardier
bombe *f.* bomb, shell; feast; **— de cobalt** cobalt bomb; **— glacée** molded ice cream; **faire la —** to have a gay time
bombé *a.* arched, rounded
bomber *vt.* to make round; **—** *vi.* to become round
bon *a.* good; kind; sound; wholesome; valid; fir; **à quoi —?** what's the use (of)?; **à la —ne heure!** fine!; well done; **de —ne heure** early; **—** *m.* (com.) bond, coupon
bonace *f.* calm sea; calm
bonasse *a.* simple; innocent; good-natured; **—ment** *adv.* simply; simple-mindedly
bonbec *m.* gossip
bonbon *m.* candy
bonbonne *f.* demijohn
bonbonnière *f.* candy dish
bond *m.* bound, leap; bounce
bonde *f.* bung hole; bung; plug; sluice gate
bondé *a.* crowded, jammed
bondir *vi.* to bound, leap; bounce
bondon *m.* bung; plug
bonheur *m.* happiness; good fortune, luck; **par —** luckily
bonhomie *f.* kindness; credulity
bonhomme *m.* fellow, good-natured man
boni *m.* surplus; bonus
bonification *f.* improvement; discount
bonifier *vt.* to improve; give a discount to
boniment *m.* misleading talk, empty talk; quack's show
bonite *f.* bonito
bonjour *m.* good day, good morning, hello
bonne *f.* maid, servant girl
bonnement *adv.* honestly; truly; **tout —** simply; plainly
bonnet *m.* cap; woman's hat; **gros —** (fig. & coll.) important person
bonneterie *f.* hosiery, knitwear
bonsoir *m.* good evening; good night
bonté *f.* goodness, kindness
borborygme *m.* growling of the stomach
bord *m.* edge, brink; shore; **à —** on board; **— de la mer** seashore; **faux —** *m.* (naut.) list; **hors —** outboard
bordage *m.* boards, planking; bulwarks; curb
bordeaux *m.* Bordeaux wine, claret
bordée *f.* (naut.) broadside, volley; tack; watch
bordel *m.* brothel

bordelais *a.* from Bordeaux; **sauce —e** *f.* Bordeau wine sauce
border *vt.* to border, edge; tuck in (bed); **— un lit** make a bed
bordereau *m.* itemized account; memorandum, note
bordure *f.* border; curb
bore *m.* boron
boréal *a.* northern
borgne *a.* one-eyed; suspicious (in appearance)
borinage *m.* soft coal mining *or* miner
borique *a.* boric
borne *f.* boundary, limit, milestone
borné *a.* limited, narrow
borner *vt.* to bound, limit
bosquet *m.* small wood, grove
bosse *f.* hump, bump, hunch
bosseler *vt.* to emboss
bossu *a.* hunchbacked
bot *a.,* clubfooted; **—** *m.* clubfooted person; **pied —** *m.* clubfoot
botanique *f.* botany; **—** *a.* botanical
botte *f.* boot; bunch, bundle; sword thrust
botteler *vt.* to bunch, tie in bunches
botter *vt.* to shoe, put on shoes; to boot, kick
bottier *m.* bootmaker (to order)
bottine *f.* high shoe (with buttons or elastic)
boubouler *vi.* to hoot like an owl
bouc *m.* billy goat; **— émissaire** scapegoat
boucan *m.* smokehouse; (coll.) noise, tumult; **—er** *vt.* to smoke meat
boucanier *m.* buccaneer
boucharde *f.* roller; hammer (having points on the head)
bouche *f.* mouth; muzzle of a gun; opening; **— d'incendie** fire hydrant
bouchée *f.* mouthful; patty filled with creamed food
boucher *m.* butcher
boucher *vt.* to cork; block, stop up
boucherie *f.* butcher shop; slaughter, butchery
bouche-trou *m.* stopgap
bouchon *m.* cork, stopper
boucle *f.* buckle; curl; bend; loop, bow; **— d'oreille** earring
boucler *vt.* to buckle; curl, loop; tie; **—** *vi.* to curl; buckle
bouclier *m.* shield
bouddhisme *m.* Buddhism
bouddhiste *m.* Buddhist
bouder *vi.* to pout, sulk
boudeur *a.* pouting
boudin *m.* blood sausage; spring (coach); flange
boudiner *vt.* to twist

boudoir *m.* boudoir
boue *f.* mud, filth; (fig.) humiliation, abjection
bouée *f.* buoy; — **de sauvetage** life preserver
boueur *m.* garbage collector
boueux *a.* muddy
bouffant *a.* puffed
bouffe *a.* comical; **opéra** — light opera
bouffée *f.* puff; gust
bouffer *vt.* to puff; (coll.) gulp down food; — *vi.* to swell, puff
bouffette *f.* bow of ribbon; tassel (on harness)
bouffi *a.* swollen, puffed, bloated
bouffir *vt.* & *vi.* to expand, swell, bloat
bouffissure *f.* swelling; extreme vanity
bouffon *m.* clown; — *a.* comic, burlesque
bouffonnerie *f.* buffoonery, burlesque
bouge *m.* (coll.) burlesque; den; evil place; bulge
bougeoir *m.* short candlestick
bouger *vi.* to budge, stir, move
bougie *f.* candle; sparkplug; probe
bougran *m.* buckram
bouillabaisse *f.* fish stew
bouillant *a.* boiling; (fig.) ardent
bouilleur *m.* still (liquor); small nuclear reactor
bouilli *m.* boiled meat
bouillie *f.* cooked cereal, pap; pulp
bouillir *vi.* to boil; bubble
bouilloire *f.* teakettle
bouillon *m.* broth; **à gros** **-s** at a rolling boil
bouillonnement *m.* boiling; (fig.) agitation
bouillonner *vi.* to boil up
bouillotte *f.* hot-water bottle
boulanger *m.* baker; — *vi.* to bake bread
boulangerie *f.* bakery
boule *f.* ball
bouleau *m.* birch
bouledogue *m.* bulldog
bouler *vt.* to roll like a ball; (coll.) to muff, fail at; send (someone) packing
boulet *m.* cannon ball
boulette *f.* little ball, pellet; — **de viande** meatball
bouleversement *m.* upset, upheaval
bouleverser *vt.* to overthrow; upset
boulier *m.* kind of abacus
boulingrin *m.* lawn (edged with trees); bowling green
boulodrome *m.* bowling alley, bowling green
boulon *m.* metal bolt; **-ner** *vt.* to bolt
boulot *a.* fat, round; — *m.* (coll.) work; cylindrical loaf of bread
bouquet *m.* bunch, bouquet; clump; aroma (of wine); large shrimp; hare

bouquetier *m.* vase
bouquetière *f.* flower seller
bouquiner *vi.* to shop for old books
bouquiniste *m.* dealer in old books
bourbe *f.* mire, mud, slush
bourbeux *a.* muddy
bourbier *m.* mire; difficulty
bourde *f.* fib; sham; (coll.) error, stupidity
bourdon *m.* bumblebee; great bell; bourdon; pilgrim's staff; **faux** — drone
bourdonnement *m.* buzz, buzzing
bourdonner *vi.* to buzz, hum
bourg *m.* large village, small town
bourgade *f.* little village
bourgeois *m.* bourgeois; commoner; — *a.* middle-class
bourgeoisie *f.* middle class, bourgeoisie
bourgeon *m.* bud; pimple; **-ner** *vi.* to bud
bourgeonnement *m.* budding
bourgeron *m.* smock
bourguignon *a.* from Burgundy
Bourgogne *f.* Burgundy; — *m.* Burgundy wine
bourlinguer *vi.* to roll (ship); (coll.) gad about, travel
bourrade *f.* sharp blow; poke
bourrage *m.* stuffing; cramming
bourrasque *f.* squall; fit, attack, spasm
bourre *f.* wad; stuffing
bourreau *m.* executioner
bourreler *vt.* to torment, torture
bourrelet *m.* pad; weather stripping
bourrer *vt.* to stuff, pad, cram; beat, drub
bourrique *f.* she-ass; (coll.) stupid person
bourru *a.* rough; brusque; unfermented (wine)
bourse *f.* purse, bag; scholarship; stock exchange; **-s** *pl.* scrotum
boursier *m.* scholarship student; purse maker; stock dealer
boursouflé *a.* swollen, puffed up; bombastic
boursoufler *vt.* to swell, bloat, puff up
bousculer *vt.* to jostle; throw into disorder
bouse *f.* dung
bousiller *vt.* to bungle
boussole *f.* compass
boustifaille *f.* feasting; good food
bout *m.* end, tip; bit, piece; **pousser à** — to push to the limit; **être à** — to be exhausted; **venir à** — **de** to succeed in
boutade *f.* outburst, fit; whim
boutefeu *m.* firebrand; (fig.) trouble maker
bouteille *f.* bottle; — **isolante** vacuum bottle
boutique *f.* shop
boutiquier *m.* shopkeeper
bouton *m.* button, knob, handle; bud; pimple; — **d'or** buttercup

boutonner vt. to button; — vi. to bud
boutonneux a. pimply
boutonnière f. buttonhole
bouture f. cutting (from a plant)
bouturer vi. to take root; — vt. to root (cuttings)
bouvier m. cowherd
bouvillon m. young steer
bouvreuil m. bullfinch
bovin a. bovine
bow-window m. bay window
boxe f. boxing; **-r** vi. to box; **-ur** m. boxer
boy m. houseboy
boyau m. gut, intestine, bowel; narrow passage; tube
boycotter vt. to boycott
bracelet m. bracelet; — **de caoutchouc** rubber band
bracelet-montre m. wristwatch
braconnage m. poaching
braconner vi. & vt. to poach
braconnier m. poacher
braguette f. fly (pants); codpiece
Brahmane m. Brahman
brai m. resin, pitch
braille m. Braille
brailler vi. to bawl, yell
braiment m. bray
braire vi. to bray
braise f. embers, coals
braiser vt. to braise
brancard m. stretcher; shaft
brancardier m. stretcher-bearer
branche f. branch, bough
brancher vt. to connect, plug in; — vi. perch
branchies f. pl. gills
brande f. broom (plant); brand
brandebourg m. braid; facing
brandevin m. brandy
brandir vt. to brandish; wave
brandon m. torch; firebrand
branlant a. shaking, tottering; loose
branle m. impetus; oscillation; **mettre en** — to put in motion; **-r** vt. & vi. to shake, oscillate
braquer vt. to aim, point
bras m. arm; shaft; handle; — **dessus** — **dessous** arm in arm
braser vt. to braise, solder
brasero m. brazier, charcoal burner
brasier m. brazier; very hot charcoal fire
brasiller vt. to grill over charcoal; — vi. to spark, sparkle
brassage m. brewing; mixing
brassard m. brassard, armband
brasse f. (naut.) fathom; breast stroke (swimming)
brassée f. armful; stroke (swimming)
brasser vt. to brew; mix completely;

(naut.) brace
brasserie f. brewery; bar, café
brasseur m. brewer; — **d'affaires** (fig.) one with many irons in the fire
brassière f. baby shirt; shoulder strap; breast support; — **de sauvetage** life-jacket
bravache m. braggart; bold front, false bravery; bully
bravade f. bravado
brave a. worthy; honest; courageous, brave
braver vt. to brave, face, defy
bravoure f. bravery; intrepidity
brebis f. ewe; — **galeuse** black sheep
brèche f. breach; gap
brèche-dent a. snaggle-toothed; missing one front tooth
bréchet m. breastbone (of a bird)
bredouille f. (fig.) sheepishness (as a result of returning empty-handed)
bredouiller vi. to stutter, sputter
bref (**brève**) a. brief, short; — adv. in short; — m. (eccl.) pastoral letter of the Pope
brelan m. three-of-a-kind; gaming house
breloque f. trinket, watch charm; **battre la** — to work irregularly; (fig.) go off the track
brème f. bream; flat calm-water fish
Brésil m. Brazil
Brésilien m. & a. Brazilian
Bretagne f. Brittany
bretelle f. sling, strap; (mil.) line of defense; **-s** pl. suspenders
Breton m. & a. Breton
bretzel m. pretzel
breuvage m. brew, potion; beverage
brevet m. diploma; license; patent
brevetable a. patentable
breveté a. certified, approved, licensed
breveter vt. to patent
bréviaire m. (eccl.) breviary
bribe f. scrap, bit; oddments
bric-à-brac m. bric-a-brac, odds and ends
brick m. brig (ship)
bricole f. trifle; strap, harness; something without importance
bricoler vi. to putter; — vt. (coll.) to cook up
bricoleur m. putterer
bride f. bridle; strap; clamp; **à** — **abattue** at full speed
brider vt. to bridle, check
bridge m. bridge (cards, teeth)
bridger vi. to play bridge
bridgeur m. bridge player
brièvement adv. briefly
brièveté f. brevity
brigade f. brigade; **général de** — m. briga-

dier general
brigadier *m.* corporal (cavalry)
brigand *m.* robber, brigand
brigue *f.* plot; **−r** *vt.* to plot to obtain
brigueur *m.* plotter, schemer
brillamment *adv.* brilliantly
brillant *a.* brilliant; sparkling; **—** *m.* brilliance; diamond
brillantine *f.* brilliantine
briller *vi.* to shine, sparkle, glitter
brimade *f.* hazing
brimborion *m.* small object of little value
brimer *vt.* to haze
brin *m.* bit, sprig; **— d'herbe** blade of grass
brindille *f.* twig; sprig
brio *m.* spirit
brioche *f.* brioche; rich, light roll
brique *f.* brick
briquet *m.* lighter; **pierre à —** *f.* flint
briquetage *m.* brickwork
briqueteur *m.* bricklayer
briquetier *m.* brickmaker
briquette *f.* fuel briquette
brisant *m.* breakers, reef
brise *f.* breeze
brisé *a.* broken; folding; jagged; **chaise −e** *f.* folding chair; **pâte −e** *f.* puff paste
brise-bise *m.* weather stripping; café curtains
brise-glace *m.* ice breaker
brise-jet *m.* deflector
brise-lames *m.* breakwater
briser *vt.* to break, shatter, crush
brisque *f.* service stripe (army)
bristol *m.* cardboard
brisure *f.* break; joint
britannique *a.* British
broc *m.* jug
brocanteur *m.* secondhand dealer
brocard *m.* taunt, gibe
brocart *m.* brocade
brocatelle *f.* imitation brocade; variegated marble
broche *f.* brooch (jewelry); spit; spindle; peg
broché *a.* brocaded; **livre —** *m.* paperbound book
brocher *vt.* to brocade; bind in paper; sew a binding; be slipshod (in working); nail the shoe of a horse
brochet *m.* pike (fish)
brochette *f.* skewer
brocheuse *f.* stapler
brochure *f.* pamphlet, brochure
brocoli *m.* broccoli
brodequin *m.* buskin; torture boot
broder *vt.* to embroider; **−ie** *f.* embroidery
brome *m.* bromine
bromure *f.* bromide

broncher *vi.* to stumble, falter; flinch; budge
bronches *m. pl.* bronchial tubes
bronchite *f.* bronchitis
bronzer *vt.* to tan; bronze
brook *m.* brook; waterjump (steeplechase
broque *m.* broccoli
broquette *f.* tack
brossage *m.* brushing
brosse *f.* brush; **−r** *vt.* to brush
brou *m.* walnut shell
brouet *m.* thin broth, stew
brouette *f.* wheelbarrow
brouillage *m.* radio jamming
brouillard *m.* fog, mist
brouille *f.* quarreling, falling out
brouillé *a.* confused, mixed up; on the outs with; **œufs −s** *m. pl.* scrambled eggs
brouiller *vt.* to mix up, tangle, confuse; **se —** to have a falling out, quarrel; become confused
brouillon *m.* mischief-making; rough draft; muddled person; **—** *a.* muddled
broussailles *f. pl.* brush, underbrush
broussailleux *a.* overgrown; thick, heavy
brousse *f.* brush
brouter *vt.* to graze
broyer *vt.* to grind, crush, pulverize
bru *f.* daughter-in-law
brucelles *f. pl.* tweezers
brugnon *m.* clingstone peach
bruine *f.* drizzle; **−r** *vi.* to drizzle
bruire *vi.* to sound, make a confused noise, rustle
bruissement *m.* rustling
bruit *m.* noise; rumor; uproar; fuss, ado
brulé *a.* burned; **—** *m.* smell of something burned
brûle-gueule *m.* short pipe
brûle-parfums *m.* incense burner
brûle-pourpoint *adv.* **à —** point-blank; (fig.) brusquely
brûler *vt.* to burn; singe; sting; **—** *vi.* to burn; **se — la cervelle** to blow out one's brains
brûleur *m.* burner
brûloir *m.* roaster
brûlure *f.* burn; scald
brumailleux *a.* misty
brume *f.* mist, fog; **−r** *vi.* to be foggy
brumeux *a.* misty, foggy
brun *a.* brown; dark; **—** *m.* brown; **−e** *f.* twilight
brunâtre *a.* brownish
brunet *a.* brownish; **−te** *f.* brunette
bruni *a.* burnished; **—** *m.* polish
brunir *vt.* to burnish; brown, tan; **—** *vi.* become dark; tan
brusque *a.* abrupt, brusque, blunt

brusquer *vt.* to treat roughly; be abrupt with

brut *a.* rough, raw; rude; crude; dry

brutal *a.* brutal, brutish; coarse

brutaliser *vt.* to treat roughly

brutalité *f.* brutality, brutishness; cruelty

Bruxelles, Brussels; choux de — *m. pl.* Brussels sprouts

bruyamment *adv.* noisily; clamorously

bruyant *a.* noisy, loud

bruyère *f.* heath; (bot.) heather; briar

buanderie *f.* laundry room

buandière *f.* laundress

bubonique *a.* bubonic; **peste —** *f.* bubonic plague

bûche *f.* firewood, log; (fig.) stupid person; **— de Noël,** log-shaped Christmas cake

bûcher *vi.* to chop wood; work hard; **—** *m.* woodshed; stake; pyre

bûcheron *m.* woodcutter

bûchette *f.* stick of wood

bûcheur *m.* hard worker, eager beaver (U.S. coll.)

bucolique *a.* bucolic

budgétaire *a.* budgetary

buée *f.* steam; mist, vapor

buffet *m.* buffet; refreshment room; sideboard

buffle *m.* buffalo

building *m.* very large, modern building

buis *m.* boxwood

buisson *m.* bush; thicket

buissonier *a.* hidden in bushes; (fig.) **faire l'école —ère** to play hooky

bulbe *f.* bulb

bulbeux *a.* bulbous

Bulgare *n. & a.* Bulgarian

Bulgarie *f.* Bulgaria

bulle *f.* bubble; (eccl.) papal bull; **papier — ** *m.* wrapping paper

bulletin *m.* bulletin; ballot; **— de bagages** baggage check; **— scolaire** report card

bure *f.* monk's cloth; mine shaft

bureau *m.* office; writing desk; bureau; officers

bureaucrate *m.* bureaucrat

bureaucratie *f.* bureaucracy

bureaucratique *a.* bureaucratic

burette *f.* cruet; burette; oilcan

burin *m.* engraving; burin, engraving tool

burlesque *a.* comical

busc *m.* metal stay, whalebone

buse *f.* buzzard; millrace; shaft, tube

business *m.* work; complicated business

busqué *a.* arched; aquiline

buste *m.* bust (sculpture)

but *m.* mark, aim, purpose, design; goal; **de — en blanc** *adv.* abruptly; point-blank

butane *m.* butane

buté *a.* obstinate, unmoving, set

butée *f.* abutment

buter *vi.* to abut; **— contre** bump into, stumble on; **—** *rt.* to prop, support

butin *m.* booty; prize

butiner *vi.* to pillage; **—** *vt.* to gather nectar

butoir *m.* buffer

butor *m.* (fig.) lout, good-for-nothing

butte *f.* bluff; hill; **en —** à exposed to

butter *vt.* to heap earth around (asparagus, celery)

buvable *a.* drinkable

buvard *m.* blotter

buvette *f.* bar; taproom

buveur *m.* drinker; drunkard

Byzance *f.* Byzantium

Byzantin *m. & a.* Byzantine

C

ça *pron.* (coll.) that; **c'est —** that's it

çà *adv.* here; **— et là** here and there

cabale *f.* plot, cabal

cabaler *vi.* to plot, cabal

cabalistique *a.* cabalistic; mysterious

cabane *f.* cabin; hut; kennel

cabanon *m.* cabin; padded cell

cabas *m.* basket

cabestan *m.* capstan

cabillaud *m.* fresh cod

cabine *f.* boat cabin; booth; beach cabana

cabinet *m.* closet; study; lawyer's office; cabinet; collection; **-s** *pl.* toilets, bathrooms

câble *m.* cable

câbler *vi.* to twist; cord; send a cable

câblier *m.* cable-layer

câblogramme *m.* cable

cabochard *a.* obstinate

caboche *f.* hobnail; (coll.) big head

cabochon *m.* upholstery nail

cabot in *m.* strolling comedian; ham actor

cabrer *vt.* put into a passion; **se —** *vi.* to rear up

cabri *m.* kidskin

cabriole *f.* caper

cabrioler *vi.* to caper

cabriolet *m.* gig; **place de —** *m.* cabstand

cacao *m.* cocoa

cacaouète, cacaouette, cacauète *f.* peanut

cache *f.* cache, hiding place

cache-cache *m.* hide-and-go-seek

cachemire *m.* cashmere

cache-nez *m.* scarf, muffler

cacher *vt.* to hide, conceal

cache-radiateur *m.* radiator cover

cache-sexe *m.* loin cloth, shorts

cachet *m.* seal, distinctive mark; fee

cacheter vt. to seal; close an envelope
cachette f. hiding place; **en — ** adv. secretly
cachot m. dungeon; cell
cacophonie f. cacophony
cadastre m. land-survey register
cadavre m. cadaver, corpse
cadeau m. gift, present
cadenas m. padlock; **—ser** vt. to padlock
cadencer vt. to cadence; put into rhythm
cadet a. younger, junior; **— ** m. younger son; caddie (golf)
cadmium m. cadmium
cadrage m. framing
cadran m. dial; **— solaire** sundial
cadre m. frame; limit(s); (mil.) cadre
cadrer vi. to conform, agree, tally
caduc a. old, decrepit; null and void
caducée m. (med.) caduceus, symbol of Hermes
caducité f. decrepitude
cafard m. hypocrite; (coll.) melancholy; cockroach
café m. coffee; coffee shop, café
caféier m. coffee plant
caféière f. coffee plantation
caféine f. caffeine
cafetière f. coffeepot
cage f. cage; stair well; casing
cagnard a. indolent, lazy
cagneux a. knock-kneed
cagot m. & a. bigot; bigoted
cagoule f. hood, cowl
cahier m. notebook
cahot m. jerk, bump, jolt
cahoter vi. to jerk, bump, jolt
cahoteux a. bumpy
cahute f. hut
caille f. quail
caillé m. curdled milk, curds
caillebotis m. (mil.) duckboard; wooden trellis
cailler vt. & vi. to curdle, clot
caillot m. blood clot
caillou m. pebble
cailloutage m. paving with pebbles, gravelling
caillouteux a. pebbly
cailloutis m. mass of broken stones, gravel
caiman m. crocodile
caisse f. chest; till; cashier's desk; chassis, body; **— d'épargne** savings bank; **grosse — ** bass drum
caissier m. cashier
caisson m. caisson, ammunition wagon; **maladie des —s** f. (med.) the bends
cajoler vt. to wheedle, cajole
cajolerie f. wheedling, cajolery
calamine f. calamine; sludge
calamiteux a. calamitous

calandre f. mangle, roller
calcaire a. calcarious, chalky; **— ** m. limestone; **eau — ** f. hard water
calcédoine f. chalcedony
calciner vt. to burn, reduce to powder
calcium m. calcium
calcul m. calculation; calculus; (med.) stone
calculateur m. calculator; **— ** a. calculating
calculatrice digitale f. digital computer
calculer vt. to calculate; **machine à — ** f. adding machine
cale f. wedge; (naut.) hold; **— sèche** dry dock
calé a. smart
calebasse f. gourd
calèche f. old-style open carriage
caleçon m. undershorts; swimming trunks
calembour m. pun
calendrier m. calendar
caler vt. to prop up; give in; stop; stall, jam
calfater vt. to caulk
calfeutrer vt. to stop up; **se — to shut** oneself up
calibre m. caliber, quality; cylinder diameter (gun)
calibrer vt. to calibrate
calice m. chalice; calyx
calicot m. calico
calife m. caliph
californium m. californium
califourchon, (à) adv. astride, astraddle
câlin a. coaxing, cajoling
câliner vt. to coax; cajole
calleux a. callous; callused
calligraphie f. calligraphy, penmanship
callosité f. callus
calmant m. (med.) sedative
calmar m. squid
calme a. & n. calm, calmness
calmer vt. to calm, appease, quiet; **se — ** to calm down
calomnie f. calumny, slander
calorifère m. radiator; heater
calorifuge a. heat-retaining; insulating
calot m. cap, policeman's hat
calotte f. skullcap; (coll.) blow on the head
calotter vt. to hit on the head
calquer vt. to trace, copy
calumet m. pipe, peace pipe
calvados m. applejack
calvaire m. Calvary; Stations of the Cross
calviniste n. & a. Calvinist
calvitie f. baldness
camarade m. & f. comrade, friend
camaraderie f. companionship
camard a. snub-nosed
Cambodge m. Cambodia
cambouis m. sludge; axle grease

cambrer *vt.* to curve, arch
cambrioler *vt.* to burgle
cambrioleur *m.* burglar
cambrure *f.* arch; curve
cambuse *f.* (naut.) storeroom; canteen
came *f.* cam
camée *m.* cameo
caméléon *m.* chameleon
camélia *m.* camellia
camelot *m.* peddler; paper boy
camelote *f.* junk, rubbish
camembert *m.* cheese of Camembert
caméra *f.* camera (movies, pictures) television camera
camion *m.* truck; paint bucket
camion-citerne *m.* tank truck
camionnage *m.* trucking
camionnette *f.* light truck; **— sanitaire** mobile health unit
camionneur *m.* truck driver, teamster
camisole *f.* camisole; **— de force** strait jacket
camomille *f.* camomile
camouflage *m.* camouflage
camoufler *vt.* to camouflage
camp *m.* camp; camp site; **ficher le —** (coll.) to clear out
campagnard *m.* country dweller; **— a.** rustic
campagne *f.* country; countryside; campaign
campé *a.* built, constructed; established
campement *m.* encampment
camper *vt. & vi.* to encamp
campeur *m.* camper
camphre *m.* camphor
camus *a.* flat-nosed
Canada *m.* Canada
Canadien *n. & a.* Canadian
canadienne *f.* mackintosh, jacket; canoe with raised ends
canaille *f.* rabble; scoundrel
canal *m.* canal; irrigation drain
canalisation *f.* canalization; canal system
canapé *m.* sofa; canapé
canard *m.* duck; rumor; newspaper; sugar soaked in alcohol
canari *m.* canary
cancan *m.* can-can (dance); gossip
cancaner *vi.* to quack; gossip
cancer *m.* cancer; **-eux** *a.* cancerous
candélabre *m.* candelabrum; sconce
candeur *f.* candor, innocence
candi *m.* rock candy; **— a.** candied
candidat *m.* candidate
candidature *f.* candidacy
candide *a.* naïve, innocent
candir *v.*, **se** — to crystallize; go to sugar
cane *f.* female duck
caneton *m.* duckling

canette *f.* cane; beer bottle
canevas *m.* canvas
canezou *m.* lace blouse, usually sleeveless
caniche *f.* poodle
canicule *f.* dog days
canif *m.* penknife
canin *a.* canine; **dent –e** *f.* canine tooth
cannaie *f.* sugar-cane plantation
canne *f.* cane; reed; **— à pêche** fishing rod
canneler *vt.* to flute (a column)
cannelle *f.* cinnamon; spigot
cannelure *f.* fluting (of a column)
canner *vt.* to cane a chair
cannibale *n.* cannibal
canoë *m.* canoe
canon *m.* cannon; barrel of a gun; **— m.** (eccl.) decree; **— a.** canon; **droit — m.** canon law
cañon *m.* canyon
canonial, canonique *a.* canonical
canoniser *vt.* to canonize
canonnade *f.* volley, barrage
canonner *vt.* to fire cannons on
canonnier *m.* cannoneer
canonnière *f.* popgun; gunboat
canot *m.* rowboat, dinghy; **— de sauvetage** lifeboat
canotier *m.* rower; sailor hat, straw hat
cantaloup *m.* cantaloupe
cantate *f.* cantata
cantatrice *f.* professional singer
cantine *f.* canteen
cantique *m.* canticle, hymn
canton *m.* canton, district
cantonade *f.*, **à la — adv.** (theat.) in (to) the wings
cantonnement *m.* cantonment, billet(ing)
cantonner *vt.* to billet; district
canular *m.* practical joke
canule *f.* tube of a syringe
caoutchouc *m.* rubber
caoutchoutier *a.* rubber
cap *m.* cape, headland; (naut.) course
capacité *f.* capacity; ability; aptitude
cape *f.* cape; **rire sous —** to laugh up one's sleeve
capillaire *a.* capillary; **vaisseau — m.** capillary
capitaine *m.* captain
capital *m.* capital; stock; **— a.** capital; main, principal
capitale *f.* chief city, capital; capital letter
capitaliste *m.* capitalist; **— a.** capitalistic
capitation *f.* poll tax
capiteux *a.* heady wine or beer
capitonner *vt.* to stuff, upholster
capitulation *f.* capitulation, surrender
capituler *vt.* to capitulate
capon *a.* shameful, bashful; **— m.** coward, sneak

caporal *m.* corporal; shag (tobacco)
capot *m.* (auto.) hood; cover; casing; — *a.* trickless (cards); confused
capotage *m.* (auto.) overturning
capote *f.* hooded cloak; (mil.) greatcoat; (auto.) top of convertible
capoter *vi.* (auto.) to turn over; (naut.) capsize
câpre *f.* (bot.) caper
caprice *m.* caprice, whim
capricieux *a.* capricious
capsule *f.* capsule; bottle cap; pod; percussion cap
capsuler *vt.* to cap a bottle; — *vi.* to misfire
capter *vt.* to obtain, get hold of insidiously; to tap, bring in a water supply; (rad.) to tune in
captieux *a.* insidious; specious
captif *a. & n.* captive
captivant *a.* captivating
captiver *vt.* to captivate
captivité *f.* captivity
capture *f.* capture; —r *vt.* to capture
capuchon *m.* hood; cover; cap
capucine *f.* nasturtium; Capuchin nun
caque *f.* keg, barrel
caquet *m.* cackling; gossip, slander
caquetage *m.* cackling; gossiping
caqueter *vi.* to cackle; gossip
car *conj.* for, because; — *m.* sightseeing bus
carabe *m.* beetle
carabine *f.* carbine, rifle
carabinier *m.* cavalryman, rifleman; Italian policeman
caraco *m.* loose bodice; jacket
caractère *m.* character; feature; nature
caractériser *vt.* to characterize; distinguish
carafe *f.* decanter, bottle, carafe
carafon *m.* small carafe
Caraïbe *n. & a.* Carib; Mer — *f.* Caribbean Sea
carambolage *m.* jostling, bumping
caramboler *vi.* to carom (billiards)
caramel *m.* drop, chewy candy; — mou caramel
caraméliser *vt.* to caramelize
carapace *f.* turtle shell, carapace
caravane *f.* caravan; convoy; house trailer
caravansérail *m.* caravansary
caravelle *f.* (naut.) caravel
carbonate *m.* carbonate
carbonation *f.* carbonation
carbone *m.* carbon; — 14 (chem.) carbon 14; papier — *m.* carbon paper
carboné *a.* carbonated
carbonique *a.* carbonic

carboniser *vt.* to carbonize
carbonnade *f.* stew, pot roast
carborundum *m.* carborundum
carburant *m.* motor fuel
carburateur *m.* (auto.) carburetor
carbure *m.* carbide
carburéacteur *m.* jet fuel
carcasse *f.* carcass; skeleton
carcinogénique *a.* (med.) carcinogenic
cardamome *m.* cardamon
cardan *m.* (mech.) universal joint
carder *vt.* to card wool or flax
cardiaque *a.* cardiac; — *n.* heart patient
cardinal *m. & a.* cardinal
cardiographe *m.* cardiograph; — électrique electrocardiograph
carême *m.* Lent
carême-prenant *m.* Shrovetide
carence *f.* lack; failure
carène *f.* hull
caréner *vt.* to careen
caresse *f.* caress; endearment
caresser *vt.* to caress, fondle
cargaison *f.* cargo, shipload
cargo *m.* freighter, cargo ship
cari *m.* curry powder
caricature *f.* caricature
caricaturer *vt.* to caricature
caricaturiste *m.* caricaturist
carie *f.* caries, decay; —r *vt.* to decay
carillonner *vi.* to chime
carlingue *f.* (avi.) cockpit
carmin *m. & a.* carmine
carnage *m.* carnage
carnassier *a.* carniverous
canassière *f.* bag for game
carnation *f.* flesh coloring; flesh color
carnaval *m.* carnival
carné *a.* flesh-colored; meaty
carnet *m.* notebook; ticket book; — de chèques checkbook
carnier *m.* hunting sack
carnivore *a.* carnivorous
carolingien *a.* Carolingian
carotide *f. & a.* carotid
carotte *f.* carrot; sampling (of rock from a mine)
carpe *f.* carp
carpette *f.* rug, mat
carquois *m.* quiver (for arrows)
carre *f.* shape; crown; breadth
carré *a.* square; sensible; firm; obstinate; — *m.* square; patch; — de papier slip of paper
carreau *m.* tile; flagstone; diamond (at cards); pane of glass; à —x checked;
carrefour *m.* crossroads
carrelage *m.* tiling, flooring
carreler *vt.* to tile
carrément *adv.* squarely; frankly

carrer *vt.* to square
carrier *m.* quarry worker
carrière *f.* career, course; race; quarry; open-pit mine
carriole *f.* cart
carrossable *a.* passable for vehicles
carrosse *m.* coach, carriage
carrosserie *f.* (auto.) body
carrousel *m.* cavalry parade; carousel
carrure *f.* width (of shoulders)
cartable *m.* cardboard portfolio; briefcase
carte *f.* card; map; chart; menu; jeu de —s *m.* deck of cards; — **blanche** free hand; — **grise** automobile registration
cartel *m.* wall clock; cartel, monopoly, trust; challenge
carte-lettre *f.* correspondence card
carter *m.* case, casing; (auto.) crankcase; bicycle-chain guard
cartésien *a.* cartesian, relative to Descartes
cartilagineux *a.* cartilagenous
cartographe *m.* cartographer, mapmaker
cartomancie *f.* fortune telling with cards
carton *m.* cardboard; cardboard box; cartoon
carton-pâte *m.* papier-mâché
cartonnage *m.* cardboard construction; cardboard binding
cartonner *vt.* to bind in cardboard
cartonnier *m.* cardboard file; chest of cardboard drawers
cartouche *f.* cartridge; cartouche; — **chargée à balle** rifle cartridge; — **chargée à plomb** shotgun shell
cartouchière *f.* cartridge bag
cas *m.* case, circumstance; matter; **en tout** — in any case, in any event; **faire peu de** — **de** to pay little attention to; consider unimportant
casanier *m.* homebody; — *a.* retired, domestic
casaque *f.* jacket; jockey's jacket
cascade *f.* cascade, waterfall
cascader *vt.* to cascade
case *f.* compartment; square, box; hut, cabin; — **postale** post-office box
caséine *f.* caseine
casemate *f.* underground fortification
caser *vt.* to get someone settled in a job; to put in order; **se** — to get settled, be established
caserne *f.* (mil.) barracks
caserner *vt.* to lodge in barracks
casier *m.* set of pigeonholes; cabinet of small drawers; — **judiciaire** police record
casque *m.* helmet; headpiece, headphones
casquette *f.* cap
cassant *a.* brittle; rigid

cassation *f.* reversal of a court decision; breaking of a noncommissioned officer; **cour de** — *f.* supreme court
casse *f.* breakage; type case; cassia
cassé *a.* broken, broken-down; hesitant voice
casse-cou *m.* daredevil; dangerous point in a road
casse-croûte *m.* snack
casse-noisette, casse-noix *m.* nutcracker
casser *vt.* to break, crack; reverse; reduce in rank
casserole *f.* saucepan
casse-tête *m.* club; cudgel; (fig.) work requiring close application
cassette *f.* strongbox
cassis *m.* black currant; black-currant liqueur; dip in a road
cassolette *f.* incense burner
cassonade *f.* brown sugar
cassoulet *m.* stew with white beans
cassure *f.* fracture, crack
castagnettes *f. pl.* castanets
caste *f.* caste, class
castor *m.* beaver
castrat *m.* something castrated
castration *f.* castration
castrer *vt.* to castrate
casuel *a.* chance, accidental; — *m.* supplementary income
casuiste *m.* casuist
cataclysme *m.* cataclysm
catacombes *f. pl.* catacombs
catafalque *m.* bier
catalepsie *f.* catalepsy
cataleptique *a.* cataleptic
catalogue *m.* catalog
cataloguer *vt.* to catalog
catalyse *f.* catalysis
catalyseur *m.* catalyst
catalytique *a.* catalytic
cataplasme *m.* poultice
catapulte *f.* catapult
cataracte *f.* cataract, waterfall
catarrhe *m.* catarrh
catastrophique *a.* catastrophic
catch *m.* wrestling
catcheur *m.* wrestler
catéchisme *m.* catechism
catégorie *f.* category
catégorique *a.* categorical
caterpillar *m.* caterpillar tread
cathartique *a.* cathartic
cathédrale *f.* cathedral
cathode *f.* cathode
catholique *m. & a.* Catholic
cati *m.* glaze, gloss
catir *vt.* to glaze
Caucasien *m. & a.* Caucasian
cauchemar *m.* nightmare

cause *f.* cause; source; reason; **à — de** on account of (law), for the sake of
causer *vt.* to cause; **— *vi.*** chat
causerie *f.* chat, talk; gossiping; unpretentious conference, informal lecture
causeur *a.* chatty, having art of conversation
causeuse *f.* love seat
caustique *m. & a.* caustic
cautérisation *f.* cauterization
cautériser *vt.* to cauterize
caution *f.* bail, security; (fig.) guarantee
cautionnement *m.* bail
cautionner *vt.* to provide bail for, bail out
cavalcade *f.* cavalcade; parade
cavalerie *f.* cavalry
cavalier *m.* horseman, rider; cavalier; gentleman; knight (chess); **— *a.*** cavalier; unceremonious; **piste cavalière** *f.* bridle path
cave *f.* cellar; crypt
caveau *m.* cellar
caver *vt.* to dig, excavate
caverne *f.* cavern; cave, den
caverneux *a.* cavernous
caviar *m.* caviar
caviarder *vt.* to cross out; censor
cavité *f.* cavity, hollow
cawcher, kasher *a.* kosher
ce, (cet) *a. m.* this, that; **— *pron.*** it, that, this; he, she; **— qui, — que** what, that which
céans *adv.* herein
ceci *pron.* this; the latter
cécité *f.* blindness
céder *vt. & vi.* to cede, yield, give up
cédille *f.* (gram.) cedilla
cédrat *m.* citron, citron tree
cèdre *m.* cedar
cédule *f.* rate, schedule
ceindre *vt.* to buckle on, gird; encircle
ceinture *f.* belt; waist, waistline; circle
cela *pron.* that, it; this; the former
célébrant *m.* priest officiating at Mass
célébration *f.* celebration; solemn commemoration
célèbre *a.* celebrated, famous
célébrer *vt.* celebrate; commemorate
célébrité *f.* celebrity
celer *vt.* to hide, conceal
céleri *m.* celery root; celery; **— en branches** celery stalks
célérité *f.* rapidity, promptness
céleste *a.* celestial, heavenly; **mécanique — *f.*** celestial mechanics
célibat *m.* celibacy; bachelorhood
célibataire *a.* unmarried; **— *m.*** bachelor
celle *pron.* the one, she; **-ci** this one; the latter; **-là** that one; the former
cellier *m.* storeroom; wine cellar

cellulaire *a.* cellular
cellule *f.* cell, cellule; **— photo-électrique** (phot.) exposure meter
celluloïd *m.* celluloid
celte *a. & m.* celt; celtic
celui *pron. m.* he, the one; **-ci** the latter, this one; **-là** the former; that one
cénacle *m.* group, club, circle
cendre *f.* ashes; **couleur de —** ashen
cendrée *f.* shot, buckshot; cinder track
cendrier *m.* ash tray
Cendrillon *f.* Cinderella
Cène *f.* Last Supper
cénobite *m.* cenobite
cénotaphe *m.* cenotaph
cens *m.* census; minimum tax for voting qualification
censé *a.* supposed, reputed; **-ment** *adv.* supposedly, reputedly
censeur *m.* censor, censurer; auditer
censurable *a.* censurable; blameworthy
censure *f.* censorship; censure; audit (govt.)
censurer *vt.* to censor; censure, criticize, find fault with
cent *a. & m.* one hundred; **pour —** per cent
centenaire *m.* centenary
centennal *a.* centennial
centiare *m.* 1/100 are, 1 square meter
centième *a. & m.* hundredth
centigramme *m.* centigram
centilitre *m.* centiliter
centime *m.* centime
centimètre *m.* centimeter
centipède *m.* centipede
central *a.* central; middle; main, principal; **— *m.*** center
centraliser *vt.* to centralize
centre *m.* center; middle
centrer *vt.* to center; focus, adjust
centrifuge *a.* centrifugal
centripète *a.* centripetal
centuple *m.* hundredfold (100 times); **au — *adv.*** a hundredfold
cep *m.* vine, vine stock
cèpe *m.* edible mushroom
cependant *adv.* meanwhile; **— *conj.*** however; but; still, yet
céramique *a.* ceramic; **— *f.*** ceramics; ceramic piece; ceramic tile
cerbère *m.* watchdog; guard
cerceau *m.* hoop, ring; **-x** *m. pl.* pin feathers
cercle *m.* circle, ring; club, group; dial
cercler *vt.* to ring, encircle
cercueil *m.* coffin
céréale *a. & f.* cereal plant
cérébral *a.* cerebral
cérémonial *a.* ceremonial; **— *m.*** ceremo-

nial, ceremony
cérémonie f. ceremony, formality; **faire des —s** to stand on ceremony
cérémonieux a. ceremonious; formal
cerf m. stag
cerf-volant m. kite
cerisaie f. cherry orchard
cerise f. cherry; — a. & m. cherry-colored, cerise
cerisier m. cherry tree
cerne m. annual ring (of a tree); circle, ring
cerner vt. to surround, ring, encircle; **avoir les yeux cernés** to have rings under one's eyes
certain a. certain, sure; some; **—ement** adv. certainly; of course
certes adv. indeed; certainly
certificat m. certificate
certification f. certification
certifier vt. to certify; authenticate
certitude f. certainty
cérumen m. ear wax
céruse f. lead carbonate, white lead
cerveau m. brain; mind
cervelet m. cerebellum
cervelle f. brain, brains; mind
cervical a. cervical, of the neck
ces a. pl. these, those
césar m. Caesar, occidental emperor
césarienne a. (med.) Caesarean (operation)
cesse f. cessation, rest; **sans —** unceasingly, incessantly, continually
cesser vt. & vi. to cease, stop, discontinue (com.) stop payment
cession f. relinquishing, giving up
cessez-le-feu n. cease-fire
c'est-à-dire conj. that is to say, in other words
césure f. caesura
cette a. f. this, that
ceux pron., m. pl. these, those, the ones
Ceylan m. Ceylon
chablis m. Chablis wine
chacal m. jackal
chacun pron. each; everyone
chadburn m. public address system (ship)
chagrin m. grief, sorrow; worry; goat leather; sheepskin; **-é** a. sad, worried, upset
chagriner vt. to grieve; worry
chah m. shah
chaîne f. chain; (naut.) cable; mountain range; fabric warp
chaînette f. small chain; **point de — chain-stitch**
chaînon m. link of a chain
chair f. flesh; pulp; meat; **— de poule** goose flesh

chaire f. pulpit; professorship, chair
chaise f. chair, seat; **— longue** reclining chair
chaland n. river or canal barge
Chaldée f. Chaldea
Chaldéen m. & a. Chaldean
châle m. shawl
chalet m. cottage, chalet; **— de nécessité** public toilet
chaleur f. heat, warmth; zeal
chaleureux a. warm, heated
châlit m. bedstead
chaloupe f. launch
chalumeau m. straw, reed; **— oxyacétylénique** acetylene torch
chalut m. seine, net
chalutier m. trawler
chamailler v., se — to squabble
chamarrer vt. to deck, ornament
chambellan m. chamberlain
chambre f. room; chamber; **— à coucher** bedroom; **— à air** (auto.) inner tube
chambré a. at room temperature (wine); chambered; honeycombed
chambrée f. roommates (army)
chameau m. camel
chamois m. chamois, shammy; **—** a. buff, chamois
champ m. field; ground; scope; range; subject; **— de courses** race track; **— de tir** firing range; **— libre** clear field
Champagne f. (province) Champagne; **—** m. champagne
champêtre a. rural
champignon m. mushroom (edible or ineddible)
champignonner vi. to mushroom
championnat m. championship
chance f. chance; luck, good luck, good fortune; **avoir de la —** to be lucky, be fortunate
chancelant a. staggering; wavering; unsteady
chanceler vi. to stagger, waver
chancelier m. chancellor
chancellerie f. chancery; chancellery
chanceux a. risky; lucky
chancre m. canker
chandail m. sweater
chandelier m. candlestick
chandelle f. candle, taper; prop, stay; **— de glace** icicle
change m. exchange; **agent de —** stockbroker; **cours du —** rate of exchange; **donner le — à** to throw off the track
changeable a. changeable; exchangeable
changeant a. changing, changeable
changement m. change; turn; alteration
changer vt. to change; exchange; turn; alter; **— vi.** change; **— d'avis** change

one's mind
changeur *m.* changer
chanoine *m.* (eccl.) canon
chanson *f.* song
chansonnier *m.* song writer; song book
chant *m.* singing, song; chant; canto; crowing (rooster)
chantage *m.* blackmail
chanter *vt. & vi.* to sing; praise
chanteur *m.*, chanteuse *f.* singer, vocalist; blackmailer
chantier *m.* workshop; woodyard; shipyard
chantonner *vt. & vi.* to sing softly; hum
chantoung *m.* shantung
chantourner *vt.* to cut out; cut in profile, silhouette
chantre *m.* singer; poet
chanvre *m.* hemp; couleur de — flax color
chaos *m.* chaos, confusion, disorder
chaotique *a.* chaotic
chape *f.* cover, covering; coping; (eccl.) cope; cap; tire tread
chapeau *m.* hat; cap; cover
chapelet *m.* rosary, beads
chapelier *m.* hatmaker, hat seller, hatter
chapelle *f.* chapel; choir
chapellerie *f.* hat trade, hats; hat shop
chapelure *f.* bread crumbs
chaperon *m.* hood, riding hood; chaperon; coping
chaperonner *vt.* to chaperon
chapiteau *m.* capital of a column; top
chapitre *m.* chapter; item, subject
chapitrer *vt.* to reprimand, lecture someone
chapon *m.* capon; head of garlic
chaque *a.* each, every
char *m.* chariot; cart; (mil.) tank
charabia *m.* gibberish
charançon *m.* weevil
charbon *m.* coal, ember; (med.) carbuncle; — de bois charcoal; carbon
charbonnage *m.* coal mining; coal mine
charbonnier *m.* charcoal-burner; coaldealer
charcuter *vt.* to butcher, botch; mangle
charcuterie *f.* delicatessen
charcutier *m.* owner of a delicatessen; pork shop
chardon *m.* thistle
chardonneret *m.* goldfinch
charge *f.* load, burden; charge; commission; duty, responsibility; — *prep.* à — de provided that
chargé *a.* loaded, laden; full; overcast; lettre —e *f.* registered letter; — *m.* assistant, deputy; — d'affaires diplomatic representative
chargement *m.* loading, lading; charging; cargo

charger *vt.* to load, burden; entrust; charge; se — de to be responsible for, to take it upon oneself to
chargeur *m.* loader; stoker; shipper
chariot *m.* wagon; baby walker; typewriter carriage; — élévateur fork-lift; le grand — Ursa Major; le petit — Ursa Minor
charitable *a.* charitable
charité *f.* charity, love of neighbor
charivari *m.* noise; cacophony
charlatan *m.* charlatan, quack
charlatanisme *m.* charlatanism, quackery
charlemagne *m.*, king (cards); faire — to quit while winning
charmant *a.* charming
charme *m.* charm, spell
charmer *vt.* to charm, bewitch; delight
charmeur *m.* charmer
charmille *f.* bower, arbor
charnel *a.* carnal; sensual
charnière *f.* hinge
charnu *a.* fleshy, pulpy; plump
charogne *f.* carrion
charpente *f.* framework; bois de — *m.* lumber
charpenter *vt.* to square (off); construct; frame; shape, cut
charpenterie *f.* carpentry
charpentier *m.* carpenter
charpie *f.* lint
charretée *f.* cartload
charretier *m.* driver of a cart
charrette *f.* cart
charriage *m.* cartage
charrier *vt.* to cart, haul
charroi *m.* cartage
charron *m.* cartmaker
charrue *f.* plow
charte *f.* charter
chartiste *m. & f.* student of the École des Chartes
chartreuse *f.* chartreuse liqueur; Carthusian monastery
chas *m.* eye of a needle
chasse *f.* hunting; chase; pursuit; — d'eau flush of water
châsse *f.* shrine; reliquary; (coll.) frame of eyeglasses
chasse-clou *m.* tool for countersinking; nail puller
chasse-mouches *m.* fly swatter
chasse-neige *m.* snowplow
chasse-pierres *m.* cowcatcher (train)
chasser *vt.* to hunt; put to flight, drive out; discharge, dismiss, fire; — *vi.* hunt
chasseresse *f.* huntress
chasseur *m.* hunter; bellhop; busboy; fighter plane; fighter pilot; — *a.* hunting

châssis *m.* frame, chassis; window frame; hotbed

châssis-presse *m.* (phot.) printing frame

chasteté *f.* chastity

chasuble *f.* chasuble

chat *m.*, **chatte** *f.* cat; darling; — **en poche** pig-in-a-poke

châtaigne *f.* chestnut

châtaignier *m.* chestnut tree

châtain *a.* chestnut color, brown

château *m.* castle, fort; estate, manor; palace

chateaubriand, châteaubriant *m.* grilled beef steak

châtelain *m.* lord of a manor; **–e** *f.* lady of a manor; decorative chain

châtelet *m.* small chateau

chat-huant *m.* screech owl

châtier *vt.* to chastise, punish

châtiment *m.* punishment, chastisement

chatoiement *m.* sparkle; play of colors

chaton *m.* kitten; setting; set stone; (bot.) catkin

chatouillement *m.* tickling

chatouiller *vt.* to tickle

chatouilleux *a.* ticklish; sensitive, touchy

chatoyer *vi.* to shine, glisten like cat's eye

châtrer *vt.* to castrate

chatterie *f.* cajoling, coaxing

chatterton *m.* friction tape, insulating tape

chaud *a.* hot, warm; **il fait** — it is warm (weather); — *m.* heat, warmth; **avoir** — to be **warm** (of body)

chaud-froid *m.* jellied poultry (chicken) covered with jellied mayonnaise

chaudière *f.* large kettle, steam boiler

chaudron *m.* caldron, boiler

chaudronnier *m.* boilermaker

chauffage *m.* fuel; heating; stoking

chauffe *f.* heating; stoking

chauffe-assiette *m.* hot plate

chauffe-bain *m.* bathroom water heater

chauffe-eau *m.* water heater

chauffe-lit *m.* bed warmer

chauffe-pieds *m.* foot warmer

chauffe-plat *m.* dish warmer

chauffer *vt.* to heat, warm; — *vi.* get warm; overheat

chaufferette *f.* chafing dish; car heater; foot warmer

chauffeur *m.* driver, chauffeur; stoker

chaume *m.* stubble; thatch;

chaumière *f.* thatched cottage

chausse *f.* professor's robe insignia; **–s** *pl.* breeches

chaussée *f.* causeway; road, pavement

chausse-pied *m.* shoehorn

chausser *vt.* to put on footwear; **se —** put on one's shoes

chaussette *f.* sock

chausson *m.* slipper, pump; gym shoe; stocking; savate, French boxing; — **aux pommes** apple turnover

chaussure *f.* shoes, footwear; shoe

chauve *a.* bald

chauve-souris *f.* (zool.) bat

chauvin *a.* chauvinist(ic); — *m.* chauvinist

chaux *f.* lime; **blanchir à la** — to white-wash; **lait de —, blanc de —** whitewash; **pierre à —** *f.* limestone

chef *m.* chief, head, leader; chef; (mus.) conductor; sports captain; — **de gare** stationmaster

chef-d'œuvre *m.* masterpiece

chef-lieu *m.* chief town of a department

cheik *m.* sheik

chelem (schelem) *m.* slam (at cards)

chemin *m.* way, path, road; means; — **de fer** railroad, railway; — **de traverse** crossroad

chemineau *m.* tramp, vagabond, vagrant

cheminée *f.* fireplace; mantelpiece; chimney

cheminer *vi.* to walk, trudge, tramp

cheminot *m.* railway employee

chemise *f.* shirt; chemise; cover, folder; book jacket; **–tte** *f.* short-sleeved shirt

chemisier *m.* shirtmaker; tailored blouse

chenal *m.* channel

chenapan *m.* bandit, good-for-nothing

chêne *m.* oak

chéneau *m.* rain spout

chêne-liège *m.* cork oak

chenet *m.* andiron

chenil *m.* dog kennel

chenille *f.* caterpillar; chenille; caterpillar tread

chenillé *a.* with a caterpillar tread

chenu *a.* hoary; white with age

chèque *m.* check; **toucher un —** to cash a check

chéquier *m.* checkbook

cher (chère) *a.* dear; beloved; expensive; high; — *adv.* dear(ly), a great deal

chercher *vt.* to look for, seek; try; **aller** — to go and get; **envoyer** — to send for

chercheur *m.* seeker; researcher

chère *f.*, **faire bonne** — to live well

chéri (chérie) *a.* cherished, dear; — *n.* dear, darling

chérir *vt.* to cherish

cherté *f.* dearness, expensiveness

chérubin *m.* cherub

chétif *a.* puny, sickly; poor; wretched

cheval *m.* (*pl.* chevaux) horse; **à** — on horseback; — **de course** race horse; — **de race** thoroughbred

chevaleresque *a.* chivalrous

chevalerie *f.* chivalry; knighthood
chevalet *m.* sawhorse; easel; frame, stand; violin bridge
chevalier *m.* knight; rider; — **d'industrie** adventurer; swindler
chevalière *f.* signet ring
chevalin *a.* horse; **boucherie —e** *f.* horse-meat shop
cheval-vapeur *m.* horsepower
chevauchée *f.* ride on horseback; cavalcade
chevaucher *vi.* to ride a horse; overlap, cross; — *vt.* ride, straddle
chevelu *a.* hairy; long-haired
chevelure *f.* head of hair
chevet *m.* headboard; bolster; **livre de —** *m.* favorite book, constant reference; **table de —** *f.* bedside table
cheveu *m.* (*pl.* **cheveux**) hair of the head
cheville *f.* ankle; peg; pin, bolt; skewer
cheviller *vt.* to pin, bolt together
chèvre *f.* goat; derrick
chevreau *m.* kid, kidskin
chèvrefeuille *m.* honeysuckle
chevrette *f.* kid, goat; andiron; tripod
chevreuil *m.* roebuck; **peau de —** *f.* buckskin
chevron *m.* stripe, chevron; rafter
chevronné *a.* experienced; chevroned
chevrotant *a.* trembling, tremulous
chevrotine *f.* buckshot
chez *prep.* at, to, in one's house; among, with; — **soi** at home
chez-soi *m.* home
chiasse *f.* metal scum, dross; flyspecks
chic *m.* style; — *a.* stylish, smart, fashionable; **un — type** a good egg (U.S. coll.)
chicane, chicanerie *f.* chicanery; quibbling, quarrel
chicaner *vt. & vi.* to quibble (with)
chiche *a.* stingy; lacking; **pois — m.** chick-pea; dwarf pea
chichon *m.* romaine lettuce
chicorée *f.* chicory; curly endive
chicot *m.* stump, stub
chien *m.* dog; gun hammer; — **d'arrêt** pointer; — **couchant** setter; — **de garde** watchdog; **temps de — m.** bad weather
chienlit *m.* mask; disguise
chien-loup *m.* wolf hound
chienne *f.* bitch
chienner *vi.* to whelp
chiffe *f.* rag; (fig.) man without character
chiffon *m.* rag; scrap; chiffon
chiffonnade *f.* shredded greens
chiffonner *vt.* to crimple, rumple, wrinkle; to ruffle, anger
chiffonnier *m.* ragpicker; chest of drawers
chiffre *m.* figure, number; total; code; monogram

chiffrer *vt.* to number, mark; code, put into code; — *vi.* to calculate
chignole *f.* punch; (coll.) jalopy
chignon *m.* chignon, bun of hair
Chili *m.* Chile
chimère *f.* chimera, fancy
chimérique *a.* chimerical; fancied, fanciful
chimie *f.* chemistry; — **polymère** polymer chemistry
chimique *a.* chemical; **produit — m.** chemical
chimiste *m.* chemist
chimpanzé *m.* chimpanzee
Chine *f.* China; **encre de — f.** India ink
Chinois *m. & a.* Chinese
chinoiserie *f.* oriental objet d'art; **-s** *pl.* complications
chiot *m.* pup
chiquenaude *f.* flip, flick
chiromancie *f.* palm reading
chirurgical *a.* surgical
chirugie *f.* surgery; **-n** *m.* surgeon
chiure *f.* flyspeck
chlorate *m.* chlorate
chlore *m.* chlorine
chlorer *vt.* to chlorinate
chlorhydrique *a.* hydrochloric
chloroformer, chloroformiser *vt.* to chloroform
chlorophylle *f.* chlorophyll
chlorose *f.* anemia; (med.) chlorosis, green sickness; yellowing of plant leaves
chlorure *m.* chloride
chlorurer *vt.* to chlorinate, chlorinize
choc *m.* shock, collision; clash; clink of glasses
chocolat *m.* chocolate
chocolaterie *f.* chocolate factory
chocolatière *f.* chocolate pot
chœur *m.* choir; chorus
choir *vi.* to fall
choisi *a.* choice, select
choisir *vt.* to choose, select, pick
choix *a.* choice, option, selection; — *a.* **de —** choice, prime, best, first-class
choléra *m.* cholera; (coll.) evil person
cholestérol *m.* cholesterol
chômage *m.* unemployment; **en — un**-employed
chômé *a.* nonworking
chômer *vi.* to be unemployed
chômeur *m.* unemployed worker
chope *f.* beer mug, stein
chopine *f.* small mug; half-liter measure
chopper *vi.* to stumble; blunder
choquant *a.* shocking
choquer *vt.* to shock; strike against, knock; clink; **se —** to collide; be shocked
choral *a.* choral; — *m.* religious chant; **-e**

f. choral group, chorus
chorégraphie *f.* choreography
choriste *m. & f.* member of the chorus
chorus *m.* chorus; **faire —** to repeat in chorus
chose *f.* thing; matter, case; **autre —** something else, another thing, another matter; **quelque —** something
chou *m.* cabbage; cream puff; dear, darling; **— de Bruxelles** Brussels sprout
chou-fleur *m.* cauliflower
chou-rave *m.* kohlrabi
choucroute *f.* sauerkraut; **— garnie** sauerkraut with sausages, ham
chouette *f.* owl
chow-chow *m.* chow dog
choyer *vt.* to pamper
chrème *m.* holy oil
chrestomathie *f.* anthology
chrétien (chrétienne) *a. & n.* Christian
chrétienté *f.* Christianity, Christendom
Christ *m.* Christ; Christus; crucifix
christianiser *vt.* to christianize
christianisme *m.* Christianity
chromatique *a.* chromatic
chrome *m.* chromium; chrome
chromer *vt.* to chrome-plate
chromosome *m.* chromosome
chronique *f.* chronicle; **—** *a.* chronic
chroniqueur *m.* chronicler; reporter
chronologique *a.* chronological
chronomètre *m.* chronometer; stop watch
chronométrer *vt.* to time
chronométreur *m.* timekeeper
chrysalide *f.* chrysalis, pupa
chrysanthème *m.* chrysanthemum
chuchotement *m.* whisper, whispering
chuchoter *vt. & vi.* to whisper
chuchoterie *f.* whispering; gossip
chuchoteur *m.* whisperer; **—** *a.* whispering
chut! *interj.* sh!, quiet!
chute *f.* fall, downfall; drop; **— d'eau** cataract
chuter *vt.* to quiet; shush
Chypre *f.* Cyprus
ci *adv.* here; **par —, par là** here and there
ci-après *adv.* hereafter
ci-bas *adv.* below
cible *f.* target
ciboire *m.* ciborium
ciboule *f.* scallion; **-tte** *f.* chive
cicatrice *f.* scar
cicatriser *vt. & vi.* to scar; heal
cicérone *m.* guide
ci-dessous *adv.* hereafter; underneath
ci-dessus *adv.* aforesaid
ci-devant *a.* former; **—** *adv.* formerly
cidre *m.* cider; **— bouché, — mousseux** sparkling cider
ciel *m.* (*pl.* **cieux**) sky, heaven

cierge *m.* wax candle, church candle
cigale *f.* grasshopper; cicada
cigare *m.* cigar
cigogne *f.* stork
ciguë *f.* hemlock
ci-inclus *a.* enclosed
ci-joint *a.* herewith, enclosed
cil *m.* eyelash
cilice *m.* hair shirt
ciller *vt. & vi.* to blink, wink
cime *f.* top, summit
ciment *m.* cement; concrete; **-er** *vt.* to cement
cimeterre *m.* scimitar
cimetière *m.* cemetery
ciné *m.* movies
cinéaste *m.* movie technician
ciné-club *m.* film group, film club
cinégraphiste *m.* scenarist
cinéma *m.* movie theater; movies; cinema
cinémascope *m.* cinemascope
cinémathèque *f.* film library
cinématographique *a.* film, motion-picture, cinematographic
cinéphile *m. & f.* movie lover, movie fan
cinéprojecteur *m.* motion-picture projector
cinérama *m.* cinerama
cinétique *a.* kinetic; **—** *f.* kinetics
Cingalais *m. & a.* Cingalese, of Ceylon
cinglant *a.* biting, cutting; scathing
cingler *vt.* to cut, bite, sting; lash; **—** *vi.* to sail
cinq *a. & m.* five
cinquantaine *f.* fifty, about fifty; **avoir la —** be fifty years old
cinquante *a.* fifty
cinquantenaire *m.* fiftieth (golden) anniversary
cinquantième *a. & m.* fiftieth
cinquième *a. & m.* fifth
cintre *m.* arch, curve; hanger
cintrer *vt.* to arch, bend, curve
cirage *m.* shoe polish; wax; polishing, waxing
circoncire *vt.* to circumcise
circoncision *f.* circumcision
circonférence *f.* circumference
circonflexe *a.* circumflex
circonlocution *f.* circumlocution
circonscription *f.* circumscription, district
circonscrire *vt.* to circumscribe, circle; limit
circonspect *a.* circumspect, cautious
circonspection *f.* circumspection, caution, prudence
circonstance *f.* circumstance; case, situation; **—** *a.* **de —** occasional; improvised
circonstancié *a.* detailed
circonstanciel *a.* circumstantial; (gram.)

adverbial
circonvenir vt. to circumvent
circuit m. circuit; lap (sports)
circulaire a. & f. circular
circulation f. circulation; traffic; movement; action
circulatoire a. circulatory
circuler vi. to circulate; move about; pass from one to another
circumnavigation f. circumnavigation
cire f. wax; **-r** vt. to wax; polish
ciré a. waxed, polished; **toile -e** f. oilcloth
cireur m. polisher, waxer; bootblack
cireuses f. (mech.) floor waxer
cireux a. waxy
ciron m. mite, tiny animal infesting food
cirque m. circus
cirrhose f. cirrhosis
cirrus m. cirrus cloud
cisaille(s) f. (pl.) shears (for metal, branches); cuttings, metal shearings
cisailler vt. to shear
ciseau m. chisel; **-x** pl. scissors, shears, chisels
ciseler vt. to chisel; cut, carve; chase; emboss, tool
citadelle f. citadel
citadin m. townsman, citizen
citation f. citation; quotation; summons
cité f. city; fortified city; group of apartment buildings; **— universitaire** university dormitories; **-s ouvrières** housing project
citer vt. to quote; cite; summon, subpoena
citerne f. cistern
cithare f. zither
citoyen m., **citoyenne** f. citizen
citoyenneté f. citizenship
citrate m. citrate
citrique a. citric
citron m. lemon; **— a.** lemon-colored **— pressé**, lemonade
citronnade f. lemonade, lemon drink
citronnelle f. citronella
citronnier m. lemon tree
citrouille f. gourd; pumpkin
cive f. scallion
civet m. stew; **— de lièvre** jugged hare
civette f. civet cat
civière f. stretcher, litter; bier
civil a. civil; civic; polite; **droit — m.** civil rights, common law; **— m.** civilian
civilisateur a. civilizing
civilisation f. civilization
civiliser vt. to civilize; **se — to become** civilized
civilité f. civility, politeness
civique a. civic; civil
civisme m. civic pride, civic duty
clabauder vi. to clamor, bawl

claie f. wicker work; trellis; screen
clair a. clear, bright; evident, plain; light; pale; **— m.** light, brightness, highlight; **— de lune** moonlight
clairet a. light; pale
claire-voie f. skylight; lattice; (arch.) clerestory
clairière f. clearing
clair-obscur m. chiaroscuro (art)
clairon m. bugle; bugler
claironner vi. to sound the bugle; **— vt. to** announce
clairsemé a. scattered; sparse, thin
clairvoyance f. clairvoyance, second sight
clairvoyant a. clear-sighted; clairvoyant
clamer vt. to cry out
clameur f. clamor, outcry
clamp m. surgical clamp
clan m. clan, tribe
clandestin a. clandestine; secret
clapet m. (mech.) valve
clapier m. rabbit warren; hutch
clapotement m. lapping, splashing
clapoter vi. to lap, splash (water)
claque f. (theat.) claque; slap; **— m.** opera hat
claquemurer vt. to shut up, confine; **s'—** to shut oneself up at home
claquer vi. to clap; slap; bang; click; crack; snap; chatter (teeth); **— vt. slap;** applaud
claqueur m. member of the claque
clarifier vt. to clarify; **se — become clear**
clarine f. cowbell
clarinette f. clarinet
clarté f. clearness, clarity, brightness; light
classe f. class, order, rank; school
classement m. classification; filing
classer vt. to class, classify; sort; file; **— selon le groupe sanguin** to blood-type
classeur m. sorter; file, filing cabinet
classification f. classification
classifier vt. to classify; sort
classique a. classic(al); **livre — m.** schoolbook, textbook; **— m.** classic; classicist
claudication f. limp, limping
clause f. clause, stipulation
claustration f. confinement; cloistering
clavecin m. harpsichord
claveciniste m. & f. harpsichordist
clavette f. (mech.) retaining pin
clavicule f. clavicle, collarbone
clavier m. keyboard; key ring
clayère f. oyster bed
clé, clef f. key; wrench; clue; (mus.) clef; **donner un tour de — à** to lock; **fermer à — to lock; sous — locked, under lock** and key
clémence f. clemency, leniency, mercy

clément a. lenient, merciful; mild
clenche, clenchette f. latch
cleptomane m. & f. kleptomaniac
cleptomanie f. kleptomania
clerc m. cleric; clergyman; clerk; scholar
clergé m. clergy
clérical a. (eccl.) clerical
cléricalisme m. clericalism
cliché m. stencil; negative; (print.) cut; cliché; photograph, picture; (coll.) banality
clicher vt. to stereotype
client m. client; customer; patient
clientèle f. customers, clientele; practice
clignement m. blinking; wink, winking
cligner vt. & vi. to wink; blink
clignotant m. (auto.) direction signal
clignotement m. twinkling, flickering; blinking
clignoter vi. to twinkle; flicker; wink; blink
climat m. climate
climatisation f. air-conditioning
climatisé a. air-conditioned
climatiser vt. to air-condition
clin d'œil m. twinkling of an eye
clinicien m. clinician
clinique a. clinical; — f. hospital
clinquant m. tinsel; foil; gaudiness, showiness
clip m. clip, pin (jewelry)
clique f. group, band, clique; drum and bugle corps; —s pl. wooden shoes
cliquet m. pawl, ratchet
cliqueter vi. to click; clink; jingle
cliquetis m. click(ing); clink(ing); jingling
clisse f. draining rack; wicker bottle-wrapping
cliver vt. to cleave, cut a gem
cloaque f. cesspool; sewer
cloche f. bell; glass-bell; blister (skin); — de sauvetage escape hatch (submarine)
clochement m. limp, limping
clocher vi. to limp
clocher m. steeple; bell tower, belfry
cloche-pied adv. à — hopping
clocheton m. small steeple, spire
clochette f. small bell
cloison f. partition, wall; — étanche ship's watertight door
cloisonner vt. to partition
cloître m. cloister; monastery
cloîtrer vt. to cloister; confine
clopiner vi. to limp
cloque f. blister
cloquer vt. & vi. to blister
clore vt. to close, shut; enclose; conclude, end
clos a. closed; concluded; — m. closing, end; enclosure

clôture f. fence, enclosure; cloture; closure; conclusion
clôturer vt. to fence, enclose; conclude
clou m. nail; boil; highlight; — de girofle clove
clouer vt. to nail, tack; pin, hold down
clouter vt. to trim with nails; passage clouté m. crosswalk
club m. club, society
clystère m. enema
coadjuteur m. coadjutor
coagulation f. coagulation
coaguler vt. to coagulate, congeal; se — to clot, coagulate, congeal
coaliser v., se — to form a coalition
coalition f. coalition; combination
coasser vi. to croak
coauteur m. coauthor
coaxial a. coaxial; câble — m. coaxial cable
cobalt m. cobalt
cobaye m. guinea pig
cobra m. cobra
cocaïne f. cocaine
cocaïnomane m. & f. cocaine addict
cocarde f. cockade
cocasse a. funny, ridiculous
coccinelle f. wood louse; lady bug (U.S.)
coche m. coach, stagecoach, 2-door sedan; barge; — f. notch
cocher m. coachman, driver; — vt. to check; notch; tally
cochère, porte — f. carriage entrance
cochon m. hog, pig; (fig.) swine; — de lait suckling pig; — d'Inde guinea pig
cockpit m. (avi.) cockpit
cocktail m. cocktail; cocktail party
coco m., noix de — f. coconut
cocon m. cocoon
cocotier m. coconut palm
cocotte f. saucepan, casserole; (coll.) hussy, streetwalker
code m. code; law; — postale d'arrondissement zip code number; — de district area code number
codéine f. codeine
codicille m. codicil
codifier vt. to codify; code
coefficient m. coefficient; factor
coercitif a. coercive
coercition f. coercion
cœur m. heart; feeling(s); courage; center, middle; à contre — against one's will; avoir mal au — to be sick to one's stomach; donner mal au — to nauseate
coffre m. chest, box, trunk, coffer
coffre-fort m. safe, strongbox
coffrer vt. to place in safety; (coll.) lock up, jail
coffret m. small box; — à bijoux jewel case

cognac *m.* brandy from Cognac
cognassier *m.* quince tree
cognée *f.* axe, hatchet
cogner *vt.* to hammer, knock; bump; —
  vi. knock; bump
cohérence *f.* coherence
cohérent *a.* coherent
cohéritier *m.* joint heir
cohésion *f.* cohesion, cohesiveness
cohorte *f.* cohort
cohue *f.* crowd, throng
coi, (coite) *a.* calm, quiet, peaceful
coiffer *vt.* to put on a head covering; cap;
  to dress the hair; se — to arrange one's
  hair or hat
coiffeur *m.* hairdresser; barber
coiffeuse *f.* hairdresser; dressing table
coin *m.* corner; nook; quiet place, spot;
  wedge
coincer *vt.* to wedge; se — *vi.* to jam, stick
coïncidence *f.* coincidence
coïncider *vi.* to coincide
coing *m.* quince
col *m.* collar; neck; (geog.) mountain pass
coléoptère *m.* beetle
colère *f.* anger; en — angry; mettre en —
  to anger; se mettre en — become very
  angry, lose one's temper
coléreux *a.* quick-tempered
colibri *m.* hummingbird
colifichet *m.* trinket
colimaçon *m.* snail; en — spiral
colin-maillard *m.* blindman's buff
colique *f.* colic
colis *m.* package, parcel
côlite *f.* colitis
collaborateur *m.*, collaboratrice *f.* collaborator; contributor; associate
collaboration *f.* collaboration
collaborer *vi.* to collaborate; contribute
collage *m.* pasting, gluing, mounting; collage; sizing; (coll.) common-law marriage
collant *a.* tight-fitting; sticky
collatéral *a. & m.* collateral
collation *f.* light meal; collation; confer-
  ring
collationner *vi.* to have a snack; — *vt.* to
  collate; confer
colle *f.* glue, paste
collecteur *m.* collector; (elec.) commutator; tuyau — sewage collector
collectif *a.* collective; joint, cooperative
collection *f.* collection, collecting
collectionner *vt.* to collect
collectionneur *m.* collector
collectivisme *m.* collectivism
collectivité *f.* collectivity
collège *m.* secondary school; college
collégial *a.* collegiate; (eccl.) of the chap-

ter (canon); —e *f.* collegiate church
collègue *m.* colleague
coller *vt.* to paste, glue; stick; press; —
  vi. stick; cling
collerette *f.* cloth collar; metal flange;
  ring, pipe joint
collet *m.* collar; flange; neck; snare
colleter *vt.* to collar; s'— wrestle, scuffle
  with
collier *m.* necklace; harness collar; metal
  ring; (fig.) coup de — great effort
colline *f.* hill
collision *f.* collision
colonnade *f.* collonade
colloque *m.* conversation; conference
collusion *f.* collusion
colocataire *m. & f.* co-tenant
colombe *f.* dove
colombophile *m. & f.* pigeon raiser, pigeon
  fancier
colon *m.* colonist; settler
côlon *m.* (anat.) colon
colonial *a. & m.* colonial; soldier of colonial army
colonialisme *m.* colonialism
colonie *f.* colony; settlement
colonisation *f.* colonization
coloniser *vt.* to colonize; settle
colonne *f.* column, pillar
colophane *f.* colophony, rosin
coloration *f.* color, coloring
coloré *a.* colored; ruddy
colorer, colorier *vt.* to color
coloris *m.* coloring
colossal *a.* colossal, huge
colosse *m.* colossus, giant
colporter *vt.* to peddle; spread news
colporteur *m.* peddler
columbarium *m.* columbarium
comateux *a.* comatose
combat *m.* battle, fight, combat, struggle;
  hors de — out of action
combattant *m.* combatant
combattre *vt. & vi.* to fight
combien *adv.* how much, how many
combinaison *f.* combination; coveralls;
  (chem.) compound; machination; — s
  f. pl. lady's undergarment
combiné *m.* compound; — *a.* combined,
  joint
combiner *vt.* to combine, unite; contrive
comble *m.* top, summit; roofing; limit,
  end; — *a.* full, packed
combler *vt.* to fill; heap; overwhelm
combustible *a.* inflammable; — *m.* fuel;
  — exotique exotic fuel
combustion *f.* combustion
comédie *f.* comedy
comédien *m.* actor; —ne *f.* actress
comédon *m.* blackhead

comestible *m.* food, provision; — *a.* edible

comète *f.* comet

comique *a.* comic(al), funny; — *m.* comic, comedian; comic author; comedy

comité *m.* committee

commandant *m.* commander; major; commanding officer

commande *f.* order for goods; control, lever; control panel; **fait sur** — made to order

commandement *m.* command, order; commandment

commander *vt. & vi.* to command, order; control

commandeur *m.* (mil.) cavalry commander

commanditaire *m.* backer, financier

commandite *f.* joint-stock company

commanditer *vt.* to back, finance

commando *m.* (mil.) detachment, detail; commando group

comme *adv.* as, like; how; sort of; — *conj.* as, since

commémoraison *f.* commemoration (of a saint)

commémoratif *a.* commemorative; memorial

commémoration *f.* commemoration

commémorer *vt.* to commemorate

commençant *m.* beginner

commencement *m.* beginning

commencer *vt. & vi.* to begin, commence

comment *adv.* how; —! *interj.* what!

commentaire *m.* comment, commentary; —s *pl.* memoirs

commentateur *m.* commentator; author of commentaries

commenter *vt.* to comment on; annotate

commérage *m.* gossip

commerçant *m.* merchant, businessman; — *a.* commercial, business

commercer *vi.* to deal, trade, do business

commercial *a.* commercial, business; —e *f.* station wagon

commère *f.* gossip, busybody

commettre *vt.* to commit; do, make

commis *m.* clerk; **grand** — **de l'État** high official; — **voyageur** traveling salesman

commisération *f.* commiseration, pity

commissaire *m.* commissioner; commissar; purser

commissaire-priseur *m.* appraiser; auctioneer

commissariat *m.* commissariat; function of a commissioner; — **ae police** police station

commission *f.* commission; committee, board; errand; (com.) payment for selling

commissionnaire *m.* factor; agent; messenger

commissionner *vt.* to delegate; authorize

commode *f.* chest of drawers; — *a.* convenient, comfortable, spacious; accommodating

commodité *f.* comfort, convenience, accommodation

commotion *f.* concussion (brain); commotion; shock

commuer *vt.* to commute (law)

commun *a.* common, ordinary, usual; commonplace; **en** — in common; co-operative(ly)

communal *a.* common; communal

communauté *f.* community

commune *f.* township, commune

communiant *m.* (eccl.) communicant

communicant *a.* communicating

communicatif *a.* communicative

communication *f.* communication; message; phone call; **fausse** — wrong number

communier *vi.* to take communion; commune

communiqué *m.* press release; official communication

communiquer *vt. & vi.* to communicate

communisant *m.* communist sympathizer

communisme *m.* communism

communiste *m. & f.* communist

commutation *f.* commutation

commutateur *m.* (elec.) switch, commutator

commutatrice *f.* (elec.) transformer

compact *a.* compact, solid

compagne *f.* female companion; spouse

compagnie *f.* company

compagnon *m.* companion, associate; worker, co-worker

comparable *a.* comparable

comparaison *f.* comparison

comparaître *vi.* (law) to appear

comparatif *a. & m.* comparative

comparé *a.* comparative; compared

comparer *vt.* to compare

comparoir *vi.* to appear in court

comparse *m. & f.* (theat.) supernumerary

compartiment *m.* compartment; division

comparution *f.* court appearance

compas *m.* compass; calipers; (fig.) standard

compassé *a.* stiff, set; formal; regularized

compasser *vt.* to measure with compass; weigh, consider

compatible *a.* compatible; — *f.* compatability

compatir *vi.* to sympathize

compatissant *a.* compassionate; sympathetic

compatriote *m.* fellow countryman

compensateur a. compensating; equalizing; — m. compensator; equalizer
compensation f. compensation; equalization; adjustment; **chambre de —** f. clearing house
compenser vt. to compensate, make up for; equalize; adjust
compérage m. gossip; plotting
compétence f. competence; competency; (fig.) jurisdiction
compétent a. competent; reliable
compilateur m. compiler
compilation f. compilation, compiling
compiler vt. to compile
complainte f. lament
complaire vi. to please; **se — à** take pleasure in, delight in
complaisance f. kindness, goodness, obligingness; complacency
complaisant a. obliging; compliant; complacent
complément m. complement
complémentaire a. complementary
complet (complète) a. complete; full; — m. man's suit; **au —** full; **au grand —** in force; at full strength
compléter vt. to complete; finish
complexe a. complex, complicated; (math.) compound; — m. complex
complexion f. constitution, disposition
complexité f. complexity
complice m. & f. accomplice, accessory
complicité f. complicity
compliment m. compliment
complimenter vt. to compliment; congratulate
compliqué a. complicated, intricate
compliquer vt. to complicate; **se —** become complicated
complot m. plot, conspiracy
comploter vt. to plot, conspire
comploteur m. plotter, conspirator
componction f. compunction
comportement m. behavior
comporter vt. to permit; comprise; **se —** to behave
composant a. & m. component
composé a. composed; compound, composite; — m. compound
composer vt. & vi. to compose; compound; write; set (type); **se — de** consist of, be composed of
compositeur m. composer; compositor
composition f. composition; composing; compound; typesetting
compost m. compost
composteur m. (print.) composing stick
compotier m. compote dish; dish for sauce
compréhensible a. comprehensible
compréhensif a. comprehensive; understanding
compréhension f. comprehension, understanding
comprendre vt. to understand; include, comprise; **se faire —** make oneself understood
compresse f. compress
compresseur m. compressor; **rouleau —** m. steam roller
compression f. compression; repression
comprimé m. tablet, pill; — a. compressed
comprimer vt. to compress; repress
compris a. understood, included; **y —** including
compromettre vt. & vi. to compromise; expose, put in embarrassment or peril
compromis m. compromise, mutual agreement
comptabilité f. accounting, bookkeeping
comptable m. accountant, bookkeeper; — a. accountable
comptant a. counted on, prompt; **argent —** m. ready money, cash
compte m. account, computation; value; profit; **à — on** account; **à bon —** cheap; **— rendu** m. report; review; **se rendre — de** to realize, be aware of; **tenir — de** take into account; bear in mind
compte-fils m. magnifier
compte-gouttes m. medicine dropper
compter vt. to count; number; expect; — vi. count, rely; **sans — to** say nothing of, not to mention, not counting
compte-tours m. revolution counter
compteur m. meter; speedometer; counter; comptometer
comptoir m. counter; cashier's desk
compulser vt. to subpoena records; **to examine records**
computation f. computation
computer vt. to compute
comte m. count, earl
comté m. county, earldom
comtesse f. countess
concasser vt. to crush
concasseur m. stone crusher, crushing machine
concéder vt. to concede, grant, admit
concentration f. concentration
concentré a. concentrated; (fig.) taciturn
concentrer vt. to concentrate, condense, repress; **se —** concentrate
concentrique a. concentric
concept m. concept, idea
conception f. conception; idea; image
concernant prep. concerning, about
concerner vt. to concern
concert m. concert; harmony; **de — avec** together with, hand in hand with
concertant a. performing together

concerté *a.* concerted
concerter *vt.* to plan, concert
concession *f.* concession; grant
concevable *a.* conceivable
concevoir *vt.* to conceive; imagine, understand
concierge *m. & f.* doorkeeper, janitor
concile *m.* (eccl.) council
conciliateur *a.* conciliating, conciliatory
conciliation *f.* conciliation; reconciliation
concilier *vt.* to conciliate; reconcile
concis *a.* concise, short
concision *f.* conciseness, brevity
concitoyen *m.* fellow citizen
conclave *m.* conclave
concluant *a.* conclusive
conclure *vt.* to conclude; decide; end, finish; drive or strike a bargain
conclusif *a.* conclusive
conclusion *f.* conclusion; decision; end, ending
concombre *m.* cucumber
concordance *f.* concordance; (gram.) agreement
concordat *m.* concordat, agreement
concorde *f.* harmony, concord, agreement
concorder *vi.* to agree
concourir *vi.* to compete; converge; cooperate
concours *m.* competitive examination; concourse; assistance, aid; concurrence
concret *a.* concrete
concupiscence *f.* lust
concurremment *adv.* concurrently; jointly
concurrence *f.* competition; concurrence
concurrencer *vt.* to rival; compete with
concurrent *a.* competitive; — *m.* competitor
concussion *f.* extortion, embezzlement
condamnable *a.* blameworthy
condamnation *f.* condemnation; blame, censure; legal sentence *or* judgment
condamner *vt.* to condemn, sentence; blame, censure, criticize
condensateur *m.* condenser
condensation *f.* condensation; gas liquidation; condensing
condensé *m.* resumé
condenser *vt.* to condense, liquify gas; se — condense (fig.) to group, assemble
condenseur *m.* condenser
condescendance *f.* condescension
condescendre *vi.* to condescend
condiment *m.* condiment, seasoning, spice
condisciple *m.* fellow student
condition *f.* condition, state; circumstance(s); position; rank; status; station; à — on approval; à — que on condition that; sans — unconditional
conditionnel *a.* conditional; — *m.* (gram.)

conditional
conditionner *vt.* to condition
condoléance *f.* condolence
conducteur *m.*, **conductrice** *f.* leader; driver; motorman; (elec.) conductor; overseer, foreman; — *a.* conducting; driving
conduire *vt.* to conduct, lead; drive; se — to behave; permis de — *m.* driver's license
conduit *m.* conduit, pipe, main
conduite *f.* conduct, behavior; driving; direction, supervision; flue; main; tubing; pipeline
cône *m.* cone
confection *f.* making; manufacturing; ready-made clothes
confectionner *vt.* to make; manufacture
confédération *f.* confederation, confederacy
confédérer *vt.* to confederate
conférence *f.* lecture; conference
conférencier *m.* lecturer
conférer *vt.* to compare; confer, bestow; — *vi.* confer, discuss
confesser *vt.* to confess; se — (eccl.) to confess
confesseur *m.* (eccl.) confessor
confession *f.* confession
confiance *f.* confidence; reliance; trust; (digne) de — reliable, trustworthy
confiant *a.* confiding; confident
confidamment *adv.* confidently, in confidence
confidence *f.* confidence, trust; secrecy; secret
confident *m.*, **confidente** *f.* trusted friend, confidant
confidentiel *a.* confidential
confier *vt.* to confide; trust, entrust; se — à to put one's trust in
configuration *f.* configuration
confiner *vt.* to confine; — *vi.* to border, verge on
confins *m. pl.* confines, limits
confire *vt.* to preserve, pickle, candy
confirmation *f.* confirmation
confirmer *vt.* to confirm
confiserie *f.* confectionary
confiseur *m.* confectioner
confisquer *vt.* to confiscate
confit *a.* preserved; candied
confiture *f.* jam, preserve(s)
confiturière *f.* jam dish; dealer in preserves
conflagration *f.* conflagration
conflit *m.* conflict, clash, struggle
confluence *f.* confluence
confluer *vi.* to meet, come together
confondre *vt.* to confound, mingle, con-

fuse, mistake; disconcert, upset; **se —** to mix, blend
conformation *f.* conformation
conforme *a.* conformable, consistent; **— à** corresponding to; according to; **copie — f.** true copy
conformément *adv.* in conformity; **— à** in accordance with, according to
conformer *vt.* to form; conform; **se —** to conform, comply
conformiste *m. & f.* conformist
conformité *f.* conformity; similarity
confort *m.* comfort
confortable *a.* comfortable
confrère *m.* colleague
confrérie *f.* brotherhood
confronter *vt.* to confront, compare
confus *a.* confused; embarassed; blurred; overcome
confusément *adv.* confusedly; vaguely
confusion *f.* confusion; embarrassment
congé *m.* leave, furlough; dismissal; vacation; **jour de — m.** holiday
congédiement *m.* dismissal
congédier *vt.* to discharge, dismiss
congélation *f.* freezing; congealing, coagulation
congeler *vt.* to congeal, freeze
congère *f.* snowdrift
congestion *f.* congestion; accumulation in blood vessels
congestionné *a.* flushed face
congestionner *vt.* to congest; **se —** to become congested
conglomérat *m.* conglomerate
conglomérer *vt.* to conglomerate
congre *m.* conger eel
congrégation *f.* congregation
congrès *m.* congress
congressiste *m.* delegate
congru *a.* precise; sufficient; suitable
conifère *a.* coniferous; **— m.** conifer
conique *a.* conic(al)
conjecturer *vt.* to conjecture, guess
conjoindre *vt.* to join in marriage; unite
conjoint *a.* joined, joint; married
conjoncteur *m.* automatic switch
conjonctif *a.* (gram.) conjunctive; relative; (anat.) connective
conjonction *f.* conjunction; connection, joining, union
conjoncture *f.* contingency, conjuncture, juncture
conjugaison *f.* conjugation
conjugal *a.* conjugal; **vie —e f.** marriage, married life
conjuguer *vt.* to join; (gram.) to conjugate
conjurateur *m.* conjurer
conjuration *f.* conspiracy, plot; exorcism
conjuré *m.* conspirator, plotter

conjurer *vt.* to implore, beg, beseech; conspire, plot
connaissance *f.* knowledge; acquaintance; consciousness; **faire la — de** to meet, become acquainted with a person; **perdre — to** lose consciousness; **sans —** unconscious
connaissement *m.* bill of lading
connaisseur *m.* connoisseur, judge, expert
connaître *vt.* to know; be acquainted with; **se — à, se — en** be an expert in, be a good judge of
connecter *vt.* (elec.) to connect
connecteur *m.* (elec.) connector
connexe *a.* connected; related
connexion *f.* connection; relation
connexité *f.* relationship, connection
connivence *f.* connivance
connu *a.* known, well-known
conque *f.* conch; conch shell; (anat.) concha
conquérant *a.* conquering; **— m.** conqueror
conquérir *vt.* to conquer; gain
conquête *f.* conquest; acquired property, acquisition
consacré *a.* consecrated; hallowed, sacred; time-honored
consacrer *vt.* to consecrate; ordain; sanctify; dedicate, devote
consanguin *a.* related on the father's side
consciemment *adv.* consciously
conscience *f.* conscience, consciousness; conscientiousness; **avoir — de** to be aware of, be conscious of; **avoir de la —** be conscientious; **en — adv.** in truth
consciencieux *a.* conscientious
conscient *a.* conscious, aware
conscrit *m.* recruit, conscript, draftee
consécration *f.* consecration; dedication
consécutif *a.* consecutive
conseil *m.* counsel, advice; council, committee; **— d'administration** board of directors; **— d'Etat** legislative advisory group; **— de guerre** court-martial; **— de révision** draft board; **— de prud'hommes** labor-management arbitration committee; **— des ministres** cabinet; **— général** local (departmental) legislature
conseiller *m.* counsellor; councillor; adviser
conseiller *vt.* to counsel, advise, recommend
consensus *m.* consensus
consentement *m.* consent; approval
consentir *vi.* to consent, agree; approve; **— vt.** to grant; approve
conséquemment *adv.* consequently
conséquence *f.* consequence, conclusion,

result; importance; inference

conséquent *a.* consistent; (coll.) important; par — consequently

conservateur *a.* preserving; conservative; — *m.* keeper; curator; librarian; conservative

conservation *f.* conservation, preservation; keeping

conservatisme *m.* conservatism

conservatoire *m.* conservatory, school of music

conserve *f.* preserved food, canned food; de — preserved; canned; —s *pl.* preserves, canned goods

conserver *vt.* to conserve, preserve; keep, hold, maintain; se — to keep, remain preserved

conserverie *f.* canning factory *or* industry

considérable *a.* considerable; extensive, large; important

considérant *m.* motive

considération *f.* consideration; regard, respect

considérer *vt.* to consider; regard

consignataire *m.* (com.) consignee; legal trustee

consignation *f.* (com.) consignment

consigne *f.* (mil.) order, instructions; password; (rail.) checkroom

consigner *vt.* to consign; confine; deposit money; check baggage

consistance *f.* consistency; stability

consistant *a.* firm, set

consister *vi.* to consist

consolateur *a.* consoling; — *m.* consoler

console *f.* bracket; console table

consoler *vt.* to console, comfort

consolidation *f.* consolidation; (med.) buildup

consolider *vt.* to consolidate; se — to heal

consommateur *m.* consumer; café customer

consommation *f.* consummation; consumption; drink, beverage

consommé *a.* consummate, perfect; — *m.* consommé

consommer *vt.* to consummate; consume

consomptif *a.* consumptive

consonance *f.* consonance

consonne *f.* (gram.) consonant

consort *a.* consort; prince — *m.* prince consort; —s *m. pl.* interested parties

consortium *m.* association, company, group

conspirateur *m.* conspirator, plotter

conspirer *vt. & vi.* to conspire, plot

constable *m.* constable, policeman

constamment *adv.* constantly

constance *f.* constancy; perseverance

constant *a.* constant; unchanging, steady; uniform; (math.) invariable

constat *m.* official declaration, examination

constatation *f.* proof; statement, declaration; authentication

constater *vt.* to declare; take note of; certify; establish

constellé *a.* spangled, star-spangled

consteller *vt.* to bespangle

consterner *vt.* to consternate, dismay

constipant *a.* constipating

constipation *f.* constipation

constituant *a.* constituent, component; — *m.* voter, constituent

constituer *vt.* to constitute, set up; make, take; — prisonnier to take prisoner, take into custody

constitutif *a.* constituant

constitution *f.* constitution; composition

constitutionnalité *f.* constitutionality

constitutionnel *a.* constitutional

constricteur *a. & m.* constrictor

constriction *f.* constriction; compression of diameter

constructeur *m.* constructor; builder, engineer

constructif *a.* constructive

construction *f.* construction, building; — mécanique mechanical engineering

construire *vt.* to construct; build; (gram.) to construe

consulaire *a.* consular

consulat *m.* consulate; consulship

consultant *a.* consulting; — *m.* consultant

consultation *f.* consultation

consulte *f.* (pol. & eccl.) consultation

consulter *vt.* to consult

consumer *vt.* to consume, destroy; use up

contact *m.* contact; touch; connection, switch

contacter *vt.* to contact, come in contact with

contagieux *a.* contagious

container *m.* case

contamination *f.* contamination

contaminer *vt.* to contaminate

conte *m.* tale, story

contemplateur *m.* contemplator

contemplatif *a.* contemplative

contemplation *f.* contemplation; meditation, thought

contempler *vt.* to contemplate; meditate

contemporain *a. & m.* contemporary

contempteur *a.* contemptuous

contenance *f.* countenance; content(s), capacity

contenant *m.* container

contenir *vt.* to contain; restrain

content *a.* content, satisfied, happy, glad

contentement *m.* contentment, satisfaction

contenter vt. to content, satisfy; **se — de** to be content with, be satisfied with

contentieux a. contentious

contention f. contention; contest

contenu m. contents

conter vt. to relate, tell

contestable a. disputable, debatable

contestation f. dispute

conteste, sans — adv. incontestably

contester vt. & vi. to dispute, contest

conteur m. storyteller

contexte m. context

contexture f. structure, arrangement

contigu (contiguë) a. adjoining, adjacent, contiguous

contiguïté f. contiguity

continence f. continence

continent m. continent; **–al** m. continental

contingence f. contingency

contingent a. contingent; **—** m. contingent; quota

continu a. continual, continuous

continuel a. continual; continuous

continûment adv. continually; continuously

continuer vt. & vi. to continue

continuité f. continuity

contondant a. blunt

contorsion f. contortion

contorsionner vt. to contort

contortionniste m. & f. contortionist

contour m. outline, contour

contourné a. twisted; affected

contournement m. detour, bypass

contourner vt. to outline, shape; bypass, skirt; twist, distort; **— la loi** to get around the law

contractant m. person contracting; **—** a. contracting

contracte a. contracted, agreed

contracté a. contracted (made shorter)

contracter vt. to contract; acquire; **se —** to contract, narrow

contractuel a. contractual; stipulated by contract

contradiction f. contradiction

contradictoire a. contradictory

contraindre vt. to compel, restrain, constrain, force

contraint a. constrained, forced

contrainte f. restraint; force, constraint

contraire a. contrary, opposite; against; **au —** on the contrary

contrarier vt. to thwart; vex, annoy; go against

contrariété f. contrariness; annoyance

contraste m. contrast

contraster vt. & vi. to contrast

contrat m. contract, agreement

contravention f. violation, misdemeanor; traffic ticket

contre prep. against; contrary to; near by; **—** adv. against; near by; **—** m. counter, opposite; **le pour et le —** the pros and cons; **par —** on the other hand

contre-amiral m. rear admiral

contre-appel m. second appeal

contre-attaque f. counterattack

contre-attaquer vt. to counterattack

contre-avions a. antiaircraft

contrebalancer vt. to counterbalance

contrebande f. contraband; smuggling

contrebandier m. smuggler

contrebas, en — adv. downwards

contrebasse f. double bass; tuba; double bass player

contrebassiste, contrebassier m. double bass player

contrebasson m. contrabassoon

contre-boutant m. buttress

contre-bouter, contre-buter vt. to buttress

contrecarrer vt. to foil, thwart; oppose

contre-chant m. counter theme

contrecœur m. back of a fireplace; fireplace plaque; (rail.) guard rail; **à —** adv. unwillingly, reluctantly

contrecoup m. rebound; backfire; result

contredanse f. contredanse, country dance

contrée f. country, region

contre-écrou m. lock nut

contre-épaulette f. epaulette without fringe

contre-espion m. counterspy

contre-espionnage m. counterespionnage

contrefaçon f. counterfeit; forgery; counterfeiting; plagiarism

contrefacteur m. forger, counterfeiter

contrefaction f. counterfeiting

contrefaire vt. to counterfeit, forge, imitate; disguise

contre-feu m. reverse fire (fire fighting)

contre-fil m. opposite direction

contrefort m. buttress; spur; foothill(s); reinforcement

contre-haut, en — adv. up, upwards, above

contre-jour m. (photo.) light from opposite side of an object; **à —** adv. against the light

contremaitre m. foreman; (naut.) petty officer

contremander vt. to countermand

contremarque f. countersign; pass-out check

contrepartie f. counterpart; return match (sports)

contre-pas m. rapid half-step; change in step (marching)

contre-plaqué a. laminated; **bois —** m.

plywood
contre-plaquer *vt.* to laminate, manufacture plywood
contrepoids *m.* counterweight, counterbalance
contre-poil *m.* opposite direction; **à —** *adv.* against the grain
contrepoint *m.* (mus.) counterpoint
contre-pointer *vt.* to quilt
contrepoison *m.* antidote
contrer *vt.* to counter; **—** *vi.* to double (at cards)
contre-rail *m.* guard rail
contre-révolution *f.* counterrevolution
contre-révolutionnaire *a. & m. & f.* counterrevolutionary
contresens *m.* misinterpretation
contresigner *vt.* to countersign
contretemps *m.* mishap; delay; (mus.) syncopation; **à —** inopportunely
contre-torpilleur *m.* destroyer (navy)
contrevenant *m.* lawbreaker; nonconformer
contrevenir *vt.* to break a law; act contrarily
contrevent *m.* window shutter
contribuable *m. & f.* taxpayer
contribuer *vi.* to contribute
contribution *f.* contribution; tax
contrister *vt.* to sadden
contrit *a.* contrite, grieved
contrôle *m.* inspection, verification; auditing; ticket-taking
contrôler *vt.* to supervise; check; inspect-audit; verify; control, restrain
contrôleur *m.* ticket collector; auditor; in; spector; comptroller
controuvé *a.* made-up, invented, imagined
controversable *a.* controversial
controverse *f.* controversy; discussion
controverser *vt.* to debate; controvert
contumace *f.* contempt of court; nonappearance; default
contus *a.* bruised; **–ion** *f.* contusion, bruise
contusionner *vt.* to bruise
convaincant *a.* convincing
convaincre *vt.* to convince; convict
convalescent *a. & m.* convalescent
convenable *a.* suitable, proper, appropriate, becoming
convenance *f.* suitability; expediency; propriety, convention; conformity
convenir *vi.* to agree; fit, suit
convention *f.* convention; agreement; **de —** conventional
conventionnel *a.* conventional
convenu *a.* agreed, arranged, settled
convergeance *f.* convergence
converger *vi.* to converge
conversation *f.* conversation

converser *vi.* to converse, talk
converti *m.* convert
convertibilité *f.* convertibility
convertible *a.* (law) convertible
convertir *vt.* to convert; **se — (en)** to become converted; turn into, change into
convertissable *a.* convertible
convertisseur *m.* converter; transformer
convexe *a.* convex
convexité *f.* convexity
conviction *f.* conviction; belief
convié *m.* one guest
convier *vt.* to invite
convive *m.* guest; table companion
convocation *f.* convocation; convening
convoi *m.* funeral procession; convoy
convoiter *vt.* to covet, want, desire
convoiteur *a.* covetous
convoitise *f.* covetousness; cupidity; immoderate desire
convoquer *vt.* to convoke; summon
convoyer *vt.* to convoy
convoyeur *a.* convoying, escorting; **— m.** escort, convoy; conveyor
convulser *vt.* to convulse
convulsif *a.* convulsive
convulsionner *vt.* to convulse
coopérateur *m.* co-operator; member of a co-operative
coopératif *a.* co-operative
coopération *f.* co-operation
coopérer *vi.* co-operate
coordination *f.* co-ordination
coordonnateur *m.* co-ordinator; **— a.** co-ordinating
coordonné *a.* co-ordinate; co-ordinated; **–es** *f. pl.* co-ordinates
copeau *m.* chip, wood shaving
copie *f.* copy; imitation; reproduction; **— conforme** true copy, authenticated copy
copier *vt.* to copy, imitate; reproduce
copieux *a.* copious; hearty
copilote *m.* copilot
copiste *m.* copyist; copier; clerk; **faute de — f.** clerical error
coposséder *vt.* to own jointly
copra(h) *m.* copra
copte *m. & f.* Copt; **— a.** coptic
copulatif *a.* co-ordinating
coq *m.* rooster, cock; weathervane; sea cook; **— de bruyère** grouse; **poids —** bantamweight (boxing)
coq-à-l'âne *m.* confused speech; farce, cock-and-bull story
coque *f.* shell; cocoon; hull; **œuf à la — m.** soft-boiled egg
coquelicot *m.* (bot.) poppy
coqueluche *f.* whooping cough

coquerie *f.* galley, ship's kitchen
coqueriquer *vi.* to crow
coquet *a.* coquettish; natty
coqueter *vi.* to flirt
coquetier *m.* egg cup; egg and chicken wholesaler
coquetière *f.* egg cooker
coquette *f.* coquette, flirt
coquetterie *f.* flirtation, coquetry
coquillage *m.* shellfish; shell
coquille *f.* shell; case, casing; typographical error; — Saint-Jacques creamed scallops; huîtres en — *f. pl.* scalloped oysters
coquin *m.* rogue, rascal; — *a.* roguish
cor *m.* horn; French horn; corn (foot); — de chasse hunting horn
corail *m.* coral
corbeau *m.* raven; crow
corbeille *f.* basket; wedding presents; — à papier wastepaper basket
corbillard *m.* hearse
cordage *m.* rope; string
corde *f.* cord, rope, line; string; thread; wire; chord
cordé *a.* heart-shaped
cordeau *m.* string, lace
cordée *f.* cord (of wood); group of mountain climbers (roped together)
cordelier *m.* Franciscan friar
corder *vt.* to cord; make into rope; string
cordial *a.* cordial, warm, hearty; stimulating; — *m.* cordial; stimulant
cordialité *f.* cordiality
cordier *m.* ropemaker
cordon *m.* strand; cord; ribbon; tape; door pull; cordon; — bleu expert chef; — de soulier shoelace
cordonnerie *f.* shoemaking; shoe repairing
cordonnier *m.* shoemaker
Corée *f.* Korea; -n *m. & a.* Korean
coriace *a.* tough, leathery
Corinthe *f.* Corinth; raisin de — *m.* currant
corinthien *a.* Corinthian
cormoran *m.* cormorant
cornac *m.* elephant boy; guide
corne *f.* horn; dog-ear a page; — à souliers shoehorn
corné *a.* horny
cornée *f.* cornea
corneille *f.* crow
cornemuse *f.* bagpipes
corner *vt. & vi.* to blare out; (auto.) to blow the horn
cornet *m.* horn; trumpet; cornet; paper cone; — acoustique ear trumpet; — à pistons cornet with valves; glace en — ice-cream cone
cornette *f.* nun's headdress

corniche *f.* cornice; ledge
cornichon *m.* gherkin, pickle
Cornouailles *f. pl.* Cornwall
cornouiller *m.* dogwood
cornu *a.* horned
cornue *f.* (chem.) retort
corollaire *m.* corollary
coronaire *a.* coronary
corporatif *a.* corporate
corporel *a.* corporal; corporeal; bodily
corps *m.* body; substance; corpse; corps; font (type); — à — hand-to-hand; — simple (chem.) element; — composé (chem.) compound; prendre — to develop, take shape; saisir au — to arrest (law)
corps-à-corps *m.* hand-to-hand combat; clinch (boxing)
corpulent *a.* corpulent, fat
corpuscule *m.* corpuscle
correct *a.* correct; accurate; right; proper
correcteur *m.* corrector; proofreader
correctif *a.* corrective
correction *f.* correction, correcting; correctness, propriety; proofreading; punishment; reprimand
correctionnel *a.* relating to a misdemeanor; —le *f.* misdemeanor court
corrélatif *a.* correlative
corrélation *f.* correlation
correspondance *f.* correspondence; interchange, transfer
correspondant *a.* corresponding; — *m.* correspondent
correspondre *vi.* to correspond; communicate
corriger *vt.* to correct; proofread; punish
corroborer *vt.* to corroborate
corrodant *a. & m.* corrosive
corroder *vt.* to corrode
corrompre *vt.* to corrupt; spoil; bribe
corrompu *a.* corrupt; spoiled
corrosif *a. & m.* corrosive
corroyer *vt.* to plane (wood); solder, weld; prepare (leather)
corrupteur *a.* corrupting; — *m.* corrupter
corruption *f.* corruption; corruptness; bribery
corsage *m.* bust, bodice; blouse
corsaire *m.* corsair, pirate
Corse *f.* Corsica; — *m. & f. & a.* Corsican
corsé *a.* full-bodied; (fig.) scabrous
corselet *m.* bodice
cortège *m.* cortege, train, retinue, procession; funeral
cortisone *f.* cortizone
corvée *f.* drudgery; unpleasant task; hard labor; tenue de — *f.* (mil.) fatigues
corvette *f.* corvette; capitaine de — lieutenant commander

cosignataire *m. & f.* cosigner
cosinus *m.* (math.) cosine
cosmétique *a. & m.* cosmetic
cosmique *a.* cosmic
cosmopolite *a.* cosmopolitan
cosmos *m.* cosmos
cosse *f.* pod, husk, shell
costume *m.* costume, dress, suit
costumer *vt.* to costume
cosy *m.* cosy corner; studio bed
cote *f.* number; quota; mark; classification; (com.) price, quotation
côte *f.* rib; seacoast; hill; chop; — à — side by side
côté *m.* side; way; à — near, by, on one side; à — de beside, next to; d'un — on one hand; de l'autre — on the other hand; on the other side; across; de — aside, to one side; du — de in the direction of
coteau *m.* hill, hillside; slope
côtelé *a.* ribbed cloth; corded; corduroy
côtelette *f.* chop, cutlet
coter *vt.* to mark; number; classify; quote a price; assess
coterie *f.* group, set, coterie
cothurne *m.* buskin
côtier *a.* coastal
cotisation *f.* share; dues, fee; assessment
cotiser *vi.* to pay one's share
coton *m.* cotton
cotonnade *f.* cotton goods
cotonner *vt.* to pad, stuff with cotton; (se) — *vi.* to become fluffy, downy
cotonnerie *f.* cotton field; cotton raising; cotton factory
cotonneux *a.* fluffy; downy
cotonnier *a.* cotton; relating to cotton; — *m.* cotton plant
côtoyer *vt.* to border on; stay close to, hug (the shore)
cotre *m.* (naut.) cutter
cotte *f.* short skirt; — à bretelles overalls; — de mailles coat of mail
cou *m.* neck; couper le — à to behead
couard *a.* cowardly; — *m.* coward
couardise *f.* cowardice
couchage *m.* bedding; coating; sac de — *m.* sleeping bag
couchant *a.* setting; — *m.* sunset, west; decline
couche *f.* bed; confinement; layer, coat; fausse — miscarriage
couché *a.* lying; in bed
coucher *vt.* to put to bed; put down, lay down; — en joue to aim at; se — to go to bed; lie down; — *m.* setting of sun; going to bed; bed, lodging
couchette *f.* berth; crib
coucou *m.* cuckoo; (bot.) daffodil

coude *m.* elbow; bend; angle; coup de — *m.* nudge, poke
cou-de-pied *m.* instep
couder *vt.* to bend like an elbow
coudoyer *vt.* to elbow, jostle
coudre *vt. & vi.* to sew; machine à — *f.* sewing machine
couenne *f.* rind; skin; birthmark
couette *f.* (coll.) feather bed; grating (on escape valve); strainer
couguar *m.* cougar
coulage *m.* pouring; leaking; (naut.) scuttling; waste
coulant *a.* flowing, smooth; nœud — *m.* slipknot
coulé *a.* cast or poured metal
coulée *f.* flow; casting; pouring
couler *vi.* to flow, run; leak; founder, sink; — *vt.* pour; sink, scuttle
couleur *f.* color; paint; complexion; suit at cards
couleuvre *f.* snake, serpent
coulisse *f.* groove; slide; (theat.) wing à — sliding
coulisseau *m.* slide, runner
couloir *m.* passage, corridor; lobby
coup *m.* blow, throw, stroke; knock, tap, rap; thrust; shot; attempt, coup; — de feu gun shot; — de froid chill, cold; — d'œil glance, look; — de sang (med.) stroke; — de téléphone telephone call; — de tête butt; rash action; — de vent gust of wind; encore un — once again; en venir aux —s to come to blows; sur le — on the spot, right off, outright; tout à — suddenly, all of a sudden; tout d'un — at one shot; at once
coupable *a.* guilty; culpable; sinful, wrong; — *m. & f.* culprit, guilty one
coupant *a.* sharp, cutting; — *m.* sword edge
coup-de-poing *m.* brass knuckles (U.S.); fist blow
coupe *f.* cut, cutting; haircut; cross section; cup, champagne glass
coupé *a.* cut, broken; — *m.* (auto.) coupe
coupe-circuit *m.* circuit-breaker; fuse
coupe-coupe *m.* machete
coupe-feu *m.* fire break
coupe-fil *m.* wirecutters
coupe-gorge *m.* hazard, danger spot
coupe-jarret *m.* assassin
coupe-légumes *m.* vegetable cutter
coupe-ongles *m.* nail clippers
coupe-papier *m.* paper knife
couper *vt.* to cut; cross; interrupt, cut off, break; turn off; trump cards; cut wine, water down; se — to cut oneself; intersect
couperet *m.* chopper, cleaver; guillotine

blade
couperose *f.* (med.) acne; (chem.) blue vitriol
coupeur *m.* cutter
coupe-vent *m.* windbreaker
couple *m.* couple, pair; —*f.* couple; yoke; brace
coupler *vt.* to couple, connect, join
couplet *m.* stanza, verse
coupleur *m.* coupler
coupoir *m.* cutter, cutting tool
coupole *f.* cupola
coupon *m.* remnant, cutting; coupon
coupure *f.* cut, slit; cutting, clipping; banknote (under 1000 francs)
cour *f.* court; yard; courtship; **faire la —** à to court
courage *m.* courage, bravery, valor; (fig.) heart, spirit
courageux *a.* courageous, brave
courailler *vi.* to run around, run from side to side
couramment *adv.* fluently; easily; currently
courant *a.* current, running; present; **prix — ** *m.* price list; **— ** *m.* current, flow, stream; course; **— d'air** draft; **être au — de** to know about, be informed about
courbature *f.* aching, stiffness
courbaturé *a.* aching, stiff
courbe *f.* curve; **— ** *a.* curved, crooked, bent
courber *vt.* to bend, bow; curve; **— ** *vi.* to bend, sag, droop; **se — ** to bend, stoop
courbure *f.* curve, curvature, bend
courette *f.* small courtyard
coureur *m.* runner, racer; wanderer; adventurer; **— de spectacles** playgoer
courge *f.* gourd, squash
courgette *f.* zucchini
courir *vi.* to run; race; **— ** *vt.* to run, run after, hunt, pursue; run, take a risk
courlis *m.* plover
couronne *f.* crown; coronet; wreath
couronnement *m.* coronation; crowning
couronner *vt.* to crown; cap; (fig.) honor, pay
courrier *m.* courier; mail; column, section of a newspaper
courriériste *m.* columnist, feature editor
courroie *f.* strap; drive-belt
courroucer *vt.* to irritate; anger
courroux *m.* anger, wrath
cours *m.* course; current, stream; way; price, rate; lecture; **au — de** during, in the course of; **— du change** rate of exchange; **en — de route** on the way, along the way
course *f.* running; racing; race; trip; errand; flight, course, path; **champ de —s**

racetrack; **faire des —s** to go shopping
coursier *m.* messenger; steed
coursive *f.* passageway to ship cabin
court *a.* short; concise; brief; **— ** *adv.* short; **à — de** short of; **— ** *m.* tennis court
courtage *m.* brokerage; fee, commission
courtaud *a.* short, stocky
court-circuit *m.* short circuit
courtepointe *f.* quilt
courtier *m.* broker; jobber; agent
courtisan *m.* courtier; **-e** *f.* courtesan
courtiser *vt.* to court; woo
courtois *a.* courteous, polite; courtly
courtoisie *f.* courtesy, politeness
couru *a.* sought after; (fig. & coll.) sure thing
couseuse *f.* seamstress; sewing machine
cousin *m.*, **cousine** *f.* cousin; **— germain(e)** first cousin
cousinage *m.* relatives
coussin *m.* cushion
coussinet *m.* small cushion; (mech.) bearing
coût *m.* cost, price
couteau *m.* knife
coutelas *m.* cutlass
coutellerie *f.* cutlery
coûter *vi.* to cost; **— cher** to be expensive
coûteux *a.* costly, expensive
coutil *m.* twill, duck; mattress ticking
coutume *f.* custom, habit; common law
coutumier *a.* customary, usual; **droit — ** *m.* common law
couture *f.* sewing; seam; suture; scar
couturer *vt.* to seam, scar
couturier *m.* designer of women's clothes
couturière *f.* seamstress, dressmaker
couvaison *f.* incubation period
couvée *f.* brood of chickens; group of eggs under brood hen; (coll.) all the family
couvent *m.* convent; monastery
couver *vt.* to hatch; sit on; **— ** *vi.* to smolder; brew; develop
couvercle *m.* cover, lid, cap
couvert *m.* table place setting; **cover charge**; shelter, cover; **mettre le — ** to set the table; **ôter le — ** to clear the table; **— ** *a.* covered; shady, wooded; clothed, clad; overcast (weather)
couverture *f.* cover; wrapper; blanket
couveuse *f.* brood hen; incubator
couvre-feu *m.* curfew
couvre-lit *m.* bedspread, coverlet
couvre-pieds *m.* bedspread; quilt
couvreur *m.* roofer
couvrir *vt.* to cover; clothe; **se — ** to put one's hat on; clothe oneself
coyote *m.* coyote
crabe *m.* crab
crachat *m.* spit; sputum

cracher *vt. & vi.* to spit out
crachin *m.* light drizzle
crachoir *m.* spittoon
crachoter *vi.* to spit frequently
craie *f.* chalk
craindre *vt.* to fear, be afraid of
crainte *f.* fear; de — de for fear of; de — que for fear that
craintif *a.* timid; fearful
cramoisi *a.* crimson
crampe *f.* cramp
crampillon *m.* small hook
crampon *m.* clamp; crampon; stud
cramponner *vt.* to clamp; (coll.) to pester, bother
cran *m.* cog, tooth, catch; notch
crâne *m.* skull; — *a.* bold, swaggering
crâner *vi.* to swagger
crânerie *f.* bravado; daring
cranien *a.* cranial
cranter *vt.* to notch, tally; cog
crapaud *m.* toad
crapule *f.* mob, rabble; lewdness; filth
crapuleux *a.* lewd; foul, filthy
craqueler *vt.* to crack
craquelure *f.* crack
craquement *m.* cracking, snapping
craquer *vi.* to crack; creak; crackle; crunch
crasse *f.* filth; squalor; stinginess; — *a.* crass
crasseux *a.* dirty, filthy; stingy
cratère *m.* crater
cravacher *vt.* to whip
cravate *f.* necktie; cravat, scarf
crayeux *a.* chalky
crawl(e) *m.* crawl (swimming stroke)
crayon *m.* pencil; crayon; stick; — hémostatique styptic pencil
crayonnage *m.* pencil sketch, pencil drawing
crayonner *vt.* to draw, sketch
créance *f.* trust, credit; credence; debt
créancier *m.* creditor
créateur *m.*, **créatrice** *f.* creator; inventor; author; — *a.* creative
création *f.* creation, creating; establishment, establishing
créature *f.* creature; creation
crécelle *f.* rattle
crèche *f.* crib, manger; nursery school
crédence *f.* credenza, buffet
crédibilité *f.* credibility; probability
crédit *m.* credit; credence; prestige, repute; à — on credit
créditer *vt.* to credit
créditeur *m.* creditor
credo *m.* creed, belief
crédule *a.* credulous
crédulité *f.* credulity

créer *vt.* to create; produce; engender
crémaillère *f.* pothook; pendre la — to have a housewarming
crémation *f.* cremation
crématoire *a.* pertaining to cremation
crème *f.* cream; custard, pudding; cream soup; — fouettée whipped cream
crémer *vt.* to cremate
crémerie *f.* dairy; grocery; creamery
crémeux *a.* creamy
crémier *m.* dairyman, grocer
crénelé *a.* notched (as coin edge), toothed; crenate; crenellated; milled
créneler *vt.* to crenelate; cog; notch
créole *a. & n.* creole, French-colonial born
créosol *m.* creosol
créosote *f.* creosote
crêpe *f.* pancake; — *m.* crepe, crape; mourning band
crépitation *f.*, **crépitement** *m.* crepitation; crackling
crépiter *vi.* to crackle
crépu *a.* fuzzy, frizzy; crinkled
crépusculaire *a.* twilight, crepuscular
crépuscule *m.* twilight
cresson *m.* watercress
crête *f.* crest, comb; ridge
crétin *m.* cretin; idiot
crétois *a. & n.* Cretan
creuser *vt.* to dig, excavate; look deeply into, study carefully; se — la tête to rack one's brains
creuset *m.* crucible; melting pot
creux (creuse) *a.* hollow; deep; sunken; — *m.* hollow; pit; hole
crevaison *f.* bursting; (auto.) puncture, blowout
crevasse *f.* crevice, chink, crack, crevasse
crevasser *vt.* to crack; to chap hands
crève-cœur *m.* heartbreak
crever *vi.* to break; burst; (coll.) die; — *vt.* to burst; puncture
crevette *f.* shrimp; prawn
cri *m.* cry, shout; dernier — latest thing, latest style
criaillement *m.* shrill sound; shouting; shreiking
criailler *vi.* to shout; bawl; whine; nag
criaillerie *f.* shouting; bawling; whining; nagging
criant *a.* outrageous, crying
criard *a.* noisy, shrill; loud color
crible *m.* sieve; screen
criblé *a.* riddled; pitted face; saddled with debts
cribler *vt.* to sift; riddle
cribleur *m.*, **cribleuse** *f.* sifter (machine)
cricri *m.* cricket; chirping
criée *f.* auction, public selling
crier *vi.* to proclaim; shout, cry out;

scream; squeal; chirp; creak; — *vt.*
shout, cry; peddle

crieur *m.* shouter, crier; peddlar; town
crier

crime *m.* crime

criminalité *f.* crime rate; criminality

criminel *a.* criminal; guilty; — *m.* criminal

criminologie *f.* criminology

crin *m.* horsehair

crinière *f.* mane

crinoline *f.* crinoline, hoop skirt

crique *f.* cove; creek

criquet *m.* locust; cricket

crise *f.* crisis; attack, fit; problem

crispant *a.* irritating, annoying

crispation *f.* puckering, shriveling; tic,
twitching; clenching; fidgeting

crisper *vt.* to contract; clench; make
fidgety

crissement *m.* grating, rasping, grinding;
squeaking

crisser *vt. & vi.* to grate, rasp, grind;
squeak

cristal *m.* crystal; glass; — **taillé** cut glass

cristallin *a.* crystalline; clear, transparent

cristallisation *f.* crystalization

cristalliser *vt. & vi.* to crystallize

critère, critérium *m.* criterion; standard;
test

critiquable *a.* censurable

critique *f.* criticism, critique; — *m.* critic;
— *a.* critical

critiquer *vt.* to criticize

croasser *vi.* to croak; caw

croate *a. & n.* Croatian

Croatie *f.* Croatia

croc *m.* hook; fang; tusk

croc-en-jambe *m.* trip, fall; **faire un — à**
to trip

croche *f.* (mus.) eighth-note

crocher *vt.* to hook

crochet *m.* small hook; (print.) square
bracket; sharp turn; fang; pick, key

crocheter *vt.* to pick a lock; crochet

crochu *a.* hooked; crooked

crocodile *m.* crocodile

crocus *m.* crocus

croire *vt. & vi.* to believe, think; — **à** to
believe in; **en — to take someone's
word for it**

croisade *f.* crusade

croisé *a.* crossed; twilled; double-breas-
ted; **mots –s** *m. pl.* crossword puzzle; —
m. crusader; twill

croisée *f.* crossing; casement window;
crossed filaments in a bomb sight

croisement *m.* crossing; cross; intersection

croiser *vt.* to cross; to fold arms; meet;
pass; — *vi.* to cruise; **se — to cross,**

meet, intersect

croisette *f.* small cross

croiseur *m.* cruiser

croisière *f.* cruise

croissance *f.* growth

croissant *a.* growing; increasing; — *m.*
crescent moon; crescent roll

croître *vi.* to grow; increase

croix *f.* cross, crucifix; — **ou pile heads or
tails**

croquant *a.* crisp, crunchy; tasty

croque-mitaine *m.* bugaboo, bugbear,
bogyman

croque-mort *m.* funeral attendant

croquer *vt. & vi.* to crunch, munch; sketch

croquette *f.* croquette

croquis *m.* rough sketch; draft, outline

crosse *f.* crook, club, stick; gun butt;
crozier

crotale *m.* rattlesnake

crotte *f.* mud; dung

crotter *vt.* to dirty; cover with mud

crottin *m.* horse manure

croulant *a.* crumbling, falling, tottering

crouler *vi.* to crumble, totter; collapse

croupe *f.* croup, crupper, rump

**croupetons, à — ** *adv.* squatting

croupier *m.* croupier

croupion *m.* rump

croupir *vi.* to stagnate; wallow

croustade *f.* crusty food

croustillant *a.* crisp, crusty

croustiller *vi.* to crunch

croustilleux *a.* risqué

croûte *f.* crust; rind; scab; **casser la — to
have a snack; faire — to form a crust**

crouton *m.* piece of crust; crouton

croyable *a.* credible, believable

croyance *f.* belief

croyant *a.* believing; — *m.* believer

cru *m.* place of origin of a wine; vintage;
— *a.* raw; rough; crude

cruauté *f.* cruelty

cruche *f.* pitcher, jug

cruchon *m.* small pitcher

crucial *a.* cruciform; crucial

cruciement *m.* crucifixion

crucifier *vt.* to crucify

crucifix *m.* crucifix

crucifixion *f.* crucifixion

cruciforme *a.* cross-shaped, cruciform

crudité *f.* crudeness; crudity; rawness;
roughness, coarseness

crue *f.* rise, rising, flood

cruel *a.* cruel

cruellement *adv.* cruelly

crûment *adv.* roughly; crudely; harshly

crustacé *m.* crustacean

cryogénique *f.* cryogenics

crypte *f.* crypt

cryptogénétique *a.* of unknown origin
cryptogramme *m.* cryptogram
cryptographie *f.* cryptography
Cuba *n.* Cuba
cubage *m.* cubic volume, capacity, space
Cubain *n. & a.* Cuban
cube *m.* cube; block
cuber *vt.* (math.) to cube
cubique *a.* cubic, cubical
cubisme *m.* cubism
cubital *a.* cubital
cubitus *m.* (anat.) ulna
cueillage *m.* gathering, picking; harvest time
cueillaison *f.* gathering, picking
cueilleur *m.* gatherer, picker, fruitpicker
cueillir *vt.* to gather, pluck, pick; (coll.) grab, take
cuiller, cuillère *f.* spoon; ladle; scoop; — **à bouche** tablespoon; — **à café** teaspoon
cuillerée *f.* spoonful
cuilleron *m.* bowl of a spoon
cuir *m.* leather, hide; — **chevelu** scalp; — **verni** patent leather; — **vert** untanned leather; rawhide
cuirasse *f.* armor, plate; cuirass
cuirassé *m.* battleship
cuirasser *vt.* to armor; protect; **se** — to steel oneself
cuire *vt. & vi.* to cook
cuisant *a.* biting, stinging, smarting
cuisine *f.* kitchen; cuisine, cooking; food; **faire la** — to do the cooking
cuisiner *vt.* to cook; (coll.) doctor, falsify; question, grill
cuisinier *m.* cook
cuisinière *f.* cook; stove, range
cuisse *f.* thigh; drumstick
cuisseau *m.* leg of veal
cuisson *f.* cooking; firing; burning
cuissot *m.* leg of game
cuistre *m.* (coll.) pedant
cuite *f.* firing (ceramics)
cuivre *m.* copper; — **jaune** brass
cuivré *a.* copper-colored; bronzed; brassy
cuivrer *vt.* to copper; bronze; — *vi.* to blare, sound
cuivreux *a.* cuprous
cuivrique *a.* cupric
cul *m.* posterior, bottom; rump
culasse *f.* gun breech; bolt; (mech.) cylinder head
culbute *f.* fall, tumble; somersault
culbuter *vt.* to overturn, overthrow, knock over — *vi.* to tumble; somersault
cul-de-sac *m.* dead-end street
culée *f.* abutment
culinaire *a.* culinary
culminant *a.* culminating, culminant;

point — *m.* height, zenith
culminer *vi.* to culminate
culot *m.* base, bottom; dottle; (coll.) youngest child
culotte *f.* breeches; panties; shorts; rump meat
culotter *vt.* to color; — **une pipe** to cure a pipe
culpabilité *f.* guilt, culpability
culte *m.* worship; cult; religion
cultivable *a.* suitable for farming; arable
cultivateur *m.* farmer; grower; plow, cultivator
cultivé *a.* cultivated; cultured person
cultiver *vt.* to cultivate; grow; farm; raise
cultural *a.* agricultural
culture *f.* cultivation, tillage; culture
culturel *a.* cultural
cumin *m.* cumin
cumul *m.* accumulation
cumulatif *a.* cumulative
cumuler *vt.* to accumulate
cumulus *m.* cumulus
cunéiforme *a.* cuneiform
cupide *a.* greedy
cupidité *f.* greed, cupidity
Cupidon *m.* Cupid
cuprifère *a.* copper-bearing
curable *a.* curable
curaçao *m.* curaçao, orange-peel liqueur
curage *m.* cleansing
curare *m.* curare
curatelle *f.* guardianship, trusteeship
curateur *m.* guardian, trustee
curatif *a.* curative
cure *f.* care; (med.) treatment; ministry; presbytery, rectory
curé *m.* parish priest
cure-dent *m.* toothpick
curée *f.* quarry (hunting); spoils
cure-pipe *m.* pipe cleaner
curer *vt.* to cleanse; pick; dredge
curieux *a.* curious; interested; indiscreet; inquisitive; odd
curiosité *f.* curiosity; inquisitiveness; curio; oddness; —s *pl.* sights; **visiter les** —s to go sightseeing
curium *m.* curium
curseur *m.* slide, runner
cursif *a.* cursory; handwritten
cursive *f.* handwriting
cutané *a.* cutaneous; pertaining to the skin
cuticule *f.* cuticle
cuve *f.* vat, tank for fermenting grapes
cuveau *m.* small vat *or* tank
cuver *vt. & vi.* to ferment wine
cuvette *f.* basin, pan
cuvier *m.* washtub
cyanose *f.* (med.) cyanosis

cyanure *m.* cyanide
cybernétique *f.* cybernetics
cyclable *a.* piste — *f.* bicycle path
cycle *m.* cycle; bicycle
cyclique *a.* cyclic, cyclical
cyclisme *m.* cycling, bicycling
cycliste *m. & f.* cyclist, bicyclist
cycloïde *f.* cycloid
cyclomoteur *m.* motorbike
cyclone *m.* cyclone
cyclope *m.* cyclops; giant
cyclotron *m.* cyclotron
cygne *m.* swan
cylindre *m.* cylinder; drum; roller
cylindrer *vt.* to roll; mangle
cylindrique *a.* cylindrical
cymbale *f.* cymbal
cynique *a.* cynical; — *m.* cynic
cynisme *m.* cynicism
cyprès *m.* cypress
cyste *m.* cyst
cytologie *f.* cytology
cytoplasme *m.* cytoplasm

D

dactyle *m.* dactyl
dactylique *a.* dactylic
dactylo, dactylographe *m. & f.* typist
dactylographie *f.* typing, typewriting
dactylographié *a.* typed, typewritten
dactylographier *vt.* to typewrite
dada *m.* hobbyhorse; (coll.) hobby; obsession
dadais *m.* idiot, stupid fellow
dague *f.* dagger
daguerréotype *m.* daguerrotype
dahlia *m.* dahlia
daigner *vt.* to deign, condescend
daim *m.* deer; buckskin; suede
dais *m.* canopy
dallage *m.* floor tile; flagstone surface
dalle *f.* flagstone, slab of marble, tile
daller *vt.* to tile, pave
dalmate *a. & n.* Dalmatian
dalot *m.* scupper
daltonien *a.* color-blind
daltonisme *m.* color blindness
Damas *m.* Damascus
damas *m.* damask; damson plum
damassé *a.* damask; Damascus steel
dame *f.* lady; queen (at cards); jeu de –s *pl.* game of checkers; pion du jeu de –s checkers man
damier *m.* chessboard, checkerboard
damnation *f.* damnation
damné *a.* damned
damner *vt.* to damn
damoiseau *m.* dandy; fop
dancing *m.* dance hall; public dance, ball

dandiner *vt.* to dandle; (fig.) pamper; se — to waddle
Danemark *m.* Denmark
danger *m.* danger; risk, peril
dangereux *a.* dangerous
danois *a.* Danish; — *m.* Dane; Danish language
dans *prep.* in, into, at, within; from, out of
dansant *a.* dancing; soirée –e *f.* dance; thé — *m.* tea dance
danse *f.* dance, dancing
danser *vt. & vi.* to dance
danseur *m.*, danseuse *f.* dancer, ballet dancer
dard *m.* dart; forked tongue; pain, sting
darder *vt.* to shoot, throw, flash
dardillon *m.* small dart
darne *f.* slice of fish
datation *f.* dating
date *f.* calendar date; sans — undated
dater *vt. & vi.* to date
datif *a. & m.* (gram.) dative
datte *f.* (bot.) date
dattier *m.* date palm
daube *f.* braising; bœuf en — braised beef
dauber *vt. & vi.* to braise; make fun of
dauphin *m.* dolphin; Dauphin
davantage *adv.* more, any more; more time
davier *m.* (naut.) davit; (dent.) forceps
de *prep.* of; from; by; with; in; — *art.* some, any
dé *m.* thimble; die; domino; golf tee; –s *m. pl.* dice
déambuler *vi.* to stroll, saunter
débâcle *m.* debacle, disaster, rout; collapse, downfall
déballer *vt.* to unpack
déballeur *m.* peddler
débandade *f.* dispersal; à la — in disorder
débander *vt.* to unbend, relax; unbandage; se — to disband, disperse
débaptiser *vt.* to change the name of
débarbouiller *vt.* to wash someone's face; se — to wash one's face; clear up (weather)
débarcadère *m.* landing place; wharf
débardage *m.* unloading
débarder *vt.* to unload
débardeur *m.* stevedore
débarquement *m.* landing; arrival; unloading
débarquer *vt.* to land, disembark; unload; — *vi.* to land, disembark, get off
débarras *m.* riddance
débarrasser *vt.* to clear; rid, disencumber; relieve; se — de to get rid of
débarrer *vt.* to unbar

débat *m.* debate; discussion; dispute

débattre *vt.* to discuss; debate; **se —** to struggle

débauche *f.* debauchery

débauché *a.* debauched

débaucher *vt.* to debauch; corrupt; lead astray

débile *a.* weak, sick

débilitant *a.* debilitating

débilité *f.* debility, weakness

débiliter *a.* to debilitate

débit *m.* debit; sale; store, shop; flow, output

débitant *m.* retailer

débiter *vt.* to retail, sell; deliver; produce; speak, pronounce, utter; debit

débiteur *m.* debtor; teller, speaker

déblayer *vt.* to clear away

débloquer *vt.* to unblock

déboire *m.* unpleasant aftertaste

déboisement *m.* deforestation

déboiser *vt.* to deforest

déboîtement *m.* (med.) dislocation

déboîter *vt.* to disconnect; dislocate

débonnaire *a.* easy-tempered, kind, good-natured, weak

débordant *a.* overflowing; blooming; protruding

debordé *a.* overflowing; (coll.) rushed, busy, snowed under

débordement *m.* overflowing; outburst

déborder *vt. & vi.* to overflow, run over; protrude; trim (adorn)

débouché *m.* outlet, exit

déboucher *vt.* to uncork; open; clear; — *vi.* to flow; open on; emerge

déboucler *vt.* to unbuckle; uncurl

débourser *vt.* to disburse, lay out

debout *adv.* standing up, upright; alive; **à dormir —** boring; **se tenir —** to stand

déboutonner *vt.* to unbutton

débraillé *a.* untidy, unkempt; loose

débrayage *m.* (auto.) clutch

débrayer *vt.* to disengage from gear; disconnect

débrider *vt.* to unbridle; stop

débris *m. pl.* remains; ruins; debris

débrouillard *a. & m.* resourceful, (coll.) smart person

débrouiller *vt.* to disentangle; clear up; decipher; **se —** to clear up; get along, manage

début *m.* beginning; debut; coming out

débutant *m.* beginner; new performer **—e** *f.* beginner in society

débuter *vi.* to begin; do, appear for the first time

deçà *prep. & adv.* on this side

décacheter *vt.* to unseal

décadence *f.* decay, decline, decadence

décadent *a.* decadent

décaféiné *a.* decaffeinated, caffeine-free

décaisser *vt.* to uncrate; pay out, disburse

décalcomanie *f.* decalcomania, transfer

décaler *vt.* to change, shift

décalitre *f.* decaliter

décalogue *m.* Ten Commandments

décalque *m.* tracing, transfer

décalquer *vt.* to trace, transfer

décamètre *m.* ten meters

décamper *vi.* to decamp

décanat *m.* office of dean, deanship

décanter *vt.* to decant, pour (off)

décaper *vt.* to scour, clean

décapitation *f.* decapitation

décapiter *vt.* to behead, decapitate

décapotable *a.* (auto.) convertible

décatir *vt.* to remove cloth shine by steaming

décathlon *m.* decathlon

décavé *a.* (coll.) broke, ruined, cleaned out

décédé *a.* deceased, departed

décéder *vi.* to decease, die

déceler *vt.* to disclose, betray

décélération *f.* deceleration

décembre *m.* December

décemment *adv.* decently

décence *f.* decency; propriety

décennal *a.* decennial

décent *a.* decent; proper

décentralisation *f.* decentralization

décentraliser *vt.* to decentralize

déception *f.* disappointment; deception

décerner *vt.* to award, confer

décès *m.* decease, death; **acte de — *m.*** death certificate

décevant *a.* disappointing; deceptive

décevoir *vt.* disappoint; to deceive

déchaînement *m.* unchaining; outburst, wave

déchaîner *vt.* to unchain; let loose; **se —** to break out

décharge *f.* discharge; discharging, unloading; rebate; release; acquittal (at law)

déchargement *m.* discharging, unloading

décharger *vt.* to unload, discharge; unburden; fire a gun; **se —** to discharge; go off; **se — de** to get rid of; relieve oneself of

déchargeur *m.* unloader

décharné *a.* skinny; emaciated; gaunt

déchaussé *a.* barefoot

déchausser *vt., se —* to take off one's shoes

déchéance *f.* forfeiture; downfall; term, expiration

déchet *m.* loss; waste

déchiffrable *a.* legible, readable, decipherable

déchiffrer *vt.* to decipher; decode; read, make out

déchiqueté *a.* jagged, torn

déchirant *a.* heartrending

déchirement *m.* tearing; rift; sorrow

déchirer *vt.* to tear; rend

déchirure *f.* tear, rip, rent

déchloruré *a.* salt-free

déchoir *vi.* to fall; go down; decline in condition

déchu *a.* fallen; forfeited; expired

décibel *m.* decibel

décidé *a.* decided; resolved, determined

décidément *adv.* decidedly, positively; firmly, resolutely

décider *vt.* to decide; persuade; determine; se — to resolve, decide

décigramme *m.* ½ gram

décilitre *m.* ⅒ liter

décimal *a.* decimal; —e *f.* decimal

décimer *vt.* to decimate

décisif *a.* decisive; positive, firm; critical, crucial

décision *f.* decision; resolution

déclamation *f.* declamation; declaiming

déclamer *vt.* to declaim; rant, harangue

déclaration *f.* declaration; affadavit; statement; announcement

déclarer *vt.* to declare, proclaim; state, assert; notify

déclassé *m.* social outcast; — *a.* socially lowered; obsolete

déclasser *vt.* to lower in rank, class; demote; make obsolete; disarrange; declassify

déclencher *vt.* to unleash; (fig.) set in motion, release; trigger (mech.) disengage

déclic *m.* catch; trigger

déclin *m.* decline, decay; wane; ebb; fall

déclinaison *f.* (gram.) declension; (ast.) declination

décliner *vt.* to decline; shun, refuse; — *vi.* decline, diminish, fall, wane

déclive *a.* sloping; — *f.* slope

décliver *vi.* to slope, incline

déclivité *f.* slope, incline

décoder *vt.* to decode

décoiffer *vt.* to undo, disarrange (the hair)

décollage *m.* unsticking; (avi.) take-off

décollation *f.* decapitation, beheading

décoller *vt.* to unstick; loosen; — *vi.* (avi.) to take off

décolleté *a.* in a low-cut dress

décolorer *vt.* to fade; bleach; discolor

décombres *m. pl.* rubbish, refuse, debris

décommander *vt.* to cancel, countermand

décomposer *vt.* to decompose; se — to become decomposed; decay, rot; become distorted

décomposition *f.* decomposition

décompression *f.* decompression

décomprimer *vt.* to decompress

décompter *vt.* to deduct

déconcertant *a.* disconcerting

déconcerter *vt.* to disconcert; baffle, confound; upset

déconfit *a.* baffled, confused

décongeler *vt.* to defrost, thaw

déconseiller *vt.* to dissuade; advise against

déconsidérer *vt.* to discredit

décontenancer *vt.* to discountenance, upset, mortify

déconvenue *f.* disappointment

décor *m.* decoration; scenery, setting

décorateur *m.* decorator; (theat.) designer

décoratif *a.* decorative

décoration *f.* decoration; scenery; medal, ribbon

décorer *vt.* to decorate, adorn

décorum *m.* decorum; propriety, decency

découdre *vt.* to unsew, unstitch, rip; gore

découler *vi.* to flow, proceed; drip, trickle

découper *vt.* to carve; cut up; couteau à — *m.* carving knife; scie à — *f.* jigsaw; se — sur to stand out against

découpler *vt.* to uncouple

découpure *f.* cutting out; clipping, cutout; indentation

découragé *a.* discouraged

décourageant *a.* discouraging

découragement *m.* discouragement

décourager *vt.* to discourage; se — to become discouraged

découronner *vt.* to dethrone; untop a tree

décours *m.* wane, ebb, decline

décousu *a.* unsewed, unstitched, ripped; rambling, incoherent; disjointed; loose

découvert *m.* deficit; overdraft; mettre à — to reveal, expose; — *a.* uncovered; open

découverte *f.* discovery

découvreur *m.* discoverer

découvrir *vt.* to uncover; discover; disclose; expose; show; se — to take off one's hat; be discovered, be revealed; come to light

décrasser *vt.* to scour, cleanse; (auto.) remove carbon

décréditer *vt.* to discredit

décrépi *a.* dilapidated

décrépit *a.* decrepit; dilapidated

décret *m.* decree

décréter *vt.* to decree

décri *m.* disrepute

décrier *vt.* to decry, disparage

décrire *vt.* to describe

décrocher *vt.* to unhook; lift the receiver (telephone); disconnect

décroiser *vt.* to uncross

décroissance *f.* decrease; decline
décroître *vi.* to decrease; decline; diminish
décrotter *vt.* to clean; scrape clean
décrotteur *m.* bootblack
décrottoir *m.* scraper; doormat
décrue *f.* fall, drop, subsiding
décuple *a.* tenfold
dédaigner *vt.* to disdain, scorn
dédaigneux *a.* disdainful, scornful
dédain *m.* disdain, scorn
dédale *m.* labyrinth, maze, confusion
dedans *adv.* in, within; — *m.* inside
dédicace *f.* dedication
dédicacer *vt.* to dedicate; autograph a book
dédicatoire *a.* dedicatory
dédier *vt.* to dedicate; inscribe
dédire *v.*, se — de to take back, go back on, retract
dédit *m.* retraction; forfeit
dédommagement *m.* indemnity, damages, compensation
dédommager *vt.* to indemnify, compensate
dédouaner *vt.* to clear through customs
dédoublement *m.* dividing, sectioning into two parts; duality; duplication
dédoubler *vt.* to divide; remove lining; unfold; se — to divide; unfold
déduction *f.* deduction; discount
déduire *vt.* to deduct; discount; deduce
déesse *f.* goddess
défaillance *f.* failing; failure; weakness; lapse; faint
défaillant *a.* failing; weakening; faint
défaillir *vi.* to fail, faint; grow weak
défaire *vt.* to unmake, undo; defeat; rid of; untie; unpack; se — de to get rid of
défait *a.* lean; worn; pale
défaite *f.* defeat
défaitiste *a. & n.* defeatist
défalquer *vt.* to deduct, take away
défaut *m.* defect; fault, failing; default; lack, want; à — de, au — de for want of
défaveur *f.* disfavor
défavorable *a.* unfavorable
défavoriser *vt.* to handicap, put at a disadvantage
défectif *a.* (gram.) defective verb
défection *f.* defection; faire — to defect
défectueux *a.* defective
défectuosité *f.* defectiveness; defect
défendeur *m.* defendant (at law)
défendre *vt.* to defend; protect; prohibit; se — to defend oneself; protect oneself
défense *f.* defense; prohibition; — civile civil defense; — de fumer no smoking, smoking prohibited; légitime — self-defense (at law); –s *pl.* tusks

défenseur *m.* defender; protector; defense counsel (law)
défensif *a.* defensive
déférence *f.* deference; consideration, respect
déférent *a.* deferent; respectful
déférer *vt.* to confer, award; hand over (at law); refer; swear (in); — *vi.* to defer, comply
déferler *vt.* to unfurl; set sail; — *vi.* to break (waves)
défeuiller *vt.* to remove the leaves from
défi *m.* defiance; challenge
défiance *f.* diffidence; distrust, mistrust
défiant *a.* mistrustful, distrustful; suspicious
déficeler *vt.* to untie
déficit *m.* deficit
déficience *f.* lack, deficiency
déficitaire *a.* unbalanced, with a deficit
défier *vt.* to defy; challenge; se — de to mistrust, distrust, be suspicious of, beware of
défigurer *vt.* to disfigure, deform
défilé *m.* defile, narrow passage; pass; parade, procession; — de voitures autocade, motorcade
défiler *vi.* to parade, march by
défini *a.* definite; well-defined
définir *vt.* to define; se — to become clear
définissable *a.* definable
définitif *a.* definitive; final; permanent; definite
définition *f.* definition
définitivement *adv.* finally; permanently; once and for all, for good; definitely
déflatation *f.* deflation; deflating
défloraison *f.* time of falling of flowers, falling of petals
défoncé *a.* battered; crumpled; bumpy
défoncer *vt.* to smash in; break up
déformation *f.* deformation; warping
déformer *vt.* to deform, distort; warp; se — to become deformed, lose shape; warp
défraichi *a.* shopworn; faded
défrayer *vt.* to defray
défricher *vt.* (agr.) to clear ground
défriser *vt.* to uncurl
défroncer *vt.* remove the wrinkles from
défunt *a.* deceased, late
dégagé *a.* disengaged, free; nonchalant
dégagement *m.* disengagement; clearing, freeing from obligation; release; relief; redeeming (pawned article); exit
dégager *vt.* to disengage, free; clear; release; relieve; redeem; se — to free oneself; clear oneself; appear, emerge, come out
dégaine *f.* (coll.) gait; ridiculous attitude

dégainer *vt.* to draw a sword; unsheathe

déganter *vt.* to unglove; **se —** to take off one's gloves

dégarnir *vt.* to strip, take apart; remove, take away; **se —** to lose (hair, leaves); be depleted, emptied, stripped

dégâts *m. pl.* damage

dégauchir *vt.* to straighten

dégel *m.* thaw; **—er** *vt. & vi.* to thaw

dégénération *f.* degeneration; deterioration

dégénéré *a.* degenerate

dégénérer *vi.* to degenerate; decline

dégivrer *vt.* to deice; defrost

dégivreuse *f.* defroster

déglacer *vt.* to thaw; defrost

dégonfler *vt.* to deflate; reduce; **se —** lose air, go flat; diminish, subside

dégorger *vt.* to disgorge; clear, open; scour; **— vi.** to flow into; overflow

dégourdi *a.* lively; sharp, alert

dégourdir *vt.* to revive, quicken; warm, take the chill from; **se —** to stretch one's limbs; get warm

dégoût *m.* disgust; dislike

dégoûtant *a.* disgusting; disagreeable, unpleasant

dégoûter *vt.* to disgust; **se — de** to become disgusted with; be fed up with

dégouttant *a.* trickling; dripping

dégoutter *vi.* to drip, trickle

dégradation *f.* degradation; erosion; defacement; wear; damage

dégrader *vt.* to degrade; damage, deface; **se —** to degrade oneself, lower oneself; become dilapidated

dégrafer *vt.* to unhook, unclasp, undo

dégraisser *vt.* to remove fat from; scour, clean, dry-clean

dégraisseur *m.* cleaner, dry cleaner

degré *m.* degree; stair step

dégriser *vt.* to sober up; (fig.) to disillusion

déguenillé *a.* ragged, in rags

déguerpir *vi.* to move out; clear out; **faire — to evict**

déguisement *m.* disguise

déguiser *vt.* to disguise; hide, conceal

dégustation *f.* tasting, art of tasting

déguster *vt.* to taste; sip, savor

dehors *adv.* out, outdoors, outside; **— m.** outside; external appearance

déifier *vt.* to deify

déisme *m.* deism

déité *f.* deity

déjà *adv.* already

déjeter *vt.* to warp; make uneven

déjeuner *m.* lunch; **petit — breakfast; — vi.** to breakfast; lunch

déjouer *vt.* to baffle; frustrate, foil

delà *prep. & adv.* beyond, on the other side; **au — (de)** beyond

délabré *a.* broken, dilapidated

délabrer *vt.* to ruin, dilapidate

délacer *vt.* to unlace

délai *m.* delay; interval; respite; (com.) time extension; **sans —** immediately

délaissement *m.* legal abandonment, desertion; loneliness; helplessness

délassement *m.* rest, relaxation

délaisser *vt.* to abandon, forsake; relinquish

délasser *vt.* to rest, relax

délavé *a.* faded, washed out; soaked

délayer *vt.* to dilute, thin, water

délébile *a.* erasable

délectable *a.* delectable

délectation *f.* delight, pleasure

délecter *vt.* to delight; **se — à** to delight in, enjoy

délégation *f.* delegation

délégué *m.* delegate

déléguer *vt.* to delegate

délester *vt.* to unburden, relieve

délétère *a.* deleterious; harmful; poisonous

délibération *f.* deliberation

délibéré *a.* deliberate

délibérer *vt. & vi.* to deliberate; resolve

délicat *a.* delicate; sensitive; fine; difficult; dainty; touchy; tactful

délicatesse *f.* delicacy; daintiness; nicety; fineness; difficulty

délice *m.* delight; **—s** *f. pl.* delight, pleasure

délicieux *a.* delicious; delightful

délié *a.* slender, slim; sharp; glib

délier *vt.* to untie, release; **se —** to come loose

délinéer *vt.* to delineate

délinquant *m.* delinquent, offender

délirant *a.* delirious

délire *m.* delirium, frenzy

délirer *vi.* to be delirious; rave

délit *m.* offense, wrong; misdemeanor

délivrance *f.* deliverance, rescue; delivery

délivre *m.* afterbirth, placenta

délivrer *vt.* to deliver, free; rescue; **se — de** to free oneself from; get rid of

déloger *vi.* to move out; go away; **— vt.** to eject, dislodge, drive out

déloyal *a.* disloyal, unfaithful; unfair; foul, unsporting

déloyauté *f.* disloyalty; treachery; foul play

déluge *m.* deluge, flood

déluré *a.* lively

démagnétiser *vt.* to demagnetize

démagogie *f.* demagogy

démagogue *m.* demagog

démailler *vt.* to undo links *or* mesh
démailloter *vt.* to unswathe
demain *adv. & m.* tomorrow; à — good-by, until tomorrow, see you tomorrow
demande *f.* question, claim; request; demand; application; petition; proposal, offer
demander *vt.* to ask, ask for; claim; request; want, require, need; demand
demandeur *m.* plaintiff (at law)
démangeaison *f.* itch, itching; desire
démanger *vi.* to itch
démarcation *f.* demarcation
démarche *f.* step, pace; gait; measure; procedure
démarquer *vt.* to remove the mark; imitate; reduce, put on sale
démarrer *vt. & vi.* (naut.) to cast off; (auto.) start; (coll.) leave
démarreur *m.* (auto.) starter
démasquer *vt.* to unmask
démêlé *m.* dispute, strife
démêler *vt.* to disentangle, separate comb out; clear up; make out, see
démembrement *m.* dismemberment
démembrer *vt.* to dismember; divide up
déménagement *m.* moving, removal; voiture de — *f.* moving van
déménager *vi.* to move, change residence; (fig.) (coll.) to become childish
déménageur *m.* mover of household goods
démence *f.* insanity, madness
démener *v.*, se — to struggle, be agitated
dément *a. & m.* lunatic
démenti *m.* denial, contradiction
démentir *vt.* to deny; contradict; belie
démérite *m.* lack of merit
démériter *vi.* to lose esteem, lose favor
démesure *f.* lack of measure, lack of moderation, excess
démesuré *a.* excessive; immoderate; inordinate
démettre *vt.* to dislocate; se — (de) to resign (from)
démeubler *vt.* to remove the furniture from
demeurant *adv.*, au — furthermore, besides, moreover
demeure *f.* dwelling, residence; delay (law)
demeurer *vi.* to live; stay, remain; delay
demi *a.* half; — *m.* half; football halfback; à — half, by half
demi-cercle *m.* semicircle
demi-dieu *m.* demigod
demi-finale *f.* semi-final (sports)
demi-frère *m.* half brother; stepbrother
demi-heure *f.* half hour
demi-jour *m.* half-light; gray; twilight
démilitarisé *a.* demilitarized

demi-lune *f.* half-moon
demi-mesure *f.* half measure
demi-monde *m.* shady society
demi-mot *m. adv.*, entendre à —, comprendre à — to take a hint
déminer *vt.* to demine, clear of mines
demi-pension *f.* partial board (two meals per day)
demi-pensionnaire *m. & f.* boarder (for breakfast and supper)
demi-place *f.* half price; half fare
demi-saison *f.* periods between winter and summer (spring *and* fall); vêtements de — *m. pl.* spring *or* fall clothing
demi-sœur *f.* half sister; stepsister
demi-solde *f.* army pension; — *m.* pensioned officer
démission *f.* resignation
démissionner *vi.* to resign
demi-tasse *f.* small coffee cup (after-dinner size)
demi-teinte *f.* medium shade (color)
demi-ton *m.* (mus.) half tone
demi-tour *m.* half turn; about-face; faire — to turn back, turn around
démobilisation *f.* demobilization
démobiliser *vt.* to demobilize
démocrate *m. & f.* democrat
démocratie *f.* democracy
démocratique *a.* democratic
démodé *a.* out of style; obsolete, old-fashioned
demoiselle *f.* young lady; dragonfly; — d'honneur bridesmaid; nom de — *m.* maiden name
démolir *vt.* to demolish
démolition *f.* demolition
démon *m.* demon, devil
démonétiser *vt.* to devalue, depreciate
démoniaque *a.* demoniac(al), devilish
démonstrateur *m.* demonstrator
démonstratif *a.* demonstrative
démonstration *f.* demonstration
démontable *a.* collapsible; detachable; portable
démonter *vt.* to dismantle; unhorse; upset
démontrable *a.* demonstrable
démontrer *vi.* to demonstrate
démoralisant, démoralisateur *a.* demoralizing
démoraliser *vt.* to demoralize
démuni *a.* out, sold out; unprovided; deprived
dénationaliser *vt.* to denationalize
dénaturer *vt.* to denature; make unnatural; pervert
dénégation *f.* denial
déni *m.* denial at law, refusal
dénicher *vt.* to dislodge; discover
denier *m.* money; penny, denier (of

fibers); interest money
dénier *vt.* to deny, refuse
dénigrer *vt.* to disparage
dénombrement *m.* enumeration; census
dénombrer *vt.* to enumerate, count
dénominateur *m.* denominator
dénomination *f.* denomination; name
dénommer *vt.* to name
dénoncer *vt.* to denounce
dénonciateur *m.* denouncer; informer; — *a.* revealing
dénonciation *f.* denunciation
dénoter *vt.* to denote
dénouement *m.* untying; end, ending, outcome, result
dénouer *vt.* to untie, undo, clear up
denrée *f.* commodity, product; **–s** *pl.* provisions; produce
dense *a.* dense; thick; close
densité *f.* density
dent *f.* tooth; notch; cog; prong; **coup de** — *m.* bite; **–s de lait** baby teeth; **mal de –s** *m.* toothache; **avoir mal aux –s** to have a toothache
dentaire *a.* dental
dental *a.* dental (phonetics)
dent-de-lion *f.* dandelion
denté *a.* notched; cogged; toothed
dentelle *f.* lace, lacework
dentelure *f.* notching; perforation
dentier *m.* row of teeth; denture
dentifrice *m.* dentifrice; **pâte** — *f.* toothpaste
dentine *f.* dentine
dentiste *m.* dentist
dénuder *vt.* to strip, denude
dénué *a.* devoid, lacking; out, without
dénuement *m.* destitution, want, poverty
dénuer *vt.* to deprive, strip
déodoriser *vt.* to deodorize
dépannage *m.* repair service
dépanner *vt.* to repair a breakdown
dépanneur *m.* (auto.) repair man
dépanneuse *f.* wrecker, tow truck
dépaqueter *vt.* to unpack; unwrap
dépareiller *vt.* to remove one of a pair; spoil a pair
déparer *vt.* to strip; remove adornment from
départ *m.* departure; start; division, separation
département *m.* department, administrative department
départemental *a.* departmental
départir *vt.* to divide; **se** — **de** to depart from; part with, to cease, desist
dépasser *vt.* to go beyond, overreach, overstep; overtake; transcend; exceed
dépaysé *a.* out of place
dépecer *vt.* to carve, cut in pieces

dépêche *f.* dispatch; telegram
dépêcher *vt.* to dispatch; **se** — to hurry, hasten
dépeindre *vt.* to paint, portray, depict
dépendance *f.* dependence, dependency
dépendant *a.* dependent
dépendre *vi.* to depend on; result; belong; — *vt.* to unhang, take down
dépens *m. pl.* (com.) cost; costs (law); **aux** — **de** at the expense of
dépense *f.* expense, expenditure; pantry
dépenser *vt.* to spend, expend
dépensier *a. & m.* extravagant; spendthrift
dépérir *vi.* to waste away; pine; decline; die out
dépeupler *vt.* to depopulate; unstock
dépilatoire *a.* hair-removing, depilatory
dépiler *vt.* to remove hair from
dépister *vt.* to track, hunt down
dépit *m.* spite; vexation
dépiter *vt.* to vex; spite
déplacé *a.* misplaced, out of place
déplacement *m.* moving; travelling; displacement
déplacer *vt.* to move; displace; transfer
déplaire *vi.* to displease; offend
déplaisant *a.* unpleasant
déplaisir *m.* displeasure
déplanter *vt.* to dig up for transplanting
dépliant *m.* folder, brochure
déplier *vt.* to unfold
déplisser *vt.* to remove the pleats *or* wrinkles from
déploiement *m.* deployment; unfolding
déplorable *a.* deplorable
déplorer *vt.* to deplore
déployé *a.* unfolded; **rire à gorge –e to** laugh heartily
déployer *vt.* to unfold; display; deploy
déplumer *vt.* to pluck the feathers of
dépolariser *vt.* to depolarize
dépolarisation *f.* depolarization
dépolir *vt.* to take off the polish; **verre dépoli** *m.* frosted glass
dépopulation *f.* depopulation
déportation *f.* deportation
déportements *m. pl.* misdeeds
déporter *vt.* to deport; — *vi.* to swerve
déposant *m.* depositor; deponent (law), witness; — *a.* testifying
dépose *f.* removal
déposer *vt. & vi.* to depose; deposit; give testimony
dépositaire *m. & f.* depository
déposition *f.* deposition
déposséder *vt.* to dispossess
dépôt *m.* deposit; storehouse, warehouse, trust
dépouille *f.* spoil; remains; cast-off skin;

—s *pl.* booty

dépouiller *vt.* to strip, skin an animal; examine, study

dépourvu *a.* unprovided for, destitute, lacking; **au — ** *adv.* unawares

dépravation *f.* depravity, corruption

dépraver *vt.* to deprave

déprécier *vt.* to depreciate, disparage

déprédation *f.* depradation, pillage

déprendre *v.,* **se — ** to separate, detach oneself

dépression *f.* depression

déprimer *vt.* to depress; disparage

depuis *prep.* since, for; **— longtemps** for a long time; **— ** *adv.* since; **— que** *conj.* since

dépurer *vt.* to purify

députation *f.* deputation

député *m.* deputy

députer *vt.* to send as representative

déraciner *vt.* to root out, uproot

dérailler *vi.* to be derailed; go off the track

déraison *f.* unreasonableness, folly

déraisonnable *a.* unreasonable

déraisonner *vi.* to be unreasonable

dérangement *m.* derangement; breakdown

déranger *vt.* to derange; put out of order; disturb

déraper *vi.* to detach; skid; aweigh (anchor)

dératé *m.* lively individual; **courir comme un — ** to run like a deer

derechef *adv.* again, anew

déréglé *a.* out of order; disorderly

dérèglement *m.* disorder; irregularity

dérégler *vt.* to put out of order

dérider *vt.* to unwrinkle; (fig.) to cheer up

dérision *f.* derision; **tourner en — ** to ridicule, deride

dérisoire *a.* derisive, ridiculous

dérivatif *m. & a.* derivative

dérivation *f.* derivation; drift; diversion

dérive *f.* drift; **à la — ** adrift

dérivé *m.* derivative

dériver *vi.* to derive; **— ** *vt.* to divert

dermatologie *f.* dermatology

dermatologiste *m.* dermatologist

dernier *a.* last; preceding; final

dernièrement *adv.* recently, lately

dernier-né *m.* youngest (in a family)

dérobée *f.,* **à la — ** secretly

dérober *vt.* to rob, steal; hide, conceal; **se — ** to steal away; disappear; hide

dérogation *f.* derogation

déroger *vi.,* **— à** to depart from, not conform to; detract from

dérouiller *vt.* to remove the rust from; limber up; polish

dérouler *vt.* to unroll, unfold

déroute *f.* rout, disorder

dérouter *vt.* to rout

derrière *prep. & adv.* behind; **— ** *m.* back, rear; behind

derviche *m.* dervish

dès *prep.* from, since, starting with; **— que** *conj.* as soon as

désabonner *v.,* **se — ** to cancel a subscription

désabuser *vt.* to disabuse, undeceive

désaccord *m.* disagreement, discord

désaccorder *vt.* to cause discord in

désaffecter *vt.* to deconsecrate, eliminate the original function of

désaffection *f.* loss of affection

désagréable *a.* disagreeable, unpleasant

désagrégation *f.* dissolution, separation; breaking up

désagréger *vt.* to separate, break up

désagrément *m.* unpleasantness

désaltérer *vt.* to quench one's thirst

désamorcer *vt.* to disarm a bomb; (elec.) cut the current

désappointement *m.* disappointment

désappointer *vt.* to disappoint; dull

désapprendre *vt.* to unlearn, forget

désapprobateur *a.* disapproving

désapprobation *f.* disapproval

désapprouver *vt.* to disapprove (of)

désarçonner *vt.* to unsaddle, unseat, throw from horse; (fig. & coll.) to disconcert; confuse in a discussion

désarmement *m.* disarmament

désarmer *vt.* to disarm; appease

désarroi *m.* disorder, confusion

désastre *m.* disaster

désastreux *a.* disastrous

désavantage *m.* disadvantage

désavantager *vt.* to put at a disadvantage, handicap

désavantageux *a.* disadvantageous

désaveu *m.* disavowal, denial

désavouer *vt.* to disavow

desceller *vt.* to unseal

descendance *f.* descent, descendants

descendant *a.* descending; **— ** *m.* descendant

descendre *vi.* to descend, come downstairs; **— à un hotel** stay at a hotel; **— ** *vt.* to bring down; (coll.) depose; (avi.) bring down an enemy plane

descente *f.* descent; decline; hernia; **— de lit** bedside rug

descriptible *a.* describable

descriptif *a.* descriptive

désemballer *vt.* to unpack, unwrap

désemparé *a.* disconcerted

désemparer *vi.,* **sans — ** immediately;

continuously
désenchanter vt. to disillusion, disenchant
désencombrer vt. to free, disencumber
désengager vt. to release from a commitment
désennuyer vt. to divert, cheer
désensabler vt. to free from the sand
désensibiliser vt. to desensitize
désentortiller vt. to straighten; sort
déséquilibrer vt. to unbalance
désert m. desert, wilderness; — a. deserted, solitary, abandoned
déserter vt. & vi. to desert
déserteur m. deserter
désertion f. desertion
désespérance f. despair, loss of hope
désespéré a. desperate, hopeless
désespérer vi. to despair; — vt. to be the despair of
désespoir m. despair
déshabillé m. housecoat
déshabiller vt. to undress
déshérité a. disinherited; downtrodden
déshériter vt. to disinherit
déshonnête a. improper, unseemly
déshonneur m. dishonor, disgrace
déshonorer vt. to dishonor
déshydratant m. dehumidifier
déshydrater vt. to dehydrate
désignation f. designation
désigner vt. to designate; appoint
désillusion f. disappointment, disillusion
désillusionner vt. to disillusion
désinence f. (gram.) ending of word
désinfecter vt. to disinfect
désinfection f. disinfection
désintégrable a. fissionable
désintégration f. disintegration; fission
désintégrer vt. to disintegrate
désintéressé a. disinterested; unselfish
désintéressement m. impartiality; unselfishness
désintéresser vt. to idemnify; buy out
désinviter vt. to withdraw an invitation
désinvolte a. unconstrained; impertinent
désinvolture f. ease, gracefulness
désir m. desire, wish
désirable a. desirable
désirer vt. to desire, wish for
désireux a. desirous, anxious
désister v., se — to desist; **se** — **de** to waive, renounce
désobéir vi. to disobey
désobéissance f. disobedience; — **civile** civil disobedience
désobligeant a. disobliging
désobliger vt. to displease
désodorisant m. deodorant
désodoriser vt. to clear of odor, deodorize
désœuvré a. idle, unoccupied

désœuvrement m. idleness, lack of occupation
désolant a. distressing, sad
désolation f. desolation; desolateness; grief
désolé a. very sorry; desolate
désoler vt. to desolate, ruin, destroy
désopilant a. very funny, hilarious
désordonné a. disordered; disorderly
désordonner vt. to disorder
désordre m. disorder, confusion
désorganiser vt. to disorganize
désorienter vt. to mislead; cause to become lost
désormais adv. henceforth
désoxyder vt. to deoxidize
despote m. despot; — a. despotic
despotisme m. despotism
dessaisir vt. to dispossess
dessécher vt. to dry; wither
dessein m. design, purpose; scheme, plan; **à** — on purpose; **sans** — unintentionally; aimlessly
desserrer vt. to loosen
dessert m. dessert
desserte f. sideboard
dessertir vt. to remove a gem from its setting
desservant m. parish priest
desservir vt. to serve; clear the table; harm, be of disservice to
dessiller vt. to open the eyes
dessin m. drawing; plan; pattern; — **de vol** (avi.) flight pattern
dessinateur m. designer; draftsman
dessiner vt. to draw, design, sketch
dessouler vt. & vi. to sober up
dessous prep. & adv. under, below; underneath, undermost; **au** — **(de)** below; — m. underpart; wrong side
dessus prep. & adv. on, upon, uppermost; **au** — **(de)** above, beyond; — m. upper part; advantage
destin m. destiny, fate
destinataire m. receiver, addressee, consignee
destinée f. destiny, doom, fate
destiner vt. to destine; intend
destitué a. destitute, devoid
destituer vt. to dismiss, discharge
destitution f. destitution, dismissal
destrier m. charger, war horse
destructeur a. destructive; — m. destroyer
destructif a. destructive
désuet a. obsolete
désuétude f. obsolescence, disuse
désunion f. lack of harmony, discord; misunderstanding
désunir vt. to separate, unjoin

détaché *a.* loose, indifferent, detached

détachement *m.* detachment

détacher *vt.* to detach, loosen; clean, remove spots from

détail *m.* detail; (com.) retail; au — (com.) at retail

détaillant *m.* retailer

détailler *vt.* to cut up; detail; retail

détartrer *vt.* remove tartar from teeth

detaxer *vt.* to remove the tax from, exempt from tax

détecter *vt.* to detect

détecteur *m.* detector

détective *m.* detective; (phot.) box camera

déteindre *vi.* to fade *or* run (colors)

dételer *vt.* to unharness; give up, cease

détendre *vt.* to relax, loosen; take down

détenir *vt.* to detain, withhold; hold, possess

détente *f.* trigger; (fig.) relaxation; expansion

détention *f.* detention, custody

détenu *m.* prisoner

déterger *vt.* to clean

détérioration *f.* deterioration

détériorer *vt.* to deteriorate

déterminant *a.* determining; — *m.* determinant

déterminatif *a.* determining

détermination *f.* determination

déterminé *a.* determined; definite

déterminer *vt.* to determine, settle, decide; cause

déterminisme *m.* determinism

déterrer *vt.* to disinter; unearth, discover

détersif *m.* detergent

détestable *a.* detestable

détestation *f.* detestation

détester *vt.* to detest, abhor, hate

détonant *a. & m.* explosive

détonateur *m.* detonating cap

détonation *f.* detonation, explosion

détoner *vi.* to explode

détonner *vi.* to sing *or* play off key; to clash

détordre *vt.* to untwist

détorquer *vt.* to distort, misrepresent

détorsion *f.* distortion

détortiller *vt.* to untwist

détour *m.* turning, roundabout way; evasion, excuse, subterfuge; turn, bend; prendre des —s to beat about the bush

détourné *a.* off the beaten track; isolated; secret

détournement *m.* diverting, turning away; embezzlement

détourner *vt.* to turn aside; divert, change; avert

détracteur *m.* detractor; — *a.* detracting

détraquer *vt.* to lead astray, distract,

divert; break, put out of commission; se — to break down

détrempe *f.* distemper (art)

détremper *vt.* to dilute; soften, remove the temper

détresse *f.* distress; danger

détriment *m.* detriment

détritus *m.* waste, rubbish, debris

détroit *m.* strait, channel

détromper *vt.* to undeceive

détrôner *vt.* to dethrone

détrousser *vt.* to undo; rob

détruire *vt.* to destroy, ruin

dette *f.* debt

deuil *m.* mourning, mourning clothes

deutérium *m.* deuterium

deux *a.* two; tous les — both

deuxième *a.* second

deux-points *m.* colon

dévaler *vi.* to go down(ward)

dévaliser *vt.* to rob

dévaloriser *vt.* to devaluate

dévaluation *f.* devaluation

dévaluer *vt.* to devaluate

devancer *vt.* to go before, precede; anticipate

devancier *m.* predecessor; -s *pl.* ancestors

devant *m.* front, forepart; aller au — de to go and meet; — *prep. & adv.* in front of, before

devanture *f.* store window; window display

dévastateur *m.* devastator; — *a.* devastating

dévastation *f.* devastation

dévaster *vt.* to devastate

déveine *f.* bad luck

développement *m.* development

développer *vt.* to develop; unfold

devenir *vi.* to become; grow, turn

dévergondage *m.* shamelessness; excesses

dévergonder *v.*, se — to become dissolute, commit excesses, be shameless

dévernir *vt.* to remove the varnish

déverrouiller *vt.* to unbolt

devers *prep.* towards; par — in the possession of; in the eyes of

dévers *a.* out of alignment

déverser *vt.* to slope, bank; pour, divert; — *vi.* lean; become lopsided

dévêtir *vt.* to undress; divest

déviation *f.* deviation, deflection; detour

dévider *vt.* to wind onto

dévier *vt.* to turn aside; — *vi.* to make a detour; deviate

deviner *vt.* to divine, guess

devinette *f.* riddle

dévisager *vt.* to stare at

devise *f.* motto; -s *pl.* foreign currency

deviser *vi.* to chat

dévisser *vt.* to unscrew
dévoiler *vt.* to unveil, discover
devoir *vt. & vi.* to owe, be indebted to; be bound, be obliged; must, ought; be necessary; — *m.* duty, obligation, task
dévorateur *a.* devouring
dévorer *vt.* to devour; (fig.) consume
dévot *a.* devout; pious; bigoted
dévouement *m.* devotion; religious devotion
dévouer *vt.* to devote, dedicate
dévoyé *m. & a.* stray
dextérité *f.* dexterity
diabète *m.* (med.) diabetes
diabétique *a. & n.* diabetic
diable *m.* devil; hand truck for baggage
diablerie *f.* deviltry
diablotin *m.* little devil
diabolique *a.* diabolic(al)
diaconesse *f.* deaconess
diacre *m.* deacon
diacritique *a.* diacritic(al)
diadème *m.* diadem
diagnose *f.* (med.) diagnosis
diagnostique *a.* diagnostic
diagnostiquer *vt.* to diagnose
diagramme *m.* diagram
dialectal *a.* dialectical
dialecte *m.* dialect
dialectique *a.* dialectic; — *f.* dialectics
dialogue *m.* dialog
dialoguer *vi.* to converse
diamant *m.* diamond
diamantaire, diamantin *a.* diamond-like
diamétral *a.* diametrical
diamètre *m.* diameter
diane *f.* (mil.) reveille
diantre *interj.* devil, dickens
diapason *m.* diapason
diaphane *a.* transparent
diaphragme *m.* diaphragm
diapositif *m.*, diapositive *f.* (phot.) transparency
diaprer *vt.* to ornament, color with many hues
diarrhée *f.* diarrhea
diastolique *a.* (med.) diastolic
diathermie *f.* diathermy
diatomée *f.* diatom
diatonique *a.* (mus.) diatonic
dichromatique *a.* dichromatic
dictateur *m.* dictator
dictatorial *a.* dictatorial
dictature *f.* dictatorship
dictée *f.* dictation
dicter *vt.* to dictate
diction *f.* diction
dictionnaire *m.* dictionary
dicton *m.* saying, proverb
didactique *a.* didactic

diérèse *f.* diaeresis
dièse *a. & m.* (mus.) sharp
diesel *m.* diesel engine
diéser *vt.* (mus.) to sharp
diète *f.* diet
diéticien *m.* dietician
diététique *f.* dietetics
Dieu *m.* God; — merci! thank God!; plût à —! God grant it!; à — ne plaise! God forbid!
diffamation *f.* defamation
diffamatoire *a.* defamatory
diffamer *vt.* to defame, slander; libel
différemment *adv.* differently
différence *f.* difference
différenciation *f.* differentiation
différencier *vt.* to distinguish
différend *m.* difference, source of argument
différentiel *a. & m.* differential
différer *vt.* to defer, put off; — *vi.* to differ
difficile *a.* difficult; hard
difficulté *f.* difficulty
difficultueux *a.* difficult
difforme *a.* deformed
difformité *f.* deformity
diffracter *vt.* to diffract
diffraction *f.* diffraction
diffus *a.* diffuse; wordy
diffuser *vt.* to diffuse, spread
diffusion *f.* diffusion; spreading
digérer *vt. & vi.* to digest; stomach; simmer
digest *m.* digest, abridgment, résumé
digestif *m.* (med.) digestive; liqueur, brandy; — *a.* digestive
digestion *f.* digestion
digitaline *f.* (med.) digitalis
digne *a.* worthy (of); dignified
dignitaire *m.* dignitary
dignité *f.* dignity, title, rank
digression *f.* digression
digue *f.* dike
dilacérer *vt.* to lacerate
dilapidation *f.* dilapidation
dilapider *vt.* to dilapidate; embezzle; squander
dilation *f.* dilation, expansion
dilater *vt.* to dilate, expand, widen
dilatoire *a.* dilatory
dilemme *m.* dilemma
dilettante *m.* dilettante, amateur
diligemment *adv.* diligently
diligence *f.* diligence; haste; stagecoach
diluer *vt.* to dilute
diluvien *a.* diluvian; diluvial
dimanche *m.* Sunday
dîme *f.* tithe
diminuer *vt. & vi.* to diminish

diminutif *a.* diminutive

dinde *f.* hen turkey; (fig.) goose; foolish woman

dindon *m.* tom turkey; **—neau** *m.* young turkey

dîner *m.* dinner; **—** *vi.* to dine

dînette *f.* family supper; children's evening meal

dîneur *m.* dinner guest; diner

dinosaure, dinosaurien *m.* dinosaur

diocèse *m.* diocese

diphthérie *f.* diphtheria

diphthongue *m.* diphthong

diphtonguer *vt.* to diphthongize

diplomate *m.* diplomat

diplomatie *f.* diplomacy

diplomatique *a.* diplomatic

diplôme *m.* diploma

diplômé *a.* graduate, licensed

dipsomanie *f.* compulsive drinking

dire *vt.* to tell, say, relate; think; mean; **pour ainsi —** as it were; **vouloir — to** mean; **—** *n.* words, statement

directeur *m.* director, manager

direction *f.* direction; management; steering gear

directionnel *a.* directional

directive *f.* directive

directoire *m.* directory

directorat *m.* directorship

dirigeable *m.* dirigible

diriger *vt.* to direct, manage, guide, lead **— par radio** (avi.) to vector

discernable *a.* discernible, perceptible

discernement *m.* discernment

discerner *vt.* to discern

disciple *m.* disciple

disciplinaire *a.* disciplinary; **—** *m.* disciplinarian

discipliner *vt.* to discipline

discobole *m.* discus thrower

discontinu *a.* discontinuous

discontinuation *f.* discontinuation

discontinuer *vt.* to interrupt, discontinue

discontinuité *f.* interruption, discontinuity

disconvenance *f.* disproportion, disparity; unsuitableness

disconvenir *vi.* to disagree

discophile *m.* & *f.* amateur record collector *or* maker

discordant *a.* discordant

discorde *f.* discord

discorder *vi.* to be out of harmony, not to harmonize; clash

discothèque *f.* collection of phonograph records, record library

discourir *vi.* to discourse

discours *m.* discourse; speech

discourtois *a.* discourteous

discourtoisie *f.* discourtesy, impoliteness

discrédit *m.* discredit; disfavor

discréditer *vt.* to discredit

discret *a.* discreet; prudent; quiet

discrétion *f.* discretion

discrétionnaire *a.* discretionary

discrimination *f.* discrimination

disculper *vt.* to clear, exonerate

discussion *f.* argument, debate; discussion

discutable *a.* moot, debatable

discuter *vt.* to discuss, argue, debate

disert *a.* fluent, eloquent

disette *f.* want, poverty; famine

diseur (diseuse) *m.* & *f.* speaker, teller; **— de bonne aventure** fortune teller

disgrâce *f.* disgrace, disfavor

disgracié *a.* fallen from favor

disgracieux *a.* ungraceful, awkward; disagreable; rude

disjoindre *vt.* to disjoin, disjoint

disjoncteur *m.* circuit breaker

disjonctif *a.* disjunctive

disloquer *vt.* to dislocate

disparaître *vi.* to disappear

disparate *a.* incongruous; unmatched; **—** *f.* incongruity, sharp contrast

disparité *f.* disparity

disparition *f.* disappearance

dispendieux *a.* costly, expensive

dispensaire *m.* dispensary, clinic

dispensation *f.* dispensing, dispensation

dispense *f.* dispensation; exemption

dispenser *vt.* to dispense; excuse, **exempt**

disperser *vt.* to disperse, scatter

dispersion *f.* dispersion, dispersal

disponibilités *f. pl.* available funds

disponible *a.* available; free, unoccupied

dispos *a.* well-disposed; in good condition

disposé *a.* disposed, inclined

disposer *vt.* & *vi.* to dispose; **— de to** have at one's disposal

dispositif *m.* apparatus; terms; assembly of machinery pieces

disposition *f.* disposition; arrangement; **–s** *pl.* preparation; **— de vol** flight pattern

disproportionné a. disproportionate

dispute *f.* dispute, quarrel

disputer *vt.* & *vi.* to dispute, quarrel, **argue**

disqualification *f.* disqualification

disquaire *m.* record seller, record dealer

disqualifier *vt.* to disqualify

disque *m.* disk, discus; phonograph record; (rail.) safety signal; **— longue durée** long-playing record

dissection *f.* dissection

dissemblable *a.* unsimilar, different

dissémination *f.* dissemination

disséminer *vt.* to disseminate

dissension *f.* dissension, discord

dissentiment *m.* difference of opinion

disséquer *vt.* to dissect
dissertation *f.* dissertation; essay on a certain subject
disserter *vi.* to expound
dissident *a.* dissident
dissimulateur *m.* dissembler; — *a.* dissembling, hiding
dissimulation *f.* dissimulation, dissembling
dissimulé *a.* secretive, deceptive
dissimuler *vt. & vi.* to conseal; hide; dissemble
dissipation *f.* dissipation
dissiper *vt.* to dissipate; disperse
dissociation *f.* dissociation
dissocier *vt.* to dissociate, separate
dissolu *a.* dissolute
dissolution *f.* dissolution; dissoluteness; dissolving
dissonance *f.* disssonance
dissonant *a.* dissonant
dissoudre *vt.* to dissolve
dissuder *vt.* to dissuade
distance *f.* distance; interval
distancer *vt.* to outdistance; to stagger (racing); to disqualify (racing)
distant *a.* distant
distendre *vt.* to distend
distension *f.* distension
distillat *m.* distillate
distillateur *m.* distiller
distillation *f.* distillation
distiller *vt.* to distill; —ie *f.* distillery
distinct *a.* distinct, clear
distinctif *a.* distinctive
distinction *f.* distinction
distingué *a.* distinguished
distinguer *vt.* to distinguish; single out
distordre *vt.* to distort, twist
distors *a.* distorted, twisted
distorsion *f.* distortion
distraction *f.* distraction, abstraction; absent-mindedness; amusement
distraire *vt.* to distract, divert
distrait *a.* inattentive, absent-minded
distribuer *vt.* to distribute
distributeur *a.* distributing; — *m.* distributor
distribution *f.* distribution; (theat.) cast
district *m.* district
dit *a.* said, appointed, fixed; prendre pour — to take for granted; — *m.* saying
dito *adv.* ditto
diurétique *a. & m.* diuretic
diurne *a.* daily; day-blooming; active in daylight
divaguer *vi.* to go astray, wander, ramble
divan *m.* divan, couch
divergence *f.* divergency, divergence
divergent *a.* divergent

diverger *vi.* to diverge
divers *a.* diverse; various; different
diversifier *vt.* to diversify, vary
diversion *f.* diversion
diversité *f.* diversity
divertir *vt.* to divert, entertain; se — to have a good time
divertissement *m.* recreation, pastime, diversion
dividende *f.* dividend
divin *a.* divine; heavenly
divination *f.* divination, soothsaying
diviniser *vt.* to deify
divinité *f.* divinity
diviser *vt.* to divide; separate
diviseur *m.* divider; (math.) divisor, factor
divisible *a.* divisible
division *f.* division; dividing; section; disagreement; hyphen
divorcer *vi.* to divorce, be divorced
divulguer *vt.* to divulge
dix *a.* ten
dix-huit *a.* eighteen
dixième *a.* tenth
dix-neuf *a.* nineteen
dix-sept *a.* seventeen
dizaine *f.* about ten
djinn *m.* jinni, genie
do *m.* (mus.) do; first scale syllable; French key of C
docile *a.* docile, submissive
docilité *f.* docility
dock *m.* dock
docker *m.* dock worker
docte *a.* learned, scholarly
docteur *m.* doctor
doctorat *m.* doctor's degree, doctorate
doctrinal *a.* doctrinal
doctrine *f.* doctrine, dogma
document *m.* document; written proof
documentaire *a. & m.* documentary; documentative, educational film
documentation *f.* documentation
documenter *vt.* to document
dodeliner *vi.* to sway, rock; — *vt.* to dandle a baby, balance gently
dogmatique *a.* dogmatic
dogmatiser *vi.* to pontificate; speak in a pre-emptory tone
dogmatisme *m.* dogmatism
dogme *m.* dogma, tenet
dogue *m.* bullgod; watchdog
doigt *m.* finger; — du pied toe; montrer du — to point at
doigter *vt.* to finger, strum, play
doigtier *m.* finger guard
doit *m.* (com.) debit
doléance *f.* complaint; grievance
dolent *a.* sad, doleful; painful

dolmen *m.* dolmen (archeology)

domaine *m.* domain; estate; property

dôme *m.* dome; — **géodésique** geodesic dome

domestication *f.* domestication

domesticité *f.* domesticity

domestique *m. & f.* domestic, servant; — *a.* domestic

domestiquer *vt.* to tame, domesticate

domicilier *vt.* to domicile; **se** — to establish residence

dominant *a.* dominant; **-e** *f.* dominant trait

dominateur *a.* dominant, dominating

dominer *vt.* to dominate, rule, control; overlook; — *vi.* to rule, prevail

dominical *a.* dominical; Sunday; **oraison -e** *f.* Lord's prayer

domino *m.* domino; robe; disguise

dommage *m.* damage, loss; **c'est** — it is a pity

dommageable *a.* damaging; damageable

domptable *a.* conquerable; tamable, trainable

dompter *vt.* to tame; subdue, vanquish, conquer

dompteur *m.* conqueror; animal trainer

don *m.* gift, present; (fig.) knack, talent

donataire *m. & f.* recipient, beneficiary

donateur *m.* donor

donation *f.* donation, gift

donc *conj.* then, thus, therefore, so

donjon *m.* castle keep; isolated tower for castle watchman; tiered metal tower (modern battleship)

donne *f.* card deal

donnée *f.*, **-s** *pl.* information; data

donner *vt. & vi.* to give; impart; grant; deal cards; — **sur** to open onto, look out on

donneur *m.* donor; dealer at cards

dont *pron.* whose, of which, of whom

donzelle *f.* woman of easy virtue

dorade, daurade *f.* goldfish

dorénavant *adv.* henceforth

dorer *vt.* to gild; to glaze pastry

doreur *m.* gilder

dorique *a.* Doric

dorlotement *m.* coddling, pampering

dorloter *vt.* to pamper, coddle

dormant *a.* sleeping; dormant

dormeur *m.* sleeper

dormir *vi.* to sleep; **à** — **debout** boring

dortoir *m.* dormitory

dorure *f.* gilding; application of pastry glaze

dos *m.* back; — **du nez** bridge of the nose

dosage *m.* dose, dosage

dossier *m.* chair back; file, folder; dossier

dot *f.* dowry

dotation *f.* endowment

doter *vt.* to endow; furnish with a dowry

douaire *m.* widow's dowry

douairière *f.* dowager

douane *f.* custom house, duty, customs

douanier *m.* customs officer; — *a.* concerning customs

doublage *m.* lining; doubling; dubbing (movie film)

double *m.* double; spare; copy; — *a.* double

doublé *m.* plated metal; metal plating (gold *or* silver); bank shot (billiards); — *a.* lined

doublement *adv.* doubly

doubler *vt.* to double; line; pass (a car); hasten; begin over; dub (a film)

doublon *m.* doubloon

doublure *f.* lining; (theat.) understudy

doucement *adv.* softly; slowly

doucereux *a.* unpleasantly sweet

douceur *f.* sweetness; softness, gentleness; docility

douche *f.* shower bath; (med.) douche

doucir *vt.* to polish, rub

doué *a.* gifted, endowed

douer *vt.* to bestow, endow

douille *f.* socket; cartridge shell; casing

douillet *a.* soft, delicate; (fig.) oversensitive

douleur *f.* pain, sorrow

douloureux *a.* painful; sorrowful

doute *m.* doubt; suspicion; skepticism; **mettre en** — to doubt, question; **sans** — without doubt, probably; of course

douter *vi.* to doubt; **se** — **de** to suspect

douteur *a.* doubting

douteux *a.* doubtful; dubious, suspicious

douve *f.* moat; plank, stave

doux (douce) *a.* sweet; soft, smooth; fresh; quiet; mild; timid

douzaine *f.* dozen

douze *a.* twelve

douzième *a.* twelfth

doxologie *f.* doxology

doyen *m.* dean

doyenneté *f.* seniority

dragée *f.* Jordan almond; buckshot; sugar-coated pill

drageon *m.* (bot.) sucker, shoot (tree root)

dragon *m.* dragon; (mil.) dragoon

drague *f.* dredge; seine; minesweeping apparatus; — **à vapeur** steam shovel

draguer *vt.* to dredge

dragueur *m.* dredge (boat); minesweeper

drain *m.* drain pipe; (med.) drain

drainage *m.* drainage

drainer *vt.* to drain

dramatique *a.* dramatic

dramatiser *vt.* to dramatize

dramaturge *m.* dramatist
drame *m.* drama, play
drap *m.* cloth; bed sheet; **–ie** *f.* drapery
drapeau *m.* flag
draper *vt.* to drape
drapier *m.* cloth merchant, cloth manufacturer; draper
drelin *m.* sound of ringing, ting-a-ling (bell)
dressage *m.* training of animals
dresser *vt.* to raise; build; train animals; set up; trim; — **les oreilles** prick up ears; **se** — to stand, straighten up, rise; sit up
dresseur *m.* animal trainer
dressoir *m.* sideboard, buffet; dresser
drisse *f.* halyard, rope
drogue *f.* drug; chemical
droguer *vt.* to drug; physic
droguerie *f.* drug business
droguiste *m.* druggist
droit *m.* right, justice; prerogative, privilege; law; tax; **de** — by rights, rightfully; — *a.* right; straight; just; honest; upright; — *adv.*, **tout** — straight ahead
droite *f.* right; **à** — to the right
droitier *a.* right-hand(ed)
droiture *f.* integrity
drolatique *a.* droll, funny, amusing
drôle *a.* droll, funny; odd, peculiar
drôlesse *f.* wench, hussy
dromadaire *m.* dromadary
dru *a.* vigorous, heavy; — *adv.* thickly, heavily
dû *a. & m.* due; what is owed
dualisme *m.* dualism
dualité *f.* duality
duc *m.* duke; horned owl
duché *m.* duchy
duchesse *f.* duchess; (coll.) woman with airs; 18th century couch; Duchess pear
ductile *a.* ductile
duègne *f.* duenna, chaperon
duel *m.* duel
duelliste *m.* duelist
dulcifier *vt.* to sweeten; neutralize
dûment *adv.* duly
dune *f.* dune
dunette *f.* (naut.) poop
duo *m.* (mus.) duet
duodécimal *a.* duodecimal
duodénum *m.* duodenum
dupe *f.* dupe; — *a.* duped
duper *vt.* to dupe; fool
duperie *f.* deception, trickery
duplicata *m.* duplicate
duplicateur *m.* duplicator, duplicating machine
duplication *f.* duplication
duplicité *f.* duplicity

duquel *pron.* of which, of whom, whose
dur *a. & adv.* hard; tough, difficult
durabilité *f.* durability
durable *a.* durable, lasting
durant *prep.* during
durcir *vt. & vi.* to harden
durcissement *m.* hardening; stiffening
durée *f.* duration
durer *vi.* to last, endure
dureté *f.* hardness, toughness; cruelty
durillon *m.* callus, corn
duvet *m.* down; fuzz
duveté *a.* downy
duveteux *a.* downy
dynamique *a.* dynamic
dynamisme *m.* dynamism
dynamite *f.* dynamite; **–r** *vt.* to dynamite
dynamo *f.* dynamo
dynastie *f.* dynasty
dynastique *a.* dynastic
dyne *f.* dyne
dysenterie *f.* dysentery
dyspepsie *f.* dispepsia, indigestion

E

eau *f.* water; — **de Cologne** cologne; — **douce** soft water; fresh water; **cours d'** — *m.* stream; **jet d'** — *m.* fountain
eau-de-vie *f.* brandy; spirits
eau-forte *f.* nitric acid; etching
ébahir *vt.* to stupify, amaze
ébahissement *m.* astonishment, amazement
ébats *m. pl.* frolics, revels
ébattre *v.*, **s'** — to frolic, revel
ébaubir *v.*, **s'** — to be astonished
ébauche *f.* rough draft, sketch
ébaucher *vt.* to sketch, make a rough draft of
ébène *f.* ebony
ébenier *m.* ebony tree
ébéniste *m.* cabinetmaker
éberluer *vt.* to astonish
éblouir *vt.* to dazzle; bewitch
éblouissement *m.* dazzlement; glare
ébouillanter *vt.* to scald
éboulement *m.* landslide; cave-in (earth)
ébouler *vt.* to cause to fall; to crumble; **s'** — to tumble down
ébouriffant *a.* amazing
ébouriffer *vt.* to disorder, mess up; amaze
ébrancher *vt.* to prune
ébranlement *m.* shaking; shock
ébranler *vt.* to shake, shock; set in motion; **s'** — to waver, shake
ébrécher *vt.* to breach; notch; — **sa fortune** cut into one's fortune
ébriété *f.* inebriation
ébroer *v.* **s'** — to snort

ébruiter *vt.* to spread about; make public

ébullition *f.* boiling; boiling point

éburnéen *a.* ivory

écaille *f.* scale, shell; tortoise shell

écailler *vt. & vi.* to scale fish

écale *f.* shell, hull

écaler *vt.* to shell, hull

écarlate *f. & a.* scarlet

écarquiller *vt.* to spread, open wide

écart *m.* stepping aside; swerving; discard; digression; **à l'** — *adv.* aside; secluded; aloof **à l'** — **de** *prep.* far from

écarté *a.* lonely, secluded

écartèlement *m.* quartering

écarteler *vt.* to quarter

écartement *m.* removal, separation

écarter *vt.* to put aside; separate; avert

ecchymose *f.* bruise, black-and-blue mark

ecclésiastique *a. & m.* ecclesiastic

écervelé *a.* brainless, flighty; — *m.* scatterbrain

échafaud *m.* scaffold; platform

échafaudage *m.* scaffolding

échafauder *vt.* to put up a scaffold; plan, set up, build up

échalote *f.* (bot.) shallot

échancrer *vt.* to hollow out; indent

échange *m.* exchange; **libre** — free trade

échanger *vt.* to exchange, barter

échanson *m.* cupbearer

échantillon *m.* sample, specimen

échappatoire *f.* way out; loophole

échappée *f.* escape; space, short period; **à l'** — stealthily

échappement *m.* escapement (watch); leak, leakage, escape; exhaust

échapper *vt.* to escape; avoid; **s'** — to escape; leave

écharde *f.* splinter

écharpe *f.* scarf; sash; sling; **en** — *adv.* diagonally

écharper *vt.* to slash, cut up

échasse *f.* stilt

échauder *vt.* to scald

échauffement *m.* heating; overexcitement

échauffer *vt.* to warm; excite; **s'** — to get warm; grow angry

échauffourée *f.* blunder; riot; rash project

échéance *f.* expiration, falling due; **tomber à** — to fall due

échéant *a.* falling due; **le cas** — if such should be the case

échec *m.* check; failure; **-s** *pl.* chess; chessmen; — **et mat** checkmate

échelle *f.* ladder, scale; stocking run; —

échelon *m.* rung; echelon

échelonnement *m.* spreading out

échelonner *vt.* to spread out; space out; (mil.) arrange in echelon

écheniller *vt.* to exterminate caterpillars

écheveau *m.* skein

échevelé *a.* dishevelled, tangled

écheveler *vt.* to dishevel

échine *f.* spine; backbone

échiner *vt.* to break the back of; beat; **s'** — to tire oneself out

échiquier *m.* chessboard; exchequer

écho *m.* echo

échoir *vi.* to fall due; happen

échopper *vt.* to gouge, scoop out

échotier *m.* gossip columnist, newsmonger

échouer *vt. & vi.* (naut.) to run aground, strand; be stranded; fail; **faire** — **to** wreck

échu *a.* expired

éclabousser *vt.* to splash, splatter

éclaboussure *f.* splash, splatter

éclair *m.* lightning flash; eclair (pastry)

éclairage *m.* lighting, lamps; (fig.) point of view

éclaircie *f.* bright spot (sky); clearing (forest)

éclaircir *vt.* to clear, thin, brighten; explain, elucidate

éclaircissement *m.* clearing up; explanation

éclairer *vt. & vi.* to light, illuminate, enlighten

éclaireur *m.* scout

éclaireuse *f.* girl scout

éclat *m.* splinter; brightness; splendor; explosion; peal of thunder; (fig.) glory

éclatant *a.* glittering, brilliant

éclatement *m.* explosion, bursting

éclater *vi.* to split, burst; sparkle, glitter; break out, blow up

éclectique *a. & n.* eclectic

éclectisme *m.* eclecticism

éclipser *vt.* to eclipse; **s'** — to be eclipsed, vanish

éclisse *f.* splinter; (med.) splint

éclisser *vt.* (med.) to use a splint

éclopé *a.* lame, crippled

éclore *vi.* to be hatched; blossom; open

éclosion *f.* blooming; manifestation; advent; hatching

écluse *f.* floodgate; canal lock

écluser *vt.* to close by a lock; — **un bateau** to take a boat through a lock

écœurer *vt.* to sicken; dishearten; cause aversion

école *f.* school; — **maternelle** nursery school; — **mixte** school for boys *and* girls

écolier *m.* schoolboy

écolière *f.* schoolgirl

écologie *f.* ecology

éconduire *vt.* to show out; get rid of

économat *m.* treasurer's office; bureau **of** economies

économe *a.* economical; — *m. & f.* housekeeper; accounts keeper; treasurer
économie *f.* economy; saving; — domestique home economics
économique *a.* economic; economical
économiser *vt.* to economize, save
économiste *m.* economist
écope *f.* (naut.) bailing scoop
écoper *vt.* (naut.) to bail out
écorce *f.* bark (tree), rind, peel; outside
écorcer *vt.* to peel
écorcher *vt.* to flay; scrape; scorch
écorchure *f.* scrape, abrasion
écorner *vt.* to dog-ear; curtail, reduce
écornifleur *m.* parasite, moocher
écossais *a.* Scotch, Scottish; — *n.* Scot, Scotsman
Ecosse *f.* Scotland
écosser *vt.* to shell
écot *m.* share, part, portion; tree stump
écoulement *m.* drain, discharge; sale
écouler *vt.* to sell; **s'** — to flow out, drain off; elapse, go by
écourter *vt.* to shorten; crop
écoute *f.* listening post; monitor; être aux —s to be listening (in), be eavesdropping
écouter *vt.* to listen (to); pay attention
écouteur *m.* listener; telephone receiver
écoutille *f.* hatch
écran *m.* fire screen; (phot.) filter
écrasant *a.* crushing
écrasement *m.* crushing; defeat, disaster
écraser *vt.* to crush; **s'** — to crash; flock over
écrémer *vt.* to skim milk
écrémeuse *f.* cream separator
écrevisse *f.* crayfish
écrier *v.*, **s'** — to cry out, exclaim
écrin *m.* jewel box, casket
écrire *vt.* to write, compose; write down
écrit *m.* writing, written word, written examination; — *a.* written
écriteau *m.* sign, placard
écritoire *f.* writing set; desk set
écriture *f.* handwriting; document; account
Ecriture *f.*, l' — sainte Scriptures
écrivailleur *m.* scribbler, hack writer
écrivain *m.* writer, author of books
écrou *m.* screw nut; lever l' — to liberate
écrouelles *f. pl.* scrofula
écrouer *vt.* to imprison
écroulement *m.* fall, collapse; (fig.) complete ruin
écrouler *v.*, **s'** — to collapse, crumble
écroûter *vt.* to remove the crust from
écru *a.* unbleached; raw silk
ectoplasme *m.* ectoplasm
écu *m.* shield; crown (coin); **–s** *pl.* (fig.) money

écueil *m.* reef, rock
écuelle *f.* bowl, basin
éculer *vt.* to wear down a heel
écumant *a.* foaming; fuming
écume *f.* foam; froth; scum; (fig.) dregs (of humanity); — de mer meerschaum
écumer *vt.* to skim; — *vi.* to foam
écumeux *a.* scummy; foamy, frothy
écumoire *f.* skimmer
écurage *m.* scouring
écurer *vt.* to scour, cleanse
écureuil *m.* squirrel
écurie *f.* stable; string of horses (same owner)
écusson *m.* shield (heraldry); escutcheon; bud (grafting)
écuyer *m.* horseman, squire
écuyère *f.* horsewoman
eczéma *m.* eczema
éden *m.* Garden of Eden; paradise
édenté *a.* toothless
édicule *m.* small building on the street, shelter
édifiant *a.* edifying
édification *f.* erecting, building; edification
édifier *vt.* to edify; build, found
édile *m.* town councillor
édit *m.* edict
éditer *vt.* to edit; publish
éditeur *m.* editor, publisher; — *a.* publishing
édition *f.* edition; publishing
éditorial *a. & m.* editorial
édredon *m.* eiderdown; feather quilt
éducation *f.* upbringing; education; breeding
édulcorer *vt.* to sugar-coat; water down; make inoffensive
éduquer *vt.* to rear, bring up
effacement *m.* effacement, erasing, obliteration
effacer *vt.* to efface, erase; **s'** — to be obliterated; stand aside; (fig.) to bow to superiority
effarement *m.* fright
effarer *vt.* to frighten
effaroucher *vt.* to scare away; frighten, alarm
effectif *m.* effective force; (mil.) complement; manpower; size; — *a.* effective, actual
effectivement *adv.* actually, in fact
effectuer *vt.* to effect, accomplish
efféminé *a.* effeminate
effervescence *f.* effervescence, excitement
effervescent *a.* effervescent
effet *m.* effect, result; impression; **–s** *pl.* belongings; **–s publics** public bonds; **en** — indeed

effeuillaison *f.* falling of leaves
effeuiller *vt.* to strip of leaves, petals
efficace *a.* effective, efficacious
efficacité *f.* efficiency, effectiveness, efficacy
efficience *f.* effectiveness; efficiency
effigie *f.* effigy
effilé *a.* slender; — *m.* fringe
effiler *vt.* to unravel; taper
effilocher *vt.* to unravel
efflanqué *a.* lean, skinny, thin
effleurer *vt.* to graze, touch lightly
effluve *m.* effluvium, emanation
effondrement *m.* collapse, collapsing, destruction
effondrer *vt.* to break open; break up ground **s'** — to sink down, cave in
efforcer *v.*, **s'** — to strive, try to do one's best
effort *m.* effort, work; stress, strain
effraction *f.* housebreaking, burglary
effranger *vt.* to unravel the edges
effrayant *a.* frightful, dreadful
effrayer *vt.* to frighten; **s'** — to be frightened
effréné *a.* unbridled; frantic
effroi *m.* fright, terror
effronté *a.* bold, shameless, impudent
effronterie *f.* impudence, insolence, effrontery
effroyable *a.* frightful
effusion *f.* effusion; outpouring; — **de sang** bloodshed
égal *a.* equal; alike; indifferent; even, level; — *m.* equal; **cela m'est** — it's all the same to me, I don't care, all right
egaler *vt.* to equal, match, value the same
égalisation *f.* equalisation, equalizing
égaliser *vt.* to equalize, make even
égalitaire *a.* equalitarian
égalité *f.* equality; evenness
égard *m.* respect, consideration; **à l'** — **de** in reference to, toward; **en** — **à** considering that
égaré *a.* stray, lost
égarement *m.* losing, misplacing; deviation; straying, wandering; mental disorder
égarer *vt.* to mislead; mislay; bewilder; **s'** — to go astray, wander
égayer *vt.* to cheer up; **s'** — to make merry
égéen *a.* Aegean
églantier *m.* (plant), **églantine** *f.* (flower) eglantine; sweetbrier; wild rose
église *f.* church
égocentrique *a.* egocentric
égoïne *f.* handsaw
égoïsme *m.* selfishness
égoïste *a.* selfish; — *m.* egotist
égorger *vt.* to cut the throat (of), slaughter

égotisme *m.* egotism
égotiste *m. & f.* egotist
égout *m.* drainage; sewer
égoutier *m.* sewer worker
égoutter *vt. & vi.* to drain
égouttoir *m.* draining rack
égratigner *vt.* to scratch
égratignure *f.* scratch
égrener *vt.* to shell; pick off (grapes); **gin**
égrillard *a.* fancy-free
égrugeoir *m.* mortar
égruger *vt.* to pound, pulverize
égueuler *vt.* to break the neck of
Égypte *f.* Egypt
égyptien *m. & a.* Egyptian
égyptologie *f.* Egyptology
éhonté *a.* shameless
éjaculation *f.* ejaculation
éjaculer *vt.* to ejaculate
éjecter *vt.* to eject
éjection *f.* ejection
élaboration *f.* elaboration
élaborer *vt.* to elaborate
élaguer *vt.* to prune, trim; (fig.) to curtail (literary work)
élan *m.* impetus, impulse; bound; outburst; elk
élancé *a.* slender, slim
élancement *m.* twinge; yearning
élancer *vi.* to throb; dart; **s'** — **to rush** upon; shoot forward *or* up
élargir *vt.* to widen; free
élasticité *f.* elasticity
élastique *a.* elastic; — *m.* elastic, rubber band
électeur *m.* elector, **voter**
électif *a.* elective
élection *f.* election
électoral *a.* electoral
électricien *m.* electrician
électricité *f.* electricity
électrification *f.* electrification
électrifier *vt.* to electrify
électrique *a.* electric, electrical
électriser *vt.* to electrify
électro-aimant *m.* electromagnet
électrocardiogramme *m.* cardiogram
électrochoc *m.* shock treatment
électrocuter *vt.* to electrocute
électrocution *f.* electrocution
électrode *f.* electrode
électrodynamique *a.* electrodynamic; — *f.* electrodynamics
électro-encéphalogramme *m.* electroencephalogram
électrolyse *f.* electrolysis
électromagnétique *a.* electromagnetic
électromètre *m.* electrometer
électron *m.* electron
électronique *a.* electronic

électroscope *m.* electroscope
électrostatique *a.* electrostatic
élégamment *adv.* elegantly
élégance *f.* elegance
élégant *a.* elegant, stylish
élégie *f.* elegy
élément *m.* element; (elec.) cell —s *pl.*
    natural forces
élémentaire *a.* elementary, basic
éléphant *m.* elephant
éléphantesque *a.* enormous
élevage *m.* animal husbandry; ranching
élévation *f.* elevation
élève *m. & f.* pupil
élevé *a.* high; brought up; **bien** — well-
    bred, well-mannered; **mal** — ill-bred
élever *vt.* to raise, bring up; **s'** — to rise,
    arise
éleveur *m.* animal raiser
elfe *m.* elf
élider *vt.* to elide
éligibilité *f.* eligibility
éligible *a.* eligible
élimer *vt.* to wear out
élimination *f.* elimination
éliminatoire *a.* preliminary (sports)
éliminer *vt.* to eliminate; cancel
élire *vt.* to elect
élisabéthain *a.* Elizabethan
élision *f.* elision
élite *f.* élite; choice
élixir *m.* elixir
elle *pron.* she, her, it; —s *pl.* they
elle-même *pron.* herself, itself
ellipse *f.* ellipse
elliptique *a.* elliptical
élocution *f.* elocution
éloge *m.* eulogy, praise
élogieux *a.* full of praise
éloigné *a.* distant, faraway, remote; re-
    moved
éloignement *m.* absence, remoteness;
    aversion; postponement
éloigner *vt.* to remove; drive away; defer;
    s' — to move off, away, deviate
élongation *f.* elongation
éloquemment *adv.* eloquently
éloquence *f.* eloquence
éloquent *a.* eloquent
élu *n.* chosen one; —s *pl.* elect
élucidation *f.* elucidation
élucider *vt.* to elucidate
éluder *vt.* to elude
émaciation *f.* emaciation
émacié *a.* emaciated
émail *m.* enamel, glaze
émailler *vt.* to enamel
émailleur *m.* enameller
émanation *f.* emanation
émancipation *f.* emancipation

émanciper *vt.* to emancipate
émaner *vi.* to emanate
émarger *vt.* to note in the margin, initial
    to prove reading; trim; receive pay
émasculer *vt.* to emasculate
emballage *m.* packing, crating
emballer *vt.* to pack, wrap; crate; excite
emballeur *m.* packer
embarcadère *m.* wharf; (rail.) platform
embarcation *f.* small boat, launch
embardée *f.* lurch; (naut.) yaw; (auto.)
    swerve
embarquement *m.* embarcation; shipment
embarquer *vt. & vi.* to embark
embarras *m.* obstruction; difficulty; per-
    plexity; confusion
embarrasser *vt.* to trouble; perplex; con-
    fuse; embarass
embaucher *vt.* to hire
embauchoir *m.* shoe tree
embaumement *m.* embalming
embaumer *vt.* to embalm; perfume
embellir *vt. & vi.* to embellish; become
    beautiful
embellissement *m.* embellishment
embêtement *m.* annoyance
embêter *vt.* (coll.) to bother, annoy
emblée, d' — *adv.* first, on the spot; with-
    out difficulty
emblématique *a.* emblematic
emblème *m.* emblem
embobiner *vt.* to wind (up), put on a
    spool *or* reel
emboîter *vt.* to fit in; copy, take after; set
    a bone; — **le pas à** fall into step with
embonpoint *m.* plumpness
embouche *f.* pasture
embouché *a.*, **mal** — foulmouthed
embouchoir *m.* (mus.) instrument mouth-
    piece
embouchure *f.* mouth of a river; mouth-
    piece
embourber *vt.* to stick in the mud, impli-
    cate
embout *m.* handle (cane, umbrella)
embouteillage *m.* bottling up; bottleneck;
    traffic jam
embouteiller *vt.* to bottle up; (fig.) to
    block
embranchement *m.* branch, division; road
    junction
embrasement *m.* conflagration, burning
embraser *vt.* to set on fire
embrassade *f.* embrace
embrasse *f.* curtain tieback; armrest
embrassement *m.* embrace; kiss
embrasser *vt.* to embrace; kiss
embrasure *f.* opening; port
embrayage *m.* clutch; coupling, engaging
embrayer *vt.* to connect, engage; (auto.)

to let in the clutch

embrocher vt. to spit (meat cookery)

embrouiller vt. to tangle, mix up; **s' —** to get confused; become intricate

embroussaillé a. busy; complex, tangled

embrumé a. misty, hazy

embrun m. spray; fog

embryologie f. embryology

embryon m. embryo

embryonnaire a. embryonic

embûche f. trap

embuscade f. ambush

embusqué m. soldier at the rear; person lying in ambush

embusquer vt. to ambush, trap

émeraude f. emerald

émergence f. emergence

émerger vi. to emerge

émeri m. emery

émerillonné a. lively

émérite a. eminent, experienced; emeritus

émerveillement m. wonderment

émerveiller vt. to astonish, amaze

émétique m. emetic

émetteur m. radio transmitter

émettre vt. to emit, issue; transmit, broadcast

émeute f. riot

émietter vt. to crumble

émigration f. emigration

émigré m. emigrant; refugee; emigrated nobleman (history)

émigrer vt. to emigrate

émincé m. minced meat, mincemeat

émincer vt. to slice thinly; hash

éminemment adv. eminently

éminence f. eminence

éminent a. eminent; distinguished

émissaire m. emissary

émission f. emission, issue; transmission, broadcast; **— transmise en direct** live broadcast; **— de télévision transmise en couleurs** colorcast

emmagasiner vt. to store up, stockpile

emmailloter vt. to swathe, swaddle

emmêler vt. to entangle, mat; disturb

emménagement m. moving in, installation

emménager vi. to move into

emmener vt. to take away, lead away

emmitoufler vt. to muffle up

emmurer vt. to wall up

émoi m. emotion, agitation, turmoil

émoluments m. pl. emoluments

émonder vt. to prune, trim

émotif a. emotive; emotional

émotion f. emotion, feeling; excitement

émotionnable a. emotional

émotionner vt. to move, thrill; **s' —** to get excited

émouchoir m. fly swatter

émoudre vt. to sharpen, grind

émoulage m. grinding, sharpening

émoulu a. sharpened; **frais — de fresh** from, just out of

émousser vt. to dull (senses), blunt; weaken

émouvoir vt. to move, affect; rouse; **s' —** to be moved

empailler vt. to cover, stuff, pack

empailleur m. taxidermist

empaler vt. to impale

empan m. span (measure)

empanacher vt. to plume

empaqueter vt. to package

emparer v., **s' — de** to take possession of, seize

empâter vt. to make sticky; destroy harmony

empattement m. foundation, platform; (auto.) wheelbase

empaumer vt. to take in hand; overcome

empêchement m. obstacle, hindrance

empêcher vt. to hinder, prevent; **s' — de** to keep from, help, refrain from

empêcheur m. preventer; **— de danser en rond** (coll.) wet blanket

empeigne f. top leather of shoes

empennage m. stabilizing fins; feathers on an arrow

empenné a. plumed, feathered

empereur m. emperor

empeser vt. to starch

empester vt. to infect, make foul; **— vi. to** reek, smell

empêtrer vt. to bind, involve, hinder

emphase f. overemphasis; bombast

emphatique a. emphatic, bombastic

emphysème m. emphysema

empiècement m. yoke (clothing)

empierrer vt. to pave with stone (road); ballast (tracks, roads, etc.)

empiétement m. incursion, usurpation

empiéter vi., **— sur** to usurp; encroach on

empiler vt. to pile up, stack

empire m. empire, rule; mastery

empirer vt. to make worse; aggravate; **—** vi. grow worse

empirique a. empirical

empirisme m. empiricism

emplacement m. place, location, site

emplâtre m. (med.) plaster, salve; (fig.) apathetic person

emplette f. purchase; **aller faire des —s to** go shopping

emplir vt. to fill up

emploi m. use; employment; **— du temps** schedule; **mode d' —** instructions for use

employé m. employee; clerk; white-collar

worker

employer vt. to employ; use; **s'** — to occupy oneself

employeur m. user, employer

empocher vt. to pocket

empoigner vt. to grasp; seize; arrest

empois m. starch

empoisonnement m. poisoning

empoisonner vt. to poison; ruin; make bitter; (coll.) bore, annoy

empoisonneur m. poisoner, (coll.) bore, annoying person

empoissonner vt. to stock with fish

emporté a. quick-tempered, hasty

emporte-pièce m. punch tool

emportement m. temper, anger

emporter vt. to take away, carry away; prevail; **s'** — to lose control of oneself

empoter vt. to pot (plant)

empourprer v., **s'** — to turn crimson; flush

empreindre vt. to imprint, stamp

empreinte f. imprint; — **digitale** fingerprint

empressé a. bustling, eager

empressement m. eagerness, zeal, readiness

empresser v., **s'** — to be eager; hasten

emprise f. seizure; influence

emprisonnement m. imprisonment

emprisonner vt. to imprison

emprunt m. loan, borrowing

emprunté a. feigned; constrained

emprunter vt. to borrow; (fig.) plagiarize

emprunteur m. borrower

ému a. moved; affected

émulation f. emulation

emule m. emulator; rival

émulsion f. emulsion

émulsionner vt. to emulsify

en prep. in, into; at; by; — pron. of him, of her, of it, of them; some, any; — adv. from it, thence

enamourer v., **s'** — (de) to fall in love (with)

encadrement m. frame, framework

encadrer vt. to frame

encager vt. to cage

encaisse f. cash in hand; cash balance

encaissé a. banked, with high banks

encaissement m. taking in of money; boxing, crating; embankment

encaisser vt. to pack, box; deposit; take in

encan m. auction

encanailler vt. to degrade; **s'** — to lose caste

encapuchonner vt. to hood

encart, encartage m. insert

encarter vt. to insert

en-cas m. snack, potluck meal; emergency supply

encastrement m. groove; fitting

encastrer vt. to fit in, imbed

encaustique f. furniture wax, floor wax

encaustiquer vt. to wax

encaver vt. to put away, store (in a cellar)

enceindre vt. to surround, gird, encircle; enclose

enceinte f. enclosure; — a. pregnant

encens m. incense

encenser vt. to incense, perfume

encensoir m. incense burner

encéphalite f. encephalitis

encerclement m. encirclement

encercler vt. to encircle

enchaînement m. chain(ing); series

enchaîner vt. to chain; connect

enchanter vt. to enchant, delight; charm

enchanteur a. enchanting; — m. enchanter

enchâsser vt. to enclose; fit in; enshrine; set a jewel

enchère f. bid, bidding; **vente aux —s** f. auction sale

enchérir vt. to raise prices; — vi. go up in price; — **sur** outdo, exceed

enchevêtrer vt. to bind; entangle

enchifrener vt. to stop up, stuff up (with a cold)

enclave f. enclave; enclosed land

enclaver vt. to enclose; dovetail

enclin a. inclined, prone

enclos m. enclosure

enclume f. anvil

encoche f. notch; **—s** pl. thumb index

encocher vt. to notch, nick

encoignure f. corner building; corner furniture

encollage m. size (glue); sizing

encoller vt. to size

encolure f. neck opening; collar size; horse collar

encombre, encombrement m. encumbrance; hindrance; cumbersomeness; congestion

encombrer vt. to encumber, clog

encontre, à l' — prep. counter to

encore adv. yet; still; — **une fois again**

encorner vt. to horn; gore

encourageant a. encouraging

encourager vt. to encourage

encourir vt. to incur

encrasser vt. to make dirty, soil; clog

encre f. ink; — **de Chine** India ink

encrer vt. to ink

encroûter vt. to crust; plaster (walls); (fig.) make stupid

encrier m. inkwell

encyclique f. encyclical

encyclopédie f. encyclopedia

encyclopédique a. encyclopedic

endémique *a.* endemic

endenter *vt.* to tooth, cog; mesh

endetter *vt.* to put into debt; s' — to go into debt

endiablé *a.* bedeviled

endimancher *v.,* s' — to put on Sunday clothes; get dressed up

endive *f.* French endive

endocrinologie *f.* endocrinology

endoctrinement *m.* indoctrination

endoctriner *vt.* to indoctrinate

endolorir *vt.* to make painful, cause pain in

endommagement *m.* damage

endommager *vt.* to damage, injure

endormi *a.* asleep, sleepy

endormir *vt.* to put to sleep; lull; s' — to fall asleep

endos, endossement *m.* endorsement

endosser *vt.* to endorse; take on

endosseur *m.* endorser

endroit *m.* place, spot; right side of cloth

enduire *vt.* to spread, cover, coat

enduit *m.* layer, coat, plastering

endurable *a.* endurable, bearable, tolerable

endurant *a.* patient

endurci *a.* hardened, inveterate, calloused

endurcir *vt.* to harden

endurcissement *m.* hardening

endurer *vt.* to endure, suffer, bear, tolerate

en entier *adv.* fully, in detail

énergie *f.* energy

énergique *a.* energetic

énergumène *m. & f.* enthusiast, avid fanatic, madman

énervant *a.* weakening, debilitating; nerve-racking

énervement *m.* enervation

énerver *vt.* to enervate

enfance *f.* childhood; children; dotage; première — infancy

enfant *m. & f.* child; — naturel illegitimate child; — trouvé foundling

enfantement *m.* childbirth; (fig.) creation

enfanter *vt.* to give birth to

enfantillage *m.* childishness

enfantin *a.* childish; juvenile; infantile

enfariner *vt.* to flour, cover with flour

enfer *m.* hell

enfermé *m.* mustiness

enfermer *vt.* to shut up, lock up; enclose

enferrer *vt.* to pierce; s' — to be caught

enfiévrer *vt.* to make feverish; inflame

enfilade *f.* file, string, series

enfiler *vt.* to thread (needle); string (beads); (fig.) put on (clothes); pierce; start down a street

enfin *adv.* after all, at last, finally; in short

enflammer *vt.* to inflame; s' — to catch

fire; become inflamed

enfler *vt. & vi.* to swell, bloat; (fig.) exaggerate

enflure *f.* swelling

enfoncé *a.* sunken, deep

enfoncement *m.* hollow; recess; breaking down; breaking in

enfoncer *vt. & vi.* to thrust, drive in; break open; sink; s' — to plunge; sink

enfouir *vt.* to bury; hide

enfourcher *vt.* to climb on; straddle

enfourchure *f.* crotch (tree *or* trousers)

enfourner *vt.* to put in the oven

enfreindre *vt.* to violate, break, infringe on

enfuir *v.,* s' — to run away; elope

enfumé *a.* smoked; smoky

enfumer *vt.* to smoke, blacken

engagé *m.* (mil.) volunteer, enlisted man

engageant *a.* engaging, prepossessing

engagement *m.* commitment, obligation; pawning; promise; hiring; enlistment; (mil.) engagement

engager *vt.* to pawn; pledge; hire; (mech.) engage; enter into; s' — to commit oneself; enlist

engainer *vt.* to sheathe, envelop

engazonner *vt.* to sod

engeance *f.* breed; race

engelure *f.* chilblain

engendrer *vt.* to engender

engin *m.* engine; machinery; device

englober *vt.* to unite; comprise

engloutir *vt.* to swallow up, engulf

engloutissement *m.* swallowing (up)

engluer *vt.* to glue; lime; catch; take in

engorgement *m.* obstruction

engorger *vt.* to obstruct; block

engouement *m.* infatuation

engouer *v.,* s' — to become infatuated

engouffrer *vt.* to engulf

engourdi *a.* dull, numbed

engourdir *vt.* to numb; lull

engourdissement *m.* numbness

engrais *m.* fertilizer, manure; enriched fodder

engraisser *vt.* to fatten; fertilize; — *vi.* to grow fat

engramme *m.* engram

engrenage *m.* gear, system of gears

engrener *vt.* to engage gears

engueuler *vt.* (coll.) to bawl out; insult

enhardir *vt.* to make bold; s' — to venture, be bold enough

enharnacher *vt.* to harness; (fig.) to deck out

énigmatique *a.* enigmatic

énigme *f.* riddle; enigma

enivrant *a.* intoxicating

enivrement *m.* intoxication

enivrer *vt.* to intoxicate; (fig.) carry away;

enjambée 93 entité

s' — to get drunk
enjambée *f.* stride
enjamber *vt. & vi.* to stride over, straddle; encroach
enjeu *m.* stake, bet
enjoindre *vt.* to enjoin, call on; order
enjôler *vt.* to coax, cajole, wheedle
enjôleur *a.* coaxing, cajoling
enjoliver *vt.* to make pretty, ornament, embellish
enjoué *a.* cheerful, lively, playful
enjouement *m.* cheerfulness
enlacer *vt.* to entwine; clasp; hem in
enlaidir *vt.* to make ugly; disfigure; — *vi.* to grow ugly
enlèvement *m.* removal; kidnapping; elopement
enlever *vt.* to remove; take away; abduct
enliser *vt.* to swallow up in sand, suck in
enluminer *vt.* to illuminate a manuscript
ennemi *m.* enemy; — *a.* hostile
ennoblir *vt.* to make noble, ennoble, dignify
ennui *m.* boredom, worry
ennuyeux *a.* annoying; boring, tiresome
ennuyer *vt.* to annoy; worry; bore; s' — to be bored, weary
énoncé *m.* terms, data; statement
énoncer *vt.* to state, announce
énonciation *f.* enunciation; stating, announcing
enorgueillir *vt.* to make proud; s' — de to pride oneself on
énorme *a.* enormous
énormément *adv.* enormously; a great deal
énormité *f.* enormity
enquérir *v.,* s' — de to inquire about
enquête *f.* inquiry, investigation
enquêter (sur) *vi.* to investigate
enraciner *vt.* to implant s' — to take root
enragé *m.* enthusiast; madman; — *a.* mad; enthusiastic; inveterate
enrager *vt.* to madden; — *vi.* to be mad
enrayer *vt.* to halt, stop, brake; suspend
enrégimenter *vt.* to regiment
enregistrement *m.* recording, registering, transcribing; transcription
enregistrer *vt.* to register, record
enrhumer *v.,* s' — to catch cold
enrichir *vt.* s' — to enrich; adorn; develop
enrichissement *m.* enrichment
enrober *vt.* to cover, coat; wrap
enrôler *vt.* to enroll; enlist
enrouement *m.* hoarseness
enrouer *v.,* s' — to become hoarse
enrouler *vt.* to roll up
ensabler *vt.* to cover with sand; run aground
ensacher *vt.* to bag

ensanglanter *vt.* to stain with blood
enseignant *a.* teaching; — *m.* teacher
enseigne *f.* distinctive sign; insignia designating particular firm; ensign; — *m.* ensign (rank)
enseignement *m.* teaching; education
enseigner *vt.* to teach, show
ensemble *adv.* together; — *m.* whole, entirety; d' — comprehensive; combined
ensemencer *vt.* to sow
ensevelir *vt.* to bury; shroud
ensevelissement *m.* burial, interment
ensiler *vt.* to put in a silo
ensoleillé *a.* sunny
ensommeillé *a.* sleepy
ensorceler *vt.* to bewitch
ensorcellement *m.* enchantment, charm, spell; sorcery
ensuite *adv.* afterwards, then, after
ensuivre *v.,* s' — to result; follow; be the consequence
entacher *vt.* to soil, stain, taint
entailler *vt.* to notch, nick, gash
entamer *vt.* to cut; open; begin
entassement *m.* heaping, piling up, accumulation
entasser *vt.* to heap up, accumulate
ente *f.* plant graft; handle
entendement *m.* understanding, judgment
entendre *vt.* to hear; understand; mean; s' — to be heard; understand each other; get along
entendu *a.* heard, understood; c'est — all right, agreed
entente *f.* understanding; agreement
enter *vt.* to graft; s' — to be related by blood
entériner *vt.* to ratify
entérique *a.* enteric
entérite *f.* enteritis
enterrement *m.* funeral, burial, interment
enterrer *vt.* to bury, inter
en-tête *m.* heading, headline; letterhead
entêté *a.* obstinate, headstrong
entêtement *m.* obstinacy
entêter *v.,* s' — to persist, be obstinate
enthousiasme *m.* enthusiasm
enthousiasmer *vt.* to fill with enthusiasm; s' — to be enthusiastic about
enthousiaste *m. & f.* enthusiast; fanatic; — *a.* enthusiastic
entichement *m.* infatuation
enticher *v.,* s' — to become infatuated
entier *a.* entire, whole, intact; — *m.* totality
entièrement *adv.* completely, entirely, wholly
entité *f.* entity

entomologie *f.* entomology
entomologiste *m.* entomologist
entonner *vt.* to intone; begin to sing
entonnoir *m.* funnel
entorse *f.* sprain
entortiller *vt.* to twist, wind; warp, deform
entour *m.* à l' — (de) around, in the vicinity (of); **–s** *pl.* vicinity, surrounding area
entourage *m.* surroundings; set, circle, associates
entourer *vt.* to surround
entraccuser *v.*, **s'** — to accuse each other, accuse one another
entracte *m.* intermission, interval
entradmirer *v.*, **s'** — to admire each other, admire one another
entraide *f.* mutual aid
entraider *v.*, **s'** — to help one another
entrailles *f. pl.* entrails, bowels; feeling
entr'aimer *v.*, **s'** — to love each other, love one another
entrain *m.* spirit, gusto
entraînement *m.* carrying away; enthusiasm; training
entraîner *vt.* to drag, carry away; lead astray; entail
entraîneur *m.* trainer
entrave *f.* shackle; hindrance
entraver *vt.* to shackle; hinder
entre *prep.* between, among
entre- *prefix* inter-; partially; reciprocally, mutually
entrebâiller *vt.* to open partially, open slightly
entrebâilleur *m.* doorstop
entrecôte *f.* ribsteak, beef rib
entrecouper *vt.* to interrupt; intersect
entre-deux *m.* space between; partition
entrée *f.* entry, entrance, admission; course (usually fish or eggs) preceding main course; **porte d'** — *f.* front door
entrefaites *f. pl.*, **sur ces** — meanwhile
entrefermer *vt.* to close partially
entrefilet *m.* note, item in a newspaper
entregent *m.* tact, confidence; resourcefulness
entrejambes *m.* crotch; **longueuer d'** — length from crotch to heel
entrelacer *vt.* to interlace
entrelarder *vt.* to lard
entre-ligne *m.* space between the lines
entremêler *vt.* to mix, mingle; intersperse
entremets *m.* dessert, sweet
entremetteur *m.* go-between
entremetteuse *f.* B-girl
entremettre *v.* **s'**— to intervene
entremise *f.* intervention, mediation
entrepont *m.* (naut.) between decks
entreposer *vt.* to place in a warehouse

entrepôt *m.* warehouse
entreprenant *a.* enterprising
entreprendre *vt.* to undertake; **contract** for
entrepreneur *m.* contractor
entreprise *f.* enterprise, contract(ing)
entrer *vi.* to enter, come in
entreregarder *v.*, **s'** — to look at each other, look at one another
entresol *m.* mezzanine floor
entre-temps *adv.* meanwhile; — *m.* interval
entretenir *vt.* to maintain, support; entertain, converse with
entretien *m.* maintenance; conversation
entre-tuer *v.*, **s'** — to kill each other, kill one another
entrevoir *vt.* to glimpse; foresee
entrevue *f.* interview
entrouvrir *vt.* to open partially
énumérer *vt.* to enumerate
envahir *vt.* to invade
envahissement *m.* invasion
envaser *vt.* to fill with mud
enveloppe *f.* envelope, wrapper, **casing**
enveloppement *m.* enveloping
envelopper *vt.* to envelop, wrap up
envenimer *vt.* to poison, ruin
envergure *f.* wingspread; spread; scope, power
envers *m.* wrong side, reverse; **à l'** — inside out; upside down; — *prep.* towards
envi, à l' — **(de)** *adv.* vying (with)
envie *f.* desire, longing; envy; birthmark, hangnail; **avoir** — **de** to feel like, want to
envier *vt.* to envy, be jealous of; covet
envieux *a.* envious
environ *adv.* about, approximately; **–s** *m. pl.* outskirts, vicinity
environner *vt.* to surround
envisager *vt.* to envisage
envoi *m.* dispatch; consignment, **shipment**; envoy (poetry)
envol *m.*, **envolée** *f.* flight; take-off
envoler *v.*, **s'** — to fly away, take off
envoûtement *m.* voodoo, spell
envoûter *vt.* to dominate; to harm **by a** wax image used to cause a person to suffer (voodoo)
envoyé *m.* envoy
envoyer *vt.* to send
enzyme *m.* enzyme
épagneul *m.* spaniel
épais *a.* thick
épaisseur *f.* thickness
épaissir *vt. & vi.* to thicken
épanchement *m.* pouring out; effusion
épancher *vt.* to pour out, pour forth; **s'** —

to open up, overflow
épandre *vt.* to scatter, spread
épanouir *v.*, **s'** — to bloom; beam
épanouissement *m.* blossoming
épargne *f.* saving, thrift; **caisse d'** — *f.* savings bank
épargner *vt.* to spare, save
éparpillement *m.* scattering
éparpiller *vt.* to scatter
épars *a.* scattered, sparse
épatant *a.* amazing; (coll.) wonderful
épaté *a.* flattened; flat-nosed
épaule *f.* shoulder
épaulement *m.* breastworks
épauler *vt.* to help; put against the shoulder; put behind breastworks
épaulette *f.* epaulette; shoulder strap
épave *f.* wreck, wreckage; stray; (fig.) debris in general
épée *f.* sword
épéiste *m.* fencer, swordsman
épeler *vt.* to spell
épellation *f.* spelling
éperdu *a.* distracted; desperate
éperdument *adv.* desperately, wildly, madly
éperlan *m.* smelt
éperon *m.* spur
éperonner *vt.* to spur
épervier *m.* sparrow hawk; fishnet
épeuré *a.* fearful, frightened
éphémère *a.* ephemeral; — *m.* May fly
épi *m.* ear, head of grain; tuft, cowlick; cluster
épice *f.* spice; **pain d'** — gingerbread
épicer *vt.* to spice
épicerie *f.* grocery
épicier *m.* grocer
épicurien *a.* Epicurean
épidémie *f.* epidemic
épidémique *a.* epidemic
épiderme *m.* epidermis
épier *vt.* to watch, spy on
épieu *m.* pike
épiglotte *f.* epiglottis
épigramme *f.* epigram
épigraphe *f.* epigraph; quotation, motto
épilepsie *f.* epilepsy
épileptique *m. & f. & a.* epileptic
épiler *vt.* to pluck hair; depilitate
épilogue *m.* epilogue
épiloguer *vi.* to criticize, harp (on); split hairs
épinard *m.* spinach
épine *f.* thorn; spine
épinette *f.* spinet, clavichord
épineux *a.* thorny; difficult
épingle *f.* pin; — **de sûreté** safety pin
épingler *vt.* to pin; (fig., coll.) to pin down
épinière *a. & f.* spinal

Epiphanie *f.* Epiphany
épique *a.* epic
épiscopal *a.* episcopal, of the bishop
épiscopat *m.* bishopric; body of bishops, episcopacy
épisode *m.* episode
épisodique *a.* episodic
épisser *vt.* to splice
épissure *f.* splice
épistémologie *f.* epistemology
epistolaire *a.* epistolary
épistolier *m.* letter writer
épitaphe *f.* epitaph
épithète *f.* epithet
épitoge *f.* shoulder band (equivalent of French doctor's hood)
épitomé *m.* digest, abridgment
épître *f.* epistle, letter
éploré *a.* weeping, sad
éployé *a.* outspread
éplucher *vt.* to peel, pare, clean; (fig.) examine closely
épluchoir *m.* paring knife
epluchure *f.* peeling, waste
épode *f.* epode
épointer *vt.* to dull the point of
éponge *f.* sponge
éponger *vt.* to sponge
épopée *f.* epic poem, epic
époque *f.* epoch, period, era; — **de l'espace** air age, space age
épouiller *vt.* to delouse
épousailles *f. pl.* wedding
épouse *f.* wife, spouse
épouser *vt.* to marry; espouse
époussetage *m.* dusting
épousseter *vt.* to dust
époussette *f.* duster
épouvantable *a.* dreadful, frightful
épouvantail *m.* scarecrow
épouvante *f.* fright, terror
épouvanter *vt.* to terrify, frighten
époux *m.* husband; — *pl.* married couple
éprendre *v.*, **s'** — **de** to fall in love with
épreuve *f.* trial, proof, test; (phot.) print
épris (de) *a.* in love (with)
éprouver *vt.* to try; experience
éprouvette *f.* test tube, gauge
epsomite *f.* Epsom salts
épucer *vt.* to deflea
épuisant *a.* exhausting
épuisement *m.* exhaustion
épuiser *vt.* to exhaust; drain; wear out; use up
épuration *f.* purification, purifying, refining
épurer *vt.* to purify, filter
équanimité *f.* equanimity
équarrir *vt.* to square off; cut up, quarter
équateur *m.* equator

Équateur *m.* Ecuador
équation *f.* equation
équatorial *a.* equatorial
Equatorien *m. & a.* Ecuadorian
équerre *f.* T-square, angle iron
équestre *a.* equestrian
équidistant *a.* equidistant
équilatéral *a.* equilateral
équilibrage *m.* balancing
équilibre *m.* equilibrium; balance
équilibrer *vt.* to poise, balance
équilibriste *m. & f.* acrobat, tight-rope performer
équin *a.* equine
équinoxe *m.* equinox
équipage *m.* (naut.) crew; retinue; apparel, equipment
équipe *f.* team; travail d' — *m.* teamwork
équipée *f.* wild time, mad frolic
équipement *m.* equipment
équiper *vt.* to equip, fit out, man
équipier *m.* member of a team
équitable *a.* equitable
équitation *f.* horseback riding
équité *f.* equity, justice
équivalence *f.* equivalent, equivalence
équivalent *a.* equivalent
équivaloir *vt.* to be equivalent to
équivoque *f.* ambiguity; misunderstanding; — *a.* ambiguous; doubtful
équivoquer *vi.* to be ambiguous, be equivocal
érable *m.* maple; sucre d' — maple sugar
érafler *vt.* to graze, scratch
éraflure *f.* graze, scratch
éraillé *a.* bloodshot; frayed
ère *f.* era, epoch
érectile *a.* erectile
érection *f.* erection
éreinter *vt.* to exhaust; break from fatigue
érémitique *a.* ascetic, pertaining to hermits
erg *m.* erg
ergot *m.* rooster's spur; (agr.) ergot
ergotage *m.*, ergoterie *f.* quibbling, hair-splitting
ergoter *vi.* to quibble
ériger *vt.* to erect, raise
ermitage *m.* hermitage
ermite *m.* hermit
éroder *vt.* to erode
érosif *a.* erosive
érosion *f.* erosion
érotique *a.* erotic
érotisme *m.* eroticism
errant *a.* wandering; stray; errant
erratique *a.* erratic
errements *m. pl.* erring ways, habits
errer *vi.* to wander
erreur *f.* error. mistake; delusion

erroné *a.* erroneous
éructation *f.* belch
éructer *vi.* to belch
érudit *a.* learned; — *m.* scholar
érudition *f.* erudition
éruptif *a.* eruptive
éruption *f.* eruption
ès *prep.* in; docteur — lettres *m.* doctor of letters
escabeau *m.* stool; stepladder
escabelle *f.* stool; stepstool
escadre *f.* (navy) squadron
escadrille *f.* escadrille; small squadron
escadron *m.* (army) squadron
escalade *f.* scaling
escalader *vt.* to scale
escale *f.* (naut., avi.) port of call, stop; vol sans — *m.* nonstop flight
escalier *m.* staircase, stairs
escalope *f.* cutlet
escamotable *a.* concealable; retractable
escamoter *vt.* to hide, conceal; make away with; (fig.) side step a question
escarbille *f.* cinder, clinker
escarboucle *f.* carbuncle
escarcelle *f.* purse
escargot *m.* snail
escarmouche *f.* skirmish
escarmoucher *vt.* to skirmish
escarole *f.* escarole
escarpe *f.* scarp, escarpment; — *m.* thief, cutthroat
escarpé *a.* steep
escarpement *m.* escarpment; steep incline
escarpin *m.* pump (shoe)
escarpolette *f.* swing
escarre *f.* scab
esche *f.* bait
escient, à bon — with full knowledge
esclaffer *v.*, s' — to burst out laughing
esclandre *m.* scandal
esclavage *m.* slavery; bondage
esclave *m. & f.* slave
escompte *m.* (com.) discount; rebate
escompter *vt.* (com.) to discount
escopette *f.* blunderbuss
escorte *f.* escort; (naut.) convoy
escorter *vt.* to escort, convoy
escouade *f.* squad
escrime *f.* fencing
escrimer *vi.* to fence
escrimeur *m.* fencer
escroc *m.* crook, swindler
escroquer *vt.* to swindle, cheat
escroquerie *f.* swindle, fraud
ésotérique *a.* esoteric
espace *m.* space, room; interval; time lapse; — interplanétaire aerospace
espacer *vt.* to space; separate
espadon *m.* swordfish

espadrille *f.* tennis shoe; beach sandal
Espagne *f.* Spain
Espagnol *m.* Spaniard
espagnol *a.* Spanish
espagnolette *f.* window catch
espalier *m.* row of espaliered trees
espèce *f.* species, kind; **—s** *pl.* cash
espérance *f.* hope, expectation
espéranto *m.* esperanto
espérer *vt. & vi.* to hope, expect
espiègle *a.* mischievous; **—** *m. & f.* mischievous person
espièglerie *f.* prank, mischievousness
espionnage *m.* espionage, spying
espionner *vt.* to spy (on)
esplanade *f.* esplanade, promenade
espoir *m.* hope
esprit *m.* spirit; mind; wit, intelligence
esquif *m.* skiff
esquimau *a. & n.* Eskimo
esquisse *f.* sketch; outline, rough plan
esquisser *vt.* to sketch, outline
esquiver *vt.* to avoid; **— de la tête to** duck; **s' —** to steal away
essai *m.* test, trial; assaying metal; attempt
essaim *m.* swarm; host, multitude
essaimage *m.* swarming
essaimer *vt.* to swarm
essarter *vt.* to clear
essarts *m. pl.* clearing(s)
essayage *m.* fitting; testing; trying on, trying out
essayer *vt.* to try, attempt; try on; try out, test
essayiste *m.* essayist
essence *f.* essence; gasoline
essentiel *a.* essential; most important, basic, fundamental; **— *m.*** most important thing; gist
esseulé *a.* left alone, abandoned
essieu *m.* axle
essor *m.* flight; soaring; (fig.) development
essorer *vt.* to dry; wring
essoreuse *f.* dryer; wringer
essoufflé *a.* breathless
essoufflement *m.* breathlessness
essuie-glace *m.* windshield wiper
essuie-main(s) *m.* towel
essuie-pieds *m.* doormat
essuie-plume *m.* penwiper
essuyer *vt.* to wipe, dry; suffer, endure, undergo
est *m.* east
estacade *f.* stockade
estafette *f.* runner, messenger
estafier *m.* armed servant; bully
estaminet *m.* bar, café
estampe *f.* print, engraving

estampille *f.* trademark; seal; impression; tax stamp
ester *vi.* to appear in court
esthète *m.* esthete
esthéticienne *f.* beauty shop attendant
esthétique *a.* esthetic; **—** *f.* esthetics
estimateur *m.* estimator, appraiser
estimation *f.* evaluation; estimation
estime *f.* esteem, estimation
estimer *vt.* to esteem; estimate; value; deem
estival *a.* summer
estivant *m.* summer resident
estiver *vi.* to spend the summer
estomac *m.* stomach
Estonie *f.* Esthonia
estrade *f.* platform for chairs
estragon *m.* tarragon
estropié *a.* crippled
estropier *vt.* to cripple
estuaire *m.* estuary
estudiantin *a.* student, pertaining to students
esturgeon *m.* sturgeon
et *conj.* and; **— ... —** both ... and
étable *f.* cattle shed; sty
établer *vt.* to stable; place in a stall
établi *m.* workbench
établir *vt.* to establish; create
établissement *m.* establishment; institution
étage *m.* story, floor; stage; condition
étagère *f.* set of shelves; whatnot
étai *m.* prop, stay, support
étain *m.* tin
étal *m.* butcher's block
étalage *m.* display, show
étalagiste *m.* window dresser, window trimmer
étaler *vt.* to display, show
étalon *m.* standard; stallion
étalonner *vt.* to verify, control, test; standardize; scale, graduate, calibrate
étamer *vt.* to tin; tin-plate; silver (a mirror)
étamine *f.* stamen; cheesecloth; etamine
étampe *f.* punch, stamp, die
étamper *vt.* to punch, stamp
étanche *a.* watertight
étancher *vt.* to stop; appease
étang *m.* pond
étape *f.* stage, stop
état *m.* state, condition; estate; **— civil** vital statistics
étatiser *vt.* to nationalize, put under state control
étatisme *m.* state control
état-major *m.* staff, headquarters
étau *m.* vise
étayer *vt.* to prop, stay

été *m.* summer
éteignoir *m.* candle snuffer
éteindre *vt.* to extinguish, put out; calm; fade; s' — to go out; become extinct
éteint *a.* extinguished, out, extinct
étendard *m.* standard, flag
étendoir *m.* clothesline, drying room
étendre *vt.* to extend, spread, stretch; s' — to stretch out; extend
étendu *a.* extended; stretched (out); adulterated, watered; vast, extensive
étendue *f.* extent, expanse, range, scope
éternel *a.* eternal
éterniser *vt.* to drag out, make last a long time
éternité *f.* eternity
éternuement *m.* sneeze, sneezing
éternuer *vi.* to sneeze
étêter *vt.* to top, remove the top of
éteule *f.* stubble
éther *m.* ether
éthéré *a.* ethereal
Ethiopie *f.* Ethiopia
éthiopien *a. & m.* Ethiopian
éthique *a.* ethical; — *f.* ethics
ethnique *a.* ethnic
ethnographie *f.* ethnography
ethnologie *f.* ethnology
ethnologue *m. & f.* ethnologist
éthyle *m.* ethyl
éthylène *m.* ethylene
étiage *m.* low-water point; low water
étincelant *a.* sparkling, glittering
étinceler *vi.* to sparkle, glitter
étincelle *f.* spark, flash
étincellement *m.* sparkling, glittering; twinkling
étioler *v.*, s' — to wither away
étique *a.* lean, emaciated
étiqueter *vt.* to label, ticket, mark
étiquette *f.* label; etiquette
étirer *vt.* to lengthen, elongate
étoffe *f.* material, fabric
étoile *f.* star
étoiler *vt.* to bespangle
étole *f.* stole
étonnamment *adv.* astonishingly
étonnant *a.* astonishing
étonnement *m.* astonishment
étonner *vt.* to astonish; s' — to be astonished
étouffant *a.* stifling; sweltering
étouffée *f.* cuire à l' — to braise
étouffement *m.* suffocation; choking
étouffer *vt. & vi.* to stifle, suffocate, choke, smother
étouffoir *m.* piano damper; stuffy room
étoupe *f.* oakum, hemp fiber
étourderie *f.* inadvertance; oversight, stupidity

étourdi *a.* thoughtless, scatterbrained
étourdir *vt.* to stun, daze; deaden
étourdissement *m.* dizziness; numbing
étourneau *m.* starling
étrange *a.* strange
étranger *m.* foreigner; stranger, outsider; à l' — abroad; — *a.* strange, foreign
étrangeté *f.* strangeness
étrangler *vt. & vi.* to strangle; choke; strangulate
étrangleur *m.* strangler
être *vi.* to be, exist; — à belong to; y — understand; *m.* being, existence
étreindre *vt.* to embrace; grip
étreinte *f.* grasp; embrace
étrenner *vt.* to use for the first time
étrier *m.* stirrup
étrille *f.* currycomb
étriller *vt.* to curry; thrash; ransom
étriper *vt.* to gut, clean
étriquer *vt.* to make too narrow
étroit *a.* narrow; strict
étroitement *adv.* closely, intimately; strictly
étroitesse *f.* narrowness; closeness; — d'esprit narrow-mindedness
Étrusque *m. & f. & a.* Etruscan
étude *f.* study, research; study hall; lawyer's office; (mus.) etude
étudiant *m.* student
étudié *a.* studied, calculated
étudier *vt.* to study
étui *m.* case, box
étuve *f.* steam room; drying oven; sterilizer
étuver *vt.* to stew; steam; heat
étymologie *f.* etymology
étymologique *a.* etymological
étymologiste *m.* etymologist
eucalyptus *m.* eucalyptus
eucharistie *f.* eucharist
eugénique *f.*, eugénisme *m.* eugenics
eunuque *m.* eunuch
euphémisme *m.* euphemism
euphonie *f.* euphony
eurasien *a. & m.* Eurasian
Europe *f.* Europe
Européen *m. & a.* European
euthanasie *f.* euthanasia
eux *pron., m. pl.* them, they
évacuation *f.* evacuation
évacuer *vt.* to evacuate; vacate
évader *v.*, s' — to escape; break loose
évaluation *f.* evaluation
évaluer *vt.* to value, appraise
évangélique *a.* evangelical
évangéliser *vt.* to evangelise
évangeliste *m.* evangelist
évangile *m.* Gospel
évanouir *v.*, s' — to faint; vanish

evanouissement *m.* faint; disappearance; (rad.) fading

évaporation *f.* evaporation

évaporé *a.* flighty, fickle

évaporer *vt.* to evaporate

évaser *vt.* to enlarge, widen

évasif *a.* evasive

évasion *f.* escape, evasion; (fig.) distraction

évêché *m.* bishopric, diocese; bishop's palace

éveil *m.* alertness; warning; awakening; wakefulness

éveillé *a.* awake, alert

éveiller *vt.* to awaken, wake up

événement *m.* event; outcome

évent *m.* vent

éventail *m.* fan

éventer *vt.* to fan, ventilate, air; sense, suspect; s' — to get stale; fan oneself

éventrer *vt.* to disembowel; rip open

éventualité *f.* eventuality

éventuel *a.* possible; eventual

évêque *m.* bishop

évertuer *v.*, s' — to strive, exert oneself

évidement *m.* hollowing out; hollowness

évidemment *adv.* evidently, obviously

évidence *f.* evidence

évident *a.* obvious, evident

évider *vt.* to hollow out

évier *m.* kitchen sink

évincer *vt.* to evict; oust

éviter *vt.* to avoid; dodge

évocateur *a.* evocative

évocation *f.* evocation; recollection

évocatoire *a.* evocative

évoluer *vi.* to evolve; revolve

évolution *f.* evolution

évoquer *vt.* to evoke

exacerber *vt.* to exacerbate

exact *a.* exact; correct; punctual

exaction *f.* exacting; exaction

exactitude *f.* exactness, correctness; punctuality

exagération *f.* exaggeration

exagérer *vt.* to exaggerate

exalté *a.* exalted

exalter *vt.* to exalt; excite

examen *m.* examination; survey; — de conscience self-examination

examinateur *m.* examiner

examiner *vt.* to examine

exaspérant *a.* exasperating

exaspération *f.* exasperation

exaspérer *vt.* to exasperate

exaucer *vt.* to grant prayer *or* request; — un vœu to fulfill a desire

excavateur *m.* steam shovel

excaver *vt.* to excavate

excédant *a.* excessive

excédent *m.* excess, surplus

excéder *vt.* to exceed; wear out

excellemment *adv.* excellently

excellence *f.* excellence; Excellency

exceller *vt.* to excel

excentricité *f.* eccentricity

excentrique *a.* eccentric

excepté *prep.* except, save

excepter *vt.* to except

exceptionnel *a.* exceptional

excès *m.* excess; abuse; (phot.) — de pose overexposure

excessif *a.* excessive; unreasonable

exciper (de) *vi.* to allege; take exception to

exciser *vt.* to excise, cut off

excitabilité *f.* excitability

excitant *m.* stimulant; — *a.* stimulating

excitateur *a.* exciting

excitation *f.* excitement

exciter *vt.* to excite, arouse, stimulate

exclamation *f.* exclamation; point d'— *m.* exclamation point

exclamer *v.*, s'— to exclaim

exclure *vt.* to reject; exclude; (fig.) to be incompatible

exclusif *a.* exclusive

exclusivité *f.* exclusivity, exclusiveness; en — first-run movies

excommunier *vt.* to excommunicate

excorier *vt.* to excoriate

excrément *m.* excrement

excréter *vt.* to excrete

excrétion *f.* excretion

excroissance *f.* growth, tumor

excursionner *vi.* to take a trip, go on an excursion

excuse *f.* excuse; —s *pl.* apology; faire ses —s to apologize

excuser *vt.* to excuse; apologize for; s'— excuse oneself, apologize

exécrable *a.* execrable

exécration *f.* execration

exécrer *vt.* to execrate

exécutant *m.* performer

exécuter *vt.* to execute, perform

exécuteur *m.* executor

executif *a.* executive

exécution *f.* execution

exégèse *f.* exegesis

exemplaire *m.* copy, sample; — *a.* exemplary

exemple *m.* example; precedent; par — for example; indeed!

exempter *vt.* to exempt

exemption *f.* exemption

exercé *a.* practiced, experienced

exercer *vt.* to exercise; train; exert; s'— to practice

exercice *m.* exercise, practice; drill

exfolier *vt.* to scale, exfoliate

exhalaison *f.* exhalation, vapor
exhalation *f.* exhalation, exhaling
exhaler *vt.* to exhale; breathe out; give off
exhaussement *m.* raising; rise
exhausser *vt.* to raise; **s'—** to rise
exhaustif *a.* exhaustive
exhaustion *f.* exhaust
exhiber *vt.* to exhibit, display, show
exhibition *f.* exhibition; show, showing, exposition, display
exhibitionniste *m. & f.* exhibitionist
exhorter *vt.* to exhort, urge, encourage
exhumation *f.* exhumation
exhumer *vt.* to exhume, disinter; unearth, dig up
exigeant *a.* exacting, hard to please, demanding
exigence *f.* exigence, exigency, requirement, demand
exiger *vt.* to exact, require, demand
exigible *a.* required, due, exigible
exigu *a.* very small, tiny; slim, scanty
exiguïté *f.* smallness; scantiness; relative poverty
exil *m.* exile, banishment
exilé *m.* exiled person
exiler *vt.* to exile, banish
existant *a.* existent, existing, extant; living; present; available
existence *f.* existence; life, living; being; (com.) stock, inventory
existentialiste *m. & f.* existentialist
existentiel *a.* existential; pertaining to existence
exister *vi.* to exist, be; live
exode *m.* exodus
exonération *f.* exoneration; exemption
exonérer *vt.* to exonerate; exempt
exorable *a.* exorable, flexible
exorciser *vt.* to exorcize
exorcisme *m.* exorcism; exorcizing
exotique *a.* exotic
expansif *a.* expansive
expansion *f.* expansion; expansiveness
expatrié *m.* expatriate, exile
expatrier *vt.* to expatriate
expectant *a.* expectant
expectative *f.* expectancy, expectation; prospect
expectoration *f.* expectoration; sputum
expectorer *vt.* to expectorate
expédient *a.* expedient; **— m.** expedient; resource; device
expédier *vt.* to expedite; send off; dispatch; clear, get through
expéditeur *m.* sender, shipper
expéditif *a.* expeditious
expédition *f.* expedition; shipment, consignment; dispatch; copy
expéditionnaire *a.* expeditionary; **— m.**

sender; shipper; forwarding agent
expérience *f.* experience; experiment
expérimental *a.* experimental
expérimentateur *m.* experimenter
expérimentation *f.* experimentation
expérimenté *a.* experienced; **peu — in**experienced
expérimenter *vt.* to try, test; **— vi.** to experiment
expert *a.* expert; trained; skilled; competent; **— m.** expert; appraiser
expert-comptable *m.* certified public accountant
expertise *f.* expert appraisal or evaluation
expertiser *vt.* to appraise
expiable *a.* expiable
expiation *f.* expiation, atonement
expier *vt.* to expiate, atone for
expirant *a.* expiring, dying
expiration *f.* expiration; termination
expirer *vi.* to expire; die; terminate; exhale
explétif *a. & m.* expletive
explicable *a.* explainable, explicable
explicatif *a.* explanatory
explication *f.* explanation, interpretation; accounting
explicite *a.* explicit
expliciter *vt.* to make explicit
expliquer *vt.* to explain; comment on, interpret; account for; **s'— to explain** oneself; have an argument
exploit *m.* exploit, deed; (law), writ summons
exploitable *a.* exploitable, workable
exploitant *m.* operator of an enterprise; cultivator; developer; **— a.**, **huissier — m.** process server
exploitation *f.* exploitation; working, cultivation; improvement; development
exploiter *vt.* to exploit; operate; work; cultivate; develop
explorateur *m.* explorer; **— a.** exploratory
exploratif *a.* exploratory
exploration *f.* exploration, exploring
explorer *vt.* to explore; examine; probe; **— au scaphandre autonome** to skin-dive
exploser *vi.* to explode, blow up
explosible *a.* explosive
explosif *a. & m.* explosive
explosion *f.* explosion, exploding, blowing up; outburst
exportateur *m.* exporter
exporter *vt.* to export
exposant *m.* exhibitor; petitioner; (math.) exponent
exposé *a.* exposed; open; subject to, liable; **— m.** statement, account
exposer *vt.* to expose; exhibit, display, show; explain

exposition *f.* exposition; exhibition, display, showing; exposure; **salle d'— ** *f.* showroom

exprès (expresse) *a.* express, explicit; **par — special delivery; — ** *adv.* on purpose, intentionally, expressly

express *m.* local-express train

expressément *adv.* expressly, clearly

expressif *a.* expressive

expression *f.* expression; show, display; term, language, words; squeezing, extracting

expressivement *adv.* expressively

exprimable *a.* expressible

exprimer *vt.* to express; show; squeeze out, extract

expropriation *f.* expropriation

exproprier *vt.* to expropriate

expugnable *a.* pregnable

expulser *vt.* to expel; evict; eject, throw out

expulsion *f.* expulsion; eviction; ejection; deportation

expurger *vt.* to expurgate

exquis *a.* exquisite; of extreme beauty

exsangue *a.* bloodless, anemic

exsuder *vt. & vi.* to exude

extase *f.* ecstasy; rapture; trance

extasier *v.*, **s'— ** to go into ecstasy, go wild, be wild

extatique *a.* ecstatic

extenseur *m.* stretcher, expander; extensor muscle

extensible *a.* extendable, expandable

extensif *a.* extensive; tensile

extension *f.* extension; stretching; spread, expansion; extent

exténuation *f.* extenuation; exhaustion

exténuant *a.* extenuating, exhausting

exténuer *vt.* to extenuate; exhaust; **s'— ** to exhaust oneself

extérieur *a.* exterior, external; outside; foreign; — *m.* exterior, outside; outward appearance; surface

extérieurement *adv.* externally; outwardly; superficially, on the surface

exterminateur *m.* exterminator

extermination *f.* extermination

exterminer *vt.* to exterminate; wipe out

externat *m.* day school

externe *a.* external, exterior, outside; — *m.* nonresident pupil; (med.) nonresident assistant interne

extincteur *m.* fire extinguisher

extinction *f.* extinction; extinguishing; slaking; abolition; loss

extirpateur *m.* uprooter, extirpator; remover

extirpation *f.* uprooting, extirpation; removal

extirper *vt.* to extirpate, uproot; remove

extorquer *vt.* to extort

extorqueur *m.* extortionist

extorsion *f.* extortion

extra *adv.* extra, additional; — *m.* (*pl.*) extra(s)

extracteur *m.* extractor

extraction *f.* extraction; pulling out; origin, ancestry, birth

extrader *vt.* to extradite

extradition *f.* extradition

extra-fin *a.* superfine, very fine

extraire *vt.* to extract, draw out; pull out; pull a tooth

extrait *m.* extract, excerpt; abstract

extra-légal *a.* extralegal

extraordinaire *a.* extraordinary, out of the ordinary

extrapoler *vt.* to extrapolate

extra-sensoriel *a.* extrasensory

extravagance *f.* extravagance; exorbitance; foolishness

extravagant *a.* extravagant; exorbitant; foolish

extravaguer *vi.* to rave, talk nonsense

extrême *a.* extreme; excessive; severe; farthest; — *m.* extreme

extrêmement *adv.* extremely, very highly

extrême-onction *f.* (eccl.) extreme unction

Extrême-Orient *m.* Far East

extrémist *m. & f.* extremist

extrémité *f.* extremity; tip, end; urgency; dying moment; extreme

extrinsèque *a.* extrinsic

extroverti *m.* extrovert

exubérance *f.* exuberance

exubérant *a.* exuberant, luxuriant

exultation *f.* exultation

exulter *vi.* to exult, rejoice

ex-voto *m.* (eccl.) votive offering; ex-voto

F

fable *f.* fable, story; laughing stock

fablier *m.* collection of fables

fabricant *m.* manufacturer

fabricateur *m.* fabricator; forger

fabrication *f.* manufacturing, manufacture; fabrication; forging

fabrique *f.* manufacture; factory; paper mill

fabriquer *vt.* to manufacture, produce, make; fabricate; forge

fabuleux *a.* fabulous

façade *f.* façade, front

face *f.* front, face; aspect; side; **en — de** opposite; **faire — à** to face, confront, meet; **pile ou — ** heads or tails

face-à-main *m.* lorgnette

facétie *f.* prank, joke, trick

facétieux a. facetious
facette f. facet
facetter vt. to cut in facets
fâché a. angry; sorry
fâcher vt. to anger; afflict, grieve; **se —** to get angry; be offended
fâcheux a. tiresome, annoying; troublesome; unfortunate
faciès m. facies; appearance, facial aspect
facile a. easy; facile; glib
facilité f. facility; ease, easiness; aptitude; glibness
faciliter vt. to facilitate
façon f. fashion; fashioning, making, creation; way, manner; fuss, ceremony; **à la — de** like; **de — que** so that; **de cette —** in this way, thus; **de toute —** in any event, in any case; **faire des —s** to stand on ceremony; **sans —(s)** without fuss or ceremony; unceremoniously
faconde f. glibness, fluency
façonner vt. to fashion, make; shape, form
façonnier a. overly fussy
facsimilé m. facsimile, reproduction, duplicate
factage m. delivery, delivery service
facteur m. (math.) factor; mailman, postman; agent; maker, manufacturer
factice a. imitation, factitious
factieux a. factious
factionnaire m. sentry; picket
factorielle f. (math.) factorial
factotum m. factotum; jack-of-all-trades; handyman
facturation f. billing, invoicing
facture f. (com.) invoice, bill; workmanship, make; making, manufacture
facturer vt. to invoice
facturier m. invoice book; billing clerk
facultatif a. optional
faculté f. faculty; ability, capacity; option; school within a university
fadaise f. silliness, foolishness, nonsense
fade a. insipid, tasteless, flat
fadeur f. insipidity; lack of taste, flatness
fagot m. faggot, bundle of sticks
fagotin m. small faggot, small bundle
faible a. feeble, weak; faint; poor; low; thin; — m. foible, weakness
faiblesse f. weakness; feebleness; failing, frailty; faint
faiblir vi. to weaken, fail; abate, diminish
faïence, (faïencerie) f. earthenware, pottery
faille f. (geol.) fault, crack, break
faillibilité f. fallibility
faillible a. fallible
faillir vi. to fail; go bankrupt; be on the point of; — **faire quelque chose** almost to do something

faillite f. failure, bankruptcy; **faire — to** go bankrupt
faim f. hunger; **avoir — to** be hungry; hunger
fainéant a. lazy; — m. loafer, idler; good-for-nothing
fainéanter vi. to idle, loaf, do nothing
fainéantise f. laziness, loafing, idleness
faire vt. to make; do; perform, execute, accomplish; be, come to, amount to; say, remark; play (music), act, pretend; matter, be of importance; see to, attend to, arrange; cause something to be done, have someone do something; have something done; — **le mort** play dead; — **le tour de** circumnavigate; round; — **son droit** study law; — **une malle** pack a trunk; — **une pièce** clean a room; — **une promenade** take a walk, go for a walk; **cela ne fait rien** it doesn't matter, never mind; **il fait beau** it's nice out (weather); **il fait chaud** it's warm, hot; **il fait froid** it's cold; **il fait mauvais** the weather is bad; **il fait du soleil** it's sunny; **il fait du vent** it's windy; **se —** become, grow; develop, be formed; get used to, adjust to; be, happen
faire-part m. notification, notice
faisable a. feasible, practical
faisan m., **–(de)** f. pheasant
faisceau m. bundle, bunch, cluster
faiseur m. maker, doer
fait a. made, done; matured, ripe; — m. fact; feat, act, deed; **mettre au — to** inform, bring up to date; **sur le — in** the act
fait-divers m. news item
faîte m. top, summit; ridge; (fig.) in highest point
faix m. load, burden, weight
falaise f. cliff
fallacieux a. fallacious
falloir v. to be necessary; to be lacking; **il faut —** it is necessary, one must, one should; it takes; **il me faut** I must, I have to; I need; **comme il faut** proper, properly; **il s'en faut de beaucoup, tant s'en faut** far from it; **peu s'en faut** almost, nearly
falot a. pale, colorless; quaint; — m. lamp, lantern, light
falsificateur m. falsifier, forger
falsifier vt. to falsify; adulterate; forge
famé a. noted; **bien —** of good repute
famélique a. famished, starving, starved
fameux a. famous; distinguished; wonderful, excellent
familial a. of the family; domestic
familiariser vt. to familiarize; **se — avec**

to become accustomed to, familiarize oneself with; become familiar with
familiarité *f.* familiarity; intimacy
familier *a.* familiar, intimate; of the family, domestic; colloquial
familièrement *adv.* familiarly, in a familiar manner
famille *f.* family; **soutien de — m.** breadwinner
famine *f.* famine; starvation
fanal *m.* light, lantern, beacon; headlight
fanatique *a. & n.* fanatic
fanatiser *vt.* to make fanatic, make a fanatic of
fanatisme *m.* fanaticism
fanchon *f.* scarf, kerchief
faner *vt.* to fade; pitch (hay); **se — to** fade, wither
fanfare *f.* fanfare, flourish; brass band, military band
fanfaron *a.* boasting, bragging; — *m.* braggart
fanfaronnade *f.* boasting, bragging
fanfaronner *vi.* to boast, brag, swagger
fanfreluche *f.* frill; trifle
fange *f.* mire, mud, dirt, filth; vice
fangeux *a.* muddy, dirty, filthy
fanion *m.* pennant, flag
fanon *m.* fetlock, dewlap, wattle; pendant; whalebone; (eccl.) maniple; **-s** *pl.* streamers of a bishop's mitre
fantaisie *f.* fantasy; fancy, imagination; whim, caprice; vagary; **de — fancy;** imaginary
fantaisiste *a.* fanciful, whimsical, imaginary
fantasmagorique *a.* fantastic, grotesque, weird
fantasque *a.* whimsical; temperamental; odd
fantassin *m.* foot soldier
fantastique *a.* fantastic; fanciful; unbelievable; weird
fantoche *m.* puppet, marionette
fantôme *m.* phantom, spectre, ghost, spirit
faon *m.* fawn
faonner *vi.* to fawn
faquin *m.* rascal, scoundrel
farce *f.* farce; trick, joke; stuffing (for food)
farceur *m.* joker, buffoon
farcir *vt.* to stuff (in cooking)
fard *m.* rouge; cosmetics, makeup; embellishment; pretense
fardeau *m.* burden, load, weight
farder *vt.* to make up; disguise, mask; **se — to** put on make-up
farfouiller *vt. & vi.* to search, look around, rummage
farine *f.* flour, meal; — **lactée** malted

milk
farineux *a.* starchy, mealy; covered with flour
farouche *a.* wild, savage; cruel; timid, shy
fascicule *m.* cluster, bunch; section, part of a publication
fascinant, fascinateur *a.* fascinating
fasciner *vt.* to fascinate; charm; bewitch
fascisme *m.* Fascism
fasciste *m. & f.* Fascist
faste *m.* pomp; ostentation
fastidieux *a.* tedious, tiresome; dull
fastueux *a.* ostentatious; pompous; sumptuous
fat *a.* conceited, vain
fatal *a.* fatal; mortal; inevitable
fatalisme *m.* fatalism
fataliste *a.* fatalistic; — *m. & f.* fatalist
fatalité *f.* fatality, fate
fatidique *a.* fateful
fatigant *a.* fatiguing, tiring, tiresome
fatigue *f.* fatigue, weariness; strain, wear
fatiguer *vt.* to fatigue, tire; strain, overwork; — *vi.* to labor, strain; **se — to** get tired
fatras *m.* rubbish, trash, jumble
fatuité *f.* conceitedness
faubourg *m.* suburb
faubourien *a.* suburban; — *m.* suburbanite
faucher *vt.* to mow, cut down; reap
faucheuse *f.* harvester, mower, reaper
faucille *f.* sickle
faucon *m.* falcon; hawk
fauconnerie *f.* falconry
faufil *m.* thread for basting
faufiler *vt.* to baste, tack; weave in and out; slip in; **se — thread one's way;** slip in *or* out, sneak in *or* out; curry favor
faune *m.* faun; — *f.* (zool.) fauna
faussaire *m. & f.* forger
faussement *adv.* falsely
fausser *vt.* to falsify; bend, warp; force (a lock); **se — to** bend, warp, crack, break down
fausset *m.* falsetto
fausseté *f.* falseness, falsehood, untruth
faute *f.* fault; error, mistake; blame; fowl (in sports); lack, need, want; **faire — to** be lacking; — **de** for lack of, for want of; **sans — without fail**
fauteuil *m.* armchair; chair; (theat.) seat
fauteur *m.* instigator, agitator
fautif *a.* faulty; offending
fauvette *f.* warbler
faux *f.* scythe
faux *m.* falsehood, lie; forgery, imitation; — **(fausse)** *a.* false, untrue; imitation, counterfeit, forged; wrong
faux-col *m.* removable collar

faux-filet *m.* steak
faux-fuyant *m.* evasion, subterfuge
faux-monnayeur *m.* counterfeiter
faux-semblant *m.* pretext
faveur *f.* favor; preference; liking, good graces; **billet de — m.** complimentary ticket, pass
favori *m.* favorite; **–s** *m. pl.* side whiskers; **— (favorite)** *a.* favorite
favoriser *vt.* to favor; encourage, promote; like
favoritisme *m.* favoritism
fébrile *a.* feverish, febrile
fébrilité *f.* feverishness
fécal *a.* fecal
fèces *f. pl.* feces, stool
fécond *a.* fecund, fertile, productive, fruitful; rich
féconder *vt.* to fecundate, impregnate
fécondité *f.* fecundity, fertility; richness
fécule *f.* flour-like consistency; **— de maïs** cornstarch
féculent *a.* starchy; **— m.** starchy food
fédéral *a.* federal
fédéraliser *vt.* to federalize
fédéraliste *a. & n.* federalist
fédératif *a.* federated, confederate
fédération *f.* federation
fédérer *vt.* to federate
fée *f.* fairy; **conte de –s** *m.* fairy tale
féerie *f.* fairyland; enchantment; fantasy
féerique *a.* fairy; magic
feindre *vt.* to feign, pretend, simulate
feinte *f.* feint, pretense, pretending; limp
feinter *vi.* to feint
feldspath *m.* felspar
fêlé *a.* cracked; crazy
fêler *vt.* to crack
félicitations *f. pl.* congratulations
félicité *f.* felicity, happiness
féliciter *vt.* to congratulate
félin *a. & m.* feline
félonie *f.* treason
fêlure *f.* crack, chink; break, fracture
femelle *f. & a.* female
féminin *a.* feminine; **— m.** (gram.) feminine
féminisme *m.* feminism
femme *f.* woman, wife; female; **— de charge** housekeeper; **— de chambre** chambermaid
fémur *m.* femur
fenaison *f.* harvesting of hay
fendille *f.* crack, break, fissure
fendiller *vt.* to crack; **se — to crack, peel**
fendoir *m.* cleaver, chopper
fendre *vt.* to split; crack; cleave; rend
fenêtre *f.* window
fenil *m.* hayloft
fenouil *m.* fennel

fente *f.* crack, split, crevice, fissure; slot; lunge
féodal *a.* feudal
féodalité *f.* feudalism
fer *m.* iron; (fig.) sword, blade; **coup de — m.** pressing, ironing; **— à cheval** horseshoe; **— à friser** curling iron; **— à marquer** branding iron; **— à repasser** flatiron; **— à souder** soldering iron; **— de fonte** cast iron; **— forgé** wrought iron; **marquer au —** to brand; **–s irons, chains**
ferblanterie *f.* tinware
ferblantier *m.* tinsmith
férié *a.,* **jour — m.** public holiday
férir *vt.* to strike; **se — de** be struck with, ' stricken with; fall in love with
ferler *vt.* to furl
fermage *m.* tenant farming
ferme *a.* firm, fixed, steady; **— adv.** fast; hard; firmly; with assurance
ferme *f.* farm; (theat.) flat (scenery mounted on frame)
fermé *a.* closed; exclusive, restricted
fermentation *f.* fermentation, ferment
fermenter *vi.* to ferment
fermer *vt.* to shut, close; turn off; **— vi.** shut, close; **— à clef** to lock
fermeté *f.* firmness, steadiness
fermeture *f.* closing; shutting; fastening; lock; bolt of a gun; lockout; **— éclair** zipper
fermier *m.* farmer
fermoir *m.* fastener, snap, clasp
féroce *a.* ferocious, savage, wild
férocité *f.* ferocity, wildness
ferraille *f.* scrap iron; junk
ferrailler *vi.* to rattle
ferré *a.* ironclad, ironshod; hobnailed (shoe sole); (coll.) good, well versed; **route –e** *f.* paved road; **voie –e** *f.* railway
ferrer *vt.* to shoe (horse); equip, fit with iron; pave
ferret *m.* tab, tag
ferreux *a.* ferrous
ferrique *a.* ferric
ferronnerie *f.* wrought iron; ironworks
ferroviaire *a.* railroad, railway, train
ferrure *f.* iron fittings
fertilisant *a.* fertilizing; **— m.** fertilizer
fertiliser *vt.* to fertilize; enrich
fertilité *f.* fertility, fruitfulness; richness
féru *a.* in love; wrapped up, obsessed
férule *f.* stick, cane, rod
fervent *a.* fervent, ardent; **— m.** devotee
ferveur *f.* fervor; ardor
fesse *f.* buttock
fessée *f.* spanking
fesse-mathieu *m.* miser, skinflint; usurer

fesser vt. to spank

festin m. feast, banquet

festiner vt. & vi. to feast

festivité f. festivity

feston m. festoon; scallop (sewing, edging)

festonner vt. to festoon; scallop

festoyer vt. & vi. to feast

fête f. feast, festival; holiday; saint's day; birthday; festivity; **jour de** — m. holiday

fête-Dieu f. (eccl.) Corpus Christi

fêter vt. to celebrate; entertain

fétiche m. fetish

fétide a. fetid, repulsive

fétidité f. fetidness

fétu m. straw; (fig.) something of no value

feu m. (pl. **feux**) fire, burning; flame; match, light; — **de joie** bonfire; — **d'artifice** fireworks; — **rouge** red light; **au** —! fire!; **à petit** — on a slow fire; by inches; **armes à** — f. pl. firearms; **coup de** — m. gunshot; **mettre** — **à** to set fire to; **prendre** — to catch fire; **faire** — to fire; **faire du** — to make a fire; **faire long** — hang fire

feu a. late, defunct

feudataire m. vassal

feuillage m. foliage

feuillaison f. appearance of leaves

feuille f. leaf; sheet; page; paper, newspaper

feuillée f. foliage; **-s** pl. (mil.) latrine

feuiller vi. to produce leaves

feuilleté a. laminated, foliated; — m. puff pastry

feuilleter vt. to leaf through; turn the pages of; foliate, form into leaves or thin layers

feuilleton m. serial; **roman** — serialized novel

feuillette f. small leaf; leaflet

feuillu a. leafy; — m. foliage

feutre m. felt; felt hat

feutré a. soft, quiet, velvet-like; muffled

feutrer vt. to cover with felt; make into felt

fève f. lima bean

février m. February

fi interj. fie! for shame!; — m., **faire** — **de** dislike, scorn

fiacre m. horse-drawn cab, hack

fiançailles f. pl. engagement, betrothal

fiancé a. engaged, betrothed; — m. fiancé, bridegroom; **-e** f. fiancée, bride

fiancer v., **se** — to become engaged

fibre f. fiber, grain, thread

fibreux a. fibrous

ficeler vt. to tie (up); wrap and tie

ficelle f. string, cord, twine

fiche f. index card, note card; case history; (elec.) plug; pin; microscope slide

ficher vt. to drive, thrust in; (coll.) cheat, trick; throw out; **se** — **de** to laugh at, make fun of; care nothing about

fichier m. file, card file; filing cabinet

fichu m. scarf, shawl, kerchief

fictif a. fictitious, invented, imaginary

fiction f. fiction; invention; story; — **interplanétaire** space fiction

fidéicommis m. trust (law)

fidèle a. faithful, true, loyal

fidélité f. fidelity, faithfulness; loyalty

fiduciaire a. fiduciary; paper money; — m. fiduciary, trustee

fief m. fief, fee

fiel m. gall; bitterness, malice

fielleux a. galling, bitter

fiente f. droppings, manure, dung

fier (**fière**) a. proud; haughty

fier vt. to entrust; **se** — **à** to rely upon, trust, depend on, count on

fier-à-bras m. braggart, swaggerer

fièrement adv. proudly

fierté f. pride; dignity

fièvre f. fever; heat; temperature

fiévreux a. feverish, fevered

figement m. clotting, coagulation, congealing

figer vt. to coagulate, congeal; curdle; thicken, solidify; **se** — to clot, coagulate; become frozen

figue f. fig; — **de Barbarie** prickly pear

figuier m. fig tree

figurant n. (theat.) extra; **-e** f. ballet dancer

figuratif a. figurative

figuration f. figuration; (theat.) extras

figure f. face; figure, form, shape

figuré a. figured; figurative

figurer vt. to represent; portray; — vi. to figure; **se** — to imagine

fil m. thread; line; cutting edge; grain (of wood); — **de fer** wire; — **de l'eau** current, stream

filasse f. tow; oakum

filature f. spinning

file f. file, row, line; **à la** — in file; in succession, on end

filé m. thread

filer vt. to spin; draw out, prolong; follow, shadow; — vi. pass, go by; move along, get going; leave; — **à l'anglaise** to take French leave

filet m. net; fillet; thread; bit, small amount, trickle; snaffle (harness part)

fileter vt. to stretch, draw metal; thread a screw

fileur m. spinner

filial a. filial; **-e** f. branch, subsidiary

filiation *f.* filiation; relationship; ancestry

filigrane *m.* filigree; watermark

fille *f.* daughter; girl; (eccl.) sister; **fille d'honneur** bridesmaid; maid of honor; **jeune —** girl; **vieille —** old maid, spinster

fillette *f.* young girl, little girl

filleul *m.* godson; **-e** *f.* goddaughter

film *m.* film; **— fixe** filmstrip

filmer *vt.* to film

filoche *f.* netting

filon *m.* vein, lode, strike

filou *m.* pickpocket; cheat, thief

filouter *vt.* to rob, cheat

fils *m.* son; junior (after a name); the younger

filtrant *a.* filtering; filterable; **bout — m.** filter tip

filtrat *m.* filtrate

filtration *f.* filtration, filtering

filtre *m.* filter; strainer; individual coffee-maker (strainer type)

filtrer *vt.* to filter, strain; **— vi.** to filter through; drip, leak

fin *f.* end, extremity, conclusion, close; aim, purpose; **en — de compte** in the end, as it turned out; to get to the point; **sans —** endless

fin *a.* fine; delicate, small, thin; clear, pure; ingenious; clever, subtle

final *a.* final, last, concluding

finalement *adv.* finally, lastly

finaliste *m. & f.* finalist

finalité *f.* finality

financement *m.* financing

financer *vt.* to finance, back

financier *a.* financial; **— m.** financier

finasser *vi.* to finesse, use finesse

finasserie *f.* finesse, shrewdness

finaud *a.* clever, shrewd, cunning

finesse *f.* fineness; finesse; delicacy, artifice; artfulness; ingenuity, subtlety; shrewdness

fini *a.* finished, ended, over, done, concluded; skilled, experienced; finite

finir *vt.* to finish, end, conclude; **— vi.** finish, end; **en — avec** be done with, get something over with; **— de** finish, stop

finissage *m.* finishing, final step, finishing touch

finisseur *m.* finisher

finlandais *a.* Finnish; **— m.** Finn

Finlande *f.* Finland

fiole *f.* phial, flask, bottle

fioriture *f.* flourish, curlicue

firmament *m.* firmament, heavens, sky

firme *f.* firm, house, company; imprint

fisc *m.* treasury, internal revenue

fiscal *a.* fiscal; pertaining to revenue

fiscaliser *vt.* to tax, make subject to tax

fiscalité *f.* tax collecting

fissurer *vt.* to fissure, split, cleave

fistule *f.* fistula

fixatif *m.* fixative

fixation *f.* fixation; fixing, setting, placing; determining

fixe *a.* fixed, steady, set; **prix —** set price; **— m.** regular salary

fixer *vt.* to fix; make firm, set, hold; stare at

fixité *f.* fixity

flaccidité *f.* flaccidity; flabbiness

flacon *m.* flask, bottle, decanter; flagon

flagellant *m.* flagellant

flagellation *f.* flagellation; flogging, whipping

flagelier *vt.* to flagellate; flog, whip

flageoler *vi.* to quiver, tremble, buckle

flageolet *m.* (mus.) flageolet, flute; kidney bean

flagorner *vt.* to flatter, be obsequious toward

flagrance *f.* flagrancy

flagrant *a.* flagrant; **en — délit** in the act

flair *m.* scent; perspicacity; flair, knack

flairer *vt.* to smell, scent, sniff; sense

flamand *a. & m.* Flemish

flamant *m.* flamingo

flambant *a.* flaming

flambé *a.* flamed with brandy

flambeau *m.* torch, brand; light; candle; candlestick

flambée *f.* fire, blaze

flambement *m.* collapse, buckling

flamber *vi.* to flame, blaze; collapse, buckle, fall in; **— vt.** to singe, char

flamboyant *a.* flaming; flamboyant

flamboyer *vi.* to blaze

flamme *f.* flame; love

flammèche *f.* spark, ember

flan *m.* custard

flanc *m.* flank, side; (fig.) womb

flanchet *m.* meat flank

Flandre *f.* Flanders

flanelle *f.* flannel

flâner *vi.* to stroll; idle, loiter

flânerie *f.* idling, loitering; strolling

flâneur *m.* idler; loiterer; stroller

flanquer *vt.* to flank; throw; **— à la porte** throw out, kick out

flaque *f.* puddle

flash *m.* (photo.) flash attachment, flash bulb

flasque *a.* flaccid; flabby; **— f.** powder flask

flatter *vt.* to flatter, caress; please

flatterie *f.* flattery

flatteur *a.* flattering; pleasing; **— m.** flatterer

flatueux *a.* flatulent
flatulence *f.* flatulence
fléau *m.* scourge; flail; (fig.) plague
flèche *f.* arrow; church spire; pole; rise; (avi.) direction indicator
fléchette *f.* dart
fléchir *vt. & vi.* to bend; submit; give way
flegmatique *a.* phlegmatic; stolid
flegme *m.* phlegm
flet *m.* flounder
flétan *m.* halibut
flétrir *vt.* to fade, wither; tarnish, stain; se — to fade, wither
flétrissure *f.* fading; withering; tarnish; stigma
fleur *f.* flower; blossom; prime; à — de level with
fleuraison *f.* flowering, blooming
fleuret *m.* fencing foil
fleurette *f.* little flower
fleuri *a.* in bloom; flowery; florid
fleurir *vt.* to decorate with flowers; — *vi.* to flower, bloom: flourish
fleuriste *m. & f.* florist
fleuve *m.* river
flexibilité *f.* flexibility
flexible *a.* flexible; pliant, pliable
flexion *f.* bending, flexion; inflexion
flibuster *vt.* to rob; — *vi.* to steal; commit piracy
flibustier *m.* buccaneer, pirate
flirt *m.* flirting, flirtation
flirter *vi.* to flirt
flocon *m.* snowflake; tuft; fleece
floconner *vi.* to form flakes; become fleecy
floconneux *a.* fleecy, fluffy
floraison *f.* blossoming, flourishing
flore *f.* flora
florentin *a.* Florentine; à la—e served with spinach
florissant *a.* flourishing
flot *m.* wave; flood, tide; floating; raft; à — floating, afloat
flottabilité *f.* buoyancy
flottable *a.* buoyant
flottant *a.* floating; vacillating, undecided
flotte *f.* fleet; float
flottement *m.* vacillation, wavering; undulation; flapping, waving
flotter *vt.* to float; — *vi.* to float; vacillate, waver; wave
flotteur *m.* float; buoy
flottille *f.* flotilla
flou *a.* light and soft; blurred, hazy; fluffy
fluctuer *vi.* to fluctuate
fluer *vi.* to flow
fluet *a.* thin, slender
fluide *m. & a.* fluid; liquid
fluidifier *vt.* to liquefy
fluidité *f.* fluidity

fluor *m.* fluorine
fluorescent *a.* fluorescent
fluoridation *f.* fluoridation
fluorure *m.* fluoride
flûte *f.* flute; tube, shaft
flûter *vi.* to play the flute
flux *m.* flow; flux; ebb
fluxion *f.* fluxion; — de poitrine pneumonia
foc *m.* (naut.) jib
foetal *a.* foetal
foetus *m.* foetus
foi *f.* faith; fidelity; belief; trust, confidence; de bonne — sincere, honest; digne de — trustworthy, reliable
foie *m.* liver; — gras goose liver paste
foin *m.* hay
foire *f.* fair, market
fois *f.* time; à la — at once, simultaneously, at a time; une — que once; encore une — once again; une — pour toutes definitely
foison *f.* abundance
foisonnant *a.* plentiful, abundant
folâtre *a.* frisky, playful
folâtrer *vi.* to play, frolic, romp
folie *f.* folly; insanity, madness
folié *a.* foliated
folio *m.* folio; page number
folklorique *a.* concerning folklore
follement *adv.* madly, foolishly
follet *a.* merry, gay
follicule *m.* follicle
fomentateur *m.* fomenter, agitator
fomenter *vt.* to foment
foncé *a.* dark, deep, somber (color)
foncer *vt.* to drive (in); deepen, darken — *vi.*, — sur to charge, rush
foncier *a.* pertaining to land or property; (fig.) fundamental; biens — *m. pl.* real property, real estate
foncièrement *adv.* fundamentally, basically
fonction *f.* function, duty, office
fonctionnaire *m. & f.* civil servant, petty official
fonctionnarisme *m.* bureaucracy
fonctionnel *a.* functional
fonctionnement *m.* functioning; order
fonctionner *vi.* to function, work, run
fond *m.* bottom; foundation; back; end; à — thoroughly; au — basically; de — fundamental, main, most important; sans — bottomless
fondamental *a.* fundamental, (fig.) essential
fondant *a.* melting; — *m.* flux for soldering; candy, bonbon
fondateur *m.* founder
fondation *f.* founding; foundation

fondé a. founded; justified; — m. agent; manager

fondement m. foundation; basis, base

fonder vt. to found; lay the foundation of; establish

fonderie f. foundry; casting; smelting

fondre vt. to melt, dissolve; smelt (iron); cast; — vi. to melt

fondrière f. quagmire; mud hole

fonds m. land; landed property; capital; funds

fondu a. melted, molten; — m. fadeout (films)

fontaine f. fountain, spring, well, source

fonte f. melting; cast iron; casting; smelting; alloy; (print.) font, type of one style and size

footing m. walk, hike, walking

forage m. drilling, boring

forain a., **fête** f. — f. fair

forban m. pirate

forçat m. galley slave; convict, one condemned to hard labor

force f. force, strength, power; **à — de** by means of, by dint of; **–s** f. pl. shears (for metal, hedges, etc.)

forcé a. forced

forcément adv. necessarily

forcement m. forcing

forcené a. frantic, mad

forcer vt. to force, compel; break into; break out of

forer vt. to drill, bore

forestier a. of the forest; — m. forest ranger

foret m. drill

forêt f. forest; — **pluvieuse** rain forest

foreuse f. drilling machine, drill, borer

forfaire vt. to forfeit; — **à** to be remiss in

forfait m. crime; forfeit; contract

forfaitaire a. contractual

forfanterie f. bragging, boasting

forgé a. forged; **fer — m.** wrought iron

forgeage m. forging

forger vt. to forge; (fig.) invent, imagine

forgeron m. blacksmith

forgeur m. forger, inventor

formaldéhyde m. formaldehyde

formaliser v., **se —** to be offended

formaliste m. & f. formalist

formalité f. formality; form, ceremony

format m. size, format

formatif a. formative

formation f. formation; forming

forme f. form, shape; formality; politeness; **sous la — de** in the form of

formel a. formal; express; strict

formellement adv. formally; strictly

former vt. to form; formulate; model; bring up, train, educate

formidable a. formidable; tremendous

formique a. formic

formulaire m. set of rules or regulations

formule f. formula; form, blank

formuler vt. to formulate

forniquer vi. to fornicate

forsythia m. forsythia

fort a. strong, vigorous; high (wind); loud; heavy (sea); large, great; — adv. very, extremely; loudly; strongly; — m. strong point; strong man; fort

forteresse f. fortress

fortifiant a. fortifying; — m. tonic

fortification f. fortification

fortifier vt. to fortify, strengthen

fortuit a. chance, casual, fortuitous

fortune f. fortune; chance; destiny; **faire —** to become rich

fortuné a. fortunate, happy; well-off

forum m. forum

fosse f. pit, hole; grave

fossé m. ditch; moat

fossette f. dimple

fossile a. & m. fossil

fossilisation f. fossilization

fossiliser vt. to fossilize

fossoyeur m. gravedigger

fou m. fool; madman; jester; bishop (chess)

fou, fol (folle) a. mad, foolish; **in love**

foucade f. impulse, whim

foudre f. thunderbolt; thunder; lightning; **coup de — m.** love at first sight

foudroyant a. crushing, overwhelming

foudroyer vt. to strike with lightning; strike down; blast; dumbfound

fouet m. whip

fouettement m. whipping

fouetter vt. to whip, flog; — vi. to whip, lash; flap

fougère f. fern

fougue f. spirit, fire, mettle

fougueux a. firery, impetuous, spirited

fouille f. digging, excavation

fouiller vt. to dig, excavate; search, look through; — vi. search

fouillis m. jumble, disorder

fouiner vi. to pry, ferret

fouir vt. to burrow, dig

foulard m. scarf, foulard cloth

foule f. crowd; pressing, milling

foulée f. tread; stride; track, spoor

fouler vt. to tread on; press; crush, trample; sprain; **se — la cheville** to sprain one's ankle

foulure f. sprain

four m. oven; kiln; **faire —** to fail; **petit — cooky**, pastry; — **soufflé** blast furnace

fourbe m. deceiver, cheat; — a. deceitful

fourberie f. deceit; cheating
fourbir vt. to furbish, polish
fourbissage m. polishing, furbishing
fourbu a. exhausted
fourche f. fork, pitchfork
fourcher vt. & vi. to fork
fourchetée f. forkful of food
fourchette f. fork
fourchon m. prong, tine
fourchu a. forked; cloven
fourgon m. wagon, van; baggage car; truck; poker
fourmi f. ant; — **blanche** termite
fourmilier m. anteater
fourmilière f. ant hill
fourmillement m. swarming; pricking sensation
fourmiller vi. to swarm, teem
fournaise f. furnace
fourneau m. cooking stove; furnace; **haut** — blast furnace
fournée f. batch, ovenful
fourni a. bushy, thick
fournir vt. to furnish, provide, supply; produce
fournisseur m. contractor, supplier, caterer
fourniture f. furnishing; —**s** pl. supplies
fourrage m. fodder; foraging
fourrager vi. to forage; search; — vt. to ravage
fourreau m. scabbard, sheath; case
fourré a. fur-lined, furry; densely wooded; — m. thicket
fourrer vt. to put in; stuff, cram, poke
fourre-tout m. duffel bag
fourreur m. furrier
fourrière f. dog pound
fourrure f. fur; hair; skin; lining
fourvoyer vt. to lead astray
foyer m. hearth; home; center, source, seat; foyer, lobby; focus
frac m. dress coat
fracas m. bustle, noise
fracasser vt. to break in pieces, shatter
fraction f. fraction
fractionner vt. to split, divide
fracture f. fracture; breaking
fracturer vt. to fracture; break open
fragilité f. fragility; frailty
fragment m. fragment
fragmentaire a. fragmentary
fragmenter vt. to break into fragments
fraîchement adv. freshly; coolly; recently, lately
fraîcheur f. freshness; coolness; chill
fraîchir vi. to freshen; become cooler
frais (fraîche) a. fresh; cool; recent; — m. fresh air; cool(ness)
frais m. pl. expenses; cost

fraise f. strawberry
framboise f. raspberry
franc (franche) a. free; frank; open; sincere; — adv. frankly
franc (franque) a. Frankish, of the Franks
franc m. franc (currency)
français m. the French language; — a. French; **à la** —**e** in the French fashion
Français m. Frenchman
France f. France
franchement adv. frankly, sincerely
franchir vt. to leap over; clear; overcome; cross
franchise f. frankness, sincerity; immunity, exemption; — **académique** academic freedom
franchissement m. crossing
francique a. Frankish
franciscain a. & m. Franciscan
franciser vt. to gallicize
francium m. francium
franc-maçon m. freemason
franc-maçonnerie f. freemasonry
franco adv. postpaid
franco-bord m. & adv. free on board (F.O.B.)
franc-parler m. frankness
franc-tireur m. sniper
frange f. fringe; —**r** vt. to fringe
frangible a. breakable, fragile
frappant a. striking, surprising
frappe f. minting, striking of coins
frappé a. cooled, chilled (wine)
frapper vt. to strike, hit; knock; mint stamp; ice
frasque f. escapade
fraternel a. fraternal; brotherly
fraternisation f. fraternizing
fraterniser vi. to fraternize
fraternité f. fraternity, brotherhood
fratricide m. & f. fratricide
fraude f. deceit, imposture; fraud; — **fiscale** tax evasion
frauder vt. to defraud, cheat
fraudeur m. cheat, defrauder
frauduleux a. fraudulent
frayer vt. to scrape; open, clear, trace; — vi. to associate with; spawn (fish)
frayeur f. fright, terror
fredaine f. frolic, prank
fredonner vt. & vi. to hum
frégate f. frigate
frein m. brake; bit; bridle; **sans** — unbridled, unchecked
freiner vt. to brake, apply the brakes; check
frelater vt. to adulterate
frêle a. frail, weak
frelon m. hornet
frémir vi. to shudder, tremble, quiver

frémissement *m.* shivering, shuddering, quivering
frêne *m.* (bot.) ash
frénésie *f.* frenzy
frénétique *a.* frantic; frenzied
fréquemment *adv.* frequently
fréquence *f.* frequency
fréquent *a.* frequent
fréquentation *f.* frequenting; association, company
fréquenter *vt.* to frequent, haunt; associate with
frère *m.* brother
fresque *f.* fresco
fret *m.* (naut.) freight, cargo; chartering; (naut.) charge for freight transportation by boat
fréter *vt.* (naut.) to load freight; charter
frétillant *a.* brisk, lively; frisky; wagging; wriggling
frétiller *vi.* to wriggle; fidget
fretin *m.* menu — small fish thrown back; small fry
frette *f.* hoop, iron ring; fret
freudien *a.* Freudian
freudisme *m.* Freudianism
friable *a.* friable, capable of being pulverized
friand *a.* dainty, nice; fond
friandise *f.* daintiness; **-s** *pl.* dainties, delicacies
fricassée *f.* fricassee
fricasser *vt.* to fricassee; squander
fricatif *a.* fricative (phonetics)
friche *f.* fallow land; **en** — fallow
friction *f.* rub, massage; friction
frictionner *vt.* to rub, massage
frigide *a.* frigid
frigidité *f.* frigidity
frigorification *f.* refrigeration
frigorifier *vt.* to refrigerate
frigorifique *a.* refrigerating
frimas *m.* rime, hoarfrost
fringale *f.* hunger pang
fringant *a.* frisky, lively; dapper
fringuer *vi.* to frisk, frolic
fripé *a.* rumpled, mussed
friper *vt.* to rumple, wrinkle
friperie *f.* secondhand clothes; rubbish
fripier *m.* secondhand clothier, ragman
fripon *m.* rogue
friponnerie *f.* roguery
frire *vi.* to fry
frise *f.* frieze
frisé *a.* curly, crisp
friser *vt. & vi.* to curl
frisoir *m.* hair curler
frisson *m.* shivering, shaking; thrill
frissonnement *m.* shiver; thrill
frissonner *vi.* to shiver, shudder; be thrilled

frisure *f.* curliness
frit *a.* fried; **-es** *f. pl.* French fried potatoes
friture *f.* frying; fritter; any fried food; fat for frying; radio static
frivole *a.* frivolous, trifling
frivolité *f.* frivolity
froc *m.* frock (of a monk)
froid *m.* coldness, chilliness; **il fait** — **it is cold** (weather); **avoir** — **to be cold** (person); — *a.* cold; cool
froideur *f.* coldness; coolness
froidure *f.* coldness; frostbite
froissant *a.* hurting, hurtful, injurious
froissement *m.* rumpling; rustling; clash, jostling
froisser *vt.* to bruise; rumple; jostle; hurt (feelings); **se** — to take offense
frôlement *m.* rustling sound
frôler *vt.* to touch lightly, brush
fromage *m.* cheese
froment *m.* wheat
fronce *f.* crease, fold, pucker
froncement *m.* frown, frowning; wrinkling
froncer *vt.* to pucker, wrinkle; — **le sourcil** to frown
frondaison *f.* foliage; foliation
fronde *f.* slingshot; (bot.) frond
fronder *vt.* to sling
front *m.* forehead, brow, face, head; front; boldness, impudence, nerve
frontal *a.* frontal
frontière *f.* frontier, border
frontispice *m.* frontispiece
fronton *m.* façade
frottement *m.* rubbing, friction; chafing
frotter *vt.* to rub, polish; — *vi.* to rub
frotteur *m.* polisher
frottoir *m.* polisher; brush; sandpaper on a matchbox
froufrou *m.* swish, rustling; pomp, show
fructifère *a.* fruit-bearing
fructification *f.* fruition
fructifier *vi.* to bear fruit
fructueux *a.* fruitful, profitable
frugal *a.* frugal
frugalité *f.* frugality
fruit *m.* fruit; profit; **sans** — fruitless(ly)
fruiterie *f.* fruit dealer's, fruit and vegetable store
fruitier *m.* fruit dealer
frumentaire *a.* pertaining to wheat
fruste *a.* rough; worn
frustration *f.* frustration; cheating
frustrer *vt.* to frustrate, disappoint; cheat
fugace *a.* fleeting
fugitif *a.* fugitive; transitory, fleeting; — *m.* fugitive
fugue *f.* fugue; flight

fuir *vi.* to flee; leak; — *vt.* to avoid
fuite *f.* flight; avoiding; leak
fulgurant *a.* flashing
fulgurer *vi.* to flash, shine
fuligineux *a.* sooty, smoky
fulminant *a.* fulminating
fulminer *vt. & vi.* to fulminate
fumage *m.* smoking (of meat)
fumage, fumaison *m.* manuring, fertilizing
fumant *a.* smoking, steaming
fume-cigarette *m.* cigarette holder
fumée *f.* smoke, steam; fumes
fumer *vt.* to smoke; fertilize, manure; — *vi.* to smoke, steam; fume
fumet *m.* bouquet (of wine); aroma; scent
fumeur *m.* smoker
fumeux *a.* smoky; heady
fumier *m.* dung, manure
fumigation *f.* production of smoke *or* steam; treatment using a vaporizer
fumiger *vt.* to fumigate
fumoir *m.* smoking room, smoker; smoke house
funambule *m. & f.* tightrope artist
funambulesque *a.* fantastic
funèbre *a.* funeral; dismal, funereal
funerailles *f. pl.* funeral ceremony
funéraire *a.* funereal, funeral urn
funeste *a.* fatal
funiculaire *a. & m.* (rail.) funicular
fur *m.*, **au — et à mesure que** as, in proportion to
furet *m.* ferret; (coll.) busybody
fureter *vi.* to ferret, pry about, search
fureur *f.* fury, rage, craze, passion
furibond *a.* furious
furie *f.* fury; rage
furieux *a.* furious, wild, raging
furoncle *m.* (med.) boil, furuncle
furtif *a.* furtive
furtivement *adv.* furtively, stealthily
fusain *m.* art charcoal; charcoal drawing
fuseau *m.* spindle; time zone
fusée *f.* rocket; fuse; axle; **avion à — m.** rocket plane
fuselage *m.* fuselage
fuselé *a.* tapered; streamlined
fuseler *vt.* to taper
fuser *vi.* to fuse, melt; run (color)
fusible *m.* (elec.) fuse; — *a.* fusible
fusil *m.* gun, rifle; whetstone; — **à deux coups** double-barreled gun; **coup de — m.** gunshot, report; **pierre à — f.** flint
fusillade *f.* rifle fire, fusillade, volley
fusiller *vt.* to shoot; execute by firing squad
fusion *f.* fusion, melting; (com.) merger
fusionner *vt. & vi.* to unite, blend; (com.) to merge

fustiger *vt.* to beat, whip, thrash
fût *m.* stock of a gun; bole of a tree; cask, barrel; shaft of a column, stem
futaie *f.* forest of tall trees
futaille *f.* cask, barrel
futé *a.* smart, cunning, shrewd
futile *a.* futile
futilité *f.* futility
futur *a.* future; — *m.* (gram.) future; fiancé, husband-to-be
fuyant *a.* fleeing; fleeting
fuyard *m.* runaway, fugitive

G

gabare *f.* barge, lighter
gabarit *m.* mold; model; gauge
gabelle *f.* salt tax (history)
gâche *f.* catch; notch; clip; staple
gâcher *vt.* to spoil; bungle; squander
gâchette *f.* catch, pawl; trigger
gâcheur *a. & m.* spoiling, bungling; bungler
gâchis *m.* slush; mud; unhardened cement; (coll.) mess
gaélique *a. & m.* Gaelic
gaffe *f.* boat hook; blunder; **faire une —** to put one's foot in it
gaffer *vt.* to hook; — *vi.* to put one's foot in it
gage *m.* pawn, pledge; token; **mettre en — to pawn; –s** *pl.* wages; **prêteur sur —** pawnbroker
gagé *a.* salaried
gager *vt.* to hire, pay wages to; bet, wager
gageur *m.* bettor, wagerer
gageure *f.* bet, wager
gagiste *m.* pledger (law); (theat.) bit player, extra
gagnant *m.* winner
gagne-pain *m.* livelihood, living; breadwinner
gagner *vt.* to gain; win, earn; reach; — *vi.* gain, improve
gai *a.* gay, lively, cheerful
gaité *f.* gaiety
gaillard *a.* hearty; fresh; strong; ribald; — *m.* (naut.) quarterdeck; fellow; strong, attractive man; quick-witted man
gaillardise *f.* cheerfulness; risqué remark
gain *m.* gain, earnings, profit
gaine *f.* sheath, casing; holster
gainer *vt.* to sheath, cover
gala *m.* gala, celebration, festivity
galamment *adv.* gallantly; politely
galant *a.* gallant; gay; elegant; — *m.* wooer, suitor, lover
galanterie *f.* politeness; gallant talk; escapade, love affair

galaxie *f.* galaxy; Milky Way
galbe *m.* curve; curving shape, outline
gale *f.* itch; scab; mange
galère *f.* (naut.) galley; (fig.) labor
galerie *f.* gallery; (theat.) balcony; arcade; cornice
galérien *m.* galley slave; convict
galet *m.* pebble; shingle; roller
galetas *m.* garret; hovel
galette *f.* flat thin cake; pancake
galeux *a.* mangy
galimatias *m.* nonsense, jumble
galion *m.* galleon
galle *f.* gall
Galles *f.* Wales
gallois *a.* Welsh; — *m.* Welshman; Welsh language
galoche *f.* clog; overshoe
galon *m.* braid, stripe, chevron
galonner *vt.* to braid, trim with braid
galop *m.* gallop; petit — canter
galopade *f.* gallop, galloping
galoper *vt. & vi.* to gallop
galopin *m.* rascal; (coll.) mischievous child
galuchat *m.* sharkskin
galvanique *a.* galvanic
galvaniser *vt.* to galvanize; electroplate
galvanomètre *m.* galvanometer
galvanoplastie *f.* electroplating
galvauder *vt.* (coll.) to smear; botch; — *vi.* roam
galvaudeux *m.* (coll.) tramp
gambade *f.* gambol, frolic, caper
gambader *vi.* to gambol, frolic, caper
gambit *m.* gambit
gamelle *f.* mess kit
gamin *m.* street urchin, rascal, youngster
gaminer *vt.* to play in the streets
gaminerie *f.* urchin's prank
gamme *f.* gamut; scale; range
ganglion *m.* ganglion
gangrène *f.* gangrene; (bot. *and* med.) canker
gangrener *vt.* to gangrene
ganse *f.* braid, piping, cord
gant *m.* glove
gantelet *m.* gauntlet
ganter *vt.* to glove; se — to put on one's gloves
ganterie *f.* glovemaking; glove department; glove shop
gantier *m.* glover
garage *m.* garage; parking place; boathouse; docking, dock; (rail.) siding
garagiste *m.* garageman; auto mechanic
garant *m.* guarantee; surety; security
garantie *f.* guarantee; warranty; deposit, security; underwriting
garantir *vt.* to guarantee, vouch for; insure, protect

garce *f.* trollop
garçon *m.* boy; fellow, young man; bachelor; waiter; — d'honneur best man
garçonnière *f.* tomboy; bachelor's apartment
garde *m.* guard, watchman; — *f.* keeping; guard; guarding; care, custody; watch; watching; fly-leaf; chien de — *m.* watchdog; prendre — (de) to be careful (not to)
garde-à-vous *m.* (mil.) attention
garde-barrière *m.* gatekeeper; crossing guard
garde-boue *m.* mudguard
garde-chasse *m.* gamekeeper
garde-corps *m.* railing, guardrail; parapet, barrier; (naut.) life line
garde-côte *m.* coast guardsman; coast guard cutter
garde-feu *m.* fire screen
garde-fou *m.* guardrail; parapet
garde-frein *m.* (rail.) brakeman
garde-magasin *m.* warehouseman
garde-malade *m. & f.* nurse
garde-manger *m.* pantry, larder
garde-meuble *m.* furniture warehouse
garde-nappe *m.* table mat, place mat
gardénia *m.* gardenia
garde-pêche *m.* fishing warden
garde-phare *m.* lighthouse keeper
garde-place(s) *m.* (rail.) reservations office
garder *vt.* to keep; guard; protect, watch over; preserve; — le lit to stay in bed, be confined to bed, be ill; se — de to beware of, take care not to
garderie *f.* nursery school
garde-robe *f.* wardrobe
gardeur *m.* keeper; herder
garde-vue *m.* eyeshade; lamp shade
gardien *m.* guardian, keeper; prison guard; policeman; goal tender
gare *f.* railway station; chef de — *m.* stationmaster
gare *interj.* watch out!, look out!
garer *vt.* to dock; shunt; put in the garage; se — to get out of the way
gargariser *v.*, se — to gargle
gargarisme *m.* gargle
gargote *f.* ordinary, cheap restaurant (in lower-class area)
gargouille *f.* spout of a gutter; drainpipe; (arch.) gargoyle
gargouiller *vi.* to gurgle; rumble
garnement *m.* scamp, rogue
garni *a.* garnished; served with parsley or watercress; plat — *m.* main dish with potatoes or vegetable; chambre -e *f.* furnished room; choucroute -e *f.* sauerkraut with frankfurters; — *m.* fur-

nished room
garnir vt. to furnish; strengthen; trim; garnish; line; (mil.) garrison
garnison f. garrison
garniture f. garnish, ornaments, trimming; lining; complete set; — **de lit** bedding; — **de feu,** — **de foyer** set of fire irons; — **de frein** brake lining
garrot m. (med.) tourniquet; withers of a horse
garrotte f. garrote; garroting, strangling
garrotter vt. to garrote, strangle; secure, pinion
garrulité f. garrulity, garrulousness, loquacity
Gascogne f. Gascony; **Golfe de** — m. Bay of Biscay
gascon a. & m. Gascon
gasconner vi. (coll.) boast, brag
gasoil m. Diesel fuel
gaspiller vt. to waste, squander
gastrique a. gastric
gastrite f. gastritis
gastronome m. epicure, gourmet
gastronomie f. gastronomy
gastronomique a. gastronomical
gâté a. spoiled; pampered
gâteau m. cake; honeycomb
gâte-papier m. hack writer; scribbler
gâter vt. to spoil, harm, damage; pamper, overindulge
gâterie f. spoiling, overindulgence
gâtisme m. senility
gauche a. left; crooked; awkward; **à** — to the left; — m. left; left wing
gaucher a. left-handed; leftist, left-wing
gaucherie f. awkwardness; blunder; left-handedness
gauchir vt. to warp; — vi. to warp, buckle; flinch
gaufrage m. fluting; embossing; corrugating
gaufre f. honeycomb; waffle, wafer
gaufrer vt. to flute; emboss; corrugate
gaufrette f. wafer
gaufrier m. waffle iron
gaule f. pole, rod, stick
Gaule f. Gaul
gaulois a. Gallic
gauloiserie f. risqué joke or story
gausser vt. & vi., **se** — to scoff; jest, banter
gaver vt. to cram; forcefeed; **se** — to gorge with food
gaz m. gas; **compteur à** — gas meter
gaze f. gauze
gazéifier vt. to carbonate; ærate
gazelle f. gazelle
gazer vt. to gas; cover with gauze; gloss over

gazeux a. gaseous; fizzy, carbonated
gazon m. turf, lawn, sod
gazonner vt. to cover with sod
gazouillement m. warbling; babbling
gazouiller vi. to warble; babble
gazouillis m. warbling
geai m. jay
géant m. giant; — a. gigantic
geignard a. (coll.) whining; — m. habitual whiner
geignement m. whine, whining, whimpering
geindre vi. to whine, whimper
gel m. frost, freezing
gélatine f. gelatin
gélatineux a. gelatinous
gelé a. frozen; frostbitten
gelée f. frost; jelly
geler vt. & vi. to freeze; jelly
gélose f. agar-agar
gelure f. frostbite
géminé a. twin
gémir vi. to groan, moan
gémissement m. groan, moan; groaning, moaning
gemme f. gem, precious stone; resin; **sal** — m. rock salt
gemmer vi. to bud; — vt. to cut, tap for resin
gênant a. troublesome, embarrassing
gencive f. (anat.) gums
gendarme m. policeman
gendarmer vt. to arouse, stir up
gendarmerie f. police; police headquarters; gendarmes
gendre m. son-in-law
gêne f. discomfort, embarrassment; **sans** — unconstrained
gêné a. embarrassed, troubled; having difficulty; short of money
généalogie f. genealogy; pedigree
généalogique a. genealogical; **arbre** — m. family tree
gêner vt. to pinch; obstruct; hinder, inconvenience, embarrass
général a. general; **en** — generally, in general; — m. general; **-e** f. general alert, general quarters
généralement adv. generally, in general
généralisateur a. generalizing; — m. generalizer
généralisation f. generalization
généraliser vt. to generalize
généralissime m. generalissimo
généralité f. generality
générateur (génératrice) a. generating; — n. generator
génératif a. generative
génération f. generation
générer vt. to generate

généreux *a.* generous, liberal
générique *a.* generic
générosité *f.* generosity, liberality
Gênes *f.* Genoa
genèse *f.* genesis, origin
genêt *m.* (bot.) broom plant
génétique *f.* genetics
genevois *a.* of Geneva
genévrier *m.* juniper
génial *a.* brilliant, ingenious
génie *m.* genius; spirit; genie; engineering; (mil.) engineers
genièvre *m.* (bot.) juniper; gin
génisse *f.* heifer
génital *a.* genital
géniteur *m.* sire, father
génitif *m.* (gram.) genitive
génocide *m.* genocide
génois *a.* of Genoa
genou *m.* knee; (mech.) joint; ball and socket
genouillère *f.* knee guard, knee pad, knee-cap
genre *m.* genus; (gram.) gender; kind, type, manner; style; genre; — humain man, mankind
gens *m. pl.* people, men; servants; jeunes — young people; young men
gentil (gentille) *a.* nice; pretty; *m.* gentile
gentilhomme *m.* gentleman, nobleman
gentilité *f.* pagans
gentillesse *f.* graciousness, kindness
gentillet *a.* rather nice
gentiment *adv.* nicely; gracefully
génuflexion *f.* (eccl.) kneeling, genuflexion
géocentrique *a.* geocentric
géodésique *a.* geodetic; geodesic
géographie *f.* geography
géographique *a.* geographic(al)
geôle *f.* jail
geôlier *m.* jailor
géologie *f.* geology
géologique *a.* geological
géologue *m.* geologist
géométrie *f.* geometry
géomètrique *a.* geometric(al)
géophysique *a.* geophysical; — *f.* geophysics
gérance *f.* management; board of directors
géranium *m.* geranium
gérant *m.* manager; director; — d'une publication managing editor
gerbe *f.* sheaf; column, cone
gerbée *f.* straw (rye *or* corn)
gerber *vt.* to bind in sheaves; stack
gerce *f.* crack, split; chap; clothes moth
gercer *vt.* to crack, split; chap
gerçure *f.* crack, cracking; chap, chapping
gérer *vt.* to manage, operate, run

gériatrie *f.* geriatrics
germain *a.* german; cousin — *m.* first cousin
germain *a. & m.* German
germanique *a.* Germanic
germanium *m.* germanium
germe *m.* germ, seed; sprout, shoot
germer *vi.* to germinate, sprout
germicide *a. & m.* germicide
germination *f.* germination
gérondif *m.* (gram.) gerundive
gérontologie *f.* geriatrics; gerontology
gésier *m.* gizzard
gésir *vi.* to lie; lie dead
gesse *f.* (bot.) vetch; — odorante sweet pea
gestation *f.* gestation
geste *m.* gesture, movement, motion; wave, waving
geste *f.* heroic exploit; chanson de — *f.* medieval French epic
gesticuler *vi.* to gesticulate
gestion *f.* management, administration
gestionnaire *m. & f.* manager
geyser *m.* geyser
gibbeux *a.* hunchbacked; humped
gibecière *f.* game bag; satchel
gibelotte *f.* rabbit stew
giberne *f.* cartridge pouch; satchel
gibet *m.* gibbet; gallows
gibier *m.* game; gros — big game; — de potence jailbird
giboulée *f.* shower, squall of sleet or hail
gicelée *f.* spurt of liquid; squirt
giclement *m.* spurting
gicler *vi.* to squirt, spurt
gicleur *m.* jet, nozzle; sprayer; carburetor opening
gifle *f.* slap, smack; humiliation
gifler *vt.* to slap, smack; affront
gigantesque *a.* gigantic
gigone *a.*, table — *f.* stack-table (nested tables)
gigot *m.* leg of lamb
gigue *f.* jig
gilet *m.* vest, cardigan, waistcoat; — de force strait jacket; — de sauvetage life jacket
gingembre *m.* ginger
gingivite *f.* gingivitis
girafe *f.* giraffe
girandole *f.* cluster; centerpiece, candelabrum; earring
giration *f.* gyration
giratoire *a.* turning, gyratory
girofle *m.* clove
giron *m.* lap; — de l'Eglise bosom of the church
girouette *f.* weather vane
gisant *a.* lying; lying dead

gît (*from* gésir), ci-gît here lies
gitan *a.* Gypsy
gîte *m.* lodging, resting place; refuge, lair; stratum, layer, (mining)
gîte *f.* (naut.) list, heeling
gîter *vt.* to shelter, lodge; — *vi.* to lie; perch; (naut.) list; run aground
givre *m.* hoarfrost
givrer *vt.* to frost
glabre *a.* smooth shaven, beardless; (fig.) smooth
glace *f.* ice; plate glass; mirror; windshield; glaze; icing; ice cream
glacé *a.* frozen; cold; iced; icy; chilled; glazed; glossy
glacer *vt.* to freeze; glaze; frost; ice
glacerie *f.* glass factory
glaciaire *a.* glacial
glacial *a.* icy, cold, freezing, frigid
glacier *m.* (geol.) glacier; ice-cream vendor
glacière *f.* icehouse; refrigerator, icebox
glacis *m.* slope; colorless glaze (art); tacking (sewing)
glaçon *m.* ice floe; icicle
glaçure *f.* ceramic glaze, glazing
gladiateur *m.* gladiator
glaïeul *m.* gladiolus
glaire *f.* white of egg; mucus
glaise *f.* clay; potter's earth
glaisière *f.* clay pit
glaive *m.* sword
gland *m.* acorn; tassel
glande *f.* gland
glandulaire, glanduleux *a.* glandular
glaner *vt.* to glean
glanure *f.* gleaning
glapir *vi.* to yelp; scream
glas *m.* knell
glaucome *m.* glaucoma
glauque *a.* blue-green
glèbe *f.* clod, sod; soil
glène *f.* (naut.) coil of rope; (anat.) socket
glissade *f.* slip, slide, sliding; glide
glissant *a.* slippery; sliding; unstable
glissement *m.* slipping, sliding; landslide
glisser *vt. & vi.* to slip, slide; skid; glide; se — to glide, steal, slip
glisseur *m.* glider; slider
glissière *f.* slide, groove; shoot; porte à —s *f.* sliding door
glissoir *m.* icy slide
glissoire *f.* sliding, slide on ice
global *a.* global; total; lump (sum)
globe *m.* globe, ball, sphere
globulaire *a.* globular
globuleux *a.* globular
globulin *m.* globulin
gloire *f.* glory; halo; pride; vanity
gloria *m.* coffee with brandy

gloriette *f.* arbor, summerhouse
glorieux *a.* glorious; proud; vain
glorification *f.* glorification
glorifier *vt.* to glorify; se — to boast
gloriole *f.* vainglory, vanity
glose *f.* gloss; commentary
gloser *vt.* to gloss, comment on; — *vi.* to find fault; criticize
glossaire *m.* glossary
glotte *f.* (anat.) glottis; coup de — *m.* glottal stop (phonetics)
glouglou *m.* gurgle, gurgling sound; coo, cooing; gobble
glouglouter *vi.* to gurgle; gobble; coo
glousser *vi.* to cluck; (coll.) chuckle
glouton *m.* glutton; — *a.* gluttonous
gloutonnerie *f.* gluttony
glu *f.* birdlime; glue; (fig.) trap, snare
gluant *a.* sticky, viscous; (fig.) tenacious
glucose *f.* glucose
glutineux *a.* glutinous
glycérine *f.* glycerin
glycine *f.* wistaria
go (tout de) *adv.* at once; easily; at one shot; suddenly
goal *m.* goal tender, goalie
gobelet *m.* goblet, cup, tumbler
gobe-mouches *m.* flycatcher (bird) (fig.) gullible person
gober *vt.* to swallow greedily, gulp down; (fig.) believe credulously se — to be conceited
gobeter *vt.* to plaster; fill in cracks
gobeur *a. & m.* easily fooled person
goder *vi.* to wrinkle, pucker
godet *m.* mug; bowl; basin; pan; scoop; flare of a skirt
godille *f.* oar, scull
godiller *vi.* to scull
goéland *m.* sea gull
goélette *f.* (naut.) schooner
goguenard *a.* jeering, mocking
goguenarder *vi.* to mock; banter
goitre *m.* goiter
golf *m.* golf; terrain de — golf course
golfe *m.* gulf
gomme *f.* gum; — élastique gum eraser; — laque shellac
gommelaquer *vt.* to shellac
gommer *vt.* to gum; erase; — *vi.* to stick, become stuck
gommeux *a.* gummy
gommier *m.* gum tree
gonade *f.* gonad
gond *m.* door hinge; sortir de ses —s to fly off the handle
gondole *f.* gondola
gondoler *vi.* to warp, buckle
gondolier *m.* gondolier
gonfalon *m.* gonfalon, pennant

gonflage *m.* inflating
gonflement *m.* inflating, inflation
gonfler *vt.* to inflate; fill with air; pump up; bulge; puff up; swell; — *vi.* to be inflated, become inflated
gonfleur *m.* (auto.) air pump
goret *m.* young pig; (coll.) dirty person
gorge *f.* throat; bosom; bust; gorge; **avoir mal à la** — to have a sore throat
gorgée *f.* mouthful, gulp
gorger *vt.* to gorge, stuff
gorille *m.* gorilla
gosier *m.* throat; gullet
gosse *m. & f.* (coll.) youngster; child
gothique *a. & m.* Gothic
gouape *f.* (coll.) good-for-nothing person; hoodlum
gouaper *vi.* to loaf, idle
goudron *m.* tar
goudronner *vt.* to tar
gouffre *m.* gulf, abyss; whirlpool
gouge *f.* gouge, chisel
gouger *vt.* to gouge
goujat *m.* lout, boor
goujon *m.* gudgeon; (fig.) bait
goulasch *m.* goulash
goule *f.* ghoul
goulet *m.* (naut.) channel, narrows
goulot *m.* neck of a bottle
goulu *a.* gluttonous; greedy
goupille *f.* peg, pin, bolt
goupillon *m.* brush; (eccl.) holy water sprinkler
gourd *a.* benumbed, numb
gourde *f.* gourd; metal flask
gourdin *m.* club, bludgeon
gourmand *m.* greedy person; glutton; — *a.* greedy, gluttonous
gourmander *vi.* to guzzle; — *vt.* rebuke
gourmandise *f.* greediness, gluttony; sweets
gourme *f.* rash; impetigo
gourmé *a.* formal, stiff; stuck up (U.S. coll.)
gourmet *m.* connoisseur of food and drink; epicure
gourmette *f.* curb (of a harness); watch chain
gousse *f.* pod, husk; — **d'ail** clove of garlic
gousset *m.* watch pocket, vest pocket
goût *m.* taste; flavor; aroma; liking; style
goûter *vt.* to taste, like, enjoy; — *m.* afternoon snack
goutte *f.* drop; speck, spot, bit; nothing, anything; (med.) gout
gouttelette *f.* droplet
goutteux *a.* gouty
gouttière *f.* gutter; rainspout; —s *pl.* eaves
gouvernail *m.* rudder; helm, steering wheel

gouvernante *f.* housekeeper; governess; governor's wife
gouverne *f.* guidance; —s *pl.* (avi.) controls
gouvernement *m.* government; management; control; steering
gouvernemental *a.* governmental
gouverner *vt.* to govern, manage; direct; control; (naut.) to steer
gouverneur *m.* governor
grabat *m.* pallet, litter; sickbed
grâce *f.* grace; gracefulness; favor; pardon; mercy; thanks; **actions de** — *f. pl.* thanksgiving; **avec** — gracefully; **de** —! please!, I beg of you!; **de bonne** — graciously, willingly; — **à** thanks to; **faire** — to pardon, reprieve
graciable *a.* pardonable
gracier *vt.* to pardon, reprieve
gracieusement *adv.* graciously; gracefully; gratuitously
gracieuseté *f.* graciousness, kindness
gracieux *a.* gracious; graceful; **à titre** — free, gratis; as a favor
gracile *a.* slender, svelte
gracilité *f.* slenderness
gradation *f.* gradation
grade *m.* grade, rank, degree
gradé *m.* noncommissioned officer
gradient *m.* gradient, variation
gradin *m.* tier, row; tiered seating
gradué *a.* graduated, measured, graded
graduel *a.* gradual (eccl.) verse between epistle and gospel
graduelement *adv.* gradually
graduer *vt.* to graduate, scale; grade
graillement *m.* hoarseness, huskiness
grailler *vi.* to speak in a hoarse manner; cough up phlegm
grain *m.* grain; berry, bean; bead; particle, iota, speck; (naut.) squall; — **de beauté** beauty mark
grain-d'orge *m.* (coll.) sty of the eye
graine *f.* seed
grainer *vt.* to grain; granulate
graissage *m.* greasing, lubrication
graisse *f.* grease, fat; — **de rôti** meat drippings
graisser *vt.* to grease, oil, lubricate
graisseux *a.* greasy, oily; fatty
grammaire *f.* grammar
grammairien *m.* grammarian
grammatical *a.* grammatical
gramme *m.* gram
grand *a.* great; large, tall, high; important, big; main, chief, principal; — *m.* great person; grownup; grandee
grand-chose *m.* something important; something significant
Grande-Bretagne *f.* Great Britain
grandelet *a.* rather big

grandeur *f.* greatness, tallness, largeness, magnitude; size; nobility; grandeur
grandiloquence *f.* grandiloquence
grandiose *a.* grandiose, impressive
grandir *vi.* to grow, grow up; — *vt.* to increase; magnify
grandissant *a.* growing
grandissement *m.* growth, growing; magnification
grand-livre *m.* ledger
grand'mère *f.* grandmother
grand-messe *f.* (eccl.) high mass
grand-oncle *m.* great-uncle
grand-père *m.* grandfather
grand'route *f.* main highway
grand'rue *f.* main street
grands-parents *m. pl.* grandparents
grand-tante *f.* great-aunt
grange *f.* barn; building for keeping straw *or* hay
granit *m.* granite
granulaire *a.* granular
granuler *vt.* to granulate
granuleux *a.* granular
graphique *a.* graphic; — *m.* graph
graphite *m.* graphite
graphologue *m.* graphologist
grappe *f.* bunch, cluster of fruit
grappillon *m.* little bunch *or* cluster
grappin *m.* grapnel, grappling hook
gras (grasse) *a.* fat, stout; fatty, greasy; thick; containing meat; caractères — *m. pl.* bold-faced type; jours — *m.* (eccl.) carnival days (pre-lenten) temps — *m.* foggy weather; — *m.* fat
gras-double *m.* tripe
grassement *adv.* comfortably; generously
grassouillet *a.* plump, chubby
gratification *f.* tip; bonus; reward
gratifier *vt.* to confer, bestow
gratin *m.* breading, crust; au — served *or* cooked with cheese and bread crumbs
gratiné *a.* au gratin; breaded
gratis *adv.* gratis, free
gratitude *f.* gratitude
gratte-ciel *m.* skyscraper
gratte-papier *m.* (coll.) hack writer; copyist
gratte-pieds *m.* doormat; scraper for shoes
gratter *vt.* to scrape, scratch; scratch out, erase
grattoir *m.* scraper; eraser
gratuit *a.* gratuitous; free; unmotivated à titre — free of charge
gratuité *f.* gratuitousness
grave *a.* grave, serious, important; (phy.) heavy; (mus.) flat; (gram.) accent grave
graveler *vt.* to gravel
graveleux *a.* gravelly, gritty

gravelle *f.* gravel
gravement *adv.* gravely, seriously
graver *vt.* to engrave; carve; — à l'eau forte etch
graveur *m.* engraver; etcher
gravier *m.* gravel; grit
gravir *vt.* to climb with effort
gravité *f.* gravity; graveness; seriousness; (mus.) lowness, flatness
graviter *vi.* to gravitate
gravure *f.* engraving, etching; print; carving
gré *m.* will, liking; de bon — willingly; bon — mal — willy-nilly; de son propre — freely, of one's own free will; savoir (bon) — de to be grateful for; — *adv.* de — à — amiably; de son pleine — voluntarily
grec (grecque) *a.* Greek, Grecian; — *m.* Greek
Grèce *f.* Greece
gredin *m.* scoundrel
gréement *m.* (naut.) rig, rigging
gréer *vt.* (naut.) to rig
greffe *f.* (med., bot.) graft, grafting; — épidermique *f.* skin graft
greffer *vt.* to graft
greffier *m.* recorder, clerk of the court
grégaire *a.* gregarious
grégorien *a.* Gregorian
grêle *f.* hail; hailstorm; — *a.* shrill
grêlé *a.* pock-marked
grelin *m.* (naut.) hawser
grêlon *m.* large hailstone
grelot *m.* little bell
grelotter *vi.* to shiver, tremble; jingle
grenade *f.* pomegranate; grenade
grenadier *m.* grenadier; pomegranate tree
grenadine *f.* grenadine syrup
grenailler *vt.* to granulate
grenat *a. & m.* garnet
grené *a.* stippled (art); — *m.* stipple
grenier *m.* granary; hayloft; attic
grenouille *f.* frog
grenouillère *f.* swamp, marsh
grenu *a.* granular, grainy, rough-grained
grès *m.* sandstone; stoneware
grésil *m.* sleet
grésiller *vi.* to crackle; sizzle; patter
grève *f.* sandy shore, beach; strike (labor); faire — to strike, go out on strike
grever *vt.* to entail legally, encumber
gréviste *m. & f.* worker on strike, striker
gribouillage *m.* scribble, scrawl
gribouiller *vt.* to scribble, scrawl
grief *m.* grievance; injury, wrong
grièvement *adv.* grievously, seriously, gravely
griffe *f.* claw, talon; clamp, clip; coup de — *m.* scratch; — à papiers paper clip;

marteau à — claw hammer
griffer vt. to claw, scratch
griffonnage m. scribble, scribbling, scrawl
griffonner vt. to scrawl, scribble
grignoter vt. to pick at, nibble
gril m. grill, gridiron
grillade f. grilled meat
grillage m. grating, latticework; grilling, toasting
grille f. iron bars; gate, grate; grid
grille-pain m. toaster
griller vt. & vi. to grill; toast; broil; bar, grate
grillon m. cricket
grimacer vi. to grimace
grimacier a. grimacing; affected
grimer vt. (theat.) to apply makeup, make up
grimper vt. & vi. to climb up; scale
grimpeur a. climbing; — m. climber
grincement m. gnashing
grincer vi. to gnash; grind; scratch; — des dents grit one's teeth in anger
grincheux a. grumpy, crabby; — m. grumbler, crab
gringalet m. weakling, runt
grippe f. influenza; (fig.) dislike
grippé a. having influenza; stuck together
gripper vt. to grab, seize; — vi. to grab, stick, jam
grippe-sou m. miser, skinflint
gris a. gray; gray-haired; drunk, tipsy; cloudy, overcast (weather)
grisailler vt. to daub with gray; — vi. to turn gray (hair)
grisâtre a. grayish
griser vt. to intoxicate; se — to become intoxicated
griserie f. intoxication, drunkenness, tipsiness
grisonner vi. to become gray (hair)
grive f. thrush
grivelé a. speckled
grivois a. risqué, off-color
grizzly m. grizzly bear
Groenland m. Greenland
grog m. grog, toddy
grognard a. grumbling; — m. grumbler
grognement m. grumbling, growling; grunt, grunting
grogner vi. to grunt, grumble, growl
grognerie f. grumbling, growling
grognon a. grumbling; — m. grumbler
grognonner vi. to grumble, complain, whine
groin m. snout of a pig
grommeler vi. to grumble, mutter
grondement m. rumbling, roaring; growling; — sonique sonic boom
gronder vt. to scold; — vi. to grumble,

growl; rumble
gronderie f. scolding
grondeur a. grumbling; scolding; — m.
grumbler
grondeuse f. nag, shrew
gros (grosse) a. big, bulky, large; rich; heavy; thick; loud; coarse; vulgar; pregnant, swollen; — sel m. coarse salt; — jeu m. high stakes; — temps m. bad weather; — m. bulk, main part; — adv. en — in bulk, wholesale; rough, roughly
gros-bec m. grosbeak
groseille f. currant; gooseberry
grosse f. (com.) gross, twelve dozen
grossesse f. pregnancy
grosseur f. size; bulk; swelling; largeness
grossier a. coarse, rough; rude; vulgar
grossièreté f. grossness, coarseness, rudeness, vulgarity
grossir vt. & vi. to enlarge, increase
grossissant a. growing, increasing, swelling; verre — m. magnifying glass
grossissement m. increase, growth, swelling; enlargement; magnification
grossiste m. wholesaler
grotte f. grotto; cavern
grouiller vi. to swarm, teem, crawl
groupe m. group; unit; set, section; — sanguin blood type
groupement m. group, grouping; coupling
grouper vt. to group; bring together; couple; se — to form a group
gruau m. oatmeal; fine flour; small crane
grue f. crane
grumeler v., se — to curdle, clot
grumeleux a. curdled; gritty, grainy
gruyère m. variety of Swiss cheese; crème de — f. processed gruyère cheese
gué m. ford, crossing
guéable a. fordable
guéer vt. to ford; water
guelte f. (com.) commission, percentage, fee
guenille f. ragged garment, tatters
guenilleux a. ragged, in rags
guenipe f. whore, trollop
guenon f. monkey
guépard m. cheetah
guêpe f. wasp
guêpier m. wasps' nest; (fig.) hornets' nest
guère adv., not much; not long; but little; ne . . . — hardly
guéret m. (agr.) unsown land
guéridon m. small table
guérilla f. guerilla warfare; guerilla army
guérillero m. guerilla, guerilla fighter
guérir vt. to cure, heal; — vi. to recover, be cured, healed
guérison f. cure, recovery; healing

guérissable *a.* curable
guérisseur *a.* healing; — *m.* healer; quack
guérite *f.* turret, sentry box; shack, hut (for watchman); (rail.) signal box; — téléphonique call box
guerre *f.* war, warfare; struggle, strife; en — at war
guerrier *a.* warlike; — *m.* warrior
guerroyant *a.* warlike, bellicose
guerroyer *vi.* to make war
guerroyeur *a.* fighting; — *m.* fighter
guet *m.* watch, lookout; au — on the lookout
guet-apens *m.* ambush; (fig.) premeditation
guêtre *f.* gaiter; legging; (auto.) tire patch
guetter *vt.* to watch for; (coll.) lie in wait for
guetteur *m.* lookout
gueulard *m.* furnace mouth, gun muzzle; powerful loudspeaker
gueule *f.* mouth; muzzle; avoir la — de bois to have a hangover
gueule-de-loup *f.* snapdragon
gueuse *f.* beggar; hussy; fer en — *m.* pig iron
gueuser *vi.* to beg in the streets
gueuserie *f.* begging; wretchedness
gueux (gueuse) *a.* beggarly, wretched, poor; — *m.* beggar
gui *m.* mistletoe; (naut.) guy; boom
guichet *m.* grilled window; ticket window; box-office window
guide *m.* guide, guidebook; — *f.* rein
guide-âne *m.* manual, set of instructions; travel guide
guider *vt.* to guide, lead; steer; drive
guidon *m.* handlebar; gun sight *or* bead; (naut.) pennant
guigne *f.* white-heart cherry; (coll.) bad luck
guigner *vt.* to ogle; eye
guignol *m.* Punch and Judy show; puppet theater
guignolet *m.* cherry liqueur
guillemeter *vt.* to put in *or* between, quotation marks
guillemets *m. pl.* quotation marks
guiller *vi.* to ferment
guilleret *a.* gay, lively
guillotine *f.* guillotine; fenêtre à — sash window
guillotiner *vt.* to guillotine
guindé *a.* stiff, affected, stuck-up
guindeau *m.* windlass; hoist
guinder *vt.* to hoist; se — to act superior
Guinée *f.* Guinea
guingan *m.* gingham
guingois (de) *adv.* askew
guipage *m.* wrapping, covering, winding;
tape, taping
guiper *vt.* to wrap, cover; wind; tape
guipure *f.* lace
guirlande *f.* garland, wreath
guirlander *vt.* to garland
guise *f.* manner, fashion, wax; en — de by way of
guitare *f.* guitar
guppy *m.* guppy
gustation *f.* taste, tasting; eating
Guyane *f.* Guiana
gymnase *m.* gymnasium
gymnaste *m. & f.* gymnast
gymnastique *a.* gymnastic; — *f.* gymnastics
gynécologie *f.* gynecology
gynécologue, gynécologiste *m.* gynecologist
gypse *m.* gypsum; plaster of Paris
gyrocompas *m.* gyrocompass
gyroscope *m.* gyroscope

H

* Indicates a word which allows neither elision nor linking

habile *a.* clever, skilful; capable
habileté *f.* cleverness; skill, ability
habilité *f.* ability (law), title
habillé *a.* dressed
habillement *m.* clothing, clothes
habiller *vt.* to dress; clothe; put together; s' — to get dressed
habit *m.* suit, full-dress suit; evening clothes; (eccl.) habit; frock; –s *pl.* clothes; prendre l' — to become a nun *or* monk
habitabilité *f.* habitability
habitable *a.* habitable
habitacle *m.* cockpit; (naut.) binnacle
habitant *m.* inhabitant, dweller
habitat *m.* habitat
habitation *f.* habitation; housing; dwelling
habiter *vt. & vi.* to inhabit; live in
habitude *f.* habit, custom; avoir l' — de to be used to; be in the habit of; d' — usually; comme d' — as usual
habitué *m.* regular customer, frequenter
habituel *a.* habitual; usual, regular
habituer *vt.* to habituate, accustom; s' — à to get used to
*hâbler *vi.* to brag
*hâblerie *f.* bragging
*hâbleur *m.* braggart
*hache *f.* axe, hachet
*haché *a.* chopped; choppy, jerky
*hacher *vt.* to hash, chop, mince; hack
*hachette *f.* hatchet
*hachis *m.* hash, minced meat
hachisch *m.* hashish, hasheesh

*hachoir m. chopper; cleaver; chopping board
*hachurer vt. (art) to shade
*hagard a. haggard, drawn
*haie f. hedge; hurdle
*haillon m. rag, tatter
*haillonneux a. ragged, in rags
*haine f. hate, hatred
*haineux a. full of hate
*haïr vt. to hate; loathe; feel repugnance for
*haïssable a. hateful; odious
*halage m. towing
halcyon m. kingfisher
*hâle m. sunburn, tan; searing wind
*hâlé a. sunburned, tanned
haleine f. breath, wind
halenée f. whiff
*haler vt. to tow; (naut.) heave; — vi. to heave, haul
*hâler vt. to burn, tan; se — to be burned by the sun, become tanned
*haletant a. breathless, out of breath, panting
halètement m. breathlessness, panting
*haleter vi. to pant; puff
*hall m. hall, hallway; lounge; shop in a factory
*halle f. covered market place
*hallier m. thicket
hallucination f. hallucination
halluciner vt. to hallucinate, delude
*halo m. halo (meteorology)
*halte f. halt, stop; faire — to halt, come to a halt; —! (mil.) interj. halt! stop!
haltère m. dumbbell (gymnastics)
*hamac m. hammock
*hameau m. hamlet
hameçon m. hook, fishhook; (fig.) bait
*hamman m. Turkish bath(s)
*hampe f. pole, shaft; stem
*hamster m. hamster
*hanche f. hip, haunch; (naut.) lee quarter
*hanché a. (mil.) at ease
*handicap m. handicap
*handicaper vt. to handicap (sports)
*hangar m. shed; boathouse; (avi.) hangar
*hanter vt. to haunt, frequent; obsess
*hantise f. obsession
*happe f. tongs; staple
*happer vt. to grab, snatch, seize; — vi. to stick
*harangue f. speech, harangue
*haranguer vt. to harangue
*harasser vt. to harass; exhaust
*harceler vt. to harass, harry; torment; nag, pester
*harde f. flock, herd; dog leash

*hardes f. pl. ordinary clothes
*hardi a. hardy, bold, daring
*hardiesse f. boldness, daring, audacity
*harem m. harem
*hareng m. herring; — saur smoked herring
*harenguet m. sprat
*hargne f. irritation, peevishness, ill temper
*hargneux a. surly, snapping; ill-tempered, cross; nagging
*haricot m. bean; — vert string bean; — de mouton mutton stew
*haricot-beurre m. butter bean
harmonie f. harmony; accord
harmonieux a. harmonious; melodious
harmonique a. & m. harmonic
harmonisation f. harmonizing, harmonization
harmoniser vt. to harmonize; s'— to harmonize; blend; agree
*harnachement m. harness, harnessing; saddlery
*harnacher vt. to harness; rig, deck out
*harnais m. harness, armor; gears
harpagon m. miser
*harpe f. harp
*harpie f. harpy
*harpin m. boat hook
*harpiste m. & f. harpist
*harpon m. harpoon
*harponner vt. to harpoon
*hasard m. hazard, chance, luck, accident; au — at random; coup de — m. stroke of luck; par — by chance, accidentally
*hasardé a. risky, hazardous; rash; indiscreet
*hasarder vt. to risk, hazard, venture
*hasardeux a. risky, hazardous
*hâte f. haste, speed; à la — hastily; avoir — de to be in a hurry to; be anxious to, be eager to
*hâter vt. to hasten, hurry, quicken; se — to hurry oneself
*hâtif (hâtive) a. hasty; early, premature
*hâtivement adv. hastily, hurriedly
*hauban m. (naut.) shroud; stay
*haubert m. coat of mail, hauberk
*hausse f. rise, increase; (mil.) elevation, range
*haussement m. raising; — d'épaules shrug
*hausser vt. to raise, lift, elevate; — vi. to rise; — les épaules shrug
*haussier m. bull stock
*haussière f. hawser
*haut a. high; tall; elevated; great; loud; upper, higher; — adv. high, up; loud(ly), aloud; back (in time); — m. height; top; au — de at the top of; de — en

bas from top to bottom; condescend-
ingly; en — above; upstairs
*hautain a. haughty, proud, arrogant
*hautbois m. oboe
*hautboïste m. & f. oboist
*haut-de-chausses m. breeches
*haut-de-forme m. top hat
*hautement adv. highly; nobly; loudly
*hauteur f. height, elevation; rise; hill;
haughtiness, scorn; (mus.) pitch; à la
— de level with
*haut-fond m. shallows, shoal
*haut-fourneau m. blast furnace
*haut-le-cœur m. nausea
*haut-le-corps m. start, jump
*haut-parleur m. speaker, loudspeaker
*havana m. Havana cigar
la Havane f. Havana
*hâve a. gaunt, sunken; pale and sickly
*havre m. haven, harbor
*havresac m. bag, kit; knapsack
hawaiien a. & m. Hawaiian
la Haye f. the Hague
hebdomadaire a. weekly; — m. weekly
paper
héberger vt. to lodge, shelter
hébété a. dazed, bewildered
hébêtement m. daze, bewilderment, stupor
hébéter vt. to dull, blunt; daze, stupefy
hébraïque a. Hebrew, Hebraic
hébreu a. Hebrew
hectare m. hectare (about 2½ acres)
hédonisme m. hedonism
hégémonie f. hegemony
*hein interj. what?; right?
*hélas interj. alas!
*héler vt. to hail, call
hélianthe m. sunflower
hélice f. (naut.) screw; helix, spiral; (avi.)
propeller; — en drapeau feathered propeller
hélicoptère m. helicopter
hélio f. heliogravure
héliocentrique a. heliocentric
héliothérapie f. sun-lamp treatment
héliotrope m. heliotrope
héliport m. heliport
hélium m. helium
hélix m. helix
hellène a. Hellenic
hellénique a. Hellenic, Hellenistic
hellénisme m. Hellenism
hellénistique a. Hellenistic
helvétique a. Swiss
hématie f. red blood corpuscle
hémisphère m. hemisphere
hémisphérique a. hemispherical
hémistiche m. hemstitch
hémoglobine f. hemoglobin

hémophile a. & n. hemophiliac
hémophilie f. hemophilia
hémorragie f. hemorrhage
hémorroïdes f. pl. hemorrhoids
hémostatique a. styptic
*henné m. henna
*hennir vi. to neigh, whinny
*hennissement m. neigh, whinny
hépatique a. hepatic
hépatite f. hepatitis
heptagone a. heptagonal; — m. heptagon
heptemètre m. heptameter
héraldique a. heraldic; — f. heraldry
*héraut m. herald; sign, harbinger
herbacé a. (bot.) herbaceous
herbage m. grass; pasture, meadow
herbe f. grass; herb; weed; en — budding;
green (unripe); mauvaises –s pl. weeds;
fines –s seasoning herbs
herbeux a. grassy
herbivore a. herbivorous
herbu a. grassy
herculéen a. Herculean
*hère m. wretch
héréditaire a. hereditary
hérédité f. inheritance; heredity
hérésie f. heresy
hérétique a. heretical; — m. & f. heretic
*hérissé a. bristling; brushy, shaggy
*hérisser vt. to bristle
*herisson m. hedgehog; series of bristles
or spikes; bottle brush; pinwheel; —
de mer sea urchin
heritable a. inheritable
héritage m. heritage, inheritance, legacy
hériter vt. & vi. to inherit
héritier m., héritière f. heir, heiress
hermétique a. hermetic, tight; hermeti-
cally sealed
hermine f. ermine
herminette f. adze
hermite m. hermit, recluse
*herniaire a. hernial; bandage — m. truss
*hernie f. (med.) hernia, rupture
*hernieux a. ruptured
héroïne f. heroine; (chem.) heroin
héroïque a. heroic
héroïsme m. heroism
*héron m. heron
*héros m. hero
hésitant a. hesitant, hesitating
hésitation f. hesitation
hésiter vi. to hesitate; falter
hétéroclite a. unusual, odd; eccentric
hétérodoxe a. heterodox
hétérogène a. heterogeneous
*hêtre m. beech tree
heur m. luck, good luck
heure f. hour; time; moment; à l'— on
time; de bonne — early; à la bonne —!

well!, fine!; **tout à l'**— in a little while; a little while ago; **à tout à l'**— see you soon!, see you later!, so long!

heureusement adv. fortunately

heureux a. happy, fortunate, lucky, successful

*heurt m. blow, bump, shock; **sans** — without a hitch

*heurtement m. shock, clash

*heurter vt. & vi. to strike against, hit against, knock; bump into; conflict with

*heurtoir m. bumper, stop; knocker of a door

hexagone a. hexagonal; — m. hexagon

hiatus m. hiatus; gap, break

hibernant a. hibernating

hiberner vi. to hibernate

hibiscus m. hibiscus

*hibou m. owl

*hideur f. hideousness, ugliness

*hideux a. hideous, ugly

hiémal a. pertaining to winter

hier adv. yesterday; — **soir** last night

*hiérarchie f. hierarchy

*hiérarchique a. hierarchical

hiéroglyphe m. hieroglyph; –s pl. hieroglyphics

hilarant a. producing laughter; **gaz** — m. laughing gas

hilare a. hilarious

hilarité f. hilarity, laughter

hindou a. & m. Hindu

hippique a. equine; pertaining to horses

hippisme m. horse racing

hippocratique a. Hippocratic

hippodrome m. race track; hippodrome

hippopotame m. hippopotamus

hirondelle f. swallow

hirsute a. hirsute, hairy

hispanique a. Hispanic, Spanish

hispano-américain a. Spanish-American

*hisser vt. (naut.) to hoist; raise, pull up

histoire f. history; story

histologie f. histology

historien m. historian

historier vt. to illuminate a book; illustrate

historiette f. short story, anecdote

historique a. historic(al)

histrion m. histrion, actor

histrionique a. histrionic

hiver m. winter

hivernage m. winter quarters; winter season

hivernal a. of the winter

hiverner vi. to hibernate; winter

*hoche f. notch, cut, nick

*hochement m. head shaking, affirmative nod

*hocher vt. to shake, nod; notch, nick

*hochet m. toy, teething ring

*holà interj. stop!; hello!

*holding m. (com.) holding company

*hollandais a. & m. Dutch

*Hollande f. Holland

holocauste m. holocaust

*homard m. lobster

homélie f. homily

homérique a. Homeric, epic

homicide m. homicide (person or the act); — **involontaire** manslaughter; — a. homicidal; murderous

hommage m. homage; present; testimony; tribute; –s pl. respects

homme m. man; — **d'affaires** businessman

homogène a. homogeneous

homologation f. probating

homologuer vt. confirm (law); probate

homonyme m. homonym

homosexuel a. & m. homosexual

*hongre m. gelding, castrated horse

*hongrer vt. to geld

*Hongrie f. Hungary

*hongrois a. & m. Hungarian

honnête a. honest, sincere; respectable; gentlemanly; proper, decent, mannerly; reasonable

honnêteté f. honesty, integrity; respectability; courtesy; decency

honneur m. honor; respect

honorabilité f. respectability

honorable a. honorable, respectable

honoraire a. honorary; — m. honorarium, fee; royalty

honorer vt. to honor, respect

honorifique a. honorary

*honte f. shame, dishonor, disgrace; **avoir** — to be ashamed

*honteux a. shameful; disgraceful; shamefaced

hôpital m. hospital

*hoquet m. hiccup; gasp

*hoqueter vi. to hiccup, have the hiccups

horaire m. timetable, schedule

horizon m. horizon

horizontal a. horizontal

horloge f. timeclock

horloger m. watchmaker, clockmaker

horlogerie f. clocks, watches; watch business; watch factory; watch and clock shop

*hormis prep. except, save, but

hormone f. hormone

horoscope m. horoscope

horreur f. horror, terror; abhorrence; **avoir** — **de** to abhor; **faire** — **à** to horrify

horrible a. horrible; horrid

horrifier vt. to horrify

horrifique a. horrific

horripilant *a.* hair-raising
horripilation *f.* goose flesh
*hors *prep.* except, out of; — de out of, outside of; — de combat out of action; — de soi beside oneself
*hors-bord *m.* outboard motorboat
*hors-caste *m. & f.* untouchable, outcast
*hors-d'œuvre *m.* outwork; digression; first course, hors d'œuvres
*hors-jeu *m.* offside (sports)
*hors-la-loi *m.* outlaw
hortensia *m.* hydrangea
horticole *a.* horticultural
horticulture *f.* horticulture
hosanna *m.* hosanna, praise
hospice *m.* charitable institution; asylum, home; poorhouse
hospitalier *a.* hospitable; pertaining to charitable institutions
hospitalisation *f.* hospitalizing, hospitalization, hospital care
hostie *f.* (eccl.) host
hostile *a.* hostile, inimical; opposed
hostilité *f.* hostility
hôte *m.* host; landlord; guest; table d'—*f.* fixed menu
hôtel *m.* hotel; mansion; building; — de ville city hall; — meublé lodginghouse; maître d' — head waiter
hôtel-Dieu *m.* main hospital
hôtelier *m.* innkeeper
hôtellerie *f.* hostelry; inn
hôtesse *f.* hostess; guest; — de l'air airline stewardess
*hotte *f.* hod; basket; (chem.) hood
*houache *f.* (naut.) wash, wake
*houblon *m.* (bot.) hops
*houe *f.* hoe
*houer *vt.* to hoe
*houille *f.* coal; — blanche water power
*houillère *f.* coal mine
*houilleur *m.* coal miner
*houle *f.* surge; swell
*houlette *f.* crook, staff; trowel
*houleux *a.* stormy, surging
*houppe *f.* tuft; puff, powder puff; tassel; crest on an animal
*houppelande *f.* overcoat, greatcoat
*houppette *f.* powder puff
*houspiller *vt.* to jostle; abuse
*housse *f.* cover; slipcover; dust cover; (auto.) seat cover
*housser *vt.* to dust
*houssine *f.* furniture and rug beater; switch (for punishment)
*houssoir *m.* brush, whiskbroom
*houx *m.* (bot.) holly
*hoyau *m.* pickax; hoe used to flatten
*hublot *m.* porthole; verre de — *m.* bull's-eye

*huche *f.* bin; hopper; trough
*huer *vt. & vi.* to hoot, shout, boo
*huguenot *a. & m.* Huguenot
huile *f.* oil
huiler *vt.* to oil, grease
huileux *a.* oily; greasy
huilier *m.* oiler; oilcan; oil seller *or* maker
huis *m.* door
huisserie *f.* door frame
huissier *m.* usher; bailiff
*huit *a. & m.* eight; d'aujourd'hui en — a week from today; — jours a week
*huitaine *f.* about eight; week
*huitième *a. & m.* eighth
huître *f.* oyster
*huit-reflets *m.* top hat
huîtrière *f.* oyster bed
humain *a.* human; humane; — *m.* human being
humanisation *f.* humanization
humaniser *vt.* to humanize
humaniste *m.* humanist; classicist
humanitaire *a. & n.* humanitarian
humanité *f.* humanity; mankind; –s *pl.* humanities
humble *a.* humble
humecter *vt.* to moisten
*humer *vt.* to suck in, breathe in
humérus *m.* (anat.) humerus
humeur *f.* humor; disposition, mood; temper
humide *a.* humid, moist, damp
humidifier *vt.* to humidify, moisten
humidistat *m.* humidistat
humidité *f.* humidity, moisture, dampness; — absolue absolute humidity; — relative relative humidity
humiliant *a.* humiliating
humiliation *f.* humiliation
humilier *vt.* to humiliate, humble
humilité *f.* humility
humoriste *m.* humorist; — *a.* humorous
humoristique *a.* humorous
humour *m.* comic irony, humor
humus *m.* humus
*hune *f.* (naut.) top; — de vigie crow's nest
*hunter *m.* hunting horse, jumper
*huppé *a.* crested; well-dressed
*hurlement *m.* howl, howling, roar, yell
*hurler *vi.* to howl, roar, yell
*hurleur *a.* howling, yelling; — *m.* howler; powerful loudspeaker
hurluburlu *m.* silly person, scatterbrain
*hussard *m.* hussar
*hussarde *f.* Hungarian dance; à la — *adv.* roughly, unceremoniously
*hutte *f.* hut, cabin, shack
hyalin *a.* glassy
hybridation *f.* crossbreeding

hybride a. & m. hybrid
hybrider vt. to cross breeds or strains
hydratation f. hydration
hydrate m. hydrate; — **de carbone** carbohydrate; **−r** vt. to hydrate
hydraulique a. hydraulic; — f. hydraulics
hydravion m. seaplane
hydre f. hydra
hydrocarbure m. hydrocarbon
hydrodynamique a. hydrodynamic; — f. hydrodynamics; — **magnétique** magnetohydrodynamics
hydroélectrique a. hydroelectric
hydrofuge a. waterproof
hydrofuger vt. to make waterproof or watertight
hydrogène m. hydrogen; — **liquide** liquid hydrogen
hydroglisseur m. speedboat
hydrologie f. hydrology
hydrolyse f. hydrolysis
hydrophile a. absorbent
hydrophobie f. hydrophobia, fear of the water
hydropisie f. dropsy
hydrosphère f. hydrosphere
hydrothérapie f. hydrotherapy, water cure
hydrure m. hydride
hyène f. hyena
hygiène f. hygiene, health; sanitation
hygiènique a. hygienic; sanitary
hygiéniste m. & f. hygienist
hymnaire m. hymnal
hymne m. hymn; song, anthem
hyperbole f. hyperbole; (math.) hyperbola
hypercritical a. hypercritical
hypergolique a. hypergolic
hypersensibilité f. hypersensitivity
hypersensible a. hypersensitive
hypersonique a. hypersonic
hypertension f. hypertension
hypertrophie f. hypertrophy; (fig.) excessive development
hypnose f. hypnosis
hypnotique a. hypnotic
hypnotiser vt. to hypnotize
hypnotisme m. hypnotism
hypocondriaque a. & n. hypochondriac
hypocondrie f. hypochondria
hypocrisie f. hypocrisy
hypocrite m. hypocrite; — a. hypocritical
hypodermique a. hypodermic
hypotension f. (med.) hypotension
hypoténuse f. hypotenuse
hypothécable a. mortgageable
hypothécaire a. mortgage; — n. mortgagee
hypothèque f. mortgage
hypothéquer vt. to mortgage
hypothèse f. hypothesis
hypothétique a. hypothetical

hystérie f. (med.) hysterics
hystérique a. hysterical

ïambique a. iambic
ibère, ibérique a. & n. Iberian
ibis m. ibis
ichtyologie f. ichthyology
ichtyologiste m. ichthyologist
ici adv. here; **d'**— from hence, hence; **par** — this way; **d'**— **là** between now and then; **jusqu'**— until now; this far
ici-bas adv. here on earth
icone f. icon, ikon
iconoclaste a. iconoclastic; — m. iconoclast
ictère m. (med.) jaundice
idéal m. & a. ideal; **−iser** vt. to idealize
idéalisme m. idealism
idéaliste m. & f. idealist; — a. idealistic
idéation f. ideation
idée f. idea, thought, opinion; **changer d'**— to change one's mind; — **fixe** obsession
identification f. identification
identifier vt. to identify
identique a. identical
identité f. identity; **carte d'**— f. identification card
idéologie f. ideology
idéologique a. ideological
idéologue m. ideologist
ides f. pl. ides
idiomatique a. idiomatic
idiome m. language, speech, idiom, dialect
idiosyncrasie f. idiosyncrasy
idiot a. idiot; idiotic; — m. idiot; fool
idiotie f. idiocy; stupidity
idiotisme m. (gram.) idiom, idiomatic expression
idolâtre a. idolatrous; — m. idolater
idolâtrer vt. to worship, idolize
idole f. idol, god
idylle f. idyl
idyllique a. idyllic
if m. (bot.) yew
igname f. Chinese yam
ignare a. ignorant; uninstructed
igné a. igneous
ignifuge a. fireproof
ignoble a. ignoble, base
ignominie f. ignominy, shame
ignominieux a. ignominious, shameful
ignorance f. ignorance
ignorant a. ignorant; unaware; — m. ignoramus, dunce
ignoré a. unknown
ignorer vt. to be ignorant of, not to know
iguane m. iguana

il *pron.* he, it; — **y a** there is, there are; ago; **—s** they
île *f.* island
iléon *m.* (anat.) ileum
ilex *m.* holm oak
iliaque *a.* iliac
illégal *a.* illegal; unlawful
illégalité *f.* illegality
illégitime *a.* illegitimate; unlawful
illégitimité *f.* illegitimacy; unlawfulness
illettré *a.* illiterate
illicite *a.* illicit, illegal
illimité *a.* unlimited
illisibilité *f.* illegibility
illisible *a.* illegible, unreadable
illogique *a.* illogical
illuminant *a.* illuminating
illuminateur *m.* illuminator
illumination *f.* illumination; light; lighting
illuminer *vt.* to illuminate, enlighten
illusion *f.* illusion, delusion; self-deception
illusionner *vt.* to delude; deceive
illusionnisme *m.* conjuring, conjurer's art
illusionniste *m. & f.* conjurer
illusoire *a.* illusive; fallacious
illustrateur *m.* illustrator
illustration *f.* illustriousness; glorification; glory; explanation; illustration
illustre *a.* illustrious
illustré *m.* tabloid; — *a.* illustrated
illustrer *vt.* to make illustrious; illustrate
îlot *m.* small island, islet; block of houses
ilote *m.* helot
image *f.* picture; image; metaphor
imagé *a.* metaphorical
imager *vt.* to embellish with metaphors, images
imagerie *f.* imagery
imaginable *a.* imaginable
imaginaire *a.* imaginary
imaginatif *a.* imaginative
imagination *f.* imagination, fancy
imaginer *vt.* to imagine, conceive, contrive; picture; **s'—** imagine, think
imbattable *a.* unbeatable
imbattu *a.* unbeaten
imbécile *m. & f.* imbecile; idiot, fool
imbécillité *f.* imbecility; stupidity
imberbe *a.* beardless; very young
imbiber *vt.* to imbue, soak, steep; imbibe, absorb
imbrifuge *a.* waterproof
imbrisable *a.* unbreakable
imbrûlable *a.* fireproof
imbu *a.* imbued, steeped, soaked
imbuvable *a.* undrinkable
imitateur *m.* imitator; — *a.* imitative
imitatif *a.* imitative
imitation *f.* imitation; copy; forgery; counterfeit
imiter *vt.* to imitate; copy; forge, counterfeit
immaculable *a.* stainless
immaculé *a.* immaculate; (fig.) untarnished; stainless
immanent *a.* immanent
immangeable *a.* uneatable, inedible
immanquable *a.* infallible, inevitable
immatériel *a.* immaterial
immatriculation *f.* registration; enrollment
immatricule *f.* registration number
immatriculer *vt.* to matriculate; register; enroll
immaturité *f.* immaturity
immédiat *a.* immediate; imminent; urgent
immédiatement *adv.* immediately, right away
immémorial *a.* immemorial
immense *a.* immense; vast
immensément *adv.* immensely
immensité *f.* immensity
immensurable *a.* immeasurable
immerger *vt.* to immerse; (naut.) submerge
immérité *a.* undeserved
immersion *f.* immersion; plunging; submersion
immesurable *a.* immeasurable
immeuble *a.* real (law); **biens —s** *m. pl.* real estate; — *m.* real estate; building, apartment house
immigrant *a. & m.* immigrant
immigré *m.* immigrant
immigrer *vi.* to immigrate
imminence *f.* imminence
imminent *a.* imminent, impending
immiscer *vt.* to involve; mix up; **s'—** to meddle; intrude
immixtion *f.* interference, meddling
immobile *a.* immovable, motionless
immobilier *a.* pertaining to real property; **agent —** *m.* realtor
immobiliser *vt.* to immobilize
immobilité *f.* immobility
immodéré *a.* immoderate
immodeste *a.* immodest
immodestie *f.* immodesty
immolation *f.* immolation, sacrifice
immoler *vt.* to immolate, sacrifice
immonde *a.* unclean, foul
immondices *f. pl.* rubbish, refuse, filth
immoral *a.* immoral
immoralité *f.* immorality
immortaliser *vt.* to immortalize
immortalité *f.* immortality
immortel *a.* immortal, everlasting
immotivé *a.* unmotivated
immuable *a.* immutable, unchangeable

immunisation *f.* immunization
immuniser *vt.* to immunize
immunité *f.* immunity
immutabilité *f.* immutability
impact *m.* impact
impair *a.* odd, uneven; — *m.* blunder
impalpabilité *f.* impalpability
impalpable *a.* impalpable
impardonnable *a.* unpardonable, unforgivable
imparfait *a.* imperfect; incomplete; — *m.* (gram.) imperfect
imparité *f.* inequality; (math.) oddness
impartial *a.* impartial; without prejudice
impartialité *f.* impartiality
impartir *vt.* (law), to grant accord
impassable *a.* impassable
impasse *f.* dead end; deadlock
impassibilité *f.* impassibility
impassible *a.* impassible; impassive; without emotion
impatiemment *adv.* impatiently, eagerly
impatience *f.* impatience, eagerness
impatient *a.* impatient, eager
impatienter *vt.* to make impatient; **s'—** to fret, grow impatient
impavide *a.* fearless
impayable *a.* invaluable, inestimable, priceless
impayé *a.* unpaid
impeccabilité *f.* impeccability
impeccable *a.* impeccable; flawless
impécunieux *a.* impecunious
impédance *f.* impedance
impénétrabilité *f.* impenetrability, inscrutability
impénétrable *a.* impenetrable; inscrutable
impénitent *a.* unrepentant
impensable *a.* unthinkable
impératif *a.* imperative; — *m.* (gram.) imperative
impératrice *f.* empress
imperceptible *a.* imperceptible
imperfection *f.* imperfection; incompleteness
impérial *a.* imperial
impériale *f.* style of beard; upper deck of a two-decker bus
impérialisme *m.* imperialism
impérialiste *m.* imperialist
impérieux *a.* imperious; imperative
impérissable *a.* imperishable
impéritie *f.* incapacity, lack of experience
imperméabiliser *vt.* to waterproof
imperméable *a.* impervious, waterproof; — *m.* raincoat
impersonnel *a.* impersonal
impertinemment *adv.* impertinently
impertinence *f.* impertinence, impropriety; irrelevance

impertinent *a.* impertinent; rude; irrelevant
imperturbable *a.* imperturbable
impétueux *a.* impetuous, impulsive
impétuosité *f.* impetuosity, impulsiveness
impie *a.* impious, irreligious
impiété *f.* impiety; blasphemy
impitoyable *a.* unmerciful, merciless; pitiless
implacabilité *f.* implacability
implacable *a.* implacable, unforgiving
implanter *vt.* to implant, insert; graft; **s'—** to take root
implication *f.* implication; suggestion of contradiction
implicite *a.* implicit
impliquer *vt.* to implicate; imply
imploration *f.* imploring, beseeching
implorer *vt.* to implore, beseech
imployable *a.* unyielding, unbending, inflexible
impoli *a.* impolite, rude, discourteous
impolitesse *f.* impoliteness, rudeness, discourtesy
impolitique *a.* ill-advised
impondérable *a.* imponderable
impopulaire *a.* unpopular
impopularité *f.* unpopularity
importable *a.* unbearable; importable
importance *f.* importance, consequence; seriousness; authority; social standing, self-conceit
important *a.* important; having authority; — *m.* essential point
importateur *m.* importer
importer *vt.* to import; — *v.* to be of importance; be of consequence, to concern; **n'importe** it does not matter; **n'importe qui** no matter who, anyone; **n'importe quoi** no matter what, anything; **qu'importe?** what does it matter?
importun *a.* importunate; annoying, bothersome
importuner *vt.* to importune; annoy, bother
imposable *a.* taxable
imposant *a.* imposing, impressive
imposé *m.* taxpayer
imposer *vt.* to impose; inspire, command; tax; — *vi.* to command respect; — **à** impose on; deceive; **s'—** command, inspire; assert oneself; force oneself on someone
imposition *f.* imposition; imposing; tax; assessment
impossibilité *f.* impossibility
impossible *a.* impossible
imposte *f.* transom; (arch.) impost
imposteur *m.* imposter

imposture *f.* imposture; swindle

impôt *m.* tax, duty; — sur le revenu income tax

impotence *f.* impotence, infirmity, helplessness

impotent *a.* impotent; infirm, crippled; — *m.* cripple

impraticable *a.* impracticable, impractical; impassable

impratiqué *a.* unused, out-of-the-way

imprécation *f.* curse, imprecation

imprécis *a.* not precise, indefinite

imprécision *f.* lack of precision

imprégner *vt.* to impregnate

imprenable *a.* impregnable

impréparation *f.* lack of preparation

imprésario *m.* impresario

impression *f.* impression; printing process; print; mark; edition; faute d'— *f.* typographical error, misprint

impressionnable *a.* impressionable; sensitive

impressionnant *a.* impressive

impressionner *vt.* to impress; make an impression upon; s'— to get excited; be moved

impressionniste *m.* impressionist

imprévisible *a.* unpredictable, unforeseeable

imprévision *f.* lack of foresight

imprévoyable *a.* unpredictable, unforeseeable

imprévoyance *f.* improvidence; lack of foresight

imprévoyant *a.* improvident

imprévu *a.* unforeseen, unexpected; — *m.* contingency

imprimé *m.* printed paper; –s *p.* printed matter

imprimer *vt.* to print, stamp; impart

imprimerie *f.* printing; print shop; typography

imprimeur *m.* printer

imprimeuse *f.* printing press

improbabilité *f.* improbability

improbable *a.* improbable, unlikely

improbatif *a.* disapproving

improbation *f.* lack of approval, disapproval

improbité *f.* lack of probity; dishonesty

improductif *a.* unproductive

improductivité *f.* unproductiveness

impromptu *m. & a.* impromptu; à l'— extemporaneously

imprononçable *a.* unpronounceable

impropre *a.* improper; incongruous; unfit

impropriété *f.* impropriety

improuvable *a.* unprovable

improvisateur *m.* improviser

improviser *vt. & vi.* to extemporize, impro-

vise

improviste *adv.*, a l'— unawares, unexpectedly

improvoqué *a.* unprovoked

imprudemment *adv.* imprudently

imprudence *f.* imprudence, indiscretion

imprudent *a.* imprudent; indiscreet; unwise

impubliable *a.* unpublishable; not fit for publication

impudemment *adv.* impudently

impudence *f.* impudence

impudent *a.* impudent; immodest; shameless

impudeur *f.* shamelessness, immodesty; lewdness

impudicité *f.* lack of chastity; act of lust

impudique *a.* immodest, unchaste

impuissance *f.* impotence, inability; vainness

impuissant *a.* impotent, powerless; vain

impulsif *a.* impulsive, without deliberation

impulsion *f.* impulse, impetus, urge

impulsivité *f.* impulsiveness

impunément *adv.* with impunity

impuni *a.* unpunished

impunité *f.* impunity

impur *a.* impure, tainted; (fig.) unchaste

impureté *f.* impurity; (fig.) immorality

impurifié *a.* unpurified

imputable *a.* attributable, imputable; (com.) chargeable; creditable

imputation *f.* imputation, charge; (com.) deduction

imputer *vt.* to impute, attribute, charge; deduct; (com.) credit; debit

inabondance *f.* scarcity, short supply

inabordable *a.* inaccessible; too costly

inabrité *a.* unsheltered

inaccentué *a.* unaccented, unstressed

inacceptable *a.* unacceptable

inacceptation *f.* nonacceptance, refusal

inaccessible *a.* inaccessible; unattainable

inaccompagné *a.* unaccompanied

inaccompli *a.* unaccomplished, unfulfilled

inaccordable *a.* irreconcilable; untunable; inadmissible

inaccoutumé *a.* unaccustomed, unused; unusual

inachevé *a.* unfinished, not completed

inachèvement *m.* state of incompletion

inactif *a.* inactive; inert

inaction *f.* inaction; lack of business activity

inactivité *f.* inactivity; inertness

inadéquat *a.* inadequate

inadmissibilité *f.* inadmissibility

inadmissible *a.* inadmissible; nonqualify-

ing
inadvertance *f.* oversight, inadvertance, carelessness
inadvertant *a.* inadvertent
inaliénable *a.* inalienable
inaliéné *a.* unalienated
inaltérabilité *f.* unchanging nature; permanence
inaltérable *a.* unchangeable; incorruptible; unalterable
inamical *a.* unfriendly, hostile; discourteous
inamovible *a.* irremovable; permanent
inanimé *a.* inanimate, lifeless; unconscious
inanité *f.* inanity; inane remark
inapaisable *a.* inappeasable, unquenchable
inapaisé *a.* unappeased, unquenched
inapercevable *a.* unperceivable
inaperçu *a.* unperceived, unnoticed, unseen
inapparent *a.* unapparent
inappétence *f.* lack of appetite
inapplication *f.* lack of application
inappliqué *a.* unapplied; lacking in application
inappréciable *a.* invaluable, inestimable; unperceivable; inappreciable
inapprécié *a.* unappreciated
inapprivoisable *a.* untamable
inapprivoisé *a.* untamed
inapte *a.* inapt, inept; unfit
inaptitude *f.* lack of aptitude
inarticulé *a.* inarticulate; inarticulated
inassociable *a.* incompatible, unmixable
inassouvi *a.* unsatisfied, unquenched
inassouvissable *a.* insatiable
inattaquable *a.* unquestionable; unassailable
inattendu *a.* unexpected; unforeseen
inattentif *a.* inattentive
inattention *f.* carelessness; lack of attention
inauguration *f.* inauguration; unveiling
inaugurer *vt.* to inaugurate; unveil a monument; (fig.) mark a beginning
inauthenticité *f.* lack of authenticity
inauthentique *a.* unauthentic
inautorisé *a.* unauthorized
inaverti *a.* uninformed; unwarned
inavouable *a.* shameful
inavoué *a.* unconfessed; unacknowledged
incalculable *a.* incalculable
incandescence *f.* incandescence
incandescent *a.* white-hot, incandescent
incapable *a.* incapable, unable, unfit
incapacité *f.* incapacity, incapability, inability, unfitness; disability
incarcération *f.* incarceration

incarcérer *vt.* to incarcerate
incarnadin *a.* pink, rosy
incarnat *m.* flesh color; — *a.* rosy, pink
incarné *a.* incarnate; ingrown
incarner *vt.* to incarnate; s'— to become incarnate; grow into, embody
incartade *f.* tirade; prank
incassable *a.* unbreakable
incendiaire *m.* arsonist; (coll.) firebug
incendie *m.* fire, arson, conflagration; pompe à — *f.* fire engine
incendié *m.* victim of a fire
incendier *vt.* to burn, set fire to
incertain *a.* uncertain; doubtful, undecided
incertitude *f.* uncertainty, doubt, indecision
incessamment *adv.* incessantly, continually; shortly, without delay
incessant *a.* incessant, unceasing
incessible *a.* inalienable
inceste *m.* incest
incestueux *a.* incestuous
inchangé *a.* unchanged
incidemment *adv.* incidently
incidence *f.* (phy.) incidence
incident *a.* incidental; parenthetical; — *m.* incident; difficulty
incinérateur *m.* incinerator
incinération *f.* incineration; cremation
incinérer *vt.* to incinerate; cremate
incirconcis *a.* uncircumcized
inciser *vt.* to cut, make an incision in
incisif *a.* incisive
incisive *f.* (dent.) incisor
incision *f.* incision, cut, cutting
incitant *a.* stimulating; — *m.* tonic, stimulant
incitation *f.* incitement, inciting
inciter *vt.* to incite; urge
incivil *a.* uncivil, rude
incivilisé *a.* uncivilized
incivilité *f.* incivility, rudeness
incivique *a.* uncivil
inclassable *a.* unclassifiable
inclémence *f.* inclemency
inclément *a.* inclement
inclinaison *f.* inclination; incline, slope; tilt, slant
inclination *f.* inclination; bowing, stooping; love; mariage d'— *m.* love match
incliné *a.* inclined; bowed
incliner *vt. & vi.* to incline, bow; tilt, slant; s'— bow, yield; slope, slant; (avi.) bank; (naut.) heel
inclure *vt.* to enclose; insert
inclus *a.* enclosed
inclusif *a.* inclusive
inclusion *f.* enclosing; inclusion; enclosure

inclusivement *adv.* inclusively
incohérence *f.* incoherence
incohérent *a.* incoherent, unconnected
incohésion *f.* lack of cohesion
incolore *a.* colorless
incomber *vi.* to be incumbent
incombustible *a.* fireproof
incomestible *a.* inedible
incommensurable *a.* incommensurate; immeasurable
incommodant *a.* disagreeable, annoying
incommode *a.* uncomfortable, inconvenient
incommodé *a.* indisposed
incommoder *vt.* to annoy, trouble, inconvenience; upset
incommodité *f.* inconvenience; discomfort
incommunicable *a.* incommunicable
incommutable *a.* nontransferable (at law)
incomparablement *adv.* incomparably
incompatibilité *f.* incompatibility
incompatible *a.* incompatible
incompétence *f.* incompetency, lack of authority
incompétent *a.* incompetent; unauthorized, unqualified
incomplaisant *a.* disobliging
incomplet *a.* unfinished, incomplete
incomplètement *adv.* incompletely
incompréhensibilité *f.* incomprehensibility
incompréhensible *a.* incomprehensible
incompréhension *f.* lack of understanding
incompris *a.* not understood; unappreciated
inconcevable *a.* inconceivable
inconciliable *a.* irreconcilable
inconditionnel *a.* unconditional
inconduite *f.* misconduct (law); misbehavior
inconfort *m.* lack of comfort
inconfortable *a.* uncomfortable
incongru *a.* incongruous; inappropriate
incongruité *f.* incongruity; impropriety
inconnu *a.* unknown; strange; — *m.* unknown; unknown person, stranger
inconsciemment *adv.* unconsciously, unknowingly
inconscience *f.* unconsciousness, unawareness
inconscient *a.* unconscious, unaware
inconséquence *f.* inconsequence
inconséquent *a.* inconsequent, inconsistent; inconsequential
inconsidération *f.* lack of consideration
inconsidéré *a.* inconsiderate; thoughtless; ill-considered
inconsistance *f.* inconsistency; lack of solidity
inconsistant *a.* inconsistent; loose, soft

inconsolable *a.* inconsolable; disconsolate
inconstance *f.* inconstancy; fickleness; changeability
inconstant *a.* inconstant, changeable, fickle
inconstitutionnalité *f.* unconstitutionality
inconstitutionnel *a.* unconstitutional
incontestable *a.* incontestable, indisputable
incontesté *a.* uncontested, undisputed
incontinence *f.* incontinence
incontinent *a.* incontinent; — *adv.* at once, immediately
incontrôlable *a.* impossible to check or verify
incontrôlé *a.* unchecked, unverified
incontroversé *a.* uncontroverted, undisputed
inconvaincu *a.* unconvinced
inconvenance *f.* impropriety; indecency; lack of suitability
inconvenant *a.* unbecoming, improper; indecent
inconvénient *m.* inconvenience; disadvantage, objection
inconvertissable *a.* beyond conversion
inconvié *a.* uninvited
incoordination *f.* lack of co-ordination
incorporal *a.* incorporeal
incorporer *vt.* to incorporate
incorrect *a.* incorrect; wrong; unseemly, improper
incorrection *f.* incorrectness; mistake, error; inaccuracy
incorrigibilité *f.* incorrigibility
incorruptibilité *f.* incorruptibility
incrédibilité *f.* incredibility
incrédule *a.* incredulous; unbelieving; — *m. & f.* infidel, unbeliever
incrédulité *f.* incredulity; disbelief
incrément *m.* increment
increvable *a.* puncture-proof
incrimination *f.* incrimination; indictment; accusation
incriminer *vt.* to incriminate; indict; accuse
incrochetable *a.* burglarproof
incroyable *a.* incredible, unbelievable
incroyant *a.* unbelieving; — *m.* unbeliever
incrustation *f.* incrustation; inlaying; scale, crust
incruster *vt.* to incrust; inlay
incubateur *m.* incubator
incubation *f.* incubation; hatching
incuber *vt.* to incubate (eggs)
incuit *a.* uncooked
inculpabilité *f.* blamelessness, innocence; liability to indictment (law)
inculpable *a.* liable to indictment (law)
inculpation *f.* indictment, charge

inculpé *m.* defendant (law), accused
inculper *vt.* to accuse, charge; indict
inculquer *vt.* to inculcate
inculte *a.* uncultivated, untilled
incultivé *a.* uncultivated, untilled; uncultured; rude
incurable *a. & n.* incurable
incurie *f.* lack of concern; negligence, carelessness
incurieux *a.* not curious
incuriosité *f.* lack of curiosity
incursion *f.* inroad, incursion
incurvé *a.* incurvated, concave
Inde *f.* India; —s *pl.* Indies
inde *m.* indigo plant, indigo blue
indébrouillable *a.* tangled
indécemment *adv.* indecently; immodestly; improperly
indécence *f.* indecency
indécent *a.* indecent; unbecoming, immodest; improper
indéchiffrable *a.* undecipherable; illegible
indéchirable *a.* untearable
indécis *a.* undecided; vague; hesitating, doubtful
indécisif *a.* indecisive
indécision *f.* indecision; irresolution
indéclinable *a.* not refusable; indeclinable
indécousable *a.* rip-proof
indécouvrable *a.* undiscoverable, hidden
indécrottable *a.* uncleanable
indédoublable *a.* indecomposable
indéfendable *a.* indefensible
indéfini *a.* indefinite; undefined
indéfinissable *a.* indefinable
indéformable *a.* not capable of losing shape *or* form
indéfrisable *a.* permanent (curls); — *f.* permanent wave
indélébile *a.* indelible
indélébilité *f.* indelibility
indélibéré *a.* undeliberated, unpremeditated
indélicat *a.* indelicate; tactless; unscrupulous
indélicatesse *f.* indelicacy; tactlessness; unscrupulousness
indémaillable *a.* run-proof
indemne *a.* undamaged, unhurt; without loss
indemnisable *a.* entitled to damages *or* compensation
indemnisation *f.* indemnification
indemniser *vt.* to indemnify, compensate, pay damages to
indemnité *f.* indemnity, compensation, damages; grant, benefit; expenses
indémontrable *a.* undemonstrable
indéniable *a.* undeniable

indénouable *a.* secure, fast, tight; not able to be untied
indépendamment *adv.* independently
indépendance *f.* independence
indépendant *a.* independent
indéracinable *a.* firmly rooted; not able to be uprooted; impossible to eradicate
indéréglable *a.* foolproof; impossible to upset
Indes *f. pl.* Indies
indescriptible *a.* indescribable
indésirable *a. & n.* undesirable
indesserrable *a.* self-locking (nut); very tight
indestructible *a.* indestructible
indéterminable *a.* indeterminable
indétermination *f.* indetermination, lack of determination; indefiniteness
indéterminé *a.* indeterminate, undetermined; indefinite; undecided
indévinable *a.* unguessable; mysterious
indévot *a.* undevout, irreligious
indévotion *f.* irreligion
index *m.* table of contents, index; index finger; indicator, pointer
indicateur *a.* indicatory; telltale; **doigt —** *m.* index finger; **poteau —** *m.* signpost; **—** *m.* indicator; gauge; speedometer; timetable; spy, informer
indicatif *a.* indicative, indicating, indicatory; **—** *m.* (gram.) indicative; (rad.) program theme music
indication *f.* indication, sign; information; **—s** *pl.* directions, instructions
indice *m.* sign, mark; clue; index; indication; (com.) trace
indicible *a.* unspeakable, indescribable
indien *a. & m.* Indian
indienne *f.* print; calico; chintz; overarm swimming stroke
indiennerie *f.* printed cotton fabric
indifféremment *adv.* indifferently, indiscriminately
indifférence *f.* indifference
indifférent *a.* indifferent, unconcerned; immaterial
indigence *f.* indigence, poverty
indigène *a. & m.* native
indigent *a.* indigent, poor, needy; **—** *m.* pauper; **— s** *pl.* the poor, needy, destitute
indigeste *a.* indigestible; undigested
indigestion *f.* indigestion
indignation *f.* indignation
indigne *a.* unworthy, undeserving; odious
indigné *a.* indignant
indigner *vt.* to make indignant, shock; **s'—** to be indignant
indignité *f.* indignity; unworthiness
indigo *m.* indigo dye *or* color

indigotier *m.* (bot.) indigo plant
indiquer *vt.* to indicate, point out, show; appoint
indirect *a.* indirect; underhand(ed); circumstantial (law)
indirectement *adv.* indirectly
indiscernable *a.* indistinguishable
indisciplinable *a.* intractable
indiscipliné *a.* undisciplined, unmanageable
indiscret *a.* indiscreet, tactless; — *m.* indiscreet, tactless person
indiscrètement *adv.* indiscreetly
indiscrétion *f.* indiscretion; tactlessness
indiscutable *a.* indisputable
indisponibilité *f.* unavailability
indisponible *a.* unavailable; inalienable (law)
indisposé *a.* indisposed, unwell; unfriendly, angry
indisposer *vt.* to indispose; make unwell; turn against
indisposition *f.* indisposition, mild illness
indisputable *a.* indisputable, unquestionable
indissolubilité *f.* indissolubility; insolubility
indissoluble *a.* indissoluble; insoluble
indistinct *a.* indistinct; vague, hazy, faint, blurred
indistinguible *a.* indistinguishable
individu *m.* individual; person, fellow; character
individualiser *vt.* to individualize
individualiste *a.* individualistic; — *m. & f.* individualist
individualité *f.* individuality
individuel *a.* individual; private, personal
indivisibilité *f.* indivisibility
indivisible *a.* indivisible
indivulgué *a.* undivulged, unrevealed
Indo-Chine *f.* Indo-China
indochinois *a. & m.* Indochinese
indocile *a.* indocile, intractable
indocilité *f.* indocility, intractability
indo-européen *a. & m.* Indo-European
indolemment *adv.* indolently, lazily
indolence *f.* indolence, laziness
indolent *a.* indolent, lazy
indolore *a.* painless
indomptable *a.* untamable, unmanageable, unconquerable; indomitable
indompté *a.* untamed, unconquered
Indonésie *f.* Indonesia
indonésien *a. & m.* indonesian
indu *a.* undue; unowed; not due
indubitable *a.* indubitable, unquestionable
inductance *f.* (elec.) inductance; inductance coil

inducteur *a.* (elec.) inductive; — *m.* inductor
inductif *a.* inductive
induire *vt.* to induce; infer; lead
induit *a.* (elec.) induced; — *m.* armature
indulgence *f.* indulgence
indulgent *a.* indulgent
indûment *adv.* unduly
indurer *vt.* to harden
industrialisation *f.* industrialization
industrialiser *vt.* to industrialize
industrialisme *m.* industrialism
industrie *f.* industry; ingenuity, skill
industriel *a.* industrial; — *m.* industrialist
industrieux *a.* industrious; skillful
inébranlable *a.* firm; unshakable; resolute
inéchangeable *a.* unexchangeable
inéclairci *a.* unexplained, unelucidated
inéclairé *a.* unlighted, unlit; unenlightened
inédit *a.* unpublished; new, latest, original
ineffaçable *a.* ineffaceable, unforgettable; indelible
inefficace *a.* ineffectual, unavailing
inefficacité *f.* inefficacy, inefficiency
inégal *a.* unequal; uneven; irregular
inégalité *f.* inequality; unevenness; irregularity, disparity
inélégance *f.* inelegance
inélégant *a.* inelegant
inéligibilité *f.* ineligibility
inéligible *a.* ineligible
inéluctable *a.* ineluctable; unescapable, irrevocable
inéludable *a.* unescapable, inevitable
inemployé *a.* unemployed, unused
inentamé *a.* uncut; whole, intact
inepte *a.* inept, unfit; foolish
ineptie *f.* ineptness, ineptitude
inépuisable *a.* inexhaustible
inépuisé *a.* unexhausted, unused, remaining
inéquitable *a.* inequitable, unfair, unjust
inerte *a.* inert; passive; dull
inertie *f.* inertia; dullness
inespéré *a.* unhoped for, unexpected
inessayé *a.* untried, untested
inestimable *a.* inestimable, invaluable
inétudié *a.* unstudied, natural
inévitable *a.* inevitable; unavoidable
inexact *a.* inexact, inaccurate; wrong, incorrect; careless, remiss; unpunctual
inexactitude *f.* inexactitude, inaccuracy; incorrectness; error, mistake; carelessness, remissness; unpunctuality
inexécutable *a.* impracticable; impossible to do
inexécuté *a.* undone, unfulfilled, unperformed; not carried out
inexécution *f.* inexecution; nonfulfillment

inexercé *a.* unexercised; unpracticed, untrained
inexistant *a.* nonexistent
inexistence *f.* nonexistence
inexpérience *f.* inexperience, lack of experience
inexpérimenté *a.* inexperienced; untested, untried
inexpiable *a.* unatonable, inexpiable
inexpié *a.* unatoned
inexplicable *a.* inexplicable, unaccountable
inexpliqué *a.* unexplained
inexploitable *a.* unexploitable; unworkable
inexploité *a.* unexploited, undeveloped; unworked
inexploré *a.* unexplored
inexplosible *a.* nonexplosive
inexpressif *a.* expressionless; inexpressive
inexprimable *a.* inexpressable; ineffable, unspeakable
inexprimé *a.* unexpressed
inexpugnable *a.* impregnable
in-extenso (en entier) *adv.* fully, in detail
inextinguible *a.* inextinguishable; unquenchable; irrepressible
infaillibilité *f.* infallibility
infaillible *a.* infallible; unfailing; certain
infaisable *a.* impracticable, not feasable
infamant *a.* dishonorable, defamatory
infâme *a.* infamous; vile, fowl, base
infamie *f.* infamy; infamous action
infanterie *f.* infantry
infantilisme *m.* infantilism
infatigable *a.* indefatigable, tireless
infatuation *f.* infatuation, self-satisfaction
infatué *a.* self-satisfied
infécond *a.* sterile, barren
infécondité *f.* sterilty
infect *a.* foul, filthy; smelly, noisome, stinking
infecter *vt.* to infect; taint, corrupt; pollute
infectieux *a.* infectious
infection *f.* infection; smell, stench
inférence *f.* inference
inférer *vt.* to infer
inférieur *a.* inferior, lower; of poor(er) quality; — *m.* subordinate, underling
infériorité *f.* inferiority
infertile *a.* sterile; infertile; unfruitful
infertilité *f.* sterility, infertility; unfruitfulness
infester *vt.* to infest
infidèle *a.* unfaithful; faithless; dishonest; inexact, incorrect; heathenish; — *m.* infidel, unbeliever
infidélité *f.* infidelity, unfaithfulness; faithlessness; dishonesty; inexactitude,

inaccuracy; unbelief
infiltration *f.* infiltration; filtering; seepage
infiltrer *vt.*, **s'** — to infiltrate; seep
infime *a.* lowest; smallest; infinitesimal, minute
infini *a.* infinite; endless; unlimited; — *m.* infinite; infinity; **à l'** — ad infinitum, to infinity; **–té** *f.* infinity
infiniment *adv.* infinitely
infinitésimal *a.* infinitesimal
infinitif *a. & m.* (gram.) infinitive
infinitude *f.* infiniteness
infirme *a.* infirm; frail, feeble; crippled
— *m. & f.* cripple; invalid
infirmer *vt.* to weaken; invalidate; annul (law); set aside
infirmerie *f.* infirmary, sickroom
infirmier *m.* male nurse; hospital attendant
infirmière *f.* nurse
infirmité *f.* infirmity; disability
inflammabilité *f.* inflammability
inflammation *f.* inflammation; firing; igniting
inflammatoire *a.* inflammatory
inflation *f.* inflation
inflationniste *a.* inflationary; — *m.* inflationist
infléchir *vt.* to inflect, bend
infléchissable *a.* unbendable; unbending, inflexible
inflexibilité *f.* inflexibility
inflexible *a.* inflexible; unbending, unyielding
inflexion *f.* inflexion, inflection; modulation; bending
infliger *vt.* to inflict, impose
influençable *a.* able to be influenced
influence *f.* influence, sway; effect
influencer *vt.* to influence, sway
influent *a.* influential
influer (sur) *vi.* to influence
influx *m.* influx
informateur *m.* informant
informatif *a.* informative
information *f.* inquiry; information; news; legal investigation; proceedings; **prendre des** —s to make inquiries
informe *a.* shapeless, formless; unshapely; informal
informer *vt.* to inform, tell, apprise; — *vi.* to inform; investigate (law); **s'** — to make inquiries, ask
informulé *a.* unformulated
infortune *f.* misfortune
infortuné *a.* unfortunate, unhappy, unlucky
infraction *f.* infraction, violation; infringement
infranchissable *a.* impassable

infrangible *a.* unbreakable
infrarouge *a.* infrared
infrastructure *f.* substructure; undercarriage, underframe
infréquent *a.* infrequent, unusual, rare
infréquenté *a.* unfrequented
infructueux *a.* unfruitful, unprofitable; fruitless
infus *a.* infused, innate
infusé *m.* infusion
infuser *vt.* to infuse, steep; instill
infusion *f.* infusion, tea
ingambe *a.* active, alert, nimble
ingénier *v.*, **s'—** to tax one's ingenuity
ingénieur *m.* engineer
ingénieusement *adv.* ingeniously
ingénieux *a.* ingenious
ingéniosité *f.* ingenuity
ingénu *a.* ingenuous; naïve, artless; **—e** *f.* naïve girl; (theat.) ingénue
ingénuité *f.* ingenuousness
ingérence *f.* interference, meddling
ingérer *vt.* to ingest; **s'— de** to interfere in, meddle in
inglorieux *a.* inglorious
ingouvernable *a.* ungovernable, unmanageable
ingrat *a.* ungrateful; thankless; unpleasant; unproductive
ingratitude *f.* ingratitude, ungratefulness; thanklessness
ingrédient *m.* ingredient, component
inguéable *a.* unfordable
inguérissable *a.* incurable; chronic
ingurgitation *f.* swallowing, gulping
ingurgiter *vt.* to swallow
inhabile *a.* unfitted, unskilled, inept; clumsy, awkward; legally incompetent
inhabileté *f.* clumsiness, awkwardness; lack of skill *or* knack; incapability
inhabilité *f.* legal incompetency, incapacity
inhabitable *a.* uninhabitable
inhabité *a.* uninhabited
inhabitude *f.* lack of familiarity *or* experience
inhabitué *a.* accustomed, not used to
inhabituel *a.* not habitual, unusual
inhalateur *m.* inhalator
inhalation *f.* inhalation
inhaler *vt.* to inhale
inharmonieux *a.* inharmonious, unmelodious; discordant
inhérent *a.* inherent
inhiber *vt.* to inhibit
inhibiteur, inhibitif *a.* inhibiting, inhibitive
inhibition *f.* inhibition
inhospitalier *a.* inhospitable
inhumain *a.* inhuman

inhumanité *f.* inhumanity
inhumation *f.* inhumation, burial
inhumer *vt.* to inter, bury, inhume
inimaginable *a.* unimaginable, inconceivable
inimitable *a.* inimitable
inimitié *f.* enmity, hatred, hostility
inimprimé *a.* unprinted, unpublished
ininflammable *a.* fireproof; noninflammable
inintelligemment *adv.* unintelligently
inintelligence *f.* lack of intelligence
inintelligent *a.* unintelligent
inintelligibilité *f.* unintelligibility
inintelligible *a.* unintelligible
inintéressant *a.* uninteresting
ininterrompu *a.* uninterrupted, unbroken
inique *a.* unjust, iniquitous; sinful
iniquité *f.* iniquity
initial *a.* initial; **— e** *f.* first letter (name, word, person's name); **-ement** *adv.* originally
initiateur *m.* initiator
initiative *f.* initiative
initié *m.* initiate
initier *vt.* to initiate
injecté *a.* injected; bloodshot
injecter *vt.* to inject; **s'—** become bloodshot
injecteur *m.* injector
injection *f.* injection
injonction *f.* injunction, formal order
injouable *a.* unplayable
injudicieux *a.* injudicious, unwise
injure *f.* insult; wrong, injury; tort (law)
injurier *vt.* to insult, abuse
injurieux *a.* insulting, abusive, outrageous
injuste *a.* unjust, unfair
injustice *f.* injustice; wrong; unfairness
injustifiable *a.* unjustifiable
injustifié *a.* unjustified
inlassable *a.* untiring; tireless
innavigable *a.* unnavigable; unseaworthy
inné *a.* innate, inborn; **-ité** *f.* innateness
innocemment *adv.* innocently, foolishly
innocence *f.* innocence; simplicity
innocent *a.* innocent; harmless; simple; **—** *m.* simpleton
innocenter *vt.* to find innocent, clear; excuse
innocuité *f.* harmlessness, innocuousness
innombrable *a.* innumerable, numberless
innovateur *m.* innovator
innover *vi.* to innovate
inobservance *f.* nonobservance
inobservation *f.* nonobservance, disregard
inobservé *a.* unobserved; disregarded
inoccupation *f.* inoccupation, idleness, unemployment
inoccupé *a.* unoccupied; vacant; not busy,

idle; not in use

inoculer *vt.* to inoculate; infect

inodore *a.* odorless

inoffensif *a.* inoffensive, harmless

inondation *f.* flood, inundation

inondé *a.* flooded; deluged; — *m.* flood victim

inonder *vt.* to flood, inundate

inopérable *a.* inoperable

inopérant *a.* inoperative

inopiné *a.* unexpected, unforeseen

inopportun *a.* inopportune; not appropriate

inopportunité *f.* inopportuneness

inopposable *a.* unanswerable

inorganique *a.* inorganic

inoubliable *a.* unforgettable; memorable

inoublié *a.* unforgotten

inouï *a.* unheard of; unbelievable; fantastic

inoxydable *a.* rustproof; stainless (steel)

inqualifiable *a.* unqualifiable; unspeakable

inquiet (inquiete) *a.* uneasy, anxious, disturbed, nervous, restless, upset, concerned

inquiétant *a.* disturbing, upsetting

inquiéter *vt.* to disturb, upset, make uneasy; **s'—** to be anxious, worry, be uneasy

inquiétude *f.* uneasiness, anxiety, nervousness, concern

inquisiteur *m.* inquisitor; — *a.* inquisitive

inquisition *f.* inquisition

inrouillable *a.* rustproof, stainless

insaisissable *a.* unseizable, difficult to grasp; fleeting, imperceptible

insalubre *a.* unhealthy, unwholesome

insalubrité *f.* unhealthiness, unwholesomeness

insanité *f.* insanity

insatiabilité *f.* insatiability

insatiable *a.* insatiable

insatisfaction *f.* lack of satisfaction

insatisfait *a.* unsatisfied

insciemment *adv.* unknowingly, unwittingly

inscripteur *m.* recorder, recording apparatus

inscriptible *a.* inscribable

inscription *f.* inscription; inscribing; registration, enrolling; recording

inscrire *vt.* to inscribe; register, enroll; **s'—** to register, sign up

inscrutable *a.* inscrutable

insécable *a.* indivisible

insecte *m.* insect

insécurité *f.* insecurity

insémination *f.* insemination

insensé *a.* insane, mad, senseless; — *m.*

madman

insensiabilisation *f.* local anesthesia, removal of sense of feeling

insensibiliser *vt.* to anesthetize

insensibilité *f.* lack of sensitivity, lack of feeling(s); insensibility; coldness, indifference

insensible *a.* insensitive; unfeeling; insensible; cold, indifferent; imperceptible

inséparable *a.* inseparable

inséparablement *adv.* inseparably

insérer *vt.* to insert; wedge, sandwich in

insertion *f.* insertion

inserviable *a.* not obliging, disobliging

insidieusement *adv.* insidiously

insidieux *a.* insidious

insigne *a.* notorious; unusual; distinguished; — *m.* sign of membership, authority, dignity

insignes *m. pl.* insignia

insignifiance *f.* insignificance

insignifiant *a.* insignificant

insincère *a.* insincere

insincérité *f.* insincerity

insinuant *a.* insinuating

insinuation *f.* insinuation, implication; hint

insinuer *vt.* to insinuate; insert; **s'—** (dans) to steal (into); penetrate; insinuate oneself

insipide *a.* insipid; tasteless; uninteresting; flat

insipidité *f.* insipidity; lack of taste; flatness

insistance *f.* insistence

insistant *a.* insisting, insistent

insister *vt.* to insist; emphasize; persist

insobriété *f.* lack of sobriety, intemperance

insociabilité *f.* unsociableness

insociable *a.* unsociable

insolation *f.* sunstroke; insolation

insolemment *adv.* insolently

insolence *f.* insolence, impudence

insolent *a.* insolent, impudent; rude

insoler *vt.* to expose to the sun; **s'—** to sunbathe

insolite *a.* unusual

insolubilité *f.* insolubility

insoluble *a.* insoluble; unsolvable

insolvabilité *f.* insolvency

insolvable *a.* insolvent

insomnie *a.* insomnia

insondable *a.* unfathomable, mysterious; unsoundable

insonore *a.* soundproof

insonorisation *f.* soundproofing

insonoriser *vt.* to soundproof, insulate

insonorité *f.* lack of sonority

insouciance *f.* lack of care *or* concern, un-

concern; carelessness, thoughtlessness
insouciant *a.* unconcerned; careless; thoughtless
insoucieux *a.* unmindful, heedless
insoumis *a.* unsubdued, unruly
insoumission *f.* unruliness, lack of submissiveness; insubordination
insoupçonnable *a.* above suspicion
insoupçonné *a.* unsuspected
insoutenable *a.* untenable, unmaintainable; unbearable
inspecter *vt.* to inspect; survey
inspecteur *m.* inspector; examiner; surveyor, supervisor
inspection *f.* inspection; examining
inspirant *a.* inspiring
inspirateur *a.* inspiring; — *m.* inspirer
inspiration *f.* inspiration; prompting; inhaling
inspiré *a.* inspired
inspirer *vt.* to inspire; motivate; inhale, breathe in; s'— de be inspired by
instabilité *f.* instability; uncertainty
instable *a.* unstable, unsteady; uncertain
installation *f.* installation; arranging; setting up; moving in; equipment; plant, shop; apparatus, set
installer *vt.* to install; arrange; settle; set up; equip; s'— to install oneself; settle; move in; make oneself comfortable
instammant *a.* urgently, insistently; immediately
instance *f.* instance, instancy; request; immediacy, urgency; legal proceedings, action
instant *a.* urgent; — *m.* instant, moment; à l'— immediately, at once; just now, a moment ago
instantané *a.* instantaneous; — *m.* snapshot
instar, à l'— de in the manner of
instaurateur *m.* founder of an institution
instauration *f.* founding, establishment
instaurer *vt.* to found, establish
instigateur *m.* instigator
instigation *f.* instigation; suggestion
instiller *vt.* to instill, pour by drops
instinct *m.* instinct; d'— instinctively
instinctif *a.* instinctive
instinctivement *adv.* instinctively
instituer *vt.* to institute, establish, found; appoint
institut *m.* institute
instituteur *m.*, **institutrice** *f.* grade school teacher; tutor; founder
institution *f.* institution; establishment
institutionnel *a.* institutional
instructeur *m.* instructor
instructif *a.* instructive

instruction *f.* instruction; direction; training, education, schooling; lesson; legal investigation; **juge d'**— *m.* examining magistrate
instruire *vt.* to instruct, educate, teach, inform, train; investigate legally, examine
instruit *a.* educated; trained; learned; informed, aware
instrument *m.* instrument, tool
instrumentation *f.* instrumentation, orchestration
instrumenter *vt.* to score, orchestrate; — *vi.* to order proceedings (law)
instrumentiste *m.* instrumentalist
insu *m.*, **à l'**— **de** unknown to, without the knowledge of
insubmersible *a.* unsinkable
insubordonné *a.* insubordinate
insuccès *m.* lack of success; failure
insuffisamment *adv.* insufficiently
insuffisance *f.* insufficiency, deficiency; inadequacy; incapacity; — **de pose** (phot.) underexposure
insuffisant *a.* insufficient, inadequate; incapable
insuffler *vt.* to inflate, blow up; breathe in; insufflate; (med.) spray
insulaire *a.* insular; — *m. & f.* islander
insularité *f.* insularity
insuline *f.* insulin
insultant *a.* insulting
insulte *f.* insult, affront
insulter *vt.* to insult
insupportable *a.* unbearable; intolerable; insufferable
insurgé *a. & m.* insurgent
insurger *v.*, s'— to rebel
insurmontable *a.* insuperable, insurmountable
insurpassable *a.* unsurpassable; incomparable
insurrection *f.* insurrection, rebellion
intact *a.* intact, untouched; undamaged; whole
intangibilité *f.* intangibility
intarissable *a.* inexhaustible; endless
intégral *a.* integral; whole; full, in full, unexpurgated
intégrale *f.* (math.) integral
intégralement *adv.* wholly, fully, in full
intégralité *f.* wholeness, entireness
intégrant *a.* integral
intégration *f.* integration
intègre *a.* upright, honest; ethical; incorruptible
intégrer *vt.* to integrate
intégrité *f.* integrity, honesty; entirety, wholeness
intellect *m.* intellect

intellectualité *f.* intellectuality
intellectuel *a. & m.* intellectual
intellectuellement *adv.* intellectually
intelligemment *adv.* intelligently
intelligence *f.* understanding, intellect, intelligence, comprehension; être d'— to have an understanding together; —s *pl.* relations, connections, dealings
intelligent *a.* intelligent
intelligentsia *f.* intelligentsia, intellectuals
intelligibilité *f.* intelligibility
intelligible *a.* intelligible
intempérance *f.* intemperance
intempérant *a.* intemperate
intempéré *a.* immoderate, intemperate; inclement
intempérie *f.* inclement weather
intempestif *a.* untimely, inopportune
intemporel *a.* timeless, eternal
intenable *a.* untenable
intendance *f.* direction, management
intendant *m.* steward, manager; intendant
intense *a.* intense; intensive; severe; high; deep
intensément *adv.* intensely
intensif *a.* intensive
intensifier *vt.* to intensify
intensité *f.* intensity; strength; depth; force; severity
intensivement *adv.* intensively
intenter *vt.* to bring legal suit
intention *f.* intention; intent; purpose; wish; à l'— de for, for the sake of; designed for, destined for; in honor of; avoir l'— de to intend to
intentionné *a.* intentioned
intentionnel *a.* intentional, deliberate
intentionnellement *adv.* intentionally
interallié *a.* interallied, interrelated
interastral *a.* interstellar
interattraction *f.* mutual attraction
intercalaire *a.* interpolated
intercalation *f.* interpolation, intercalation
intercaler *vt.* to intercalate, interpolate
intercéder *vi.* to intercede
intercellulaire *a.* intercellular
intercepter *vt.* to intercept
intercepteur *m.* (avi.) interceptor
interception *f.* interception
intercesseur *m.* intercessor, mediator
intercession *f.* intercession
interchangeable *a.* interchangeable
intercontinental *a.* intercontinental
intercostal *a.* intercostal
interdépartemental *a.* interdepartmental
interdépendance *f.* interdependence
interdépendant *a.* interdependent
interdiction *f.* interdiction, prohibition
interdire *vt.* to forbid, ban, prohibit; bewilder
interdit *a.* speechless, taken aback; prohibited, forbidden; — *m.* (eccl.) interdict, prohibitory decree
intéressant *a.* interesting
intéressé *a.* interested; selfish; — *m.* interested party
intéresser *vt.* to interest; be interesting to; concern; s'— à to take an interest in
intérêt *m.* interest, concern, self-interest; share; advantage
intérieur *a.* interior; internal; inner; — *m.* interior, inside
intérieurement *adv.* internally; inwardly; inside
intérim *m.* interim
intérimaire *a.* temporary, provisional
interindividuel *a.* among individuals, group
injecter *vt.* to utter, ejaculate
interjection *f.* interjection
interjeter *vt.* to interject; — appel (law) lodge an appeal
interligne *f.* space between lines; (print.) leading
interligner *vt.* to interline; write between the lines
interlinéaire *a.* interlinear
interlocuteur *m.* interlocutor
interlocutoire *a.* interlocutory
interlope *a.* illegal; unauthorized; suspect
interloquer *vt.* to make speechless, confuse
intermède *m.* intermediary; (theat.) interlude
intermédiaire *a.* intermediate; — *m.* intermediary, agent, middleman
intermezzo *m.* (mus.) intermezzo
interminable *a.* interminable, endless
intermittence *f.* intermittency; par — intermittently
internat *m.* living-in, residing; internship; boarding school
international *a.* international
internationaliser *vt.* internationalize
internationaliste *m. & f.* internationalist
internationalité *f.* internationality
interne *m.* resident student; intern; boarder; — *a.* internal, interior, inner
internement *m.* internment
interner *vt.* to intern; confine
internissable *a.* untarnishable
interpellation *f.* interpellation; question, challenge
interpeller *vt.* to challenge, demand an accounting; interpellate
interplanétaire *a.* interplanetary
interpolation *f.* interpolation
interpoler *vt.* to interpolate
interposer *vt.* to interpose; s'— to intervene

interposition f. intervention; interposition
interprétable a. interpretable
interprétateur m. commentator, interpreter (of a work of art)
interprétation f. interpretation
interprète m. & f. interpreter
interpréter vt. to interpret; render, perform; read, make out, translate
interrègne m. interregnum
interrogateur a. questioning, interrogatory; — m. questioner, interrogator
interrogatif a. interrogative
interrogation f. interrogation, questioning, examination; **point d'**— m. question mark
interrogatoire m. questioning, examination, cross-examination
interroger vt. to interrogate, question, examine
interrompre vt. to interrupt; break; break off; stop
interrupteur m. interrupter; (elec.) switch, circuit-breaker
interruption f. interruption; break, breaking; disconnecting
inter-saison f. offseason (sports)
intersecté a. intersecting
intersection f. intersection
intersession f. intersession, break, recess
intersidéral, **interstellaire** a. interstellar
interstitiel a. interstitial
interurbain a. interurban
intervalle m. interval; period; space, distance
intervenir vi. to intervene, interfere; happen
intervention f. intervention; interference
interventionniste m. interventionist
interversion f. inversion
intervertir vt. to invert, reverse, transpose
interviewer vt. to interview
intestat a. intestate
intestin a. internal, intestine; civil; — m. intestine, bowel
intestinal a. intestinal
intimation f. notice, notification
intime a. intimate, close; inner; — n. close friend
intimement adv. intimately, closely
intimer vt. to notify; summon at law
intimidant a. intimidating
intimidateur a. intimidating; — m. intimidator
intimidation f. intimidation; threat, threatening
intimider vt. to intimidate; threaten, frighten; s'— to become nervous
intimité f. intimacy, closeness, privacy; inner being

intitulé m. title, heading
intituler vt. to entitle
intolérable a. intolerable, unbearable
intolérance f. intolerance
intolérant a. intolerant
intouchable a. & n. untouchable
intoxicant a. toxic, poisonous
intoxication f. poisoning
intoxiquer vt. to poison
intraduisible a. untranslatable
intraitable a. intractable, unmanageable
intra-muros a. intramural
intransférable a. untransferable
intransigeance f. intransigence
intransigeant a. intransigent, uncompromising, inflexible
intransitif a. intransitive
intraveineux a. intravenous
intrépide a. intrepid, fearless, undaunted
intrépidité f. intrepidity
intrigant a. intriguing, scheming; — m. intriguer, schemer
intrigailler vi. to scheme, plot
intrigue f. intrigue, plot
intriguer vt. to perplex; intrigue; — vi. to intrigue, scheme, plot
intrinsèque a. intrinsic
introducteur m. introducer, usher
introductif a. introductory
introduction f. introduction; insertion; induction
introduire vt. to bring in, show in; insert, introduce; s'— to enter, penetrate
intronisation f. enthronement; founding, establishment
introniser vt. to enthrone; found, establish
introspectif a. introspective
introspection f. introspection
introuvable a. which cannot be found, undiscoverable; incomparable
introverti a. introverted; — m. introvert
intrus a. intruding; trespassing; — m. intruder; trespasser
intrusion f. intrusion; trespassing
intuitif a. intuitive
intuition f. intuition
inusable a. that will never wear out; everlasting
inusité a. not in use; unusual; obsolete
inutile a. useless, needless, vain, unavailing
inutilisable a. unusable, unserviceable
inutilisé a. unused, unutilized
inutilité f. uselessness, inutility
invaincu a. unvanquished, unconquered
invalidation f. invalidating, invalidation
invalide a. invalid; disabled; void; — m. invalid, disabled veteran
invalider vt. to invalidate

invalidité *f.* disability; ill-health; invalidism; invalidity
invariabilité *f.* invariability
invariable *a.* invariable
invariablement *adv.* invariably
invasion *f.* invasion
invective *f.* invective
invectiver *vi.* to inveigh; — *vt.* to insult, abuse
invendable *a.* unsaleable
invendu *a.* unsold
inventaire *m.* inventory, stock
inventer *vt.* to invent; make up
inventeur *m.* inventor, discoverer
inventif *a.* inventive
invention *f.* invention, discovery; inventiveness; lie
inventorier *vt.* to inventory, take stock of
invérifiable *a.* unverifiable
invérifié *a.* unverified
inverse *a. & m.* inverse, opposite, reverse
inversement *adv.* inversely
inverser *vt.* to reverse
inversion *f.* inversion; reversing
invertébré *a.* invertebrate
invertir *vt.* to reverse, invert
investigateur *a.* investigating; — *m.* investigator
investigation *f.* investigation
investir *vt.* to invest
investissement *m.* investment, investing
investiture *f.* investiture
invétéré *a.* inveterate, confirmed
invétérer *v.*, s'— to become inveterate
invincibilité *f.* invincibility
invincible *a.* invincible; insurmountable
inviolabilité *f.* inviolability
inviolable *a.* inviolable; sacred
invisibilité *f.* invisibility
invisible *a.* invisible
invitant *a.* inviting
invitation *f.* invitation
invite *f.* signal, cue (cards); discard conveying information to one's partner
invité *m.* guest
inviter *vt.* to invite
involontaire *a.* involuntary
involontairement *adv.* involuntarily
involuté *a.* involute(d)
involution *f.* involution
invoquer *vt.* to invoke
invraisemblable *a.* improbable, unlikely
invraisemblance *f.* unlikelihood, improbability
invulnérabilité *f.* invulnerability
invulnérable *a.* invulnerable
iode *m.* iodine
ioder *vt.* to iodize
iodure *m.* iodide
iodurer *vt.* to iodize

ion *m.* ion
ionien *a.* Ionian
ionique *a.* (arch.) Ionic; (phy.) ionic
ionisation *f.* ionization
ioniser *vt.* to ionize
ionosphère *f.* ionosphere
iota *m.* iota; bit, scrap, speck
iouler *vi.* to yodel
ipréau *m.* white poplar
Irak *m.* Iraq
irakien *a. & m.* Iraqi
Iran *m.* Iran
iranien *a. & m.* Iranian
irascibilité *f.* irascibility, irritability
irascible *a.* irascible, irritable
ire *f.* anger
iridescence *f.* iridescence
iridium *m.* iridium
iris *m.* iris; rainbow; halo; — *m. or f.* (bot.) iris
irisation *f.* iridescence
irisé *a.* iridescent; rainbow-colored
irlandais *a.* Irish; Erse
Irlande *f.* Ireland
ironie *f.* irony
ironique *a.* ironical
ironiser *vi.* to speak *or* write ironically
irraccommodable *a.* unrepairable, unmendable
irrachetable *a.* irredeemable
irradiation *f.* irradiation, radiation
irradier *vi.* to irradiate, radiate; spread, increase, advance
irraisonnable *a.* irrational
irrassasiable *a.* insatiable
irrationalisme *m.* irrationalism
irrationalité *f.* irrationality
irrationnel *a.* irrational
irréalisable *a.* unrealizable; impossible
irrecevable *a.* unacceptable, inadmissible
irréconciliable *a.* irreconcilable
irrécusable *a.* irrecusable, unimpeachable
irréductible *a.* irreducible; firm, unyielding, inflexible
irréel *a.* unreal
irréfléchi *a.* thoughtless, unthinking, hasty
irréflexion *f.* thoughtlessness, haste
irréfragable *a.* unimpeachable
irréfutable *a.* irrefutable
irréfuté *a.* unrefuted
irrégularité *f.* irregularity; unevenness; unpunctuality
irrégulier *a.* uneven; unpunctual; (gram.) irregular; — *m.* irregular, guerilla
irrégulièrement *adv.* irregularly
irréligieux *a.* irreligious
irréligion *f.* irreligion
irréligiosité *f.* irreligiousness
irrémédiable *a.* irremediable, incurable

irrémédiablement *adv.* irremediably, incurably
irremplaçable *a.* irreplaceable
irréparable *a.* irreparable
irrépréhensible *a.* not reprehensible, blameless
irrépressible *a.* irrepressible
irréprimable *a.* irrepressible
irréprochable *a.* irreprochable
irrésistible *a.* irresistible
irrésolu *a.* irresolute; uncertain; hesitant, undecided; unsteady; unsolved
irrésoluble *a.* irresolvable; unsolvable
irrésolution *f.* irresolution; hesitation; indecision
irrespect *m.* disrespect, lack of respect
irrespectueux *a.* disrespectful
irrespirable *a.* unbreathable
irresponsabilité *f.* irresponsibility
irresponsable *a.* irresponsible
irrévérence *f.* irreverence
irrévérencieusement *adv.* irreverently
irrévérencieux *a.* irreverent
irréversible *a.* irreversible
irrévocabilité *f.* irrevocability
irrévocable *a.* irrevocable
irrigateur *m.* watering hose
irrigation *f.* irrigation; watering; flooding; spraying
irriguer *vt.* to irrigate; water; flood; spray
irritabilité *f.* irritability; sensitivity
irritable *a.* easily irritable; sensitive
irritant *a.* irritating; — *m.* irritant
irriter *vt.* to irritate; s'— to become irritated; get angry
irruption *f.* irruption; inrush; inroad, invasion; bursting in; flooding
Islam *m.* Islam
islamique *a.* Islamic
islandais *a. & m.* Icelandic
Islande *f.* Iceland
isobare *f.* isobar
isocèle *a.* isosceles
isolant *a.* isolating; insulating; bouteille —e *f.* vacuum bottle, Thermos bottle
isolateur *a.* (elec.) insulating; — *m.* insulator
isolation *f.* insulating, insulation
isolationnisme *m.* isolationism
isolationniste *m. & f.* isolationist
isolé *a.* isolated; apart; lonely, desolate; insulated
isolement *m.* isolation, loneliness; (elec.) insulation
isolément *adv.* individually, singly, separately; solitarily
isoler *vt.* to isolate; segregate; (elec.) insulate
isoloir *m.* insulator; voting booth
isomère *m.* isomer

isométrique *f.* isometrics
isomorphe *m.* isomorph
isotherme *m.* isotherm
isotope *m.* isotope
isotrope *m.* isotrope
Israël *m.* Israel
israélien *a. & m.* Israeli
issu *a.* descended, born; (fig.) resulting
issue *f.* outlet, exit; conclusion; issue; —s *pl.* by-products
isthme *m.* isthmus
Italie *f.* Italy
italien *a. & m.* Italian
italique *a.* Italic; — *m.* italics
itération *f.* iteration, repetition
itinéraire *m.* itinerary, route; — *a.* pertaining to roads
itinérant *a.* itinerant
ivoire *m.* ivory
ivoirin *a.* resembling ivory
ivre *a.* inebriated, intoxicated, drunk
ivresse *f.* intoxication; (fig.) ecstasy
ivrogne *a.* drunken; — *m.* drunkard
ivrognerie *f.* chronic drunkenness

J

jabot *m.* bird's crop; ruffle, neck frill
jabotage *m.* chatter, talk, gossip
jaboter *vi. & vt.* to jabber; chatter; talk unintelligibly
jacasse *f.* gossip, chatterbox; magpie
jacasser *vi.* to jabber, chatter; gossip
jacasserie *f.* chatter, gossip
jachère *f.* fallow land
jacinthe *f.* (bot.) hyacinth
jack *m.* (elec.) jack
jacobée *f.* (bot.) ragwort
jacobin *m.* Dominican friar; Jacobin
Jacques (*m.*) James
jacquet *m.* backgammon
jactance *f.* boasting, bragging
jade *m.* jade
jadis *adv.* of old, formerly
jaguar *m.* jaguar
jaillir *vi.* to spout out, spurt, gush, squirt; fly up; flash; (fig.) show liveliness
jaillissant *a.* gushing, spurting; flying
jaillissement *m.* spurt, spurting, gushing
jais *m.* jet; noir comme du — jet-black
jalon *m.* marker (post, stake, rod, staff); landmark
jalonner *vt.* to mark; stake (out); blaze
jalouser *vt.* to envy, be jealous of
jalousie *f.* jealousy; chagrin; Venetian blind
jaloux *a.* jealous, envious; desirous
Jamaïque *f.* Jamaica
jamais *adv.* ever; ne . . . — never; à —, pour — for ever

jambage *m.* jamb of a door; side

jambe *f.* leg; shank; stem of a glass; brace, support; **à toutes —s** at full speed

jambière *f.* elastic stocking; **—s** *pl.* leggings; shin guards (sports)

jambon *m.* ham

jamboree *m.* jamboree, international scout meeting

janissaire *m.* janissary; 14th century Turkish soldier

jansénisme *m.* Jansenism

janséniste *a. & n.* Jansenist

jante *f.* rim of wheel

janvier *m.* January

Japon *m.* Japan

japonais *a. & m.* Japanese

japonaiseries *f. pl.* Japanese art objects

jappement *m.* yelp, yelping

japper *vi.* to yelp, yap

jaquemart *m.* jack, figure which strikes the hours

jaquette *f.* jacket, coat

jardin *m.* garden; **— d'enfants** kindergarten; **— des plantes** botanical garden(s); **— potager** vegetable garden; truck farm

jardinage *m.* gardening; gardening products; produce

jardiner *vi.* to garden

jardinet *m.* small garden

jardinier *m.* gardener

jardinière *f.* gardener; flower stand; **à la —** served with various vegetables

jardiniste *m.* landscape gardener

jargon *m.* jargon

jargonner *vi.* to speak in jargon; use jargon

jarre *f.* large jar

jarret *m.* shin; hock; knuckle; part of leg back of the knee joint

jarretelle *f.* garter

jarretière *f.* garter; rope

jars *m.* (zool.) gander

jaser *vi.* to prattle, chatter, talk; gossip

jaserie *f.* chatter, gossip, talk

jaseur *a.* talkative, gossipy; **— m.** talker, chatterbox; gossip

jasmin *m.* jasmine

jaspe *m.* jasper

jasper *vt.* to marble

jatte *f.* bowl, basin

jattée *f.* bowlful

jauge *f.* gauge; (naut.) tonnage

jaugeage *m.* gauging, measuring

jauger *vt.* to gauge, measure

jaunâtre *a.* yellowish

jaune *a.* yellow; **— m.** yellow; (coll.) non-union worker; **— d'œuf** egg yolk; **race — yellow** race

jaunir *vt.* to make yellow; **— vi.** grow yellow

jaunisse *f.* (med.) jaundice

javanois *a. & m.* Javanese

javeline *f.* javelin

javellisation *f.* chlorination

javelliser *vt.* to chlorinate; add bleach to

javelot *m.* javelin, spear

je, (j') *pron.* I

Jean (*m.*) John

Jeanne (*f.*) Jane, Joan, Jean

jeannette *f.* small gold crucifix (pendant)

jérémiade *f.* lament, complaint, jeremiad

jersey *m.* jersey material

jésuite *m.* Jesuit

Jésus *m.* Jesus depicted as infant

jet *m.* throwing, casting; jet, spurt, spout, gush; blast, burst; jettisoning; (bot.) shoot; **premier —** rough draft, first attempt; **— d'eau** fountain

jetée *f.* pier, jetty

jeter *vt.* to throw, cast, fling, toss, hurl; utter

jeton *m.* counter, chip, token

jeu *m.* (*pl.* jeux) play, game, sport, performance; acting; gambling; slack, play, looseness; set; **en —** at stake; in action; **— de cartes** pack of cards; **— d'esprit** witticism; **— de mots** pun; **— de paume** tennis court; **maison de — f.** gambling house; **table de — f.** card table; gambling table

jeudi *m.* Thursday

jeun, *adv.* **à —** fasting; without having eaten

jeune *a.* young, youthful; green (not ripe)

jeûne *m.* fast, fasting

jeûner *vi.* to fast

jeunesse *f.* youth, young people; youthfulness

jeunet *a.* (coll.) very young

joaillerie *f.* jewelry

joaillier *m.* jeweller

jobard *a. & m.* (coll.) easy mark, fool, dupe

jocrisse *m.* fool, dupe

jodler *vi.* to yodel

joie *f.* joy, gladness; **feu de — m.** bonfire

joindre *vt.* to join, put together, connect; meet; adjoin; add; combine; weld; **se — to join**; meet; adjoin

joint *a.* joined, united **— m.** joint

jointif *a.* joined

jointure *f.* joint; juncture

joker *m.* joker (cards)

joli *a.* pretty

joliment *adv.* nicely; very

jonc *m.* rush, rattan, reed

joncher *vt.* to strew, scatter; litter, be spread over

jonction *f.* junction; joining

jongler *vi.* to juggle
jonglerie *f.* juggling
jongleur *m.* juggler; jongleur
jonque *f.* (naut.) junk
jonquille *f.* jonquil
jouable *a.* playable
joue *f.* cheek; flange; **coucher en** — to aim at, point a gun at
jouer *vt.* to play; perform; act; bet on; feign; trick; — *vi.* to play; gamble; act, work; come into play, operate; **faire** — to bring into play
jouet *m.* plaything, toy
joueur *m.* player, gambler; performer; **mauvais** — poor sport
joug *m.* yoke; slavery
jouir *vi.* to enjoy; possess
jouissance *f.* enjoyment; possession
joujou *m.* plaything, toy
jour *m.* day, daylight, light; opening; **du** — **au lendemain** at any moment; soon; **faire** — to grow light; **grand** — broad daylight; **mettre au** — to bring to light; give birth to; **petit** — early dawn; **plein** — broad daylight; **-s** *pl.* days; life; **de nos** **-s** today, nowadays
Jourdain *m.* Jordan
journal *m.* (*pl.* **journaux**) journal, diary; log; newspaper
journalier *a.* daily, everyday; — *m.* daylaborer
journalisme *m.* journalism
journaliste *m.* & *f.* journalist; reporter
journalistique *a.* journalistic
journée *f.* daytime; day's work; day's pay; day's march; **à la** — by the day; **toute la** — all day long
journellement *adv.* daily
joute *f.* joust, jousting; competition, contest
jouter *vi.* to joust, fight
jouvence *f.* youth
jovialité *f.* joviality
joyau *m.* jewel
joyeusement *adv.* joyfully
joyeuseté *f.* prank, joke
joyeux *a.* joyful; glad, merry
jubilation *f.* jubilation
jubilé *m.* jubilee; golden anniversary
jubiler *vi.* to jubilate, be jubilant, exult
jucher *vi.* & *vt.* to perch
juchoir *m.* perch, roost
judaïque *a.* Judaic, Jewish
judaïsme *m.* Judaism
judas *m.* traitor; peephole
judéo-allemand *a.* & *m.* Yiddish
judiciaire *a.* judicial, judiciary
judicieusement *adv.* judiciously
judicieux *a.* judicious
juge *m.* judge; — **d'instruction** examining

magistrate
jugement *m.* judgment, understanding; trial; sentence, decision, verdict; opinion; sense
jugeotte *f.* (coll.) common sense
juger *vt.* to judge, try; pass sentence; think; consider, deem
jugoslave *a.* & *n.* Yugoslav(ian), Jugoslav
jugulaire *a.* jugular; — *f.* jugular vein; chin strap
juguler *vt.* to strangle; cut the throat of
juif (juive) *a.* Jewish
juillet *m.* July
juin *m.* June
Jules (*m.*) Julius
julien *a.* Julian
julienne *f.* consommé Julienne (made with herbs and vegetables)
jumeau (jumelle) *a.* & *n.* twin
jumelé *a.* paired, coupled; twin; dual
jumeler *vt.* to pair
jumelles *f. pl.* binoculars
jument *f.* mare
jumping *m.* steeplechase (racing)
jungle *f.* jungle
junior *a.* & *m.* junior
junte *f.* junta
jupe *f.* skirt
jupon *m.* petticoat
juré *a.* sworn; — *m.* juror; **les –s** *pl.* the jury
jurement *m.* cursing, swearing
jurer *vt.* to swear, vow; — *vi.* curse; to clash (color)
juridiction *f.* jurisdiction
juridictionnel *a.* jurisdictional
juridique *a.* judicial, juridical
jurisconsulte *m.* lawyer, law expert
jurisprudence *f.* jurisprudence
juriste *m.* jurist
juron *m.* oath, swear word
jury *m.* jury, board, panel
jus *m.* juice; gravy
jusant *m.* ebb tide
jusque, jusqu'à *prep.* until; as far as; even; **jusqu'ici, jusqu'à present** till now, hitherto; **jusqu'à ce que** *conj.* until
justaucorps *m.* doublet
juste *a.* just, equitable, right, fair; precise, exact; **au** — exactly, precisely; — *adv.* right, very, exactly; — *m.* just person; person in state of grace
juste-milieu *m.* moderation, golden mean
justesse *f.* exactness, accuracy; fairness
justice *f.* justice; law; **faire** — to treat as one deserves; **se faire** — to punish oneself; avenge oneself
justiciable *a.*, — **de** under the jurisdiction of
justicier *m.* officer of justice, judge; — *vt.*

to punish
justifiable *a.* justifiable
justificateur *a.* justifying
justicatif *a.* justificative
justification *f.* justification
justifier *vt.* to justify, vindicate; — **de** to give proof of
juteux *a.* juicy
juvénile *a.* juvenile
juvénilité *f.* character of what is juvenile
juxtaposer *vt.* to juxtapose

K

kaki *a.* khaki-colored
kaléidoscope *m.* kaleidoscope
kangourou *m.* kangaroo
kaolin *m.* kaolin
kapok *m.* kapok
kayac *m.* kayak
keepsake *m.* album, scrapbook
képi *m.* military cap
kermesse *f.* village fair
kérosène *m.* kerosene
kitchenotte *f.* peasant's bonnet
kidnapper *vt.* to kidnap
kidnappeur *m.* kidnapper
kilo(gramme) *m.* kilogram
kilomètre *m.* kilometer
kilométrer *vt.* to mark off in kilometers
kilométrique *a.* kilometric
kilowatt *m.* kilowatt
kilt *m.* kilt
kimono *m.* kimono
kinescope *m.* kinescope; picture tube
kiosque *m.* kiosk; newsstand; conning tower
kirsch *m.* Kirsch, cherry brandy
klaxon *m.* (auto.) horn
klaxonner *vi.* to blow the horn
kleptomanie (cleptomanie) *f.* kleptomania
knock-out *m.* boxing knockout
knockouter *vt.* to knock out
kodak *m.* camera
krach *m.* financial crash
krypton *m.* krypton
kyrie *m.* (eccl.) Kyrie eleison (invocation)
kyrielle *f.* (coll.) tirade, avalanche of words
kyste *m.* (med.) cyst

L

la *art. f.* the; — *pron.* her, it; — *m.* (mus.) French key of A; 6th note of a scale
là *adv.* there, that, that way; then
là-bas *adv.* over there; yonder
label *m.* guarantee; inspection mark
labeur *m.* labor, work
laborantine *f.* laboratory technician

laboratoire *m.* laboratory
laborieusement *adv.* laboriously
laborieux *a.* hard-working; painstaking, difficult
labour *m.* tillage, plowing
labourable *a.* arable
labourage *m.* plowing
labourer *vt.* to till, plow
laboureur *m.* plower; farm hand
labyrinthe *m.* labyrinth, maze
lac *m.* lake
laçage *m.* lacing
lacer *vt.* to lace; **se** — to tie one's shoelaces, lace one's shoes
lacération *f.* laceration
lacérer *vt.* to lacerate
lacet *m.* shoelace; hairpin turn; snare; route en —s winding road
lâche *a.* loose, lax; cowardly; — *m.* coward
lâcher *vt.* to release, loosen; let go, drop; — prise to let go
lâcheté *f.* cowardice; cowardly action
lâcheur *m.* (coll.) quitter
lacis *m.* network
laconique *a.* laconic
lacrymal *a.* teary
lacrymogène *a.*, **gaz** — *m.* tear gas
lacs *m.* knotted cord; trap, snare
lacté *a.* lacteal, milky; **voie** -e *f.* Milky Way
lactique *a.* lactic
lactose *m.* lactose, milk sugar
lacune *f.* gap, void, lacuna
lad *m.* stable boy
là-dessus *adv.* thereupon
ladre *a.* mean, stingy; leprous
lagon *m.* lagoon of an atoll
lagune *f.* lagoon
là-haut *adv.* up above, up there
lai *m.* lay, song; — *a.* lay; **frère** — *m.* lay brother
laïc *a.* lay, secular
laid *a.* ugly
laideron *f.* ugly young woman
laideur *f.* ugliness
lainage *m.* wool goods
laine *f.* wool
laineux *a.* woolly, fleecy
lainier *a.* wool; — *m.* wool merchant
laïque *a.* laic, lay; — *m.* layman
laisse *f.* leash
laissé-pour-compte *m.* unsold item; unwanted thing
laisser *vt.* to let, allow; leave behind, leave alone
laisser-aller *m.* unconstraint
laissez-passer *m.* pass, permit
lait *m.* milk; — écrémé skim milk; **cochon de** — *m.* suckling pig; **dents de** — *f. pl.* milk teeth, baby teeth; **petit** — whey

laitance *f.* milt
laiterie *f.* dairy, dairy store
laiteux *a.* milky
laitier *m.* milk seller, milkman; — *m.* vitrified slag
laitière *f.* milkmaid; dairy cow
laiton *m.* brass
laitue *f.* lettuce
laize *f.* cloth width
lamaserie *f.* lamasery
lambeau *m.* rag, tatter; shred
lambin *a.* slow; loitering
lambiner *vi.* to move slowly, dawdle
lambourde *f.* studding
lambrequin *m.* valence, hanging
lambris *m.* wainscoting, paneling, wall plaster
lame *f.* knife blade; slat; wave
lamentation *f.* lamentation
lamenter *v.*, **se** — to lament, complain
laminage *m.* laminating
laminer *vt.* to laminate
lampadaire *m.* lamppost; floor lamp
lampe *f.* lamp; light; bulb; (rad.) tube; — **éclair** photoflash bulb, flash bulb
lampion *m.* oil lamp; lantern
lampiste *m. & f.* lampmaker; lamp seller
lamproie *f.* lamprey
lampyre *m.* firefly
lance *f.* lance; lancer; nozzle
lance-flammes *m.* flame-thrower
lance-fusées *m.* rockèt launcher
lance-grenades *m.* grenade launcher
lancement *m.* throw, throwing; start, send-off
lance-pierres *m.* slingshot
lancer *vt.* to fling, hurl, throw, start; launch
lance-torpille *m.* torpedo tube
lancette *f.* lancet
lancier *m.* lancer
lanciner *vi.* to shoot (pain)
lande *f.* heath, moor
langage *m.* language, speech
lange *m.* swaddling cloth
langer *vt.* to swaddle
langoureux *a.* languishing, languid
langouste *f.* spiny lobster
langoustine *f.* very small lobster
langue *f.* tongue; speech, language
languette *f.* tongue, tab; (mus.) instrument reed
langueur *f.* languor
languir *vi.* to languish, pine; — **pour** to long for
languissant *a.* languishing
lanière *f.* strap
lanoline *f.* lanolin
lanterne *f.* lantern, light; projector
lanterner *vi.* to loaf, idle, waste time

lapement *m.* lapping
laper *vt. & vi.* to lap
lapereau *m.* young rabbit
lapidaire *m. & a.* lapidary
lapidation *f.* stoning, lapidation
lapider *vt.* to stone
lapin *m.* rabbit, (coll.) brave man, cunning man
lapis *m.* lapis lazuli
Laponie *f.* Lapland
lapsus *m.* error, slip of the tongue
laquais *m.* lackey; flunky
laque *f.* lac; — **en feuilles** shellac; — *m.* lacquer
laquelle *pron. f.* who, which, that
laquer *vt.* to lacquer
larcin *m.* larceny, theft
lard *m.* bacon; pork, fat
larder *vt.* to lard; interlard, sprinkle; pierce, riddle
lardon *m.* bit of fat
large *a.* wide, broad; liberal, generous; large; — *m.* room, space; width; open sea
largesse *f.* liberality, generosity
largeur *f.* breadth, width
largue *a.* slack; (naut.) on the quarter
larguer *vt.* to slacken
larme *f.* tear; drop
larmioement *m.* weeping, tears
larmoyant *a.* weeping, tearful
larmoyer *vt.* to weep constantly
larron *m.* thief, robber
larvaire *a.* larval
larve *f.* larva
laryngite *f.* laryngitis
laryngologiste *m.* throat specialist
lasl *interj.* alas!
las (lasse) *a.* tired, weary
lascif *a.* lascivious
lasciveté *f.* lasciviousness
lassant *a.* tiring; tedious
lasser *vt.* to tire; **se** — to grow tired
lassitude *f.* weariness, fatigue, lassitude
latent *a.* latent
latéral *a.* lateral; **–ement** *adv.* on the side
Latin *m. & a.* Latin
latiniser *vt.* to latinize
latiniste *m. & f.* latinist
latino-américain *a. & m.* Latin-American
latrines *f. pl.* latrines
lattage *m.* lathwork
latte *f.* lath, slat
latter *vt.* to lath
lattis *m.* lathwork; latticework
latvien *a. & m.* Latvian
laudatif *a.* laudatory
lauré *a.* crowned with laurel, laureate
lauréat *m.* laureate, winner
Laurent (*m.*) Lawrence

laurier *m.* laurel
lavable *a.* washable
lavabo *m.* wash basin, sink; lavatory; (eccl.) priest's prayer
lavage *m.* washing
lavallière *f.* necktie with large flat knot
lavande *f.* lavender
lavandière *f.* washerwoman
lave *f.* lava
lavé *a.* washed out; water-color wash (art)
lavement *m.* washing; enema
laver *vt.* to wash
lavette *f.* dishcloth
laveur *m.* washer; **raton — raccoon**
laveuse *f.* washing machine
lavis *m.* wash (art)
lavoir *m.* wash house, laundry
laxatif *a. & m.* laxative
lazaret *m.* quarantine station
lazzi *m. pl.* (theat.) tricks, jokes
le *art. m.* the; **—** *pron. m.* him, it
leader *m.* political leader; editorial
lèche *f.* thin slice (food)
lèchefrite *f.* dripping pan
lécher *vt.* to lick; polish; polish excessively
lècherie *f.* gluttony
leçon *f.* lesson, assignment; reading, version
lecteur *m.* reader
lecture *f.* reading
légal *a.* legal
légalement *adv.* legally
légalisation *f.* legalization
légaliser *vt.* to legalize; authenticate
légalité *f.* legality
légat *m.* papal legate
légataire *m. & f.* heir, legatee; **— universel** residual heir
légation *f.* legation
légendaire *a.* legendary
légende *f.* legend
léger *a.* light; slight; active; agile; frivolous
légèrement *adv.* lightly
légèreté *f.* lightness, levity, triviality
légion *f.* legion
légionnaire *m.* legionary; member of the Foreign Legion; member of the Legion of Honor
législateur *m.* legislator
législatif *a.* legislative
législation *f.* legislation
législature *f.* legislature
légiste *m.* jurist, legist
légitime *a.* legitimate; lawful
légitimer *vt.* to recognize, legitimatize
légitimité *f.* legitimacy, lawfulness
legs *m.* legacy

léguer *vt.* to leave, bequeathe
légume *m.* vegetable; **—** *f.* (coll.) very important person
légumeuse *f.* legume
légumier *m.* vegetable dish; **— a.** vegetable; vegetable garden
légumineux *a.* leguminous
lendemain *m.* next day, tomorrow
lénifier *vt.* to mitigate, attenuate
lénitif *a.* soothing
lent *a.* slow
lente *f.* nit
lentement *adv.* slowly
lenteur *f.* slowness
lenticulaire *a.* lenticular
lentille *f.* lentil; lens; **— s** *pl.* freckles
léonin *a.* leonine; **part —e** *f.* lion's share
léopard *m.* leopard
léopardé *a.* spotted
lèpre *f.* leprosy
lépreux *a.* leprous; **—** *m.* leper
lequel *pron. m.* which, who, that
les *art.* (*pl. of* **le, la**); **—** *pron.* them
lès *prep.* near
lesbien *a.* Lesbian
lèse-humanité *f.* crime against humanity
lèse-majesté *f.* high treason
léser *vt.* to wrong, injure
lésine *f.* stinginess
lésiner *vi.* to be stingy, be niggardly
lésion *f.* wrong, damage, hurt; lesion
lessivage *m.* washing
lessive *f.* lye; laundry, washing powder
lessiver *vt.* to launder
lest *m.* (naut.) ballast
lestage *m.* ballasting
leste *a.* nimble, brisk, agile
lester *vt.* to ballast, weight
léthargie *f.* lethargy
léthargique *a.* lethargic
Lette *m. & f. & a.* Lett, Latvian
letton *a. & m.* Lett, Latvian
Lettonie *f.* Latvia
lettrage *m.* lettering
lettre *f.* letter; **à la —, au pied de la —** literally
lettré *a.* literate; learned
lettrine *f.* large initial capital letter; reference letter at head of dictionary column
leucémie *f.* leukemia
leucocyte *m.* leucocyte, white blood cell
leur *a.* their; **—** *pron.* to them, for them; **le —, la —** theirs
leurre *m.* lure, decoy
leurrer *vt.* to lure, trap, decoy
levain *m.* leaven, yeast; **poudre —** *f.* baking powder
levant *a.* rising; **—** *m.* east
Levantin *m. & a.* Levantine

levée f. raising, lifting; adjourning; harvesting; levying; mail collection; trick (at cards); removal; levee, dike
lever m. rising; — du soleil sunrise
lever vt. to lift, raise; collect; levy; remove; draw (a plan); — vi. to come up (plants); to rise (dough)
levier m. lever; crowbar; — articulé toggle switch
lévitation f. levitation
levraut m. young hare
lèvre f. lip; rim
lévrette f., **lévrier** m. greyhound
levure f. yeast; — chimique baking powder
lexicographe m. lexicographer
lexicologie f. lexicology
lexique m. lexicon; glossary; vocabulary
lézard m. lizard
lézarde f. crevice, crack
lézarder vt. to crack
liaison f. binding, joining, relation; intimacy, affair
liane f. liana, vine
liant a. good-natured, engaging; flexible; — m. flexibility, affability
liard m. ¼ sou; tiny sum, cent; **un rouge** — a red cent
liasse f. bundle, wad, file
Liban m. Lebanon
Libanais m. & a. Lebanese
libation f. libation
libelle m. lampoon, satire; libel
libellé m. composition, wording (judiciary or administrative)
libeller vt. to draw up, compose, word
libelliste m. satirist
libellule f. dragonfly
libéral a. & m. liberal
libéralement adv. liberally
libéralisation f. liberalization
libéraliser vt. to liberalize
libéralisme m. liberalism
libéralité f. liberality, generosity
libérateur m. liberator
libération f. liberation
libérer vt. to free, liberate, discharge
libertaire m. & f. anarchist
liberté f. liberty, freedom
libertin a. libertine, licentious; — m. libertine; freethinker (history)
libertinage m. licentiousness, debauchery; libertinage
libidineux a. libidinous, lascivious
libraire m. & f. bookseller
librairie f. bookstore; book trade; publishing house
libre a. free; unoccupied
libre-échange m. free trade
librement adv. freely

libre-service m. self-service; **restaurante de** — cafeteria
librettiste m. librettist
Libye f. Libya
lice f. lists, jousting field; bitch; **entrer en** — to undertake, enter upon
licence f. license; Master's degree
licencié m. holder of a Master's degree
licenciement m. dismissal, firing
licencier vt. to dismiss, fire
licencieux a. licentious
lichen m. lichen
licitation f. sale at auction
licite a. lawful
liciter vt. to sell at auction
licorne f. unicorn
licou, licol m. halter (of a harness)
licteur m. lictor
lie f. lees, (dregs) — **de vin** wine dregs; red-violet color
lié a. tied, united; intimate
liège m. cork, cork oak; **à bout(s) de** — cork-tipped
lien m. tie, bond
lier vt. to tie, bind, fasten; establish; bind, thicken (cooking); **se** — to become close friends, become intimate; thicken
lierre m. ivy
liesse f. joy, gaiety
lieu m. place; cause, reason; — **x** pl. premises; **au** — **de** instead of; **avoir** — **to** take place; **avoir** — **de** to have reason to; — **commun** commonplace, banality; **tenir** — **de** to replace
lieue f. league (2 ½ miles)
lieutenance f. lieutenancy
lieutenant-colonel m. lieutenant-colonel
lièvre m. hare
liftier m. elevator operator
ligament m. ligament
ligaturer vt. to ligature, bind
lignage m. lineage
ligne f. line
lignée f. issue, stock; **chien de bonne** — m. pedigreed dog
ligneux a. ligneous
lignite m. lignite
ligoter vt. to bind, tie up
ligue f. league
liguer vt. to bind together, unite
ligueur m. member of the League (historical)
ligurien a. & m. Ligurian
lilas m. lilac; lilac color, light purple
lilliputien a. Lilliputian, tiny
limace f. (zool.) slug
limaçon m. snail
limande f. straight edge (carpentry)
limbe m. border; — **s** pl. limbo
lime f. file

limer vt. to file; (fig.) to polish, rework
limier m. bloodhound; sleuth
liminaire a. prefatory, introductory
limitable a. limitable
limitatif a. limiting
limitation f. limitation; — **sur la natalité** birth control
limite f. boundary, limit
limiter vt. to limit
limitrophe a. surrounding, bordering
limon m. lime; mud, slime; silt; shaft; support of a stair step
limonade f. lemon soda, lemonade
limoneux a. slimy; full of mud; silted
limousine f. limousine
limpide a. limpid
limpidité f. limpidness, clearness
lin m. flax; linen; **graine de** — f. linseed
linceul m. shroud
linéaire a. linear
linéal a. lineal
linéament m. feature; stoke; line; element
linette f. linseed
linge m. linen; table linen; underclothing; soiled clothes
lingerie f. linen goods; underclothing; linen closet; **vente de** — f. white-goods sale
lingot m. ingot
linguiste m. linguist
linguistique a. linguistic; — f. linguistics
liniment m. liniment
linoléum m. linoleum
linon m. batiste
linotype f. linotype machine
linotypiste m. & f. linotypist
linteau m. lintel
lion m. lion; — **ne** f. lioness
lionceau m. lion cub
lippe f. protruding lower lip; **faire la** — to pout
liquéfaction f. liquefying, liquefaction
liquéfier vt. to liquefy
liqueur f. liqueur; liquor, liquid; (chem.) solution
liquidation f. settlement, liquidating of debts
liquide a. liquid; — m. liquid; — f. liquid consonant
liquider vt. to liquidate; settle
liquoriste m. dealer in liqueurs
lire vt. to read
lire f. lira
lis, lys m. (bot.) lily; (fig.) **teint de** — very white
Lisbonne f. Lisbon
lise f. quicksand
liséré m. piping; a sewed-on border
lisérer vt. to edge, border
liseur m. reader; bookmark

liseuse f. reader; protective cover of a book
lisibilité f. legibility
lisible a. legible, readable
lisière f. selvage; border, edge; support
lisse a. sleek, smooth, glossy
lisser vt. to smoothe, make glossy
lisseuse f. polishing machine
liste f. list
listel m. edging, frame
lit m. bed; layer; — **de sangle** folding bed
litanie f. litany
litée f. litter of young animals
literie f. bedding
lithium m. lithium
lithographe m. lithographer
lithographie f. lithograph; **lithography**
lithographier vt. to lithograph
litière f. litter
litige m. litigation
litigieux a. litigious; contentious (law)
litre m. liter
lit-sac m. sleeping bag
littéraire a. literary
littéral a. literal
littéralement adv. literally
littérateur m. literary man, man of letters
littérature f. literature
littoral m. & a. coast; littoral
Lituanie f. Lithuania
Lituanien m. & a. Lithuanian
liturgie f. liturgy
liturgique a. liturgical
livarot m. livarot cheese
livide a. livid
lividité f. lividness, lividity
Livourne f. Leghorn
livrable a. deliverable
livraison f. delivery; part, installment (of book)
livre f. pound (weight or Eng. money)
livre m. book, register; **grand** — ledger
livrée f. livery; colors
livrer vt. to deliver; hand over; betray; **se** — **à** to give oneself over to; devote oneself to; go in for, indulge in; surrender to
livresque a. relating to books
livret m. small book; passbook; **libretto**
livreur m. delivery man
livreuse f. delivery truck
lobaire a. lobar
lobe m. lobe
local m. premises; — a. local
localisation f. localization
localiser vt. to localize
localité f. locality
locataire m. & f. tenant
locatif m. (gram.) locative
location f. renting; **bureau de** — m. box

office
loch *f.* (naut.) log; **table de — *f.*** log book
locomoteur *a.* locomotive
locomotion *f.* locomotion
locuste *f.* locust
locution *f.* locution; phrase
logarithme *m.* logarithm
logarithmique *a.* logarithmic
loge *f.* (theat.) box; dressing room; janitor's apartment; loggia
logement *m.* lodging, housing
loger *vt.* to lodge, house; — *vi.* to reside
logeur *m.* landlord
logicien *m.* logician
logique *a.* logical; — *f.* logic
logis *m.* home, dwelling
logistique *f.* logistics
loi *f.* law
loin *adv.* far, far off, at a distance
lointain *a.* far, remote, distant; — *m.* distance
loir *m.* dormouse
loisible *a.* permissible
loisir *m.* leisure; time-off
lombago *m.* lumbago
lombaire *a.* lumbar
lombes *m. pl.* lumbar region
lombric *m.* earthworm
londonien *m.* Londoner; — *a.* of London
Londres *m.* London
long (longue) *a.* long, lengthy; **à la — ue** in the long run; — *m.* length; **de — en large** up and down, back and forth; **le — de** *prep.* along
longanimité *f.* longanimity; forbearance
long-courrier *m.* ocean-going ship
longe *f.* tether; loin
longer *vt.* to go along, skirt
longeron *m.* crossbeam; boom (avi.)
longévité *f.* longevity
longitudinal *a.* longitudinal
longtemps *adv.* a long time
longue *f.* long vowel
longuement *adv.* for a long time, at length
longuet *a.* rather long; — *m.* long roll
longueur *f.* length
longue-vue *f.* telescope
looping *m.* (avi.) loop
lopin *m.* bit, piece
loquace *a.* loquacious
loquacité *f.* loquaciousness
loque *f.* rag, tatter
loquet *m.* latch
loqueteau *m.* small latch
loqueteux *a.* ragged, dressed in rags
loquette *f.* scrap, waste
lorgner *vt.* to ogle, stare at
lorgnette *f.* opera glasses
lorgnon *m.* lorgnette
loriot *m.* oriole

lorrain *a.* Lorraine
lors *adv.* at the time; **dès — from that time; — de** at the time of
lorsque *conj.* when
losange *f.* lozenge
lot *m.* lot, part, share; jack pot; prize (gambling)
loterie *f.* lottery
loti *a.* favored; divided
lotion *f.* lotion; hair tonic
lotionner *vt.* to lotion, bathe
lotir *vt.* to divide into lots; sort out; provide for
loto *m.* lotto
lotus *m.* lotus
louable *a.* praiseworthy
louage *m.* letting out; hiring
louange *f.* praise
louanger *vt.* to praise
louangeur *a.* praising, laudatory
louche *f.* soup ladle; — *a.* cross-eyed, squinting; shady, suspect, unwholesome
loucher *vi.* to squint; be cross-eyed
louchet *m.* spade
louer *vt.* to praise; hire, rent; **se — de to** be pleased with
loufoque *m.* crank
lougre *m.* (naut.) lugger
louis *m.* 20-franc gold piece
loulou *m.* Pomeranian dog
loup *m.* wolf; evil person; mask; defect
loupe *f.* magnifying glass; cyst, wen, tree gnarl
louper *vt.* to botch
loup-garou *m.* werewolf
lourd *a.* heavy, weighty, dull
lourdaud *a.* clumsy
lourdement *adv.* heavily
lourdeur *f.* heaviness; dullness; sultriness
loutre *f.* otter
louveteau *m.* wolf cub
louveterie *f.* wolf hunt; hunting gear
louvoyer *vi.* dodge, be evasive; (naut.) to tack
lover *vt.* to coil
loyaliste *a. & n.* loyalist
loyauté *f.* loyalty
loyer *m.* rent, rental
lubie *f.* whim, fancy
lubricité *f.* lewdness, inclination toward obscenity
lubrifiant *m.* lubricant; — *a.* lubricating
lubrificateur *a.* lubricating
lubrifier *vt.* to lubricate
lubrique *a.* lewd
Luc (*m.*) Luke
lucarne *f.* skylight, dormer window
lucide *a.* lucid
lucidité *f.* lucidity

luciole *f.* firefly
lucratif *a.* lucrative
lucre *m.* profit, love of profit
luette *f.* uvula
lueur *f.* gleam, glimmer
luge *f.* sled
lugubre *a.* lugubrious, gloomy
lui *pron.* he, him, to him, to her, to it
luire *vi.* to shine, gleam
luisance *f.* shininess, glossiness
luisant *a.* shining, gleaming; glossy
lumière *f.* light, illumination
lumignon *m.* small light; wick
luminaire *m.* luminary; lights, lighting
luminescent *a.* luminescent
lumineux *a.* luminous
luminosité *f.* luminosity
lunaire *a.* lunar
lunaison *f.* lunation, lunar month
lunatique *a.* fantastic; — *m. & f.* lunatic
luncher *vi.* to have lunch
lundi *m.* Monday
lune *f.* moon; clair de — *m.* moonlight; — de miel honeymoon
luné *a.* crescent-shaped
lunetier *m.* optician
lunette *f.* glass, telescope; hole; — de tir telescopic gunsight; — s *pl.* eyeglasses
lunetterie *f.* optician's trade
lustre *m.* luster, gloss; chandelier; 5-year period, lustrum
lustrer *vt.* to gloss; glaze
lustrine *f.* cotton satin
luth *m.* lute
Luthérien *m.* Lutheran
luthier *m.* maker of stringed instruments
lutin *m.* sprite, elf
lutiner *vt.* to tease, torment
lutrin *m.* lectern
lutte *f.* struggle, wrestling
lutter *vi.* to wrestle, struggle
lutteur *m.* wrestler
luxation *f.* dislocation
luxe *m.* luxury
luxer *vt.* to dislocate
luxmètre *m.* light meter
luxueux *a.* luxurious
luxure *f.* lewdness, lust
luxuriant *a.* luxuriant
luxurieux *a.* lustful, lewd
luzerne *f.* alfalfa
lycée *m.* secondary school, junior college
lycéen *m.* schoolboy, student, lycée student
lymphatique *a.* lymphatic
lymphe *f.* lymph
lynchage *m.* lynching
lyncher *vt.* to lynch
lynx *m.* lynx
lyonnais *a.* from Lyons

lyre *f.* lyre
lyrique *a.* lyrical

M

ma *a. f.* my
macabre *a.* macabre, deathly; danse — *f.* dance of death
macadamiser *vt.* to pave with macadam
macaron *m.* macaroon
macaronis *m. pl.* macaroni
macédoine *f.* mixed salad; mixed vegetables
Macédonie *f.* Macedonia
Macédonien *m. & a.* Macedonian
macération *f.* maceration
macérer *vt.* to macerate; se — to mortify the flesh
mâchefer *m.* clinker, dross, slag
mâchelier *a.* molar
mâcher *vt.* to chew
machette *f.* machete
machin *m.* thing, gadget
machinal *a.* mechanical; instinctive
machinalement *adv.* mechanically
machine *f.* machine, engine; — à coudre sewing machine; — à écrire typewriter
machiner *vt.* to machinate, put together, prepare; to handle scenery
machinerie *f.* machinery; machine works; engine room
machiniste *m.* bus driver; (theat.) stagehand
mâchoire *f.* jaw, jawbone
mâchonner *vt.* to munch, chew slowly; mutter, mumble
mâchure *f.* bruise; defect in cloth
mâchurer *vt.* to daub, blacken
macis *m.* mace (spice)
maçon *m.* mason, bricklayer
maçonnage *m.* masonry
maçonner *vt.* to construct with masonry
maçonnerie *f.* masonry; free-masonry
maçonnique *a.* masonic
macrocosme *m.* macrocosm, the Universe
maculation, maculature *f.* macule; spotted sheet; poorly printed sheet
macule *f.* spot, stain
maculer *vt.* to spot, stain
Madagascar *m.* Madagascar
madame *f.* madam, Mrs.
madécasse *a.* Malagasy
Madeleine (*f.*) Magdalen
madeleine *f.* small sponge cake
mademoiselle *f.* miss
Madère *f.* Madeira; — *m.* Madeira wine
madone *f.* madonna
madras *m.* madras
madré *a.* cunning, sly
madrier *m.* thick plank

madrigal m. madrigal

madrilène a. of Madrid, from Madrid

magasin m. store; warehouse; magazine of a rifle; **grand — ** department store

magasinage m. warehousing

magasinier m. warehouse clerk; stock clerk; library stack boy

mage m. magus, wizard; **les — s, les rois — s** the Magi, the Wise Men

magicien m. magician

magie f. magic

magique a. magic

magister m. country teacher

magistère m. mastery; teaching

magistral a. imposing; authoritative; magisterial

magistrat m. magistrate

magistrature f. magistrate's position; the bench; magistrates

magnanarelle f. silkworm raiser; mulberry-leaf picker

magnanerie f. silkworm house

magnanime a. magnanimous

magnanimité f. magnanimity

magnat m. magnate

magnésie f. magnesia

magnésium m. magnesium

magnétique a. magnetic

magnétisation f. magnetization, magnetizing

magnétiser vt. to magnetize

magnétisme m. magnetism

magnéto f. magneto; **–hydrodynamique** magnetohydrodynamics

magnétophone m. tape or wire recorder

magnificat m. Magnificat

magnificence f. magnificence

magnifier vt. to glorify, magnify

magnifique a. magnificent

magnitude f. magnitude

magnolia m. magnolia

magnum m. magnum, two-liter bottle

magot m. ape, monkey; treasure; grotesque figurine

Mahométan m. & a. Mohammedan

mahométisme m. Mohammedanism

mai m. May

maie f. kneading trough

maigre a. thin, lean; meager; **jour — ** m. fast day, meatless day

maigrelet a. somewhat thin

maigreur f. thinness; meagerness

maigrir vt. to make thin; **— ** vi. to grow thin, lose weight

mail m. mall; public walk

maille f. stitch; mesh; link mail; **avoir — à partir** to have a disagreement, have a bone to pick (U.S. coll.)

maillechort m. German silver

maillet m. mallet

mailloche f. large mallet

maillon m. link of a small chain

maillot m. swaddling clothes; tights; swim suit; jersey

main f. hand; handwriting; **coup de — ** m. aid, **de longue — ** for a long time; **battres des — s** to applaud; **en venir aux — s** to come to blows

main-d'oeuvre f. manual labor, manpower

main-forte f. help, assistance

mainmise f. legal seizure

mainmorte f. mortmain, perpetual possession

maint a. many, undetermined number; **—es fois** on many occasions, often

maintenant adv. now, at present

maintenir vt. to maintain, support

maintien m. maintenance, support

maire m. mayor; **— sse** f. mayor's wife

mairie f. town hall

mais conj. but

maïs m. corn

maison f. house, home

maisonnée f. household, houseful

maisonnette f. small house

maître m. master, teacher; lawyer's title; **— d'hôtel** head waiter

maître-autel m. high altar

maîtresse f. mistress

maîtrise f. mastery; lectureship; choir school; choir boys; master's degree

maîtriser vt. to master, control

majesté f. majesty

majestueusement adv. majestically

majestueux a. majestic

majeur a. major; of age; f. force **— e** absolute necessity; **— ** m. middle finger; **— e** f. major premise

major m. (mil.) executive officer of a regiment; medical officer

majoration f. increase in price

majordome m. majordomo, butler

majorer vt. to increase the price

majoritaire a. majority, of the majority

majorité f. majority

Majorque f. Majorca

majuscule f. capital letter

mal m. (pl. **maux**) evil, harm, wrong; pain, ailment; **— de tête, — à la tête** headache; **— de mer** seasickness; **— du pays** homesickness; **— ** adv. ill, badly; **pas — de** (coll.) many, a great deal of

malade a. sick, ill

maladie f. sickness, illness

maladif a. sickly

maladresse f. awkwardness, clumsiness

maladroit a. awkward

malaga m. Malaga wine

malaire a. (anat.) of the cheek

Malais m. & a. Malay

malaise *m.* uneasiness; indisposition
malaisé *a.* difficult
Malaisie *f.* Malaya
malandrin *m.* vagabond
malappris *a.* ill-bred
malavisé *a.* ill-advised
malaxer *vt.* to mix, knead
malaxeur *m.* mixer; concrete mixer
malbâti *a.* ill-formed; ill-shaped
malchance *f.* bad luck, mishap
malchanceux *a.* unlucky
maldonne *f.* misdeal (at cards)
mâle *a.* male, manly; — *m.* male
malédiction *f.* curse
maléfice *m.* witchcraft
maléfique *a.* harmful, malignant
malemort *f.* violent death, tragic death
malencontre *f.* mishap
malencontreux *a.* unfortunate, unlucky
malendurant *a.* impatient
mal-en-point *adv.* in a bad way, badly off
malentendu *m.* misunderstanding
malfaçon *f.* defect
malfaire *vi.* to do evil
malfaisance *f.* evil-doing
malfaisant *a.* harmful; evil-minded
malfaiteur *m.* malefactor, evildoer, criminal
malfamé *a.* ill-famed, infamous, notorious
malgache *a.* from Madagascar
malgracieux *a.* ungraceful
malgré *prep.* in spite of, notwithstanding; — *que conj.* in spite of the fact that
malhabile *a.* awkward
malheur *m.* misfortune; ill luck, bad luck
malheureusement *adv.* unfortunately
malheureux *a.* unhappy, unfortunate, unlucky
malhonnête *a.* dishonest; rude; indecent
malhonnêteté *f.* dishonesty; rudeness
malicieusement *adv.* maliciously
malicieux *a.* malicious
malignité *f.* malignity
malin (maligne) *a.* malicious, malignant; shrewd, sharp; — *m.* devil
malingre *a.* sickly
malintentionné *a.* ill-disposed, evil-intentioned
mal-jugé *m.* miscarriage of justice
malle *f.* trunk; faire une — to pack a trunk
malléabilité *f.* malleability
malléable *a.* malleable
malle-poste *f.* mail coach
mallette *f.* small trunk
malmener *vt.* to mistreat, abuse
malodorant *a.* malodorous, foul-smelling
malotru *m.* uncouth individual
malpropre *a.* slovenly; dirty; improper
malpropreté *f.* dirtiness; impropriety; dis-honesty

malsain *a.* unhealthy, unwholesome
malséance *f.* unseemliness; inopportune-ness
malséant *a.* unbecoming, unseemly
malsonnant *a.* clashing; unseemly
malt *m.* malt
maltais *a. & m.* Maltese
Malte *f.* Malta
malthusianisme *m.* theory of birth control
maltose *m.* maltose
maltraiter *vt.* to mistreat
malveillamment *adv.* malevolently
malveillance *f.* ill will, malevolence
malveillant *a.* malevolent
malvenu *a.* uncalled for, unwarranted
malversation *f.* embezzlement of public funds
maman *f.* mama, mother
mamelle *f.* breast; udder
mamelon *m.* nipple; hillock
mammaire *a.* mammary
mammouth *m.* mammoth
manager *m.* trainer, athlete's manager
manant *m.* peasant; uncouth individual
manche *f.* sleeve; hose; air shaft; channel; (avi.) wind sock — *m.* handle; — à balai broomstick; (avi.) control stick
Manche, La *f.* English Channel
manchette *f.* cuff; marginal note; head-line
manchon *m.* muff; casing, sleeve; mantle of gas light
manchot *a.* one-armed, one-handed — *m.* penguin
mandarine *f.* mandarin orange; tangerine
mandat *m.* mandate; warrant; power of attorney; proxy; order; — poste postal money order; — lettre money order with space for message
mandataire *m. & f.* representative, agent, proxy
Mandchourie *f.* Manchuria
mandement *m.* mandamus; bishop's charge
mander *vt.* to send for; send word
mandibule *f.* mandible
mandoline *f.* mandolin
manège *m.* horsemanship; riding school; mill, treadmill; merry-go-round, carousel; intrigue
mânes *m. pl.* manes, dead souls (Roman history)
manette *f.* handle, lever
manganèse *m.* manganese
mangeable *a.* eatable
mangeoire *f.* manger, crib
mangeotter *vt.* to pick at one's food
manger *vt. & vi.* to eat, eat up; — *m.* food

mange-tout *m.* bean, pea with which pods are eaten
mangeur *m.* eater; wastrel
mangouste *f.* mongoose
mangue *f.* mango
manguier *m.* mango tree
maniabilité *f.* maneuverability; suppleness
maniable *a.* tractable, pliable; supple; maneuverable
maniaque *m. & f.* maniac; — *a.* maniacal
manie *f.* mania; passion
maniement *m.* handling; maneuvering
manier *vt.* to handle; feel; manage; work, use, drive, activate
manière *f.* manner, way; **de — que** so that; **de — à** so as to
maniéré *a.* affected
maniérisme *m.* mannerism, affectedness
manieur *m.* handler, manager
manifestant *m.* demonstrator
manifestation *f.* manifestation
manifeste *m.* manifesto; — *a.* obvious, evident, manifest
manifester *vt.* to manifest, show; — *vi.* to make a demonstration
manifold *m.* notebook; sales book
manigance *f.* intrigue, plot, trick
manigancer *vt.* to plot, scheme, be up to something
Manille *f.* Manila
manille *f.* link; manilla (card game); — *m.* cigar originating in Manila; hat of manilla straw
manioc *m.* manioc, source of tapioca
manipulateur *m.* manipulator
manipule *m.* (eccl.) maniple
manipuler *vt.* to manipulate; wield
manivelle *f.* handle, crank; winch
manne *f.* manna; two-handled basket
mannequin *m.* model, mannequin; fashion model; — **de couturière** dressmaker's dummy
manœuvrabilité *f.* maneuverability
manœuvrable *a.* maneuverable
manœuvre *f.* working, handling (boat); maneuver; (mil.) drill, maneuvers; — *m.* common laborer
manœuvrer *vt.* to maneuver, work; — *vi.* to maneuver
manœuvrier *m.* tactician; able seaman
manoir *m.* manor
manomètre *m.* pressure gauge
manqué *a.* which has failed, who has failed; inadequate; defective; short of the mark
manquement *m.* failing; infraction
manquer *vt.* to miss, fail; — *vi.* want, lack; — **à quelqu'un** to be missed by someone
mansarde *f.* mansard roof; attic; dormer

mansardé *a.* with dormers, dormered
mansuétude *f.* mildness, gentleness, indulgence
mante *f.* mantle; mantis
manteau *m.* coat, overcoat, cloak; mantle
mantelet *m.* short coat
mantille *f.* mantilla
manucure *f.* manicurist
manuel *a.* manual, hand; — *m.* manual
manuellement *adv.* manually, by hand
manufacture *f.* factory; manufacture
manufacturer *vt.* to manufacture
manufacturier *a.* manufacturing; — *n.* factory owner
manumission *f.* manumission, freeing of slaves
manutention *f.* maintenance; handling; manipulation; administration; (mil.) bakery
manutentionner *vt.* to handle, manipulate
mappemonde *f.* world map (global projection)
maquereau *m.* mackerel; pimp
maquette *f.* sketch, design; model; **d'après la — de** designed by
maquignon *m.* horse dealer; (fig.) go-between
maquignonner *vt.* to deal underhandedly
maquillage *m.* make-up
maquiller *vt.* to put on make-up
maquilleur *m.* make-up man
maquis *m.* underbrush, scrub; (pol.) underground unit *or* movement
maquisard *m.* member of the underground
maraîcher *m.* truck farmer; — *a.* of truck farming
marais *m.* marsh, bog, swamp; truck-garden land; — **salants** saltern, salt bed
marasme *m.* apathy; atrophy
marasque *f.* maraschino cherry
marasquin *m.* maraschino liqueur
marâtre *f.* stepmother; cruel mother
maraud *a.* rascal
maraude *f.* marauding; petty thievery from gardens; **taxi en —** cruising taxi
marauder *vi.* to maraud; prowl
maraudeur *m.* marauder
marbre *m.* marble
marbré *a.* marbled, veined
marbrer *vt.* to marble, vein
marbrière *f.* marble quarry
marc *m.* marc, residue; dregs (from wine making); — **de café** coffee grounds; **eau-de-vie de —** brandy made from marc
marcassin *m.* young boar
marchand *m.* merchant, shopkeeper, dealer
marchander *vt. & vi.* to bargain, haggle
marchandise *f.* merchandise

marche *f.* step; march; functioning, running (machine); (mus.) march (fig.) progress **se mettre en —** to start out; **— arrière** reverse motion

marché *m.* market, market place; bargain; deal; shopping, marketing; **bon —** cheapness; **— noir** black market **bon —** *a.* cheap, inexpensive, low-cost

marchepied *m.* stepladder; running board; step of a carriage; (fig.) stepping stone

marcher *vi.* to march, walk; move, function

marcheur *m.* walker

mardi *m.* Tuesday; **— gras** Shrove Tuesday

mare *f.* stagnant pond

marécage *m.* marsh, swamp

marécageux *a.* swampy

maréchal *m.* (mil.) marshal; **— des logis** master sergeant (cavalry, artillery)

maréchale *f.* marshal's wife

maréchal-ferrant *m.* blacksmith

maréchaussée *f.* constabulary, state police

marée *f.* tide; salt-water fish

marelle *f.* hopscotch

marémoteur *a.* tide-powered

mareyeur *m.* wholesale fishmonger

marge *f.* page margin; edge, rim; leeway

margelle *f.* stone rim around a well

marger *vt.* to feed into a press

Margot (*f.*) Marjorie

marguerite *f.* daisy

Marguerite (*f.*) **Margaret**

marguillier *m.* churchwarden, deacon

mari *m.* husband

mariable *a.* marriageable

mariage *m.* marriage, wedding

marial *a.* pertaining to the Virgin Mary

Marie (*f.*) Mary

marié *a.* married; **— m.** bridegroom; **— e** *f.* bride; **nouveaux — s** *m. pl.* newlyweds

marier *vt.* to marry off; wed, unite; match; **se — (avec)** to get married (to), marry

marin *a.* marine, nautical; **— m.** sailor, seaman

marine *f.* navy

mariner *vt.* to marinate, pickle

marinier *a.* marine; **— m.** sailor, bargeman

marinière *f.* middy, blouse

marionnette *f.* marionette, puppet

maritime *a.* maritime; **gare — f.** boatside railway terminal

maritorne *f.* (coll.) slut, wench

marivaudage *m.* banter, witty patter

marjolaine *f.* marjoram

mark *m.* German mark

marmaille *f.* (coll.) brood of children

marmelade *f.* marmelade, preserves

marmite *f.* pot, pan; **— norvégienne** fireless cooker; **petite — vegetable soup**

marmitée *f.* potful

marmiton *m.* kitchen boy, apprentice cook

marmonner *vt.* to mutter, mumble

marmoréen *a.* marble, marblelike

marmot *m.* lad; youngster

marmotte *f.* marmot; babushka; sample case

marmottement *m.* mumbling

marne *f.* marl; chalk and clay mixture used as fertilizer

Maroc *m.* Morocco

marocain *a.* Moroccan

maroquinerie *f.* leather goods

maroquinier *m.* dealer in Morocco leather goods

marotte *f.* whim, hobby; fool's sceptre; dummy head

maroufle *m.* rascal

marquage *m.* marking process

marque *f.* mark; trademark, brand; score; **— déposée** registered trademark

marquer *vt.* to mark, stamp, brand

marqueter *vt.* to splatter; inlay

marqueterie *f.* marquetry, inlay work

marquisat *m.* marquisate, marquis' lands

marquise *f.* marchioness; marquee

marquoir *m.* sampler; marker

marraine *f.* godmother; sponsor

marri *a.* sorry, grieved

marron *m.* chestnut; **— a.** maroon, brown; **— a. & m.** runaway, fugitive

marronnier *m.* chestnut tree

mars *m.* March

marseillais *a. & m.* of Marseilles, from Marseilles

Marseillaise *f.* Marseillaise, French national anthem

marsouin *m.* porpoise

marteau *m.* hammer; **— pneumatique** air-pressure hammer

marteau-pilon *m.* pile driver

martelage *m.* hammering operation

martèlement *m.* hammering, result of hammering

marteler *vt.* to hammer, pound; (fig.) to torment

martien *a.* martian

martinet *m.* trip hammer; cat-o'-nine-tails, lash; swift

martingale *f.* martingale; **jouer à la — to** play double or nothing

martin-pêcheur *m.* kingfisher

martre *f.* marten

martyr *m.*, **martyre** *f.* martyr

martyre *m.* martyrdom

martyriser *vt.* to martyr, martyrize

marxisme *m.* Marxism

marxiste *m. & f.* Marxist
maryland *m.* Maryland tobacco
mas *m.* farmhouse, country house (southern France)
mascarade *f.* masquerade
mascotte *f.* charm, mascot
masculin *a.* masculine, male
masculinité *f.* masculinity
masochisme *m.* masochism
masochiste *m. & f.* masochist
masque *m.* mask; masked person
masquer *vt.* to mask, conceal
massacrant *a.* disagreeable
massacrer *vt.* to massacre
massage *m.* massage
masse *f.* mass, lump; sledge hammer; mace; group; fund; en — in a body, all at once
massepain *m.* marzipan
masser *vt.* to mass; massage
massette *f.* bullrush; sledge hammer
massier *m.* mace-bearer; seargeant-at-arms
massif *a.* massive, massy; solid; argent — *m.* solid (sterling) silver
massivement *adv.* massively
massivité *f.* massiveness
massue *f.* club
mastic *m.* putty
mastiquer *vt.* to masticate; putty
mastoc *m.* heavy metal
mastodonte *m.* mastodon
mastoïdien *a.* mastoid
mastoïdite *m.* mastoid infection
masure *f.* hut; house in ruins
mat *a.* unpolished, dull; — *m.* mate (chess); être — to be in check
mât *m.* (naut.) mast
matador *m.* matador
matamore *m.* braggart
match *m.* match, game
matelas *m.* mattress
matelasser *vt.* to pad, stuff
matelassure *f.* stuffing
matelot *m.* seaman, sailor
matelote *f.* fish stew using red wine
mater *vt.* to check (chess); (fig.) to check, overcome
matérialisation *f.* materialization, realization
matérialiser *vt.* to materialize
matérialisme *m.* materialism
matérialiste *m.* materialist; — *a.* materialistic
matérialité *f.* materiality, reality
matériaux *m. pl.* materials
matériel *a.* material, corporeal; — *m.* materials; apparatus; equipment
matériellement *adv.* materially
maternel *a.* maternal; école –le *f.* kinder-

garten
maternellement *adv.* maternally
maternité *f.* maternity; lying-in hospital
mathématicien *m.* mathematician
mathématique *a.* mathematical; —s *f. pl.* mathematics
matière *f.* matter, materials, body, subject
matin *m.* morning; — *adv.* early
mâtin *m.* mastiff
matinal *a.* morning, early
mâtiné *a.* crossbred
matinée *f.* morning, forenoon; morning's occupation; afternoon performance; morning dress; faire la grasse — to sleep late
mâtiner *vt.* to crossbreed (dogs)
matines *f. pl.* Matins
matineux *a.* early-rising
matinière *a. f.* morning; étoile — morning star
matité *f.* dullness
matois *a.* sharp, cunning, foxy
matoiserie *f.* cunning
matou *m.* tomcat
matraque *f.* bludgeon
matraquer *vt.* to club, bludgeon
matriarcal *a.* matriarchal
matrice *f.* matrix; womb
matricide *m. & f.* matricide
matricule *f.* matriculation; — *m.* (auto.) license number; serial number
matriculer *vt.* to register, matriculate
matrimonial *a.* matrimonial
matrone *f.* matron
mâture *f.* (naut.) masts
maturité *f.* maturity, ripeness
matutinal *a.* morning, of the morning
maudire *vt.* to curse
maudit *a.* cursed; very bad
maugréer *vi.* to fume, be angered, grumble
Maure *m. & f.* Moor; — *a.* Moorish
mauresque *a.* Moorish
mausolée *m.* mausoleum
maussade *a.* sulky, sullen
maussaderie *f.* sullenness
mauvais *a.* bad, ill, evil; il fait — (temps) the weather is bad
mauve *f.* mallow; — *f. & a.* mauve
mauviette *f.* lark
maxillaire *a.* maxillary
maxima *a. & f.* maximum
maximal *a.* maximal
maxime *f.* maxim
maximum *m. & a.* maximum
Mayence *f.* Mainz
mazout *m.* oil residue
me *pron.* me, to me
méandre *m.* meander; winding
mécanicien *m.* mechanic, machinist;

(rail.) engineer

mécanique *f.* mechanics; — *a.* mechanical

mécaniquement *adv.* mechanically

mécanisation *f.* mechanization

mécaniser *vt.* to mechanize

mécanisme *m.* mechanism

mécène *m.* patron

méchamment *adv.* wickedly, maliciously

méchanceté *f.* wickedness, malice

méchant *a.* wicked, bad; poor, sad, worthless

mèche *f.* wick; fuse; bit, drill; cloth filter; plot; — **de cheveux** lock of hair

mécompte *m.* miscalculation, mistake

méconnaissable *a.* unrecognizable

méconnaissance *f.* lack of appreciation, lack of recognition, lack of awareness

méconnaître *vt.* not to know; disown; ignore

méconnu *a.* unappreciated, unrecognized

mécontent *a.* dissatisfied

mécontentement *m.* discontent

mécontenter *vt.* to discontent

Mecque *f.* Mecca

mécréant *m.* miscreant

médaille *f.* medal

médaillé *a.* decorated; — *m.* decorated soldier, decorated individual

médailler *vt.* to decorate

médaillier *m.* medal collection

médaillon *m.* medallion

médecin *m.* physician, doctor, medic

médecine *f.* medicine; — **aérienne** aeromedicine

médial *a.* median, middle

médian *a.* median; **-e** *f.* median

médianoche *f.* midnight supper; midnight supper following a meatless day

médiateur *m.* mediator

médiation *f.* mediation

médical *a.* medical

médicament *m.* medicine

médicamenter *vt.* to dose, administer medicine to

médicamenteux *a.* medicinal

médicastre *m.* quack doctor, charlatan

médication *f.* medication

médicinal *a.* medicinal

médiéval *a.* medieval

médiévisme *m.* Medieval studies

médiéviste *m. & f.* medievalist

médiocre *a.* mediocre, moderate; indifferent

médiocrité *f.* mediocrity

médire *vi.* to slander

médisance *f.* slander, scandal

méditatif *a.* meditative

méditation *f.* meditation

méditer *vt. & vi.* to meditate

Méditerranée, Mer — *f.* Mediterranean Sea

méditerranéen *a.* Mediterranean

médium *m.* medium, spiritualist; (mus.) middle voice

médius *m.* middle finger

médoc *m.* Medoc (a Bordeaux wine)

médullaire *a.* medullar

médulle *f.* medulla

méduse *f.* jellyfish

meeting *m.* political meeting, sports meet

méfaire *vi.* to do wrong

méfait *m.* misdeed

méfiance *f.* mistrust, distrust

méfiant *a.* distrustful, suspicious

méfier *v.*, **se —** (de) to mistrust, distrust

mégacycle *m.* megacycle

mégalithique *a.* megalithic

mégalomanie *f.* megalomania

mégaphone *m.* megaphone

mégarde *f.* inadvertency; **par —** inadvertently

mégère *f.* shrew, vixen

mégisserie *f.* leather dressing

mégissier *m.* leather dresser

mégot *m.* cigarette butt; cigar stump

méhari *m.* camel

méhariste *m.* camel-mounted soldier

meilleur *a.* better; **le —** best

méjuger *vi.* to misjudge, be mistaken

mélancolie *f.* melancholy

méloncolique *a.* melancholy

mélanésien *a. & m.* Melanesian

mélange *m.* mixture; **-s** *pl.* miscellany

mélanger *vt.* to mix

mélangeur *m.* mixer

mélasse *f.* molasses

mêlée *f.* conflict; scuffle

mêler *vt.* to mix, mingle; **se —** to mingle, blend; **se — de** to meddle in; pay attention to

méli-mélo *m.* (coll.) combination, jumble

mélinite *f.* melinite

mélisse *f.* balm

mellifue *a.* mellifluous

mélodie *f.* melody

mélodieusement *adv.* melodiously

mélodieux *a.* melodious

mélodique *a.* melodic

mélodiste *m. & f.* melodist, composer of melodies

mélodramatique *a.* melodramatic

mélodrame *m.* melodrama

mélomane *m.* music lover

melon *m.* melon; — **d'eau** watermelon; **chapeau —** *m.* derby

melonnière *f.* melon patch

membrane *f.* membrane

membre *m.* member; limb

membru *a.* long-legged, long-armed; with large arms and legs

même *pron.* same, self, itself; — *adv.* same, like; very; even, also; **de** — in the same way; **tout de** — all the same; **de** — **que** as well as; **à** — **de** in a position to

mémento *m.* notebook, memorandum book; résumé, compendium; memento

mémoire *f.* memory, remembrance; — *m.* memorandum; memorial; bill, statement; report, monograph, dissertation; —**s** *pl.* proceedings, reports; memoirs

mémorable *a.* memorable

mémorandum *m.* memorandum, notebook

mémoratif *a.* memorative

mémorial *m.* report; memorabilia

mémorialiste *m.* author of memoirs

mémorisation *f.* memorization, memorizing

menacer *vt.* to menace, threaten

ménage *m.* household; housekeeping; married couple; family; **femme de** — *f.* cleaning woman, maid

ménagement *m.* care, prudence

ménager *vt.* to spare; handle, treat with tact; humor; arrange

ménager *a.* household; sparing, prudent; **arts** —**s** *m. pl.* home economics

ménagère *f.* housekeeper

ménagerie *f.* menagerie

mendiant *m.* beggar; — *a.* begging, mendicant

mendicité *f.* begging; beggars (collectively)

mendier *vt. & vi.* to beg

meneau *m.* (arch.) mullion

menée *f.* plot, intrigue

mener *vt.* to lead, conduct, govern; steer; manage (an enterprise); treat

ménestrel *m.* minstrel

ménétrier *m.* country fiddler

meneur *m.* leader; head, chief

méningite *f.* meningitis

ménopause *m.* menopause

menotter *vt.* to handcuff

menottes *f. pl.* handcuffs

mensonge *m.* lie, falsehood

mensonger *a.* lying, deceitful

menstruation *f.* menstruation

mensualité *f.* monthly payment

mensuel *a.* monthly

mensuellement *adv.* monthly, by the month

mensurabilité *f.* mensurability

mensurer *vt.* to measure

mental *a.* mental

mentalement *adv.* mentally

mentalité *f.* mentality; state of mind

menterie *f.* lie, lying

menteur *m.* liar; — *a.* deceitful, false

menthe *f.* mint

menthol *m.* menthol

mentholé *a.* mentholated

mentionner *vt.* to mention

mentir *vi.* to lie

menton *m.* chin

mentonnet *m.* catch of a lock

mentonnière *f.* chin strap

mentor *m.* mentor, guide

menu *m.* menu; table d'hote, fixed menu; — *a.* small, thin; — **peuple** *m.* lowest class; —**s plaisirs** *m. pl.* pocket money, mad money (U.S. coll.); — *adv.* fine, in small pieces

menuet *m.* minuet

menuiser *vi.* to do woodworking

menuiserie *f.* woodwork; carpentry

menuisier *m.* carpenter, cabinet maker

méplat *a.* thicker on one side

méprendre *v.*, **se** — to be mistaken

mépris *m.* contempt, scorn, disdain

méprisable *a.* despicable, contemptible

méprise *f.* mistake

mépriser *vt.* to despise, scorn, slight

mer *f.* sea; **pleine** —, **haute** — high seas; **basse** — low tide; **d'outre** — oversea; **mal de** — *m.* seasickness

mercanti *m.* dishonest businessman

mercantile *a.* mercantile, commercial

mercenaire *m. & a.* mercenary

mercerie *f.* notions, knick-knacks

merceriser *vt.* to mercerize

merci *m.* thanks; — *f.* mercy; —! thank you; no thank you; — **bien!** thank you very much!

mercier *m.* notions salesman

mercredi *m.* Wednesday; — **des Cendres** Ash Wednesday

mercure *m.* mercury

mercuriale *f.* grain market prices; reprimand, rebuke

mercuriel *a.* mercurial

mercurique *a.* mercuric

merde *f.* excrement

mère *f.* mother

méridien *a. & n.* meridian

méridional *a.* southern

mérinos *m.* merino sheep; merino wool

merisier *m.* wild cherry tree

méritant *a.* worthy, meritorious

mérite *m.* merit

mériter *vt.* to merit, deserve; — *vi.* to be deserving

méritoire *a.* meritorious

merlan *m.* whiting

merle *m.* blackbird

merlin *m.* cleaver; club

merluche *f.* dried cod

Mérovingien *m. & a.* Merovingian

merrain *m.* stave; clapboard

merveille *f.* marvel; **à** — wonderfully

merveilleusement *adv.* marvelously, wonderfully

merveilleux a. marvellous; wonderful
mes a. pl. my
mésalliance f. misalliance
mésallier v., **se —** to marry beneath one's station
mésange f. titmouse, tomtit
mésaventure f. misadventure
mesdames f. pl. ladies, women
mesdemoiselles f. pl. young ladies; misses
mésentente f. misunderstanding
mésestime f. poor opinion of someone, lack of consideration, scorn
mésestimer vt. to underrate, scorn
mésintelligence f. incompatibility, lack of understanding
mésinterpréter vt. to misinterpret
mesmérisme m. mesmerism
mésopotamien a. & m. Mesopotamian
mesquin a. stingy, shabby, low, mean
mesquinerie f. stinginess, meanness
messager m. messenger
messagerie f. steamship line; transport line; parcel delivery service
messe f. (eccl.) Mass
messianique a. Messianic
Messie m. Messiah
messieurs m. pl. gentlemen, sirs
mesurable a. measurable
mesurage m. measuring
mesure f. measure, proportion; restraint; mean(s); **à — que** conj. in proportion as; **sur —** made to order
mesuré a. measured, cautious
mesurer vt. to measure, consider, calculate; **se — avec** to compete with; compare oneself with
métabolisme m. metabolism; **— basal** basal metabolism
métairie f. farm of a sharecropper
métal m. metal
métallifère a. metal-bearing
métallique a. metallic
métalliser vt. to plate, metallize
métallurgie f. metallurgy
métallurgique a. metallurgical
métallurgiste m. metallurgist
métamorphique a. metamorphic
métamorphisme m. metamorphism
métamorphose f. metamorphosis
métamorphoser vt. to transform, metamorphose
métaphore f. metaphor
métaphorique a. metaphorical
métaphysicien m. metaphysician
métaphysique f. metaphysics
métapsychique f. psychic research
métastase f. metastasis
métatarse m. metatarsus
métatarsien a. metatarsal
metathèse f. metathesis

métayage m. tenant farming, sharecropping
métayer m. tenant farmer, sharecropper
méteil m. mixture of wheat and rye
métempsycose f. metempsychosis, transmigration of souls
météore m. meteor
météorique a. meteoric
météoriser vt. to distend
météorisme m. gas, flatulence
météorite f. meteorite
météorologie f. meteorology
météorologique a. meteorological
météorologiste, **météorologue** m. meteorologist
métèque m. foreigner
méthane m. methane
méthode f. method, system
méthodique a. methodical
méthodisme m. methodism
méthodiste m. Methodist
méthodologie f. methodology
méthyle m. methyl
méthylène m. methylene; (com.) methyl or wood alcohol
méthylique a. methyl
méticuleusement adv. meticulously
méticuleux a. meticulous
méticulosité f. meticulousness
métier m. trade, profession; loom
métis a. & m. half-breed, half-caste
métissage m. crossbreeding
métisser vt. to cross, crossbreed
métrage m. measuring by the meter
mètre m. meter; yardstick
métrer vt. to measure out by the meter
métreur m. surveyor; measurer
métrique a. metrical; metric; **tonne —** metric ton (1000 kg.); **— f.** metrics
Métro m. Paris subway
métromanie f. mania for writing verse
métronome m. metronome
métropole f. metropolis; continental France
métropolitain a. metropolitan; **chemin de fer — m.** Paris subway
mets m. dish; cooked or prepared food
mettable a. wearable
metteur m. one who places; **— en pages** (print.) make-up man; **— en scène** (theat.) director
mettre vt. to put, place; put on; suppose; **— en drapeau** (avi.) to feather (an engine); **— en vedette** to highlight; **se — à** to begin to
meuble m. piece of furniture; **—s** pl. furniture
meubler vt. to furnish; stock
meuglement m. bellow
meugler vi. to bellow

meule *f.* millstone; haystack; round, wheel of cheese
meulière *f.* flint
meunier *m.* miller
meunière *f.* miller's wife; **à la — sautéed** in butter
meurtre *m.* murder
meurtrier *m.* murderer; **—** *a.* murderous, dangerous
meurtrière *f.* gun slit
meurtrir *vt.* to bruise
meurtrissure *f.* bruise
meute *f.* pack, band
mévendre *vt.* to sell at a loss
mévente *f.* sale at a loss
Mexicain *m. & a.* Mexican
Mexico *m.* Mexico City
Mexique *m.* Mexico
miasme *m.* miasma, evil odor
miaulement *m.* mew, meow
miauler *vi.* to mew, meow
miche *f.* round loaf of bread
Michel (*m.*) Michael
micheline *f.* (rail.) diesel car *or* train
**mi-chemin, à — ** *adv.* halfway, at the halfway point
micro *m.* microphone
microbiologie *f.* microbiology
microcircuit *m.* microcircuit
microcosme *m.* microcosm
microfilm *m.* microfilm
microfilmer *vt.* to microfilm
micrographie *f.* micrography
micromètre *m.* micrometer
micron *m.* micron, 1-millionth meter
micro-organisme *m.* micro-organism
microphone *m.* microphone
microphotographie *f.* microphotography
microphysique *f.* microphysics
microscope *m.* microscope; **— électronique** electron microscope
microscopique *a.* microscopic
microsillon *m.* record microgroove; long-playing record
midi *m.* noon; south
midinette *f.* seamstress, shop girl
mie *f.* inside part of bread; **pain de — ** *m.* sandwich bread, American-style bread; **ma — ** (coll.) my dear, my darling; **— ** *adv.* not at all
miel *m.* honey
mielleux *a.* honeyed, honey-like
mien *pron.*, **le —**, **la –ne** mine
miette *f.* bread crumb, bit
mieux *adv.* better, rather; **le — ** best; **de — en — ** better and better; **aimer — ** prefer
mièvre *a.* affected; roguish
mièvrerie *f.* affectedness; roguishness
mignard *a.* nice, delicate, sweet

mignarder *vt.* to indulge, coddle; **be overnice to**
mignardise *f.* delicacy, daintiness
mignon *a.* delicate, cute, nice, slight; **—** *m.* favorite
mignonnerie *f.* niceness; cuteness; delicateness
migraine *f.* headache
migraineux *a.* migraine
migrateur *a.* migrating
migratoire *a.* migratory
mijaurée *f.* finicky woman; **faire la — to** be finicky
mijoter *vi.* to simmer
mil *a.* thousand; **—** *m.* millet
milady *f.* lady, wife of a lord; **my lady** (salutation)
milan *m.* kite (bird)
milanais *a.* of Milan, from Milan
milice *f.* militia
milicien *m.* militiaman
milieu *m.* middle; environment; area; **au — de** in the middle of; **au beau — in the** very middle
militaire *m.* soldier; **—** *a.* military
militariser *vt.* to militarize
militarisme *m.* militarism
militariste *m. & f.* militarist
militer *vi.* to militate, work, fight
mille *m.* mile; **—** *a.* thousand
mille-feuille *f.* napoleon (pastry); milfoil
millénaire *m.* 1000 years; 1000th anniversary; **—** *a.* 1000-year-old
millésime *m.* date
milliaire *a.*, **pierre —** *f.* milestone
milliard *m.* billion
milliardaire *m. & f. & a.* billionaire
millibar *m.* millibar
millième *m. & a.* thousandth
millier *m.* about a thousand; **–s** *pl.* thousands
milligramme *m.* milligram
millimètre *m.* millimeter
millionnaire *m. & f. & a.* millionnaire
milord *m.* lord; my lord (salutation)
mime *m.* mime, pantomime
mimer *vt. & vi.* to mime, mimic
mimi *m.* kitty, pussycat (baby talk); darling
mimique *a.* mimetic; **—** *f.* mimicry; pantomime
mimodrame *m.* pantomime play
mimosa *m.* acacia
minable *a.* pitiful, shabby
minaret *m.* minaret
minauder *vi.* to mince, be or act affected, smirk
minauderie *f.* mincing manner; affectedness
minaudier *a.* mincing

mince *a.* thin, slender
minceur *f.* thinness, slenderness, scantiness
mine *f.* look, appearance; mine, excavation; mina (Greek coin); pencil lead;
(mil.) mine; **avoir bonne (mauvaise)** —
to look well (bad)
miner *vt.* to mine; wear away, undermine
minerai *m.* ore
minéral *a. & m.* mineral
minéralisation *f.* mineralization
minéraliser *vt.* to mineralize
minéralogie *f.* mineralogy
minéralogique *a.* mineralogical
minéralogiste *m.* mineralogist
minestrone *m.* minestrone soup
minet *m.*, **minette** *f.* (coll.) kitty, pussy
mineur *m.* minor; miner; — **e** *f.* minor
premise
miniature *f.* miniature
miniaturer *vt.* to paint in miniature
minier *a.* mining
minimal *a.* minimal
minime *a.* insignificant, trifling
minimiser *vt.* to minimize
minimum *m.* minimum
ministère *m.* ministry, office; cabinet
ministériel *a.* of the ministry, of the cabinet, pro-government
ministre *m.* minister, secretary (government)
minium *m.* red lead
minoritaire *a.* minority, belonging to the
minority
minorité *f.* minority
Minorque *f.* Minorca
minoterie *f.* flour milling
minotier *m.* miller
minuit *m.* midnight
minuscule *a.* tiny; — *f.* lower-case letter
minute *f.* minute, moment; rough draft;
original copy
minuter *vt.* to take minutes; limit
minuterie *f.* (elec.) time-switch (which
stays on for only a short time)
minutie *f.* minutia; minuteness
minutieusement *adv.* minutely
minutieux *a.* minute; detailed
mioche *m. & f.* (coll.) brat; young child
mi-parti *a.* half
mi-partition *f.* dividing in half
mirabelle *f.* small yellow plum; mirabelle
liqueur
miracle *m.* miracle
miraculeusement *adv.* miraculously
miraculeux *a.* miraculous
mirador *m.* watchtower
mirage *m.* mirage
mire *f.* gun sight; aim
mirer *vt. & vi.* to aim at; **se** — to look at

oneself
mirliton *m.* reed flute; **vers de** — doggerel
mirmillon *m.* gladiator
miroir *m.* mirror, looking glass
miroitant *a.* reflecting, sparkling
miroitement *m.* mirroring, reflection,
sparkling
miroiter *vi.* to shine, glisten
miroitier *m.* dealer in mirrors
miroton *m.* onion stew
misaine *f.* (naut.) foremast
misanthrope *m. & f.* misanthrope
misanthropie *f.* misanthropy
miscellanées *f. pl.* miscellanea, miscellany
miscible *a.* miscible, which can be mixed
mise *f.* putting, placing; dress, clothing,
appearance; game stake; investment;
bid; — **en plis** finger wave; — **en scène**
(theat.) direction
miser *vt.* to bet; bid
misérable *a.* miserable; wretched; wicked;
poverty-stricken
misérablement *adv.* miserably, wretch-
edly
misère *f.* misery, poverty
miséreux *m.* pauper
miséricorde *f.* mercy, pardon
miséricordieux *a.* merciful
misogyne *m.* mysogynist
missel *m.* missal
missionnaire *m.* missionary
missive *f.* missive, letter
mistral *m.* cold north wind of Provence
mitaine *f.* mitten, mitt
mite *f.* clothes moth
mité *a.* moth-eaten
miteux *a.* pitiful
mitigation *f.* mitigation
mitiger *vt.* to mitigate, soften
mitonner *vi.* to simmer; — *vt.* to coddle
mitoyen *a.* intermediate, joint, dividing
(line)
mitraille *f.* (mil.) grapeshot, canister shot
mitrailler *vt.* to machine gun
mitraillette *f.* tommy gun
mitrailleur *m.* machine gunner
mitrailleuse *f.* machine gun
mitre *m.* miter
mitré *a.* mitered
mitron *m.* baker's boy
mi-voix, à — *adv.* in a low voice
mixte *a.* mixed; **école** — *f.* coeducational
school
mixtion *f.* mixture
mixtionner *vt.* to mix
mnémonique *a.* mnemonic
mnémotechnie *f.* memory training
mobile *m.* spring; motive; — *a.* movable;
quick
mobilier *m.* furniture

mobilisation *f.* mobilization, mobilizing
mobiliser *vt.* to mobilize
mobilité *f.* mobility
mocassin *m.* moccasin
moche *f.* skein, hank
modal *a.* (gram.) modal
modalité *f.* modality
mode *m.* (gram.) mood; mode; — *f.* fashion, custom, way; **–s** *pl.* millinery; **à la —** in fashion; **à la — de . . . in the . . .** fashion
modelage *m.* modelling
modèle *m.* model
modeler *vt.* to model
modeleur *m.* modeller
modéliste *m. & f.* model designer
modérantisme *m.* (pol.) moderation in political matters
modérantiste *m. & f.* (pol.) moderate
modérateur *m.* moderator; governor
modération *f.* moderation
modéré *a.* moderate
modérer *vt.* to moderate, regulate, reduce
moderne *a.* modern
modernisation *f.* modernization
moderniser *vt.* to modernize
modernisme *m.*, **modernité** *f.* modernity
moderniste *m. & f.* modernist
modeste *a.* modest
modestement *adv.* modestly
modestie *f.* modesty
modicité *f.* smallness, lowness
modifiable *a.* modifiable
modification *f.* modification
modifier *vt.* to modify
modique *a.* moderate, small in importance, low in price
modiste *f.* milliner, modiste
module *m.* modulus; module; diameter of coins; thickness of bells
moduler *vt. & vi.* to modulate
moelle *f.* marrow; pith
moelleux *a.* pithy; soft, mellow
moellon *m.* small stone used in walls
mœurs *f. pl.* manners, morals, customs, mores
mofette *f.* poison gas
mogol *m.* mogul
moi *pron.* I, me; — *m.* self, ego
moignon *m.* stump, stub
moindre *a.* less, lesser; **le —** least, slightest
moine *m.* monk, friar; warming pan
moineau *m.* sparrow
moins *adv.* less; minus; **au —, pour le —, du —** at least; **à — que** *conj.* unless; **— le —** least; **à — at** a lower price; *prep.* minus, less
moins-perçu *m.* underpayment
moins-value *f.* depreciation, loss of value
moire *f.* watered silk, moire

moirer *vt.* to water silk
mois *m.* month; monthly salary, monthly payment
moïse *m.* cradle, baby basket
Moïse (*m.*) Moses
moise *f.* tie beam, brace
moisi *a.* moldy, musty; — *m.* mustiness
moisir *vt. & vi.* to mildew
moisissure *f.* mold, mildew
moisson *f.* harvest
moissonnage *m.* reaping, harvesting
moissonner *vt.* to reap, harvest
moissonneur *m.*, **moissonneuse** *f.* reaper; (person)
moisonneuse *f.* reaper, harvester (machine)
moite *a.* moist, clammy
moiteur *f.* moistness
moitié *f. & a.* half; **à — prix** *adv.* half-price
moitir *vt.* to moisten
moka *m.* mocha coffee; mocha cake
mol *a.* soft
molaire *a. & n.* molar
môle *m.* mole, pier
moléculaire *a.* molecular
molécule *f.* molecule
moleskine *f.* leatherette
molestation *f.* molesting, molestation
molester *vt.* to molest
molette *f.* roller; serrated roller; rowel; trimming tool; edging tool; **clé à — f.** adjustable wrench
mollesse *a.* apathetic, flabby
mollesse *f.* softness; flabbiness
mollet *m.* calf of the leg; — *a.* soft; **œuf — m.** soft-boiled egg
molletière *f.* legging
molleton *m.* flannel
mollification *f.* mollification, mollifying
mollir *vt. & vi.* to soften, grow soft; give way, slacken
mollusque *m.* mollusk
molosse *m.* mastiff, watchdog
molybdène *m.* molybdenum
momentané *a.* momentary
momentanément *adv.* momentarily
momie *f.* mummy
momification *f.* mummification
momifier *vt.* to mummify
mon *a. m.* my
monacal *a.* monkish
monarchie *f.* monarchy
monarchique *a.* monarchical
monarchisme *m.* monarchism
monarchiste *m. & f. & a.* monarchist
monarque *m.* monarch
monastère *m.* monastery; convent
monastique *a.* monastic
monceau *m.* heap, pile

mondain *a.* worldly; mundane; society; — *m.* society person

mondanité *f.* mundaneness, mundanity, worldliness; **-s** *pl.* social events (newspaper)

monde *m.* world; society; people; **tout le** — everybody

monder *vt.* to clean; husk

mondial *a.* worldwide

monégasque *a.* from Monaco

monétaire *a.* monetary

Mongol *m. & a.* Mongol; **purée -e** *f.* tomato and pea soup

Mongolie *f.* Mongolia

mongolien *a.* (med.) Mongolian

Mongoloïde *a.* Mongoloid

moniteur *m.* monitor

monnaie *f.* money, coin; mint; change; — **légale** legal tender

monnayage *m.* coinage, minting

monnayer *vt.* to coin, mint

monnayeur *m.* coiner, minter

monobloc *a.* in one piece

monochrome *a.* monochromatic

monoculture *f.* one-crop farming

monodie *f.* (mus.) unaccompanied solo

monogame *a.* monogamous

monogamie *f.* monogamy

monogramme *m.* monogram

monographie *f.* monograph

monolithe *a.* monolithic

monologue *m.* monologue

monologuer *vi.* to talk to oneself; soliloquize

monomane, monomaniaque *m. & f.* monomaniac

monomanie *f.* monomania

monôme *m.* student parade, demonstration, snake dance; (math.) monomial

monophasé *a.* (elec.) single-phase

monoplace *a.* in one place; **voiture —** *f.* one-seater

monoplan *m.* monoplane

monopole *m.* monopoly

monopolisation *f.* monopolization

monopoliser *vt.* to monopolize

monosyllabe *m.* monosyllable

monosyllabique *a.* monosyllabic

monothéisme *m.* monotheism

monothéiste *m. & f.* monotheist; — *a.* monotheistic

monotone *a.* monotonous

monotonie *f.* monotony

monotype *f.* (print.) typesetting machine

monovalent *a.* univalent

monseigneur *m.* highness; monsignor; lock pick

monsieur *m.* sir, gentleman; Mister, Mr.

monstre *m.* monster

monstrueux *a.* monstrous

monstruosité *f.* monstruousness; monstrosity

mont *m.* mount, mountain

montage *m.* carrying up; layout; (elec.) wiring; editing (movie film)

montagnard *m.* mountaineer

montagne *f.* mountain

Montagnes Rocheuses *f. pl.* Rocky Mountains

montagneux *a.* mountainous

montant *m.* amount, sum; goal post; upright; side piece of a ladder; odor, taste; — *a.* rising, uphill; high-cut (dress)

mont-de-piété *m.* municipal pawn shop

monte-charge *m.* freight elevator

montée *f.* rise, ascent

monte-plats *m.* dumb waiter

monter *vt. & vi.* to go up, climb, rise; carry up, take up; mount, sit on a horse; to set up; arouse, excite

monteur *m.* mounter

montgolfière *f.* hot-air balloon

monticule *m.* hillock

montmorency *f.* variety of sour cherry

montoir *m.* stepping-stone for mounting a horse

montrable *a.* showable

montre *f.* watch; display, shop window

montre-bracelet *m.* wristwatch

montrer *vt.* to show, exhibit

montreur *m.* displayer; showman

montueux *a.* hilly

monture *f.* mount; setting; frame

monument *m.* monument; curiosity, sight; **visiter les -s** to sightsee

moquer *v.*, **se —** **de** to mock, laugh at; not to care

moquerie *f.* mockery, derision

moquette *f.* velvet carpet, carpeting

moqueur *a.* mocking; — *m.* mocker

moral *a.* moral, ethical; — *m.* state of mind; morale

morale *f.* morals, ethics; morale

moralement *adv.* morally

moralisateur *a.* moralizing

moraliser *vi. & vt.* to moralize; lecture

moraliste *m. & f.* moralist

moralité *f.* morality, morals; moral; morality play

morasse *f.* (print.) final proof

moratoire *m.* moratorium

morave *a. & n.* Moravian

morbide *a.* morbid

morbidesse *f.* morbidezza; suppleness, delicacy of skin (fine arts)

morbidité *f.* morbidness

morceau *m.* bit, piece

morceler *vt.* to break, divide into pieces

morcellement *m.* fragmentation, breaking-up

mordacité *f.* bitterness; corrosiveness
mordancer *vt.* to size, varnish
mordant *a.* biting; corrosive; — *m.* sizing, varnish; bitterness
mordicus *adv.* stoutly, tenaciously
mordiller *vt.* to nibble
mordorer *vt.* to give a russet color to
mordre *vt.* to bite, corrode; — *vi.* to engage, take hold
morfondre *vt.* to chill, freeze, benumb
morganatique *a.* morganatic
morgue *f.* haughtiness; morgue
moribond *a.* moribund
moricaud *a.* black, dark-skinned
morigéner *vt.* to reprimand
morille *f.* morel (edible mushroom)
morne *a.* gloomy, dull, dejected
morosité *f.* moroseness
morphine *f.* morphine
morphinomane *m. & f.* morphine addict
morphologie *f.* morphology
morphologique *a.* morphological
mors *m.* curb, bit
morse *m.* walrus
morsure *f.* bite
mort *f.* death; — *a. & m.* dead, deceased; dummy (at cards)
mortadelle *f.* large Italian sausage
mortaise *f.* dovetail
mortaiser *vt.* to dovetail
mortalité *f.* mortality; death rate
mort-aux-rats *f.* rat poison
mort-bois *m.* deadwood
mortel *a.* mortal, fatal
mortellement *adv.* mortally
morte-saison *f.* off-season
mortier *m.* mortar
mortifère *a.* death-dealing
mortifiant *a.* mortifying
mortification *f.* mortification
mortifier *vt.* to mortify
mort-né *a.* stillborn
mortuaire *a.* mortuary
morue *f.* codfish
morve *f.* nasal discharge; glanders
morveux *a.* one with a clogged or running nose; sick with glanders; — *m.* brat
mosaïque *f.* mosaic
mosaïquer *vt.* to decorate with mosaic tile
Moscou *m.* Moscow
Moscovite *m. & f. & a.* Muscovite
mosquée *f.* mosque
mot *m.* word; **bon** — witticism; **en un** — *a.* briefly
moteur *m.* motor, engine; moving force; (fig.) instigator; — *a.* motivating
moteur-fusée *m.* rocket motor
motif *m.* motive, reason, motif, theme
motion *f.* parliamentary motion
motivation *f.* motivation

motiver *vt.* to motivate, justify
motoculture *f.* mechanized farming
motocyclette *f.* motorcycle
motocycliste *m. & f.* motorcyclist
motorcade *f.* autocade, motorcade
motorisation *f.* motorization
motoriser *vt.* to motorize
mots-croisiste *m. & f.* crossword-puzzle fan
motte *f.* clod; mound; butter pat
motus! *interj.* quiet!
mou, (mol, molle) *a.* soft, mellow; weak; (fig.) effeminate; limp; muggy; — *m.* edible animal lungs
mouche *f.* fly; speck, stain; bull's-eye; beauty spot; vandyke beard; secret policeman; — **à miel** bee
moucher *vt.* to wipe the nose; **se** — **to** blow one's nose
moucheron *m.* fly
moucheter *vt.* to spot; polka dot
mouchette *f.* candle snuffer
moucheture *f.* spot; polka dot
mouchoir *m.* handkerchief
mouchure *f.* nasal mucus
moudre *vt.* to grind, mill
moue *f.* pout; **faire la** — to pout
mouette *f.* sea gull
mouffette *f.* skunk
moufle *f.* mitten; block and tackle; — *m.* kiln, furnace
mouflon *m.* wild sheep, moufflon
mouillage *m.* wetting; watering, adulteration with water; (naut.) anchor, anchorage
mouiller *vt.* to wet, soak; water, adulterate; (naut.) heave (anchor); lay (mine)
mouilleur *m.* moistener; — **de mines** minelayer
mouillure *f.* wetting; water spot; wet spot
moulage *m.* molding, casting; grinding
moule *m.* mold, cast; — *f.* mussel
moulé *a.* well-molded, well-made; tight-fitting; — *m.* printed letter, printing
mouler *vt.* to mold, cast
mouleur *m.* molder, caster
moulin *m.* mill; — **à vent** windmill; — **à café** coffee grinder
moulinet *m.* wheel; paddle wheel; reel; turnstile; winch
moulu *a.* ground, powdered
moulure *f.* molding
mourant *a.* dying; fading
mourir *vi.* to die; **se** — **to be dying**
mousquet *m.* musket
mousquetaire *m.* musketeer
mousqueton *m.* carbine
mousse *f.* (bot.) moss; foam, lather; whipped dessert; — *m.* cabin boy; — *a.*

dull, calm

mousseline *f.* muslin; **pommes —** mashed potatoes

mousser *vi.* to foam, lather, whip; sparkle

mousseux *a.* mossy; foamy; **—** *m.* sparkling wine

moussoir *m.* beater, whipper, eggbeater

mousson *f.* monsoon

moussu *a.* mossy

moustache *f.* mustache

moustiquaire *f.* mosquito net

moustique *m.* mosquito

moût *m.* grape juice, unfermented fruit juice

moutarde *f.* mustard

moutardier *m.* mustard pot; mustard maker

mouton *m.* sheep; mutton; sheepskin; pile driver, rammer, **-s** *pl.* (naut.) whitecaps

moutonné *a.* fleecy; frizzy

moutonner *vt.* to curl; **—** *vi.* to form whitecaps

moutonneux *a.* fleecy; (naut.) whitecapped

moutonnier *a.* sheeplike

mouture *f.* grinding, milling; mixture of wheat, rye, barley

mouvant *a.* moving; shifting; **sable —** *m.* quicksand

mouvement *m.* motion, movement

mouvementé *a.* agitated, animated; hilly, undulating

mouvoir *vt.* to move, propel

moyen *m.* means, way; **au — de** by means of; **—** *a.* middle, intermediate; average, mean; **le — âge** Middle Ages

moyenâgeux *a.* medieval

moyennant *prep.* on condition that, in return for; by means of

moyenne *f.* average

moyennement *adv.* to an average degree

moyeu *m.* hub

muable *a.* mutable, changeable

mucilagineux *a.* mucilaginous

mucosité *f.* mucosity, mucus

mue *f.* moulting, moulting time; adolescent change of voice

muer *vi.* to moult; have an adolescent change of voice

muet *a.* mute, dumb, speechless; **—** *m.* mute

mufle *m.* snout; (fig.) cad, coarse individual

muflerie *f.* coarseness

muge *m.* mullet

mugir *vi.* to bellow, low (cattle); roar; howl (wind)

mugissant *a.* roaring

mugissement *m.* roaring, bellowing; of cattle; howling of wind

muguet *m.* lily of the valley

muid *m.* hogshead

mulâtre *a. & n.* mulatto

mule *f.* mule; backless slipper

mulet *m.* mule; mullet

muletier *m.* mule driver

mulot *m.* field mouse

mulsion *f.* milking

multicolore *a.* multicolored

multiforme *a.* multiform, many-formed

multimillionnaire *m. & f.* multimillionaire

multiplicande *m.* multiplicand

multiplicateur *m.* multiplier

multiplication *f.* multiplication

multiplicité *f.* multiplicity

multiplier *vt.* to multiply

multitude *f.* multitude

municipalité *f.* municipality

munificence *f.* munificence

munificent *a.* munificent

munir *vt.* to provide, furnish; **se — de to** procure, provide oneself with

munitionnaire *m.* commissary

munitions *f. pl.* munitions, stores, supplies

muqueuse *f.* mucous membrane

muqueux *a.* mucous

mur *m.* wall

mûr *a.* ripe, mature

murage *m.* walling, walling up

muraille *f.* outer wall

mural *a.* mural, wall

mûre *f.* blackberry

murène *f.* marine eel

murer *vt.* to wall in, wall up, block up

muret *m.*, **murette** *f.* small wall

muriatique *a.* muriatic

mûrier *m.* blackberry bush; mulberry tree

mûrir *vt. & vi.* to ripen, mature

murmurant *a.* murmuring

murmure *m.* murmur

murmurer *vi.* to murmur; grumble

musaraigne *f.* shrew mouse

musard *a.* dawdling; **—** *m.* dawdler

musarder *vt.* to dawdle

musc *m.* musk

muscade *f.* nutmeg; **fleur de —** *f.* mace

muscadier *m.* nutmeg tree

muscat *m.* muscatel wine, muscatel grape

muscle *m.* muscle

musclé *a.* muscled

muscler *vt.* to develop the muscles of

musculaire *a.* muscular

musculature *f.* musculature

musculeux *a.* muscular, brawny

muse *f.* muse

museau *m.* animal snout, **muzzle**

musée *m.* museum

museler *vt.* to muzzle

muselière *f.* muzzle
muser *vi.* to loiter, loaf
musette *f.* bagpipe; bag, musette bag; **bal** — dance, small dance, country dance, dance to accordion
muséum *m.* museum, natural history museum
music-hall *m.* vaudeville theater
musicien *m.* musician
musique *f.* music; band
musqué *a.* musk-scented; **rat** — *m.* muskrat
Musulman *m.* & *a.* Moslem
mutabilité *f.* mutability
mutable *a.* mutable
mutation *f.* mutation
muter *vt.* to transfer; transform
mutilateur *m.* mutilator
mutilation *f.* mutilation
mutiler *vt.* to mutilate
mutin *a.* disobedient, unruly; mutinous
mutiner *v.*, **se** — to mutiny; be disobedient
mutinerie *f.* mutiny
mutisme *m.* muteness
mutualité *f.* mutualness; mutuality; mutual-aid society
mutuel *a.* mutual
mutuellement *adv.* mutually
myope *a.* nearsighted
myopie *f.* myopia; near-sightedness
myosotis *m.* forget-me-not
myriade *f.* myriad
myriapode *m.* myriapod, millipede
myrrhe *f.* myrrh
myrte *m.* myrtle
myrtille *f.* blueberry
mystère *m.* mystery; mystery play
mystérieusement *adv.* mysteriously
mystérieux *a.* mysterious
mysticisme *m.* mysticism
mystificateur *a.* mystifying; — *m.* mystifier
mystification *f.* mystification, hoax
mystifier *vt.* to mystify, hoax
mystique *a.* & *n.* mystic
mythe *m.* myth
mythique *a.* mythical
mythologie *f.* mythology
mythologique *a.* mythological

N

nabab *m.* nabob
nabot *m.* small person
nacelle *f.* small boat; (avi.) nacelle
nacre *f.* mother-of-pearl
nacré *a.* pearl-colored, pearly
naevus *m.* birthmark
nage *f.* swimming; rowing; à la — by swimming; être **tout en** — to be soaking with perspiration
nageoire *f.* fin of a fish
nager *vi.* to swim, float; row
naguère *adv.* a short time ago
naïade *f.* naiad, water nymph
naïf *a.* artless, ingenuous, innocent, inexperienced
nain *m.* & *a.* dwarf
naissance *f.* birth, origin, beginning; **acte de** — *m.* birth certificate
naissant *a.* dawning; incipient
naître *vi.* to be born; arise, come about
naïvement *adv.* naively
naïveté *f.* artlessness, ingenuousness
naja *m.* cobra
nanan *m.* goodies (baby talk); delight; something exquisite
nantir *vt.* to give as security, pledge; provide
nantissement *m.* pledge, security
naphte *m.* naphtha
napoléon *m.* gold 20-franc piece
napoléonien *a.* Napoleonic
napolitain *a.* & *m.* Neapolitan
nappe *f.* tablecloth, cloth, cover; sheet
napper *vt.* to cover with a cloth
napperon *m.* tea-table cloth; **petit** — doily
narcisse *m.* narcissus
narcose *f.* narcosis
narcotique *a.* & *m.* narcotic
narguer *vt.* to harrass; flout; jeer at
narguilé *m.* Turkish water pipe
narine *f.* nostril
narquois *a.* sly, cunning; mocking
narrateur *m.* narrator
narratif *a.* narrative
narration *f.* narration, narrative
narrer *vt.* to narrate, tell of
narthex *m.* narthex, vestibule
nasal *a.* nasal; —e *f.* nasal consonant
nasaliser *vt.* to nasalize
nasarde *f.* blow on the nose; affront
naseau *m.* animal nostril
nasillard *a.* nasal
nasiller *vi.* to speak through the nose
nasonnement *m.* nasal voice, nasal speech
nasse *f.* fish trap
natal *a.* native; **jour** — *m.* birthday; **pays** — *m.* native country
natalité *f.* birth rate
natation *f.* swimming
natatoire *a.* pertaining to swimming
natif *a.* native; natural
national *a.* national
nationaliser *vt.* to nationalize
nationaliste *m.* & *f.* nationalist; — *a.* nationalistic
nationalité *f.* nationality
nativement *adv.* natively, by nature

nativité *f.* nativity; (eccl.) celebration of the birthday of a saint
Nativité *f.* Christmas
natte *f.* mat; braid
natter *vt.* to weave, braid
naturalisation *f.* naturalization
naturaliser *vt.* to naturalize
naturaliste *m.* naturalist; naturalist author; — *a.* naturalistic
nature *f.* nature; character; kind; **d'après** — from nature, from life; **contre** — unnatural; — **morte** still life; **café** — *m.* black coffee
naturel *m.* nature, disposition; — *a.* natural; **au** — plain; **enfant** — illegitimate child
naturellement *adv.* naturally
naufrage *m.* shipwreck
naufrager *vi.* to be wrecked, sink
nauséabond *a.* nauseating
nausée *f.* nausea
nauséeux *a.* nauseous
nautique *a.* nautical, aquatic
navarin *m.* mutton stew prepared with turnips and potatoes
navet *m.* turnip
navette *f.* shuttle; **faire la** — to shuttle back and forth; — **hélicoptère** helibus
navigabilité *f.* navigability
navigable *a.* navigable
navigateur *m.* navigator
navigation *f.* navigation
naviguer *vi. & vt.* to navigate, sail
navire *m.* ship, vessel
navrant *a.* heartrending
navrer *vt.* to grieve, break the heart of
ne *adv.* no, not; — . . . . **pas** not
né *a.* born
néanmoins *conj.* nevertheless, still, yet
néant *m.* nothingness, nothing
nébuleux *a.* nebulous, cloudy
nébulosité *f.* nebulousness, nebulosity
nécessaire *a.* necessary; — *m.* necessities of life; kit, set
nécessairement *adv.* necessarily
nécessité *f.* necessity
nécessiter *vt.* to necessitate
nécessiteux *a.* needy
nécrologie *f.* necrology, obituary
nécromancie *f.* necromancy
nécromancien *m.* necromancer
nécrose *f.* necrosis
nectar *m.* nectar
néerlandais *a.* Dutch
nef *f.* nave of a church
néfaste *a.* ill-fated, fatal, harmful
négatif *a.* negative; — *m.* (phot.) negative
négative *f.* negative side (debating)
négation *f.* negation
négativement *adv.* negatively

négligé *a.* neglected, careless, informal
négligeable *a.* negligeable
négligemment *adv.* negligently, indifferently
négligence *f.* negligence
négligent *a.* negligent; indifferent
négliger *vt.* to neglect
négoce *m.* negotiation
négociable *a.* negotiable
négociant *m.* merchant, dealer, trader
négociateur *m.* negotiator
négociation *f.* nogotiation
négocier *vt. & vi.* to negotiate; trade; deal
nègre, négresse *n. & a.* Negro; ghost writer; **petit** — *m.* pidgin French
négrier *m.* slave ship; slave dealer
négroïde *a.* negroid
neige *f.* snow; **battre en** — to beat stiff
neiger *vt.* to snow
neigeux *a.* snowy
ne-m'oubliez-pas *m.* forget-me-not
nénuphar *m.* water lily
Néo-caledonien *m. & a.* New Caledonian
néolithique *a.* neolithic
néon *m.* neon
neophyte *m. & f.* neophyte
Néo-zélandais *m.* New Zealander; — *a.* of New Zealand
néphrite *f.* nephritis
néo-platonicien *a.* neo-Platonic; — *m.* neo-Platonist
néo-platonisme *m.* neo-Platonism
népotisme *m.* nepotism
neptunien *a.* Neptunian
néréide *f.* Nereid
nerf *m.* nerve; sinew, (coll.) tendon; leaf vein
nerveusement *adv.* nervously
nerveux *a.* nervous, high-strung; sinewy, vigorous
nervosité *f.* nervousness
nervure *f.* leaf rib; nervure, cording of a book binding
net *a.* clean; clear, clear-cut; net; — *adv.* flatly, outright; **s'arrêter** — to stop dead; — *m.*, **mettre au** — to put in final form
nettement *adv.* cleanly; clearly; flatly
netteté *f.* cleanness, clearness; neatness
nettoiement, nettoyage *m.* cleaning, cleansing; **nettoyage au sec** dry-cleaning
nettoyer *vt.* to clean, cleanse, scour
nettoyeur *m.* cleaner
neuf *a.* nine; new, fresh
neurasthénie *f.* neurasthenia
neurasthénique *a.* neurasthenic
neurologie *f.* neurology
neurologue, neurologiste *m.* neurologist
neurone *m.* neuron

neutralisation *f.* neutralization
neutraliser *vt.* to neutralize
neutraliste *m. & f.* neutralist
neutralité *f.* neutrality
neutre *a.* neuter; neutral
neutron *m.* neutron
neuvaine *f.* novena
neuvième *a.* ninth
neveu *m.* nephew
névralgie *f.* neuralgia
névrite *f.* neuritis
névropathie *f.* nervous disorders
névrose *f.* neurosis
névrosé *a.* neurotic
nez *m.* nose; cape of land; prow; — à —
   face to face; **piquer du** — to nose-dive
ni *conj.* neither, nor
niable *a.* deniable
niais *a.* silly; foolish
niaiserie *f.* silliness
niche *f.* prank, trick; niche; — à chien
   doghouse
nichée *f.* nestful
nicher *vi.* to nestle
nickel *m.* nickel
nickelage *m.* nickel-plating
nickeler *vt.* to nickel-plate
nicotine *f.* nicotine
nid *m.* nest
nidifier *vi.* to make a nest
nièce *f.* niece
nielle *m.* enamel inlay; cereal blight;
   cockleweed
nier *vt.* to deny
nigaud *a.* simple; — *m.* simpleton, idiot
nigauderie *f.* stupidity
nihilisme *m.* nihilism
nihiliste *m. & f.* nihilist; — *a.* nihilistic
Nil *m.* Nile
nimbe *f.* halo, nimbus
nimber *vt.* to halo
nimbus *m.* numbus cloud
nippes *f. pl.* things, old clothes, possessions
nippon *a.* Nipponese
nique *f.* gesture of scorn; **faire la** — à to
   make fun of, scorn
nirvanâ *m.* nirvana
nitouche *f.* apparently *or* falsely innocent
   person
nitrate *m.* nitrate
nitre *m.* saltpeter, niter
nitreux *a.* nitrous
nitrique *a.* nitric
nitrite *m.* nitrite
nitroglycérine *f.* nitroglycerin
niveau *m.* level; — **de vie** standard of
   living; **passage à** — *m.* level crossing
nivelage *m.* leveling
niveler *vt.* to level

nivellement *m.* leveling
nobiliaire *a.* of the nobility
noble *a. & m. & f.* noble
noblesse *f.* nobility
noce, noces *f.* wedding; **faire la** — (coll.)
   to be living it up, living riotously
nocif *a.* harmful
nocivité *f.* noxiousness, harmfulness
noctambule *m. & f.* sleepwalker; person
   active at night
nocturne *a.* nocturnal
nocuité *f.* noxiousness
nodal *a.* nodal
nodosité *f.* node; knot
nodule *m.* nodule
Noé (*m.*) Noah
Noël *m.* Christmas; **veille de —** *f.* Christmas Eve
nœud *m.* knot
noir *a.* black, dark
noirâtre *a.* blackish
noiraud *a.* black-haired, dark
noirceur *f.* blackness, darkness
noircir *vt. & vi.* to blacken, darken
noircissement *m.* blackening
noircissure *f.* black spot
noire *f.* (mus.) quarter note
noise *f.* quarrel
noisetier *m.* hazelnut tree
noisette *f.* hazelnut
noix *f.* nut, walnut; — **de veau veal**
   shoulder
noliser *vt.* to charter, rent
nom *m.* name; surname; (gram.) noun;
   au — **de** in the name of; **petit** — given
   name; nickname; — **et prénoms full**
   name
nomade *a.* nomadic, wandering; — *m. & f.*
   nomad
nombrable *a.* countable
nombre *m.* number
nombrer *vt.* to number, count
nombreux *a.* numerous, many
nombril *m.* navel
nomenclature *f.* nomenclature, list
nominal *a.* nominal
nominalement *adv.* nominally
nominatif *m. & a.* nominative
nomination *f.* nomination
nommer *vt.* to name; **se** — to be called
non *adv.* no, not
nonagénaire *m. & f.* nonagenarian
non-agression *f.* nonaggression
nonante *a.* ninety (in Belgium and Switzerland)
nonce *m.* nuncio, papal legate
nonchalamment *adv.* nonchalantly
nonchalance *f.* nonchalance
nonchalant *a.* negligent, unconcerned
non-combattant *a. & m.* noncombattant

non-conformisme *m.* non-conformity, non-conformism
non-conformiste *a. & n.* nonconformist
non-être *m.* (phil.) non-existence
non-intervention *f.* non-intervention
non-lieu *m.* no grounds for prosecution
nonne *f.* nun; pet de — *m.* apple turnover
nonobstant *prep. & adv.* notwithstanding
non-paiement *m.* nonpayment
nonpareil *a.* peerless, without equal
non-pesanteur *f.* weightlessness
non-réussite *f.* failure
non-sens *m.* nonsense
non-syndiqué *a.* nonunion
non-violence *f.* nonviolence
nord *m.* north
nord-africain *a.* North African
nord-américain *a.* North American
nord-est *m.* northeast
nordique *a.* Nordic
nord-ouest *m.* northwest
normal *a.* normal; école **—e** *f.* teachers' college
normalement *adv.* normally
normalien *m.* normal school student
normalisation *f.* normalization
normand *a.* Norman
Normandie *f.* Normandy
norme *f.* norm, standard
Norvège *f.* Norway
norvégien *a. & m.* Norwegian
nos *a. pl.* our
nostalgie *f.* homesickness; nostalgia
notabilité *f.* notability; notable
notable *a. & m. & f.* notable
notaire *m.* notary
notamment *adv.* especially
notarié *a.* notarized
notation *f.* notation
note *f.* note, memorandum; mark, grade; bill, invoice
noter *vt.* to note, mark; signify
notice *f.* account, review
notification *f.* notification
notifier *vt.* to notify
notion *f.* notion, acquaintance, slight knowledge
notoire *a.* notorious, well-known
notoriété *f.* notoriety
notre *a.* our
nôtre *pron.*, le (la) — ours
notule *f.* gloss, short note
nouer *vt.* to tie, knot; stiffen; se — to kink, twist; knit
noueux *a.* knotty, gnarled
nouilles *f. pl.* noodles
nourrice *f.* wet nurse
nourricier *a.* nutritive; père — *m.* foster father
nourrir *vt. & vi.* to nourish; nurse; feed;

bring up; foster
nourrissant *a.* nourishing
nourrisseur *m.* cattle feeder
nourrisson *m.* infant at the breast
nourriture *f.* nourishment, food
nous *pron. pl.* we, us, to us
nouveau (nouvel, nouvelle) *a.* new, recent; novel, different; de — again, anew
nouveau-né *a. & m.* new-born child
nouveauté *f.* novelty, newness; something new
nouvelle *f.* news; short story
Nouvelle-Écosse *f.* Nova Scotia
nouvellement *adv.* lately, recently
nouvelliste *m.* short-story writer
novateur *m.* innovator
novembre *m.* November
novice *m. & f.* novice
noviciat *m.* noviciate
noyade *f.* drowning
noyau *m.* pit, core, stone; nucleus; (pol.) cell, unit
noyautage *m.* forming of political units
noyauter *vt.* to form political cells
noyer *vt.* to drown; inundate; — *m.* walnut tree
nu *a.* naked, bare, nude; mettre à — to expose; — *m.* nude; nudity
nuage *m.* cloud; — artificiel smoke screen
nuageux *a.* cloudy
nuance *f.* shade, tinge; suggestion
nuancer *vt.* to shade, blend, vary
nubile *a.* nubile, marriageable
nucléaire *a.* nuclear
nucléé *a.* having a nucleus
nucléique *a.* nucleic
nucléon *m.* nucleon
nudisme *m.* nudism
nudiste *m. & f.* nudist
nudité *f.* nudity
nuée *f.* cloud; (fig.) swarm
nuer *vt.* to shade colors in embroidery
nuire *vi.* to injure, harm, wrong, prejudice
nuisible *a.* detrimental, injurious
nuit *f.* night; darkness; (fig.) — blanche sleepless night
nuitamment *adv.* by night, at night
nul *a.* null, void; no, not one; match —, partie —e *f.* tie game, draw
nullement *adv.* not at all, by no means
nullifier *vt.* to nullify
nullité *f.* nullity, nothing, negative quantity
nûment *adv.* openly, frankly
numéraire *m.* coin, coined money, cash
numéral *a.* numeral
numérateur *m.* numerator
numération *f.* numbering
numérique *a.* numerical
numéro *m.* number; issue of a periodical

numérotage *m.* numbering
numéroter *vt.* to number; (print.) page
numéroteur *m.* numbering stamp
numismate *m.* numismatist, coin collector
nuptualité *f.* marriage rate
nuque *f.* nape of the neck
nurse *f.* child's nurse
nutritif *a.* nutritive
nutrition *f.* nutrition
nymphe *f.* nymph
nymphéa *m.* water lily

O

oasis *m.* oasis
obéir(à) *vi.* to obey, comply
obéissance *f.* obedience; compliance
obéissant *a.* obedient
obélisque *m.* obelisk
obérer *vt.* to burden with debt
obèse *a.* obese
obésité *f.* obesity
obi *f.* Japanese sash
obit *m.* memorial service
obituaire *a. & m.* obituary
objecter *vt.* to object
objecteur *m.* objector; — **de conscience** conscientious objector
objectif *a.* objective; — *m.* lens; objective
objection *f.* objection
objectivement *adv.* objectively
objectiver *vt.* to make objective
objectivité *f.* objectivity
objet *m.* object; subject; (gram.) complement
objurgation *f.* objurgation
oblat *m.* oblate
obligataire *m. & f.* bondholder
obligation *f.* obligation; bond
obligatoire *a.* obligatory, compulsory
obligé *a.* obliged, compelled
obligeamment *adv.* obligingly
obligeance *f.* kindness
obligeant *a.* kind, obliging
obliger *vt.* to oblige, compel; bind
oblique *a.* oblique, slanting
obliquer *vi.* to strike at an angle; go off at an angle, swerve
oblitération *f.* obliteration; cancellation
oblitérer *vt.* to obliterate; cancel (stamp); obstruct
obole *f.* obole, bit; (fig.) penny, red cent
obscène *a.* obscene, smutty
obscénité *f.* obscenity
obscur *a.* obscure; abstruse; of humble birth
obscurcir *vt.* to obscure, darken; **s'—** to become dark, cloud over
obscurcissement *m.* obscuring, darkening

obscurément *adv.* obscurely, dimly
obscurité *f.* obscurity, darkness
obséder *vt.* to obsess
obsèques *f.* funeral, obsequies
obséquieusement *adv.* obsequiously
obséquieux *a.* obsequious
obséquiosité *f.* obsequiousness
observable *a.* observable
observance *f.* observance
observateur *m.* observer
observation *f.* observation
observatoire *m.* observatory; observation post
observer *vt.* to observe; **s'—** to be careful, watch one's step
obsession *f.* obsession
obsolète *a.* obsolete
obstacle *m.* obstacle
obstétrical *a.* obstetric(al)
obstétrique *f.* obstetrics
obstination *f.* obstinacy
obstiné *a.* obstinate
obstinément *adv.* obstinately
obstiner *v.*, **s'—** (à) to persist in
obstruction *f.* obstruction
obstructionnisme *m.* obstructionism
obstructionniste *m. & a.* obstructionist
obstruer *vt.* to obstruct
obtempérer *vi.* to obey, yield
obtenir *vt.* to obtain
obtention *f.* attainment, obtaining
obturateur *m.* (phot.) shutter
obturer *vt.* to close, stop
obtus *a.* obtuse
obus *m.* (mil.) shell
obusier *m.* howitzer
obvier *vi.*, — à to obviate
oc *m.*, langue d'— southern-French dialect, old Provençal
ocarina *m.* ocarina
occasion *f.* occasion, opportunity; bargain; d'— secondhand
occasionnel *a.* occasional; chance
occasionner *vt.* to occasion, cause, bring about, result in
occident *m.* Occident
occidental *a.* Western, Occidental
occipital *a.* occipital
occis *a.* killed
occlure *vt.* to occlude
occlusif *a.* occlusive
occlusion *f.* occlusion
occulte *a.* occult
occupant *m.* occupant; — *a.* occupying
occupé *a.* busy, occupied
occuper *vt.* to occupy; busy; **s'—** to keep busy; be interested in
occurrence *f.* occurrence; chance happening
océan *m.* ocean

océanide *f.* sea nymph
Océanie *f.* Oceania
océanien *a.* of Oceania, from Oceania
océanique *a.* oceanic
océanographie *f.* oceanography
ocelot *m.* ocelot
ocre *f.* ochre
ocré *a.* ochre-colored
octaèdre *m.* octahedron
octante *a.* eighty (in Belgium and Switzerland)
octave *f.* (mus., poet.) octave; week following a festival
Octave (*m.*) Octavius
octobre *m.* October
octogénaire *m.* octogenarian
octogonal *a.* octagonal
octogone *a.* octagonal; — *m.* octagon
octroi *m.* grant, granting; city tariff; city customs
octroyer *vt.* to grant, accord
oculaire *a.* ocular; — *m.* eye piece of microscope; témoin — *m.* eyewitness
oculiste *m. & f.* oculist, ophthalmologist
odalisque *f.* odalisk
ode *f.* ode
odelette *f.* short ode
odeur *f.* odor, smell, scent
odieux *a.* odious, hateful; heinous; — *m.* odiousness, hatefulness
odomètre *m.* odometer, mileage meter
odontalgie *f.* toothache
odorant *a.* odorous, fragrant
odorat *m.* sense of smell
odorer *vt.* to smell
odoriférant *a.* sweet-smelling
odyssée *f.* odyssey
œdème *m.* edema
œdipe *m.* œdipus
œil *m.* (*pl.* yeux) eye; sight; à vue d'— visibly; coup d'— *m.* glance, look
œil-de-boeuf *m.* (arch.) bull's-eye window; oxeye daisy
œillade *f.* ogling, ogle, glance
œillère *f.* eyecup; horse blinder
œillet *m.* carnation; eyelet
œsophage *m.* esophagus
œuf *m.* egg; — à la coque soft-boiled egg; — brouillé scrambled egg; — sur le plat fried egg
œuvre *m. & f.* work, working; literary production
œuvrer *vi.* to produce, turn out
offensant *a.* offensive
offense *f.* offense
offenser *vt.* to offend; s'— de to take offense at
offenseur *m.* offender
offensif *a.* offensive
offensivement *adv.* offensively

offertoire *m.* offertory
office *m.* office, function; church service; d'— officially; — *f.* pantry
officiant *m.* officiating priest
officiel *a.* official
officiellement *adv.* officially
officier *m.* officer; — *vt.* to officiate; — *vi.* to say a divine service
officieusement *adv.* officiously
officieux *a.* officious
offrande *f.* offering; (eccl.) offertory
offrant *adj. & m.*, au plus — to the highest bidder
offre *f.* offer
offrir *vt.* to offer
offset *m.* offset printing
offusquer *vt.* to cloud; dazzle; offend
ogival *a.* (arch.) Gothic
ogive *f.* Gothic arch; warhead
ogre *m.* ogre
ohé! *interj.* hey!
ohm *m.* ohm
oie *f.* goose
oignon *m.* onion; bunion
oïl *adv.*, langue d'— *f.* Northern French
oindre *vt.* to anoint; (eccl.) to consecrate sacramental oil
oint *a.* anointed; consecrated; — *m.* something that has been consecrated
oiseau *m.* bird; à vol d'— *a.* in a straight line, as the crow flies; vue à vol d'— *f.* bird's eye view
oiseau-mouche *m.* hummingbird
oiseleur *m.* bird trapper
oiselier *m.* bird seller
oisellerie *f.* bird store; bird farm
oiseux *a.* idle, useless
oisif *a.* lazy; idle, unemployed
oisillon *m.* little bird
oisiveté *f.* idleness
oison *m.* gosling
oléagineux *a.* oleaginous, oily
oléandre *m.* oleander
olfactif *a.* olfactory
oligarchie *f.* oligarchy
oligophrénie *f.* mental retardation
olivacé *a.* olive-colored
olivaie *f.* olive orchard
olivâtre *a.* olive-colored, greenish
olive *f.* olive
olivette *f.* olive orchard
olivier *m.* olive tree
Olivier Oliver
olographe *a.* holographic, handwritten by testator
Olympe *m.* Olympus; — *f.* Olympia
olympiade *f.* Olympiad
olympique *a.* Olympic
ombilic *m.* navel
ombilical *a.* umbilical

omble *m.* fresh-water salmon
ombrage *m.* shade; umbrage, suspicion
ombrager *vt.* to shade
ombrageux *a.* skittish; umbrageous, suspicious
ombre *f.* shadow; shade; darkness; ghost; sienna
ombrelle *f.* parasol
ombrer *vt.* to shade
ombreux *a.* shaded, shadowed
omelette *f.* omelet
omettre *vt.* to omit; neglect
omission *f.* omission, oversight
omnibus *a.*, train — *m.* local train
omnipotence *f.* omnipotence
omniprésence *f.* omnipresence
omniprésent *a.* omnipresent
omniscience *f.* omniscience
omniscient *a.* omniscient
omnivore *a.* omnivorous
omoplate *f.* shoulder blade
on *pron.* one, we, they, people
onagre *m.* wild ass
onanisme *m.* onanism
once *f.* ounce
oncle *m.* uncle
onction *f.* unction, annointing
onctueusement *adv.* unctuously
onctueux *a.* unctuous; oily
onctuosité *f.* unctuousness
onde *f.* wave; — ultracourte microwave
ondé *a.* waved, wavy, with wavy lines
ondée *f.* shower, passing storm
ondoiement *m.* undulation; baptism
ondoyer *vi.* to undulate, billow
ondulant *a.* undulant, undulating
ondulation *f.* wave; undulation; — permanente permanent wave
ondulatoire *a.* undulating
onduler *vt. & vi.* to wave the hair; undulate
onéreux *a.* onerous, burdensome
ongle *m.* nail; claw; coup d'— *m.* scratch
onglé *a.* nailed
onglée *f.* numbness, frostbite of the fingers
onglet *m.* tab; boîte à –s miter box
onglier *m.* manicure set; –s *pl.* nail scissors
onguent *m.* ointment
ongulé *a.* having hoofs, nails
oniromancie *f.* dream interpretation
ontologie *f.* ontology
O.N.U. *f.* United Nations
onyx *m.* onyx
onze *a.* eleven
onzième *a.* eleventh
opacifier *vt.* to make opaque
opacité *f.* opaqueness
opale *f.* opal

opalescence *f.* opalescence
opalescent *a.* opalescent
opalin *a.* opaline
opaque *a.* opaque
opéra *m.* opera, grand opera; opera house
opéra-comique opera with alternate songs and spoken dialogue
opérable *a.* operable
opérateur *m.* operator
opération *f.* operation
opérationnel *a.* operational
opercule *m.* cover, lid
opérer *vt.* to operate, effect, perform; s'— to take place; se faire — to undergo an operation
opérette *f.* operetta, musical comedy
ophtalmie *f.* ophthalmy
ophtalmologue, ophtalmologiste *m.* ophthalmologist
opiacé *a.* containing opium
opiner *vi.* to be of the opinion; — de la tête to nod approval
opiniâtre *a.* obstinate, stubborn
opiniâtrer *v.*, s'— to be obstinate
opinion *f.* opinion
opiomane *m. & f.* opium addict
opium *m.* opium
opossum *m.* opossum
oppidum *m.* fortified city
opportun *a.* opportune
opportunément *adv.* opportunely
opportunisme *m.* opportunism
opportuniste *m. & f.* opportunist
opportunité *f.* opportuneness
opposable *a.* opposable
opposant *a.* opposing; — *m.* opponent
opposé *a.* opposing, opposite; — *m.* opposite
opposer *vt.* to oppose; s'— to be against
opposite *m.* opposite
opposition *f.* opposition
oppresser *vt.* to oppress; weigh on
oppresseur *m.* oppressor
oppressif *a.* oppressive
oppression *f.* oppression
opprimer *vt.* to oppress
opprobre *m.* shame, disgrace
opter *vi.* to chose, make a choice
opticien *m.* optician
optimisme *m.* optimism
optimiste *m. & f.* optimist; — *a.* optimistic
optimum *a. & m.* optimum
option *f.* option
optique *a.* optical; — *f.* optics
optométrie *f.* optometry
opulence *f.* opulence
opulent *a.* opulent
opuscule *m.* short work; pamphlet, booklet

or *m.* gold; — *conj.* now
oracle *m.* oracle
orage *m.* electrical storm
orageux *a.* stormy, violent
oraison *f.* oration; prayer
oral *a.* oral
oralement *adv.* orally
orange *f.* orange; — **pressée** orangeade; — *m.* orange color
orangé *a.* orange-colored
orangeade *f.* orange drink
oranger *m.* orange tree
orangeraie *f.* orange grove
orangerie *f.* hothouse for orange trees
orang-outan *m.* orangutang
orateur *m.* orator
oratoire *a.* oratorical; — *m.* oratory, chapel
orbe *m.* orb; sphere
orbital *a.* orbital; **décrire une courbe -e** to orbit
orbite *f.* orbit; **décrire une —** to orbit
orchestral *a.* orchestral
orchestration *f.* orchestration
orchestre *m.* orchestra
orchestrer *vt.* to orchestrate
orchidée *f.* orchid
ordalie *f.* ordeal, trial by ordeal
ordinaire *a.* ordinary, common, usual; — *m.* custom, practice; **d'—** *adv.* usually
ordinairement *adv.* ordinarily
ordinal *a.* ordinal
ordination *f.* ordination
ordonnance *f.* order; class; ordinance; prescription; (mil.) orderly
ordonner *vt.* to order, put in order; ordain
ordre *m.* order; **numéro d'—** *m.* serial number; **de premier —** first-class, first-rate; **billet à —** *m.* promissory note
ordure *f.* filth, dirt; excrement; garbage
ordurier *a.* filthy
orée *f.* border, edge
oreille *f.* ear; hearing
oreiller *m.* pillow
oreillette *f.* auricle
oreillons *m. pl.* mumps
ores *adv.*, **d'— et déjà** from now on
orfèvre *m.* goldsmith, silversmith
orfèvrerie *f.* jewelry; goldsmith's shop; goldsmith's trade
orfraie *f.* osprey
organdi *m.* organdy
organe *m.* organ
organique *a.* organic
organisateur *m.* organizer
organisation *f.* organization
organiser *vt.* to organize
organisme *m.* organism
organiste *m. & f.* organist
orge *f.* barley; **sucre d'—** *m.* barley sugar

orgelet *m.* (med.) sty on the eye
orgie *f.* orgy
orgue *m.* (mus.) organ; — **de barbarie** barrel organ, hand organ
orgueil *m.* pride
orgueilleusement *adv.* proudly
orgueilleux *a.* proud
Orient *m.* Orient, East
oriental *a.* oriental, eastern
orientation *f.* orientation
orienter *vt.* to orient, direct; **s'—** to become oriented; get one's bearings
orifice *m.* orifice
origan *m.* marjoram
originaire *a.*, — **(de)** native (to)
original *a.* original; eccentric
originalité *f.* originality; eccentricity
origine *f.* origin
originel *a.* original, inherited
orignal *m.* moose
orillon *m.* handle, ear, grip of a bowl
oripeau *m.* tinsel; trash
ormaie *f.* elm grove
orme *m.* elm
orne *m.* ash tree
ornement *m.* ornament
ornemental *a.* ornamental
ornementation *f.* ornamentation
ornementer *vt.* to ornament
orner *vt.* to adorn, ornament
ornière *f.* rut, groove
ornithologie *f.* ornithology
ornithologue *m.* ornithologist
orpailleur *m.* prospector who pans for gold
orphelin *m.* orphan
orphelinat *m.* orphanage
orteil *m.* toe; **gros —** big toe
orthodentiste *m.* orthodontist
orthodoxe *a.* orthodox
orthodoxie *f.* orthodoxy
orthographe *f.* spelling
orthographier *vt.* to spell
orthographique *a.* orthographic, spelling
orthopédie *f.* orthopedics
orthopédique *a.* orthopedic
orthopediste *m.* orthopedist
ortie *f.* nettle
os *m.* bone
oscillation *f.* oscillation
oscillatoire *a.* oscillating
osciller *vi.* to oscillate; hesitate
osé *a.* bold, daring
oseille *f.* sorrel
oser *vt. & vi.* to dare, venture
oseraie *f.* willow grove
oseur *a.* daring
osier *m.* (bot.) willow; wicker work
osmium *m.* osmium
osmose *f.* osmosis
ossature *f.* bones, bone structure; frame

osselet *m.* little bone, osselet; knuckle-bone

ossements *m. pl.* bones

osseux *a.* bony

ossification *f.* ossification

ossifier *vt.* to ossify

ossu *a.* bony

ossuaire *m.* ossuary; bone pile

ostensible *a.* ostensible

ostensoir *m.* monstrance

ostentateur *a.* ostentatious

ostentation *f.* ostentation

ostéomyélite *f.* osteomyelitis

ostracisme *m.* ostracism

ostréiculture *f.* oyster farming

otage *m.* hostage; guarantee

otalgie *f.* earache

otarie *f.* sea lion

ôter *vt.* to take away, take off; remove

otique *a.* pertaining to the ear

ottoman *m. & a.* ottoman

ou *conj.* or; **ou . . . ou** either . . . or

où *adv.* where, on which, when; **d'—** whence, from where; **par —** which way; **— que** wherever

ouaille *f.* member of a spiritual flock

ouate *f.* cotton batting

ouater *vt.* to stuff with cotton batting; pad

oubli *m.* oblivion, forgetfulness, neglect

oubliable *a.* forgettable

oublier *vt.* to forget

oubliette *f.* dungeon, cell

oublieux *a.* forgetful

ouest *m.* west

oui *adv.* yes

ouï-dire *m.* hearsay

ouïe *f.* hearing

ouïr *vt.* to hear

ouragan *m.* hurricane

ourdir *vt.* to plot; weave (intrigue)

ourler *vt.* to hem; **— à jour** to hemstitch

ourlet *m.* hem

ours *m.* bear

**Ourse, la Grande — ** Ursa Major; **la Petite — ** Ursa Minor

oursin *m.* sea urchin

ourson *m.* bear club

out *adv.* out; out of bounds (sports)

outarde *f.* bustard

outil *m.* tool, implement

outillage *m.* tools, tool kit; apparatus

outiller *vt.* to tool; furnish, supply

outrage *m.* outrage, abuse, insult

outrageant *a.* insulting, abusive

outrager *vt.* to outrage

outrageusement *adv.* insultingly; outrageously

outrageux *a.* outrageous; insulting

outrance *f.* excess

outrancier *a.* excessive

outre *adv.* further, beyond; **en — ** moreover, besides; **— prep.** beyond; **— f.** goatskin waterbag

outré *a.* overdone, exaggerated

outrecuidance *f.* presumption, conceit

outrecuidant *a.* conceited, self-satisfied

outremer *m.* ultramarine; lapis lazuli

outre-mer *adv.* overseas

outrepasser *vt.* to overtake, go beyond

outrer *vt.* to overdo, exaggerate; anger

ouvert *a.* open; candid; sincere

ouvertement *adv.* openly, frankly

ouverture *f.* opening; beginning; overture

ouvrable *a.* workable, capable of being worked; working; **jour — ** *m.* working day

ouvrage *m.* work, piece of work

ouvrager *vt.* to work on, work over

ouvre-boîtes *m.* can opener

ouvrer *vt.* to work

ouvreuse *f.* (theat.) usher

ouvrier *m.* laborer, worker

ouvrir *vt.* to open

ouvroir *m.* workroom

ovaire *m.* ovary

ovale *a. & m.* oval

ovarien *a.* ovarian

ovation *f.* ovation

ovationner *vt.* to applaud, give an ovation to

ove *m.* egg, egg-shaped ornament; ovum

ové *a.* egg-shaped

oviducte *m.* oviduct

ovin *a.* ovine

ovipare *a.* oviparous

ovoïde *a.* ovoid

ovulation *f.* ovulation

ovule *m.* ovule

oxalide *f.* oxalis

oxalique *a.* oxalic

oxhydrique *a.* oxyhydric

oxyacétylénique *a.* oxyacetylene

oxydant *a.* oxidizing; **— m.** oxidizer

oxygène *m.* oxygen

oxyure *f.* tapeworm

P

pacage *m.* pasture

pacager *vt.* to put to pasture

pachyderme *m.* pachyderm

pacificateur *m.* pacifier; **— a.** pacifying

pacification *f.* pacifying

pacifier *vt.* to pacify, appease

pacifique *a.* peaceful; mild

pacifisme *m.* pacifism

pacifiste *m.* pacifist; **— a.** pacifistic

pacotille *f.* cheap merchandise, trash

pacte *m.* pact

pactiser *vi.* to make a pact; compromise

pactole *m.* source of great wealth
padou *m.* narrow tape
Padoue *f.* Padua
pagaie *f.* paddle
pagaille, pagaye *f.* disorder, confusion
paganisme *m.* paganism
pagayer *vt. & vi.* to paddle
pagayeur *m.* paddler
page *f.* page; (fig.) epoch; **à la** — up to date; — *m.* page boy (court)
pagination *f.* pagination
paginer *vt.* to paginate
pagne *m.* loincloth
pagode *f.* pagoda
paie *f.* pay; paying off; salary
paiement *m.* payment, paying
païen *m. & a.* pagan, heathen
paierie *f.* paymaster's office
paillard *a.* lecherous
paillasse *f.* straw mattress; — *m.* pagliaccio, clown
paillasson *m.* straw mat
paille *f.* straw; flaw; — **de fer** steel wool; **tirer à la courte** — to draw straws
pailler *vt.* to cover with straw
pailleté *a.* spangled, sequined
pailleter *vt.* to spangle
paillette *f.* sequin, spangle; gold nugget; flake
paillon *m.* spangle; straw basket; straw wrapping (of a bottle); large gold nugget
pain *m.* bread, loaf; **petit** — roll
pair *m.* peer, equal; equality; **au** — at par; without salary, with board and lodging in exchange for services; — *a.* even, equal; **nombre** — *m.* even number; **de** — *adv.* on the same level
paire *f.* pair
pairesse *f.* peeress
paisible *a.* peaceable; peaceful, calm
paitre *vi.* to browse; — *vt.* to put to pasture
paix *f.* peace, quiet
pal *m.* stake; pale
palabre *f.* talk, conference
paladin *m.* paladin, knight
palais *m.* palace; (anat.) palate; — **de justice** courthouse
palan *m.* block of a pulley; tackle
palanche *f.* yoke
palanque *f.* stockade
palanquin *m.* palanquin
palatalisation *f.* palatalization
pale *f.* post, stake, pale; (mech.) blade
pâle *a.* pale, wan, pallid
palefrenier *m.* horse's groom
palefroi *m.* palfrey; parade horse (Middle Ages)
paléographie *f.* paleography

paléolithique *a.* paleolithic
paleron *m.* part of an animal's shoulder; cut of meat
palestinien *a. & m.* Palestinian
palet *m.* quoit
paletot *m.* topcoat, overcoat
palette *f.* pallette; paddle; oar blade
palétuvier *m.* mangrove
pâleur *f.* paleness, pallor
palier *m.* landing of a staircase; (fig.) level; degree
palindrome *m.* palindrome
palinodie *f.* retraction
pâlir *vi.* to turn pale, wane; fade; — *vt.* make pale
palis *m.* picket; picket fence; pale, enclosure
palissade *f.* fence, fencing; palisade; stockade
palissader *vt.* to fence in, enclose; palisade
palliatif *a. & m.* palliative
pallier *vt.* to palliate, alleviate
palmarès *m.* list of honors and awards
palme *f.* palm; palm tree; **-s** *pl.* honors *or* insignia
palmé *a.* palmate; web-footed
palmeraie *f.* palm grove
palmette *f.* (arch.) palm-leaf design
palmier *m.* palm tree
palmiste *m.* palmetto
palombe *f.* wood pigeon
palourde *f.* clam
palpable *a.* palpable, obvious
palpe *f.* feeler, palp of an insect
palper *vt.* to feel with the hand
palpitation *f.* palpitation
palpiter *vi.* to palpitate; flutter; thrill
paludéen *a.* pertaining to marshes **or** swamps; **fièvre –e** *f.* malaria
paludisme *m.* malaria
pâmer *v.*, **se** — to be overcome, faint; be excessively happy
pâmoison *f.* faint, fainting
pamphlet *m.* lampoon, satire
pamphlétaire *m.* lampooner, pamphleteer
pamplemousse *f.* grapefruit
pampre *m.* branch of a fruit vine
pan *m.* section, piece; flap; wall panel; — *interj.* bang!
panacée *f.* panacea
panache *m.* decorative plume, stripe; swagger
panaché *a.* plumed; streaky; varied
panacher *vt.* to plume; decorate with different colors
panais *m.* parsnip
Panama *m.* Panama; Panama hat
panaméricain *a.* Pan-american
pancarte *f.* placard, sign, folder

panchromatique *a.* panchromatic
pancréas *m.* pancreas
panda *m.* panda
pandémonium *m.* pandemonium
pandit *m.* pundit
pané *a.* breaded
panégyrique *m.* panegyric, eulogy
paner *vt.* to bread
panerée *f.* basketful
panier *m.* basket; hoop skirt
panique *f.* panic
panne *f.* breakdown, failure; lard; plush; être en — to be out of order, not to work
panneau *m.* wood panel; trap, snare; (naut.) hatch
panneton *m.* window catch
panoplie *f.* suit of armor; panoply
panoramique *a.* panoramic
panse *f.* paunch, (coll.) belly
pansement *m.* bandage, dressing
panser *vt.* to bandage, dress
pantalon *m.* pair of pants, trousers
panteler *vi.* to pant
panthéisme *m.* pantheism
panthéiste *m.* pantheist; — *a.* pantheistic
panthéon *m.* pantheon
panthère *f.* panther, leopard, jaguar
pantin *m.* puppet; jumping jack
pantographe *m.* pantograph
pantomime *f.* pantomime; — *m.* pantomimist
pantoufle *f.* house slipper
panure *f.* bread crumbs
paon *m.* peacock
paonner *vi.* to strut
papal *a.* papal
papauté *f.* papacy
pape *m.* pope
paperasse *f.* old paper
paperasserie *f.* red tape
papeterie *f.* paper mill; stationery; stationery store
papetier *m.* stationer; papermaker
papier *m.* paper; — à lettres stationery; — hygiénique toilet tissue; — peint wallpaper; — de soie tissue paper; — de verre sandpaper
papier-cuir *m.* imitation leather, leatherette
papille *f.* papilla
papillon *m.* butterfly; leaflet; amendment; — de nuit moth; nœud — *m.* bow tie
papillonner *vi.* to flit, flutter
papillote *f.* curlpaper
papillotement *m.* fluttering, flickering
papilloter *vi.* to flicker, twinkle; glitter
papoter *vi.* to talk, chatter, gossip
paprika *m.* paprika
papule *f.* papule, rash, blemish

papyrus *m.* papyrus
Pâque *f.* Passover
paquebot *m.* liner, ship; mail boat
Pâques *f. pl.* Easter
paquet *m.* bundle, parcel, pack
paquetage *m.* packaging
paqueter *vt.* to bale, package, tie up
par *prep.* by, through; by means of; per; in; on; finir — (faire quelque chose) to end up doing something; — ici this way; — là that way; — où? which way? — trop much too much
parabole *f.* parable; parabola
parachever *vt.* to complete to perfection
parachutage *m.* parachuting, air-drop
parachute *m.* parachute; — de traînage drogue
parachuter *vt.* to parachute
parachutiste *m.* parachutist, paratrooper; — du corps médecin paramedic
parade *f.* display, show, pomp; parade
parader *vi.* to display, show off; parade
paradis *m.* paradise; (theat.) gallery
paradisier *m.* bird of paradise
paradoxe *m.* paradox
paradoxal *a.* paradoxical
parafe *m.* initials; flourish
parafer *vt.* to initial; sign
paraffine *f.* paraffin
paraffiner *vt.* to coat with paraffin
parage *m.* trimming, paring; lineage, birth —s *m. pl.* ocean localities, vicinity
paragraphe *m.* paragraph
paraître *vi.* to appear, seem; be apparent; be published
parallèle *a. & m.* parallel
parallélogramme *m.* parallelogram
paralogisme *m.* fallacy
paralysant *a.* paralyzing
paralyser *vt.* to paralyze
paralysie *f.* paralysis; — agitante shaking palsy; — cérébrale cerebral palsy
paralytique *a. & n.* paralytic
paramécie *f.* (zool.) paramecium
paramètre *m.* parameter
paramilitaire *a.* paramilitary
parangon *m.* paragon, model, example
paranoïa *f.* paranoia
parapet *m.* parapet
paraphrase *f.* paraphrase
paraphraser *vt.* to paraphrase; stretch
paraplégique *a.* paraplegic
parapluie *m.* umbrella
parapsychologie *f.* parapsychology
parasite *m.* parasite; —s *pl.* (coll.) static
parasitaire, parasitique *a.* parasitic
parasol *m.* parasol
paratonnerre *m.* lightning rod
paravent *m.* folding screen
parc *m.* park; grounds; parking space;

parcage *m.* parking

parcelle *f.* piece; plot, parcel, lot; bit, scrap

parceller *vt.* to divide into parcels

parce que *conj.* because

parchemin *m.* parchment

parcimonie *f.* parsimony

parcimonieux *a.* parsimonious; sparing; stingy

parcourir *vt.* to travel over; (fig.) run through, read over

parcours *m.* trip, distance; route, course

par-dessous *adv. & prep.* under, underneath

pardessus *m.* overcoat, topcoat

par-dessus *adv. & prep.* over, on top of

pardon *m.* pardon, forgiveness

pardonnable *a.* pardonnable, forgivable

pardonner *vt.* to pardon, forgive

paré *a.* dressed up; adorned

pare-boue *m.* mudguard

pare-brise *m.* windshield

pare-bruit *m.* (auto.) muffler

pare-chocs *m.* (auto.) bumper

pare-étincelles *m.* fire-screen

parégorique *a. & m.* paregoric

pareil (pareille) *a.* like, alike; equal, same; similar; such; — *m.* equal, peer, like; sans — without equal, peerless

pareillement *adv.* similarly; in the same way; also

parement *m.* adornment, ornament; ornamentation; curb; facing of outer wall

parent *m.* relative, relation; -s *pl.* parents; family, relatives

parentage *m.* parentage, lineage; family, relatives

parenté *f.* relationship; relatives

parenthèse *f.* parenthesis, parenthetical phrase; en –s *adv.* parenthetically

parer *vt.* to adorn; trim; prepare; parry, avoid; se — to adorn oneself; dress up

pare-soleil *m.* visor, shade

paresse *f.* laziness

paresseux *a.* lazy; sluggish, slow

parfaire *vt.* to perfect

parfait *a.* complete, perfect; absolute; — *m.* (gram.) perfect tense

parfaitement *a.* completely, perfectly; absolutely, certainly

parfois *adv.* sometimes

parfum *m.* perfume, scent, fragrance

parfumer *vt.* to perfume, scent

pari *m.* wager, bet

paria *m.* pariah, outcast

parier *vt.* to bet, wager

parieur *m.* bettor

Paris *m.* Paris

parisien *a. & m.* Parisian

parité *f.* parity, equality

parjure *a.* perjured; — *m.* perjury; perjurer

parjurer *vt.*, se — to perjure oneself, commit perjury

parking *m.* garage, parking place

parlant *a.* speaking; expressive

parlé *a.* spoken

parlement *m.* parliament; court

parlementaire *a.* parliamentary; **drapeau** — *m.* flag of truce

parlementer *vi.* to confer, parley

parler *vi.* to speak, talk; **entendre** — **de** to hear about; — *m.* speech, language

parleur *m.* speaker, talker

parloir *m.* parlor

Parme *f.* Parma

parmesan *a.* from Parma; — *m.* Parmesan cheese

parmi *prep.* among

parnassien *a. & m.* Parnassian

parodie *f.* parody

parodier *vt.* to parody

paroi *f.* partition, wall; (anat.) lining

paroisse *f.* parish

paroissial *a.* parochial, parish

paroissien *m.* parishioner; prayer-book

parole *f.* word, spoken word, parole, promise; speech, speaking; **avoir la** — to be speaking, have the floor

paroxysme *m.* paroxysm

Parque *f.*, les –s *pl.* the Fates

parquer *vt.* to pen up; park

parquet *m.* floor, flooring; court, **bar of** justice; pit, trading floor

parqueter *vt.* to parquet a floor

parqueterie *f.* parquet floor, inlaid floor

parrain *m.* godfather; sponsor

parricide *m. & f.* parricide

parsemer *vt.* to sow, scatter; intersperse

part *f.* portion, share; à — aside; peculiar; autre — elsewhere; de — et d'autre on both sides; nulle — nowhere; quelque — somewhere; de ma — from me; for me; de la — de on behalf of; d'une — on one hand; d'autre — on the other hand; faire — de to announce; inform, notify

partage *m.* share, portion; sharing, dividing

partager *vt.* to share, divide

partance *f.* (naut.) leaving, departure, sailing; en — pour bound for

partant *conj.* therefore; consequently

partenaire *m. & f.* partner

parterre *m.* flower bed; (theat.) orchestra, rear of orchestra, audience

parti *m.* party, faction, cause; decision; profit; match, prospective husband or wife; du — de on the side of; **prendre son** — to make up one's mind; — **pris** prejudice; closed mind; **prendre le —** de to take the side of; to decide to; **tirer — de** to take advantage of

partialement adv. partially, in a prejudiced manner

partialité f. prejudice, partiality

participant m. participant

participation f. participation; sharing

participe m. participle

participer vi. to participate, share

participial a. participial

particulariser vt. to specify; go into detail about

particularité f. particularity; peculiarity; particular, detail

particule f. particle; **— bêta** beta particle

particulier a. particular; special; peculiar; characteristic; private, personal; **en —** privately; **— m.** individual, private party

particulièrement adv. particularly, especially

partie f. part, portion; game, match; party (law); **— civile** plaintiff; **en —** in part, partly; **en grande —** for the most part

partiel a. partial, part, incomplete

partiellement adv. partially, in part

partir vi. to depart, leave, go away; start, come, emanate; come off; go off (gun); **à — d'aujourd'hui** from this day on; **— à l'anglaise** to take French leave

partisan m. partisan; believer, follower

partitif a. partitive

partition f. division; (mus.) score

partout adv. everywhere; **— ailleurs** anywhere else

parure f. dress, ornament; decoration; necklace

parution f. appearance of a published work

parvenir vi. to arrive, reach; manage, succeed

parvenu m. upstart

parvis m. church square

pas m. step, footstep, pace; threshold; narrow passage; defile; (fig.) precedence; **faux —** stumble, slip, mistake; **mauvais —** scrape, difficulty; **— de ce —** immediately; **à — de loup** stealthily; **— à —** step by step, slowly

pas adv. no, not, none; **— du tout** not at all; **— mal de** many, quite a few

Pas de Calais m. Straits of Dover

pascal a. (eccl.) Paschal

passable a. passable, fair

passage m. passage; passing; voyage; crossing; **droit de — m.** right of way; **— clouté** crosswalk

passager a. transient, transitory, fleeting;

momentary; migratory (bird); **— m.** passenger

passant m. passer-by

passavant m. (naut.) gangway; pass, permit

passe f. pass; passing; permit; fencing thrust; **mauvaise —** difficult situation

passé a. past, over, gone by; **— m.** past time; (gram.) past tense

passement m. braid, lace

passementerie f. braid or lace trimming

passe-partout m. skeleton key, master key

passe-passe m. sleight of hand, magic

passepoil m. braid, braiding

passeport m. passport

passer vi. to pass, go by; go over; go through; pass away; pass on; **— vt.** to pass; exceed, go beyond; strain; go over, pass over, cross; hand, give; put; put on; spend time; sign an agreement; **se —** to happen, occur, go on; go by; pass away; **se — de** to do without

passereau m. sparrow

passerelle f. foot bridge

passe-temps m. pastime

passe-thé m. tea strainer

passeur m. ferryman

passible a. liable, subject

passif a. passive; **— m.** passive; (com.) liabilities, debt

passion f. passion

passionnant a. exciting, moving, thrilling

passionnel a. pertaining to passion(s); **crime — m.** crime committed in the heat of jealousy

passionner vt. to excite; impassion; thrill

passivité f. passivity

passoire f. strainer

pastel m. pastel color or drawing

pastèque f. watermelon

pasteur m. shepherd; pastor, minister

pasteuriser vt. to pasteurize

pastiche m. parody, pastiche, imitation

pasticher vt. to parody, imitate

pastille f. drop, candy; cough drop; rubber patch

pastoral a. pastoral

pat m. stalemate

patate f. sweet potato; (coll.) potato

pataud a. & m. clumsy person

pataugeage, pataugement m. floundering

patauger vi. to flounder; splash, wade

pâte f. paste, dough; pasta, spaghetti products; **— dentifrice** toothpaste

pâté m. pâté of meat; ink blot; clump; block of houses

pâtée f. mash for animals

patelinage m. glib talk, smooth talk

patenôtre f. Lord's prayer

patent a. patent, obvious, clear

patente *f.* license, permit, certification, authorization

patenter *vt.* to license, authorize

patère *f.* clothing peg; curtain hook

paterne *a.* benevolent, kindly

paternel *a.* paternal; fatherly

paternité *f.* paternity, fatherhood

pâteux *a.* pasty; thick

pathétique *a.* pathetic; — *m.* pathos

pathologie *f.* pathology

pathologiste *m.* pathologist

patiemment *adv.* patiently

patience *f.* patience; jeu de — *m.* jigsaw puzzle; solitaire (cards)

patient *a.* patient; — *m.* patient

patienter *vi.* to have patience, be patient

patin *m.* skate; runner; brake shoe; —s à roulettes roller skates

patine *f.* patina

patiner *vi.* to skate; slip

patinette *f.* child's scooter

patineur *m.* skater

patinoire *f.* skating rink

pâtir *vi.* to suffer

pâtis *m.* pasture

pâtisser *vi.* to make pastry

pâtisserie *f.* pastry; pastry shop

pâtissier *m.* pastry cook, baker of cake and pastry

patois *m.* dialect; jargon

patouiller *vi.* to flounder in mud

pâtre *m.* shepherd

Patrice (*m.*) Patrick

patricien *a. & m.* patrician

patrie *f.* native country

patrimoine *m.* patrimony

patrimonial *a.* patrimonial

patriote *a.* patriotic; — *n.* patriot

patriotique *a.* patriotic

patriotisme *m.* patriotism

patron *m.* patron; employer, boss, chief, proprietor; skipper; pattern; — à jour stencil

patronage *m.* patronage; church social group

patronal *a.* pertaining to employers; pertaining to a patron saint

patronne *f.* patroness; owner, proprietress

patronner *vt.* to patronize, support; pattern; stencil

patrouiller *vi.* to patrol

patrouilleur *m.* soldier on patrol; patrol boat

patte *f.* paw, foot; tab, strap; à quatre —s four-footed; on all fours

patte-d'oie *f.* wrinkle, crow's foot

pâturage *m.* pasture, grazing

pâture *f.* feed, fodder; pasture

pâturer *vi. & vt.* to graze, feed

paume *f.* palm of the hand; jeu de — *m.* tennis court (history)

paumer *vt.* to strike, slap with the palm

paupière *f.* eyelid

pause *f.* pause, stop, respite, interval; (mus.) rest

pauser *vi.* to pause

pauvre *a.* poor; wretched, unfortunate; — *n.* poor person

pauvresse *f.* poor woman, beggar

pauvreté *f.* poverty, poorness

pavage *m.* pavement; paving

pavaner *v., se* — *vi.* to strut, parade

pavé *m.* pavement; slab, block of paving stone; street; sidewalk

paver *vt.* to pave

pavillon *m.* pavillion; lodge; flag; — de golf golf clubhouse

pavoiser *vt.* to trim, adorn with bunting

pavot *m.* poppy

payable *a.* payable

payant *a.* paying; — *m.* payer

paye *f.* wages, pay

payement *m.* payment

payer *vt.* to pay, pay for, pay back; treat; se — to treat oneself to

payeur *m.* payer; bursar; bank teller; paymaster

pays *m.* country, land, region; avoir le mal du — to be homesick

paysage *m.* landscape; scenery; countryside

paysagiste *m. & f.* landscape painter

paysan *m.* peasant

paysannerrie *f.* peasantry

Pays-Bas *m. pl.* Netherlands

péage *m.* toll; pont à — *m.* toll bridge

péan *m.* paean

peau *f.* skin, hide; pelt; peel; à fleur de — skin-deep

Peau-Rouge *m.* Indian, redskin

pécari *m.* peccary

pechblende *f.* pitchblende

pêche *f.* peach; fishing

pêcher *vt.* to fish, fish up, catch; — *m.* peach tree

pécher *vi.* to sin

pécheresse *f.* sinner; trespasser; — *a.* sinning

pêcherie *f.* fishery

pêcheur *m.* angler, fisherman; fishing boat

pécheur *m.* sinner

pectine *f.* pectin

pectoral *a. & m.* pectoral

péculat *m.* embezzlement

péculateur *m.* embezzler

pécule *m.* nest egg, savings

pécuniaire *a.* pecuniary

pédagogique *a.* pedagogic(al)

pédagogue *m.* pedagogue

pédale *f.* pedal; frein à — *m.* foot brake;

— d'embrayage (auto.) clutch
pédaler *vi.* to pedal
pédaleur *m.* bicyclist
pédant *a.* pedantic; — *m.* pedant
pédanterie *f.*, **pédantisme** *m.* pedantry
pédantesque *a.* pedantic
pédestre *a.* pedestrian
pédiatre *m.* pediatrician
pédiatrie *f.* pediatrics
pédicure *m.* chiropodist
pedigree *m.* pedigree
peigne *m.* comb
peigné *a.* combed; **bien** — well-groomed; **mal** — unkempt
peigner *vt.* to comb, card wool; (coll.) beat, thrash; **se** — to comb one's hair
peignoir *m.* dressing gown, wrapper
peindre *vt.* to paint, portray, depict
peine *f.* pain, punishment, penalty; difficulty; trouble; **à** — hardly, scarcely; **faire de la** — **à** to trouble, disturb, distress; **se donner (de) la** — to take the trouble
peiner *vt.* to pain, trouble, distress; — *vi.* to work hard, struggle, labor
peintre *m.* painter; artist; — **en bâtiments** house painter
peinture *f.* painting; paint; picture
peinturer *vt.* to paint, coat with paint
péjoratif *a.* pejorative
péjorativement *adv.* pejoratively
pekinois *m.* Pekinese
pelage *m.* fur, coat of an animal; skinning
pelé *a.* hairless; skinless; peeled
pêle-mêle *adv.* pell-mell; hastily; in confusion; — *m.* jumble, disorder
peler *vt.* to peel, pare, skin; remove the hair from; — *vi.* to peel; **se** — peel; lose hair
pèlerin *m.* pilgrim
pèlerinage *m.* pilgrimage
pèlerine *f.* cape, tippet
pélican *m.* pelican
pelisse *f.* pelisse, cloak
pellagre *f.* pellagra
pelle *f.* shovel, scoop; blade of a paddle
pelletée *f.* shovelful
pelleter *vt.* to shovel
pelleterie *f.* furs, fur trade
pelletier *m.* furrier
pellicule *f.* skin, film; (phot.) film; **-s** *pl.* dandruff
pelote *f.* wad, ball; pincushion; pelota
peloter *vt.* to wind into a ball
peloton *m.* group; (mil.) platoon; wad, ball; cluster
pelotonner *v.*, **se** — to group together; huddle; roll up, curl up
pelouse *f.* lawn, grass, a green
peluche *f.* plush, shag

pelucher *vi.* to shed the nap (fabric), become nappy
pelucheux *a.* fluffy
pelure *f.* paring, peel; rind; **papier** — *m.* onionskin paper
pelvien *a.* pelvic
pénal *a.* penal
pénalisation *f.* sports penalty
pénaliser *vt.* to penalize
pénalité *f.* penalty
penaud *a.* sheepish, crestfallen
penchant *a.* sloping, inclined; — *m.* slope; inclination, leaning, bent
penché *a.* bent, leaning
pencher *vt. & vi.* to incline, tilt, lean over; **se** — bend, stoop; lean out
pendable *a.* deserving of hanging
pendaison *f.* hanging on the gallows
pendant *a.* hanging; pending; — *m.* pendant; match, one of a pair; — *prep.* during, for; — **que** *conj.* while
pendeloque *f.* earring; crystal of a chandelier
pendiller *vi.* to dangle, hang
pendre *vt. & vi.* to hang, hang up
pendule *f.* clock with pendulum; — *m.* pendulum
pêne *m.* bolt of a lock
pénétrabilite *f.* penetrability
pénétrable *a.* penetrable
pénétrant *a.* penetrating, sharp, keen, searching, deep, profound
pénétration *f.* penetration; insight
pénétrer *vt.* to penetrate, pierce; fill; — *vi.* penetrate, enter, get into
pénible *a.* painful; difficult, hard, rough
péniblement *adv.* painfully
péniche *f.* canalboat, barge
pénicilline *f.* penicillin
péninsulaire *a.* peninsular
péninsule *f.* peninsula
pénis *m.* penis
pénitence *f.* penitence, penance; repentance
pénitencier *m.* penitentiary
pénitent *a. & m.* penitent
pénitentiaire *a.* penitentiary
penne *f.* feather, plume
pennon *m.* pennant
pénombre *f.* semidarkness, half-light
pensant *a.* thinking
pensée *f.* thought, idea; (bot.) pansy
penser *vi.* to think; remember; — *vt.* to think, believe, conceive, imagine
penseur *m.* thinker
pensif *a.* pensive, thoughtful, thinking
pension *f.* pension; boardinghouse, boarding school; room and board; — **alimentaire** alimony
pensionnaire *m. & f.* boarder; pensioner;

inmate
pensionnat *m.* boarding school
pensionner *vt.* to pension
pensivement *adv.* pensively
pensum *m.* task, chore (as punishment)
pentagone *m.* pentagon; — *a.* pentagonal
pentamètre *m.* pentameter
pentathlon *m.* pentathlon
pente *f.* slope, incline, grade
Pentecôte *f.* Pentecost
pénultième *a. & f.* penultimate, last but one
pénurie *f.* penury, poverty; scarcity
pépiement *m.* cheeping, chirping
pépin *m.* pip, seed
pépinière *f.* nursery garden
pépite *f.* nugget
pepsine *f.* pepsin
percale *f.* percale
perçant *a.* piercing; penetrating; biting, sharp; shrill
perce *f.* drill, punch; boring implement
perce-bois *m.* teredo, ship worm, borer
percée *f.* opening, break
percepteur *m.* tax collector; — *a.* discerning
perceptible *a.* perceptible
perception *f.* perception; revenue collection
percer *vt.* to pierce; go through, penetrate; bore, drill, sink; — *vi.* to pierce, come through
perceur *m.* driller, borer
perceuse *f.* drill, drilling machine
percevable *a.* perceivable; collectable
percevoir *vt.* to perceive; collect taxes
perche *f.* fresh-water perch; pole
percher *vi.* to perch, roost; **se** — to come to rest, alight
percheron *m.* percheron
perchoir *m.* perch, roost
perclus *a.* stiff-jointed, crippled
perçoir *m.* awl; punch; borer
percolateur *m.* percolator
percussion *f.* percussion
percutant *a.*, **fusée –e** *f.* percussion fuse
percuter *vt.* to percuss, tap
percuteur *m.* hammer of a gun
perdant *a.* losing; — *m.* loser
perdition *f.* perdition; (naut.) sinking
perdre *vt.* to lose; ruin, destroy; waste time; — *vi.* lose; lose value; fall; leak; **se** — be lost; get lost
perdrix *f.* partridge
perdu *a.* lost, ruined; wasted
père *m.* father
pérégrination *f.* peregrination
péremptoire *a.* peremptory
perfection *f.* perfection
perfectibilité *f.* perfectibility

perfectionnement *m.* improvement; perfecting
perfectionner *vt.* to perfect; improve
perfide *a.* perfidious, treacherous
perfidie *f.* perfidy, treachery
perforateur *m.* drill, punch
perforation *f.* perforation; drilling; puncture
perforer *vt.* to perforate; drill; puncture
pergola *f.* pergola
péri *m. & f.* genie, peri
péricarde *m.* pericardium
périclitant *a.* risky, shaky
péricliter *vi.* to be in danger
périgée *f.* perigee
péril *m.* peril, risk, danger
périlleusement *adv.* perilously
périlleux *a.* perilous, dangerous
perimé *a.* overdue; expired; out of date
périmer *vi.* to lapse, expire
périmètre *m.* perimeter
période *f.* period; age, era; (elec.) cycle
périodicité *f.* periodicity
périodique *a. & m.* periodical
périodiquement *adv.* periodically
péripatétique *a.* peripatetic
péripétie *f.* sudden turn of fortune; **–s** *pl.* vicissitudes, up and downs
périphérie *f.* periphery; circumference
périphérique *a.* peripheral
périr *vi.* to perish, die
périscope *m.* periscope
périscopique *a.* periscopic
périssable *a.* perishable
péristyle *m.* peristyle
péritoine *m.* peritoneum
péritonite *f.* peritonitis
perle *f.* pearl, bead
perlé *a.* pearled; pearly; beaded
perler *vt.* to husk; — *vi.* to bead
permanence *f.* permanence; **en** — permanent; without cessation; permanently
permanent *a.* permanent; lasting; open continuously; open day and night; **spectacle** — *m.* continuous performance
permanganate *m.* permanganate
perméable *a.* permeable; porous
permettre *vt.* to permit, allow
permis *a.* permitted; — *m.* permit, license; — **de conduire** *m.* driver's license
permission *f.* permission; (mil.) leave, pass
permissionnaire *m.* soldier on leave
permutable *a.* interchangeable
permutation *f.* permutation; transfer, exchange of positions
permutatrice *f.* (elec.) rectifier, commutator

pernicieusement adv. perniciously
pernicieux a. pernicious, harmful, injurious
perniciosité f. perniciousness
péroné m. fibula
péroraison f. peroration
pérorer vi. to harangue
Pérou m. Peru
peroxyde m. peroxide
perpendiculaire a. perpendicular
perpétration f. perpetration
perpétrer vt. to perpetrate
perpétuel a. perpetual; endless; for life
perpétuellement adv. perpetually
perpétuer vt. to perpetuate
perpétuité f. perpetuity; à — for life, forever
perplexe a. perplexed; perplexing
perplexité f. perplexity
perquisition f. search; **mandat de** — m. search warrant
perquisitionner vi. to search, conduct a search
perron m. flight of steps to a house
perroquet m. parrot
perruche f. parakeet
perruque f. wig
pers a. gray-green
persan a. & m. Persian
perse f. chintz
Perse f. Persia; — n. & a. Persian
persécuter vt. to persecute; harass; annoy
persécuteur m. persecutor
persécution f. persecution
persévérance f. perseverance
persévérant a. persevering
persévérer vi. to persevere, persist
persienne f. outside shutter
persiflage m. persiflage, banter
persifler vt. to treat lightly, banter
persil m. parsley
persillé a. marbled, streaked
persique a. Persian
persistance f. persistence, persistency
persistant a. persistent
persister vi. to persist
personnage m. personage, important person; (theat.) character, role
personnalité f. personality; personage; individuality
personne f. person; **en** — in person, personified; — pron. nobody, no one; anybody, anyone
personnel a. personal; — m. personnel
personnellement adv. personally
personnifier vt. to personify; impersonate
perspective f. perspective; prospect; view
perspicacité f. perspicacity
persuadant a. persuasive, convincing
persuadé a. positive, convinced, sure

persuader vt. to persuade, convince
persuasif a. persuasive, convincing
persuasion f. persuasion, conviction
persuasivement adv. persuasively, convincingly
perte f. loss, damage, ruin; leakage; falling off, drop; (med.) discharge; **à — de vue** as far as the eye can see
pertinence f. pertinence, relevance
pertinent a. pertinent, relevant
pertuis m. channel, narrows; opening; narrow pass, passage; sluice
perturbateur a. disturbing; — m. disturber
perturbation f. perturbation; disturbance
perturber vt. to perturb; disturb
péruvien a. & m. Peruvian
pervenche f. periwinkle
pervers a. perverse
perversement adv. perversely
perversion f. perversion
perversité f. perversity
pervertir vt. to pervert; **se** — to become perverted
pesage m. weighing in
pesamment adv. heavily
pesant a. heavy, weighty; — m. weight
pesanteur f. weight; gravity; heaviness
pèse-alcool m. alcometer
pèse-bébé m. baby scale(s)
pesée f. weighing; leverage
pèse-lettres m. postal scale(s)
peser vt. to weigh, consider; measure; — vi. to weigh; press
pessimisme m. pessimism
pessimiste m. & f. pessimist; — a. pessimistic
peste f. plague, pestilence
pester vi. to rage, storm; curse
pestiféré a. stricken with the plague
pétale m. petal
pétarade f. backfire
pétard m. firecracker; detonator
pétarder vt. to blast; — vi. backfire
péter vi. to backfire, explode, pop
pétillant a. sparkling; crackling
pétillement m. crackling sound
pétiller vi. to sparkle; crackle; bubble
petit a. small, little; young; petty; minor, of humble origin, lesser; **à** — little by little; — m. child; little boy; **-e** f. little girl; **-s** m. pl. children, little ones; **en** — adv. shortened
petit-cheval m. donkey engine
petit-cousin m. second cousin
petite-fille f. granddaughter
petitesse f. smallness, littleness; pettiness
petit-fils m. grandson
pétition f. petition
pétitionnaire m. & f. petitioner

pétitionner vi. to petition
petit-lait m. whey
petit-maître m. fop
petit-neveu m. grandnephew
petite-nièce f. grandniece
petits-enfants m. pl. grandchildren
petit-suisse m. cream cheese
pétoire f. popgun
pétoncle m. scallop
pétrel m. petrel
pétri a. kneaded, shaped; full of
pétrifier vt. to petrify
pétrin m. container for dough (bakery); (coll.) in trouble, difficulty
pétrir vt. to knead; shape
pétrole m. petroleum, oil
pétrolier m. (naut.) tanker
pétrolifère a. oil-yielding, oil-bearing
pétulance f. friskiness, vivacity
pétulant a. frisky, vivacious
pétunia m. petunia
peu adv. little; not very; — de few; — à — gradually; depuis — lately; quelque — somewhat; — m. small quantity; un — (de) a little
peuplade f. tribe, people
peuple m. people, nation; masses, lower class
peuplé a. populated
peupler vt. to people, populate, settle; stock with fish
peuplier m. poplar
peur f. fear, fright; **avoir** — to be afraid; **de** — de for fear of; **de** — que for fear that; **faire** — à to frighten; **prendre** — become afraid
peureux a. fearful; timid, shy
peut-être adv. perhaps, maybe
phalange f. phalanx
phalène f. moth
pharaon m. Pharaoh; faro
phare m. lighthouse, beacon; (auto.) headlight
pharisien m. pharisee
pharmacie f. pharmacy
pharmacien m. pharmacist, druggist
pharyngite f. pharyngitis
pharynx m. pharynx
phase f. phase, stage
Phénicie f. Phoenicia
phénicien a. & m. Phoenician
phénique a. carbolic
phénix m. phoenix
phénol m. phenol; carbolic acid
phénoménal a. phenomenal
phénomène m. phenomenon
philanthrope m. philanthropist
philanthropie f. philanthropy
philanthropique a. philanthropic
philatéliste m. & f. philatelist, stamp col-

lector
philharmonique a. philharmonic
Philippe (m.) Philip
philistin a. & m. Philistine
philologie f. philology
philologue m. philologist
philosophe m. philosopher; — a. philosophical
philosopher vi. to philosophize
philosophie f. philosophy
philosophique a. philosophical
philtre m. philter, magic potion
phlébite f. phlebitis
phlogistique m. phlogiston
phlyctène f. blister, vesicle
phobie f. phobia, dread
phonème m. phoneme
phonétique a. phonetic; — f. phonetics
phonique a. acoustic, phonic
phonographe m. phonograph
phonologie f. phonology
phoque m. (zool.) seal
phosphate m. phosphate
phosphore m. phosphorus
phosphorescence f. phosphorescence
phosphorescent a. phosphorescent
phosphure m. phosphide
photo f. photo, photograph
photocalque m. blueprint
photocopie f. photocopy
photo-électrique a. photoelectric
photogénique a. photogenic
photographe m. photographer
photographie f. photography; photograph; — aérienne aerial photography
photographier vt. to photograph
photographique a. photographic
photogravure f. photoengraving
photostat m. photostat
photosynthèse f. photosynthesis
phrase f. sentence; phrase
phraséologie f. phraseology
phrénologie f. phrenology
phrénologiste m. phrenologist
phtisie f. pulmonary tuberculosis
phtisique a. tubercular, consumptive
physicien m. physicist
physico-chimie f. physical chemistry
physiologie f. physiology
physiologique a. physiological
physiologiste m. physiologist
physionomie f. face, features, character
physique a. physical; — f. physics; — m. physique; — **plasmatique** plasma physics
physiquement adv. physically
piaffer vi. to step, prance, paw the ground
piaillard a. bawling, crying; chirping
piailler vi. to bawl, squall, cry; chirp
piaillerie f. bawling, crying; whining;

chirping

pianiste *m. & f.* pianist

piano *m.* piano; — **à queue grand piano;** — **à demi-queue** baby grand piano

piaulard *a.* crying, whining; chirping

piauler *vi.* to whine, cry; chirp

piaulis *m.* chirping

pic *m.* pickax; mountain peak; wood-pecker; **à** — precipitous, sheer, abrupt

picard *a. & m.* native of Picardy

Picardie *f.* Picardy

picaresque *a.* picaresque

piccolo *m.* piccolo

pichet *m.* pitcher, jug

picorer *vi.* to peck, pick up food (birds)

picot *m.* splinter; picot

picotement *m.* pricking sensation, prickle; pins and needles (coll. U.S.)

picoter *vt.* to prick; pick at, peck at; — *vi.* sting, smart, burn

picrique *a.* picric

pictural *a.* pictorial

pie *f.* magpie; (coll.) chatterbox; — *a.* piebald

pièce *f.* piece; patch; room in a house; (theat.) play; coin; cask; part; — **de rechange** spare part

piécette *f.* one-act play; small coin

pied *m.* foot; footing; base; leg of a chair; support, stand; tripod; **à** — on foot; **an** — **de la lettre** literally; **coup de** — *m.* kick; **en** — full-length (portrait) **mettre** — **à terre** to dismount; step down from, get out of a vehicle; — **de laitue** head of lettuce; **lâcher** — to turn tail

pied-bot *m.* clubfooted person

pied-d'alouette *m.* larkspur, delphinium

pied-de-biche *m.* forceps; nail claw; bell pull

piédestal *m.* pedestal

piège *m.* snare, trap, pitfall

piéger *vt.* to trap

pie-grièche *f.* shrike

Piémont *m.* Piedmont

pierraille *f.* rubble, stones; ballast

pierre *f.* stone; flint; — **à fusil** flint; — **d'achoppement** stumbling block; — **de touche** touchstone

Pierre (*m.*) Peter

pierreries *f. pl.* precious stones, jewels

pierrette *f.* small stone

pierreux *a.* stony; gritty; gravelly

piété *f.* piety; devotion

piétinement *m.* trampling; treading

piétiner *vt.* to trample, tread on; — *vi.* to stamp

piéton *m.* pedestrian, person on foot

piètre *a.* poor, miserable, paltry

pieu *m.* stake, post, pile

pieusement *adv.* piously

pieuvre *f.* octopus

pieux *a.* pious, devoted, reverent

pige *f.* measuring stick

pigeon *m.* pigeon, dove; — **voyageur** homing pigeon

pigeonneau *m.* squab

pigeonnier *m.* dovecote, pigeon roost

piger *vt.* to measure, check; (coll.) nab, grab

pigmentation *f.* pigmentation

pigne *f.* pine cone

pignon *m.* house gable; chain-sprocket; pine seed

pilaf *a.* pilaf

pilastre *m.* pilaster, newel

pilau *m.* rice, pilaf

pile *f.* pile, heap; battery; — **ou face** heads or tails

piler *vt.* to pound, grind by pounding

pilet *m.* pintail duck

pileux *a.* hairy

pilier *m.* pillar, column

pillage *m.* pillage, plunder, sacking, loot-ing; pilfering, stealing

pillard *a.* pillaging, looting; pilfering, stealing; — *m.* pillager, looter; pilferer, thief

piller *vt.* to pillage, plunder, sack, loot, steal from; plagiarize

pilleur *a.* pillaging; pilfering; — *m.* pil-lager

pilon *m.* hammer, rammer; pestle; crush-ing implement

pilonner *vt.* to ram, pound, crush

pilori *m.* pillory

pilot *m.* bridge pile

pilotage *m.* piloting; flying; pile driving

pilote *m.* pilot

piloter *vt.* to pilot, fly

pilotis *m.* piling

pilou *m.* cotton flannel

pilule *f.* pill

piment *m.* red pepper, allspice; — **vert** green pepper

pimenter *vt.* to spice, season with red pepper

pin *m.* pine tree; fir tree

pinacle *m.* pinnacle

pince *f.* pincers, tweezers, tongs; pliers; forceps; clip, clamp; lever, crowbar; claw of a lobster; hand grip; — **à linge** clothespin

pincé *a.* pinched; wry; — *m.* pizzicato

pinceau *m.* paint brush; beam of light

pincée *f.* pinch, small quantity

pincement *m.* pinching, pinch

pince-monseigneur *m.* jimmy

pince-nez *m.* pince-nez, nose glasses

pincer *vt.* to pinch; (mus.) pluck; clip; hold, grip; catch, nab

pincettes *f. pl.* pincers, tongs, tweezers
pingouin *m.* penguin; auk
pingre *a.* miserly, stingy; — *m.* miser
pinière *f.* pine forest
pinson *m.* finch
pintade *f.* guinea hen
pinte *f.* pint
pioche *f.* pickax
piocher *vt.* to dig; — *vi.* work hard
piocheur *m.* digger; (with a pick); plodder hard worker
piolet *m.* ice axe; piolet
pion *m.* checker; pawn; monitor (coll.) school disciplinary officer
pionnier *m.* pioneer
pipe *f.* pipe
pipeau *m.* (mus.) pipe
pipée *f.* snaring birds with artifical bird calls
pipe-line *m.* pipeline
piper *vi.* to chirp, cheep, peep; — *vt.* to snare; lure birds; decoy
piquant *a.* sharp; spicy; witty; interesting; pricking, stinging; — *m.* sharpness; pointedness; best part, main point (of a story)
pique *f.* pike, lance; pique; — *m.* spade (at cards)
piqué *a.* piqued; stung, pricked, stuck; spotted, dotted; quilted; (mus.) stac-cato; (avi.) nose dive
pique-assiette *m.* parasite, sponger (per-son)
pique-nique *m.* picnic
pique-niquer *vi.* to picnic
piquer *vt.* to prick, sting; stick; inject; quilt; stimulate; irritate, pique; — *vi.* (avi.) to nose dive; **se** — prick oneself; be irritated, be offended; pride onself; become pitted
piquet *m.* picket, post, stake; piquet (at cards)
piqueter *vt.* to picket; stake out; spot, dot
piqueur *m.* machine sewer, stitcher; out-rider; digger
piqûre *f.* puncture, sting; prick; injec-tion; shot (U.S.); quilting, stitching; — **de rappel** (med.) booster shot
pirater *vi.* to pirate
piraterie *f.* piracy
pire *a.* worse; **le** — the worst
pirogue *f.* pirogue, canoe
pirouette *f.* pirouette, whirling
pirouetter *vi.* to pirouette; whirl
pis *adv.* worse; **le** — the worst; **de** — **en** — worse and worse
pis *m.* udder
pis-aller *m.* worst alternative, last resort
pisan *a.* of Pisa, from Pisa
piscine *f.* pool, swimming pool

pissenlit *m.* dandelion
pisser *vi.* to urinate
pissoir *m.* urinal
pistache *f.* pistachio nut
piste *f.* path; track; trail; — **d'atter-rissage** airstrip, landing strip; — **cava-lière** bridle path; — **cyclable** bicycle path
pister *vt.* to track, trail; follow; shadow
pisteur *m.* tracker, follower
pistolet *m.* pistol; (naut.) davit
piston *m.* piston; influence, pull; (mus.) cornet valve
pistonner *vt.* to use one's influence to help another; sponsor, back
pitance *f.* pittance, allowance, bare living
piteusement *adv.* piteously
piteux *a.* piteous, pitiable
pithécanthrope *m.* pithecanthropus
pitié *f.* pity, compassion, mercy
piton *m.* ring bolt; screw eye
pitoyable *a.* pitiful, pitiable
pitre *m.* clown
pittoresque *a.* picturesque
pituitaire *a.* pituitary
pivert *m.* woodpecker
pivoine *f.* peony
pivot *m.* pivot, fulcrum, axis; **à** — revol-ving, swivel
pivoter *vi.* to pivot, revolve, turn
placage *m.* veneering; plating
placard *m.* placard; poster; closet; cup-board; (print.) proof
placarder *vt.* to post a bill, placard
place *f.* square; seat; place, room, space; job, employment; — **d'armes** parade ground; **faire** — **à** to make room for; — **marchande** shopping plaza
placement *m.* investment; placement; **bureau de** — employment agency
placer *vt.* to place; sell; invest
placeur *m.* placer; usher; seller
placide *a.* placid, calm
placidité *f.* placidity, calmness
placier *m.* traveling salesman; agent
plafond *m.* ceiling; limit, maximum; top
plafonner *vt.* to equip with a ceiling
plage *f.* beach
plagiat *m.* plagiarism
plagier *vt.* to plagiarize
plaid *m.* plaid
plaider *vt. & vi.* to plead a case
plaideur *m.* party in a lawsuit, litigant
plaidoirie *f.* legal plea, pleading
plaidoyer *m.* legal plea, remarks by de-fense attorney
plaie *f.* wound
plaignant *m.* plaintiff at law
plain-chant *m.* (mus.) plainsong
plaindre *vt.* to pity; **se** — to complain

plaine *f.* plain, field
plain-pied *m.*, de — *adv.* on a level; even; smoothly, evenly
plainte *f.* complaint; moan
plaintif *a.* plaintive
plaintivement *adv.* plaintively
plaire *vi.* to please; **s'il vous plaît** please; **plût à Dieu!** would to God!; **à Dieu ne plaise!** God forbid!; **se** — enjoy oneself, take pleasure, be pleased
plaisamment *adv.* pleasantly, agreeably
plaisance *f.* pleasure; **maison de** — *f.* country home
plaisant *a.* amusing, funny; — *m.* joker; **mauvais** — practical joker
plaisanter *vi.* to joke, fool; — *vt.* to make fun of, tease
plaisanterie *f.* joke; trick
plaisir *m.* pleasure; enjoyment; **faire** — **à** to please
plan *m.* plane; plan; map, diagram; project; — **de vol** flight plan; **gros** — movie closeup; **premier** — foreground; — *a.* flat, even, plane
planage *m.* planing; smoothing
planche *f.* plank, board; plate, illustration; **faire la** — to float on one's back; — **à repasser** ironing board; — **de bord** dashboard; **-s** *pl.* (theat.) stage
planchéier *vt.* lay a wooden floor
plancher *m.* floor; flooring; planking
planchette *f.* small plank
plancton *m.* plankton
plane *m.* plane tree
plané *m.* glide, gliding; rolled gold
planer *vt.* to plane, smooth; — *vi.* to glide soar; hover, hang
planétaire *a.* planetary; — *m.* planetarium
planète *f.* planet
planeur *m.* glider
planquer *vt.*, **se** — to fall flat on the ground; take cover
plant *m.* sapling, seedling; grove, clump
plantage *m.* planting
plantain *m.* plantain
plantation *f.* plantation; planting
plante *f.* plant; sole of the foot
planter *vt.* to plant; place, put; stick
planteur *m.* planter
plantoir *m.* dibble
plantureux *a.* abundant, fertile; plump
planure *f.* wood shaving(s)
plaque *f.* plate; metal sheet; badge; tag
plaqué *a.* plated
plaquemine *f.* persimmon
plaquer *vt.* to plate; veneer; cover; cake; plaster; tackle (sports); **se** — to lie flat, fall flat
plaquette *f.* small plate or sheet; brochure
plasticité *f.* plasticity

plastique *a.* plastic; **matière** — *f.* plastic
plastron *m.* breastplate, protective pad; front of a shirt, dickey; butt of a joke
plat *a.* flat; smooth; level; dull; **à** — flat; tired, run down; — *m.* flat surface, flat part; dish, course; plate
platane *m.* plane tree
plat-bord *m.* (naut.) gunwale
plateau *m.* tray; plateau; platform; plate; stage
plate-bande *f.* border, bed of flowers or grass
platée *f.* plateful, dishful
plate-forme *f.* platform
platine *m.* platinum; — *f.* gun lock; platen
platiner *vt.* to coat, plate with platinum
platitude *f.* platitude, dullness
Platon *m.* Plato
platonique *a.* platonic (love)
platonisme *m.* Platonism
plâtrage *m.* plastering
plâtras *m.* plaster rubbish
plâtre *m.* plaster; plaster cast
plâtrer *vt.* to plaster; cover over, smooth over
plâtrier *m.* plasterer
plausibilité *f.* plausibility
plausible *a.* plausible
plèbe *f.* common people, masses
plébéien *a. & m.* plebeian
plébiscite *m.* plebiscite
plein *a.* full, filled; complete; **en** — . . . in the middle of; **en** — **air** in the open air, out of doors; **en** — **jour** in broad daylight; — *m.* fullness, fill, plenum
pleinement *adv.* fully
plénière *a. & f.* plenary, full; complete
plénipotentiaire *a. & m.* plenipotentiary
plénitude *f.* plenitude, fullness
pléonasme *m.* pleonasm
pléthore *f.* plethora
pleur *m.* tear; **-s** *pl.* tears, crying
pleurard *a.* whimpering; — *m.* whimperer, whiner
pleurer *vi.* to cry, weep; run, water (eyes); drip, leak; — *vt.* to cry for, mourn
pleurésie *f.* pleurisy
pleureur *m.* whimperer, weeper; — *a.* whimpering, weeping
pleurnicher *vi.* to whine, whimper
pleuviner *v.* to drizzle
pleuvoir *vi.* to rain
plexus *m.* plexus
pli *m.* fold; wrinkle; crease; wave; tuck; pleat; cover, envelope; bend; **sous ce** — enclosed herewith
pliable *a.* pliable; folding
pliant *a.* pliant; tractable; folding; — *m.* folding chair
plier *vt.* to fold, bend; warp; discipline;

— *vi.* to bend; yield, give in, submit;
se — yield; obey

plinthe *f.* (arch.) plinth

plissement *m.* folding, pleating; creasing;
wrinkling

plisser *vt.* to pleat; crease; wrinkle

ploiement *m.* folding, bending

plomb *m.* lead; plumb line; shot; (elec.)
fuse; à — vertical, plumb

plombage *m.* leading; (dent.) filling

plombagine *f.* graphite, black lead

plombé *a.* leaden; lead-coated; livid

plomber *vt.* to lead, cover with lead;
plumb; se — to become leaden

plomberie *f.* plumbing

plombier *m.* plumber; — *a.* leaden, about
lead

plombières *f.* ice cream with glacé fruit

plongée *f.* plunge, dive; dip

plongement *m.* plunging

plongeoir *m.* diving board

plongeon *m.* dive, plunge

plonger *vt.* to plunge, immerse; — *vi.* to
plunge, dive; dip; submerge

plongeur *m.* diver; washer of dishes; — *a.*
diving

ploutocrate *m.* plutocrat

ployable *a.* pliable, tractable

pluie *f.* rain

plume *f.* feather; pen; quill

plumeau *m.* feather duster

plumer *vt.* to pluck; — *vi.* to feather oars

plumet *m.* plume

plumeux *a.* feathery

plupart *f.* most, majority; **pour la —**
mostly

pluralité *f.* plurality, majority

pluriel *a. & m.* (gram.) plural

plus *adv.* more; plus; **ne** — no more, no
longer; **au** — at most, maximum; —
tôt sooner; **le** — the most; **de** — besides,
moreover; more, additional, extra; **de
— en** — more and more; **non** — either,
neither; — *m.* more; most, best;
greatest number; (math.) plus sign

plusieurs *a. pl.* several

plus-que-parfait *m.* (gram.) pluperfect

plutonium *m.* plutonium

plutôt *adv.* rather; better, preferably

pluvial *a.* rainy; pertaining to rain

pluvieux *a.* rainy

pluviosité *f.* precipitation, rainfall

pneu *m.* tire

pneumatique *a.* pneumatic; — *m.* tire;
letter sent by pneumatic tube

pneumonie *f.* pneumonia

pochade *f.* work done hastily

pochard *m.* drunk, drunkard

poche *f.* pocket; pouch; sac; bag, sack;
ladle

pochée *f.* pocketful, contents of a pocket

pocher *vt.* to bruise, blacken; poach;
sketch; stencil

pochetée *f.* pocketful

pochette *f.* small pocket; pouch

podagre *f.* gout; — *a.* gouty

podium *m.* podium

podomètre *m.* pedometer

poêle *f.* frying pan, pan; — *m.* stove,
cooker; pall

poêlée *f.* panful

poêlette *f.* small frying pan

poêlon *m.* saucepan

poème *m.* poem

poésie *f.* poetry; poem

poète *m.* poet

poétique *a.* poetical, poetic; — *f.* poetics

poids *m.* weight; load, burden; consequence, importance; — **utile** payload

poignant *a.* poignant, gripping

poignard *m.* dagger

poignarder *vt.* to stab

poigne *f.* grip, hold, grasp

poignée *f.* handful; handle; grip, hold;
hilt, haft; — **de main** handshake

poignet *m.* wrist; cuff

poil *m.* hair; bristle; nap; down; (coll.); **à**
— *a.* naked; bareback; **être de mauvais**
— bad humored

poilu *a.* hairy; — *m.* soldier of the First
World War

poinçon *m.* punch; awl; die, stamp; hall-
mark

poinçonner *vt.* to stamp; punch

poinçonneuse *f.* punch, punching machine, hole punch

poindre *vi.* to appear, come into view;
dawn; sprout

poing *m.* fist, hand; **coup de** — *m.* punch,
blow; **menacer du** — to shake a fist at

point *m.* point; period, dot; mark; (med.)
stitch; **à** — cooked to a turn, medium; **à
— apropos; au** — ready, in shape; in
tune; in focus; **deux** —**s** (gram.) colon;
— **d'appui** fulcrum; basis; (mil.) bridgehead; — **d'interrogation** question mark;
— **du jour** dawn, daybreak; — **et virgule**
semicolon; **sur le** — **de** on the point of;
— *adv.* no, not

pointage *m.* checking, checking off, ticking off; scoring; timing; aiming, point-
ing

pointe *f.* point; pointed tool; promontory;
tip; diaper, kerchief; (fig.) sharpness

pointer *vt.* to sharpen; prick; check a list;
aim, point; — *vi.* to appear; rise; sprout

pointeur *m.* checker, scorer; **chien** — *m.*
pointer (dog)

pointiller *vt.* to stipple, dot; harass; —
vi. quibble

pointillerie *f.* quibbling
pointilleux *a.* fastidious; finicky; touchy
pointu *a.* pointed; sharp
pointure *f.* size, fit
poire *f.* pear
poireau *m.* leek
poirier *m.* pear tree
pois *m.* pea; — **chiche** chick pea; **petits —** *pl.* green peas
poison *m.* poison
poissard *a.* common, vulgar speech
poisser *vt.* to cover with a sticky substance; make sticky; pitch, tar
poisseux *a.* sticky, gummy
poisson *m.* fish; — **rouge** goldfish
poissonnerie *f.* fish market
poissonneux *a.* full of fish
poissonnier *m.* fishmonger, operator of a fish market
Poitevin *m. & a.* native of Poitou
poitrail *m.* breast of a horse
poitrinaire *a. & m.* consumptive, tubercular person
poitrine *f.* chest; breast, bust, bosom; brisket
poivre *m.* pepper; **grain de** — *m.* peppercorn; — **de Cayenne** red pepper
poivré *a.* peppered; peppery, spicy
poivrer *vt.* to pepper, season, spice
poivrier *m.* pepperbox; pepper plant
poivrière *f.* pepper shaker
poivron *m.* green pepper; allspice
poix *f.* pitch, resin
polaire *a.* polar
polarisateur *a.* polarizing; — *m.* polarizer
polarisation *f.* polarization
polariser *vt.* to polarize
polarité *f.* polarity
pôle *m.* (elec., geog.) pole
polémique *f.* polemic; — *a.* polemical
poli *a.* polished; polite; — *m.* polish
police *f.* police; policy; — **d'assurance** insurance policy; **agent de** — *m.* policeman; **bonnet de** — *m.* overseas cap
policer *vt.* to regulate, organize, police
polichinelle *m.* Punch, buffoon; **théâtre de** — *m.* Punch and Judy show
policier *a.* police; **roman** — *m.* detective novel; — *m.* detective, policeman
poliment *adv.* politely
poliomyélite *f.* poliomyelitis, infantile paralysis
polir *vt.* to polish; refine
polisseur *m.* one who polishes, buffer
polisseuse *f.* polishing machine, buffing machine
polissoir *m.* polishing implement, buffer
polisson *m.* rascal; mischievous child
polissonnerie *f.* mischief, mischievousness; lewdness

politesse *f.* politeness, courtesy
politicien *m.* politician
politique *a.* political; politic; diplomatic; — *f.* policy; politics; — *m.* politician
polka *f.* polka
polker *vi.* to polka
pollinisation *f.* pollinization
polluer *vt.* to pollute
pollution *f.* pollution
Pologne *f.* Poland
polonais *a. & m.* Polish; — *m.* Pole
poltron *m.* coward; — *a.* cowardly
poltronnerie *f.* cowardice
polycopier *vt.* to duplicate, reproduce
polyèdre *m.* polyhedron; — *a.* polyhedral
polygame *a.* polygamous; — *m.* polygamist
polygamie *f.* polygamy
polyglotte *a.* polyglot
polygone *m.* polygon; — *a.* polygonal
polygraphe *m. & f.* versatile author, writer on varied subjects
polymorphe *a.* polymorphous
Polynésie *f.* Polynesia
Polynésien *m. & a.* Polynesian
polynôme *m.* polynomial
polype *m.* polyp
polyphasé *a.* multi-phase
polyphonique *a.* polyphonic
polysoc *m.* gangplow
polysyllabe *a.* polysyllabic
polytechnicien *m.* student at the École Polytechnique
polytechnique *a.* polytechnic
polythéiste *m. & f.* polytheist; — *a.* polytheist; — *a.* polytheistic
polyvalent *a.* polyvalent, multivalent
pommade *f.* pomade; salve, ointment
pommader *vt.* to pomade
pomme *f.* apple; knob; — **d'arrosoir** sprinkler; — **de pin** pine cone; — **de terre** potato; **-s à l'huile** potato salad; **-s frites** French fried potatoes; **-s en purée, purée de -s** mashed potatoes; **-s vapeur** boiled potatoes; **-s rissolées** roast potatoes
pommé *a.* round; consummate
pommeau *m.* knob; pummel of a sword
pommelé *a.* dappled, mottled
pommelle *f.* grating
pommeraie *f.* apple orchard
pommette *f.* cheekbone; knob
pommier *m.* apple tree
pompadour *m.* flowered cloth
pompe *f.* pump; pomp, splendor; **-s funèbres** *pl.* funeral
pomper *vt.* to pump
pompeux *a.* pompous
pompier *m.* fireman
pompon *m.* pompon; puff

pomponner *vt.* to ornament, adorn, deck out, festoon

ponant *m.* Occident

ponce *f.* pumice

ponceau *m.* culvert; corn poppy, red poppy

poncer *vt.* to sand, sandpaper; rub with pumice

poncho *m.* poncho

ponction *f.* (med.) opening, pricking; puncture

ponctualité *f.* punctuality

ponctuation *f.* punctuation

ponctué *a.* punctuated; having dotted line

ponctuel *a.* punctual

ponctuer *vt.* to punctuate; accentuate

pondaison *f.* egg laying

pondérable *a.* ponderable, weighable

pondérateur *a.* stabilizing

pondération *f.* ponderation; poise, balance

pondéré *a.* well-balanced; collected, cool

pondérer *vt.* to balance, stabilize

pondeuse *f.* laying hen

pondre *vt.* to lay (eggs)

poney *m.* pony

pongé *m.* pongee

pont *m.* bridge; deck of a ship; axle, shaft; platform; — **aérien** airlift; — **élévateur** (auto.) grease rack; **tête de —** *f.* bridgehead

ponte *f.* egg laying

ponté *a.* equipped with a deck

pontée *f.* deck cargo

ponter *vt.* to lay a deck (on a ship); — *vi.* play against the bank (at cards)

pontet *m.* trigger guard

pontife *m.* pontiff; pope

pontifical *a.* pontifical

pontificat *m.* pontificate

pontifier *vi.* to pontificate

pont-levis *m.* drawbridge

ponton *m.* pontoon; hulk

popeline *f.* poplin

populace *f.* populace, mob, rabble

populacier *a.* vulgar, common, low

populaire *a.* of the people; popular; **chanson —** *f.* folk song

populariser *vt.* to popularize

popularité *f.* popularity

population *f.* population

populeux *a.* populous

poquet *m.* hole for seeds

porc *m.* hog, pig; pork

porcelaine *f.* porcelain, china

porcelet *m.* piglet; wood louse

porc-épic *m.* porcupine

porche *m.* porch

porcher *m.* swineherd

poreux *a.* porous

pornographie *f.* pornography

pornographique *a.* pornographic

porosité *f.* porosity

porphyre *m.* porphyry

port *m.* port, harbor; postage; charge for transportation; carriage, deportment

portable *a.* portable; wearable

portage *m.* portage; transport, transporting; (mech.) bearing

portail *m.* portal, front gate

portant *a.* bearing; **bien —** in good health; **mal —** not well; — *m.* support; handle

portatif *a.* portable

porte *f.* door, gate; doorway; entrance; — **cochère** *f.* carriage entrance, gate at beginning of a driveway; — **d'entrée** front door

porté *a.* inclined; carried; worn; — **à** inclined to

porte-à-faux *m.* overhang; **en —** in a dangerous position

porte-affiches *m.* bulletin board; billboard

porte-aiguilles *m.* needle case

porte-allumettes *m.* matchbox

porte-amarre *m.* gun for shooting mooring lines

porte-avions *m.* aircraft carrier

porte-bagages *m.* baggage rack, luggage carrier

porteballe *m.* peddlar

porte-bannière *m. & f.* standard bearer

porte-bât *m.* pack animal

porte-billets *m.* billfold

porte-bonheur *m.* good luck charm

porte-cartes *m.* card case

porte-chapeaux *m.* hat rack

porte-cigarette *m.* cigarette holder

porte-clefs *m.* guard, turnkey

porte-copie *m.* copy stand

porte-couteau *m.* knife rest

porte-documents *m.* zippered portfolio

porte-drapeau *m.* flag bearer

portée *f.* brood, litter; scope, range, reach, extent; comprehension; implication, meaning; (mus.) staff

portefaix *m.* porter; stevedore

porte-fenêtre *f.* French door, French window

portefeuille *m.* portfolio; billfold, wallet

portemanteau *m.* coat rack; suitcase; saddlebag

porte-mine *m.* automatic pencil

porte-monnaie *m.* coin purse, change purse

porte-musique *m.* music case

porte-objet *m.* microscope slide

porte-parapluies *m.* umbrella stand

porte-parole *m.* spokesman

porte-pipes *m.* pipe rack

porte-plat *m.* trivet, hot pad; hot-pan holder
porte-plume *m.* penholder
porter *vt.* to carry, bear; raise, lift; indicate, mark; bring; take; wear; — *vi.* to bear, have an effect; **se** — **bien** to be well
porte-serviettes *m.* towel rack
porteur *m.* porter, carrier, bearer
porte-vent *m.* wind tunnel, air duct
porte-vêtement(s) *m.* clothes hanger
porte-voix *m.* megaphone; speaking tube
portier *m.* doorman; porter; janitor
portière *f.* door of a vehicle
portillon *m.* gate, barrier
portionner *vt.* to apportion
portique *m.* portico
portland *m.* Portland cement
Porto *m.* port wine
portrait *m.* portrait
portraitiste *m. & f.* portrait painter
portraiturer *vt.* to paint the portrait of
Portugais *m. & a.* Portuguese
Portugal *m.* Portugal
pose *f.* pose, posing, posture; (phot.) exposure; — **instantanée** snapshot
posé *a.* steady, even, sedate
posemètre *m.* (phot.) exposure meter
poser *vt.* to put, place; — *vi.* to pose; **une question** to ask a question; **se** — (avi.) to land; **se** — **en** set oneself up as
poseur *a.* posing, putting on airs, affected; — *m.* affected person; — **de mines** (naut.) minelayer
positif *a.* positive
position *f.* position, location; standing, status; stance; post, job
positivisme *m.* positivism
possédé *a.* possessed; — *m.* person possessed by the devil
posséder *vt.* to possess, have, own
possesseur *m.* possessor
possessif *a. & m.* possessive
possession *f.* possession, ownership; property
possibilité *f.* possibility
possible *a.* possible; — *m.* everything possible, utmost
postage *m.* packing for mailing; mailing
postdater *vt.* to postdate
poste *f.* post, mail; post office; **mettre (une lettre) à la poste** to mail a letter; — **recommandée** *f.* registered mail; — **restante** general delivery; — *m.* post; station; job, position; entry in a ledger; — **de TSF** radio set
poster *vt.* to post, station
postérieur *a.* posterior; back, hind; later; — *m.* posterior
postérité *f.* posterity

posthume *a.* posthumous
postiche *a.* false, imitation
postier *m.* postal worker
postillon *m.* postilion
postopératoire *a.* post-operative
postscolaire *a.* postgraduate; after-school
post-scriptum *m.* postscript
postsynnchronisation *f.* dubbing
postsynchroniser *vt.* to dub movies
postulant *m.* candidate, applicant
postulat *m.* postulate
postuler *vt.* to apply for
posture *f.* posture, position
pot *m.* pot; jug, jar; — **d'échappement** (auto.) muffler; — **pourri** stew; mixture
potable *a.* drinkable; **eau** — *f.* drinking water
potage *m.* soup
potager *a.* culinary; **jardin** — *m.* vegetable garden; truck farm
potasse *f.* potash
potassium *m.* potassium
pot-au-feu *m.* boiled or pot-roasted beef and vegetables
pot-de-vin *m.* tip; bribe
poteau *m.* post, stake, pole; — **indicateur** signpost
potée *f.* potful, jugful
potelé *a.* plump, chubby
potence *f.* gallows; bracket, support
potentat *m.* potentate
potentiel *a.* potential; — *m.* potential, potentialities
poter *vt. & vi.* to putt (in golf)
poterie *f.* pottery
poterne *f.* postern
potiche *f.* porcelain vase
potier *m.* potter
potin *m.* pewter; (coll.) talk, gossip; ado, fuss
potion *f.* potion
potiron *m.* pumpkin
pou *m.* louse, tick
pouah! *interj.* ugh!
poubelle *f.* garbage can, refuse can
pouce *m.* thumb; big toe; inch; (fig.) very small quantity
poucettes *f. pl.* thumbscrew
poudre *f.* powder; gunpowder; **en** — powdered, ground; — **de riz** face powder
poudrer *vt.* to powder
poudreux *a.* dusty, powdery
poudrière *f.* powder magazine; powder horn
poudrin *m.* spindrift, sea spray, fine spray
poudroyant *a.* dusty
poudrier *m.* powder box; compact
poudroyer *vt.* to cover with dust; — *vi.* to raise dust

pouf *m.* pouf, ottoman; — *interj.* phew! plop!

pouffer *vi.* to burst out laughing

pouillerie *f.* place infested with lice; hovel; poverty

pouilleux *a.* lousy, lice-ridden; wretched, filthy

poulailler *m.* henhouse; poulterer

poulain *m.* colt, foal

poulaine *f.* (naut.) latrine

poularde *f.* chicken

poule *f.* hen; gambling pool

poulet *m.* chicken

poulette *f.* pullet

pouliche *f.* filly

poulie *f.* pulley; block

pouliner *vi.* to foal

poulinière *f.* brood mare

pouliot *m.* windlass

poulpe *m.* octopus

pouls *m.* pulse

poumon *m.* lung

poupard *m.* baby; doll; — *a.* baby-like; chubby

poupe *f.* poop, stern

poupée *f.* doll; puppet

poupin *a.* baby-like, pink, rosy

pouponnière *f.* nursery school, day nursery

pour *prep.* for, in order to; for the sake of; because of; with regard to; — ainsi — dire so to speak; — que *conj.* in order that; — *m.* pros, advantages; le — et le contre pros and cons

pourboire *m.* gratuity, tip

pourceau *m.* hog, pig

pour-cent *m.* per cent; —age percentage

pourchasser *vt.* to pursue; harass

pourfendre *vt.* to attack, tilt with

pourlécher *v.*, se — to lick one's lips

pourparlers *m. pl.* parleys, conferences, negotiations

pourpier *m.* (bot.) purslane

pourpre *m.* dark red; — *f.* purple, symbol of royalty

pourpré *a.* dark red

pourquoi *adv.* why

pourri *a.* rotten; putrid

pourrir *vt. & vi.* to rot

pourriture *f.* rot, decay; rottenness

poursuite *f.* pursuit; —s *pl.* legal action

poursuivant *m.* plaintiff at law

poursuivre *vt.* to pursue, chase; prosecute; continue

pourtant *adv.* however, still, nevertheless

pourtour *m.* circumference, periphery

pourvoi *m.* appeal at law

pourvoir *vt.* to provide, supply, furnish

pourvoyeur *m.* provider; purveyor; caterer

pourvu que *conj.* provided

pousse *f.* shoot, sprout; growth

poussé *a.* deep; comprehensive; elaborate

poussée *f.* push, thrust, shove; growth, sprouting; buoyancy

pousse-pousse *m.* rickshaw

pousser *vt.* to push, urge, drive; utter; — *vi.* push; grow; sprout

poussier *m.* coal dust

poussière *f.* dust; spray

poussiéreux *a.* dusty

poussin *m.* spring chicken; baby chick

poussinière *f.* incubator for chicks; chicken coop

poussoir *m.* push button

poutrage *m.* beams, rafters

poutre *f.* beam, girder

poutrelle *f.* small beam

pouvoir *vt.* to be able; be possible; — *m.* power, authority

pragmatique *a.* pragmatic

prairie *f.* meadow; grassland, prairie

pralin *m.* kind of fertilizer; burnt-sugar frosting

praline *f.* burnt almond candy, praline

praliner *vt.* to brown (in sugar)

praticabilité *f.* practicability, feasibility

praticable *a.* practicable, feasible; sociable, easy-going

praticien *m.* practitioner

pratiquant *a.* practicing, (eccl.) orthodox

pratique *f.* practice, exercise, use; application; custom; experience; — *a.* practical

pratiquer *vt.* to practice, use, exercise; effect; frequent

pré *m.* meadow

préalable *a.* previous; preliminary; au — previously, beforehand

préambule *m.* preamble

préau *m.* yard, playground, recreation area

préavis *m.* advance notice

préaviser *vt.* to give advance notice to

prébendier *m.* (eccl.) prebendary

précaire *a.* precarious

précaution *f.* precaution, caution, care

précautionner *vt.* to warn, caution; se — to take precautions

précautionneux *a.* cautious, careful

précédemment *a.* before, previously

précédence *f.* precedence, priority

précédent *a.* preceding, previous, having priority; — *m.* precedent

précéder *vt.* to precede; have precedence of

précellence *f.* superiority

précepte *m.* precept

précepteur *m.* tutor

préceptoral *a.* tutorial, preceptorial

préchauffage *m.* preheating
prêche *f.* sermon
prêcher *vt.* to preach
prêcheur *m.* (coll.) preacher; — *a.* preaching, sermonizing
précieux *a.* precious; affected
préciosité *f.* affectation; preciosity
précipice *m.* precipice
précipitamment *adv.* headlong, in haste, precipitately
précipitation *f.* precipitation, haste; rain, rainfall
précipité *a.* precipitate; precipitous, hasty; hurried, rushed; headlong; — *m.* (chem.) precipitate
précipiter *vt.* to precipitate, hurry; **se** — to rush upon, rush into
précis *a.* precise, exact; — *m.* brief summary
précisément *adv.* precisely, just, exactly
préciser *vt.* to specify
précision *f.* precision, preciseness, exactness; specification, detail
précité *a.* above, aforementioned
précoce *a.* precocious; maturing early
précocité *f.* precociousness, precocity
préconception *f.* preconception
préconcevoir *vt.* to preconceive
préconiser *vt.* to advocate
préconnaissance *f.* prior knowledge, foreknowledge
précurseur *m.* precursor, forerunner
prédateur *a.* predatory
prédécéder *vi.* to die first
prédécesseur *m.* predecessor
prédestination *f.* predestination
prédestiner *vt.* to predestine
prédéterminer *vt.* to predetermine
prédicat *m.* predicate
prédicateur *m.* preacher
prédicatif *a.* predicative
prédiction *f.* prediction, forecast
prédilection *f.* predilection; **de** — favorite
prédire *vt.* to predict, foretell
prédisposer *vt.* to predispose; prejudice
prédisposition *f.* predisposition; prejudice
prédominance *f.* predominance
prédominant *a.* predominant, prevailing
prédominer *vt. & vi.* to predominate
prééminence *f.* pre-eminence
prééminent *a.* pre-eminent
préemptif *a.* pre-emptive
préemption *f.* pre-emption
préétabli *a.* pre-established
préétablir *vt.* to pre-establish
préexister *vi.* to pre-exist
préfabrication *f.* prefabrication
préfabriqué *a.* prefabricated
préface *f.* preface
préfacer *vt.* to preface

préfecture *f.* prefecture; police headquarters in Paris; administrative headquarters of a Department
préférable *a.* preferable, better
préféré *a.* preferred; — *m.* favorite
préférence *f.* preference; **de** — preferential; (com.) preferred; preferably
préférer *vt.* to prefer
préfet *m.* prefect; — **de police** chief of police
préfixe *m.* prefix
préfixer *vt.* to prefix; determine in advance
préhenseur *a.* prehensile
préhistorique *a.* prehistoric
préjudice *m.* prejudice, wrong, detriment
préjudiciable *a.* prejudicial, injurious
préjudicier *vi.* to be injurious, be prejudicial
préjugé *m.* prejudice, bias; presumption; legal precedent
préjuger *vt.* to prejudge
prélart *m.* tarpaulin
prélasser *v.*, **se** — to act important
prélat *m.* prelate
prélèvement *m.* deduction; sample
prélever *vt.* to deduct, take off
préliminaire *a.* preliminary
prélude *m.* prelude
prématuré *a.* premature, inopportune
préméditation *f.* premeditation
préméditer *vt.* to premeditate
prémices *f. pl.* first fruits; (fig.) beginnings
premier *a.* first; — **ministre** *m.* Prime Minister, premier; **le** — **venu** anyone
première *f.* first performance, opening night
premièrement *adv.* first, in the first place
premier-né *a. & m.* first-born
premier-paris *m.* lead article in newspaper
prémisse *f.* premise
prémonition *f.* premonition
prémunir *vt.* to forewarn; **se** — **contre be** prepared for
prenable *a.* pregnable, accessible
prenant *a.* attractive; adhesive; — *m.* taker
prénatal *a.* prenatal
prendre *vt.* to take; seize, grab; get; acquire; take on; catch; pick up, call for; take in; influence, gain, win; — *vi.* to take, set; be effective, work; succeed; freeze; — **corps** take form; — **le change** be mistaken; — **le large** flee; **se** — **to** catch, be caught; **s'en** — **à to** blame; **s'y** — to go about it, manage
preneur *m.* taker; purchaser; catcher
prénom *m.* first name
prénommé *a.* above-named

préoccupation f. preoccupation, care, concern; absent-mindedness
préoccupé a. preoccupied; absentminded
préoccuper vt. to preoccupy, concern; **se —** be preoccupied, be busy
préopiner vi. to speak or vote first
préordonné a. preordained
préparateur m. preparer; coach
préparation f. preparation
préparatoire a. preparatory
préparer vt. to prepare, get ready; **se —** to get ready; be in the process, be developing
prépondérance f. preponderance
prépondérant a. preponderant, major, key
préposé m. person in charge
préposer vt. to name, appoint
prépositif a. (gram.) prepositive, prepositional
préposition f. preposition
prérogative f. prerogative
près adv. near, close; **à cela —** except for that; **à peu —** almost, nearly; roughly, approximately; **— de** prep. near; nearly; ready to, about to
présage m. presage, omen, foreboding
présager vt. to forebode, presage, predict
presbyte a. far-sighted
presbytère m. parsonage, rectory
prescience f. prescience
prescient a. prescient
prescription f. regulation(s); direction(s); prescription (at law)
prescrire vt. to prescribe, call for, ordain
préséance f. priority, precedence
présence f. presence; **— d'esprit** presence of mind
présent a. present; **— m.** present time; (gram.) present tense; **à —** at present, right now
présentable a. presentable
présentateur m. introducer, presenter
présentation f. presentation, introduction
présentement adv. at the moment, right now
présenter vt. to present; introduce; **se —** to present oneself; appear; introduce oneself; arise, come about
préservateur a. preservative
préservatif a. & m. preservative; preventive; contraceptive; **— oral** m. oral contraceptive
préservation f. preservation, conservation, saving
préserver vt. to preserve, save, protect
présidence f. presidency, chairmanship
président m. president, chairman, presiding officer
présidentiel a. presidential
présider vt. & vi. to preside over

présomptif a. presumptive
présomption f. presumption
présomptueux a. presumptuous
presque adv. almost, nearly
presqu'île f. peninsula
pressant a. pressing, urgent
presse f. press; crowd; haste; impressment (history)
pressé a. pressed; crowded; squeezed; in a hurry; **citron —** lemonade
presse-citron m. lemon squeezer
presse-fruits m. fruit press
pressentiment m. presentiment, feeling, foreboding
pressentir vt. to have a presentiment of, sense in advance
presse-papiers m. paperweight
presse-purée f. vegetable masher
presser vt. & vi. to press, squeeze; urge; hurry; **se —** to hurry; crowd
pressier m. pressman
pression f. pressure; (elec.) tension
pressoir m. wine press; push button
pressurer vt. to press, extract, squeeze
prestance f. bearing, carriage of a person
prestation f. prestation; oath; lending, loaning
preste a. quick, nimble, agile
prestesse f. nimbleness, quickness, agility
prestidigitateur m. prestidigitator, magician
prestige m. prestige, renown; wonder, marvel
prestigieux a. marvelous, amazing
présumer vt. to presume, assume; allege
présupposer vt. to presuppose
prêt a. ready, prepared; **— m.** loan
prétendant m. aspirant, candidate, applicant
prétendre vt. to claim, maintain; aspire
prétendu a. so-called, alleged; **— n.** (coll.) future spouse, intended
prête-nom m. figurehead, front
prétentieux a. pretentious
prétention f. pretension, claim
prêter vt. to lend; attribute; **— attention** to pay attention; **— serment** to take an oath; **se — à** to lend oneself to, agree to; indulge in
prétérit m. preterite
prétexte m. pretext, excuse; **sous — de** supposedly, presumably
prétexter vt. to offer as a pretext
prétoire m. courtroom
prêteur m. lender; **— sur gages** pawnbroker
prêtre m. priest; **—sse** f. priestess
prêtrise f. priesthood
preuve f. proof, evidence
preux a. valiant, courageous

prévaloir *vi.* to prevail; se — to avail one-self
prévaricateur *a.* dishonest public official
prévarication *f.* malfeasance, dishonesty
prévenance *f.* kind attention, considera-tion
prévenant *a.* considerate, attentive; en-gaging, prepossessing
prévenir *vt.* to anticipate; prevent; pre-judice; warn, inform
préventif *a.* preventive; pre-emptive (cards)
prévention *f.* prejudice; custody
prévenu *a.* prejudiced, accused (at law)
prévision *f.* forecast, estimate
prévoir *vt.* to foresee; forecast; provide for, anticipate
prévôt *m.* provost
prévoyance *f.* foresight, precaution
prévoyant *a.* foreseeing, looking ahead, farsighted
prie-dieu *m.* prayer desk
prier *vt.* to pray; ask; invite; **je vous (en) prie** please, if you please
prière *f.* prayer; request
prieuré *m.* priory
primaire *a.* primary
primauté *f.* priority; primacy
prime *f.* premium; bonus, gift; (eccl.) prime; — *a.* first, earliest; **de — abord** first of all
primer *vt.* to surpass; give a prize to
primerose *f.* hollyhock
primesaut *m.* first impulse
prime-sautier *a.* impulsive; quick
primeur *f.* newness, earliness; early crop
primevère *f.* (bot.) primrose; cowslip
primitif *a.* primitive; primary; early; ear-liest; crude
primo *adv.* first of all, firstly
primogéniture *f.* primogeniture
primordial *a.* primordial, primeval
prince *m.* prince; ruler, monarch
princeps *a.*, **édition —** *f.* first edition
princesse *f.* princess
princier *a.* princely, royal
principal *a.* principal, main, chief; — *m.* principal; main point, main thing
principauté *f.* principality
principe *m.* principle
printanier *a.* spring, springlike
printemps *m.* spring, springtime
priorité *f.* priority, precedence
pris *a.* taken, caught; busy, occupied; **bien — having a good figure** *or* shape
prise *f.* taking, capture; hold, grip; set-ting, hardening; engaging of gears; valve, intake; (naut.) prize; **en venir aux −s** to come to blows, come to grips; **hors de — out of gear; lâcher —**

to let go; — **de corps** arrest; — **de courant** (elect.) plug, outlet; — **de tabac** pinch of snuff; — **de vue** view-finder
prisée *f.* evaluation, appraisal
priser *vt.* to appraise, value, prize; **to take snuff**
priseur *m.* appraiser; auctioneer; user of snuff
prismatique *a.* prismatic
prisme *m.* prism
prisonnier *m.* prisoner
privation *f.* privation; deprivation; pov-erty; hardship
privautés *f. pl.* familiarity, liberties
privé *a.* private; privy; tame
priver *vt.* to deprive; se — to do without, stint
privilège *m.* privilege; authorization, license
privilégié *a.* privileged; authorized, li-censed; preferred (stock)
privilégier *vt.* to privilege; authorize, li-cense
prix *m.* price, value, cost; prize, award; **à tout — at any price; au — de at the** price of; compared with, in comparison with; — **dirigé** (econ.) price control; **hors de — prohibitive; — fixe set price**
prix-courant *m.* price list, catalog
probable *a.* probable, likely
probabilité *f.* probability, likelihood
probe *a.* honest, upright, of integrity
problème *m.* problem
procéde *m.* proceeding, procedure; process
procéder *vi.* to proceed
procédure *f.* procedure; proceedings
procès *m.* lawsuit; trial; ceremony, for-mality, ado; process
processif *a.* pertaining to courtroom procedure
processionnel *a.* processional
processionner *vi.* to file by (as in a pro-cession)
processus *m.* process; development
procès-verbal *m.* report, record, minutes
prochain *a.* next; neighboring, nearest; imminent; — *m.* neighbor, fellow man
prochainement *adv.* in the near future, shortly, soon
proche *a.* near, close; **–es** *m. pl.* relatives
proclamation *f.* proclamation
proclamer *vt.* to proclaim
proconsul *m.* proconsul
procréateur *a.* procreative; — *m.* pro-creator
procréation *f.* procreation
procréer *vt.* to procreate
procurable *a.* procurable, obtainable
procuration *f.* power of attorney; proxy

procurer *vt.* to procure, obtain
procureur *m.* attorney; prosecuting attorney, prosecutor
prodigalité *f.* prodigality; extravagance
prodige *m.* prodigy, marvel
prodigieux *a.* prodigious
prodigue *a. & m.* prodigal; spendthrift
prodiguer *vt.* to waste, squander; lavish
producer *m.* movie producer
producteur *a.* productive; — *m.* producer
productif *a.* productive
production *f.* production; producing; yield; product
productivité *f.* productivity
produire *vt.* to produce; yield, give, bear; se — to happen, take place, occur
produit *m.* product; proceeds
proéminence *f.* prominence; protuberance
proéminent *a.* prominent; protuberant
profanateur *m.* profaner
profanation *f.* profanation, desecration
profane *a.* profane; sacrilegious; secular, lay; — *m.* layman, uninitiated person; something profane
profaner *vt.* to profane, desecrate
proférer *vt.* to utter
professer *vt.* to profess; teach
professeur *m.* professor, teacher
profession *f.* profession; occupation, business
professionnel *a. & m.* professional
professoral *a.* professorial
professorat *m.* professorship
profil *m.* profile, side view; outline, shape, contour
profilé *a.* in sections, sectional; streamlined
profilée *f.* side view
profiler *vt.* to profile; shape; se — to be silhouetted, be outlined
profitable *a.* profitable, advantageous
profiter *vi.* to profit, be profitable; gain by; grow, develop
profiteur *m.* profiteer
profond *a.* profound; deep; — *m.* deepest part, depth(s)
profondeur *f.* profundity, depth
profus *a.* profuse
profusion *f.* profusion, abundance
progéniture *f.* progeny, offspring
prognostique *a.* prognostic
programme *m.* program; plan; curriculum
progrès *m.* progress
progresser *vi.* to progress
progressif *a.* progressive
progressiste *a. & m. & f.* (pol.) progressive
progression *f.* progress, progression
prohiber *vt.* to prohibit, forbid
prohibitif *a.* prohibitive

proie *f.* prey; en — à prey to; subject to; affected by
projecteur *m.* projector; searchlight
projectile *a. & m.* projectile; — balistique ballistic missile
projection *f.* projection; (phot.) slide; beam, shaft of light
projecture *f.* projection
projet *m.* project, plan; — de vol flight plan
projeter *vt.* to project; plan
prolétaire *a. & m.* proletarian
prolétariat *m.* proletariate
prolifération *f.* proliferation
prolifère *a.* proliferous
prolifique *a.* prolific
prolixe *a.* prolix, verbose
prolixité *f.* prolixity, verbosity
prolongateur *m.* extension cord
prolongation *f.* prolongation; extension of time
prolongé *a.* prolonged, long
prolongement *m.* prolongation; extension
prolonger *vt.* to prolong, extend, lengthen
promenade *f.* walking, walk, stroll; promenade; faire une — take a walk; — en auto auto ride; — en bateau boat ride
promener *vt.* to take for a walk; se — to take a walk
promeneur *m.* walker
promenoir *m.* promenade; (theat.) standing room
promesse *f.* promise
prometteur *a.* promising
promettre *vt. & vi.* to promise
promis *a.* promised; — *m.* fiancé; -e *f.* fiancée
promiscuité *f.* promiscuity
promontoire *m.* promontory, cape
promoteur *m.* promoter
promotion *f.* promotion
promouvoir *vt.* to promote
prompt *a.* prompt, ready, quick minded
promptitude *f.* promptitude; readiness, quickness
promu *a.* promoted
promulgation *f.* promulgation
promulguer *vt.* to promulgate, publish
pronation *f.* prone position
prône *m.* sermon
prôner *vt.* to praise; preach
pronom *m.* pronoun
pronominal *a.* pronominal; verbe — *m.* reflexive verb
prononçable *a.* pronounceable
prononcé *a.* pronounced, marked, decided, definite; — *m.* decision, verdict
prononcer *vt.* to pronounce; deliver; declare
prononciation *f.* pronunciation

pronostic *m.* prognostic, prognostication; (med.) prognosis
pronostiquer *vt.* to prognosticate, predict
propagande *f.* publicity, advertising, propaganda
propagandiste *m. & f.* propagandist
propagateur *a.* propagating; — *m.* propagator
propager *vt.* to propagate; se — to spread; be propagated
propédeutique *f.* first year of university studies
propension *f.* propensity
prophétie *f.* prophecy
prophétique *a.* prophetic
prophétiser *vt.* to prophesy; forecast
prophylactique *a.* prophylactic
prophylaxie *f.* prophylaxis
propice *a.* propitious, auspicious
propitiatoire *a.* propitiatory, conciliatory
proportionné *a.* proportioned; proportionate
proportionnel *a.* proportional
proportionner *vt.* to proportion
propos *m.* discourse, talk, words; design; purpose; subject; à — suitable, appropriate; by the way; à — de on the subject of; hors de — inopportune, out of place
proposer *vt.* to propose, present, recommend, suggest
proposition *f.* proposition, proposal, motion; clause
propre *a.* one's own; clean; proper; fit, suitable
proprement *adv.* properly; cleanly; appropriately
propreté *f.* cleanliness, neatness
propriétaire *m. & f.* proprietor, owner; landlord
propriété *f.* property; ownership; propriety; quality, characteristic
propulser *vt.* to propel
propulseur *a.* propelling; — *m.* propellant
propulsion *f.* propulsion; — à réaction jet propulsion
prorata *m.* share; au — pro rata
proroger *vt.* to extend, prolong; adjourn
prosaïque *a.* prosaic
prosateur *m.* prose writer
proscenium *m.* (theat.) proscenium
proscription *f.* proscription, proscribing
proscrire *vt.* to proscribe, outlaw; abolish, forbid
proscrit *a.* proscribed, outlawed; — *m.* proscript, outlaw
prosélyte *m. & f.* proselyte
prospecter *vt.* to prospect
prospecteur *m.* prospector
prospectus *m.* prospectus; leaflet, handbill

prospérer *vi.* to prosper, thrive
prospérité *f.* prosperity
prostate *f.* prostate
prosternation *f.* prone position; prostration; bowing
prosterné *a.* prone, prostrate
prosternement *m.* prone position, prostration; bowing
prosterner *vt.*, se — to prostrate oneself; bow down
prostituée *f.* prostitute, call girl
prostitution *f.* prostitution
prostration *f.* prostration, exhaustion, breakdown; prone position
prostré *a.* prostrate, exhausted
protagoniste *m.* protagonist
protane *m.* methane
protase *f.* (theat.) protasis, exposition
protecteur *m.* protector, guard; patron; — *a.* protective
protection *f.* protection, patronage
protectionisme *m.* protectionism
protectionniste *m. & f.* protectionist
protectorat *m.* protectorate
protéger *vt.* to protect, guard; patronize
protège-vue *m.* eyeshade
protéine *f.* protein
protestant *a. & m.* Protestant
protestantisme *m.* Protestantism
protestateur *m.* protestor
protestation *f.* protest; protestation
protester *vt. & vi.* to protest
protêt *m.* legal protest
prothèse *f.* prosthesis, artificial limb or part
protocolaire *a.* pertaining to protocol
protocole *m.* protocol, etiquette
proton *m.* proton
protoplasme *m.* protoplasm
prototype *m.* prototype
protozoaire *m.* protozoan
protubérance *f.* protuberance; bump; knob
protubérant *a.* protuberant
proue *f.* (naut.) prow, bow
prouesse *f.* prowess; feat
prouver *vt.* to prove, establish
provenance *f.* origin, source; production; en — de coming from
provençal *a.* Provençal, of Provence; — *m.* Provençal
Provence *f.* Provence
provende *f.* fodder, provender
provenir *vi.* to proceed, arise, come, result, issue
proverbe *m.* proverb
providence *f.* providence
providentiel *a.* providential
province *f.* province; country; de — provincial

provincial *a. & m.* provincial
proviseur *m.* school principal
provision *f.* provision; supply; stock; deposit; reserve; funds
provisoire *a.* provisional, temporary, acting
provocant *a.* provocative
provocateur *a.* provocative; — *m.* provoker, instigator
provocatif *a.* provocative
provoquer *vt.* to provoke, instigate; arouse; challenge
proximité *f.* proximity, nearness
prude *a.* prudish; — *f.* prude
prudemment *adv.* prudently
prudence *f.* prudence, caution, discretion
prudent *a.* prudent, cautious, discreet
pruderie *f.* prudery, prudishness
prud'homme *m.* elected arbiter
prune *f.* plum
pruneau *m.* prune
prunelle *f.* pupil of the eye; sloe
prunier *m.* plum tree
prurit *m.* itching
Prusse *f.* Prussia
Prussien *m. & a.* Prussian
psalmiste *m.* psalmist
psalmodier *vt. & vi.* to intone
psaume *m.* psalm
psautier *m.* psalm book, Psalter
pseudonyme *m.* pseudonym
pseudopode *n.* pseudopod
psychanalyse *f.* psychoanalysis
psychanalyser *vt.* to psychoanalyze
psychanalyste *m. & f.* psychoanalyst
psychiatre *m.* psychiatrist
psychiatrie *f.* psychiatry
psychique *a.* psychic
psychologie *f.* psychology; — industrielle industrial psychology
psychologique *a.* psychological
psychologue *m. & f.* psychologist
psychose *f.* psychosis
psychosomatique *a.* psychosomatic
psychothérapie *f.* psychotherapy
ptomaïne *f.* ptomaine
P.T.T.: Postes Télégraphes Téléphones postal and telegraph service
puant *a.* smelly, stinking
pubère *a.* in puberty, pubescent
puberté *f.* puberty
public (publique) *a.* public; open; — *m.* public, the people
publication *f.* publication, publishing
publiciste *m.* publicist, newspaperman
publicitaire *m.* (com.) adman
publicité *f.* advertising
publier *vt.* to publish
puce *f.* flea
pucelle *f.* maid, virgin

puceron *m.* aphid
pudeur *f.* decency, modesty
pudibond *a.* prudish, excessively modest
pudibonderie *f.* prudishness
pudique *a.* chaste
puer *vi.* to stink, smell
puériculture *f.* raising, rearing of children
puéril *a.* childish, puerile
puérilité *f.* puerility
puffisme *m.* publicity, boosting
puffiste *m.* booster
pugilat *m.* pugilism, boxing
pugiliste *m.* pugilist, boxer
puîné *a.* younger
puis *adv.* then, afterwards; moreover, besides
puisage *m.* pumping; droit de — *m.* water rights
puisard *m.* cesspool; sump
puisatier *m.* well digger
puisette *f.* scoop, ladle
puisoir *m.* large industrial scoop
puisque *conj.* since, as; but
puissamment *adv.* powerfully
puissance *f.* power, force, strength; authority, control
puissant *a.* powerful, strong, potent
puits *m.* well; shaft; hole
pullman *m.* luxury car; parlor car
pulluler *vi.* to multiply; swarm; pullulate
pulmonaire *a.* pulmonary
pulmonie *f.* lung disease
pulpe *f.* pulp
pulper *vt.* to pulp
pulpeux *a.* pulpy
pulsatif *a.* throbbing
pulsation *f.* pulsation, throbbing
pulvérisateur *m.* pulverizer; atomizer
pulvérisation *f.* pulverization
pulvériser *vt.* to pulverize, crush, grind; atomize
pulvériseur *m.* disc plow
puma *m.* puma
punaise *f.* bedbug; thumbtack
punch *m.* punch (beverage)
punir *vt.* to punish
punition *f.* punishment, punishing; penalty
pupe *f.* pupa, chrysalis
pupille *m. & f.* legal ward; — *f.* pupil of the eye
pupitre *m.* desk; lectern; music stand
pur *a.* pure; simple; clear
purée *f.* thick soup; mashed vegetable
pureté *f.* purity, pureness
purgatif *a. & m.* purgative
purgation *f.* purgation, purging
purge *f.* purge; purgative; purging; draining; cleaning; redeeming; paying off
purger *vt.* to purge, cleanse; clear; redeem,

pay off; drain
purificateur *a.* purifying; — *m.* purifier
purification *f.* purification
purifier *vt.* to purify, refine; clean
puriste *m.* purist
purpurin *m.* crimson, dark red
pur-sang *m.* thoroughbred, race horse
purulent *a.* purulent
pus *m.* pus
pusillanime *a.* pusillanimous
pusillanimité *f.* pusillanimity
pustule *f.* pustule
putatif *a.* putative, supposed
putois *m.* skunk, polecat
putréfaction *f.* putrefaction
putréfier *vt.* to putrify
putride *a.* putrid, rotten
puzzle *m.* jigsaw puzzle
pygmée *m. & f.* pygmy
pyjama *m.* pajamas
pylône *m.* pylon, tower
pylore *m.* pyloris
pyorrhée *f.* pyorrhea
pyramidal *a.* pyramidal
pyramide *f.* pyramid
Pyrénées *f. pl.* Pyrenees
pyrite *f.* pyrite
pyrotechnie *f.* pyrotechnics
pyrotechnique *a.* pyrotechnic
python *m.* python

Q

Quadragésime *f.* old name of Lent; dimanche de la — *m.* first Sunday in Lent
quadrangulaire *a.* quadrangular
quadratique *a.* quadratic
quadrature *f.* squaring
quadriennal *a.* quadrennial
quadrilatéral *a.* quadrilateral
quadrilatère *m.* quadrilateral
quadrillage *m.* squaring, checkering, cross-ruling
quadrillé *a.* squared, checked, cross-ruled
quadriller *vt.* to cross-rule
quadrimoteur *a.* four-engined
quadrupède *m.* quadruped
quadrupler *vt. & vi.* to quadruple
quai *m.* quay, wharf; embankment; (rail.) platform
qualificatif *a.* qualifying
qualification *f.* qualification; qualifying; character; naming, calling, designating
qualifier *vt.* to qualify; call, designate; se — to qualify; call oneself
qualitatif *a.* qualitative
qualité *f.* quality; rank; characteristic, property; qualification; occupation

quand *adv.* when; depuis — how long; — *conj.* when; although, though, even if; — même even though; in spite of all; just the same
quant à *prep.* as to, as for
quant-à-moi, quant-à-soi *m.* reserve, aloofness
quantième *m.* a day of the month
quantitatif *a.* quantitative; (gram.) quantity
quantité *f.* quantity, amount
quantum *m.* quantum; amount
quarantaine *f.* forty, around forty, two score; quarantine
quarante *a.* forty
quarantième *a.* fortieth
quart *m.* quarter, fourth; (naut.) watch; ¼ liter; — d'heure quarter-hour, fifteen minutes
quarte *f.* quart; (mus.) fourth
quarteron *a. & m.* quadroon
quartier *m.* quarter, district; piece, part, portion; barracks, camp; — commerçant shopping plaza; — général headquarters
quarto *adv.* fourthly; in fourth place
quartz *m.* quartz
quasi *adv.* almost
quatorze *a.* fourteen; fourteenth
quatorzième *a.* fourteenth
quatrain *m.* quatrain
quatre *a.* four; fourth
quatre-saisons *f.* strawberry plant bearing very small fruit; marchand des — *m.* pushcart vendor of seasonal fruits and vegetables
quatre-vingts *a.* eighty
quatrième *a.* fourth
quatuor *m.* quartet
que *conj.* that; if, when, as, than, till, until, whether, than; afin —, de sorte — so that; ne . . . . — only; — *pron.* that, whom, which; — *interr. pron.* what; how; — de how many, how much; ce — that which, what; which; (with exclamations)
quel (quelle) *a. interr.* which, what; what (a) (in exclamations); — *pron.* whatever
quelconque *a.* any, whatever, any at all; mediocre
quelque *a.* some, any; a few; — chose something, anything; — part somewhere; — *adv.* however; — *pron.* whatever
quelquefois *adv.* sometimes
quelqu'un, quelqu'une *indefinite pron.* one; somebody, someone; quelques-uns, quelques-unes *pl.* some
quémander *vi. & vt.* to beg for, solicit
quenelle *f.* meatball, fishball

quenouille *f.* distaff; bedpost; bulrush
querelle *f.* quarrel, row, feud
quereller *vt.* to quarrel with; **se — to** quarrel; have a strong difference of opinion; have a falling out
querelleur *a.* quarrelsome; **—** *m.* quarreler
quérir *vt.* to find, get, bring, fetch
qu'est-ce que *interr. pron.* what (as object of verb)
qu'est-ce qui *interr. pron.* what (as subject of verb)
question *f.* question; matter; **poser une —, faire une —** to ask a question
questionnaire *m.* questionnaire; questions
questionner *vt.* to question, interrogate
questionneur *a.* inquisitive; **—** *m.* interrogator
quetsche *f.* purple plum
quête *f.* quest, search; (eccl.) collection
quêter *vt.* to collect; look for
queue *f.* tail; line; handle; stalk; train of a garment; **piano à —** *m.* grand piano; **faire la —** to line up
queue-d'aronde *f.* dovetail
queue-de-chat *f.* cat-o'-nine-tails; cirrus cloud
queue-de-rat *f.* round *or* rat-tail file
qui *interr. pron.* who, whom; **à —** whose, to whom; **de —** whose, of whom; **—** *rel. pron.* who, which, that; the one who, he who; **ce —** that which, what; which; **— que** whoever; **— que ce soit** anyone
quiconque *pron.* whoever; anyone
quidam *m.* unidentified person, someone; unknown party (law)
qui est-ce que *interr. pron.* whom
qui est-ce qui *interr. pron.* who
quiétude *f.* quietude
quignon *m.* hunk, chunk
quille *f.* ninepin, tenpin; (naut.) keel; **jeu de –s** *m.* bowling
quincaillerie *f.* hardware, hardware store
quincaillier *m.* hardware dealer
quinconce *f.*, **en —** alternately; staggered, zigzag
quinine *f.* quinine
quinquennal *a.* quinquennial, five-year
quintal *m.* hundredweight, quintal
quinte *f.* (mus.) fifth; fit of coughing
quintette *f.* quintet
quinteux *a.* fitful, restive
quintuple *a.* quintuple
quintupler *vt. & vi.* to quintuple
quintuplés *m. pl.* quintuplets
quinzaine *f.* about fifteen; two-week period, fortnight
quinze *a.* fifteen; fifteenth; **— jours** two weeks
quinzième *a.* fifteenth

quiproquo *m.* mistake, mistaken identity
quittance *f.* receipt
quitte *a.* free, clear; rid; quits, even; **jouer à — ou double** to play double or nothing
quitter *vt.* to leave; take off; abandon
qui-vive *m.* (mil.) challenge by a sentry, **être sur le —** to be on the watch, be alert
quoi *interr. pron.* what; **— de nouveau** what's new; **un je ne sais —** a certain something; **—** *rel. pron.* what; **de —** enough; wherewithal; reason, cause, justification; **il n'y a pas de —** you're welcome, don't mention it; **— que** whatever; **— qu'il en soit** be that as it may; **sans —** or else, otherwise
quoique *conj.* though, although
quolibet *m.* gibe, jeering remark
quote-part *f.* quota, share
quotidien *a.* daily; **—** *m.* daily newspaper
quotidiennement *adv.* every day, daily
quotient *m.* quotient; quota

R

rabâcher *vi.* to repeat, rehash
rabais *m.* reduction, discount, rebate
rabaisser *vt.* to lower, reduce, humiliate, deprecate
rabat *m.* flap
rabat-joie *m.* killjoy
rabattre *vt.* to turn down; lower; fold back; flatten; lower, reduce the price; **—** *vi.* to turn off; **se —** to fall back; fold
rabbin *m.* rabbi
râblé *a.* strong, strong-backed
rabonnir *vt. & vi.* to improve
rabot *m.* plane (tool)
raboter *vt.* to plane, smooth
raboteux *a.* rough, uneven; knotty
rabougrir *vt.* to stunt
rabouter *vt.* to place end to end
rabrouer *vt.* to snub; become very angry at, become surly toward
racaille *f.* rubbish, trash; social outcast
raccommodage *m.* mending, repairing; darning
raccommodement *m.* reconciliation
raccommoder *vt.* to mend, repair; darn; reconcile; **se —** to be reconciled, make up
raccord *m.* joint, coupling, connection; tieing together, joining
raccordement *m.* connecting, joining; junction
raccorder *vt.* to connect, join, tie together, link; **se —** to join, fit
raccourci *a.* abridged, shortened; **—** *m.* abridgment; short cut; book digest; **en**

— briefly

raccourcir *vt.* to shorten; abridge; — *vi.* to become shorter

raccourcissement *m.* shortening; shrinking

raccoutrer *vt.* to repair, mend

raccroc *m.* stroke of luck, fluke, chance

raccrocher *vt.* to hook up; hang up (telephone); **se** — to grab hold; regain, recover

race *f.* race, family, breed; **de** — thoroughbred

racé *a.* thoroughbred

rachat *m.* buying back, repurchase; redemption

rachetable *a.* redeemable

racheter *vt.* to buy back, repurchase; redeem; ransom

rachitisme *m.* rickets

racine *f.* root

raciste *m.* racist

racketter *m.* racketeer

raclage *m.* scraping

racle *f.* scraper

racler *vt.* to scrape; rake

raclette *f.* scraper; hoe

racloir *m.* scraping implement

raclure *f.* scrapings

racoler *vt.* to recruit, enlist, enroll

racoleur *m.* recruiter

racontage *m.* recounting, telling; gossip

raconter *vt.* to relate, tell

raconteur *m.* storyteller

racornir *vt.* to harden, make horny

racquitter *v.*, **se** — to recoup

radar *m.* radar

radariste *m.* radar operator

rade *f.* (naut.) roadstead, basin, harbor

radeau *m.* raft, float

radiateur *m.* radiator; — *a.* radiating

radiation *f.* radiation; cancellation; erasure, crossing out; disbarment

radical *a. & m.* radical

radicelle *f.* (bot.) radicle

radier *m.* frame, foundation floor

radier *vi.* to radiate; — *vt.* to erase, cross out; strike off

radieux *a.* radiant, bright

radio *f.* radio; — *m.* radio operator

radio-actif *a.* radioactive

radio-activité *f.* radioactivity

radio-astronomie *f.* radioastronomy

radiobalisage *m.* (avi.) radio beam

radiocommunication *f.* radio communication

radiodiffuser *vt.* to broadcast

radiodiffusion *f.* radio program; broadcast

radio-émission *f.* broadcast; broadcasting

radiogoniomètre *m.* direction finder

radiogramme *m.* radiogram, radio message

radiographie *f.* X-ray photography, radiography

radiographier *vt.* to X-ray

radiographique *a.* X-ray, radiographic

radiojournal *m.* radio newscast

radiologie *f.* radiology

radiologique *a.* radiological, X-ray

radiologue *m. & f.* radiologist, X-ray technician

radioreportage *m.* radio report, program

radioreporter *m.* radio commentator

radioscopie *f.* radioscopy

radiotéléscope *m.* radio telescope

radiothérapie *f.* X-ray therapy

radium *m.* radium

radius *m.* (anat.) radius

radotage *m.* dotage; raving; nonsense

radoter *vi.* to be in one's dotage; talk nonsense

radoteur *m.* dotard

radoub *m.* (naut.) repair; **bassin de** — *m.* drydock

radouber *vt.* to repair; put in drydock

radoucir *vt.* to soften, appease; calm; **se** — to relent, soften; turn mild

rafale *f.* gust, flurry; burst, volley

raffermir *vt.* to strengthen, make firm(er), reinforce; harden; **se** — to become firmer, become stronger; harden

raffinage *m.* refining

raffiné *a.* refined

raffinement *m.* refinement

raffiner *vt.* to refine; **se** — to become refined

raffinerie *f.* refinery; refining

raffoler (de) *vi.* to be wild about; be infatuated with; dote on

raffûter *vt.* to sharpen, resharpen

rafistoler *vt.* to patch up

rafle *f.* raid; loot; looting; police roundup

rafler *vt.* to loot, clean out (a house); round up (criminals)

rafraîchir *vt.* to refresh, cool; renovate; touch up; remind; trim hair; **se** — to refresh oneself; drink; become cooler (weather)

rafraîchissant *a.* cooling, refreshing

rafraîchissement *m.* refreshment, cooling; touching up; brushing up

rage *f.* rage, madness; passion, **mania**; rabies; **à la** — *adv.* excessively

rager *vi.* (coll.) to rage, fume

ragot *a.* stocky, squat; — *m.* (coll.) gossip, talk

ragoût *m.* stew, ragout; relish

ragoûter *vt.* to revive the appetite

rai *m.* radius; beam of light; spoke

raid *m.* raid; endurance contest; (avi.) long flight, trip

raide *a.* stiff; inflexible; steep; firm; —

adv. quickly; on the spot

raideur *f.* stiffness; steepness

raidir *vt.* to stiffen; **se —** to get stiff, stiffen, become tight

raie *f.* line, stripe; part in the hair; furrow; ray, skate (fish)

raifort *m.* horseradish

rail *m.* rail

railler *vt.* to laugh at, make fun of; **—** *vi.* to joke

raillerie *f.* raillery, mockery, joking

railleur *a.* jeering, scoffing, joking; **—** *m.* scoffer, joker

rainer *vt.* to groove

rainette *f.* tree frog

rainure *f.* groove; channel

raiponce *f.* rampion

rais *m.* spoke

raisin *m.* grape, grapes; **grappe de —** *f.* bunch of grapes; **— sec** raisin; **— de Corinthe** currant

raison *f.* reason, cause, motive; justification; satisfaction, amends; (math.) ratio; **à — de** at the rate of; **à plus forte —** all the more; **avoir —** to be right; **en — de** by reason of, because of; **— d'être** rational explanation, justification

raisonnable *a.* reasonable, rational; just, fair

raisonné *a.* founded on reason, methodical

raisonnement *m.* reasoning; argument

raisonner *vi.* to reason; **—** *vt.* to think out, study

rajeunir *vt.* to make young again; rejuvenate; **—** *vi.* to grow young again; be rejuvenated

rajustement *m.* readjustment; setting in order

rajuster *vt.* to readjust, set in order again, straighten, fix

râle *m.* death rattle; rail

ralenti *a.* slow, slower, slowed down; **—** *m.* slow motion

ralentir *vt.* to slacken, lessen, slow down

ralentissement *m.* slackening, slowing down, abatement

râler *vi.* give the death rattle; grumble

ralliement *m.* rally, rallying

rallier *vt.* to rally; assemble, bring together

rallonge *f.* extension; table leaf

rallongement *m.* lengthening, extending

rallonger *vt.* to lengthen, extend; thin a sauce

rallumer *vt.* to light again, rekindle

ramage *m.* warbling of birds; prattle; flowering; floral pattern

ramas *m.* heap, accumulation, collection

ramassé *a.* stocky; compact

ramasse-miettes *m.* silent butler, crumb tray

ramasse-poussière *m.* dustpan

ramasser *vt.* to pick up, gather, collect; **se —** to gather together; pick oneself up; crouch

ramassis *m.* collection, accumulation

rambarde *f.* railing

rame *f.* oar; ream of paper; (rail.) train, string of cars; convoy; wooden support for plants

ramé *a.* supported by sticks

rameau *m.* bough, branch; **dimanche des Rameaux** *m.* Palm Sunday

ramée *f.* boughs, arbor

ramener *vt.* to bring back, lead back, take back; pull down one's hat; restore

ramequin *m.* filled pastry shell

ramer *vi.* to row; grow antlers

rameur *m.* rower, oarsman

rameux *a.* ramose, having many branches

ramification *f.* ramification; branch

ramifier *v.*, **se —** to ramify, branch out

ramille *f.* twig

ramoindrir *vt.* to lessen, diminish, reduce

ramollir *vt.* to soften; weaken; **se —** to become soft

ramollissement *m.* softening

ramonage *m.* chimney sweeping

ramoner *vt.* to sweep a chimney

ramoneur *m.* chimney sweep

rampant *a.* creeping, crawling; rampant (heraldry)

rampe *f.* flight of stairs; balustrade, banister, handrail; slope; ramp; footlights of a stage

ramper *vi.* to crawl, creep; grovel; toady

ramure *f.* branches; antlers

rance *a.* rancid

ranch *m.* ranch

rancidité *f.* rancidness

rancir *vi.* to become rancid

rancœur *f.* bitterness, rancor

rançon *f.* ransom

rançonner *vt.* to ransom

rancune *f.* grudge, ill-feeling, rancor, spite

rancunier *a.* rancorous, spiteful, vindictive

randonnée *f.* trip, outing, excursion

rang *m.* row, file, line; rank, standing

rangé *a.* ranged; steady, regular, orderly; pitched battle

rangée *f.* row, file, line

ranger *vt.* to range; rank, put in ranks; arrange, set in order; put away; **se —** to line up; pull up; take sides; settle down

ranimer *vt.* to restore, revive; rouse; **se —** to become animated again; enliven

Raoul (*m.*) Ralph

rapace *a.* rapacious; grasping; ravenous

rapacité *f.* rapacity

râpage *m.* grating, filing
rapatriement *m.* repatriation
rapatrier *vt.* to repatriate
râpe *f.* grater; file, rasp
râpé *a.* threadbare; grated
râper *vt.* to grate; file; wear out (clothing)
rapetasser *vt.* to patch up clothing; mend extensively
rapetisser *vt.* to make smaller, shorten; shrink; — *vi.* to become shorter, become smaller
raphia *m.* raffia
rapide *a.* rapid, swift, fast; — *m.* express train; –s *pl.* rapids in a river
rapidité *f.* rapidity, speed
rapiéçage *m.* patching, mending
rapiécer *vt.* to piece; patch, mend
rapière *f.* rapier
rapine *f.* pillage, pillaging
rapiner *vt. & vi.* to pillage
rappareiller *vt.* to match
rapparier *vt.* to pair, match
rappel *m.* recall; calling in; call to arms; (theat.) curtain call; reminder; revocation, repeal; back spacer of a typewriter
rappeler *vt.* to recall, call back; remind; **se —** to remember, recall
rapport *m.* report; return, profit; relation, connection; ratio; **par — à, sous le — de** with regard to, with respect to
rapportable *a.* attributable
rapporter *vt.* to bring back, carry back; return, produce, bring in; report, tell of; revoke; attribute; **se —** to refer, relate, have to do with; **s'en — à** to rely on
rapporteur *m.* reporter; tattletale; (math.) protractor; sponsor, introducer
rapprendre *vt.* to learn again; teach again
rapproché *a.* close, near; connected, related; close-set (eyes)
rapprochement *m.* reconciliation; bringing together; comparison, comparing; closeness
rapprocher *vt.* to draw near again, bring near; bring together; compare
rapsodie *f.* rhapsody
rapt *m.* abduction, kidnapping
râpure *f.* gratings, scrapings
raquette *f.* racket; snowshoe
rare *a.* rare; thin, sparse; unusual, uncommon
raréfaction *f.* rarefaction; scarcity
raréfier *vt.* to rarefy; make scarce
rareté *f.* rarity; scarcity; unusualness
rarissime *a.* very rare
ras *a.* short-haired, close-cut; smooth-shaven; bare; plain, smooth; open; flat; **au — de** on a level with; **à — de** level with; **faire table —e** start from scratch;

make a clean sweep
rasant *a.* grazing, skimming, staying close to; boring, dull
rase-mottes *m.* (avi.) low-level flying, hedge-hopping
raser *vt.* to shave; raze; graze, skim; stay close to; bore; **se —** to shave; be bored
raseur *m.* shaver; bore
rasoir *m.* razor; **— à lame** straight razor; **cuir à — m.** razor strop; **— de sûreté** safety razor
rassasiant *a.* satisfying, filling
rassasiement *m.* satisfying, satiety
rassasier *vt.* to satiate, fill, satisfy; **se —** to fill up, eat one's fill
rassemblement *m.* assembling; assemblage
rassembler *vt.* to collect, assemble; unite; **se —** to meet; assemble
rasseoir *vt.* to seat again
rasséréner *vt.* to calm; **se —** to brighten, clear up
rassir *vi.* to harden (bread)
rassis *a.* calm, sedate; stale (bread)
rassortir *vt.* (com.) to restock
rassurer *vt.* to reassure; strengthen; **se —** be reassured
rat *m.* rat; **— musqué** muskrat
rataplan *m.* roll of a drum
ratatiner *vt.* to dry up; shrink, shrivel
rate *f.* spleen
raté *a.* failed, missed; — *m.* failure; dud
râteau *m.* rake
râteler *vt.* to rake
rater *vi.* to miss; fail; misfire; — *vt.* miss, fail in
ratière *f.* rat trap
ratifier *vt.* to ratify
rationaliser *vt.* to rationalize
rationnel *a.* rational
rationner *vt.* to ration
ratisser *vt.* to scrape, rake
ratissoire *f.* rake; scraper
raton *m.* small rat; **— laveur** raccoon
rattacher *vt.* to tie again, attach, fasten; **se —** to be tied to, be connected with
ratteindre *vt.* to overtake; retake
rattraper *vt.* to catch again, retake; overtake, catch up with; get back, recover; **se —** to make up, recoup
rature *f.* erasure; scraping
raturer *vt.* to scratch out, erase
raucité *f.* hoarseness
rauque *a.* hoarse, harsh, raucous
ravager *vt.* to ravage, pillage, devastate; pit by smallpox
ravages *m. pl.* devastation; havoc
ravalement *m.* scraping, cleaning; resurfacing
ravaler *vt.* to reswallow; (fig.) hold back;

take back, retract; **se —** to debase oneself

ravaudage *m.* mending, patching; bungling

ravauder *vt.* to mend, patch

ravi *a.* delighted

ravier *m.* hors-d'œuvres dish

ravigote *f.* sauce with shallots

ravillir *vt.* to vilify

ravin *m.* ravine

raviner *vt.* to furrow

ravir *vt.* to ravish, abduct, steal; delight

raviser *v.*, **se —** to change one's mind

ravissant *a.* delightful, ravishing

ravissement *m.* ravishing, abduction; delight, rapture

ravisseur *m.* ravisher, abductor, kidnapper

ravitaillement *m.* supplying, provisioning, revictualing; refueling

ravitailler *vt.* to supply, provision; **se —** to take in fresh supplies

ravitailleur *m.* supply ship

raviver *vt.* to revive; renew, touch up; reopen a wound

ravoir *vt.* to have again; recover, get back

rayé *a.* striped; rifled; (fig.) suppressed; erased

rayer *vt.* to erase, cross out, strike out; rule, line; rifle a gun

rayon *m.* ray, beam; spoke; radius; furrow, row; shelf; department (in a store); **chef de —** floorwalker; **— X** X ray

rayonnant *a.* radiant, beaming; radiating

rayonne *f.* rayon

rayonnement *m.* radiation, radiancy

rayonner *vi.* to radiate, beam

rayure *f.* erasure, crossing out; scratch; stripe; groove, furrow; rifling

raz *m.* race, current; **— de marée** tidal wave

razzia *f.* raid

razzier *vt.* to raid

réabonnement *m.* renewal of a subscription

réabonner *vt.* to renew a subscription

réabsorber *vt.* to reabsorb

réaccoutumer *vt.* to reaccustom

réacteur *m.* reactor; **— nucléaire** nuclear reactor

réactif *m.* (chem.) reagent; **— a.** reactive

réaction *f.* reaction; **avion à — ** *m.* jet plane; **— en chaîne** chain reaction; **fusée à — ** *f.* jet-propelled missile; **moteur à — ** *m.* jet engine

réactionnaire *m. & a.* reactionary

réadmettre *vt.* to readmit

réaffirmer *vt.* to reaffirm

réagir *vi.* to react

réalisable *a.* realizable; practicable, feasible

réalisation *f.* realization, fulfilling, execution; **— de** produced by (movie credit)

réaliser *vt.* to realize, fulfil, execute; convert into money; **se —** to be realized; come true

réalisme *m.* realism

réaliste *m. & f.* realist; **— a.** realistic

réalité *f.* reality

réapparaître *vi.* to reappear

réapparition *f.* reappearance

réapprovisionner *vt.* to restock; revictual

réarmer *vt.* to rearm; refit; recock

réassurer *vt.* to reinsure

rébarbatif *a.* surly, grim

rebâtir *vt.* to rebuild

rebattre *vt.* to beat again; (fig.) repeat uselessly

rebattu *a.* repeated; trite; **sentier — ** *m.* beaten track

rebelle *m. & f.* rebel; **— a.** rebellious

rebeller *v.*, **se —** to rebel, resist

rébellion *f.* rebellion, revolt

rebobiner *vt.* to rewind

reboire *vt.* to drink again

reboisement *m.* reforestation, tree conservation

reboiser *vt.* to reforest

rebond *m.* rebound, bounce

rebondi *a.* plump, chubby

rebondir *vi.* to rebound, bounce

rebord *m.* edge, border, rim; ledge

reboucher *vt.* to stop up again; recork

rebours *m.* wrong side; reverse; **à —, au —** against the grain; backwards; the wrong way

rebouter *vt.* to set (a broken bone)

reboutonner *vt.* to rebutton

rebrousse-poil (à) *adv.* **—** against the grain

rebrousser *vt.* to turn back; **— chemin** to retrace one's steps

rebuffade *f.* rebuff, snub

rébus *m.* rebus, puzzle

rebut *m.* outcast; reject; scrap, trash, rubbish

rebutant *a.* discouraging, tedious; repellent

rebuter *vt.* to reject, repulse, refuse, rebuff; dishearten

récalcitrance *f.* recalcitrance

récalcitrant *a.* recalcitrant

récapitulation *f.* recapitulation, summary

récapituler *vt.* to recapitulate, summarize

recel, recèlement *m.* concealment (law); receiving of stolen goods

recéler *vt.* to conceal stolen goods; harbor

recéleur *m.* receiver of stolen goods, fence

récemment *adv.* recently, lately

recensement *m.* census

recenser *vt.* to make a census; tally, count

recenseur *m.* census taker (counter)

récent *a.* recent, new, late

récépissé *m.* receipt, acknowledgment

réceptacle *m.* receptacle

récepteur *m.* receiver; — *a.* receiving

réception *f.* reception; receiving; receipt; **accusé de** — *m.* receipt, acknowledgment

réceptionnaire *m.* (com.) consignee; — *a.* receiving

recette *f.* receipt of money; receiving, collection; recipe; **–s** *pl.* receipts

recevable *a.* acceptable, allowable, admissible

receveur *m.* receiver; tax collector; postmaster

recevoir *vt.* to receive; accept; entertain

rechange *m.* spare, replacement; **pièce de** — spare part; **pneu de** — *m.* spare tire

rechaper *vt.* to recap, retread a tire

réchappé *m.* survivor of a disaster

réchapper *vi.* to escape, survive

recharger *vt.* to recharge, reload

réchaud *m.* chafing dish; heater; stove; — **électrique** hot plate

réchauffer *vt.* to warm up *or* over, rekindle; **se** — to get warm, warm oneself

rechausser *vt.* to put footwear on again

rêche *a.* harsh, rough; bitter

recherche *f.* search, inquiry, investigation; finery, care; **à la** — **de** in search of; **–s** *pl.* research

recherché *a.* choice, rare; much in demand; affected; studied

rechercher *vt.* to seek again; search for; court

rechigné *a.* sulky, crabby

rechigner *vi.* to look unhappy; balk

rechuter *vi.* to relapse; have a relapse

récidive *f.* recurrence, relapse; second offense

récidiver *vi.* to recur; relapse (crime)

récif *m.* reef, shelf of rocks

récipient *m.* receptacle, container

réciprocité *f.* reciprocity

récit *m.* recital, relation, narrative, story; (mus.) solo

récital *m.* recital

récitant *m.* (mus.) solo, solo part

récitatif *m.* (mus.) recitative

récitation *f.* recitation

réciter *vt.* to recite

réclamant *m.* legal claimant

réclamation *f.* claim; protest; complaint

réclame *f.* advertising; **article de** — feature article

réclamer *vt.* to claim, call for, demand; — *vi.* to protest, complain

reclasser *vt.* to reclassify, rearrange

reclus *m.* recluse

réclusion *f.* reclusion; solitary confinement (penal)

récognition *f.* recognition (of a nature *or* quality)

recoin *m.* corner, nook, cranny

récoler *vt.* to verify, audit, check

recoller *vt.* to paste together again, put together again; **se** — to mend, knit, or heal (a fracture); cling together

récolte *f.* crop; harvest

récolter *vt.* to reap, gather, harvest

recommandable *a.* commendable, praiseworthy

recommandation *f.* recommendation; registration of mail

recommandé *a.* registered (mail)

recommander *vt.* to recommend; register a letter

recommencer *vt.* & *vi.* to recommence, begin again

récompense *f.* reward, recompense

récompenser *vt.* to reward, recompense

réconciliable *a.* reconcilable

réconciliation *f.* reconciliation

réconcilier *vt.* to reconcile; **se** — to be reconciled

reconduire *vt.* to lead back, see someone home, drive home; show out, usher out

réconfort *m.* consolation, comfort; relief

réconfortant *a.* comforting, consoling; stimulating

réconforter *vi.* to comfort, cheer; strengthen, refresh

reconnaissable *a.* recognizable

reconnaissance *f.* recognition; gratitude, thankfulness; recompense, reward; acknowledgment; note, pawn ticket; (mil.) reconnaissance

reconnaissant *a.* thankful, grateful

reconnaitre *vt.* to recognize, acknowledge; (mil.) to reconnoiter; **se** — to acknowledge; become oriented; (fig.) take one's bearings

reconquérir *vt.* to reconquer, regain

reconstituant *m.* tonic, stimulant, restorative

reconstituer *vt.* to reconstitute; restore

reconstruire *vt.* to rebuild

reconvention *f.* countersuit

recopier *vt.* to copy over, recopy

record *m.* sports record

recorder *vt.* to retie; restring

recordman *m.* record holder

recoucher *vt.*, **se** — to go back to bed, lie down again

recoudre *vt.* to sew in place again; sew up; (fig.) reunite

recoupement *m.* cross-check, verification

recouper *vt.* to cut again; mix, blend (wines)

recourber vt. to bend back

recourir vi. to run again; have recourse, resort to

recours m. recourse, resort

recouvrement m. recovery, getting back; recovering; cover

recouvrer vt. to recover, regain

recouvrir vt. to cover again, re-cover; cover

recracher vt. to spit out

récréatif a. recreational, entertaining

récréation f. recreation; recess

recréer vt. to create again, re-create

récréer vt. to entertain; please; **se** — to enjoy oneself, relax; be entertained

récrier v., **se** — to exclaim; protest

récrimination f. recrimination

récriminer vi. to recriminate

récrire vt. to rewrite

recroqueviller v., **se** — to retract; (fig.) to curl up, shrivel, wilt

recru a. worn out

recrû m. annual growth

recrue f. recruit, draftee

recruter vt. to recruit, enlist

rectal a. rectal

rectangle m. rectangle; — a. right-angled

rectangulaire a. rectangular

recteur m. rector; university president

rectificateur m. (elec.) rectifier; — dentaire dental brace

rectificatif a. rectifying; — m. correction

rectifier vt. to rectify, adjust, correct; straighten

rectifieuse f. rectifier

rectitude f. rectitude, uprightness; correctness; straightness

rectorat m. rectorate; university presidency

rectum m. rectum

reçu m. receipt; — a. received; usual; customary; **être** — to pass; graduate

recueil m. collection; anthology

recueillement m. contemplation, pious meditation

recueilli a. contemplative

recueillir vt. to gather, collect; shelter; **se** — to meditate

recuire vt. to recook, reheat; temper, anneal

recuit a. tempered, annealed

recul m. gun recoil; setback; backing up

reculade f. moving back; retreat

reculé a. remote, distant (in time); isolated

reculée f. space in which to move backward

reculement m. moving back, backing up; postponement

reculer vi. to move back; retreat; recoil;

— vt. to move back; postpone; hesitate

reculons, à — adv. backwards

récuperable a. recuperable

récupération f. recuperation, recovery

récupérer vt. to retrieve, recoup, recover; **se** — to recuperate, recover

récurage m. scouring, cleansing

récurer vt. to scour, cleanse

récurrence f. recurrence

récurrent a. recurrent, recurring

récusable a. exceptionable (at law)

récusation f. legal exception, objection

récuser vt. to object to, challenge; **se** — to disqualify oneself

rédacteur m. editor, compiler; writer; — en chef editor-in-chief

rédaction f. editorship, compiling; editorial staff; theme, composition

rédactionnel a. editorial

reddition f. surrender; rendering

redécouvrir vt. to rediscover

redemander vt. to ask again, ask return of something

rédempteur m. redeemer; — a. redeeming

rédemption f. redemption, redeeming

redescendre vi. to go down again; go back down; — vt. to bring down, take down

redevable a. indebted; bound by gratitude

redevance f. fee, tax; royalty

redevenir vi. to become again

rédiger vt. to phrase, draw up, write; edit

redingote f. frock coat

redire vt. to repeat, say again; **trouver à** — à to find fault with, criticize

redistribuer vt. to redistribute

redite f. repetition; redundancy

redondance f. redundancy

redondant a. redundant

redonder vi. to be redundant

redonner vt. to give again, give back

redorer vt. to re-gild

redoublé a. redoubled; **pas** — m. (marching) double-time, quick-step

redoublement m. doubling, redoubling

redoubler vt. to redouble; reline clothing; — vi. to redouble; increase

redoutable a. formidable, redoubtable; dreadful

redoute f. redoubt

redouter vt. to dread, fear; be afraid

redressé a. upright, erect

redressement m. making erect again, righting; straightening, rectifying; recovery

redresser vt. to make straight again; set upright; mend, correct; straighten, rectify; **se** — become upright again; sit up again

redresseur m. rectifier; righter

redû *m.* balance due
réducteur *m.* reducer; reducing agent; —
  a. reducing
réductible *a.* reducible
réduction *f.* reduction, reducing
réduire *vt.* to reduce, subdue, conquer
réduit *m.* redoubt; retreat; shack, hovel;
  — *a.* reduced, obliged
réduplication *f.* reduplication
réédifier *vt.* to rebuild
rééditer *vt.* to republish
réédition *f.* reprinting, republication
rééducatif *a.*, thérapie rééducative *f.* oc-
  cupational therapy
rééducation *f.* rehabilitation
rééduquer *vt.* to re-educate; rehabilitate
réel *a.* real; — *m.* reality
réélection *f.* re-election
réélire *vt.* to re-elect
réellement *adv.* really, actually
réensemencer *vt.* to reseed
refaçonner *vt.* to refashion
réfaction *f.* (com.) allowance, rebate; re-
  pairs
refaire *vt.* to do again; remake; se — to
  recover, recuperate
réfection *f.* rebuilding; repairing, restoration
réfectoire *m.* refectory, dining room
refend *m.* (arch.) pierre de — *f.* cornerstone
refendre *vt.* to split
référence *f.* reference
référendum *m.* referendum
référer *vi.* to refer; — *vt.* to attribute; impute; se — à to refer to; s'en — to confide
refermer *vt.* to reclose, shut again
refiler *vt.* (coll.) to pass, pass off
réfléchi *a.* thoughtful; considered; pre-
  meditated; peu — hasty; verbe — *m.*
  reflexive verb
réfléchir *vt.* to reflect, reverberate; — *vi.*
  reflect, think; se — to be reflected
réfléchissement *m.* reflection, reflecting
réfléchissant *a.* reflecting
réflecteur *m.* reflector; — *a.* reflecting
reflet *m.* reflection
refléter *vt.* to reflect
refleurir *vi.* to flower again, flourish again
réflexe *a. & m.* reflex
réflexion *f.* reflection; thought; toute —
  faite all things considered
refluer *vi.* to ebb, flow back
reflux *m.* ebb, reflux, flowing back
refondre *vt.* to remelt, recast
refonte *f.* remelting, recasting
réformateur *m.* reformer
réformation *f.* reformation
réforme *f.* reform, reformation; (mil.)

discharge
réformé *m.* Protestant; rejected serviceman, soldier discharged for wounds or
  unfitness
reformer *vt.* to re-form, form again
réformer *vt.* to reform; (mil.) discharge,
  retire
refoulement *m.* forcing back; repression;
  output
refouler *vt.* to force back; repress
réfractaire *a.* refractory, rebellious; fire
  resistant
réfracter *vt.* to refract
réfracteur *m.* refractor
réfraction *f.* refraction
refrain *m.* refrain; song; chorus
réfranger *vt.* to refract
réfréner *vt.* to check, curb, bridle, restrain
réfrigérant *a.* refrigerating; cooling; — *m.*
  refrigerator; cooler
réfrigération *f.* refrigeration
réfrigérer *vt.* to refrigerate
refroidir *vt.* to cool, chill; — *vi.* to grow
  cool, grow cold
refroidissement *m.* cooling; chill
réfugié *m.* refugee
réfugier *v.*, se — to take refuge
refus *m.* refusal
refuser *vt.* to refuse, deny; reject; fail (a
  student); se — to object; refuse
réfutable *a.* refutable
réfutation *f.* refutation
réfuter *vt.* to refute
regagner *vt.* to regain, recover; reach
  again, return to
regain *m.* (agr.) aftergrowth; renewal
régal *m.* feast; treat
régalade *f.* regaling, feasting; treat
régalant *a.* entertaining, diverting
régale *a.*, eau — (chem.) aqua regia
régalement *m.* leveling
régaler *vt.* to treat, entertain; level,
  smooth out
régalien *a.* royal, regal
regard *m.* look, glance; eyes; aperture,
  opening; peephole; manhole
regardant *m.* onlooker; — *a.* particular,
  fussy; stingy
regarder *vt.* to look at; regard, concern;
  face
regarnir *vt.* to regarnish, restock, replenish
regate *f.* regatta, boat race
regel *m.* refreezing; new freeze
regeler *vt. & vi.* to refreeze, freeze again
régence *f.* regency
régénérateur *a.* regenerative; — *m.* hair
  restorer
régénération *f.* regeneration
régénérer *vt.* to regenerate

régent *m.* regent
régenter *vt.* to dominate
régicide *m.* regicide
régie *f.* administration, management; public corporation
regimbement *m.* recalcitrance
regimber *vi.* to balk, object
régime *m.* regime, administration; system; bunch of dates; diet; (gram.) object; **être au** — to be on a diet
régiment *m.* regiment
régimentaire *a.* regimental
région *f.* region, area
régional *a.* regional; local
régir *vt.* to govern, manage, supervise
régisseur *m.* administrator, manager; (theat.) stage manager
registre *m.* register, ledger, account book
réglable *a.* adjustable
réglage *m.* way of ruling paper; adjustment of machinery, tuning
règle *f.* rule, ruler; order; — **à calcul** slide rule; **en** — in order
réglé *a.* ruled, regular, orderly; **vent** — *m.* tradewind
règlement *m.* regulation; rule; adjustment, settlement; payment
réglementaire *a.* prescribed by law
réglementation *f.* regulating
réglementer *vt.* to regulate
régler *vt.* to rule; regulate; adjust, set; settle
réglet *m.* moulding
réglette *f.* small ruler; metal strip
régleur *m.* adjuster
réglisse *f.* licorice
réglure *f.* ruling of paper
règne *m.* reign; kingdom
régnant *a.* reigning; dominant
régner *vi.* to reign; prevail
regommer *vt.* to retread
regonfler *vt.* to pump up again, reinflate
regorgeant *a.* overflowing, brimming
regorger *vi.* to overflow, abound, be full, be packed; — *vt.* to regurgitate
regoûter *vt.* to taste again
regrat *m.* peddling used *or* retail articles
regrattage *m.* scraping
regratter *vi.* to peddle, hawk; — *vt.* rescrape, scrape clean
régressif *a.* regressive
régression *f.* regression, retrogression; recession
regret *m.* regret; **à** — regretfully, reluctantly
regretter *vt.* to regret, be sorry; miss
régularisation *f.* regularizing
régulariser *vt.* to regularize
régularité *f.* regularity; evenness
-égulateur *a.* regulating; — *m.* regulator;

governor
régulation *f.* regulating
régulier *a.* regular; even; steady; punctual
régurgitation *f.* regurgitation
régurgiter *vt.* to regurgitate
réhabilitation *f.* rehabilitation
réhabiliter *vt.* to rehabilitate; reinstate
réhabituer *vt.* to reaccustom
rehaussement *m.* raising; enhancing
rehausser *vt.* to raise; enhance, accentuate
réimperméabiliser *vt.* to waterproof again
réimposer *vt.* to reimpose
réimpression *f.* reprint, reprinting
réimprimer *vt.* to reprint
rein *m.* kidney; **–s** *pl.* lower part of back
réincarnation *f.* reincarnation
réincarner *v.*, **se** — to be reincarnated
réincorporer *vt.* to reincorporate
reine *f.* queen
reine-claude *f.* greengage plum
réinscrire *vt.* to reinscribe; re-enter
réintégrer *vt.* to reinstate
réitération *f.* reiteration
réitérer *vt.* to reiterate
rejaillir *vi.* to spurt out; rebound; be reflected
rejet *m.* rejection; plant shoot, sprout; throwing out; enjambement
rejeter *vt.* to throw back; reject; **se** — move back, fall back
rejeton *m.* offspring, shoot
rejetonner *vi.* to throw off shoots (plants)
rejoindre *vt.* to rejoin; overtake; **se** — to meet again
rejouer *vt.* to play again, replay
réjoui *a.* jovial, joyful, happy
réjouir *vt.* to gladden; entertain; **se** — to rejoice, be happy
réjouissance *f.* rejoicing, merrymaking
réjouissant *a.* pleasing, entertaining, giving pleasure
relâchant *a.* (med.) laxative
relâche *m.* rest, respite; (theat.) no performance; interruption; (naut.) port of call
relâché *a.* loose, slack; relaxed
relâchement *m.* relaxation, loosening; abatement
relâcher *vt.* to relax; release, slacken; — *vi.* (naut.) to put into port; **se** — to become loose, slacken; diminish, abate; become milder
relais *m.* relay, shift
relancer *vt.* to throw again, throw back; start again; hunt
relater *vt.* to relate, tell of, give, state
relatif *a.* relative; pertinent, relating
relation *f.* relation, connection; report, statement, account

relationné *a.* having contacts *or* connections

relativité *f.* relativity

relaxation *f.* legal release; lessening, reduction

relaxer *vt.* to release, discharge at law

relayer *vt.* to relieve, relay; — *vi.* to relay; **se** — to take turns, work in shifts

relégation *f.* life sentence to penal colony

relégué *m.* convict serving life sentence

reléguer *vt.* to relegate; sentence for life, transport

relent *m.* musty smell, staleness

relevage *m.* lifting, raising; collecting of letters from a mail box

relevant *a.* pertaining; dependent

relevé *a.* raised, high; highly seasoned; — *m.* abstract, summary, statement; survey; meter reading

relève *f.* (mil.) relief, changing of the guard

relevée *f.* afternoon

relèvement *m.* raising, lifting; increase; restoration, recovery; (mil.) relieving; (naut.) bearing; (com.) statement

relever *vt.* to raise again, lift up, turn up; increase; enhance, heighten; season; point out; (mil.) relieve; (naut.) take the bearings of; (com.) bill; read a meter; — *vi.* be dependent, be responsible; recover from illness; **se** — get up again; revive, recover

relief *m.* relief, embossing, enhancement; **-s** *pl.* left-over food

relier *vt.* to tie again; bind, connect, join

relieur *m.* bookbinder

religieux *a.* religious; — *m.* monk

reliquaire *m.* (eccl.) shrine, reliquary

reliquat *m.* left-over portion, remainder; aftereffects; balance due

relique *f.* relic

relire *vt.* to read again; reread

reliure *f.* binding of a book; bookbinding trade

relouer *vt.* to sublet, relet

reluctance *f.* (elec.) reluctance

reluire *vi.* to shine, glitter, gleam

reluisant *a.* shining, glittering, gleaming; glossy

reluquer *vt.* to look at sideways, look at from the corner of the eyes

remâcher *vt.* to chew again; mull over

remailler *vt.* to mend (knitted or meshed garments)

remaniement *m.* alteration; reshaping, rehandling

remanier *vt.* to handle again, alter; reshape

remarier *vt.*, **se** = to marry again, remarry

remarquable *a.* remarkable; noteworthy

remarque *f.* remark; **digne de** — noteworthy

remarquer *vt.* to observe, notice, remark; mark again; **se faire** — to be noticed, attract attention

remballer *vt.* to repack

rembarquer *vt. & vi.* to re-embark

remblai *m.* fill for construction; earth; embankment

remblaver *vt.* to reseed

remblayer *vt.* to fill; embank

rembobinage *m.* rewinding

rembobiner *vt.* to rewind

remboîter *vt.* to repack, recase; reassemble; (med.) set a bone

rembourrer *vt.* to stuff, wad; pad, upholster

rembourrure *f.* stuffing material

remboursable *a.* refundable

remboursement *m.* reimbursement, redemption; refund; **livraison contre** — *f.* C.O.D.

rembourser *vt.* to reimburse, repay, refund

rembrunir *vt. & vi.* to darken; make gloomy; **se** — grow dark

remède *m.* remedy, cure

remédiable *a.* remediable, curable

remédier *vt.* to remedy, cure

remêler *vt.* to mix again, remix

remembrer *vt.* to assemble, consolidate

remémoratif *a.* commemorative

remémorer *vt.* to remind; **se** — to remember

remerciement *m.* thanks

remercier *vt.* to thank; discharge, dismiss

réméré *m.* (com.) repurchase

remettant *m.* sender, remitter

remetteur *vt.* remitting; — *m.* remitter

remettre *vt.* to put back; put on again; restore; hand over, remit; postpone; **se** — recover one's health; **se** — à to start again; **s'en** — à rely on, depend on

remeubler *vt.* to refurnish

réminiscence *f.* reminiscence

remise *f.* putting back; remitting, remittance; remission; rebate, discount; shed, garage, *or* coachhouse; — **en état** repair, restoration; **voiture de grande** — *f.* rentable limousine

remiser *vt.* to house; put back in a garage, shed, *or* coachhouse; (coll.) to pension

rémissible *a.* remissible

rémission *f.* remission

remmener *vt.* to lead back, take back

rémois *a.* from Rheims

remontant *a. & m.* tonic, stimulant

remonte *f.* remounting; return, ascent of salmon

remontée *f.* going up again, ascent, climb
remonter *vi.* to go up again; remount; reascend; go back; — *vt.* go up again, climb again; take up again; pull up; wind up; remount, reassemble; (theat.) perform again, put on again, redo; **se** — recover one's strength *or* spirit
remontoir *m.* watch winder
remontrance *f.* remonstrance
remontrer *vt.* to show again; indicate, point out; **en** — **à** to remonstrate with
remords *m.* remorse, conscience
remorquage *m.* towing
remorque *f.* towing, tow; tow rope; (auto.) trailer; **à la** — in tow
remorquer *vt.* to tow, pull
remorqueur *m.* tugboat; tractor
remoudre *vt.* to grind again, regrind
rémoudre *vt.* to resharpen, regrind
rémouleur *m.* knife grinder
remous *m.* eddy, swirl, backwash
rempailler *vt.* to repair, recane, replace chair reeds
rempailleur *m.* repairer of chairs
rempart *m.* rampart
remplaçable *a.* replaceable
remplaçant *m.* replacement, substitute
remplacement *m.* replacing, substitution
remplacer *vt.* to replace, substitute for
rempli *m.* fold, tuck
remplier *vt.* to make a fold *or* tuck in
remplir *vt.* to refill, fill in; fill out; fill up; fulfill, do, carry out
remployer *vt.* to use again
remplumer *v.*, **se** — to grow new feathers
rempoissonner *vt.* to stock with fish
remporter *vt.* to carry back, carry away; win, achieve, obtain
rempoter *vt.* to repot a plant
remuant *a.* moving; agitated
remue-ménage *m.* bustle, to-do, movement, agitation, stir, stirring
remuement *m.* movement, agitation, stir
remuer *vt.* to move, stir up; arouse, agitate; turn (earth); — *vi.* move, budge, stir
remugle *m.* musty odor, stale odor
rémunérateur *a.* remunerative, rewarding, profitable; — *m.* remunerator
rémunération *f.* remuneration
rémunérer *vt.* to remunerate, reward, pay for
renâcler *vi.* to snort; shirk; be hesitant, be reluctant
renaissance *f.* rebirth, revival
renaissant *a.* renascent
renaître *vi.* to be born again; revive; reappear
rénal *a.* renal, kidney
renard *m.* fox

renarde *f.* vixen
rencaisser *vt.* to recase, rebox; receive as a refund
renchaîner *vt.* to chain up again
renchéri *a.* fastidious
renchérir *vi.* to increase in price; — **sur** to outdo; outbid
renchérissement *m.* increase in price
renchérisseur *m.* one who outbids, highest bidder
rencogner *vt.* to drive into a corner; **se** — be pushed, retreat into a corner
rencontre *f.* meeting, encounter; occasion; **aller à la** — **de** to go to meet; **de** — chance, random, haphazard
rencontrer *vt.* to meet, come across, run into, encounter; **se** — meet, meet by chance; collide; come together, agree, check
rendement *m.* yield, profit, return; efficiency, output
rendez-vous *m.* appointment; meeting place, rendezvous
rendormir *vt.* to put back to sleep; **se** — to fall asleep again, go back to sleep
rendosser *vt.* to put on again
rendre *vt.* to give back; return; produce, yield; give up; vomit; render; make; **se** — to go, proceed; surrender
rendu *a.* tired out, exhausted, spent; — *m.* rendering; (com.) return of an article
rêne *f.* rein
renégat *m.* renegade
rêner *vt.* to rein in
renfaîter *vt.* to repair a roof
renfermé *a.* stuffy, close; uncommunicative
renfermer *vt.* to shut up, lock up, confine; contain, include, comprise; enclose; conceal
renflammer *vt.* to set fire to again, rekindle; **se** — catch fire again, be rekindled
renflement *m.* swelling, bulge
renfler *vt. & vi.* to swell
renflouer *vt.* to reinflate; refloat
renfoncé *a.* recessed; sunken
renfoncer *vt.* to drive in, hammer in; indent, recess
renforcé *a.* reinforced, strengthened, strong; absolute
renforcer *vt.* to reinforce, strengthen, brace; intensify; **se** — grow stronger
renfort *m.* reinforcement; backing, support
renfrogné *a.* frowning, scowling
renfrogner *v.*, **se** — to frown, scowl
rengager *vt.* to engage again; pawn again; — *vi.* to re-enlist
rengaine *f.* refrain, old story
rengainer *vt.* to sheathe, put back (a

sword)
rengorgement *m.* swagger, strutting
rengorger *v.*, se — to strut, swagger
reniement *m.* denial, repudiation, disavowal
renier *vt.* to deny, disown, disavow, repudiate, abjure
reniflard *m.* air valve; sniffer, sniffler
reniflement *m.* sniffing, snorting, snort; sniffle, sniffling
renifler *vi.* to sniff, snivel, snuffle, snort; — *vt.* to sniff
reniveler *vt.* to level again
renne *m.* reindeer
renom *m.* renown, fame, repute
renommé *a.* renowned, famous, famed, celebrated, well-known
renommée *f.* fame, reputation, renown, repute
renommer *vt.* to renominate, rename
renonce *f.* renege, revoke (at cards)
renoncement *m.* renunciation; renouncing; self-denial
renoncer *vi.* to renounce, give up, waive; renege, revoke (at cards); — *vt.* to renounce
renonciation *f.* renunciation
renoncule *f.* buttercup
renouer *vt.* to tie again, knot again; renew
renouveau *m.* revival, renewal; springtime
renouvelable *a.* renewable
renouveler *vt.* to renew; revive; repeat; change, alter; se — be renewed; renew again; happen again
rénover *vt.* to renew, give a new form
renseignement *m.* piece of information; —s *pl.* information; (mil.) intelligence; prendre des —s sur to inquire about
renseigner *vt.* to inform; se — to inquire, ask
rente *f.* income, revenue; annuity, pension
renté *a.* endowed; of independent means, having a private income
renter *vt.* to endow, provide with an income
rentier *m.* person of independent means, stockholder, bondholder
rentrant *m.* recess in a wall; new participant, new player
rentré *a.* hollow, sunken; suppressed
rentrée *f.* return, homecoming; reopening of school; gathering, collecting, bringing in
rentrer *vi.* to re-enter, return, come home; reopen; bring in, take in
renverse *f.* (naut.) turn, change in weather; tomber à la — to fall backwards
renversement *m.* reversing, reversal, inversion; turn, turning, change; overturning, overthrowing
renverser *vt.* to reverse, invert; knock over, turn over, overturn, upset; overthrow; — *vi.* to overturn; (naut.) capsize; se — to fall down; turn over; lean back; capsize
renvoi *m.* sending back, returning; throwing back; reflection; discharge, dismissal; postponement; reference mark; caret; belch; (mus.) repetition
renvoyer *vt.* to send back, return, throw back; reflect; discharge, dismiss; postpone; refer
réoccupation *f.* reoccupation
réoccuper *vt.* to reoccupy
réordonner *vt.* to reorder
réorganisation *f.* reorganization
réorganiser *vt.* to reorganize
réorientation *f.* reorientation
réorienter *vt.* to reorient
réouverture *f.* reopening
repaire *m.* lair, den
repaître *vt.* to feed, se — de to eat one's fill of; delight in
répandre *vt.* to spread; spill, shed; give off; strew, scatter; se — to spread, spill, spill over
répandu *a.* widespread; fashionable
reparaître *vi.* to reappear
réparation *f.* reparation; repairing; amends, satisfaction
réparer *vt.* to repair, fix, mend; make up for, make amends for
repartie *f.* repartee, reply, retort
repartir *vi.* to reply, retort; start out again, set out again
répartir *vt.* to divide, distribute; allocate, allot, apportion; assess
répartiteur *m.* distributor; assessor
répartition *f.* dividing, distribution; allocation, apportionment; assessment
repas *m.* meal
repassage *m.* ironing, pressing; sharpening
repasser *vi.* to pass by again; — *vt.* to pass again, pass over; go over; sharpen grind, strop; iron; planche à — *f.* ironing board
repasseur *m.* grinder, sharpener; finisher
repasseuse *f.* ironer
repavage *m.* repaving
repaver *vt.* to repave
repayer *vt.* to pay for again
repêcher *vt.* to fish out again, fish up; rescue
repeindre *vt.* to paint again, repaint
rependre *vt.* to hang up again
repenser *vt.* to think over again
repenti *a. & m.* repentant

repentir v., se — repent, be sorry about, rue; — m. repentance
repérable a. locatable, findable
repérage m. finding, locating
répercussion f. repercussion, reverberation; consequence, effect
répercuter vt. to reflect, reverberate; se — to have repercussions
reperdre vt. to lose again
repère m. reference mark; point de — point of reference, guidemark; landmark
repérer vt. to mark with points of reference (blaze a trail); fix, locate; se — to take one's bearings
répertoire m. index, list; directory; (theat.) stock, repertory
répertorier vt. to list; index; catalog
répéter vt. to repeat; rehearse; se — to repeat, be done again, recur
répétiteur m. tutor, helper, coach
répétition f. repetition; duplicate; rehearsal, practice; tutoring lesson; (TV) rerun
repeupler vt. to repopulate; restock
repiquer vt. to prick again; restitch; repair, mend; transplant
répit m. respite, delay
replacer vt. to put back, replace; reinvest
replanter vt. to replant
replâtrer vt. to replaster; patch up
replet a. plump, chubby
réplétion f. repletion; plumpness
repli m. fold; coil; bend; (mil.) retreat
replier vt. to fold again, fold up; tuck; coil cord; se — fold up; wind; (mil.) fall back, retreat
réplique f. answer, reply, retort, replica; (theat.) cue
répliquer vi. to reply, answer back, retort
replonger vt. to plunge again; — vi. dive again; sink again
repolir vt. to repolish
répondant m. guarantor, surety; (eccl.) server at mass
répondre vt. to answer, reply; — vi. to answer; respond; reciprocate; correspond
réponse f. answer, reply
report m. carry over, amount brought forward (bookkeeping)
reportage m. reporting, newspaper writing, commentary
reporter vt. to carry back, carry over; postpone; se — à refer to
repos m. rest, repose, tranquility; landing of a stairway; au — (mil.) at ease; en — resting, at rest
reposant a. restful
reposé a. rested; tranquil, calm; à tête

—e adv. calmly, coolly, deliberately
reposer vt. to put back, replace; rest; — vi. to rest, lie; se — rest, repose; come to rest, alight; se — sur rely on
reposoir m. resting place; (eccl.) temporary parade altar; repository
repoussage m. stamping of sheet metal
repoussant a. repulsive; offensive
repousse f. new growth
repoussé a. embossed; chased; — m. embossing; chasing
repoussement m. repulse, repulsing; rejecting, rejection; dislike; recoil
repousser vt. to repulse, repel, reject; deny; postpone; recoil; emboss; chase; — vi. produce new plant growths
repoussoir m. embossing punch; contrast, foil
répréhensible a. reprehensible
reprendre vt. to retake, take again, take back; resume; regain; reply; continue; reprove, criticize; — vi. return, come back; recover; se — take hold of oneself, regain composure; correct oneself
représailles f. pl. reprisals, retaliation
représentant a. & m. representative; — de commerce salesman
représentatif a. representative
représentation f. representation; agency; protest; (theat.) performance; — à grand spectacle (TV) spectacular
représenter vt. to represent; reintroduce; present again; show, depict; perform; point out; se — present oneself again; represent oneself; recur, reappear
répressif a. repressive
répression f. repression
réprimable a. repressible
réprimandable a. censurable, worthy of censure
réprimande f. reprimand
réprimander vt. to reprimand, censure
réprimer vt. to repress; hold back, check
repris m., — de justice habitual criminal
reprise f. retaking; recapture; renewal; recovery; repetition; mending, darning; (theatre) revival; (mus.) chorus, refrain; (auto.) trade-in; à plusieurs —s repeatedly
repriser vt. to darn, mend
réprobateur a. reproachful
réprobation f. reprobation, censure; rejection
reproche m. reproach, blame; —s pl. blame, criticism, censure
reprocher vt. to reproach, blame, find fault with; grudge, begrudge
reproducteur a. reproductive; — m. reproducer; stud, sire
reproductif a. reproductive

reproduction *f.* reproduction; — **en miniature** miniaturization

reproduire *vt.* to reproduce; **se** — to reproduce; recur, occur again

réprouvé *m.* reprobate

réprouver *vt.* to disapprove of; reject

reptation *f.* crawling

reptile *m. & a.* reptile

repu *a.* sated, satiated, full

républicain *a. & m.* republican

républicanisme *m.* republicanism

republier *vt.* to republish

république *f.* republic

répudiation *f.* repudiation

répudier *vt.* to repudiate, renounce

repue *f.* **franche** — free dinner

répugnance *f.* repugnance, loathing, aversion, dislike; reluctance

répugnant *a.* repugnant, loathsome; loath, reluctant

répugner *vi.* to feel repugnance; be repugnant; be reluctant

répulsif *a.* repulsive

répulsion *f.* repulsion

réputation *f.* reputation, repute, name, renown

réputé *a.* of repute, well-known, famous

réputer *vt.* to repute, consider, think

requérable *a.* demandable

requérant *m.* legal petitioner, plaintiff

requérir *vt.* to demand, petition; ask

requête *f.* request, petition

requin *m.* shark; **peau de** — *f.* shagreen

requis *a.* requisite, required

réquisition *f.* requisition; requisitioning

réquisitionner *vt.* to requisition

réquisitoire *m.* legal indictment, charge

rescapé *a.* rescued, delivered

rescinder *vt.* to rescind

rescousse *f.* rescue

réseau *m.* network; net; (rad., rail.) system

réséda *m.* mignonette

réservation *f.* reservation

réserve *f.* reserve, reservation; **à la** — **de** except for; **sans** — unqualified, without exception; **sous** — **de** subject to

réservé *a.* reserved; shy; guarded

réserver *vt.* to reserve, save

réservoir *m.* reservoir; tank; well

résidence *f.* residence; dwelling

résider *vi.* to reside, dwell; consist

résidu *m.* residue; (com.) balance

résiduel *a.* residual

résignation *f.* resignation; submission, submissiveness

résigné *a.* resigned; submissive

résigner *vt.* to resign; submit; give up; **se** — to resign oneself, submit

résiliation *f.* cancellation, termination of an agreement

résilience *f.* resilience

résilier *vt.* to cancel, terminate an agreement

résille *f.* hair net, snood; lattice

résine *f.* resin

résiner *vt.* to resin; tap for resin

résineux *a.* resinous

résistance *f.* resistance; stamina, strength; **pièce de** — *f.* main dish, main course; highlight, main feature

résistant *a.* resistant, strong; — *m.* member of the resistance

résister *vi.* to resist, withstand, endure

résolu *a.* resolute, determined

résoluble *a.* solvable; terminable

résolument *adv.* resolutely, determinedly

résolution *f.* resolution; resolve; solution; termination, cancellation

résonance *f.* resonance

résonnement *m.* resonance, reverberation

résonner *vi.* to resound, reverberate

résorber *vt.* to absorb again, reabsorb; imbibe

résoudre *vt.* to resolve; solve; dissolve; terminate, cancel; **se** — to make up one's mind

respect *m.* respect; **rendre ses –s à** to pay one's respects to

respectabilité *f.* respectability

respecter *vt.* to respect, have respect for; **se** — to act in a seemly fashion

respectif *a.* respective

respectueux *a.* respectful

respirateur *m.* respirator

respiration *f.* respiration, breathing

respiratoire *a.* respiratory

respirer *vt. & vi.* to breathe; inhale; (fig.) to pause for breath

resplendir *vi.* to shine, glow, be resplendent

responsabilité *f.* responsibility; liability

responsable *a.* responsible; liable

ressac *m.* surf; undertow

ressaigner *vi.* to open, start bleeding again

ressaisir *vt.* to seize again; retake, recapture; **se** — to recover, regain one's composure

ressasser *vt.* to repeat incessantly

ressaut *m.* projection; rise

ressauter *vi.* to rise; jump again

ressayer *vt.* to try again

resseller *vt.* to resaddle

ressemblance *f.* resemblance, likeness

ressembler *vi.* to resemble, look alike; be like; **se** — to be the same, be alike

ressemeler *vt.* to resole

ressentiment *m.* resentment

ressentir *vt.* to resent; feel, experience

resserre *f.* storing, storage; storeroom;

resserré *a.* tight, narrow, confined

resserrement *m.* tightening, contracting; oppression, heaviness; constipation

resserrer *vt.* to contract, constrict, tighten; confine; compress; lock up again; se — to become tighter; contract

resservir *vt. & vi.* to serve again

ressort *m.* spring; elasticity, resilience; motive; legal jurisdiction, competence; resort; (fig.) function

ressortir *vi.* to go out again, emerge again; stand out, appear, be evident; — à belong to legally, be under the jurisdiction of; faire — make evident, bring out, stress, emphasize

ressouder *vt.* to solder *or* weld again; se — to heal, mend, *or* knit bone

ressource *f.* resource; expedient, resort; –s *pl.* resources, means; funds

ressouvenance *f.* remembrance, recollection

ressouvenir *v.* se — to remember, recollect; — *m.* memory, remembrance

ressuer *vi.* to sweat

ressusciter *vt.* to ressuscitate, revive, restore; — *vi.* to ressuscitate, come back to life, revive

ressuyer *vt.* to dry

restant *a.* remaining; poste –e *f.* general delivery; — *m.* remainder, balance, residue

restaurant *m.* restaurant; — *a. & m.* restorative

restaurateur *m.* restorer; restaurant proprietor

restauration *f.* restoration, restoring

restaurer *vt.* to restore; refresh; se — take refreshment; refresh oneself (fig.) to regain strength

reste *m.* remainder, rest, remains; au —, du — besides; de — left over; et le — and so forth

rester *vi.* to remain, be left; stay

restituer *vt.* to restore; give back; rehabilitate

restreindre *vt.* to restrict, limit; se — to limit oneself, retrench

restreint *a.* restricted, limited

restrictif *a.* restrictive

restringent *a. & m.* astringent

résultant *a.* resulting, resultant

résultat *m.* result

résulter *vi.* to result, follow

résumé *m.* summary, résumé, abstract; en — in short, in brief

résumer *vt.* to sum up, summarize

résurgence *f.* resurgence, reappearance

résurgin *vi.* to rise, reappear

résurrection *f.* resurrection

retable *m.* retable, shelf or screen above an altar

rétablir *vt.* to re-establish, restore; recover, regain; se — to re-establish oneself; regain one's health

rétablissement *m.* re-establishment; restoration; recovery

retaille *f.* chip, portion removed

retailler *vt.* to cut again, recut; resharpen

retaillure *f.* cutting; sharpening

rétameur *m.* tinker

retaper *vt.* to fix, adjust, straighten; retype; se — to get well

retard *m.* delay; backwardness; slowness, lateness; en — late, behind, in arrears

retardataire *a.* late; backward; slow; in arrears; — *m. & f.* latecomer; person in arrears

retarder *vt.* to delay, retard; put back; defer; — *vi.* be late, be slow

reteindre *vt.* to dye again, redye

retendre *vt.* to stretch again; set (a trap) again

retenir *vt.* to retain, detain, keep back; hold back, withhold; restrain; se — to restrain oneself

rétenteur *a.* retaining

rétention *f.* retention, holding in

retentir *vi.* to resound, reverberate

retentissant *a.* resounding, loud

retentissement *m.* resounding, reverberation, effect, repercussion

retenu *a.* circumspect, prudent; reserved; booked; detained

retenue *f.* holding back; deduction; detention; reserve, modesty; restraint

réticence *f.* reticence

réticulaire *a.* reticular, netlike

réticule *m.* cross hairs in an eyepiece, reticle; reticule, bag, handbag

rétif *a.* restive, stubborn

rétiforme *a.* netlike, retiform

rétine *f.* retina

retirer *vt.* to withdraw, pull out; take off; take away; derive; reprint; se — to retire, withdraw; recede

rétivité *f.* stubbornness, obstinacy

retombant *a.* sagging, hanging, drooping

retomber *vi.* to fall again, sink again; hang down; droop

retordre *vt.* to twist again

rétorquer *vt.* to retort

retors *a.* wily, clever, crafty; twisted in weaving

retoucher *vt.* to retouch, touch up

retoucheur *m.* alterer; (phot.) retoucher

retour *m.* return; turn, twist; billet d'aller et — round-trip ticket; billet de — return ticket; être de — to be back

retournage *m.* turning, reversing

retourner *vt.* to turn, turn over; turn inside out; return; — *vi.* to return, go back; **se** — to turn around; **s'en** — return, be on the way back

retracer *vt.* to retrace

rétractation *f.* retraction, recantation

rétractable *a.* retractable

rétracter *vt.* to retract; recant; **se** — to retract

retrait *m.* withdrawal; shrinkage; recess, indentation

retraite *f.* retreat; retirement; refuge, lair; (mil.) **battre en** — to beat a retreat; **prendre sa** — to retire

retraiter *vt.* to pension off, retire

retranché *a.* entrenched, fortified

retranchement *m.* entrenchment; cutting off

retrancher *vt.* to retrench, entrench, fortify; cut off, cut out

retransmettre *vt.* to retransmit; broadcast

retransmission *f.* rebroadcast

retravailler *vt.* to rework

retraverser *vt.* to cross again, recross, cross back

rétréci *a.* narrow, shrunken

rétrécir *vt.* to narrow, contract; shrink; take in; — *vi.* grow narrow

retremper *vt.* to soak again; retemper; **se** — to be invigorated

rétribuer *vt.* to remunerate, reward, pay

rétribution *f.* remuneration, reward, pay

rétroactif *a.* retroactive

rétroaction *f.* (elec.) feedback; retroactivity

rétrogradation *f.* retrogression; reduction in rank

rétrograde *a.* retrograde, reverse(d)

rétrograder *vt.* to reduce in rank; — *vi.* to retrogress; shift to a lower gear

rétrogressif *a.* retrogressive

rétrogression *f.* retrogression

rétrospectif *a.* retrospective

retroussé *a.* turned up; snub-nosed

retroussement *m.* curling

retrousser *vt.* to turn up, tuck up; roll up; **se** — tuck up a dress; lift out of the mud

retrouver *vt.* to find again, recover; meet, rejoin; **se** — to recover oneself, find oneself again, meet again

rétroviseur *m.* rear-view mirror; reflector

rets *m.* net, snare

réunion *f.* bringing together, meeting, gathering; reunion

réunir *vt.* to reunite, unite, assemble; bring together; **se** — to meet, gather

réussi *a.* successful, well-done

réussir *vi.* to succeed, have a happy outcome; — *vt.* to carry out, succeed in, bring off

réussite *f.* success; result, outcome, issue

revacciner *vt.* to revaccinate

revaloir *vt.* to pay back, get even with

revaloriser *vt.* to revalue

revanche *f.* revenge; return; return match; **en** — on the other hand; in return

rêvasser *vi.* to dream, daydream, be lost in thought

rêvasserie *f.* dreaming, daydreaming

rêve *m.* dream

revêche *a.* rough, harsh; crabby, ill-tempered

réveil *m.* waking, awakening; alarm clock; (mil.) reveille; (eccl.) revival

réveille-matin *m.* alarm clock

réveiller *vt.* to awaken, wake up; **se** — wake up, awake

réveillon *m.* midnight supper (Christmas Eve and New Year's Eve)

réveillonner *vi.* to celebrate Christmas *or* the New Year at a midnight supper

révélateur *a.* revealing; — *m.* revealer; (phot.) developer

révélation *f.* revelation

révéler *vt.* to reveal, show, display, disclose; (phot.) develop; **se** — to be revealed, appear

revenant *a.* pleasing; — *m.* ghost

revendeur *m.* secondhand dealer; retailer

revendication *f.* claim, demand, petition

revendiquer *vt.* to claim, demand

revendre *vt.* to sell again, resell

revenir *vi.* to come back, return, go back; recover, get over; **s'en** — to return, be coming back

revente *f.* resale

revenu *m.* revenue, income; profit, yield

rêver *vt. & vi.* to dream

réverbération *f.* reverberation

réverbère *m.* reflector; street light

réverbérer *vt. & vi.* to reverberate, reflect

revercher *vt.* to patch, solder

reverdir *vi.* to become green again; — *vt.* to make green again

révéremment *adv.* reverently

révérence *f.* reverence; bow, curtsey

révérenciel *a.* reverential

révérencieux *a.* ceremonious, overly formal

révérendissime *a.* very reverend, most reverend

révérer *vt.* to revere

rêverie *f.* musing, dreaming, reverie

revernir *vt.* to revarnish

revers *m.* reverse, back; lapel; **coup de** — *m.* backhand stroke; (fig.) setback

reverser *vt.* to pour again, pour back; shift, assign blame

réversible a. reversible
réversion f. reversion
réversoir m. irrigation dam
revêtement m. covering, casing, coating
revêtir vt. to clothe, reclothe, dress; **se —** put on again; put on; cover, case
rêveur a. pensive, musing, dreaming, dreamy; **— m.** dreamer
revient m., **prix de —** cost price
revigorer vt. to reinvigorate
revirement m. sudden change; reversal; (com.) assignment, transfer
réviser, reviser vt. to revise; audit; overhaul; re-examine
réviseur, reviseur m. reviser; auditor; proofreader
révision, revision f. revision; examination, inspection; proofreading; overhauling; **conseil de — m.** draft board
revisser vt. to screw tight, tighten
revivification f. revival
revivifier vt. to revive
revivre vi. to live again, come back to life
révocable a. revokable
révocation f. revocation, repeal; dismissal
revoir vt. to see again; revise, review; **— m., au —** good-bye
revoler vi. to fly again, fly back
révolte f. revolt, rebellion, uprising
révolté m. rebel
révolter vt. to cause to revolt; shock; **se — to** rebel, revolt
révolu a. completed, accomplished
révolution f. revolution; revolving
révolutionnaire a. & n. revolutionary
révolutionner vt. to revolutionize
revolver m. revolver
revomir vt. to vomit, throw up
révoquer vt. to revoke, repeal; dismiss
revue f. review, inspection; revue
rez-de-chaussée m. ground floor, street floor, first floor
rhabiller vt. to dress again, reclothe; repair, fix, mend; **se — to** get dressed again, put on one's clothes again
rhabilleur m. repairer
rhabituer vt. to reaccustom
rhapsodie f. rhapsody
rhénan a. pertaining to the Rhine, Rhenish
rhénium m. rhenium
rhéostat m. rheostat
rhésus m. rhesus monkey; **facteur — m.** RH factor
rhétorique f. rhetoric
Rhin m. Rhine
rhinite f. rhinitis
rhinocéros m. rhinoceros
rhodanien a. pertaining to the Rhone
rhodium m. rhodium

rhodedendron m. rhododendron
rhombe m. rhombus
rhomboïdal a. rhomboid
rhomboïde m. rhomboid
rhubarbe f. rhubarb
rhum m. rum
rhumatisant a. & m. rheumatic person
rhumatisme m. rheumatism
rhume m. (med.) cold
riant a. laughing, smiling
ribaud a. ribald
riblons m. pl. scrap metal
ricanement m. sneering, snickering, scoffing
ricaner vi. to sneer, laugh derisively
ricaneur a. derisive, snickering; **— m.** derider
riche a. rich, wealthy
richesse f. riches, richness, wealth
ricin m. castor-oil plant; **huile de — f** castor oil
ricocher vi. to rebound; ricochet
ricochet m. rebound; ricochet
ride f. wrinkle; ripple; (naut.) lanyard
ridé a. wrinkled, lined; corrugated
rideau m. curtain; screen; (phot.) shutter; **— de fer** iron curtain
ridelle f. side panel of a truck, or cart
rider vt. to wrinkle, line; ripple; corrugate; **se —** become wrinkled, become lined
ridicule a. ridiculous, absurd, laughable; **— m.** ridicule, ridiculousness; **tourner en — to** ridicule, make fun of
ridiculiser vt. to ridicule
rien pron. nothing, anything; **de — you're** welcome, don't mention it; **— que** only, merely; **ne . . . — nothing**, not anything; **— m.** nothing; bagatelle, trifle
rieur a. laughing; **— m.** laughter
riflard m. file; plastering trowel; jackplane; (coll.) very large umbrella
rifler vt. to file; plane; pare
rigide a. rigid, stiff; fixed, in place; tense
rigidité f. rigidity, stiffness; **— cadavérique** rigor mortis
rigole f. trench, gutter, drain
rigoleur a. fun-loving; laughing; **— m.** laugher; gay person
rigorisme m. absolute strictness
rigoriste a. very strict, rigorous; **— m. & f.** very strict person
rigoureux a. rigorous, strict, severe; hard, harsh
rigueur f. rigor, strictness, severity, harshness; **à la — strictly**; if necessary; **de —** required, obligatory
rillettes f. pl. minced pork
rillons m. pl. greaves, fryings
rimailler vi. to write verse, write second-

rate poetry
rimailleur *m.* rhymester, writer of verse
rime *f.* rhyme, verse
rimer *vt. & vi.* to rhyme
rimeur *m.* rhymer, writer of verse
rinçage *m.* rinsing
rince-bouteilles *m.* bottle-washer
rince-doigts *m.* finger bowl
rincer *vt.* to rinse, wash
rinçure *f.* dirty water, waste water, wash water
ringard *m.* poker, fire iron
ripaille *f.* feast, celebration, party
ripailler *vi.* to feast, celebrate
ripe *f.* scraper
riper *vt. & vi.* to scrape, rub
ripolin *m.* enamel
ripoliner *vt.* to enamel
riposte *f.* retort; repartée; counter
riposter *vi.* to retort, counter, riposte
riquiqui *m.* little finger; tiny person
rire *vi.* to laugh; joke; — à smile at, smile upon; — de laugh at, laugh about; **éclater de** — burst out laughing; **il n'y a pas de quoi** — it's not at all funny; **se** — de laugh at, make fun of; — *m.* laugh, laughing, laughter
ris *m.* laugh; (naut.) reef in a sail; — de veau sweetbreads
risée *f.* mockery, laughing stock; (naut.) gust, squall
risette *f.* smile of a child, little smile
risible *a.* laughable, ludicrous
risque *m.* risk, peril, danger
risqué *a.* risqué, risky
risquer *vt.* to risk, chance, endanger; **se** — to dare, venture; take risks
risque-tout *m.* daredevil
rissoler *vt.* to brown
ristourne *f.* refund, rebate; kickback
ristourner *vt.* to refund, rebate
ritournelle *f.* (mus.) ritournelle, short instrumental passage; (coll.) same old story
ritualiste *a.* ritualistic; — *m. & f.* ritualist
rituel *a. & m.* ritual
rivage *m.* bank, shore
rivaliser (avec) *vi.* to rival, compete (with)
rivalité *f.* rivalry
rive *f.* bank, shore; edge, border, side
rivelaine *f.* pick (tool)
river *vt.* to rivet, clinch
riverain *a.* riparian; bordering on a waterway *or* road
riveraineté *f.* riparian rights
rivet *m.* rivet; clinch
rivetage *m.* riveting
riveter *vt.* to rivet
riveur *m.* riveter

riveuse *f.* riveting machine
rivière *f.* river, stream
rivoir *m.* riveting hammer
rivure *f.* riveting; riveted work
rixe *f.* scuffle, melee, brawl
riz *m.* rice; — au lait rice pudding; **poudre de** — face powder
rizière *f.* rice field
robe *f.* dress, gown, frock; robe; husk, animal coat; **gens de** — bar, legal profession
robinet *m.* spigot, faucet, tap
rob, robre *m.* rubber (at cards)
robuste *a.* robust, strong, sturdy
robustesse *f.* robustness, strength, sturdiness
roc *m.* rock
rocaille *f.* rocks; rubble; **jardin de** — *m.* rock garden
rocailleur *m.* ornamental stonemason
rocailleux *a.* rocky; rough, harsh
rocambolesque *a.* fantastic
roche *f.* rock, stone
rocher *m.* rock, crag; — *vi.* to froth
rochet *m.* ratchet
rocheux *a.* rocky
rochier *m.* rockfish
rococo *a. & m.* rococo, baroque
rodage *m.* grinding; polishing; wear, wearing away; breaking-in of an automobile motor
rodailler *vi.* to wander, loaf
roder *vt.* to grind, polish; break in (a motor)
rôder *vi.* to roam, prowl
rôdeur *a.* roaming, prowling, idling; — *m.* prowler, idler, loafer
rodoir *m.* grinder, grinding implement
rodomont *m.* boaster
rœntgenthérapie *f.* X-ray treatment
rogatons *m. pl.* scraps, bits of food
rogner *vt.* to pare, clip, trim
rognoir *m.* parer, paring implement
rognon *m.* edible animal kidney
rognures *f. pl.* cuttings, parings, trimmings; leftovers, scraps
rogue *a.* haughty
roi *m.* king
roide *a.* stiff; steep; firm
roideur *f.* stiffness
rôle *m.* roll, roster, list; (theat.) part, role; **à tour de** — in turn
Romain *m. & a.* Roman
romaine *f.* balance, scale; romaine lettuce
roman *m.* novel; romance; — *a.* Romance; (arch.) Romanesque
romance *f.* (mus.) ballad, song
romancier *m.* novelist
romand *a.*, **Suisse –e** *f.* French-speaking Switzerland

romanesque *a.* romantic
roman-feuilleton *m.* serialized novel
romanichel *m.* gypsy, wanderer
romaniste *m.* specialist in Romance languages; (eccl.) Romanist
romantique *a.* romantic (literature, art); — *m.* romanticist
romantisme *m.* romanticism
romarin *m.* rosemary
rompre *vt.* to break, break off, break up; break in, train; disrupt, interrupt; — *vi.* break; **se** — to break off, break up; break oneself in, become accustomed
rompu *a.* broken; broken in, trained, experienced; fatigued, worn out
romsteck *m.* rump steak
ronce *f.* bramble; blackberry bush
ronce-framboise *f.* loganberry
ronceux *a.* thorny, brambly
ronchonner *vi.* to grumble, complain
rond *a.* round; plump; straightforward; — *m.* round, circle, ring; — **de serviette** napkin ring
rondache *f.* round shield
rond-de-cuir *m.* (coll.) bureaucrat, petty official
ronde *f.* (mus.) round; patrol
rondeau *m.* (mus.) rondo; rondeau (literature)
rondelet *a.* round, roundish; plump
rondelle *f.* ring, washer; disk; circular piece; round
rondement *adv.* roundly; promptly; in a straightforward manner
rondeur *f.* roundness; rotundity; frankness, straightforwardness
rondin *m.* log; stick; beam
rond-point *m.* circular intersection, circus
ronflant *a.* snoring; booming; rumbling; pretentious
ronflement *m.* snoring, snore; buzzing; booming cannon; rumbling
ronfler *vi.* to snore; roar; whirr; boom; rumble
ronfleur *m.* snorer
rongeant *a.* gnawing, eating away; corroding
ronger *vt.* to gnaw, nibble, eat away; erode; corrode; torment
rongeur *a.* gnawing; corroding; tormenting; — *m.* rodent
ronron *m.* hum, purr
ronronner *vi.* to hum, purr
roquer *vt.* to castle (chess)
roquet *m.* mongrel, cur, dog
rosaire *m.* (eccl.) rosary, beads
rosâtre *a.* pinkish
rosbif *m.* roast beef
rose *f.* rose; — *a.* pink; rosy
rosé *a.* light red

roseau *m.* (bot.) reed
rosée *f.* dew
roselet *m.* ermine fur
roséole *f.* (med.) roseola; German measles
roseraie *f.* rose garden
rosette *f.* rosette; ribbon, bow
rosier *m.* rose bush
rosir *vi.* to turn pink *or* rosy
rossard *m.* good-for-nothing
rossée *f.* beating, thrashing, licking
rosser *vt.* to thrash, whip, beat
rossignol *m.* nightingale
rossinante *f.* nag, old horse
rôt *m.* roast
rotative *f.* rotary press
rotatoire *a.* rotary
roter *vi.* to belch, eructate
rôti *m.* roast
rôtie *f.* toast
rotin *m.* rattan
rôtir *vt. & vi.* to roast; toast
rôtissage *m.* roasting
rôtisserie *f.* roaster's shop
rôtissoire *f.* Dutch oven; roaster
rotonde *f.* rotunda
rotondité *f.* rotundity, roundness
rotor *m.* rotor
rotule *f.* kneecap; knee joint; (mech.) knuckle
roture *f.* low estate; commoners
roturier *m. & a.* plebeian, commoner
rouage *m.* wheels, gears, workings
rouan *a.* roan
roublard *a. & m.* shrewd, crafty person
roublardise *f.* skulduggery
roucouler *vi.* to coo
roue *f.* wheel
roué *m.* rake, profligate, roué; — *a.* clever, shrewd, crafty, sly
rouelle *f.* round piece, slice; filet of veal
rouennerie *f.* printed fabrics
rouer *vt.* to torture on a wheel; beat, thrash
rouerie *f.* cheating, trickery, sharping
rouet *m.* spinning wheel; pulley wheel
rouge *a.* red; — *m.* red; rouge; lipstick
rougeâtre *a.* reddish
rougeaud *a.* red-faced, ruddy
rouge-gorge *m.* robin
rougeole *f.* measles
rougeoyer *vi.* to turn red
rougeur *f.* redness; blush
rougir *vt.* to redden, turn red; heat, cause to glow; — *vi.* to grow red, turn red; blush
rouille *f.* rust; blight
rouillé *a.* rusty, rusted; blighted
rouiller *vt.* to rust, blight; **se** — to become rusty, rust
rouilleux *a.* rust-colored

rouillure *f.* rust, rustiness
roulade *f.* trill, roll
roulage *m.* rolling; hauling, transporting; traffic
roulant *a.* rolling; moving; smooth; **fauteuil —** wheel chair
rouleau *m.* roll; roller; coil; cylinder; rolling pin; **— compresseur** steam roller
roulement *m.* rolling; functioning, running; rotation, alternation; **— à billes** ballbearing
rouler *vt.* to roll; roll up; carry, haul; consider, turn over; **—** *vi.* roll; run; turn; move along; rove; rumble; rotate, alternate
roulette *f.* small wheel; roller; caster; roulette; **patins à -s** *m. pl.* roller skates
roulier *m.* hauler, trucker, carter
roulis *m.* (naut.) roll
roulotte *f.* caravan, house trailer
Roumain *m. & a.* Roumanian
Roumanie *f.* Roumania
roupie *f.* rupee
roussâtre *a.* reddish
rousselet *m.* russet pear
rousseur *f.* reddishness, redness; **tache de —** freckle
roussi *a.* burned; burning; browned
roussin *m.* draft horse, plow horse
roussir *vt. & vi.* to redden; turn brown; singe, burn
routage *m.* newspaper delivery *or* distribution
route *f.* route, road, way; **grande —** highway; **en —** on the way; go on; let's go; **se mettre en —** to start out, set out
router *vt.* to deliver, distribute
routier *a.* of roads; **—** *m.* long-distance trucker; long-distance cyclist; **-s** *pl.* highwaymen; **carte routière** *f.* road map
routine *f.* routine, habit
routinier *a.* routine
rouvrir *vt.* to open again, reopen
roux (rousse) *a.* reddish, red-headed
royal *a.* royal; regal
royaliste *m. & f.* royaliste
royaume *m.* kingdom, realm
royauté *f.* royalty
ru *m.* streamlet
ruade *f.* attack; kicking of an animal
ruban *m.* ribbon; tape; band, strip; **— magnétique** magnetic recording-tape
rubané *a.* striped
rubaner *vt.* to adorn with ribbons; cut into strips
rubéole *f.* German measles
rubicond *a.* rubicund
rubiette *f.* robin
rubigineux *a.* rusty; rust-colored

rubis *m.* ruby; watch jewel
rubrique *f.* rubric; red chalk; category, heading
ruche *f.* beehive; frill, ruche, ruffle
ruché *m.* ruche, frilling
ruchée *f.* bees of a hive
rucher *m.* apiary; **—** *vt.* to gather (sewing); trim with ruching
rude *a.* rough, rugged; hard, harsh; coarse; steep; brusque; primitive
rudement *adv.* roughly, harshly
rudesse *f.* roughness, ruggedness; harshness; coarseness; abruptness
rudiment *m.* rudiment
rudimentaire *a.* rudimentary, elementary
rudoyer *vt.* to treat roughly
rue *f.* street
ruée *f.* rush, stampede; attack, onslaught
ruelle *f.* narrow street, lane, alley
ruer *vi.* to kick; **se — (sur)** to rush upon, stampede
rufian *m.* ruffian
ruginer *vt.* to clean, scale teeth
rugir *vi.* to roar, bellow
rugissement *m.* roar, roaring, bellow, bellowing
rugosité *f.* roughness, ruggedness; wrinkle
rugueux *a.* rough, rugged; wrinkled, gnarled
ruine *f.* ruin; downfall; destruction
ruiner *vt.* to ruin, destroy; **se —** to be ruined; go to ruin; fall to ruins
ruineux *a.* ruinous; disastrous
ruisseau *m.* stream, brook; gutter
ruisseler *vi.* to stream, gush out, run; drip, trickle
ruisselet *m.* little brook *or* stream
rumba *f.* rhumba
rumen *m.* first stomach of a ruminant
rumeur *f.* noise, din, sound; rumor
ruminant *a. & m.* ruminant
rumination *f.* rumination
ruminer *vt. & vi.* to ruminate
rumsteck *m.* rump steak
runes *f. pl.* runes
runique *a.* Runic
rupteur *m.* (elec.) circuit breaker
rupture *f.* breaking, rupture; fracture; breaking up; breaking in two; breaking off; breach
ruse *f.* ruse, trick
rusé *a.* sly, cunning, crafty
ruser *vi.* to use trickery
Russe *m. & a.* Russian
Russie *f.* Russia
rustaud *m.* boor; hick, bumpkin; **—** *a.* boorish
rusticité *f.* rusticity
rustique *a.* rustic; strong, robust
rustre *m.* boor, lout; **—** *a.* boorish, loutish

ruthénium *m.* ruthenium
rutilant *a.* glowing, gleaming, red
rutiler *vi.* to glow, gleam, redden
rythme *m.* rhythm
rythmé, rythmique *a.* rhythmic, rhythmical

S

sa *a. f.* his, her, its; one's
Saba *m.* Sheba
sabbat *m.* Sabbath
sabbatique *a.* sabbatical
sabin *a. & m.* Sabine
sable *m.* sand; — **mouvant** quicksand
sablé *a.* sanded, covered with sand *or* gravel; — *m.* shortbread cookie
sabler *vt.* to sand, gravel, cover with sand *or* gravel; sand-blast; drink dry
sableux *a.* sandy
sablier *m.* hourglass
sablière *f.* sandbox; sand pit, gravel pit; — *f.* beam, plate, templet
sablon *m.* sand for cleaning *or* scouring
sablonner *vt.* to clean, scour with sand
sablonneux *a.* sandy
sabord *m.* port hole, gun port
saborder *vt.* to hit below the water line; se — to scuttle
sabot *m.* wooden shoe; hoof; (auto.) brake shoe; **-s en caoutchouc** rubbers
sabotage *m.* sabotage; manufacture of sabots
saboter *vt.* to sabotage
sabotier *m.* maker of sabots
sabre *m.* saber, sword
sabrer *vt.* to saber, cut down
sac *m.* sack, sac, bag, pouch; sackcloth; sacking (a place); — **à main** handbag, purse
saccade *f.* jerk, jolt
saccadé *a.* by jerks; abrupt; irregular, uneven
saccader *vt.* to jerk, jolt
saccager *vt.* to plunder, sack, pillage; ransack
saccageur *m.* plunderer
saccharine *f.* saccharine
sacerdotal *a.* priestly
sachée *f.* sackful, bagful
sachet *m.* sachet; small sack *or* bag
sacoche *f.* bag; handbag; satchel; saddlebag; tool kit
sacre *m.* coronation; consecration
sacré *a.* sacred, holy; confounded; (anat.) sacral
sacrement *m.* sacrament
sacrer *vt.* to crown; consecrate
sacrificateur *m.* sacrificer
sacrificatoire *a.* sacrificial

sacrifice *m.* sacrifice; oblation
sacrifier *vt.* to sacrifice; devote
sacrilège *m.* sacrilege; — *a.* **sacrilegious**
sacristain *m.* sexton, sacristan
sacristie *f.* vestry
sacro-saint *a.* sacrosanct
sacrum *m.* (anat.) sacrum
sadique *a.* sadistic
sadisme *m.* sadism
sadiste *m. & f.* sadist
safran *m.* saffron, crocus
safrané *a.* saffron-colored
sagace *a.* sagacious
sagacité *f.* sagacity
sage *a.* wise; good, well-behaved; — *m.* sage, wise man
sage-femme *f.* midwife
sagesse *f.* wisdom; good behavior; discretion
sagittaire *m.* archer; (astrol., ast.) Saggitarius
sagittal *a.* arrow-shaped
sagou *m.* sago
Sahara *m.* Sahara
saharien *a.* of the Sahara
saie *f.* cape; hog-bristle brush
saignant *a.* bleeding, bloody; rare (meat)
saignée *f.* (med.) bleeding, bloodletting; drainage ditch; groove
saigner *vt. & vi.* to bleed
saigneux *a.* bloody
saillant *a.* projecting, prominent; salient; **dents -es** *f. pl.* buck teeth
saillie *f.* protrusion, projection; start; sally; spurt; gushing
saillir *vi.* to jut out, project; stand out, be prominent; spurt, gush; rush forth
sain *a.* sound, healthy; wholesome; sane; — **et sauf** safe and sound
sainfoin *m.* hay, forage
saindoux *m.* lard
saint *a.* saint; sacred, holy; saintly, godly; consecrated; — *m.* saint
saint-cyrien *m.* army cadet
Saint-Domingue *m.* Santo Domingo; Dominican Republic
Saint-Esprit *m.* (eccl.) Holy Ghost
sainte-nitouche *f.* hypocrite
sainteté *f.* sanctity, holiness
saint-frusquin *m.* possessions
Saint-Laurent *m.* St. Lawrence River
Saint-Marin *m.* San Marino
Saint-Père *m.* (eccl.) Pope, Holy Father
Saint-Siège *m.* (eccl.) Holy See
Saint-Sylvestre *m.* New Year's Eve
saisie *f.* seizure; attachment, foreclosure
saisie-arrêt *f.* legal garnishment, attachment
saisir *vt.* to seize, catch, grip, grasp; understand, apprehend; attach legally

saisissable *a.* perceptible
saisissant *a.* striking; startling; thrilling, gripping; keen, sharp
saisissement *m.* sudden shock, attack, seizure
saison *f.* season; **de —** in season; timely, opportune; **hors de —** out of season; untimely, inopportune
saisonnier *a.* seasonal
salacité *f.* salaciousness
salade *f.* salad
saladier *m.* salad bowl
salaire *m.* salary, wages, pay; fee; reward
salaison *f.* salting, curing; salted meat
salamandre *f.* salamander, newt
salanque *f.* salt marsh
salariat *m.* wage earners, salaried class
salarier *vt.* to pay, salary
sale *a.* dirty; foul; filthy; coarse
salé *m.* salt pork; **petit —** ham hock; **— a.** salted; risqué
saler *vt.* to salt; season; pickle, cure
saleté *f.* dirtiness, dirt, filth; obscenity
salicoque *f.* shrimp, prawn
salière *f.* salt cellar, salt shaker
salin *a.* saline, briny, salty
saline *f.* salt flats, salt mine
salinité *f.* salinity
salir *vt.* to soil, dirty; tarnish
salissure *f.* spot, stain, dirt mark
salivaire *a.* salivary
salive *f.* saliva
saliver *vi.* to salivate
salle *f.* hall, room; auditorium; audience; **— à manger** dining room; **— d'attente** waiting room; **— de bain** bathroom; **— de conférences** lecture hall
Salomon (*m.*) Solomon
salon *m.* living room, parlor; exhibition; **— de thé** tearoom; **— de beauté** beauty shop; **— de coiffure** barber shop
salopette *f.* dungarees, overalls
salpêtre *m.* saltpeter
salsepareille *f.* sarsaparilla
salsifis *m.* salsify, oysterplant
saltimbanque *m.* quack, charlatan; mountebank; tumbler
salubre *a.* salubrious, wholesome, healthy
salubrité *f.* salubrity, wholesomeness, healthiness; health, hygiene
saluer *vt.* to salute, greet, bow
salure *f.* saltiness, salinity
salut *m.* bow, greeting, salutation, salvation; safety; welfare; **—!** *interj.* hello!
salutaire *a.* salutary, beneficial
salve *f.* salvo, salute
samaritain *m.* samaritan
samedi *m.* Saturday
samovar *m.* samovar, tea urn
sanctifier *vt.* to sanctify, hallow

sanction *f.* sanction; approval, consent; penalty, punitive action
sanctionner *vi.* to sanction, approve; penalize
sanctuaire *m.* sanctuary
sandale *f.* sandal
sandaraque *f.* sandarac
sang *m.* blood; lineage; **coup de —** (med.) stroke; **pur —** thoroughbred
sang-froid *m.* composure, self-control, calmness, coolness
sanglant *a.* bloody, covered with blood; cutting, keen
sangle *f.* strap; **lit de —** *m.* cot, camp bed
sangler *vt.* to strap; whip, lash
sanglier *m.* wild boar
sanglot *m.* sob
sangloter *vi.* to sob
sangsue *f.* leech
sanguin *a.* sanguine, blood-red; of blood
sanguinaire *a.* sanguinary; bloody; blood-thirsty
sanguine *f.* blood orange; bloodstone; red chalk
sanguinelle *f.* dogwood
sanitaire *a.* sanitary; medical
sans *prep.* without; were it not for; free of; **— doute** without a doubt; probably; perhaps
sans-cœur *m.* heartless person
sanscrit, sanskrit *a. & m.* Sanskrit
sans-façon *m.* lack of formality, straightforwardness
sans-fil *m.* wireless, radio
sans-gêne *m.* excessive familiarity; lack of ceremony
sans-le-sou *m.* penniless person
sans-logis *m. pl.* homeless persons
sansonnet *m.* starling
sans-souci *m.* lack of concern; **— m. & f.** carefree person
sans-travail *m. pl.* unemployed persons
santal *m.* sandalwood
santé *f.* health
saoul *a.* (See soûl)
saouler *vt.* (See soûler)
sape *f.* (mil.) sap, sapping; undermining
saper *vt.* to sap, undermine
sapeur *m.* (mil.) sapper
sapeur-pompier *m.* fireman, fire fighter
saphir *m.* sapphire
sapide *a.* savory, flavorful
sapience *f.* wisdom
sapin *m.* fir tree; **–ette** *f.* spruce tree
sapine *f.* scaffolding; fir board; construction crane
sapinière *f.* fir forest
saponacé *a.* soapy
sarbacane *f.* blowpipe; pea shooter

sarcasme *m.* sarcasm
sarcastique *a.* sarcastic
sarcler *vt.* to weed; hoe
sarcleur *m.* weeder
sarcloir *m.* hoe
sarclure *f.* weeds
sarcome *m.* (med.) sarcoma
sarcophage *m.* sarcophagus
Sardaigne *f.* Sardinia
Sarde *m. & a.* Sardinian
sardinerie *f.* sardine cannery
sardinier *m.* sardine fishermen, cannery worker
sardoine *f.* sardonyx
sardonique *a.* sardonic
sargasse *f.* sargasso; mer des –s *f.* Sargasso Sea
S.A.R.L.: Société à Responsabilité Limitée incorporated
sarment *m.* shoot of a vine
sarracenique *a.* Saracen
sarrasin *m.* buckwheat
Sarrasin *m. & a.* Saracen
sarrasine *f.* portcullis
sarrau *m.* smock; overalls
Sarre *f.* Saar Basin
sariette *f.* savory
sas *m.* sifter, sieve, screen; lock of a dam
sasser *vt.* to sift, screen; (naut.) lock a vessel (in a canal)
Satan *m.* Satan, the Devil
satanique *a.* diabolical, devilish, satanic
satellite *m.* satellite
satiété *f.* satiety, repletion, fullness
satiné *a.* satin-like; glossy
satiner *vt.* to satin, gloss, glaze
satinette *f.* sateen
satire *f.* satire
satirique *a.* satirical; — *m.* satirist
satiriser *vt.* to satirize
satisfaction *f.* satisfaction; amends
satisfaire *vt.* to satisfy; please; make amends to; — *vi.* to satisfy, carry out, fulfil
satisfaisant *a.* satisfactory; satisfying
satisfait *a.* satisfied; pleased
satrape *m.* satrap
saturation *f.* saturation
saturer *vt.* to saturate
saturnin *a.* saturnine
saturnisme *m.* lead poisoning
satyre *m.* satyr
sauce *f.* sauce; gravy; dressing
saucer *vt.* to dip into sauce; soak, drench
saucière *f.* gravy boat; sauce dish
saucisse *f.* sausage; — de Francfort frankfurter
saucisson *m.* sausage, salami
sauf *prep.* except, except for, but; barring; — (sauve) *a.* safe

sauf-conduit *m.* safe conduct, pass, permit
sauge *f.* sage
saugrenu *a.* absurd, ridiculous
saule *m.* willow; — pleureur weeping willow
saumâtre *a.* brackish; salty; bitter
saumon *m.* salmon; ingot, bar; — de fonte pig iron; — *a.* salmon, pink
saumoné *a.* pink-fleshed; truite –e *f.* salmon trout
saumurage *m.* curing in brine
saumure *f.* brine
saupiquet *m.* spicy sauce
saupoudrer *vt.* to sprinkle; powder; dust with
saupoudroir *m.* shaker
saur *a.*, hareng — *m.* smoked red herring
saure *a.* sorrel
saurer *vt.* to smoke, cure fish
saut *m.* jump, leap; waterfall; — à la perche pole vault; — d'obstacles hurdles
saut-de-lit *m.* dressing gown; bedroom scatter rug
saut-de-mouton *m.* overpass, underpass
saute *f.* jump, leap; rise, increase
sauté *a.* fried; — *m.* food fried rapidly
saute-mouton *m.* leapfrog
sauter *vt.* to leap, jump; skip, omit; — *vi.* leap, jump; skip; explode, blow up; fail; — au cou de throw one's arms around; — aux yeux to be very obvious; faire — to blow up, explode; pop open
sauterelle *f.* grasshopper
sauterie *f.* leaping, jumping; hopping, hop; dance, dancing
sauternes *m.* Sauterne wine
sauteur *a.* leaping, jumping; — *m.* leaper, jumper
sautiller *vt.* to skip, leap, hop
sautoir *m.* X-shaped cross; frying pan; sports hurdle; bar of a jump *or* vault; en — crosswise
sauvage *a.* wild; savage; barbarous, uncivilized; shy, unsociable
sauvagerie *f.* wildness, savagery; shyness, unsociability
sauvegarde *f.* safeguard, protection; bodyguard; safe-conduct; (naut.) lifeline
sauvegarder *vt.* to protect, safeguard
sauve-qui-peut *m.* wild flight, stampede
sauver *vt.* to save, preserve; rescue; se — to escape; run away, flee
sauvetage *m.* salvage; saving, rescue; canot de — lifeboat; ceinture de — *f.* life preserver
sauveteur *m.* saver, rescuer; salvager
sauvette; à la — *adv.* hastily
sauveur *m.* deliverer; saviour, redeemer
savamment *adv.* in a learned *or* scholarly

manner; knowingly
savane *f.* savanna
savant *a.* learned, scholarly, erudite; knowing; — *m.* scholar; scientist
savarin *m.* rum cake
savate *f.* old shoe; foot boxing (French style); (fig.) bungler
savetier *m.* cobbler, shoe repairer
saveur *f.* flavor, savor, taste
Savoie *f.* Savoy; **gâteau de** — *m.* sponge cake
savoir *vt.* to know, know how, be able, find out; **à** — namely, viz., to wit; **faire** — to inform; **reste à** — it remains to be seen; — *m.* knowledge, learning, erudition
savoir-faire *m.* skill, ability, know-how; tact
savoir-vivre *m.* manners, breeding, social poise
savoisien *a.* of Savoy
savon *m.* soap; **pain de** — *m.* cake of soap; **pierre de** — *f.* soapstone
savonnage *m.* soaping, washing
savonner *vt.* to soap; lather; wash
savonnette *f.* toilet soap
savonneux *a.* soapy
savourer *vt.* to relish, taste, savor, enjoy
savoureux *a.* savory, flavorful, tasty; spicy
Saxe *f.* Saxony; **porcelaine de** — *f.* Dresden china
saynète *f.* comic play, farce
Saxon *m. & a.* Saxon
saxophone *m.* saxophone
scabieux *a.* scabby
scabreux *a.* scabrous; risky, dangerous; risqué
scalpe *m.* scalp
scalper *vt.* to scalp
scandale *m.* scandal, disgrace
scandaleux *a.* scandalous, disgraceful, shocking
scandaliser *vt.* to scandalize
scander *vt.* to scan (poetry); stress, accentuate, measure
Scandinave *m. & a.* Scandinavian
Scandinavie *f.* Scandinavia
scansion *f.* scanning
scaphandre *m.* diving suit; aqualung
scaphandrier *m.* deep-sea diver
scapulaire *m.* (eccl.) scapular
scarabée *m.* beetle, scarab
scarlatine *f.* scarlet fever
scarole *f.* escarole
sceau *m.* seal; stamp, mark, imprint
scélérat *a.* villainous, wicked; sly, crafty; — *m.* villain, scoundrel
scélératesse *f.* villainy, wickedness
scellage *m.* sealing

scellé *m.* legal seal
scellement *m.* fixing in cem?
sceller *vt.* to seal; fasten
scénario *m.* scenario, screenr
scénariste *m. & f.* author of a
scène *f.* scene; stage; scenery; met? — *m.* director; **mettre en** — to direc?, stage; **mise en** — *f.* direction, staging
scénique *a.* scenic; of the stage
scepticisme *m.* skepticism
sceptique *a.* skeptical; — *m. & f.* skeptic
sceptre *m.* scepter
schelem *m.* slam (in bridge)
schelling *m.* shilling
schéma *m.* plan, sketch, diagram
schématique *a.* schematic
schisme *m.* schism
schiste *m.* shale
schizophrène *a.* schizophrenic
schizophrénie *f.* schizophrenia
schnorchel *m.* snorkel
sciage *m.* sawing
sciatique sciatic; — *f.* sciatica
scie *f.* saw; — **à chantourner** jigsaw; — **à métaux** hack saw; — **à refendre** ripsaw; — **à ruban** band saw; — **de mer** sawfish
sciemment *adv.* knowingly; purposely
science *f.* science; knowledge, learning; — **des fusées** rocketry
scientifique *a.* scientific
scientiste *m.* scientist
scier *vt.* to saw
scierie *f.* sawmill
scinder *vt.* to split, divide
scintillant *a.* scintillating; twinkling
scintillation *f.* scintillation; twinkling; (phot.) flickering
scintiller *vi.* to scintillate; twinkle; flicker
scion *m.* scion, shoot, sprout
scission *f.* secession; division, split
sciure *f.* sawdust
sclérose *f.* sclerosis; — **multiple** multiple sclerosis
scléroser *vt.* (med.) to harden
scolaire *a.* scholastic, academic, school
scolarisation *f.* teaching; school attendance
scolarité *f.* length of study; **certificat de** — *m.* attendance certificate
scolastique *a.* scholastic
scolopendre *f.* centipede
scombre *m.* mackerel
scorbut *m.* scurvy
scorie *f.* slag, dross
scoutisme *m.* scouting, boy scout movement
scrofules *f. pl.* (med.) scrofula
scrupule *m.* scruple, qualm, doubt; **sans -s** unscrupulous

scrupuleux a. scrupulous
scruter vt. to scrutinize; examine at length
scrutin m. ballot, vote, voting
scrutiner vi. to vote, ballot
sculpter vt. to sculpt, sculpture, carve, chisel
sculpteur m. sculptor
scythe a. & n. Scythian
se pron. oneself, himself; herself, itself, themselves; each other, one another
séance f. sitting, session, meeting; showing, performance; **lever la —** to adjourn
séant a. sitting; in session; fitting, proper, becoming
seau m. pail, bucket
sébacé a. fatty
sébile f. wooden bowl
sec (sèche) a. dry, dried; lean; sharp, curt; barren; **argent —** m. hard cash; **coup —** m. snap; clean, hard blow; **à —** dry; aground; **mettre à —** to dry up, drain, pump out; **— adv.**, **boire —** to drink straight; **parler —** to speak plainly, in a straightforward manner
sèche-cheveux m. hair dryer
sécheresse f. dryness; leanness; curtness; drought
sécher vt. to dry; (coll.) cut a class; fail a student; **— vi.** dry
sécheur m. drier
séchoir m. drier; towel rack
second a. second; **en — lieu** secondly, in the second place; **sans —** peerless, unequalled; **— m.** second in command; first mate
secondaire a. secondary
seconde f. second; second class
seconder vt. to second, assist, support, promote
secouer vt. to shake, shake off
secourable a. helpful; ready to help
secourir vt. to succor, help, assist, aid
secours m. succor, aid, assistance, help; **crier au —** to call for help; **premiers —** pl. first aid
secousse f. shake, shock, jolt
secret a. secret; concealed, hidden; **— m.** secret; secrecy
secrétaire m. & f. secretary
secrétariat m. secretariat; secretary's office
sécréter vt. to secrete
sécréteur a. secreting
sécrétion f. secretion
sectaire m. sectarian
sectateur m. member of a sect
secte f. sect, party, faction
secteur m. sector; area, district; segment
sectionner vt. to divide into sections

séculaire a. century-old, secular
sécularisation f. secularization
séculariser vt. to secularize
séculier a. secular, worldly; **— m.** layman
sécurité f. security; safety
sédatif a. & m. sedative
sédentaire a. sedentary
sédiment m. sediment
séditieux a. seditious
sédition f. sedition
séducteur a. enticing, seductive; **— m.** enticer; seducer
séduction f. seductiveness, charm; bribery; seduction
séduire vt. to charm; bribe; seduce
séduisant a. charming; enticing, seductive
segment m. segment; **— de piston** piston ring
segmenter vt. to divide into segments
ségrégation f. segregation
ségrégationiste m. segregationist
seiche f. cuttlefish; floodwave
seigle m. rye; **pain de — m.** rye bread
seigneur m. lord, nobleman
seigneurie f. lordship; domain
seille f. wooden bucket
seillon m. shallow tub
sein m. breast; bosom
seing m. signature; **acte sous — privé** simple contract
séisme m. earthquake
seize a. sixteen
seizième a. sixteenth
séjour m. sojourn, stay; abode, dwelling
séjourner vi. to stay, sojourn; reside
sel m. salt; (fig.) wit; **— anglais** m. Epsom salts; **— blanc** table salt; **— gemme** rock salt
sélecteur a. selective; **— m.** selector
sélection f. selection, choice, choosing
sélectivité f. selectivity
sélénium m. selenium
selle f. saddle; stool
seller vt. to saddle
sellette f. stool; saddle
selon prep. according to, by
seltz m., **eau de — f.** seltzer, soda water
semailles f. pl. sowing, seeding
semaine f. week; week's pay; week's work; **— anglaise** five and one-half-day week
semaison f. seeding time
sémantique a. semantic; **— f.** semantics
sémaphore m. semaphore
semblable a. like, similar; such; **— n.** like, equal, fellow man
semblablement adv. likewise, similarly
semblant m. semblance, appearance; **faire — (de)** to pretend (to)
sembler vi. to seem, appear, look

semelle *f.* sole of a shoe; **battre la —** to be on the move, be roving
semence *f.* seed
semer *vt.* to sow; seed; spread, scatter
semestre *m.* semester, term; six-month period
semestriel *a.* six months long; taking place every six months, semi-annual
semeur *m.* sower; spreader
semi-circulaire *a.* semicircular
sémillant *a.* sprightly; light, gay
sémi-mensuel *a.* bimonthly
séminaire *m.* seminary
semis *m.* sowing, seeding; seed bed
sémitique *a.* Semitic
semi-voyelle *f.* semivowel
semoir *m.* mechanical sower, seeder
semonce *f.* summons; warning; lecture, talking-to
semoncer *vt.* to lecture, reprimand
semoule *f.* semolina
sempiternel *a.* eternal
sénat *m.* senate
sénateur *m.* senator
sénatorial *a.* senatorial
séné *m.* senna
senestrorsum *adv.* counterclockwise
sénévé *m.* mustard seed
sénile *a.* senile
sénilité *f.* senility
sens *m.* sense; judgment; meaning; direction; consciousness; **bon —** common sense; **— interdit** one-way street
sensation *f.* sensation; feeling; excitement
sensationnel *a.* sensational, exciting
sensé *a.* sensible, aware
sensibilisateur *a.* sensitizing; **— m.** sensitizer
sensibiliser *vt.* to sensitize
sensibilité *f.* sensitiveness, feeling; sensibility
sensible *a.* sensitive; sympathetic; tender, painful, sore; perceptible
sensiblement *a.* perceptibly, measurably
sensiblerie *f.* sentimentality
sensitif *a.* sensory; sensitive
sensualiste *a.* sensual; **— m.** sensualist
sensualité *f.* sensuality
sensuel *a.* sensuous, sensual
sentant *a.* sentient
sente *f.* path, footpath, trail
sentence *f.* maxim, saying; penal sentence; **— de mort** sentence of death
sentencieux *a.* sententious
senteur *f.* scent, perfume, fragrance; **pois de — m.** sweet pea
sentier *m.* path, track
sentiment *m.* septiment, feeling; sensation, sense
sentimentalité *f.* sentimentality

sentinelle *f.* sentinel; sentry
sentir *vt.* to feel; sense; smell; **— vi.** smell; smell of, reek of; **se —** feel
seoir *vi.* to suit, become; be located
sépale *m.* sepal
séparable *a.* separable
séparateur *m.* separator
séparatif *a.* separating, dividing
séparation *f.* separation; partition, division; parting
séparé *a.* separate; apart, separated
séparément *adv.* separately
séparer *vt.* to separate; divide; part; **se — to** separate, divide, part; break up; branch off
sépia *f.* sepia; cuttlefish
sept *a.* seven; seventh
septante *a.* seventy
septembre *m.* September
septicémie *f.* blood poisoning
septième *a.* seventh
septique *a.* septic; **fosse — f.** septic tank
sépulcral *a.* sepulchral
sépulcre *m.* sepulcher
sépulture *f.* burial; tomb; cemetery
séquence *f.* sequence
séquestration *f.* seclusion; sequestration (law)
séquestre *m.* sequestration (law); depository
séquestrer *vt.* to sequester; isolate, confine
sérail *m.* seraglio, harem
séraphin *m.* seraph
séraphique *a.* seraphic, angelic
Serbe *m. & f. & a.* Serb, Serbian
Serbo-Croate *m. & f. & a.* Serbo-Croatian
serein *a.* serene, calm, peaceful
sérénade *f.* serenade
sérénissime *a.* most serene
sérénité *f.* serenity, calm, calmness
sergent *m.* sergeant; **— de ville** policeman
sériculture *f.* silkworm raising
série *f.* series, succession, string, run; **fin de — f.** (com.) remainder, remnant
sérier *vt.* to arrange in series
sérieux *a.* serious, grave; genuine; **— m.** seriousness
sérigraphie *f.* (print.) silk screen process
serin *m.* canary
seringue *f.* syringe
seringuer *vt.* to syringe; squirt
serment *m.* oath; **faux —** perjury; **prêter — to** take an oath
sermonner *vi. & vt.* to sermonize, lecture
serpe *f.* billhook, pruning hook; rough work
serpent *m.* snake
serpenter *vi.* to wind, meander, twist

serpentin *a.* serpentine; — *m.* coil
serpette *f.* billhook, pruning hook
serpillière *f.* sacking; apron
serpolet *m.* thyme
serrage *m.* tightening, clamping
serre *f.* grip; bird claw; squeezing; forceps; greenhouse; — **chaude** hothouse
serré *a.* tight, compact, dense, close
serre-frein *m.* brakeman
serre-livres *m.* book ends
serrement *m.* squeezing, gripping; — **de cœur** pang; — **de main** handshake
serre-papiers *m.* paper clip; paperweight; file, folder
serrer *vt.* to squeeze, tighten, clasp, grip; lock up; keep close to, hug; — **la main (à)** to shake hands (with); — **les freins** to put on the brakes; **se —** tighten; press, mill, be close together
serre-tête *m.* headband; kerchief; crash helmet
serrure *f.* lock
serrurerie *f.* locksmith's establishment; works, workings of a lock; iron work
serrurier *m.* locksmith; ironworker
sertir *vt.* to set; mount (jewel)
sertissure *f.* bezel; setting
sérum *m.* serum
servage *m.* bondage, slavery, serfdom
servant *m.* server (sports)
servante *f.* servant; serving tray
serveur *m.* server; bartender; card dealer
serveuse *f.* waitress
serviabilité *f.* obligingness, usefulness
serviable *a.* obliging
service *m.* service; military service; **chef de — ** *m.* department head; — **compris** service charge included; **être de —** be on duty
serviette *f.* napkin; towel; briefcase
servilité *f.* servility
servir *vi.* to serve, be useful; — **de** to serve as; — *vt.* serve, wait on; **se — de** to use, make use of
serviteur *m.* servant
servo-frein *m.* power brakes
servo-moteur *m.* servomotor
ses *a. pl.* his, her, its
sésame *m.* sesame
session *f.* session, sitting; term
set *m.* tennis, movies; set of games (tennis); (theat.) scenery
sétacé *a.* bristly
séton *m.*, **blessure en —** *f.* flesh wound
seuil *m.* sill, threshold
seul *a.* sole, single; only; alone
seulement *adv.* only; even; merely
sève *f.* sap, juice; vitality
sévère *a.* severe, hard, harsh; strict
sévérité *f.* severity

sévices *m. pl.* maltreatment (law)
sévir *vi.* to be severe; rage
sevrer *vt.* to wean
sexe *m.* sex
sextuor *m.* (mus.) sextet
sexualité *f.* sexuality
sexuel *a.* sexual
seyant *a.* becoming, suitable
shake-hand *m.* handshake
shaker *m.* cocktail shaker
shampooing *m.* shampoo; liquid shampoo
shantung *m.* shantung
short *m.* movie short subject; clothing shorts
shunter *vt.* (elec.) to shunt
si *conj.* if; whether; suppose, **how about,** what if; — *adv.* so; yes; — **. . . que** however, no matter how
siamois *a. & m.* Siamese
Sibérie *f.* Siberia
sibilant *a.* sibilant
sicaire *m.* hired cutthroat
siccatif *a.* siccative, drying; — *m.* siccative, dryer
siccité *f.* dryness
Sicile *f.* Sicily
Sicilien *m. & a.* Sicilian
sidéral *a.* sidereal
sidération *f.* apoplectic stroke; sideration
sidéré *a.* struck, killed by lightning *or* apoplexy; thunderstruck
siècle *m.* century; age, time, period
siège *m.* seat; chair; (eccl.) see; center, focus; — **social** (com.) central office
siéger *vi.* to sit, be seated; (com.) have a central office
sien *pron.*, **le —, la -ne** his, hers, its; **les -s** *m. pl.* one's family, one's close friends
Sienne Sienna; **terre de —** *f.* burnt Sienna
sieste *f.* siesta, nap
sifflant *a.* whistling, hissing, sibilant
sifflante *f.* sibilant, consonant
sifflement *m.* whistling, hissing; sizzling; wheezing
siffler *vi.* to whistle, hiss; sizzle; **wheeze;** — *vt.* to whistle; hiss, hoot
sifflet *m.* whistle; hiss, hoot
siffleur *a.* whistling, hissing; — *m.* whistler, hisser
siffloter *vi.* to whistle quietly, whistle to oneself
signalé *a.* conspicuous; notorious; signal; well-known
signalement *m.* description
signaler *vt.* to signal; signalize, point out, report; **se —** distinguish oneself
signaleur *m.* signalman

signalisateur *m.* traffic signal; burglar alarm; — **de direction** direction indicator
signataire *m. & f.* signer, subscriber
signe *m.* sign, mark, symbol, indication; omen; gesture; **faire** — **à** to signal to; motion to; — **de tête** nod; — **des yeux** wink
signer *vt.* to sign; mark
signet *m.* bookmark
significatif *a.* significant, meaningful
signification *f.* signification; meaning, sense; service of a legal writ
signifier *vt.* to signify, mean; declare, notify; serve a legal writ
silence *m.* silence; secrecy; (mus.) rest
silencieux *a.* silent, still, taciturn; — *m.* auto muffler
silex *m.* flint, silex
silhouette *f.* silhouette, outline
silhouetter *vt.* to silhouette, outline; **se** — be silhouetted, stand out
silicate *m.* silicate
silice *f.* silica
silicium *m.* silicon
sillage *m.* (naut.) wake, wash; headway; — **de fumée** (avi. coll.) contrail
sillon *m.* furrow; wrinkle, groove; wake, path
sillonner *vt.* to furrow, wrinkle; streak
simagrée *f.* affectation; **faire des** —**s** to make faces, fuss
simiesque *a.* simian, monkey-like
similaire *a.* similar, like
similarité *f.* similarity, likeness
similateur *m. & f.* pretender, malingerer
simili *m.* imitation
similicuir *m.* imitation leather
similigravure *f.* half-tone
similitude *f.* similitude; similarity, likeness; simile
similor *m.* imitation gold
simoun *m.* desert storm, sandstorm
simple *a.* simple; single; plain, ordinary; simple-minded; **corps** — *m.* (chem.) element
simplet *a.* ingenuous
simplicité *f.* simplicity; simpleness; ingenuousness
simplificateur *a.* simplifying; — *m.* simplifier
simplification *f.* simplification, simplifying
simpliste *a.* oversimple, simplistic
simulacre *m.* semblance, show; image
simulateur *m.* simulator, pretender; faker
simulation *f.* simulation, pretense
simulé *a.* simulated, pretended, feigned
simuler *vt.* to simulate, pretend, feign
simultané *a.* simultaneous

sinapisme *m.* mustard plaster
sincère *a.* sincere, genuine; frank
sincérité *f.* sincerity, genuineness; frankness
sinécure *f.* sinecure
singe *m.* monkey, ape; imitator
singer *vt.* to ape, imitate, mimic
singerie *f.* aping, imitation; monkey-like behavior; mimicry
singeur *a.* aping, imitating; — *m.* aper, imitator
singulariser *vt.* to singularize, make distinguished, make conspicuous; **se** — stand out, be conspicuous
singularité *f.* singularity; oddness, peculiarity
singulier *a.* singular; peculiar; odd; conspicuous
sinistre *a.* sinister, threatening; dismal; fatal; — *m.* disaster, catastrophe
sinistré *m.* victim of a disaster
sinon *conj.* if not, otherwise; except; — **que** except that
sinueux *a.* sinuous, winding
sinuosité *f.* sinuosity; bending, winding
sinus *m.* sinus; sine
sinusite *f.* sinus infection, sinusitis
siphonner *vt.* to siphon
sire *m.* lord, sire
sirène *f.* siren, mermaid; horn
siroc *m.* sirocco
sirop *m.* syrup
siroter *vt. & vi.* to sip
sirupeux *a.* syrupy
sisal *m.* sisal (hemp)
sismique *a.* seismic
sismographe *m.* seismograph
site *m.* site, location
sitôt *adv.* immediately; **de** — soon; — **que** *conj.* as soon as
situation *f.* situation; position, location; condition; circumstances
situé *a.* situated, located
situer *vt.* to situate, locate
six *a.* six
sixième *a.* sixth
sketch *m.* short theatrical sketch
ski *m.* ski, skiing; **faire du** — to ski
skier *vi.* to ski
skieur *m.* skier
Slave *m.* Slav; — *a.* Slavic, Slavonic
sleeping *m.* Pullman sleeper
slip *m.* shorts, briefs; — **(de bain)** bathing trunks, bathing suit
Slovaque *m. & f.* Slovak; — *a.* Slovakian
slovène *a. & m. & f.* Slovenian
smoking *m.* dinner jacket
snow-boot *m.* overshoe
sobre *a.* temperate; restrained, sober
sobriété *f.* sobriety, temperance, modera-

tion, restraint
sobriquet *m.* nickname
soc *m.* plowshare
sociabilité *f.* sociability
sociable *a.* sociable, companiable
socialiser *vt.* to socialize
socialisme *m.* socialism
socialiste *m. & f.* socialist; — *a.* socialistic
sociétaire *m. & f.* member; stockholder
société *f.* society; company; association, club; partnership; — **anonyme** corporation
sociologie *f.* sociology
sociologique *a.* sociological
sociologue *m.* sociologist
socle *m.* base, pedestal; stand
socque *m.* clog; (fig.) (theat.) sock; comedy
socquettes *f. pl.* bobby socks, anklets
socratique *a.* socratic
soda *m.* soda water
sodium *m.* sodium
sœur *f.* sister; nun
soi *pron.* himself, herself, oneself, itself
soi-disant *a.* so-called, supposed, self-styled; — *adv.* supposedly
soie *f.* silk; **papier de** — *m.* tissue paper
soierie *f.* silk goods; silk factory
soif *f.* thirst; **avoir** — to be thirsty
soigné *a.* carefully done; well cared for; neat, well-groomed
soigner *vi.* to look after, take care of; attend, nurse
soigneux *a.* careful; neat, tidy
soi-même *pron.* oneself
soin *m.* care; attention; **avec** — carefully; **premiers** —**s** *pl.* first aid; **aux bons** —**s de** in care of
soir *m.* evening, late afternoon; **hier** — last night
soirée *f.* evening; evening out; evening performance; party
soit *interj.* all right, so be it; — *conj.*, — **(que)** . . . — **(que)** either . . . or; **tant** — **peu** *adv.* very little
soixantaine *f.* about sixty
soixante *a.* sixty
soixante-dix *a.* seventy
soixantième *a.* sixtieth
soja *m.* soy bean
sol *m.* soil, ground, earth; (mus.) key of G; 5th note of a scale
solaire *a.* solar; **cadran** — *m.* sundial
soldat *m.* soldier
solde *m.* (com.) balance; surplus; **(en)** — at reduced prices; **vente de** —**s** *f.* clearance sale
solder *vt.* (com.) to settle, balance; sell, put on sale; (mil.) pay

sole *f.* sole; animal hoof
soleil *m.* sun; sunshine; **coucher du** — *m.* sunset; **coup de** — *m.* sunstroke; **il fait du** — it's sunny; **lever du** — *m.* sunrise; (coll.) **piquer un** — blush; **prendre du** — to sun oneself
solennel *a.* solemn; ceremonial, formal, official
solenniser *vt.* to solemnize; mark, celebrate
solennité *f.* solemnity; formality, ceremony
solidage *f.* goldenrod
solidaire *a.* responsible; integral; interlocked
solidariser *vt.* to make responsible; cause to interlock; **se** — join together in a common responsibility *or* cause
solidarité *f.* solidarity; joint responsibility
solide *a.* solid; strong; sound; reliable; — *m.* solid
solidification *f.* solidification, solidifying
solidifier *vt.* to solidify
solidité *f.* solidity; strength; soundness; reliability
soliloque *m.* soliloquy
soliloquer *vi.* to soliloquize
soliste *m. & f.* soloist
solitaire *a.* solitary, lonely; — *m.* solitaire; hermit
solitude *f.* solitude, loneliness
solive *f.* beam, joist, rafter, girder
soliveau *m.* small beam *or* joist
sollicitation *f.* solicitation, plea, request; pull of a magnet
solliciter *vt.* to solicit, canvass; request, beg, pull, attract
solliciteur *m.* canvasser; petitioner
sollicitude *f.* solicitude, concern, care
solubilité *f.* solubility; solvability
solution *f.* solution; solving; (med.) termination
solutionner *vt.* to solve
solvabilité *f.* solvency
solvable *a.* solvent
Somalie *f.* Somaliland
sombre *a.* dark, gloomy, somber; melancholy; overcast, cloudy; **faire** — to be dark
sombrer *vi.* to sink, go down
sommaire *a. & m.* summary
sommation *f.* legal summons, legal notice
somme *m.* sleep, nap; —*f.* sum, amount; **en** — in short; — **toute** all in all, on the whole; **bête de** — pack animal, beast of burden
sommeil *m.* sleep; **avoir** — to be sleepy
sommeiller *vi.* to slumber, doze, be dormant, lie dormant
sommer *vt.* to summon; sum up

Ian Longfield

sommet *m.* summit, top
sommier *m.* pack animal; transom; balance beam; mattress; register, file (law) — **élastique** spring mattress
sommité *f.* summit
somnambule *m.* somnambulist, sleepwalker
somnifère *a. & m.* soporific
somnolence *f.* somnolence, sleepiness
somnolent *a.* somnolent, sleepy
somnoler *vi.* to doze, drowse
somnose *f.* sleeping sickness; hypnotic sleep
somptuaire *a.* sumptuary
somptueux *a.* sumptuous
somptuosité *f.* sumptuousness
son *m.* sound; bran
son (sa) *a.* his, her, its
sonar *m.* sonar
sonate *f.* sonata
sondage *m.* (naut.) sounding; (med.) probing
sonde *f.* (naut.) lead; (med.) probe; (mining) boring apparatus
sonder *vt.* to probe; (naut.) sound; examine, explore
sondeur *m.* (naut.) sounder; prober; borer, driller
sondeuse *f.* drilling apparatus
songe *m.* dream
songe-creux *m.* dreamer, visionary
songer *vi.* to dream; think; imagine
songerie *f.* daydreaming
songeur *a.* dreamy, musing, pensive; — *m.* dreamer
sonique *a.* sonic; **vitesse** — *f.* speed of sound
sonnaille *f.* cow bell
sonnailler *m.* bellwether; — *vi.* to toll; ring incessantly
sonnant *a.* ringing, striking; hard (money); **à . . . . heures −es** at the stroke of . . .
sonné *a.* past; completed
sonner *vi. & vt.* to sound; ring; strike
sonnerie *f.* ringing; chimes; bell clapper
sonnette *f.* little bell; doorbell; **coup de** — *m.* ring, ringing; **serpent à −s** *m.* rattlesnake
sonneur *m.* sounder, ringer; bell-ringer; bugler
sonore *a.* sonorous, resonant; ringing; loud; voiced; **film** — *m.* sound film; **onde** — *f.* sound wave
sonoriser *vt.* to make resonant; add sound to
sonorité *f.* sonority, resonance
sophisterie *f.* sophistry
sophistication *f.* alteration, adulteration
sophistique *a.* sophistic; — *f.* sophistry

sophistiquer *vi.* to quibble; — *vt.* adulterate
soporatif *a. & m.* soporific
soporifique *a.* soporific, causing sleep
sopraniste *m.* male soprano, castrato
soprano *m. & f.* soprano
sorbet *m.* sherbet
sorbetière *f.* ice cream freezer
Sorbonne *f.* University of Paris
sorcellerie *f.* sorcery, witchcraft
sorcier *m.* sorcerer
sorcière *f.* sorceress, witch
sordide *a.* sordid; grubby; mean
sordidité *f.* sordidness
sornettes *f. pl.* foolishness, nonsense
sort *m.* fate, destiny, lot; spell, charm; **coup du** — *m.* stroke of fate; **tirage au** — *m.* drawing of a lottery; **tirer au** — to draw lots
sortable *a.* suitable
sortant *a.* outgoing, coming out, going out; **numéro** — *m.* winning number
sorte *f.* sort, kind; way, manner; **de la** — thus, in this manner; **de** — **que so** that; **en quelque** — in a certain way
sortie *f.* going out; exit; excursion; (com.) exporting; (mil.) sortie
sortilège *m.* spell, charm
sortir *vi.* to go out, come out, be out; leave; come from, issue; stand out; — *vt.* take out, bring out; pull out; put out; — *m.* coming out, going out, emerging
sosie *m.* double, image, twin
sot (sotte) *a.* stupid; silly, foolish; — *n.* fool
sottise *f.* foolishness, silliness; stupidity
sou *m.* sou, five-centime coin; cent, penny; **cent −s** five francs
soubresaut *m.* start, jolt; leap; gasp; **−s** *pl.* trembling
soubresauter *vi.* to jolt, start, leap
soubrette *f.* maid, chambermaid
souche *f.* stump; stub; shaft of a chimney; lineage, ancestry; founder of a family; **faire** — to found a family
souci *m.* care, anxiety, worry; marigold; **sans** — carefree
soucier *vt.* to trouble; **se** — **(de)** to concern oneself (about), care (for)
soucieux *a.* uneasy, concerned, anxious, worried
soucoupe *f.* saucer
soudain *a.* sudden; — *adv.* suddenly
Soudan *m.* Sudan
Soudanais *m. & a.* Sudanese
soude *f.* soda; **bicarbonate de** — *m.* bicarbonate of soda, baking soda
souder *vt.* to solder; weld; **lampe à** — *f.* blowtorch; **se** — to be welded; fuse,

join; mend, knit (bone)

soudoir *m.* soldering iron

soudoyer *vt.* to hire (for criminal purposes); bribe

soudure *f.* solder; soldering; welding

soue *f.* pigsty

soufflage *m.* blowing, blasting (of a furnace); glassblowing

souffle *m.* breath; breathing; blast. puff; **à bout de —** out of breath ⟋

soufflé *a.* puffed, puffy; unvoiced vowel; **— *m.*** soufflé

souffler *vi.* to blow; puff, pant, be short of breath; **— *vt.*** to blow, blow up, blow out; breathe; (theat.) prompt

soufflerie *f.* blower, bellows

soufflet *m.* bellows, blower; slap, box on ears; insult

souffleter *vt.* to slap; insult

souffleur *m.* blower; (theat.) prompter

soufflure *f.* air or gas blister, bubble

souffrance *f.* suffering, pain; abeyance

souffrant *a.* suffering, in pain; ailing, ill

souffre-douleur *m. & f.* butt, scapegoat

souffreteux *a.* suffering, poor, destitute; sickly

souffrir *vt.* to suffer, tolerate, endure, bear; allow; **— *vi.*** suffer, be in pain

soufre *m.* sulfur

souhait *m.* wish, desire; **à —** according to one's wish

souhaitable *a.* desirable

souhaiter *vt.* to wish, desire

souillarde *f.* laundry room

souiller *vt.* to dirty, stain; sully, taint

souillure *f.* stain, spot; blot, taint

soûl *a.* drunk; full, gorged, sated

soulagement *m.* relief, comfort, comforting

soulager *vt.* to ease, relieve, alleviate

soûler *vt.* to fill, gorge, stuff; make drunk; **se —** to get drunk; overeat, stuff oneself

soulèvement *m.* rising; uprising; **— de cœur** nausea

soulever *vt.* to lift, raise; stir up, arouse, excite; **se —** rise, swell; heave; revolt, rise up

soulier *m.* shoe, slipper

souligner *vt.* to underline, emphasize

soulte *f.* balance, balance due; settlement; difference between declared and actual value

soumettre *vt.* to submit; subdue

soumis *a.* submissive, compliant

soumission *f.* submission, obedience, compliance; tender, contract

soumissionner *vt.* to contract for, tender

soupape *f.* valve; plug; **— de sûreté** safety valve

soupçon *m.* suspicion; bit, tiny amount

soupçonner *vt.* to suspect; question

soupçonneux *a.* suspicious; suspecting

soupe *f.* soup; meal, mess

soupente *f.* attic, attic ceiling

souper *m.* supper; **— *vi.*** to eat supper

soupeser *vt.* to weigh, judge, heft

soupière *f.* soup tureen

soupir *m.* sigh; (mus.) quarter rest; **dernier —** last breath

soupirail *m.* vent; cellar window

soupirant *m.* suitor

soupirer *vi.* to sigh; **— après** to long for

souple *a.* supple

souplesse *f.* suppleness, flexibility

souquenille *f.* long smock

souquer *vi.* to strive, strain

source *f.* source, spring, fountain

sourcier *m.* dowser, user of a divining rod

sourcil *m.* eyebrow

sourciller *vi.* to knit the brow; frown

sourcilleux *a.* haughty, severe

sourd *a.* deaf; dull; dark; hollow; **— *m.*** deaf person

sourdine *f.* (mus.) mute; **à la —, en —** muted, soft; slyly

sourd-muet *a.* deaf and dumb; **— *m.*** deaf and dumb person

sourdre *vi.* to spring, well up, gush out (water)

souricier *m.* mouser, mouse catcher

souricière *f.* mousetrap; stake-out, police ambush; trap

sourire *vi.* to smile; be favorable

sourire, souris *m.* smile

souris *f.* mouse

sournois *a.* sly, cunning

sournoiserie *f.* cunning, slyness

sous *prep.* under, beneath, below; (in compound words) assistant, sub; **— peu** *adv.* shortly, soon, in a little while

sous-alimentation *f.* insufficient food supply

sous-bois *m.* underbrush

sous-chef *m.* assistant manager, second-in-command

souscripteur *m.* subscriber

souscription *f.* subscription; signature

souscrire *vt. & vi.* to subscribe

sous-cutané *a.* subcutaneous, under the skin

sous-développé *a.* underdeveloped

sous-diacre *m.* subdeacon

sous-directeur *m. or f.* assistant manager, assistant director

sous-entendre *vt.* to understand, leave unexpressed

sous-estimer *vt.* to undervalue

sous-évaluer *vt.* to undervalue

sous-garde *m.* trigger guard

Ian longfield

sous-lieutenant *m.* second lieutenant
sous-locataire *m. & f.* subletter, subtenant
sous-location *f.* subletting, sublease
sous-louer *vt.* to sublet
sous-main *m.* desk blotter; **en — ** *adv.* secretly
sous-marin *a. & m.* submarine
sous-marinier *m.* submarine crewman
sous-mentonnière *f.* chin strap
sous-nappe *m.* table pad
sous-officier *m.* noncommissioned officer
sous-préfecture *f.* subprefecture, second administrative capital of a department
sous-produit *m.* by-product
sous-secrétaire *m.* undersecretary, assistant secretary
sous-secretariat *m.* work of a undersecretary
soussigné *a.* undersigned
sous-sol *m.* subsoil; basement
sous-titre *m.* subtitle
soustraction *f.* subtraction; abstraction
soustraire *vt.* to subtract, deduct; remove, protect
sous-ventrière *f.* cinch, strap
sous-verre *m.* bound slide, bound picture, picture covered with glass but unframed
sous-vêtements *m. pl.* underclothing
soutacher *vt.* to trim with braid
soutane *f.* cassock
soute *f.* magazine of a ship
soutenable *a.* supportable
soutenance *f.* oral exam covering a thesis, defense
soutènement *m.* retaining, support
souteneur *m.* upholder; white-slaver, procurer
soutenir *vt.* to support; bear
soutenu *a.* elevated, lofty; sustained
souterrain *a.* underground; **— ** *m.* tunnel; underground passage, cave
soutien *m.* support
soutien-gorge *m.* brassière
soutirer *vt.* to draw off, obtain by deception
souvenance *f.* memory; remembrance
souvenir *m.* remembrance, memory; **— ** *v.,* **se — (de)** to remember
souvent *adv.* often
souverain *m. & a.* sovereign
souveraineté *f.* sovereignty
soviétique *a.* Soviet
soya *m.* soybean
soyeux *a.* silky
spacieux *a.* spacious
spahi *m.* North African trooper
sparadrap *m.* adhesive plaster, adhesive tape

Sparte *f.* Sparta
Spartiate *m. & f. & a.* Spartan
spasme *m.* spasm
spasmodique *a.* spasmodic
spatule *f.* spatula; spoonbill
speaker *m.* radio announcer
speakerine *f.* woman radio announcer
spécial *a.* special
spécialisation *f.* specialization
spécialiser *vt.* to specialize
spécialiste *m. & f.* specialist; **— ** *a.* specialized, specializing
spécialité *f.* speciality
spécieux *a.* specious
spécification *f.* specification
spécifier *vt.* to specify
spécifique *m.* medication, remedy; **— ** *a.* specific
spécimen *m.* specimen; sample
spectacle *m.* spectacle, show
spectaculaire *a.* spectacular
spectateur *m.* spectator
spectral *a.* spectral
spectre *m.* apparition, ghost; spectrum
spectroscope *m.* spectroscope
spéculateur *m.* speculator
spéculatif *a.* speculative
spéculation *f.* speculation
spéculer *vi.* to speculate
spéléologie *f.* cave exploration
sphère *f.* sphere
sphéricité *f.* sphericity, roundness
sphérique *a.* spherical
sphéroïde *m.* spheroid
spider *m.* (auto.) rumble seat
sphincter *m.* sphincter
sphinx *m.* sphinx
spinelle *m.* spinel
spiral *a.* spiral; **— ** *m.* watch hairspring
spirale *f.* spiral
spire *f.* spiral line, helix
spirée *f.* spiraea
spirite *m. & f. & a.* spiritualist
spiritisme *m.* spiritualism
spiritualiser *vt.* to spiritualize
spiritualisme *m.* spiritualism
spiritualiste *m. & f. & a.* spiritualist
spiritualité *f.* spirituality
spirituel *a.* witty; religious; spiritual
spiritueux *a.* alcoholic, spiritous
spleen *m.* boredom, bitter melancholy
splendeur *f.* splendor
splendide *a.* splendid
spoliateur *m.* despoiler; **— ** *a.* despoiling
spolier *vt.* to despoil
spongieux *a.* spongy
spontané *a.* spontaneous
spontanéité *f.* spontaneity
sporadique *a.* sporadic
sportif *a.* sportive, sporting; **— ** *m.* sports-

man

sportivité *f.* sportsmanship; loyalty

spot *m.* spotlight

spoutnik *m.* sputnik, satellite

sprinter *vi.* to sprint

spumeux *a.* foamy, frothy

squale *m.* shark

squame *f.* skin scale

squameux *a.* scaley

square *m.* small public square

squelette *m.* skeleton

stabilisateur *m.* stabilizer; — *a.* stabilizing

stabaliser *vt.* to stabilize

stabilité *f.* stability

stable *a.* stable

staccato *adv.* staccato

stade *m.* stadium

stage *m.* preparatory period, development stage; probationary period

stagiaire *a.* preparatory, probationary; — *m. & f.* probationer; apprentice

stagnant *a.* stagnant

stagnation *f.* stagnation

stagner *vi.* to stagnate

stalactite *f.* stalactite

stalagmite *f.* stalagmite

stalle *f.* choir stall; stall

stance *f.* stanza

stand *m.* display, stand; grandstand

standard *m.* standard; switchboard

standardisation *f.* standardization

standardiser *vt.* to standardize

standardiste *m. & f.* switchboard operator

standing *m.* standard of living; level of luxury

stase *f.* blood stagnation

station *f.* stop; station; resort; position

stationnaire *a.* stationary

stationnement *m.* parking; — **interdit** no parking

stationner *vt. & vi.* to park; stand

station-service *f.* service station

statique *f.* statics; — *a.* static

statisticien *m.* statistician

statistique *f.* statistics; — *a.* statistical

statuaire *m.* statuary (person); — *f.* statuary (art)

statuer *vt.* to decree; enact

statuette *f.* statuette

statu quo *m.* status quo

stature *f.* stature, height

statut *m.* statute, ordinance

statutaire *a.* statutory

stéatite *f.* soapstone

steeple *m.* steeplechase

stèle *f.* stele, monument, stone

stellaire *a.* stellar

sténo *m. & f.* stenographer; — **dactylo** stenographer-typist

sténographe *m. & f.* stenographer

sténographie *f.* stenography

sténographier *vt.* to take down in shorthand

sténographique *a.* stenographic

sténopé *m.* pinhole camera

sténotype *f.* stenotype machine

sténotypie *f.* stenotypy

stentor *m.* stentor; **voix de** — stentorian voice

stère *m.* cubic meter

stéreographique *a.* stereographic

stéreophonie *f.* stereophonic sound, stereophonic music

stéréophonique *a.* stereophonic

stéréoscope *m.* stereoscope; **stereo camera**

stéréoscopique *a.* stereoscopic

stéréotype *a.* stereotyped

stéréotyper *vt.* to stereotype

stéréotypie *f.* stereotyping

stérile *a.* sterile, barren

stérilisateur *m.* sterilizer

stérilisation *f.* sterilization

stériliser *vt.* to sterilize

stérilité *f.* sterility

sternum *m.* breastbone, sternum

stéthoscope *m.* stethoscope

stick *m.* hockey stick; walking stick

stigmate *m.* scar; stigma; stigmata

stigmatiser *vt.* to stigmatize, brand

stilligoutte *f.* medicine dropper

stimulant *a.* stimulating; — *m.* stimulant

stimulation *f.* stimulation

stimuler *vt.* to stimulate

stipendiaire *a.* hired

stipendier *vt.* to hire

stipulation *f.* stipulation

stipuler *vt.* to stipulate

stockage *m.* stocking up

stocker *vt.* to stock up, **stockpile**

stoïcien *a.* stoical

stoïcisme *m.* stoicism

stoïque *a.* stoic

stoppage *m.* repair

stopper *vi. & vt.* to stop; repair a stocking

store *m.* blind, shutter, venetian blind, curtain; windowshade, awning, metal curtain

strabisme *m.* crossed eyes

strangulation *f.* strangulation

strapontin *m.* folding seat

strass *m.* paste jewels

stratagème *m.* strategem

stratège *m.* strategist

stratégie *f.* strategy

stratégique *a.* strategic

stratification *f.* stratification

stratifier *vt.* to stratify

stratosphère *f.* stratosphere

stratosphérique *a.* stratospheric

stratus *m.* stratus cloud
streptococcie *f.* streptococcus infection
streptocoque *m.* streptococcus
streptomycine *f.* streptomycin
strette *f.* (mus.) stretta, fugue passage
strict *a.* strict, severe; exact
strident *a.* shrill, strident, harsh
strié *a.* streaked, striate(d)
strier *vt.* to streak
strige *f.* vampire
strontium *m.* strontium; — 90 strontium 90
strophe *f.* stanza
structure *f.* structure
strychnine *f.* strychnine
stuc *m.* stucco
studieux *a.* studious
studio *m.* studio; studio apartment
stupéfaction *f.* stupefaction
stupéfait *a.* stupefied, nonplussed
stupéfiant *a.* stupefying; — *m.* stupefactive
stupéfier *vt.* to stupify
stupeur *f.* stupor
stupide *a.* stupid; stupefied
stupidité *f.* stupidity
stuquer *vt.* to cover with stucco
stygien *a.* Stygian
style *m.* stylus; style
styler *vt.* to style
stylet *m.* stiletto
styliser *vt.* to stylize
styliste *m. & f.* stylist
stylo(graphe) *m.* fountain pen
suaire *m.* shroud
suave *a.* smooth, suave
suavité *f.* suavity, sweetness
subalterne *a. & m. & f.* subaltern
subconscience *f.* subconscious
subdiviser *vt.* to subdivide
subdivision *f.* subdivision, secondary division
subéreux *a.* corky
subir *vt.* to undergo, submit to
subit *a.* sudden
subjectif *a.* subjective
subjectivité *f.* subjectivity
subjonctif *m.* (gram.) subjunctive mood
subjuguer *vt.* to subjugate
sublimation *f.* sublimation
sublime *a.* sublime
sublimé *m.* sublimate
sublimer *vt.* to sublimate
subliminal *a.* subliminal
sublimité *f.* sublimity
submerger *vt.* to submerge
submersible *a.* submersible
submersion *f.* submersion
subodorer *vt.* to smell from afar
subordination *f.* subordination

subordonné *a. & m.* subordinate
subordonner *vt.* to subordinate
suborner *vt.* to suborn, bribe, tamper with
subreptice *a.* surreptitious, furtive
subrogé *a.* replacement, substitute
subroger *vt.* to replace
subséquent *a.* subsequent
subside *m.* subsidy
subsidiaire *a.* subsidiary
subsistance *f.* subsistence
subsister *vi.* to subsist, last
substantiel *a.* substantial
substantif *m.* noun
substantivement *adv.* as a noun
substituer *vt.* to substitute
substitut *m.* substitute
substrat(um) *m.* substratum
subterfuge *m.* subterfuge
subtil *a.* subtle, thin, sharp
subtiliser *vt.* to refine, make subtle; — *vi.* to be subtle
subtilité *f.* subtlety
subtropical *a.* subtropical
suburbain *a.* suburban
subvenir *vi.* to relieve, assist
subvention *f.* subsidy
subventionner *vt.* to subsidize
subversif *a.* subversive
subversion *f.* subversion
subvertir *vt.* to subvert, overthrow
suc *m.* juice, sap; cellular liquid
succéder *vi.* to follow
succès *m.* success, issue
successeur *m.* successor
successif *a.* successive
succession *f.* inheritance; estate; succession
succinct *a.* succinct
succion *f.* sucking
succomber *vi.* to succumb
succulence *f.* succulence
succulent *a.* succulent, juicy
succursale *f.* branch-office; regional office
sucer *vt.* to suck
sucette *f.* lollipop, sucker; child's pacifier
suçoir *m.* sucker
sucre *m.* sugar
sucré *a.* sugared; sweet
sucrer *vt.* to sugar, sweeten
sucrerie *f.* sugar factory; —s *pl.* candy
sucrier *m.* sugar bowl; sugar manufacturer; — *a.* sugary
sud *m.* south; — -est *m.* southeast; — -ouest *m.* southwest
Sud-Africain *m. & a.* South African
Sud-Américain *m. & a.* South American
sudiste *m.* southerner
Suède *f.* Sweden; — *m.* suede
Suédois *m. & a.* Swedish
suée *f.* sweating

suer *vt. & vi.* to perspire, sweat
sueur *f.* sweat, perspiration
suffire *vi.* to suffice, be sufficient
suffisamment *adv.* sufficiently
suffisance *f.* sufficiency
suffisant *a.* sufficient, conceited
suffixe *f.* suffix
suffocant *a.* suffocating
suffocation *f.* suffocation
suffoquer *vt. & vi.* to suffocate
suffrage *m.* suffrage, vote
suffragette *f.* suffragette
suggérer *vt.* to suggest
suggestif *a.* suggestive
suggestion *f.* suggestion
suicide *m.* act of suicide
suicidé *m.* person who commits suicide
suicider *v., se* — to commit suicide
suie *f.* soot
suif *m.* tallow, suet
suint *m.* grease, lanolin
suintement *m.* oozing
suinter *vi.* to leak, ooze; trickle
Suisse *f.* Switzerland; — *m. & a.* Swiss;
— *m.* beadle; porter; Swiss guard;
petit — cream cheese
Suissesse *f.* Swiss woman
suite *f.* consequence; series; set; continuation; train, attendants; **à la** — de after,
behind; **de** — without stopping; **par** —
de as a result of; **tout de** — immediately
suivant *m.* follower; -**e** *f.* servant; — *a.*
following, subsequent, next; — *prep.*
according to
suivi *a.* connected, coherent; popular
suivre *vt. & vi.* to follow
sujet *m.* subject; reason; **au** — **de** about;
— *a.* subject, exposed; — **à** apt to
sujétion *f.* subjection
sulfate *m.* sulfate
sulfure *m.* sulfide
sulfurer *vt.* to combine with sulfur
sulfureux *a.* sulfurous
sulfurique *a.* sulfuric
sultanat *m.* sultanate
sultane *f.* sultana
sunnite *m. & f.* orthodox Moslem
superbe *a.* superb; proud, haughty
supercarburant *m.* high-octane gas, ethyl
supercherie *f.* fraud, deceit
superfétation *f.* redundancy
superficie *f.* superficies, surface, area
superficiel *a.* superficial; shallow
superfin *a.* superfine
superflu *a.* superfluous
superfluité *f.* superfluity
supérieur *a.* superior, upper, higher; — *m.*
superior
supériorité *f.* superiority
superlatif *a.* superlative

superposer *vt.* to place on top of one another
supersonique *a.* supersonic
superstitieux *a.* superstitious
superstition *f.* superstition
superstructure *f.* superstructure
superviser *vt.* to supervise
supin *a.* supine
supination *f.* supine position
supplanter *vt.* to supplant
suppléant *m.* substitute, assistant
suppléer *vt. & vi.* to supply, make up;
substitute for; — **à** to remedy
supplément *m.* supplement, addition, supplemental charge; second helping
supplémentaire *a.* supplementary, additional
supplication *f.* supplication
supplice *m.* torture; punishment; death
penalty
supplicier *vt.* to execute; torture; cause to
suffer
supplier *vt.* to implore
supplique *f.* petition
support *m.* prop; assistance
supportable *a.* bearable
supporter *vt.* to bear, tolerate, support
supposé *a.* supposed, pretended; — **que**
conj. supposing that
supposer *vt.* to suppose
supposition *f.* supposition
suppositoire *m.* suppository
suppôt *m.* supporter, upholder, partisan
suppression *f.* suppression, elimination,
cancellation
supprimer *vt.* to suppress, cancel, eliminate; conceal
suppuration *f.* festering, suppuration
suppurer *vi.* to form pus
supputation *f.* calculation, evaluation
supputer *vt.* to calculate, evaluate
suprématie *f.* supremacy
suprême *a.* supreme; crowning; — *m.*
chicken in cream sauce
sur *prep.* on, upon, over, in, by, near,
about, towards
sur *a.* sharp tasting
sur- *prefix* super-, over-
sûr *a.* sure, certain
surabondance *f.* superabundance
surabondant *a.* superabundant
surabonder *vi.* to be superabundant
suractivité *f.* hyperactivity
surajouter *vt.* to add on
suralimenter *vt.* to overfeed, oversupply
suranné *a.* superannuated, old, obsolete
surcharge *f.* surcharge; excess load, overload; word written over another word
surcharger *vt.* to overload; surcharge;
supercharge; write over another word

surchauffer *vt.* to overheat
surchoix *m.* first choice, first quality
surclasser *vt.* to outclass
surcontrer *vt.* to redouble (at bridge)
surcroît *m.* addition, increase, surplus; de — extra
surdi-mutité *f.* deafness and dumbness
surdité *f.* deafness
sureau *m.* elder tree
surélever *vt.* to raise, raise excessively
surenchère *f.* higher bid
surenchérir *vt.* to outbid
surestimer *vt.* to overvalue
suret *a.* sharp, somewhat sour
sûreté *f.* surety, security, safety
Sûreté *f.* security police
surévaluer *vt.* to overvalue
surexcitable *a.* overexcitable
surexcitation *f.* overexcitement
surexciter *vt.* to overexcite
surexposer *vt.* (phot.) overexpose
surexposition *f.* (phot.) overexposure
surface *f.* surface
surfaire *vt.* to overvalue, overcharge; overpraise
surfiler *vt.* to weave in and out
surfin *a.* superfine
surgeon *m.* offshoot
surgir *vt.* to arise, rise up; reach port
surhausser *vt.* to elevate; exaggerate
surhomme *m.* superman
surhumain *a.* superhuman
surimposer *vt.* to superimpose
surimposition *f.* superimposing; (phot.) double exposure
surintendance *f.* superintendence
surintendant *m.* superintendent; **-e** *f.* superintendent; morale officer
surir *vi.* to sour, become acid
surjeter *vt.* to overcast
sur-le-champ *adv.* immediately, instantly
surlendemain *m.* the second day after
surmenage *m.* overwork, overactivity
surmener *vt.* to overwork
sur-moi *m.* superego
surmonter *vt.* to surmount; overcome
surmulet *m.* red mullet
surnager *vi.* to float on the surface; survive, remain
surnaturel *a.* supernatural
surnom *m.* surname
surnombre *m.* excess
surnommer *vt.* to name, give a surname to
surnuméraire *a. & m. & f.* supernumerary
suroît *m.* southwest wind; sou'wester hat; jacket
surpaye *f.* extra pay
surpayer *vt.* to pay dearly for, overpay
surpasser *vt.* to surpass; exceed

surpeuplé *a.* overpopulated
surpeuplement *m.* overpopulation
surplis *m.* surplice
surplomb *m.* overhang; **en** — overhanging
surplomber *vt.* to overhang
surplus *m.* surplus; **au** — moreover
surprendre *vt.* to surprise
surpris *a.* surprised
surprise *f.* surprise
surproduction *f.* overproduction
surréalisme *m.* surrealism
surréaliste *m. & f.* surrealist; — *a.* surrealistic
sursaturer *vt.* to supersaturate
sursaut *m.* start; jump; **en** — *adv.* suddenly
sursauter *vi.* to somersault; jump, start
surseoir *vt.* to suspend
sursis *m.* suspension, delay; **avec** — with sentence suspended
surtaxe *f.* surtax
surtaxer *vt.* to overtax
surtension *f.* hypertension
surtout *adv.* especially; — *m.* overcoat
surveillant *m.* inspector, overseer
surveille *f.* second day previous
surveiller *vt. & vi.* to oversee, superintend, watch over
survenir *vi.* to come unexpectedly; happen unexpectedly
survenue *f.* unexpected arrival
survie *f.* survival; afterlife
survivance *f.* survival
survivre *vi.* to survive
survoler *vt.* to fly over
survolté *a.*, **lampe -e** *f.* photoflood lamp
sus *prep.* upon; **en** — besides, in addition
susceptibilité *f.* susceptibility
susceptible *a.* susceptible, likely; — d'accidents accident-prone
susciter *vt.* to create, cause
susdit *a.* aforementioned
susmentionné *a.* aforementioned
susnommé *a.* aforenamed
suspect *a.* suspected, suspicious
suspecter *vt.* to suspect
suspendre *vt.* to suspend, hang; put off
suspendu *a.* suspended, hanging; **pont** — suspension bridge
suspens *a.* suspended; **en** — in suspense
suspension *f.* suspension; hanging; ceiling fixture; **points de** — *m. pl.* elipsis
suspensoir *m.* suspensory
suspicion *f.* suspicion
sustentateur *m.* sustainer; — *a.* sustaining
sustenter *vt.* to sustain
susurrement *m.* murmur, buzz
susurrer *vt.* to murmer, buzz
suturer *vt.* to suture

suzerain *a.* paramount; — *m.* suzerain
svastike *m.* swastika
svelte *a.* svelte, slender
sveltesse *f.* slenderness, slimness
S.V.P.: s'il vous plaît please
sycophante *m.* sycophant, deceiver
syllabaire *m.* spelling book
syllabe *f.* syllable
syllabique *a.* syllabic
syllogisme *m.* syllogism
sylvestre *a.* sylvan
sylviculture *f.* forestry
symbiotique *a.* (biol.) symbiotic
symbolique *a.* symbolic(al)
symbolisme *m.* symbolism
symboliste *a. & m.* symbolist
symétrie *f.* symmetry
symétrique *a.* symmetrical
sympathie *f.* sympathy, feeling; liking
sympathique *a.* sympathetic; likeable
sympathiser *vi.* to sympathize
symphonie *f.* symphony
symphonique *a.* symphonic
symposion *m.* symposium
symptomatique *a.* symptomatic
symptôme *m.* symptom
synchrone *a.* synchronized
synchronisation *f.* synchronization
synchroniser *vt.* to synchronize
syncope *f.* faint; syncope; syncopation; **tomber en** — to faint
syncoper *vt.* to syncopate
syndic *m.* syndic, chief, mayor; receiver of a business in receivership
syndical *a.* union, trade union
syndicalisme *m.* trade unionism
syndicaliste *a. & m. & f.* unionist
syndicat *m.* syndicate; trade union
syndiquer *vt.* to syndicate; unionize; **se** — to join a union
synecdoque *f.* synecdoche
synode *m.* synod
synonyme *a.* synonymous; — *m.* synonym
synonymie *f.* synonymy
synoptique *a.* synoptic
syntaxe *f.* syntax
syntaxique *a.* syntactical
synthèse *f.* synthesis
synthétique *a.* synthetic; synthesizing
synthétiser *vt.* to synthesize
syntonisation *f.* (rad.) tuning
syphilitique *a. & m. & f.* syphilitic
Syrie *f.* Syria
Syrien *m. & a.* Syrian
systématique *a.* systematic
systématiser *vt.* to systematize
système *m.* system
systole *f.* systole

T

ta *a. f.* your
tabac *m.* tobacco
tabagie *f.* smoke-filled room
tabatière *f.* snuffbox
tabellion *m.* notary
tabernacle *m.* tabernacle
table *f.* table; board; list; — **de jeu** card table; **mettre la** — to set the table; — **des matières** table of contents; — **volante** end table
tableau *m.* picture, painting; blackboard; — **de bord** (auto.) dashboard; (elec.) switchboard
tablée *f.* group at table
tablette *f.* tablet, notebook; shelf; slab; bar; — **de cheminée** mantel
tablier *m.* apron; dashboard; bridge roadway
tabou *m. & a.* taboo
tabouret *m.* stool; footstool
tabulaire *a.* tabular
tabulateur *m.* tabulator, tab key
tache *f.* spot, stain; blemish
tâche *f.* task; job
tacher *vt.* to spot, stain
tâcher *vi.* to endeavor, try
tâcheron *m.* pieceworker; taskmaster
tacheté *a.* spotted, speckled
tacheter *vt.* to speckle
tachymètre *m.* tachometer, speedometer
tacite *a.* tacit
tact *m.* touch; tact
tacticien *m.* tactician
tactique *a.* tactical; — *f.* tactics
taffetas *m.* taffeta
taie *f.*, — **d'oreiller** pillowcase
taillable *a.* subject to head tax
taillade *f.* slash
taillader *vt.* to slash
taillandier *m.* maker of cutting tools
taillant *m.* cutting edge
taille *f.* cut, cutting, trimming; height; size; waist; figure; head tax; cutting edge; tenor; new growth
taille-crayons *m.* pencil sharpener
taille-douce *f.* engraving
taille-ongles *m.* nail clippers
tailler *vt.* to cut, trim; sharpen
taillerie *f.* gem cutting
tailleur *m.* tailor; cutter; lady's suit
tailleuse *f.* dressmaker, cutter
taillis *m.* copse
tailloir *m.* platter, meat-chopping block; (arch.) abacus
tain *m.* tinfoil; silver on a mirror; **glace sans** — *f.* plate glass
taire *vt.* to conceal, say nothing about, hush up; **se** — to stop talking, be si-

lent; keep silent
talaire *a.* ankle-length (dress)
talc *m.* talc; talcum powder
talé *a.* bruised (of fruit)
talent *m.* talent, capacity
talentueux *a.* talented
talion *m.* retaliation
talisman *m.* talisman
talon *m.* heel; tub; pile, deck (at cards); keel; foot
talonner *vt.* to tread on with the heel; to follow close upon; — *vi.* to go aground
talonnette *f.* heel reinforcement; heel lift
talonnières *f. pl.* talaria, Mercury's heel wings
talquer *vt.* to spread with talcum
talus *m.* slope; embankment; **en** — at an angle
tamarin *m.* tamarind
tamarinier *m.* tamarind tree
tamaris *m.* tamarisk
tambour *m.* drum; drummer; cylinder; section of a column; spool; eardrum; embroidery hoop; — **de basque** tambourine; — **de frein** brake drum; **sans** — **ni trompette** quietly
tambourin *m.* tambourine; bongo drum, long narrow drum
tambourinaire *m.* drummer
tambouriner *vi.* to drum
tambour-major *m.* drum major
tamis *m.* sieve
tamisage *m.* sifting
Tamise *f.* Thames
tamiser *vt. & vi.* to sift; filter; sieve
tampon *m.* bung, stopper; stamp pad; surgical sponge; (rail.) buffer
tamponnement *m.* collision; (rail.) bump
tamponner *vt.* to plug; collide with; (rail.) to bump
tam-tam *m.* tom-tom; gong
tan *m.* bark used to tan leather
tancer *vt.* to repriᵐand
tandem *m.* tandem carriage, tandem bicycle
tandis que *conj.* whereas, while
tangage *m.* pitch of a boat
tangent *a.* tangeant; -**e** *f.* tangent
Tanger Tangiers
tango *m.* tango; — *a.* yellow-orange
tanguer *vi.* (naut.) to pitch
tanière *f.* den, lair
tannage *m.* tanning; dressing
tanné *a.* tan, tanned
tanner *vt.* to tan (leather)
tannerie *f.* tannery
tanneur *m.* tanner
tan(n)in *m.* tannin
tannique *a.* tannic
tan-sad *m.* extra saddle of a motorcycle

tant *adv.* so much, so many; — **soit peu** somewhat; — **pis** so much the worse; — **mieux** so much the better; — **s'en faut** far from it; — **que** as long as; **en** — **que** as
tantale *m.* tantalum; tantalus
tantaliser *vt.* to tantalize
tante *f.* aunt
tantinet *m.* small amount, mite
tantôt *adv.* soon, presently; just now; — ... — sometimes ... sometimes
taon *m.* horsefly, gadfly
tapage *m.* noise, din
tapageur *a.* noisy; showy; — *m.* noisemaker
tape *f.* slap, tap, pat
tapé *a.* dried (fruit)
tape-à-l'œil *a.* gaudy
tapecul *m.* jolting vehicle
taper *vt.* to tap, slap; typewrite
tapette *f.* tap, light tap; swatter
tapin *m.* drummer
tapinois, en — *adv.* secretly
tapioca *m.* tapioca
tapir *m.* tapir
tapir *v.*, **se** — to squat, crouch, cower
tapis *m.* carpet; cloth; — **roulant** conveyor belt; **sur le** — under discussion; — **vert** gambling table
tapisser *vt.* to paper, hang
tapisserie *f.* tapestry; wallpaper; **faire** — be a wallflower
tapissier *m.* upholsterer; paper hanger; tapestry maker
taponner *vt.* to stopper
tapoter *vt.* to pat, rap; strum
taquet *m.* wedge, block
taquin *a.* teasing
taquiner *vt.* to tease; tantalize
taquinerie *f.* teasing
tarabiscoter *vt.* to overadorn, overornament
taraud *m.* threading tool
tarauder *vt.* to thread, make a thread
taraudeuse *f.* threading machine
tard *adv.* late
tarder *vi.* to delay; be long in; **il me tarde (de)** I am anxious (to)
tardif *a.* tardy, late; backward
tare *f.* defect, taint; (com.) depreciation
tarentelle *f.* tarentella
tarentule *f.* tarantula
tarer *vt.* to damage; tarnish
targette *f.* slide bolt
targuer *v.*, **se** — **(de)** to pride oneself **(on)**
tarière *f.* auger; borer (of an insect)
tarif *m.* tariff; price list, rate; fare
tarifer *vt.* to set the price of
tarir *vt. & vi.* to dry up
tarissement *m.* drying up, exhausting

tarse *m.* instep
tarsier *m.* tarsus
tartane *f.* (naut.) tartan, small fishing boat
tarte *f.* tart
tartine *f.* slice of bread and butter, bread and jam
tartiner *vt.* to spread
tartre *m.* tartar
tartufe *m.* hypocrite
tas *m.* heap, pile
tasse *f.* cup
tasseau *m.* bracket, brace; lug; lathe
tasser *vt.* to compress, pack; se — to sink, settle; crowd together
tâter *vt.* to feel, handle
tâtonner *vi.* to grope; (fig.) to fumble
tâtonneur *a.* groping
tâtons, à — *adv.* gropingly
tatou *m.* armadillo
tatouage *m.* tattoo
tatouer *vt.* to tattoo
taudis *m.* hovel; — *pl.* slums
taupe *f.* mole
taupinière *f.* molehill
taure *f.* heifer
taureau *m.* bull
tauromachie *f.* bullfighting
taux *m.* rate, set price
tavelage *m.* fruit bruise, spot
taveler *vt.* to bruise, spot
taverne *f.* tavern
tavernier *m.* tavern keeper
taxatif *a.* taxable
taxe *f.* tax, duty, rate, charge; toll
taxer *vt.* to tax, regulate; — de to accuse; lettre taxée *f.* postage-due letter
taxi *m.* taxicab
taxidermie *f.* taxidermy
taximètre *m.* meter of a taxi
taxiphone *m.* telephone booth
Tchécoslovaque *m. & f. & a.* Czechoslovakian
Tchécoslovaquie *f.* Czechoslovakia
tchèque *a.* Czech
te *pron.* you, to you, yourself
té *m.* T-shape; T-square
technicien *m.* technician
technicité *f.* technical nature, technical complexity
technique *a.* technical; — *f.* technique
technologie *f.* technology
teck *m.* teakwood
teckel *m.* dachshund
teigne *f.* moth; dandruff, scaliness; (coll.) scurvy fellow
teigneux *a.* scurvy
teindre *vt.* to dye, stain
teint *m.* dye; complexion
teinte *f.* tint

teinter *vt.* to tint
teinture *f.* dye; dyeing; tinting; tincture; slight knowledge
teinturerie *f.* dye shop; dyeing
teinturier *m.* dyer
tel *a.* such, like; — que such as, like; — quel just as it is; — *pron.* such a one
télécommandé *a.* remote-controlled
télécommunication *f.* long-distance communication
télégramme *m.* telegram; — sous-marin cablegram
télégraphe *m.* telegraph
télégraphie *f.* telegraphy; — sans fil wireless
télégraphier *vt. & vi.* to telegraph
télégraphique *a.* telegraphic
télégraphiste *m. & f.* telegrapher; telegram messenger
téléguidage *m.* radio control
téléguider *vt.* to control by radio
téléimprimeur *m.* teleprinter, teletype machine
télémécanique *f.* remote control
télémètre *m.* range finder
téléobjectif *m.* telephoto lens
télépathie *f.* telepathy
téléphérage *m.* aerial transport
téléphérique *m.* cable car
téléphone *m.* telephone; coup de — phone call
téléphoner *vt. & vi.* to telephone
téléphonique *a.* telephonic; cabine — *f.* phone booth
téléphoniste *m. & f.* telephonist, telephone operator
téléphotographie *f.* wire photo-transmission
télescopage *m.* telescoping, collision
télescope *m.* telescope
télescoper *vt.* to telescope, crash into
téléscripteur *m.* teletype machine
téléski *m.* ski lift
téléspectateur *m.* TV viewer
télétype *m.* teletype machine
télévisé *a.* televized
téléviser *vt.* to televize
téléviseur *m.* television set
télévision *f.* television; appareil de — television set
tellement *adv.* so, in such a manner
tellière *m.* foolscap paper
téméraire *a.* rash, bold
témérité *f.* rashness, boldness
témoignage *m.* testimony, evidence
témoigner *vt. & vi.* to testify; show
témoin *m.* witness
tempe *f.* (anat.) temple of the head
tempérament *m.* temperament
tempérant *a.* temperate

température *f.* temperature
tempéré *a.* temperate, moderate
tempérer *vt.* to temper, moderate
tempête *f.* tempest, storm
tempêter *vi.* to storm, fume
tempétueux *a.* stormy; tempestuous
temple *m.* protestant church; temple
temporaire *a.* temporary
temporal *a.* (anat.) relating to the temple of the head
temporel *a.* temporal; — *m.* temporals, church income; temporal power
temporisateur *a.* delaying, postponing
temporisation *f.* delay, postponement
temporiser *vt.* to delya, postpone
temps *m.* time; weather; tense; à — in time; **avant le** — prematurely; **de** — **en** —, **de** — **à autre** from time to time; **de tout** — always; **en même** — together, at the same time; **entre** — meanwhile
tenable *a.* tenable
tenace *a.* tenacious; clinging; stubborn
ténacité *f.* tenacity
tenaille *f.* pincers
tenancier *m.* tenant operator *or* director of rented property
tenant *a.*, **séance** –e forthwith; — *m.* defender, supporter; –s *pl.* details, particulars; –s **et aboutissants** contiguous lands
tendance *f.* tendency
tendancieux *a.* tendentious; suggestive; prejudiced
tendeur *m.* spreader; shoe tree
tendoir *m.* clothesline
tendon *m.* tendon
tendre *vt. & vi.* to stretch out; hold out; hang; tend, lead; paper a room; — *a.* tender, soft; affectionate; — *m.* tenderness; love
tendresse *f.* tenderness, affection
tendreté *f.* tenderness of meat
tendron *m.* shoot; (coll.) very young girl; –s *pl.* cartilage
tendu *a.* stretched, strained, tight
ténèbres *f. pl.* darkness; (fig.) ignorance
ténébreux *a.* dark, gloomy
teneur *f.* tenor, literal text; — *m.* keeper
ténia *m.* tapeworm
tenir *vt. & vi.* to hold; have; keep; hold out, endure; — à to value, be anxious to, be determined, want; **se** — to remain, be, stand, stay; contain oneself
tennis *m.* tennis; tennis court
tenon *m.* bolt
ténor *m.* tenor
ténoriser *vi.* to sing tenor
tension *f.* tension, tenseness; pressure
tentacule *m.* tentacle

tentateur *m.* temptor; — *a.* tempting
tentation *f.* temptation
tentative *f.* attempt
tentatrice *f.* temptress
tente *f.* tent
tente-abri *f.* shelter tent
tenter *vt.* to tempt; try
tenture *f.* wallpaper; hanging(s)
tenu *a.* kept; obliged; firm
ténu *a.* tenuous, thin
tenue *f.* holding, keeping; behavior; dress, clothes, uniform
ténuité *f.* tenuousness
ter *adv.* thrice, three times; B, third entrance (house numbers)
térébenthine *f.* turpentine
térébrant *a.* boring, piercing
tergiversation *f.* hesitation, beating about the bush
tergiverser *vi.* to hesitate, beat about the bush
terme *m.* term, limit; end; rental period, quarter
terminaison *f.* ending
terminer *vt.* to terminate, end
terminologie *f.* terminology
terminus *m.* terminal point, end of the line, terminus
termite *m.* termite
termitière *f.* termite's nest
terne *a.* dull, leaden; colorless
ternir *vt.* to tarnish, dull
ternissure *f.* tarnished spot; tarnishing
terrain *m.* ground; playing field
terrasse *f.* terrace; sidewalk in front of a café
terrassement *m.* earth removal; ditch-digging
terrasser *vt.* to throw down; embank; dismay
terrassier *m.* ditchdigger, excavation worker
terre *f.* earth, ground, land; property; — à — earthy, common; **ventre à** — at full speed
terreau *m.* compost
terre neuve *m.* Newfoundland dog
Terre-Neuve *f.* Newfoundland
terre-neuvien *a.* of Newfoundland; — *m.* Grand Banks fishing boat; Grand Banks fisherman
terre-plein *m.* platform; terre-plein; terrace
terrer *vt.* to put dirt around a plant; **se** — to live in the ground; hide
Terre-Sainte *f.* Holy Land
terrestre *a.* terrestrial, earthly
terreur *f.* terror, dread
terreux *a.* earthen; earth-colored; earthy
terrien *a.* earth-inhabiting, ground-living;

propriétaire — landed proprietor
terrier *m.* lair, burrow
terrifier *vt.* to terrify
terrine *f.* earthenware pot; casserole; potted meat
territoire *m.* territory
terroir *m.* soil, land
terroriser *vt.* to terrorize
terrorisme *m.* terrorism
terroriste *m.* terrorist
tertiaire *a.* tertiary
tertio *adv.* thirdly
tertre *m.* hillock, knoll
tes *a. pl.* your
tesson *m.* potsherd, pottery fragment
test *m.* testa; test
testacé *a.* testaceous; — *m.* testacean
testament *m.* will, testament
testamentaire *a.* testamentary
testateur *m.* maker of a will
tester *vi.* to make one's will; — *vt.* to test
testicule *m.* testicle
testimonial *a.* testimonial
tétanos *m.* tetanus, lockjaw
têtard *m.* polliwog, tadpole
tête *f.* head; mind; chief, leader; top; signe de — *m.* nod; avoir mal à la — to have a headache
tête-à-queue *m.* sharp full turn of a vehicle
tête-à-tête *m.* private conversation, intimate meeting; love seat
tête-bêche *adv.* upside-down
têtée *f.* act of suckling
téter *vt. & vi.* to suck, feed at the breast
tétin *m.* nipple
tétine *f.* udder; nipple of a nursing bottle
tétraèdre *m.* tetrahedron
tétralogie *f.* tetralogy
tette *f.* teat, dug
têtu *a.* stubborn, headstrong
Teuton *m.* Teuton; — *a.* teutonic
texte *m.* text
textile *a.* textile
textuel *a.* textual
texture *f.* texture
thaï *a.* Thai; — *n.* Thai language
Thaïlande *f.* Thailand
thé *m.* tea
théâtral *a.* theatrical
théâtre *m.* theater
thébaïde *f.* solitude
théier *m.* tea plant
théière *f.* teapot
thématique *a.* thematic
thème *m.* theme; translation into a foreign language
théocrate *m.* theocrat
théocratique *a.* theocratic
théologal *a.* theological

théologie *f.* theology
théologien *m.* theologian
théologique *a.* theological
théorème *m.* theorem
théoricien *m.* theorist
théorie *f.* theory
théorique *a.* theoretical
théosophie *f.* theosophy
thérapeute *m.* therapist
thérapeutique *a.* therapeutic
thermal *a.* thermal; station -e hot springs resort
thermes *m. pl.* hot springs resort; Roman baths
thermique *a.* thermic, thermal
thermite *f.* thermite
thermodynamique *f.* thermodynamics
thermo-électrique *a.* thermoelectric
thermogène *a.* warming, irritating
thermographe *m.* recording thermometer
thermomètre *m.* thermometer
thermométrique *a.* thermometric
thésauriser *vi.* to hoard
thésauriseur *m.* hoarder
thèse *f.* thesis; argument
thiamine *f.* thiamine
thomiste *m.* Thomist
thon *m.* tuna
thonier *m.* tuna boat
thoracique *a.* thoracic
thorax *m.* thorax
thorium *m.* thorium
thrombose *f.* thrombosis
thuriféraire *m.* incense bearer; (fig.) flatterer
thym *m.* thyme
thymus *m.* thymus
thyroïde *a.* thyroid
tiare *f.* tiara
Tibet *m.* Tibet
Tibétain *m. & a.* Tibetan
tic *m.* tic, twitch; mania
ticket *m.* ration ticket; ticket; — modérateur patient's share of payment for health insurance
tiède *a.* lukewarm, tepid
tiédeur *f.* lukewarmness
tiédir *vt. & vi.* to make tepid, grow tepid
tien *pron.*, le —, la -ne yours
tierce *f.* (eccl.) tierce (also, in fencing); triplet, three of a kind (at cards); (mus.) third
tiers *m.* third part; un — one third
tiers-point *m.* point of an arch; triangular file; triangular sail
tige *f.* tree trunk, stem; stalk; shaft
tignasse *f.* matted hair
tigre *m.* tiger; -sse *f.* tigress
tigré *a.* striped, tiger-striped
tillac *m.* (naut.) deck

tilleul *m.* lime tree, linden tree
timbale *f.* (mus.) kettledrum; mold, ring mold; food cooked in a ring mold; metal goblet; **–s** *pl.* timpani
timbalier *m.* tympanist
timbrage *m.* stamping
timbre *m.* stamp; bell; timbre; stamp bureau
timbré *a.* stamped; sonorous; (coll.) crazy; **papier —** paper with imprinted revenue stamp
timbre-poste *m.* postage stamp
timbre-quittance *m.* revenue stamp
timbrer *vt.* to stamp
timbreur *m.* stamper
timide *a.* timid
timidité *f.* timidity
timonerie *f.* steerage
timonier *m.* helmsman; wheel horse
timoré *a.* timorous
tin *m.* (naut.) block, support
tine *f.* water cask
tinette *f.* large bucket, cask
tintamarre *m.* noise, uproar
tinter *vt. & vi.* to ring, tinkle; tingle
tintinnabuler *vi.* to tinkle
tique *f.* (ent.) tick
tiqueté *a.* spotted
tir *m.* shooting, firing; rifle range; shooting gallery; **— à la cible** target shooting
tirage *m.* drawing, pulling; printing
tiraillement *m.* sniping, shooting; spasm; friction
tirailler *vt. & vi.* to snipe, shoot at intervals; pull in two directions
tirailleur *m.* sharpshooter
tirant *m.* (naut.) draft; bootstrap; drawstring
tire *f.* pull, tug; **vol à la —** pocket picking
tiré *a.* drawn; tired; **— à quatre épingles** dapper, neat; **— par les cheveux** far-fetched, unlikely
tire-botte *m.* bootjack
tire-bouchon *m.* corkscrew
tire-bouton *m.* buttonhook
tire-clou *m.* claw hammer
tire-d'aile, à — *adv.* rapidly, with rapid flapping of wings
tire-fond *m.* French railway spike; ceiling ring for light fixture
tirelire *f.* coin bank
tirer *vt. & vi.* to draw, pull; extract; derive; shoot; stick out; draw, trace; draw off, print; (phot.) print; (naut.) draw, have a draft of; deliver; **se — d'affaire** to get along, manage
tire-sou *m.* penny pincher, petty profiteer
tiret *m.* hyphen, dash
tirette *f.* drawstring, cord; table leaf
tireur *m.* drawer; shooter; fortune teller

tireuse *f.* (phot.) printing box
tiroir *m.* drawer
tisane *f.* infusion, tea
tison *m.* hot coal, ember
tisonner *vi.* to stir the fire
tisonnier *m.* poker
tissage *m.* weaving
tisser *vt.* to weave
tisserand *m.* weaver
tisseur *m.* weaver
tissu *m.* fabric
tissu-éponge *m.* terry cloth
tissure *f.* weave
titan *m.* titan
titane *m.* titanium
titanesque, titanique *a.* titanic
titillation *f.* titillation, tickling
titiller *vt. & vi.* to titillate, tickle
titrage *m.* quantitive analysis
titre *m.* title; quality, right; deed; headline; **–s** *pl.* degree, credentials; **–s flamboyants** banner headlines; **à — de** *prep.* as, in the capacity of; **à juste —** *adv.* deservedly, rightly
titrer *vt.* to title
tituber *vi.* to titubate, stagger
titulaire *m. & f. & a.* titular
toaster *vi.* to make a toast
toasteur *m.* toaster
toboggan *m.* toboggan; slide, chute
toc *m.* (coll.) imitation (of valuable objects); **en —** false, fake
toge *f.* toga; robe
tohu-bohu *m.* tumult, disorder
toi *pron.* you
toile *f.* cloth; curtain; painting, canvas; **— cirée** oilcloth; **— d'araignée** cobweb; **— de fond** backdrop
toilette *f.* toilet, comfort station; dress; dressing table
toise *f.* toise (6½ feet, 2 meters); measuring scale
toisé *m.* measuring
toiser *vt.* to measure; evaluate; disdain
toison *f.* fleece; **— d'or** golden fleece
toit *m.* roof
toiture *f.* roofing
tokai *m.* Tokay wine
tôle *f.* sheet iron
tolérable *a.* tolerable
tolérance *f.* tolerance
tolérant *a.* tolerant
tolérantisme *m.* religious tolerance
tolérer *vt.* to tolerate
tôlerie *f.* sheet metal trade; sheet metal factory
tôlier *m.* sheet metal worker
tollé *m.* outcry
tomaison *f.* volume number
tomate *f.* tomato

tombal *a.* tomb; **pierre —e** tombstone
tombe *f.* tomb
tombeau *m.* tomb, grave, gravestone
tombée *f.* fall
tomber *vi.* to fall, fall down; — *vt.* to fell
tombereau *m.* cart
tombola *f.* lottery
tome *m.* volume
ton *a.* your; — *m.* tune, note; tone; style
tonalité *f.* tonality; tone control
tondaison *f.* shearing
tondeur *a.* shearing
tondeuse *f.* shearing machine; lawn mower; hair clippers
tondre *vt.* to shear, clip; mow
tondu *a.* shorn, fleeced
tonicité *f.* tonicity, tone
tonifier *vt.* to tone; invigorate
tonique *a. & m.* tonic
tonitruant *a.* thundering
tonnage *m.* tonnage
tonnant *a.* thundering
tonne *f.* metric ton
tonneau *m.* cask
tonnelet *m.* small cask, keg
tonnelier *m.* cooper
tonnelle *f.* arbor; tunnel vault; hunting net
tonnellerie *f.* cooperage
tonner *vi.* to thunder; (fig.) to speak with fervor
tonnerre *m.* thunder
tonsure *f.* tonsure
tonsurer *vt.* to tonsure
tonte *f.* shearing
tonture *f.* clipping
tonus *m.* muscle tone
topaze *f.* topaz
toper *vi.* to shake hands in agreement
topinambour *m.* Jerusalem artichoke
topique *a.* topic, topical; — *m.* topic
topographe *m.* topographer
topographie *f.* topography
topographique *a.* topographical
toponymie *f.* study of place names
toquade *f.* whim
toque *f.* cap, bonnet
toquer *v.*, **se — de** to fall in love with
torche *f.* torch
torcher *vt.* to wipe
tochère *f.* torchere, torch holder, candelabrum
torchis *m.* mortar of adobe and straw
torchon *m.* cleaning cloth, rag
torchonner *vt.* to wipe
tordant *a.* very funny
tordeur *m.* twister
tordeuse *f.* twisting machine
tordre *vt.* to twist, wring
tore *m.* (arch) tore, torus, twisted column

toréador *m.* bullfighter
toréer *vi.* to fight bulls
toréro *m.* bullfighter
tornade *f.* tornado
toron *m.* cable strand
torpeur *f.* torpor
torpide *a.* torpid
torpillage *m.* torpedoing
torpille *f.* torpedo; bomb; **mine**
torpiller *vt.* to torpedo
torpilleur *m.* torpedo boat
torque *f.* coil; twist of tobacco
torréfacteur *m.* roaster
torréfaction *f.* roasting
torréfier *vt.* to roast; grill; scorch
torrentiel *a.* torrential
torrentueux *a.* torrentuous
torride *a.* torrid
tors *a.* twisted; crooked
torsade *f.* twisted braid
torse *m.* torso, trunk
torsion *f.* twisting
tort *m.* wrong, injury, harm; **à — wrongly**; **à — et à travers** helter skelter, indiscriminately; **avoir —** to be wrong; **faire — à** to harm
torticolis *m.* stiff neck
tortillage *m.* twisting
tortillard *m.* interurban train
tortillement *m.* twisting
tortiller *vt. & vi.* to twist
tortionnaire *m.* torturer; — *a.* torturing
tortu *a.* crooked, twisted
tortue *f.* turtle, tortoise
tortueux *a.* tortuous; winding
torturer *vt.* to torture
torve *a.* threatening
Toscan *m. & a.* Tuscan
Toscane *f.* Tuscany
tôt *adv.* soon
total *a. & m.* total; whole
totaliser *vt.* to total
totalitaire *a.* totalitarian
totalitairisme *m.* totalitarianism
totalité *f.* totality
toton *m.* top (toy)
touage *m.* towing
touchant *a.* touching, moving; — *prep.* relating to, concerning
touche *f.* (mus.) stop, key; touch, stroke; assay; touchstone; goad
touche-à-tout *m.* busybody
toucher *vt. & vi.* to touch, feel; play a musical instrument; cash, receive money; — *m.* touch, sense of touch
toucheur *m.* animal driver
toue *f.* tow, towing
touer *vt.* to tow
touffe *f.* tuft; cluster
touffeur *f.* stifling heat

touffu *a.* tufted, thick; full, luxuriant
touiller *vt.* to stir up
toujours *adv.* always; still
toundra *f.* tundra
toupet *m.* tuft of hair; toupee
toupie *f.* top (toy)
toupiller *vi.* to spin like a top
toupillon *m.* tuft
tour *m.* turn, turning; excursion, trip, circuit; lathe; trick; — *f.* tower; castle (chess); — **de contrôle** (avi.) control tower
tourbe *f.* peat, turf; crowd, throng
tourbière *f.* peat bog
tourbillon *m.* whirlwind
tourbillonnement *m.* whirling
tourbillonner *vi.* to whirl
tourelle *f.* turret
tourie *f.* demijohn
tourisme *m.* tourism; **agence de** — travel bureau
touriste *m.* tourist
touristique *a.* tourist, of tourist interest
tourment *m.* torment
tourmente *f.* tempest, storm
tourmenter *vt.* to torment, torture
tourmenteur *m.* tormentor; — *a.* tormenting
tournailler *vi.* to turn about
tournant *m.* turning, turning point, curve; roundabout way; — *a.* turning
tourné *a.* turned; spoiled; **bien** — well-shaped
tourne-à-gauche *m.* wrench
tournebroche *m.* spit for roasting
tourne-disque *m.* record player, turntable
tournedos *m.* filet steak
tournée *f.* round, circuit; journey
tournemain, en un — *adv.* in a moment
tourner *vt. & vi.* to turn, turn over, turn out, go around; produce (movie), film; play a role
tournesol *m.* heliotrope
tourneur *m.* lathe man; — *a.* whirling, turning
tournevis *m.* screwdriver
tourniquet *m.* turnstile
tournoi *m.* tournament
tournoiement *m.* rotation, whirling
tournoyer *vi.* to turn, whirl
tornure *f.* turn; shape, figure; expression
tourte *f.* tart; pie
tourtière *f.* tart pan, pie pan
Toussaint *f.* All-Saints'-Day
tousser *vi.* to cough
toussoter *vi.* to cough intermittently
tout *m.* whole, all; **du** — not at all; — *a. & pron.* all, whole, any, every; — *adv.* all, any, wholly, quite; — **à coup** suddenly; — **à fait** entirely; — **à l'heure**

in a little while; a little while ago; — **de suite** immediately
toute-épice *f.* allspice
toutefois *conj.* yet, however
toute-présence *f.* omnipresence
toute-puissance *f.* omnipotence
tout-puissant *a.* omnipotent
toux *f.* cough; coughing
toxicologie *f.* toxicology
toxicomane *m.* drug addict
toxicomanie *f.* drug addiction
toxine *f.* toxin
toxique *m. & a.* poison
trabe *f.* flagstaff
trac *m.* stage fright
traçage *m.* tracing
tracas *m.* bustle, fuss
tracasser *vt.* to trouble, worry
tracasserie *f.* annoyance, worry
trace *f.* trace, mark, footstep
tracé *m.* outline, draft
tracement *m.* tracing
tracer *vt.* to trace, outline
trachéal *a.* tracheal
trachée (artère) *f.* trachea
trachéen *a.* trachial
tract *m.* tract, pamphlet
tractation *f.* treatment, procedure
tracteur *m.* tractor
traction *f.* traction; — **avant** *f.* small front-wheel-drive auto
tradition *f.* tradition
traditionalisme *m.* traditionalism
traditionaliste *m. & f.* traditionalist; — *a.* traditionalistic
traditionnel *a.* traditional
traducteur *m.* translator; — **juré** official translator
traduction *f.* translation
traduire *vt.* to translate; transfer
traduisible *a.* translatable
trafic *m.* traffic, trade
trafiquant *m.* dealer
trafiquer *vi.* to traffic, trade, deal
tragédie *f.* tragedy
tragédien *m.* tragedian, tragic actor
tragi-comédie *f.* tragi-comedy
tragique *a.* tragic
trahir *vt.* to betray, reveal
trahison *f.* treason, treachery
train *m.* (rail.) train; rate, pace; attendants; bustle, noise; rear, hind part; front, forepart; — **d'atterrissage** (avi.) landing gear; undercarriage; — **avant** (auto.) front assembly; — **arrière** rear assembly; — **de marchandises** freight train; — **de voyageurs** passenger train; — **de plaisir** excursion train; — **express** ordinary express; — **omnibus** local train; — **poste** mail train; — **rapide**

fast express; — **de maison** housekeeping; — **de vie** way of life; — **des équipages** (army) transportation corps; **en — (de)** in spirits; in the act of; busy; — **mixte** combination freight and passenger train

traînage m. dragging

traînard m. straggler; slow poke (U.S. coll.)

traînasser vi. to loiter; — vt. to drag out

traîne f. train of a dress; seine; dragging; **à la —** in tow

traîneau m. sled; seine

traînée f. powder train; trail

traîner vt. & vi. to drag, drag out; loiter

traire vt. to milk

trait m. arrow, shaft, dart, bolt; line, leash; stroke; gulp; feature; trait; — **d'union** hyphen; — **d'esprit** witticism

traitable a. easy to deal with, tractable; treatable

traite f. trade, trading

traité m. treaty, agreement; treatise

traitement m. treatment; salary

traiter vt. & vi. to treat, negotiate; — **de** to call, style

traiteur m. caterer

traître m. traitor; — **(traîtresse)** a. traitorous, treacherous

traîtrise f. treachery

trajectoire f. trajectory

trajet m. distance, journey; passage, crossing

tramer vt. to plot

tramontane f. north wind; **perdre la —** to lose one's bearings

tranchant a. sharp; decisive; — m. blade, cutting edge

tranche f. slice; fore edge of a book; series; rim, edge; **doré sur** — gilt-edged

tranchée f. trench; -s pl. colic; labor pains

tranchelard m. kitchen knife

tranche-montagne m. swaggerer

trancher vt. & vi. to slice; cut off; decide, determine

tranchoir m. chopping block

tranquille a. tranquil; quiet; still; calm

tranquilliser vt. to quiet, calm

tranquillité f. tranquility, quiet

transalpin a. transalpine

transat m. deck chair

Transat f. French Line

transatlantique a. transatlantic; — m. ocean liner; deck chair

transbordement m. transshipping

transborder vt. to transship

transbordeur m. transshipper; transporter; — a. transporting; **pont —** transporter bridge, bridge which carries passengers on a moving platform

transcendence f. transcendency

transcendant a. transcendent

transcendantal a. transcendental

transcontinental a. transcontinental

transcripteur m. transcriber

transcription f. transcription

transcrire vt. to copy; transcribe

transe f. apprehension; trance

transept m. transept

transfèrement m. transfer of a prisoner

transférer vt. to transfer

transfert m. transfer

transfiguration f. transfiguration

transfigurer vt. to transfigure

transformable a. transformable

transformateur m. transformer

transformation f. transformation; conversion

transformer vt. to transform

transfuge m. fugitive, deserter

transfuser vt. to transfuse; give a transfusion

transfusion f. transfusion

transgresser vt. to transgress against

transgresseur m. transgressor; trespasser

transgression f. transgression

transi a. numb, benumbed

transiger vi. to make concessions

transir vt. & vi. to chill, numb; be chilled

transistor m. transistor

transiter vt. & vi. to transit in bond

transitif a. (gram.) transitive

transition f. transition

transitoire a. transitory

translation f. removal; transfer

translucide a. translucid

transmetteur m. transmitter; — a. transmitting

transmettre vt. to transmit; forward

transmissible a. transmissible

transmission f. transmission; transmittal

transmu(t)able a. transmutable

transmuer vt. to transmute

transmutabilité f. transmutability

transocéanique a. transoceanic

transparaître vi. to be visible through, to be guessed

transparence f. transparency

transpercer vt. to pierce

transpiration f. perspiration

transpirer vt. to perspire

transplantation f. transplanting

transplanter vt. to transplant

transport m. transport; ecstasy, rapture

transportable a. transportable

transportation f. transfer of a prisoner

transporter vt. to transport, excite, upset

transporteur a. transporting; — m. transporter

transposer vt. to transpose

transposition *f.* transposition
transsonique *a.* of the speed of sound
transsuder *vt.* to transsude
transvasement *m.* decanting
transvaser *vt.* to decant
transversal *a.* transversal
transvider *vt.* to empty the contents from one vessel into another
trapèze *m.* trapezoid; trapeze; trapezium
trapézoïdal *a.* trapezoidal
trappe *f.* trap; trap door; pitfall
Trappe, la — *f.* Trappist order; Trappist monastery
trappeur *m.* trapper
trappiste *m.* trappist
trapu *a.* short and fat
traquenard *m.* snare, trap
traquer *vt.* to flush (game); pursue
traqueur *m.* tracker
traumatique *a.* traumatic
traumatisme *m.* traumatism
travail (*pl.* travaux) *m.* work; travaux forcés *m. pl.* penal servitude
travailler *vt. & vi.* to work, toil
travailleur *m.* laborer, workman
travailliste *m.* laborite
travée *f.* (arch.) bay of a vault
travers *m.* breadth; à —, au — across; en — across, sideways; de — crosswise
traverse *f.* traverse, crossarm; crossroad, short cut; (rail.) tie; obstacle
traversée *f.* voyage, crossing
traverser *vt.* to cross
traversier *a.* transverse; transversal
traversin *m.* bolster; cross bar
travesti *a.* costumed as the opposite sex; costumed
travestir *vt.* to disguise; travesty
travestissement *m.* disguise, travesty
trayon *m.* teat, dug
trébuchant *a.* stumbling; espèces sonnantes et –es *f. pl.* hard cash
trébucher *vi.* to stumble; trip; — *vt.* to weigh
trébuchet *m.* snare, trap; balance, scales
tréfilage *m.* drawing of wire
tréfiler *vt.* to draw wire
trèfle *m.* clover; cloverleaf; clubs (at cards)
tréfonds *m.* mineral rights; secret ḥasis
treillage *m.* trellis
treille *f.* vine growing on a trellis
treillisser *vt.* to trellis, interweave
treize *a.* thirteen
treizième *a. & m.* thirteenth
tremble *m.* aspen
tremblement *m.* trembling, shaking; — de terre earthquake
trembler *vi.* to tremble
trembloter *vi.* to shiver

trémie *f.* loading device
trémousser *vt.* to stir up
trempe *f.* temper of iron; character; soaking
trempée *f.* tempering
tremper *vt. & vi.* to dip, soak; temper iron
tremplin *m.* trampoline; diving board; (fig.) stepping stone
trentaine *f.* about thirty
trente *a.* thirty
trentenaire *m.* thirtieth anniversary; — *a.* thirty-year old
trentième *m. & a.* thirtieth
trépaner *vt.* to trepan
trépas *m.* death
trépasser *vi.* to die
trépidant *a.* terror stricken
trépidation *f.* trepidation
trépied *m.* trivet; tripod
trépigner *vi.* to stamp on the ground
très *adv.* very
trésor *m.* treasure; treasury
trésorerie *f.* treasury
trésorier *m.* treasurer
tressaillement *m.* start, leap, shudder
tressaillir *vi.* to start; leap, thrill
tressauter *vi.* to jump, start
tresser *vt.* to braid, twist
tréteau *m.* platform; (theat.) the stage
treuil *m.* windlass
trève *f.* truce
tri *m.* sorting, choosing
triage *m.* choice; sorting
triangle *m.* triangle
triangulaire *a.* triangular
tribord *m.* (naut.) starboard
tribordais *m.* starboard watch
tribu *f.* tribe
tribulation *f.* tribulation
tribune *f.* tribune; gallery, stands; parliament; de la — parliamentary
tribut *m.* tribute; retribution
tributaire *m. & a.* tributary
tricher *vt. & vi.* to cheat
tricherie *f.* cheating
tricheur *m.* cheater
trichine *f.* trichina
trichinose *f.* trichinosis
trichromie *f.* (print.) three-color process
tricolore *a. & m.* tricolor
tricorne *m.* three-cornered hat
tricot *m.* knit fabric, tricot; knit ware
tricotage *m.* knitting, knitted work
tricoter *vt.* to knit
tricoteur *m.* knitter
trictrac *m.* backgammon
tricycle *m.* tricycle
tridimensionnel *a.* three-dimensional
trièdre *a.* three-sided
triennal *a.* triennial; three-year

trier *vt.* to pick, sort
trieur *m.* sorter
trigonométrie *f.* trigonometry
trigonométrique *a.* trigonometric
trilatéral *a.* three-sided
trille *m.* trill
triller *vi.* to trill
trilogie *f.* trilogy
trimestre *m.* quarter, three months
trimestriel *a.* quarterly
trimoteur *a.* trimoter
tringle *f.* rod; curtain rod
Trinité *f.* Trinity; Trinidad
trinquer *vi.* to toast, clink glasses
triomphal *a.* triumphal
triomphateur *a.* triumphant
triomphe *m.* triumph
triompher *vi.* to triumph
triparti(te) *a.* tripartite
tripatouiller *vt.* to tamper with a literary work; mishandle, butcher
triplace *a.* three-seater
triple *a.* triple; treble
triplex *m.* safety glass
triplicata *m.* second copy, second carbon
tripoli *m.* Tripoli; rottenstone
triporteur *m.* bicycle delivery truck
tripot *m.* gambling house, disorderly house
tripotage *m.* mess; intrigue; influence peddling; shady dealings
tripoter *vt.* to misuse, speculate with
triptyque *m.* triptych; international automobile documents
trisaïeul *m.* great-great-grandfather
trisannuel *a.* three-year; triannual
trisection *f.* trisection
trisme, trismus *m.* lockjaw
triste *a.* sad
tristesse *f.* sadness
triturer *vt.* to crush, grind
trivial *a.* trivial; vulgar
trivialité *f.* triviality; vulgar expression
troc *m.* barter
troène *m.* privet
troglodyte *m.* troglodyte, cave dweller
trognon *m.* fruit *or* vegetable core, stalk
trois *a.* three; –ième *a. & m.* third
trolleybus *m.* trolleybus, trackless trolley
trombe *f.* waterspout; arriver en — to arrive unexpectedly
tromblon *m.* blunderbuss
trombone *m.* trombone; trombone player; (coll.) paper clip
trompe *f.* hunting horn; elephant's trunk; — d'Eustache Eustachian tube
trompe-la-mort *m. & f.* unexpectedly recovered invalid
trompe-l'œil *m.* deceptively real painting; vain appearance, surface glitter
tromper *vt.* to deceive, delude; se — to be

mistaken
tromperie *f.* deceit, cheat
trompeter *vt.* to trumpet, cry
trompette *f.* trumpet; — *m.* trumpet player
trompettiste *m.* trumpeter
trompeur *a.* deceitful
tronc *m.* trunk, stump, stem; poor box; — de cône truncated cone
troncature *f.* truncation
tronçon *m.* stump, piece, fragment
tronçonner *vt.* to cut to pieces
trône *m.* throne
trôner *vi.* to reign supreme
tronqué *a.* cut short, cut off, cut down, truncated
tronquer *vt.* to truncate, curtail
trop *adv.* too, too much, too many
trophée *m.* trophy
tropicalisé *a.* packed for the tropics
tropique *m.* tropic; — du Cancer Tropic of Cancer; — du Capricorne Tropic of Capricorn; — *a.* tropical
trop-perçu *m.* overcharge, overpayment
trop-plein *m.* overflow
troquer *vt.* to barter
troqueur *m.* barterer
trotte *f.* distance, way
trotte-menu *a.* short-stepping
trotter *vi.* to trot, trot along
trotteur *m.* trotter
trotteuse *f.* watch's second hand; fast walker
trottin *m.* errand boy
trottiner *vi.* to trot about
trottinette *f.* scooter
trottoir *m.* sidewalk, pavement
trou *m.* hole
troubadour *m.* troubadour
trouble *m.* confusion; uneasiness; — *a.* cloudy, dim; confused
trouble-fête *m.* kill-joy, wet blanket
troubler *vt.* to disturb, upset; confuse; se — to become overcast; become confused
trouée *f.* hole, opening
trouer *vt.* to make a hole, perforate
troupe *f.* troop, company
troupeau *m.* flock, herd
troupier *m.* soldier
troussage *m.* trussing of poultry
trousse *f.* bundle; case, kit; truss
troussé *a.* built, turned
trousseau *m.* bunch of keys; trousseau; layette
trousser *vt.* to tuck, turn up; finish off polish off
troussis *m.* tuck
trouvable *a.* findable
trouvaille *f.* find; godsend

trouver *vt.* to find; think; **se —** to be, be found; feel; happen
trouvère *m.* troubadour of Northern France
Troyen *m. & a.* Trojan
truand *m.* beggar, thief
truanderie *f.* beggars, vagrants; begging
truc *m.* trick; knack; thing, gadget
trucage *m.* faking; special effects (movies); camouflage; counterfeit
truchement *m.* go-between
truc(k) *m.* (rail.) flat-car
truculence *f.* truculence
truculent *a.* truculent
truelle *f.* trowel; fish server
truellée *f.* trowelful
truffe *f.* truffle; nose of a dog
truffer *vt.* to stuff with truffles
truffier *a.* of truffles, truffled; **cochon —** pig trained to hunt truffles
truffière *f.* truffle patch
truie *f.* female pig, sow
truisme *m.* truism
truite *f.* trout
trumeau *m.* pier glass; mirror surmounted by a picture; picture surmounting a mirror; panel between two windows
truquage *m.* falsifying; false aging; special effects (movies)
truquer *vt. & vi.* to fake
truqueur *m.* faker
trust *m.* trust, cartel
truster *vt.* to monopolize
tsar *m.* czar; **–ine** *f.* czarina
tsé-tsé *f.* tsetse fly
T.S.F. *f.* radio
tu *pron.* you
tube cathodique *m.* cathode-ray tube
tuber *vt.* to tube
tubercule *m.* tuber, tubercle
tuberculeux *a.* tuberculous, tubercular
tuberculose *f.* tuberculosis
tubéreuse *f.* tuberose
tubéreux *a.* tuberous
tubulaire *a.* tubular
tubulé *a.* tubular, tubulated
tudesque *a.* German
tue-mouches *a.*, **papier —** flypaper; **tapette —** fly swatter
tuer *vt.* to kill
tuerie *f.* massacre
tue-tête, à — *adv.* at the top of one's voice
tueur *m.* killer
tuffeau *m.* chalk
tuilerie *f.* tile factory
tuilier *m.* tilemaker
tularémie *f.* tularemia
tulipe *f.* tulip
tuméfaction *f.* swelling
tuméfier *vt.* to grow, swell

tumescent *a.* tumescent
tumeur *f.* tumor, swelling
tumulaire *a.* tumular, pertaining to a grave
tumulte *m.* tumult
tumultueux *a.* tumultuous
tungstène *m.* tungsten
tunique *f.* tunic; envelope, covering
Tunisie *f.* Tunisia
Tunisien *m. & a.* Tunisian
tunnel *m.* tunnel
turbine *f.* turbine
turboréacteur *m.* turbojet
turbot *m.* turbot
turbulence *f.* turbulence
turbulent *a.* turbulent
turc (turque) *m. & f.* Turk; **— a.** Turkish
turf *m.* race track; racing
turfiste *m.* follower of horse races
turlupin *m.* punster, poor joker
turlupinade *f.* pun, poor joke
turlutaine *f.* mania
Turquie *f.* Turkey
turquoise *f.* turquoise
tutélaire *a.* tutelary, guardian
tutelle *f.* guardianship
tuteur *m.*, **tutrice** *f.* guardian; plant support, stake
tuteurer *vt.* to prop up, put on stakes
tutoiement *m.* use of familiar address
tutu *m.* ballet skirt
tuyau *m.* tube, pipe; hose; (coll.) tip, information
tuyautage *m.* pipes, pipe system; pleating
tuyauter *vt.* to pleat; (coll.) to inform
tuyauterie *f.* pipes, pipe system
tuyère *f.* furnace vent
tympan *m.* eardrum; panel between mouldings, tympanum
tympaniser *vt.* to decry; annoy; cry out
type *m.* type; fellow, chap, individual
typhique *a.* typhous; typhoid; **— m. & f.** typhus victim; typhoid victim
typhoïde *a.* typhoid
typhoïdique *a.* typhoid
typhon *m.* typhoon
typhus *m.* typhus
typification *f.* standardization
typique *a.* typical
typographe *m.* typographer, printer
typographie *f.* typography
typographique *a.* typographical
tyran *m.* tyrant
tyrannie *f.* tyranny
tyrannique *a.* tyrannical
tyranniser *vt.* to tyrannize
Tyrol *m.* Tyrol
Tyrolien *m. & a.* Tyrolean
tzigane *m. & f. & a.* Gypsy

U

ubiquité f. ubiquity
ulcération f. ulceration
ulcère m. ulcer; sore
ulcérer vt. to ulcerate
ultérieur a. ulterior; later
ultimatum m. ultimatum
ultime a. final, last, ultimate
ultimo adv. lastly
ultra-sonore a. supersonic
ultra-violet a. ultraviolet
ululement m. hooting
ululer vi. to hoot
un (une) a. a, an; one
unanime a. unanimous
uni a. united; even; plain
unification f. unification
unifier vt. to unify
uniforme m. & a. uniform
uniformément a. uniformly
uniformiser vt. to standardize; make uniform
uniformité f. uniformity
unilatéral a. unilateral
unioniste m. unionist
unique a. only, sole; unique
unir vt. to unite, join, level; **s'— à** join forces with; marry
unisson m. unison; agreement
unitaire a. unitarian
unitarien m. Unitarian
unité f. unity; unit
univers m. universe
universalité f. universality
universel a. universal
universitaire a. university, academic; **cité — ** university dormitories
université f. university
uranium m. uranium
urbain a. urban
urbanisme m. city planning
urbaniste m. city planner
urbanité f. urbaneness
urée f. urea
urémie f. uremia
urémique a. uremic
uretère m. ureter
urgence f. urgency; **d'—** immediately
urgent a. urgent; **cas — ** m. emergency
urinaire a. urinary
urinal m. urinal
uriner vi. to urinate
urinoir m. urinal
urique a. uric
urne f. urn; ballot box
us m. pl. customs, usage
usage m. use; practice, custom
usagé a. used
usager m. user

usé a. worn, worn out, threadbare; frayed
user vt. & vi. to wear out; consume; use; **s'—** to wear out; be spent; decay; **— de** make use of
usine f. factory, works, mill
usiner vt. to tool, machine
usinier a. industrial; **— ** m. industrialist
usité a. used, in use
ustensile m. utensil
usuel a. usual, ordinary
usure f. usury; erosion; wear and tear
usurier m. usurer, money-lender
usurpateur m. usurper; **— ** a. encroaching; usurping
usurpation f. usurpation
usurper vt. to usurp
ut m. (mus.) C, do
utérin a. uterine; of the same mother by different fathers
utérus m. uterus
utile a. useful; profitable; convenient
utilisable a. usable, utilizable
utilisation f. use, utilization
utiliser vt. to utilize; make use of
utilitaire a. utilitarian, useful
utilité f. utility
utopie f. utopia
uval a. grape
uvulaire a. uvular
uvule f. uvula

V

va interj. go ahead; **— pour cent francs a** hundred francs is acceptable
vacance f. vacancy; **-s** pl. holidays, vacation; **grandes —s** summer vacation
vacant a. vacant; tenantless
vacarme m. uproar, din
vacation f. court hearing; **-s** pl. suspension of court
vaccin m. vaccine
vaccination f. vaccination
vacciner vt. to vaccinate, inoculate
vache f. cow; cowhide
vacher m. cowherd
vacherie f. cowbarn
vachette f. calfskin
vacillation f., **vacillement** m. vacillation
vaciller vi. to vacillate, reel, waver
vacuité f. emptiness
vade-mecum m. constant companion or accompaniment
va-et-vient m. seesaw; swinging motion; coming and going
vagabond m. & a. vagabond
vagabondage m. vagabonding, roving
vagabonder vi. to rove
vagir vi. to cry, wail
vagissement m. cry, wail of an infant

vague f. wave; — a. vague, indefinite
vaguemestre m. (mil.) regimental mail clerk
vaguer vi. to wander, rove
vaillamment adv. valiantly
vaillance f. valor, bravery
vaillant a. valiant, courageous; brave
vain a. vain; **en** — adv. uselessly
vaincre vt. to vanquish; conquer
vainqueur a. conquering, victorious; — m. conqueror, victor
vair m. fur, squirrel's fur
vairon m. minnow; — a. wall-eyed; having eyes unmatched in color
vaisseau m. vessel, ship; church nave
vaisselier m. china cupboard
vaisselle f. dishes, tableware
val m. valley, vale
valable a. valid
Valence f. Valencia
valence f. valence; Valencia orange
valenciennes f. Valenciennes lace
valériane f. valerian
valet m. valet; jack (at cards); clamp
valétudinaire a. sickly
valeur f. value, worth; valor; **-s** pl. securities, stocks
valeureux a. valorous
valgus a. bow-legged
valide a. valid; able-bodied
valider vt. to validate; authenticate
valise f. suitcase, valise; — **diplomatique** diplomatic pouch
vallée f. valley
vallon m. small valley
vallonné a. valleyed
valoir vt. & vi. to be worth, be of value; produce, yield; — **mieux** to be better; **faire** — to make the most of; **à** — on account
valorisation f. valuation
valse f. waltz
valser vi. to waltz
valve f. valve; scallop shell
valvulaire a. valvular
valvule f. valve, valvule
vampire m. vampire; vampire bat; (fig.) leech, bloodsucker
van m. winnowing basket; van
vanadium m. vanadium
vandale m. vandal
vandalisme m. vandalism
vanille f. vanilla
vanillé a. vanilla-flavored
vanilline f. vanillin, artificial vanilla
vanité f. vanity
vaniteux a. vain, conceited
vannage m. winnowing
vanne f. sluice
vanner vt. to winnow

vannerie f. basketry; basket making
vanneur m. winnower
vannier m. basketmaker; basket seller
vannure f. chaff
vantail m. leaf, panel
vantard m. boaster; — a. boasting, boastful
vantardise f. boasting
vanter vt. to praise, extol; **se** — to boast, brag
vanterie f. boasting
vapeur f. vapor, steam; gas, fumes; **à toute** — at full steam; full speed ahead; — m. (naut.) steamer
vaporeux a. vaporous, nebulous
vaporisateur m. vaporizer, atomizer, sprayer
vaporisation f. vaporizing, atomizing
vaporiser vt. to vaporize, atomize
vaquer vi. to be vacant; not to be in session; — **à** vt. to take care of, busy oneself with, pay attention to
varech m. seaweed
varenne f. game preserve, warren
vareuse f. blazer, jacket, middy blouse
variabilité f. variability
variable a. variable
variante f. variant
varice f. varicose vein
varicelle f. chicken pox
varier vt. & vi. to vary; variegate; fluctuate
variété f. variety
variole f. smallpox
variolé a. pockmarked
varioleux a. concerning smallpox; — m. smallpox victim
variqueux a. varicose
varlet m. squire; clamp
varlope f. jointing plane (tool)
varloper vt. to plane
Varsovie f. Warsaw
varus (vara) a. knock-kneed; pigeon-toed
vasculaire a. vascular
vase m. vase, receptacle; — f. slime, mud
vaseux a. muddy, slimy; (coll.) tired, lazy
vasistas m. transom
vaso-constricteur a. vaso-constrictor
vaso-dilateur a. vaso-dilator
vaso-moteur a. vasomotor
vasque f. basin of a fountain
vaste a. vast
Vatican m. Vatican; **Cité du** — Vatican City
vaticane a. Vatican
vaticiner vi. to prophesy, vaticinate
va-tout m. all or nothing (gambling)
vaudeville f. musical comedy; comedy
vaudevilliste m. musical comedy author
vaudou m. voodoo

vau-l'eau, à — *adv.* adrift, with the current
vaurien *m.* good-for-nothing
vautour *m.* vulture
vautrer *v.*, **se** — to wallow, sprawl
veau *m.* calf; veal; calfskin
vecteur *m.* (avi.) vector
vedette *f.* (theat.) star; speedboat; cavalry sentinel; (fig.) prominent position
végétal *a.* vegetable
végétarien *m. & a.* vegetarian
végétation *f.* vegetation; growth, tumor
végéter *vi.* to vegetate
véhemence *f.* vehemence
véhément *a.* vehement
véhicule *m.* vehicle
véhiculer *vt.* to transport, cart
veille *f.* staying up; watch, lookout; vigil; wakefulness; eve, day before
veillée *f.* watching, vigil, wake; social evening
veiller *vt. & vi.* to stay up, stay awake; watch, watch over
veilleur *a.* watchman
veilleuse *f.* night light; pilot light
veinard *m.* (coll.) lucky person; — *a.* lucky
veine *f.* vein, lode; luck
veiner *vt.* to vein; grain, streak, marble
veineux *a.* veined; veinous; veining; venal
veinule *f.* small vein
vêlage, vêlement *m.* calving
vêler *vi.* to calve
vélin *m.* vellum
velléitaire *a.* fanciful
velléité *f.* fancy, desire
véloce *a.* rapid, lively
vélocipède *m.* bicycle
vélodrome *m.* cycling arena
vélomoteur *m.* light motorcycle
velot *m.* sheepskin
velours *m.* velvet
velouté *a.* velvety; soft, downy; — *m.* creamed soup
velouter *vt.* to make like velvet
veloutine *f.* velveteen
velu *a.* hairy
vélum *m.* velum; awning; circus tent
venaison *f.* venison
vénal *a.* venal; bought, mercenary
vénalité *f.* venality
venant *a.* arriving; — *m.* comer; **à tout** — to the first comer
vendable *a.* sellable
vendange *f.* vintage, vine harvest
vendanger *vt.* to harvest (grapes)
vendangeur *m.* grape harvester; vintner
vendeur *m.* seller, salesperson
vendre *vt.* to sell; (fig.) betray; **à** — **for** sale

vendredi *m.* Friday; — **saint** Good Friday
vendu *a.* sold; in the pay of
venelle *f.* small street
vénéneux *a.* poisonous
vénérable *a.* venerable
vénération *f.* veneration
vénérer *vt.* to venerate
vénerie *f.* hunting; hunting with a pack of hounds
vénérien *a.* venerial
veneur *m.* master of the hunt; master of the hounds
vengeance *f.* vengeance, revenge
venger *vt.* to avenge; **se** — to be revenged, take vengeance
vengeur *m.* avenger; — *a.* avenging
véniel *a.* venial; slight
venimeux *a.* venimous
venin *m.* venom, poison
venir *vi.* to come; occur; reach; **faire** — to send for; — **à (faire quelque chose)** to happen to (do something); — **de to** have just
Venise *f.* Venice
Vénitien *m. & a.* Venetian
vent *m.* wind; **coup de** — *m.* gust of wind; **faire du** — to be windy; **sous le** — leeward; **avoir** — **de** get wind of
ventail *m.* visor of a helmet
vente *f.* sale; **en** — being sold
venteaux *m. pl.* vents
venter *vi.* to blow; be windy
venteux *a.* windy
ventilateur *m.* electric fan; **ventilator**
ventilation *f.* ventilation
ventiler *vt.* to ventilate
ventis *m. pl.* blown-down trees
ventosité *f.* gas in the stomach
ventouse *f.* suction cup; sucker; **cup for** bloodletting
ventouser *vt.* to cup, bleed
ventral *a.* ventral
ventre *m.* belly, stomach, womb; **à plat** — lying face down; **bas** — abdomen
ventriculaire *a.* ventricular
ventricule *m.* ventricle
ventrière *f.* bellyband
ventriloque *m.* ventriloquist
ventriloquie *f.* ventriloquism
ventru *a.* fat, pot-bellied, paunchy
venu *a.* received; successful; arrived; — *m.* comer; **le premier** — anyone; **bien** — welcome; **mal** — unwelcome
venue *f.* coming, arrival; advent
vénusté *f.* charm, beauty, elegance
vêpres *f. pl.* vespers
ver *m.* worm; maggot; — **solitaire** tapeworm
véracité *f.* veracity
véranda *f.* porch, veranda

verbalisation *f.* report, minutes
verbaliser *vi.* to prepare a detailed report
verbe *m.* verb; word
verbeux *a.* verbose, wordy
verbiage *m.* verbosity, wordiness
verdâtre *a.* greenish
verdeur *f.* greenness; tartness; vigor youth
verdict *m.* verdict
verdir *vt.* to make green; — *vi.* to become green
verdoyant *a.* verdant, green
verdoyer *vi.* to be verdant
verdunisation *f.* chlorination
verduniser *vt.* to chlorinate
verdure *f.* greenness; greens; verdure
véreux *a.* wormy; lowdown; no-good; false
verge *f.* rod, switch, whip; penis
vergé *a.* lined, corded with same material
verger *m.* orchard
vergeter *vt.* to whisk clean; stripe with strokes of a rod
vergette *f.* whisk; little rod
vergeture *f.* lash mark, whip mark
vergeure *f.* lines in the substance of cloth, paper
verglacé *a.* covered with freezing rain
verglas *m.* glazed frost; freezing rain
vergne *m.* alder tree
vergogne *f.* shame
vergue *f.* (naut.) yard
véridique *a.* veracious
vérifiable *a.* verifiable, checkable
vérificateur *m.* verifier
vérification *f.* verification, checking
vérifier *vt.* to verify; check
vérin *m.* jack, hoist
véritable *a.* true, genuine
vérité *f.* truth
verjus *m.* juice of green grapes, verjuice
vermeil *a.* vermilion-colored; ruby-colored; — *m.* gilt
vermiculaire *a.* vermiform; wormlike
vermiforme *a.* vermiform
vermifuge *a. & m.* worm medicine
vermillon *m.* vermilion
vermine *f.* vermin
vermineux *a.* caused by intestinal worms; covered with vermin, buggy
vermisseau *m.* small worm
vermouler *v.*, **se** — to become worm-eaten
vermoulu *a.* worm-eaten
vermoulure *f.* worm hole
vermouth *m.* vermouth
vernaculaire *m. & a.* vernacular
vernier *m.* vernier, slide rule
verni *a.* varnished; **cuir** — *m.* patent leather
vernir *vt.* to varnish; polish
vernis *m.* varnish, polish, glaze

vernissage *m.* varnishing; premier, opening of an art show
vernisser *vt.* to glaze
vernisseur *m.* glazer
vérole *f.* syphilis; **petite** — smallpox
verrat *m.* boar, pig
verre *m.* glass; lens; crystal; — **à vitre** sheet glass; — **de sûreté** safety glass
verrerie *f.* glassware
verrière *f.* stained glass window; glass covering a picture
verroterie *f.* glass bibelots, glass figurines
verrou *m.* bolt
verrouiller *vt.* to bolt
verrue *f.* wart
verrugueux *a.* warty, covered with warts
vers *m.* verse; line; — *pl.* poetry, verses; **–s blancs** blank verse; **–s libres** lines of different lengths; **–s libres modernes** free verse
vers *prep.* toward(s); about
versage *m.* pouring; tilling of a fallow field
versant *m.* slope
versatile *a.* versatile; changeable, fickle
versatilité *f.* versatility; fickleness
verse *f.*, **il pleut à** — it's pouring;
versé *a.* versed
versement *m.* payment, installment
verser *vt. & vi.* to pour; shed; pay; overturn
verseur *m.* pourer, server
verseuse *f.* straight-handled coffee pot
versicolore *a.* many-colored
versificateur *m.* versifier
versifier *vt. & vi.* to versify
version *f.* version; translation from a foreign language to one's own language
vert *a.* green; unripe; tart; fresh; lively, young, active; **langue –e** *f.* slang
vert-de-gris *m.* verdigris
ver-de-grisé *a.* covered with verdigris
vertébral *a.* vertebral
vertèbre *f.* vertebra
vertébré *a. & m.* vertebrate
vertical *a.* vertical; **–e** *f.* vertical line
verticalité *f.* verticalness
verticille *m.* whorl
verticillé *a.* in a whorl
vertige *m.* dizziness, giddiness
vertigineux *a.* dizzy, giddy
vertigo *m.* staggers (horses); whim, caprice
vertu *f.* virtue
vertueux *a.* virtuous
vertugadin *m.* farthingale
verve *f.* zest, life, spirit
verveine *f.* verbena
vervelle *f.* band, leg band on birds
verveux *a.* lively, spirited'

vésanie *f.* insanity
vésical *a.* vesical
vesicant *a.* blistering, blister-forming
vésicatoire *a.* blistering, vesicatory
vésicule *f.* vesicle; bladder
vespasienne *f.* street urinal
vespéral *a.* evening
vesse-de-loup *m.* puffball mushroom
vessie *f.* bladder
vestale *f.* vestal virgin
veste *f.* jacket
vestaire *m.* checkroom
vestibule *m.* vestibule, entrance hall
vestimentaire *a.* clothing
veston *m.* suit coat; — **intérieur** smoking jacket
Vésuve *m.* Vesuvius
vêtement *m.* article of clothing
vétéran *a.* veteran
vétérinaire *m.* veterinarian; — *a.* veterinary
vétille *f.* trifle
vétilleux *a.* picayune, interested in trifles
vêtir *vt.* to clothe; **se** — to get dressed
vêture *f.* investiture, taking the habit, taking the veil
vétuste *a.* old, worn
vétusté *f.* oldness, age, deterioration
veuf *m.* widower
veule *a.* weak; awkward
veulerie *f.* weakness, lack of energy
veuvage *m.* widowhood
veuve *f.* widow
vexation *f.* vexation
vexatoire, vexatéure *a.* vexing
vexer *vt.* to vex
viabilité *f.* viability, ability to live; good condition
viable *a.* viable, durable
viaduc *m.* viaduct
viager *a.* lifelong; **rente –ère** life annuity
viande *f.* meat, flesh
vibrant *a.* vibrating; vibrant
vibration *f.* vibration
vibratoire *a.* vibratory
vibrer *vi.* to vibrate
vibreur *m.* vibrator
vibrion *m.* microbe
vicaire *m.* curate; vicar
vice *m.* vice; fault, imperfection
vice-amiral *m.* vice-admiral
vice-chancelier *m.* vice chancellor
vice-consul *m.* vice-consul
vice-consulat *m.* vice-consulate; vice-consulship
vicennal *a.* of 20 years' duration
vice-présidence *f.* vice-presidency
vice-président *m.* vice-president
vice-recteur *m.* university vice-president
vice-roi *m.* viceroy

vice-versa *adv.* vice versa
vichy *m.* Vichy water; **toile de** — cotton or cotton-rayon cloth
viciable *a.* corruptible; spoilable
viciateur *a.* corrupting
viciation *f.* spoiling; corruption; fouling
vicier *vt.* to vitiate, invalidate; corrupt; spoil
vicieux *a.* vicious; defective
vicinal *a.* local; parochial
vicinalité *f.* local character
vicissitude *f.* vicissitude
vicomte *m.* viscount; **–sse** *f.* vicountess
victime *f.* victim
victoire *f.* victory
victorien *a.* Victorian
victorieux *a.* victorious
victuailles *f. pl.* victuals
vidage *m.* emptying
vidange *m.* emptying; **en** — being emptied, opened
vidanger *vt.* to empty
vide *m.* void, vacuum, emptiness; — *a.* empty, void, vacant
vide-bouteille *m.* roadhouse
vide-cave *m.* cellar pump, sump pump
vide-citron *m.* fruit reamer
vide-gousset *m.* pickpocket
videlle *f.* darn; fruit pitter; pastry cutter
vide-ordures *m.* incinerator chute
vide-poches *m.* nightstand
vide-pomme *m.* apple corer
vider *vt.* to empty; leave; clean, dress; finish, settle; core; bore; gut; exhaust
vidimer *vt.* to certify as exact
vidoir *m.* dump
viduité *f.* widowhood
vie *f.* life, lifetime; **à** — for life
vieillard *m.* old man
vieille *f.* old woman
vieilleries *f. pl.* old things, old ideas
vieillesse *f.* old age
vieillir *vt. & vi.* to age; grow old
vieillot *a.* oldish, old-looking
vièle *f.* viol
vielle *f.* hurdy-gurdy
vieller *vi.* to play the hurdy-gurdy
Vienne *f.* Vienna
Viennois *m. & a.* Viennese; **–e** *f.* filled doughnut
vierge *f. & a.* virgin
vieux (vieil, vieille) *a.* old
vif *a.* live, alive, living; quick, lively
vif-argent *m.* quicksilver
vigie *f.* (naut.) lookout; watch tower
vigilamment *adv.* vigilant
vigilance *f.* vigilance
vigile *f.* vigil, eve; — *m.* night watchman
vigne *f.* vine, vineyard
vigneron *m.* vine grower, vintner

vignette *f.* engraving, cut; vignette; poster stamp, seal
vignoble *m.* vineyard, vines
vigoreux *a.* vigorous, sharp
vigogne *f.* vicuna
vigueur *f.* vigor, power
vil *a.* vile; mean; low, paltry
vilain *a.* villanous; ugly; base
vilebrequin *m.* brace, drill; cam shaft
vilenie *f.* vileness, low act, dastardly deed
vilipender *vt.* to vilify, decry, scorn
villa *f.* summer house, country house
village *m.* village
villageois *m.* villager
villanelle *f.* kind of pastoral poetry; kind of dance
ville *f.* town, city; **en** — downtown; **diner en** — to dine out
villégiateur *m.* vacationer
villégiature *f.* vacation
villégiaturer *vi.* to vacation
villeux *a.* hairy
villosité *f.* villosity; roughness; hairiness
vin *m.* wine
vinaigre *m.* vinegar
vinaigrer *vt.* to flavor with *or* add vinegar
vinaigrerie *f.* vinegar works
vinaigrette *f.* oil and vinegar sauce
vinaigrier *m.* vinegar cruet; vinegar manufacturer; vinegar seller
vinasse *f.* residue after distillation; poor wine
vindicatif *a.* vindicative
vindicte *f.* prosecution
viner *vt.* to fortify wine
vineux *a.* wine-producing; tasting of wine, winey; strong with alcohol
vingt *a.* twenty; **-ième** *m. & a.* twentieth
vingtaine *f.* score, about twenty
vinicole *a.* wine-growing
viniculture *f.* wine making; vine growing
vinification *f.* wine-making
vinylique *a.* vinyl
viol *m.* rape
violacé *a.* purplish
violateur *m.* violator
violation *f.* violation, breach
violâtre *a.* purplish
viole *f.* viol; viola
violemment *adv.* violently
violence *f.* violence
violenter *vt.* to force, do violence to
violer *vt.* to violate, rape
violet *a.* purple; — **te** *f.* violet (flower)
violine *f.* red violet, red purple; violine
violon *m.* violin, violinist; (coll.) jail
violoncelle *m.* cello; cellist
violoncelliste *m.* cellist
violoneux *m.* fiddler
violoniste *m. & f.* violinist

vipère *f.* viper
vipérin *a.* viperine
virage *m.* curve, turn; turning; (phot.) fixing; fixing-bath
virago *f.* virago, tomboy
viral *a.* virus
virement *m.* transfer; transfer payment
virer *vi.* to turn about; change; — **de bord** to tack, turn about; — *vt.* to transfer funds; (phot.) to fix
virevolte *f.* rapid movement back and forth
virevolter *vi.* to move back and forth
virginité *f.* virginity
virgule *f.* comma; **point et** — *m.* semicolon
viril *a.* virile
virilité *f.* virility
virole *f.* ferrule, ring
viroler *vt.* to attach a ferrule to
virtualité *f.* virtuality; potentiality
virtuel *a.* virtual; potential
virtuose *m. & f.* virtuoso
virtuosité *f.* virtuosity
virulence *f.* virulence
virulent *a.* virulent
vis *f.* screw; **escalier à** — circular staircase; **pas de** — thread of a screw
visa *m.* visa; certification, authentification
visage *m.* face
vis-à-vis *adv.* opposite; face to face
viscéral *a.* visceral
viscère *m.* viscera
viscose *f.* viscose
viscosité *f.* viscosity
visé *a.* certified
visée *f.* aim, end, design
viser *vt. & vi.* to aim, view; visa; certify; authenticate; — **à** to aim for
viseur *m.* aimer; viewer; — **de bombardement** bomb sight
visibilité *f.* visibility
visible *a.* visible, discernible; evident
visière *f.* visor
vision *f.* vision
visionnaire *a.* visionary
visionneuse *f.* slide viewer; film editor
visite *f.* visit; search; inspection; **rendre** — **à** to visit
visiter *vt.* to inspect; visit
vison *m.* mink
visqueux *a.* viscous
vissage *m.* screwing
visser *vt.* to screw
visserie *f.* nuts, bolts, and screws; manufacture of screws
visuel *a.* visual
vital *a.* vital
vitalisme *m.* vitalism
vitalité *f.* vitality
vitamine *f.* vitamin

vite *a. & adv.* quick(ly); fast
vitesse *f.* quickness, rapidity; — **relative** air speed
viticole *a.* wine-producing, grape-growing
viticulteur *m.* grape grower
viticulture *f.* vine growing
vitrage *m.* glazing; windows
vitrail (*pl.* **vitraux**) *m.* stained glass window
vitre *f.* pane of glass, window
vitrer *vt.* to glaze; install windows in
vitrerie *f.* glazing, glass trade
vitreux *a.* vitrous, glassy, glasslike
vitrier *m.* glazier, glassworker
vitrifiable *a.* vitrifiable
vitrifier *vt.* to vitrify
vitrine *f.* store window
vitriol *m.* vitriol, sulphuric acid
vitrioler *vt.* to throw acid in the face of
vitupération *f.* vituperation
vitupérer *vt.* to vituperate
vivace *a.* long-lived, perennial
vivacité *f.* vivacity, vivaciousness
vivandier *m.* clerk, seller in an army canteen
vivant *a.* lively; alive; lifelike; **langue –e** modern language; — *m.* living person; — *pl.* the living
vivat *m.* cheer; —! *interj.* bravo!
vivement *adv.* bridly, vigorously, quickly
viveur *m.* playboy, rake
vivier *m.* fishpond
vivifiant *a.* animating
vivifier *vt.* to animate, recreate, make come alive
vivipare *a.* viviparous
vivisection *f.* vivisection
vivoter *vi.* to live from hand to mouth, eke out one's existence
vivre *m.* food; **–s** *pl.* provisions, food
vivre *vi.* to live
vlan! *interj.* bang!, slam!
vocable *m.* word, term
vocabulaire *m.* vocabulary; vocabulary list
vocalisation *f.* vocalization; vocalizing; vocal exercise
vocaliser *vi.* to do a vocal exercise
vocalisme *m.* vowel system
vocatif *m.* vocative case
vocation *f.* vocation
vocifération *f.* vociferation
vociférer *vi.* to vociferate
vœu *m.* vow, wish
vogue *f.* fashion, popularity
voguer *vi.* to sail, wander
voici *adv.* here is, here are
voie *f.* way, means, road; wheelbase; (anat.) canal; trail; **–s de fait** assault and battery; **être en —** de to be on the way to, be in the act of; — **ferrée** railroad
voilà *adv.* there is, there are
voile *m.* veil; — *f.* sail
voiler *vt.* to veil; **se** — to become bent, bow
voilette *f.* small veil on a hat
voilier *m.* sailing ship
voilure *f.* sails, canvas; (avi.) wings
voir *vt. & vi.* to see
voire *adv.* indeed, verily, even
voirie *f.* highway department; dump, sewer
voisin *m.* neighbor; — *a.* neighboring
voisinage *m.* neighborhood, vicinity
voisiner *vi.* to visit with the neighbors
voiturage *m.* trucking, hauling
voiture *f.* carriage, coach; automobile; — **commune** carpool
voiturer *vt.* to haul, cart
voiturier *m.* hauler
voix *f.* voice; vote; **à haute** — loudly; **à** — **basse** in a whisper
vol *m.* flight; robbery, theft; **à** — **d'oiseau** bird's-eye view
volage *a.* flighty, fickle
volaille *f.* poultry
volailler *m.* poultry store, poultry dealer; poultry yard
volant *a.* flying, winged; **pont** — *m.* movable bridge; **table –e** *f.* end table, light table; — *m.* steering wheel; balance wheel; flounce, ruffle; shuttlecock; badminton
volatil *a.* volatile
volatile *m.* bird; winged creature
volatilisation *f.* volatilization
volatiliser *vt.* to volatilize; **se** — (coll.) to disappear, get out
vol-au-vent *m.* filled patty shell
volcan *m.* volcano
volcanique *a.* volcanic
volcaniser *vt.* to vulcanize
vole *f.* grand slam; **faire la** — to take all the tricks (at cards)
volée *f.* flight of birds, flying; volley; class, rank; **à la** — in flight
voler *vt. & vi.* to rob, steal; fly; — **à** l'aveuglette blind flying; — **sans visibilité** blind flying
volerie *f.* petty theft
volet *m.* shutter; (avi.) flap
voleter *vi.* to fly about
voleur *m.* thief, robber
volière *f.* bird cage, aviary
volige *f.* scantling, board
volleyeur *m.* volley ball player
volontaire *a.* voluntary; — *m.* volunteer
volontariat *m.* (mil.) enlistment (as contrasted to the draft)

volonté *f.* will; willingness; **payable à —**
payable at will
volontiers *adv.* willingly, gladly
voltaïque *a.* voltaic
voltaire *m.* high-backed chair
volte-face *f.* about face
voltiger *vi.* to fly about
voltigeur *m.* trapeze or equestrian performer
voltmètre *m.* voltmeter
volubile *a.* volubilate, spiraling
volubilité *f.* volubility, fluency
volumineux *a.* voluminous
volupté *f.* voluptuousness
voluptueux *a.* voluptuous
volute *f.* spiral, curl, scroll
vomir *vt. & vi.* to vomit
vomissement *m.* vomiting; vomit
vomitif *a.* vomitive; — *m.* emetic
vorace *a.* voracious, ravenous
voracité *f.* voraciousness
vos *a. pl.* your
votation *f.* voting
votif *a.* votive
votre *a* your
vôtre *pron.*, **le —, la —** yours
vouer *vt.* to devote; consecrate; pledge
vouloir *vt. & vi.* to wish; intend; — **bien** to be willing; — **dire** to mean; **en — à** to hold a grudge against; — *m.* will
voulu *a.* intentional; desired
vous *pron.* you
voussoir, vousseau *m.* stone of an arch, wedge-shaped stone
voussure *f.* curve of an arch, a vault
voûte *f.* vault, arched roof
voûté *a.* vaulted; crooked; round-shouldered
voûter *vt.* to vault, cover with vaulting; bend
voyage *m.* trip, journey, tour; — **à forfait** prepaid tour
voyager *vi.* to travel; migrate (birds)
voyageur *m.* traveller; passenger; **commis** — *m.* traveling salesman
voyant *a.* showy, gaudy; — *m.* sight, target; — *m.* seer
voyelle *f.* vowel
voyou *m.* scum, cad, hoodlum (U.S. coll.)
vrac, en — *adv.* in disorder; unpacked
vrai *a.* true, real
vraisemblable *a.* likely, probable
vraisemblance *f.* verisimilitude
vrille *f.* tendril of a vine; gimlet
vriller *vt.* to pierce with a gimlet; — *vi.* ascend in spiral; twist
vrombir *vt.* to rumble
vrombissement *m.* rumble
vu *a.* seen; — *prep.* in view of, considering; — **que** *conj.* considering that

vue *f.* sight; view
vulcanisation *f.* vulcanization
vulcaniser *vt.* to vulcanize
vulcanite *f.* vulcanite
vulgaire *a.* common
vulgarisateur *a.* popularizing; — *m.* popularizer
vulgarisation *f.* popularizing; **ouvrage de — *m.*** work for popular consumption
vulgariser *vt.* to popularize
vulgarité *f.* vulgarity
vulnérable *a.* vulnerable
vulnéraire *a.* vulnerary
vultueux *a.* flushed of face
vulve *f.* vulva

W

wagon *m.* railway car
wagon-bar *m.* club car
wagon-lit *m.* sleeping car
wagon-poste *m.* mail car
wagon-réservoir *m.* tank car
wagon-restaurant *m.* dining car
wagon-salon *m.* parlor car
wagonnet *m.* cart, handcart
warrant *m.* warrant, guarantee
warranter *vt.* to warrant
wattman *m.* motorman of a streetcar

X

xénophobie *f.* xenophobia
xérophagie *f.* xerophagy
xérophile *adv.* xerophilous
xérophyte *a.* xerophyte
xylographie *f.* wood engraving
xylophone *m.* xylophone

Y

y *adv.* there, here; **il — a** there is, there are; **vous — êtes** you are right, that's it; — *pron.* to it, to them
yachting *m.* yachting
yack *m.* yak
yaourt, yogourt *m.* yoghurt
yeuse *f.* ilex, holly oak
yeux *m. pl.* eyes
yole *f.* yawl
Yougoslave *m. & f. & a.* Yugoslavian
Yougoslavie *f.* Yugoslavia
youyou *m.* sampan, small boat

Z

zazou *m.* bobby-soxer, teen-ager
zèbre *m.* zebra
zébu *m.* zebu

zélateur *a.* zealous
zèle *m.* zeal, warmth; **avec —** zealously
zélé *a.* zealous
zénith *m.* zenith
zéro *m.* cipher, nought, zero
zeste *m.* citrous peel; **–r** *vt.* to peel
zézaiement *m.* lisp
zézayer *vt. & vi.* to lisp
zibeline *f.* sable; sable fur
zigzag *m.* zigzag; **—** *m. & a.* (coll.) drunk
zigzaguer *vi.* to zigzag
zinc *m.* zinc; (coll.) bar, counter
zinguer *vt.* to zinc-plate

zingueur *m.* zinc worker
zinnia *m.* zinnia
zinzolin *m.* red-violet
zircon *m.* zircon
zodiaque *m.* zodiac
zona *f.* (med.) shingles
zoologie *f.* zoology
zoologique *a.* zoological; **parc — zoo**
zoologiste *m.* zoologist
zoonose *f.* zoonosis
zostère *f.* seaweed
zouave *m.* North African trooper
zut! *interj.* curses!

English-French

A

a, an *art.* un, une
Aachen *n.* Aix-la-Chapelle
aback, to be taken — être surpris
abandon *vt.* abandonner; to — oneself to
s'abandonner à; **–ed** *a.* dissolu; **–ment**
n. abandon *m.*
abase *vt.* avilir; **–ment** *n.* avilissement,
abaissement *m.*
abate *vi.* diminuer, se calmer, s'apaiser;
baisser; **–ment** *n.* diminution *f.*
abbess *n.* abbesse *f.*
abbey *n.* abbaye *f.*
abbot *n.* abbé *m.*
abbreviate *vt.* abréger
abbreviation *n.* abréviation *f.*
ABC *n.* abc *m.*; abécédaire *m.*
abdicate *vt. & vi.* abdiquer
abdication *n.* abdication, renonciation *f.*
abdomen *n.* abdomen, bas-ventre *m.*
abduct *vt.* enlever; **–ion** *n.* enlèvement
m.; **–or** *n.* ravisseur *m.*
aberration *n.* égarement *m.*, aberration *f.*
abet *vt.* encourager; soutenir
abeyance *n.* attente *f.*; in — en suspens
abhor *vt.* abhorrer; **–rence** *n.* horreur *f.*;
–rent *a.* répugnant
abide *vi.* demeurer, rester; — *vt.* supporter; — by respecter
abiding *a.* permanent, constant
ability *n.* habileté, capacité *f.*; to the
best of one's — de son mieux
abject *a.* bas, abject, vil; **–ion** *n.* bassesse, abjection *f.*
abjuration *n.* abjuration *f.*
abjure *vt.* abjurer
ablative *a.* ablatif *m.*
ablaze *a.* en flammes
able *a.* capable; to be — pouvoir; savoir;

être à même de
able-bodied *a.* propre au service; en
bonne santé
ablution *n.* ablution *f.*
ably *adv.* bien, habilement
abnegate *vt.* renier, renoncer à
abnegation *n.* abnégation *f.*, renoncement *m.*
abnormal *a.* anormal; **–ity** *n.* anormalité *f.*
aboard *adv.* à bord; to go — s'embarquer;
to take — embarquer; all —! *interj.* à
bord!; en voiture!
abode *a.* demeure, habitation *f.*; domicile
m.
abolish *vt.* abolir
abolition *n.* abolissement *m.*, abolition *f.*;
–ist *n.* abolitionniste, antiesclavagiste
m. & f.
A-bomb *n.* bombe atomique *f.*
abominable *a.* abominable
abominate *vt.* avoir en abomination
abomination *n.* abomination *f.*
aboriginal *a.* aborigène
abort *vi.* avorter; **–ion** *n.* avortement *m.*;
–ive *a.* avorté, manqué
abound *vi.* abonder; **–ing** *a.* abondant
about *adv.* çà et là; à peu près, environ;
come — arriver; bring — causer;
be — to être sur le point de; — *prep.*
autour de, près de; parmi, par; vers;
au sujet de; sur le point de
about-face *n.* volte-face *f.*
above *adv.* en haut, là-haut, plus haut;
— *prep.* au-dessus de, plus haut que; —
all surtout; over and — en outre
aboveboard *a.* franc, légitime
above-mentioned *a.* ledit, susdit
abrade *vt.* frotter, user en frottant

253

abrasion n. abrasion f., frottement m.
abrasive a. abrasif, qui use en frottant; — n. émeri m.; abrasif m.
abreast adv. à côté l'un de l'autre; au courant; two — par deux
abridge vt. abréger
abridgment n. abrégé m.; résumé m.
abroad adv. à l'étranger; to get — se répandre
abrogate vt. abroger
abrogation n. abrogation, revocation f.
abrupt a. abrupte, précipité, brusque; —ness n. brusquerie f.; précipitation f.
abscess n. abcès m.
abscond vi. échapper, disparaître; –ing n. évasion, fuite f.
absence n. absence f.; leave of — congé m.
absent a. absent; — vt., to — one's self s'absenter; –ee n. absent (de son poste) m.; –eeism n. absentéisme m.
absent-minded a. distrait; –ness n. distraction f.
absolute a. absolu; –ly adv. tout à fait; absolument
absolute altitude n. (avi.) altitude absolue f.
absolution n. absolution f.
absolve vt. absoudre; dégager
absorb vt. absorber; –ent a. & n. absorbant m.;–ent cotton coton hydrophile m.
abstain vi. s'abstenir
abstemious a. abstinent, sobre, modéré
abstention n. abstention, abstinence f.
abstinence n. abstinence, privation volontaire f.; day of — jour maigre m.
abstract n. résumé, sommaire m.; — vt. résumer, abréger; faire abstraction de; — a. abstrait; –ion n. abstraction f.; –ionism n. (art) abstractionnisme m.
abstruse a. abstrus; –ness n. complexité f.
absurd a. absurde; –ity n. absurdité f.
abundance n. abondance f.
abundant a. abondant
abuse n. abus, outrage m.; — vt. abuser (de), tromper; injurier
abusive a. abusif, injurieux; –ness n. grossièreté f.; abus m.
abut vi. buter (contre); aboutir (à); –ment n. butée, culée f.
abysmal a. sans fond; profond
abyss n. abîme, gouffre m.
Abyssinia n. Abyssinie f.
academic a. académique; universitaire; — freedom n. franchise académique f.
academy n. académie, école f.
accede vi. accéder
accelerate vt. accélérer; précipiter; — vi. s'accélérer

acceleration n. accélération f.
accelerator n. accélérateur m.
accent vt. accentuer, souligner, donner de l'emphase à; — n. accent, accent tonique m.; –uate vt. accentuer; –uation n. accentuation f.
accept vt. accepter; agréer; –able a. acceptable; –ance n. acceptation, réception f.; –ation n. acception, signification f.
access n. accès m., entrée f.; –ible a. accessible, abordable; –ibility n. accessibilité f.; –ion n. avènement m.; acquisition f.; –ory n. & a. complice m.; accessoire m.
accident n. accident m.; by — par hasard; –al a. accidentel, fortuit; –ally adv. par hasard, fortuitement
accident-prone d. susceptible d'accidents
acclaim vt. acclamer, applaudir; — n. acclamation f., applaudissements m. pl.
acclamation n. acclamation f.
acclimate vt. acclimater
accommodate vt. accommoder, régler; pourvoir; loger; recevoir; obliger
accommodating a. accommodant, serviable, obligeant, complaisant
accommodation n. adaptation f.; accommodement m.; arrangement m., convenance, commodité f.; logement m.
accompaniment n. accompagnement m.
accompany vt. accompagner
accomplice n. complice m. & f.
accomplish vt. accomplir, exécuter, achever; –ed a. accompli, habile, expert; –ment n. accomplissement, talent m.
accord n. accord m., union f.; convention f.; consentement m.; of one's own — de son propre gré, de plein gré; with one accord d'un commun accord; — vt. accorder; –ance n. conformité f.; in –ance with selon; –ing prep., –ing to d'après, selon; –ingly adv. conformément
accost vt. aborder, accoster
account n. compte, calcul m.; valeur, considération f.; importance f.; raison f.; rapport, récit m.; on — (com.) à valoir; on — of à cause de; on no — d'aucune façon; to take into — tenir compte de; to keep –s tenir des comptes; — book n. livre de comptes m.; — vt. compter, calculer; estimer; rendre compte de, rendre raison de, être responsable de; –able a. responsable; –ant n. comptable m.; –ing n. comptabilité f.
accoutrement n. équipement m.; ornement m.
accredit vt. croire; accréditer; –ed a.

approuvé, agréé
accrue *vi.* accroître; résulter
accumulate *vi.* s'accumuler; — *vt.* amasser
accumulation *n.* accumulation *f.*, entassement *m.*
accuracy *n.* exactitude, justesse *f.*
accurate *a.* exact, juste; –ly *adv.* exactement, avec justesse; –ness *n.* précision,
justesse *f.*
accusation *n.* accusation *f.*
accusative *n.* accusatif *m.*
accuse *vt.* accuser; –d *n.* accusé *m.*; –r *n.*
accusateur *m.*
accustom *vt.* accoutumer, habituer; **to become** –ed s'habituer, s'accoutumer; –ed
a. accoutumé, habituel
ace *n.* as *m.*; expert *m.*; champion *m.*
acetate *n.* acétate *m.*
acetone *n.* acétone *f.*
acetylene *n.* acétylène *m.*
ache *n.* mal *m.*, douleur *f.*; — *vi.* faire
mal, souffrir; **my head** –s j'ai mal à la
tête
achievable *a.* réalisable
achieve *vt.* atteindre; achever, exécuter;
–ment *n.* réalisation *f.*; fait, exploit *m.*
aching *n.* peine *f.*; — *a.* douloureux
acid *n.* & *a.* acide *m.*; — test épreuve
déterminante *f.*; –ity *n.* acidité *f.*
acidulate *vt.* aciduler
acknowledge *vt.* reconnaître; avouer; —
receipt accuser réception; –d *a.* reconnu
acknowledgment *n.* reconnaissance *f.*,
aveu, *m.*; concession *f.*; accusé de
réception *m.*
acme *n.* sommet *m.*; apogée *f.*; comble *m.*
acorn *n.* gland *m.*
acoustic *a.* acoustique; –s *n.* *pl.* acoustique *f.*
acquaint *vt.* informer, faire savoir; **be** –ed
with connaître; **become** –ed **with** connaître, faire la connaissance de; –ance
n. connaissance *f.*
acquiesce *vi.* acquiescer; –nce *n.* soumission *f.*; –nt *a.* soumis, consentant
acquire *vt.* acquérir, obtenir
acquisition *n.* acquisition *f.*
acquisitive *a.* capable d'acquérir; qui aime
acquérir
acquit *vt.* acquitter, absoudre; –tal *n.*
acquittement *m.*
acre *n.* acre *f.* (= 40.5 ares); arpent, demi-
hectare *m.*
acreage *n.* superficie *f.*, terrain, arpentage
m.
acrid *a.* âcre; –ity, –ness *n.* âcreté *f.*
acrimonious *a.* acrimonieux
acrimony *n.* acrimonie *f.*
acrobat *n.* acrobate *m.*; –ic *a.* acrobatique;
–ics *n.* acrobatie *f.*

across *adv.* de travers; — *prep.* à travers,
au travers de; — **the street** de l'autre
côté de la rue, en face; **come** — rencontrer; **go** — traverser, passer, franchir
act *n.* acte *m.*, action *f.*, fait, exploit *m.*;
loi *f.*; **be in the** — **of** être en train de;
put on an — faire semblant; **Acts** (eccl.)
Actes des apôtres *m.* *pl.*; — *vt.* agir,
opérer; faire; se comporter; — *vt.* jouer,
représenter; — **on** suivre; agir d'après;
–ing *a.* provisoire; intérimaire; –ing *n.*
(theat.) jeu *m.*; –ing *a.* par intérim;
–or *n.* acteur *m.*; –ress *n.* actrice *f.*
actin *n.* (chem.) actinium *m.*
actinic *a.* actinique
action *n.* action *f.*, fait *m.*; bataille *f.*;
procès *m.*; **out of** — hors de service;
(mil.) hors de combat; **take** — agir
activate *vt.* activer; mettre en marche
activator *n.* (chem.) activeur *m.*
active *a.* actif, agile; vif
activity *n.* activité, vivacité *f.*
actual *a.* réel, véritable, vrai; –ity *n.*
réalité *f.*; –ly *adv.* réellement, véritablement
actuate *vt.* mettre en action; actionner;
animer
acuity *n.* acuité *f.*
acumen *n.* finesse *f.*
acute *a.* aigu, pointu; subtil; fin; intense;
–ness *n.* aiguité *f.*; acuité *f.*
A.D. (Anno Domini) de l'ère chrétienne
adage *n.* adage, proverbe *m.*
adamant *a.* inflexible
adapt *vt.* adapter, accommoder; –able
a. adaptable, applicable; –ability *n.*
qualité de pouvoir s'adapter *f.*; –ation
n. adaptation *f.*
add *vt.* ajouter, joindre; **to** — **up** additionner; se résumer; –ing **machine** *n.*
machine à calculer *f.*
adder *n.* vipère *f.*
addict *vt.* adonner, vouer; — *n.* toxicomane *m.*; –ion *n.* manie, disposition *f.*,
penchant *m*
addition *n.* addition *f.*, accroissement *m.*;
in — en outre, en sus; –al *a.* additionnel, supplémentaire; de plus
addled *a.* fou; gâté
address *n.* adresse *f.*; allocution *f.*, discours *m.*; plaidoyer *m.*; dextérité,
habileté *f.*; — **book** carnet d'adresses
m.; — *vt.* adresser; parler à; –ee *n.*
destinataire *m.* & *f.*
addressograph *n.* machine à adresser
adenoids *n.* *pl.* adénoïdes *m.* *pl.*
adept *a.* habile; adepte; –ness *n.* habileté
f.
adequacy *n.* suffisance *f.*
adequate *a.* suffisant; –ness *n.* suffisance *f.*

adhere *vi.* adhérer, s'attacher; **–nce** *n.*
adhésion *f.*; **–nt** *n.* partisan *m.*
adhesion *n.* adhérence, adhésion *f.*
adhesive *a.* adhérent; collant; — *n.* colle
f.; timbre-poste *m.*; — tape *n.* sparadrap *m.*; **–ness** *n.* adhésion *f.*
ad infinitum *adv.* à l'infini
adipose *a.* adipeux
adjacent *a.* adjacent, voisin, contigu
adjective *n. & a.* adjectif *m.*
adjoin *vt.* être contigu à, avoisiner; donner
sur; **–ing** *a.* contigu
adjourn *vt.* ajourner, remettre; lever,
clore (une séance); **–ment** *n.* ajournement *m.*; suspension *f.*
adjudicate *vt.* adjuger
adjudge *vt.* adjuger, condamner
adjunct *n.* accessoire *m.*, appartenance *f.*
adjoint *m.*
adjust *vt.* ajuster, arranger, régler;
corriger; mettre à point; **–able** *a.*
réglable; **–ment** *n.* réglement *m.*;
réglage *m.*; adjustage *m.*; correction
adjutant *n.* adjudant major *m.*; — general
général chef des archives militaires *m.*
ad-lib *vi. & vt.* improviser
adman *n.* (com.) publicitaire *m.*
administer, administrate *vt.* administrer,
gouverner, gérer
administration *n.* administration *f.*, gouvernement *m.*
administrative *a.* administratif
administrator *n.* administrateur *m.*
admiral *n.* amiral *m.*; rear — contre-
amiral *m.*; **–ty** *n.* ministère de la marine
m.
admire *vt.* admirer; **–r** *n.* admirateur *m.*
admiring *a.* admiratif
admission *n.* admission, réception *f.*;
confession *f.*, aveu *m.*; — charge entrée
f., tarif *m.*
admit *vt.* admettre; permettre; avouer;
reconnaître; laisser entrer; **–tance** entrée *f.*; no **–tance** entrée interdite;
–ted *a.* avoué, reconnu; **–tedly** *adv.*
reconnu comme; de son propre aveu
admonish *vt.* exhorter; admonester
admonition *n.* exhortation *f.*; admonestation *f.*
ado *n.* bruit *m.*, cérémonies *f. pl.*; difficulté, peine *f.*
adolescent *n. & a.* adolescent *m. & a.*
adopt *vt.* adopter; **–ed** *a.* adoptif, d'adoption; **–ion** *n.* adoption *f.*; **–ive** *a.*
adoptif, d'adoption
adorable *a.* adorable
adoration *n.* adoration *f.*
adore *vt.* adorer; **–r** *n.* adorateur *m.*;
soupirant *m.*
adorn *vt.* orner, décorer; parer; embellir;

–ment *n.* ornement *m.*; ornementation *f.*; parure *f.*
adrenalin *n.* adrénaline *f.*
Adriatic Sea *n.* Mer Adriatique *f.*
adrift *adv.* à la dérive
adroit *a.* adroit; habile; **–ness** *n.* adresse,
dextérité *f.*
adulate *vt.* aduler
adulation *n.* adulation *f.*
adulatory *a.* adulateur
adult *n. & a.* adulte *m. & f.*
adulterate *vt.* adultérer; couper; falsifier,
corrompre
adulteration *n.* falsification *f.*; adultération *f.*
adulterer, adulteress *n.* adultère *m. & f.*
adultery *n.* adultère *m.*
advance *n.* avance *f.*, avancement *m.*,
approche *f.*; progrès *m.*; — guard
avant-garde *f.*; in — d'avance, préalablement; — *vt.* avancer; faire avancer,
pousser; approcher; — *vi.* s'avancer;
–d *a.* avancé; **–ment** *n.* avancement *m.*
advantage *n.* avantage *m.*, supériorité *f.*;
to take — of profiter de; abuser de;
turn to one's — mettre à profit; **–ous** *a.*
avantageux; profitable
advent *n.* venue *f.*, avènement *m.*; Avent
m.
adventure *n.* aventure *f.*, accident, hasard
m.; — *vt.* risquer; **–r** *n.* aventurier *m.*;
–some *a.* aventureux
adventurous *a.* aventureux
adverb *n.* adverbe *m.*; **–ial** *a.* adverbial
adversary *n.* adversaire *m.*
adverse *a.* adverse, contraire; défavorable; **–ly** *adv.* au contraire; d'une façon
défavorable
adversity *n.* adversité *f.*
advertise *vt.* annoncer; — *vi.* faire de la
publicité; **–ment** *n.* annonce
advertising *n.* publicité *f.*; réclame *f.*;
annonces *f. pl.*
advice *n.* conseil *m.*; avis *m.*; piece of —
conseil *m.*; on the — of sur l'avis de;
take someone's — suivre le conseil de
quelqu'un
advisability *n.* convenance, opportunité *f.*
advisable *a.* prudent, judicieux; convenable; opportun
advise *vt. & vi.* conseiller; — against déconseiller; **–r**, advisor *n.* conseiller *m.*
advisory *a.* consultatif
advocacy *n.* appui *m.*; soutien *m.*
advocate *n.* défenseur *m.*; avocat *m.*; —
vt. soutenir; défendre
Aegean Sea *n.* Mer Egée *f.*
aegis *n.* égide *f.*
aeon *n.* éternité *f.*; éon *m.*
aerate *vt.* aérer; gazéifier

aeration n. aération f.
aerial a. aérien; — n. antenne f.; — photography n. photographie aérienne f.
aerodynamics n. pl. aérodynamique f.
aeromedicine n. médecine de l'aviation f.
aeronaut n. aéronaute m.; –ics n. pl. aéronautique f.
aerosol n. aérosol m.; bombe, vaporisateur à insecticide f.
aerospace n. espace interplanétaire m.
aerothermodynamics n. aérothermodynamique f.
aesthetic a. esthétique; –s n. esthétique f.
afar adv. loin; from — de loin
affability n. affabilité f.
affable a. affable, gracieux
affair n. affaire f.; love — liaison f.; foreign –s affaires étrangères f. pl.
affect vt. affecter; émouvoir, toucher; feindre; –ation n. affectation f.; –ed a. affecté; –ing a. touchant
affection n. affection f.; tendresse f.; –ate a. affectueux, tendre; affectionné
affiance vt. fiancer
affidavit n. déclaration f., affidavit m.
affiliate vt. affilier
affiliation n. affiliation f.; relation f.
affinity n. affinité f.; rapport m.
affirm vt. affirmer; –ation n. affirmation f.; –ative n. affirmative f.; –ative a. affirmatif
affix vt. fixer, apposer, attacher
afflict vt. affliger; –ion n. affliction f.
affluence n. affluence, opulence f.; abondance f.
affluent a. abondant, riche; — n. affluent m.
afford vt. pouvoir se payer, se permettre; fournir
affront n. affront m., insulte f.; — vt. affronter; insulter
afghan n. couverture f.
afire, **aflame** adv. en flammes, en feu
afloat adv. à flot, flottant
afoot adv. à pied, sur pied, en train
aforementioned, **aforesaid** a. précité, susdit
afraid a. éffrayé; to be — avoir peur
Africa n. Afrique f.; –n a. & n. africain m.; **North** — n. Afrique du Nord f.; **North** –n n. & a. Nord-Africain m.
aft adv. à l'arrière
after adv. après, plus tard; derrière; — prep. après; derrière; à la suite de; d'après; à la poursuite de; — all après tout; enfin; be — chercher; day — tomorrow après-demain; take — tenir de; time — time bien des fois; — conj. après que; — a. arrière, d'arrière; futur, untérieur

afterbirth n. arrière-faix, délivre m.
aftereffect n. résultat m.; suite f.; ré-percussion f.; contre-coup m.
afterglow n. lueur (qui subsiste) f.
afterlife n. vie future f.
aftermath n. regain m.; conséquences, suites f. pl.
afternoon n. après-midi m. & f.
aftertaste n. arrière-goût m.
afterthought n. réflexion après coup f.
afterwards adv. après
again adv. encore, de nouveau; — and — sans cesse; now and — de temps en temps, de temps à autre; once — encore une fois; then — d'autre part
against prep. contre; vers, sur; — the grain à contre-poil; — the will à contre-cœur; come up — se heurter contre; as — comparé à
agape adv. bouche bée
agar-agar n. gélase f.
agate n. agate f.; (print.) corps 5.5 m.
age n. âge m.; génération f.; vieillesse f.; under — a. mineur; of — majeur; over — a. trop vieux, périmé; to be ten years of — avoir dix ans; — vi. vieillir; –d a. âgé; middle –d a. d'un certain âge
agency n. agence f.; intermédiaire m. & f.; entremise f.; action f.
agenda n. ordre du jour, programme m.
agent n. agent m.
agglomeration n. agglomération f.
agglutination n. agglutination f.
aggrandizement n. agrandissement m.
aggravate vt. aggraver; agacer
aggravating a. aggravant; agaçant
aggravation n. aggravation f.; provocation f., agacement m.
aggregate n. masse f., rassemblement m.; in the — dans l'ensemble; — a. collectif
aggregation n. rassemblement m., réunion f.
aggression n. agression f.
aggressive a. agressif; entreprenant; –ness n. caractère agressif m.; entreprise f.
aggressor n. agresseur m.
aghast a. stupéfait
agile a. agile, leste
agility n. agilité, légèreté f.
agitate vt. agiter, remuer; troubler; — vi. faire de l'agitation
agitation n. agitation f., trouble m.
agitator n. agitateur m.; (pol.) fauteur m.
aglow a. incandescent, luisant
agnostic n. & a. agnostique m. & f.; –ism n. agnosticisme m.
ago adv. il y a; passé; long — il y a long-temps

agog *a.* en train; en émoi

agonize *vi.* agoniser; — *vt.* torturer; **-ed** *a.* d'angoisse

agonizing *a.* angoissant; atroce

agony *n.* agonie *f.*; angoisse *f.*

agrarian *a.* agraire

agree *vi.* convenir; se mettre d'accord; tomber d'accord; être d'accord; s'accorder; **-d** *a.* convenu; d'accord; **-able** *a.* agréable; consentant; **be -able** vouloir bien; **-ment** *n.* accord *m.*; acte *m.*; contrat *m.*; entente *f.*; **be in -ment** être d'accord

agricultural *a.* agricole

agriculture *n.* agriculture *f.*

agriculturist *n.* agriculteur *m.*

agronomy *n.* agronomie *f.*

aground *adv.* à la côte; **to run —** s'échouer

ahead *adv.* en avant; **get — réussir; go —** continuer, persévérer; **aller en avant; straight —** tout droit

aid *n.* aide, assistance *f.*, secours *m.*; aide *m.*; — *vt.* aider, assister, secourir

ail *vt.* chagriner, causer de la peine; **what -s you?** qu'avez-vous?; **-ing** *a.* souffrant; **-ment** *n.* maladie *f.*, mal *m.*

aileron *n.* aileron *m.*

aim *n.* visée *f.*; but *m.*; objet, dessein *m.*; **-less** *a.* sans but; — *vt.* viser, diriger; mettre en joue; (cannon) pointer

air *n.* air *m.*; chant *m.*; (of a person) mine *f.*; apparence *f.*, aspect *m.*; **on the —** (radio) en train d'être radio-diffusé; à la radio; **give oneself -s, put on -s** se donner des airs; **in the open —** en plein air, à la belle étoile; **— base** terrain d'aviation *m.*; **— blast** coup de vent *m.*; **— brake** frein à air comprimé *m.*; **— chamber** chambre à air *f.*; **— corps** aviation *f.*; **— cushion** matelas pneumatique *m.*; **— force** aviation *f.*; **— freight** frêt aérien; *m.* **— gun** fusil à air comprimé *m.*; **— hole** évent, soupirial *m.*; **— letter** aérogramme *m.*; **— passage** route aérienne *f.*; passage aérien *m.*; **— pocket** trou d'air *m.*; **— power** forces aériennes *f. pl.*; **— pressure** pression atmosphérique *f.*; **— pump** pompe à air *f.*; **— raid** raid (aérien) *m.*; **— shaft** puits d'aérage *m.*; **— valve** soupape à air *f.*; — *vt.* aérer; exhiber, montrer; **-ily** *adv.* légèrement; **-iness** *n.* abondance d'air et d'espace dans une pièce *f.*; légèreté *f.*; **-ing** *n.* promenade *f.*; aération *f.*; aérage *m.*; ventilation *f.*; **-y** *a.* aéré; exposé à l'air; léger; chimérique

air age *n.* époque de l'espace *f.*

airborne *a.* porté par les airs; **— troops**

parachutistes *m. pl.*

airbrake *n.* aérofrein *m.*

airbrush *n.* pinceau pneumatique *m.*

air-condition *vt.* climatiser; **-ing** *n.* climatisation *f.*

air-cooled *a.* refroidi par air

aircraft *n.* avion *m.*; **— carrier** *n.* porte-avions *m.*

airfield *n.* terrain d'aviation *m.*; aérodrome *m.*

air letter *n.* aérogramme *m.*

airlift *n.* pont aérien *m.*

airline *n.* ligne aérienne *f.*; **-r** *n.* avion pour passagers *m.*

airmail *n.* poste aérienne *f.*; — *adv. & a.* par avion

airman *n.* aviateur, soldat de l'air *m.*

airplane *n.* avion *m.*

airport *n.* aéroport, aérodrome *m.*

airship *n.* dirigeable *m.*

air speed *n.* vitesse relative *f.*

airstrip *n.* petit aérodrome *m.*; **piste d'atterrissage** *f.*

air terminal *n.* aérogare *f.*

airtight *a.* étanche, hermétique

airway *n.* route aérienne *f.*; ligne aérienne *f.*

aisle *n.* passage *m.*

ajar *a.* entr'ouvert

akimbo *adv.* les mains sur les hanches

akin *a.* parent; allié

alabaster *n.* albâtre *m.*

alacrity *n.* vivacité, gaieté *f.*; empressement *m.*

alarm *n.* alarme, épouvante *f.*; réveil *m.*; alerte *f.*; **— signal,** avertisseur *m.*; **sound an —** sonner l'alarme; **— bell** *n.* tocsin *m.*; **— clock** *n.* réveille-matin, réveil *m.*; — *vt.* alarmer; **-ing** *a.* inquiétant; **-ist** *n.* alarmiste *m.*

Albania *n.* Albanie *f.*

albatross *n.* albatros *m.*

albeit *adv.* quoique, bien que

albino *n.* albinos *m.*

album *n.* album *m.*

albumen *n.* (egg) albumine *f.*; (bot.) albumen *m.*

alchemist *n.* alchimiste *m.*

alchemy *n.* alchimie *f.*

alcohol *n.* alcool *m.*; **-ic** *n. & a.* alcoolique *m. & f.*; **-ism** *n.* alcoolisme *m.*

alcove *n.* alcôve *f.*; niche *f.*

alderman *n.* conseiller municipal *m.*

alert *a.* alerte, éveillé; vif; — *n.* alerte *f.*; **on the —** en éveil; sur le qui-vive; — *vt.* avertir, prévenir; alerter; **-ness** *n.* état d'éveil *m.*, vigilance *f.*; vivacité *f.*

Aleutian Islands *n. pl.* Aléoutiennes *f. pl.*

Alexandria *n.* Alexandrie *f.*

alga (algae) *n.* (*pl.*) algue *f.*

algebra *n.* algèbre *m.*; **–ic** *a.* algébrique

Algeria *n.* Algérie *f.*; **–n** *a.* & *n.* algérien *m.*

alias *n.* faux nom *m.*; — *adv.* autrement dit

alien *n.* & *a.* étranger *m.* & *a.*; **–ate** *vt.* aliéner; **–ist** *n.* médecin aliéniste *m.*

alight *vi.* descendre, mettre pied à terre; (birds) s'abattre; — *a.* allumé, illuminé

align *vt.* aligner; **–ment** *n.* alignement *m.*

alike *a.* semblable; pareil; — *adv.* également, de même

alimentary *a.* alimentaire

alimony *n.* pension alimentaire *f.*

alive *a.* vivant; gai; en vie; **be — with** foisonner de, fourmiller de; grouiller de; **dead or —** mort ou vif

alkali *n.* alcali *m.*; **–ne** *a.* alcalin; **–ze** *vt.* alcaliser

alkaloid *n.* alcaloïde *m.*

all *n.* tout *m.*; — *a.* tout, tous *m. pl.*; — *adv.* tout; entièrement; **— aboard!** en voiture!; **— along** tout le temps; **— but** presque; **— clear** (mil.) fin d'alerte; il n'y a personne; **— day** toute la journée; **— in** (coll.) fatigué, épuisé; **— in —** somme toute; **— of a sudden** tout à coup; **— of us** nous tous; **— over** (*adv.*) partout; (coll.) fini; **— right** (*adv.*) bien, pas mal; eh bien; alors; honnête; **— set** tout prêt; **— the better** tant mieux; **— the same** tout de même; **— together** tous ensemble; **above —** surtout; **at — hours** à toute heure; **by — means** certainement; mais oui; **not at —** pas du tout, point du tout; **on — fours** à quatre pattes; **once and for —** une fois pour toutes; **one — (sports)** un à un; **one and —** tout le monde

allay *vt.* apaiser, calmer; modérer, tempérer; dissiper

allegation *n.* allégation *f.*

allege *vt.* alléguer; citer; **–d** *a.* allégué; présumé

allegiance *n.* obéissance *f.*; fidélité *f.*

allegoric(al) *a.* allégorique

allegory *n.* allégorie *f.*

allergen *n.* (med.) allergène *m.*

allergic *a.* allergique

allergy *n.* allergie *f.*

alleviate *vt.* alléger; soulager; apaiser

alleviation *n.* soulagement *m.*

alley *n.* ruelle *f.*; **blind —** cul-de-sac *m.*

alliance *n.* alliance *f.*; parenté *f.*

allied *a.* allié; parent; voisin

alligator *n.* alligator *m.*; **— pear** poire d'avocat *f.*

all-night *a.* ouvert toute la nuit; de toute la nuit

allocate *vt.* attribuer; distribuer, allouer

allocation *n.* (com.) allocation *f.*; attribution *f.*

allot *vt.* accorder, attribuer; **–ment** *n.* allocation *f.*; part, portion *f.*; (mil.) délégation de solde *f.*

allow *vt.* permettre; laisser; autoriser; allouer; avouer; **— for** avoir égard à; **— oneself** se permettre; **–able** *a.* permis; **–ance** *n.* argent de poche *m.*; allocation *f.*; indulgence *f.*; part *f.*; **make –ances for** faire la part de; tenir compte de; **–ing for** vu, eu égard à

alloy *n.* alliage *m.*; — *vt.* allier

all-powerful *a.* tout-puissant

all-purpose *a.* à tout faire; universel

all-round *a.* universel, varié, complet

All Saints' Day *n.* la Toussaint *f.*

allspice *n.* toute épice *f.*; piment *m.*

all-time *a.* de tous les temps

allude *vi.* faire allusion

allure *vt.* séduire, attirer

alluring *a.* attrayant, séduisant

allusion *n.* allusion *f.*

allusive *a.* figuré, fait par allusion

alluvial *a.* alluvien

ally *n.* allié *m.*; — *vt.* allier

almanac *n.* almanach *m.*

almighty *a.* tout-puissant

almond *n.* amande *f.*; **— tree** *n.* amandier *m.*

almost *adv.* presque; à peu près

alms *n. pl.* aumône, charité *f.*

aloft *adv.* en haut, en l'air

alone *a.* seul; **let me —!** laissez-moi tranquille!; — *adv.* seulement

along *adv.* de compagnie; avec; en avant; — *prep.* le long de; **get — with** s'accomoder avec; s'entendre; **go — suivre,** longer; **go — with** accompagner

alongside *prep.* le long de; — *adv.* bord à bord; **come — aborder**

aloof *a.* à l'écart, distant; **–ness** réserve *f.*; désintéressement *m.*

aloud *adv.* à haute voix

alpaca *n.* (zool.) alpaca *m.*; (material) alpaga *m.*

alphabet *n.* alphabet *m.*; **–ical** *a.* alphabétique; **–ize** *vt.* alphabétiser

alpine *a.* alpin; alpestre

Alps *n.* Alpes *f. pl.*

already *adv.* déjà

Alsace *n.* Alsace *f.*

Alsatian *a.* & *n.* alsatien *m.*

also *adv.* aussi, également, encore

altar *n.* autel *m.*

alter *vt.* altérer; changer; modifier; — *vi.* s'altérer; changer; **–ation** *n.* changement *m.*; altération *f.*; modification *f.*

alternate *a.* alternatif, alternant, alterné;

(rhyme) croisé; — *n.* suppléant, remplaçant *m.*; **-ly** *adv.* tour à tour, alternativement; — *vi.* alterner; — *vt.* faire alterner

alternating *a.* alternant; — **current** courant alternatif *m.*

alternation *n.* alternation *f.*; alternance *f.*

alternative *n.* alternative *f.*, choix *m.*; — *a.* alternatif

although *conj.* quoique, bien que; encore que

altimeter *n.* altimètre *m.*

altitude *n.* élévation, hauteur *f.*; altitude *f.*

altogether *adv.* entièrement, tout à fait

altruism *n.* altruisme *m.*

altruist *n.* altruiste; **-ic** *a.* altruiste

alum *n.* alun *m.*

aluminum *n.* aluminium *m.*

alumnus *n.* ancien élève *m.*

always *adv.* toujours

A.M. (ante meridiem) du matin

amalgam *n.* amalgame *m.*; **-ate** *vt.* amalgamer; **-ation** *n.* almagamation, fusion, union *f.*

amass *vt.* amasser

amateur *n.* nonprofessionnel, amateur *m.*; **-ish** *a.* gauche, inexpérimenté

amatory *a.* amoureux, d'amour, sentimental

amaze *vt.* étonner, émerveiller; **-ment** *n.* étonnement *m.*

amazing *a.* étonnant

amazon *n.* amazone *f.*

ambassador *n.* ambassadeur *m.*; **-ship** *n.* ambassade *f.*

amber *n.* ambre *m.*

ambidextrous *a.* ambidextre

ambiguity *n.* ambiguïté *f.*

ambiguous *a.* ambigu; confus; équivoque; **-ness** *n.* ambiguïté *f.*

ambition *n.* ambition *f.*

ambitious *a.* ambitieux

amble *vi.* aller doucement; (horses) ambler; — *n.* amble *m.*

ambling *a.* à l'amble

ambrosia *n.* ambroisie *f.*

ambulance *n.* ambulance *f.*

ambulatory *a.* ambulatoire; ambulant

ambush *n.* embuscade *f.*; guet-apens *m.*; **in** — en embuscade, embusqué; à l'affût; — *vt.* embusquer

ameliorate *vt.* améliorer; — *vi.* s'améliorer

amelioration *n.* amélioration *f.*

amen *interj.* amen; (prayer books) ainsi soit-il

amenable *a.* docile, traitable; responsable

amend *vt.* amender, corriger; — *vi.* s'amender; se corriger; **-ment** *n.* amendement *m.*

amends *n. pl.* compensation *f.*, dédommagement *m.*; **to make** — faire amende honorable

amenity *n.* aménité *f.*; **amenities** civilités *f. pl.*; commodités *f. pl.*

America *n.* Amérique *f.*; **North** — Amérique du Nord *f.*; **South** — Amérique du Sud *f.*; **Central** — Amérique Centrale *f.*; **-n** *a. & n.* américain *m.*; — **plan** (hotels) prix qui comprend chambre et trois repas *m.*, pension complète *f.*

Americanize *vt.* américaniser

amiability *n.* amabilité *f.*

amiable *a.* aimable; **-ness** *n.* amabilité *f.*

amicability *n.* cordialité, amabilité *f.*

amicable *a.* amical, bienveillant

amidships *adv.* par le travers

amid(st) *prep.* au milieu de, parmi

amiss *adv.* mal, en mal, mal à propos; **take** — prendre en mauvaise part

amity *n.* amitié *f.*

ammeter *n.* ampère-mètre *m.*

ammonia *n.* ammoniaque *f.*; — **gas** *n.* ammoniaque *m.*

ammunition *n.* cartouches *f. pl.*; munitions *f. pl.*

amnesia *n.* amnésie *f.*

amnesty *n.* amnistie *f.*; — *vt.* amnistier

amoeba *n.* amibe *f.*

among(st) *prep.* parmi, entre

amoral *a.* amoral

amorous *a.* amoureux

amorphous *a.* amorphe

amortization *n.* amortissement *m.*

amortize *vt.* amortir

amount *n.* montant, total *m.*; somme, quantité *f.*; — *vi.*, — **to** s'élever à revenir à; valoir

amour *n.* amourette *f.*; intrigue *f.*

amperage *n.* ampérage *m.*

ampere *n.* ampère *m.*

ampersand *n.* symbole typographique pour *et m.*

amphibian, amphibious *a.* amphibie

amphitheater *n.* amphithéâtre *m.*

ample *a.* ample, large; **-ness** *n.* ampleur, étendue *f.*

amplification *n.* amplification *f.*

amplifier *n.* amplificateur *m.*

amplify *vt.* amplifier, augmenter

amplitude *n.* largeur *f.*; étendue *f.*; amplitude *f.*

amply *adv.* amplement

amputate *vt.* amputer

amputation *n.* amputation *f.*

amputee *n.* amputé *m.*

amuck *adv.* comme un furieux

amulet *n.* amulette *f.*

amuse *vt.* amuser, divertir; — **onself** s'amuser; **-ment** *n.* amusement *m.*;

divertissement *m.*; **–ment park fête**
foraine *f.*
amusing *a.* amusant; divertissant
an *art.* un, une
anachronism *n.* anachronisme *m.*
anachronistic *a.* anachronique
anaconda *n.* boa (de l'Amérique du Sud)
m.
anal *a.* anal
analgesic *a. & n.* analgésique *m.*
analogical *a.* analogique
analogous *a.* analogue
analogy *n.* analogie *f.*
analysis *n.* analyse *f.*
analyst *n.* analyste *m.*
analytic(al) *a.* analytique
analyze *vt.* analyser
anarchist *n.* anarchiste *m. & f.*
anarchy *n.* anarchie *f.*
anathema *n.* anathème *m.*; **–tize** *vt.* ana-
thémiser
anatomical *a.* anatomique
anatomist *n.* anatomiste *m.*
anatomy *n.* anatomie *f.*
ancestor *n.* ancêtre, aïeul *m.*; **–s** *pl.* aïeux
m. pl.
ancestral *a.* ancestral; héréditaire
ancestry *n.* lignée *f.*; aïeux *m. pl.*
anchor *n.* ancre *f.*; **cast —** jeter l'ancre;
weigh — lever l'ancre; **ride at —** être
à l'ancre; — *vt.* ancrer; — *vi.* jeter
l'ancre; **–age** *n.* ancrage, mouillage *m.*
anchovy *n.* anchois *m.*
ancient *a.* antique; ancien; **–ness** *n.*
ancienneté *f.*
and *conj.* et; (both) — . . . . — et . . . .
et; **— so on** et ainsi de suite
Andalusia *n.* Andalousie *f.*
Andes *n.* Andes *f. pl.*
andiron *n.* chenet *m.*
Andorra *n.* Andorre *f.*
androgen *n.* (biol.) androgène *m.*
anemia *n.* anémie *f.*
anemic *a.* anémique
anemometer *n.* anémomètre *m.*
aneroid *a.* anéroïde
anesthesia *n.* anesthésie *f.*
anesthetic *n.* anesthétique *m.*
anesthetist *n.* anesthésiste *m.*
anesthetize *vt.* anesthésier
anew *adv.* de nouveau; encore; **à neuf**
angel *n.* ange *m.*; **–ic** *a.* angélique
anger *n.* colère *f.*; — *vt.* mettre en colère
angle *n.* angle *m.*; coin *m.*; (coll.) point
de vue *m.*; **— iron** cornière *f.*; **—** *vi.*
pêcher à la ligne; **–r** *n.* pêcheur (à la
ligne) *m.*
angleworm *n.* ver de terre *m.*
Anglican *a.* anglican
Anglicism *n.* anglicisme *m.*

Anglicize *vt.* angliciser
angling *n.* pêche à la ligne *f.*
Anglo-Saxon *a. & n.* anglo-saxon *m.*
Angola *n.* Angola *m.*
angora *n.* angora *m.*
angry *a.* fâché, irrité; **become —** se
mettre en colère; **be — with** être fâché
contre
anguish *n.* angoisse *f.*
angular *a.* anguleux; **–ity** *n.* angularité *f.*
aniline *n.* aniline *f.*
animal *n. & a.* animal *m.*
animate *vt.* animer; encourager; **—, –d**
a. animé
animation *n.* animation *f.*
animosity *n.* animosité *f.*
animus *n.* animosité *f.*
anise *n.* anis *m.*
ankle *n.* cheville *f.*; **turn one's —** se
fouler la cheville
anklet *n.* chaussette courte *f.*; bracelet de
cheville *m.*
annals *n. pl.* annales *f. pl.*
anneal *vt.* recuire, tempérer
annex *n.* annexe *f.*; — *vt.* annexer; **–ation**
n. annexion *f.*
annihilate *vt.* annihiler, anéantir
annihilation *n.* anéantissement *m.*
anniversary *n.* anniversaire *m.*
annotate *vt.* annoter
annotation *n.* annotation *f.*
annotator *n.* annotateur *m.*
announce *vt.* annoncer; **–ment** *n.* annonce
f.; faire-part *m.*; avis *m.*; **–r** *n.* speaker
m.
annoy *vt.* ennuyer, troubler, gêner; **–ance**
n. ennui *m.*; **–ing** *a.* ennuyeux
annual *n.* annuaire *m.*; plante annuelle
f.; **— a.** annuel
annuity *n.* rente *f.*; **life —** rente viagère *f.*
annul *vt.* annuler, casser; **–ment** *n.* annulation *f.*; (marriage) dissolution *f.*
Annunciation *n.* Annonciation *f.*
anode *n.* anode *f.*
anodyne *n.* remède anodin *m.*
anoint *vt.* oindre; consacrer, sacrer; **–ing**
n. onction *f.*
anomalous *a.* anomal, hétéroclite
anomaly *n.* anomalie *f.*
anon *adv.* bientôt, tout à l'heure
anonymity *n.* anonymat *m.*
anonymous *a.* anonyme
another *a.* un autre; encore un; **one —**
l'un l'autre; les uns les autres **— pron.**
autrui
answer *n.* réponse, réplique *f.*; raison *f.*;
solution *f.*; — *vt.* répondre; réfuter; **—**
for être responsable de; répondre de
–able *a.* responsable
ant *n.* fourmi *f.*

antagonism *n.* antagonisme *m.*
antagonist *n.* antagoniste *m.*; **–ic** *a.* antagoniste; opposé
antagonize *vt.* contrarier, opposer
antarctic *a.* & *n.* antarctique *m.*
anteater *n.* fourmilier *m.*
antecedence *n.* antécédence *f.*; priorité *f.*
antecedent *n.* & *a.* antécédent *m.*
antechamber *n.* antichambre *f.*
antedate *vt.* précéder; antidater
antediluvian *a.* antédiluvien
antelope *n.* antilope *f.*
antenna *n.* antenne *f.*
anterior *a.* antérieur
anteroom *n.* vestibule *m.*, salle d'attente *f.*
anthem *n.* antienne *f.*; hymne *m.*
anthill *n.* fourmilière *f.*
anthology *n.* anthologie, chrestomathie *f.*
anthracite *n.* anthracite *m.*
anthrax *n.* charbon *m.*
anthropological *a.* anthropologique
anthropologist *n.* anthropologiste *m.*
anthropology *n.* anthropologie *f.*
anthropomorphous *a.* anthropomorphe
antiaircraft *a.* antiavion
antibiotic *n.* & *a.* antibiotique *m.*
antibody *n.* anticorps *m.*
antic *n.* singerie, gambade *f.*
anticipate *vt.* anticiper; devancer, aller au-devant de; prévenir
anticipation *n.* anticipation *f.*; prévision *f.*
anticipatory *a.* par anticipation
anticlerical *a.* anticlérical
anticlimax *n.* dénouement décevant *m.*
antidote *n.* antidote *m.*
anti-electron *n.* anti-électron *m.*
antifreeze *n.* antigel *m.*
antihistamine *n.* antihistamine *f.*
anti-particle *n.* (phy.) antiparticule *f.*
antipathy *n.* antipathie *f.*
antiphony *n.* contre-chant *m.*
antiproton *n.* antiproton *m.*
antiquarian, antiquary *n.* antiquaire *m.*
antiquated *a.* suranné, vieilli
antique *n.* antiquité *f.*; — *a.* ancien
antiquity *n.* antiquité *f.*
antisemitism *n.* antisémitisme *m.*
antiseptic *n.* & *a.* antiseptique *m.*
antisocial *a.* antisocial
antisubmarine *a.* anti-sousmarin
antitank *a.* antichar
antithesis *n.* antithèse *f.*
antitoxin *n.* antitoxine *f.*
antitrust *a.* anticartel
antler *n.* andouiller *m.*
antonym *n.* antonyme *m.*
Antwerp *n.* Anvers *m.*
anus *n.* anus *m.*
anvil *n.* enclume *f.*

anxiety *n.* anxiété, inquiétude *f.*
anxious *a.* inquiet, soucieux: désireux; **be — to** tenir à; avoir hâte de
any *adj.* du, de la, des; quelque; (**ne . . .**) aucun; n'importe quel; tout; — *pron.* en; (**ne . . .**) aucun; n'importe lequel
anybody *pron.* (**ne . . .**) personne; quelqu'un; n'importe qui; le premier venu
anyhow *adv.* n'importe comment; en tout cas
anyone *pron.* (**ne . . .**) personne; quelqu'un; n'importe qui; le premier venu
anything *pron.* (**ne . . .**) rien; quelque chose; n'importe quoi, quoi que ce soit; **not for —** pour rien au monde
anyway *adv.* n'importe comment; en tout cas
anywhere *adv.* n'importe où, où que ce soit, partout; quelque part, (**ne . . .**) nulle part
aorta *n.* aorte *f.*
apart *adv.* à part, séparément; **— from** en dehors de; **come —** se défaire; **take —** démonter; **tell —** distinguer (entre)
apartment *n.* appartement *m.*; **— building** *n.* immeuble d'habitation *f.*
apathetic *a.* apathique
apathy *n.* apathie *f.*
ape *n.* singe *m.*; **—** *vt.* singer, imiter
aperture *n.* ouverture *f.*
apex *n.* sommet *m.*, pointe *f.*
aphasia *n.* aphasie *f.*
aphorism *n.* aphorisme *m.*
aphoristic *a.* aphoristique
aphrodisiac *a.* aphrodisiaque
apiary *n.* rucher *m.*
apiece *adv.* par pièce, par tête, chacun
apish *a.* de singe; bouffon
aplomb *n.* aplomb *m.*
Apocalypse *n.* apocalypse *f.*
apocalyptic(al) *a.* apocalyptique
apocryphal *a.* apocryphe
apogee *n.* apogée *f.*
apologetic *a.* d'excuse; apologétique
apologist *n.* apologiste *m.*
apologize *vi.* s'excuser
apology *n.* excuses *f. pl.*; (**defense)** apologie *f.*
apoplectic *a.* apoplectique
apoplexy *n.* apoplexie *f.*
apostasy *n.* apostasie *f.*
apostate *a.* & *n.* apostat *m.*
apostle *n.* apôtre *m.*
apostolic *a.* apostolique
apostrophe *n.* apostrophe *f.*
apothecary *n.* pharmacien *m.*
appall *vt.* effrayer, consterner; **–ing** *a.* épouvantable
apparatus *n.* appareil *m.*
apparel *n.* vêtements, habits *m. pl.*

apparent *a.* apparent, visible; évident; (of heirs) présomptif; **–ly** *adv.* apparemment, évidemment

apparition *n.* apparition *f.*

appeal *n.* appel *m.*; charme, attrait *m.*; — *vt.* faire appel (à); se reporter (à); être séduisant; (law) interjeter appel; **–ing** *a.* séduisant, attrayant; sympathique

appear *vi.* apparaître, paraître; sembler; **–ance** *n.* apparition *f.*; aspect *m.*; air *m.*; apparence *f.*; — (book) parution *f.*; **to all –ances** apparemment

appease *vt.* apaiser, calmer; **–ment** *n.* apaisement *m.*

appellate *a.* d'appel; **— court** cour d'appel *f.*

append *vt.* apposer, ajouter; **–age** *n.* dépendance *f.*, accessoire *m.*

appendicitis *n.* appendicite *f.*

appendix *n.* appendice *m.*; (anat.) appendice *m.*

appertain *vi.* appartenir (à), concerner

appetite *n.* appétit *m.*

appetizer *n.* amuse-gueule, hors-d'œuvre *m.*; (drink) apéritif *m.*

appetizing *a.* appétissant

applaud *vt.* applaudir

applause *n.* applaudissements *m. pl.*

apple *n.* pomme *f.*; **— brandy** calvados *m.*; **— core** trognon de pomme *m.*; **— dumpling** *n.* chausson *m.*; **— orchard** *n.* pommeraie *f.*; **— pie** tarte aux pommes *f.*; **— tree** *n.* pommier *m.*; **baked —** pomme cuite *f.*

**apple-pie order, in — impeccable; tout ce qu'il y a de mieux

applesauce *n.* compote de pommes *f.*

appliance *n.* appareil *m.*; application *f.*

applicability *n.* applicabilité *f.*

applicant *n.* pétitionneur, soliciteur *m.*; candidat, postulant *m.*

application *n.* application *f.*; demande *f.*; emploi, usage *m.*; attention *f.*; **— blank** *n.* formule *f.*

applied *a.* appliqué; **— arts** arts industriels *m. pl.*

apply *vt.* appliquer; employer; **— for** soliciter; **— to** s'adresser à

appoint *vt.* fixer, nommer, désigner; **–ed** *a.* désigné, dit, convenu; **–ee** *n.* fonctionnaire nommé *m.*; **–ment** *n.* rendez-vous *m.*; nomination *f.*; équipement *m.*

apportion *vt.* répartir, partager; **–ment** *n.* répartition *f.*, partage *m.*

apposite *a.* convenable, à propos

appraisal *n.* évaluation, estimation, expertise *f.*

appraise *vt.* priser, évaluer, estimer

appraiser *n.* estimateur, commissaire-priseur *m.*

appreciable *a.* appréciable; sensible

appreciably *adv.* sensiblement

appreciate *vt.* apprécier, évaluer; comprendre, se rendre compte de

appreciation *n.* appréciation *f.*; évaluation, estimation *f.*; augmentation de valeur *f.*

appreciative *a.* reconnaissant; sensible

apprehend *vt.* appréhender; saisir; redouter

apprehension *n.* appréhension, crainte *f.*

apprehensive *a.* craintif, inquiet; **become — about** redouter

apprentice *n.* apprenti *m.*; — *vt.* mettre en apprentissage; **–ship** *n.* apprentissage *m.*

apprise *vt.* apprendre; informer

approach *n.* approche *f.*, accès, abord *m.*; — *vt.* approcher; s'approcher de; **–able** *a.* abordable

appropriate *vt.* approprier; **— to oneself** s'approprier; — *a.* approprié, convenable; à propos; **–ness** *n.* convenance, justesse *f.*

appropriation *n.* affectation *f.*; appropriation *f.*

approval *n.* approbation *f.*; **on —** (envoi) au choix, à condition

approve *vt.* approuver; **–r** *n.* approbateur *m.*

approving *a.* approbateur

approximate *vt.* approcher; s'approcher de; — *a.* approximatif

approximation *n.* approximation *f.*

appurtenance *n.* dépendance *f.*, accessoire *m.*

apricot *n.* abricot *m.*; **— tree** *n.* abricotier *m.*

April *n.* avril *m.*; **— Fool's Day** premier avril *m.*; **— fool's joke** poisson d'avril *m.*

apron *n.* tablier *m.*; **he is tied to his mother's — strings** il est pendu aux jupes de sa mère

apropos *a.* à propos

apt *a.* apte; propre, enclin à; prompt, porté à; à propos; **–ness** *n.* aptitude, convenance *f.*

aptitude *n.* aptitude, disposition *f.*, talent *m.*

aqualung *n.* aquapoumon *m.*

aquamarine *n.* aigue-marine *f.*

aquaplane *n.* aquaplane *m.*

aquarium *n.* aquarium *m.*

aquatic *n.* aquatique

aqueduct *n.* aqueduc *m.*

aquiline *a.* aquilin

Arab *n.* Arabe *m. & f.*; **–ia** *n.* Arabie *f.*; **Saudi –ia** *n.* Arabie Soudite *f.*; **–ian** *a. & n.* arabe *m.*; **–ic** *a. & n.* arabe *m.*

arable *a.* labourable

arbiter *n.* arbitre *m.*

arbitrary *a.* arbitraire
arbitrate *vt.* arbitrer, déterminer, juger
arbitration *n.* arbitrage *m.*
arbitrator *n.* arbitre *m.*
arbor *n.* berceau *m.*; tonnelle, treille *f.*
arbutus *n.* aubépine *f.*
arc *n.* arc *m.*; — **light** arc voltaïque *m.*
arch *n.* arche *f.* voûte *f.*; arc *m.*; **fallen —es** pied bot *m.*; — *vt.* voûter; arrondir — *a.* espiègle; **–ed** *a.* cintré; voûté
archaeologist *n.* archéologue *m.*
archaeology *n.* archéologie *f.*
archaic *a.* archaïque
archaism *n.* archaïsme *m.*
archangel *n.* archange *m.*
archbishop *n.* archevêque *m.*
archduchess *n.* archiduchesse *f.*
archduke *n.* archiduc *m.*
archer *n.* archer *m.*; **–y** *n.* tir à l'arc *m.*
archetype *n.* archétype, prototype *m.*
archipelago *n.* archipel *m.*
architect *n.* architecte *m.*; **–ural** *a.* architectural; **–ure** *n.* architecture *f.*
archives *n. pl.* archives *f. pl.*
archivist *n.* archiviste *m. & f.*
archway *n.* voûte *f.*
arctic *a.* arctique
arc-weld *vt.* souder à l'arc
ardent *a.* ardent, violent; **–ly** *adv.* ardemment
ardor *n.* ardeur *f.*
arduous *a.* ardu; rude; difficile; **–ness** *n.* difficulté *f.*
area *n.* région *f.*; surface *f.*; superficie *f.*; aire *f.*; zone *f.*
area code number *n.* code de district *m.*
arena *n.* arène *f.*; arènes *f. pl.*
Argentina *n.* Argentine *f.*
Argentine *n. & a.* Argentin *m.*
argon *n.* argon *m.*
arguable *a.* discutable
argue *vt.* discuter; soutenir; démontrer; — *vi.* discuter, disputer; argumenter
argument *n.* argument *m.*; discussion *f.*; **–ation** *n.* argumentation *f.*; **–ative** *a.* disposé à argumenter
aria *n.* air *m.*
arid *a.* aride; **–ity** *n.* aridité *f.*
arise *vi.* s'élever; provenir, résulter
aristocracy *n.* aristocratie *f.*
aristocrat *n.* aristocrate *m.*; **–ic** *a.* aristocratique
Aristotle *n.* Aristote *m.*
arithmetic *n.* arithmétique *f.*; **–al** *a.* arithmétique; **–ian** *n.* arithméticien *m.*
ark *n.* arche *f.*; — **of the covenant** arche d'alliance *f.*; **Noah's —** arche de Noé *f.*
arm *n.* bras *m.*; arme *f.*; — **in —** bras dessus, bras dessous; **bear –s** porter les armes; **be up in –s** être en rébellion;

fold one's –s croiser les bras; **small –s** armes portatives *f. pl.*; — *vt.* armer; s'armer; **–s** *n. pl.* armoiries *f. pl.*
armada *n.* armada *f.*
armadillo *n.* tatou *m.*
armament *n.* armement *m.*
armature *n.* armature *f.*
armband *n.* brassard *m.*
armchair *n.* fauteuil *m.*
Armenia *n.* Arménie *f.*
armful *n.* brassée *f.*
armhole *n.* entournure *f.*
armistice *n.* armistice *m.*, trêve *f.*
armor *n.* armure *f.*; blindage *m.*, cuirasse *f.*; — **plate** plaque de blindage *f.*; — *vt.* blinder, cuirasser; **–ed** *a.* blindé; **–er** *n.* armurier *m.*; **–ial** *a.* armorial; d'armoiries; **–y** *n.* arsenal *m.*; fabrique d'armes
armor-plated *a.* blindé, cuirassé
armpit *n.* aisselle *f.*
arm-rest *n.* accoudoir *m.*
army *n.* armée *f.*
aroma *n.* arome *m.*; **–tic** *a.* aromatique
around *prep.* autour de; — *adv.* autour, à la ronde; quelque part; (approximation) à peu près, environ
arouse *vt.* soulever; éveiller; exciter
arraign *vt.* (law) accuser; **–ment** *n.* accusation *f.*
arrange *vt.* arranger, mettre en ordre; ranger; régler; disposer; **–ment** *n.* arrangement *m.*; disposition *f.*; (mus.) adaptation *f.*
array *n.* ordre de bataille *m.*; rang *m.*, rangée *f.*; étalage *m.*; parure *f.*; — *vt.* ranger
arrears *n. pl.* arriéré *m.*; **be in —** avoir de l'arriéré
arrest *n.* arrestation *f.*; arrêt *m.*; **place under —** mettre aux arrêts; — *vt.* arrêter
arrival *n.* arrivée *f.*
arrive *vi.* arriver; parvenir; — **at** arriver à; gagner, atteindre
arrow *n.* flèche *f.*
arrowhead *n.* pointe de flèche *f.*
arson *n.* crime d'incendie volontaire *m.*
art *n.* art *m.*; habileté *f.*; artifice *m.*; **–s and crafts** arts et métiers *m. pl.*; **the fine –s** les beaux-arts; **–ful** *a.* habile; artificieux; fait avec art; **–isan** *n.* artisan *m.*; **–ist** *n.* artiste *m.*; peintre *m.*; **–istic** *a.* artistique; **–istry** *n.* art *m.*; **–less** *a.* sans art, simple; **–lessness** *n.* ingénuité, candeur, naïveté *f.*
arterial *a.* artériel
arteriosclerosis *n.* artériosclérose *f.*
artery *n.* artère *f.*
artesian *a.* artésien
arthritic *a.* arthritique

arthritis *n.* arthrite *f.*
artichoke *n.* artichaut *m.*
article *n.* article *m.*; condition, stipulation *f.*
articulate *vt.* articuler; énoncer; — *a.* articulé
articulation *n.* articulation *f.*
artifice *n.* artifice *m.*
artificial *a.* artificiel; factice; –ity caractère artificiel *m.*
artillery *n.* artillerie *f.*; –man *n.* artilleur
Aryan *n. & a.* Aryen *m.*
as *conj.* comme; aussi; que; selon que; suivant, tandis que; puisque; — far — jusqu'à; — far — I am concerned quant à moi; — for quant à; — good — aussi bon que; — is tel quel; — of en date du; — well — aussi bien que; comme; — if comme si; — it were pour ainsi dire; — regards en ce qui concerne; — soon — aussitôt que; — though comme si; — yet jusqu'ici; act — servir de; agir en
asbestos *n.* asbeste, amiante *m.*
ascend *vi. & vt.* monter; — *vt.* s'élever; –ancy, –ent *n.* ascendant *m.*
ascension *n.* ascension *f.*
ascent *n.* montée *f.*; ascension *f.*
ascertain *vt.* s'assurer de; prouver; constater, reconnaître; s'informer, vérifier; –able *a.* vérifiable, reconnaissable
ascetic *n.* ascète *m.*; — *a.* ascétique; –ism *n.* ascétisme *m.*
ascribable *a.* imputable
ascribe *vt.* attribuer, imputer
aseptic *n. & a.* aseptique *m.*
ash *n.* cendres *f. pl.*; (bot.) frêne *m.*; — tray cendrier *m.*; Ash Wednesday mercredi des cendres *m.*; –en *a.* couleur de cendre
ashamed *a.* honteux; be — avoir honte
ash-blond *a.* blond cendré
ashore *adv.* à terre; go — débarquer
Asia *n.* Asie *f.*; — Minor Asie Mineure *f.*; –n, –tic *n. & a.* Asiatique *m.*
aside *adv.* de côté, à part; à l'écart; — from à part; lay, put, set — mettre de côté; to turn — (se) détourner; — *n.* aparté *m.*
asinine *a.* d'âne
ask *vt.* demander; réclamer; — a question poser une question; — for demander; demander à voir
askance *adv.* obliquement, de travers
askew *adv.* de biais
asleep *adv.* endormi; be — dormir, être endormi; fall — s'endormir
asp *n.* aspic *m.*
asparagus *n.* asperges *f. pl.*
aspect *n.* aspect *m.*, mine *f.*, air *m.*

aspen *n.* tremble *m.*
asperity *n.* aspérité, âpreté *f.*
aspersion *n.* aspersion *f.*; diffamation *f.*
asphalt *n.* asphalte *m.*; bitume *m.*; — *vt.* asphalter
asphyxia *n.* asphyxie *f.*; –te *vt.* asphyxier
aspic *n.* gelée *f.*
aspirant *n.* candidat, aspirant, *m.*
aspirate *vt.* aspirer; — *a.* aspiré
aspiration *n.* aspiration *f.*, désir ardent *m.*
aspire *vi.* souhaiter ardemment; prétendre (à); aspirer (à)
aspirin *n.* aspirine *f.*
aspiring *a.* qui aspire; ambitieux
ass *n.* âne *m.*, ânesse *f.*
assail *vt.* assaillir, attaquer; –able *a.* attaquable; –ant *n.* assaillant *m.*
assassin *n.* assassin *m.*; –ate *vt.* assassiner; –ation *n.* assassinat *m.*
assault *n.* assaut *m.*; attaque *f.*; atteinte *f.*; viol *m.*; — and battery menaces et voies de fait *f. pl.*; — *vt.* assaillir; attaquer; violer
assay *n.* essai, examen *m.*; — *vt.* essayer, éprouver; –er *n.* essayeur *m.*; –ing *n.* essai *m.*
assemblage *n.* assemblage *m.*; réunion *f.*
assemble *vt.* assembler, rassembler; — *vi.* s'assembler, se rassembler
assembly *n.* assemblée, réunion *f.*; assemblage, montage *m.*; — line production fabrication en série *f.*
assemblyman *n.* député *m.*
assent *n.* consentement *m.*; assentiment *m.*; — *vi.* consentir (à); — to approuver
assert *vt.* affirmer, maintenir, défendre; revendiquer; faire valoir; –ion *n.* affirmation *f.*; –ive *a.* assuré; –iveness *n.* assurance *f.*
assess *vt.* taxer, imposer, évaluer; –ment *n.* répartition *f.* (d'impôts); évaluation *f.*; cote *f.*; –or *n.* contrôleur-répartiteur *m.*
asset *n.* bien *m.*; –s *pl.* actif *m.*; avoir *m.*
assiduity *n.* assiduité *f.*
assiduous *a.* assidu; –ly *adv.* assidûment; –ness *n.* assiduité *f.*
assign *vt.* assigner, désigner; attribuer; –ment *n.* attribution, désignation *f.* (school) devoir *m.*
assimilate *vt.* assimiler; — *vi.* s'assimiler
assimilation *n.* assimilation *f.*
assist *vt.* aider, secourir; –ance *n.* aide *f.*, secours *m.*; –ant *n. & a.* assistant, adjoint *m.*
assizes *n. pl.* assises *f. pl.*
associate *n. & a.* associé, adjoint *m.*; — *vt.* associer; — *vi.* s'associer; — with fréquenter
association *n.* association, alliance *f.*;

union, société *f.*

assort *vt.* assortir; **–ment** *n.* assortiment *m.*

assuage *vt.* apaiser, soulager

assume *vt.* présumer, supposer; se charger de; prendre; **–d** *a.* d'emprunt; feint; supposé

assuming *a.* prétentieux; — **(that)** en supposant que

assumption *n.* présomption *f.*; (eccl.) Assomption *f.*

assurance *n.* assurance, confiance *f.*; promesse *f.*

assure *vt.* assurer, garantir; **–dly** *adv.* assurément

asterisk *n.* astérisque *m.*

astern *adv.* à l'arrière, en arrière

asteroid *n.* astéroïde *m.*

asthma *n.* asthme *m.*; **–tic** *a.* asthmatique

astigmatic *a.* astigmate

astigmatism *n.* astigmatisme *m.*

astonish *vt.* étonner; **–ing** *a.* étonnant; **–ment** *a.* étonnement *m.*

astound *vt.* étonner, ahurir, stupéfier

astraddle *adv.* à califourchon

astray *a. & adv.* égaré; **go** — s'égarer; **lead** — égarer

astride *adv.* à califourchon

astringency *n.* astringence *f.*

astringent *n. & a.* astringent *m.*

astrologer *n.* astrologue *m.*

astrological *a.* astrologique

astrology *n.* astrologie *f.*

astronaut *n.* astronaute *m.*

astronomer *n.* astronome *m.*

astronomical *a.* astronomique

astronomy *n.* astronomie *f.*

astute *a.* fin, rusé; **–ness** *n.* finesse, astuce *f.*

asunder *adv.* à part l'un de l'autre

asylum *n.* asile. refuge *m.*; hospice *m.*; **insane, lunatic** — asile d'aliénés *f.*

asymmetric(al) *a.* asymétrique

at *prep.* à, dans; en; sur; après; contre; — **all** du tout; — **all costs** à tout prix; — **all events** en tout cas; — **first** d'abord; — **home** à la maison; — **large** libre; — **last** enfin; — **least** au moins; — **length** in extenso; à la longue; — **once** tout de suite; — **peace** en paix; — **pleasure** à loisir; — **your house** chez vous; — **sea** en pleine mer; — **stake** en jeu; — **times** à moments; — **war** en guerre; — **will** à volonté; — **work** au travail; — **your service** à votre service

atavistic *a.* atavique

Athenian *a. & n.* athénien *m.*

Athens *n.* Athènes

atheism *n.* athéisme *m.*

atheist *n.* athée *m.*; **–ic** *a.* athée

athlete *n.* athlète *m.*; **–'s foot** favus (du pied) *m.*

athletic *a.* athlétique; **–s** *n. pl.* athlétisme *m.*

Atlantic Ocean *n.* Océan Atlantique *m.*

atmosphere *n.* atmosphère *f.*; ambiance *f.*

atmospheric *a.* atmosphérique

atom *n.* atome *m.*; **–(ic) bomb** bombe atomique *f.*; **–ic** *a.* atomique; **–ic pile** réacteur atomique *m.*

atomizer *n.* vaporisateur *m.*

atone *vi. & vt.*; — **(for)** expier; racheter; **–ment** *n.* expiation *f.*

atonic *a.* atone; (anat.) atonique

atop *adv.* en haut, au sommet

atrocious *a.* atroce

atrocity *n.* atrocité *f.*

atrophy *n.* atrophie *f.*; — *vi.* s'atrophier

attach *vt.* attacher, fixer; saisir; **be –ed to** se rattacher à; **–ment** *n.* attachement *m.*; accessoire *m.*

attaché *m.* attaché *m.*; — **case** mallette *f.*, porte-documents *m.*

attack *n.* attaque *f.*, assaut *m.*; crise *f.*, accès *m.*; — *vt.* attaquer, assaillir; **–er** *n.* attaquant *m.*

attain *vt.* atteindre, obtenir; — *vi.* parvenir (à); **–able** *a.* qu'on peut atteindre; **–ment** *n.* talent *m.*, connaissance *f.*; réalisation *f.*

attar *n.* essence (de rose) *f.*

attempt *n.* essai *m.*; tentative *f.*, effort *m.*; — *vt.* tenter, essayer; **–ed** *a.*, **–ed murder** tentative d'assassinat *f.*

attend *vt.* assister à; servir, soigner; — **to** s'occuper de; se charger de; **–ance** *n.* assistance *f.*; présence *f.*; **–ant** *n.* serviteur, aide *m.*; **–ant** *a.* attenant, qui accompagne

attention *n.* attention *f.*; (mil.) garde à vous *m.*; **attract** — se faire remarquer; **pay** — faire attention

attentive *a.* attentif; prévenant; **–ness** *n.* attention *f.*

attenuate *vt.* atténuer

attenuation *n.* atténuation *f.*

attest *vt.* attester, certifier; **–ation** *n.* attestation, certification *f.*

attic *n.* mansarde *f.*; comble *m.*

attire *n.* vêtement, habillement *m.*, parure *f.*; — *vt.* vêtir, parer

attitude *n.* attitude, posture *f.*

attorney *n.* avocat *m.*; avoué *m.*; **district** — procureur *m.*; notaire *m.*; — **general** ministre de la justice *m.*; **power of** — procuration *f.*

attract *vt.* attirer; entraîner; séduire; **–ion** *n.* attraction *f.*, attrait *m.*; **–ive** *a.* séduisant; attrayant; attractif; **–ive-**

ness *n.* attrait, charme *m.*
attributable *a.* attribuable, imputable
attribute *vt.* attribuer, imputer; — *n.* attribut *m.*
attribution *n.* attribution *f.*
attributive *a.*, — adjective adjectif qualificatif *m.*
attrition *n.* attrition *f.*; usure *f.*
attune *vt.* accorder
auburn *n. & a.* châtain clair *m.*
auction *n.* vente aux enchères *f.*; — *vt.* vendre aux enchères; —eer *n.* commissaire-priseur *m.*; crieur *m.*
audacious *a.* audacieux
audacity *n.* audace *f.*; hardiesse *f.*
audible *a.* distinct (à l'oreille)
audience *n.* auditoire *m.*, assistance *f.* audience *f.*
audiology *n.* audiologie *f.*
audiometer *n.* audiomètre *m.*
audit *n.* vérification de comptes *f.*; — *vt.* vérifier; visiter (un cours universitaire); —or *n.* vérificateur *m.*; (school) visiteur *m.*
audio *a.* (coll.) qui se rapporte au son radiodiffusé d'une émission télévisée
audition *n.* audition *f.*; ouïe *f.*
auditorium *n.* salle *f.*
auditory *a.* auditif
auger *n.* tarière *f.*
augment *vt.* augmenter; — *vi.* s'accroître; —ation *n.* augmentation *f.*; —ative *a.* augmentatif
augur *vt.* augurer; — *n.* augure *m.*
August *n.* août *m.* ˙
august *a.* auguste
aunt *n.* tante *f.*
aura *n.* émanation *f.*; souffle *m.*
aural *a.* de l'oreille
aureomycin *n.* auréomycin *m.*
auricle *n.* auricule *f.*; (anat.) oreillette *f.*
auspices *n. pl.* auspices *m. pl.*
auspicious *a.* propice, favorable
austere *a.* austère, sévère
austerity *n.* austérité *f.*
Australia *n.* Australie *f.*; —n *n. & a.* Australien *m.*
Austria *n.* Autriche *f.*; —n *n. & a.* Autrichien *m.*
authentic *a.* authentique; vrai, véritable; conforme; —ate *vt.* vérifier, certifier; viser; —ity *n.* authenticité *f.*
author *n.* auteur *m.*; —ess *n.* femme auteur *f.*; —ship *n.* paternité (littéraire) *f.*
authoritarian *a. & n.* autoritaire *m.*
authoritative *a.* autoritaire; —ness *n.* autorité *f.*
authority *n.* autorité *f.*; mandat, pouvoir *m.*; on good — de bonne source
authorization *n.* autorisation *f.*

authorize *vt.* autoriser
autobiographer *n.* autobiographe *m.*
autobiographical *a.* autobiographique
autobiography *n.* autobiographie *f.*
autocade *n.* défieé des voitures *m.*
autocrat *n.* autocrate *m.*; –ic *a.* autocratique
autogiro *n.* hélicoptère *m.*
autograph *n.* autographe *m.*; — *vt.* signer
automatic *a.* automatique; — tracking *n.* poursuite automatique *f.*
automation *n.* automation *f.*
automaton *n.* automate *m.*
automobile *n.* automobile *f.*
automotive *a.* automobile
autonomous *a.* autonome
autumn *n.* automne *m.*; –al *a.* automnal
auxiliary *n. & a.* auxiliaire, assistant *m.*
avail *n.* utilité *f.*, secours *m.*; — *vt.* servir; — oneself of se servir de, profiter de; –able *a.* disponible; utilisable; –ibility *n.* disponibilité *f.*
avaricious *a.* avare
avenge *vt.* venger; –r *n.* vengeur *m.*
avenue *n.* avenue *f.*; boulevard *m.*
aver *vt.* affirmer
average *n.* moyenne *f.*; on the — en moyenne; — *vt.* calculer la moyenne; — *vi.* atteindre une moyenne de (vitesse, distance, consommation); — *a.* moyen
averse *a.* contraire, opposé
aversion *n.* aversion *f.*; répugnance *f.*
avert *vt.* détourner, écarter
aviator *n.* aviateur *m.*
avid *a.* avide; –ity *n.* avidité *f.*
avocado *n.* poire d'avocat *f.*
avocation *n.* occupation *f.*; distraction *f.*, délaissement *m.*
avoid *vt.* éviter; –able *a.* évitable; –ance *n.* action d'éviter *f.*
avow *vt.* avouer, confesser; –al *n.* aveu *m.*
await *vt.* attendre
awake *vi.* se réveiller; s'éveiller; — *a.* éveillé; –n *vt.* éveiller, réveiller; –ning *n.* réveil *m.*
award *n.* jugement *m.*; récompense *f.*, prix *m.*; — *vt.* décerner; adjuger
aware *a.* conscient, au courant; –ness *n.* conscience *f.*
awash *a.* à fleur d'eau; surnageant
away *a.* absent; loin; — *adv.* au loin, loin; go — s'en aller; take — enlever; send — renvoyer; right — tout de suite
awe *n.* crainte *f.*, respect *m.*; — *vt.* effrayer, impressionner
awe-inspiring, awesome *a.* impressionnant
awe-struck *a.* effrayé, impressionné

awful *a.* terrible; affreux; imposant

awhile *adv.* un peu, un moment

awkward *a.* gauche; maladroit; (situation) gênant; **-ness** *n.* maladresse *f.*

awl *n.* alène *f.*, poinçon *m.*

awning *n.* tente *f.*; abri *m.*; store *m.*

awry *adv.* de travers

ax, axe *n.* hache *f.*

axiom *n.* axiome *m.*; **-atic** *a.* axiomatique

axis *n.* axe *m.*

axle *n.* essieu *m.*; arbre *m.*

ay, aye *n.* & *adv.* oui *m.*; — *adv.* toujours

Azores *n.* Açores *f. pl.*

azure *n.* azur *m.*; — *a.* azuré, d'azur

B

B.A.: Bachelor of Arts *n.* bachelier ès lettres *m.*

babble *n.* babil *m.*; — *vi.* bavarder, parler avec incohérence; babiller, murmurer; **-r** *n.* babillard *m.*

babbling *a.* babillard; (brook) murmurant; — *n.* babil *m.*

babe *n.* bébé *m.*

babel *n.* tumulte *m.*; confusion *f.*

baboon *n.* babouin *m.*

babushka *n.* fichu (porté à la tête) *m.*

baby *n.* bébé *m.*; — *a.* de bébé; — carriage *n.* landau *m.*, poussette *f.*; — grand piano piano à queue *m.*; **-hood** première enfance *f.*; **-ish** *a.* enfantin; — *vt.* traiter d'enfant; amadouer

baccalaureate *n.* baccalauréat *m.*

bachelor *n.* célibataire, garçon *m.*; (educ.) bachelier *m.*; **-hood** *n.* célibat *m.*; **-'s-button** *n.* (bot.) bluet *m.*; **-'s degree** baccalauréat *m.*

bacillus *n.* bacille *m.*

back *n.* dos *m.*, derrière *f.*; dossier *m.*; verso *m.*; fond *m.*; revers *m.*; — to — dos à dos; behind one's — à l'insu de; — talk (coll.) impertinence, réponse, impertinente *f.*; turn one's — tourner le dos; — *a.* de derrière; dorsal; — door porte de derrière *f.*; — number numéro ancien (d'un journal) *m.*; — payment arriéré *m.*; — seat siege de derrière *m.*; — stairs escalier de service *m.*; **-street** ruelle *f.*; — *adv.* en arrière, à l'arrière; de retour; en retour; — and forth de long en large; (in) — of derrière; bring — rapporter; come — revenir; give — rendre; go — retourner; go — on ne pas tenir (la parole donnée); — *vt.* soutenir, subventionner, seconder; parier pour; mettre un dos à; servir de dos (fond) à; — *vi.* reculer; faire reculer; aller (faire aller) en marche arrière; — down, — out se

dédire; se soustraire (à); — up reculer; **-er** *n.* soutien *m.*; **-ing** *n.* appui *m.*; subvention *f.*

backbite *vt.* calomnier

backboard *n.* dossier *m.*

backbone *n.* épine dorsale *f.*

backbreaking *a.* dur; éreintant

backdrop *n.* toile de fond *f.*

backfire *n.* (engine) contre-allumage *m.*; (firefighting) contre-feu *m.*; — *vi.* pétarder; (fig.) retomber

backgammon *n.* trictrac *m.*

background *n.* fond *m.*

backhanded *a.* donné avec le revers de la main; (fig.) immoral

backlash *n.* contre-coup *m.*

backlog *n.* accummulation de travail *f.* (qui reste à faire)

backpedal *vi.* contre-pédaler; (fig.) reculer

backslide *vi.* retomber

backstage *adv.* dans les coulisses

backstroke *n.* brasse (sur le dos) *f.*

backtrack *vi.* rebrousser chemin

backward *adv.* en arrière, à la renverse; — *a.* arriéré; **-ness** *n.* retard *m.*

backwash *n.* remous *m.*

backwoodsman *n.* homme des forêts, homme des frontières *m.*

bacon *n.* lard *m.*; bacon *m.*

bacteria *n. pl.* bactéries *f. pl.*

bacteriologist *n.* bactériologiste *m.*

bacteriology *n.* bactériologie *f.*

bad *a.* mauvais, méchant; grave, sérieux; from — to worse de mal en pire; too — dommage; — debt mauvaise créance *f.*; **-ly** *adv.* mal; gravement; want **-ly** avoir grande envie de

badge *n.* plaque *f.*; insigne *m.*

badger *n.* blaireau *m.*; — *vt.* harceler

badminton *n.* badminton *m.*

baffle *vt.* confondre, déjouer

bag *n.* sac *m.*; sleeping — sac de couchage *m.*; be left holding the — être dupé; — *vt.* mettre en sac; (hunting) prendre; faire une poche; **-gy** *a.* qui font une poche

bagful *n.* sachée *f.*

baggage *n.* bagage *m.*; to be off bag and — plier bagage; — car fourgon *m.*; — check bulletin des bagages *m.*; excess — excédent de bagages *m.*

Bahamas *n.* Bahamas *m. pl.*

bagpipe *n.* cornemuse *f.*

bail *n.* caution *f.*; be out on — être libre sous caution; put up — se porter caution (pour); — *vt.* cautionner; — out (law) se porter caution pour; (avi.) sauter en parachute; (naut.) écoper

bailiff *n.* huissier *m.*; bailli *m.*

bailiwick *n.* bailliage *m.*; rayon *m.*

bait n. appât m., amorce f.; — vt. amorcer; appâter, leurrer; harceler

bake vt. & vi. cuire au four; faire le pain, boulanger; **half –d** prématuré, pas assez mûri; **–r** n. boulanger m.; **–r's dozen** treize; **–ry** n. boulangerie f.

baking n. cuisson au four f.; — **powder** levure chimique f.; — **soda** bicarbonate de soude m.

balance n. balance f.; équilibre m.; solde d'un compte m.; — **sheet** n. bilan m.; — vt. peser, balancer; équilibrer; — vi. hésiter; **–d** a. équilibré

balancing n. balancement m.; équilibre m.; (com.) solde m.

balcony n. balcon m.; galerie f.

bald a. chauve; nu; **–ness** n. calvitie f.

bale n. balle f. paquet m.; — vt. emballer

balearic a. baléare

baleful a. triste; fatal, funeste

balk vt. désappointer, frustrer; — vi. regimber; hésiter; reculer; **–y** a. rétif: hésitant, récalcitrant

Balkans n. Balkans m. pl.

ball n. balle, boule f., ballon m.; globe m.; bal m.; — **bearing** bille f.; roulement à billes m.; **masked** — bal masqué

ballad n. romance, chanson populaire f.

ballast n. lest m.; (rail.) ballast m.; — vt. lester; (rail.) empierrer

ballerina n. danseuse f.; **prima** — première danseuse f.

ballistic a. balistique; **–s** n. balistique f. — **missile** n. projectile balistique m.

balloon n. ballon m.; aérostat m.; **–ist** n. aérostier m.

ballot n. scrutin m.; bulletin de vote m.; — **box** urne f.; — vi. voter; **–ing** n. vote, scrutin m.

ballroom n. salle de danse f.

ballyhoo n. publicité extravagante f.

balm n. baume m.; (fig.) soulagement m.; **–y** a. balsamique; (coll.) loufoque

balsam n. baume m.

Baltic Sea n. Mer Baltique f.

bamboo n. bambou m.

ban vt. empêcher, interdire; — n. interdiction f.

banal a. banal; **–ity** n. banalité f.

banana n. banane f.; — **tree** bananier m.

band n. lien m.; ruban m.; bande f.; clique f.; musiciens m. pl.; musique, fanfare f.; (mus.) (coll.) orchestre m.; **military** — musique militaire f.; — vt. entourer de bandes, bander; marquer de bandes; **together** se grouper

bandbox n. carton de modiste m.

bandage n. pansement m.; — vt. panser

bandleader n. chef d'orchestre m.

bandstand n. kiosque m.

bandwagon n. char des victorieux m.; majorité victorieuse f.; **climb, jump on the** — suivre la majorité

bandy vt. discuter

bane n. poison m.; ruine f.; **–ful** a. funeste, nuisible

bang n. coup m., tape f.; — vt. rosser; fermer avec bruit; —! pan!

bangle n. bijou, bracelet m.

bangs n. pl. frange f. (de cheveux)

banish vt. bannir, exiler; **–ment** n. bannissement, exil m.

banister n. rampe f.

bank n. digue f.; bord, rivage m.; banc m.; banque f.; — vt. terrasser; déposer (de l'argent dans une banque); (avi.) virer; — **on** compter sur; **–er** n. banquier m.; **–ing** n. actions de banque f. pl.

bankbook n. carnet de banque m.

bank note n. billet de banque m.

bankrupt a. en faillite; — n. banqueroutier m.; **go** — faire banqueroute; — vt. réduire à la faillite; **–cy** n. banqueroute f.

banner n. bannière f.

banquet n. banquet, festin m.; — vi. banqueter

bantamweight n. poids bantam m.

banter n. raillerie, plaisanterie f.; — vt. railler, plaisanter

baptism n. baptême m.; **–al** a. de baptême, baptismal

baptistry n. baptistère m.

baptize vt. baptiser

bar n. barre, barrière f.; (mus.) mesure f.; barreau m.; (fig.) empêchement m.; obstacle m.; **candy** — n. tablette f.; bar m.; **be admitted to the** — être reçu avocat; **prisoner at the** — prisonnier devant le banc des accusés m.; — vt. empêcher, interdire; barrer; excepter; **–red** a. barré, à barreaux; **–ring** prep. sauf

barb n. barbillon m.; **–ed** a. pointu; **–ed wire** fil de fer barbelé m.

Barbados n. Barbade f.

barbarian n. & a. barbare m.

barbaric a. barbare

barbarous a. barbare; **–ness** n. barabarie f.

barbecue vt. faire rôtir en entier; griller à la sauce piquante; — n. pique-nique m., grillade (faite en plein air) f.

barber n. coiffeur m.; — **shop** salon de coiffure m.

barbiturate n. & a. barbiturique m.

bard n. barde, poète m.

bare a. nu, découvert; simple; — vt.

mettre à nu; **–ly** *adv.* à peine; juste

bareback *adv.* à nu

barefaced *a.* impudent, effronté

barefoot(ed) *a.* nu-pieds

bareheaded *a.* nu-tête

barelegged *a.* nu-jambes

bargain *n.* marché, contrat *m.*; bonne affaire *f.*; — **counter** rayon des marchandises soldées *m.*; — *vt. & vi.* marchander

barge *n.* chaland *m.*; péniche *f.*; — *vi.* entrer sans façons

baritone *n.* baryton *m.*

barium *n.* baryum *m.*

bark *n.* écorce *f.*; barque *f.*, bateau *m.*; (dog) aboiement *m.*; — *vi.* aboyer; **–er** aboyeur *m.*; sideshow **–er** barnum *m.*

barley *n.* orge *f.*

barmaid *n.* fille de comptoir *f.*

barn *n.* grange *f.*; écurie, étable *f.*

barnacle *n.* barnache *f.*

barnstorm *vi.* aller en tournée

barnyard *n.* cour, basse-cour *f.*

barometer *n.* baromètre *m.*

barometric *a.* barométrique

baron *n.* baron *m.*; **–ess** *n.* baronne *f.*; **–et** *n.* baronnet *m.*; **–y** *n.* baronnie *f.*

barracks *n.* caserne *f.*

barrage *n.* barrage *m.*

barrel *n.* baril *m.*, barrique *f.*; tonneau *m.*; (gun) canon *m.*; — **organ** orgue de barbarie *m.*; — *vt.* mettre en tonneau

barren *a.* stérile; **–ness** *n.* stérilité *f.*

barricade *n.* barricade *f.*; — *vt.* barricader

barrier *n.* barrière *f.*

barroom *n.* cabaret *m.*

barrow *n.* brouette *f.*

bartender *n.* barman *m.*

barter *vt.* échanger; — *n.* échange *m.*

basal metabolism *n.* métabolisme basique *m.*

basalt *n.* basalte *m.*

base *n.* base *f.*, piédestal *m.*; — *a.* bas, vil; — *vt.* baser; **–ness** *n.* bassesse *f.*

baseball *n.* baseball *m.*

basement *n.* cave *f.*

bash *vt.* (coll.) cogner, assommer

bashful *a.* timide; **–ness** *m.* timidité *f.*

basic *a.* fondamental; basique; — **English** *n.* anglais basique *m.*

basil *n.* (spice) basilic *m.*

basilica *n.* basilique *f.*

basin *n.* bassin *m.*; bol *m.*; cuvette *f.*

basis *n.* base *f.*, fondement *m.*

bask *vt.* se chauffer (au soleil)

basket *n.* panier *m.*, corbeille *f.*; **wastepaper —** *n.* panier *m.*

Basque *n. & a.* Basque *m. & f.*

bas-relief *n.* bas-relief *m.*

bass *n.* (fish) bar *m.*; (mus.) basse *f.*; —

clef clef de fa *f.*; — **drum** grosse caisse *f.*; — **horn** basse *f.*; — **viol** contrebasse *f.*; — *a.* de basse; bas, grave

bassinette *n.* barcelonnette *f.*

bassoon *n.* basson *m.*

basswood *n.* tilleul (d'Amérique) *m.*

bastard *n. & a.* bâtard *m.*; **–ize** *vt.* abâtardir, avilir

baste *vt.* (cooking) arroser; (sewing) faufiler

basting *n.* (cooking) arrosage *m.*; (sewing) faufilure *f.*

bastion *n.* bastion *m.*

bat *n.* chauve-souris *f.*; bâton *m.*; (baseball) batte *f.*; **be at —** tenir la batte; **go to — for** (coll.) appuyer; — *vt.* tenir la batte; battre; **without –ting an eye** sans battre l'œil; (fig.) impassible; **–ter** *n.* joueur qui tient la batte

batch *n.* fournée *f.*; lot *m.*

bath *n.* bain *m.*; **shower —** douche *f.*

bathe *vt.* baigner; — *vi.* se baigner; **–r** *n.* baigneur *m.*

bathhouse *n.* établissement de bains *m.*

bathing *n.* bain *m.*, baignade *f.*; — **beach** plage *f.*; — **suit** costume de bain *m.*; — **trunks** slip de bain, caleçon de bain *m.*

bath mat *n.* descente de bain *f.*

bathrobe *n.* peignoir *m.*

bathroom *n.* salle de bain *f.*

bathtub *n.* baignoire *f.*

baton *n.* bâton (de chef d'orchestre) *m.*

battalion *n.* bataillon *m.*

batter *n.* pâte *f.*; — *vt.* battre; renverser

battering-ram *n.* bélier *m.*

battery *n.* batterie *f.*; pile *f.*; (law) voies de fait *f. pl.*

battle *n.* bataille *f.*, combat *m.*; — *vi.* livrer combat; lutter, se battre

battle-ax *n.* hache d'armes; (coll.) harpie *f.*

battlefield *n.* champ de bataille *m.*

battlement *n.* créneau *m.*

battleship *n.* cuirassé *m.*

bauble *n.* babiole, bagatelle *f.*

Bavaria *n.* Bavière *f.*; **–n** *a. & n.* bavarois *m.*

bawl *vi.* brailler, crier; — **out** réprimander

bay *n.* laurier *m.*; baie *f.* (sea) golfe *m.*; **at —** aux abois; — **window** *n.* fenêtre en saillie *f.*; (coll.) bedaine *f.*; — *vi.* aboyer; — *a.* bai

bayberry *n.* baie *f.*; (tree) laurier *m.*

bayonet *n.* baïonnette *f.*; — *vt.* blesser à coups de baïonnette

bayou *n.* anse *f.*

bazaar *n.* bazar *m.*; vente de charité *f.*

bazooka *n.* (mil.) fusil à fusées antichar *m.*

be *vi.* être, exister; devoir; **so — it** ainsi soit-il; **–ing** *n.* être *m.*; **for the time –ing** pour le moment

beach *n.* rivage *m.*; plage *f.*; grève *f.*; — *vt.* échouer

beachcomber *n.* vagabond des plages *m.*

beachhead *n.* débarquement *m.*; (mil.) tête de pont *f.*

beacon *n.* signal, phare *m.*

bead *n.* grain (de collier) *m.*; perle *f.*; **–s** *n. pl.* (eccl.) chapelet *m.*

beak *n.* bec *m.*; pic *m.*

beaker *n.* verre à expériences *m.*

beam *n.* (arch.) poutre *f.*; (naut.) bau *m.*; travers *m.*; (light) rayon *m.*; (rad.) signal *m.*; — *vi.* rayonner; sourire; **–ing** *a.* radieux; rayonnant

bean *n.* haricot *m.*; **kidney —** haricot de Soissons *m.*; **lima —** fève *f.*; **navy —** haricot *m.*; **string —** haricot vert *m.*

bean pole *n.* perche à fèves *f.*

bear *n.* ours *m.*; (stock market) baissier *m.*; **–ish** *a.* brutal, d'ours; (stocks) favorable à la baisse

bear *vi.* porter; supporter; — *vt.* porter; souffrir; **— a grudge against** en vouloir à; **— down** appuyer; **— in mind** tenir présent à l'esprit; **— witness** témoigner; **–able** *a.* supportable; **–er** *n.* porteur *m.*; **–ing** *n.* mine *f.*; (mech.) roulement *m.*; **get one's –ings** s'orienter; **have –ing** on avoir à faire avec; **lose one's –ings** se perdre

beard *n.* barbe *f.*; **–ed** *a.* barbu; **–less** *a.* imberbe; sans barbe

beast *n.* animal *m.*; bête *f.*; **— of burden** bête de somme *f.*; **–liness** *n.* bestialité, brutalité *f.*; **–ly** *a.* brutal, bestial

beat *n.* coup *m.*; battement *m.*; ronde *f.*; — *vt. & vi.* frapper, battre; vaincre; **— a path** frayer un chemin; **— around the bush** éviter la matière à traiter, esquiver; **— back, — off** repousser; **— up** battre sévèrement; **that –s me** je n'y comprends rien; **–er** *n.* pilon, battoir, batteur *m.*; **–ing** *n.* battement *m.*; raclée *f.*; défaite *f.*

beatify *vt.* béatifier

beatitude *n.* béatitude *f.*

beatnik *n.* bohémien *m.*

beau *n.* beau, galant *m.*

beautician *n.* coiffeur *m.*, coiffeuse *f.*

beautiful *a.* beau (belle)

beautify *vt.* embellir

beauty *n.* beauté *f.*; **— salon, — shop** salon de beauté *m.*; **— spot** tache de beauté *f.*

beaver *n.* castor *m.*

becalm *vt.* accalminer, déventer

because *conj.* parce que; **— of** *prep.* à

cause de

beck *n.* signe de tête *m.*; **be at one's — (and call)** être aux ordres de quelqu'un

beckon *vi.* faire un signe

become *vi.* devenir; — *vt.* convenir à; **what has — of him?** qu'est-ce qu'il est devenu?

becoming *a.* convenable, joli

bed *n.* lit *m.*; **to go to — se coucher; to put to —** coucher; **flower — plate-bande** *f.*; **folding —** lit escamotable *m.*; **four-poster —** lit à quenouilles *m.*; **mineral —** gisement *m.*; **oyster —** parc d'huîtres *m.*; **road — encaissement** *m.*; — *vt.* coucher; **— down** coucher; se coucher

bedbug *n.* punaise *f.*

bedding *n.* literie *f.*

bedeck *vt.* parer, orner

bedevil *vt.* ensorceler, harceler

bedfellow *n.* camarade de lit *m.*

bed head *n.* chevet *m.*

bedjacket *n.* liseuse *f.*

bedlam *n.* tumulte *m.*

bedpan *n.* bassin de lit *m.*

bedpost *n.* pied de lit *m.*

bedraggled *a.* crotté; échevelé

bedridden *a.* alité

bedrock *n.* roche de fond *f.*

bedroom *n.* chambre à coucher *f.*

bedside *n.* bord du lit *m.*

bedspread *n.* dessus de lit *m.*

bedspring *n.* sommier *m.*

bedstead *n.* bois de lit *m.*

bedtime *n.* heure de coucher *f.*

bee *n.* abeille *f.*; **spelling — concours** d'orthographe *m.*

beef *n.* bœuf *f.*; **— tea** consommé *m.*; **roast —** rosbif, rôti de bœuf *m.*

beefsteak *n.* biftek, steak *m.*

beehive *n.* ruche *f.*

beekeeper *n.* apiculteur *m.*

beeline *n.* route la plus courte *f.*

beer *n.* bière *f.*

beeswax *n.* cire d'abeille *f.*

beet *n.* betterave *f.*; **— sugar** sucre de betterave *m.*; **sugar —** betterave à sucre *f.*

beetle *n.* scarabée *m.*; coléoptère *m.*

beetle-browed *a.* à sourcils épais

befall *vi.* arriver, survenir

befit *vt.* convenir à, être propre à; **–ting** *a.* convenable

befog *vt.* obscurcir

before *adv.* avant, auparavant; en avant; **the day —** la veille *f.*; **the evening —** la veille au soir *f.*; — *prep.* avant; devant; **the day — yesterday** l'avant-veille *f.*; — *conj.* avant que

beforehand *adv.* d'avance, préalablement

auparavant
befoul *vt.* souiller, salir
befriend *vt.* venir en aide à; traiter en ami
beg *vt.* mendier; prier, supplier; — *vi.* mendier; **I** — **of you!** je vous en prie!, de grâce!; –**gar** *n.* mendiant, gueux *m.*: –**ging** *n.* mendicité *f.*
beget *vt.* engendrer
begin *vt. & vi.* commencer; débuter; se mettre à; **to** — **with** tout d'abord; –**ner** *n.* commençant, débutant *m.*; novice *m. & f.*; –**ning** *n.* commencement, début *m.*, origine *f.*; **in the** –**ning** au commencement
begrudge *vt.* envier; donner à contre-cœur
begrudgingly *adv.* à contre-cœur
beguile *vt.* tromper; charmer
behalf *n.* faveur, part *f.*; **on** — **of** au nom de, de la part de
behave *vi.* se conduire, se comporter; être sage
behavior *n.* conduite, tenue *f.*, comportement *m.*
behead *vt.* décapiter; –**ing** *n.* décapitation *f.*
behest *n.* ordre *m.*; demande *f.*
behind *adv.* derrière, par derrière; en retard; **be** — être en retard; **fall** — traîner en arrière; — *prep.* derrière; en arrière de
behold *vt.* voir, contempler
behoove *vt.* convenir
belabor *vt.* rosser, battre; trop insister sur
belated *a.* attardé; tardif
belch *vi.* éructer; — *n.* éructation *f.*
beleaguer *vt.* cerner; investir
belfry *n.* beffroi, clocher *m.*
Belgian *a. & n.* belge *m. & f.*
Belgian East Africa *n.* Ruanda-Urundi *m.*
Belgium *n.* Belgique *f.*
belie *vt.* démentir
belief *n.* croyance, foi *f.*; **to the best of my** — autant que je sache
believable *a.* croyable
believe *vt. & vi.* croire, penser; **make** — faire semblant; –**r** *n.* croyant *m.*
belittle *vt.* déprécier
bell *n.* cloche, clochette *f.*; (house) sonnette *f.*; — *vt.* attacher un grelot à
bellboy, bellhop *n.* chasseur *m.*; garçon d'hôtel *m.*
belle *n.* beauté *f.*
bell glass, bell jar *n.* cloche (de verre) *f.*
belligerent *a. & n.* belligérant *m.*
bellow *vi.* beugler, mugir; — *n.* beuglement, mugissement *m.*
bellows *n. pl.* soufflet *m.*
bellpull *n.* cordon de sonnette *m.*

bell tower *n.* campanile, clocher *m.*
bellwether *n.* sonnailler *m.*
belly *n.* ventre *m.*; –**ful** *n.* rassasiement, soûl *m.*
bellyband *n.* (horse) sous-ventrière; (baby) brassière *f.*
belong *vi.* appartenir (à), être (à); faire partie (de); –**ings** *n. pl.* biens, effets *m. pl.*
beloved *a.* bien-aimé, chéri
below *adv.* en bas, (au) dessous; ci-dessous, ci-après; — *prep.* au dessous de, sous
belt *n.* ceinture *f.*; zone *f.*; **transmission** — courroie *f.*; — *vt.* ceindre, entourer; –**ed** *a.* à ceinture; –**ing** *n.* ceinture *f.*
bemoan *vt.* déplorer
bench *n.* banc *m.*, banquette *f.*; (law) siège *m.*; magistrature *f.*
bend *n.* courbure *f.*; courbe *f.*; coude, tournant *m.*; — *vt. & vi.* courber; plier, fléchir; tourner; — **down** se courber, se baisser
bends *n. pl.* (coll.) mal des caissons *m.*
beneath *adv.* en bas, (au-) dessous; — *prep.* au-dessous de, sous
benedictine *n.* (monk) bénédictin *m.*; (liqueur) bénédictine *f.*
benediction *n.* bénédiction *f.*
benefaction *n.* bienfait *m.*
benefactor *n.* bienfaiteur *m.*
benefactress *n.* bienfaitrice *f.*
beneficence *n.* bienfaisance *f.*
beneficent *a.* bienfaisant
beneficial *a.* avantageux, profitable; salutaire
beneficiary *n.* bénéficiaire *m. & f.*
benefit *n.* avantage, profit *m.*; bénéfice *m.*; — *vt.* être avantageux, profiter à; bénéficier
benevolence *n.* bienveillance *f.*; bienfait *m.*
benevolent *a.* bienveillant; charitable; bienfaisant; –**ly** *adv.* avec bienveillance
benign *a.* bénin, bénigne
benignant *a.* bienveillant; bénin
bent *n.* penchant *m.*; inclination *f.*; — *a.* courbé; fléchi; résolu, déterminé
benumb *vt.* engourdir
benzine *n.* benzine *f.*
bequeath *vt.* léguer
bequest *n.* legs *m.*
berate *vt.* gronder
bereave *vt.* priver; –**d** *a. & n.* affligé *m.*; –**ment** *n.* deuil *m.*
Bermuda *n.* Bermudes *m. pl.*
berry *n.* baie *f.*; raisin *m.*; grain *m.*
berserk *a.* forcené, affolé
berth *n.* couchette *f.*; emplacement *m.*
beseech *vt.* supplier; –**ing** *a.* suppliant

beset *vt.* assiéger, assaillir
beside *prep.* à côté de, auprès de; **be —**
oneself être hors de soi; être transporté;
—s *adv.* en outre, d'ailleurs, en plus
besiege *vt.* assiéger; **—r** *n.* assiégeant *m.*
besmear *vt.* barbouiller, enduire
besmirch *vt.* souiller, salir
best *a.* le meilleur, la meilleure; **— man**
témoin *m.*; **do one's —** faire de son
mieux; **get the — of it** l'emporter;
avoir le dessus; **make the — of** s'accomoder de; **— adv.** le mieux; **at —**
pour dire le mieux; **— vt.** l'emporter sur
bestial *a.* bestial; **–ity** *n.* bestialité *f.*
bestow *vt.* donner, accorder; conférer; **–al**
n. don *m.*, donation *f.*
best seller *n.* livre à gros tirage *m.*
bet *n.* pari *m.*, gageure *f.*; **— vt.** parier;
–ting *n.* paris *m. pl.*; **–tor** *n.* parieur *m.*
beta particle *n.* particule bêta *f.*
betray *vt.* trahir; révéler; **–al** *n.* trahison
f.; révélation *f.*; **–er** *n.* traître *m.*;
traîtresse *f.*
betroth *vt.* fiancer; **–al** *n.* fiançailles *f. pl.*
better *a.* meilleur; supérieur; **— adv.**
mieux; **so much the —** tant mieux;
be — aller mieux; **get —** guérir;
s'améliorer; **get the — of** l'emporter
sur; **it is —** il vaut mieux; **think — of**
se raviser; **— vt.** améliorer; **— vi.**
s'améliorer; **–ment** *n.* amélioration *f.*
between *prep.* entre; **— (us)** entre nous
bevel *adj.* en biseau; **— vt.** couper en
biseau, biaiser; **–ed** *a.* coupé en biseau
beverage *n.* breuvage *m.*, boisson *f.*
bevy *n.* troupe, bande *f.*; (quail) volée *f.*
bewail *vt.* pleurer, regretter
beware *vi.* se garder de, se méfier de
bewilder *vt.* confondre, égarer; **–ed** *a.* confondu, abasourdi; **–ment** *n.* abasourdis-
sement, trouble *m.*
bewitch *vt.* ensorceler, enchanter; **–ing** *a.*
enchanteur; ravissant
beyond *adv.* au delà; **— prep.** au delà de;
be —, go — dépasser; **it is — me** je n'y
comprends rien; **— (a) doubt** hors de
doute; **— n.** au-delà *m.*
B-girl *n.* entremetteuse *f.*
biannual *a.* semi-annuel
bias *n.* biais *m.*; penchant *m.*; prévention
f., préjugé *m.*; **on the —** en biais, de
biais; **— vt.** prévenir; **–ed** *a.* prédisposé,
partial
bib *n.* bavette *f.*
Bible *n.* Bible *f.*
biblical *a.* biblique
bibliographer *n.* bibliographe *m.*
bibliography *n.* bibliographie *f.*
bicarbonate *n.* bicarbonate *m.*; **— of soda**
bicarbonate de soude *m.*

biceps *n.* biceps *m.*
bicker *vi.* se quereller, disputer; **–ing** *a.*
querelleur; **–ing** *n.* querelle(s) *f.* (*pl.*)
bicuspid *n.* prémolaire *f.*
bicycle *n.* bicyclette *f.*; vélo *m.*; **— vi.**
faire de la bicyclette; aller à bicyclette
bicycling *n.* cyclisme *m.*
bicyclist *n.* cycliste *m. & f.*
bid *n.* enchère, offre *f.*; (cards) demande
f.; **— vt.** commander, ordonner; dire;
offrir; (cards) demander; **— vi.** faire
une offre; **–der** *n.* offrant, enchérisseur
m.; **–ding** *n.* commandement ordre *m.*;
enchères *f. pl.*
bide *vt.* attendre
biennial *a.* bisannuel
bier *n.* cercueil *m.*
bifocal *a.* bifocal
big *a.* gros, grand; **get –(ger)** grossir;
grandir; **talk —** faire l'important; **–ness**
n. grosseur *f.*; grandeur *f.*; **— wheel**
(coll.) gros bonnet *m.*
bigamist *n.* bigame *m. & f.*
bigamy *n.* bigamie *f.*
Big Dipper *n.* Grande Ourse *f.*
bigot *n.* sectaire *m. & f.*; fanatique *m. & f.*;
bigot *m.*, bigote *f.*; **–ed** *a.* fanatique;
étroit; **–ry** *n.* fanatisme *m.*; étroitesse *f.*
bike *n.* bécane *f.*, vélo *m.*
bilateral *a.* bilatéral
bilge *n.* sentine *f.*; **— water** eau de cale *f.*
bilingual *a.* bilingue
bilious *a.* bilieux
bilk *vt.* tromper, escroquer
bill *n.* (bird) bec *m.*; (com.) facture, note
f.; (restaurant) addition *f.*; affiche *f.*,
placard *m.*; (law) projet de loi *m.*; **—**
of fare carte *f.*; **— of lading** connaissement *m.*; **— of sale** facture *f.*, acte de
vente *m.*; **post no –s** défense d'afficher;
— vt. facturer
billboard *n.* panneau d'affichage *m.*;
enseigne *f.*
billet *n.* billet, logement *m.*; **— vt.** loger,
cantonner
billfold *n.* portefeuille *m.*
billiard ball *n.* bille *f.*
billiards *n. pl.* billard *m.*
billion *n.* milliard *m.*
billionaire *n.* milliardaire *m.*
billow *n.* vague *f.*, flot *m.*; **— vi.** ondoyer;
–y *a.* onduleux, ondoyant
billy (stick) *n.* bâton d'agent de police *m.*
billy goat *n.* (coll.) bouc *m.*
bimonthly *a.* bimensuel
bin *n.* huche *f.*; coffre *m.*
binary *a.* binaire
binaural *a.* stéréophonique
bind *vt.* lier; relier; obliger; bander;
attacher; **–er** lieur *m.*; relieur *m.*;

–ery *n.* atelier de reliure *m.*; –ing *a.* obligatoire; (med.) astringent; –ing *n.* reliure *f.*
binoculars *n. pl.* jumelle(s) *f. pl.*
binomial *a. & n.* binôme *m.*
biochemistry *n.* biochimie *f.*
biogenetics *n.* biogénétique *f.*
biogenesis *n.* biogenèse *f.*
biographer *n.* biographe *m.*
biographical *a.* biographique
biography *n.* biographie *f.*
biological *a.* biologique; — **warfare** guerre bactériologique *f.*
biologist *n.* biologiste *m.*
biology *n.* biologie *f.*
biophysical *a.* biophysique
bipartisan *a.* (pol.) dit d'une politique approuvée par les deux partis
biped *n.* bipede *m.*
birch *n.* bouleau *m.*; verge *f.*
bird *n.* oiseau *m.*; — **cage** *n.* cage *f.*
bird's-eye view *n.* vue à vol d'oiseau *f.*
birth *n.* naissance *f.*; **give** — **to** donner naissance à, donner le jour à, mettre au monde; — **certificate** acte de naissance *m.*; — **control** *n.* limitation sur la natalité *f.*; — **rate** natalité *f.*
birthday *n.* anniversaire *m.*
birthmark *n.* tache, envie *f.*
birthplace *n.* lieu de naissance *m.*
birthright *n.* droit de naissance *m.*
biscuit *n.* biscuit *m.*; (genre de) petit pain *m.* (à la levure chimique)
bisect *vt.* couper en deux
bishop *n.* évêque *m.*; (chess) fou *m.*; –ric *n.* évêché *m.*
bit *n.* (bridle) mors *m.*; (drill) mèche *f.*; morceau, bout, brin *m.*; **a** — **(of)** un peu (de); — **by** — peu à peu, petit à petit
bitch *n.* chienne *f.*; (coll.) garce *f.*
bite *n.* bouchée *f.*; morsure, piqûre *f.*; (fishing) touche *f.*; –*vt.* mordre, piquer
biting *a.* mordant, piquant
bitter *a.* amer; aigre, âpre; acerbe; –ness *n.* amertume *f.*; acrimonie *f.*, rancune *f.*
bittersweet *a.* aigre-doux
bituminous *a.* bitumineux; — **coal** houille *f.*
biweekly *a.* bihebdomadaire; — *adv.* deux fois par mois
black *a.* noir; sombre; — **eye** œil poché *m.*; — **and blue** (tout) meurtri; — **market** marché noir *m.*; — **sheep** brebis galeuse *f.*; — *n.* noir *m.*; **in** — **and white** par écrit; **in the** — (com.) bénéficiaire; — *vi. & vt.* noircir; –**en** *vt.* noircir; obscurcir; calomnier; –**ish** *a.* noirâtre; –**ness** *n.* noirceur *f.*; obscurité *f.*
blackball *vt.* blackbouler

blackberry *n.* mûre *f.*; mûre de ronce *f.*; (bush) mûrier sauvage *m.*, ronce *f.*
blackbird *n.* merle *m.*
blackboard *n.* tableau noir *m.*
blackguard *n.* goujat, vaurien *m.*
blackhead *n.* point noir *m.*
blackjack *n.* assommoir *m.*; (cards) vingt-et-un *m.*
black list *n.* index *m.*, liste des personnes interdites *f.*; — *vt.* boycotter, interdire
blackmail *n.* chantage *m.*; — *vt.* faire chanter
blackout *n.* obscurcissement *m.*; blackout, camouflage des lumières *m.*
blacksmith *n.* forgeron *m.*
bladder *n.* vessie *f.*
blade *n.* lame *f.*; brin (d'herbe) *m.*; (mech.) aile, ailette, pale *f.*; (man) gaillard *m.*
blamable *a.* blâmable, coupable
blame *n.* blâme *m.*; reproches *m. pl.*; faute *f.*; — *vt.* blâmer, reprocher; **s'en prendre (à)**; –**less** *a.* innocent, irréprochable; –**worthy** *a.* blâmable
blanch *vt.* blanchir; — *vi.* pâlir
bland *a.* doux; affable; narquois; –ness *n.* douceur *f.*
blandish *vt.* flatter; –**ment** *n.* flatterie *f.*
blank *a.* blanc (blanche); — *n.* blanc, vide *m.*; lacune *f.*; formule *f.*
blanket *n.* couverture *f.*; — *a.* général; — *vt.* envelopper, couvrir
blare *vi.* sonner; — *n.* sonnerie *f.*; bruit *m.*
blaspheme *vt. & vi.* blasphémer; –**r** *n.* blasphémateur *m.*
blasphemous *a.* blasphémateur; blasphématoire
blasphemy *n.* blasphème *m.*
blast *n.* bouffée *f.*; souffle *m.*; jet *m.*; charge *f.*; coup *m.*; **full** — (fig.) en pleine activité; — **furnace** haut fourneau *m.*; — *vt.* détruire; faire sauter; foudroyer; –**ing** *n.* abattage à la poudre *m.*
blatant *a.* vulgaire; criant
blaze *n.* flamme *f.*, incendie *m.*; feu *m.*; — *vi.* flamber; flamboyer; — **a trail** tracer un chemin; frayer un chemin
blazer *n.* jacquette *f.*, veston *m.*
blazing *a.* en feu, embrasé; flambant
bleach *vt.* blanchir; — *n.* blanchiment *m.*; eau de Javel *f.*
bleachers *n.* gradins *m. pl.*
bleak *a.* froid, désert, triste, morne; –ness *n.* tristesse *f.*; nudité *f.*
bleary *a.* chassieux; larmoyant
bleat *vi.* bêler; –**ing** *n.* bêlement *m.*
bleed *vt. & vi.* saigner; –**ing** *a.* saignant; –**ing** *n.* saignement *m.*; saignée *f.*

blemish n. tache f.; défaut m.; — vt. tacher; souiller

blend n. mélange m.; — vt. mêler, mélanger

bless vt. bénir; **–ed** a. saint; bienheureux; béni; **–ing** n. bénédiction f.

blight n. influence néfaste f.; (agr.) rouille f.; — vt. flétrir, frustrer, anéantir

blimp n. dirigeable m.

blind a. aveugle; — **alley** cul-de-sac m.; — **flying** n. vol sans visibilité, vol à l'aveuglette m.; — **person** aveugle m. & f.; **–ly** adv. aveuglément; — vt. aveugler; éblouir; — n. store m.; jalousie, persienne f.; (fig.) feinte f., subterfuge m.; **–ness** n. cécité f.; (fig.) aveuglement m.

blindfold n. bande f.; — vt. bander les yeux; **–(ed)** a. & adv. les yeux bandés

blink n. clignotement m.; — vi. cligner, clignoter, battre (des yeux); **–er** n. feu clignotant m.; (horses) œillère f.

bliss n. félicité f.; **–ful** a. heureux, bienheureux; **–fullness** n. béatitude, félicité f.

blister n. ampoule f.; cloque f.; boursouflure f.; — vi. se couvrir d'ampoules

blithe a. gai, heureux

blizzard n. tourmente de neige f.

bloat vt. & vi. enfler, bouffir; **–ed** a. enflé; congestionné

blob n. pâté (d'encre) m.; goutte f.

block n. bloc m.; pâté de maisons m.; (com.) tranche f.; (toy) cube m.; — vt. bloquer, barrer; — **up** boucher; murer

blockade n. blocage m.; — vt. bloquer

blockhead n. sot, imbécile m.

blood n. sang m.; parenté f.; race f.; — **bank** réserve de sang f.; — **donor** donneur de sang m.; — **orange** sanguin; — **plasma** plasma du sang m.; — **platelet** (med.) plaquette sanguine f.; — **poisoning** septicémie f.; — **pressure** tension artérielle f.; **high** — **pressure** hypertension f.; — **stream** cours du sang m.; — **vessel** vaisseau sanguin m.; **in cold** — de sang-froid

bloodhound n. limier m.

bloodshed n. effusion de sang f.; carnage m.

bloodshot a. injecté de sang; éraillé

bloodstain n. tache de sang f.; **–ed** a. taché de sang

bloodthirsty a. sanguinaire m.

blood type n. groupe sanguin

blood-type vt. classer selon le groupe sanguin

bloody a. sanglant

bloom n. fleur f.; épanouissement m.; **in** — en fleur, épanoui; — vi. fleurir; **–ing**

a. fleurissant, florissant; **–ing** n. fleuraison, floraison f.

bloomers n. pl. (sorte de) culotte de femme f.

blooper n. (coll.) gaffe, bévue f.

blossom n. fleur f.; — vi. fleurir

blot n. tache d'encre f.; pâté m.; — vt. tacher; sécher; — vi. boire; **–ter** n. buvard m.; **–ting paper** papier buvard m.

blotch n. pustule f.; tache f.; **–y** a. brouillé; tacheté

blouse n. blouse f.; corsage m.

blow n. coup m.; **at a** — d'un coup; **come to –s** en venir aux coups; — vi. souffler; — **one's nose** se moucher; — **away** emporter; — **out** (auto.) éclater; — **over** passer; — **up** éclater, sauter; (coll.) se mettre en colère; (phot.) agrandir; **–er** n. ventilateur m.

blowout n. (auto.) crevaison f.

blowpipe n. chalumeau m.

blowtorch n. lampe à braser f.

blubber n. graisse de baleine f.; — vi. pleurnicher

bludgeon n. assommer, rouer de coups; — n. assommoir m.; massue, matraque f.

blue a. bleu; (fig.) triste, mélancolique; — **cheese** espèce de fromage genre roquefort m.; — **chips** (stocks) premières valeurs f. pl.; — n. bleu m.; azur m.; **light** — bleu clair; **navy** — bleu marine; **–s** n. mélancolie f.; (mus.) blues m. pl.; — vt. & vi. bleuir

blueberry n. airelle myrtille f.

bluebird n. oiseau bleu m.

blue-eyed a. aux yeux bleus

blueprint n. négatif, bleu m.; plan m.

bluff a. escarpé; — n. falaise f.; à-pic m.; bluff m.; — vt. bluffer

bluing, blueing n. bleu m.

bluish a. bleuâtre

blunder n. bévue, gaffe f.; — vi. faire une bévue, gaffer; — **into** se heuter contre; **–ing** a. maladroit

blunt a. émoussé; brusque; — vt. émousser

blur n. tache f.; ternissure f.; — vt. barbouiller; brouiller; rendre indistinct

blurb n. annonce publicitaire f.

blurt vt., — **out** laisser échapper

blush n. rougeur f.; — vi. rougir

bluster vi. tempêter, tonner; — n. fracas, tapage m.; emportement m.

boar n. cochon mâle, verrat m.; **wild** — sanglier m.

board n. planche f.; table f.; tableau m.; (chess) tablier m.; commission f.; **ironing** — planche à repasser f.; **room and** — pension f.; — **of directors** conseil d'administration m.; **on** — à

bord; — *vi.* être en pension, prendre la pension; — *vt.* s'embarquer; monter dans; — **up** boucher; **-er** *n.* pensionnaire *m.* & *f.*; (schools) interne *m.* & *f.*
boardinghouse *n.* pension *f.*
boardwalk *n.* promenade (faite de planches) au bord de la mer *f.*
boast *n.* vanterie *f.*; — *vi.* se vanter (de); **-ful** *a.* arrogant, vantard; **-ing** *n.* jactance *f.*
boat *n.* bateau *m.*; barque *f.*; canot *m.*; embarcation *f.*; **-ing** *n.* canotage *m.*; **to go -ing** faire du canotage, canoter
boat hook *n.* gaffe *f.*
boathouse *n.* hangar, garage *m.*
boatload *n.* batelée *f.*
boatman *n.* batelier *m.*
boat race *n.* régate *f.*
boatswain *n.* maître d'équipage *m.*
bob *vi.* s'agiter, danser; **-bed** *a.* coupé court
bobbin *n.* bobine *f.*
bobby pin *n.* épingle à cheveux *f.*
bobby-socks *n. pl.* chaussettes courtes *f. pl.*
bobby-soxer *n.* zazou *m.*
bobsled, bobsleigh *n.* bob *m.*
bode *vt.* & *vi.* présager
bodily *a.* corporel, physique; — *adv.* corporellement; en corps
body *n.* corps *m.*; cadavre *m.*; substance *f.*; — (auto.) carrosserie *f.*
bodyguard *n.* garde du corps *m.*
bog *n.* marécage *m.*; fondrière *f.*; — *vt.* enliser; — **(down)** *vi.* s'enliser
bogus *a.* faux, fausse; simulé
Bohemia *n.* Bohême; **-n** *a.* & *n.* bohémien *m.*
boil *n.* ébullition *f.*; (med.) furoncle, clou *m.*; — *vi.* bouillir, bouillonner; — *vt.* faire bouillir; **-er** *n.* chaudière *f.*; **-ing** *a.* bouillant; **-ing** *n.* ébullition *f.*, bouillonnement *m.*; **-ing point** point d'ébullition *m.*
boilermaker *n.* chaudronnier *m.*
boisterous *a.* bruyant, débordant; **-ly** *adv.* bruyamment
bold *a.* audacieux, téméraire; hardi; effronté; **-ness** *n.* audace, témérité, hardiesse, effronterie *f.*
boldface (type) *n.* caractères gras *m. pl.*
bold-faced *a.* effronté
Bolivia *n.* Bolivie *f.*
boll weevil *n.* hélothis *m.*
Bolshevik *a.* & *n.* bolchevique *m.* & *f.*
bolster *n.* traversin *m.*; — *vt.* soutenir
bolt *n.* verrou, pêne *m.*; rouleau, coupon *m.*; coup de foudre *m.*; **screw** — boulon *m.* (à écrou); **thunder** — fuite *f.*; — *vt.* verrouiller; (food) gober; — *vi.* dé-

camper
bomb *n.* bombe *f.*; — **shelter** abri-voûte *m.*; — *vt.* bombarder; **-er** *n.* bombardier *m.*; **-ing** *n.* bombardement *m.*
bombardier *n.* bombardier *m.*
bombardment *n.* bombardement *m.*
bombast *n.* boursouflage *m.*; enflure *f.*; **-ic** *a.* boursouflé; enflé
bombproof *a.* à l'épreuve des bombes
bombshell *n.* (fig.) sensation *f.*
bombsight *n.* viseur de bombardement, appareil de visée *m.*
bonanza *n.* aubaine *f.*; trouvaille *f.*
bond *n.* lien *m.*; obligation *f.*; (com.) bon *m.*; titre *m.*; **in** — (com.) à l'entrepôt; — *vt.* (com.) entreposer, mettre à l'entrepôt; **-age** *n.* esclavage *m.*; servitude *f.*
bondholder *n.* obligataire *m.* & *f.*
bondsman *n.* (law) répondant *m.*
bone *n.* os *m.*; (fish) arête *f.*; **have a** — **to pick** avoir maille à partir; — *vt.* désosser; **-less** *a.* désossé, sans os, sans arêtes
bonfire *n.* feu de joie *m.*
bonnet *n.* bonnet, chapeau *m.*
bonus *n.* boni *m.*; prime *f.*; gratification *f.*
bony *a.* osseux; décharné
booby *n.* nigaud *m.*; — **prize** prix qu'on donne au plus mauvais joueur *m.*; — **trap** attrape-nigaud *m.*
book *n.* livre *m.*; bouquin *m.*; livret *m.*; carnet *m.*; **telephone** — annuaire *m.*; — **ends** serre-livres *m. pl.*; — **review** compte rendu *m.*; — *vt.* louer, réserver; **-ing** *n.* réservation *f.*; (theat.) location *f.*
bookbinder *n.* relieur *m.*
bookcase *n.* bibliothèque *f.*; étagère *f.*
bookkeeper *n.* comptable *m.* & *f.*
bookkeeping *n.* comptabilité *f.*
booklet *n.* livret *m.*; opuscule *m*; brochure *f.*
bookmark *n.* signet *m.*
bookmobile *n.* bibliobus *m.*
bookseller *n.* libraire *m.* & *f.*
bookshelf *n.* étagère *f.*, rayon (de bibliothèque) *m.*
bookshop, bookstore *n.* librairie *f.*
bookworm *n.* ciron *m.*; (fig.) bibliomane, mangeur de livres *m.*
boom *n.* barrage *m.*; (naut.) bout-dehors, tangon, mât de charge *m.*; (avi.) longeron *m.*; retentissement *m.*; (com.) boom *m.*; vogue *f.*; **sonic** — grondement du son *m.*; — *vi.* retentir, gronder; (com.) être en hausse, prospérer; **-ing** *a.* (com.) florissant
boomerang *n.* boumerang *m.*; — *vi.* revenir vers soi; réagir sur soi

boon *n.* don *m.*, faveur *f.*
boor *n.* rustre *m.*; goujat *m.*; **–ish** *a.* grossier, rustre; **–ishness** *n.* grossièreté, rusticité *f.*
boost *n.* relèvement *m.* aide *f.*; — *vt.* soulever par derrière; faire du battage, de la réclame pour; (elec.) survolter; **–er** *n.* réclamiste *m.*; (elec.) survolteur *m.*; **–er rocket** fusée de lancement, fusée porteuse *f.*; **–er shot** (med.) piqûre de rappel *f.*; **–ing** *n.* battage *m.*, réclame *f.*
boot *n.* botte, bottine *f.*; **to** — *adv.* en sus; — *vt.* botter
bootee *n.* chausson de bébé *m.*
bootblack *n.* cireur *m.*
booth *n.* tente *f.*; cabine *f.*
bootie *n.* chausson de bébé *m.*
bootleg *a.* de contrebande; — *vt.* faire la contrebande (de l'alcool); **–ger** *n.* contrebandier *m.*; **–ging** *n.* contrebande
booty *n.* butin *m.*
border *n.* bord *m.*, bordure *f.*; frontière *f.*; galon *m.*; — *vi.* border; — **on** toucher; approcher
borderline *n.* frontière *f.*; — *a.* limite
bore *n.* trou *m.*; calibre *m.*; (person) raseur *m.*; ennui *m.*; — *vt.* percer; sonder; ennuyer, raser; **–dom** *n.* ennui
boric *a.* borique
boring *a.* ennuyant, ennuyeux; (coll.) assommant
born, to be — naître; — *a.* né
boron *n.* bore *m.*
borough *n.* bourg *m.*
borrow *vt.* emprunter; **–er** *n.* emprunteur *m.*
bosom *n.* sein *m.*; poitrine *f.*; (fig.) giron *m.*
boss *n.* chef, patron *m.*; — *vt.* diriger, régenter; **–y** *a.* autoritaire
botanical *a.* botanique
botanist *n.* botaniste *m.*
botany *n.* botanique *f.*
botch *vt.* saboter; ravauder; mal faire
both *a.* les deux; — *pron.* tous les deux; — . . . **and** et . . . et
bother *n.* ennui *m.*; — *vt.* déranger; ennuyer, gêner; **–some** *a.* importun
bottle *n.* bouteille *f.*; bocal *m.*; — **brush** *n.* goupillon *m.*; **nursing** — biberon *m.*; — *vt.* mettre en bouteille; — **up** embouteiller
bottleneck *n.* goulot *m.*; embouteillage *m.*
bottling *n.* mise en bouteilles *f.*
bottom *n.* fond *m.*; bas *m.*; dessous *m.*; **at** — au fond; — **dollar** dernier sou *m.*; **–less** *a.* sans fond
bough *n.* rameau *m.*
boulder *n.* bloc, rocher *m.*
bounce *n.* bond, rebond *m.*; — *vi.*

rebondir; — *vt.* faire rebondir; (coll.) flanquer à la porte; **–r** *n.* (coll.) agent, souteneur *m.*
bound *n.* bornes, limites *f.* *pl.*; bond, saut *m.*; **out of –s** hors des limites; défendu; — *vi.* borner, limiter; sauter, bondir; — *a.* lié; engagé, obligé; — **for en route** pour; **–less** *a.* sans bornes; illimité
boundary *n.* borne, limite *f.*; frontière *f.*
bounteous, bountiful *a.* bienfaisant; généreux
bounty *n.* bonté, munificence *f.*; prime, subvention *f.*
bouquet *n.* bouquet *m.*
bout *n.* (sport) match, assaut *m.*; épreuve *f.*
bovine *a.* bovin
bow *n.* arc *m.*; (mus.) archet *m.*; (saddle) arçon *m.*; (ribbon) nœud *m.*; révérence *f.*; inclinaison *f.*; (naut.) avant *m.*; — **tie** nœud papillon *m.*; — *vi.* s'incliner; — *vt.* courber
bowels *n.* *pl.* entrailles *f.* *pl.*
bower *n.* tonnelle *f.*, berceau *m.*
bowie-knife *n.* couteau-poignard *m.*
bowl *n.* bol *m.*; (spoon) cuilleron *m.*; (pipe) fourneau *m.*; (stadium) stade *m.*; — *vt.* jeter, lancer; — *vi.* jouer aux boules; (U.S.) jouer aux quilles; — **over** renverser; **–er** *n.* joueur (de boules, de quilles) *m.*; chapeau melon *m.*; **–ing** *n.* jeu de boules *m.*; **–ing pin** *n.* quille *f.*
bowlegged *a.* arqué, bancal; **to be** — avoir les jambes arquées
bowman *n.* archer *m.*
bowsprit *n.* beaupré *m.*
bowstring *n.* corde d'arc *f.*; cordon *m.*
box *n.* boîte *f.*; coffre, coffret *m.*; carton *m.*; caisse *f.*; cabine *f.*; (theat.) loge, baignoire *f.*; — **on the ear** claque *f.*; — **camera** détective *m.*; — **office** bureau de location *m.*; — *vt.* mettre en boîte; emboîter, encartonner; claquer; — *vt.* & *vi.* (sports) boxer; **–er** *n.* boxeur *m.*; **–ing** *n.* boxe *f.*
boxcar *n.* wagon de marchandises *m.*
boy *n.* garçon, enfant *m.*; gamin *m.*; **scout** scout, éclaireur *m.*; **–hood** *n.* enfance *f.*; **–ish** *a.* d'enfant, de garçon; enfantin
boycott *n.* boycottage *m.*; — *vt.* boycotter
brace *n.* attache *f.*, lien *m.*; écharpe *f.*; paire *f.*; vilebrequin *m.*; — *vt.* ancrer; fortifier
bracer *n.* tonique *m.*; brassard *m.*
bracing *n.* tonique
bracket *n.* console *f.*; (print.) crochet *m.*
brackish *a.* saumâtre
brad *n.* clou (sans tête) *m.*
brag *n.* vanterie *f.*, jactance *f.*; — *vi.* se

vanter; **–gart** *n.* vantard, fanfaron *m.*

braid *n.* tresse *f.*; galon *m.*; passementerie *f.*; — *vt.* tresser; galonner; passementer

brain *n.* cerveau *m.*, cervelle *f.*; **rack one's** — se creuser la cervelle; **–storm** inspiration *f.*; — *vt.* casser la tête à; **–less** *a.* stupide, sans intelligence; **–y** *a.* intelligent

brainwashing *n.* (coll.) indoctrination idéologique (imposée aux prisonniers politiques ou de guerre) *f.*

brake *n.* frein *m.*; — *vt.* freiner, serrer les freins

brakeman *n.* (rail.) serre-frein *m.*

bramble *n.* ronce *f.*

bran *n.* son *m.*

branch *n.* branche *f.*; succursale *f.*; embranchement *m.*; — *v.*, — **off** s'embrancher, se bifurquer; — **out** se ramifier

brand *n.* brandon, tison *m.*; fer chaud *m.*; flétrissure *f.*; (com.) marque *f.*; — *vt.* marquer au fer chaud, flétrir; **–ing iron** *n.* fer (à flétrir) *m.*

brandish *vt.* brandir

brand-new *a.* tout neuf

brandy *n.* eau-de-vie *f.*

brash *a.* impertinent, insolent

brass *n.* cuivre jaune, laiton *m.*; airain *m.*; (mus.) cuivre *m.*

brassiere *n.* soutien-gorge *m.*

brat *n.* (coll.) gosse, marmot *m.*

bravado *n.* bravade *f.*

brave *a.* brave, courageux; — *vt.* braver; **–ry** *n.* bravoure *f.*

brawl *n.* bagarre *f.*; querelle *f.*; — *vi.* brailler; se quereller

brawn *n.* muscles *m. pl.*; **–y** *a.* musclé

bray *n.* braîment *m.*; — *vi.* braire

braze *vt.* braser; souder

brazen *a.* d'airain; impudent, effronté

brazier *n.* chaudronnier *m.*

Brazil *n.* Brésil *m.*; **–ian** *a. & n.* brésilien *m.*

breach *n.* brèche *f.*; rupture *f.*; infraction, violation *f.*; — **of promise** manque de parole *m.*; — **of trust** abus de confiance *m.*; — *vt.* ouvrir une brèche; battre en brèche

bread *n.* pain *m.*; — **crumbs** chapelure *f.*; — *vt.* paner, gratiner

breadbasket *n.* corbeille à pain *f.*; (coll.) estomac *m.*

breadboard *n.* planche à pain *f.*

breadth *n.* largeur *f.*

breadwinner *n.* gagne-pain *m.*; soutien de famille *m.*

break *n.* rupture, ouverture *f.*; cassure, fracture *f.*; lacune *f.*; interruption *f.*; répit, battement *m.*; — **of day** pointe du jour *f.*; aube *f.*; — *vt.* briser, casser, rompre; amortir; ruiner; — **one's word** manquer de parole; — **in** enfoncer; rompre; interrompre; — **into** entrer de force; cambrioler; — **open** forcer, enfoncer; — **out** éclater; s'échapper; — **through** percer; — **up** disperser; fragmenter; diviser; **–able** *a.* fragile; **–age** *n.* fracture *f.*; casse *f.*; **–er** *n.* (naut.) brisant *m.*

breakdown *n.* arrêt *m.*; épuisement *m.*; (auto) panne *f.*

breakfast *n.* petit déjeuner *m.*

breakthrough *n.* découverte scientifique ou technologique *f.*

breakwater *n.* brise-lames *m.*; digue *f.*

breast *n.* sein *m.*; mamelle *f.*; poitrine *f.*; — *vt.* affronter

breastbone *n.* sternum *m.*

breastplate *n.* cuirasse *f.*

breastwork *n.* parapet *m.*

breath *n.* haleine *f.*, souffle *m.*; **out of** — essoufflé, à bout de souffle; **–e** *vt. & vi.* respirer, souffler; **–ing** *n.* respiration *f.*, souffle *m.*; **–ing space** répit *m.*; **–less** *a.* essoufflé, haletant

breech *n.* (gun) culasse *f.*; **–es** *n. pl.* culotte *f.*, pantalon *m.*

breed *n.* race *f.*; — *vt.* engendrer, produire; élever, faire de l'élevage; — *vi.* se reproduire; **–ing** *n.* éducation *f.*; élevage *m.*; **–er** *n.* éleveur *m.*; reproduction *f.*; manières *f. pl.*; savoir-vivre *m.*

breeze *n.* brise *f.*; vent *m.*

breezy *a.* venteux; jovial

brethren *n. pl.* frères *m. pl.*

brevity *n.* brièveté *f.*

brew *n.* breuvage *m.*; brassage *m.*; infusion *f.*; — *vt.* brasser; — *vi.* s'infuser; **–er** *n.* brasseur *m.*; **–ery** *n.* brasserie *f.*; **–ing** brassage *m.*

bribe *n.* pot-de-vin *m.*; — *vt.* corrompre, suborner; **–ry** *n.* corruption *f.*

brick *n.* brique *f.*; — *vt.* briqueter

brickbat *n.* briquaillon *m.*; **hurl –s at** (fig.) lapider

bricklayer *n.* maçon *m.*

brickyard *n.* briqueterie *f.*

bridal *a.* nuptial

bride *n.* épousée *f.*; future *f.*

bridegroom *n.* marié *m.*; futur *m.*

bridesmaid *n.* demoiselle d'honneur *f.*

bridge *n.* pont *m.*; (naut.) passerelle *f.*; (cards) bridge *m.*; — *vt.* construire un pont sur; — **a gap** combler une lacune

bridgehead *n.* (mil.) point d'appui *m.*

bridle *n.* bride *f.*; frein *m.*; — **path** piste *f.*; — *vt.* brider; maîtriser

brief *a.* bref; court; concis; **–ly** en résumé;

— *n.* résumé, abrégé *m.*; dossier *m.*; — *vt.* mettre au courant; **–ing** *n.* mise au courant *f.*; **–ness** *n.* brièveté *f.*; **–s** *n. pl.* sous-vêtement court *m.*

brief case *n.* serviette *f.*

brig *n.* brick *m.*; prison navale *f.*

brigadier general *n.* général de brigade *m.*

brigantine *n.* brigantin *m.*

bright *a.* clair; brillant; lumineux; éclatant; vif; **–en** *vt.* faire briller; **–en** *vi.* s'éclaircir; **–ness** *n.* éclat *m.*; clarté *f.*; vivacité *f.*; intelligence *f.*

Bright's disease *n.* néphrite albumineuse *f.*

brilliance, brilliancy *n.* éclat *m.*, splendeur *f.*

brilliant *a.* brillant, éclatant; **–ly** *adv.* brillamment

brilliantine *n.* brillantine *f.*

brim *n.* bord *m.*; — *vi.* déborder; **–ful, –ming** *a.* débordant

brimstone *n.* soufre *m.*

brine *n.* saumure *f.*

bring *vt.* apporter, amener; — **about** causer, opérer; — **along** amener; — **back** ramener; rapporter; — **down** descendre; faire crouler; — **in** introduire; — **out** sortir; faire ressortir; — **together** réunir; — **up** éduquer, élever; monter; **–ing** *n.*, **–ing up** éducation *f.*

brink *n.* bord *m.*

briny *a.* salé, amer, saumâtre

brisk *a.* actif; vif; rapide; vivifiant; **–ness** *n.* vivacité; activité *f.*

brisket *n.* poitrine *f.*

bristle *n.* soie *f.*; poil *m.*; — *vi.* se hérisser

bristling *a.* hérissé

Britain *n.*, **Great** — Grande Bretagne *f.*

British *a.* britannique; anglais

Brittany *n.* Bretagne *f.*

brittle *a.* fragile, cassant; **–ness** *n.* fragilité *f.*

broad *a.* large; grand; général; — **daylight** plein jour *m.*; — **jump** saut (en longeur) *m.*; **–en** *vt.* élargir; **–en** *vi.* s'élargir; **–ness** *n.* largeur *f.*

broadcast *n.* radiodiffusion, émission *f.*; — *vt.* radiodiffuser, émettre; répandre; **–ing** *n.* radiodiffusion *f.*; **–er** *n.* (instrument) émetteur *m.*; (person) microphoniste *m.*

broadcloth *n.* popeline *f.*

broad-minded *a.* aux idées larges; tolérant

broadside *n.* bordée *f.*; côté *m.*; (print.) placard *m.*

brocade *n.* brocart *m.*; **–d** *a.* de brocart

broccoli *n.* brocoli *m.*

brochure *n.* brochure *f.*

brogue *n.* accent *f.* (irlandais) *m.*; patois *m.*; (shoe) brogue *f.*

broil *vt. & vi.* griller; **–er** gril *m.*

broke *a.* (coll.) fauché

broken *a.* brisé, cassé, rompu

broker *n.* agent *m.*; courtier *m.*; (stock) agent de change *m.*; **–age** *n.* courtage *m.*

bromide *n.* bromure *m.*

bromine *n.* brome *m.*

bronchi, bronchia *n. pl.* bronches *f. pl.*

bronchial *a.* bronchique

bronchitis *n.* bronchite *f.*

bronco *n.* cheval sauvage (américain) *m.*

brooch *n.* broche, épingle *f.*

brood *n.* couvée *f.*; — **hen** couveuse *f.*; — **mare** poulinière *f.*; — *vi.* couver; rêver (noir)

brook *n.* ruisseau *m.*; — *vt.* souffrir

broom *n.* balai *m.*

broomstick *n.* manche à balai *m.*

broth *n.* bouillon, consommé *m.*

brothel *n.* bordel *m.*

brother *n.* frère *m.*; **–hood** *n.* fraternité, confrérie *f.*; **–ly** *a.* fraternel; **–ly** *adv.* fraternellement

brother-in-law *n.* beau-frère *m.*

brow *n.* front *m.*; sourcil *m.*; **to knit one's** — froncer les sourcils

browbeat *vt.* intimider

brown *a.* brun; marron; châtain; bruni; — **paper** papier d'emballage *m.*; — **sugar** cassonade *f.*; — *n.* brun *m.*; — *vt.* dorer; brunir; rissoler; **–ish** *a.* brunâtre

browse *vt. & vi.* brouter; butiner (dans), feuilleter

bruise *n.* meurtrissure *f.*; bleu *m.*; — *vt.* meurtrir; **–r** *n.* costaud, fort, boxeur *m.*

brunette *n.* brune *f.*

brunt *n.* choc *m.*

brush *n.* brosse *f.*; (paint) pinceau *m.*; (elec.) balai *m.*; (bot.) brousse *f.*; — *vt.* brosser; — **against** frôler; — **aside** écarter; — **up (on)** repasser, rafraîchir

brushwood *n.* broussailles *f. pl.*; brindilles *f. pl.*

Brussels *n.* Bruxelles; — **sprouts** choux de Bruxelles *m. pl.*

brutal *a.* brutal; **–ity** *n.* brutalité *f.*; **–ize** *vt.* abrutir

brute *n.* brute *f.*; — *a.* brutal; sauvage

brutish *a.* brutal; **–ness** *n.* brutalité *f.*

bubble *n.* bulle *f.*; — **gum** gomme à bulles *f.*, bubble-gum *m.*; — *vi.* bouillonner; — **over** déborder

buccaneer *n.* boucanier *m.*

buck *n.* daim, chevreuil *m.*; (coll.) dollar *m.*; — *a.*, — **private** (mil.) simple soldat *m.*; — **teeth** dents saillantes *f. pl.*

bucket *n.* seau *m.*

buckle n. boucle, agrafe f.; — vt. boucler, agrafer; — vi. arquer, gauchir; — **down** s'appliquer

buckram n. bougran m.

buckshot n. gros plomb m.

buckskin n. peau de daim f.

buckwheat n. sarrasin m.; — **cakes** n. pl. crêpes de sarrasin f. pl.

bud n. bouton, bourgeon m.; — vi. boutonner; bourgeonner; –**ding** a. en bouton; en germe; en herbe

Buddhism n. bouddhisme m.

Buddhist n. bouddhiste m.

buddy n. copain m.

budge vi. bouger; reculer

budget n. budget m.; –**ary** a. budgétaire

buff a. & n. couleur chamois f.; — vt. polir, émeuler

buffalo n. buffle m.; bison m.

buffer n. (rail.) tampon m.; (polishing) brunissoir m.

buffet vt. frapper, jeter çà et là

buffoon n. bouffon m.; –**ery** n. bouffonnerie f.

bug n. insecte m.; (coll.) idée fixe f.

bugaboo, bugbear n. croque-mitaine m.

buggy n. buggy, boghei m.; **baby** — landau m., poussette f.

bugle n. (mil.) cor de chasse; clairon m.; –**r** n. clairon m.

build vt. bâtir, construire m.; –**er** n. entrepreneur, constructeur m.; (fig.) fondateur m.; –**ing** n. bâtiment, édifice m.; maison f.; construction f.

buildup n. construction; (med.) consolidation f.

bulb n. bulbe f., oignon m.; (elec.) ampoule f.; lampe f.; –**ous** a. bulbeux

bulge n. bosse, protubérance f.; bombement, renflement m.; — vi. faire une bosse, bomber; –**ing** a. bombé; protubérant; bourré

bulk n. masse, quantité f.; volume m.; **in** — en volume, en bloc, en gros; en quantité; –**y** a. volumineux; gros

bulkhead n. cloison f.

bulldoze vt. intimider; –**r** n. bulldozer m.

bullet n. balle f.

bulletin n. bulletin m.; communiqué m.; — **board** tableau d'affichage m.

bulletproof a. à l'épreuve des balles

bullfight n. course de taureaux f.; –**er** n. toréador m.

bullfrog n. grosse grenouille f.

bullion n. or en lingot m.; **argent en** lingot m.

bullock n. bœuf m.

bull's-eye n. (target) noir, centre m.; (window) œil-de-bœuf m.

bully n. brutal, tyran m.; — vt. brutaliser, malmener

bulwark n. rempart m.

bumblebee n. bourdon m.

bump n. bosse f.; choc m.; cahot m.; — vt. cogner; — vi. se cogner; –**er** n. (auto.) pare-choc(s); (rail.) tampon m.; –**er** a., –**er crop** récolte magnifique f.; –**y** a. cahoteux

bumpkin n. rustre, lourdaud m.

bun n. petit pain m.; chignon m.

bunch n. botte f., bouquet m.; grappe f.; (keys) trousseau m.; bande f., groupe m.; — vt. grouper; — vi. se serrer

bunco n. mystification, escroquerie f.; tricherie f.

bundle n. paquet m.; liasse f.; ballot m.; — vt. empaqueter, mettre en paquet

bung n. bondon m.; — vt. bondonner

bungalow n. rater; gâcher; –**r** n. maladroit, gâcheur m.

bungling a. gauche, maladroit; — n. maladresse f.

bunion n. oignon (au pied) m.

bunk n. couchette f.; (coll.) balivernes f. pl.; — vi. se coucher

bunker n. soute f.; (golf) banquette f.

Bunsen burner n. bec Bunsen m.

bunting n. drapeaux m. pl.; étamine f.; (bird) bruant m.

buoy n. (naut.) bouée f.; — vt. faire flotter; soutenir; –**ancy** n. flottabilité f.; –**ant** a. flottable

burden n. fardeau m., charge f.; (mus.) refrain m.; **beast of** — bête de somme f.; — vt. charger; –**some** a. onéreux

bureau n. bureau m.; secrétaire m.; commode f.

bureaucracy n. bureaucratie f.

bureaucrat n. bureaucrate, rond-de-cuir m.; –**ic** a. bureaucratique

burgess, burgher n. bourgeois, citoyen m.

burglar n. cambrioleur m.; — **alarm** signalisateur antivol m.; –**ize** vt. cambrioler; –**y** n. cambriolage m.

Burgundy n. Bourgogne f.; — **wine** bourgogne m.; vin de bourgogne m.

burial n. enterrement m.

burlap n. toile d'emballage f.

burlesque a. burlesque; — n. burlesque m.; parodie f.; variété f.; — vt. parodier

burly a. solide, costaud

Burma n. Birmanie f.

burn n. brûlure f.; — vt. & vi. brûler; –**er** n. bec de gaz m.; brûleur m.; –**ing** a. brûlant; embrasé; en feu

burnish vt. brunir, polir

burro n. âne, baudet m.

burrow n. terrier m.; — vt. creuser; — vi. se terrer

bursar n. économe (d'une université) m.

burst *n.* explosion *f.*; éclat *m.*; jet *m.*; — *vi.* éclater, exploser; crever; — **out** laughing éclater de rire; — **into tears** se mettre à pleurer

bury *vt.* enterrer, inhumer

bus *n.* autobus, autocar, car *m.*

busboy *n.* garçon de restaurant (chargé d'enlever le couvert) *m.*

bush *n.* buisson *m.*; arbuste, arbrisseau *m.* —**y** *a.* buissonneux; touffu

bushel *n.* demi-boisseau *m.* (= 36 litres)

bushing *n,* garniture *f.*; fourrure *f.*; paroi intérieur *m.*

busily *adv.* d'un air affairé; activement

business *n.* affaire(s) *f.* (*pl.*); **it's none of your** — cela ne vous regarde pas

businesslike *a.* capable, sérieux

businessman *n.* commerçant, homme d'affaires *m.*

bust *n.* (sculpture) buste *m.*; gorge, poitrine *f.*

bustle *n.* remue-ménage, affairement *m.*; — *vi.* se remuer, s'affairer

bustling *a.* affairé

busy *a.* occupé, affairé; — *vt.*, — **oneself with** s'occuper à

busybody *n.* officieux *m.*

but *conj.* mais; toutefois; — *prep.* sauf, excepté; sinon

butcher *n.* boucher *m.*; — **shop** boucherie *f.*; — *vt.* massacrer, égorger; —**y** *n.* massacre *m.*, tuerie *f.*

butler *n.* maître d'hôtel *m.*

butt *n.* bout *m.*; (gun) crosse *f.*; (cigarette) mégot *m.*; (of a remark) plastron *m.*; (blow) coup de tête *m.*; — **end** gros bout *m.*; — *vt. & vi.* buter (contre); donner des coups de la tête (contre); — **in** intervenir sans façon

butter *n.* beurre *m.*; — **dish** beurrier *m.*; — *vt.* beurrer; — **up** (coll.) flatter; — **fat** gras de beurre *m.*

butterfingered *a.* maladroit

butterfly *n.* papillon *m.*

buttermilk *n.* petit lait *m.*; babeurre *m.*

buttock *n.* fesse *f.*

button *n.* bouton *m.*; — *vt.* boutonner

buttonhole *n.* boutonnière *f.*; — *vt.* interpeller, prendre à part, aborder

buttonhook *n.* tire-bouton *m.*

buttress *n.* arc-boutant *m.*; contrefort *m.*; — *vt.* arc-bouter

buxom *a.* plantureux

buy *vt.* acheter; —**er** *n.* acheteur

buzz *n.* bourdonnement *m.*; — **saw** scie circulaire *f.*; — *vi.* bourdonner; —**er** *n.* sonnerie *f.*

buzzard *n.* busard *m.*; vautour *m.*

by *prep.* par; près de; en; — *adv.* là; par là; **close** — tout près; — **and** — tout à l'heure; **to stand** — être là

bygone *a.* d'autrefois, passé

bylaws *n. pl.* ordonnances *f. pl.*; règlements *m. pl.*

by-line *n.* signature de journaliste *f.*

bypass *n.* contournement *m.*, déviation *f.*; — *vt.* contourner, dévier, éviter

byplay *n.* jeu muet *m.*

by-product *n.* dérivé, sous-produit *m.*

bystander *n.* assistant, spectateur *m.*

byway *n.* chemin obscur *m.*

byword *n.* proverbe *m.*

Byzantine *a.* byzantin; — **Empire** Bas-Empire *m.*

C

cab *n.* taxi *m.*; fiacre *m.*; cabine *f.*; — **driver** *n.* chauffeur de taxi *m.*

cabal *n.* cabale *f.*; — *vi.* cabaler; —**istic** *a.* cabalistique

cabaret *m.* boîte de nuit *f.*

cabbage *n.* chou *m.*

cabin *n.* case, cabane *f.*; (naut.) cabine *f.*; — **boy** mousse *m.*; — **class** deuxième classe *f.*

cabinet *n.* cabinet *m.*; conseil des ministres *m.*

cabinetmaker *n.* ébéniste *m.*

cable *n.* câble *m.*; chaîne *f.*; — *vt.* câbler

cable car *n.* funiculaire *m.*; téléférique *m.*

cablegram *n.* câblogramme *m.*

cable length *n.* encablure *f.*

caboose *n.* (train) fourgon de queue *m.*

cabstand *n.* taxiplace *f.*

cackle *n.* caquet *m.*; — *vi.* caqueter

cacophony *n.* cacophonie *f.*

cad *n.* mufle *m.*

cadaver *n.* cadavre *m.*

caddie, caddy *n.* (golf) caddie, cadet *m.*

cadence *n.* cadence *f.*, rythme *m.*

cadet *n.* cadet *m.*; élève-officier *m.*

Cadiz *n.* Cadix

cadmium *n.* cadmium *m.*

cæsarian *a.* césarienne

café *n.* café, restaurant *m.*; — **curtains** demi-rideaux *m. pl.*

cafeteria *n.* self-service, libre-service *m.*

caffein *n.* caféine *f.*

cage *n.* cage *f.*; — *vt.* mettre en cage; en**cager**

cagey *a.* (coll.) malin, rusé, fin

Cairo *n.* Le Caire

caisson *n.* caisson *m.*

cajole *vt.* cajoler, enjôler

cajoling *a.* cajoleur

cake *n.* gâteau *m.*; pâtisserie *f.*; croûte *f.*; — **of soap** pain de savon *m.*; — *vi.* s'agglutiner, se prendre; faire croûte

calabash *n.* calebasse *f.*
calamitous *a.* calamiteux, désastreux
calamity *n.* calamité *f.*; malheur *m.*; désastre *m.*
calcify *vt.* calcifier; — *vi.* se calcifier
calcimine *n.* chaux *f.*
calcite *n.* calcaire *m.*
calcium *n.* calcium *m.*
calculate *vt.* calculer; compter
calculating *a.* calculateur
calculation *n.* calcul *m.*
calculator *n.* machine à calculer *f.*
calculus *n.* calcul, cacul infinitésimal *m.*
caldron *n.* chaudron *m.*
calendar *n.* calendrier *m.*
calf *n.* veau *m.*; (of the leg) mollet *m.*
calfskin *n.* veau *m.*, peau de veau *f.*
caliber, calibre *n.* calibre *m.*
calibrate *vt.* calibrer; graduer
calipers *n. pl.* compas à calibrer *m.*
calisthenics *n. pl.* callisthénie *f.*
calk, caulk *vt.* calfater
call *n.* appel *m.*; cri *m.*; visite *f.*; **curtain** — rappel *m.*; **telephone** — coup de téléphone *m.*; — *vt.* appeler; crier; convoquer; — *vi.* faire une visite; (naut.) faire escale; — **for** venir chercher; demander; — **off** rompre; — **up** donner un coup de téléphone; (mil.) mobiliser; **–ing** *n.* vocation, profession *f.*, métier *m.*; **–ing card** carte de visite *f.*
call girl *n.* prostituée *f.*
callous *a.* calleux; insensible, dur
callow *a.* jeune, inexpérimenté
callus *n.* callosité *f.*
calm *vt.* calmer; tranquilliser; — **down** *vt.* pacifier; — **down** *vi.* se calmer; — *a.* calme, tranquille; —, **–ness** *n.* calme *m.*; tranquillité *f.*
calorie, calory *n.* calorie *f.*
calumny *n.* calomnie, diffamation *f.*
caluminate *vt.* calomnier
calvary *n.* calvaire *m.*
calve *vi.* vêler
calyx *n.* calice *m.*
cam *n.* came *f.*; **–shaft** arbre de distribution *m.*
Cambodia *n.* Cambodge *m.*
cambric *n.* batiste *f.*
camel *n.* chameau *m.*
cameo *n.* camée *m.*
camera *n.* appareil (photographique) *m.*; **movie** — caméra *m.*
cameraman *n.* photographe *m.*
Cameroons *n. pl.* Cameroun *m.*
camouflage *n.* camouflage *m.*; — *vt.* camoufler
camp *n.* camp *m.*; — **bed** lit de sangle *m.*; — **chair** chaise pliante *f.*; — *vi.* camper, faire du camping

campaign *n.* campagne *f.*; — *vi.* faire une campagne; **–er** *n.* ancien combattant, vétéran *m.*
camphor *n.* camphre *m.*
campus *n.* parc d'une université *m.*
camshaft *n.* arbre à cames *m.*
can *n.* boîte *f.*; bidon *m.*; — **opener** ouvre-boîtes *m.*; — *vi.* pouvoir; savoir; — *vt.* mettre en boîtes, conserver; **–ned** *a.* conservé; **–ned goods** conserves *f. pl.*; **–ned music** musique enregistrée *f.*; **–nery** conserverie *f.*
Canadian *n. & a.* Canadien *m.*
canal *n.* canal *m.* (*pl.* canaux); **–ize** *vt.* canaliser
canary *n.* serin *m.*
cancel *vt.* annuler; rescinder; infirmer; rapporter; biffer; **–lation** *n.* annulation *f.*; oblitération *f.*
cancer *n.* cancer *m.*; **–ous** *a.* cancéreux
candelabrum *n.* candélabre *m.*
candid *a.* sincère; franc (franche); — **camera** *n.* petit appareil pour photographies impromptus *m.*
candidacy *n.* candidature *f.*
candidate *n.* candidat, aspirant *m.*
candied *a.* confit, glacé, candi
candle *n.* bougie *f.*; chandelle *f.*; (eccl.) cierge *f.*: — **power** bougie *f.*
candlestick *n.* chandelier, bougeoir *m.*
candor *n.* franchise, sincérité *f.*
candy *n.* confiserie *f.*, sucreries *f. pl.*; — *vt.* glacer, faire candir
cane *n.* canne *f.*; jonc *m.*; bâton *m.*, badine *f.*; — **sugar** sucre de canne *m.*; **sugar** — canne à sucre *f.*; — *vt.* battre, bâtonner; (chair) canner
canine *a.* canin, de chien; — **tooth** canine, œillère *f.*
canister *n.* boîte *f.*; (mil.) mitraille *f.*
canker *n.* chancre *m.*; (fig.) plaie *f.*; — *vt.* ronger corrompre
cannibal *n.* cannibale, anthropophage *m. & f.*; **–ism** *n.* cannibalisme *m.*, anthropophagie *f.*; **–istic** *a.* cannibale
cannon *n.* canon *m.*; — **ball** *n.* boulet de canon *m.*; — **shot** *n.* coup de canon *m.*
canoe *n.* canoë *m.*; pirogue *f.*; — *vi.* faire du canoë; pagayer; **to go –ing** faire du canoë; **–ist** *n.* canotier *m.*
canon *n.* canon *m.*, règle *f.*; (person) chanoine *m.*; — **law** droit canon *m.*; **–ize** *vt.* canoniser
canopy *n.* dais, baldaquin *m.*; marquise *f.*
cant *n.* inclinaison *f.*; (arch.) pan coupé *m.*; argot, jargon *m.*; hypocrisie *f.*; — *vt.* incliner; **–ing** *a.* hypocrite
cantaloupe *n.* cantaloup *m.*
cantankerous *a.* revêche, acariâtre
cantata *n.* cantate *f.*

canteen *n.* cantine *f.*; bidon *m.*

canter *n.* petit galop *m.*; — *vi.* aller au petit galop

canto *n.* chant *m.*

canton *n.* canton *m.*

canvas *n.* toile *f.*; canevas *m.*; –back duck *n.* canard américain *m.*

canvass *vt.* solliciter; faire une tournée électorale; (com.) faire la place; –er *n.* solliciteur *m.*; placier *m.*; –ing *n.* sollicitation *f.*

canyon *n.* cañon *m.*, gorge *f.*

cap *n.* bonnet *m.*, casquette *f.*; toque *f.*; chapeau *m.*; capuchon *m.*; — and gown costume académique *m.*; — *vt.* coiffer; capsuler; couronner; (shell) amorcer

capability *n.* capacité *f.*; faculté *f.*

capable *a.* capable; habile; susceptible

capacious *a.* spacieux, vaste, ample

capacity *n.* capacité *f.*; intelligence, aptitude *f.*; contenance *f.*

capacitate *vt.* rendre capable

cape *n.* cap, promontoire *m.*; pèlerine, cape *f.*; manteau *m.*

Cape of Good Hope Cap de Bonne Espérance *m.*

caper *n.* cabriole *f.*; (bot.) câpre *f.*; — *vi.* faire des cabrioles

capillary *a.* capillaire

capital *a.* capital (*pl.* capitaux); — punishment peine capitale *f.*; — *n.* capital, fonds *m.*; (city) capitale *f.*; (letter) majuscule *f.*; (arch.) chapiteau *m.*; –ism *n.* capitalisme *m.*; –ist *n.* capitaliste *m.* & *f.*; –ize *vt.* écrire avec une majuscule; capitaliser

Capitol *n.* Capitole *m.*; — *a.* capitolin

capitulate *vi.* capituler

capitulation *n.* capitulation *f.*

capon *n.* chapon *m.*

caprice *n.* caprice *m.*, lubie *f.*

capricious *a.* capricieux

capsize *vi.* chavirer; capoter; — *vt.* faire chavirer

capsizing *n.* chavirement, capotage *m.*

capstan *n.* cabestan *m.*

capsule *n.* capsule *f.*

captain *n.* capitaine *m.*; chef *m.*; (sports) chef d'équipe *m.*; — *vt.* commander, diriger, conduire; –cy *n.* grade de capitaine *m.*; direction *f.*, commandement *m.*

caption *n.* rubrique *f.*; sous-titre *m.*; (law) arrestation *f.*

captious *a.* captieux, pointilleux

captivate *vt.* captiver, fasciner, charmer

captivating *a.* captivant; séduisant, charmant

captive *a.* captif; — *n.* captif, prisonnier *m.*

captivity *n.* captivité *f.*

captor *n.* preneur, ravisseur *m.*

capture *n.* prise *f.*; capture *f.*; — *vt.* prendre; capturer

car *n.* auto, automobile, voiture *f.*; (rail.) wagon *m.*; — pool système coopératif de voyage entre la maison et le travail en employant des voitures particulières *m.* used — *n.* voiture d'occasion *f.*

caramel *n.* caramel *m.*; caramel mou *m.*

caravan *n.* caravane *f.*; roulotte *f.*

caravansary *n.* caravansérail *m.*

caraway *n.* carvi, cumin *m.*

carbide *n.* carbure *m.*

carbine *n.* carabine *f.*

carbohydrate *n.* hydrate de carbone *m.*

carbolic *a.* phénique; — acid phénol *m.*

carbon *n.* carbone *m.*; — copy double *m.*, copie *f.*; — dioxide anhydride carbonique *m.*; — 14 (chem.) carbone 14 *m.*; — monoxide oxyde de carbone *m.*; — paper papier carbone *m.*

carborundum *n.* carborundum *m.*

carbuncle *n.* carboncle *m.*; (stone) escarboucle *f.*

carburetor *n.* carburateur *m.*

carcass *n.* cadavre, corps *m.*; carcasse *f.*

carcinogen *n.* (med.) carcinogénique *m.*

card *n.* carte *f.*; index — fiche *f.*; (coll.) original *m.*; (racing) programme *m.*; dance — carnet de bal *m.*; deck of –s jeu de cartes *m.*; — index fichier, classeur *m.*; — sharp *n.* tricheur *m.*; — table table de jeu *f.*; — *vt.* carder, peigner

cardboard *n.* carton *m.*

cardiac *a.* cardiaque

cardigan *n.* gilet *m.*

cardinal *a.* cardinal, fondamental; pourpre; — *n.* cardinal *m.*

cardiogram *n.* cardiogramme *m.*

cardiology *n.* cardiologie *f.*

care *n.* souci *m.*; attention *f.*; soins *m. pl.*; sollicitude *f.*; préoccupation *f.*; take — not to se garder de, prendre garde de; take — of se charger de; arranger; soigner; — *vi.* se soucier; se préoccuper; I don't — cela m'est égal; — for soigner; aimer; –ful *a.* soigneux; attentif; prudent; –ful! faites attention!; –fully *adv.* soigneusement, avec soin; attentivement; –fulness *n.* soin *m.*, attention *f.*; –less *a.* négligent; insouciant; –lessly *adv.* négligemment; –lessness *n.* négligence *f.*; inattention *f.*; insouciance *f.*

careen *vi.* donner de la bande

career *n.* carrière *f.*

carefree *a.* sans souci; insouciant

caress *n.* caresse *f.*; — *vt.* caresser; –ing *a.* caressant

caret *n.* signe d'omission *m.*

caretaker n. concierge m. & f.; intendant m.; gardien m.; — **government** régime intérimaire m.

carfare n. prix d'un billet, tarif, billet de tramway m.

cargo n. cargaison f.; chargement m.; — **ship** cargo m.

Caribbean Sea n. mer des Caraïbes f.

caricature n. caricature f.; — vt. caricaturer

caricaturist n. caricaturiste m.

caries n. carie f.

carmine n. carmin m.; — a. carmin; carminé

carnage n. carnage m.

carnal a. charnel; sexuel; sensuel; — **sin** péché de la chair m.

carnation n. (bot.) œillet m.; — a. & n. (color) incarnat m.

carnival n. carnaval m.; fête foraine f.

carnivorous a. carnivore; carnassier

carol n. chant m.; **Christmas** — noël m.; — vt. & vi. chanter

carom n. carambolage m.; — vi. caramboler

carouse vi. faire la bombe

carp n. carpe f.; — vi. critiquer, trouver à redire, épiloguer; –ing a. pointilleux; –ing n. critique pointilleuse f.

carpenter n. charpentier m.; menuisier m.

carpentry n. charpenterie f.

carpet n. tapis m.; — **sweeper** balayeuse f.; **lay a** — poser un tapis; — vt. recouvrir d'un tapis; –ed a. (re)couvert d'un tapis; tapissé; –ing n. tapis m.

carpool n. voiture commune f.

carport n. garage ouvert m.; remise f.

carriage n. voiture f.; port m., maintien m.; (gun) affût m.; (typewriter) chariot m.; — **entrance** porte cochère f.

carrier n. porteur m.; voiturier m.; — **pigeon** pigeon voyageur m.; **aircraft** — porte-avions m.; **letter** — facteur m.; **luggage** — porte-bagages m.

carrion n. charogne f.

carrot n. carotte f.

carry vt. porter; emporter; vendre, avoir; conduire; pousser; adopter; (math.) retenir; — **away** (emotion) entraîner, transporter; — **forward** avancer; reporter; — **off** enlever; emporter; réussir; — **on** continuer; soutenir; se comporter; — **out** exécuter; remplir; **be carried** être voté; **be carried away** (fig.) être entraîné; s'emporter; — n. portée f., trajet m.; –ing n. port, transport m.

carryall n. charrette, carriole f.

cart n. charrette f.; tombereau m.; — vt. charrier; –age n. charriage, transport m.; –er n. camionneur m.; charretier m.;

voiturier m.

Cartesian a. cartésien

Carthusian a. & n. chartreux m.; chartreuse f.

cartilage n. cartilage m.

cartographer n. cartographe m

cartography n. cartographie f.

carton n. carton m.; boîte f.

cartoon n. caricature f.; (movies) dessin animé m.; –ist n. caricaturiste m.

cartridge n. cartouche f.; (record-player) cellule de lecture f.

cartwheel n. roue f.; **do** –s faire les roues

cartwright n. charron m.

carve vt. découper; graver, sculpter; tailler

carving n. découpage m.; gravure, sculpture f.; — **knife** n. couteau à découper m.; — **set** service à découper m.

cascade n. cascade, chute d'eau f.; — vi. cascader

case n. cas m.; (law) cause f.; caisse f.; colis m.; écrin m.; trousse f.; étui m.; boîte f.; (glass) vitrine f.; (med.) malade m. & f.; (typ.) casse f.; (watch) boîtier m.; **in any** — en tout cas; **upper** — haut de casse m.; — vt. encaisser; envelopper; (coll.) observer, épier

casehardened a. aciéré, cimenté; (person) endurci

casement window n. croisée f.

cash n. argent comptant m.; espèces f. pl.; — **box** n. caisse f.; cassette f.; — **on delivery** contre remboursement; — **register** caisse enregistreuse f.; — vt. toucher, escompter

cashew n. noix d'acajou f.

cashier n. caissier m., caissière f.; — vt. casser; –'s **check** chèque bancaire m.

cashmere n. cachemire m.

casing n. enveloppe f.; chemise f.

cask n. tonneau, fût m., barrique f.

casket n. cassette f.; cercueil m.

Caspian Sea n. Mer Caspienne f.

cassava n. cassave f.

cassock n. soutane f.

cast n. jet m.; coup m.; coulée f.; moulage m.; (theat.) distribution f.; — vt. lancer, jeter; fondre; mouler; couler; (theat.) distribuer; — **lots** tirer au sort; — **aside** mettre de côté; — **off** rejeter; (naut.) abattre; — **out** mettre à la porte; exorciser; — a. moulé; coulé; — **iron** fonte (de fer) f.; –ing n. fonte f., moulage m.; jet m.; pièce de fonte f.

castanet n. castagnette f.

castaway n. naufragé m.

caster n. roulette f.

castigate vt. châtier, corriger

castigation n. châtiment m., correction f.

Castile n. Castille f.; — **soap** savon blanc

m.
castle n. château m.; château fort m.; (chess) tour f.; — vt. (chess) roquer
castoff a. jeté, rejeté; vieux; — n. rejeté m.
castor oi! n. huile de ricin f.
castrate vt. châtrer m.
castration n. castration f.
casual a. accidentel, fortuit; indifférent; désinvolte; insouciant; -ly adv. par hasard, fortuitement; négligemment
casualty n. blessé m.; mort m.; accidenté m.
cat n. chat m., chatte f.; let the — out of the bag vendre la mèche; -ty a. cancanier, méchant
cataclysm n. cataclysme m.; -ic a. cataclysmique
catacombs n. pl. catacombes f. pl.
catalepsy n. catalepsie f.
cataleptic a. cataleptique
catalog, catalogue n. catalogue m.; prix-courant m.; liste f.; — vt. cataloguer
Catalonia n. Catalogne f.
catalyst n. catalyseur m.
catalytic a. catalyseur, catalytique
catapult n. catapulte f.; lance-pierres m.; — vt. lancer
cataract n. cataracte f.
catastrophe n. catastrophe f.
catcall n. huée f.; sifflet m.
catch n. prise f.; (door) loquet m.; (clothing) agrafe f.; (buckle) ardillon m.; (fishing) pêche f.; attrape f.; — vt. attraper; saisir; prendre; surprendre; accrocher; — vi. prendre, s'engager; s'accrocher; — on réussir, prendre; comprendre; — up with rattraper; — cold s'enrhumer; — fire s'enflammer, prendre feu; -ing a. contagieux; communicatif; -y a. entraînant, facile à retenir
catchall n. sac ou panier pour recevoir tout m.; catégorie qui comporte un mélange de choses f.
catechism n. catéchisme m.
categorical a. catégorique
category n. catégorie f.
cater vi. pourvoir, approvisionner; -er n. approvisionneur, pourvoyeur m.; -ing n. approvisionnement m.
cater-cornered, catty-cornered a. diagona
caterpillar n. chenille f.
catfish n. loup marin m.
catgut n. corde de boyau f.
cathartic a. cathartique, purgatif
cathedral n. cathédrale f.
catheter n. cathéter m.
cathode n. cathode f.
cathode-ray tube n. tube cathodique m.
catholic a. universel; éclectique
Catholic n. & a. (eccl.) catholique m. & f.;

-ism n. catholicisme m.
catkin n. (bot.) chaton m.
catnap n. petit somme m.
catnip n. cataire f.
cat's-paw n. (fig.) dupe f.
catsup n. sauce tomaille f.
cattle n. bétail m.; bêtes f. pl.; bestiaux m. pl.
cattleman n. éleveur de bétail m.
catwalk n. coursive f.
caucus n. réunion f. (d'une clique politique)
cauliflower n. chou-fleur m.
cause n. cause f.; raison f.; sujet m.; procès m.; have -(to) avoir lieu (de); — vt. causer; faire; occasionner
causeway n. chaussée f.
caustic a. caustique; mordant
cauterize vt. cautériser
caution n. prudence, précaution f.; circonspection f.; avertissement m.; — interj. attention! — vt. avertir
cautious a. prudent; circonspect; -ly adv. prudemment; avec circonspection
cavalcade n. cavalcade f.
cavalier n. cavalier m.; — a. cavalier, désinvolte
cavalry n. cavalerie f.
cave n. grotte f., souterrain m.; caverne f., antre m.; — man troglodyte m.; — vi., — in s'effondrer
cavern n. caverne f.; -ous a. caverneux
cavil vi. ergoter, chicaner
cavity n. cavité f.; creux m.; trou m.; (tooth) carie f.
cavort vi. gambader, caracoler
caw vi. croasser; —, -ing n. croassement m.
cease vt. & vi. cesser; (s')arrêter; — fire cesser le feu; — fire n. trêve f.; -less a. incessant, continuel; sans arrêt; -lessly adv. sans cesse
cedar n. cèdre m.
cede vt. & vi. céder
cedilla n. cédille f.
ceiling n. plafond m.; (avi.) ciel, plafond m.; — price prix maximum m.
celebrate vt. fêter; célébrer; commémorer; -ed a. célèbre, renommé
celebration n. fête f.; commémoration f.; célébration f.
celebrity n. célébrité f.; vedette f.
celery n. céleri m.
celestial a. céleste; — mechanics n. mécanique céleste f.
celibacy n. célibat m.
celibate a. & n. célibataire m. & f.
cell n. cellule f.; cachot m.; (pol.) noyau m.; (elec.) élément m.; pile f.
cellar n. cave f.; sous-sol m.

cello, 'cello *n.* violoncelle *m.*
cellophane *n.* cellophane *f.*
cellular *a.* cellulaire
celluloid *n.* celluloïd *m.*
cellulose *a.* celluleux; — *n.* cellulose *f.*
Celt *n.* Celte *m.* & *f.*; –ic *a.* celte; celtique; –ic *n.* celtique
cement *n.* ciment *m.*; cément *m.*; — *vt.* cimenter; cémenter; consolider
cemetery *n.* cimetière *m.*
cenotaph *n.* cénotaphe *m.*
censer *n.* (eccl.) encensoir *m.*
censor *n.* censeur *m.*; — *vt.* interdire; supprimer; –ing, –ship *n.* censure *f.*; contrôle *m.*
censurable *a.* blâmable, censurable
censure *n.* censure *f.*; blâme *m.*; — *vt.* censurer, blâmer
census *n.* recensement *m.*
cent *n.* cent *m.*; sou, liard *m.*; per — pour cent
centennial *a.* & *n.* centenaire *m.*
center *n.* centre *m.*; milieu *m.*; foyer *m.*; — *vt.* centrer; placer au centre; — *vi.* se concentrer
centerpiece *n.* surtout, milieu *m.*
centigrade *a.* centigrade
centigram *n.* centigramme *m.*
centimeter *n.* centimètre *m.*
centipede *n.* centipède *m.*; myriapode *m.*; mille-pattes *m.*
central *a.* central; –ization *n.* centralisation *f.*; –ize *vt.* centraliser
Central America *n.* Amérique Centrale *f.*
centrifugal *a.* centrifuge
centrifuge *n.* centrifugeuse *f.*
centripetal *a.* centripète
century *n.* siècle *m.*; — old *a.* séculaire
cereal *a.* & *n.* céréale *f.*
cerebellum *n.* cervelet *m.*
cerebral *a.* cérébral; — palsy *n.* paralysie cérébrale *f.*
cerebrum *n.* cerveau *m.*
ceremonial *a.* cérémonial, de cérémonie; — *n.* cérémonial *m.*
ceremonious *a.* cérémonieux
ceremony *n.* cérémonie *f.*; stand on — faire des façons; without — sans façon(s)
certain *a.* certain, sûr; make — s'assurer; –ly *adv.* certainement, assurément; parfaitement; certes; –ty *n.* certitude *f.*
certificate *n.* certificat *m.*; attestation *f.*; acte *m.*; titre *m.*; diplôme *m.*; birth — acte de naissance *m.*
certification *n.* certification, attestation *f.*
certified *a.* certifié; — check chèque visé *m.*; — public accountant expert-comptable diplômé *m.*
certify *vt.* certifier; attester; authentiquer,

homologuer, légaliser; constater; diplômer
certitude *n.* certitude *f.*
cessation *n.* cessation *f.*
cesspool *n.* fosse d'aisance *f.*
Ceylon *n.* Ceylan *m.*
chafe *vt.* échauffer; frotter; frictionner; irriter; — *vi.* s'énerver, s'irriter
chaff *n.* paille menue *f.*; balle *f.*; (coll.) raillerie *f.*; — *vt.* railler, persifler
chafing *n.* écorchement, frottement *m.*; irritation *f.*; — dish réchaud de table *m.*
chagrin *n.* chagrin *m.*; mortification *f.*; dépit *m.* to be –ed être mortifié
chain *n.* chaîne *f.*; chaînette *f.*; enchaînement *m.*; — gang chaîne de forçats *f.*; — smoker fumeur à la file *m.*; — reaction réaction en chaîne *f.*; — stitch point de chaînette *m.*; — store succursale *f.*; — stores grand magasin à succursales *m.*; société coopérative *f.*; — *vt.* enchaîner; attacher
chair *n.* chaise *f.*; siège *m.*; fauteuil *m.*; (academic) chaire *f.*
chairman *n.* président *m.*; –ship *n.* présidence *f.*
chalice *n.* calice *m.*
chalk *n.* craie *f.*; (geol.) calcaire *m.* (billiards) blanc *m.*; French — *n.* talc *m.*; — *vt.*, marquer à la craie; — up marquer; attribuer; –y *a.* crayeux
challenge *n.* défi *m.*; (mil.) qui-vive *m.*, interpellation *f.*; (sports) challenge *m.*; — *vt.* défier; interpeller; provoquer; disputer, mettre en doute
challenging *a.* de défi; provocateur; provocant; (coll.) très intéressant
chamber *n.* chambre *f.*; salle *f.*, pièce *f.*; — music musique de chambre *f.*
chamberlain *n.* chambellan *m.*
chambermaid *n.* femme de chambre *f.*
chameleon *n.* caméléon *m.*
champ *vt.* & *vi.* mâcher, ronger
champagne *n.* (vin de) champagne *m.*
champion *n.* champion, recordman *m.*; — *vt.* défendre, soutenir; –ship *n.* championnat *m.*
chance *n.* hasard *m.*, chance *f.*; sort *m.*; accident *m.*; occasion *f.*; risque *m.*; by — par hasard; off — chance moyenne; take a — encourir un risque; — *vt.* risquer: — *vi.* venir à; — *a.* fortuit; de rencontre
chancellor *n.* chancelier *m.*; ministre *m.*
chandelier *n.* lustre *m.*
change *n.* changement *m.*; monnaie *f.*; revirement *m.*; — of address changement de domicile *m.*; for a — comme distraction; — of clothes vêtements de rechange *m. pl.*; — *vt.* changer; échanger;

donner la monnaie; transformer; modifier; — **clothes** changer de vêtements; — **the subject** changer de sujet; — **color** changer de visage; — *vi.* (se) changer; tourner; **–ability** *n.* mobilité *f.*; variabilité *f.*; **–able** *a.* mobile; variable; **–less** *a.* immuable; éternel

changing *a.* changeant; — *n.* changement *m.*; — **of the guard** relève *f.*

channel *n.* canal *m.*; lit *m.*; chenal *m.*; conduit *m.*; rigole *f.*; voie *f.*; — *vt.* canneler; creuser des rigoles

chant *n.* chant *m.*; (eccl.) psalmodie *f.*; — *vt.* chanter; (eccl.) psalmodier

chanty *n.* chanson (de bord) *f.*

chaos *n.* chaos *m.*

chaotic *a.* chaotique

chap *n.* type, individu *m.*

chap *vt.* crevasser, gercer; — *n.* crevasse, gerçure *f.*; **–ped hands** des crevasses aux mains

chapel *n.* chapelle *f.*; oratoire *m.*

chaplain *n.* aumônier *m.*

chapter *n.* chapitre *m.*; bureau régional ou local d'une société *m.*

char *vt.* carboniser; — *vi.* se carboniser

character *n.* caractère *m.*; marque *f.*; lettre *f.*; personnage *m.*; sujet *m.*; type *m.*; — **actor** acteur de genre *m.*; **be in —** s'accorder, s'harmoniser; **–istic** *a.* caractéristique; **–istic** *n.* trait *m.*; **–istically** *adv.* d'une manière caractéristique; **–ization** *n.* caractérisation *f.*; **–ize** *vt.* caractériser, dépeindre

charcoal *n.* charbon de bois *m.*; (art) fusain *m.*; — **burner** *n.* charbonnier *m.*

charge *n.* prix *m.*; charge *f.*; soin *m.*; accusation; devoir *m.*; fonction *f.*; (of a judge) résumé *m.*; **free of —** gratis; **exempt de frais**; **take —** of se charger de; — **account** compte courant *m.*; — *vt.* charger; accuser; imputer; débiter; demander; porter; **–able** *a.* accusable; imputable; **–r** *n.* cheval de bataille *m.*; (elec.) chargeur *m.*

chariot *n.* char *m.*

charitable *a.* charitable

charity *n.* charité *f.*; aumônes *f. pl.*; bienfaisance *f.*

Charley horse *n.* crampe musculaire, raideur musculaire *f.* (comme résultat d'un exercice violent)

charm *n.* charme, sortilège *m.*; porte-bonheur *m.*; breloque *f.*; — *vt.* charmer, enchanter; ensorceler; **–ing** *a.* charmant

chart *n.* carte *f.*; diagramme *m.*; — *vt.* dresser la carte de; **–er** *n.* charte *f.*; privilège *m.*; (naut.) affrètement *m.*; **–er member** membre fondateur *m.*; **–er** *vt.* accorder une charte à; (naut.) affré-

ter; **–ered** *a.* à charte; privilégié; affrété

chase *n.* chasse, poursuite *f.*; — *vt.* chasser; poursuivre; (gold) ciseler; (metal) repousser; (gem) enchâsser; — **away** chasser; **–r** *n.* chasseur *m.*; pousse-café *m.*; boisson (d'ordinaire) non-alcoolique prise après un verre de whisky *f.*

chasm *n.* gouffre *m.*; chasme *m.*; abîme *m.*

chassis *n.* châssis *m.*

chaste *a.* chaste; pudique; pur; **–n** *vt.* châtier

chastise *vt.* châtier, corriger; **–ment** *n.* châtiment *m.*

chastity *n.* chasteté, pureté *f.*

chat *n.* causerie *f.*; — *vi.* causer, jaser; **–ty** *a.* causeur

chattel *n.* bien mobilier *m.*

chatter *n.* bavardage *m.*; caquetage *m.*; — *vi.* bavarder, caqueter, jaser; claquer; **–ing** *n.* (teeth) claquement *m.*; (people) bavardage *m.*; (birds) caquetage *m.*

chatterbox *n.* bavard, babillard *m.*

chauffeur *n.* chauffeur *m.*

chauvinism *n.* chauvinisme *m.*

cheap *a.* bon marché; (coll.) honteux; **–en** *vt.* baisser le prix de; **–er** *a.* meilleur marché; **–ly** *adv.* bon marché; **–ness** *n.* bon marché, bas prix *m.*; qualité inférieure *f.*; médiocrité *f.*

cheat *n.* tricheur, escroc *m.*; trompeur *m.*; — *vt.* tricher; tromper; frauder; **–ing** *n.* tricherie *f.*; tromperie *f.*

check *n.* chèque *m.*; billet, bulletin, ticket *m.*; contrôle *m.*; vérification *f.*; arrêt *m.*; frein *m.*; (chess) échec *m.*; carreau *m.*; — **list** liste de controle *f.*; — *vt.* vérifier; contrôler; arrêter; freiner; retenir, refouler; (chess) faire échec; (baggage) faire enregistrer; — **off** pointer; — *vi.* s'arrêter; hésiter; — **in** (hotel) s'inscrire dans le registre d'un hôtel; — **out** quitter l'hôtel; **–ed** *a.* (material) à carreaux; **–er** *n.* contrôleur *m.*; **–ing** *n.* contrôle *m.*; vérification *f.*; enregistrement *m.*; **–ing account** compte en banque *m.*

checkbook *n.* carnet de chèques *m.*

checkerboard *n.* damier *m.*

checkered *a.* à carreaux, quadrillé; — **career** vie mouvementée *f.*

checkers *n. pl.* dames *f. pl.*

checkmate *n.* échec et mat *m.*; — *vt.* faire échec et mat à

checkroom *n.* vestiaire *m.*; consigne *f.*

checkup *n.* examen *m.*; vérification *f.*

cheddar *n.* cheddar *m.*

cheek *n.* joue *f.*; (coll.) impertinence *f.*, toupet *m.*; **–bone** *n.* pommette *f.*

cheep *vi.* piauler; —, **–ing** *n.* piaulement *m.*

cheer *n.* humeur, disposition *f.*; encouragement *m.*; ban *m.*; acclamation *f.*; — *vt.*

encourager; égayer; acclamer; — **up** se ragaillardir; — up! courage!; –**ful** *a.* de bonne humeur, gai, égayant; –**fully** *adv.* gaiement; volontiers, de bon cœur: –**ing** *a.* réjouissant; encourageant; –**ing** *n.* acclamation *f.*; –**less** *a.* triste, morne

cheerleader *n.* étudiant qui organise et dirige les bans aux événements sportifs *m.*

cheese *n.* fromage *m.*

cheesecake *n.* pâtisserie au **fromage** *f.*; (phot.) (coll.) cheesecake *m.*

cheesecloth *n.* gaze *f.*

chef *n.* chef de cuisine *m.*

chemical *a.* chimique; — *n.* produit chimique *m.*

chemist *n.* chimiste *m.*; –**ry** *n.* chimie *f.*

cherish *vt.* chérir; nourrir, caresser

cherry *n.* cerise *f.*; — **orchard** cerisaie *f.*; — **tree** cerisier *m.*; — *a.* cerise, vermeil; **wild** — merise *f.*

cherub *n.* chérubin *m.*; –**ic** *a.* chérubique

chess *n.* échecs *m. pl.*

chessboard *n.* échiquier *m.*

chessman, chesspiece *n.* pièce *f.*

chest *n.* poitrine *f.*; coffret *m.*, caisse *f.*; — **of drawers** commode *f.*

chestnut *n.* châtaigne *f.*; marron *m.*; (tree) châtaignier, marronnier *m.*; — *a.* châtain, châtaigne

cheviot *n.* cheviote *f.*

chew *vt.* mâcher; (tobacco) chiquer; (fig.) méditer; — *n.* morceau *m.*; –**ing** *n.* mastication *f.*; –**ing gum** gomme à mâcher *f.*; chewing-gum *m.*

chicanery *n.* chicane, chicanerie *f.*

chicken *n.* poulet *m.*; **spring** — poussin *m.*; — **pox** *n.* varicelle *f.*

chick-pea *n.* pois chiche *m.*

chicory *n.* chicorée *f.*; endive *f.*

chide *vt.* reprocher; gronder

chief *n.* chef *m.*; patron *m.*; — **of staff** chef de l'état-major *m.*; — **justice** président du tribunal *m.*; — *a.* principal; en chef; –**ly** *adv.* surtout; principalement

chieftain *n.* chef *m.*

chiffon *n.* chiffon *m.*, gaze *f.*

chilblain *n.* engelure *f.*

child *n.* enfant *m. & f.*; **with** — enceinte; –**ish** *a.* enfantin, d'enfant; puéril; –**ishness** *n.* puérilité *f.*

childbirth *n.* accouchement *m.*

childhood *n.* enfance *f.*

Chile *n.* Chili *m.*

chill *n.* froid *m.*; coup de froid *m.*; froidure *f.*; refroidissment *m.*; frisson *m.*; **take the** — **off** (faire) tiédir; — *vt.* glacer, refroidir; réfrigérer; faire frissonner; –**ed** *a.* glacé; –**iness** *n.* froideur *f.*; fraîcheur *f.*; –**ing** *a.* glacial; –**y** *a.* frais, froid; feel

–**y** avoir froid; **be** –**y** (behavior) être froid

chime *n.* carillon *m.*; — *vt. & vi.* carillonner; — **in** intervenir

chimerical *a.* chimérique

chiming *n.* carillonnement *m.*; sonnerie *f.*

chimney *n.* cheminée *f.*; — **sweep** *n.* ramoneur *m.*; — **sweeping** *n.* ramonage *m.*

chimpanzee *n.* chimpanzé *m.*

chin *n.* menton *m.*

China *n.* Chine *f.*

china *n.* porcelaine *f.*

Chinese *a. & n.* chinois *m.*

chink *n.* fente, crevasse *f.*

chip *n.* copeau, éclat *m.*; brisure *f.*; fragment *m.*; (cards) jeton *m.*; — *vt.* ébrécher; enlever un copeau (un fragment) à; — *vi.* s'écailler; — **in** contribuer, cotiser

chipmunk *n.* tamias *m.*

chipper *a.* gai, heureux

chiropodist *n.* pédicure *m.*

chiropracter *n.* chiropracteur *m.*

chirp *n.* gazouillement *m.*; grésillement *m.*; chant *m.*; — *vi.* pépier, gazouiller; grésiller

chisel *n.* ciseau *m.*; — *vt.* ciseler

chitchat *n.* conversation *f.*; bavardage *m.*

chivalrous *a.* chevaleresque, de chevalerie

chivalry *n.* chevalerie *f.*

chive *n.* ciboulette *f.*

chloride *n.* chlorure *m.*

chlorinate *vt.* chlorurer

chlorination *n.* chloruration *f.*

chlorine *n.* chlore *m.*

chloroform *n.* chloroforme *m.*; — *vt.* chloroformer, chloroformiser

chlorophyll *n.* chlorophylle *f.*

chock-full *a.* bondé, comble; bourré

chocolate *n.* chocolat *m.*

choice *n.* choix *m.*; alternative *f.*; préférence *f.*; — *a.* de choix

choir *n.* chœur *m.*

choke *n.* (auto.) étrangleur *m.*; — *vt. & vi.* suffoquer, étouffer, étrangler; boucher; — **back** refouler; –**r** *n.* foulard *m.*; (necklace) collier court *m.*

choking *n.* étranglement, étouffement *m.*; suffocation *f.*

choleric *a.* colérique

cholesterol *n.* cholestérol *m.*

choose *vt.* choisir; élire; préférer; opter; vouloir

choosing *n.* choix *m.*

choosy *a.* (coll.) difficile à plaire

chop *n.* côtelette *f.*; coup de hache *m.*; **lick one's** –**s** se lécher les babines; — *vt.* hacher; couper; — *vi.* clapoter; — **down** abattre; — **off** trancher, couper; –**ped meat** viande hachée *f.*; –**per** *n.*

couperet, hachoir *m.*; **-py** *a.* clapoteux *m.*
chopsticks *n. pl.* baguettes *f. pl.*, bâton-nets *m. pl.*
chord *n.* accord *m.*
chore *n.* devoir *m.*; corvée *f.*; **-s** *n. pl.* travaux de ménage *m. pl.*
choreography *n.* chorégraphie *f.*
chorister *n.* choriste *m.*; enfant de chœur *m.*
chortle *vi.* glousser
chorus *n.* chœur *m.*; refrain *m.*; — *vt.* répéter en chœur
chosen *a.* choisi, élu
Christ *n.* Le Christ, Jésus-Christ *m.*
christen *vt.* baptiser; **-ing** *n.* baptême *m.*
Christendom *n.* chrétienté *f.*
Christian *n. & a.* chrétien *m.*; — **name** prénom *m.*, nom de baptême *m.*; **-ity** *n.* christianisme *m.*
Christmas *n.* Noël *m.*; **Merry** — joyeux Noël; — **card** carte de Noël *f.*; — **carol** chant de Noël *m.*; — **Eve** la veille de Noël *f.*; — **presents** cadeaux de Noël *m. pl.*
chromatic *a.* chromatique
chrome *n.* acier chromé *m.*; chromage *m.*
chromium *n.* chrome *m.*; chromium *m.*
chromosome *n.* chromosome *m.*
chronic *a.* chronique; continuel, constant
chronicle *n.* chronique *f.*; **-r** *n.* chroniqueur *m.*
chronological *a.* chronologique; **in** — **order** chronologiquement, par ordre des dates
chronometer *n.* chronomètre *m.*
chrysalis *n.* chrysalide *f.*
chrysanthemum *n.* chrysanthème *m.*
chubby *a.* rondelet; joufflu
chuck *vt.* jeter, lancer; flanquer; — *n.* petite tape sous le menton *f.*; — **steak** steak coupé à l'épaule du bœuf *m.*
chuckle *n.* petit rire *m.*; — *vi.* rire tout bas
chum *n.* copain *m.*, camarade *m.*; **-my** *a.* copain; intime, familier
chunk *n.* (gros) morceau *m.*
church *n.* église *f.*; (Protestant) temple *m.*; — **service** office *m.*
churchman *n.* ecclésiastique *m.*
churchyard *n.* cimetière *m.*
churlish *a.* grossier; mal élevé
churn *n.* baratte *f.*; — *vt.* battre, baratter
chute *n.* glissière *f.*; couloir, conduit *m.*; coulisse *f.*, coulisseau *m.*
cicada *n.* cigale *f.*
Cicero *n.* Cicéron *m.*
cider *n.* cidre *m.*
cigar *n.* cigare *m.*; — **store** bureau de tabac *m.*
cigarette *n.* cigarette *f.*; — **butt** mégot

m.; — **holder** porte-cigarettes *m.*; — **lighter** *n.* allume-cigarette *m.*
cinch *n.* (saddle) sangle *f.*; (coll.) quelque chose de très facile
cinder *n.* cendre *f.*; — **track** piste cendrée *f.*
cinnamon *n.* cannelle *f.*
cipher *n.* chiffre *m.*; (math.) zéro *m.*; — *vt.* chiffrer
circle *n.* cercle *m.*; milieu, monde *m.*; — *vt.* entourer, ceindre; faire le tour de; — *vi.* tournoyer
circuit *n.* circuit *m.*; détour *m.*; tournée *f.*; **short** — court-circuit *m.*; — **breaker** *n.* coupe-circuit *m.*; **-ous** *a.* détourné
circular *a.* circulaire; — *n.* feuille publicitaire *f.*; **-ize** *vt.* prospecter
circulate *vi.* circuler; — *vt.* faire circuler
circulation *n.* circulation *f.*; (newspaper) tirage *m.*
circumcise *vt.* circoncire; **-d** *a.* circoncis
circumcision *n.* circoncision *f.*
circumference *n.* circonférence *f.*; périphérie *f.*
circumflex *a. & n.* circonflexe *m.*
circumnavigate *vt.* faire le tour de
circumnavigation *n.* circumnavigation *f.*
circumscribe *vt.* circonscrire; limiter
circumscription *n.* circonscription *f.*
circumspect *a.* circonspect, prudent; **-ion** *n.* circonspection, prudence *f.*
circumstance *n.* circonstance(s) *f.* (*pl.*); cas *m.*; incident *m.*; détail *m.*; situation *f.*; pompe, cérémonie *f.*
circumstantial *a.* circonstanciel; circonstancié, détaillé; accidentel; — **evidence** preuves indirectes *f. pl.*
circumvent *vt.* circonvenir
circus *n.* cirque *m.*
cirrus *n.* cirrus *m.*, (coll.) queue de vache *f.*
cistern *n.* citerne *f.*; réservoir *m.*
citadel *n.* citadelle *f.*
citation *n.* citation *f.*
cite *vt.* citer; assigner
citizen *n.* citoyen *m.*; citadin *m.*; **fellow** — concitoyen *m.*; **-ry** *n.* citoyens *m. pl.*; **-ship** *n.* nationalité *f.*; droit de cité *m.*
citric *a.* citrique
citron *n.* cédrat *m.*
citrus *n. & a.* citron *m.*
city *n.* ville *f.*; cité *f.*; — **hall** hôtel de ville *m.*
civet *n.* civette *f.*
civic *a.* civique; **-s** *n. pl.* instruction civique *f.*
civil *a.* civil; courtois, poli; — **defense** *n.* défense civile *f.*; — **disobedience** désobéissance civile *f.*; — **rights** droits civils *m. pl.*; — **service**

administration publique *f.*; fonction de l'Etat *f.*; **–ian** *a. & n.* civil *m.*; **–ian** life civil *m.*; **–ity** *n.* civilité *f.*; politesse *f.*; **–ization** *n.* civilisation *f.*; **–ize** *vt.* civiliser

clad *a.* vêtu, habillé, couvert

claim *n.* prétention *f.*; titre *m.*; réclamation, revendication *f.*; (prospecting) concession *f.*; — *vt.* prétendre; réclamer, revendiquer; demander; faire valoir; soutenir; **–ant** *n.* prétendant *m.*; réclamant, revendicateur *m.*; demandeur *m.*

clairvoyant *a. & n.* voyant *m.*; clairvoyant *m.*

clam *n.* palourde *f.*

clamber *vi.* grimper; — **over**, — **up** escalader

clamminess *n.* moiteur froide *f.*

clammy *a.* humide, moite; collant

clamor *n.* clameur *f.*, bruit *m.*; — *vi.* vociférer; — **for** réclamer; **–ous** *a.* bruyant

clamp *n.* crampon *m.*; main de fer *f.*; agrafe *f.*; attache *f.*; — *vt.* fixer, attacher

clan *n.* clan *m.*; **–nish** *a.* de clan; **–nishness** *n.* étroitesse *f.*, esprit de corps étroit *m.*

clandestine *a.* clandestin

clang *n.* son métallique, résonnement *m.*; **–or** son métallique, résonnement (des cloches) *m.*

clap *n.* battement *m.*; coup *m.*; applaudissements *m. pl.*; — *vt.* battre (des mains); taper, donner une tape à; — *vi.* applaudir; **–per** *n.* battant *m.*; applaudisseur *m.*; claqueur *m.*; **–pers** (theat.) claque *f.*; **–ping** *n.* applaudissements *m. pl.*

claret *n.* (vin de) bordeaux *m.*

clarify *vt.* éclaircir, clarifier

clarinet *n.* clarinette *f.*

clarion *n.* clairon *m.*

clarity *n.* clarté *f.*

clash *n.* choc *m.*; conflit *m.*; dispute *f.*; (color) disparate *f.*; — *vi.* se heurter, s'opposer; s'entre-choquer; faire disparate

clasp *n.* agrafe *f.*; fermoir *m.*; fermeture *f.*; étreinte *f.*; **hand—** serrement de mains *m.*; — **knife** couteau pliant *m.*; — *vt.* agrafer; étreindre, serrer; tenir

class *n.* classe *f.*; cours *m.*; genre *m.*, sorte *f.*; catégorie *f.*; type *m.*; caste *f.*; **lower** — prolétariat *m.*; **middle** — bourgeoisie *f.*; — *vt.* classer; **–ic** *a. & n.* classique *m.*; **–ical** *a.* classique; **–ics** *n.* classiques *m. pl.* humanités *f. pl.*; **–ification** *n.* classement *m.*; classifica-

tion *f.*; **–ified** *a.* classé; **–ified** advertisement petite annonce *f.*; **–ified** information document(s) déclaré(s) secret(s) par le gouvernement *m. (pl.)*; **–ify** *vt.* classer, classifier; **–y** *a.* chic

classmate *n.* camarade de classe *m.*

classroom *n.* salle de classe *f.*

clatter *n.* bruit, cliquetis *m.*; — *vi.* faire du bruit

clause *n.* clause *f.*; article *m.*; (gram.) proposition *f.*

clavicle *n.* clavicule *f.*

claw *n.* griffe *f.*, serre *f.*; pince *f.*; (hammer) panne fendue *f.*; — *vt.* griffer, déchirer

clay *n.* argile *f.*; glaise *f.*; — **pipe** pipe en terre *f.*; — **pit** argilière, glaisière *f.*; **–ey** *a.* argileux

clean *a.* propre; net; — *adv.* net; tout à fait; — *vt.* nettoyer; faire; récurer; (fish) vider; (streets) balayer; — **out** curer; ranger; (person) mettre à sec; — **up** nettoyer; se laver, se débarbouiller; **–er** *n.* nettoyeur *m.*; **–ing** *n.* nettoyage *m.*; **dry –ing** nettoyage à sec; **–liness** *n.* propreté *f.*; netteté *f.*

cleanse *vt.* nettoyer; purifier, écurer; assainir

cleansing *n.* nettoyage *m.*; curage *m.*

clear *a.* clair; net; dégagé; libre; certain; (property) franc d'hypothèque; **all —** (civil defense) fin d'alerte *f.*; **keep —of** éviter; — *vt.* éclaircir; clarifier; franchir; dégager; déblayer; liquider; faire un bénéfice; (com.) solder; (land) défricher; (customs) dédouaner; — **away** écarter, enlever; — **oneself** se disculper; — **the table** desservir; enlever le couvert; — **up** éclaircir; — *vi.* s'éclaircir; se dégager; — **out** filer; **–ance** *n.* jeu *m.*; espace *m.*; **–ance sale** vente de soldes *f.*; **–ing** *n.* (forest) éclaircie *f.*; dégagement *m.*; (banking) compensation de chèques *f.*; **–ing house** comptoir de règlement *m.*; **–ly** *adv.* clairement, nettement; clair; évidemment; **–ness** *n.* clarté *f.*; netteté *f.*

clear-cut *a.* net

clearheaded *a.* lucide; perspicace

clear-sighted *a.* clairvoyant

cleat *n.* taquet *m.*

cleavage *n.* fendage *m.*; scission *f.*

cleave *vt.* fendre; — *vi.* se fendre; s'attacher, adhérer; **–r** *n.* couperet *m.*

cleft *n.* fente, crevasse *f.*; — *a.*, — **palate** palais fendu *m.*

clemency *n.* clémence *f.*; (weather) douceur *f.*

clement *a.* clément; doux

clench *vt.* serrer, crisper
clergy *n.* clergé *m.*; **—man** *n.* ecclésiastique *m.*; pasteur *m.*
clerical *a.* clérical, de copiste; **— error** faute de copiste *f.*; **— work** travail de bureau *m.*
clerk *n.* commis *m.*; employé de bureau *m.*; (court) greffier *m.*; (eccl.) clerc *m.*
clever *a.* habile; adroit; fort; intelligent; **—ness** *n.* habileté *f.*; adresse *f.*; intelligence *f.*
cliché *n.* cliché *m.*
click *n.* clic, cliquet, cliquetis *m.*; clappement *m.*; **—** *vt. & vi.* cliqueter; claquer; **—** *vi.* (coll.) réussir; aller ensemble
cliff *n.* falaise *f.*; escarpement *m.*
climate *n.* climat *m.*
climatic *a.* climatique, climatérique
climax *n.* point culminant *m.*; comble *m.*
climb *n.* montée *f.*; ascension *f.*; **—** *vt. & vi.* monter, gravir; grimper; **— down** descendre; **-er** *n.* grimpeur *m.*; (bot.) plante grimpante *f.*; **mountain —er** alpiniste *m. & f.*; **-ing** *a.* grimpant; **-ing** *n.* montée *f.*; escalade *f.*; **mountain -ing** alpinisme *m.*
clinch *n.* crampon, rivet *m.*; (boxing) corps-à-corps *m.*; **—** *vt.* river; **—** *vi.* se prendre corps-à-corps; **-er** *n.* argument sans réplique *m.*
cling *vi.* adhérer; coller; s'attacher, s'accrocher alberge, pavie *f.*
clinic *n.* clinique *f.*; **-al** *a.* clinique
clink *n.* tintement (de verres) *m.*; **—** *vi.* tinter; **—** *vt.* trinquer; **-er** *n.* mâchefer *m.*
clip *n.* agrafe, **griffe**, attache, **pince** *f.*; attache-papiers *m.*; (rifle) chargeur *m.*; **—** *vt.* couper; tondre; découper; agrafer, pincer, attacher; **-per** *n.* (naut., avi.) clipper *m.*; **-pers** *m. pl.* tondeuse *f.*; **-ping** *n.* coupe *f.*; coupure *f.*; tondage *m.*
clique *n.* coterie *f.*
cloak *n.* manteau *m.*; (fig.) voile *m.*; **— and dagger** *a.* de cape et d'épée; **—** *vt.* (fig.) masquer
cloakroom *n.* vestiaire *m.*; (rail.) consigne *f.*
clock *n.* horloge, pendule *f.*; **alarm —** réveil *m.*; **one o'—** une heure; **two o'—** deux heures; **twelve o'—** (noon) midi *m.*, (midnight) minuit *m.*; **—** *vt.* chronométrer
clockwise *a.* dextrorsum; à droite
clockwork *n.* mouvement, rouage *m.*; **like —** comme sur des roulettes
clod *n.* motte *f.*; (person) rustre *m.*
clog *n.* entrave *f.*; galoche *f.*; **—** *vt.*

entraver; boucher; **—** *vi.* se boucher
cloister *n.* cloître *m.*; **—** *vt.* cloîtrer
close *n.* fin *f.*; bout *m.*; clôture *f.*; **—** *vt.* fermer; terminer; clore; serrer; **—** *vi.* se fermer; se terminer; **— down** fermer; **— up** boucher; se serrer; **—** *a.* renfermé; intime; proche; serré; étroit; **at — quarters** de près; **have a — call** l'échapper belle; **—** *adv.* (de) près; **— by** tout près; **-d** *a.* fermé; (theat.) relâche; **-d shop** usine où la main-d'œuvre est tout à fait syndiquée *f.*; **-ly** *adv.* étroitement; attentivement; **-ness** *n.* proximité *f.*; intimité; exactitude *f.*; réserve *f.*; (weather) lourdeur *f.*
close-cropped *a.* coupé ras
closefisted *a.* ladre, avare
close-fitting *a.* collant
closemouthed *a.* peu communicatif
closet *n.* placard *m.*; armoire *f.*; **—** *vt.*, **be -ed** être enfermé
close-up *n.* vue prise de près *f.*; **—** *n.* (movies) gros plan *m*
closing *n.* fermeture *f.*; clôture *f.*; **—** *a.* final, dernier
closure *n.* clôture, fermeture *f.*
clot *n.* caillot *m.*; embolie *f.*; **—** *vi.* se coaguler; se cailler; se figer
cloth *n.* étoffe *f.*; drap *m.*; tissu *m.*; toile *f.*; **-e** *vt.* habiller, vêtir, revêtir; **-es** *n. pl.* vêtements, habits *m. pl.*; effets *m. pl.*; **-ier** *n.* drapier *m.*; **-ing** *n.* vêtements *m. pl.*
clothesbrush *n.* brosse à habits *f.*
clothes closet *n.* garde-robe *f.*
clothes hanger *n.* cintre *f.*
clothesline *n.* étendoir *m.*
clothespin *n.* pince *f.*; épingle à lingne *f.*
cloud *n.* nuage *m.*; nue, nuée *f.*; voile *m.*; **—** *vt.* voiler, obscurcir; troubler; **— up** se voiler, se couvrir; **-less** *a.* sans nuages; **-y** *a.* nuageux; couvert; trouble
cloudburst *n.* averse, trombe *f.*
clout *n.* linge *m.*; (coll.) claque *f.*
clove *n.* clou de girofle *m.*; **— of garlic** gousse d'ail *f.*
cloven *a.*, **— hoof** pied fourchu *m.*
clover *n.* trèfle *m.*
clown *n.* clown, pitre *m.*; fou *m.*; bouffon *m.*; **—** *vi.* faire le clown
cloy *vt.* rassasier
club *n.* club, cercle *m.*, société *f.*; cénacle *m.*; (weapon) massue *f.*; (cards) trèfle *m.*; **—** *vt.* assommer, frapper; **—** *vi.* se réunir, se cotiser
clubfoot *n.* pied bot *m.*
clubhouse *n.* pavillon *m.*
clubroom *n.* salle de réunion *f.*
club steak *n.* aloyau de bœuf *m.*

cluck *vi.* glousser

clue *n.* indice *m.*; piste *f.*; clef *f.*; indication *f.*

clump *n.* bouquet *m.*; massif *m.*; bloc *m.*; pas lourd *m.*; — *vi.* se grouper; marcher d'un pas lourd

clumsiness *n.* maladresse *f.*; gaucherie *f.*

clumsy *a.* maladroit, gauche

cluster *n.* bouquet *m.*; massif *m.*; groupe *m.*; (grapes) grappe *f.*; — *vt.* grouper; — *vi.* se grouper

clutch *n.* griffe, patte *f.*; (auto.) embrayage *m.*; let in the — embrayer; **release the** — débrayer; in the –es of sous la patte de; — *vt.* saisir; — **at** se raccrocher à

clutter *n.* désordre *m.*; encombrement *m.*; — *vt.*, — **up** mettre en désordre; encombrer

coach *n.* voiture *f.*; carrosse *m.*; (rail.) wagon *m.*; (sports) entraîneur *m.*; — *vt.* entraîner; (theat.) faire répéter

coachhouse *n.* remise *f.*

coachman *n.* cocher *m.*

coagulant *n.* coagulant *m.*

coagulate *vt. & vi.* (se) figer, (se) coaguler

coagulation *n.* coagulation *f.*

coal *n.* charbon *m.*; houille *f.*; — **gas** gaz d'éclairage *m.*; — **mine** mine de houille *f.*; houillère *f.*; — **miner** mineur *m.*; — **mining** exploitation de la houille *f.*

coalesce *vi.* s'unir, se combiner; fusionner; –**nce** *n.* coalescence, fusion *f.*

coalition *n.* bloc *m.*; coalition *f.*

coarse *a.* grossier; gros; rude; –**ness** *n.* grossièreté *f.*; rudesse *f.*; grosseur *f.*; gros grain *m.*

coarse-grained *a.* à gros grain; à gros fil

coast *n.* côte *f.*, rivage *m.*; littoral *m.*; — **guard** *n.* gardes-côte *m.*; — **guardsman** garde-côte *m. s.*; — *vi.* descendre en roue libre; –**ing** *n.* descente en roue libre *f.*; (naut.) cabotage *m.*

coaster *n.* dessous *m.*

coat *n.* habit *m.*; veston *m.*; pardessus, manteau *m.*; (paint) couche *f.*; (animal) robe *f.*; — **of arms** armes, armoiries *f. pl.*; — **of mail** cotte de mailles *f.*; — **hanger** *n.* porte-vêtements *m.*; –**room** *n.* vestiaire *m.*; — *vt.* couvrir, enduire; –**ed** *a.* enduit, couvert, recouvert; –**ed tongue** langue chargée *f.*; –**ing** *n.* enduit *m.*; couche *f.*; (anat.) paroi *f.*

coauthor *n.* coauteur, collaborateur *m.*

coax *vt.* câliner, cajoler, enjôler; –**ing** *a.* câlin, cajoleur; –**ing** *n.* cajolerie *f.*

coaxial *a.* coaxial; — **cable** *n.* câble coaxial *m.*

cobalt *n.* cobalt *m.*; — **bomb** bombe au cobalt *f.*

cobbler *n.* savetier, cordonnier *m.*

cobblestone *n.* caillou, galet *m.*

cobweb *n.* toile d'araignée *f.*

cocaine *n.* cocaïne *f.*

cock *n.* coq *m.*; robinet *m.*; (weapons) chien *m.*; **crow of the** — chant du coq *m.*; — *vt.* armer; dresser; (hat) retrousser; –**iness** *n.* suffisance *f.*; –**y** *a.* suffisant

cockade *n.* cocarde *f.*

cock-and-bull *a.*, — **story** coq-à-l'âne *m.*

cockeyed *a.* de travers, de biais; insensé

cockfight *n.* combat de coqs *m.*

cockpit *n.* cockpit *m.*; carlingue *f.*

cockroach *n.* blatte *f.*, cafard *m.*

cocktail *n.* cocktail *m.*; apéritif *m.*

cocoa *n.* cacao *m.*

coconut *n.* noix de coco *f.*; — **palm** cocotier *m.*

cocoon *n.* cocon *m.*

cod *n.* morue *f.*

C.O.D. contre remboursement

coddle *vt.* gâter, dorloter, choyer

code *n.* code *m.*; chiffre *m.*; — *vt.* chiffrer

codfish *n.* morue *f.*

codicil *n.* codicille *m.*

codification *n.* codification *f.*

codify *vt.* codifier

cod-liver oil *n.* huile de foie de morue *f.*

coeducational *a.* mixte

coefficient *n.* coefficient *m.*

coerce *vt.* contraindre, forcer

coercion *n.* contrainte *f.*; coercition *f.*

coercive *a.* coercitif

coeval *a.* contemporain

coexist *vi.* coexister; –**ence** *n.* coexistence *f.*

coffee *n.* café *m.*; **black** — café nature, café noir; — **bean** grain de café *m.*; — **cup** tasse à café *f.*; — **grinder**, — **mill** moulin à café *m.*; — **grounds** marc de café *m.*; — **plantation** *n.* caféière *f.*

coffeepot *n.* cafetière *f.*

coffer *n.* coffre *f.*

cofferdam *n.* bâtardeau *m.*

coffin *n.* cercueil *m.*

cog *n.* dent *f.*; — *vt.* denter

cogency *n.* force, puissance *f.*

cogent *a.* puissant

cogitate *vi.* réfléchir, méditer

cogitation *n.* réflexion, méditation *f.*

cognac *n.* cognac *m.*

cognizance *n.* connaissance *f.*

cognizant *a.* instruit

cogwheel *n.* roue dentée *f.*

cohabit *vi.* cohabiter

cohere *vi.* adhérer, se tenir; –**nce** *n.* cohérence *f.*; –**nt** *a.* cohérent; –**ntly** *adv.*

avec cohérence
cohesion *n.* cohésion *f.*
cohesive *a.* cohésif
cohort *n.* cohorte *f.*
coif *n.* (headdress of a nun) cornette *f.*
coil *n.* pli *m.*, repli, rouleau *m.*; anneau *m.*; (elec.) bobine *f.*, enroulement *m.*; — *vt.* rouler, bobiner; enrouler; — *vi.* serpenter; s'enrouler, boucler
coin *n.* pièce *f.*; monnaie *f.*; espèces *f. pl.*; — collector numismate *m.*; — *vi.* battre (monnaie), frapper; inventer; **–age** *n.* monnayage *m.*; monnaie *f.*
coincide *vi.* coïncider; s'accorder; **–nce** *n.* coïncidence *f.*
coke *n.* coke *m.*
colander *n.* passoire *f.*
cold *a.* froid; indifférent, insensible; **be** — (person) avoir froid; (weather) faire froid; **grow** — se refroidir; — **cream** crème de beauté *f.*; — **cuts** charcuterie *f.*; assiette anglaise *f.*; — **feet** (coll.) trac *m.*, peur *f.*; — **storage** entrepôt frigorifique *m.*; — *n.* froid; (med.) rhume *m.*; **catch (a)** — attraper un rhume, s'enrhumer; **have a** — être enrhumé; **–ness** *n.* froideur *f.*
cold-blooded *a.* (animal) à sang froid; insensible; prémédité
coleslaw *n.* salade de choux *f.*
colic *n.* colique *f.*
Coliseum *n.* Colisée *m.*
colitis *n.* colite *f.*
collaborate *vi.* collaborer
collaboration *n.* collaboration *f.*
collaborator *n.* collaborateur *m.*
collapse *n.* effondrement, écroulement *m.*; débâcle *f.*; chute *f.* affaissement *m.*, prostration *f.*; — *vi.* s'effondrer, s'écrouler; s'affaisser
collapsible *a.* pliant; démontable
collar *n.* col *m.*; collet *m.*; collier *m.*; (mech.) anneau *m.*; **detachable** — **faux** col *m.*; — *vt.* saisir; colleter
collarbone *n.* clavicule *f.*
collate *vt.* collationner
collateral *a.* collatéral; — *n.* garantie *f.*
colleague *n.* collègue *m.*; confrère *m.*
collect *vt.* rassembler; recueillir; collectionner; — **oneself** se reprendre; — *vi.* s'assembler, se rassembler; **–ed** *a.* recueilli; calme; **–ion** *n.* recueil *m.*; collection *f.*; (taxes) perception *f.*; (postal) levée *f.*; assemblage *m.*; **–ive** *a.* collectif, commun; **–ivity** *n.* collectivité *f.*; **–or** *n.* (tickets) contrôleur *m.*; (taxes) percepteur *m.*; collectionneur *m.*; receveur *m.*; encaisseur *m.*; collecteur *m.*
collective bargaining *n.* discussion entre les patrons et les ouvrers *f.*

college *n.* collége *m.* (établissement d'enseignement supérieur aux États-Unis)
collegiate *a.* collégial; de collège
collide *vi.* entrer en collision; se heurter
collision *n.* collision *f.*, choc *m.*; (naut.) abordage *m.*; (rail.) tamponnement *m.*
colloquial *a.* familier; vulgaire; **–ism** *n.* expression familière *f.*
collusion *n.* collusion *f.*; complicité *f.*
Colombia *n.* Colombie *f.*
colon *n.* (gram.) deux points *m.* *pl.*; (anat.) côlon *m.*
colonel *n.* colonel *m.*
colonial *a.* colonial
colonization *n.* colonisation *f.*
colonize *vt.* coloniser; **–r** *n.* colonisateur *m.*
colony *n.* colonie *f.*
color *n.* couleur *f.*; coloris *m.*; teint *m.*; **–s** *n. pl.* (mil., naut.) drapeau, pavillon *m.*; **be off** — être pâle; **lose** — devenir pâle; — *vt.* colorer; colorier; imager; — *vi.* se colorer; rougir; **–ation** *n.* coloration *f.*; **–ed** *a.* coloré, colorié; de couleur; en couleurs; **–ing** *n.* coloris *m.*; coloration *f.*; teint *m.*; **–ful** *a.* coloré; **–less** *a.* incolore; sans couleur
color-blind *a.* daltonien
color blindness *n.* daltonisme *m.*
colorcast *n.* émission de télévision transmise en couleurs *f.*
color television *n.* télévision en couleurs *f.*
colossus *n.* colosse *m.*
colt *n.* poulain *m.*
column *n.* colonne *f.*; (newspaper) rubrique *f.*; **–ist** *n.* journaliste *m.*; chroniqueur *m.*
comatose *a.* comateux
comb *n.* peigne *m.*; carde *f.*; (cock) crête *f.*; — *vt.* peigner; — *vi.* se peigner; — **one's hair** se peigner les cheveux; — **out** démêler; éliminer
combat *n.* combat *m.*; — *vt.* combattre; **–ant** *n.* combattant *m.*; **–ive** *a.* combatif
combination *n.* combinaison *f.*; combiné, mélange *m.*
combine *n.* cartel *m.*, combinaison *f.*; (agr.) machine qui bat et qui vanne le grain en même temps; fau cheuse-batteuse *f.*; — *vt.* combiner; joindre; — *vi.* se combiner, s'unir; **–d** *a.* réuni
combustible *a.* combustible, inflammable
combustion *n.* combustion *f.*; **spontaneous** — inflammation spontanée *f.*
come *vi.* venir, arriver; advenir; — **about** arriver, se passer; (naut.) virer de bord; — **across** tomber sur, rencontrer; — **after** suivre; succéder à; — **again** revenir; — **along** venir, arriver; accompagner; — **apart** se défaire; — **back**

revenir; — **before** précéder; — **between** intervenir, s'interposer; — **by** passer; obtenir; — **down** descendre; tomber; baisser; se résumer; — **for** venir chercher; — **forward** s'avancer; — **home** rentrer, revenir; — **in** entrer; arriver; — **off** se détacher; avoir lieu; réussir; — **out** sortir; paraître, se découvrir; débuter; — **through** traverser, passer par; pénétrer; — **to** reprendre connaissance; — **together** se réunir, s'assembler; — **up** monter; — **upon** tomber sur, rencontrer; — **now!** allons!

comeback n. retour à la célébrité m.; riposte f.

comedian n. comique m.; comédien m.

comedy n. comédie f.

come on n. (coll.) leurre m., attrape f.

comet n. comète f.

comfort n. confort m.; consolation f., soulagement m.; — vt. consoler, soulager; bien-être m.; aise, aisance f.; **be —able** a. (things) confortable; (persons) être bien, être à l'aise; **—er** n. consolateur m.; couverture piquée f.; **—ing** a. réconfortant, de consolation

comfort index n. relation entre humidité et température f.

comfort station n. toilette f.

comic a. comique; — **opera** n. opéra bouffe, opéra comique m.; — n. comique; comédien m.; **—al** a. comique, drôle

coming a. qui vient; prochain; futur; — n. venue, arrivée f.; avènement m.; — **out** n. début m.; sortie f.; parution f.; apparition f.

comma n. virgule f.

command n. commandement, ordre m.; gouvernement m.; disposition f.; maîtrise, connaissance f.; **have at one's —** avoir à sa disposition; **be at someone's —** être aux ordres de quelqu'un; — vt. commander, ordonner; inspirer; dominer; **—ant** n. commandant m.; **—eer** vt. réquisitionner; **—er** n. commandant m.; **—ing** a. imposant; d'autorité; **—ing officer** n. commandant m.; **—ment** n. commandement m.

commander-in-chief n. commandant en chef m.

commando n. commando m.

commemorate vt. commémorer, célébrer

commemoration n. commémoration f.; **in —** of en mémoire de

commence vt. & vi. commencer; **—ment** n. commencement m.; (school) distribution des prix f.; réception (d'un grade universitaire) f.

commend vt. louer; recommander, confier; **—able** a. louable; **—ation** n. louange f.

commensurate a. proportionné

comment n. commentaire m.; remarque f.; — vi. faire des observations; critiquer; commenter; **—ary** n. commentaire m.; reportage m.; **—ator** n. commentateur m.; speaker, reporter m.

commercial a. commercial, de commerce; — n. annonce publicitaire f.; **—ize** vt. commercialiser

commingle vt. mêler (ensemble); — vi. se mêler

commiserate vt. & vi.; — **with** avoir de la compassion pour

commiseration n. commisération, compassion f.

commissary n. (mil.) grand magasin à l'usage des militaires et de leurs familles m.

commission n. commission, charge f.; pourcentage, pot de vin m.; perpétration f.; — vt. commissioner; charger; (naut.) armer (un vaisseau); (painting) commander; **—er** n. commissaire m.; membre d'une commission m.; directeur m.; préfet m.

commit vt. commettre; confier; engager; — **to prison** envoyer en prison; — **to memory** apprendre par cœur; **—ment** n. engagement m.; **—tal** n. perpétration f.; mise en prison f.

committee n. comité m.; commission f., conseil m.

commodious a. spacieux, ample

commodity n. produit m.; denrée f.; marchandise f.

common a. commun; ordinaire; courant; vulgaire; — **stock** action(s) ordinaire(s) f. (pl.); — n. terrain commun m.; **in —** en commun; **—er** n. bourgeois m.; homme du peuple m.; **—ness** n. banalité f.; fréquence f.; **House of C—s** Chambre des Communes f.

commonplace a. banal; — n. lieu commun m.; banalité f.

commonwealth n. république f.; état m.

commotion n. commotion, agitation, confusion f.; bruit m.

communal a. communal

commune n. commune f.; — vi. s'entretenir

communicable a. communicable; contagieux

communicant n. (eccl.) communiant m.; informateur m.

communicate vt. & vi. communiquer; (eccl.) communier

communication n. communication f.

communicative a. communicatif

communion n. communion f.

communism n. communisme m.

communist n. communiste m. & f.; **-ic** a. communiste

community n. communauté f.; voisinage m.; société f.

commutation n. commutation f.; — ticket carte d'abonnement au chemin de fer f.

commutator n. (elec.) commutateur m.

commute vt. commuer; — vi. voyager régulièrement entre la maison dans la banlieue et le bureau en ville; **-r** n. habitant de banlieue qui travaille en ville m.

compact a. serré, compact; — n. pacte, accord m.; convention f.; (cosmetics) poudrier m.; **-ness** n. compacité f.; concision f.

companion n. compagnon m., compagne f.; **-able** a. sociable; **-ship** n. camaraderie f.; compagnie f.

company n. compagnie f.; assemblée f.; monde m.; (com.) société f.; (theat.) troupe f.; (naut.) équipage m.; **keep someone** — tenir compagnie à quelqu'un; **part** — (with) se séparer (de)

comparable a. comparable

comparative a. comparé; comparatif; relatif; **-ly** adv. relativement; par comparaison

compare vt. comparer; **-d to** en comparaison de; auprès de

comparison n. comparaison f.; **in** — **with** en comparaison de; auprès de

compartment n. compartiment m.; case f.

compass n. boussole f.; (mech.) compas m.; portée f.; — vt. entourer; comploter

compassion n. compassion f.; **-ate** a. compatissant

compatibility n. compatibilité, convenance f.

compel vt. contraindre, forcer; obliger; imposer, inspirer; **-ling** a. puissant, irrésistible; compulsif

compendium n. abrégé m.; manuel m.; recueil m.

compensate vt. compenser, dédommager; rémunérer; **-for** compenser; remplacer

compensation n. compensation f.; honoraires m. pl.; dédommagement m.

compensatory a. compensateur

compete vi. concourir; — **with** faire concurrence à

competence, competency n. compétence f.

competent a. compétent; capable

competition n. concurrence, compétition f.; concours m.; rivalité f.

competitor n. concurrent m.

compilation n. compilation f.

compile vt. compiler; **-r** n. compilateur m.

complacence, complacency n. complai-

sance f.; suffisance f.

complacent a. complaisant; suffisant

complain vi. se plaindre; faire des réclamations; **-ant** n. plaignant m.

complaint n. complainte f.; réclamation f.; (med.) mal m.; **cause for** — n. grief m.

complaisant a. complaisant, obligeant

complement n. complément m.; (mil.) effectif m.; — vt. compléter; **-ary** a. complémentaire

complete vt. compléter; achever; remplir; — a. complet, entier; achevé, terminé; parfait, accompli

completion n. accomplissement, achèvement m.

complex a. complexe; — n. complexe m.; **inferiority** — complexe d'infériorité m.; **-ity** n. complexité f.

complexion n. complexion f.; teint m.; caractère, aspect m.

compliance n. complaisance f.; acquiescement m.; conformité f.; **in** — **with** conformément à

compliant a. complaisant, obligeant; soumis

complicate vt. compliquer, embrouiller; **-d** a. compliqué

complication n. complication f.

complicity n. complicité f.

compliment n. compliment m.; flatterie f.; **to pay a** — faire un compliment; — vt. complimenter; flatter; **-ary** a. complimenteur; gratuit

comply vi. se soumettre; se conformer; obéir, accéder

component n. partie constituante f.; composant m.; — a. composant; — **parts** éléments constitutifs m. pl.

compose vt. composer; arranger; calmer; — **oneself** se calmer; **-d** a. tranquille, calme; **be -d of** se composer de; **-r** n. compositeur m.

composite a. & n. composé m.

composition n. composition f.; rédaction f., thème m.; constitution f.; composé m.

compositor n. compositeur, typographe m.

compost n. engrais, compost m.

composure n. tranquillité f.; sang-froid m.

compound n. composé m.; (mil.) enceinte f.; — vt. composer, arranger; — a. composé; — **interest** intérêts composés m. pl.; — **number** n. nombre composé m.

comprehend vt. comprendre

comprehensible a. compréhensible

comprehension n. compréhension f.

comprehensive a. compréhensif; étendu; d'ensemble

compress *n.* compresse *f.*; — *vt.* comprimer; condenser; **–ion** *n.* compression *f.*

comprise *vt.* comprendre, contenir; comporter; renfermer; **be –d** of se composer de

compromise *n.* compromis *m.*; accomodement *m.*; — *vi.* faire un compromis; transiger; — *vt.* compromettre

compromising *a.* compromettant

comptometer *n.* machine à calculer *f.*

comptroller *n.* comptable *m.*; vérificateur *m.*

compulsion *n.* contrainte *f.*

compulsory *a.* forcé, obligatoire

compunction *n.* remords *m.*, componction *f.*

computation *n.* calcul *m.*

compute *vt.* compter, calculer, computer

comrade *n.* camarade *m.*; **–ship** *n.* camaraderie *f.*

con *n.* contre *m.*; **pros and –s** le pour et le contre; — *vt.* étudier; (naut.) gouverner

concave *a.* concave, creux

conceal *vt.* cacher, dissimuler; masquer, voiler; dérober; recéler; **–ment** *n.* dissimulation *f.*; (law) recel *m.*

concede *vt.* concéder, accorder, admettre

conceit *n.* vanité *f.*; amour-propre *m.*; **–ed** *a.* vaniteux, vain

conceivable *a.* concevable, imaginable

conceive *vt.* & *vi.* concevoir; — of imaginer

concentrate *vt.* concentrer

concentration *n.* concentration *f.*; — **camp** camp de concentration *m.*

concentric *a.* concentrique

concept *n.* concept *m.*; **–ion** *n.* conception *f.*; idée *f.*

concern *n.* affaire, cause *f.*; intérêt, égard *m.*; inquiétude *f.*, trouble *m.*; importance *f.*; compagnie, société anonyme *f.*; maison *f.*; — *vt.* regarder, concerner; inquiéter; toucher, intéresser; **–ed** *a.* inquiet; intéressé; **as far as I am –ed** quant à moi; **–ing** *prep.* touchant, au sujet de, concernant; en ce qui concerne

concert *n.* concert *m.*; **in** — de concert; (mus.) à l'unisson; — *vt.* concerter; **–ed** *a.* concerté

concertmaster *n.* premier violon *m.*; chef d'orchestre *m.*

concession *n.* concession *f.*; **–naire** *n.* concessionnaire *m.* & *f.*

concessive *a.* concessif

conciliate *vt.* concilier, réconcilier

conciliator *n.* conciliateur *m.*; **–y** *a.* conciliatoire, conciliant

concise *a.* concis, succinct; **–ness** *n.* concision *f.*

conclave *n.* conclave *m.*, assemblée *f.*

conclude *vt.* conclure, terminer, achever; — *vi.* conclure, se terminer

concluding *a.* final, dernier

conclusion *n.* conclusion *f.*; fin *f.*; décision *f.*; **in** — pour conclure

conclusive *a.* concluant, décisif; **–ly** *adv.* d'une manière décisive

concoct *vt.* préparer, combiner; confectionner, composer; **–ion** *n.* breuvage *m.*, boisson *f.*; mélange *m.*; confectionnement *m.*

concomitant *a.* concomitant

concord *n.* accord *m.*, harmonie *f.*; concorde *f.*; **–ance** *n.* concordance *f.*; **–ant** *a.* concordant, d'accord

concourse *n.* concours *m.*, foule *f.*; place publique *f.*

concrete *a.* concret; — *n.* béton *m.*; **reinforced** — béton armé *m.*; — **mixer** malaxeur *m.*, bétonnière *f.*; **–ly** *adv.* d'une manière concrète

concur *vi.* concourir; s'accorder, être d'accord; **–rence** *n.* accord *m.*; approbation *f.*; simultanéité *f.*; **–rent** *a.* concourant; simultané

concussion *n.* ébranlement *m.*, secousse *f.*; **brain** — *n.* commotion cérébrale *f.*

condemn *vt.* condamner; censurer; **–ation** *n.* condamnation *f.*; censure *f.*

condense *vt.* condenser; abréger; — *vi.* se condenser; **–r** *n.* condenseur *m.*; condensateur *m.*

condescend *vi.* condescendre, daigner; **–ing** *a.* condescendant

condescension *n.* condescendance *f.*

condiment *n.* assaisonnement, condiment *m.*

condition *n.* condition *f.*, état, rang *m.*; stipulation *f.*; **on** — **that** à condition que, pourvu que; — *vt.* conditionner; habituer, accoutumer; **–al** *a.* & *n.* conditionnel *m.*; **–ed** *a.* conditionné; habitué

condolence *n.* condoléance *f.*

condone *vt.* pardonner; permettre, approuver

conducive *a.* contribuant, contributif; favorable

conduct *n.* conduite *f.*, comportement *m.*; — *vt.* conduire; mener, diriger; — **oneself** se comporter; **–ion** *n.* conduction *f.*; **–ive** *a.* conducteur; **–ivity** *n.* conductivité *f.*; **–or** *n.* conducteur *m.*; (train, bus) contrôleur, receveur *m.*; (mus.) chef d'orchestre *m.*

conduit *n.* conduit, tuyau *m.*

cone *n.* cône *m.*; **ice cream** — glace en cornet *f.*; **pine** — pomme de pin *f.*

confection *n.* confiserie *f.*; **-er** *n.* confiseur *m.*; **-ery** *n.* confiserie *f.*
confederacy *n.* confédération *f.*
confederate *n.* & *a.* confédéré *m.*; complice *m.*; — *vi.* se confédérer
confer *vt.* conférer; — *vi.* consulter; **-ence** *n.* consultation, conférence *f.*; (sport) groupement (d'équipes) *m.*
confess *vt.* confesser, avouer; — *vi.* se confesser; **-ion** *n.* confession *f.*; aveu *m.*; (eccl.) confesse, confession *f.*; **-ional** *n.* confessionnal *m.*; **-ional** *a.* confessionnel; **-or** *n.* confesseur *m.*
confidant *n.* confident *m.*; confidente *f.*
confide *vt.* confier; — *vi.* se confier (à), se fier (à); **-nt** *a.* assure, confiant; **-nt** *n.* confident *m.*; **-ntial** *a.* confidentiel; particulier.
confidence *n.* confiance *f.*; **have — in** avoir confiance en
confiding *a.* confiant
configuration *n.* configuration *f.*
confine *n.* confins *m. pl.*, frontière *f.*; — *vt.* enfermer, renfermer; — **oneself to** se borner à; **-ment** *n.* emprisonnement *m.*; accouchement *m.*, couches *f. pl.*
confirm *vt.* confirmer, assurer; corroborer; **-ation** *n.* confirmation *f.*; **-ed** *a.* invétéré, endurci
confiscate *vt.* confisquer, saisir
conflagration *n.* incendie *m.*, conflagration *f.*
conflict *n.* conflit *m.*; — *vi.* être en contradiction; se heurter; **-ing** *a.* contradictoire; opposé
confluence *n.* confluent *m.*
conform *vt.* rendre conforme; conformer; — *vi.* se conformer; obéir, se soumettre; **-ation** *n.* conformation *f.*; **-ity** *n.* conformité *f.*; **in -ity with** conformément à
confound *vt.* confondre; **—l** *interj.* diable!; **-ed** *a.* sacré
confraternity *n.* confraternité *f.*; confrérie *f.*
confront *vt.* confronter; faire face à, affronter; **-ation** *n.* confrontation *f.*
confuse *vt.* confondre, troubler; brouiller; embrouiller; **-d** *a.* confondu; confus; embrouillé; trouble; **-dly** *adv.* confusément
confusion *n.* confusion *f.*; désordre *m.*
congeal *vt.* geler, congeler; coaguler; figer; — *vi.* geler; se congeler; se figer
congenial *a.* sympathique, agréable
congenital *a.* congénital, inné; de naissance
congest *vt.* congestionner; encombrer; **-ed** *a.* congestionné; encombré; (traffic) embouteillé; **-ion** *n.* congestion *f.*;

encombrement *m.*
conglomerate *vt.* conglomérer; — *vi.* se conglomérer; — *a.* conglomére
congratulate *vt.* féliciter
congratulation *n.* félicitation *f.*
congratulatory *a.* de félicitations
congregate *vt.* rassembler; — *vi.* s'assembler, se rassembler
congregation *n.* congrégation *f.*; assistance *f.*; rassemblement *m.*; **-al** *a.* de congrégation; (eccl.) indépendant; **-alist** *a.* & *n.* congrégationaliste *m.*
congress *n.* congrès *m.*; assemblée *f.*; réunion *f.*; **-man** *n.* député *m.*; **-ional** *a.* parlementaire
congruent *a.* congruent; conforme
congruity *n.* congruité *f.*; conformité *f.*
congruous *a.* conforme
conifer *n.* conifère *m.*
conjecture *n.* conjecture *f.*; — *vt.* & *vi.* conjecturer
conjugate *vt.* conjuguer; — *a.* conjugué
conjugation *n.* conjugaison *f.*
conjunction *n.* conjonction *f.*
conjunctive *a.* conjonctif
conjuncture *n.* conjoncture *f.*
conjure *vt.* conjurer; comploter; évoquer; — *vi.* conjurer, faire de la sorcellerie; **-r** *n.* sorcier *m.*
connect *vt.* joindre, lier; unir, réunir, rattacher, relier; — *vi.* se joindre, s'unir; se réunir, se lier; **-ed** *a.* suivi; connexe; **-ing rod** *n.* bielle *f.*; **-ion** *n.* connexion *f.*; liaison *f.*, rapport *m.*, correspondance *f.*; **in -ion with** à propos de, au sujet de
connive *vi.* conniver
connoisseur *n.* connaisseur *m.*
connotation *n.* connotation, signification *f.*
connote *vt.* signifier (en delà du sens littéral)
connubial *a.* conjugal
conquer *vt.* & *vi.* conquérir, vaincre; **-ing** *a.* conquérant, triomphant, victorieux; **-or** *n.* vainqueur *m.*; conquérant *m.*
conquest *n.* conquête, victoire *f.*
consanguinity *n.* consanguinité *f.*; parenté *f.*
conscience *n.* conscience *f.*
conscience-stricken *a.* pris de remords
conscientious *a.* consciencieux; **— objector** *n.* réformé de guerre *m.* (pour cause de convictions religieuses); **-ness** *n.* conscience *f.*; assiduité *f.*
conscionable *a.* juste, raisonnable
conscious *a.* conscient; **be —** (awareness) avoir conscience; (physical state) avoir la connaissance; **-ly** *adv.* sciemment; **-ness** *n.* connaissance *f.*; conscience *f.*;

sentiment *m.*; lose −ness perdre connaissance; regain −ness reprendre connaissance

conscript *n.* conscrit *m.*, recrue *f.*; — *a.* conscrit; — *vt.* recruter, enrôler; −ion *n.* conscription *f.*, enrôlement *m.*

consecrate *vt.* consacrer; bénir; −d *a.* consacré, béni, saint

consecration *n.* consécration *f.*; dévouement *m.*; sacre *m.*

consecutive *a.* consécutif, successif; de suite; −ly *adv.* de suite, consécutivement

consensus *n.* accord *m.*; orientation de l'opinion générale *f.*

consent *n.* consentement *m.*; accord *m.*; — *vi.* consentir (à)

consequence *n.* conséquence *f.*; importance *f.*; suite *f.*; by —, in — par conséquent

consequent *a.* conséquent; −ial *a.* important; consécutif, conséquent; −ly *adv.* conséquemment, par conséquent

conservation *n.* conservation, garde *f.*

conservative *n.* & *a.* conservateur *m.*

conservatory *n.* serre *f.*; (mus.) conservatoire *m.*

conserve *vt.* préserver, conserver; −s *n. pl.* conserves, confitures *f. pl.*

consider *vt.* considérer, regarder; estimer, penser; avoir égard à; — *vi.* réfléchir; −able *a.* considérable; −ate *a.* attentif, prévenant, soucieux; −ateness *n.* égards *m. pl.*; −ation *n.* considération *f.*; importance *f.*; égard *m.*; be under −ation être à l'étude; take into −ation tenir compte de; −ing *prep.* vu, étant donné

consign *vt.* consigner; livrer; −ee *n.* consignataire *m.*; −ment *n.* livraison *f.*; expédition *f.*; on −ment en consignation; −or *n.* consignateur *m.*

consist *vi.* consister; être composé (de); −ency *n.* consistance, substance *f.*; suite *f.*; −ent *a.* consistant; conséquant; d'accord; −ently *adv.* conséquemment

consistory *n.* consistoire *m.*

consolable *a.* consolable

console *n.* console *f.*; — *vt.* consoler; −r *n.* consolateur *m.*

consolidate *vt.* consolider; unifier; réunir; — *vi.* se consolider

consolidation *n.* consolidation *f.*; unification *f.*

consoling *a.* consolateur, consolant

consonance *n.* consonance *f.*; accord *m.*

consonant *n.* consonne *f.*; — *a.* consonant; conforme (à), d'accord

consort *n.* compagnon *m.*; époux *m.*, épouse *f.*; — *vi.* s'associer; — with

fréquenter

conspicuous *a.* apparent, frappant; become — se signaler, se faire remarquer

conspiracy *n.* conspiration *f.*

conspirator *n.* conspirateur *m.*

conspire *vi.* conspirer, comploter

constable *n.* constable *m.*; agent de police *m.*; connétable *m.*

constabulary *n.* police, gendarmerie *f.*

constancy *n.* constance *f.*; fidélité *f.*

constant *a.* constant, ferme; continuel; fidèle; — *n.* constante *f.*; −ly *adv.* constamment; continuellement

consternation *n.* consternation *f.*

constipate *vt.* constiper

constipation *n.* constipation *f.*

constituency *n.* circonscription (électorale) *f.*; électeurs *m. pl.*

constituent *a.* constituant; — *n.* constituant, composant *m.*; électeur *m.*

constitute *vt.* constituer

constitution *n.* constitution *f.*; tempérament *m.*; −al *a.* constitutionnel; −al *n.* promenade *f.*; −ality *n.* conformité (à la constitution) *f.*

constrain *vt.* contraindre, forcer; −ed *a.* contraint, force; −t *n.* contrainte, force *f.*; retenue *f.*

constrict *vt.* resserrer, contracter; gêner; −ion *n.* constriction *f.*; resserrement *m.*; −or *n.* constricteur *m.*; boa −or boa (constricteur) *m.*

construct *vt.* construire, bâtir; −ion *n.* construction *f.*; interprétation *f.*; under — en construction; −ive *a.* constructif; −or *n.* constructeur *m.*

construe *vt.* expliquer, interpréter

consul *n.* consul *m.*; −ar *a.* consulaire; −ate *n.* consulat *m.*

consult *vt.* consulter; — *vi.* délibérer, se consulter; demander conseil; −ant *n.* conseiller, consultant *m.*; −ation *n.* consultation *f.*; -ing *a.* consultant; conseil

consume *vt.* consumer; brûler; épuiser; dévorer; consommer; −r *n.* consommateur *m.*

consummate *vt.* consommer; terminer; — *a.* consommé, parfait, achevé

consummation *n.* consommation *f.*, achèvement *m.*; couronnement, comble *m.*

consumption *n.* consommation *f.*; (med.) phthisie *f.*

consumptive *a.* & *n.* phthisique, poitrinaire *m.* & *f.*

contact *n.* contact *m.*; rapport *m.*; — lens verre de contact *m.*; — *vt.* se mettre en relations avec; entrer en communication avec; parler à; écrire à

contagious *a.* contagieux; communicatif; **–ness** *n.* contagiosité *f.*

contain *vt.* contenir; comporter, comprendre; retenir; **–er** *n.* contenant *m.*; boîte *f.*

contaminate *vt.* contaminer, corrompre

contamination *n.* contamination *f.*

contemplate *vt.* contempler; méditer; envisager; — *vi.* contempler; méditer

contemplation *n.* contemplation *f.*; méditation *f.*; recueillement *m.*

contemplative *a.* contemplatif

contemplator *n.* contemplateur *m.*

contemporaneous, contemporary *a.* & *n.* contemporain *m.*

contempt *n.* mépris, dédain *m.*; — **of court** *n.* contumace *f.*; **hold in** — mépriser; **–ible** *a.* méprisable; **–ibly** *adv.* d'une manière méprisable; **–uous** *a.* dédaigneux; **–uously** *adv.* avec mépris

contend *vi.* disputer, combattre; — *vt.* prétendre, soutenir

content *n.* contentement *m.*; contenu *m.*; **–s** *n. pl.* contenu *m.*; **table of –s** table des matières *f.*; **to one's heart's** — à volonté; — *a.* content, tranquille; — *vt.* contenter; **be –(ed) with** se contenter de; **–ment** *n.* contentement *m.*

contention *n.* contention, dispute *f.*; prétention *f.*; **bone of** — pomme de discorde *f.*

contentious *a.* litigieux, querelleur

contest *vt.* disputer; contester; — *n.* concours *m.*; dispute *f.*; combat *m.*; **–able** *a.* contestable; **–ant** *n.* concurrent *m.*; **–ation** *n.* contestation *f.*

context *n.* contexte *m.*

contiguity *n.* contiguïté *f.*

contiguous *a.* contigu

continence *n.* continence *f.*

continent *n.* & *a.* continent *m.*; **–al** *a.* continental

contingency *n.* contingence *f.*; éventualité *f.*; cas imprévu *m.*

contingent *a.* contingent; éventuel, accidentel; imprévu; **be** — **on** dépendre de; — *n.* contingent

continual *a.* continuel; **–ly** *adv.* continuellement, sans cesse

continuance, continuation *n.* continuation *f.*; suite *f.*

continue *vt.* & *vi.* continuer; **to be –d** à suivre

continuity *n.* continuité, suite *f.*

continuous *a.* continu

contort *vt.* tordre; **–ed** *a.* tordu, contorsionné; **–ion** *n.* contorsion *f.*; **–ionist** *n.* contorsionniste *m.* & *f.*

contour *n.* contour *m.*; profil *m.*

contraband *n.* contrebande *f.*

contraceptive *n.* préservatif *m.*

contract *n.* contrat, pacte *m.*; acte *m.*; entreprise *f.*; — *vt.* contracter; crisper; prendre, entreprendre; — *vi.* se contracter; faire un contrat; s'engager; entreprendre, mettre à l'entreprise; **–ing** *n.* entreprise *f.*; **–ion** *n.* contraction *f.*; **–or** *n.* entrepreneur *m.*; adjudicataire *m.*; **–ual** *a.* de contrat, contractuel

contradict *vt.* contredire; démentir; **–ion** *n.* contradiction *f.*; **–ory** *a.* contradictoire

contrail *n.* (avi.) sillage de fumée *m.*

contraption *n.* machin, appareil *m.*

contrapuntal *a.* en contrepoint

contrariness *n.* contrariété *f.*

contrariwise *adv.* au contraire

contrary *n.* contraire, opposé; **on the** — au contraire; — *a.* contraire; **to** contrairement à

contrast *n.* contraste *m.*; — *vi.* contraster; — *vt.* opposer, faire contraster; **–ing** *a.* opposé, en contraste

contravene *vt.* contrevenir à

contravention *n.* contravention *f.*

contribute *vt.* & *vi.* contribuer; collaborer

contribution *n.* contribution *f.*; apport *m.*

contributor *n.* collaborateur *m.*; contribuant *m.*; **–y** *a.* contribuant, contributif

contrite *a.* contrit, pénitent

contrivance *n.* projet *m.*; appareil *m.*; invention *f.*

contrive *vt.* inventer, projeter, essayer; combiner; — *vi.* parvenir à; s'arranger

control *n.* contrôle *m.*; autorité, direction *f.*; empire *m.*; **–s** *n. pl.* commandes *f. pl.*; — **stick** *n.* (avi.) manche à balai *m.*; — **tower** *n.* (avi.) tour de contrôle *f.*; — *vt.* contrôler; diriger; commander; — **oneself** se maîtriser; se retenir; **–lable** *a.* gouvernable; maîtrisable

controller *n.* comptable *m.*; contrôleur *m.*

controversial *a.* de controverse, discutable

controversy *n.* controverse *m.*, polémique *f.*

controvert *vt.* disputer; controverser; **–ible** *a.* controversible

contumely *n.* outrage *m.*, insulte *m.*; honte *f.*

contuse *vt.* contusionner

convalesce *vi.* guérir; se remettre; **–nce** *n.* convalescence *f.*; **–nt** *a.* convalescent

convection *n.* convection *f.*

convene *vt.* assembler, réunir, convoquer; — *vi.* s'assembler, se réunir

convenience *n.* aise, commodité *f.*; convenance *f.*; **at your earliest** — aussitôt que possible; **at your own** — quand il vous plaira; **–s** *pl.* confort *m.*

convenient *a.* commode, aisé

convent *n.* couvent *m.*

convention *n.* rassemblement, congrès *m.*; convention *f.*; bienséance *f.*; contrat *m.*; **-al** *a.* conventionnel; ordinaire, normal

converge *vi.* converger; **-nce** *m.* convergence *f.*; **-nt** *a.* convergent

converging *a.* convergent

conversant *a.* familier; versé (dans)

conversation *n.* conversation *f.*, entretien *m.*; **-al** *a.* de conversation

converse *n.* & *a.* converse *f.*; réciproque *f.*; — *vi.* causer, s'entretenir; **-ly** *adv.* réciproquement

convert *n.* converti *m.*; — *vt.* convertir; changer, transformer; — *vi.* se convertir; **-er** *n.* convertisseur *m.*; **-ibility** *n.* convertibilité *f.*; **-ible** *a.* (auto) décapotable; convertible; convertissable

convex *a.* convexe

convey *vt.* transporter; communiquer; transmettre; **-ance** *n.* voiture *f.*; moyen de transport *m.*; transmission *f.*; **-er, -or** *n.* transporteur *m.*; courroie *f.*; tapis roulant *m.*

convict *n.* condamné *m.*; forçat *m.*; — *vt.* convaincre, condamner; **-ion** *n.* condamnation *f.*; conviction *f.*

convince *vt.* convaincre, persuader

convincing *a.* convainquant

convivial *a.* sociable, joyeux

convocation *n.* convocation, assemblée *f.*

convoke *vt.* convoquer

convolution *n.* circonvolution *f.*

convoy *n.* convoi *m.*, escorte *f.*; — *vt.* escorter, convoyer

convulse *vt.* convulsionner; ébranler; **-d** *a.* convulsé

convulsive *a.* convulsif

coo *vi.* roucouler; **-ing** *n.* roucoulement *m.*

cook *n.* cuisinier *m.*; cuisinière *f.*; chef *m.*; — *vi.* faire la cuisine; — **up** (coll.) comploter; **-er** *n.* réchaud *m.*; cuisinière *f.*; **-ery** *n.* cuisine; **-ing** *n.* cuisine *f.*; **-ing** utensils batterie de cuisine *f.*; **-book** *n.* livre de cuisine *m.*

cookie, cooky *n.* gâteau sec, biscuit, petit four *m.*

cool *n.* frais *m.*, fraîcheur *f.*; — *a.* frais (fraîche); indifferent; tranquille; — *vt.* & *vi.* refroidir; — **off** se refroidir; — one's heels attendre; **-er** *n.* frigorifique *m.*; (coll.) prison *f.*; **-ing** *a.* rafraîchissant; **-ing** *n.* refroidissement *m.*; **-ness** *n.* frais *m.*; indifference *f.*; froideur *f.*; clame, sang-froid *m.*

cooling-off period (com.) *n*, trêve *f.*, arrangée pour empêcher une grève

coop *n.* cage *f.*, poulailler *m.*; **fly the** — s'évader; — **up** *vi.* enfermer

co-op *n.* (coll.) entreprise coopérative *f.*

cooper *n.* tonnelier *m.*; **-age** *n.* tonnellerie *f.*

co-operate *vi.* coopérer, collaborer

co-operation *n.* coopération *f.*

co-operative *n.* entreprise coopérative *f.*; — *a.* coopératif

co-ordinate *vt.* coordonner; — *a.* coordonné; — *n.* coordonné *m.*

co-ordination *n.* coordination *f.*

coot *n.* foulque *f.*

cope *vi.* combattre, lutter, se tirer d'affaire

copier *n.* copiste *m.* & *f.*; imitateur *m.*

coping *n.* faîte *m.*; — saw porte-scies *m.*

copious *a.* copieux, abondant; **-ly** *adv.* copieusement; **-ness** *n.* abondance *f.*

copilot *n.* copilote *m.*

copper *n.* cuivre *m.*; monnaie de cuivre *f.*; (coll.) flic *m.*; — *a.* de cuivre, en cuivre; — *vt.* cuivrer

copperhead *n.* (variété de) serpent vénéneux *m.*; partisan du sud *m.* (guerre de sécession, USA)

copperplate *n.* gravure sur cuivre *f.*; plaque de cuivre *f.*

coppersmith *n.* chaudronnier *m.*

copse *n.* taillis *m.*

copulate *vi.* s'accoupler

copulation *n.* copulation *f.*

copulative *a.* copulatif

copy *n.* copie, reproduction *f.*; exemplaire *m.*; numéro *m.*; **-book** *n.* cahier *m.*; **-cat** *n.* imitateur, singe *m.*; — **writer** (com.) *n.* rédacteur d'annonces publicitaires *m.*; **rough** — brouillon *m.*; — *vt.* copier; imiter; **-ist** *n.* copiste *m.*

copyright *n.* copyright, droit d'auteur *m.*; — *vt.* déposer; **-ed** *a.* dont tous les droits sont réservés

coquette *n.* coquette *f.*

coquettish *a.* coquet

cord *n.* corde *f.*; cordon *m.*, ficelle *f.*; stère *m.*, mesure *f.* (pour le bois: 128 pieds[3]); — *vt.* corder; ligoter; **-age** *n.* cordage *m.*; **-ed** *a.* à cordes; côtelé

cordial *a.* cordial; — *n.* liqueur *f.*, digestif *m.*; **-ity** *n.* cordialité *f.*

Cordoba *n.* Cordoue *f.*

cordovan *n.* cuir de Cordoue *m.*

corduroy *n.* velours (rayé) *m.*

core *n.* cœur, intérieur *m.*; noyau *m.*; (apple) trognon *m.*; — *vt.* vider

corespondent *n.* coaccusé *m.*

cork *n.* liège, bouchon (de liège) *m.*; — *vt.* boucher; **-age** *n.* débouchage *m.*

corkscrew *n.* tire-bouchon *m.*

cormorant *n.* cormorant *m.*

corn *n.* maïs *m.*; (foot) cor *m.*; — **cob** *n.* épi de maïs; **-crib** *n.* dépôt de maïs *m.*; — **pone** *n.* (sorte de) polenta *f.*; —

popper appareil pour faire éclater le maïs *m.*; — *vt.* saler; **-ed beef** bœuf salé *m.*; **-starch** *n.* fécule de maïs *f.*; amidon *m.*

cornea *n.* cornée *f.*

corner *n.* coin, angle *m.*; extrémité *f.*; tournant, virage *m.*; — *vt.* attraper; acculer; (com.) accaparer

cornerstone *n.* pierre angulaire *f.*; pierre de refend *f.*

cornice *n.* corniche *f.*

Cornish *a.* cornouaillais

cornucopia *n.* corne d'abondance *f.*

Cornwall *n.* Cornouailles *m.*

corolla *n.* corolle *f.*

corollary *n.* corollaire *m.*

corona *n.* couronne *f.*

coronation *n.* couronnement, sacre *m.*

coronet *n.* petite couronne *f.*

corporal *n.* caporal *m.*; — *a.* corporel (eccl.) corporal

corporate *a.* incorporé

corporation *n.* société anonyme *f.*; (coll.) ventre *m.*, bedaine *f.*

corporeal *a.* corporel, matériel

corps *n.* corps, corps d'armée *m.*

corpse *n.* cadavre *m.*; corps *m.*

corpsman *n.* (mil.) infirmier *m.*

corpulence *n.* corpulence *f.*

corpulent *a.* corpulent

corpuscle *n.* corpuscule, *m.*

corral *n.* enclos *m.*; — *vt.* mettre dans l'enclos

correct *vt.* corriger; châtier, punir; retoucher; — *a.* correct; exact; bienséant; **-ion** *n.* correction *f.*; **-ive** *a.* correctionnel; correctif; **-ly** *adv.* correctement, exactement; **-ness** *n.* correction *f.*; exactitude *f.*

correlate *vi.* correspondre; — *vt.* marquer la corrélation

correlation *n.* corrélation *f.*

correlative *a.* corrélatif, réciproque

correspond *vi.* correspondre; **-ence** *n.* correspondance *f.*; **-ent** *n.* correspondant *m.*; **-ing** *a.* correspondant; conforme

corridor *n.* couloir, corridor *m.*

corroborate *vt.* corroborer

corroboration *n.* corroboration *f.*

corroborator *n.* témoin *m.*

corrode *vt.* corroder, ronger; — *vi.* se corroder

corrosion *n.* corrosion *f.*

corrugate *vt.* rider, froncer, plisser; **-ed iron** tôle ondulée *f.*

corrupt *vt.* corrompre, gâter, séduire, suborner; — *a.* corrompu; **-ible** *a.* corruptible; **-ion** *n.* corruption *f.*

corsage *n.* fleur *f.*, bouquet *m.* (porté au corsage)

Corsica *n.* Corse *f.*; **-n** *a.* & *n.* corse *m.* & *f.*

cortex *n.* substance corticale *f.*

cortisone *n.* cortisone *m.*

corundum *n.* corindon *m.*

cosmetic *n.* cosmétique *m.*; fard *m.*; — *a.* cosmétique

cosmic *a.* cosmique; — **ray** rayon cosmique *m.*

cosmopolitan *n.* & *a.* cosmopolite *m.*

Cossack *n.* Cosaque *m.*

cost *n.* prix *m.*, frais *m.* *pl.*, dépense *f.*; — **price** prix de revient *m.*; — **of living** coût de la vie *m.*; **whatever the** — coûte que coûte; — *vi.* coûter; **-liness** *n.* (haut) prix *m.*; cherté *f.*; **-ly** *a.* cher; coûteux

Costa Rica *n.* Costa Rica *m.*

costume *n.* costume *m.*; **-r** *n.* costumier *m.*

cot *n.* lit de sangle *m.*

cote *n.* pigeonnier, colombier *m.*

cottage *n.* cabane, chaumière *f.*; villa *f.*; — **cheese** lait caillé, fromage blanc *m.*

cotton *n.* coton *m.*; **absorbent** — coton hydrophile *m.*; — **batting** coton cardé *m.*; ouate *f.*; — **flannel** *n.* flanelle de coton *f.*; — **goods** cotonnades *f.* *pl.*; — **mill** filature de coton *f.*

couch *n.* lit *m.*; divan *m.*; canapé *m.*; — *vt.* coucher; — *vi.* se tapir

cougar *n.* couguar *m.*

cough *n.* toux *f.*; — **drop** pastille *f.*; — *vi.* tousser; **-ing** *n.* toux *f.*

council *n.* conseil *m.*; concile *m.*; **city** — conseil minucipal *m.*; **-or** *n.* conseiller *m.*

counsel *n.* conseil, avis *m.*; consultation *f.*; avocat *m.*; — *vt.* & *vi.* conseiller; **-or** *n.* conseiller *m.*; avocat *m.*

count *n.* nombre, compte *m.*; (title) comte *m.*; — *vi.* compter; — **on** compter su :; **-er** *n.* compteur *m.*; jeton *m.*; contre *m.*; comptoir *m.*; **Geiger -er** *n.* compteur de Geiger *m.*; **-er** *adv.* contre; **-er** *a.* contraire; **-less** *a.* innombrable

count-down *n.* (coll.) longue vérification finale avant de lancer un projectile dans l'espace

countenance *n.* contenance *f.*, visage *m.*; air, regard *m.*; — *vt.* soutenir, favoriser; approuver; encourager

counter *vt.* opposer, agir contre; riposter

counteract *vt.* contrebalancer

counterattack *n.* contre-attaque *f.*; — *vt.* contre-attaquer

counterbalance *vt.* contre-balancer; — *n.* contre-poids *m.*

countercharge *n.* contre-accusation *f.*

counterclockwise *adv.* au sens inverse des aiguilles d'une montre

counterfeit *n.* contrefaçon, fausse monnaie

f.; — *vt.* contrefaire; –ing *n.* contrefait; –er *n.* contrefaiteur, faux-monnayeur *m.*

counterintelligence *n.* contre-espionnage *m.*

countermand *vt.* contremander; décommander

countermarch *n.* contremarche *f.*

counteroffensive *n.* contre-offensive *f.*

counterpane *n.* courtepointe *f.*

counterpart *n.* contre-partie *f.*; pendant *m.*

counterpoint *n.* contre-point *m.*

counterreformation *n.* contre-réforme *f.*

counterrevolution *n.* contre-révolution *f.*

countershaft *n.* contre-arbre *m.*

countersign *n.* contre-seing *m.*; (mil.) mot d'ordre *m.*; — *vt.* contresigner

countersink *vt.* fraiser; — *n.* fraise *f.*

countertenor *n.* haute-contre *f.*

counterweight *n.* contre-poids *m.*

countess *n.* comtesse *f.*

country *n.* pays *m.*; contrée, compagne *f.*; **native** — patrie *f.*; –man *n.* compatriote *m.*; compagnard *m.*

countryside *n.* paysage *m.*; région *f.*

county *n.* comté, département, canton *m.*; — **seat** chef-lieu *m.*

coupe *n.* coupé *m.*

couple *n.* couple *m.*, paire *f.*; — *vt.* coupler; accoupler; embrayer; grouper; — *vi.* s'accoupler

coupling *n.* accouplement *m.*; couplage *m.*; attelage *m.*

coupon *n.* coupon *m.*; (com.) bon-prime *m.*

courage *n.* courage *m.*; –ous *a.* courageux

courier *n.* courrier *m.*

course *n.* course, carrière *f.*; cours *m.*; plat, service *m.*; chemin *m.*, route *f.*; terrain *m.* (naut.) cap *m.*; **as a matter of** — comme affaire routinière; **in due** — en temps voulu; **in the** — **of time** avec le temps; **of** — bien entendu; **give a** — faire un cours; **take a** — suivre un cours; — *vi.* courir

court *n.* cour *f.*; cour de justice *f.*, tribunal *m.*; (sport) terrain *m.*; — *vt.* faire la cour (à), courtiser

courteous *a.* poli, courtois; –ness *n.* politesse *f.*

courtesan *n.* courtisane *f.*

courtesy *n.* courtoisie, politesse *f.*

courthouse *n.* palais de justice *m.*

courtier *n.* courtisan *m.*; homme de la cour *m.*

court-martial *n.* conseil de guerre *m.*; — *vt.* traduire en conseil de guerre

courtroom *n.* salle du tribunal *f.*

courtship *n.* cour *f.*

courtyard *n.* cour (de maison) *f.*

cousin *n.* cousin *m.*, cousine *f.*; **first** — *m.*; **cousin** germain *m.*

cove *n.* crique *f.*; abri *m.*; anse *f.*

covenant *n.* contrat, accord *m.*

cover *n.* couvert *m.*, enveloppe *f.*; couverture *f.*; couvercle *m.*; abri *m.*, protection *f.*; prétexte *m.*; — **charge** couvert *m.*; **take** — se mettre à l'abri; **under separate** — sous pli séparé; — *vt.* couvrir; recouvrir; cacher; parcourir; (newspaper) assurer un reportage; –age *n.* reportage *m.*; assurance *f.*; (insurance) *n.* couverture d'assurance *f.*; –ing *n.* couverture *f.*

coverlet *n.* (bed) couvre-lit *m.*, (foot) couvre-pieds *m.*

covert *a.* couvert, caché

covet *vt.* & *vi.* convoiter; désirer ardemment; –ous *a.* cupide, désireux; avide; –ousness *n.* convoitise, cupidité *f.*

covey *n.* couvée, volée *f.*

cow *n.* vache *f.*; — *vt.* intimider

coward *n.* lâche *m.*; –ice *n.* lâcheté *f.*; –ly *a.* lâche

cowboy *n.* vacher, cow-boy *m.*

cower *vi.* s'accroupir, se tapir

cowhide *n.* vache, peau de vache *f.*

cowl *n.* capuchon *m.*; capot *m.*; –ing *n.* capuchonnement *m.*; capotage *m.*

cowlick *n.* épi de cheveux *m.*

co-worker *n.* collaborateur *m.*

cowslip *n.* primevère *f.*

coxcomb *n.* fat, petit-maître *m.*

coxswain *n.* patron de chaloupe *m.*; barreur *m.*

coy *a.* modeste; réservé; –ness *n.* modestie, timidité, réserve *f.*

coyote *n.* (genre de) loup *m.*

coziness *n.* confortable *m.*

C.P.A.: Certified Public Accountant comptable diplômé *m.*

crab *n.* crabe *m.*; tourteau *m.*; personne désagréable *f.*; — **(apple)** pomme sauvage *f.*; — *vi.* se plaindre, être désagréable; –by *a.* désagréable, grognon, revêche

crack *n.* fente *f.*; craquement, bruit *m.*; fêlure *f.*; — **of dawn** pointe du jour *f.*; — *a.* expert, de premier ordre; — *vi.* se fendre; — *vt.* fendre; — **a joke** faire une plaisanterie; –down (coll.) mesure très stricte; –ed *a.* fendu; (coll.) fou; –er *n.* biscuit *m.*; –ling *n.* friton *m.*; craquement *m.*

crackle *vi.* craqueter, pétiller; — *n.* craquement *m.*

crackpot *n.* (coll.) original, excentrique, tapé *m.*

crack-up *n.* collision *f.*; accident *m.*;

écrasement *m.*; écroulement *m.*; accident d'avion *m.*

cradle *n.* berceau *m.*; — *vt.* bercer

craft *n*, métier *m.*, profession *f.*; artifice *m.*, fourberie *f.*; barque *f.*, vaisseau *m.*; **–iness** *n.* ruse *f.*; **–y** *a.* rusé

craftsman *n.* artisan *m.*

crag *n.* rocher escarpé *m.*; **–ged, –gy** *a.* escarpé

cram *vt.* fourrer; farcir; — *vi.* (coll.) étudier à la dernière heure; bûcher

cramp *n.* crampe *f.*; — *vt.* gêner, entraver; **–ed** *a.* serré; gêné

cranberry *n.* airelle *f.*; — **sauce** compote d'airelles *f.*

cranial *a.* cranien

cranium *n.* crâne *m.*

crank *n.* manivelle *f.*; (coll.) excentrique *m.*; — *vt.* tourner la manivelle (de); **–iness** *n.* irritabilité, mauvaise humeur *f.*; **–y** *a.* irritable, de mauvaise humeur

crankcase *n.* carter *m.*

crankshaft *n.* arme de manivelle, arbre-manivelle *m.*

cranny *n.* fente, crevasse *f.*; coin *m.*; niche *f.*

crape *n.* crêpe *m.*

crash *n.* craquement, fracas *m.*; écrasement *m.*; (com.) krach *m.*; — *vt.* briser, fracasser; — *vi.* retentir

crash-landing *n.* (avi.) atterrissage violent *m.* (exécuté par le pilote dans un cas urgent)

crass *a.* grossier

crate *n.* emballage à claire-voie *m.*; — *vt.* emballer

crater *n.* cratère *m.*

cravat *n.* foulard *m.*; cravate *f.*

crave *vt.* implorer, solliciter; désirer

craven *a.* lâche *m.*

craving *n.* désir ardent *m.*; soif *f.*

crawfish, crayfish *n.* écrevisse *f.*

crawl *vi.* ramper; se traîner; **be –ing with** fourmiller de; — *n.* rampement *m.*; (swimming) crawl *m.*

crayon *n.* couleur *f.*; crayon (de pastel) *m.*; — *vt.* crayonner

craze *n.* manie *f.*; vogue *f.*; — *vt.* rendre fou

craziness *n.* folie *f.*

crazy *a.* fou (folle); —, **(funny), bone** *n.* nerf du coude *m.*; — **quilt** courte-pointe multicolore *f.*

creak *vi.* crier, craquer; — *n.* cri *m.*; **–y** *a.* criard

cream *n.* crème *f.*; meilleur, élite *m.*; **whipped** — crème fouettée *f.*; — **cheese** fromage à la crème, fromage blanc *m.*; — **puff** chou à la crème *m.*; — *vt.* mélanger (beurre et sucre); **–ery** *n.*

crèmerie, laiterie *f.*; **–y** *a.* crémeux

crease *n.* pli, faux pli *m.*; — *vt.* plisser, faire un faux pli; — *vi.* se plisser

create *vt.* créer, produire; inventer

creation *n.* création *f.*; invention *f.*

creative *a.* créateur, inventif

creator *n.* créateur *m.*

creature *n.* créature *f.*; être *m.*; (animal) bête *f.*

credence *n.* créance, foi *f.*

credentials *n. pl.* lettres de créance *f. pl.*, documents, papiers *m. pl.*

credibility *n.* crédibilité *f.*

credible *a.* croyable, digne de foi

credit *n.* crédit *m.*; foi, croyance *f.*; témoignage *m.*; influence *f.*; **to be a** — to faire honneur à; — *vt.* croire, ajouter foi à; donner à crédit; porter au crédit de; **–able** *a.* estimable; **–or** *n.* créditeur *m.*

credulity *n.* crédulité *f.*

credulous *a.* crédule; **–ness** *n.* crédulité *f.*

creed *n.* croyance *f.*; profession de foi *f.*

creek *n.* ruisseau *m.*; crique *f.*

creel *n.* panier de pêche *m.*

creep *vi.* ramper; se traîner; **–er** *n.* (bot.) plante rampante *f.*; **–y** *a.* (coll.) mystérieux

cremate *vt.* incinérer

cremation *n.* incinération *f.*

Creole *n.* Louisianais *m.* (d'origine française ou espagnole)

creosote *n.* créosote *f.*; — *vt.* créosoter

crepe *n.* crêpe *m.*; — **paper** papier crêpe *m.*

crepitation *n.* crépitation *f.*

crescent *a. & n.* croissant *m.*

cress *n.* cresson *m.*

crest *n.* crête *f.*; cimier *m.*; sommet *m.*; **–ed** *a.* huppé; à crête

crestfallen *a.* abattu, decouragé, penaud

Crete *n.* Crète *f.*

crevice *n.* crevasse, fente *f.*

crew *n.* troupe, bande *f.*; équipage *m.*; équipe *f.*

crib *n.* mangeoire, crèche, étable *f.*; petit lit *m.*; (grain) coffre *m.*; — *vt.* copier; **–bing** *n.* (coll.) emploi frauduleux d'un aide-mémoire pour réussir à un examen *m.*

cricket *n.* grillon *m.*; (sports) cricket *m.*

crier *n.* crieur *m.*

Crimea *n.* Crimée *f.*

criminal *n. & a.* criminel *m.*

criminologist *n.* criminaliste *m.*

criminology *n.* criminologie *f.*

crimp *vt.* friser; gaufrer; — *n.* (coll.) obstacle *m.*

crimson *n. & a.* cramoisi *m.*

cringe *vi.* ramper, s'abaisser

cringing a. craintif; servile; — n. crainte f.; servilité f.
crinkle n. pli m.; — vt. froisser, plisser
cripple n. estropié m.; — vt. estropier; paralyser
crisis n. crise f.
crisp a. croustillant; vif; brusque; frais; **–ness** n. qualité croustillante f.; netteté f.
crisscross a. en zigzag; en quinconce; — vt. & vi. aller en zigzag, (s')entrecroiser
criterion n. critérium, critère m.
critic n. critique m.; **–al** a. critique; **–ism** n. critique f.; **–ize** vt. critiquer; blâmer
croak vi. coasser; (coll.) crever; — n. coassement m.
Croatia n. Croatie f.
crochet n. ouvrage au crochet m.; — vt. faire au crochet; — vi. faire du crochet
crock n. pot de terre m.; **–ery** n. poterie f.
crocodile n. crocodile m.
crone n. vieille femme f.
crony n. copain m.
crook n. crochet m.; courbure f.; (eccl.) crosse f.; (coll.) escroc, malfaiteur, filou m.; — vt. courber; — vi. se courber; **–ed** a. courbé; tortueux; (coll.) malhonnête, filou; **–edness** n. nature tortueuse f.
croon vi. chantonner doucement; chanter d'une maniere sentimentale; **–er** n. chanteur dont la voix est douce et sentimentale f.
crop n. récolte, moisson f.; (bird) jabot m.; (whip) manche m.; — vt. couper court; — up apparaître; **–per, share –er** n. métayer m.
cross n. croix f.; mélange, croisement m.; — a. fâché; contraire; — purpose opposition f.; — reference renvoi m.; — section coupe f.; — vt. & vi. traverser; croiser; — out rayer; **–ing** n. traversée f.; passage m.; level **–ing** (rail.) passage à niveau m.; pedestrian **–ing** passage clouté m.
crossbill n. bec-croisé m.
crossbow n. arbalète f.; **–man** n. arbalétrier m.
crossbreed n. personne de race croisée f.; — vt. croiser la race
cross-check vt. vérifier tous les éléments de
cross-country a. à travers campagne
crosscut a. qui coupe en travers
cross-examination n. contre-interrogatoire m.
cross-eyed a. louche
cross fire n. feu croisé m.
cross-legged a. les jambes croisées
cross-purposes n. pl. malentendu m.

crossroad n. carrefour m.; chemin de traverse m.
crosswise, crossways a. en travers
crossword puzzle n. mots croisés m. pl.
crotch n. entre-jambes m.
crotchety a. irritable, désagréable, revêche; capricieux
crouch vi. se baisser, s'accroupir; — n. accroupissement m.; (boxing) crouch m.
croup n. croupion n.; (med.) croup m.; croupe (d'un cheval) f.
crouton n. croûton m.
crow n. corneille f.; chant du coq m.; as the — flies à vol d'oiseau; — vi. chanter; se vanter
crowd n. foule, presse f.; (coll.) bande, côterie f.; — vt. encombrer; — vi. se presser, s'assembler en foule; **–ed** a. bondé
crown n. couronne f.; sommet m.; forme (d'un chapeau) f.; — prince prince héritier m.; — vt. couronner, sacrer; **–ing** a. suprême; **–ing** n. couronnement m.
crow's-foot n. patte-d'oie f.
crow's-nest n. (naut.) vigie f.
crucial a. crucial, décisif
crucible n. creuset m.
crucifix n. crucifix m.; **–ion** n. crucifixion f.
cruciform a. cruciforme, en forme de croix
crucify vt. crucifier
crude a. cru; rude; brut; fruste; grossier; — oil pétrole brut m.; **–ness** n. crudité f.; grossiereté f.; rudesse f.
crudity n. crudité f.
cruel a. cruel; **–ty** n. cruauté f.
cruet n. burette f., huilier, vinaigrier m.
cruise n. croisière f.; — vi. faire une croisière; **–r** n. croiseur m.
cruller n. beignet m.
crumb n. mie, miette f.; **bread –s** chapelure f.; — vt. paner; **–ed** a. pané
crumble vt. émietter; — vi. s'écrouler; crouler; s'émietter
crumbling n. écroulement m.
crumple vt. froisser
crunch vt. croquer; — vi. craquer
crupper n. croupe f.
crusade n. croisade f.; **–r** n. croisé m.
crush n. écrasement m.; choc m.; foule f.; (coll.) amourette f.; — vt. écraser; opprimer; **–ing** a. écrasant; accablant; **–ing** n. écrasement m.
crust n. croûte f.; incrustation f.; — vt. encroûter; **–y** a. couvert d'une croûte; vieux, maussade
crustacean n. crustacé m.
crutch n. béquille f.

crux *n.* crise *f.*; point central *m.*
cry *n.* cri *m.*; **a far — from** bien eloigné de; **—** *vt.* crier; **—** *vi.* pleurer; crier, s'écrier; **–ing** *n.* pleurs *f. pl.*; cri *m.*
crybaby *n.* pleurnicheur *m.*
cryogenics *n.* cryogénique *f.*
crypt *n.* crypte *f.*; **–ic** *a.* secret; énigmatique
cryptography *n.* cryptographie *f.*
crystal *n.* cristal *m.*; (of a watch) verre *m.*; **—** *a.* de cristal; **–line** *a.* cristallin; **–lize** *vt.* cristaliser; **–lization** *n.* crystallisation *f.*
C.S.T.: **Central Standard Time** heure du centre (des USA)
cub *n.* petit d'un animal *m.*; (scout) louveteau *m.*; **— reporter** reporter débutant *m.*
cubbyhole *n.* case *f.*
cube *n.* cube *m.*; **—** *vt.* **cuber**
cubic *a.* cube; cubique
cubicle *n.* cabine *f.*
cuckoo *n.* coucou *m.*; **—** *a.* (coll.) fou
cucumber *n.* concombre *m.*
cud, **to chew the —** ruminer
cuddle *vt.* serrer, presser; **—** *vi.* se serrer
cudgel *n.* massue *f.*; **—** *vt.* rosser; **— one's brains** se casser la tête
cue *n.* (billiards) queue *f.*; (theat.) réplique *f.*; **—** *vt.* donner la réplique
cuff *n.* (blow) coup *m.*; (shirt) manchette *f.*; (trousers) revers *m.*; **— links** boutons de manchette *m. pl.*; **—** *vt.* battre, talocher
culinary *a.* de cuisine, culinaire
cull *vt.* cueillir; choisir; trier
culminate *vi.* culminer
culmination *n.* point culminant *m.*
culottes *n. pl.* pantalon court de femme *m.*
culpability *n.* culpabilité *f.*
culpable *a.* coupable
culprit *n.* coupable *m.*
cult *n.* culte *m.*
cultivate *vt.* cultiver
cultivation *n.* cultivation, culture *f.*
cultivator *n.* cultivateur *m.*
cultural *a.* culturel
culture *n.* culture *f.*; **–d** *a.* cultivé
culvert *n.* ponceau *m.*
cumbersome *a.* embarrassant, incommode
cumulative *a.* cumulatif
cuneiform *a.* cunéiforme
cunning *n.* ruse *f.*, artifice *m.*; **—** *a.* adroit; rusé; (coll.) délicieux, charmant
cup *n.* tasse *f.*; coupe *f.*; (med.) ventouse *f.*
cupboard *n.* armoire *f.*; placard *m.*
cupcake *n.* petit gâteau *m.*
Cupid *n.* Cupidon *m.*

cupidity *n.* cupidité *f.*
cupola *n.* coupole *f.*
cur *n.* chien hargneux *m.*
curable *a.* guérissable
curate *n.* vicaire, curé *m.*
curative *a.* curatif
curator *n.* conservateur *m.*
curb *n.* frein *m.*; restreinte *f.*; bordure (de trottoir) *f.*; **—** *vt.* restreindre; brider
curbstone *n.* bordure (de trottoir) *f.*
curd *n.* lait caillé *m.*; **–le** *vt.* cailler; **–le** *vi.* se cailler
cure *n.* cure *f.*; guérison *f.*, traitement *m.*; **—** *vt.* guérir; mariner, saler; préparer, travailler
cure-all *n.* panacée *f.*
curfew *n.* couvre-feu *m.*
curio *n.* bibelot *m.*
curiosity *n.* curiosité *f.*
curious *a.* curieux
curl *n.* boucle (de cheveux) *f.*; (fig.) ondulation *f.*; **—** *vt. & vi.* friser; **— up** enrouler; **–y** *a.* frisé, en boucles
curlicue *n.* parafe *m.*
currant *n.* groseille *f.*; **black —** cassis *m.*
currency *n.* circulation *f.*, cours *m.*, continuité *f.*; papier-monnaie *m.*
current *n.* courant *m.*; **alternating —** courant alternatif *m.*; **direct —** courant continu *m.*; **—** *a.* courant
curriculum *n.* cours d'études *m.*
curry *n.* cari *m.*; **— powder** cari *m.*; **—** *vt.* étriller; **— favor (with)** chercher à s'insinuer dans les bonnes grâces (de)
curse *n.* malédiction *f.*; **—** *vt.* maudire; **—** *vi.* jurer
cursing *n.* jurons *m. pl.*
cursory *a.* précipité; léger
curt *a.* court, brusque; **–ness** *n.* brusquerie *f.*
curtail *vt.* écourter; retrancher; **–ment** *n.* restriction *f.*
curtain *n.* rideau *m.*; **— call** rappel *m.*; **— raiser** lever de rideau *m.*; **— rod** monture *f.* (pour rideaux); **—** *vt.* garnir de rideaux
curtsy *n.* révérence *f.*; **—** *vi.* faire la révérence
curvature *n.* courbure *f.*
curve *n.* courbe *f.*; virage *m.*; **—** *vt.* courber; **—** *vi.* se courber; **–d** *a.* courbe, courbé
cushion *n.* coussin *m.*; **—** *vt.* rembourrer; amortir
custard *n.* flan *m.*; crème *f.*
custodian *n.* gardien *m.*
custody *n.* garde *f.*; emprisonnement *m.*
custom *n.* coutume, habitude *f.*; **–s** *pl.* douane *f.*; **–ary** *a.* habituel, ordinaire;

–er n. client m.; (coll.) type m.

custom-built, custom-made a. fait sur commande, fait sur mesure

customhouse n. douane f.

cut n. coupure f.; coupe f.; morceau m.; tranche f.; (print.) gravure f.; baisse f.; **short** — raccourci m.; — vt. couper, tailler; trancher; baisser; (prices) réduire; (records) enregistrer; (teeth) faire; — **across** traverser; — **class** sécher un cours; — **down** faucher, abattre; — **out** découper; (coll.) cesser; — **short** couper court (à); — **up** couper en petits morceaux; découper; (coll.) faire la noce; — a. coupé; taillé; tranché; baissé; — **and dried** décidé, fixé; — **glass** cristal taillé m.; –ting a. tranchant; mordant; cinglant; –ting n. coupe f.; découpage m.; coupon m.; coupure f.

cutaneous a. cutané

cutaway n. frac m.

cutback n. réduction de la force ouvrière d'une usine f.

cute a. joli, délicieux

cuticle n. pellicule f., épiderme m.

cutlass n. coutelas m.

cutlery n. coutellerie f.

cutlet n. (with bone) côtelette f.; (without bone) escalope f.

cutoff n. interrupteur m.; soupape f.; bifurcation f.; chemin plus court m.

cutout n. (elec.) coupe-circuit m. coupure f.

cut-rate a. à prix réduit

cutthroat n. coupe-gorge m.; — a. acharné

cwt. : hundredweight n. un demi quintal m.

cyanide n. cyanure m.

cybernetics n. cybernétique f.

cycle n. cycle m.; — vi. aller à bicyclette; pédaler

cyclist n. cycliste m. & f.

cyclotron n. cyclotron m.

cylinder n. cylindre m.

cylindrical a. cylindrique

cymbal n. cymbale f.

cynic n. cynique n.; –al a. cynique; –ism n. cynisme m.

cypress n. cyprès m.

Cyprus n. Chypre f.

cyst n. kyste m.; sac m.

Czar n. tsar m.; –ina n. tsarine f.

Czech a. & n. tchèque m. & f.

Czechoslovakia n. Tchécoslovakie f.

D

D.A.: District Attorney procureur m.

dab n. éclaboussure f.; tache f.; petit coup, petit morceau m.; — vt. éclabousser; tacher; tamponner

dabble vi. s'occuper en amateur

Dacron (trademark) n. dacron m.

dactyl n. dactyle m.; pied de trois syllabes dont la première accentuée m.

dad, daddy n. papa m.

daffodil n. asphodèle m.

daft a. idiot, fou

dagger n. poignard m.

daily n. quotidien m.; — a. journalier, quotidien; — adv. tous les jours; quotidiennement;

daintiness n. délicatesse f.

dainty n. friandise f.; — a. délicat

dairy n. laiterie f.; — **farm** vacherie f.; — **industry** industrie laitière f.

dairyman n. laitier, crémier m.

daisy n. marguerite f.

dale n. val m.

dalliance n. affaire f.; flirtage m.

dally vi. badiner, perdre son temps, s'amuser

Dalmatia n. Dalmatie f.

dam n. barrage m.; (zool.) mère f.; — vt. barrer

damage n. dommage m.; dégats m. pl.; avarie f.; — vt. endommager, avarier

damaging a. nuisible

damascene vt. damasquiner

Damascus n. Damas m.

damask n. damas m.

dame n. dame f.; (coll.) femme f.

damn vt. damner, condamner; —! interj. zut!; –able a. damnable; –ation n. damnation f.; –ed a. damné; (coll.) sacré

damp n. humidité f.; — a. humide; –en vt. humidifier; humecter; étouffer; –er n. registre m.; étouffoir m.; –ness n. humidité f.

damsel n. demoiselle f.

damson n. prune de damas f.

dance n. danse f.; bal m.; dancing m.; — **hall**, salle de danse f.; dancing m.; — vi. danser; –er n. danseur m., danseuse f.

dandelion n. pissenlit m.

dander n. colère f.

dandle vt. bercer, dorloter

dandruff n. pellicules f. pl.

dandy n. dandy m.; — a. (coll.) épatant

Dane, Danish a. & n. Danois m.

danger n. danger m.; –ous a. dangereux, périleux; –ously adv. dangereusement

dangle vi. être suspendu; pendre, pendiller; — vt. suspendre

dank a. humide, moite

dapper a. vif; élegant

dapple a. pommele, bigarré; — vt. tacheter

dare n. défi m.; — vt. donner le défi (à); provoquer; oser; risquer; — vi. oser

daredevil *n.* casse-cou *m.*

daring *a.* hardi; audacieux; — *n.* audace *f.*

dark *a.* sombre, obscur; noir; (color) foncé; — **horse** candidat obscur *m.*; — *n.* obscurité, nuit *f.*; **–en** *vi.* faire nuit; **–en** *vt.* noircir; **–ness** *n.* nuit *f.*; obscurité *f.*

Dark Ages *n.* Moyen-Âge *m.*

darkroom *n.* chambre noire *f.*

darling *n.* favori *m.*, favorite *f.*, chéri *m.*, chérie *f.*; — *a.* chéri, favorite

darn *vt.* raccommoder; repriser; — *n.* raccommodage *m.*; reprise *f.*; —! *interj.* zut!; **–ing** *n.* raccommodage *m.*; **–ing needle** *n.* aiguille à repriser *f.*; demoiselle *f.*

dart *n.* dard, trait *m.*; — *vt.* darder, lancer; jeter; — *vi.* voler comme un trait

dash *n.* trait *m.*; petit brin, grain *m.*; course *f.*; ruée *f.*; (gram.) tiret *m.*; — *vt.* jeter; plonger; précipiter; éclabousser; — *vi.* se briser, se heurter; se ruer; — **off** esquisser; **–ing** *a.* élégant

dastard *n.* lâche *m.*; **–ly** *a.* lâche

data *n.* données *f. pl.*

date *n.* date *f.*; époque *f.*; (bot.) datte *f.*; (coll.) rendez-vous *m.*; **up to** — à la page; — *vt. & vi.* dater; **–d** *a.* vétuste, démodé

dative *n.* datif *m.*

daub *vt.* barbouiller; enduire; peinturer; — *n.* barbouillage *m.*; enduit *m.*

daughter *n.* fille *f.*

daughter-in-law *n.* belle-fille *f.*

daunt *vt.* intimider, abattre; **–less** *a.* intrépide

davenport *n.* divan, canapé *m.*

davit *n.* (naut.) davier *m.*

dawdle *vi.* muser; flâner; **–r** *n.* traînard *m.*

dawdling *a.* musard, flâneur; — *n.* musarderie, flânerie *f.*

dawn *n.* aube, aurore *f.*, point du jour *m.*; — *vi.* paraître, naître; poindre

day *n.* jour *m.*; journée *f.*; **a** — par jour; **by the** — à la journée; **carry the** — vaincre; — **after** lendemain *m.*; — **after** — d'un jour à l'autre; — **before** yesterday avant-hier; — **by** — au jour le jour; jour par jour; **every** — tous les jours; **every other** — tous les deux jours; **from** — **to** — au jour le jour; **on the following** — le lendemain; — **laborer** manœuvrier *m.*; — **nursery** garderie d'enfants *f.*; — **school** externat *m.*; — **shift** équipe du jour *f.*

daybreak *n.* pointe du jour *f.*; aube *f.*

daydream *n.* rêverie *f.*; — *vi.* faire des châteaux en Espagne

daylight *n.* jour *m.*; — **saving time** *n.* heure d'été *f.*

daytime *n.* jour *m.*, journée *f.*

daze *vt.* éblouir; étourdir; — *n.* éblouissement *m.*, étourdissement *m.*

dazzle *vt.* éblouir

dazzling *a.* éblouissant

d.c.: direct current courant continu *m.*

deacon *n.* diacre *m.*

deactivate *vt.* déactiver

dead *a.* mort, sans vie; sourd; — **body** *n.* cadavre *m.*; — **calm** calme plat *m.*; — **center** point mort *m.*; — **end** impasse *f.*, cul-de-sac *m.*; — **heat** manche à manche; — **letter** rebut *m.*; — **line** *n.* experation d'un délai *f.*; — **reckoning** route estimée *f.*; — **shot** bon tireur *m.*; — **silence** silence total *m.*; — **weight** poids inerte *m.*; **–wood** *n.* bois mort *m.*; coulée d'un navire *f.*; **the** — *n.*; **les morts** *m. pl.*; — *adv.* tout à fait, entièrement; **–en** *vt.* assourdir; amortir; **–ly** *a.* mortel; vénéneux

dead line *n.* heure-limité *f.*

deadlock *n.* impasse *f.*

Dead Sea *n.* (la) Mer Morte *f.*

deaf *a.* sourd; insensible; **stone** — complètement sourd; — **and dumb** sourd-muet; **–en** *vt.* rendre sourd; **–ening** *a.* assourdissant; **–ness** *n.* surdité *f.*

deaf-mute *n.* sourd-muet *m.*

deal *n.* quantité, partie *f.*; (cards) donne *f.*; affaire *f.*; **a great** —, **a good** — beaucoup; — *vt.* (cards) donner, distribuer; — *vi.* avoir affaire. traiter; **–er** *n.* commerçant *m.*; (cards) donneur *m.*; **–ings** *n. pl.* affaires *f. pl.*

dean *n.* doyen *m.*

dear *a.* cher; côuteux; bien aimé; **–ly** *adv.* cher, chèrement; **–ness** *n.* cherté *f.*

dearth *n.* rareté *f.*; pénurie *f.*

death *n.* mort *f.*, trépas *m.*; — **rate** mortalité *f.*; **at** — **'s door** à deux doigts de la mort; **–blow** *n.* coup de mort *m.*; — **penalty** *n.* peine capitale *f.*; — **warrant** ordre d'exécution *m.*; **put to** — exécuter, mettre à mort; **–less** *a.* immortel; **–ly** *a.* mortel

deathbed *n.* lit de mort *m.*

deathtrap *n.* coupe-gorge *m.*

debar *vt.* exclure, priver

debase *vi.* abaisser, avilir; falsifier; **–ment** *n.* avilissement *m.*

debatable *a.* contestable

debate *n.* débat *m.*, dispute *f.*; — *vt. & vi.* débattre; disputer

debauch *vt.* débaucher; **–ery** *n.* débauche *f.*; libertinage *m.*

debenture *n.* reconnaissance, obligation *f.*

debilitate *vt.* débiliter, affaiblir

debility *n.* débilité *f.*

debit *n.* débit *m.*; — *rt.* débiter

debonair *a.* élégant, gai

debris *n.* débris *m. pl.*

debt *n.* dette *f.*; **to run, get into** — faire des dettes; **–or** *n.* débiteur *m.*

debunk *vt.* démentir

debut *n.* début *m.*; **–ante** *n.* débutante *f.*

decade *n.* décade *f.*, dix ans *m. pl.*

decadence *n.* décadence *f.*

decamp *vi.* décamper, filer

decant *vt.* décanter; **–er** *n.* carafe *f.*

decapitate *vt.* décapiter

decay *n.* déclin *m.*, décadence *f.*; (teeth) carie *f.*; — *vi.* tomber en ruine; pourrir

decease *n.* décès *m.*; — *vi.* déceder; **–d** *a.* décédé

deceit *n.* tromperie *f.*; **–ful** *a.* trompeur

deceive *vt.* tromper; **–r** *n.* trompeur *m.*

deceleration *n.* décélération *f.*

December *n.* décembre *m.*

decency *n.* décence, bienséance *f.*

decent *a.* décent, convenable, bienséant

decentralization *n.* décentralisation *f.*

decentralize *vt.* décentraliser

deception *n.* tromperie *f.*

deceptive *a.* trompeur

decide *vt.* décider, résoudre; juger; — *vi.* se décider; **–ed** *a.* marqué; résolu; **–edly** *adv.* notablement; décidément

decimal *a.* décimal; — **point** virgule *f.*

decimate *vt.* décimer

decimation *n.* décimation *f.*

decipher *vt.* déchiffrer; **–able** *a.* déchiffrable

decision *n.* décision *f.*; résolution *f.*; jugement *m.*; parti *m.*; **to come to a** — prendre une décision

decisive *a.* décisif

deck *n.* tillac, pont, gaillard *m.*; (cards) jeu *m.*; — **chair** transat *m.*; — *vt.* parer, orner

declaim *vt. & vi.* déclamer; haranguer

declamation *n.* déclamation *f.*

declamatory *a.* déclamatoire

declaration *f.* déclaration *f.*; constatation *f.*

declare *vt.* déclarer; **–d** *a.* déclaré, avoué

declension *n.* déclinaison *f.*

decline *n.* déclin *m.*, décadence *f.*; — *vt.* refuser; décliner; — *vi.* déchoir; baisser; pencher

declivity *n.* déclivité *f.*

decode *vt.* déchiffrer

decompose *vt.* décomposer; — *vi.* se décomposer, pourrir

decomposition *n.* décomposition *f.*

decompression *n.* décompression *f.*

deconsecrate *vt.* séculariser

deconsecration *n.* sécularisation *f.*

decontaminate *vt.* décontaminer

decontrol *vt.* libérer du contrôle

decorate *vt.* décorer, orner

decoration *n.* décoration *f.*; décor *m.*

decorative *a.* décoratif

decorator *n.* décorateur *m.*

decorous *a.* convenable, comme il faut

decorum *n.* décorum *m.*, décence *f.*

decoy *n.* leurre *m.*; — *vt.* leurrer

decrease *n.* diminution *f.*; amoindrissement *m.*; — *vt. & vi.* diminuer; (s')amoindrir

decreasing *a.* diminuant; **–ly** *adv.* de moins en moins

decree *n.* décret, édit *m.*; arrêt, arrêté *m.*; jugement *m.*; — *vt. & vi.* décréter

decrepit *a.* décrépit; **–ude** *n.* décrepitude *f.*

decry *vt.* décrier

dedicate *vt.* dédier; dévouer; consacrer

dedication *n.* dédicace, dédication *f.*

dedicatory *a.* dédicatoire

deduce *vt.* déduire, inférer

deduct *vt.* déduire; **–ion** *n.* déduction; retranchement *m.*, remise *f.*; **–ive** *a.* déductif

deed *n.* action *f.*, acte, fait, exploit *m.*; (law) titre *m.*; — *vt.* transférer un titre

deem *vt. & vi.* juger, penser

deep *a.* profond; grave; (color) foncé; — *n.* mer *f.*; ciel *m.*; **–en** *vt.* approfondir; obscurcir; **–en** *vi.* s'approfondir; devenir plus foncé; **–ness** *n.* profondeur *f.*

Deepfreeze (trademark) *n.* frigorifique *f.*

deep-rooted, deep-seated *a.* enraciné

deep-sea *a.*, — fishing grande pêche *f.*

deface *vt.* défigurer, détériorer, mutiler; **–ment** *n.* défiguration, mutilation *f.*

defalcate *vi.* détourner de l'argent

defalcation *n.* détournement d'argent *m.*

defamation *n.* diffamation *f.*

defamatory *a.* diffamatoire

defame *vt.* diffamer; **–r** *n.* diffamateur *m.*

default *n.* défaut *m.*, faute *f.*; — *vi.* manquer; faire défaut

defeat *n.* défaite, déroute *f.*; — *vt.* vaincre, battre, défaire; **–ist** *a. & n.* défaitiste *m. & f.*

defect *n.* défaut *m.*; vice *m.*; — *vt.* faire défection; **–ion** *n.* défection *f.*; **–ive** *a.* défectueux; vicieux

defend *vt.* défendre, protéger; **–ant** *n.* accusé *m.*; **–er** *n.* defenseur *m.*

defense *n.* défense, protection *f.*; **–less** *a.* sans défense

defensible *a.* défensible

defensive *n.* défensive *f.*; — *a.* défensif

defer *vt. & vi.* différer, remettre; déférer (à); **–ence** *n.* déférence *f.*, respect *m.*; **in –ence to** par respect pour; **–ential** *a.* respectueux; **–ment** *n.* délai *m.*; (army) réformation temporaire *f.*

defiance *n.* défi *m.*; **in** — **of** au mépris de

defiant *a.* résistant, combattant; de défi

deficiency *n.* défaut *m.*, insuffisance *f.*
deficient *a.* défectueux, imparfait
deficit *n.* déficit *m.*
defile *n.* défilé *m.*; — *vt.* souiller; — *vi.* défiler: -ment *n.* souillure, tache *f.*
definable *a.* définissable
define *vt.* définir; délimiter
definite *a.* défini, exact, précis; -ly *adv.* décidément, nettement; -ness *n.* netteté *f.*
definition *n.* définition *f.*
deflate *vt.* dégonfler
deflation *n.* dégonflement *m.*; (com.) déflation *f.*
deflect *vt.* détourner; défléchir; -ion *n.* déclinaison *f.*; déflexion *f.*
deforest *vt.* déboiser; -ation *n.* déboisement *m.*
deform *vt.* défigurer, déformer; -ation *n.* déformation *f.*; -ed *a.* difforme, déformé; -ity *n.* difformité *f.*
defraud *vt.* frauder, tromper; -er *n.* fraudeur *m.*
defray *vt.* défrayer, couvrir
defrost *vt.* dégivrer; -er *n.* dégivreuse *f.*
deft *a.* adroit, preste; -ness *n.* adresse, prestesse, dextérité *f.*
defunct *a.* défunt
defy *vt.* défier, braver
degeneracy *n.* dégénération *f.*
degenerate *vi.* dégénérer; — *a.* & *n.* dégénéré *m.*
degeneration *n.* dégénération *f.*
degradation *n.* dégradation *f.*
degrade *vt.* dégrader, avilir
degrading *a.* dégradant
degree *n.* degré *m.*; qualité, condition *f.*, ordre, rang *m.*; (educ.) titre *m.*; in some — dans une certaine mesure: third — (coll.) cuisinage *m.*; by -s peu à peu, petit à petit
dehumidifier *n.* déshydratant *m.*
dehydrate *vt.* dessécher, déshydrater
deification *n.* déification *f.*
deify *vt.* déifier
deign *vi.* daigner
deist *n.* déiste *m.*
deity *n.* déité, divinité *f.*
deject *vt.* affliger, décourager; abattre; -ed *a.* découragé; abattu; -ion *n.* découragement *m.*; abattement *m.*
delay *n.* délai, retard *m.*; — *vt.* retarder; remettre, différer; — *vi.* retarder; tarder, s'attarder
delectable *a.* délectable
delegate *n.* délégué *m.*; — *vt.* déléguer
delegation *n.* délégation *f.*
delete *vt.* rayer, enlever, éliminer, supprimer, effacer
deletion *n.* rature *f.*; suppression *f.*

deliberate *vi.* délibérer; — *a.* délibéré; prémédité; voulu, calculé; réfléchi; -ly *adv.* avec préméditation; exprès; posément
deliberation *n.* délibération *f.*
delicacy *n.* délicatesse *f.*; friandise *f.*
delicate *a.* délicat; fin; friand; tendre; doux; faible
delicatessen *n.* charcuterie *f.*
delicious *a.* délicieux
delight *n.* délice *m.*, délices *f. pl.*, plaisir *m.*; joie *f.*; charme *m.*; — *vt.* réjouir, divertir; ravir; — *vi.* prendre plaisir (à); -ed *a.* ravi, enchanté; -ful *a.* charmant; ravissant: délicieux
delimit *vt.* délimiter
delineate *vt.* tracer, dessiner, décrire
delineation *n.* délinéation, esquisse *f.*
delinquency *n.* délit *m.*
delinquent *n.* délinquant *m.*
delirious *a.* en délire; be — délirer
delirium *n.* délire *m.*; — tremens delirium tremens *m.*
deliver *vt.* livrer; remettre, rendre; délivrer; (med.) accoucher; prononcer; s'acquitter de; distribuer; -ance *n.* délivrance *f.*; -er *n.* livreur *m.*; libérateur *m.*; -y *n.* livraison *f.*; (mail) distribution *f.*; (speech) débit *m.*; (med.) accouchement *m.*; (letter) general -y poste restante *f.*; special -y (letter) lettre exprès *f.*
Delphi *n.* Delphes *f.*; -c *a.* de Delphes
delude *vt.* tromper, abuser
deluge *n.* déluge *m.*; — *vt.* inonder
delusion *n.* tromperie, illusion *f.*
delusive *a.* trompeur
delve *vt.* creuser, fouir
demagogue *n.* démogogue *m.*
demand *n.* demande, requête *f.*; in great — très recherché; on — à présentation; — *vt.* réclamer, exiger
demarcate *vt.* délimiter
demarcation *n.* démarcation *f.*
demean *vt.*, — oneself se comporter; se dégrader; -or *n.* conduite, tenue *f.*
demented *a.* aliéné
demerit *n.* démérite *m.*; mauvaise note *f.*
demigod *n.* demi-dieu *m.*
demilitarization *n.* démilitarisation *f.*
demilitarize *vt.* démilitariser
demise *n.* mort *f.*, décès *m.*
demitasse *n.* café noir *m.*
demobilization *n.* démobilisation *f.*
demobilize *vt.* démobiliser
democracy *n.* démocratie *f.*
democrat *n.* démocrate *m.*; -ic *a.* démocratique
demolish *vt.* démolir, abattre
demolition *n.* démolition *f.*

demonstrability *n.* démontrabilité *f.*
demonstrable *a.* démontrable
demonstrate *vt.* démontrer; — *vi.* manifester
demonstration *n.* démonstration *f.*; (pol.) manifestation *f.*
demonstrative *a.* démonstratif
demonstrator *n.* démonstrateur *m.*; (pol.) manifestant *m.*
demoralization *n.* démoralisation *f.*
demoralize *vt.* démoraliser
demote *vt.* dégrader
demotion *n.* dégradation *f.*
demur *n.* hésitation *f* ; — *vi.* différer; hésiter
demure *a.* sobre; modeste
den *n.* caverne *f.*, repaire *m.*; étude *f.*
denaturalize *vt.* dénaturaliser
denature *vt.* dénaturer
deniable *a.* niable, reniable
denial *n.* dénégation *f.*, refus *m.*
denim *n.* étoffe croisée de coton *f.*
denizen *n.* habitant *m.*
Denmark *n.* Danemark *m.*
denominate *vt.* dénommer
denomination *n.* dénomination *f.*; culte *m.*; —al *a.* sectaire, confessionnel
denominator *n.* dénominateur *m.*
denote *vt.* dénoter, désigner
denouement *n.* dénouement *m.*
denounce *vt.* dénoncer, accuser
dense *a.* dense; épais; stupide
density *n.* densité *f.*; épaisseur *f.*
dent *n.* renfoncement *m.*; coche *f.*; — *vt.* laisser une coche, bosseler
dental *a.* dentaire, dental; — brace *n.* rectificateur dentaire *m.*
dentate *a.* denté
dentifrice *n.* dentifrice *m.*
dentist *n.* dentiste *m.*
denture *n.* dentier *m.*, fausses dents *f. pl.*
denude *vt.* dénuer, dépouiller; dénuder
denunciation *n.* dénonciation *f.*
denunciatory *a.* dénonciateur
deny *vt.* nier; dénier; désavouer, renoncer, refuser
deodorant *n.* désodorisant *m.*
deodorize *vt.* désodoriser; —r *n.* désodorisateur
depart *vi.* partir, s'en aller; —ed *a.* mort, défunt; —ure *n.* départ *m.*
department *n.* département *m.*; comptoir, rayon *m.*; — store grand magasin *m.*; —al *a.* départemental
depend *vi.* dépendre (de); résulter (de); se reposer, se fier; —able *a.* digne de confiance; —ence, —ency *n.* dépendance *f.*; —ent *a.* dépendant; —ent *n.* personne dépendante *f.*; be —ent on dépendre de
depict *vt.* dépeindre, décrire

depilation *n.* épilation *f.*
depilatory *a.* & *n.* dépilatoire *m.*
deplete *vt.* épuiser
depletion *n.* épuisement *m.*
deplorable *a.* déplorable, lamentable
deplore *vt.* déplorer, pleurer, plaindre
depolarization *n.* dépolarisation *f.*
depopulate *vt.* dépeupler
deport *vt.* déporter; (se) comporter; —ation *n.* déportation *f.*; —ment *n.* comportement *m.*
depose *vt.* déposer; mettre bas; attester
deposit *n.* dépôt, gage *m.*; (geol.) gisement *m.*; (com.) arrhes *f. pl.*; — *vt.* déposer; —ion *n.* déposition *f.*; —or *n.* déposant *m.*; —ory *n.* dépôt *m.*
depot *n.* dépôt *m.*; (rail.) gare *f.*
deprave *vt.* dépraver, corrompre
depravity *n.* corruption *f.*; perversité *f.*
deprecate *vt.* s'opposer (à); désapprouver
depreciate *vt.* déprécier; dénigrer; — *vi.* perdre sa valeur
depreciation *n.* dépréciation *f.*
depredation *n.* déprédation *f.* pillage *m.*
depress *vt.* déprimer, abaisser; —ed *a.* abattu, déprimé; —ing *a.* attristant; —ion *n.* dépression *f.*; crise financière *f.*; abattement *m.*
deprivation *n.* privation *f.*
deprive *vt.* priver; destituer
depth *n.* profondeur *f.*, abîme *m.*; milieu, cœur, fort *m.*; hauteur, obscurité *f.*; get out of one's — perdre fond; — bomb, — charge bombe sous-marine *f.*
deputation *n.* députation, délégation *f.*
depute *vt.* déléguer, députer
deputize *vt.* députer
deputy *n.* délégué *m.*; adjoint *m.*; député *m.*
derail *vt.* faire dérailler; be —ed dérailler; —ment *n.* déraillement *m.*
derange *vt.* troubler, déranger; —ment *n.* dérèglement *m.*; dérangement *m.*
derby *n.* (racing) derby *m.*; (hat) chapeau melon *m.*
derelict *n.* vaisseau abandonné *m.*; personne abandonnée *f.*; clochard *m.*; — *a.* abandonné; —ion *n.* abandon *m.*; renoncement *m.*
deride *vt.* railler, se moquer de
derision *n.* dérision *f.*; risée *f.*
derisive *a.* dérisoire
derivation *n.* dérivation *f.*; source *f.*
derivative *a.* dérivé *m.*
derive *vt.* & *vi.* dériver; — *vi.* provenir, procéder
dermatitis *n.* dermite *f.*
dermatologist *n.* dermatologiste *m.*
derogate *vi.* déroger
derogatory *a.* dérogatoire

derrick *n.* grue *f.*, derrick *m.*

descend *vi.* descendre; be –ed from descendre de; –ant, –ent *n.* descendant *m.*

descent *n.* descente *f.*; descendance *f.*

describable *a.* descriptible *a.*

describe *vt.* décrire, dépeindre

description *n.* description *f.*

descriptive *a.* descriptif

desecrate *vt.* profaner

desecration *n.* profanation *f.*

desegregate *vt.* ôter la ségrégation

desegregation *n.* intégration *f.*

desensitize *vt.* rendre insensible; désensibiliser

desert *n.* désert *m.*; — *vt.* déserter; abandonner; –er *n.* déserteur *m.*; –ion *n.* désertion *f.*

deserts *n. pl.* dû *m.*; punition *f.*; récompense *f.*

deserve *vt.* mériter

deserving *a.* méritoire, digne

desiccate *vt.* dessécher; — *vi.* se dessécher

desiccation *n.* dessiccation *f.*; dessèchement *m.*

design *n.* dessein *m.*; intention *f.*; plan *m.*; (art) dessin *m.*; — *vt.* dessiner; destiner; –er *n.* dessinateur *m.*; –ing *a.* intrigant; –ing *n.* dessin *m.*

designate *vt.* désigner, indiquer, distinguer

desirability *n.* avantage *m.*

desirable *a.* désirable, souhaitable

desire *n.* désir *m.*, envie *f.*; — *vt.* désirer; souhaiter

desirous *a.* désireux

desist *vi.* cesser; s'abstenir

desk *n.* bureau *m.*; pupitre *m.*; chaire *f.*

desolate *vt.* désoler, dépeupler; — *a.* désert, dépeuplé; désolé

desolation *n.* désolation *f.*

despair *n.* désespoir *f.*; — *vi.* désespérer (de); –ing *a.* désespéré

despatch *n.* expédition, diligence *f.*; dépêche *f.*; — *vt.* dépêcher, expédier

desperado *n.* risque-tout *m.*; hors-la-loi *m.*

desperate *a.* désespéré

desperation *n.* désespoir *m.*

despicable *a.* méprisable, bas

despise *vt.* dédaigner, détester, mépriser

despite *prep.* en dépit de, malgré

despoil *vt.* dépouiller

despondency *n.* abattement *m.*

despondent *a.* désolé; abattu; désespéré

despot *n.* despote, tyran *m.*; –ic *a.* despotique; –ism *n.* despotisme *m.*

dessert *n.* dessert, entremets *m.*

destine *vt.* destiner

destiny *n.* destinée *f.*, destin *m.*

destitute *a.* abandonné, dans la misère; destitué

destitution *n.* dénûment *m.*, misère *f.*; destitution *f.*

destroy *vt.* détruire; –er *n.* destructeur *m.*; (navy) destroyer *m.*

destruction *n.* destruction *f.*

destructive *a.* destructif; –ness *n.* caractère destructif *m.*, nature destructive *f.*

desuetude *n.* désuétude *f.*

desultory *a.* décousu, sans suite

detach *vt.* détacher, séparer; –able *a.* détachable; –ed *a.* détaché; séparé; désintéressé; –ment *n.* détachement *m.*

detail *n.* détail *m.*; — *vt.* détailler

detain *vt.* détenir, retenir

detect *vt.* repérer, découvrir; distinguer; –ion *n.* découverte *f.*; –ive *n.* détective *m.*; –or *n.* détecteur, appareil récepteur *m.*

detention *n.* retard *m.*, détention *f.*; arrêt *m.*; retenue *f.*; emprisonnement *m.*

deter *vt.* détourner, décourager; –rent *n.* empêchement *m.*

detergent *n. & a.* détersif, détergent *m.*

deteriorate *vt.* détériorer; — *vi.* se détériorer

deterioration *n.* détérioration *f.*

determinable *a.* déterminable

determinate *a.* déterminé, défini

determination *n.* détermination, décision *f.*

determinative *a.* déterminatif, déterminant

determine *vt. & vi.* déterminer, fixer, décider; –d *a.* résolu

detest *vt.* détester; –able *a.* détestable

dethrone *vt.* détrôner; –ment *n.* détrônement *m.*

detonate *vi.* détoner; — *vt.* faire détoner

detonation *n.* détonation *f.*

detonator *n.* détonateur *m.*

detour *n.* déviation *f.*; détour *m.*; — *vi.* dévier, se détourner

detract *vi.*, — from diminuer; –or *n.* détracteur *m.*

detrain *vi.* débarquer, descendre (du train)

detriment *n.* détriment *m.*, perte *f.*; –al *a.* nuisible, préjudiciable

devaluate *vt.* dévaluer

devaluation *n.* dévaluation *f.*

devalue *vt.* dévaluer

devastate *vt.* dévaster

devastating *a.* accablant; dévastateur

develop *vt.* développer; — *vi.* se développer; exploiter; contracter; –er *n.* développeur *m.*; révélateur *m.*; –ment *n.* développement *m.*; exploitation *f.*

deviate *vi.* dévier, s'égarer, dériver

deviation *n.* déviation *f.*, égarement *m.*

device *n.* appareil *m.*; moyen *m.*; ruse *f.*; devise *f.*, emblème *m.*

devil *n.* diable *m.*; — *vt.* accommoder au

poivre; –ish *a.* diabolique; espiègle; –try *n.* espièglerie *f.*

devil-may-care *a.* insouciant

devious *a.* détourné; dévié; –ness *n.* détours *m. pl.*

devise *vt.* inventer, imaginer

devoid *a.* vide, dénué

devolve *vi.* échoir; — *vt.* déléguer

devote *vt.* dévouer, dédier, consacrer; –ed *a.* dévoué

devotee *n.* amateur *m.*

devotion *n.* dévotion *f.*; dévouement *m.*; –al *a.* de dévotion

devour *vt.* dévorer

devout *a.* dévot; pieux; –ness *n.* dévotion, piété *f.*

dew *n.* rosée *f.*

dewlap *n.* fanon *m.*

dexterity *n.* dextérité, adresse *f.*

dexterous *a.* adroit; habile

dextrin *n.* dextrine *f.*

dextrose *n.* glucose *f.*, dextrose *m.*

diabetes *n.* diabète *m.*

diabetic *a.* diabétique

diabolic(al) *a.* diabolique

diacritic(al) *a.*; — **mark** *n.* marque diacritique *f.*

diadem *n.* diadème *m.*

diaeresis *n.* tréma *m.*

diagnose *vt.* diagnostiquer

diagnosis *n.* diagnostic *m.*

diagnostic *a.* diagnostique

diagonal *n.* diagonale *f.*; — *a.* diagonal

diagram *n.* diagramme *m.*; figure *f.*; schéma *m.*; –matic *a.* schématique

dial *n.* cadran *m.*; — **telephone** téléphone automatique *m.*; — *vt.* composer (un numéro)

dialect *n.* dialecte *m.*

dialog(ue) *n.* dialogue *m.*

diameter *n.* diamètre *m.*

diametrical *a.* diamétral

diamond *n.* diamant *m.*; (cards) carreau *m.*; (sport) terrain de baseball *m.*; (print.) corps 4, 5 *m.*

diapason *n.* diapason *m.*

diaper *n.* couche *f.*

diaphanous *a.* diaphane

diaphragm *n.* diaphragme *m.*

diarrhea *n.* diarrhée *f.*

diary *n.* journal *m.*

diathermy *n.* diathermie *f.*

diatom *n.* diatomée *m.*

diatribe *n.* diatribe *f.*

dice *n. pl.* dés *m. pl.*; — *vt.* couper en cubes; — *vi.* jouer aux dés

dickey, dicky *n.* faux plastron de chemise *m.*

dictaphone *n.* dictaphone *m.*

dictate *n.* règle *f.*, précepte *m.*; — *vt.* dic-

ter, prescrire, déclarer

dictation *n.* dictée *f.*

dictator *n.* dictateur *m.*; –ial *a.* dictatorial; –ship *n.* dictature *f.*

diction *n.* diction *f.*, style *m.*

dictionary *n.* dictionnaire *m.*

dictum *n.* dicton *m.*; (law) opinion *f.*

didactic *a.* didactique; –s *n. pl.* didactique *f.*

die *n.* dé *m.*; (coin) coin *m.*; (mech.) matrice *f.*

die *vi.* mourir; — **away**, — **down**, — **out** s'eteindre, se mourir

diesel engine *n.* diesel *m.*

diet *n.* nourriture *f.*; diète *f.*, régime *m.*; — *vi.* être au régime; –etic *a.* diététique; –etics *n.* diététique *f.*

differ *vi.* différer; –ence *n.* différence *f.*; différend *m.*; –ent *a.* différent; autre; –ential *a.* différentiel; –entiate *vt.* différencier; –entiation *n.* différenciation *f.*

difficult *a.* difficile; –y *n.* difficulté *f.*; inconvénient *m.*; embarras *m.*

diffidence *n.* timidité, hésitation *f.*; défiance *f.*

diffident *a.* timide, hésitant

diffract *vt.* diffracter; –ion *n.* diffraction *f.*

diffuse *vt.* diffuser, répandre; — *a.* diffus; –r *n.* diffuseur *m.*

dig *vt.* creuser; — **up** déterrer; — *n.* (coll.) insulte *f.*; remarque sarcastique *f.*; –ging *n.* excavation *f.*; fouilles *f. pl.*

digest *vt. & vi.* digérer; résumer; — *n.* résumé, digest *m.*; –ible *a.* digestible; –ion *n.* digestion *f.*; –ive *a.* digestif

digit *n.* doigt *m.*; chiffre *f.*; –al *a.* digital; –al computer *n.* calculatrice digitale *f.*

digitalis *n.* digitale *f.*

dignified *a.* plein de dignité, digne

dignify *vt.* rendre digne, honorer

dignitary *n.* dignitaire *m.*

dignity *n.* dignité *f.*

digress *vi.* faire une digression; –ion *n.* digression *f.*

dike *n.* digue *f.*

dilapidate *vt.* dilapider; –d *a.* délabré

dilapidation *n.* délabrement *m.*, dilapidation *f.*

dilate *vt.* dilater; — *vi.* se dilater

dilation *n.* dilation *f.*

dilatory *a.* dilatoire

dilemma *n.* dilemme *m.*

diligent *a.* diligent, assidu

dill *n.* aneth *m.*

dilute *vt.* délayer, diluer; –d *a.* dilué

dim *vt.* obscurcir; (lights) baisser; — *a.* obscur, pâle; sceptique; –mers *n. pl.* (headlights) feux de croisement *m. pl.*; –ness *n.* obscurité *f.*

dime *n.* pièce de dix cents *f.*; — **novel** ro-

inlaid *a.* marqueté, parqueté

inland *n. & a.* intérieur *m.*; — *adv.* vers l'intérieur

in-laws *n. pl.* parents par alliance *m. pl.*; beaux-parents *m. pl.*

inlay *vt.* marqueter; incruster; — *n.* marqueterie, incrustation *f.*

inlet *n.* anse *f.*; débouché *m.*; admission *f.*

inmate *n.* pensionnaire *m.*; prisonnier *m.*

inmost, innermost *a.* le plus intérieur; le plus intime

inn *n.* auberge *f.*

innate *a.* inné

inner *a.* intérieur; — **tube** chambre à air *f.*; **–most** *a.* le plus intime

inning *n.* (baseball) période *f.*

innkeeper *n.* aubergiste *m.*

innocence *n.* innocence *f.*

innocent *a. & n.* innocent *m.*

innocuous *a.* innocent, inoffensif

innovate *vi.* innover

innovation *n.* innovation *f.*

innuendo *n.* allusion, insinuation *f.*

innumerable *a.* innombrable

inoculate *vt.* inoculer; vacciner

inoffensive *a.* inoffensif

inoperative *a.* inefficace

inopportune *a.* mal à propos, inopportun

inordinate *a.* déréglé; irrégulier; démesuré

inorganic *a.* inorganique

inquest *n.* enquête judiciaire *f.*

inquire *vi.* s'enquérir, s'informer; demander (un avis); s'adresser

inquiry *n.* enquête, recherche *f.*, examen *m.*

inquisitive *a.* curieux; **–ness** *n.* curiosité *f.*

inquisitor *n.* inquisiteur *m.*

inroad *n.* incursion, invasion *f.*

insane *a.* insensé, fou; aliéné; — **asylum** asile des aliénés *m.*; maison de fous *f.*

insanity *n.* folie, démence *f.*

insatiability *n.* insatiabilité *f.*

insatiable *a.* insatiable

inscribe *vt.* inscrire; dédier

inscription *n.* inscription *f.*; (book) dédicace *f.*

insect *a.* insecte *m.*; **–icide** *n. & a.* insecticide *m.*

insecure *a.* mal assuré, peu sûr

insecurity *n.* insécurité, incertitude *f.*, danger *m.*

insensible *a.* insensible

insensitive *a.* insensible

inseparable *a.* inséparable

insert *vt.* insérer, introduire; — *n.* insertion *f.*; **–ion** *n.* insertion; introduction *f.*

inset *vt.* insérer (un cliché, un texte, dans un autre cliché, un autre texte); — *n.* objet inséré *m.*; hors-texte *m.*

inside *n.* intérieur *m.*; dedans *m.*; — **out**

à l'envers; **–s** *pl.* entrailles *f. pl.*; — *a.* intérieur; — **of** (time) en moins de; — **track** (coll.) avantage *m.*; — *adv.* à l'intérieur, vers l'intérieur; — *prep.* dans, à l'intérieur de; **–r** *n.* personne de la maison *f.*; initié *m.*

insidious *a.* insidieux

insight *n.* intuition *f.*; goût, jugement *m.*; aperçu *m.*

insignia *n. pl.* insignes *m. pl.*

insignificance *n.* insignifiance *f.*

insignificant *a.* insignifiant; peu important, sans importance

insincere *a.* peu sincère; faux, trompeur

insincerity *n.* manque de sincérité *m.*

insinuate *vt.* insinuer, suggérer, laisser entendre, donner à entendre

insinuating *a.* insinuant

insinuation *n.* insinuation *f.*

insipid *a.* insipide; fade; **–ity** *n.* insipidité *f.*; fadeur *f.*

insist *vi.* insister, persister; — **on** persister à; tenir à; — **that** insister pour que; **–ence** *n.* insistence *f.*; **–ent** *a.* insistant

insole *n.* semelle intérieure *f.*

insolence *n.* insolence *f.*

insolubility *n.* insolubilité *f.*

insoluble *a.* insoluble; irrésoluble

insolvency *n.* insolvabilité *f.*

insolvent *a.* insolvable

insomnia *n.* insomnie *f.*

insomuch as *conj.* dans la mesure que; à un tel pointe que

inspect *vt.* inspecter, surveiller, examiner; visiter; **–ion** *n.* inspection *f.*; visite *f.*; **–or** *n.* inspecteur *m.*

inspiration *n.* inspiration *f.*; respiration *f.*

inspire *vt.* inspirer, respirer

instability *n.* instabilité *f.*

install *vt.* installer; **–ation** *n.* installation *f.*

installment *n.* mensualité *f.*, versement, paiement, acompte *m.*

instance *n.* sollicitation *f.*; circonstance *f.*; **for** — par exemple

instant *n.* moment, instant *m.*; — *a.* immédiat, instantané; (dates) courant; **–ly** *a.* immédiatement; tout de suite; à l'instant; **–aneous** *a.* instantané

instead *adv.* à sa place; — **of** *prep.* au lieu de

instep *n.* cou-de-pied *m.*

instigate *vt.* instiguer, exciter, provoquer

instigator *n.* instigateur *m.*

instill *vt.* instiller; inculquer

instinct *n.* instinct *m.*; **–ive** *a.* instinctif

institute *n.* institut *m.*; — *vt.* instituer, établir, fonder

institution *n.* institution *f.*

instruct *vt.* instruire, enseigner; **–ion** *n.* enseignement *m.*; **–ions** *n. pl.* instruc-

tions *f. pl.*; ordres *m. pl.*; **-ive** *a.* instructif; **-or** *n.* professeur *m.*
instrument *n.* instrument *m.*; outil *m.*; (law) acte *m.*; **-al** *a.* instrumental; **be -al in** contribuer à, jouer un rôle dans; **-alist** *n.* instrumentiste *m.*; **-ation** *n.* instrumentation *f.*
insubordinate *n.* insubordonné
insubordination *n.* insubordination *f.*
insufferable *a.* intolérable, insupportable
insufficiency *n.* insuffisance *f.*
insufficient *a.* insuffisant
insular *a.* insulaire
insulate *vt.* isoler
insulator *n.* isolateur *m.*
insulin *n.* insuline *f.*
insult *n.* insulte *f.*; — *vt.* insulter
insuperable *a.* insurmontable
insupportable *a.* insupportable
insurable *a.* assurable
insurance *n.* assurance *f.*; **group —** assurance par groupe *f.*; **life —** assurance sur la vie; **fire —** assurance contre l'incendie; **— policy** police d'assurance *f.*
insure *vt.* assurer
insurgent *n. & a.* insurgé, révolté *m.*
insurmountable *a.* insurmontable
insurrection *n.* insurrection *f.*
intake *n.* adduction *f.*; robinet d'adduction *m.*; prise, entrée, admission *f.*
intangibility *n.* intangibilité *f.*
integer *n.* nombre entier *m.*
integral *n.* (math.) intégrale *f.*; — *a.* intégral, entier
integrate *vt.* intégrer
integration *n.* intégration *f.*
integrity *n.* intégrité, probité *f.*
intellect *n.* intellect *m.*; **-ual** *a. & n.* intellectuel *m.*
intelligence *n.* intelligence *f.*; nouvelle *f.*, avis, rapport *m.*
intelligent *a.* intelligent
intelligible *a.* intelligible, clair
intemperance *n.* intempérance *f.*
intemperate *a.* immodéré
intend *vi.* se proposer, compter, penser; avoir l'intention de; — *vt.* destiner; **-ed** *a.* projeté; voulu; **-ed** *a. & n.* fiancé *m.*, fiancée *f.*
intense *a.* intense, véhément; fort; **-ness** *n.* intensité *f.*
intensify *vt.* renforcer; intensifier
intensity *n.* intensité *f.*
intensive *a.* intensif
intent *a.* absorbé; appliqué, attentif; déterminé; **with —** to dans l'intention de; — *n.* intention *f.*; **-ion** *n.* intention *f.*; **-ional** *a.* intentionnel; voulu; **-ionally** *adv.* exprès, à dessein; **-ness** *n.* atten-

tion *f.*
inter *vt.* enterrer, ensevelir; **-ment** *n.* enterrement *m.*
interact *vi.* réagir réciproquement
interbreed *vt.* croiser deux espèces
intercede *vi.* intercéder
intercept *vt.* intercepter; capter; **-ion** *n.* interception *f.*; captation *f.*
interchange *n.* échange *m.*; communication *f.*; alternance *f.*; — *vt.* échanger; **-able** *a.* interchangeable
interdepartmental *a.* interdépartemental
interdict *n.* (eccl.) interdit *m.*; — *vt.* interdire; **-ion** *n.* interdiction *f.*
interest *n.* intérêt *m.*; profit *m.*; participation *f.*; **compound —** intérêts composés *m. pl.*; **rate of —** taux de l'intérêt *m.*; **take an —** in s'intéresser à; — *vt.* intéresser; **-ed** *a.* intéressé, d'intérêt; **be -ed in** s'intéresser à
interfere *vi.* intervenir; se mêler; s'interposer; **— with** gêner; **-nce** *n.* intervention *f.*; (rad.) brouillage *m.*
interim *a.* intérimaire; — *adv.* entre temps; en attendant; — *n.* intérim *m.*
interior *n. & a.* intérieur *m.*
interjection *n.* interjection *f.*
interlace *vt.* entrelacer
interlinear *a.* interlinéaire
interlining *n.* doublure intermédiaire *f.*
interlock *vi.* s'entrecroiser, s'entrelacer; **-ing** *a.* qui s'entrecroisent; — *vt.* (rail.) enclencher
interloper *n.* intrus *m.*
interlude *n.* intermède *m.*
intermarriage *n.* intermariage *m.*
intermarry *vi.* se marier les uns avec les autres
intermediary *a. & n.* intermédiaire *m.*
intermediate *a.* intermédiaire; moyen
interminable *a.* interminable
interminably *adv.* sans fin
intermingle *vt.* entremêler; — *vi.* se mêler, s'entremêler
intermission *n.* entr'acte *m.*
intermittent *a.* intermittent; **-ly** *adv.* par intervalles
intern *vt.* interner; — *n.* interne des hôpitaux *m.*; **-ment** *n.* internement *m.*; **-ship** *n.* internat *m.*
internal *a.* interne, intérieur; intestin
international *a.* international
interplanetary *a.* interplanétaire
interpolate *vt.* interpoler, intercaler
interpolation *n.* interpolation *f.*
interpret *vt.* interpréter; expliquer; **-ation** *n.* interprétation *f.*; **-er** *n.* interprète *m. & f.*
interrelated *a.* en relation mutuelle
interrelation *n.* corrélation *f.*

interrogate vt. interroger, questionner
interrogation n. interrogation f.; interrogatoire m.; — **point** point d'interrogation m.
interrogative a. interrogatif
interrupt vt. interrompre; **–er** n. (elec.)
interrupteur m.; coupe-circuit m.; **–ion**
n. interruption f.
interscholastic a. interscolaire
intersect vt. entrecouper, intersecter; —
vi. se couper, se croiser, s'intersecter;
–ion n. intersection f.; (roads) carrefour
m.; croisement m.; coin m.
intersperse vt. entremêler
interstate a. entre les états; — **commerce**
commerce dans lequel les marchandises
sont transportées au delà des frontières
de l'etat m.
interurban a. interurbain
interval n. intervalle m.; **at –s** par intervalles
intervene vi. intervenir; arriver; (time)
s'écouler
interview n. entrevue f.; interview m.; entretien m.; — vt. interviewer
interwoven a. entrelacé, entremêlé
intestate a. intestat
intestine n. intestin m.
intimacy n. intimité f.
intimate a. intime; étroit; — n. intime m.
& f.; — vt. donner à entendre; suggérer
intimation n. suggestion f.
intimidate vt. intimider
intimidation n. intimidation f.
into prep. dans, en; entre
intolerable a. intolérable; insupportable
intolerance n. intolérance f.
intolerant a. intolérant
intonation n. ton m., intonation f.
intone vt. entonner
intoxicate vt. enivrer; griser; **–d** a. ivre;
gris
intoxicating a. enivrant
intoxication n. ivresse f.; enivrement m.
intractable a. intraitable
intransitive a. intransitif
intravenous a. dans les veines, intraveineux
intrepid a. intrépide; **–ity** n. intrépidité,
hardiesse f.
intricacy n. complexité f.
intricate a. compliqué
intrigue n. intrigue f.; — vt. & vi. intriguer; **–r** n. intrigant m.
intriguing a. intrigant; très intéressant;
qui intrigue; — n. intrigues f. pl.
intrinsic a. intrinsèque
introduce vt. présenter; introduire
introduction n. présentation f.; introduction f.; (book) avant-propos m.

introductory a. préliminaire; d'introduction
introspection n. introspection f.
introspective a. introspectif
introvert n. introverti m.; **–ed** a. introverti, recueilli
intrude vi. s'ingérer; s'infiltrer; — **on** déranger; **–er** n. intrus m.
intrusion n. intrusion f.; importunité f.
intrust vt. confier
intuition n. intuition f.
intuitive a. intuitif; **–ly** adv. par intuition
inundate vt. inonder
inundation n. inondation f.
inure vt. accoutumer, habituer; endurcir
invade vt. envahir; **–r** n. envahisseur m.
invalid n. & a. (health) malade; infirme;
valétudinaire m. & f.; **–ate** vt. invalider;
vicier; infirmer
invalid a. invalide; **–idate** vt. invalider, déclarer de nul effet
invaluable a. inestimable
invariable a. invariable
invariably adv. invariablement
invasion n. invasion f., envahissement m.;
violation f.
invective n. invective f.
inveigh vi. invectiver
inveigle vt. séduire, entraîner, enjôler
invent vt. inventer; **–ion** n. invention f.;
–ive a. inventif; **–iveness** n. don d'invention m.; imagination f.; **–or** n. inventeur m.
inventory n. inventaire m.; — vt. faire l'inventaire de
inverse a. inverse; — n. inverse, contraire
m.
inversion n. (gram.) inversion f.; renversement m.
invert vt. renverser; invertir
invertebrate n. & a. invertébré m.
invest vt. (money) placer, mettre; (mil.)
investir; **–ment** n. placement, investissement m.; **–or** n. actionnaire m. & f.;
rentier m.
investigate vt. faire une enquête sur; examiner, étudier
investigation n. enquête, investigation f.;
étude f.
investigator n. investigateur m.; agent m.
inveterate a. invétéré, acharné; implacable
invigorate vt. fortifier; vivifier
invigorating a. fortifiant, vivifiant
invincibility n. invincibilité f.
invincible a. invincible
inviolable a. inviolable
invisibility n. invisibilité f.
invisible a. invisible

invite *vt.* inviter; provoquer
inviting *a.* attrayant, invitant; séduisant
invocation *n.* invocation *f.*
invoice *n.* facture *f.*; — *vt.* facturer
invoke *vt.* invoquer; évoquer
involuntarily *adv.* involontairement
involuntary *a.* involontaire
involve *vt.* envelopper; compliquer; engager; impliquer; entraîner; nécessiter; —ed *a.* compliqué; embrouillé; engagé; impliqué
invulnerable *a.* invulnérable
inward *a.* interne, intérieur; vers l'intérieur; —ly *adv.* en dedans; à l'intérieur; —s *adv.* vers l'intérieur
iodide *n.* iodure *m.*
iodine *n.* iode *m.*; **tincture of** — teinture d'iode *f.*
ion *n.* ion *m.*; —ization *n.* ionisation *f.*; —osphere ionosphère *f.*; —ize *vt.* ioniser
I.O.U. *n.* reconnaissance de dette *f.*
Iran *n.* Iran *m.*; —ian *a.* & *n.* iranien *m.*
Iraq *n.* Irak *m.*; —i *a.* & *n.* irakien *m.*
irascible *a.* irascible
irate *a.* en colère
ire *n.* colère *f.*; courroux *m.*
Ireland *n.* Irlande *f.*
iridescence *n.* iridescence *f.*
irisdescent *a.* iridescent, irisé
Irish *a.* & *n.* Irlandais *m.*; —man *n.* Irlandais; —woman *n.* Irlandaise *f.*
irk *vt.* ennuyer; —some *a.* ennuyeux
iron *n.* fer *m.*; (laundry) fer à repasser *m.*; cast — fer de fonte *m.*; curling — fer à friser *m.*; — curtain rideau de fer *m.*; — lung poumon de fer *m.*; — ore minerai de fer *m.*; pig — fonte en saumon *f.*; scrap — ferraille *f.*; wrought — fer forgé *m.*; —s *n. pl.* fers *m. pl.*, chaînes *f. pl.*; — *a.* de fer; — *vt.* repasser, donner un coup de fer à; — out faire disparaître; aplanir; —ing *n.* repassage *m.*
ironclad *a.* cuirassé; (fig.) parfait, qui ne peut être démenti
ironic(al) *a.* ironique
irony *n.* ironie *f.*
irradiate *vt.* rayonner, illuminer, éclairer
irrational *a.* déraisonnable; irrationnel
irreconcilable *a.* implacable; irréconciliable; inconciliable
irrecoverable *a.* irréparable
irreducible *a.* irréductible
irrefutable *a.* incontestable, irréfutable, irrécusable
irregular *a.* irrégulier; —ity *n.* irrégularité *f.*
irrelevance *n.* inapplicabilité *f.*
irrelevant *a.* inapplicable, hors de propos, non pertinent
irreligious *a.* irréligieux

irremediable *a.* irrémédiable
irremovable *a.* inamovible
irreparable *a.* irréparable
irreplaceable *a.* qui ne peut être remplacé
irrepressible *a.* irréprimable
irreproachable *a.* irréprochable
irresistible *a.* irrésistible
irresolute *a.* irrésolu
irrespective *a.* indépendent; — *adv.*, — of sans égard à; sans tenir compte de
irresponsibility *n.* irresponsabilité *f.*
irresponsible *a.* irréfléchi, étourdi
irretrievable *a.* irrémédiable
irreverence *n.* irrévérance *f.*
irreverent *a.* irrévérent; irrévérencieux
irreversible *a.* irrévocable
irrevocable *a.* irrévocable
irrigate *vt.* irriguer; arroser
irrigation *n.* irrigation *f.*
irritability *n.* irritabilité *f.*
irritable *a.* irritable
irritant *n.* irritant *m.*
irritate *vt.* irriter, agacer
irritating *a.* irritant, agaçant
irritation *n.* irritation *f.*
isinglas *n.* colle de poisson *f.*
island *n.* île *f.*; îlot *m.*; —er *n.* insulaire *m.* & *f.*
isle *n.* île *f.*
isolate *vt.* isoler; —ed *a.* isolé, écarté
isolation *n.* isolement *m.*; solitude *f.*; —ism (pol.) politique d'isolement *f.*
isometrics *n.* isométrique *f.*
isosceles *a.* isocèle
isotope *n.* isotope *m.*
Israel *n.* Israël *m.*; —i *a.* & *n.* israëlien *m.*; —ite *a.* & *n.* israélite *m.* & *f.*
issue *n.* question *f.*; publication *f.*; émission *f.*; délivrance *f.*; numéro *m.*; issue, sortie *f.*; résultat *m.*; fin *f.*; enfants *m. pl.*; — *vt.* publier; émettre; lancer; donner; délivrer; — *vi.* sortir, provenir
Istanbul *n.* Istamboul *m.*
isthmus *n.* isthme *m.*
it *pron.* il, elle; ce, cela; le, la
Italian *a.* & *n.* italien *m.*
italicize *vt.* mettre en italique
italics *n. pl.* italique *f.*
itch *n.* démangeaison *f.*; — *vi.* démanger
item *n.* article, détail *m.*; question *f.*; news — fait divers *m.*; —ize faire la liste de
iterate *vt.* réitérer
itinerant *a.* ambulant
itinerary *n.* itinéraire *m.*
its *a.* son, sa, ses
itself *pron.* se; lui-même, elle-même, soi-même
ivory *n.* ivoire *m.*; — *a.* d'ivoire; — tower tour d'ivoire *f.*

J

jab *n.* coup de pointe *m.*; (boxing) coup sec *m.*; — *vt.* piquer
jabber *vi.* bavardage *m.*; jacasserie *f.*; jacasser; —; –ing *n.* baragouinage *m.*
jack *n.* cric, lève-roue *m.*; (cards) valet *m.*; — *vt.*, — (up) soulever; augmenter; — **rabbit** *n.* lapin de plaine *m.*
jackass *n.* âne, baudet *m.*
jacket *n.* veston *m.*; veste *f.*; jaquette *f.*; (book) chemise, couverture *f.*
jack-in-the-box *n.* diable *m.*, boîte à surprise *f.*
jackknife *n.* couteau de poche *m.*
jack-o'-lantern *n.* feu follet *m.*
jack pot *n.* gros lot; **hit the —** (coll.) gagner le prix; faire fortune d'un seul coup
jade *n.* jade *m.*; (person) coquine *f.*; –d *a.* fatigué, éreinté
jag *vt.* ébrécher; — *n.* dent de scie *f.*
jagged *a.* dentelé, ébréché; –ness *n.* dentelure *f.*
jail *n.* prison *f.*; — *vt.* mettre en prison; –er *n.* gardien *m.*
jam *n.* confiture *f.*; presse *f.*; (traffic) embouteillage *m.*; — *vt.* presser, serrer; fourrer, enfoncer; coincer; (radio) brouiller; — *vi.* se coincer; (gun) s'enrayer
jamboree *n.* (coll.) grande réunion *f.*
jangle *vi.* cliqueter, s'entre-choquer; — *vt.* faire entre-choquer; –d *a.* agacé
janitor *n.* concierge, portier *m.*
January *n.* janvier *m.*
Japan *n.* Japon *m.*; –ese *a.* & *n.* japonais *m.*
jar *n.* bocal *m.*, pot *m.*; choc *m.*, secousse *f.*; — *vt.* choquer; agacer; — *vi.* être en désaccord; — **on** choquer, crisper
jaundice *n.* jaunisse *f.*
jaunt *n.* excursion, sortie *f.*; –y *a.* désinvolte; vif
Java *n.* Java *m.*; –nese *n.* & *a.* Javanais *m.*
javelin *n.* javeline *f.*, javelot *m.*
jaw, jawbone *n.* mâchoire *f.*
jaywalker (coll.) *n.* piéton imprudent *m.* (qui traverse la rue en dehors du passage clouté)
jealous *a.* jaloux; –y *n.* jalousie *f.*
jeans *n.* pantalon de coutil *m.*
jeep *n.* jeep *f.*
jeer *vi.* se moquer; — **at** railler; siffler; se moquer de; –ing *a.* railleur; –ing *n.* raillerie *f.*
jellied *a.* en gelée
jelly *n.* gelée *f.*; — *vt.* faire prendre en gelée; — *vi.* se prendre en gelée
jeopardize *vt.* compromettre; mettre en péril

jeopardy *n.* péril, danger *m.*
jerk *n.* saccade, secousse *f.*; — *vt.* tirer (d'un coup sec); — *vi.* se mouvoir par saccades; –ed **beef** bœuf séché *m.*; –y *a.* coupé, saccadé
jersey *n.* tricot *m.*; (sports) maillot *m.*
jest *n.* plaisanterie *f.*; — *vi.* plaisanter; –er *n.* bouffon *m.*
Jesus Christ *n.* Jésus-Christ *m.*
jet *n.* jet *m.*; brûleur, bec *m.*; (motor) réacteur *m.*; (mineral) jais *m.*; — **plane** avion à réaction *m.*; — **propulsion** propulsion à réaction *f.*
jet-black *a.* noir comme du jais
jet-propelled *a.* à réaction
jettison *vt.* jeter
jetty *n.* jetée *f.*
Jew *n.* Juif *m.*; –ish *a.* juif *m.*, juive *f.*
jewel *n.* bijou, joyau *m.*; (watch) rubis *m.*; –er *n.* bijoutier, joaillier *m.*; –ry *n.* bijouterie, joaillerie *f.*
jib *n.* (naut.) foc *m.*
jibe *vi.* s'accorder; être d'accord
jig *n.* gigue *f.*; — *vi.* danser une gigue
jigger *n.* chique *f.*; (drink measure) deux doigts *m. pl.*
jigsaw *n.* scie à chantourner *f.*; — **puzzle** jeu de patience *f.*
jilt *vt.* abandonner
jingle *n.* tintement *m.*; — *vi.* tinter; — *vt.* faire tinter
jitters *n. pl.* (coll.) nervosité *f.*; crise de nerfs *f.*
jive *n.* jive *m.*
job *n.* emploi *m.*; poste *m.*, situation *f.*; travail *m.*; métier *m.*; — **lot** lot de soldes; — **work** travail à la pièce *m.*; –ber *n.* revendeur *m.*; –less *a.* sans travail, désœuvré; –less *n.* chômeurs *m. pl.*
jockey *n.* jockey *m.*; — *vt.* & *vi.* manœuvrer
jocose *a.* plaisant, badin
jocular *a.* rieur, facétieux
jocund *a.* enjoué, jovial
jodhpurs *n. pl.* pantalon d'équitation *m.*
jog *n.* secousse *f.*; petit trot *m.*; — *vi.* aller au petit trot
join *vt.* & *vi.* joindre, unir, réunir; ajouter; relier; (club) entrer dans; — *vi.* se joindre, s'unir; — **in** prendre part; — **up** s'engager; –er *n.* (carpentry) menuisier *m.*
joint *n.* joint *m.*, jointure *f.*; articulation *f.*; **out of —** disloqué; — *a.* commun; collectif, combiné; — **account** compte conjoint, compte en participation *m.*; — **heir** cohéritier *m.*; –ly *adv.* en commun; ensemble; conjointement

joist *n.* solive *f.*

joke *n.* blague, plaisanterie *f.*; **practical — ** mystification *f.*; **play a — on** mystifier; jouer un tour a; **— ** *vi.* plaisanter; **-r** *n.* plaisant, farceur *m.*; (cards) joker *m.*; **practical -r** mauvais plaisant *m.*

joking *a.* moqueur; **-ly** *adv.* en plaisantant; **— ** *n.* plaisanterie *f.*

jolly *a.* gai, enjoué

jolt *n.* cahot *m.*, secousse *f.*; **— ** *vt.* cahoter, secouer

Jordan *n.* (river) Jourdain *m.*; (country) Jordanie *f.*

jostle *vt.* bousculer, coudoyer, serrer

jot *n.* iota *m.*; **— ** *vt.*, **— down** prendre note de, noter; **-tings** *n.* *pl.* notes *f.* *pl.*

jounce *vt.* secouer

journal *n.* journal *m.*; **-ese** *n.* (coll.) jargon des journaux *m.*; **-ism** *n.* journalisme *m.*; **yellow -ism** *n.* journalisme sensationnel *m.*; **-ist** *n.* journaliste *m. & f.*; **-istic** *a.* journalistique

journey *n.* voyage *m.*; **— ** *vi.* voyager; **-man** *n.* ouvrier, compagnon *m.*

joust *vi.* jouter; **— ** *n.* joute *f.*

jovial *a.* jovial; **-ity** *n.* jovialité, joie *f.*

jowl *n.* joue, bajoue *f.*

joy *n.* joie *f.*; **-ful** *a.* joyeux; **-fully** *adv.* joueusement; **-less** *a.* triste; **-ous** *a.* joyeux

jubilant *a.* joyeux, réjoui; triomphant

jubilate *vt.* jubiler

jubilee *n.* jubilé *m.*

Judaism *n.* judaïsme *n.*

judge *n.* juge *m.*; arbitre *m.*; connaisseur *m.*; **be a good — of** s'y connaître en; **— ** *vt.* juger; estimer, mesurer

judgment *n.* jugement *m.*; arrêt *m.*, sentence *f.*; avis *m.*, opinion *f.*; **— day** jugement dernier *m.*

judicial *a.* judiciaire; juridique

judiciary *a.* judiciaire; **— ** *n.* magistrature *f.*

judicious *a.* judicieux

jug *n.* cruche *f.*, pot, broc *m.*; **— ** *vt.* mettre en pot; **-ged hare** *n.* civet de lièvre *m.*

juggle *vi.* jongler; **-r** *n.* jongleur, bateleur *m.*

jugular *a.* jugulaire

juice *n.* jus, suc *m.*

juiciness *n.* succulence *f.*

juicy *a.* juteux, succulent; fondant

jukebox *n.* grand tourne-disque à sous, jukebox *m.*

julep *n.* julep *m.*; **mint — ** boisson au whisky et à la menthe *f.*

July *n.* juillet *m.*

jumble *n.* confusion *f.*; **— ** *vt.* brouiller

jumbo *a.* énorme

jump *n.* saut, bond *m.*; saute *f.*; (racing) obstacle *m.*; **broad — ** saut en longueur *m.*; **high — ** saut en hauteur *m.*; **— ** *vi.* sauter, bondir; **— ** *vt.* sauter, faire sauter; attaquer; **— at** saisir; **— the gun** devancer; commencer prématurément; **— the track** dérailler; **-er** *n.* sauteur *m.*; (clothes) casaquin *m.*; (elec.) connexion volante *f.*; **-iness** *n.* agitation, nervosité *f.*; **-ing** *a.* sautant, sautillant; actif; **-ing jack** pantin *m.*; **-ing** *n.* saut *m.*; **-y** *a.* nerveux, irritable

jump rope *n.* corde à sauter *f.*

junction *n.* jonction *f.*; bifurcation *f.*; **carrefour** *m.*; **— point** connexion *f.*

juncture *n.* jointure *f.*; moment *m.*

June *n.* juin *m.*

jungle *n.* jungle *f.*

junior *a.* plus jeune, cadet; (in names) fils; (mil.) subalterne; **— college** établissement qui ne fait que les deux premières années des études universitaires *m.*; **— high school** établissement qui ne fait que les deux premières années des études secondaires *m.*

juniper *n.* genièvre *m.*

junk *n.* débris, rejets *m.* *pl.*; (naut.) jonque *f.*; **— ** *vt.* mettre au rancart

junket *n.* voyage fait aux frais de l'Etat *m.*

junta *n.* junte *f.*

juridical *a.* juridique

jurisdiction *n.* juridiction *f.*; **-al** *a.* juridictionnel

jurisprudence *n.* jurisprudence *f.*

jurist *n.* juriste *m.*

juror *n.* juré, membre du jury *m.*

jury *n.* jury *m.*, jurés *m.* *pl.*; **— box** banc des jurés *m.*

just *a.* juste; équitable; **— ** *adv.* justement, juste; au juste; précisément; tout simplement; **— as** au moment où; **— now** tout à l'heure; actuellement; pour le moment; **-ly** *adv.* justement; avec justice

justice *n.* justice *f.*; (person) juge, magistrat *m.*

justifiable *a.* justifiable, légitime

justification *n.* justification *f.*

justify *vt.* justifier; motiver

jut *vi.*, **— (out)** faire saillie; **— out over** surplomber

juvenile *a.* juvénile; puéril; **— delinquent** accusé mineur *m.*; **— ** *n.* jeune *m. & f.*

juxtaposition *n.* juxtaposition *f.*; **in — ** juxtaposé

K

kale *n.* chou frisé *m.*

kaleidoscope *n.* kaléidoscope *m.*

Kashmir *n.* Cachemire *m.*
kayak *n.* kayac *m.*
keel *n.* quille *f.*
keen *a.* vif; ardent; aigu; fin; **–ness** *n.* finesse *f.*; ardeur *f.*; acuité *f.*
keep *n.* (castle-) donjon *m.*; **board and —** nourriture *f.*; **for –s** pour de bon; — *vt.* garder; tenir; entretenir, maintenir; retenir; empêcher; conserver, préserver; — *vi.* se tenir, rester; continuer; se conserver; **— an eye on** ne pas perdre de vue; **— from** s'abstenir de; empêcher de; s'empêcher de; **— in** retenir; rester dedans; rester à la maison; **— off** ne pas toucher (à); éloigner; **— on** garder; avancer; continuer; **— out** empêcher d'entrer; ne pas se mêler; rester dehors; **— quiet** rester tranquille; ne pas parler; se taire; **— up** maintenir, entretenir; faire veiller; **— waiting** faire attendre; **–er** *n.* garde, gardien *m.*; **–ing** *n.* garde *f.*; **in –ing with** en accord avec
keepsake *n.* souvenir *m.*
keg *n.* tonnelet, barillet *m.*
kelp *n.* soude de varech *f.*
ken *n.* savoir *m.*, compréhension *f.*
kennel *n.* niche *f.*; chenil *m.*
kerchief *n.* fichu *m.*
kernel *n.* grain *m.*
kerosene *n.* kérosène *m.*
kettle *n.* bouilloire, marmite *f.*
kettledrum *n.* timbale *f.*
key *n.* clé, clef *f.*; (piano) touche *f.*; **— industry** *n.* industrie-clef *f.*; **— ring** porte-clefs *m.*; **sending — manipulateur** *m.*; **— word** mot-clé *m.*; **master —** passe-partout *m.*
keyboard *n.* clavier *m.*
keyhole *n.* trou de serrure *m.*
keynote *n.* (mus.) tonique *f.*; (fig.) point principal *m.*
keystone *n.* clef de voûte *f.*
khaki *n.* khaki *m.*
kick *n.* coup de pied *m.*; (coll.) frisson *m.*; (gun) recul *m.*; — *vt.* donner un coup de pied à; (sports) botter; — *vi.* donner un coup de pied; regimber; reculer; **–back** *n.* ristourne *f.*; **— out** mettre à la porte; chasser à coups de pied
kickoff *n.* coup d'envoi *m.*
kid *n.* chevreau *m.*, chevrette *f.*; (coll.) gosse *m. & f.*; **— gloves** gants de chevreau *m. pl.*; **handle with — gloves** ménager; — *vt.* (coll.) plaisanter, faire marcher; **no –ding!** (coll.) sans blague!
kidnap *vt.* enlever, voler; **–per** *n.* kidnapper, ravisseur *m.*; **–ping** *n.* kidnapping, enlèvement, vol *m.*; rapt *m.*
kidney *n.* rein *m.*; (food) rognon *m.*; **— bean** haricot de Soissons *m.*

kidney-shaped *a.* réniforme
kidskin *n.* peau de chevreau *f.*
kill *vt.* tuer; (animal) abattre; (fig.) supprimer; **–er** *n.* assassin, meurtrier *m.*; tueur *m.*; **–ing** *n.* meurtre *m.*; tuerie *f.*, massacre *m.*; (coll.) coup *m.*
kill-joy *n.* rabat-joie *m.*
kiln *n.* four *m.*
kilocycle *n.* kilocycle *m.*
kilogram *n.* kilo, kilogramme *m.*
kilometer *n.* kilomètre *m.*
kilometric *a.* kilométrique
kilowatt *n.* kilowatt *m.*
kilowatt-hour *n.* kilowatt-heure *m.*
kilt *n.* kilt *m.*
kilter *n.* bon ordre *m.*; **out of —** détraqué, déréglé
kin *n.* parents *m. pl.*; famille *f.*; **next of —** le plus proche parent *m.*; **–ship** *n.* parenté *f.*
kind *n.* genre *m.*, espèce *f.*, sorte *f.*; **nothing of the —** rien de la sorte; **payment in —** paiement en nature *m.*; — *a.* bon; aimable; bienveillant; **–liness** *n.* bonté, bienveillance *f.*; **–ly** *a.* bon, bienveillant; **–ness** *n.* bonté, bienveillance *f.*; prévenance *f.*; service *m.*
kindergarten *n.* jardin d'enfants *m.*; école maternelle *f.*
kindhearted *a.* bon, bienveillant
kindle *vt.* allumer, enflammer; susciter; — *vi.* s'allumer, s'enflammer
kindling (wood) *n.* petit bois *m.*
kindred *a.* de la même famille; de la même nature; **— souls** âmes sœurs *f. pl.*
kinescope *n.* tube à rayons cathodiques *m.*
kinetic *a.* cinétique; **–s** *n. pl.* cinétique *f.*
king *n.* roi *m.*; (checkers) dame *f.*; **–dom** *n.* royaume *m.*; règne *m.*; **–ly** *a.* de roi royal
king-size *a.* grand, (plus) long
kink *n.* nœud *m.*; coque *f.*; faux pli *m.*; — *vi.* se nouer; **–y** *a.* crépu
kinsfolk *n.* parents *m. pl.*, famille *f.*
kinsman *n.* parent *m.*
kinswoman *n.* parente *f.*
kiosk *n.* kiosque *m.*
kiss *n.* baiser *m.*; — *vt.* embrasser; (hand) baiser
kit *n.* trousseau *m.*, trousse *f.*; nécessaire *m.*
kitchen *n.* cuisine *f.*; **–ette** *n.* petite cuisine *f.*; **— police (K.P.)** *n.* (mil.) corvée de cuisine *f.*; **— range** *n.* cuisinière *f.*; **— utensils** batterie de cuisine *f.*
kite *n.* cerf-volant *m.*; **fly a —** lancer un cerf-volant

kith n. parents, amis m. pl.

kitten n. chaton, petit chat m.; **–ish** a. enjoué, folâtre

kleptomania n. kleptomanie f.; **–c** n. kleptomane m. & f.

knack n. don m., habileté f.; coup m.; flair m.

knapsack n. sac m.

knave n. coquin, fripon m.; **–ry** n. friponnerie f.

knead vt. pétrir, travailler

knee n. genou m.; **on one's –s** à genoux, agenouillé

kneecap n. rotule f.

knee-deep a. jusqu'aux genoux

knee-high a. à la hauteur du genou

kneel vi. s'agenouiller, se mettre à genoux; **–ing** a. à genoux, agenouillé

knell n. glas m.; **death —** glas funèbre m.

knickers, knickerbockers n. (pl.) culotte f.; knickerbockers m. pl.

knicknack n. bibelot, colifichet m.

knife n. couteau m.; **— grinder** rémouleur m.; **—** vt. poignarder

knight n. chevalier m.; (chess) cavalier m.; **—** vt. armer chevalier, faire chevalier; **–hood** n. chevalerie f.; **–ly** a. chevaleresque

knight-errant n. chevalier errant m.; **–ry** n. chevalerie errante f.

knit vt. tricoter; lier, joindre; **— one's brows** froncer les sourcils; **–ted** a. tricoté, en tricot; **–ing** n. tricot m.; tricotage m.; union f.; **–ing needle** aiguille à tricoter f.

knob n. bouton m.; bosse f.

knock n. coup m.; (engine) cognement m.; **— out** knock-out m.; **—** vt. frapper, cogner; heurter; (coll.) trouver à redire; **—** vi. (engine) cogner; **–down** renverser; abattre; **— off** (coll.) finir; cesser de travailler; **— out** knockouter; supprimer; **–er** n. (door) marteau m.; **–ing** n. coups m. pl.

knock-kneed a. cagneux

knoll n. monticule, tertre, mamelon m.

knot n. nœud m.; groupe m.; **overhand —** nœud simple m.; **reef —** (naut.) nœud marin m.; **slip–** nœud coulant m.; **tie a —** faire un nœud; **—** vt. nouer; **—** vi. se nouer; **–ted** a. à nœuds; **–ty** a. noueux; **–ty question** question épineuse f.

knothole n. trou de nœud m.

know vt. savoir; connaître; apprendre; **as far as I —** autant que je sache; **–ing** a. fin; (look) entendu; **–ingly** adv. sciemment; **–n** a. connu

know-how n. connaissances techniques f. pl.; savoir-faire m.

knowledge n. science f.; savoir m.; connaissance(s) f. (pl.); **not to my —** pas que je sache; **without my —** à mon insu; **–able** a. intelligent

knuckle n. articulation du doigt f.; (animal) manche m.

Koran n. Coran m.

Korea n. Corée f.

kosher a. cawcher, kascher, cacher

kowtow vi. se prosterner; **—** vt. & vi. saluer à la chinoise

L

label n. étiquette f.; **—** vt. étiqueter

labial a. labial; **—** n. labiale f.

labor n. travail m.; labeur m.; ouvriers m. pl.; main-d'œuvre f.; (med.) couches f. pl.; **hard —** travail disciplinaire m.; **— union** syndicat ouvrier m.; **—** vi. travailler; élaborer; **–er** n. travailleur, ouvrier m.; manœuvre m.; **–ious** a. laborieux, pénible

laboratory n. laboratoire m.

laborsaving a. qui économise le travail

lace n. dentelle f.; (shoe) lacet, cordon m.; **—** vt. lacer; entrelacer

lacerate vt. lacérer; déchirer

laceration n. lacération; déchirure f.

lack n. manque, défaut m., absence f.; **for — of** faute de; **—** vt. & vi. manquer (de); **–ing** a. qui manque; dépourvu de; insuffisant

lackadaisical a. apathique; languissant

lackey n. laquais m.

laconic a. laconique

lacquer n. lacque, vernis m.; **—** vt. laquer

lacrimose a. larmoyant

lactate vi. sécréter du lait

lactation n. lactation f.

lactic a. lactique

lactose n. lactose f.

lad n. garçon, jeune homme m.

ladder n. échelle f.

lading n. chargement m.; **bill of —** connaissement m.

ladle n. louche f.; puisoir m.; **—** vt., **— out** servir

lady n. dame f.; **ladies and gentlemen** mesdames et messieurs, (coll.) messieurs-dames; **young —** jeune fille, demoiselle f.

ladylike a. de dame; comme il faut

lag n. retard, décalage m.; **—** vi. traîner, rester en arrière

lager n. bière blonde f.

laggard n. traînard m.; **—** a. tardif

lagoon n. lagune f.; (atoll) lagon m.

laid a. posé, laissé; (paper) couché

laid up a. malade; en panne

lair *n.* repaire *m.*, tanière *f.*

laity *n.* laïques *m. pl.*

lake *n.* lac *m.*

lamb *n.* agneau *m.*; — **chop** côtelette d'agneau *f.*; — *vi.* agneler

lame *a.* boiteux; estropié; (excuse) faible, pauvre; — *vt.* rendre boiteux; estropier; −ness *n.* boitement *m.*; faiblesse *f.*

lament *n.* lamentation, complainte *f.*; — *vt.* pleurer; −able *a.* déplorable, lamentable; −ation *n.* lamentation *f.*; −ed *a.* regretté

laminate *vt.* laminer

lamp *n.* lampe *f.*

lampoon *n.* libelle *m.*, satire *f.*; — *vt.* lancer des satires contre; −er *n.* libelliste, satiriste *m.*

lamppost *n.* réverbère *m.*

lamp shade *n.* abat-jour *m.*

lance *n.* lance *f.*; — *vt.* inciser, percer; −r *n.* lancier *m.*; −t *n.* lancette *f.*, bistouri *m.*

land *n.* terre *f.*; terrain *m.*; pays *m.*; — *vt.* débarquer; (plane) atterrir; (fish) amener à terre; (coll.) gagner, remporter; — *vi.* débarquer; atterrir; — **on one's feet** retomber sur ses pieds; −ed *a.* foncier; qui possède des terres; −ing *n.* débarquement *m.*; atterrissage *m.*; (stair) palier *m.*; −ing barge, −ing craft *n.* péniche de débarquement *f.*; −ing field *n.* terrain d'atterrissage *m.*; −ing strip *n.* piste d'atterrissage *f.*

landfall *n.* atterrage *m.*; aubaine *f.*

landlady *n.* propriétaire *f.*; aubergiste *f.*

landlord *n.* propriétaire *m.*; aubergiste *m.*

landlubber *n.* marin d'eau douce *m.*

landmark *n.* repère *m.*; point coté *m.*; monument *m.*

land office *n.* bureau du cadastre *m.*; **do a — business** faire des affaires inouïes, avoir un chiffre d'affaires énorme

landowner *n.* propriétaire foncier *m.*

landscape *n.* paysage *m.*; — **garden** *n.* jardin à l'anglaise *m.*; — **gardener** *n.* jardiniste *m.*; — **painter** *n.* paysagiste *m.*

landslide *n.* glissement de terre *m.*; (pol.) victoire écrasante *f.*

landward *adv.* vers la terre

lane *n.* ruelle *f.* passage *m.*; route *f.*

language *n.* langue *f.*; langage *m.*

languid *a.* languissant, langoureux; −ness *n.* langueur *f.*

languish *vi.* languir; −ing *a.* languissant, langoureux

languor *n.* langueur *f.*; −ous *a.* langoureux

lanky *a.* grand et maigre

lanolin *n.* lanoline *f.*

lantern *n.* lanterne *f.*; fanal *m.*; **Chinese —** lanterne vénitienne *f.*; — **slide** *n.* diapositive de projection *f.*

lantern-jawed *a.* aux joues creuses

lanyard *n.* garant *m.*

Laos *n.* Laos *m.*

lap *n.* genoux *m. pl.*; (sports) circuit, tour *m.*, étape *f.*; — *vt.* boucler; dépasser; — *vi.* (waves) clapoter; — **up** laper; gober

lapel *n.* revers *m.*

lapidary *a.* & *n.* lapidaire *m.*

Lapland *n.* Laponie *f.*

lapse *n.* laps *m.*; délai *m.*; intervalle *m.*; lapsus *m.*, faute *f.*; — *vi.* manquer; périmer; tomber; −d *a.* périmé; déchu; caduc

larboard *n.* bâbord *m.*

larceny *n.* larcin, vol *m.*

lard *n.* saindoux, lard *m.*; — *vt.* larder

larder *n.* garde-manger *m.*

large *a.* grand, gros; fort; nombreux; **grow −(r)** grandir, grossir; −ly *adv.* en grande partie; — *n.*, **at** — libre, en liberté; −ness *n.* grandeur *f.*; grosseur *f.*; étendue *f.*

large-scale *a.* à grande échelle, de grande échelle; de grande envergure

lariat *n.* lasso *m.*

larva *n.* larve *f.*

laryngitis *n.* laryngite *f.*

larynx *n.* larynx *m.*

lascivious *a.* lascif; −ness *n.* lascivité *f.*

lash *n.* coup de fouet *m.*; — *vt.* fouetter; cingler; attacher, lier; −ing *n.* coups de fouet *m. pl.*, flagellation *f.*; (rope) ligne d'amarrage *f.*

lass *n.* jeune fille *f.*

lassitude *n.* lassitude *f.*

last *a.* dernier; — **night** hier soir; cette nuit; — **week** la semaine passée, la semaine dernière; **next to —** l'avant-dernier; — *n.* enfin; — *vi.* durer; −ing *a.* durable; −ly *adv.* en dernier lieu

latch *n.* loquet *m.*; — *vt.* fermer à demi-tour; — **on to** (coll.) saisir

latchkey *n.* clef *f.*, passe-partout *m.*

late *a.* en retard; tard; tardif; récent; (deceased) feu; **of —** depuis peu; — *adv.* en retard; tard; −ly *adv.* récemment, depuis peu; −ness *n.* heure avancée *f.*; arrivée tardive *f.*; −r *a.* plus récent; ultérieur; −r *adv.* plus tard, après; −st *a.* le plus récent, le plus nouveau, dernier

latent *a.* latent, caché

lateral *a.* latéral

lath *n.* latte *f.*

lathe *n.* tour *m.*

lather *n.* mousse de savon *f.*; — *vt.* savonner; — *vi.* mousser

Latin a. & n. latin m.; — America Amérique latine f.
latitude n. latitude f.; (fig.) liberté f.
latrine n. latrines f. pl.
latter a. dernier; the — celui-ci; celle-ci
latter-day a. moderne
lattice n. treillis, treillage m.
Latvia n. Lettonie, Latvie f.; **-n** a. & n. letton m.; (language) lette m.
laud vt. louer; **-able** a. louable; **-atory** a. élogieux
laugh n. rire m.; — vi. rire; — **at** rire de; — **to oneself** rire tout bas; — **off** se moquer de, traiter à la légère; **-able** a. ridicule, risible; **-ing** a. riant; rieur; **it is no -ing matter** il n'y a pas de quoi rire; **-ing gas** n. gaz hilarant m.; **-ingstock** n. risée f.; **-ter** n. rires m. pl.
launch n. chaloupe f.; — vt. lancer; **-ing** n. lancement m.; mise à l'eau f.
launching pad n. plate-forme de lancement f.
launder vt. blanchir
laundress n. blanchisseuse f.
laundry n. blanchisserie f.; linge à blanchir m.; **-man** n. blanchisseur m.
lava n. lave f.
lavatory n.; lavabo; lavoir; cabinet de toilette m.
lavender a. & n. lavande f.
lavish a. prodigue; somptueux; — vt. prodiguer; **-ness** n. prodigalité f.; somptuosité f.
law n. loi f.; droit m.; **civil** — droit civil m.; **lay down the** — to faire la loi a; **-ful** a. légal, permis; légitime; valide; **-less** a. sans loi; désordonné; **-lessness** n. désordre m.; anarchie f.
law-abiding a. respectueux des lois
lawbreaker n. transgresseur de la loi m.
lawmaker n. législateur m.
lawn n. pelouse f.; gazon m.
lawn mower n. tondeuse f.
lawsuit n. procès m.
lawyer n. avocat, avoué m.
lax a. relâché; négligent, inexact; **-ity** n. relâchement m.; inexactitude f.
laxative a. & n. laxatif m.
lay n. lai m., chanson f.; (land) configuration f.; — a. lai, laïque; — vt. placer, mettre, coucher, poser; (egg) pondre; (bet) parier; — **aside**, — **away** mettre de côté; — **before** présenter à, soumettre à; — **by** mettre de côté; — **down** déposer; imposer, décréter; — **in** se faire une provision de; — **off** (labor) congédier; (coll.) laisser tranquille; — **on** appliquer; — **out** disposer, étaler; (money) débourser; — **siege to** assiéger; — **up** mettre hors de service;

tenir au lit, tenir enfermé; **-er** n. couche f.; (hen) pondeuse f.
layman n. laïque m.
layoff n. renvoi d'ouvriers en masse m.
layout n. disposition f.; dessin, schéma de montage m.; plan m.
layover n. arrêt en cours de route m. (pour attendre une correspondance)
laziness n. paresse f.
lazy a. paresseux; fainéant
lead n. (mineral) plomb m.; (pencil) mine de plomb f.; (naut.) sonde f.; — **pencil** crayon à mine de plomb; — **poisoning** saturnisme m.; **-en** a. de plomb; pesant
lead n. exemple m., direction f.; (theat.) premier rôle m.; (elec.) câble de canalisation m.; (journalism) article de fond m.; **take the** — prendre le pas; — vt. conduire, mener; guider; commander, diriger; porter, entraîner; — vi. conduire; aboutir; — **away** emmener; entraîner; — **off** commencer, être le premier; emmener; — **on** encourager; — **up to** amener à; **-er** n. conducteur, chef m.; (pol.) leader m.; (film) amorce f.; **-erless** a. sans chef; **-ership** n. direction f., commandement m.; **-ing** a. principal; important; premier; **-ing man**, **-ing lady** premier rôle m.; vedette f.; **-ing question** question tendancieuse f.
leaf n. feuille f.; (book) feuillet m.; (door) battant m.; (table) rallonge f.; **turn over a new** — faire peau neuve; — vt., — **through** feuilleter; **-age** n. feuillage m.; **-let** n. feuille f.; annonce f.; **-y** a. touffu, couvert de feuilles
league n. ligue f.; (measurement) lieue f.; (sports) groupement m., association f.; **in** — **with** d'intelligence avec; — vi., — **together** se liguer
leak n. fuite, perte f.; écoulement m.; (naut.) voie d'eau f.; — vi. fuir, couler; (naut.) faire eau; — **out** (rumor) s'ébruiter; **-age** n. fuite, perte f.; **-y** a. qui fuit, qui coule
leakproof a. étanche
lean vi. s'appuyer; (se) pencher; s'adosser; incliner; — vt. appuyer; adosser; — **back** se pencher en arrière, se renverser; — **out** se pencher à; **-ing** a. penchant, penché; **-ing** n. inclination, tendance f., penchant m.
lean a. maigré; décharné; — n. maigre m.; **-ness** maigreur f.
lean-to n. abat-vent m.; remise f.
leap n. saut m.; — **year** année bissextile f.; — vt. & vi. sauter
leapfrog n. saute-mouton m.
learn vt. apprendre; savoir; **-ed** a. ins-

truit, savant; **-ing** *n.* science, érudition *f.*; savoir *m.*
lease *n.* bail *m.*; — *vt.* louer; donner à bail; prendre à bail
leash *n.* laisse, attache *f.*
least *a.* moindre; plus petit; — *n.* le moins *m.*; **at** — au moins; du moins; **not in the** — pas du tout; — *adv.* le moins
leather *n.* cuir *m.*; — *a.* en cuir, de cuir; — **goods** maroquinerie *f.*; **-ette** *n.* simili-cuir *m.*; **-y** *a.* (food) coriace; comme de cuir
leave *n.* congé *m.*; permission *f.*; — **of absence** congé *m.*; — *vt.* laisser; quitter; partir de; — *vi.* partir; s'en aller; — **behind** laisser; oublier; — **out** omettre
leaven *n.* levain *m.*; — *vt.* faire lever
leave-taking *n.* adieux *m. pl.*
leaving *n.* départ *m.*; **-s** *n. pl.* restes *m. pl.*; reliefs *m. pl.*
Lebanon *n.* Liban *m.*
lecherous *a.* lascif, débauché; **-ness** *n.* lasciveté *f.*
lecture *n.* conférence *f.*; — *vi.* faire une conférence; — *vt.* (coll.) sermonner; **-er** *n.* conférencier *m.*
ledge *n.* rebord *m.*; corniche *f.*
ledger *n.* registre, grand livre *m.*
lee, leeward *a.* sous le vent; — *n.* côté sous le vent *m.*
leek *n.* poireau *m.*
leer *n.* œillade *f.*; — *vi.*, — **at** lancer des œillades à
lees *n. pl.* lie *f.*
leeway *n.* (naut.) dérive; (coll.) liberté *f.*; (plus de) temps *m.*; (plus de) place *f.*
left *a. & n.* gauche *f.*; — *adv.* à gauche; **on the** —, **to the** — à gauche; **-ist** *n.* partisan de la gauche *m.*
left-handed *a.* gaucher
leg *n.* jambe *f.*; patte *f.*; (fowl) cuisse *f.*; (lamb) gigot *m.*; (object) pied *m.*; **pull someone's** — faire marcher quelqu'un; **-ged** *a.* à jambes
legacy *n.* legs *m.*
legal *a.* légal; juridique; **-ity** *n.* légalité *f.*; **-ize** *vt.* légaliser, authentiquer
legatee *n.* légataire *m. & f.*
legation *n.* légation *f.*
legend *n.* légende *f.*; **-ary** *a.* légendaire
legerdemain *n.* tour d'adresse *m.*
leggings *n. pl.* jambières *f. pl.*
Leghorn *n.* Livourne *f.*
leghorn *n.* paille d'Italie *f.*; poule blanche *f.*
legibility *n.* lisibilité *f.*
legible *a.* lisible
legion *n.* légion *f.*; **-ary** *n.* légionnaire *m.*
legislate *vi.* faire des lois

legislation *n.* législation *f.*
legislator *n.* législateur *m.*
legislature *n.* législature *f.*
legitimacy *n.* légitimité *f.*
legitimize *vt.* légitimiser
legume *n.* légume *m.*
leisure *n.* loisir *m.*; **at** — à loisir, à tête reposée; **-ly** *a.* posé, mesuré; **in a -ly manner** sans se presser
lemon *n.* citron *m.*; — (tree) citronnier *m.*; **-ade** *n.* citron pressé *m.*; (lemon drink) citronnade *f.*; (carbonated) limonade *f.*; — **squeezer** *n.* presse-citron *m.*
lend *vt.* prêter; **-er** *n.* prêteur *m.*; **-ing** *n.* prêt *m.*; (com.) prestation *f.*
lend-lease *n.* prêt-bail *m.*
length *n.* longueur *f.*; bout, morceau *m.*; (fabric) coupon *m.*; (pipe) tronçon *m.*; **at** — longuement; en détail; enfin; **-en** *vt.* allonger, rallonger, prolonger; — *vi.* s'allonger; augmenter; **-y** *a.* long, prolixe
lengthwise *adv.* en long, en longueur
leniency *n.* clémence *f.*; indulgence *f.*
lenient *a.* clément; indulgent
lens *n.* lentille *f.*, verre *m.*; (phot.) objectif *m.*; — **speed** *n.* ouverture relative *f.*
Lent *n.* Carême *m.*; **-en** *a.* de Carême
lentil *n.* lentille *f.*
leprosy *n.* lèpre *f.*
leprous *a.* lépreux
lesion *n.* lésion *f.*
less *a.* moindre; moins (de); — *adv.* moins (de); **-en** *vt.* amoindrir; diminuer; — *vi.* diminuer; **-er** *a.* moindre; petit
lessee *n.* locataire *m. & f.*
lesson *n.* leçon *f.*; exemple *m.*
lessor *n.* bailleur *m.*
lest *conj.* de peur que, de crainte que
let *vt. & vi.* laisser; permettre; louer; — **go of** lâcher; — **in** laisser entrer; — **off** laisser partir; tirer, décharger; — **out** laisser sortir; faire sortir; — **up** laisser monter; ralentir, devenir moins sévère
lethargic *a.* léthargique
lethargy *n.* léthargie *f.*
letter *n.* lettre *f.*; caractère *m.*; **capital** — majuscule *f.*; — **box** boîte aux lettres; — **carrier** facteur *m.*; — **of credit** *n.* lettre de crédit *f.*; — **opener** ouvre-lettres *m.*; — *vt.* marquer avec des lettres; **-ing** *n.* lettrage *m.*; inscription *f.*
letterhead *n.* en-tête (de papier à écrire) *m.*
letter-perfect *a.* impeccable, parfait dans tous les détails
letterpress *n.* (print.) typographie *f.*

lettuce *n.* laitue *f.*
letup *n.* relâche *m.*
Levantine *n. & a.* Levantin *m.*
levee *n.* levée *f.*; (reception) lever *m.*, réception *f.*
level *n.* niveau *m.*; palier *m.*; **on a — with** de niveau avec; à la hauteur de; égal à; **— a.** égal; à niveau; **— with à ras de, à fleur de; — vt.** niveler; égaliser
levelheaded *a.* pondéré, sensé
lever *n.* levier *m.*; **-age** *n.* force de levier *f.*, bras de levier *m.*
levity *n.* légèreté *f.*
levy *n.* levée *f.*; impôt *m.*; **— vt.** lever, imposer
lewd *a.* lascif, impudique; débauché; **-ness** *n.* lascivité, luxure *f.*
lexicography *n.* lexicographie *f.*
lexicon *n.* lexique *m.*
liability *n.* responsabilité *f.*; **liabilities** *pl.* passif *m.*; dettes, obligations *f. pl.*
liable *a.* responsable; passible (de); sujet (à)
liar *n.* menteur *m.*
libel *n.* diffamation *f.*; libelle *m.*; **— vt.** diffamer; **-ous** *a.* diffamatoire
liberal *a.* libéral; généreux; large; ample; **— n.** libéral *m.*; **-ism** *n.* libéralisme *m.*; **-ity** *n.* générosité *f.*; **-ly** *adv.* libéralement; généreusement
liberal-minded *a.* large d'esprit
liberate *vt.* libérer
liberation *n.* libération *f.*
liberator *n.* libérateur *m.*
Liberia *n.* Libéria *m.*
libertine *n.* libertin *m.*
liberty *n.* liberté *f.*; **at — libre**; en liberté; **take the — of** se permettre de
librarian *n.* bibliothécaire *m. & f.*
library *n.* bibliothèque *f.*; **circulating —** cabinet de lecture *m.*
Libya *n.* Libye *f.*
license *n.* permis *m.*, permission *f.*; patente *f.*; autorisation *f.*; licence *f.*; **driver's —** permis de conduire *m.*; **number** *n.* (auto) immatriculation *f.*; numéro matricule *m.*; **— plate** *n.* plaque d'immatriculation *f.*; **— vt.** accorder un permis à
licentious *a.* licencieux; **-ness** *n.* licence *f.*, dérèglement *m.*
licit *a.* licite
lick *n.* coup de langue *m.*; **— vt.** lécher; (coll.) battre, rosser; **— one's chops** se lécher les babines
licorice *n.* réglisse *f.*
lid *n.* couvercle *m.*; (eye) paupière *f.*
lie *n.* mensonge *m.*; (of land) disposition, configuration *f.*; **— vi.** mentir; (position) être couché; se trouver, être; **—**

down se coucher; **— still** rester tranquille; **here -s** ci-gît
lie detector *n.* machine à déceler la mensonge *f.*
lien *n.* hypothèque *f.*
lieutenant *n.* lieutenant *m.*; **— commander** lieutenant de vaisseau *m.*; **— general** lieutenant de division *m.*; **second —** sous-lieutenant *m.*
life *n.* vie *f.*; existence *f.*; vivant *m.*; biographie *f.*; animation *f.*; **come to —** s'animer; **for — à vie, à perpétuité**; **it's a matter of — and death** il y va de la vie; **— annuity** rente viagère *f.*; **— insurance** assurance sur la vie, assurance-vie *f.*; **-less** *a.* sans vie; **still —** nature morte
life belt *n.* ceinture de sauvetage *f.*
lifeblood *n.* sang *m.*; (fig.) vie, âme *f.*
lifeboat *n.* canot de sauvetage *m.*
lifeguard *n.* surveillant de plage *m.*
life jacket *n.* ceinture de sauvetage *f.*
lifelong *a.* de toute la vie
life preserver *n.* appareil de sauvetage *m.*; bouée *f.*; brassière de sauvetage *f.*
lifesaving *n.* sauvetage *m.*
life-size *a.* en grand; de grandeur normale
lifetime *n.* vie *f.*; vivant *m.*; espace d'une vie *m.*
lift *n.* haussement *m.*, levée *f.*; (elevator) ascenseur *m.*; (shoe) talon *m.*; **give a — to** conduire, faire monter (dans une auto); encourager; rafraîchir; animer; **ski —** télésiège *m.*; **— vt.** lever; soulever; élever; (coll.) plagier; **— vi.** s'élever
ligament *n.* ligament *m.*
light *n.* lumière *f.*; lueur *f.*; jour *m.*; lampe *f.*; feu *m.*; phare *m.*; **electric — bulb** ampoule *f.*; **— wave** onde lumineuse *f.*; **by the — of** à la lumière de, au clair de; **bring to —** mettre au jour; **come to —** se révéler; **throw — on** éclairer; **— vt.** allumer; éclairer, illuminer; **— vi.** s'allumer; s'éclairer; **— a.** clair; blond; (weight) léger; **-en** *vt.* alléger; soulager; hausser; **-er** *n.* briquet *m.*; (naut.) péniche *f.*; **-ing** *n.* éclairage *m.*; allumage *m.*; **-ly** *adv.* légèrement; à la légère; **-ness** *n.* légèreté *f.*
light-fingered *a.* fripon, voleur
light-footed *a.* agile
lightheaded *a.* étourdi
lighthearted *a.* au cœur léger; gai
lighthouse *n.* phare (marin) *m.*
light meter *n.* (phot.) luxmètre, photomètre, posemètre *m.*
lightning *n.* foudre *f.*; éclair *m.*; **flash of — éclair** *m.*; **— rod** paratonnerre *m.*;

forked — foudre en zigzag *f.*
lightship *n.* bateau-phare *m.*
lightweight *n.* poids léger; — *a.* leger
light-year (ast.) année-lumière *f.*
likable, likeable *a.* sympathique, aimable, agréable
like *a.* pareil, semblable; tel; — *prep.* comme; **what is he** —? comment est-il?; **what is the weather** —? quel temps fait-il?; — *n.* semblable *m. & f.*; goût *m.*; — *vt.* aimer; trouver; vouloir; –lihood *n.* probabilité, vraisemblance *f.*; chance *f.*; –ly *a.* probable, vraisemblable; –ly *adv.* probablement; –n *vt.* comparer; –ness *n.* ressemblance *f.*; image *f.*, portrait *m.*
likewise *adv.* de même, autant; aussi
liking *n.* goût *m.*; gré *m.*; penchant *m.*
limb *n.* membre *m.*; branche *f.*; (math.) limbe *m.*
limber *a.* souple, flexible
limelight *n.* projecteur *m.*; **in the —** (très) en vue
limestone *n.* calcaire *m.*; pierre à chaux *f.*
limit *n.* limite, borne *f.*; — *vt.* limiter, borner; restreindre; –ation *n.* limitation *f.*; –ed *a.* borné, limité; restreint; –less *a.* sans bornes
limp *n.* boitement, clochement *m.*; — *vi.* boiter, clocher; — *a.* mou; souple; –ing *a.* boiteux; –ly *adv.* mollement; sans énergie; –ness *n.* mollesse *f.*
limpid *a.* limpide, clair; –ity *n.* limpidité, clarté *f.*
linden *n.* tilleul *m.*
line *n.* ligne *f.*; trait *m.*; forme *f.*; rangée, queue, file *f.*; (of a poem) vers *m.*; métier *m.*; compagnie *f.*; **stand in —** faire la queue; — *vt.* ligner, régler; border; (clothes) doubler; (brakes) rapetasser; — **up** aligner; faire la queue; –age *n.* lignée *f.*; –al *a.* linéal, en ligne directe; –ar *a.* linéaire; –d *a.* doublé
lineman *n.* poseur de lignes *m.*; (football) arbitre de touche *m.*; (tennis) arbitre de lignes *m.*; (railroad) garde-ligne *m.*
linen *n.* toile de lin *f.*; linge *m.*, lingerie *f.*; — **closet** lingerie *f.*
liner *n.* (ship) paquebot *n.*; garniture, bande de remplissage *f.*
line-up *n.* queue, file *f.*; disposition *f.*
linger *vi.* s'attarder; traîner; –ing *a.* lent; prolongé
lingual *a.* lingual
lingerie *n.* linge *m.*
linguist *n.* linguiste *m. & f.*; –ic *a.* linguistique; –ics *n. pl.* linguistique *f.*
liniment *n.* liniment *m.*

lining *n.* doublure *f.*; (brake) garniture *f.*; (hat) coiffe *f.*
link *n.* chaînon *m.*; anneau *m.*; lien *m.*; — *vt.* enchaîner; lier, relier
linoleum *n.* linoléum *m.*
linotype *n.* linotype *f.*
linseed *n.* graine de lin *f.*; — **oil** *n.* huile de lin *f.*
lint *n.* charpie *f.*
lintel *n.* linteau *m.*
lip *n.* lèvre *f.*; bord *m.*; — **reading** lecture sur les lèvres *f.*
lipstick *n.* rouge à lèvres *m.*
liquefaction *n.* liquéfaction *f.*
liquefy *vt.* liquéfier; — *vi.* se liquéfier
liqueur *n.* liqueur *f.*
liquid *n.* liquide *m.*; — *a.* liquide; — **assets** valeurs disponibles *f. pl.*; — **hydrogen** *n.* hydrogène liquide *m.*; –ate *vt.* liquider; –ation *n.* liquidation *f.*
liquor *n.* boisson alcoolique *f.*; alcool *m.*
Lisbon *n.* Lisbonne *f.*
lisp *n.* zézayement *m.*; — *vt. & vi.* zézayer; zozoter
list *n.* liste *f.*; état *m.*; (naut.) bande, gîte *f.*; (fabric selvage) lisière *f.*; — **price** *n.* prix marqué *m.*; — *vt.* faire une liste de; cataloguer; — *vi.* (naut.) donner de la bande
listen *vt.* écouter, prêter l'oreille, faire attention; –er *n.* auditeur *m.*; –ing *n.* écoute *f.*
listless *a.* apathique, insouciant
litany *n.* litanies *f. pl.*
liter *n.* litre *m.*
literacy *n.* capacité de lire et d'écrire *f.*
literal *a.* littéral; sans imagination; –ly à la lettre, au pied de la lettre; littéralement
literary *a.* littéraire
literate *a.* qui sait lire et écrire
literature *n.* littérature *f.*; (com.) prospectus *m. pl.*
lithe *a.* agile, souple
lithograph *n.* lithographie *f.*; — *vt.* lithographier; –er *n.*; –ic *a.* lithographique; lithographe *m.*; –y *n.* lithographie *f.*
Lithuania *n.* Lithuanie *f.*
litigate *vt. & vi.* plaider
litigation *n.* litige, procès *m.*
litmus *n.* tournesol *m.*; — **paper** *n.* papier de tournesol *m.*
litter *n.* civière, litière *f.*; encombrement *m.*; détritus, débris *m. pl.*; (of an animal) portée *f.*; — *vt.* mettre en désordre; joncher; –ed *a.* encombré
little *a.* petit; peu de; **a —** un peu de; — *adv.* peu; — *n.* peu *m.*; — **by —** peu à peu, petit à petit; –ness *n.* petitesse *f.*

liturgy *n.* liturgie *f.*
live *a.* vivant, en vie; (coal) ardent; (wire) en charge; (television) en direct; — **broadcast** *n.* émission transmise en direct *f.*; **–lihood** *n.* vie *f.*; gagne-pain *m.*; **–liness** *n.* vivacité *f.*; vie *f.*; animation *f.*; **–ly** *a.* vif (vive); animé; **–n** *vt.*, **–n up** animer
live *vi.* vivre, exister; demeurer, habiter; durer
liver *n.* foie *m.*
livery *n.* livrée *f.*; — **stable** *n.* écurie de chevaux de louage *f.*
livestock *n.* bétail *m.*, bestiaux *m. pl.*
livid *a.* livide; plombé
living *a.* vivant, en vie; vif; — **room** salon *m.*; — **wage** salaire vital *m.*; — *n.* vie *f.*; **make a** — gagner de quoi vivre, gagner sa vie; **standard of** — niveau de vie *m.*
load *n.* fardeau *m.*; charge *f.*; poids *m.*; — *vt.* charger; accabler; — *vi.* prendre charge; **–ing** *n.* chargement *m.*
loaf *n.* pain *m.*; — *vi.* fainéanter; flâner; **–er** *n.* fainéant *m.*; flâneur *m.*
loam *n.* terre grasse *f.*
loan *n.* prêt *m.*; emprunt *m.*; — **shark** *n.* usurier *m.*; — *vt.* prêter
loath *a.* fâché, peu enclin
loathe *vt.* détester, abhorrer
loathing *n.* dégoût *m.*
loathsome *a.* dégoûtant, repoussant
lobby *n.* vestibule *m.*; — *vi.* chercher à faire valoir l'influence (sur la législature); **–ist** *n.* agent, représentant (d'un groupe cherchant à faire valoir son influence) *m.*
lobe *n.* (anat.) lobe *m.*; (rad) écran du radar *m.*
lobster *n.* homard *m.*; **spiny** — langouste *f.*
local *a.* local; régional; **–e** *n.* scène *f.*; lieu *m.*; **–ity** *n.* localité *f.*; région *f.*; voisinage *m.*; **–ize** *vt.* localiser; **–ly** *adv.* localement; dans la région; dans le voisinage
locate *vt.* trouver, découvrir, localiser; situer; **be –d** se trouver, être situé
location *n.* situation *f.*; lieu, endroit *m.*
lock *n.* serrure *f.*; (rifle) platine *f.*; (dam) écluse *f.*; **air** — sas *m.*; écluse pneumatique *f.*; **pick a** — crocheter une serrure; **under** — **and key** sous clef; — *vt.* fermer à clef; enfermer; — *vi.* s'enrayer; s'enclencher; **–er** *n.* armoire *f.*; compartiment *m.*
locket *n.* médaillon *m.*
lockjaw *n.* trisme *m.*
lock nut *n.* contre-écrou *m.*
locksmith *n.* serrurier *m.*

lockup *n.* prison *f.*
locomotion *n.* locomotion *f.*
locomotive *a.* locomotif; — *n.* locomotive *f.*
locus *n.* (math.) lieu *m.*
lode *n.* filon *m.*, veine *f.*
lodge *n.* cabane *f.*; pavillon *m.*; loge *f.*; — *vt.* loger; — **a complaint** porter plainte; — *vi.* se loger; **–r** *n.* pensionnaire *m. & f.*
lodging *n.* logement *m.*
loft *n.* grenier *m.*; soupente *f.*; atelier *m.*
loftiness *n.* élévation, hauteur *f.*
lofty *a.* élevé, haut; sublime
log *n.* bûche *f.*; (naut.) livre de loch *m.*, journal de navigation *m.*; — **cabin** cabane de bois *f.*; — *vt. & vi.* exploiter (une forêt); **–ger** *n.* bûcheron *m.*
loganberry *n.* ronce-framboise *f.*
logarithm *n.* logarithme *m.*
loggerhead *n.*, **be at –s** être aux prises
logic *n.* logique *f.*; **–al** *a.* logique
logistics *n. pl.* approvisionnement, ravitaillement *m.*
loin *n.* (beef) aloyau *m.*; (veal) longe *f.*; **–s** *pl.* reins *m. pl.*
loiter *vi.* flâner; rôder; **–er** *n.* flâneur *m.*; rôdeur *m.*; **–ing** *n.* flânerie *f.*; vagabondage *m.*
loll *vi.* flâner, s'étaler; pendre
London *n.* Londres
lone *a.* seul, solitaire; **–liness** *n.* solitude *f.*; **–ly** *a.* solitaire; isolé; **–some** *a.* seul, solitaire
long *a.* long (longue); **–shot** (coll.) concurrent qui a peu de chance de gagner; **a** — **time** longtemps; **in the** — **run** à la longue; — *adv.* longtemps; **as** — **as** tant que; **be** — **in** tarder à; **how long?** (depuis) combien de temps; depuis quand; — *vi.*, — **for** avoir envie de; soupirer après; brûler de; **–ing** *n.* désir *m.*, envie *f.*
long-distance *a.* à longue distance; — **call** communication interurbaine *f.*; — **operator** inter *m.*
longevity *n.* longévité *f.*
long-faced *a.* triste, à triste mine
longhand *n.* écriture ordinaire *f.*; — *a.* non-dactylographié, écrit à main
longitude *n.* longitude *f.*
longitudinal *a.* longitudinal
long-legged *a.* aux jambes longues
long-lived *a.* à longue vie; à longue durée
long-lost *a.* perdu depuis longtemps
long-playing *a.* microsillon, à longue durée; — **record** disque microsillon *m.*
longshoreman *n.* docker, débardeur *m.*
long-standing *a.* de longue date
long-suffering *a.* endurant, patient

long-winded *a.* de longue haleine; intarissable, interminable

look *n.* regard *m.*; coup d'œil *m.*; air, aspect *m.*, apparence *f.*; — *vt.* regarder; avoir l'air, paraître; — **like** ressembler à; — **after** s'occuper de; soigner; veiller sur; — **at** regarder; — **away** détourner les yeux; — **for** chercher; — **into** étudier, examiner; — **out** prendre garde; — **over** parcourir; — **up** lever les yeux; se ranimer; consulter; (person) rechercher; –ing *a.*, –ing glass miroir *m.*, glace *f.*

lookout *n.* (person) guetteur *m.*, (naut.) vigie *f.*; **be on the —** guetter; être sur le qui-vive

loom *n.* métier à tisser *m.*; — *vi.* paraître; sortir; surgir

loop *n.* boucle *f.*; œil *m.*; attache *f.*; — *vt. & vi.* boucler

loophole *n.* meurtrière *f.*; (fig.) échappatoire *f.*

loose *a.* détaché; défait; branlant; dégagé; lâche; relâché; dissolu; **be at — ends** être sans occupation; **come —** se détacher, se dégager, se défaire; — *vt.* lâcher, libérer; –n *vt.* relâcher; dénouer; dégager; — *vi.* se défaire, se relâcher, se dégager; –ness *n.* relâchement *m.*; jeu *m.*

loose-leaf *a.* à feuilles mobiles

loot *n.* butin *m.*; — *vt.* piller; –ing *n.* pillage, sac *m.*

lop *vt.* élaguer, couper

lope *n.* galop lent *m.*; pas lent *m.*; — *vi.* aller doucement

lopsided *a.* déversé, déséquilibré

loquacious *a.* loquace

lord *n.* seigneur *m.*; châtelain *m.*; lord *m.*; — *vt.*, — **it** faire l'important; –ly *a.* noble; hautain; –ship *n.* seigneurie *f.*

Lord *n.* Seigneur; Dieu *m.*; **in the year of Our —** en l'an de grâce; –'s Prayer *n.* patenôtre *f.*; oraison dominicale *f.*

lore *n.* science *f.*, savoir *m.*

lose *vt.* perdre, égarer; — **oneself in** s'absorber dans; — **one's temper** s'emporter; — **one's way** se perdre, s'égarer; — **sight of** perdre de vue; –r *n.* battu, perdant *m.*; **bad –r** mauvais joueur *m.*

loss *n.* perte *f.*; privation *f.*; **be at a — to** avoir de la peine à; ne pas savoir

lot *n.* sort *m.*, fortune *f.*; (portion) lot *m.*, quantité *f.*; (land) terrain *m.*; **a — (of)** beaucoup (de); **draw –s** tirer au sort

lottery *n.* loterie *f.*

loud *a.* fort, haut; bruyant; (color) criard; — *adv.* à haute voix; –ness *n.* bruit *m.*; force *f.*

loud-speaker *n.* haut-parleur *m.*

lounge *n.* hall, salon *m.*; foyer *m.*; **chaise —** chaise longue *f.*; — *vi.* flâner; s'étendre

louver *n.* bande, grille *f.*, cloison *m.*; –ed *a.* à bandes, cloisonné

lovable *a.* aimable

love *n.* amour *m.*; tendresse, affection *f.*; (person) ami *m.*, amie *f.*; amour *m. & f.*; (tennis) rien, zéro *m.*; **be in — (with)** être amoureux (de), être épris (de); **fall in — (with)** tomber amoureux (de), s'éprendre (de); — **affair** liaison *f.*; — **letter** billet doux *m.*; — **song** romance, chanson d'amour *f.*; — *vt.* aimer; adorer; –less *a.* sans amour; –liness *n.* beauté *f.*; –ly *a.* beau (belle); charmant, ravissant; –r *n.* amant *m.*; amoureux *m.*; amateur *m.*

love-making *n.* cour *f.*

lovesick *a.* féru d'amour

loving *a.* aimant, affectueux; — **cup** trophée *f.*

low *a.* bas; vil; peu élevé; (dress) décolletée; (spirits) abattu; (sound) grave; — *adv.* bas; — *n.* niveau le plus bas *m.*; –er *a.* inférieur; plus bas; –er *vt.* baisser; abaisser; rabaisser; descendre; –liness *n.* humilité *f.*; –ly *a.* petit, humble, modeste; –ness *n.* petitesse *f.*; faiblesse *f.*; (action) bassesse *f.*; (spirits) abattement *m.*

low *n.* (cow) meuglement *m.*; — *vi.* meugler

lowboy *n.* commode basse *f.*

low-cut *a.* décolleté

lowland *n.* plaine basse *f.*; –s *pl.* terres basses *f. pl.*

low-pitched *a.* grave

low-pressure *a.* à basse pression

low-priced *a.* pas cher, bon marché

low-spirited *a.* triste, abattu

low-water mark *n.* niveau des basses eaux

loyal *a.* fidèle; loyal; –ist *n.* loyaliste *m. & f.*; –ty *n.* fidélité *f.*

lozenge *n.* pastille *f.*; lozenge *f.*

lubricant *n.* lubrifiant *m.*

lubricate *vt.* lubrifier, graisser

lubrication *n.* lubrification *f.*, graissage *m.*

lucid *a.* lucide; –ity *n.* lucidité *f.*

luck *n.* chance *f.*; hasard *m.*; **bad —** malheur *m.*; malchance *f.*; **good —** bonheur *m.*; bonne chance *f.*; **stroke of —** coup de veine *m.*; –ily *adv.* heureusement, par bonheur; –less *a.* infortuné, malheureux; –y *a.* fortuné; **be –y** avoir de la chance; (object) porter bonheur

lucrative *a.* lucratif

ludicrous *n.* risible; ridicule; absurde; –ness *n.* ridicule *m.*

lug *vt.* traîner; — *n.* saillie, oreille, cosse,

lamelle, patte *f.*
luggage *n.* bagages *m. pl.*
lugubrious *a.* lugubre
lukewarm *a.* tiède; **–ness** *n.* tiédeur *f.*
lull *n.* moment de calme *m.*; accalmie *f.*; — *vt.* bercer, endormir; — *vi.* se calmer
lullaby *n.* berceuse *f.*
lumber *n.* bois de charpente *m.*; — *vi.* se traîner; **–ing** *a.* lourd, lent
lumberjack *n.* bûcheron *m.*
lumberjacket *n.* gros blouson *m.*, canadienne *f.*
lumberyard *n.* dépôt de bois de charpente, chantier de bois *m.*
luminary *n.* luminaire *m.*
luminescence *n.* luminescence *f.*
luminous *a.* lumineux
lump *n.* morceau *m.*; bloc *m.*; motton *m.*; (throat) serrement *m.*; — **sum** somme grosse *f.*; prix à forfait *m.*; — *vt.* mettre en bloc; — **together** réunir ensemble; **–y** *a.* grumeleux
lunacy *n.* folie *f.*; aliénation, démence *f.*
lunar *a.* lunaire
lunatic *a.* fou; de fou; — *n.* aliéné, fou, dément *m.*
lunch *n.* déjeuner, lunch *m.*; — *vi.* déjeuner; **–eon** *n.* déjeuner, lunch *m.*
lunchtime *n.* heure du déjeuner *f.*
lung *n.* poumon *m.*; **iron —** poumon d'acier *m.*
lunge *n.* mouvement en avant *m.*; — *vi.* se jeter en avant
lurch *n.* embarras *m.*; embardée *f.*, cahot *m.*; titubation *f.*; — *vi.* embarder; marcher en titubant
lure *n.* leurre *m.*, piège *m.*; (fig.) attrait, appel *m.*; — *vt.* leurrer; attirer, séduire; — **away** détourner
lurid *a.* sensationnel, éblouissant, choquant
lurk *vi.* se cacher; rôder; **–ing** *a.* caché
luscious *a.* succulent
lush *a.* surabondant; plein de sève *n.*
lust *n.* convoitise *f.*; concupiscence *f.*; désir *m.*; luxure *f.*; soif *f.*; — *vi.* désirer ardemment; — **after** convoiter; **–ful** *a.* luxurieux; **–y** *a.* robuste, vigoureux
luster, lustre *n.* éclat, lustre, brillant *m.*
lustrous *a.* éclatant, lustré
lute *n.* luth *m.*
Luxemburg *n.* Luxembourg *m.*
luxuriant *a.* luxuriant
luxuriate *vi.* croître avec abondance; s'abandonner, vivre dans l'abondance
luxurious *a.* luxueux; somptueux; **–ness** *n.* luxe *m.*
luxury *n.* luxe *m.*
lye *n.* lessive *f.*

lying *a.* menteur; (position) couché, étendu; — *n.* mensonge *m.*
lying-in hospital *n.* (hospice de la) maternité *f.*
lymph *n.* lymphe *f.*; **–atic** *a.* lymphatique
lynch *vt.* lyncher; **–ing** *n.* lynchage *m.*
Lyons *n.* Lyon
lyre *n.* lyre *f.*
lyric(al) *a.* lyrique

M

M.A.: Master of Arts licencié ès lettres *m.*
macadam *n.* macadam *m.*
macaroni *n.* macaronis *m. pl.*
macaroon *n.* macaron *m.*
mace *n.* masse *f.*; (bot.) macis *m.*, fleur de muscade *f.*
macerate *vt.* macérer
mach *n.* mach, la vitesse du son *f.*
machination *n.* machination *f.*, complot *m.*, intrigue *f.*
machine *n.* machine *f.*; (pol.) organisation *f.*; — **gun** mitrailleuse *f.*; — **tool** machine-outil *f.*; — *vt.* usiner; **–ry** *n.* machines *f. pl.*; mécanisme *m.*
machine-gun *vt.* mitrailler
machine shop *n.* atelier de construction de machines *m.*
machinist *n.* machiniste, mécanicien *m.*
mackerel *n.* maquereau *m.*
mad *a.* fou, aliéné; insensé; furieux; enragé; **go —** devenir fou; **–den** *vt.* rendre fou; exaspérer; **–ly** *adv.* follement; furieusement; **love –ly** aimer éperdument; **–ness** *n.* folie *f.*; démence *f.*; rage *f.*
Madagascar *n.* Madagascar *m.*
madam *n.* madame *f.*
madcap *n. & a.* fou, insensé *m.*
made *a.* fait; confectionné; fabriqué
Madeira *n.* Madère *f.*
made-to-order, made to measure *a.* fait sur mesure, fait sur commande
made-up *a.* maquillé; inventé; fait; factice
madhouse *n.* maison de fous *f.*
madman *n.* fou, aliéné *m.*
madonna *n.* madone *f.*
madrigal *n.* madrigal *m.*
maestro *n.* maître *m.*
magazine *n.* revue *f.*, périodique *m.*; (mil.) magasin, dépôt *m.*; (camera) chargeur *m.*; **powder —** poudrière *f.*
maggot *n.* asticot *m.*
magic *n.* magie *f.*; —, **–al** *a.* magique; **–ian** *n.* magicien *m.*
magistrate *n.* magistrat *m.*; juge *m.*
magnanimity *n.* magnanimité *f.*
magnanimous *a.* magnanime
magnate *n.* magnat *m.*
magnesia *n.* magnésie *f.*

magnesium *n.* magnésium *m.*
magnet *n.* aimant *m.*; –**ic** *a.* magnétique, d'aimant, aimanté; –**ic (recording) tape** *n.* ruban magnétique *m.*; –**ic speaker** *n.* haut-parleur électro-magnétique *m.*; –**ism** *n.* magnétisme *m.*; –**ize** *vt.* magnétiser
magneto *n.* magnéto *m.*; –**hydrodynamics** *n.* hydrodynamique magnétique, magnétohydrodynamique *f.*
magnification *n.* amplification *f.*, grossissement *m.*
magnificence *n.* magnificence *f.*
magnificent *a.* magnifique
magnify *vt.* grossir, amplifier; –**ing glass** *n.* verre grossissant *m.*, loupe *f.*
magnitude *n.* grandeur *f.*; magnitude *f.*
maid *n.* servante, bonne *f.*; fille *f.*; **old —** vieille fille *f.*; –**en** *n.* jeune fille *f.*; vierge *f.*; –**en** *a.* de jeune fille, de demoiselle; –**en speech** discours de début *m.*
mail *n.* courrier *m.*; poste *f.*; (armor) maille *f.*; **—** *vt.* mettre (une lettre) à la poste; expédier; **— order** *n.* commande par la poste *f.*
mailbox *n.* boîte aux lettres *f.*
mailman *n.* facteur *m.*
mail-order house *n.* établissement de vente par correspondance *m.*
mailplane *n.* avion postal *m.*
maim *vt.* estropier, mutiler
main *n.* (water) canalisation maîtresse *f.*; océan *m.*, mer *f.*; **in the —** en général; **—** *a.* principal, essentiel; grand; le plus important; **— office** (com.) siège social *m.*; **— thing** essentiel *m.*; –**ly** *adv.* principalement
mainland *n.* continent *m.*; terre firme *f.*
mainspring *n.* grand ressort, ressort principal *m.*
mainstay *n.* point d'appui *m.*; appui principal *m.*
maintain *vt.* maintenir, soutenir; entretenir; garder; défendre; prétendre; subvenir aux besoins de
maintenance *n.* entretien *m.*; maintien *m.*; pension alimentaire *f.*; ménage *m.*
majestic *a.* majestueux; –**ally** *adv.* majestueusement
majesty *n.* majesté *f.*
major *n.* commandant *m.*; (age) majeur *m.*; **— general** général de division *m.*; **—** *a.* majeur, plus grand; **—** *vi.* (school) se spécialiser; –**ity** *n.* majorité *f.*; la plus grande partie *f.*
make *n.* marque *f.*; fabrication *f.*; **—** *vt.* faire; fabriquer; façonner; créer; construire; confectionner; (with adjective) rendre; causer; nommer; (cards) battre; (money) gagner; **— a living** gagner son pain; **— for** se diriger vers; (naut.) mettre le cap sur; favoriser; **— fun of** se moquer de; **— good** réussir; **— it** (coll.) réussir, y arriver; **— off** filer, décamper; **— over** céder, transmettre; **— out** faire; (list) dresser; (check) écrire, tirer; comprendre; déchiffrer; distinguer; **— up** regagner; préparer; inventer; se maquiller; se réconcilier; –**r** *n.* fabricant *m.*; faiseur *m.*
Majorca *n.* Majorque *f.*
Maker *n.* Créateur *m.*
make-believe *n.* semblant *m.*; **land of —** pays des chimères *m.*; **—** *vt.* faire semblant
makeshift *a.* improvisé; de fortune
make-up *n.* maquillage, fard *m.*; composition *f.*
making *n.* fabrication *f.*; confection *f.*; construction *f.*; composition *f.*; création *f.*; **have the –s** avoir tout ce qu'il faut; **in the —** en train de se faire; **— up** préparation, composition *f.*; compensation *f.*; réconciliation *f.*
maladjusted *a.* mal adapté, inadapté
maladjustment *n.* ajustement défectueux *m.*
malady *n.* maladie *f.*
Malay *a. & n.* malais *m.*; –**a** *n.* Malaisie *f.*
malcontent *a. & n.* mécontent *m.*
male *a. & n.* mâle *m.*
malefactor *n.* malfaiteur *m.*
malevolence *n.* malveillance *f.*
malevolent *a.* malveillant
malfeasance *n.* malfaisance *f.*
malformation *n.* malformation *f.*
malformed *a.* malformé
malice *n.* méchanceté *f.*; malice *f.*; **with — aforethought** avec préméditation
malicious *a.* méchant; malveillant; rancunier; –**ness** *n.* malice, malveillance *f.*
malign *a.* pernicieux; **—** *vt.* diffamer, calomnier; –**ancy** *n.* malignité *f.*; –**ant** *a.* malin (maligne)
mall *n.* mail *m.*
malleability *n.* malléabilité *f.*
malleable *a.* malléable, forgeable
mallet *n.* maillet *m.*
malnutrition *n.* sous-alimentation *f.*
malodorous *a.* malodorant
malpractice *n.* malversation *f.*
malt *n.* malt *m.*; –**ed milk** *n.* boisson composée de lait et de crème glacée, parfumée au malt *f.*
Malta *n.* Malte *f.*
Maltese *a. & n.* maltais *m.*
maltreat *vt.* maltraiter; –**ment** *n.* mauvais traitement *m.*
mama, mamma *n.* maman *f.*
mammal *n.* mammifère *m.*; –**ian** *a.* des

mammifères
mammary *a.* mammaire
mammoth *n.* mammouth *m.*; — *a.* géant
man *n.* homme *m.*; mari *m.*; ouvrier *m.*;
  domestique *m.*; (chess) pièce *f.*; (sports)
  joueur *m.*; **dead** — mort *m.*; **old** — vieillard *m.*; **to a** —, **to the last** — jusqu'au
  dernier; — *vt.* armer, équiper, garnir;
  –hood *n.* âge d'homme *m.*; **–kind** *n.* humanité *f.*, homme, genre humain *m.*;
  –liness *m.* virilité *f.*; **–ly** *a.* d'homme; viril
manacles *n. pl.* menottes *f. pl.*
manage *vt.* diriger, conduire; gérer, arranger; faire; savoir; arriver à; **–able** *a.*
  maniable, traitable; **–ment** *n.* direction,
  conduite *f.*; gérance *f.*; administration
  f.; **–r** *n.* directeur, gérant, administrateur *m.*; chef *m.*
managing *a.* directeur, gérant
Manchukuo *n.* Mandchoukouo *m.*
Manchuria *n.* Mandchourie *f.*
mandate *n.* mandat *m.*; commandement
  m.
mandatory *a.* obligatoire, mandatif
mandible *n.* mandibule *f.*
mandolin *n.* mandoline *f.*
mane *n.* crinière *f.*
man-eater *n.* mangeur d'hommes *m.*
maneuver *n.* manœuvre *f.*; — *vt.* manœuvrer
manganese *n.* manganèse *m.*
mange *n.* gale (de chien) *f.*
manger *n.* mangeoire, crèche *f.*
mangle *n.* calandre *f.*; — *vt.* mutiler, déchirer; (laundry) calandrer
mangy *a.* galeux
manhandle *vt.* malmener; manutentionner
manhole *n.* trou de visite *m.*, bouche d'é-
  gout *f.*
mania *n.* manie *f.*; **–c** *n.* fou *m.*, folle *f.*;
  –cal *a.* maniaque
manicure *n.* manucure *m.*; — *vt.* soigner
  les ongles (mains), se faire les ongles
  (mains)
manicurist *n.* manucure *f.*
manifest *a.* manifeste, évident; — *n.* manifeste *m.*; — *vt.* manifester; montrer,
  témoigner; **–ation** *n.* manifestation *f.*;
  –o *n.* manifeste *m.*
manifold *a.* varié, divers, multiple, nombreux; (engine) tubulure *f.*
manikin *n.* mannequin *m.*
Manila *n.* Manille *f.*
manila *n.* manille *f.*; — **paper** papier
  bulle *m.*
manipulate *vt.* manipuler; tripoter
manipulation *n.* manipulation *f.*; tripotage *m.*

manipulator *n.* manipulateur *m.*
manna *n.* manne *f.*
manner *n.* manière *f.*; façon *f.*; espèce, sorte *f.*, genre *m.*; air, maintien *m.*; **in a** —
  of speaking pour ainsi dire; **in such a**
  — that de manière que, de sorte que; **in**
  this — de cette façon, de cette manière;
  –s *pl.* manières *f. pl.*; politesse *f.*; mœurs
  f. pl.; **–ism** *n.* affectation *f.*, maniérisme *m.*; **–ly** *a.* poli; bien élevé
man-of-war *n.* vaisseau de guerre *m.*
manor *n.* château seigneurial *m.*; seigneurie *f.*
man power *n.* main-d'œuvre *f.*; (mil.) ef-
  fectifs *m. pl.*
mansard *n.* toit en mansarde *m.*
mansion *n.* hôtel (particulier) *m.*; château
  m.
manslaughter *n.* homicide involontaire *m.*
mantel *n.* manteau de cheminée *m.*; dessus de cheminée *m.*
mantle *n.* manteau *m.*, pèlerine *f.*; (fig.)
  voile *m.*; (heraldry) lambrequin *m.*; —
  vt. voiler, couvrir
manual *a.* manuel, de manœuvre; à bras,
  à main; — **training** *n.* apprentissage
  manuel *m.*; — *n.* manuel *m.*
manufacture *n.* fabrication *f.*; — *vt.* fabriquer, manufacturer; **–r** *n.* fabricant,
  manufacturier, industriel *m.*
manufacturing *n.* fabrication *n.*; — *a.* industriel
manure *n.* fumier *m.*; engrais *m.*; — *vt.* fumer, engraisser
manuscript *n.* manuscrit *m.*
Manx *n. & a.* Mannois *m.*
many *a. & n.* beaucoup (de); bien des; un
  grand nombre (de); maint; pas mal
  (de); **as** — autant (de); **how** — combien
  (de); **so** — tant (de); **too** — trop (de)
many-sided *a.* à plusieurs côtés; à de mul-
  tiples reflets; polygone
map *n.* carte *f.*; plan *m.*; — **maker** cartographe *m.*; — **making** cartographie *f.*;
  road — carte routière *f.*; — *vt.* tracer
  une carte de; — **out** arranger, projeter,
  préparer; **–ping** *n.* cartographie *f.*; action de tracer une carte *f.*
mar *vt.* gâter, troubler
maraschino *n.* marasquin *m.*
marauder *n.* maraudeur *m.*; malandrin *m.*
marble *n.* marbre *m.*; bille *f.*; — *a.* en marbre; — *vt.* marbrer; **–d** *a.* marbré
march *n.* marche *f.*; pas *m.*; — *vi.* marcher;
  — **in** entrer; — **by** défiler; — *vt.* faire
  marcher; **–ing** *n.* marche *f.*; **–ing** *a.* en
  marche
March *n.* mars *m.*
marchioness *n.* marquise *f.*
mare *n.* jument *f.*

margin *n.* marge *f.*; bord *m.*; (stock) acompte *m.*; **–al** *a.* marginal

margin release *n.* (typewriter) déclanche-marge *m.*

marimba *n.* xylophone *m.*

marine *a.* marin; maritime; — *n.* marine *f.*; soldat d'infanterie marine *m.*; **merchant** — marine marchande *f.*; **–r** *n.* marin *m.*

marital *a.* marital; matrimonial

maritime *a.* maritime

marjoram *n.* marjolaine *f.*

mark *n.* marque *f.*; signe *m.*; preuve *f.*; témoignage *m.*; trace *f.*; tache *f.*; but *m.*; (school) note *f.*; **question** — point d'interrogation *m.*; — *vt.* marquer; indiquer; (cards) maquiller, piper; (school) noter, coter; — **down** (com.) démarquer; solder; noter; — **off** mesurer; — **time** marquer le pas; — **up** défigurer, couvrir de taches; hausser le prix de; **–ed** *a.* marqué; sensible

marked-down *a.* soldé

market *n.* marché *m.*; halle *f.*; — **place** place du marché *f.*; — **price** prix courant *m.*; **on the** — en vente; — *vt.* lancer sur le marché; — *vi.* faire son marché; **–able** *a.* vendable; **–ing** *n.* marché

marksman *n.* bon tireur *m.*; **–ship** *n.* adresse au tir *f.*

markup *n.* bénéfice, profit *m.*

marmalade *n.* marmelade *f.*

marmoset *n.* marmouset *m.*

marmot *n.* marmotte *f.*

maroon *a. & n.* marron *m.*; — *vt.* abandonner (dans une île); isoler

marquee *n.* marquise *f.*

marquetry *n.* marqueterie *f.*

marquis *n.* marquis *m.*

marriage *n.* mariage *m.*; **by** — par alliance; **give (away) in** — donner en mariage; — **certificate** acte de mariage *m.*; **–able** *a.* en d'âge à (se) marier, nubile

married *a.* marié; conjugal; **get** — se marier; — **couple** ménage *m.*

marrow *n.* mœlle *f.*

marry *vt.* se marier (avec), épouser; — **into** s'allier à; — **off** marier

Marseilles *n.* Marseille *f.*

marsh *n.* marais, marécage *m.*; **–y** *a.* marécageux

marshal *n.* maréchal *m.*; maître es cérémonies *m.*; — *vt.* ranger; rassembler

marshmallow *n.* guimauve *f.*

marsupial *n.* marsupial *m.*

mart *n.* marché *m.*; entrepôt *m.*

martinet *n.* homme fort sur la discipline *m.*

Martinique *n.* Martinique *f.*

martyr *n.* martyr *m.*; **–dom** *n.* martyre *m.*

marvel *n.* merveille *f.*; — *vi.* s'étonner, s'émerveiller; **–ous** *a.* merveilleux; **–ously** à merveille, merveilleusement

Marxist *a. & n.* marxiste

marzipan *n.* massepain *m.*

mascara *n.* rimmel *m.*

mascot *n.* mascotte *f.*

masculine *a.* masculin; mâle; viril; — *n.* masculin *m.*

masculinity *n.* masculinité *f.*

mash *n.* mâche *f.*; pâtée *f.*; purée *f.*; — *vt.* brasser, broyer; mettre en purée; **–ed** *a.* en purée; **–ed potatoes** purée de pommes de terre *f.*

mask *n.* masque *m.*; — *vt.* masquer; cacher

mason *n.* maçon *m.*; franc-maçon *m.*; **–ic** *a.* maçonnique; **–ry** *n.* maçonnerie *f.*; franc-maçonnerie *f.*

masquerade *n.* mascarade *f.*; bal masqué *m.*

Mass *n.* (eccl.) Messe *f.*; **High** — Grand-messe, Messe haute *f.*; **Requiem** — Messe des morts *f.*; **hear** — assister à la Messe; — **book** missel *m.*

mass *n.* masse *f.*; multitude, foule *f.*; — **meeting** réunion en masse; — **production** fabrication en série, construction en série *f.*; **–ive** *a.* massif; en masse; — *vi.* se masser, se réunir, se rassembler; — *vt.* rassembler, réunir

massacre *n.* massacre *m.*; — *vt.* massacrer

massage *n.* massage *m.*; (head) friction *f.*; — *vt.* masser; malaxer

masses *pl.* foule *f.*; peuple *m.*

mast *n.* mât *m.*; pylône *m.*

master *n.* maître *m.*; chef, patron *m.*; (duplicator) cliché *n.*; — **key** passe-partout *m.*; — **of arts** licencié ès lettres *m.*; — **stroke** coup de maître *m.*; — *vt.* maîtriser, dompter; apprendre à fond; **–ful** *a.* autoritaire; **–ly** *a.* de maître; **–y** *n.* maîtrise *f.*; connaissance *f.*

mastermind *n.* chef, organisateur, cerveau *m.*; — *vt.* diriger, organiser

masterpiece *n.* chef d'œuvre *m.*

masticate *vt.* mâcher, mastiquer

mastiff *n.* mâtin *m.*

mastoid *a.* mastoïde

mat *n.* natte *f.*, paillasson *m.*; **picture** — passe-partout *m.*; **place** — dessous *m.*; — *vt.* natter; — *vi.* s'emmêler; **–ted** *a.* emmêlé

match *n.* allumette *f.*; mariage *m.*; (colors) assortiment *m.*; (sports) match *m.*; partie *f.*; égal, pareil *m.*; — *vt.* égaler; assortir; — *vi.* s'assortir; **–ing**, **to** — *a.* assorti; **–less** *a.* sans pareil, sans égal; incomparable

matchbox *n.* boîte à allumettes *f.*

matchmaker n. marieur m., marieuse f.
mate n. époux m., épouse f.; compagnon m., compagne f.; mâle m., femelle f.; (chess) échec et mat m.; (naut.) officier m.; first — second m.; — vt. accoupler; (chess) faire échec et mat; — vi. s'accoupler
material a. matériel; pertinent, important; — n. matière f., matériaux m. pl.; étoffe f., tissu m.; sujet m.; –ism n. matérialisme m.; –istic a. matérialiste; matériel; –ize vi. se matérialiser;.se réaliser; –ly adv. matériellement; sensiblement
maternal a. maternel
maternity n. maternité f.; — hospital n. (hospice de la) maternité f.
mathematical a. mathématique
mathematician n. mathématicien m.
mathematics n. pl. mathématiques f. pl.
matriarch n. femme chef d'une famille f.
matriculate vt. immatriculer
matriculation n. immatriculation f.
matrimonial a. matrimonial; conjugal
matrimony n. mariage m.; vie conjugale f.
matrix n. matrice f.; moule f.
matron n. matrone f.; intendante f.; –ly a. domestique, en femme mariée, d'un certain âge
matter n. matière f.; sujet m.; chose, affaire f.; question f.; as a — of fact à vrai dire; en effet; — of course chose qui va de soi f.; — of form formalité f.; — in hand chose dont il s'agit f.; what is the —? qu'y a-t-il?, qu'avez-vous?; what is the — with him? qu'a-t-il?; — vi. importer; it does not — n'importe
matter-of-course a. qui va sans dire
matter-of-fact a. positif, pratique, calme
matting n. natte f.; ouate f.
mattress n. matelas m.; (spring) sommier m.
mature a. mûr, d'âge mûr; (bond) échu; — vt. mûrir; — vi. mûrir; arriver à échéance
maturity n. maturité f.; échéance f.
maudlin a. excessivement sentimental
maul vt. meurtrir, malmener
Mauritania n. Mauritanie f.
Mauritius n. (île) Maurice f.
mausoleum n. mausolée m.
maverick n. bœuf non marqué au fer m.; solitaire, sauvage m.
maxim n. maxime f., dicton m.
maximum a. & n. maximum m.
may vi. pouvoir; it — be il se peut
May n. mai m.; — Day le premier mai m.
mayhem n. mutilation f.; (fig.) ravage, dégat m.
maybe adv. peut-être
mayor n. maire m.; président du conseil municipal m.
maypole n. arbre du premier mai m.
maze n. labyrinthe m.
M.C.: Master of Ceremonies maître des cérémonies m.
me pron. me, moi
meadow n. pré m.; prairie f.; — lark n. étourneau m.
meager, meagre a. maigre; pauvre; peu nombreux
meal n. repas m.; farine f.; –y a. farineux
mealtime n. heure du repas f.
mean a. bas, vil, méprisable; sale, vilain; mesquin; misérable; (math.) moyen; — n. milieu; (math.) moyenne f.; –s pl. moyen m. (pl.); ressources f. pl.; by all –s (mais) certainement; by no –s pas du tout; en aucune façon; by –s of au moyen de; –ness n. vilenie, mesquinerie f.; bassesse f.; petitesse f.; médiocrité f.
mean vt. vouloir dire, signifier; avoir l'intention de; –ing n. sens m., signification f.; –ingful a. significatif; –ingless a. dépourvu de sens
meander vi. serpenter; — n. méandre m.
meantime adv. & n.; in the — sur ces entrefaites; dans l'intervalle
meanwhile adv. sur ces entrefaites
measles n. pl. rougeole f.
measurable a. mesurable
measurably adv. sensiblement; modérément
measure n. mesure f.; démarche f.; in some — en partie; — vt. mesurer; métrer; avoir; –d a. compté; modéré; –less a. vaste, sans bornes; –ment n. mesure f.; mesurage m.
meat n. viande f.; nourriture f.; (fig.) moelle f.; –ball n. boulette de viande f.; –less a. (eccl.) maigre; –y a. charnu
meat market n. boucherie f.
Mecca n. Mecque f.
mechanic n. mécanicien m.; (auto) garagiste m.; –al a. mécanique; automatique;–al engineer a. ingénieur mécanicien m.; –al engineering n. mécanique f.; –s n. pl. mécanique f.
mechanism n. mécanisme m.; appareil m.
mechanize vt. mécaniser
medal n. médaille f.; –lion n. médaillon m.
meddle vi. se mêler (de), s'occuper (de); –some a. qui se mêle de tout
medial a. moyen, médial
median a. médian
mediate vi. s'interposer; servir de médiateur
mediation n. médiation f.
mediator n. médiateur m.; arbitre m.
medical a. médical; — school école de mé-

decine *f.*
medicare *n.* programme d'assurance contre la maladie pour les personnes âgées *m.*
medicate *vt.* médicamenter
medicine *n.* médicine *f.*; médicament *m.*
medicine chest *n.* pharmacie *f.*
medicine dropper *n.* compte-gouttes *m.*
medicine man *n.* médecin indien, sorcier indien *m.*
medieval *a.* médiéval; du moyen-âge
mediocre *a.* médiocre
mediocrity *n.* médiocrité *f.*
meditate *vt. & vi.* méditer
meditation *n.* méditation *f.*
meditative *a.* méditatif
Mediterranean *n.* Méditerranée *f.*
medium *n.* moyen *m.*; milieu *m.*; intermédiare *m.*; organe *m.*; (spiritualist) médium *m.*; — *a.* moyen; (cooking) à point
medium-sized *a.* de grandeur moyenne, de taille moyenne
medley *n.* mélange *m.*; (color) bigarrure *f.*; (mus.) pot-pourri *m.*
medulla *n.* moelle *f.*
meek *a.* humble, doux; timide; **–ness** *n.* humilité, douceur *f.*
meet *vt.* rencontrer; retrouver; croiser; faire la connaisance de; — *vi.* se rencontrer; se joindre; se réunir; **go to** — aller au-devant de, aller à la rencontre de; **make both ends** — joindre les deux bouts; **until we** — again au revoir; — **with** éprouver, essuyer; **–ing** *n.* réunion *f.*, meeting *m.*; rencontre *f.*; **–ing place** rendez-vous *m.*
megaphone *n.* mégaphone *m.*
melancholy *a.* mélancolique; — *n.* mélancolie *f.*
meld *n.* (cards) combinaison *f.*; — *vi.* annoncer
mellow *a.* doux (douce); mûr; moelleux; — *vt.* adoucir; mûrir; — *vi.* s'adoucir; mûrir; **–ness** *n.* moelleux *m.*; maturité *f.*; mollesse *f.*
melodious *a.* mélodieux; **–ness** *n.* mélodie *f.*
melodrama *n.* mélodrame *m.*; **–tic** *a.* mélodramatique
melody *n.* air *m.*; mélodie *f.*
melon *n.* melon *m.*
melt *vt.* fondre; — *vi.* (se) fondre; **–ing** *a.* fondant; **–ing** *n.* fonte, fusion *f.*; **–ing point** point de fusion *m.*; **–ing pot** creuset *m.*
member *n.* membre *m.*; partie *f.*; (pol.) représentant, député *m.*; **–ship** *n.* nombre des membres *m.*; qualité de membre *f.*; membres *m. pl.*

membrane *n.* membrane *f.*; tunique *f.*
memento *n.* souvenir, mémento *m.*
memo *n.* mémo, mémorandum *m.*
memoir *n.* mémoire *m.*; **–s** *pl.* mémoires *m. pl.*
memorable *a.* mémorable
memorandum *n.* mémorandum, mémo *m.*; — **pad** bloc-notes *m.*
memorial *a.* commémoratif; — *n.* monument commémoratif *m.*; **–ist** *n.* auteur de mémoires *m.*
memorize *vt.* apprendre par cœur
memory *n.* mémoire *f.*; souvenir *m.*; **commit to** — apprendre par cœur
menace *n.* menace *f.*; — *vt.* menacer
menagerie *n.* ménagerie *f.*
mend *n.* raccommodage *m.*, reprise *f.*; **on the** — en voie de guérison; — *vt.* raccommoder; réparer; — *vi.* se remettre; **–able** *a.* réparable; **–ing** *n.* raccommodage *m.*
mendicant *a. & n.* mendiant *m.*
menial *a.* bas, servile; — *n.* domestique, laquais *m.*
meningitis *n.* méningite *f.*
menopause *n.* ménopause *f.*
menstruation *n.* menstruation *f.*
mental *a.* mental; de tête; de l'esprit; — **hospital** maison de santé *f.*; asile d'aliénés *m.*; **–ity** *n.* mentalité *f.*
mention *n.* mention *f.*; — *vt.* mentionner; faire mention de; citer; **don't** — **it** il n'y a pas de quoi; de rien; **not to** — sans parler de
mentor *n.* mentor, guide *m.*
menu *n.* carte *f.*, menu *m.*
mercantile *a.* mercantile, commercial
mercenary *a. & n.* mercenaire *m.*
mercerize *vt.* merceriser
merchandise *n.* marchandise *f.*
merchant *n.* marchand *m.*; commerçant, négociant *m.*; — **marine** marine marchande *f.*
merchantman *n.* vaisseau marchand *m.*
merciful *a.* miséricordieux; clément
merciless *a.* impitoyable
mercurial *a.* mercuriel, ardent, vif
mercurochrome *n.* mercurochrome *m.*
mercury *n.* mercure *m.*
Mercury-switch *n.* interrupteur à mercure *m.*
mercury-vapor lamp *n.* lampe à vapeur de mercure *f.*
mercy *n.* miséricorde *f.*; clémence, grâce, merci *f.*; pitié *f.*; **be at someone's** — être à la merci de; **have** — **on** avoir pitié de
mere *a.* seul; simple, pur; **–ly** *adv.* seulement, (tout) simplement
merge *vt.* fondre, fusionner; — *vi.* se fon-

dre; fusionner; s'amalgamer
meridian *n.* méridien *m.*; **–al** *a.* méridional
merit *n.* mérite *m.*; **–s** *pl.* le pour et le contre; — *vt.* mériter; **–orious** *a.* méritoire
mermaid *n.* sirène *f.*
merrily *adv.* joyeusement
merriment *n.* gaieté, réjouissance *f.*
merry *a.* joyeux, gai
merry-go-round *n.* manège (de chevaux de bois) *m.*
mesa *n.* plateau élevé *m.*
mesh *n.* maille *f.*; engrenage *m.*, prise *f.*; — *vt.* engrener, endenter; — *vi.* être en prise, engrener
mesmerism *n.* mesmérisme *m.*
mesmerize *vt.* hypnotiser
mesotron *n.* électron lourd, méson *m.*
mess *n.* désordre *m.*; saleté *f.*; gâchis *m.*; (mil.) soupe *f.*, mess *m.*; **–y** *a.* sale; en désordre
message *n.* message *m.*; mot *m.*; communication *f.*
messenger *n.* messager *m.*; commissionnaire *m.*; courrier *m.*
Messiah *n.* Messie *m.*
mess hall *n.* (mil.) salle de mess *f.*, réfectoire *m.*; (navy) carré des officiers *m.*
mess kit *n.* gamelle *f.*
Messrs. MM. *n. pl.* messieurs *m. pl.*
metabolism *n.* métabolisme *m.*
metal *n.* métal; **–lic** *a.* métallique; **–lurgy** *n.* métallurgie *f.*
metamorphosis *n.* métamorphose *f.*
metaphor *n.* métaphore *f.*; **–ical** *a.* métaphorique
metaphysical *a.* métaphysique
metaphysics *n. pl.* métaphysique *f.*
metatarsal *a.* métatarsien
mete *vt.* distribuer
meteor *n.* météore *m.*; **–ic** *a.* météorique; rapide; **–ite** *n.* aérolithe *m.*; **–ological** *a.* météorologique; **–ologist** *n.* météorologiste, météo *m.*; **–ology** *n.* météorologie *f.*
meter *n.* mètre *m.*; compteur *m.*
methane *n.* méthane *m.*
method *n.* méthode *f.*; procédé *m.*; **–ical** *a.* méthodique
methyl *n.* méthyle *m.*; **–ate** *vt.* méthyler
meticulous *a.* méticuleux
metric *a.* métrique; **–al** *a.* métrique; en vers, mesuré
metronome *n.* métronome *m.*
metropolis *n.* métropole *f.*
metropolitan *a.* métropolitain
mettle *n.* courage, coeur *m.*
mew *vi.* miauler
Mexican *a. & n.* mexicain *m.*
Mexico *n.* Mexique *m.*
mezzanine *n.* entresol *m.*

microbe *n.* microbe *m.*
microbiology *n.* microbiologie *f.*
microcircuit *n.* microcircuit *m.*
microcosm *n.* microcosme *m.*
microfilm *n.* microfilm *m.*; — *vt.* microfilmer
microgroove *n.* microsillon *m.*
micrometer *n.* micromètre *m.*
micron *n.* micron *m.*
microörganism *n.* micro-organisme *m.*
microphone *n.* microphone *m.*
microphysics *n.* microphysique *f.*
microscope *n.* microscope *m.*; **electron** — microscope électronique *m.*
microscopic *a.* microscopique
microwave *n.* onde ultracourte *f.*
mid *a.* du milieu, moyen
midday *n.* midi *m.*
middle *n.* milieu *m.*; centre *m.*; **in the** — **of** au milieu de; en train de; — *a.* moyen central; du milieu; — **class** bourgeoisie *f.*
Middle Ages *n. pl.* Moyen-Âge *m.*
middle-aged *a.* d'un certain âge
middle-class *a.* bourgeois
middleman *n.* intermédiaire *m.*; revendeur *m.*; entremetteur *m.*
middleweight *n.* poids moyen *m.*
middling *a.* moyen; médiocre
middy blouse *n.* blouse de matelot *f.*
midget *n.* nain *m.*, naine *f.*
midland *a.* intérieur, de l'intérieur
midnight *n.* minuit *m.*
midriff *n.* diaphragme *m.*; tour de ceinture *m.*
midshipman *n.* aspirant de marine, midship *m.*
midst *n.*, **in the** — **of** au milieu de; parmi; en train de
midway *adv.* à mi-chemin, à mi-distance; — *n.* allée centrale *f.*; fête foraine *f.*
midwife *n.* sage-femme *f.*
mien *n.* mine *f.*, air *m.*
might *n.* puissance, force *f.*; **–y** *a.* puissant, fort; grand; — *adv.* (coll.) très, fort
migraine *n.* migraine *f.*
migrant *n.* nomade *m.*
migrate *vi.* émigrer
migration *n.* migration *f.*
migratory *a.* migrateur, de passage
mild *a.* doux (douce); léger; (climate) tempéré; **–ness** *n.* douceur *f.*
mildew *n.* moisissure *f.*; chancissure *f.*
mile *n.* mille *m.*; **–age** *n.* milles *m. pl.*; distance en milles *f.*; kilométrage *m.*
milestone *n.* borne *f.*
militarism *n.* militarisme *m.*
military *a.* militaire; — *n.* militaires *m. pl.*
militate *vi.* militer
militia *n.* milice *f.*; garde nationale *f.*;

−man *n.* milicien *m.*
milk *n.* lait *m.*; bottle of — carafe de lait *f.*; — of magnesia magnésie *f.*; — sugar *n.* sucre de lait *m.*; lactine *f.*; — tooth dent de lait *f.*; — *vt.* traire; exploiter; −y *a.* laiteux
milkmaid *n.* laitière *f.*
milkman *n.* laitier *m.*
milkweed *n.* laiteron *m.*
Milky Way *n.* voie lactée *f.*
mill *n.* moulin *m.*; fabrique, usine *f.*; — *vt.* moudre; fraiser; laminer; meuler; usiner; canneler; — *vi.* se presser; fourmiller; −er *n.* meunier *m.*
millennium *n.* millénaire *m.*; (eccl.) millénium *n.*
milligram *n.* milligramme *m.*
millimeter *n.* millimètre *m.*
milliner *n.* modiste *f.*; −y *n.* modes *f. pl.*; −y shop magasin de modes *m.*
million *n.* million *m.*; −aire *n.* millionnaire *m. & f.*; −th *a.* millionième
millrace *n.* canal de moulin *m.*
millstone *n.* meule *f.*
milt *n.* laite, laitance *f.*
mime *n.* mime *m.*; — *vi.* mimer
mimeograph *n.* machine à polycopier *f.*; — *vt.* polycopier
mimic *n.* imitateur *m.*; — *vt.* imiter, mimer; −ry *n.* imitation; mimique *f.*
minaret *n.* minaret *m.*
mince *vt.* hacher; not to — one's words parler sans phrases; −d *a.* haché; −d meat hachis *m.*
mincemeat *n.* mincemeat *m.*
mind *n.* esprit *m.*; âme *f.*; intelligence *f.*; mémoire *f.*; — reader personne qui lit dans la pensée des autres *f.*; bear in — ne pas oublier; be of one — être d'accord; bring to — rappeler; change one's — changer d'avis; have a — to avoir envie de; have in — avoir en vue; make up one's — se décider, prendre le parti (de); peace of — tranquillité d'esprit *f.*; state of — état d'âme *m.*; — *vt.* garder, surveiller; faire attention à; s'occuper de; ne pas vouloir; I don't — cela m'est égal; je veux bien; never — n'importe; ne vous inquiétez pas; −ful *a.* attentif
mine *n.* mine *f.*; — field champ de mines *m.*; — *pron.* le mien *m.*; — *a.* à moi; — layer *n.* poseur de mines *m.*; — shaft puits *m.*; — sweeper *n.* dragueur de mines, balayeur de mines *m.*; — *vt.* fouiller; (coal) exploiter; (mil.) miner; −r *n.* mineur *m.*
mineral *a. & n.* minéral *m.*; — water eau minérale *f.*; boisson gazeuse *f.*; −ogist *n.* minéralogiste *m.*; −ogy minéralogie *f.*
mingle *vi.* se mêler, se mélanger

miniature *n.* miniature *f.*; — *a.* en miniature
miniaturization *n.* reproduction en miniature
minimize *vt.* réduire au minimum
minimum *a. & n.* minimum *m.*
mining *n.* exploitation des mines, industrie minière *f.*; (naut.) pose des mines *f.*
minion *n.* mignon *m.*; (print.) corps 7 *m.*
minister *n.* ministre *m.*; pasteur *m.*; — *vi.*, — to someone's needs subvenir aux besoins de
ministry *n.* (administration) ministère; (eccl.) le saint ministère; (pol.) gouvernement *m.*
mink *n.* vison *m.*
minnow *n.* vairon *m.*
minor *a.* petit, mineur, peu important; — *n.* mineur *m.*; −ity *n.* minorité *f.*
minstrel *n.* ménestrel *m.*; chanteur, musicien *m.*
mint *n.* monnaie *f.*; (bot.) menthe *f.*; — *vt.* frapper, battre
minuet *n.* menuet *m.*
minus *prep.* moins; (coll.) sans; — *n.* moins *m.*; — *a.* négatif
minute *n.* minute *f.*; instant, moment *m.*; note *f.*; any — à tout moment; — hand grande aiguille *f.*; −s *pl.* notes *f. pl.*, procès-verbal *m.*; — *a.* menu, minuscule; moindre; minutieux
minx *n.* coquine *f.*
miracle *n.* miracle *m.*; — play *n.* miracle *m.*; — worker thaumaturge, faiseur de miracles *m.*
miraculous *a.* miraculeux
mirage *n.* mirage *m.*
mire *n.* boue, fange *f.*; — *vi.* s'enfoncer dans la boue; s'embourber
mirror *n.* miroir *m.*, glace *f.*; rear-view — rétroviseur *m.*
mirth *n.* gaieté, joie *f.*
misadventure *n.* mésaventure *f.*
misalliance *n.* mésalliance *f.*
misanthrope *n.* misanthrope *m.*
misanthropic *a.* misanthrope
misapprehension *n.* méprise *f.*, malentendu *m.*
misappropriation *n.* détournement *m.*
misbehave *vi.* se comporter mal, se conduire mal
misbehavior *n.* mauvaise conduite *f.*
miscalculate *vt.* mal calculer; — *vi.* se tromper
miscalculation *n.* mécompte *m.*, erreur de calcul *f.*
miscarriage *n.* (med.) fausse couche *f.*; avortement, insuccès *m.*; — of justice erreur judiciaire *f.*
miscarry *vi.* (med.) faire une fausse cou-

che; avorter, manquer, échouer
miscellaneous *a.* divers, varié
miscellany *n.* mélanges *m. pl.*
mischief *n.* espièglerie *f.*; mauvais tour *m.*; mal *m.*; malice *f.*
mischievous *a.* espiègle, malicieux; méchant
misconception *n.* idée fausse *f.*
misconduct *n.* mauvaise conduite *f.*; mauvaise administration *f.*
misconstrue *vt.* mésinterpréter; mal prendre
miscount *n.* erreur d'addition *f.*
miscreant *n.* mécréant *m.*
misdeal *n.* (cards) maldonne *f.*; — *vt.* faire maldonne
misdeed *n.* méfait *m.*
misdemeanor *n.* délit *m.*
misdirect *vt.* mal diriger; mal renseigner
miser *n.* avare *m.*; **–ly** *a.* avare
miserable *a.* misérable; malheureux
misery *n.* misère *f.*; souffrance *f.*
misfire *vi.* rater
misfit *n.* vêtement manqué *m.*; (person) raté *m.*; déchu *m.*
misfortune *n.* malheur *m.*, infortune *f.*
misgiving *n.* appréhension, hésitation *f.*; doute *m.*
misguide *vt.* mal guider, égarer
mishap *n.* contretemps *m.*, mésaventure *f.*; accident *m.*
misinform *vt.* mal renseigner
misinterpret *vt.* mal interpréter; **–ation** *n.* fausse interprétation *f.*
misjudge *vt.* mal juger; méconnaître
mislay *vt.* égarer
mislead *vt. ir.* égarer, tromper; **–ing** *a.* trompeur
mismanage *vt.* mal conduire, mal administrer; **–ment** *n.* mauvaise administration *f.*
mismatch *vt.* mal assortir
misnomer *n.* faux nom *m.*; nom mal approprié *m.*
misplace *vt.* mal placer; déplacer; perdre
misprint *n.* faute d'impression *f.*
mispronounce *vt.* mal prononcer
misquote *vt.* citer à faux
misrepresent *vt.* mal représenter; travestir; **–ation** *n.* faux rapport *m.*, fausse déclaration *f.*
misrule *n.* désordre m.; mauvaise administration *f.*
miss *n.* mademoiselle *f.*; jeune fille, demoiselle *f.*
miss *n.* coup manqué, coup raté *m.*; — *vt.* manquer, rater; ne pas trouver; ne pas avoir; ne pas saisir; regretter; **–ing** *a.* absent; disparu; qui manque
misshapen *a.* difforme; déformé

missile *n.* projectile *m.*; (rocket) engin *m.*; guided — engin téléguidé *m.*; intercontinental — engin intercontinental *m.*
mission *n.* mission *f.*; **–ary** *a. & n.* missionnaire *m.*
misspell *vt.* mal épeler; **–ing** *n.* faute d'orthographe *f.*
misstate *n.* mal énoncer; annoncer à faux; **–ment** rapport inexact *m.*
misstep *n.* faux pas *m.*
mist *n.* brume *f.*; buée *f.*; voile *m.*; **–y** *a.* brumeux; vague
mistake *n.* faute, erreur *f.*; méprise *f.*; **by** — par erreur; **make a** — faire une faute; se tromper; — *vt.* se tromper; mal comprendre; **–n** *a.* erroné; dans l'erreur
mister, Mr. *n.* monsieur *m.*
mistranslation *n.* erreur de traduction *f.*; contre-sens *m.*
mistress *n.* maîtresse *f.*
mistrust *n.* méfiance, défiance *f.*; — *vt.* se méfier de; **–ful** *a.* méfiant
misunderstand *vt.* mal comprendre; mal interpréter; se méprendre; méconnaître; **–ing** *n.* malentendu; quiproquo *m.*
misuse *n.* abus *m.*; mauvais usage *m.*; — *vt.* faire mauvais usage
mite *n.* mite *f.*; brin *m.*, miette *f.*
mitigate *vt.* atténuer, mitiger; adoucir
mitigating *a.* atténuant
mitre *n.* onglet *m.*; (eccl.) mitre *f.*; — *vt.* tailler à onglet
mitten *n.* mitaine *f.*
mix *vt.* mêler, mélanger; confondre; composer; malaxer; — *vi.* se mêler, se mélanger; aller (bien) ensemble; **–ed** *a.* mêlé; mixte; assorti; **–er** *n.* agitateur *m.*; malaxeur, mixer *m.*; **–ture** *n.* mélange *m.*; mixture *f.*, (med.) potion *f.*
moan *n.* gémissement *m.*; — *vi.* gémir; — *vt.* dire en gémissant
moat *n.* fossé *m.*
mob *n.* foule, cohue *f.*; populace *m.*; canaille *f.*; — *vt.* faire foule autour de; — *vi.* s'ameuter; s'attrouper
mobile *a.* mobile; changeant; — **unit** *n.* groupe mobile *m.*
mobility *n.* mobilité *f.*
mobilization *n.* mobilisation *f.*
mobilize *vt.* mobiliser
moccasin *n.* mocassin *m.*
mocha *n.* moka *m.*
mock *a.* faux; factice; feint; d'imitation; (as prefix); simili–; — **tortoise-shell** *a.* écaille imitation *f.*; — **trial** *n.* simulacre de procès *m.*; — *vt.* se moquer de, railler; imiter; **–ery** *n.* moquerie, raillerie *f.*; **–ing** *a.* moqueur, railleur
modal *a.* modal
mode *n.* mode *m.*; manière *f.*; (fashion)

mode *f.*

model *n.* modèle *m.*; patron *m.*; maquette *f.*; (person) modèle *n.* & *f.*; — *a.* modèle; — *vt.* modeler; (clothes) exposer, montrer; **–ing** *n.* modelage *m.*

moderate *vt.* modérer; tempérer; — *vi.* se modérer; — *a.* modéré; raisonnable, mesuré; modique

moderation *n.* modération *f.*; mesure *f.*

moderator *n.* président, arbitre *m.*

modern *a.* moderne; — **languages** langues vivantes *f. pl.*; **–istic** *a.* moderne; **–ize** *vt.* moderniser

modest *a.* modeste; pudique; **–y** *n.* modestie *f.*; pudeur *f.*

modicum *n.* petite quantité *f.*; un peu *m.*

modification *n.* modification *f.*

modify *vt.* modifier

modulate *vt.* & *vi.* moduler

modulation *n.* modulation *f.*

module *n.* module *m.*

Mohammedan *a.* & *n.* mahométan *m.*; **–ism** *n.* mahométisme *m.*

moist *a.* humide, moite; mouillé; **–en** *vt.* mouiller, humecter, moitir; **–ness** *n.* humidité *f.*; moiteur *f.*; **–ure** *n.* humidité *f.*

molar *a.* & *n.* molaire *f.*

molasses *n.* mélasse *f.*

mold *n.* moule *m.*, matrice *f.*; moisissure *f.*, moisi *m.*; — *vt.* mouler; pétrir; — *vi.* moisir; **–er** *vi.* tomber en poussière; **–iness** *n.* moisissure *f.*; **–ing** *n.* moulage *m.*; moulure *f.*; **–y** *a.* moisi

mole *n.* grain de beauté *m.*

molecular *a.* moléculaire; — **biology** *n.* biologie moléculaire *f.*

molecule *n.* molécule *f.*

molehill *n.* taupinière *f.*

moleskin *n.* moleskine *f.*

molest *vt.* molester

mollify *vt.* apaiser

mollusk *n.* mollusque *m.*

molt *vi.* muer; **–ing** *a.* en mue; **–ing** *n.* mue *f.*

molten *a.* fondu

molybdenum *n.* molybdène *m.*

moment *n.* moment, instant *m.*; importance *f.*; (fig.) heure *f.*; **at the** — en ce moment, pour le moment; **of** — important; **–ary** *a.* momentané; **–ous** *a.* très important

momentum *n.* force vive *f.*, moment *m.*; vitesse *f.*

Monacan *a.* & *n.* monégasque *m.*

Monaco *n.* Monaco *m.*

monarch *n.* monarque *m.*; **–ic** *a.* monarchique; **–ist** *n.* monarchiste *m.*; **–y** *n.* monarchie *f.*

monastery *n.* monastère *m.*

monastic *a.* monastique

Monday *n.* lundi *m.*

monetary *a.* monétaire

money *n.* argent *m.*; monnaie *f.*; espèces *f. pl.*; **counterfeit** — fausse monnaie *f.*; — **belt** ceinture à porte-monnaie *f.*; — **box** caisse *f.*; — **order** mandat-poste *m.*; **–ed** *a.* riche, opulent

Mongol *n.* Mongol *m.*; **–ia** *n.* Mongolie *f.*; **–ian** *a.* mongol, mongolique

mongrel *n.* bâtard *m.*; métis *m.*

monitor *vt.* contrôler, écouter; — *n.* moniteur *m.*; (school) pion *m.*; détecteur *m.*; contrôleur *m.*; **–ing** *n.* écoute *f.*; contrôle *f.*

monk *n.* moine, religieux *m.*

monkey *n.* singe *m.*; guenon *f.*; — **wrench** clé anglaise *f.*

monochromatic *a.* monochrome

monogamous *a.* monogame

monogamy *n.* monogamie *f.*

monogram *n.* chiffre, monogramme *m.*

monograph *n.* monographie *f.*

monolithic *a.* monolithe

monologue *n.* monologue *m.*

monomania *n.* monomanie *f.*; **–c** *n.* monomane *m.* & *f.*

monoplane *n.* monoplan *m.*

monopolistic *a.* de monopole, monopoleur

monopolize *vt.* monopoliser; accaparer

monopoly *n.* monopole *m.*

monorail *n.* monorail *m.*

monosyllabic *a.* monosyllabique

monotonous *a.* monotone

monotony *n.* monotonie *f.*

monoxide *n.* protoxyde *m.*; **carbon** — sous-oxyde de carbone *m.*

monsoon *n.* mousson *f.*

monster *n.* monstre *m.*

monstrance *n.* (eccl.) ostensoir *m.*

monstrosity *n.* monstruosité *f.*; monstre *m.*; énormité *f.*

monstrous *a.* monstrueux; **–ness** *n.* monstruosité *f.*

month *n.* mois *m.*; **by the** — au mois; **–'s pay** mois *m.*; **once a** — une fois par mois, mensuellement; **–ly** *a.* mensuel; **–ly payment** mensualité *f.*; **–ly** *adv.* une fois par mois, mensuellement

monument *n.* monument *m.*; **–al** *a.* monumental

moo *vi.* meugler, beugler

mood *n.* disposition, humeur *f.*; (gram.) mode *m.*; **–iness** *n.* humeur changeante *f.*; **–y** *a.* d'humeur changeante; maussade

moon *n.* lune *f.*; — *vi.* musarder

moonbeam *n.* rayon de lune *m.*

moonlight *n.* clair de lune *m.*

moon-struck, moon-stricken *a.* lunatique

moor *n.* bruyère, lande *f.*; — *vt.* amarrer;

— *vi.* s'amarrer; **–ing** *n.* amarrage *m.*; (rope) amarre *f.*

Moor *n.* Maure *m.*, Mauresque *f.*; **–ish** *a.* mauresque, maure, des Maures

moors *n. pl.* landes *f. pl.*, bruyère *f.*

moot *a.* discutable; — **court** *n.* procès simulé *m.*

mop *n.* guipon *m.*; — **of hair** tignasse *f.*; — *vt.* nettoyer avec un guipon; essuyer; éponger

mope *vi.* rêver; s'ennuyer

moral *a.* moral; — *n.* morale, moralité *f.*; **–s** *pl.* moralité *f.*; **–ist** *n.* moraliste *m. & f.*; **–ity** *n.* moralité *f.*; bonnes mœurs *f. pl.*; **–ize** *vi.* moraliser; **–ly** *adv.* moralement

morass *n.* marais *m.*

morbid *a.* morbide; maladif

more *a.* plus de; encore de, encore un; d'autres; — *n.* davantage; — *adv.* plus; davantage; **all the** — d'autant plus; — **and** — de plus en plus; **once** — encore une fois; **no** — ne . . . plus (de)

moreover *adv.* d'ailleurs, du reste

mores *n. pl.* mœurs *f. pl.*

moribund *a.* moribond

Mormon *n.* Mormon *m.*

morning *n.* matin *m.*; matinée *f.*; **good** — bonjour; **in the** — le matin; (clock time) du matin; **the next** — le lendemain matin *m.*

Moroccan *a. & n.* marocain *m.*

Morocco *n.* Maroc *m.*; — **leather** maroquin *m.*; — **leather goods** maroquinerie *f.*

moron *n.* idiot *m.*

morose *a.* morose; **–ness** *n.* morosité *f.*

morphology *n.* morphologie *f.*

Morse code *n.* alphabet Morse *m.*

morsel *n.* morceau *m.*

mortal *a.* mortel; fatal; à mort; — *n.* mortel *m.*; **–ity** *n.* mortalité *f.*; **–ly** *adv.* mortellement; à mort

mortar *n.* mortier *m.*; enduit *m.*

mortgage *n.* hypothèque *f.*; — *vt.* hypothéquer

mortician *n.* entrepreneur de pompes funèbres *m.*

mortification *n.* mortification *f.*; gangrène *f.*

mortify *vt.* mortifier; humilier; — *vi.* se mortifier; se gangrener

mortuary *a.* mortuaire; — *n.* morgue *f.*

mosaic *n.* mosaïque *f.*; — *a.* en mosaïque

Moscow *n.* Moscou *m.*

Moslem *a. & n.* mahométan, musulman *m.*

mosque *n.* mosquée *f.*

mosquito *n.* moustique *m.*; — **net** *n.* moustiquaire *f.*

moss *n.* mousse *f.*; **–y** *a.* moussu

most *a.* la plupart de; le plus de; — *n.* le plus *m.*; la plupart; — *adv.* le plus; très; **–ly** *adv.* pour la plupart

moth *n.* mite *f.*; papillon de nuit *m.*; phalène *f.*; **–y** *a.* mité

mothball *n.* boule de naphtaline *f.*

moth-eaten *a.* mité

mother *n.* mère *f.*; maman *f.*; — **tongue** langue maternelle *f.*; — *vt.* dorloter; **–hood** *n.* maternité *f.*; **–less** *a.* sans mère; **–ly** *a.* maternel

mother-in-law *n.* belle-mère *f.*

mother-of-pearl *n.* nacre *f.*

motion *n.* mouvement *m.*; signe *m.*; (debate) motion, proposition *f.*; — **picture** film *m.*; — **pictures** *n. pl.* cinéma *m.*; **set in** — mettre en marche, mettre en mouvement; — *vt. & vi.* faire signe; **–less** *a.* immobile

motion-picture *a.* cinématographique; **du cinéma**; — **camera** *n.* caméra *m.*

motivate *vt.* motiver

motive *a.* moteur (motrice); — *n.* motif, mobile *m.*

motley *a.* bigarré, bariolé

motor *a.* moteur (motrice); automobile; — *n.* moteur *m.*; **–cade** *n.* défilé de voitures *m.*; — **launch** *n.* chaloupe à moteur *m.*; — *vi.* aller en auto; **–ist** *n.* automobiliste *m. & f.*; **–ize** *vt.* motoriser

motorbike *n.* cyclomoteur *m.*

motorboat *n.* canot automobile *m.*, vedette *f.*

motorcade *n.* défilé (d'autos) *m.*

motorcycle *n.* moto, motocyclette *f.*

motorman *n.* wattman *m.*

mottle *vt.* marbrer; tacheter; **–d** *a.* marbré

motto *n.* devise *f.*

mound *n.* monticule *m.*, tertre *m.*; tas *m.*

mount *n.* mont *m.*, montagne *f.*; montage *m.*; armement *m.*; (horse) monture, monte *f.*; — *vt.* monter (sur); gravir; armer; — *vi.* monter; monter à cheval; — **up** croître; **–ed** *a.* à cheval; monté; **–ing** *n.* montage *m.*; garniture *f.*

mountain *n.* montagne *f.*; — *a.* des montagnes; montagneux; (person) montagnard; — **range** chaîne de montagnes; — **climber** *n.* alpiniste *m. & f.*; — **climbing** *n.* alpinisme *m.*; **–eer** *n.* alpiniste *m. & f.*; **–ous** *a.* montagneux

mountebank *n.* charlatan *m.*

mourn *vt. & vi.* pleurer, déplorer; **–er** *n.* affligé *m.*; personne qui est en deuil *f.*; **–ful** *a.* funèbre, lugubre; **–ing** *a.* en deuil; **–ing** *n.* deuil *m.*, affliction *f.*

mouse *n.* souris *f.*; — **trap** *n.* souricière *f.*

moustache, mustache *n.* moustache *f.*

mouth *n.* bouche *f.*; gueule *f.*; ouverture *f.*;

(river) embouchure *f.*; — organ harmonica *m.*; — wash dentifrice *m.*; — *vt. & vi.* déclamer; –ful *n.* bouchée *f.*

mouthpiece *n.* embouchure *f.*; bec, bocal *m.*

movable *a.* mobile; mobilier

move *n.* mouvement *m.*; (household) déménagement *m.*; (chess) coup *m.*; — *vt.* bouger, remuer; pousser; mouvoir; émouvoir, toucher; attendrir; déménager; (debate) proposer; (chess) jouer; — *vi.* bouger; se mouvoir, se déplacer; jouer; — off s'éloigner; — on continuer son chemin; — out déménager; –ment *n.* mouvement *m.*; transport *m.*; déplacement *m.*; –r *n.* moteur *m.*; déménageur *m.*

moving *a.* en marche, en mouvement; moteur, motrice; attendrissant; émouvant; — *n.* déménagement *m.*

mow *vt.* faucher; (lawn) tondre; –er *n.* faucheuse *f.*; (lawn) tondeuse *f.*; (person) faucheur *m.*

Mrs.: Mistress, Mme. *n.* madame *f.*

much *a.* beaucoup (de); bien (de); — *adv.* beaucoup; bien; as — autant (de); how — combien de; so — tant (de); too — trop (de); very — beaucoup

mucilage *n.* mucilage *m.*, colle *f.*

muck *n.* fange *f.*; crotte *f.*

mucous *a.* muqueux

mucus *n.* mucus *m.*

mud *n.* boue *f.*; fange *f.*; vase *f.*; –dy *a.* boueux, fangeux, vaseux; (liquid) trouble

muddle *n.* confusion *f.*; — *vt.* brouiller, embrouiller

mudguard *n.* garde-boue *m.*

muff *n.* manchon *m.*; — *vt.* rater, louper, gâcher

muffin *n.* galette *f.*; (sorte de) brioche *f.*

muffle *vt.* envelopper; emmitoufler; étouffer; –r *n.* cache-nez *m.*; (auto) pot d'échappement *m.*

mufti *n.* tenue de ville *f.*; in — en civil

mug *n.* pot *m.*, chope *f.*

muggy *a.* chaud et humide; lourd

mulatto *n.* mulâtre *m.*, mulâtresse *f.*

mule *n.* mulet *m.*, mule *f.*; –teer *n.* muletier *m.*

mulish *a.* obstiné, entêté

mull *vt.* (wine) chauffer avec des épices; — (coll.) méditer, ruminer; –ed wine vin chaud, vin chauffé *m.*

mullet *n.* (fish) mulet *m.*; red — rouget *m.*

multicolored *a.* multicolore

multigraph *n.* multigraphe *m.*, machine à imprimer *f.*

multimillionaire *n.* multimillionaire, milliardaire *m. & f.*

multiple *a. & n.* multiple *m.*

multiple sclerosis *n.* sclérose multiple *f.*

multiplication *n.* multiplication *f.*

multiplicity *n.* multiplicité *f.*

multiply *vt.* multiplier; — *vi.* se multiplier

multitude *n.* multitude *f.*; foule *f.*

mumble *vt. & vi.* marmotter; marmonner

mummify *vt.* momifier

mummy *n.* momie *f.*

mumps *n.* oreillons *m. pl.*

munch *vt.* mâcher, mâchonner, croquer

mundane *a.* du monde, mondain

municipal *a.* municipal; –ity *n.* municipalité *f.*

munificence *n.* munificence *f.*

munificent *a.* munificent, généreux

munitions *n. pl.* munitions *f. pl.*

murder *n.* meurtre *m.*; assassinat *m.*; — *vt.* assassiner; –er *n.* meurtrier, assassin *m.*; –ous *a.* meurtrier, assassin

murky *a.* brouillé; ténébreux

murmur *n.* murmure *m.*; — *vt. & vi.* murmurer, parler à voix basse

Murphy-bed *n.* (trademark) lit escamotable *m.*

muscatel *n.* muscat *m.*

muscle *n.* muscle *m.*

muscle-bound *a.* aux muscles raides

muscular *a.* musculaire; musculeux, musclé; –ity *n.* constitution musculaire *f.*

muse *n.* muse *f.*; — *vi.* méditer, rêver

museum *n.* musée *m.*

mush *n.* polenta *f.*; –y *a.* mollet, mou; (fig.) sentimental

mushroom *n.* champignon *m.*; — *vi.* faire champignon

music *n.* musique *f.*; — box boîte à musique *f.*; –al *a.* de musique; musical; mélodieux; –al comedy *n.* opérette *f.*; –ale *n.* soirée musicale *f.*; –ian *n.* musicien *m.*, musicienne *f.*

musing *n.* méditation, rêverie *f.*

musket *n.* mousquet *m.*; –eer *n.* mousquetaire *m.*

muskmelon *n.* cantaloup *m.*

muskrat *n.* rat musqué *m.*

muslin *n.* mousseline *f.*

muss *n.* désordre *m.*; — *vt.* mettre en désordre; froisser

mussei *n.* moule *f.*

must *n.* nécessité *f.*; — *vt.* devoir; falloir; I — je dois; il me faut, il faut que je . . . .

must *n.* moisi *m.*; –iness *n.* relent *m.*; odeur de moisi *f.*; –y *a.* de moisi, de relent; qui sent le renfermé

mustard *n.* moutarde *f.*; — gas *n.* gaz moutarde *m.*; — pot *n.* moutardier *m.*; — plaster *n.* cataplasme *m.*; sinapisme *m.*

muster n. revue f.; assemblée f.; rassemblement m.; — vt. rassembler; (mil.) passer en revue

mustiness n. moisi m.; renfermé m.

mutability n. mutabilité f.

mutable a. changeant, instable

mutant n. mutante f.

mutation n. changement m.

mute a. muet (muette); — n. muet m., (mus.) sourdine f.; — vt. amortir, assourdir; –d a. en sourdine; –ness n. mutisme m.

mutilate vt. mutiler, estropier

mutilation n. mutilation f.

mutineer n. mutin m.; revolté m.

mutinous a. mutin; séditieux

mutiny n. mutinerie f.; — vi. se mutiner

mutter vt. & vi. marmotter, marmonner

mutton n. mouton m.

mutual a. réciproque, mutuel; commun; — aid n. entr'aide f.

muzzle n. museau m.; muselière; (gun) bouche f.; — vt. museler

my pron. mon, ma, mes; —! interj. tiens!; –self pron. me; moi; moi-même

myopia n. myopie f.

myopic a. myope

myriad n. myriade f.

mysterious a. mystérieux; –ness n. mystère m.

mystery n. mystère m.

mystic a. mystique; occulte; — n. mystique m. & f.; –al a. mystique; –ism n. mysticisme m.

mystify vt. mystifier

myth n. mythe m.; –ical a. mythique; –ological a. mythologique; –ology n. mythologie f.

N

nab vt. arrêter, saisir, pincer

nacelle n. (avi.) nacelle f.

nag n. bidet m.; — vt. & vi. gronder, quereller; –ging a. grondeur, querelleur; agaçant

nail n. clou m.; (finger) ongle m.; — file lime à ongles f.; — vt. clouer; clouter

naive a. naïf

naked a. nu; découvert; –ness n. nudité f.

name n. nom m.; réputation f., renom m.; by — de nom; Christian —, first — prénom, nom de baptême m.; family — nom, nom de famille m.; maiden — nom de demoiselle m.; nick — sobriquet n.; my — is je m'appelle; — vt. nommer; citer; be –d s'appeler, se nommer; —less a. sans nom; anonyme; –ly adv. c'est-à-dire; à savoir

name plate n. plaque; étiquette, marque f.

namesake n. homonyme m.

nap n. somme m.; (cloth) poil, duvet m.; — vi. sommeiller

nape n. nuque f.

naphtha n. naphte m.

napkin n. serviette f.; — ring n. rond de serviette m.

narcotic a. & n. narcotique, stupéfiant m.

narrate vt. raconter, narrer

narration n. narration f.

narrator n. narrateur m.

narrow a. étroit; borné; faible; have a — escape l'échapper belle; — vt. borner, rétrécir; — vi. devenir plus étroit; se rétrécir; –ness n. étroitesse f.

narrow-minded a. borné, à l'esprit étroit; –ness n. étroitesse d'esprit f.

narrows n. détroit m.

nasal a. nasal; nasillard; –ize vt. nasaliser

nasty a. désagréable; vilain, sale; mauvais; méchant

natal a. natal, de naissance

nation n. nation f.; pays m.; –al a. national; de la nation; –alism n. nationalisme m.; –alist n. nationaliste m. & f.; –ality n. nationalité f.; –alization n. nationalisation f.; –alize vt. nationaliser

nationwide a. national, de toute la nation, à travers toute la nation, à travers le pays

native n. natif m., native f.; indigène m. & f.; originaire m. & f.; — a. natal; de naissance; indigène, originaire; inné, naturel; — land patrie f.; pays natal m.; — language langue maternelle f.

nativity n. nativité f.

natural a. naturel; inné; de la nature; — n. (mus.) bécarre m.; –ism n. naturalisme m.; –ist n. naturaliste m. & f.; –ization n. naturalisation f.; –ize vt. naturaliser; –ly adv. naturellement; de nature; –ness n. naturel m.

nature n. nature f.; naturel m.; tempérament m.; genre m., sorte, espèce f.; by — de nature; par tempérament; from — (art) d'après nature; — study n. histoire naturelle f.

naughty a. méchant, mauvais; espiègle

nausea n. nausée f.; mal au cœur m.; –te vt. écœurer; –ting a. écœurant, nauséabond

nauseous a. nauséabond

nautical a. nautique, marin

naval a. naval; de marine

nave n. nef f.

navel n. nombril m.

navigable a. navigable

navigate vi. naviguer; — vt. naviguer, gouverner

navigation n. navigation f.

navigator *n.* navigateur *m.*
navy *n.* marine *f.*; flotte *f.*; — bean *n.* haricot *m.*; — blue *a.* bleu foncé, bleu marine *m.*; — yard arsenal maritime *n.*
Nazi *a. & n.* nazi *m.*; –sm *n.* nazisme *m.*
near *a.* proche; — *adv.* près; proche; — *prep.* près de; auprès de; — *vt.* s'approcher de; –ly *adv.* à peu près; presque; près de; –ness *n.* proximité *f.*
nearby *adv.* tout près
nearsighted *a.* myope
neat *a.* soigné; rangé; net (nette); sec; –ness *n.* (bon) ordre *m.*; netteté *f.*
nebula *n.* nébuleuse *f.*
nebulous *a.* nébuleux
necessary *a.* nécessaire; indispensable; if — au besoin, s'il le faut; it is — il faut
necessitate *vt.* nécessiter
necessity *n.* nécessité *f.*; besoin *m.*
neck *n.* cou *m.*; (bottle) goulot *m.*; (dress) encolure *f.*; (land) langue *f.*
neckband *n.* collet de chemise *m.*
necklace *n.* collier *m.*; parure *f.*
necktie *n.* cravate *f.*
neckwear *n.* cravates *f. pl.*; foulards *m. pl.*
necromancy *n.* nécromancie *f.*
nectar *n.* nectar *m.*; –ine *n.* brugnon *m.*
need *n.* besoin *m.*; nécessité *f.*; indigence *f.*; — *vt.* avoir besoin de; falloir, manquer; –less *a.* inutile; –iness *n.* indigence *f.*; –y *a.* nécessiteux; indigent
needle *n.* aiguille *f.*
needlework *n.* ouvrage à l'aiguille *m.*
nefarious *a.* infâme
negation *n.* négation *f.*
negative *a.* négatif; — *n.* négative *f.*; (phot.) négatif *m.*; (gram.) négation *f.*
neglect *n.* négligence *f.*; inattention *f.*; — *vt.* négliger; omettre; –ed *a.* négligé; à l'abandon; –ful *a.* négligent
negligee *n.* négligé *m.*
negligence *n.* négligence *f.*
negligent *a.* négligent
negligible *a.* négligeable
negotiable *a.* négociable
negotiate *vt.* négocier; conclure; surmonter
negotiation *n.* négociation *f.*; in — with en pourparlers avec
negotiator *n.* négociateur *m.*
Negress *n.* négresse *f.*
Negro *a. & n.* nègre *m.*
neigh *n.* hennissement *m.*; — *vi.* hennir
neighbor *n.* voisin *m.*; (fig.) autrui *m.*; prochain *m.*; –hood *n.* voisinage *m.*; quartier *m.*; environs, alentours *m. pl.*; –ing *a.* voisin, proche; –ly *a.* amical
neither *conj.* ni; — *adv.* ni; non plus; — *pron.* ni; — . . . . nor ni . . . . ni
neon *n.* néon *m.*; — *a.* au néon; — sign *n.* enseigne au néon *f.*

neophyte *n.* néophyte *m.*
nephew *n.* neveu *m.*
nepotism *n.* népotisme *m.*
nerve *n.* nerf *m.*; sang-froid *m.*; (coll.) toupet *m.*; — cell *n.* cellule nerveuse *f.*; — center *n.* centre nerveux *m.*; — fibre *n.* fibre nerveuse *f.*
nerve-racking *a.* énervant
nervous *a.* nerveux; irrité; énervé; inquiet; –ness *n.* nervosité *f.*; inquiétude *f.*; — system *n.* système nerveux *m.*
nest *n.* nid *m.*; nichée *f.*; — egg nichet *m.*; bas de laine *m.*; — *vi.* (se) nicher; –le *vi.* se nicher; se serrer
net *n.* filet *m.*; réseau *m.*, tulle *m.*; — *vt.* prendre au filet; (com.) rapporter net; — *a.* net
Netherlands *n. pl.* Hollande *f.*; Pays-Bas
nettle *n.* ortie *f.*; — *vt.* piquer, irriter
network *n.* réseau *m.*; système *m.*
neuralgia *n.* névralgie *f.*
neuritis *n.* névrite *f.*
neurologist *n.* nevrologue *m.*
neurology *n.* névrologie *f.*
neurosis *n.* névrose *f.*
neurotic *a. & n.* névrotique, névrosé *m.*
neuter *a.* neutre
neutral *a. & n.* neutre; — *n.* (auto.) point mort *m.*; –ity *n.* neutralité *f.*; –ize *vt.* neutraliser
neutron *n.* neutron *m.*
never *adv.* jamais, ne . . . jamais; — mind n'importe
never ending *a.* perpétuel, éternel, sans fin
nevertheless *conj.* néanmoins, cependant, pourtant, toutefois; quand même
new *a.* nouveau (nouvelle); neuf (neuve); –ly *adv.* récemment, fraîchement; –ness *n.* nouveauté *f.*; inexpérience *f.*; –s *pl.* nouvelles *f. pl.*; piece of –s nouvelle *f.*
newborn *a.* nouveau-né
New Caledonia *n.* Nouvelle Calédonie *f.*
newcomer *n.* nouveau venu *m.*
Newfoundland *n.* Terre-Neuve *f.*
New Hebrides *n.* Nouvelles Hébrides *f. pl.*
newlywed *n.* nouveau marié *m.*, nouvelle mariée *f.* –s nouveaux mariés *m. pl.*
New Orleans *n.* La Nouvelle Orléans *f.*
newsboy *n.* crieur de journaux *m.*
newscast *n.* bulletin d'informations, journal parlé *m.*; –er *n.* rédacteur de journal parlé *m.*
newspaper *n.* journal *m.*
newsprint *n.* papier de journal *m.*
newsreel *n.* actualités *f. pl.*
newsstand *n.* kiosque *m.*
newsworthy *a.* d'actualité
New Year *n.* nouvel an *m.*; –'s Day jour de l'an *m.*

New Zealand *n.* Nouvelle Zélande *f.*; — *a.* néo-zélandais

New Zealander *n.* Néo-Zélandais *m.*

next *a.* prochain; voisin; d'à côté; suivant; — **day** lendemain *m.*; — **door** à côté; dans la maison voisine; — **morning** lendemain matin *m.*; — *adv.* après; ensuite, puis; — *n.* suivant *m.*; — *prep.* auprès de, à côté de

nibble *vt. & vi.* grignoter; mordre; — *n.* grignotement, petit morceau *m.*

Nicaragua *n.* Nicaragua *m.*

nice *a.* gentil (gentille); aimable; agréable; sympathique; bon; **–ly** *adv.* gentiment; agréablement; bien; **–ty** *n.* finesse *f.*; minutie *f.*

nick *n.* coche, encoche, entaille *f.*; **in the** — **of time** à pic; juste à point; — *vt.* encocher, entailler

nickel *n.* nickel *m.*; pièce de cinq cents *f.*

nickel-plated *a.* nickelé

nickname *n.* sobriquet *m.*

niece *n.* nièce *f.*

Nigeria *n.* Nigérie *f.*

niggardly *a.* mesquin, chiche

nigh *a.* proche, près; **well** — à peu près; — *adv.* presque; de près

night *n.* nuit *f.*; soir *m.*; **at** — la nuit *f.*; **by** — de nuit; **good** — bonsoir; (before retiring) bonne nuit; **last** — hier soir; **cette nuit; the** — **before** la veille au soir; — **club** *n.* boîte de nuit *f.*, cabaret *m.*; — **letter** télégramme de nuit (tarif priorité) *m.*; — **light** veilleuse *f.*; — **watchman** veilleur de nuit *m.*; **–ly** *a. & adv.* tous les soirs

nightblindness *n.* nyctalopie *f.*

nightcap *n.* bonnet de nuit *m.*; (coll.) boisson alcoolique prise avant de se coucher *f.*

nightfall *n.* tombée de la nuit *f.*; **at** — à la nuit tombante

nightgown *n.* chemise de nuit *f.*

nightmare *n.* cauchemar *m.*

nightshirt *n.* chemise de nuit *f.*

nighttime *n.* nuit *f.*

nihilist *n.* nihiliste *m.*

nil *n.* nul, zéro *m.*

Nile *n.* Nil *m.*

nimble *a.* leste, agile

nimbus *n.* nimbe *m.*; (cloud) nimbus *m.*

nincompoop *n.* sot, niais *m.*

nine *a.* neuf *f.*; **–teen** *a.* dix-neuf; **–teenth** *a.* dix-neuvième; **–tieth** *a.* quatre-vingt-dixième; **–ty** *a.* quatre-vingt-dix

ninth *a.* neuvième

nip *n.* pincement *m.*; morsure *f.*; goutte *f.*; — *vt.* pincer; piquer; mordre; — **in the bud** étouffer dans le germe; **–per** *n.* pince *f.*

nipple *n.* mamelon *m.*; (bottle) tétine *f.*

niter, nitre *n.* nitre, salpêtre *m.*

nitrate *n.* nitrate, azotate *m.*

nitric *a.* nitrique, azotique

nitrocellulose *n.* nitrocellulose *f.*

nitrogen *n.* azote *m.*

nitroglycerin *n.* nitroglycérine *f.*

nitrous *a.* nitreux, azoteux

no *adv.* non; — *a.* pas de; aucun, nul; ne . . . . pas; peu; **by** — **means** pas du tout; en aucune façon; **in** — **way** en aucune façon; — **one** personne; — **smoking** défense de fumer; — *n.* non *m.*; voix contre *f.*

nobility *n.* noblesse *f.*

noble *a.* noble; grand; — *n.* noble *m.*; **–ness** *n.* noblesse *f.*; grandeur *f.*

nobleman *n.* noble *m.*

noblewoman *n.* femme noble *f.*

nobly *adv.* noblement; superbement

nobody *pron.* personne; — *n.* nullité *f.*

nocturnal *a.* nocturne

nod *n.* signe de tête *m.*; inclination de tête *f.*; — *vt.* faire un signe de tête; incliner la tête

node *n.* nœud *m.*

nodule *n.* nodule *m.*

noise *n.* bruit *m.*; fracas, vacarme *m.*; son *m.*; **make** — faire du bruit; **–less** *a.* sans bruit; **–lessly** *adv.* sans bruit; silencieusement

noisily *adv.* bruyamment

noisiness *n.* grand bruit, tumulte *m.*

noisome *a.* infect, dégoûtant

noisy *a.* bruyant

nomad *n.* nomade *m. & f.*; **–ic** *a.* nomade

nomenclature *n.* nomenclature *f.*

nominal *a.* nominal; de nom

nominate *vt.* nommer, désigner; proposer

nomination *n.* nomination *f.*

nominative *a. & n.* nominatif *m.*

nominee *n.* candidat *m.*

nonacceptance *n.* refus *m.*, non-acceptation *f.*

nonaggression *n.* non-agression *f.*

nonattendance *n.* absence *f.*

nonchalant *a.* nonchalant

noncompliance *n.* refus d'acquiescer *m.*

noncombatant *n.* non-combattant *m.*

noncommissioned *a.* sans brevet; — **officer** gradé, sous-officier *m.*

noncommittal *a.* qui n'engage à rien

nonconductor *n.* non-conducteur *m.*

nonconformist *a. & n.* dissident *m.*

nondescript *a.* hétéroclite; inclassable

none *pron.* aucun, nul; personne; rien; — **too soon** juste à temps, juste à point

nonentity *n.* nullité *f.*

nonessential *a.* non-essentiel, peu essentiel

nonexistent a. non-existent, fictif
nonintervention n. non-intervention f.
nonobservance n. inobservance f.
nonpareil a. sans pareil
nonpayment n. non-payement m.
nonplussed a. confus, étourdi
nonresistance n. obéissance passive f.
nonsectarian a. sans esprit sectaire; sans prévention religieuse
nonsense n. non-sens m., absurdité f.
nonsensical a. absurde
nonstop a. & adv. sans arrêt; (avi.) sans escale
nonsupport n. non-support m.
nonunion a. non-syndiqué
noodle n. nouille f.
nook n. coin, recoin, enfoncement m.
noon n. midi m.; **-day** a. de midi
noose n. corde f.; (trap) lacs, nœud coulant m.
nor conj. ni; **neither . . . . — ni . . . . ni**
Nordic a. nordique
norm n. norme f.; **-al** a. normal; ordinaire; **-al school** n. école normale f.; **-alcy** n. normalité f.; **-ally** adv. normalement; d'ordinaire
Norman a. & n. normand m.; **-dy** n. Normandie f.
Norse a. norvégien m.; **-man** n. Norvégien m.
north n. nord m.; **— a.** nord, du nord; septentrional; **— adv.** au nord, vers le nord; **-erly** a. au nord, vers le nord; **-ern** a. du nord; septentrional
North America n. Amérique du Nord f.
northeast a. & n. nord-est m.; **— adv.** vers le nord-est
North Pole n. pôle du nord m.
northward a. au nord, du nord; **-s** adv. vers le nord
northwest a. & n. nord-ouest m.; **— adv.** vers le nord-ouest
Norway n. Norvège f.
Norwegian a. & n. norvégien m.
nose n. nez m.; (animals) museau m.; (ballistics) cône m.; **blow one's —** se moucher; **hold one's —** se boucher le nez; **lead by the —** mener par le bout du nez
nosebleed n. saignement du nez m.
nose dive vi. piquer du nez; **— n.** piquage du nez m.; piqué m.
nostalgia n. nostalgie f.
nostril n. narine f.; (horse) naseau m.
nostrum n. panacée f.
not adv. pas; point; ne . . . . pas; **— at all** pas du tout; **— including** sans compter; **— that** ce n'est pas que
notability n. notabilité f.

notable a. notable; remarquable; considérable; éminent; **— n.** notable m.
notably adv. notamment
notary n. notaire m.
notation n. notation f.
notch n. encoche, entaille f.; **— vt.** encocher, entailler
note n. note f.; annotation f.; remarque m.; billet, mot m., lettre f.; renom m.; son m.; (mus.) caractère m.; (piano) touche f.; **make a —** of prendre note de; **take -s** prendre des notes; **— vt.** noter, constater, remarquer; **-d** a. éminent, distingué; remarquable;
notebook n. cahier, carnet m.; **loose-leaf — n.** cahier à feuilles mobiles m.; **— filler** n. feuilles mobiles f. pl.
noteworthy a. digne d'attention
nothing n. rien m.; ne . . . . rien; rien de; zéro m.; **— but** rien que; **— else** rien d'autre; **-ness** n. néant m.
notice n. avis, avertissement m.; délai m.; affiche f.; annonce f.; attention f.; revue f.; **at short —** du jour au lendemain; à court délai; à l'instant; **give —** (to employee) donner son congé à; (to employer) donner sa démission; **take — of** faire attention à; tenir compte de; **until further —** jusqu'à nouvel avis; **— vt.** observer, remarquer, tenir compte de; **-able** a. qui se voit; perceptible, sensible
notification n. notification, faire-part m.
notify vt. notifier, faire savoir
notion n. notion, pensée, opinion f.; **-s** pl. mercerie f.
notoriety n. notoriété, évidence f.
notorious a. notoire; fameux; **-ness** n. notoriété f.
notwithstanding prep. & adv. nonobstant; **— conj.** bien que
nougat n. nougat m.
nought n. rien, néant m.; zéro m.
noun n. nom, substantif m.
nourish vt. nourrir; **-ment** n. nourriture f.; **-ing** a. nutritif
novel n. roman m.; **— a.** nouveau, neuf; **-ist** n. romancier m.; **-ty** n. nouveauté f.
November n. novembre m.
novena n. neuvaine f.
novice n. novice m.
novitiate n. noviciat m.
novocaine n. novocaïne f.
now adv. à présent, maintenant; **by —** à l'heure qu'il est; **just —** pour le moment; **— and then, — and again** de temps; **until —** jusqu'ici; **— interj.** or; eh bien; tiens
nowadays adv. de nos jours
nowhere adv. nulle part
noxious a. nuisible; pernicieux

nozzle *n.* lance *f.*, bec *m.*
nuance *n.* nuance *f.*
nuclear *a.* nucléaire
nucleic *a.* nucléique
nucleus *n.* noyau *m.*
nude *a.* nu
nudge *n.* coup de coude *m.*; — *vt.* pousser légèrement (du coude)
nudism *n.* nudisme *m.*
nudist *n.* nudiste *m. & f.*
nudity *n.* nudité *f.*
nugget *n.* pépite *f.*
nuisance *n.* incommodité *f.*; ennui *m.*
null *a.* nul, non valide; –ification *n.* annulation *f.*; –ify *vt.* annuler
numb *vt.* engourdir; — *a.* engourdi; –ness *n.* engourdissement *m.*
number *n.* nombre *m.*, quantité *f.*; numéro *m.*; chiffre *m.*; — *vt.* numéroter; –ing *n.* numérotage, calcul *m.*; –ing *a.* au nombre de; –ing machine *n.* numéroteur *m.*; –less *a.* innombrable
numeral *n.* chiffre *m.*; — *a.* numéral
numerator *n.* numérateur *m.*
numerical *a.* numérique
numerous *a.* nombreux
numskull, numbskull *n.* sot, lourdaud *m.*
nun *n.* nonne, religieuse *f.*; –nery *n.* couvent (de femmes) *m.*
nuncio *n.* (eccl.) nonce *m.*
nuptial *a.* nuptial; –s *n. pl.* noces *f. pl.*
nurse *n.* infirmière *f.*; garde-malade *f.*; male — infirmier *m.*; wet — nourrice *f.*; — *vt.* nourrir (au sein); soigner; — *vi.* téter; –ry *n.* chambre d'enfants *f.*; (bot.) pépinière *f.*; –ry school jardin d'enfants *m.*, école maternelle *f.*
nursemaid *n.* nourrice *f.*
nursing *n.* profession d'infirmière *f.*; tétée *f.*; — bottle biberon *m.*
nursling *n.* nourrisson *m.*
nurture *vt.* nourrir, élever
nut *n.* noix *f.*; (mech.) écrou *m.*; a hard — to crack un problème épineux; –s, –ty *a.* (coll.) fou
nutcracker *n.* casse-noisettes *m.*
nutmeg *n.* muscade *f.*
nutrient *n.* aliment *m.*; –a nutritif
nutriment *n.* nourriture *f.*, aliment *m.*
nutrition *f.* nutrition *f.*; nourriture *f.*, aliment *m.*
nutritious *a.* nourrissant
nutshell *n.* coquille de noix *f.*; in a — en un mot
nymph *n.* nymphe *f.*

O

oaf *n.* sot, benêt *m.*
oar *n.* rame *f.*, aviron *m.*; –sman *n.* rameur *m.*

oasis *n.* oasis *f.*
oat(s) *n.* avoine *f.*; sow one's wild — jeter sa gourme
oath *n.* serment, jurement *m.*
oatmeal *n.* bouillie d'avoine *f.*
obdurate *a.* endurci; obstiné
obedience *n.* obéissance *f.*
obedient *a.* obéissant
obeisance *n.* salut *m.*, révérence *f.*
obelisk *n.* obélisque *m.*
obese *a.* obèse
obesity *n.* obésité *f.*
obey *vt.* obéir à; — *vi.* obéir
obituary *n.* notice nécrologique *f.*
object *n.* objet *m.*, matière *f.*, sujet *m.*; (gram.) complément d'objet *m.*
object *vt.* objecter; –ion *n.* objection *f.*; –ionable *a.* désagréable; –ive *n.* objectif *m.*; — *a.* objectif; –ivity *n.* objectivité *f.*; –or *n.* objecteur *m.*; conscientious –or objecteur de conscience *m.*
obligation *n.* obligation *f.*
obligatory *a.* obligatoire
oblige *vt.* obliger; contraindre; — someone to do something obliger quelqu'un à faire quelque chose; be –d to do something être obligé de faire quelque chose
obliging *a.* obligeant
oblique *a.* oblique
obliterate *vt.* oblitérer, effacer
obliteration *n.* rature *f.*; oblitération *f.*
oblivion *n.* oubli *m.*
oblivious *a.* oublieux
oblong *a.* oblong
obnoxious *a.* nuisible, coupable, désagréable, dégoûtant
obscene *a.* obscène
obscenity *n.* obscénité *f.*
obscure *vt.* obscurcir; — *a.* obscur
obscurity *n.* obscurité *f.*
obsequious *a.* obséquieux
observable *a.* remarquable, appréciable
observance *n.* observation *f.*; observance *f.*; pratique *f.*
observant *a.* observateur, attentif; respectueux
observation *n.* observation *f.*
observatory *n.* observatoire *m.*
observe *vt.* observer; remarquer; fêter; –r *n.* observateur *m.*
observing *a.* observateur
obsess *vt.* obséder; –ion *n.* obsession *f.*
obsolescence *n.* désuétude *f.*
obsolescent *a.* qui tombe en désuétude
obsolete *a.* désuet, inusité, vieilli; become — tomber en désuetude
obstacle *n.* obstacle *m.*
obstetrician *n.* accoucheur *m.*
obstetrics *n. pl.* obstétrique *f.*
obstinacy *n.* opiniâtreté *f.*

obstinate *a.* obstiné

obstreperous *a.* déréglé, insoumis, bruyant, turbulent

obstruct *vt.* encombrer, obstruer; mettre obstacle à; **–ion** *n.* obstacle, empêchement *m.*, opposition *f.*; **–ive** *a.* embarrassant, obstructif

obtain *vt.* obtenir; **–able** *a.* trouvable, disponible

obtrusive *a.* importun

obtuse *a.* obtus

obviate *vt.* obvier à

obvious *a.* clair, évident; **–ly** *adv.* évidemment; **–ness** *n.* évidence *f.*

occasion *n.* occasion *f.*, incident *m.*; besoin *m.*; motif *m.*, cause *f.*; — *vt.* occasionner, causer; **–al** *a.* occasionnel, casuel; intermittent; **–ally** *adv.* de temps en temps

occident *n.* occident *m.*; **–al** *a.* occidental

occult *a.* occulte; **–ism** *n.* occultisme *m.*

occupancy *n.* prise de possession *f.*; habitation *f.*

occupant *n.* occupant, possesseur, habitant *m.*

occupation *n.* occupation *f.*, emploi *m.*; possession *f.*; **–al** *a.* du métier; **–al therapy** *n.* thérapie rééducative *f.*

occupier *n.* occupant *m.*

occupy *vt.* occuper, employer; habiter; prendre possession de; **be occupied with** s'occuper de

occur *vi.* arriver; avoir lieu; venir (à l'esprit); **–ence** *n.* événement *m.*

ocean *n.* océan *m.*; **–ic** *a.* océanique

Oceania *n.* Océanie *f.*

o'clock *adv.* **it is one** — il est une heure; **it is two** — il est deux heures

octagon *n.* octogone *m.*; **–al** *a.* octogonal

octane *a. & n.* (gasoline) octane *m.*

octet *n.* octuor *m.*

October *n.* octobre *m.*

ocular *a.* oculaire

oculist *n.* oculiste *m.*

odd *a.* singulier, étrange; (numbers) impair; **–ity** *n.* singularité, bizarrerie *f.*; **–s** *n. pl.* inégalité *f.*; avantage *m.*; chances *f. pl.*; **–s and ends** restes *m. pl.*, pièces diverses *f. pl.*; **be at –s** être brouillé

ode *n.* ode *f.*

odious *a.* odieux

odium *n.* haine *f.*

odor *n.* odeur *f.*; bouquet *m.*

odorous *a.* parfumé

of *prep.* de

off *a.* éloigné; loin, loin de; distant; — *adv.* au loin; à distance; — **and on** de temps en temps; **be** — partir, démarrer; **come** — tomber, se détacher; réussir; **go** — s'en aller; réussir, se passer; **put** — re-

mettre; **right** —, **straight** — (coll.) tout de suite; **set** — mettre en valeur; **take** — enlever; (avi.) décoller; **take** — **on** satiriser; **turn** — (lights) éteindre; (road) bifurquer — *prep.* de, de dessus, éloigné de; à une petite distance de; (naut.) au large; — **limits** défendu; défense d'entrer; — **the record** non-officiel

offal *n.* rebuts *m. pl.*; ordures *f. pl.*

off-color *a.* salé, risqué

offend *vt. & vi.* offenser, irriter; **–er** *n.* offenseur *m.*; **–ing** *a.* offensant, fautif

offense *n.* offense *f.*; faute *f.*; crime *m.*

offensive *a.* offensant, injurieux; — *n.* offensive *f.*

offer *vt. & vi.* offrir, présenter; — *n.* offre *f.*; **–ing** *n.* offrande *f.*; **–tory** *n.* offertoire *m.*; quête *f.*

offhand *a.* cavalier, improvisé; — *adv.* cavalièrement, sans préparation

office *n.* bureau *m.*; office *m.*; fonction, charge *f.*; **–r** *n.* officier *m.*; (police) agent *m.*; — **seeker** *n.* candidat à un poste, intrigant *m.*

official *n.* employé *m.*; fonctionnaire *m.*; officier *m.*; **–ese** *n.* jargon officiel *m.*

officiate *vi.* administrer; officier

officious *a.* officieux

offing *n.* large *m.*; **in the** — en vue

offset *n.* compensation *f.*; (print.) offset *m.*; — *vt.* contrebalancer

offshoot *n.* rejeton *m.*

offshore *adv.* vers la haute mer, en s'éloignant de la côte; — *adj.* éloigné de la côte

off side *adv.* hors des limites; de l'autre côté; hors jeu

offspring *n.* descendants *m. pl.*; lignée *f.*; rejeton *m.*

off stage *adv.* dans les coulisses

often *adv.* souvent; **how** — combien de fois

ogle *vt.* lorgner, regarder fixement

ogre *n.* ogre *m.*; **–ss** *n.* ogresse *f.*

oh! *interj.* oh!; ah!; hélas!; ouf!; aïe!

ohm *n.* ohm *m.*

oil *n.* huile *f.*; pétrole *m.*; **crude** — pétrole brut *m.*; **mineral** — huile minérale *f.*; — **paint,** — **painting** *n.* peinture à l'huile *f.*; — **well** *n.* puits à pétrole *m.*; — **slick** *n.* couche d'huile *f.*; — *vt.* huiler; **–y** *a.* huileux; — **can** *n.* broc à huile *m.*

oilcloth *n.* toile cirée *f.*

ointment *n.* onguent, baume *m.*

okra *n.* quingombo *m.*

old *a.* vieux, ancien; **become** —, **grow** — vieillir; **how** — **are you?** quel âge avez-vous?; **I am ten years** — j'ai dix ans; — **hand** vétéran *m.*; — **maid** vieille fille *f.*;

–ish *a.* plutôt vieux; –ness *n.* âge *m.*; vieillesse *f.*; ancienneté *f.*

old-fashioned *a.* démodé

old-line *a.* de vieille famille; qui remonte très loin

old-time *a.* du bon vieux temps

oleomargarine *n.* margarine *f.*

olfactory *a.* olfactif

oligarchy *n.* oligarchie *f.*

olive *n.* olive *f.*; (tree) olivier *m.*; — oil huile d'olive *f.*; — *a.* de couleur olive

Olympiad *n.* olympiade *f.*

Olympian *a.* olympien

Olympic *a.* olympique; –s *n. pl.* jeux olympiques *m. pl.*

omelet *n.* omelette *f.*

omen *n.* présage, augure *m.*

ominous *a.* de mauvais augure

omission *n.* omission *f.*

omit *vt.* omettre; négliger; oublier

omnibus *n.* omnibus *m.*; anthologie *f.*

omnipotence *n.* toute-puissance *f.*

omnipotent *a.* tout-puissant

omnipresence *n.* ubiquité *f.*; présence universelle *f.*

omnipresent *a.* présent en tous lieux

omniscient *a.* omniscient

omnivorous *a.* omnivore

on *prep.* sur; à; dans; — *adv.* en avant; and so — et ainsi de suite

once *adv.* une fois; autrefois; at — tout de suite; — and for all une fois pour toutes; — upon a time (il était) une fois

oncoming *a.* à venir, qui vient; approchant; hardi

one *a.* un, une; — *pron.* on; — another l'un l'autre, les uns les autres; — by — un à un; –'s son, sa, ses

one-eyed *a.* borgne

one-horse *a.* à un cheval; (fig.) provincial, insignifiant

onerous *a.* onéreux

oneself *pron.* soi, soi-même; se

one-sided *a.* à un seul côté; partial; –ness *n.* partialité *f.*

onetime *a.* ancien, d'autrefois

one-track *a.* à une voie; (fig.) borné

one-way *a.* à sens unique; — ticket billet simple, aller *m.*

onion *n.* oignon *m.*

onionskin (paper) *n.* papier pelure *m.*

onlooker *n.* spectateur *m.*

only *a.* seul; unique; — *adv.* ne . . . que; seulement

onomatopoeia *n.* onomatopée *f.*

onrush *n.* ruée *f.*; attaque *f.*

onset *n.* assaut, *m.*, attaque *f.*; début, commencement *m.*

onslaught *n.* attaque *f.*, assaut *m.*

on-the-job *a.* (coll.) à sur place

onto *prep.* sur; à; dans

onus *n.* fardeau, poids *m.*, charge *f.*

onward *adv.* en avant

ooze *n.* vase, bourbe *f.*; — *vi.* filtrer; suinter; s'écouler

opalescent *a.* opalescent

opaque *a.* opaque; –ness *n.* opacité *f.*

open *vt.* ouvrir; commencer; découvrir; — *vi.* s'ouvrir; — *a.* ouvert; franc, sincère; — house réception *f.*; — shop entreprise qui emploie des ouvriers syndiqués et non syndiqués; —er *n.*, can —er ouvre-boîtes *m.*; –ing *n.* ouverture *f.*; (theat.) première *f.*; débouché *m.*; –ness *n.* franchise *f.*

open-air *a.* en plein air; à la belle étoile

open-eyed *a.* les yeux écarquillés

openhanded *a.* généreux

openhearted *a.* franc

open-minded *a.* large d'esprit

openmouthed *a.* étourdi, abasourdi; bouche bée

openwork *n.* ouvrage à jour

opera *n.* opéra *m.*; — glasses jumelles de théâtre *f. pl.*; — hat chapeau claque; — house *n.* opéra *m.*; –atic *a.* d'opéra

operate *vi.* opérer, agir; — *vt.* faire marcher

operating room *n.* amphithéâtre *m.*

operation *n.* opération *f.*; have an — être opéré; –al *a.* en état de marche

operator *n.* opérateur *m.*

opiate *n.* opiat *m.*

opine *vt.* opiner

opinion *n.* opinion *f.*, sentiment *m.*; avis *m.*; in my — à mon avis; –ated *a.* opiniâtre

opium *n.* opium *m.*

opossum *n.* opossum *m.*

opponent *n.* antagoniste, adversaire *m.*

opportune *a.* opportun; à propos; –ness *n.* opportunité *f.*

opportunism *n.* opportunisme *m.*

opportunist *n.* opportuniste *m.*

opportunity *n.* occasion *f.*

oppose *vt.* & (*vi.*) (s')opposer

opposite *a.* & *n.* opposé *m.*

opposition *n.* opposition, résistance *f.*

oppress *vt.* opprimer; –ion *n.* oppression *f.*; –ive *a.* oppressif; –or *n.* oppresseur *m.*

opprobrium *n.* opprobre *m.*

optic *a.* optique, visuel; –al *a.* optique; –ian *n.* opticien *m.*; –s *n.* optique *f.*

optimism *n.* optimisme *m.*

optimist *n.* optimiste *m.* & *f.*; –ic *a.* optimiste

optimum *a.* le meilleur

option *n.* option *f.*, choix *m.*; –al *a.* facultatif

optometry *n.* optométrie *f.*

opulence *n.* opulence *f.*

opulent *a.* opulent

opus *n.* composition musicale *f.*

or *conj.* ou, **either . . . — ou . . .** ou; **— else** ou bien

oral *a.* oral; par la bouche; **—ly** *adv.* oralement, par la bouche; **— contraceptive** *n.* préservatif oral *m.*

orange *n.* orange *f.*; (tree) oranger *m.*; **—** *a.* orangé, couleur orange

orangutan *m.* orang-outan *m.*

orate *vi.* pérorer

oration *n.* discours *m.*; harangue *f.*; (funeral) oraison *f.*

orator *n.* orateur *m.*; **—ical** *a.* oratoire

orb *n.* orbe *m.*, sphère *f.*; globe *m.*

orbit *n.* orbite *f.*; **—** *vi.* décrire une courbe orbitale, décrire une orbite

orchard *n.* verger *m.*

orchestra *n.* orchestre *m.*; **— seat** fauteuil d'orchestre *m.*; **—l** *a.* orchestral; **—te** *vt.* orchestrer; **—tion** *n.* orchestration *f.*

orchid *n.* orchidée *f.*

ordain *vt.* ordonner; établir; sacrer

ordeal *n.* épreuve *f.*

order *n.* ordre, rang *m.*; commande *f.*; précepte, commandement *m.*; billet *m.*; mandat *m.*; décoration *f.*; (com.) demande *f.*; **money —** mandat-poste *m.*; **call to —** rappeler à l'ordre; **in — to** pour; **in —** en règle; par rang; **in — that** pour que, afin que; **in alphabetical —** par ordre alphabétique; **in chronological —** par ordre de date; **make to —** faire sur commande; **on —** commandé; **out of —** détraqué, déréglé; déplacé; **—** *vt.* ordonner; commander; régler, disposer; **—liness** *n.* bon ordre *m.*; **—ly** *n.* ordonnance *f.*; **—ly** *a.* bien réglé, régulier; ordonné; rangé

ordinal *a.* ordinal

ordinance *n.* ordonnance *f.*; règlement municipal *m.*

ordinarily *adv.* d'ordinaire, d'habitude

ordinary *a.* ordinaire; **—** *n.* ordinaire *m.*; **out of the —** peu ordinaire; extraordinaire

ordnance *n.* service des munitions *m.*

ore *n.* minerai *m.*

organ *n.* organe *m.*; (mus.) orgue *m.*; **— loft** *n.* tribune d'orgue *f.*; **— pipe** *n.* tuyau d'orgue *m.*; **— stop** *n.* jeu d'orgue *m.*; **—ic** *a* organique; **—ism** *n.* organisme *m.*; **—ist** *n.* organiste *m.*

organdy *n.* organdi *m.*

organ-grinder *n.* joueur d'orgue de barbarie *m.*

organization *n.* organisation *f.*

organize *vt.* organiser; **—** *vi.* s'organiser; **—r** *n.* organisateur *m.*

orgy *n.* orgie *f.*

orient *n.* orient *m.*; **—** *vt.* orienter; **—al** *a.* oriental; **—ate** *vt.* orienter; **—ation** *n.* orientation *f.*

orifice *n.* orifice *m.*, ouverture *f.*

origin *n.* origine, source *f.*; commencement *m.*; **—al** *a.* original; originaire; (eccl.) originel **—al** *n.*; original *m.*; **—ality** *n.* originalité *f.*; **—ally** *adv.* originalement; **—ate** *vt.* produire, faire naître; **—ate** *vi.* provenir, naître; **—ator** *n.* initiateur, auteur *m.*

ornament *n.* ornement *m.*; décoration *f.*; **—** *vt.* orner, parer; ornementer; **—al** *a.* ornemental; **—ation** *n.* ornementation *f.*

ornate *a.* orné; fleuri

ornithology *n.* ornithologie *f.*

orphan *n.* orphelin *m.*, orpheline *f.*; **—** *a.* orphelin; **—age** *n.* orphelinat *m.*

orthodontist *n.* orthodentiste *m.*

orthodox *a.* orthodoxe; **—y** *n.* orthodoxie *f.*

orthography *n.* orthographe *f.*

orthopedic *a.* orthopédique

orthopedist *n.* orthopédiste *m.*

oscillate *vi.* osciller

oscillation *n.* oscillation *f.*

osmosis *n.* osmose *f.*

ossification *n.* ossification *f.*

ossify *vt.* ossifier; **—** *vi.* s'ossifier

ostensible *a.* ostensible, visible; soi-disant, prétendu

ostentation *n.* ostentation *f.*; parade *f.*

ostentatious *a.* fastueux

osteopathy *n.* malaxion médicale, osteopathie *f.*

ostracism *n.* ostracisme *m.*

ostracize *vt.* ostraciser

other *pron.* autre; **each —** l'un l'autre; **—** *a.* autre; **every — day** tous les deux jours; **—** *adv.* autrement; **—s** *pron.* d'autres; autrui

otherwise *adv.* autrement

ottoman *n.* pouf *m.*

ought *vt.* devoir; **—** *vi.* falloir; **—** *n.* zéro *m.*; **—** *pron.* rien, quoi que ce soit

ounce *n.* once *f.* (30 grammes)

our *a.* notre, (*pl.* nos); **—s** *pron.* le nôtre, la nôtre, les nôtres

ourselves *pron.* nous-mêmes, nous

oust *vt.* déloger; évincer

out *adv.* dehors, au dehors; sorti; (book) paru; (flower) épanoui, en fleur; (tide) bas; (sports) hors jeu; **—** *a.* de dehors, extérieur; détaché; **— of** *prep.* hors de; en dehors de; dans; de; sur; **—er** *a.* extérieur; **—s** *n. pl.*, **ins and —s** coins et recoins *m. pl.*; **at —s, on the —s** brouillé(s)

out-and-out *a.* entier, complet; achevé

outbid *vt.* enchérir sur

outboard *n.* hors-bord *m.*

outbreak *n.* éruption *f.*
outbuilding *n.* annexe, dépendance *f.*
outburst *n.* explosion *f.*; accès *m.*
outcast *a.* exilé *m.*; rebut *m.*
outclass *vt.* surpasser; surclasser
outcome *n.* résultat *m.*, issue *f.*
outcry *n.* cri *m.*, clameur *f.*
outdated *a.* périmé; suranné
outdistance *vt.* dépasser, surpasser
outdo *vt.* l'emporter sur
outdoor *a.* du dehors; **–s** *adv.* au dehors, en plein air
outfit *n.* équipement *m.*; nécessaire *m.*; garde-robe *m.*; costume et accessoires *m. pl.*; — *vt.* équiper
outflank *vt.* déborder
outflow *n.* écoulement *m.*
outgoing *a.* sortant, partant; sociable, cordial, communicatif; sympathique
outgrow *vt.* surpasser en croissance; devenir trop grand pour; **–th** *n.* excroissance *f.*; résultat *m.*
outguess *vt.* deviner mieux que; l'emporter sur
outhouse *n.* dépendance *f.*
outing *n.* excursion *f.*; piquenique *m.*
outlandish *a.* bizarre
outlast *vt.* surpasser en durée; survivre à
outlaw *n.* proscrit *m.*; hors-la-loi *m.*; — *vt.* proscrire
outlay *n.* dépense *f.*; déboursés *m. pl.*
outlet *n.* sortie *f.*; issue *f.*; (com.) débouché *m.*
outline *n.* contour *m.*; silhouette *f.*; esquisse *f.*; plan *m.*; — *vt.* dessiner les contours de; silhouetter; esquisser; dresser un plan de
outlive *vt.* survivre à
outlook *n.* perspective *f.*, point de vue *m.*
outlying *a.* éloigné, extérieur
outmaneuver *vt.* tourner (l'ennemi); manœuvrer plus habilement que
outmoded *a.* démodé
outnumber *vt.* surpasser en nombre
out-of-date *a.* périmé, démodé
out-of-doors *adv.* au dehors
out-of-print *a.* épuisé
out-of-the-way *a.* caché, obscur
outpatient *n.* malade ambulant *m.* (traité à l'hôpital sans être hospitalisé)
outpoint *vt.* battre aux points
outpost *n.* avant-poste *m.*
outpouring *n.* effusion *f.*, épanchement *m.*
output *n.* production, chiffre de production *f.*; puissance *f.*
outrage *n.* outrage *m.*; — *vt.* outrager; **–ous** *a.* scandaleux; outrageux
outrank *vt.* surpasser de rang
outrider *n.* piqueur *m.*
outright *adv.* sur-le-champ, tout de suite;

(com.) à forfait; parfaitement; franchement; — *a.* parfait, complet
outrun *vt.* dépasser à la course, distancer
outset *n.* commencement, début *m.*
outshine *vt.* surpasser en éclat; dépasser
outside *n.* dehors *m.*, surface *f.*, extérieur *m.*; — *adv.* au dehors; dehors; en dehors, à l'extérieur; — *a.* du dehors, extérieur; — **of** *prep.* sauf; en dehors de; hors de; **–r** *n.* étranger *m.*
outskirts *n.* banlieue *f.*; environs *m. pl.*
outspoken *a.* franc
outspread *a.* étendu
outstanding *a.* éminent, remarquable; (com.) non-payé
outstare *vt.* décontenancer
outstay *vt.* rester plus longtemps que; — one's welcome rester plus longtemps qu'on ne le veut
outstretch *vt.* étendre
outstrip *vt.* dépasser, surpasser
outward *a.* extérieur; — *adv.* au dehors; — **bound** en destination pour l'étranger; **–ly** *adv.* à l'extérieur; **–s** *adv.* en dehors; vers l'extérieur
outwear *vt.* user; ne plus avoir besoin (d'un vêtement)
outweigh *vt.* peser plus que; l'emporter sur
outwit *vt.* surpasser en finesse; tromper, duper
oval *a. & n.* ovale *m.*
ovary *n.* ovaire *m.*
ovate *a.* ové
oven *n.* four *m.*; (fig.) fournaise *f.*; **Dutch** — cuisinière *f.*
over *prep.* sur, au-dessus de; par-dessus; plus de; pendant; — *adv.* au-delà; de l'autre côté; fini, passé; de nouveau; — again une fois de plus; all — partout; — and above par dessus; — and — (again) sans s'arrêter; — there là-bas; **–ly** *adv.* trop, à l'exces
overabundant *a.* surabondant
overage *a.* trop vieux
over-all *a.* complet
overalls *n.* cotte à bretelles *f.*; bleus *m. pl.*
overawe *vt.* impressionner, épouvanter
overbalance *vt.* l'emporter sur; renverser; peser plus que
overbearing *a.* arrogant, impérieux
overboard *adv.* à la mer
overburden *vt.* surcharger
overcast *vt.* obscurcir; surjeter; couvrir; — *a.* couvert (de nuages), sombre
overcharge *n.* prix exorbitant *m.*; surtaxe *f.*; — *vt.* surcharger, accabler; faire payer trop cher
overcoat *n.* pardessus *m.*
overcome *vt.* dompter, vaincre, maîtriser; — *a.* accablé

overconfidence *n.* suffisance *f.*
overconfident *a.* confiant à l'excès
overcooked *a.* trop cuit
overcrowd *vt.* encombrer, bonder
overdeveloped *a.* trop développé; (phot.) trop poussé
overdo *vt.* trop faire, outrer; — *vi.* se surmener; **–ne** *a.* trop cuit
overdose *n.* dose trop forte *f.*
overdraw *vt.* excéder son crédit, tirer à découvert
overdrive *vt.* surmener; — *n.* (auto) quatrième vitesse qui économise l'essence *f.*
overdue *a.* en retard; échu
overeat *vi.* trop manger
overestimate *vt.* surestimer
overexcite *vt.* surexciter
overexertion *n.* surmenage *m.*
overexposure *n.* excès d'exposition *m.*; (photo.) excès de pose *m.*
overfeed *vt.* surnourrir, suralimenter
overflow *n.* inondation *f.*; trop-plein *m.*; débordement ; — *vi.* déborder; surabonder; **–ing** *a.* débordant
overgrown *a.* excessivement accru, énorme; (with weeds) couvert
overgrowth *n.* couverture *f.*
overhang *vt.* surplomber; menacer
overhaul *vt.* réparer; réfectionner; — *n.* réparation *f.*; revision *f.*
overhead *adv.* au-dessus de la tête, en haut; — *n.* frais généraux *m. pl.*
overhear *vt.* entendre; surprendre
overheat *vt.* surchauffer
overindulge *vt.* gâter; **–nce** *n.* excès d'indulgence *m.*; abus *m.*
overjoyed *a.* ravi; transporté de joie, au comble de la joie
overland *a. & adv.* par voie de terre
overlap *vt. & vi.* recouvrir, chevaucher; — *n.* recouvrement, chevauchement
overload *vt.* surcharger; surmener; — *n.* surcharge *f.*
overlook *vt.* passer sous silence, négliger, mépriser; donner sur
overlord *n.* suzerain *m.*
overnight *adv.* toute la nuit; pour (toute) la nuit; jusqu'au lendemain; — *a.* de nuit
overpass *vt.* passer au-delà, franchir; — *n.* passage supérieur *m.*; pont-route *m.*
overpayment *n.* paiement en trop *m.*
overpopulate *vt.* surpeupler
overpower *vt.* dominer, opprimer, accabler; **–ing** *a.* accablant; irrésistible
overproduction *n.* surproduction *f.*
overrate *vt.* évaluer trop haut; surestimer
overreach *vt.* dépasser; — oneself aller trop loin, se duper
override *vt.* fouler; l'emporter sur

overripe *a.* trop mûr
overrule *vt.* casser, annuler
overrun *vt.* envahir, ravager
oversea *a.* d'outre-mer; **–s** *adv.* outre-mer
oversee *vt.* surveiller; **–r** *n.* inspecteur, surveillant, intendant *m.*
overshadow *vt.* ombrager; éclipser
overshoe *n.* galoche *f.*
overshoot *vt.* dépasser
oversight *n.* méprise, erreur, inadvertance *f.*
oversleep *vi.* dormir trop longtemps
overstate *vt.* exagérer; **–ment** *n.* exagération *f.*
overstep *vt.* dépasser
oversupply *n.* excédent *m.*, abondance *f.*
overt *a.* manifeste; ouvert
overtake *vt.* dépasser, surpasser; rattraper; arriver à
overtax *vt.* surtaxer; surmener
overthrow *n.* renversement *m.*; défaite *f.*; — *vt.* renverser; détruire, défaire
overtime *n.* heures de travail supplémentaires *f. pl.*
overtone *n.* note harmonique *f.*
overtrick *n.* (cards) levée en plus *f.*
overtrump *vt.* surcouper
overture *n.* ouverture *f.*
overturn *vt.* renverser; — *vi.* se renverser
overvalue *vt.* trop estimer, surestimer
overview *n.* vue, perspective *f.*
overweight *n.* excédant (de poids) *m.*; surpoids *m.*; — *a.* obèse; (baggage) en excédent; qui pèse trop
overwhelm *vt.* accabler, écraser; combler; **–ing** *a.* irrésistible; accablant
overwork *vi.* se surmener; — *vt.* surmener; trop employer; — *n.* excès de travail *m.*; surmenage *m.*
overwrought *a.* surmené; excédé
overzealous *a.* trop zélé
oviparous *a.* ovipare
ovum *n.* œuf *m.*
owe *vt.* devoir
owing *a.* dû; — to *prep.* à cause de, en raison de, par suite de
own *vt.* posséder; reconnaître, avouer; **–er** *n.* possesseur, propriétaire *m.*; **–ership** *n.* possession, propriété *f.*
own *a.* propre; my — à moi; le mien
ox *n.* bœuf *m.*
oxalic *a.* oxalique
oxide *n.* oxyde *m.*
oxidize *vt.* oxyder; — *vi.* s'oxyder
oxygen *n.* oxygène *m.*; — tent tente à oxygène *f.*
oyster *n.* huître *f.*; — bed banc d'huîtres *m.*; — plant salsifis *m.*
ozone *n.* ozone

P

pace *n.* pas *m.*; allure *f.*; (horse) amble *m.*;
keep — rester aux côtés (de quelqu'un);
rester à la page; — *vi.* aller au pas,
faire les cent pas; — off mesurer (au
pas); –r *n.* cheval qui va à l'amble *m.*
pacemaker *n.* entraîneur *m.*
pacific *a.* pacifique; –ation *n.* pacification *f.*, apaisement *m.*
Pacific Ocean *n.* Océan Pacifique *m.*
pacifist *n.* pacifiste *m.* & *f.*
pacify *vt.* pacifier, apaiser
pack *n.* paquet, ballot *m.*; fardeau *m.*;
(cards) jeu *m.*; bande, meute *f.*; —
animal *n.* bête de somme *f.*; — horse *n.*
cheval de bât *m.*; — *vt.* & *vi.* emballer,
empaqueter; fourrer; (earth) tasser;
faire (une valise); — off envoyer; — up
faire ses valises; –age *n.* colis, emballage *m.*; –er *n.* emballeur *m.*; –ing *n.*
emballage *m.*; action de faire les valises
f.; (mech.) garniture *f.*; –ing case caisse
d'emballage *f.*; –ing house abattoir *m.*
packet *n.* paquet *m.*
packsaddle *n.* bât *m.*
pact *n.* pacte, contrat *m.*
pad *n.* (paper) bloc *m.*; tampon *m.*; —
vt. rembourrer, ouater; gonfler; — *vi.*
aller doucement, aller à pas sourds;
–ding *n.* remplissage *m.*, ouate *f.*
paddle *n.* rame *f.*; pagaie *f.*; — wheel roue
à aubes *f.*; — *vt.* & *vi.* pagayer, ramer;
(coll.) fesser
paddock *n.* enclos *m.*; paddock *m.*
padlock *n.* cadenas *m.*; — *vt.* cadenasser
pagan *n.* & *a.* païen *m.*; –ism *n.* paganisme
m.
page *n.* page *f.*; (court) page *m.*; (messenger) chasseur *m.*; (book) (left) verso
(right) recto *m.*; — *vt.* chercher; crier
(le nom d'une personne), faire appeler (par un chasseur); (print.) paginer
pageant *n.* spectacle, défilé *m.*, parade *f.*;
–ry *n.* faste *m.*, pompe, parade *f.*
pagination, paging *n.* (print.) pagination
f.
pail *n.* seau *m.*
pain *n.* peine, douleur *f.*; mal *m.*; be in —
souffrir; take great –s to se donner de
la peine pour; — *vt.* peiner, donner de
la peine à; faire mal à; –ful *a.* pénible;
douloureux; –less *a.* sans douleur
painstaking *a.* soigné; laborieux; assidu
paint *n.* couleur *f.*; peinture *f.*; — *vt.*
peindre; dépeindre; –er *n.* peintre *m.*;
(naut.) amarre *f.*; house –er peintre en
bâtiments *m.*; –ing *n.* peinture *f.*;
tableau *m.*
paintbrush *n.* pinceau *m.*

pair *n.* paire *f.*; couple *m.*; — *vt.* apparier;
assortir; — off s'apparier
paisley *n.* châle écossais *m.*
pajamas *n.* pyjama *m.*
Pakistan *n.* Pakistan *m.*
palace *n.* palais *m.*
palatable *a.* agréable au goût
palate *n.* palais *m.*
palatial *a.* semblable à un palais; somptueux, magnifique
palatinate *n.* palatinat *m.*
Palatine *n.* Palatin *m.*
palaver *n.* verbiage *m.*; palabre *f.*
pale *n.* pieu *m.*; enceinte *f.*; beyond the
— inaccessible; — *a.* pâle, blême; — *vi.*
pâlir, blêmir; –ness *n.* pâleur *f.*
paleography *n.* paléographie *f.*
paleolithic *a.* paléolithique
Palestine *n.* Palestine *f.*
palette *n.* palette *f.*
palfrey *n.* palefroi *m.*
palisade *n.* palissade *f.*
pall *n.* poêle *m.*; — *vi.* affaiblir; ...enir
insipide
pallbearer *n.* porteur d'un cercueil *m*
pallet *n.* petit lit, grabat *m.*
palliate *vt.* pallier
palliative *a.* & *n.* palliatif *m.*
pallid *a.* pâle, blême
pallor *n.* pâleur *f.*
palm *n.* (tree) palmier *m.*; (leaf) palme *f.*;
(hand) paume *f.*; — *vt.* empaumer,
escamoter; — off faire accepter (une
chose pour ce qu'elle n'est pas)
Palm Sunday *n.* Dimanche des Rameaux *m.*
palmist *n.* chiromancier *m.*; –ry *n.* chiromancie *f.*
palpitate *vi.* palpiter
palpitation *n.* palpitation *f.*
palsied *a.* paralysé
palsy *n.* paralysie *f.*
paltry *a.* méprisable, bas, pauvre, mesquin
pamper *vt.* dorloter, choyer
pamphlet *n.* pamphlet *m.*; brochure *f.*,
dépliant *m.*; –eer *n.* pamphlétaire *m.*
pan *n.* poêle, casserole *f.*; cuvette *f.*; —
vt. (gold) laver; (coll.) critiquer; — out
(coll.) arriver; réussir
panacea *n.* panacée *f.*
Panama *n.* Panama *m.*
Pan-American *a.* pan-américain
pancake *n.* crêpe *f.*; — landing atterrissage à plat *m.*
panchromatic *a.* panchromatique
pancreas *n.* pancréas *m.*
pandemonium *n.* pandémonium *m.*
pander *n.* maquereau *m.*; — *vi.* faire le
maquereau
pane *n.* carreau (de vitre), panneau *m.*

panegyric *a.* panégyrique
panel *n.* panneau *m.*; jury *m.*; — *vt.* diviser en panneaux; lambrisser; –ing *n.* lambris *m.*; boiserie *f.*; –ist *n.* membre du jury *m.*
pang *n.* angoisse *f.*
panhandle *n.* queue de poêle *f.*; — *vt.* (coll.) mendier; –r *n.* (coll.) mendiant *m.*
panic *n.* panique *f.*; — *vt.* terrifier, affoler; –ky *a.* (coll.) affolé; inquiet
panic-stricken *a.* pris de panique; terrifié
panoply *n.* panoplie *f.*
panorama *n.* panorama *m.*
panoramic *a.* panoramique
pant *n.* halètement *m.*; — *vi.* palpiter; haleter; –ing *n.* halètement *m.*
pantaloons *n. pl.* pantalon *m.*
pantheism *n.* panthéisme *m.*
pantheist *n.* panthéiste *m.*
pantheon *n.* panthéon *m.*
panther *n.* panthère *f.*
pantomimist *n.* (actor) pantomime, mime *m.*
pantry *n.* office *f.*; garde-manger *m.*
pants *n. pl.* pantalon *m.*
pap *n.* mamelle *f.*; bouillie *f.*; pulpe *f.*
papacy *n.* papauté *f.*
papal *a.* papal
paper *n.* papier *m.*; journal *m.*; écrit *m.*; article *m.*; communication *f.*; **blotting —** papier buvard *m.*; **carbon —** papier carbone *m.*; **toilet —** papier hygiénique; **— bag** sac *m.*; **— boy** crieur, vendeur de journaux *m.*; **— clip** attache *f.*; **— cutter,** **— knife** coupe-papier *m.*; **— money** papier-monnaie *m.*; — *vt.* tapisser (de papier peint)
paperback *n.* livre broché, livre bon marché *m.*
paperhanger *n.* colleur *m.*
paperweight *n.* presse-papiers *m.*
papier-mâché carton-pâte *m.*; papier-mâché *m.*
papist *n.* papiste *m.*
paprika *n.* paprika; piment hongrois *m.*
Papua *n.* Papouasie *f.*
papyrus *n.* papyrus *m.*
par *n.* valeur égale *f.*; pair *m.*; niveau *m.*
parable *n.* parabole *f.*; — *vt.* répresenter par un parabole
parabola *n.* parabole *f.*
parachute *n.* parachute *m.*; — *vt. & vi.* parachuter
parachutist *n.* parachutiste *m.*
parade *n.* défilé *m.*; — *vi.* défiler; faire la parade; — *vt.* faire parade de
paradise *n.* paradis *m.*
paradox *n.* paradoxe *m.*; –ical *a.* para-

doxal
paraffin *n.* paraffine *f.*; **— oil** pétrole *m.*
paragraph *n.* paragraphe, alinéa *m.*
parallel *n.* parallèle *f.*; ressemblance *f.*; — *vt.* mettre en parallèle, comparer; — *a.* parallèle; –ism *n.* parallélisme *m.*
parallelogram *n.* parallélogramme *m.*
paralysis *n.* paralysie *f.*
paralytic *a.* paralytique
paralyze *vt.* paralyser
paramedic *n.* parachutiste du corps médecin *m.*
paramilitary *a.* paramilitaire
paramount *a.* supérieur, éminent
paramour *n.* amant, *m.*, amante *f.*
paranoia *n.* paranoïa *f.*
parapet *n.* parapet *m.*
paraphernalia *n.* attirail *m.*; équipement *m.*; outillage *m.*; effets, bagages *m. pl.*
paraphrase *vt.* paraphraser; — *n.* paraphrase *f.*
paraplegia *n.* paraplégie *f.*
parapsychology *n.* parapsychologie *f.*
parasite *n.* parasite *m.*; pique-assiette *m.*
parasitic *a.* parasite
parasol *n.* parasol *m.*, ombrelle *f.*
parboil *vt.* bouillir (avant de rôtir)
parcel *n.* paquet, colis *m.*; parcelle, quantité *f.*; **— post** *n.* colis postal *m.*; — *vt.* morceler, parceller
parch *vt.* brûler légèrement, griller; dessécher
parchment *n.* parchemin *m.*
pardon *n.* pardon *m.*, grâce *f.*; — *vt.* pardonner; gracier; –able *a.* pardonnable
pare *vt.* peler; rogner
paregoric *a. & n.* parégorique *m.*
parent *n.* père *m.*, mère *f.*; –s *pl.* parents *m. pl.*; –age *n.* parenté, parentage *m.*, naissance *f.*; –al *a.* paternel, maternel; –hood *n.* parenté *f.*
parenthesis *n.* parenthèse *f.*
parenthetical *a.* entre parenthèses
parfait *n.* glace mêlée de sirop de fruits *f.*
paring *n.* rognure, pelure, écorce *f.*; **— knife** éplucheuse *f.*
Paris *n.* Paris *m.*; –ian *a. & n.* parisien *m.*
parish *n.* paroisse *f.*; — *a.* paroissial; –ioner *n.* paroissien *m.*
parity *n.* parité *f.*
park *n.* parc *m.*; — *vt. & vi.* stationner; –ing *n.* stationnement *m.*; **no –ing** stationnement interdit; **–ing light** feu de position, feu de stationnement *m.*
parkway *n.* boulevard *m.*; autostrade *f.*
parlance *n.* langage *m.*
parley *n.* pourparler *m.*; — *vi.* discuter; (mil.) parlementer
parliament *n.* parlement *m.*; –ary *a.* parlementaire

parlor *n.* petit salon *m.*; (convents, schools) parloir *m.*; **funeral —** établissement de pompes funèbres *m.*; **— car** voiture-salon *f.*
Parnassian *a. & n.* parnassien *m.*
parochial *a.* (eccl.) paroissial; communal
parody *n.* parodie *f.*; **—** *vt.* parodier
parole *n.* parole *f.*; liberté provisoire *f.*; **—** *vt.* libérer provisoirement
paroxysm *n.* paroxysme *m.*
parquet *n.* parquet *m.*; (theat.) orchestre *m.*
parry *vt.* parer, éviter; **—** *n.* parade *f.*
parse *vt.* (gram.) expliquer (une phrase), faire l'analyse (d'une phrase)
parsimonious *a.* parcimonieux
parsimony *n.* parcimonie *f.*
parsley *n.* persil *m.*
parsnip *n.* panais *m.*
parson *n.* curé *m.*; prêtre *m.*; **–age** *n.* presbytère *m.*; cure *f.*; maison du curé *f.*
part *n.* partie, part, portion *f.*; parti, rôle *m.*; (hair) raie *f.*; **for my — pour ma** part; **quant à moi; in —** en partie; partiellement; **in great —** en grande partie; **the greater —** la plupart; **be — of** faire partie de; **play a — jouer un** rôle; **take — in** prendre part à; **take someone's — prendre le parti de;** **spare —** pièce détachée *f.*; pièce de rechange *f.*; **—** *adv.* en partie; moitié; **—** *vt.* diviser; séparer; **—** *vi.* se séparer; se diviser; se quitter; **–ing** *n.* départ *m.*; séparation *f.*; **–ly** *adv.* en partie, partiellement
partake *vi.* avoir part, participer, prendre part
partial *a.* (prejudiced) partial; (part) partiel; **–ity** *n.* partialité *f.*
participant *n.* participant *m.*
participate *vi.* participer
participation *n.* participation *f.*
participial *a.* (gram.) participial
participle *n.* (gram.) participe *m.*
particle *n.* (gram.) particule *f.*; parcelle *f.*, brin, atome *m.*
particular *n.* particularité *f.*, détail *m.*; particulier *m.*; **—** *a.* particulier; singulier; exigeant, regardant, pointilleux; **in —** notamment, en particulier; **–ity** *n.* particularité *f.*; **–ize** *vt.* particulariser, spécifier; **–ly** *adv.* en particulier, particulièrement
partisan *n.* partisan *m.*; **—** *a.* de parti
partition *n.* partition, division *f.*; cloison *f.*; (pol.) partage *m.*; **—** *vt.* diviser (par une cloison), cloisonner
partitive *a.* partitif
partner *n.* associé *m.*; compagnon *m.*;

partenaire *m.* (*& f.*); **silent — associé** commanditaire *m.*; **–ship** *n.* association *f.*; **go into — with s'associer avec**
part owner *n.* copropriétaire *m. & f.*
part-time *a.*, **— work** emploi partiel *m.*
party *n.* parti *m.*; partie *f.*; intérêt *m.*; individu *m.*; soirée *f.*, divertissement *m.*, fête *f.*; **be (a) — to prendre part à,** participer à; être complice de; **give someone a — fêter quelqu'un; — line** ligne téléphonique utilisée par plusieurs abonnés *f.*; doctrine (d'un parti politique) *f.*
pass *n.* passage étroit, défilé *m.*; situation *f.*, état *m.*; billet gratuit *m.*; laissez-passer *m.*; passe *f.*; **come to —** se passer, arriver; **—** *vt.* passer; dépasser, doubler; croiser; voter; **—** *vi.* passer; se passer; (education) être reçu (à un examen), réussir (à); **— away** décéder; **— by** passer (par); **— judgment** prononcer un jugement; **— off** faire passer; **— on** procéder; décéder; **— out** se pâmer; perdre connaissance; **— over** laisser passer, négliger; **–able** *a.* passable; praticable; **–ing** *n.* passage *m.*; mort *f.*; **–ing** *a.* passager; passant; **by–** *n.* bec-allumeur *m.*; route d'évitement *f.*
passage *n.* passage *m.*; couloir *m.*
passageway *n.* corridor, passage *m.*
passbook *n.* livret de banque *m.*
passenger *n.* passager *m.*; voyageur *m.*
passer-by *n.* passant *m.*
passion *n.* passion *f.*; **–ate** *a.* passionné
passive *a. & n.* passif *m.*; **–ness** *n.* passivité *f.*
passkey *n.* passe-partout *m.*
Passover *n.* Pâque *f.*
passport *n.* passeport *m.*
password *n.* mot d'ordre *m.*
past *n. & a.* passé *m.*; **—** *prep.* plus loin que; devant; hors de; au delà de; **—** *adv.*, **go — passer**
paste *n.* colle *f.*; pâte *f.*; (jewels) strass *m.*; **—** *vt.* coller
pasteboard *n.* carton *m.*
pasteurization *n.* pasteurisation *f.*
pasteurize *vt.* pasteuriser; **–d** *a.* pasteurisé
pastiche *n.* pastiche *m.*; **—** *vt.* pasticher
pastime *n.* passe-temps *m.*
pastor *n.* pasteur *m.*; **–al** *n.* pastorale *f.*; **—** *a.* pastoral
pastry *n.* pâtisserie *f.*; **— cook** *n.* pâtissier *m.*; **— shop** pâtisserie *f.*
pasturage *n.* pâturage *m.*
pasture *n.* pâture *f.*; pré *m.*; pâturage *m.*; **—** *vi.* paître; **—** *vt.* faire paître
pasty *a.* blême; pâteux
pat *n.* petit coup *m.*, tape *f.*; rondelle *f.*;

petit morceau (de beurre) *m.*; — *vt.*
frapper légèrement, taper; — *a.* convenable, propre, tout prêt

patch *n.* pièce *f.*, morceau *m.*; (eye) tampon *m.*; (face) mouche *f.*; terrain, plant *m.*, plantation *f.*; — *vt.* rapiécer, raccommoder

patchwork *n.* rapiéçage *m.*; travail à la pièce *m.*

pate *n.* tête *f.*

patella *n.* (anat.) rotule *f.*

patent *n.* brevet *m.*; — *a.* breveté; évident, patent; — **leather** *n.* cuir verni; — *vt.* faire breveter

paternal *a.* paternel

paternity *n.* paternité *f.*

path *n.* sentier, chemin *m.*; route *f.*

pathetic *a.* pathétique

pathfinder *n.* explorateur *m.*

pathological *a.* pathologique

pathology *n.* pathologie *f.*

pathos *n.* pathétique *m.*; pathos *m.*

pathway *n.* sentier *m.*

patience *n.* patience *f.*

patient *n.* malade *m.*; — *a.* patient; endurant; **be —** patienter

patina *n.* patine *f.*

patriarch *n.* patriarche *m.*

patrician *a. & n.* patricien *m.*

patrimony *n.* patrimoine *m.*

patriot *n.* patriote *m.*; **–ic** *a.* patriotique; **–ism** *n.* patriotisme *m.*

patrol *n.* patrouille *f.*; — *vi.* faire la ronde; — *vt.* surveiller

patrolman *n.* agent de police (qui fait la ronde) *m.*

patron *n.* patron, protecteur *m.*; — **saint** patron *m.*, patronne *f.*; **–age** *n.* patronage *m.*; clientèle *f.*; **–ize** *vt.* patronner; donner son clinetèle à; traiter avec condescendance

patter *vi.* bavarder; piétiner; faire du bruit; — *n.* bavardage *m.*; bruit *m.*

pattern *n.* patron, modèle *m.*

paucity *n.* manque *m.*, disette *f.*

paunch *n.* panse *f.*; bedaine *f.*

pauper *n.* pauvre *m.*, pauvresse *f.*

pause *n.* pause *f.*; — *vi.* faire une pause; s'arrêter; hésiter

pave *vt.* paver; frayer; (fig.) préparer; **–ment** *n.* pavé *m.*; pavage *m.*

pavilion *n.* pavillon *m.*

paving *n.* pavage *m.*; pavé *m.*

paw *n.* patte *f.*; — *vt. & vi.* frapper du pied; griffer; caresser avec la patte

pawl *n.* cliquet *m.*

pawn *n.* (chess) pion *m.*; gage *m.*; **–broker** *n.* prêteur sur gages *m.*; **–shop** *n.* mont-de-piété *m.*; — **ticket** *n.* reconnaissance de mont-de-piété *f.*; — *vt.*

engager, mettre en gage

pay *n.* solde *f.*; salaire *m.*; — *vt.* payer; acquitter; — **attention** prêter attention; — **a visit** rendre visite, faire visite; — **back** rembourser; — **for** payer; — **off** payer; réussir; — **up** solder; **–able** *a.* payable; **–day** *n.* jour de paie *m.*; **–load** *n.* poids utile *m.*; **–master** *n.* trésorier, payeur *m.*; **–ment** *n.* paiement *m.*; versement, acompte *m.*; **–roll** *n.* feuille de paie, liste de paie *f.*

pea *n.* pois *m.*; — **shooter** sarbacane *f.*; — **soup** potage Saint-Germain *m.*; purée de pois; — **soup fog** (coll.) brouillard épais

peace *n.* paix *f.*; **justice of the —** juge de paix *m.*; **–ful** *a.* paisible, tranquille; **–fulness** *n.* paix, tranquillité *f.*; — **offering** *n.* sacrifice expiatoire, cadeau de réconciliation *m.*

peace-loving *a.* pacifique

peacemaker *n.* conciliateur *m.*

peach *n.* pêche *f.*; (tree) pêcher *m.*

peak *n.* pic, sommet *m.*, cime *f.*; pointe *f.*; — *a.* meilleur; premier; **–ed** *a.* en pointe; (hat) à visière

peal *n.* carillon *m.*; bruit *m.*; coup *m.*; — *vt.* faire retentir; — *vi.* retentir; gronder

peanut *n.* arachide, cacahuète *f.*; — **brittle** caramel aux arachides *m.*; — **butter** crème d'arachides *f.*

pear *n.* poire *f.*; (tree) poirier *m.*

peasant *n.* paysan *m.*; **–ry** *n.* paysans *m. pl.*

peat *n.* tourbe *f.*

pebble *n.* caillou *m.*

pebbly *a.* caillouteux

pecan *n.* pacane *f.*; (tree) pacanier *m.*

peccadillo *n.* peccadille *f.*

peck *n.* coup de bec *m.*; (measure) peck *m.* (= 9 litres); — *vt. & vi.* becqueter, picoter

pectoral *a. & n.* pectoral *m.*

peculiar *a.* particulier, singulier, unique; **–ity** *n.* singularité *f.*

pecuniary *a.* pécuniaire

pedagogical *a.* pédagogique

pedagogue *n.* pédagogue *m.*

pedagogy *n.* pédagogie *f.*

pedal *n.* pédale *f.*; — *vi.* pédaler

pedant *n.* pédant *m.*; **–ic** *a.* pedant; **–ry** *n.* pédanterie *f.*

peddle *vt.* colporter; **–r** *n.* colporteur *m.*

pedestal *n.* piédestal *m.*

pedestrian *n.* piéton *m.*

pediatrician *n.* pédiatre *m.*

pedigree *n.* généalogie *f.*; lignage *m.*; pedigree *m.*; **–d** *a.* de race, pur-sang

pediment *n.* fronton *m.*

pedlar *n.* colporteur *m.*
pedometer *n.* podomètre *m.*
peek *n.* aperçu *m.*; coup d'œil *m.*; — *vi.* regarder furtivement
peekaboo *n.* cache-cache *m.*
peel *n.* pelure *f.*; peau *f.*; écorce *f.*; — *vt.* peler, éplucher
peep *n.* regard furtif *m.*; cri (d'un poussin) *m.*; pépiement *m.*; — *vi.* regarder furtivement; crier, pépier
peephole *n.* judas *m.*
peer *n.* pair *m.*; — *vi.* regarder longuement; **-age** *n.* pairie *f.*; **-less** *a.* incomparable, sans pareil
peevish *a.* bourru, maussade; **-ness** *n.* mauvaise humeur *f.*
peg *n.* cheville *f.*; (tent) piquet *m.*; — *vt.* cheviller
pegleg *n.* jambe de bois *f.*
pejorative *a.* péjoratif
pellagra *n.* pellagre *f.*
pellet *n.* boulette *f.*; grain de plomb *m.*, balle *f.*
pell-mell *adv.* pêle-mêle
pelt *n.* peau, fourrure *f.*; — *vt.* assaillir; battre
pelvic *a.* pelvien
pelvis *n.* bassin *m.*
pen *n.* plume *f.*; stylographe, stylo *m.*; (cattle) enclos *m.*; (poultry) poulailler; **ballpoint** — stylo à bille *m.*; — **name** nom de plume *m.*; — *vt.* écrire; — **in**, — **up** enfermer
penal *a.* pénal; **-ize** *vt.* punir; (sport) pénaliser
penalty *n.* pénalité, peine, punition, amende *f.*
penance *n.* pénitence *f.*
pencil *n.* crayon *m.*; — **sharpener** taille-crayons *m.*; — *vt.* dessiner au crayon
pendant *n.* pendant *m.*, pendeloque *f.*
pending *a.* pendant, indécis; — *prep.* en attendant
pendulum *n.* pendule *m.*
penetrate *vt. & vi.* pénétrer
penetrating *a.* pénétrant
penetration *n.* pénétration *f.*; sagacité *f.*
penholder *n.* porte-plume *m.*
penicillin *n.* pénicilline *f.*
peninsula *n.* péninsule *f.*; **-r** *a.* péninsulaire
penis *n.* pénis *m.*
penitence *n.* pénitence *f.*
penitent *a. & n.* pénitent *m.*
penitentiary *n.* prison *f.*
penknife *n.* canif *m.*
penmanship *n.* écriture *f.*
pennant *n.* banderole, flamme *f.*
penniless *a.* sans le sou
penny *n.* sou *m.*

pension *n.* pension *f.*; retraite *f.*; allocation *f.*; — *vt.*, — **off** mettre à la retraite; **-er** *n.* pensionnaire, retraité *m.*
pensive *a.* pensif
pentagon *n.* pentagone *m.*; **-al** *a.* pentagonal
pentameter *n.* pentamètre *m.*
penthouse *n.* appartement (aménagé **au** sommet d'un grand bâtiment) *m.*
pent-up *a.* (emotion) refoulé; enfermé
penumbra *n.* pénombre *f.*
penurious *a.* parcimonieux; pauvre
penury *n.* indigence, pénurie *f.*
people *n.* peuple *m.*; gens *m. pl.*; parents *m. pl.*; public *m.*; — *vt.* peupler
pepper *n.* poivre *m.*; poivron, piment *m.*; — *vt.* poivrer; (fig.) saupoudrer; **-y** *a.* poivré
peppercorn *n.* grain de poivre *m.*
peppermint *n.* menthe poivrée *f.*
pepsin *n.* pepsine *f.*
peptic *a.* digestif, gastrique
per *prep.* par, pour; — **cent** pour cent
perambulator *n.* voiture d'enfant *f.*
perceivable *a.* perceptible
perceive *vt.* apercevoir, sentir, voir
per cent *n.* pour cent *m.*
percentage *n.* pourcentage *m.*
perceptibility *n.* perceptibilité *f.*
perceptible *a.* perceptible
perception *n.* perception *f.*
perceptive *a.* perceptif
perch *n.* (fish) perche *f.*; perchoir *m.*; — *vt. & (vi.)* (se) percher
perchance *adv.* par hasard
percolate *vt. & vi.* filtrer
percolator *n.* cafetière (à l'américaine) *f.*
percussion *n.* percussion *f.*, coup *m.*; — **cap** *n.* capsule *f.*
perdition *n.* perdition *f.*; ruine *f.*
peremptory *a.* péremptoire, absolu
perennial *a.* perpétuel; (bot.), vivace; **-ly** *adv.* éternellement; tout le temps
perfect *vt.* perfectionner, achever, compléter; — *a.* parfait; complet; **-ion** *n.* perfection *f.*
perfidious *a.* perfide
perfidy *n.* perfidie *f.*
perforate *vt.* perforer, percer
perforation *n.* perforation *f.*
perforce *adv.* forcément
perform *vt. & vi.* exécuter, accomplir, faire; réussir; **-ance** *n.* accomplissement *m.*, exécution *f.*; ouvrage *m.*; exploit, fait *m.*, action *f.*; représentation *f.*; **-er** *n.* exécutant, artiste, acteur *m.*
perfume *n.* parfum *m.*; — *vt.* parfumer; **-r** *n.* parfumeur *m.*
perfunctory *a.* superficiel, négligent

perhaps *adv.* peut-être
pericardium *n.* péricarde *m.*
perigee *n.* périgée *m.*
peril *n.* péril, danger *m.*; **-ous** *a.* dangereux
perimeter *n.* périmètre *m.*
period *n.* période *f.*; époque *f.*; âge *m.*; terme *m.*; (punctuation) point *m.*; **-ic(al)** *a.* périodique; **-ical** *n.* périodique *f.*
peripatetic *a.* péripatétique; ambulant
peripheral *a.* périmétrique
periphery *n.* périphérie *f.*
periphrasis *n.* périphrase *f.*
periscope *n.* périscope *m.*
perish *vi.* périr; **-able** *a.* périssable
peristalsis *n.* mouvement péristaltique *m.*
peritoneum *n.* péritoine *m.*
peritonitis *n.* péritonite *f.*
perjure *vt.* parjurer; **-d** *a.* parjure; **-er** *n.* parjure *m.*
perjury *n.* parjure *m.*
perk *vi.* se rengorger; **— up** se ranimer; **-y** *a.* animé, vif
permanent *a.* permanent; **— wave** *n.* ondulation permanente, indéfrisable *f.*; **-ly** *adv.* d'une manière permanente
permanganate *n.* permanganate *m.*
permeable *a.* perméable
permeate *vt.* passer à travers, pénétrer, saturer
permeation *n.* pénétration *f.*
permissible *a.* admissible, tolérable
permissive *a.* qui permet; indulgent
permit *n.* permis *m.*; **—** *vt.* permettre; laisser
permutation *n.* permutation *f.*
pernicious *a.* pernicieux
peroration *n.* péroraison *f.*
peroxide *n.* peroxyde *m.*; peroxyde d'hydrogène *m.*
perpendicular *a. & n.* perpendiculaire *m.*
perpetrate *vt.* commettre, faire
perpetration *n.* perpétration *f.*
perpetrator *n.* auteur *m.*
perpetual *a.* perpétuel; sans cesse, sans fin
perpetuate *vt.* perpétuer
perpetuation *n.* perpétuation *f.*
perplex *vt.* embarrasser; confondre; embrouiller; **-ity** *n.* perplexité *f.*, embarras *m.*
perquisite *n.* casuel, émolument *m.*
persecute *vt.* persécuter
persecution *n.* persécution *f.*
persecutor *n.* persécuteur *m.*
perseverance *n.* persévérance *f.*
persevere *vi.* persévérer
persevering *a.* persévérant
Persia *n.* Perse *f.*; **-n** *a. & n.* persan *m.*;

-n Gulf Golfe Persique *m.*
persimmon *n.* plaqueminier *m.*
persist *vi.* persister; **-ence, -ency** *n.* persistance *f.*; **-ent** *a.* persistant
person *n.* personne *f.*; individu *m.*; personnalité *f.*; **-able** *a.* bien fait; aimable, sociable; **-age** *n.* personnage *m.*; personne *f.*; **-al** *a.* personnel; particulier; **-ality** *n.* personnalité *f.*; **-ification** *n.* personnification *f.*; **-ify** *vt.* personnifier
perspective *n.* perspective *f.*; **—** *a.* perspectif
perspicacity *n.* perspicacité *f.*
perspiration *n.* transpiration, sueur *f.*
perspire *vi.* transpirer, suer
persuade *vt.* persuader, convaincre
persuasion *n.* persuasion, conviction *f.*
persuasive *a.* persuasif
pert *a.* vif, pétulant, impertinent
pertain *vi.* appartenir, concerner
pertinence *n.* convenance, propriété *f.*; justesse *f.*
pertinent *a.* pertinent, convenable; juste, à propos
perturb *vt.* troubler, perturber; **-ation** *n.* perturbation *f.*, trouble *m.*
Peru *n.* Pérou *m.*
perusal *n.* lecture *f.*, examen *m.*
peruse *vt.* lire, parcourir
pervade *vt.* pénétrer
pervasive *a.* pénétrant
perverse *a.* pervers; têtu
perversion *n.* perversion *f.*
perversity *n.* perversité *f.*; méchanceté *f.*
pervert *vt.* pervertir, dépraver; **—** *n.* perverti *m.*
pervious *a.* perméable
pessimism *n.* pessimisme *m.*
pessimist *n.* pessimiste *m.*; **-ic** *a.* pessimiste
pest *n.* fléau *m.*; personne gênante *f.*; **-er** *vt.* gêner, ennuyer
pestilence *n.* peste *f.*
pestilent *a.* pestilentiel
pestle *n.* pilon *m.*
pet *n.* favori *m.*; animal favori *m.*; **— name** petit nom *m.*; **—** *vt.* caresser
petal *n.* pétale *m.*
petition *n.* pétition, supplication *f.*; demande *f.*; requête *f.*; **—** *vt.* pétitionner, supplier; demander à; réclamer à; **-er** *n.* demandeur *m.*; pétitionnaire *m. & f.*
petrel *n.* pétrel *m.*
petrify *vt. & (vi.)* (se) pétrifier
petroleum *n.* pétrole *m.*
petticoat *n.* jupon *m.*
pettiness *n.* petitesse *f.*
petty *a.* petit, inférieur; chétif; **— cash**

petite caisse *f.*; — **officer** (navy) sous-officier *m.*
petulance *n.* pétulance *f.*
petulant *a.* pétulant
pew *n.* banc d'église *m.*
pewter *n.* étain *m.*
phalanx *n.* phalange *f.*
phantom *n.* fantôme *m.*
Pharaoh *n.* Pharaon *m.*
Pharisee *n.* Pharisien *m.*
pharmaceutic(al) *a.* pharmaceutique
pharmacist *n.* pharmacien *m.*
pharmacy *n.* pharmacie *f.*
pharynx *n.* pharynx *m.*
phase *n.* phase *f.*
phenol *n.* phénol *m.*
phenomenal *a.* phénoménal
phenomenon *n.* phénomène *m.*
Philadelphia *n.* Philadelphie *f.*
philander *vi.* courir; **-er** *n.* coureur *m.*
philanthropic *a.* philanthropique
philanthropist *n.* philanthrope *m.*
philatelic *a.* philatélique
philatelist *n.* philateliste *m.*
philharmonic *a.* philharmonique
Philippines *n.* Philippines *f. pl.*
Philistine *n.* Philistin *m.*
philologist *n.* philologue *m.*
philology *n.* philologie *f.*
philosopher *n.* philosophe *m.*
philosophic(al) *a.* philosophique
philosophize *vi.* philosopher
philosophy *n.* philosophie *f.*
phlegm *n.* flegme *m.*; **-atic** *a.* flegmatique
phobia *n.* phobie *f.*
Phoenicia *n.* Phénicie *f.*; **-n** *a. & n.* phénicien *m.*
phone *n.* téléphone *m.*; — *vi.* téléphoner
phonetic *a.* phonétique; **-s** *n.* phonétique *f.*
phonic *a.* phonique
phosphate *n.* (chem.) phosphate *m.*
phosphide *n.* phosphure *m.*
phosphorescence *n.* phosphorescence *f.*
phosphoric *a.* phosphorique
phosphorus *n.* phosphore *m.*
photoelectric *a.* photo-électrique
photoengraving *n.* photogravure *f.*
photoflash lamp *n.* lampe éclair *f.*
photograph *n.* photographie *f.*; — *vt.* photographier; **-er** *n.* photographe *m.*; **-ic** *a.* photographique; **-y** *n.* photographie *f.*
photostat *n.* photocopie *f.*
photosynthesis *n.* photosynthèse *f.*
phrase *n.* phrase, expression *f.*; locution *f.*; — *vt.* exprimer, rédiger
phraseology *n.* phraséologie *f.*
phrenetic *a.* frénétique
phrenology *n.* phrénologie *f.*

physic *n.* médicament *m.*; purgatif *m.*; médecine *f.*; **-s** *n.* physique *f.*; **-al** *a.* physique; matériel
physician *n.* médecin *m.*
physicist *n.* physicien *m.*
physiognomy *n.* physionomie *f.*
physiological *a.* physiologique
physiologist *n.* physiologiste *m.*
physiology *n.* physiologie *f.*
physiotherapy *n.* physicothérapie *f.*
physique *n.* physique *m.*
pianist *n.* pianiste *m. & f.*
piano *n.* piano *m.*; **baby grand** — piano à demi-queue *m.*; **grand** — piano à queue; **upright** — piano droit *m.*
Picardy *n.* Picardie *f.*
picayune *a.* mesquin
piccolo *n.* piccolo, octavin *m.*
pick *n.* pioche *f.*; — *vi.* piquer, becqueter; — *vt.* cueillir, glaner, ramasser; éplucher, trier; choisir; — **out** choisir; — **up** ramasser; acheter à bon marché; retrouver; relever; apprendre; **-ings** *n. pl.* épluchures *f. pl.*, petits morceaux *m. pl.*; profit *m.*
pickaback *adv.* sur le dos
pickax(e) *n.* pioche *f.*
pickerel *n.* brocheton *m.*
picket *n.* piquet *m.*; pieu *m.*; (striker) piquet de grève, débaucheur *m.*; — **fence** palis *m.*; — *vt.* entourer de débaucheurs
pickle *n.* cornichon *m.*; (coll.) difficulté *f.*; mauvais pas *m.*; — *vt.* conserver au vinaigre
picklock *n.* crochet *m.*
pickpocket *n.* pickpocket *m.*
pickup *n.* (radio, television, or phonograph) pick-up *m.*; (coll.) fille, personne rencontrée dans la rue *f.*; (auto) accélération *f.*
picnic *n.* pique-nique *m.*; — *vi.* pique-niquer
picot *n.* picot *m.*; — *vt.* picoter
pictorial *a.* pittoresque, illustré
picture *n.* tableau *m.*; peinture *f.*; image *f.*; film *m.*; — **tube** *n.* kinescope *m.*; — *vt.* peindre; représenter
picturesque *a.* pittoresque
piddling *a.* insignifiant, mesquin
pidgin *a.*, — **English** jargon anglo-oriental *m.*
pie *n.* tarte *f.*
piebald *a.* pie
piece *n.* pièce *f.*, morceau *m.*; bout *m.*; partie *f.*; — *vt.* raccommoder, rapiécer; — **together** joindre, unir, réunir
piecemeal *a.* séparé, divisé; — *adv.* par petits morceaux
piecework *n.* travail à la pièce *m.*

pied *a.* pie, bigarré

pier *n.* môle *m.*; pilier, pied-droit *m.*; pile *f.*

pierce *vt. & vi.* percer, pénétrer

piercing *a.* pénétrant; aigu

piety *n.* piété, dévotion *f.*

pig *n.* cochon *m.*; porc *m.*; **buy a — in a poke** acheter chat en poche; **— iron** fer en fonte *m.*; **–gish** *a.* semblable à un cochon; glouton

pigeon *n.* pigeon *m.*; **clay —** pigeon artificiel *m.*; **homing —** pigeon voyageur *m.*

pigeon-breasted *a.* (qui a) la poitrine en saillie

pigeonhole *n.* case *f.*

pigheaded *a.* têtu, entêté; **–ness** *n.* entêtement *m.*, obstination *f.*

pigment *n.* pigment *m.*; couleur *f.*; **–ation** *n.* pigmentation *f.*

pigmy *n.* pygmée *m.*

pigpen, pigsty *n.* étable à cochons *f.*

pigskin *n.* peau de porc *f.*; (coll.) ballon de football *m.*

pigtail *n.* tresse *f.*

pike *n.* pique *f.*; pointe *f.*; (fish) brochet *m.*; (coll.) autostrade *f.*

pilaster *n.* pilastre *m.*

pilchard *n.* sardine *f.*

pile *n.* pieu, pilotis *m.*; monceau, tas *m.*; bûcher *m.*; édifice *m.*; duvet *m.*; (coll.) fortune *f.*; **—** *vt.* entasser; amonceler; amasser; **—** *vi.*, **— up** s'entasser

piles *n. pl.* hémorroïdes *f. pl.*

pilfer *vt.* voler, chiper; **–age, –ing** *n.* petits vols *m. pl.*

pilgrim *n.* pèlerin *m.*; **–age** *n.* pèlerinage *m.*

pill *n.* pilule *f.*

pillar *n.* pilier *m.*

pillbox *n.* boîte à pilules *f.*; (mil.) réduit en béton armé *m.*

pillory *n.* pilori *m.*; **—** *vt.* mettre au pilori

pillow *n.* oreiller *m.*; **—** *vt.* reposer, coucher

pillowcase *n.* taie d'oreiller *f.*

pilot *n.* pilote *m.*; **—** *vt.* piloter; **— light** *n.* veilleuse *f.*

pimento *n.* piment *m.*

pimple *n.* bouton *m.*, pustule *f.*

pimply *a.* boutonneux

pin *n.* épingle *f.*; (bowling) quille *f.*; **— money** argent de poche *m.*; **safety —** épingle de sûreté *f.*; **—** *vt.* épingler; fixer, attacher

pinafore *n.* bavette *f.*; sarrau *m.*

pincers *n. pl.* pinces, tenailles *f. pl.*

pinch *n.* pince *f.*; prise *f.*; difficulté *f.*, embarras *m.*; **—** *vt. & vi.* pincer; serrer; **–ed** *a.* tiré; à l'étroit

pinch-hit *vi.* (coll.); **— for** remplacer, suppléer (provisoirement)

pincushion *n.* pelote à épingles *f.*

pine *n.* pin *m.*; **—** *vi.* languir, soupirer

pineapple *n.* ananas *m.*

pinhole *n.* trou d'épingle *m.*; (phot.) sténopé *m.*

pinion *n.* pignon *m.*; **—** *vt.* lier

pink *n.* (bot.) œillet *m.*; rose (couleur) *f.*; **— of condition** en parfaite santé *f.*; **—** *a.* rose; **—** *vt.* denteler, découper

pinnacle *n.* pinacle, sommet *m.*; couronnement *m.*

pinpoint *vt.* localiser, mettre au net

pint *n.* demi-litre *m.*; pinte *f.*

pinwheel *n.* roue à fuseaux *f.*

pioneer *n.* pionnier *m.*

pious *a.* pieux

pip *n.* (bot.) pépin *m.*; signal *m.*

pipe *n.* tuyau *m.*; pipe *f.*; **—** *vt.* jouer; faire passer par un tuyau; **–r** *n.* joueur de flute *m.*; **–line** *n.* conduite *f.*; pipeline *m.*

pipecleaner *n.* cure-pipe *m.*

piping *n.* passe-poil *m.*; tuyauterie *f.*; **—** *a.* maladif; **— hot** tout chaud

piquant *a.* piquant

pique *n.* pique *f.*; **—** *vt.* piquer, irriter

piracy *n.* piraterie *f.*; (literature) plagiat *m.*

pirate *n.* pirate *m.*; **—** *vi.* commettre un plagiat; pirater

pirouette *n.* pirouette *f.*; **—** *vi.* pirouetter

pistachio *n.* pistache *f.*

pistol *n.* pistolet *m.*

piston *n.* piston *m.*; **— rod** *n.* tige du piston *f.*

pit *n.* fosse *f.*; trou *m.*; carrière *f.*, tombeau *m.*; (theat.) parterre; creux *m.*; **—** *vt.* opposer; grêler, marquer de trous

pitch *n.* poix *f.*; degré, point *m.*; hauteur *f.*; portée *f.*; (mus.) ton *m.*; **—** *vt.* poisser; fixer, planter, ranger; jeter, lancer; paver; obscurcir; **—** *vi.* tomber; (naut.) tanguer; **— (in)** se mettre au travail; **–er** *n.* cruche *f.*; (sport) joueur qui lance la balle *m.*

pitchblende *n.* pechblende *f.*

pitchfork *n.* fourche *f.*

pitch pipe *n.* diapason *m.*

piteous *a.* piteux, pitoyable

pitfall *n.* piège *m.*

pith *n.* moelle *f.*; **–y** *a.* plein de moelle

pitiable *a.* digne de pitié

pitiful *a.* déplorable, pitoyable; méprisable

pitiless *a.* impitoyable

pittance *n.* pitance, portion *f.*

pitter-patter *n.* bruit de la pluie sur un

toit *m.*
pituitary *a.* pituitaire
pity *n.* pitié, compassion *f.*; **it is a —** c'est dommage; **to take — on** prendre en pitié; **—** *vt.* plaindre, avoir pitié de
pivot *n.* pivot *m.*; **—** *vi.* pivoter
pixie *n.* lutin *m.*, fée *f.*
placard *n.* placard *m.*, affiche *f.*; **—** *vt.* afficher
placate *vt.* apaiser
place *n.* place *f.*; lieu *m.*; endroit *m.*; rang *m.*; emploi *m.*; demeure *f.*; position *f.*; **in — of** au lieu de; **out of —** déplacé; **take —** avoir lieu; **—** *vt.* placer, mettre; **–ment** *n.* mise *f.*; position *f.*; **— kick** *n.* (football) coup placé, coup d'envoie *m.*
placer *n.* (mining) placer *m.*; placeur *m.*
placid *a.* paisible, calme, placide; **–ity** *n.* placidité *f.*, calme *m.*
plagiarism *n.* plagiat *m.*
plagiarize *vt.* plagier
plague *n.* peste, contagion *f.*; tourment *m.*; **—** *vt.* tourmenter
plaid *n.* tartan, plaid, tissu écossais *m.*
plain *n.* plaine *f.*; **—** *a.* plat, uni, simple, sincère, franc; clair; laid; **–ness** *n.* simplicité, franchise *f.*; laideur *f.*
plainsman *n.* homme des plaines *m.*
plaintiff *n.* demandeur *m.*
plaintive *a.* plaintif
plait *n.* pli *m.*, tresse *f.*; **—** *vt.* plisser; tresser
plan *n.* plan, dessin *m.*; projet *m.*; **—** *vt.* projeter; dresser le plan de; compter; avoir l'intention de
plane *n.* plan *m.*; (tool) rabot *m.*; (avi.) avion *m.*; **—** *vt.* raboter; **—** *a.* plan, plat; **— tree** *n.* platane *m.*
planet *n.* planète *f.*; **–ary** *a.* planétaire; **–arium** *n.* planétaire *m.*
plank *n.* planche *f.*; **—** *vt.* planchéier; **–ing** *n.* planchéiage *m.*, planches *f. pl.*
plant *n.* plante *f.*; plant *m.*; (industry) usine *f.*; **—** *vt.* planter; établir; **— louse** *n.* puceron *m.*; **–er** *n.* planteur *m.*
plantain *n.* plantain *m.*
plantation *n.* plantation *f.*
plasma *n.* plasma *m.*; **—physics** *n.* physique plasmatique *f.*
plaster *n.* plâtre *m.*; emplâtre *m.*; **—** *vt.* plâtrer; **adhesive —** emplâtre resineux; sparadrap *m.*; **mustard —** sinapisme *m.*; **–board** *n.* panneau de plâtre et de papier *m.*; **— of Paris** *n.* gypse *m.*; plâtre fin *m.*; **–er** *n.* plâtrier *m.*; **–ing** *n.* plâtrage *m.*
plastic *a.* plastique; **—** *n.* matière plastique *f.*; **–ity** *n.* plasticité *f.*
plat *n.* plan *m.*, carte *f.*

plate *n.* (metal) plaque *f.*; (dish) assiette *f.*; (flatware) argenterie *f.*; (food) plat *m.*; (teeth) dentier *m.*; (engraving) gravure *f.*; **—** *vt.* plaquer, laminer; étamer; argenter; **— glass** glâce (sans tain) *f.*
plateau *n.* plateau, massif *m.*
plateful *n.* assiettée *f.*
platform *n.* plate-forme *f.*; (rail.) quai *m.*; (politics) programme politique *m.*
platinum *n.* platine *m.*
platitude *n.* platitude *f.*
platonic *a.* platonique
platoon *n.* peloton *m.*
platter *n.* plat *m.*
plaudit *n.* applaudissement *m.*
plausibility *n.* plausibilité *f.*
plausible *a.* plausible
play *n.* jeu *m.*; (theat.) pièce *f.*; **— on words** calembour *m.*; **—** *vi.* jouer; **—** *vt.* jouer; faire; **— a trick on** jouer un tour à; **— on** abuser de; **— tennis** jouer au tennis; **— the piano** jouer du piano; **— up to** courtiser; flatter; **–er** *n.* joueur *m.*; (theat.) acteur, comédien *m.*; **–er piano** piano à rouleau *m.*; **–ful** *a.* badin, espiègle; **–ing** *n.* jeu *m.*; **–ing cards** cartes à jouer *f. pl.*; **–ing field** terrain *m.*
playboy *n.* luron, libertin *m.*; homme riche qui fréquente les boîtes de nuit *m.*
playgoer *n.* habitué du théâtre *m.*
playground *n.* terrain de jeu *m.*, cour de récréation *f.*
playhouse *n.* théâtre *m.*
playmate *n.* camarade de jeu *m.*
plaything *n.* jouet *m.*
playwright *n.* auteur dramatique *m.*
plea *n.* défense *f.*; excuse *f.*; prières *f. pl.*
plead *vi.* plaider; **—** *vt.* défendre; alléguer, prétexter; **–ing** *n.* prières *f. pl.*; (law) plaidoirie *f.*
pleasant *a.* agréable; **–ness** *n.* agrément, charme *m.*; **–ry** *n. pl.* plaisanterie *f.*
please *vt. & vi.* plaire à, être agréable, contenter; **—** *interj.* s'il vous plaît; **as you —** comme il vous plaira; **if you —** s'il vous plaît; **— be seated** veuillez vous asseoir; **–d** *a.* content, heureux; **–d to meet you** enchanté de faire votre connaissance
pleasing *a.* agréable, charmant
pleasurable *a.* agréable
pleasure *n.* plaisir, gré *m.*; **with —** avec plaisir, volontiers
pleat *n.* pli, pli creux *m.*; **—** *vt.* plisser, mettre en plis
plebeian *a. & n.* plébéien *m.*
plebiscite *n.* plébiscite *m.*
pledge *n.* gage *m.*; caution *f.*; toast *m.*; vœu *m.*, promesse *f.*; **—** *vt.* engager;

promettre
plenary *a.* plein, complet, parfait
plenipotentiary *n. & a.* plénipotentiaire *m.*
plentiful *a.* abondant
plenty *n.* abondance *f.;* **have — of** ne pas manquer de, avoir beaucoup de
plethora *n.* pléthore *f.*
pleurisy *n.* pleurésie *f.*
plexus *n.* plexus *m.*
pliability *n.* souplesse, flexibilité *f.*
pliable, pliant *a.* flexible, pliable; docile
pliers *n. pl.* pince *f.*
plight *n.* condition *f.,* état *m.;* **—** *vt.* engager
plod *vi.* piocher; marcher avec peine; **–der** *n.* piocheur *m.*
plop *n. & interj.* pouf, plouf *m.;* **—** *vi.* faire plouf
plot *n.* morceau de terre *m.;* plan, complot *m.;* intrigue *f.;* **—** *vt. & vi.* comploter, conspirer, machiner; inventer; **–ter** *n.* conspirateur *m.;* **–ting** *n.* machinations *f. pl.*
plow, plough *n.* charrue *f.;* bouvet *m.;* **gang —** charrue polysoc *f.;* **—** *vt.* labourer; sillonner; **–ing** *n.* labourage *m.;* **–man** *n.* laboureur *m.*
plowshare *n.* soc de charrue *m.*
pluck *n.* action intrépide *f.;* courage *m.;* fressure (d'un animal) *f.;* **—** *vt.* arracher; (feathers) plumer; cueillir; **–y** *a.* courageux
plug *n.* tampon *m.,* cheville *f.;* piston *m ;* bouchon *m.;* prise (de courant) *f.;* fiche *f.;* **spark —** bougie *f.;* **—** *vt.* boucher; cheviller; tamponner; **— away** *vi.* (coll.) persévérer; **— in** mettre la fiche dans (la prise)
plum *n.* prune *f.;* (tree) prunier *m.*
plumb *n.* plomb *m.;* sonde *f.;* **— line** *n.* niveau *m.;* fil à plomb *m.;* **—** *vt.* mettre à plomb; **—** *adv.* à plomb; **–er** *n.* plombier *m.;* **–ing** *n.* installation sanitaire *f.*
plume *n.* plume *f.,* panache *m.;* plumet *m.;* **—** *vt.* orner d'une plume; lisser
plummet *n.* plomb *m.,* sonde *f.;* **—** *vi.* tomber
plump *vi.* s'enfler; tomber lourdement; soutenir (une candidature); **—** *a.* dodu, potelé, plantureux; **–ness** *n.* embonpoint *m.*
plunder *n.* pillage, butin *m.;* **—** *vt.* piller, spolier
plunge *vt.* plonger; **—** *vi.* se plonger; (se) jeter; **–r** *n.* plongeon *m.;* piston *m.;* (person) risque-tout *m.*
pluperfect *n.* plus-que-parfait *m.*
plural *n. & a.* pluriel *m.;* **–ity** *n.* pluralité *f.*

plus *prep.* plus
plush *n.* peluche *f.;* **—** *a.* (coll.) somptueux, élégant
plutocracy *n.* plutocratie *f.*
plutocrat *n.* ploutocrate *m.*
plutonium *n.* plutonium *m.*
ply *n.* épaisseur *f.;* **—** *vt.* se servir de; accabler, offrir
plywood *n.* bois contreplaqué *m.*
P.M. de l'après-midi, du soir
pneumatic *a.* pneumatique
pneumonia *n.* pneumonie *f.;* fluxion de poitrine *f.*
poach *vt.* pocher; **—** *vi.* piller; braconner; **–er** *n.* braconnier *m.*
pocket *n.* poche *f.;* (billiards) blouse *f.;* **— book** livre de poche *m.;* **–knife** couteau de poche *m.;* **—** *vt.* empocher; blouser; avaler (un affront)
pocketbook *n.* (ladies) sac *m.*
pock-marked *a.* grêlé
pod *n.* cosse, écale *f.*
poem *n.* poème *m*
poet *n.* poète *m.;* **–ic(al)** *a.* poétique; **–ics** *n.* art poétique *m.;* **–ry** *n.* poésie *f.*
poignancy *n.* piquant *m.*
poignant *a.* piquant; douloureux, aigu
point *n.* pointe *f.;* cap *m.;* point, moment *m.;* degré *m.;* lieu *m.;* but *m.;* sujet *m.,* idée *f.;* (math.) virgule *f.;* **—** **blank** directement, de but en blanc; **— of departure** point de départ *m.;* **— of view** point de vue *m.;* **in — of fact** en fait; **make a — of** faire un devoir de; **to the —** à propos; **to the — of** jusqu'à; **—** *vt.* pointer; aiguiser, affiler; **— out** montrer, signaler; **— up** (coll.) souligner; **–ed** *a.* pointu; piquant, mordant; marqué; **–er** *n.* (dog) chien d'arrêt *m.;* aiguille *f.;* baguette *f.;* **–less** *a.* sans pointe; sans but, sans raison
poise *vt.* tenir suspendu; tenir prêt; **—** *vi.* se tenir suspendu, se tenir prêt; **—** *n.* sang-froid, savoir-faire *m.;* équilibre *m.;* **–d** *a.* bien équilibré, suave, imperturbable
poison *n.* poison *m.;* **—** *vt.* empoisonner; **–ing** *n.* empoisonnement *m.;* **–ous** *a.* empoisonné; venimeux; (plants) vénéneux
poke *n.* coup de poing *m.;* (coll.) sac *m.;* **—** *vi.* fouiller; **—** *vt.* donner un coup de poing à; taper; (head) passer; (fire) tisonner; **–r** *n.* tisonnier *m.;* (game) poker *m.*
Poland *n.* Pologne *f.*
polar *a.* polaire; **–ity** *n.* polarité *f.;* **–ize** *vt.* polariser
pole *n.* pôle *m.;* perche *f.;* timon *m.;* poteau *m.;* **— vault** saut à la perche *m.*

Pole *n.* Polonais *m.*
polecat *n.* putois *m.*
polemic *n.* polémique *f.*
police *n.* police *f.*; — **chief, chief of** —
n. commissaire de police *m.*; — **court**
n. tribunal de police *m.*; — **dog** berger
allemand *m.*; — **headquarters,** — **station** commissariat de police *m.*; — *vt.*
surveiller, policer
policeman *n.* agent de police *m.*
policewoman *n.* femme-agent de police *f.*
policy *n.* politique *f.*; ruse *f.*; police *f.*;
plan *m.*; **insurance** — police d'assurance *f.*
polio(myelitis) *n.* poliomyélite *f.*
polish *n.* poli *m.*; élégance *f.*; — *vt.* polir; vernir; cirer
Polish *a. & n.* polonais *m.*
polite *a.* poli; courtois; —**ness** *n.* politesse
f.; courtoisie *f.*
politic *a.* politique; prudent, judicieux;
—**al** *a.* politique; —**s** *n.* politique *f.*
politician *n.* politicien *m.*
polka *n.* polka *f.*; — **dot** *n.* rond de couleur
m.; pois *m.*
poll *n.* liste électorale *f.*; enquête *f.*; voix
f., vote *m.*; —**s** *n. pl.* urnes *f. pl.*; — **tax**
n. capitation *f.*; — *vt.* consulter; voter
pollen *n.* pollen *m.*
pollinate *vt.* féconder
polling booth *n.* isoloir; bureau de scrutin
m.
pollute *vt.* polluer; souiller
pollution *n.* pollution *f.*; souillure *f.*
polo *n.* polo *m.*; — **shirt** maillot *m.*
poltroon *n.* poltron, lâche *m.*
polygamous *a.* polygame
polygamy *n.* polygamie *f.*
polyglot *n. & a.* polyglotte *m.*
polygon *n.* polygone *m.*; —**al** *a.* polygone
polygraph *n.* polygraphe *m.*
polymer chemistry *n.* chimie polymère *f.*
Polynesia *n.* Polynésie *f.*; —**n** *a. & n.*
polynésien *m.*
polyp *n.* polype *m.*
polyphonic *a.* polyphonique
polyphony *n.* polyphonie *f.*
polysyllabic *a.* polysyllabe
polysyllable *n.* polysyllabe *m.*
polytechnic *a.* polytechnique
pomade *n.* pommade *f.*
pomegranate *n.* grenade *f.*; (tree) grenadier *m.*
pommel *n.* pommeau *m.*; — *vt.* rosser
pomp *n.* pompe *f.*, éclat *m.*, faste *m.*; —**ous**
a. pompeux; ampoulé; suffisant; —**ous-
ness** *n.* suffisance *f.*; emphase *f.*
pompadour *n.* coiffure à la Pompadour *f.*
pompom *n.* (mil.) canon-mitrailleuse *m.*
pond *n.* étang *m.*; vivier *m.*; mare *f.*

ponder *vt. & vi.* peser; méditer; —**able** *a.*
pondérable; —**ous** *a.* pesant
pontiff *n.* pontife *m.*
pontifical *a.* pontifical
pontificate *n.* pontificat *m.*; — *vi.* parler
ex-cathedra; pontifier
pontoon *n.* ponton *m.*
pony *n.* poney *m.*; (educ.) traduction *f.*
(utilisée par un élève pour éviter de
traduire lui-même)
pony tail *n.* (hair) queue de cheval *f.*
poodle *n.* caniche *f.*
pool *n.* étang *m.*; mare *f.*; (swimming)
piscine *f.*; (game) billard (à blouses)
m.; (betting) poule *f.*; exploitation en
commun *f.*; dépôt *m.*; — *vt.* mettre en
commun, exploiter en commun; —
room *n.* salle de billard *f.*
poop *n.* poupe *f.*; (coll.) potins *m. pl.*
poor *a.* pauvre; indigent; mauvais; inférieur; — *n.* pauvres *m. pl.*; —**ness** *n.*
pauvreté *f.*; infériorité *f.*
poorhouse *n.* maison de charité *f.*, refuge
m.
pop *n.* petit coup *m.*; (coll.) père *m.*; (beverage) soda *m.*, boisson gazeuse; — *vi.*
éclater; — *vt.* faire éclater; — **in** (coll.)
entrer en passant; — **up** arriver; apparaître; — *interj.* crac!
popcorn *n.* maïs éclaté *m.*
Pope *n.* pape *m.*; (Greek Church) pope *m.*
popgun *n.* canonnière *f.*
poplar *n.* peuplier *m.*
poplin *n.* popeline *f.*
populace *n.* populace *f.*
popular *a.* populaire; à la mode; —**ity** *n.*
popularité *f.*; —**ize** *vt.* populariser
populate *vt.* peupler
population *n.* population *f.*
populous *a.* populeux
porcelain *n.* porcelaine *f.*
porch *n.* porche, portique *m.*, véranda *f.*
porcine *a.* de porc
porcupine *n.* porc-épic *m.*
pore *n.* pore *m.*; — *vi.* avoir les yeux
fixés; — **over** dévorer; méditer; être
absorbé dans
pork *n.* porc *m.*; — **chop** côtelette de
porc *f.*; —**er** *n.* porc, cochon *m.*
pornographic *a.* pornographique
pornography *n.* pornographie *f.*
porosity *n.* porosité *f.*
porous *a.* poreux
porphyry *n.* porphyre *m.*
porpoise *n.* marsouin *m.*
porridge *n.* bouillie *f.*
port *n.* port *m.*; (gun opening) sabord *m.*;
(wine) porto *m.*; (side) bâbord *m.*;
(hole) hublot *m.*; — *vt.* (arms) **porter;**
(naut.) mettre à bâbord

portable *a.* portatif
portage *n.* portage *m.*
portal *n.* portail *m.*, porte *f.*
portend *vt.* présager
portent *n.* présage *m.*; **-ous** *a.* de mauvais augure
porter *n.* portier *m.*; porteur, portefaix *m.*
porterhouse *n.* châteaubreant *m.*
portfolio *n.* portefeuille *m.*; carton *m.*
portico *n.* portique *m.*
portion *n.* portion, part, partie *f.*; dot *m.*; — *vt.* partager; doter
portliness *n.* embonpoint *m.*
portly *a.* corpulent
portrait *n.* portrait *m.*; — **painter** portraitiste *m.*
portray *vt.* peindre, dépeindre, décrire; **-al** *n.* portrait *m.*; peinture *f.*; description *f.*
Portugal *n.* Portugal *m.*
Portuguese *a. & n.* portugais *m.*
pose *n.* pose, attitude *f.*; — *vt.* poser; proposer; — **as** se faire passer pour; confondre (avec)
position *n.* position, situation *f.*; attitude, posture *f.*; thèse *f.*; **in a** — **to** à même de; **in** — en place; — *vt.* situer
positive *n.* positif *m.*; — *a.* positif; certain, sûr, assuré; affirmatif; vrai; **-ly** *adv.* positivement; certainement
positivism *n.* positivisme *m.*
positron *n.* positron *m.*
posse *n.* force publique d'un comté; milice *f.*
possess *vt.* posséder; jouir de; avoir; disposer de; **be -ed of** posséder; **-ion** *n.* possession *f.*; **-ive** *a.* possessif; **-or** *n.* possesseur *m.*
possibility *n.* possibilité *f.*; moyen *m.*; éventualité *f.*
possible *a.* possible; éventuel; **if** — si (c'est) possible
possibly *adv.* peut-être
post *n.* poste *f.*; courrier *m.*; poste, emploi *m.*; poteau *m.*; pilier *m.*; pieu (x) *m.* (*m. pl.*) (mil.) (lieu de) garnison *f.*; — **office** bureau de poste *m.*; — *vt.* afficher; mettre à la poste; — **no bills** défense d'afficher; **-al** *a.* postal; **-er** *n.* affiche *f.*
postage *n.* affranchissement *m.*; — **due letter** lettre taxée *f.*; — **meter** compteur d'affranchissement *m.*; — **stamp** timbre-poste *m.*
post card *n.* carte postale *f.*
postdate *vt.* postdater
posterior *a.* postérieur; — *n.* postérieur, derrière *m.*
posterity *n.* postérité *f.*
postgraduate *n.* étudiant *m.* (qui pour-

suit des études au-delà du baccalauréat)
posthaste *adv.* promptement, en grande diligence; en grand hâte
posthumous *a.* posthume
postilion *n.* postillon *m.*
postman *n.* facteur *m.*
postmark *n.* oblitération *f.*
postmaster *n.* receveur des postes *m.*
post-mortem *n.* (med.) autopsie *f.*; — *a. & adv.* après décès
postpaid *a.* port payé; — *adv.* franco
postpone *vt.* remettre, différer; **-ment** *n.* ajournement *m.*
postscript, P.S. *n.* post-scriptum *m.*
postulate *n.* postulat *m.*; — *vt.* poser, postuler
posture *n.* posture, attitude; pose *f.*
postwar *a.* d'après-guerre
pot *n.* pot *m.*; **-herb** herbe potagère *f.*; — **roast** estouffade *f.*; **take -luck** courir la fortune du pot; — *vt.* mettre en pot
potable *a.* potable
potash *n.* potasse *f.*
potato *n.* pomme de terre *f.*; **baked** — pomme au four *f.*; **boiled** — pomme à l'anglaise *f.*; **fried -es** (pommes) frites *f.*; **mashed -es** purée de pommes *f.*; **sweet** — patate *f.*; — **masher** presse-purée *m.*
potbellied *a.* ventru
potency *n.* puissance, force *f.*
potent *a.* puissant, fort; **-ate** *n.* potentat *m.*; **-ial** *a.* virtuel, potentiel, latent; **-iality** *n.* potentialité *f.*
potholder *n.* poignée pour les pots chauds *f.*
potion *n.* breuvage *m.*; philtre *m.*
potshot *n.* coup tiré sans viser *m.*
potter *n.* potier; **-y** *n.* poterie *f.*
pouch *n.* poche, pochette *f.*; bourse *f.*
poultice *a.* cataplasme *m.*
poultry *n.* volaille *f.*; — **yard** *n.* basse-cour *f.*
pounce *vi.* fondre, se précipiter
pound *n.* livre *f.*; livre sterling *f.*; (animal) fourrière *f.*; — *vt.* piler, broyer; **-age** *n.* (taux de) poids *m.*
pour *vt.* verser, épancher; — *vi.* pleuvoir à verse; couler rapidement; se précipiter avec violence; — **off** décanter; — **out** verser; épancher; sortir en foule
pout *vi.* bouder, faire la moue; — *n.* moue *f.*
poverty *n.* pauvreté, indigence *f.*; misère *f.*
poverty-stricken *a.* dans la misère
powder *n.* poudre *f.*; — **puff** houppe *f.*; — *vt.* pulvériser; poudrer, saupoudrer; **-y** *a.* poudreux

power *n.* pouvoir *m.*, puissance, faculté, force *f.*; autorité *f.*; **–ful** *a.* puissant; fort; **–less** *a.* impuissant; **–lessness** impuissance *f.*

powwow *n.* réunion, conférence *f.*; — *vi.* se réunir

practicability *n.* praticabilité *f.*

practicable *a.* praticable, faisable

practical *a.* pratique; — **joke** canular *m.*, farce *f.*; — **nurse** infirmière non-diplômée *f.*; **–ly** *adv.* en pratique; presque

practice *n.* pratique *f.*, habilité *f.*; expérience *f.*; coutume *f.*; habitude *f.*; méthode *f.*; clientèle *f.*; — *vt.* pratiquer; exercer; répéter; — *vi.* s'exercer; **–d** *a.* expérimenté; habile

practitioner *n.* praticien *m.*; **general —** médecin non-spécialisé *m.*

pragmatic *a.* pragmatique

prairie *n.* prairie *f.*; — **dog** *n.* marmotte des prairies *f.*

praise *n.* louange *f.*; éloge *m.*; — *vt.* louer; célébrer; **–worthy** *a.* louable, méritoire

praline *n.* bonbon au praliné *m.*

prance *vi.* piaffer; se pavaner; se cabrer

prancing *a.* fringant; — *n.* action de se cabrer *f.*

prank *n.* folie *f.*; farce *f.*, tour *m.*

prate *vi.* caqueter, jaser

prattle *n.* babil *m.*; — *vi.* babiller, jaser

pray *vt. & vi.* prier; **–er** *n.* prière *f.*; Lord's **–er** *n.* patenôtre, oraison dominicale *f.*

preach *vt. & vi.* prêcher; **–er** *n.* prédicateur *m.*; prêcheur *m.*; ministre *m.*; **–ing** *n.* prédication *f.*

preamble *n.* préambule *m.*

prearrange *vt.* arranger au préalable

precarious *a.* précaire

precaution *n.* précaution *f.*; **–ary** *a.* préventif

precede *vt.* précéder, devancer; préfacer; **–nce** *n.* préséance *f.*; priorité *f.*; **–nt** *n.* précédent *m.*

preceding *a.* précédent

precept *n.* précepte *m.*; **–or** *n.* précepteur *m.*

precinct *n.* borne, limite *f.*; circonscription électorale *f.*

precious *a.* précieux; **–ness** *n.* valeur *f.*

precipice *n.* précipice *m.*

precipitate *n.* précipité *m.*; — *vt.* précipiter; hâter; — *vi.* (se) precipiter; — *a.* précipité

precipitation *n.* précipitation *f.*

precipitous *a.* précipité, rapide; escarpé

precise *a.* précis, exact; scrupuleux; **–ly** *adv.* précisément; avec précision; **–ness** *n.* précision *f.*

precision *n.* précision *f.*

preclude *vt.* exclure; empêcher

precocious *a.* précoce; **–ness** *n.* précocité *f.*

precocity *n.* précocité *f.*

preconceive *vt.* concevoir d'avance; **–d** *a.* préconçu

preconception *n.* préconception *f.*

precursor *n.* précurseur *m.*; avant-coureur *m.*

predatory *a.* rapace; de rapine

predecessor *n.* prédécesseur, devancier *m.*

predestination *n.* prédestination *f.*

predestine *vt.* prédestiner

predetermine *vt.* prédéterminer, déterminer d'avance

predicament *n.* mauvais pas *m.*; situation difficile *f.*

predicate *n.* prédicat *m.*; attribut *m.*; — *vt.* affirmer

predict *vt.* prédire; **–ion** *n.* prédiction *f.*

predilection *n.* prédilection, partialité *f.*

predispose *vt.* prédisposer

predisposition *n.* prédisposition *f.*

predominance *n.* ascendant *m.*; prédomination *f.*

predominant *a.* prédominant

predominate *vi.* prédominer

pre-eminence *n.* prééminence *f.*

pre-eminent *a.* prééminent

pre-emption *n.* préemption *f.*

preen *vt.* lisser, ajuster; — **oneself faire** des grâces

pre-established *a.* pré-établi

pre-existent *a.* pré-existant

prefabricate *vt.* préfabriquer

preface *n.* préface *f.*; — *vt.* préfacer

prefatory *a.* préliminaire

prefect *vt.* préfet *m.*; **–ure** *n.* préfecture *f.*

prefer *vt.* préférer; présenter, apporter; **–able** *a.* préférable; **–ence** *n.* préférence *f.*; **–ential** *a.* privilégié; **–red** *a.* préféré; **–red stock** action de priorité *f.*

prefix *n.* préfixe *m.*; — *vt.* mettre devant

pregnant *a.* enceinte

preheat *vt.* faire chauffer au préalable

prehensile *a.* préhensile

prehistoric *a.* préhistorique

prejudge *vt.* préjuger

prejudice *n.* préjugé *m.*; prévention *f.*; — *vt.* être préjudiciable pour; prévenir; **be –d** avoir des préjugés

prejudicial *a.* préjudiciable

preliminary *a. & n.* préliminaire *m.*

prelude *n.* prélude *m.*; — *vt.* préluder

premature *a.* prématuré

premedical *a.* qui prépare la médecine; qui précède les cours de médecine

premeditate *vt.* préméditer; **–d** *a.* prémédité, réfléchi

premeditation *n.* préméditation *f.*

premier *n.* premier ministre *m.*; (France) président du conseil *m.*

première *n.* première, générale *f.*

premise *n.* prémisse *f.*; **-s** *pl.* locaux *m. pl.*; — *vt.* poser

premium *n.* prime *f.*; récompense *f.*; **at a** — à prime; en prime

premonition *n.* prémonition *f.*

prenatal *a.* prénatal

preoccupation *n.* préoccupation *f.*

preoccupy *vt.* préoccuper

preordain *vt.* préordonner, ordonner d'avance

prepaid *a.* payé d'avance; franc de port; — *adv.* franco

preparation *n.* préparation *f.*; **-s** *pl.* préparatifs *m. pl.*

preparatory *a.* préparatoire, préliminaire; — **school** lycée *m.*, école secondaire *f.*

prepare *vt.* préparer; apprêter; — *vi.* se préparer, s'apprêter; — **for** préparer

prepay *vt.* payer d'avance; envoyer franco; **-ment** *n.* paiement d'avance *m.*; affranchissement *m.*

preponderance *n.* prépondérance *f.*

preponderant *a.* prépondérant

preposition *n.* préposition *f.*; **-al** *a.* prépositif, prépositionnel

prepossess *vt.* pénétrer, préoccuper; **-ed** *a.* pénétré, imprégné; **-ing** *a.* prévenant, engageant

preposterous *a.* absurde; déraisonnable; **-ness** *n.* absurdité *f.*

prerequisite *n.* nécessité préalable *f.*; condition nécessaire *f.*; cours obligatoire *m.*

prerogative *n.* prérogative *f.*

presage *n.* présage *m.*; — *vt.* présager; augurer

prescience *n.* prescience *f.*

prescribe *vt.* prescrire; (med.) ordonner; — *vi.* (med.) faire une ordonnance; faire la loi

prescription *n.* (law) prescription *f.*; (med.) ordonnance *f.*

presence *n.* présence *f.*; — **of mind** sang-froid *m.*, présence d'esprit *f.*; **in the** — **of** en présence de

present *n.* (time) présent *m.*; (gift) cadeau *m.*; **at** — à present, actuellement, en ce moment; **-s** *pl.* (law) présentes *f. pl.*; — *vt.* présenter, offrir; — *a.* présent; actuel, courant; **-able** *a.* présentable; **-ation** *n.* présentation *f.*; **-ly** *adv.* tout à l'heure; à présent

present-day *a.* d'aujourd'hui

presentiment *n.* pressentiment *m.*

preservation *n.* préservation *f.*; conservation *f.*

preservative *a. & n.* préservatif *m.*

preserve *n.* conserve *f.*; refuge (pour animaux) *m.*; réserve *f.*; — *vt.* préserver; conserver; mettre en conserve

preside *vi.* présider

presidency *n.* présidence *f.*

president *n.* président *m.*; **-ial** *a.* présidentiel

press *n.* presse *f.*; force *f.*; (clothing) armoire *f.*; imprimerie *f.*; **in** — sous presse; — *vt.* presser, (se) serrer; appuyer; exprimer; harceler; insister; (iron) repasser; **-ing** *a.* pressant; **-ing** *n.* repassage *m.*

pressure *n.* pression *f.*; presse *f.*; urgence *f.*; **blood** — tension artérielle *f.*; **high blood** — hypertension *f.*; — **cooker** marmite norvégienne *f.*; autoclave *m.*; — **group** groupe organisé pour influencer les autres; un bloc de politique

pressurize *vt.* maintenir la pression atmosphérique (dans)

prestige *n.* prestige *m.*

presumable *a.* présumable

presumably *adv.* à ce qu'il paraît, vraisemblablement

presume *vt.* présumer, supposer

presuming *a.* présomptueux

presumption *n.* présomption *f.*

presumptive *a.* présomptif

presumptuous *a.* présomptueux; **-ness** *n.* présomption *f.*

presuppose *vt.* présupposer

pretend *vi.* faire semblant (de); — *vt.* feindre, simuler; **-er** *n.* prétendant *m*

pretense *n.* prétention *f.*; prétexte *m.*

pretension *n.* prétention *f.*

pretentious *a.* prétentieux; **-ness** *n.* prétention *f.*

preterit *n.* (gram.) prétérit, passé *m.*

preternatural *a.* surnaturel

pretext *n.* prétexte *m.*; **on the** — **of** sous prétexte de

prettiness *n.* gentillesse, élégance *f.*; beauté *f.*

pretty *a.* joli; gentil; — *adv.* assez

pretzel *n.* bretzel *m.*

prevail *vi.* prévaloir; régner; **-ing** *a.* régnant, courant; commun, ordinaire

prevalence *n.* étendue, généralité *f.*

prevalent *a.* dominant, répandu, général

prevaricate *vi.* prévariquer; tergiverser

prevaricator *n.* prévaricateur *m.*

prevent *vt.* prévenir; empêcher (de); **-able** *a.* évitable; **-ion** *n.* prévention *f.*; empêchement *m.*; **-ive** *a. & n.* préventif *m.*

preview *n.* examen préliminaire *m.*; (film) avant-première *f.*; — *vt.* examiner d'avance

previous *a.* préalable; précédant; antérieur; **-ly** *adv.* auparavant

prewar *a.* d'avant-guerre

prey *n.* proie *f.*; **fall — to** être en proie à; — *vi.* piller, ronger; — **on** tourmenter; attaquer, piller

price *n.* prix *m.*, valeur *f.*; — **control** prix dirigé *m.*; **sale** — prix de vente *m.*; prix de réclame *m.*; –**list** prix-courant *m.*; **at any** — à tout prix; — *vt.* évaluer, mettre le prix à; demander le prix de; –**less** *a.* sans prix, inestimable

prick *n.* piqûre *f.*; — *vt.* piquer, percer; éperonner; tourmenter; **to** — **up one's ears** dresser les oreilles; –**ly** *a.* piquant; –**ly heat** lichen *m.*; –**ly pear** fruit de cactus *m.*

pride *n.* orgueil *m.*; fierté *f.*; — *vt.*, — **oneself on** s'enorgueillir de, se vanter de

priest *n.* prêtre *m.*; –**hood** *n.* prétrise *f.*; sacerdoce *m.*; –**ly** *a.* de prêtre; sacerdotal

prig *n.* fat *m.*; prude *m.*; –**gish** *a.* pédant, fat

prim *a.* réservé; soigné; guindé

primacy *n.* primaute *f.*

primarily *adv.* surtout, principalement

primary *a.* primaire, primitif; principal

prime *n.* perfection *f.*; élite *f.*; fleur, force *f.*, printemps *m.*; (math.) nombre premier *m.*; — *vt.* amorcer; préparer; — *a.* premier; de meilleure qualité; principal; — **minister** premier ministre *m.*

primer *n.* premier livre, abécédaire *m.*; amorce *f.*; **great –er** (print.) corps 18 *m.*; **long –er** (print.) corps 10 *m.*

primeval *a.* primitif, vierge

priming *n.* amorce *f.*; préparation *f.*

primitive *a.* primitif; –**ness** *n.* rudesse *f.*

primordial *a.* primordial

primp *vi.* se parer

prince *n.* prince *m.*; –**ly** *a.* princier

princess *n.* princesse *f.*

principal *n.* chef *m.*; directeur *m.*; proviseur *m.*; — *a.* principal, premier

principality *n.* principauté *f.*

principle *n.* principe *m.*

print *n.* empreinte, impression; caractères d'imprimerie *m.* *pl.*; (phot.) épreuve *f.*; **out of** — épuisé; — *vt.* imprimer; (phot.) tirer (des épreuves); écrire en caractères d'imprimerie; –**ed matter** imprimés *m.* *pl.*; –**er** *n.* imprimeur *m*: –**er's devil** apprenti imprimeur *m*: –**er's ink** encre d'imprimerie *f.*; –**ing** *n.* impression; (phot.) tirage *m.*; –**ing press** presse (à imprimer) *f.*; — **shop** *n.* imprimerie *f.*

prior *a.* antérieur; — **to** avant; –**ity** *n.* priorité *f.*; — *n.* (eccl.) prieur *m.*; –**y** *n.* prieuré *m.*

prism *n.* prisme *m.*; –**atic** *a.* prismatique

prison *n.* prison *f.*; –**er** *n.* prisonnier *m.*

pristine *a.* primitif, ancien

privacy *n.* secret, isolement *m.*, retraite, solitude *f.*; intimité *f.*

private *n.* simple soldat *m.*; — *a.* privé, particulier; secret, retiré; — **house** maison particulière *f.*

privateer *n.* corsaire *m.*; –**ing** *n.* course *f.*

privilege *n.* privilège *m.*; prérogative *f.*; — *vt.* privilégier

privy *a.* privé, particulier; secret; — *n.* cabinets *m.* *pl.*

prize *n.* prix *m.*; récompense *f.*; prise *f.*; lot *m.*; — **fight** *n.* partie de boxe *f.*; — *vt.* évaluer, faire cas de; — **fighter** *n.* boxeur *m.*

pro *prep.* & *adv.* pour; — **and con** pour et contre; — *n.* professionnel *m.*

probability *n.* probabilité *f.*; vraisemblance *f.*

probable *a.* probable; vraisemblable

probate *n.* (law) vérification, homologation *f.*; — *vt.* valider (un testament)

probation *n.* épreuve *f.*; noviciat *m.*; sursis (avec surveillance) *m.*; –**ary** *a.* d'épreuve

probe *n.* sonde *f.*; — *vt.* sonder

problem *n.* problème *m.*; –**atical** *a.* problématique

procedure *n.* procédé *m.*; procédure *f.*

proceed *vi.* procéder; provenir, poursuivre; continuer; –**ings** *n.* *pl.* procédure *f*: délibérations *f.* *pl.*; –**s** *n.* *pl.* produit, revenu *m.*

process *n.* progrès, cours *m.*; procédé *m.*; procès *m.*; — *vt.* traiter; developper; –**ion** *n.* procession *f.*; cortège *m.*

proclaim *vt.* proclamer, déclarer

proclamation *n.* proclamation *f.*, édit *m.*

proclivity *n.* inclination *f.*, penchant *m.*

procrastinate *vi.* temporiser, s'attarder, hésiter

procrastinator *n.* temporisateur *m.*

procreate *vt.* procréer

procreation *n.* procréation *f.*

proctor *n.* avoué *m.*; censeur *m*: surveillant *m.*; pion *m.*

procurable *a.* qui peut se procurer

procure *vt.* procurer; –**ment** *n.* aquisition *f.*; ravitaillement *m.*; –**r** *n.* entremetteur *m.*

prod *n.* aiguillon *m.*; — *vt.* piquer; aiguillonner; pousser

prodigal *a.* & *n.* prodigue *m.*; –**ity** *n.* prodigalité *f.*

prodigious *a.* prodigieux

prodigy *n.* prodige *m.*

produce *n.* produit *m.*; denrées *f.* *pl.*; — *vt.* produire; faire, fabriquer; exhiber; (theat.) monter; –**r** *n.* producteur *m.*;

(theat.) directeur *m.*

product *n.* produit *m.;* **–ion** *n.* production *f.;* fabrication *f.;* produit *m.;* **–ive** *a.* productif; **–ivity** *n.* productivité *f.*

profane *vt.* profaner; — *a.* profane; blasphématoire

profanity *n.* juron *m.;* emploi de jurons *m.;* impiété *f.*

profess *vt.* professer, faire profession de; **–ed** *a.* déclaré; (eccl.) profès; **–edly** *adv.* ouvertement; **–ion** *n.* profession *f.;* metier *m.;* **–ional** *n.* professionnel *m.;* **–ional** *a.* professionnel; de carrière, de métier; **–or** *n.* professeur *m.;* **–orial** *a.* professoral; **–orship** *n.* professorat *m.;* chaire de professeur *f.*

proffer *n.* offre, proposition *f.;* — *vt.* proposer, offrir

proficiency *n.* capacité *f.;* connaissance *f.;* niveau *m.*

proficient *a.* habile; capable; ayant atteint un niveau déterminé

profile *n.* profil *m.;* — *vt.* profiler

profit *n.* profit, gain, avantage *m.;* produit, revenu *m.;* bénéfice *m.;* — *vt. & vi.* profiter; être utile; **— by** profiter de; **–able** *a.* profitable, avantageux; **–eer** *vi.* gagner des bénéfices démesurés; **–eer** *n.* profiteur *m.;* **–eering** *n.* mercantilisme *m.;* **–less** *a.* sans profit; **— sharing** *n.* participation aux bénéfices *f.*

profligate *n. & a.* débauché *m.*

profound *a.* profond; **–ly** *adv.* profondément

profundity *n.* profondeur *f.*

profuse *a.* prodigue; abondant; **–ness** *n.* profusion *f.;* **–ly** *adv.* excessivement

profusion *n.* profusion *f.;* abondance *f.;* prodigalité *f.*

progenitor *n.* ancêtre *m.*

progeny *n.* progéniture *f.;* lignée *f.*

prognosis *n.* (med.) prognose *f.,* pronostic *m.*

prognostic *n.* pronostic *m.;* **–ate** *vt.* prognostiquer; **–ation** *n.* prognostication *f.,* pronostic *m.*

program *n.* programme *m.;* — *vt.* établir un programme pour

progress *n.* progrès *m.;* **in —** en cours, en voie; — *vi.* faire des progrès; **–ion** *n.* progression *f.;* **–ive** *a.* progressif; (pol.) progressiste

prohibit *vt.* prohiber; défendre; interdire; **–ion** *n.* prohibition, défense *f.;* **–ive** *a.* prohibitif

project *n.* projet, dessein *m.;* — *vt.* projeter; — *vi.* saillir; **–ile** *n.* projectile *m.;* **–ion** *n.* projection *f.;* saillie *f.;* **–or** *n.* projecteur *m.*

proletarian *a.* prolétaire, prolétarien; —

n. prolétaire *m. & f.*

proletariat *n.* prolétariat *m.*

prolific *a.* prolifique, fertile

prologue *n.* prologue *m.*

prolong *vt.* prolonger; **–ation** *n.* prolongation *f.,* prolongement *m.*

promenade *n.* promenade *f.;* bal *m.;* — *vi.* se promener

prominence *n.* proéminence *f.;* éminence *f.*

prominent *a.* proéminent; éminent; prononcé; (qui est) très en vue; **–ly** *adv.* très en vue

promiscuous *a.* mêlé; confus; au hasard; libre, sans contrainte

promise *n.* promesse *f.;* espérances *f. pl.;* avenir *m.;* **break a —** manquer de parole; — *vt. & vi.* promettre

promissory *a.* qui contient une promesse; **— note** *n.* billet à ordre *m.*

promontory *n.* promontoire *m.*

promote *vt.* promouvoir, avancer; élever; encourager; **–r** *n.* homme d'affaires *m.,* animateur *m.;* auteur *m.;* promoteur *m.*

promotion *n.* promotion *f.;* avancement *m.;* publicité, réclame *f.*

prompt *vt.* souffler; suggérer; — *a.* prompt; immédiat; **–er** *n.* souffleur *m.;* **–ly** *adv.* promptement; ponctuellement; immédiatement, sur-le-champ; à l'heure; **–ness** *n.* promptitude *f.*

promulgate *vt.* promulguer, publier

promulgation *n.* promulgation *f.*

prone *a.* couché le visage contre terre; **— to** enclin à, susceptible de

prong *n.* fourchon *m.;* dent *f.;* **–ed** *a.* à fourchons, à dents

pronominal *a.* pronominal

pronoun *n.* pronom *m.*

pronounce *vt.* prononcer; articuler; **–able** *a.* prononçable; **–d** *a.* prononcé, marqué; **–ment** *n.* déclaration *f.*

pronunciation *n.* prononciation *f.*

proof *n.* preuve *f.;* épreuve *f.;* épreuves *f. pl.;* essai *m.;* — *a.* à l'épreuve (de); impénétrable

proofread *vt.* corriger les epreuves de; **–er** *n.* correcteur *m.;* **–ing** *n.* correction *f.*

prop *n.* appui, soutien *m.;* étai *m.;* (theat.) accessoire *m.;* — *vt.* appuyer, soutenir; étayer

propaganda *n.* propagande *f.*

propagandist *n.* propagandiste *m.*

propagate *vt.* propager; répandre; — *vi.* se propager, se reproduire

propagation *n.* propagation *f.;* dissémination *f.*

propel *vt.* pousser en avant; **–lant** *n.* propulseur *m.;* **–ler** *n.* hélice *f.*

propensity *n.* penchant *m.,* inclination *f.*

proper *a.* propre; bon; convenable; comme il faut; exact; **-ly** *adv.* proprement; correctement; comme il faut

property *n.* propriété, qualité *f.*; possession *f.*; (theat.) accessoire *m.*

prophecy *n.* prophétie *f.*

prophesy *vt.* & *vi.* prophétiser

prophet *n.* prophète *m.*; **-ic** *a.* prophétique

prophylactic *a.* prophylactique

prophylaxis *n.* prophylaxie *f.*

propinquity *n.* proximité *f.*

propitiate *vt.* rendre propice; apaiser

propitious *a.* propice, favorable

proponent *n.* partisan *m.*

proportion *n.* proportion *f.*; mesure *f.*; **in — as** à mesure que; **in — to** en proportion de, proportionné à; **—** *vt.* proportionner; **-al** *a.* proportionnel; **-ate** *a.* proportionné; **-ed** *a.* proportionné

proposal *n.* proposition, offre *f.*; plan, projet *m.*; demande (en mariage) *f.*

propose *vt.* proposer; avoir l'intention de; **—** *vi.* se déclarer, faire une déclaration, faire une demande en mariage

proposition *n.* proposition *f.*; offre *f.*

propound *vt.* proposer, offrir; poser

proprietary *a.* de propriété, de propriétaire

proprietor *n.* propriétaire *m.* & *f.*

propriety *n.* convenance *f.*, décorum *m.*; à-propos *m.*, opportunité *f.*

propulsion *n.* propulsion *f.*

prorate *vt.* répartir

prosaic *a.* prosaïque

proscenium *n.* (theat.) avant-scène *f.*

proscribe *vt.* proscrire, interdire

proscription *n.* proscription *f.*; interdiction *f.*

prose *n.* prose *f.*

prosecute *vt.* poursuivre

prosecution *n.* poursuite *f.*

prosecutor *n.* procureur *m.*; plaignant *m.*

proselyte *n.* prosélyte *m.* & *f.*

prospect *n.* perspective *f.*; vue *f.*, aspect *m.*; **—** *vi.* prospecter; (min.) faire des recherches; **-ive** *a.* à venir; **-or** *n.* prospecteur *m.*

prospectus *n.* prospectus *m.*

prosper *vi.* prospérer, réussir; **-ity** *n.* prospérité *f.*; **-ous** *a.* prospère

prostitute *n.* prostituée *f.*; **—** *vt.* prostituer

prostrate *vt.* renverser, abattre; prosterner; accabler; **—** *a.* prosterné; (med.) prostré; **-d** *a.* abattu

prostration *n.* prosternation *f.*; abattement *m.*; (med.) prostration *f.*

protagonist *n.* protagoniste *m.*

protect *vt.* protéger, défendre; sauvegarder; patronner; **-ion** *n.* protection, défense *f.*; sauvegarde *f.*; abri *m.*; patronage *m.*; **-ive** *a.* protecteur; préservatif; **-or** *n.* protecteur *m.*; protectrice *f.*; **-orate** *n.* protectorat *m.*

protein *n.* protéine *f.*

protest *n.* protestation *f.*; représentation *f.*; **under —** sous réserve; **—** *vt.* & *vi.* protester; **-ation** *n.* protestation *f.*

protocol *n.* protocole *m.*

proton *n.* proton *m.*

protoplasm *n.* protoplasme *m.*

prototype *n.* prototype, archétype *m.*

protozoa *n. pl.* protozoaires *m. pl.*

protract *vt.* prolonger; traîner; **-ion** *n.* prolongation *f.*; relevé *m.*; **-or** *n.* (math.) rapporteur *m.*

protrude *vi.* s'avancer, faire saillie; **—** *vt.* pousser dehors

protruding *a.* saillant; en saillie; débordant

protrusion *n.* protubérance, saillie *f.*

protuberance *n.* protubérance *f.*

proud *a.* orgueilleux, fier; superbe

provable *a.* démontrable

prove *vt.* prouver; éprouver; démontrer; vérifier; **—** *vi.* se trouver; se montrer

provender *n.* provende *f.*; fourrage *m.*; nourriture *f.*

proverb *n.* proverbe *m.*; **-ial** *a.* proverbial

provide *vt.* pourvoir, fournir, munir; **—** *vi.* (se) pourvoir; **-d** *a.* muni, pourvu; **-d that** *conj.* pourvu que; **-r** *n.* pourvoyeur, fournisseur *m.*

provident *a.* prévoyant; **-ial** *a.* providentiel

provincial *a.* provincial; de province; **—** *n.* provincial *m.*

provision *n.* clause *f.*, article *m.*; disposition *f.*; **-s** *pl.* comestibles, vivres *m. pl.*; **—** *vt.* approvisionner, ravitailler; **-al** *a.* provisoire

proviso *n.* condition *f.*

provisory *a.* provisoire

provocation *n.* provocation *f.*; défi *m.*

provocative *a.* provocateur; provocant

provoke *vt.* provoquer; exciter; inciter; irriter; contrarier; défier

provoking *a.* contrariant, irritant

provost *n.* prévôt *m.*

prow *n.* proue *f.*

prowess *n.* prouesse *f.*; vaillance *f.*

prowl *vi.* rôder; **-er** *n.* rôdeur *m.*; (inside) cambrioleur *m.*

proximity *n.* proximité *f.*

proxy *n.* procuration *f.*; mandat, mandataire *m.*; délégué *m.*

prude *n.* prude *f.*; **-ry** *n.* pruderie *f.*

prudence *n.* prudence *f.*

prudent *a.* prudent, judicieux
prudish *a.* prude; **—ness** *n.* pruderie *f.*
prune *n.* pruneau *m.*; **—** *vt.* tailler; élaguer
pruning *n.* taille *f.*; élagage *m.*; **— hook** ébranchoir *m.*; **— knife** serpette *f.*; **— shears** sécateur *m.*
pry *vt.* soulever; forcer; **—** *vi.* fouiller (dans); fureter; **—** *n.* levier *m.*; **–ing** *a.* curieux
psalm *n.* psaume *m.*
Psalter *n.* psautier *m.*
pseudonym *n.* pseudonyme *m.*
psychiatric *a.* psychiatrique
psychiatrist *n.* psychiatre *m.*
psychiatry *n.* psychiatrie *f.*
psychic *a.* psychique
psychoanalist *n.* psychanalyste *m.*
psychological *a.* psychologique
psychologist *n.* psychologue *m.*
psychology *n.* psychologie *f.*
psychopathic *a.* psychopathique
psychosomatic *a.* psychosomatique
ptomaine *n.* ptomaïne *f.*; **— poisoning** intoxication alimentaire *f.*
puberty *n.* puberté *f.*
public *n.* public, peuple *m.*; **in —** en public, publiquement; **—** *a.* public, publique; **make —** publier, rendre public; **— holiday** fête légale; **— library** bibliothèque municipale *f.*; **— official** fonctionnaire *m.*; **— school** école municipale *f.*; **— spirit** civisme *m.*; **— works** travaux publics; **–ation** *n.* publication *f.*
publicity *n.* publicité *f.*; réclame *f.*
publicize *vt.* publier; faire de la réclame pour
publish *vt.* publier; **just –ed** vient de paraître; **–er** *n.* éditeur *m.*; **–ing** *n.* publication *f.*; **–ing house** maison d'édition *f.*
puck *n.* (sport) palet; lutin *m.*
pucker *n.* pli *m.*; ride *f.*; fronce *f.*; **—** *vt.* plisser; rider; **—** *vi.* (se) froncer
puddle *n.* flaque d'eau *f.*; **—** *vt.* corroyer
pudgy *a.* rondelet; replet
puerile *a.* puéril
Puerto Rico *n.* Porto-Rico *m.*
puff *n.* bouffée *f.*; souffle *m.*; (clothes) bouffant; **powder —** houppe *f.*; **— pastry** pâte feuilletée *f.*; **—** *vt.* gonfler; fumer; **—** *vi.* souffler; haleter; **–iness** *n.* boursouflure *f.*; bouffissure *f.*; **–y** *a.* bouffi; boursouflé
pug *n.* (dog) carlin *m.*; **— nose** *n.* nez épaté *m.*
pugilism *n.* pugilat *m.*, boxe *f.*
pugilist *n.* pugiliste, boxeur *m.*
pugnacious *a.* batailleur
pull *n.* traction *f.*; attraction *f.*; appel

m.; poignée *f.*; (coll.) influence *f.*, piston, bras long *m.*; **—** *vt.* tirer; traîner; **— apart** déchirer; séparer; **— off** enlever; remporter; **— out** tirer, sortir; **— through** guérir; se tirer d'affaire; **— (oneself) together** se reprendre; **— up** remonter; hisser; hausser; s'arrêter; se ranger
pullet *n.* poulette, poularde *f.*
pulley *n.* poulie *f.*; **— block** *n.* moufle *f.*
Pullman (rail.), **— car** voiture Pullman *f.*; wagon-lit, wagon-salon *m.*
pulmonary *a.* pulmonaire
pulp *n.* pulpe *f.*; pâte *f.*; chair *f.*; **–y** *a.* charnu; pulpeux
pulpit *n.* chaire *f.*
pulsate *vi.* palpiter, vibrer, (se) battre
pulsation *n.* pulsation *f.*, battement *m.*
pulse *n.* pouls *m.*; battement *m.*, pulsation *f.*
pulverization *n.* pulvérisation *f.*
pulverize *vt.* pulvériser; atomiser
pumice *n.* ponce *f.*
pummel *vt.* battre (de coups de poing)
pump *n.* pompe *f.*; (shoe) escarpin *m.*; **air —** pompe à air; **— room** chambre des pompes; buvette *f.*; **—** *vt.* pomper; **— up** gonfler; faire monter
pumpkin *n.* citrouille *f.*, potiron *m.*
pun *n.* calembour *m.*
punch *n.* poinçon *m.*; perçoir *m.*; emporte-pièce *m.*; coup de poing *m.*; (drink) punch *m.*; **—** *vt.* poinçonner; percer; donner un coup de poing à; **–ing bag** punching *m.*
Punch and Judy show *n.* guignol *m.*
punctilious *a.* pointilleux
punctual *a.* exact, ponctuel; **–ity** *n.* ponctualité, exactitude *f.*
punctuate *vt.* ponctuer
punctuation *n.* ponctuation *f.*
puncture *n.* piqûre, perforation *f.*; (tire) crevaison *f.*; (med.) ponction *f.*; **—** *vt.* perforer, crever; ponctionner
puncture-proof *a.* increvable
pungency *n.* odeur forte *f.*; saveur *f.*
pungent *a.* piquant, âcre; mordant
puniness *n.* chétiveté *f.*
punish *vt.* punir, châtier; corriger; **–able** *a.* punissable; **–ment** *n.* punition *f.*; châtiment *m.*; peine *f.*; **capital —** peine capitale *f.*
punitive *a.* punissant; pénal
punt *n.* (sports) coup de volée *m.*; (boating) bateau plat *m.*, plate *f.*
puny *a.* chétif; faible
pup, puppy *n.* petit chien, jeune chien *m.*
pupa *n.* chrysalide *f.*
pupil *n.* (anat.) pupille *f.*; élève *m. & f.*
puppet *n.* marionnette *f.*; pantin *m.*; **—**

show théâtre de marionnettes *m.*
purchase *n.* achat *m.*, acquisition *f.*, emplette *f.*; prise *f.*, point d'appui *m.*; — *vt.* acheter; **–r** *n.* acheteur *m.*
purchasing agent *n.* acheteur *m.*
pure *a.* pur; **–ly** *adv.* purement; absolument; tout à fait
purgation *n.* purgation *f.*
purgative *a. & n.* purgatif *m.*
purgatory *n.* purgatoire *m.*
purge *n.* purgatif *m.*; purgation *f.*; — *vt.* purger; purifier; épurer
purging *n.* purgation *f.*
purification *n.* purification *f.*; épuration *f.*
purifier *n.* épurateur *m.*
purify *vt.* purifier; épurer
purist *n.* puriste *m. & f.*
puritan *a. & n.* puritain; **–ical** *a.* de puritain
purity *n.* pureté *f.*
purloin *vt.* voler
purple *a. & n.* violet *m.*; (fig.) pourpre *f.*; royal —, **imperial** — pourpre *f.*
purport *n.* sens *m.*; portée *f.*; — *vt.* avoir la prétention de
purpose *n.* but, objet, dessein *m.*; intention *f.*; fin *f.*; détermination *f.*; **for the** — of dans le but de; **on** — exprès; **to no** — en vain; **–ful** *a.* avisé; réfléchi; **–ly** *adv.* exprès; à dessein
purr *vi.* ronronner; **–ing** *n.* ronron *m.*
purse *n.* bourse *f.*; porte-monnaie *m.*; sac à main *m.*; — *vt.* pincer (les lèvres); **–r** *n.* commissaire *m.*
pursuant *adv.* conformément
pursue *vt.* poursuivre; suivre; **–r** *n.* poursuivant *m.*
pursuit *n.* poursuite *f.*; recherche *f.*; profession *f.*; occupation *f.*; **in** — of à la poursuite de; (fig.) à la recherche de
purvey *vt.* fournir; **–or** *n.* fournisseur, pourvoyeur *m.*
push *n.* poussée, impulsion *f.*; effort *m.*; — **button** poussoir, pressoir *m.*; — *vt.* pousser; bousculer; presser; — **back** repousser; **–ing** *a.* entreprenant, ambitieux
pushcart *n.* charrette à bras *f.*
pushover *n.* quelque chose de tres facile *m.*; adversaire facile à vaincre *m.*
pusillanimous *a.* pusillanime
puss(y) *n.* minette *f.*
pustule *n.* pustule *f.*
put *vt.* mettre, poser, placer; — **to bed** coucher; — **away** ranger; serrer; (money) mettre de côté; — **back** remettre; retarder; — **down** déposer; poser; supprimer; noter; — **in** faire; (naut.) entrer; — **in order** ranger; — **off** remettre; ajourner; différer; — **on**

mettre; enfiler; (shoes) chausser; — **on the light(s)** allumer; — **on weight** prendre du poids; — **out** tendre; mettre à la porte; (light) éteindre; contrarier; publier; — **oneself out** se déranger; — **together** assembler; — **up** construire, bâtir; poser; proposer; loger, descendre; — **up with** souffrir de; se résigner à
putrefaction *n.* putréfaction *f.*
putrefy *vi.* se putréfier, pourrir
putrid *a.* putride
putty *n.* mastic *m.*; — **knife** spatule *f.*; — *vt.* mastiquer
puzzle *n.* énigme *f.*; casse-tête *m.*; **crossword** — mots croisés *m. pl.*; **jigsaw** — patience *f.*; — *vt.* confondre; embarrasser; — *vi.* se casser la tête
pylon *n.* pylône *m.*
pygmy *n.* pygmée *m.*
pyorrhea *n.* pyorrhée *f.*
pyramid *n.* pyramide *f.*
pyre *n.* bûcher *m.*
Pyrenees *n. pl.* Pyrénéés *f. pl.*
pyrotechnic *a.* pyrotechnique; **–s** *n. pl.* pyrotechnie *f.*

Q

quack *n.* charlatan *m.*; (sound) couincouin *m.*; — *vi.* faire couin-couin; **–ery** *n.* charlatanisme *m.*
quadrangle *n.* cour carrée *f.*; (math.) quadrilatère *m.*
quadrangular *a.* quadrangulaire
quadrant *n.* quart, quadrant, secteur *m.*
quadratic *a.*, — **equation** équation du second degré *f.*
quadrilateral *a.* quadrilatéral, quadrilatère; — *n.* quadrilatère *m.*
quadruped *a. & n.* quadrupède *m.*
quadruple *a.* quadruple; **–ts** *n. pl.* quatre enfants nés de la même couche *m. pl.*
quaff *vt.* boire (d'un seul trait)
quagmire *n.* fondrière *f.*
quail *n.* caille *f.*; — *vi.* fléchir
quaint *a.* pittoresque; suranné; **–ness** *n.* pittoresque *m.*
quake *vi.* trembler
qualification *n.* qualité *f.*, titre *m.*; capacité *f.*; réserve, condition *f.*
qualified *a.* capable; brevcté; diplômé; conditionnel
qualify *vt.* qualifier; modifier; — *vi.* être reçu; se qualifier; **–ing** *a.* qualificatif; (sports) éliminatoire
qualitative *a.* qualitatif
quality *n.* qualité *f.*; — *a.* de qualité, de première qualité
qualm *n.* scrupule, remords; soulèvement de cœur *m.*; **–ish** *a.* qui a mal au cœur;

–ishness *n.* nausée *f.*
quandary *n.* incertitude *f.*; impasse *f.*
quantitative *a.* quantitatif
quantity *n.* quantité *f.*
quarantine *n.* quarantaine *f.*; — *vt.* mettre en quarantaine
quarrel *n.* querelle, dispute *f.*; — *vi.* se disputer, se quereller; se brouiller; –some *a.* querelleur
quarry *n.* carrière *f.*; proie *f.*; — *vt.* exploiter une carrière
quart *n.* litre *m.* 1 qt. (dry)′ = 0.95 litre (sec); 1 qt. (liquid) = 1.06 litres (liquides)
quarter *n.* (fraction) quart *m.*; quartier *m.*; trimestre *m.*; côté *m.*; (money) vingt-cinq cents *m. pl.*; a — after, a — past et quart; a — to moins le quart, moins un quart; — of an hour quart d'heure *m.*; –s *pl.* quartiers *m. pl.*, appartement, logement *m.*; (naut.) poste *m.*; — *vt.* diviser en quatre; écarteler; loger, cantonner; –ly *a.* trimestriel; –ly *adv.* par trimestre
quarter-deck *n.* gaillard arrière *m.*
quartermaster *n.* (mil.) intendant général *m.*
quartet *n.* quatuor *m.*
quasar *n.* objet quasi-stellaire *m.*
quash *vt.* étouffer; casser
quaver *vi.* trembloter; — *n.* tremblement *m.*; (mus.) trémolo *m.*; croche *f.*
queen *n.* reine *f.*; (cards) dame *f.*; — *vt.* faire la reine; (chess) damer; –ly *a.* de reine; royale
queer *a.* bizarre; étrange; drôle; original; –ness *n.* bizarrerie, étrangeté *f.*; — *vt.* gâter, gâcher
quell *vt.* étouffer, réprimer
quench *vt.* éteindre; étouffer; étancher; — one's thirst se désaltérer
query *n.* question *f.*; — *vt.* s'informer
quest *n.* recherche *f.*; quête *f.*; in — of à la recherche de
question *n.* question *f.*; demande *f.*; doute *m.*; — mark point d'interrogation *m.*; ask a — poser une question, faire une question; in — en question; dont il s'agit; it is a — of il s'agit de; out of the — impossible; without — sans aucun doute; — *vt.* interroger, questionner; mettre en doute; –able *a.* douteux; contestable; problématique; –er *n.* interrogateur *m.*; –ing *a.* interrogateur; –ing *n.* interrogation *f.*; interrogatoire *m.*
quibble *n.* chicane *f.*; argutie *f.*; — *vi.* chicaner; ergoter
quibbling *n.* chicane *f.*
quick *n.* vif *m.*; — *a.* rapide; vif, vive; prompt; agile; be —! dépêchez-vous!;

–ly *adv.* vite, rapidement; vivement; –en *vt.* accélerer, presser, hâter; animer, vivifier; –en *vi.* s'accélerer; s'animer; –ness *n.* rapidité, vitesse *f.*; vivacité *f.*; promptitude *f.*
quick-acting *a.* à action rapide
quick-freeze *vt.* congeler
quicklime *n.* chaux vive *f.*
quicksand *n.* sable mouvant *m.*
quicksilver *n.* vif-argent, mercure *m.*
quick-tempered *a.* emporté; qui s'emporte facilement
quick-witted *a.* éveillé, vif; à l'esprit prompt
quiescence *n.* quiétude *f.*
quiescent *a.* en repos
quiet *n.* tranquillité *f.*, calme *m.*; silence *m.*; repos *m.*; — *a.* tranquille, calme; silencieux; intime; simple; be —, keep — se taire; — *vt.* calmer, apaiser; faire taire; — (down) se calmer, s'apaiser; –ly *adv.* tranquillement; silencieusement, sans bruit; doucement; –ness *n.* tranquillité *f.*, calme *m.*; repos *m.*; paix *f.*; –ude *n.* quiétude *f.*
quill *n.* plume *f.*; tuyau *m.*
quilt *n.* couverture piquée *f.*; courtepointe *f.*; édredon *m.*; — *vt.* contrepointer, piquer; –ed *a.* piqué, contrepointé
quintessence *n.* quintessence *f.*
quintuple *a.* quintuple; –ts *n. pl.* cinq enfants nés de la même couche
quip *n.* repartie *f.*
quire *n.* main de papier *f.*
quirk *n.* habitude particulière *f.*; idiosyncrasie *f.*
quisling *n.* quisling, traître *m.*
quit *vt.* quitter, démissionner; — *vi.* cesser, s'arrêter; –s *a.* quitte; –ter *n.* lâcheur *m.*
quite *adv.* tout à fait; complètement, entièrement
quiver *n.* frémissement, tremblement *m.*; (archery) carquois *m.*; — *vi.* frémir, trembler; trembloter
quixotic *a.* visionnaire
quiz *n.* petit examen *m.*; — *vt.* examiner, interroger
quorum *n.* quorum *m.*
quota *n.* quote-part *f.*; contingentement *m.*
quotation *n.* citation *f.*; (com.) cote *f.*, cours *m.*; — marks guillemets *m. pl.*
quote *vt.* citer; faire un prix; coter
quotient *n.* quotient *m.*

R

rabbi *n.* rabbin *m.*
rabbit *n.* lapin *m.*

rabble *n.* canaille, populace *f.*

rabid *a.* enragé; furieux

rabies *n.* rage, hydrophobie *f.*

race *n.* course *f.*; (breed) race *f.*, sang *m.*; **human** — race humaine *f.*; humanité *f.*; homme *m.*; **foot** — course à pied *f.*; **horse** — course de chevaux *f.*; **boat** — régate *f.*; — **horse** cheval de course *m.*; — **track** *n.* champ de courses *m.*; piste *f.*; — *vi.* faire une course; courir; lutter de vitesse; — *vt.* lutter de vitesse avec; faire courir; (engine) emballer; **-r** *n.* coureur *m.*; auto de course *f.*

racing *n.* courses *f. pl.*

racist *n.* raciste *m.*

rack *n.* (luggage) porte-bagages *m.*; filet *m.*; (coat) porte-manteau *m.*; (torture) chevalet *m.*; — *vt.* torturer, tourn enter; — **one's brains** se creuser l'esprit

racket *n.* raquette *f.*; bruit, vacarme, tapage *m.*; (slang) métier, genre d'affaires *m.*, affaire louche *f.*; **-eer** *n.* gangster *m.*

racy *a.* savoureux

radar *n.* radar *m.*

radial *a.* radial

radiance *n.* rayonnement *m.*; éclat *m.*

radiant *a.* rayonnant; radieux

radiate *vi.* rayonner; — *vt.* émettre

radiation *n.* (phy.) radiation *f.*; rayonnement *m.*; — **sickness** maladie de radiation *f.*

radiator *n.* radiateur *m.*

radical *a. & n.* radical *m.*; **-ism** *n.* radicalisme *m.*

radicle *n.* (bot.) radicelle *f.*; radicule *f.*

radio *n.* radio *f.*; T.S.F. (télégraphie sans fil) *f.*; — *vt.* envoyer (un message) par radio; — **operator** radio *m.*; — **set** poste de T.S.F. *m.*; — **station** poste émetteur *m.*

radiobroadcast *n.* radiodiffusion *f.*; — *vt.* radiodiffuser, transmettre; -**er** *n.* appareil émetteur *m.*; (person) speaker *m.*, speakerine *f.*; annonceur *m.*; -**ing** *n.* radio-émission, radiophonie *f.*

radioactive *a.* radio-actif

radioastronomy *n.* radio-astronomie *f.*

radio frequency *n.* radio-fréquence *f.*

radiogram *n.* radiogramme *m.*

radiology *n.* radiologie *f.*

radiosensitive *a.* radiosensible

radiotherapy *n.* radiothérapie *f.*

radish *n.* radis *m.*

radium *n.* radium *m.*

radius *n.* rayon *m.*; **within a** — **of** dans un rayon de

raffle *n.* tombola *f.*

raft *n.* radeau *m.*; (coll.) grand nombre *m.*

rafter *n.* chevron *m.*

rag *n.* chiffon *m.*; lambeau *m.*; — **doll** pou-

pée de chiffons *f.*; **-s** *pl.* guenilles *f. pl.*, haillons *m. pl.*; -**ged** *a.* en haillons; inégal; désordonné

ragamuffin *n.* gamin *m.*; va-nu-pieds *m.*

rage *n.* fureur *f.*; rage *f.*; manie *f.*; **fly into a** — s'emporter; — *vi.* être furieux; faire rage

raging *a.* furieux

ragout *n.* ragoût *m.*

ragpicker *n.* chiffonnier *m.*

ragweed *n.* jacobée *f.*

raid *n.* raid *m.*; incursion *f.*; razzia *f.*; (police) descente *f.*; — *vt.* faire un raid à; razzier; faire une descente dans; -**er** *n.* maraudeur *m.*; attaquant *m.*

rail *n.* rail *m.*; rampe *f.*; balustrade *f.*; garde-fou *m.*; barreau *m.*; grille *f.*; **by** — par chemin de fer *m.*; **third** — rail de contact *m.*; -**ing** *n.* barrière *f.*; balustrade *f.*; garde-fou *m.*

rail *vi.*, — **at** s'en prendre à; crier contre

raillery *n.* raillerie *f.*

railroad, railway *n.* chemin de fer; — **track** voie *f.*; — **station** gare *f.*

rain *n.* pluie *f.*; **in the** — sous la pluie; — *vi.* pleuvoir; **it's** -**ing** il pleut; -**y** *a.* pluvieux; des pluies

rainbow *n.* arc-en-ciel *m.*

raincoat *n.* imperméable *m.*

rainfall *n.* pluie, précipitation *f.*

rain forest *n.* forêt pluvieuse *f.*

rainproof *a.* imperméable

rain water *n.* eau de pluie *f.*

raise *vt.* lever, soulever; hausser; relever; élever; cultiver; (salary) augmenter; — **a cry** pousser un cri

rake *n.* râteau *m.*, râtissoire *f.*; (person) roué *m.*; — *vt.* râteler, ratisser; — **off** prélever

rally *n.* ralliement *m.*; réunion *f.*; (sports) reprise *f.*; retour *m.*; — *vt.* rallier; — *vi.* se rallier; (mil.) se reformer; (med.) se remettre; (sports) se reprendre

ram *n.* (animal) bélier *m.*; pilon *m.*; — *vt.* heurter; enfoncer; (naut.) éperonner

ramble *n.* balade, promenade *f.*; — *vi.* errer, rôder; battre la campagne; parler sans suite

rambling *a.* vagabond; sans suite; — *n.* vagabondage *m.*; radotage *m.*

ramification *n.* ramification *f.*

ramify *vi.* se ramifier

ramp *n.* rampe *f.*; pont *m.*

rampage *n.* furie, folie *f.*; — *vi.* déclamer, divaguer

rampant *a.* rampant; **be** — s'étaler; se répandre

rampart *n.* rempart *m.*

ramshackle *a.* délabré

ranch *n.* grosse ferme d'élevage *f.*; ranch

m.; **–er** *n.* fermier *m.*; propriétaire de ranch *m.*

rancid *a.* rance; **–ness** *n.* rancidité *f.*

rancor *n.* rancune *f.*

random *n.* **at —** au hasard; à tort et à travers; **—** *a.* fait au hasard

range *n.* portée *f.*; étendue *f.*; champ *m.*; gamme *f.*; distance *f.*; (mountains) chaîne *f.*; (kitchen) cuisinière *f.*; **— finder** télémètre *m.*; **in —** à portée; **out of —** hors de portée; **—** *vt.* ranger; **—** *vi.* s'étendre; errer; s'échelonner; **–r** *n.* (garde) forestier *m.*

rank *n.* rang *m.*; classe *f.*; (mil.) grade *m.*; **— and file** la troupe *f.*; **—** *vi.* se ranger; être classé; **—** *a.* fétide; luxuriant; criant; parfait; **–ing** *a.* premier; en chef

ransack *vt.* piller, saccager; fouiller

ransom *n.* rançon *f.*; **—** *vt.* rançonner; racheter

rant *vi.* extravaguer

rap *n.* coup *m.*; (coll.) sou *m.*; **—** *vt.* frapper; donner sur

rapacious *a.* rapace; **–ly** *adv.* avec rapacité; **–ness** *n.* rapacité *f.*

rape *n.* viol *m.*; **—** *vt.* violer

rapid *a.* rapide; **–ly** *adv.* rapidement, vite; **–ity** *n.* rapidité *f.*; **–s** *n. pl.* rapides *m. pl.*

rapid-fire *a.* à tir rapide

rapier *n.* rapière *f.*

rapt *a.* absorbé; ravi; **–ure** *n.* transport *m.*; ravissement *m.*; extase *m.*; **–urous** *a.* d'extase

rare *a.* rare; (meat) saignant **–ness** *n.* rareté *f.*

rarefaction *n.* raréfaction *f.*

rarefied *a.* raréfié

rarefy *vt.* raréfier

rarity *n.* rareté; chose rare *f.*; objet rare *m.*

rascal *n.* coquin, fripon *m.*; **–ity** *n.* coquinerie *f.*

rash *n.* éruption *f.*; **—** *a.* irréfléchi; téméraire; **–ness** *n.* témérité *f.*

rasp *n.* (tool) râpe *f.*; grincement *m.*; **—** *vt.* râper; racler; **—** *vi.* grincer; **–ing** *a.* grinçant; âpre

raspberry *n.* framboise *f.*

rat *n.* rat *m.*; **— poison** mort aux rats *f.*; **–trap** ratière *f.*; **smell a —** se douter de quelque chose

ratchet *n.* cliquet, rochet *m.*

rate *n.* taux *m.*; cours *m.*; tarif *m.*; prime *f.*; vitesse *f.*; allure *f.*; **at any —** en tout cas, dans tous les cas; **at the — of** au taux de; à la vitesse de; sur le pied de; **birth —** natalité *f.*; **death —** mortalité *f.*; **— of exchange** cours du change *m.*; **— of interest** taux de l'intérêt *m.*; **—** *vt.* classer; considérer; estimer, évaluer; **—**

vi. être classé; se ranger

rather *adv.* plutôt; assez; **I would — . . .** j'aimerais mieux **. . .**, je préférerais **. . .**

ratification *n.* ratification *f.*

ratify *vt.* ratifier

rating *n.* classement *m.*, classification *f.*; estimation *f.*

ratio *n.* proportion *f.*; rapport *m.*

ration *n.* ration *f.*; **—** *vt.* rationner; **–ing** *n.* rationnement *m.*

rational *a.* raisonnable; raisonné; (math.) rationnel; **–ize** *vt.* rationaliser

rattle *n.* cliquetis *m.*; tapotis *m.*; (child's) hochet *m.*, hochette *f.*; (snake) sonnette *f.*; (med.) râle *m.*; **—** *vi.* cliqueter; trembler; (med.) râler; **—** *vt.* faire cliqueter; agiter; **— off** dire rapidement; **— on** continuer à parler; **–r** *n.* serpent à sonnettes *m.*

rattlesnake *n.* serpent à sonnettes *m.*

raucous *a.* rauque

ravage *n.* ravage *m.*; **—** *vt.* ravager

ravaging *a.* ravageur

rave *vi.* extravaguer; délirer; s'extasier

ravel *vt.* emmêler

ravenous *a.* vorace

ravine *n.* ravin *m.*; défilé *m.*

ravish *vt.* ravir; violer; **–ing** *a.* ravissant

raw *a.* cru; vert; inexperimenté; **–ness** *n.* crudité *f.*; inexpérience *f.*

rawhide *n.* cuir vert *m.*

ray *n.* rayon *m.*; (fish) raie *f.*

rayon *n.* rayonne *f.*

raze *vt.* raser

razor *n.* rasoir *m.*; **— blade** lame de rasoir; *f.*; **— safety —** rasoir de sûreté *m.*

re *n.*, **in —** au sujet de

reach *n.* étendue *f.*; allonge *f.*; portée *f.*; **out of —** hors de portée; **within —** à la portée de; **—** *vt.* arriver à, atteindre; parvenir; **—** *vi.* s'etendre; **— out** tendre la main

react *vi.* réagir; **–ion** *n.* réaction *f.*; **–ionary** *a. & n.* réactionnaire *m. & f.*

read *vt.* lire; étudier; parcourir; (meter) relever; **–able** *a.* lisible; **–er** *n.* lecteur *m.*, lectrice *f.*; livre de lecture *m.*; (child's) livre de lectures, abécédaire *m.*; **–ing** *n.* lecture *f.*; interprétation *f.*; observation *f.*; façon de lire *f.*; (meter) relevé *m.*; **–ing room** salle de lecture *f.*

readily *adv.* volontiers; facilement

readiness *n.* promptitude *f.*; bonne volonté *f.*; facilité *f.*; **in —** prêt

readjust *vt.* rajuster; **–ment** *n.* rajustement *m.*

ready *a.* prêt; prompt, facile; **get — se** préparer, se disposer, s'apprêter

ready-made *a.* tout fait; de confection

reaffirm vt. réaffirmer

reagent n. réactif m.

real a. réel; vrai, véritable; naturel; — **estate** propriété immobilière f.; biens immeubles m. pl.; **–ism** n. réalisme m.; **–ist** n. réaliste m. & f.; **–istic** a. réaliste; **–ity** n. réalite f.; réel m.; **–ization** n. connaissance, conception f.; réalisation f.; **–ize** vt. se rendre compte de; réaliser; **–ly** adv. vraiment; réellement; sans blague

realm n. royaume m.

realtor n. agent immobilier m.

ream n. rame f.; — vt. aléser

reanimate vt. ranimer

reap vt. moissonner; cueillir, recueillir; **–er** n. (person) moissonneur m.; (machine) moissonneuse f.; **–ing** n. moisson f.

reappear vi. reparaître; **–ance** n. réapparition f.

rear n. arrière m.; derrière m.; — a. postérieur; d'arrière; — **admiral** contre-amiral m.; — **guard** arrière-garde f.; — vt. élever; — vi. se cabrer

rearm vt. réarmer; **–ament** n. réarmement m.

rearrange vt. rarranger, arranger; **–ment** n. nouvel arrangement m.

rearview a., — **mirror** rétroviseur m.

reason n. raison f.; argument m.; sujet, lieu m.; cause f.; **have** — **to** avoir lieu de; avoir sujet à; **it stands to** — c'est évident; **listen to** — entendre raison; — **(why)** pourquoi m.; — vi. raisonner; — vt. arguer, discuter; **–able** a. raisonnable; modéré; **–ing** n. raisonnement m.

reassemble vt. rassembler; remonter; — vi. se rassembler

reassurance n. promesse f.; encouragement m.

reassure vt. rassurer

reawaken vt. & (vi.) (se) réveiller

rebate n. rabais m.; escompte m.; ristourne f.; — vt. diminuer

rebel n. rebelle, révolté, insurgé m.; — vt. & (vi.) (se) révolter, (s')insurger, (se) soulever; **–lion** n. révolte f.; **–lious** a. rebelle

rebind vt. relier de nouveau

rebirth n. renaissance f.

rebound n. ricochet m.; rebondissement m.; — vi. rebondir

rebroadcast vt. (radio) diffuser de nouveau

rebuff n. refus m.; — vt. repousser; refuser

rebuild vt. rebâtir, reconstruire

rebuke n. réprimande f.; — vt. réprimander, blâmer

recalcitrance n. récalcitrance f.

recalcitrant a. récalcitrant; réfractaire

recall n. révocation f.; rappel m.; — vt.

rappeler; se souvenir de

recant vt. rétracter; — vi. se rétracter; chanter la palinodie

recap vt. rechaper

recapitulation n. récapitulation f.

recapture vt. reprendre; — n. reprise f.

recede vi. reculer; s'éloigner; (forehead) fuir

receipt n. reçu m.; recette f.; réception f.; récépissé m., quittance f., accusé de réception m.; **acknowledge** — accuser réception; — vt. acquitter

receivable a. recevable; **bills** — effets à recevoir m. pl.

receive vt. recevoir; (welcome) accueillir; **–r** n. destinataire m. & f.; (law) administrateur m.; (stolen goods) receleur m.; (phone) récepteur m.

receiving n. réception f.; — **station** poste récepteur m.

recent a. récent, nouveau; **–ly** adv. récemment

receptacle n. réceptacle m.

reception n. réception f.; accueil m.; **–ist** n. employé de bureau chargé de recevoir les clients m.

receptive a. réceptif

recess n. (school) récréation f.; (court) vacances f. pl.; enfoncement m.; recoin m.; embrasure f.; **–ion** n. recul m.; régression f.; crise financière f.; **–ional** n. hymne de sortie m.; **–ive** a. régressif, récessif — vt. encastrer, enfoncer

recipe n. recette f.

recipient n. bénéficiaire m. & f.; destinataire m. & f.

reciprocal a. réciproque; mutuel; inverse

reciprocate vt. payer de retour; — vi. retourner un compliment, rendre la pareille

reciprocity n. réciprocité f.

recital n. récitation f.; récit m.; (mus.) récital m.

recitation n. récitation f.

recite vt. réciter, déclamer; (school) répondre (à une question)

reckless a. insouciant; imprudent

reckon vt. compter; calculer; juger; — vi. compter; calculer; — **with** compter avec; **–ing** n. calcul, compte m.; estime f.

reclaim vt. réformer; (land) défricher; mettre en valeur

reclamation n. réforme f.; défrichement m.; mise en valeur f.; réclamation f.

recline vt. appuyer, coucher; — vi. être couché; être étendu

recognition n. reconnaissance f.

recognizable a. reconnaissable

recognizance n. (law) caution personnelle

f.
recognize *vt.* reconnaître; donner la parole à
recoil *n.* recul *m.*; contre-coup *m.*; détente *f.*; — *vi.* reculer; se détendre
recollect *vt.* se rappeler; se souvenir de; –ion *n.* souvenir *m.*
recommence *vt. & vi.* recommencer
recommend *vt.* recommander; –ation *n.* recommandation *f.*
recompense *n.* récompense *f.*; dédommagement *m.*; — *vt.* récompenser; dédommager
reconcilable *a.* conciliable
reconcile *vt.* réconcilier, racommoder; concilier; mettre d'accord; — oneself to se résigner à
reconciliation *n.* réconciliation *f.*; conciliation *f.*
recondition *vt.* rénover; mettre à neuf
reconnaissance *n.* reconnaissance *f.*
reconnoiter *vt.* reconnaître; — *vi.* faire une reconnaissance
reconquer *vt.* reconquérir
reconsider *vt.* reviser; considérer de nouveau; revenir sur
reconstitute *vt.* reconstituer
reconstruct *vt.* rebâtir, reconstruire; –ion *n.* reconstruction *f.*
record *n.* registre *m.*; note *f.*; procès-verbal *m.*; document *m.*; dossier *m.*; (sports) record *m.*; (phonograph) disque *m.*; off the — non-officiel; –s *pl.* archives *f. pl.*; — *vt.* enregistrer; rapporter; graver; faire une note de; –er *n.* enregistreur *m.*; archiviste *m.*; machine à enregistrer *f.*; tape –er magnétophone *m.*; –ing *n.* enregistrement *m.*
record-breaking *a.* qui bat le record; surpassant le record
recount *vt.* raconter
re-count *vt.* recompter
recoup *vt. & (vi.)* (se) dédommager; (se) rattraper (sur); rembourser, dédommager (de)
recourse *n.* recours *m.*
recover *vt.* retrouver, regagner; (loss) réparer, reprendre; recouvrer; (oneself) revenir à soi; — *vi.* guérir, se remettre (de); –y *n.* guérison *f.*; recouvrement *m.*; reprise *f.*
re-cover *vt.* recouvrir
recreation *n.* récréation *f.*; divertissement *m.*
recrimination *n.* récrimination *f.*
recruit *n.* recrue *f.*; — *vt.* (mil.) recruter; racoler: réparer; –ing *n.* recrutement *m.*
rectal *a.* rectal
rectangle *n.* rectangle *m.*
rectangular *a.* rectangulaire

rectification *n.* rectification *f.*
rectifier *n.* (elec.) redresseur, rectificateur *m.*
rectify *vt.* rectifier; réparer, corriger; (elec.) redresser
rectilinear *a.* rectiligne
rectitude *n.* rectitude, droiture *f.*
rector *n.* recteur *m.*; curé *m.*; –y *n.* presbytère *m.*
recumbent *a.* couché
recuperate *vi.* se remettre, se rétablir; guérir
recuperation *n.* rétablissement *m.*; guérison *f.*
recur *vi.* se reproduire; revenir; –rence *n.* retour *m.*; (med.) récidive *f.*; –rent *a.* recurrent; qui revient; –ring *a.* recurrent; périodique
red *n.* rouge *m.*; in the — en déficit; — *a.* rouge; (hair) roux (rousse); pourpre; — tape paperasserie *f.*; see — voir rouge; — turn — rougir; –den *vi.* rougir; (sky) rougeoyer; –dish *a.* rougeâtre; –ness *n.* rougeur *f.*; (hair) rousseur *f.*
red-blooded *a.* robuste, vigoureux
redcap *n.* porteur (de gare) *m.*
redecorate *vt.* repeindre; refaire
redeem *vt.* racheter; amortir; dégager; –able *a.* rachetable; –er *n.* rédempteur *m.*
redemption *n.* rachat *m.*; amortissement *m.*; (eccl.) rédemption *f.*
red-eyed *a.* aux yeux éraillés
red-haired *a.* roux (rousse), aux cheveux roux
red-handed *a.* en flagrant délit
redhead *n.* personne aux cheveux roux *f.*; –ed *a.* roux (rousse), aux cheveux roux
red-hot *a.* (chauffé au) rouge
rediscover *vt.* retrouver
redistribute *vt.* redistribuer
red-letter *a.*, — day jour mémorable *m.*
redolence *n.* odeur *f.*, parfum *m.*
redolent *a.* parfumé, odorant; — of qui sent
redouble *vt. & vi.* redoubler; (cards) surcontrer
redoubtable *a.* redoutable
redound *vi.* contribuer
redress *n.* réparation *f.*; — *vt.* réparer
redskin *n.* peau-rouge *m.*
reduce *vt.* réduire; diminuer; abaisser; — *vi.* maigrir
reducible *a.* réductible
reduction *n.* réduction *f.*; diminution *f.*; baisse *f.*
redundancy *n.* redondance *f.*
redundant *a.* redondant
reduplicate *vt.* redoubler
re-echo *vi.* résonner, retentir

reed *n.* roseau *m.*; (mus.) anche *f.*

reef *n.* récif, écueil *m.*; (naut.) ris *m.*; — *vt.* prendre un ris dans

reek *n.* odeur *f.*; relent *m.*; — *vi.* sentir; suer; –ing *a.* qui sent

reel *n.* bobine *f.*, dévidoir *m.*; (fishing) moulinet *m.*; — *vt.* bobiner, dévider; — *vi.* chanceler, tournoyer; tituber; — off réciter, énumérer rapidement

re-elect *vt.* réélire; –ion *n.* réélection *f.*

re-enact *vt.* reproduire

re-enlist *vi.* se rengager

re-enter *vt.* rentrer (dans)

re-entry *n.* rentrée *f.*

re-establish *vt.* rétablir; –ment *n.* rétablissement *m.*

re-examination *n.* nouvel examen *m.*

re-examine *vt.* examiner de nouveau

refashion *vt.* refaire, refaçonner

refasten *vt.* rattacher

refectory *n.* réfectoire *m.*

refer *vt.* soumettre; renvoyer; — *vi.* se rapporter; se reporter; faire allusion; parler; –ence *n.* référence *f.*; renvoi *m.*; appel *m.*; rapport *m.*; –ence work ouvrage à consulter *m.*

referee *n.* arbitre *m.*; — *vt.* arbitrer

refill *n.* rechange *m.*; pièce de rechange *f.*; — *vt.* remplir

refine *vt.* raffiner; purifier; –d *a.* raffiné; cultivé, distingué; –ment *n.* raffinage *m.*; raffinement *m.*; –ry *n.* raffinerie *f.*

refit *vt.* remonter; (naut.) réarmer

reflect *vt.* refléter; réfléchir; — *vi.* réfléchir; méditer; se dire; faire du tort; –ion *n.* réflexion *f.*, réfléchissement *m.*; reflet *m.*; image *f.*; –or *n.* réflecteur *m.*

reflex *a.* & *n.* réflexe *m.*; –ive *a.* (gram.) réfléchi

reforestation *n.* reboisement *m.*

reform *n.* réforme *f.*; — *vt.* réformer, corriger; — *vi.* se réformer, se corriger; –ation *n.* réforme *f.*; réformation *f.*; –atory *n.* maison de correction *f.*; –er *n.* réformateur *m.*

re-form *vt.* reformer; — *vi.* se reformer

refract *vt.* réfracter; –ion *n.* refraction *f.* –ory *a.* réfractaire; insoumis

refrain *n.* (mus.) refrain *m.*; — *vi.* s'abstenir, se retenir

refresh *vt.* rafraîchir; –ing *a.* rafraîchissant; –ment *n.* rafraîchissement *m.*; boisson *f.*; quelque chose à boire (ou à manger) *m.*

refrigerate *vt.* réfrigérer, refroidir; frigorifier

refrigeration *n.* réfrigération *f.*; frigorification *f.*

refrigerator *n.* glacière *f.*, frigidaire *m.*

refuel *vi.* faire le plein d'essence

refuge *n.* refuge *m.*; abri *m.*; **take** — **se** réfugier; –e *n.* réfugié, sinistré *m.*

refulgence *n.* éclat *m.*

refund *n.* remboursement *m.*; — *vt.* rembourser; –able *a.* remboursable

refurnish *vt.* remonter

refusal *n.* refus *m.*; **first** — **première offre** *f.*

refuse *n.* rebut *m.*; — *vt.* refuser; ne pas vouloir

refutation *n.* réfutation *f.*

refute *vt.* réfuter

regain *vt.* regagner; reprendre; — consciousness reprendre connaissance

regal *a.* royal; –ia *n.* insignes *m. pl.*

regale *vt.* régaler

regard *n.* attention *f.*, égard *m.*; estime *f.*; **in** — **to** en ce qui concerne; **out of** — **for** par égard pour; **with** — **to** quant à; **have no** — **for** ne pas estimer; faire peu de cas de; **show** — témoigner de l'estime; –s *pl.* amitiés *f. pl.*; **give my** –**s to** faites mes amitiés à; — *vt.* regarder, considérer; –ing *prep.* en ce qui concerne; quant à; à l'égard de; –less *a.* sans regarder; sans se soucier; –less *adv.* en tout cas; quand même

regatta *n.* régate *f.*

regency *n.* régence *f.*

regenerate *vt.* régénérer; — *vi.* se régénérer; — *a.* régénéré

regeneration *n.* régénération *f.*

regenerator *n.* régénérateur *m.*

regent *n.* régent *m.*

regime, regimen *n.* régime *m.*

regiment *n.* régiment *m.*; –al *a.* du régiment; –ation *n.* régimentation *f.*; — *vt.* réglementer

region *n.* région *f.*; –al *a.* régional

register *n.* registre *m.*; compteur *m.*; **cash** — caisse enregistreuse *f.*; — *vt.* enregistrer; inscrire; immatriculer; (letter) recommander; (trademark) déposer; — *vi.* s'inscrire; s'immatriculer

registrar *n.* archiviste, secrétaire; teneur de registres *m.*

registration *n.* enregistrement *m.*; inscription *f.*; (school, auto) immatriculation *f.*

registry *n.* secrétariat *m.*; bureau d'enregistrement *m.*

regress *vi.* régresser; –ion *n.* régression *f.*

regret *n.* regret *m.*; — *vt.* regretter; être désolé; –ful *a.* plein de regrets; –fully *adv.* avec regret; –table *a.* regrettable; à regretter

regroup *vt.* regrouper

regular *a.* régulier; ordinaire; habituel; (officer) de carrière; (coll.) vrai; –ity *n.* régularité; –ize *vt.* régulariser; –ly *adv.* régulièrement; d'ordinaire, d'habitude

regulate vt. régler
regulation n. règlement m.; ordonnance f.
regulator n. régulateur m.
regurgitate vt. régurgiter; — vi. regorger
rehabilitate vt. réhabiliter
rehabilitation n. réhabilitation f.
rehearsal n. répétition f.
rehearse vt. répéter
reheat vt. réchauffer
reign n. règne m.; — vi. régner; –ing a. régnant
reimburse vt. rembourser; –ment n. remboursement m.
rein n. bride, rêne, guide f.; — vt. brider
reincarnation n. réincarnation f.
reincorporate vt. réincorporer
reinforce vt. renforcer; appuyer; –d a. renforcé; –d concrete béton armé m.; –ment n. renforcement m.; –ments n. pl. renfort m.
reinstate vt. réintégrer, rétablir; –ment n. réintégration f.
reinsurance n. réassurance, contre-assurance f.
reinsure vt. réassurer
reissue vt. émettre de nouveau; publier de nouveau
reiterate vt. réitérer
reiteration n. réiteration f.
reject n. pièce de rebut f.; — vt. rejeter; refuser; –ion n. rejet m.; refus m.
rejoice vt. réjouir; — vi. se réjouir (de)
rejoin vt. rejoindre; retrouver; — vi. répondre, répliquer; –der n. réplique f.
rejuvenate vt. & vi. rajeunir
rekindle vt. rallumer; ranimer
relapse n. rechute f.; — vi. rechuter, avoir une rechute; retomber (dans)
relate vt. raconter; relater; rapporter; — vi. avoir rapport (à), se rapporter; –d a. apparenté; parent; allié
relation n. (narrative) récit m.; rapport m.; relation f.; (relative) parent m.; –ship n. rapport m.; relation f.; parenté f.; in — to à l'égarde de
relative a. relatif; — n. parent m.; humidity n. humidité relative f.; — to au sujet de
relativity n. relativité f.
relax vt. détendre, relâcher; — vi. se détendre, se relâcher; –ation n. détente f.; repos m.; relâchement m.
relay n. relais m.; relève f.; — race course à relais f.; — vt. relayer
re-lay vt. reposer, poser de nouveau
release n. libération f.; élargissement m. déclencheur m.; (document) quittance f., acquit m.; — vt. libérer; élargir; lâcher; déclencher; acquitter
relegate vt. reléguer, remettre

relent vi. revenir sur; s'adoucir; –less a. impitoyable, implacable; –lessness n. implacabilité f.
relevance n. à propos m.
relevant a. à propos, pertinent; qui se rapporte à
reliability n. régularité f.; honnêteté f.
reliable a. sûr; digne de confiance
reliance n. confiance f.
reliant a., be — on dépendre de; avoir confiance en
relic n. relique f.; –s pl. restes m. pl.
relief n. soulagement m.; aide f.; secours m.; assistance publique f.; relief m.; — map carte en relief
relieve vt. soulager; aider, secourir; relever; dégager
relight vt. rallumer
religion n. religion f.; culte m.
religious a. religieux; dévot; pieux; –ly adv. religieusement; scrupuleusement
reline vt. redoubler; (brakes) regarnir
relinquish vt. renoncer; délaisser; abandonner
relish n. goût m.; assaisonnement, condiment m.; entremets m.; — vt. goûter, savourer
reload vt. recharger
relocate vt. reloger, changer de place
relocation n. relogement m.
reluctance n. regret m.; répugnance f.; hésitation f.; (elec.) reluctance f.
reluctant a. hésitant; peu disposé; –ly adv. à regret; à contre-cœur
rely vi., — on compter sur
remain vi. rester; demeurer; se tenir; –s n. pl. restes m. pl.; vestiges m. pl. –der n. reste m.; (book) solde d'édition m.
remake vt. refaire
remand n. renvoi m.; — vt. renvoyer
remark n. remarque f., observation f.; attention f.; — vt. remarquer, observer, constater; — vi. faire une remarque; –able a. remarquable
remarry vi. se remarier
remediable a. rémédiable
remedial a. réparateur; curatif
remedy n. remède m.; recours m.; — vt. remédier
remember vt. se souvenir de; se rappeler
remembrance n. souvenir m.; mémoire f.
remind vt. rappeler; faire penser; faire souvenir; –er n. rappel m.; souvenir m.; mémento m.
reminiscence n. réminiscence f.; souvenir m.
reminiscent a. qui rappelle
remiss a. négligent; –ion n. rémission f.; remise f.; –ness n. négligence f.
remit vt. remettre, envoyer; pardonner;

-tance n. remise f.; envoi m.; **-ter** n. remettant m.

remnant n. reste m.; coupon m.

remodel vt. remodeler

remonstrance n. remontrance f.

remonstrate vi. faire des remontrances; — vt. protester

remorse n. remords m.; **-ful** a. plein de remords; **-less** a. sans remords; sans pitié

remote a. lointain, éloigné; reculé; peu probable; **-ly** adv. loin; de loin; **-ness** n. éloignement m.

removable a. amovible; détachable

removal a. enlèvement m.; déplacement m.; transport m.; révocation f.

remove vt. enlever, écarter; déplacer, transporter; **-d** a. éloigné; loin

remunerate vt. rémunérer

remuneration n. rémunération f.

remunerative a. rémunérateur

renaissance n. renaissance f.

renal a. rénal

rename vt. renommer, rebaptiser

renascence n. renaissance

renascent a. renaissant

rend vt. déchirer; fendre; faire retentir

render vt. rendre; traduire; interpréter; (cooking) fondre; **-ing, rendition** n. rendu m.; traduction f.; interprétation f.

rendezvous n. rendez-vous m.

renegade n. renégat m.

renew vt. renouveler; (subscription) réabonner; — vi. renouer **-able** a. renouvelable; interchangeable; **-al** n. renouvellement m.; réabonnement m.

renounce vt. renoncer à; abandonner; répudier

renovate vt. renouveler; rénover; mettre à neuf

renovation n. rénovation f.

renown n. renom m., renommée f.; **-ed** a. renommé, célèbre, illustre

rent n. (property) loyer m.; (clothing) déchirure f.; fente, fissure f.; (income) n. pl. rentes f., revenu m.; — vt. louer, affermer; — vi. se louer; **-al** n. loyer m.; **-er** n. locataire m. & f.

renunciation n. renonciation f., renoncement m.; répudiation f.

reoccupy vt. réoccuper

reopen vt. rouvrir; — vi. (se) rouvrir; (school) rentrer; **-ing** n. réouverture f.; rentrée f.

reorder vt. commander de nouveau; — vi. renouveler une commande

reorganization n. réorganisation f.

reorganize vt. & vi. réorganiser

repair n. réparation f.; état m.; — **shop** n. atelier de réparation m.; — vt. réparer; raccommoder; — vi. aller, se rendre; **-ing** n. réparation f.; (clothes) raccommodage m.; (mech.) dépannage m.

repairman n. réparateur m.; dépanneur m.

reparable a. réparable

reparation n. réparation; satisfaction f.

repartee n. repartie f.; réplique f.

repast n. repas, festin m.

repatriate vt. rapatrier

repave vt. repaver

repay vt. rembourser; récompenser; rendre; **-able** a. payable, à rembourser; **-ment** n. remboursement m.

repeal n. révocation, abrogation f.; — vt. révoquer, (law) abroger

repeat n. répétition f.; (mus.) reprise f.; — vt. répéter; réiterer; — vi. se répéter; **-ed** a. répété; réitéré; **-edly** adv. à plusieurs reprises; **-ing** a. qui répète

repel vt. repousser; répugner à; **-lent** a. répulsif; repoussant; insect **-lent** n. chasse-insectes m.; **-ling** a. répulsif

repent vt. & vi. se repentir (de); **-ance** n. repentir m.; **-ant** a. repenti; repentant

repercussion n. répercussion f.; contrecoup m.

repertoire, repertory n. répertoire m.

repetition n. répétition f.; (mus.) reprise f.

rephrase vt. rédiger de nouveau, dire d'une autre façon

replace vt. remplacer; replacer; remettre; **-able** a. remplaçable; interchangeable; **-ment** n. remplacement m.; pièce de rechange f.; remise f.; **-ment** a. de remplacement, de rechange

replate vt. replaquer

replenish vt. remplir; se réapprovisionner (de); **-ing, -ment** n. recharge f.

replete a. rempli, plein

replica n. réplique f.; copie f.

reply n. réponse f.; réplique f.; — vt. & vi. répondre, répliquer

report n. rapport m.; compte-rendu m.; procès-verbal m.; bruit m., rumeur f.; (firearms) détonation f.; weather — bulletin météorologique m.; — vt. rapporter; rendre compte de; signaler; dire; **-er** n. reporter, journaliste m.; **-ing** n. reportage m.

repose n. repos m.; calme m., tranquillité f.; — vi. (se) reposer

repository n. dépôt m.

repossess vt. reprendre (possession); **-ion** n. rentrée en possession f.

reprehensible a. blâmable, répréhensible

represent vt. représenter; symboliser; jouer; **-ation** n. représentation f.; **-ative** a. représentatif; **-ative** n. représentant m.; député m.; House of Representatives Chambre des Représentants

f.
repress *vt.* réprimer; refouler; **–ed** *a.* réprimé; refoulé; **–ion** *n.* répression *f.*
reprieve *n.* commutation *f.*; sursis, répit *m.*; — *vt.* accorder une commutation à
reprimand *n.* réprimande *f.*; — *vt.* réprimander
reprint *n.* réimpression *f.*; tirage à part; tiré à part; *m.*; — *vt.* réimprimer; tirer à part
reprisal *n.* représaille *f.*
reproach *n.* reproche *m.*; **beyond —** irréprochable; — *vt.* faire des reproches à; **–ful** *a.* plein de reproches
reprobate *n.* vaurien *m.*; roué *m.*; — *vt.* réprouver
reproduce *vt.* reproduire; multiplier; — *vi.* se reproduire; se multiplier
reproduction *n.* reproduction *f.*; copie *f.*
reproof *n.* reproche *m.*, réprimande *f.*
reprove *vt.* réprimander, reprendre, réprouver
reproving *a.* de reproche; réprobateur
republic *n.* république *f.*; **–an** *a.* & *n.* républicain *m.*
republish *vt.* rééditer; republier
repudiate *vt.* répudier, désavouer, renier
repudiation *n.* répudiation *f.*, désaveu *m.*, reniement *m.*
repugnant *a.* répugnant
repulse *vt.* repousser, refouler
repulsion *n.* répugnance *f.*; répulsion *f.*
repulsive *a.* repoussant, dégoûtant, répulsif
repurchase *n.* rachat *m.*; — *vt.* racheter
reputable *a.* honorable, estimable
reputation *n.* réputation *f.*, renom *m.*
repute *n.* réputation *f.*; renom *m.*, renommée *f.*; estime *f.*; **–d** *a.* réputé; attribué; supposé, censé
request *n.* demande *f.*; requête *f.*; sollicitation *f.*; **on —** sur demande; — *vt.* demander; solliciter; prier
require *vt.* exiger; demander; falloir; **–d** *a.* exigé, demandé; requis, nécessaire, prescrit, voulu; **–ment** *n.* exigence *f.*; besoin *m.*; nécessité *f.*
requisite *a.* requis, nécessaire; — *n.* nécessaire *m.*, chose nécessaire *f.*
requisition *n.* réquisition, demande *f.*; — *vt.* réquisitionner
reroute *vt.* transmettre par une autre route; envoyer par une autre route
rerouting *n.* (telephone) transmission déroutée *f.*
rerun *n.* (TV) répétition *f.*
resaddle *vt.* reseller
resale *n.* revente *f.*
rescind *vt.* rescinder; abroger
rescue *n.* délivrance *f.*; sauvetage *m.*; —

vt. délivrer, sauver; **–r** *n.*, libérateur, sauveur *m.*
research *n.* recherche *f.*; enquête *f.*; investigation *f.*; travaux de recherche *m. pl.*
resemblance *n.* ressemblance *f.*
resemble *vt.* ressembler (à)
resent *vt.* ressentir; s'offenser de; **–ful** *a.* plein de ressentiment; **–ment** *n.* ressentiment *m.*
reservation *n.* réserve *f.*; place louée; chambre retenue *f.*; restriction *f.*; terres réservées *f. pl.*
reserve *n.* réserve *f.*; — **power** *n.* réserve de puissance *f.*; — *vt.* réserver; louer; retenir; **–d** *a.* réservé; loué; retenu; (person) renfermé
reservoir *n.* réservoir *m.*
reset *vt.* remettre; remonter; recomposer
resettle *vt.* réinstaller; — *vi.* se réinstaller
reside *vi.* résider, demeurer; **–nce** *n.* résidence *f.*; demeure *f.*; domicile *m.*; séjour *m.*; habitation *f.*; maison *f.*; hôtel *m.*; **–nt** *n.* habitant *m.*; résident *m.*; interne *m.*; **–ntial** *a.* d'habitation
residue *n.* résidu *m.*
resign *vt.* résigner; démissionner; — **oneself** se résigner; **–ation** *n.* démission *f.*; résignation *f.*; **–ed** *a.* résigné
resilience *n.* résilience *f.*; élasticité *f.*; rebondissement *m.*
resiliency *n.* élasticité, résilience *f.*
resilient *a.* élastique
resin *n.* résine *f.*; **–ous** *a.* résineux
resist *vt.* résister; **–ance** *n.* résistance *f.*; (elec.) impédance *f.*; — **coil** *n.* bobine de résistance *f.*; **–ant** *a.* résistant; **–ible** *a.* résistible; **–or** *n.* (elec.) résistance *f.*
resole *vt.* ressemeler
resolute *a.* résolu, ferme, déterminé; **–ness** *n.* résolution *f.*
resolution *n.* résolution *f.*; décision *f.*; détermination *f.*
resolve *n.* résolution *f.*; — *vt.* résoudre; décider; — *vi.* se résoudre; se décider; **–d** *a.* résolu; décidé
resonance *n.* résonance *f.*, retentissement *m.*
resonant *a.* résonnant; sonore; accordé
resonator *n.* résonateur *m.*
resort *n.* recours *m.*, ressource *f.*; (place) station *f.*; **summer —** station balnéaire *f.*; — *vi.* avoir recours, recourir
resound *vi.* résonner; retentir; **–ing** *a.* résonnant; retentissant
re-sound *vt.* répéter
resource *n.* ressource *f.*; **–ful** *a.* débrouillard; **–fulness** *n.* ressource *f.*
respect *n.* respect *m.*, estime, considération *f.*; égard *m.*; rapport *m.*; **in this —**

à cet égard; with — to en ce qui concerne; –s *pl.* hommages, respects *m. pl.*; — *vt.* respecter; estimer, honorer; **–ability** *n.* respectabilité *f.*; **–able** *a.* respectable; honorable; convenable, comme il faut; **–ful** *a.* respectueux; **–fully** *adv.* respectueusement; **–ive** *a.* respectif; **–ively** *adv.* respectivement

respirator *n.* respirateur *m.*; **–y** *a.* respiratoire

respite *n.* répit, relâche *m.*; délai *m.*

resplendent *a.* resplendissant

respond *vi.* répondre

response *n.* réponse, réplique *f.*; réaction *f.*; accueil *m.*; fonction *f.*, rendement *m.*

responsibility *n.* responsabilité *f.*; charge *f.*; devoir *m.*

responsible *a.* responsable; compétent

responsive *a.* sensible; sympathique; **–ness** *n.* sensibilité *f.*

rest *n.* repos *m.*; reste *m.*; (support) appui *m.*; (mus.) pause *f.*, **whole** — pause *f.*, **half** — demi-pause *f.*, **quarter** — soupir *m.*; **come to** — s'arrêter; **take a** — se reposer; **— room** lavabo *m.*; **—** *vt.* reposer; appuyer; **—** *vi.* se reposer; s'appuyer; peser; **–ful** *a.* reposant; tranquille; **–ive** *a.* inquiet; rétif; **–less** *a.* sans repos; troublé, agité; inquiet; impatient

restate *vt.* énoncer de nouveau; énoncer en d'autres termes

restive *a.* rétif; opiniâtre

restoration *n.* restitution, restauration *f.*

restore *vt.* restituer, restaurer; rendre; remettre; rétablir

restrain *vt.* retenir; contraindre; empêcher; **–t** *n.* contrainte *f.*; réserve *f.*

restrict *vt.* restreindre; **–ed** *a.* restreint; limité; **–ion** *n.* restriction *f.*; **–ive** *a.* restrictif

result *n.* résultat *m.*; **as a** — par conséquent; **as a** — **of** par suite de; **—** *vi.* résulter; s'ensuivre; **–ant** *a.* résultant

resume *vt.* reprendre; se remettre à

resumé *n.* résumé *m.*

resumption *n.* reprise *f.*

resurface *vt.* donner une nouvelle surface à; (road) refaire le revêtement de

resurgent *a.* renaissant

resurrect *vt.* ressusciter; **–ion** *n.* résurrection *f.*

resuscitate *vt.* ressusciter

resuscitation *n.* retour à la vie *m.*; renaissance *f.*

retail *n.* vente au détail *f.*; détail *m.*; — **price** prix de détail *m.*; — *vt.* vendre au détail, détailler; **–er** *n.* marchand au détail; détaillant *m.*

retain *vt.* retenir; garder, conserver; **–er**

n. avance *f.*; honoraires payés d'avance *m. pl.*; serviteur *m.*; **–ing fee** *n.* honoraires payés d'avance *m. pl.*; **–ing wall** *n.* mur de soutènement *m.*

retaliate *vi.* user de représailles

retaliation *n.* représailles *f. pl.*; talion *m.*

retaliatory *a.* de représailles

retard *vt.* retarder; **–d** *a.* attardé

retch *vi.* vomir

retell *vt.* redire, répéter

retention *n.* conservation *f.*

retentive *a.* tenace; qui retient; **–ness** *n.* ténacité *f.*

reticence *n.* réticence *f.*

reticent *a.* taciturne

retina *n.* rétine *f.*

retinue *n.* suite *f.*

retire *vi.* se retirer; prendre la retraite; se coucher; se replier; — *vt.* mettre à la retraite; **–d** *a.* retiré; retraité; en retraite; **–ment** *n.* retraite *f.*

retiring *a.* réservé; qui prend la retraite; sortant

retort *n.* réplique *f.*; (chem.) cornue *f.*; — *vt. & vi.* répliquer, riposter; renvoyer

retouch *vt.* retoucher

retrace *vt.* retracer; revenir sur

retract *vt.* rétracter; escamoter; se dédire; **–able** *a.* escamotable; **–ion** *n.* rétraction *f.*; désaveu *m.*

retread *n.* pneu rechapé *m.*; — *vt.* rechaper

retreat *n.* retraite *f.*; asile *m.*; — *vi.* battre en retraite; se retirer; **–ing** *a.* qui bat la retraite; (forehead) fuyant

retrench *vt.* restreindre; **–ment** *n.* réduction *f.*

retribution *n.* récompense *f.*; jugement *m.*

retrieve *vt.* rapporter; retrouver; **–r** *n.* chien rapporteur *m.*

retroactive *a.* rétroactif; réactif, de réaction

retrograde *a.* rétrograde; — *vi.* rétrograder

retrospect, retrospection *n.* coup d'œil rétrospectif, examen rétrospectif *m.*

return *n.* retour *m.*; profit, revenu *m.*; restitution *f.*; **in** — en tour; **in** — **for** en retour de; en échange de; moyennant; **by** — **mail** par retour du courrier; — **address** adresse de l'expéditeur *f.*; — **match** match retour *m.*; — **ticket** billet de retour *m.*; — **trip** voyage de retour *m.*; — *vi.* revenir; retourner; être de retour; tour; rentrer; — *vt.* rendre, restituer; remettre; répondre; rapporter

reunite *vt.* réunir; réconcilier; — *vi.* se réunir; se réconcilier

revamp *vt.* refaçonner, refaire, réorganiser

reveal *vt.* révéler, découvrir; laisser voir; dévoiler; mettre à jour; **–ing** *a.* révéla-

teur
reveille *n.* (mil.) diane *f.*
revel *n.* divertissement *m.*; orgie *f.*; — *vi.*
se divertir; faire bombance; **-ry** *n.* di-
vertissements *m. pl.*; bombance *f.*; orgie
f.
revelation *n.* révélation *f.*
revenge *n.* vengeance *f.*; **take** — se venger
(de); — *vt.* venger; **-ful** *a.* vengeur, vindicatif
revenue *n.* revenu *m.*; rente *f.*
reverberate *vi.* retentir; réverbérer
reverberation *n.* réverbération, répercussion *f.*
revere *vt.* révérer, honorer, vénérer; **-nce**
n. révérence, vénération *f.*; **-nd** *a.* & *n.*
révérend *m.*; **-nt** *a.* respectueux
reverie *n.* rêverie *f.*
reversal *n.* revirement *m.*; inversion *f.*;
renversement *m.*; (law) réforme *f.*
reverse *a.* opposé, contraire; inverse; —
side dos *m.*; envers *m.*; revers *m.*; verso
m. — *n.* opposé, contraire, inverse, verso *m.*; revers *m.*; verso *m.*; (auto.) marche arrière *f.*; — *vt.* renverser; invertir;
retourner; faire marche arrière; (law)
réformer, revoquer
revert *vi.* retourner, revenir
review *n.* revue *f.*; révision *f.*; examen *m.*
compte rendu *m.*; — *vt.* reviser; passer
en revue; faire le compte rendu de; **-er**
n. critique *m.*
revile *vt.* injurier, insulter
revisal *n.* revision *f.*; (print.) seconde *f.*,
(2nd) troisième épreuve d'auteur
revise *vt.* revoir, reviser; corriger
reviser *n.* réviseur *m.*
revision *n.* révision *f.*
revisit *vt.* visiter de nouveau, revisiter
revival *n.* retour à la vie *m.*; renaissance
f.; reprise *f.*; réveil *m.*; renouveau *m.*;
-ist *n.* revivaliste *m. & f.*
revive *vt.* faire revivre, ressusciter; réveiller; renouveler; ranimer; — *vi.* reprendre connaissance; ressusciter se ranimer; renaître; reprendre
revocable *a.* révocable
revocation *n.* révocation *f.*
revoke *vt.* révoquer
revolt *n.* révolte *f.*; — *vi.* se révolter,
se rebeller, s'insurger, se soulever; **-ing**
a. en révolte; repoussant, révoltant
revolution *n.* révolution *f.*; tour *m.*; **-ary**
a. & n. révolutionnaire *m. & f.*; **-ist** *n.*
révolutionnaire *m. & f.*; **-ize** *n.* révolutionner
revolve *vt.* faire tourner, retourner; — *vi.*
tourner; **-r** *n.* révolver *m.*
revolving *a.* tournant; pivotant
revulsion *n.* revirement *m.*

reward *n.* récompense *f.*; — *vt.* récompenser
rewind *vt.* rembobiner, réenrouler
reword *vt.* redire en d'autres termes; rédiger de nouveau
rewrite *vt.* récrire; refaire, remanier
rhapsody *n.* rapsodie *f.*
Rheims *n.* Reims
Rhenish *a.* rhénan, du Rhin
rhetoric *n.* rhétorique *f.*; **-al** *a.* de rhétorique; **-ian** *n.* rhétoricien, rhéteur *m.*
rheumatic *a.* rhumatismal; — **fever** *n.*
rhumatisme articulaire *m.*; — *n.* rhumatisant *m.*
rheumatism *n.* rhumatisme *m.*
Rhine *n.* Rhin *m.*
rhinestone *n.* faux diamant *m.*
rhubarb *n.* rhubarbe *f.*
rhyme *n.* rime *f.*; vers *m.*; — *vi.* rimer; —
vt. faire rimer; **neither** — **nor reason** ni
rime ni raison
rhythm *n.* rythme *m.*; **-mically** *adv.* avec
rythme; **-mical** *a.* rythmique, rythmé
rib *n.* côte *f.*; nervure *f.*; support *m.*; — *vt.*
garnir de nervures; (coll.) faire mar-
cher; taquiner; **-bed** *a.* à nervures, à
cotes
ribald *a.* libertin, obscène; **-ry** *n.* libertinage *m.*; langage licencieux *m.*
ribbon *n.* ruban *m.*; bande *f.*; **tear to -s**
déchiqueter; mettre en lambeaux
rice *n.* riz *m.*; — **field**, — **paddy** *n.* rizière
— **paper** *n.* papier de riz *m.*; — **pudding**
n. riz au lait *m.*
rich *a.* riche; fertile; gras; somptueux; —
n. riches *m. pl.*; **-es** *n. pl.* richesse *f.*;
-ness *n.* richesse *f.*; fertilité *f.*; somptuosité *f.*
rickets *n. pl.* rachitisme *m.*
rickety *a.* délabré, boiteux, bancal; (med.)
rachitique
rickrack *n.* passement en zigzag *m.*, bordure *f.*
ricochet *vi.* ricocher
rid *vt.* débarrasser; purger; délivrer; **get**
— **of** se débarrasser de, se défaire de;
-dance *n.* débarras *m.*
riddle *n.* devinette *f.*; énigme *f.*; — *vt.*
cribler
ride *n.* voyage *m.*, promenade *f.*; trajet *m.*;
go for a — (aller) faire une promenade
(en auto); — *vi.* aller, voyager, se promener; aller à cheval, monter à cheval;
— *vt.* monter; (coll.) ennuyer; harasser;
taquiner; **-r** *n.* personne qui va en auto'
passager *m. & f.*; cavalier *m.*; jockey
m.; (law) clause additionnelle *f.*, annexe, allonge *f.*
ridge *n.* arête *f.*; crête *f.*; ride *f.*
ridicule *n.* ridicule *m.*; risée *f.*; raillerie,

moquerie *f.*; — *vt.* se moquer de
ridiculous *a.* ridicule; **–ness** *n.* ridicule *m.*
riding *n.* équitation *f.*; — **boots** *n. pl.* bottes *f. pl.*; — **breeches** *n. pl.* culotte de cheval *f.*; — **habit** *n.* amazone *f.*; — **master** maître d'équitation *m.*
RH factor *n.* facteur RH *m.*
Rhodesia *n.* Rhodésie *f.*
rife *a.*, **to be** — sévir
riffraff *n.* canaille *f.*
rifle *n.* fusil *m.*; carabine *f.*; — **range** champ de tir *m.*; — **shot** coup de fusil *m.*; **within** — **shot** à portée de fusil; — *vt.* (guns) rayer; piller; fouiller
rifleman *n.* chasseur, tirailleur, fusilier *m.*
rifling *n.* pillage *m.*; (rifle bore) rayage *m.*
rift *n.* fente, fissure *f.*; (persons) brouille *f.*
rig *n.* (naut.) gréement *m.*; équipement *m.*; voiture *f.*; attelage *m.*; — *vt.* gréer; équiper; installer, monter; (coll.) truquer; **–ging** *n.* gréage *m.*; équipage *m.*; agrès *m. pl.*
right *a.* droit; juste; bon; correct; exact; (watch) à l'heure; **all** — bon; bien; entendu; — **angle** *n.* angle droit *m.*; **be** — avoir raison; **that's** — c'est cela; — **side** endroit, bon côté *m.*; — **side up** à l'endroit; — *adv.* droit; tout; **do** — faire bien; **go** — réussir; aller à droite; — **and left** de tous les côtés; — **away** tout de suite, sur-le-champ; — *n.* droit *m.*; bien *m.*; titre *m.*; droit *f.*; — **and wrong** le bien et le mal; **on the** —, **to the** — à droite; **keep to the** — tenir la droite; serrer à droite; **–s** *n. pl.* droit(s) *m. pl.*; **within one's** — **s** dans son droit; *vt.* redresser, réparer; rectifier; **–eous** *a.* droit, juste; **–eousness** *n.* droiture *f.*; **–ful** *a.* légitime; **–ist** *n.* partisan de la droite *m.*; **–fully** *adv.* à juste titre; **–ness** *n.* justesse *f.*
rightabout face *n.* demi-tour à droite *m.*; (fig.) revirement *m.*
right-hand *a.* de droite; de la main droite; — **man** bras droit *m.*; **–ed** *a.* droitier
right-of-way *n.* priorité *f.*; (rail.) voie *f.*
right-wing *a.* de droite; **–er** *n.* partisan de la droite *m.*
rigid *a.* rigide; raide; sévère; **–ity** *n.* rigidité *f.*; raideur *f.*; sévérité *f.*
rigmarole *n.* procédure compliquée *f.*; galimatias *m.*
rigor *n.* rigueur *f.*; sévérité *f.*; — **mortis** rigidité cadavérique *f.*; **–ous** *a.* rigoureux; sévère; **–ousness** *n.* rigueur *f.*
rile *vt.* troubler; faire enrager
rim *n.* bord *m.*; (eyeglasses) monture *f.*; — *vt.* border; **–less** *a.* sans monture
rind *n.* peau *f.*; pelure *f.*; écorce *f.*; croûte *f.*

ring *n.* anneau *m.*, bague *f.*; cercle *m.*; alliance *f.*; rond *m.*; groupe *m.*; bande *f.*; arène *f.*; (boxing) ring *m.*; (circuit) enceinte *f.*; sonnerie *f.*; coup de téléphone *m.*; — **finger** annulaire *m.*; **wedding** — *m.*; — **alliance** *f.*; — *vt.* entourer; sonner; — *vi.* sonner; résonner, retentir; tinter; **–ing** *n.* son *m.*; tintement *m.*; **–er** *n.* (bell) sonnette *f.*; (person) sonneur *m.*; **dead –er** (coll.) jumeau, double *m.*
ringleader *n.* chef, meneur *m.*
ringworm *n.* teigne (tonsurante) *f.*
rink *n.* patinoire *f.*
rinse *vt.* rincer; — *n.* (hair) rinçage *m.*
riot *n.* émeute *f.*; — **squad** police-secours *f.*; — *vi.* s'ameuter; **–ing** *n.* émeutes *f. pl.*; **–ous** *a.* tumultueux; déréglé, dissipé
rip *n.* déchirure *f.*; **–cord** *n.* corde d'ouverture *f.*; — *vt.* découdre, déchirer; — *vi.* se déchirer; — **open** ouvrir en déchirant
ripe *a.* mûr; prêt; **–n** *vt.* (faire) mûrir; **–n** *vi.* mûrir; **–ness** *n.* maturité *f.*
ripple *n.* ride *f.*; gazouillement *m.*; ondulation *f.*; murmure *m.*; — *vt.* rider; — *vi.* se rider; onduler; murmurer; parler
rippling *n.* murmure *m.*; clapotage *m.*; — *a.* murmurant
rise *n.* lever *m.*; hausse *f.*; élévation *f.*; (ground) éminence *f.*; (tide) montée *f.*; — *vi.* se lever; s'élever; monter; se soulever; se dresser; **–r** *n.* contremarche *f.*
rising *a.* levant; montant; en hausse; — *n.* lever *m.*; hausse *f.*
risk *n.* risque, péril *m.*; **run a** — courir un risque; — *vt.* risquer; hasarder; **–y** *a.* hasardeux; (story) risqué
rite *n.* rite *m.*; cérémonie *f.*
ritual *a.* rituel; — *n.* rituel *m.*; **rites** *m. pl.*; **–istic** *a.* rituel
rival *a. & n.* rival *m.*; émule *m. & f.*; — *vt.* rivaliser avec; **–ry** *n.* rivalité *f.*; émulation *f.*
river *n.* fleuve *m.*; rivière *f.*; **down** — en aval; **up** — en amont
riverside *n.* bord de la rivière *m.*; — *a.* qui s'étend au bord de l'eau; riverain
rivet *n.* rivet *m.*; clou (à river) *m.*; — *vt.* river, riveter; **–er** *n.* (machine) riveteuse; *f.*; **–ing** *n.* rivetage *m.*
Riviera *n.* Côte d'Azur *f.*
rivulet *n.* ruisseau *m.*
road *n.* chemin *m.*; route *f.*; voie *f.*; — **map** carte routière *f.*; **on the** — en voyage; en province
roadbed *n.* empierrement *m.*
roadblock *n.* barricade *f.*
roadhouse *n.* cabaret au bord de la route *m.*; auberge *f.*

roadside n. bord de la route m.

roadster n. coupé m.

roadway n. voie f.; chaussée f.

roam vi. errer, rôder (dans); — vt. parcourir, errer çà et là (par); **–ing** a. errant; **–er** n. vagabond m.

roar n. rugissement m.; mugissement m.; grondement m.; éclat m.; — vi. rugir; mugir; gronder; éclater; **–ing** a. mugissant, pétillant

roast a. & n. rôti m.; — **beef** rosbif m.; — vt. rôtir; griller; (coffee) torréfier; **–er** n. rôtissoire f.; (coffee) brûloir m.; **–ing** n. cuisson f.; (coffee) torréfaction f.

rob vt. voler; **–ber** n. voleur m.; **–bery** n. vol m.

robe n. robe f.; couverture f.; — vt. vêtir; — vi. se vêtir

robot n. automate m.

robust a. robuste, vigoureux; **–ness** n. vigueur, force f.

rock n. roc, rocher m., roche f., pierre f.; — **candy** n. sucre candi m.; — **crystal** cristal de roche m.; — **garden** jardin de rocaille m.; — **salt** sel gemme m.; — vt. balancer, bercer; — vi. balancer; **–er** n. bascule f.; (chair) rocking-chair, fauteuil à bascule m.; **–ing** n. bercement, balancement m.; tremblement m.; **–y** a. rocheux; rocailleux

rock-bottom a. dernier, le plus bas

rocket n. fusée, roquette f.; — **launcher** lance-fusée, lance-roquette m.; — **motor** moteur-fusée, moteur-roquette m.

rocketry n. science des fusées f.

rocking chair n. chaise à bascule f., rocking-chair m.

Rocky Mountains n. pl. Montagnes Rocheuses f. pl.

rod n. baguette, verge f.; tige f.; (measurement) perche f.; **connecting** — bielle motrice f.; **curtain** — tringle f.; **fishing** — canne à pêche f.

rodent a. & n. rongeur m.

rodeo n. concours d'équitation des cowboys m.

Roentgen n. röntgen m.; — **rays** n. pl. rayons X m. pl.; — **tube** n. tube à rayons X m.

rogue n. fripon, coquin m.

roguish a. fripon, malin; **–ness** n. friponnerie, malice f.

roil vt. troubler

role n. rôle m.

roll n. rouleau m.; petit pain m.; liste f.; roulement m.; (naut.) roulis m.; **call the** — faire l'appel; — **call** appel m.; — vt. rouler; (metal) laminer; — vi. rouler; — **over** (se) retourner; — **up** enrouler; (sleeve) retrousser; **–er** n. rouleau m.;

(metal) cylindre; **–er bearings** n. pl. roulement à rouleaux m.; **–er coaster** n. montagnes russes f. pl.; **–er skates** patins à roulettes m. pl.; **–ing** a. roulant; ondulé; **–ing** n. roulement m.; roulis m.; **–ing mill** usine de laminage f.; **–ing pin** rouleau m., bille f.

roly-poly a. dodu, potelé

romaine n. romaine f.

Roman a. & n. romain m.; — **numerals** chiffres romains m. pl.; — **type** caractères romains m. pl.; **–ic** a. roman

romance n. roman m.; aventure sentimentale f.; histoire romanesque f.; (mus.) romance f.; — vt. romancer

Romance languages n. langues romanes f. pl.

Romanesque a. & n. roman m.

Romania n. Roumanie f.; **–n** a. & n. roumain m.

romantic a. romanesque; sentimental; (lit.) romantique; **–ism** n. romantisme m.

Romany n. les gitanes m. pl.; langue des gitanes f.

romp vi. jouer, folâtrer, badiner; — n. gamine f.; (play) tapage; **–ers** m. pl. barboteuse f.

rood n. quart d'arpent m.; crucifix m.; — **screen** n. jubé m.

roof n. toit m.; toiture f.; — **of the mouth** dôme du palais m.; — vt. couvrir; **–ing** n. toiture f.; **–less** a. sans toit, sans abri

rook n. (chess) tour f.; — vt. escroquer, (se) rouler, filouter

room n. place f.; espace m.; pièce f.; salle f.; chambre f.; at — **temperature** chambré; **make** — **for** faire place à; — vi. vivre en pension, vivre en garni; habiter; **–er** n. pensionnaire m. & f.; sous-locataire m. & f.; **–y** a. ample; spacieux

roomette n. (rail.) cabine de wagon-lits f.

roommate n. compagnon de chambre m.

roost n. perchoir, juchoir m.; — vi. se percher, se jucher; **–er** n. coq m.

root n. racine f.; fond m.; source f.; — **beer** (sorte de) boisson gazeuse f.; — **square** — racine carrée f.; **take** — prendre racine; — vt. enraciner; — **for** (sports) être partisan de; — **out** déraciner; extirper; **–ed** a. cloué, figé

rope n. corde f.; cordage m.; cordon m.; — vt. lier; corder

ropemaker n. cordier m.

rosary n. rosaire m.; (eccl.) chapelet m.

rose n. rose f.; (color) rose m.; — **window** (arch.) rosace f.; **wild** — églantine f.

rosebud n. bouton de rose m.

rosebush n. rosier m.

rose-colored *a.* couleur de rose, rosé; **look through — glasses** voir la vie en rose

rosemary *n.* romarin *m.*

rosin *n.* résine, colophane *f.*

roster *n.* tableau *m.*, liste *f.*

rostrum *n.* tribune *f.*

rosy *a.* couleur de rose; rose, rosé; vermeil

rot *n.* pourriture *f.*; mildiou *m.*; (fig., coll.) blague; sottise *f.* — *vi.* pourrir; se putréfier; se décomposer; (teeth) se carier; **—ten** *a.* pourri; (eggs) gâté; sale; (coll.) de chien; (teeth) carié

rotary *a.* de rotation; rotatif; — **press** *n.* rotative *f.*

rotate *vi.* tourner tournoyer; pivoter; — *vt.* faire tourner; alterner; (crops) varier

rotation *n.* rotation *f.*; (agr.) assolement *m.*; **in** — à tour de rôle

rote *n.* routine *f.*; **by** — par routine; par cœur

rotogravure *n.* rotogravure *f.*

rotund *a.* rond, arrondi; **–ity** *n.* rondeur, rotondité *f.*

rotunda *n.* rotonde *f.*

rouge *n.* fard, rouge *m.*; — *vt.* mettre du rouge

rough *a.* rude; inégal; grossier; brutal; approximatif; — **draft,** — **sketch** ébauche *f.* croquis *m.*; premier jet *m.*; — **weather** gros temps *m.*; —, **–en** *vt.* rendre rude; —, **–en** *vi.* devenir rude; grossir; **–ly** *adv.* rudement, brutalement; à peu pres, approximativement; **treat –ly** brutaliser, malmener; **–ness** *n.* rudesse *f.*; inégalité *f.*; **–shod, ride –shod over** fouler aux pieds; traiter brutalement

roughage *n.* matières cellulosique *f.* *pl.*

round *a.* rond, circulaire; (tone) plein; — **numbers** chiffres ronds *m.* *pl.*; — **table** table ronde *f.*; — **trip** *a.* & *n.* aller et retour *m.*; — *n.* rond, cercle *m.*; tour *m.* tournée *f.*; (mil.) ronde *f.*; salve *f.*; (mus.) canon *m.*; (boxing) round *m.*; — *vt.* arrondir; — **up** *vi.* rassembler; — *adv.* autour de; à la ronde; — *prep.* par, autour de; **–ed** *a.* arrondi; rebondi; **–ness** *n.* rondeur *f.*; — **steak** *n.* bifteck pris dans le jarret *m.*

roundabout *a.* indirect, détourné

roundhouse *n.* (rail.) remise pour locomotives *f.*

round-shouldered *a.* voûté

round-the-clock *a.* jour et nuit

roundup *n.* rassemblement *m.*

rouse *vt.* réveiller, éveiller; remuer; mettre en colère; — *vi.* se réveiller

rousing *a.* entraînant; bon, grand

rout *n.* déroute *f.*; — *vt.* mettre en déroute

route *n.* route *f.*; itinéraire *m.*; direction *f.*

routine *n.* routine *f.*; — *a.* courant

rove *vi.* rôder, errer, vagabonder; — *vt.* parcourir, errer par; **–r** *n.* vagabond *n.*

roving *a.* vagabond, errant

row *n.* rang *m.*, rangée, file, ligne *f.*; (agr.) rayon *m.*; — *vi.* ramer; nager, canoter; — *vt.* conduire à l'aviron; **–er** *n.* rameur *m.*; canotier *m.*; **–ing** *n.* canotage *m.*

rowboat *n.* bateau à rames *m.*

royal *a.* royal (*pl.* royaux); du roi; princier; **–ist** *n.* royaliste *m.* & *f.*; **–ly** *adv.* royalement; **–ty** *n.* royauté *f.*; redevance *f.*, droits d'auteur *m.* *pl.*

r.p.m.: revolutions per minute *n.* tours par minute *m.* *pl.*

rub *n.* frottement *m.*; friction *f.*; difficulté *f.*; — *vt.* frotter; frictionner; — *vi.* (se) frotter; — **down** frictionner; — **out** effacer

rubber *n.* caoutchouc *m.*; gomme *f.*; (cards) robre *m.*; (person) masseur *m.*, masseuse *f.*; — **band** élastique, bracelet de caoutchouc, ruban de caoutchouc *m.*; — **stamp** timbre en caoutchouc, tampon *m.*; **–ize** *vt.* caoutchouter

rubberneck *n.* & *a.* badaud *m.*; (coll.) touriste *m.* & *f.*; — *vi.* badauder

rubbish *n.* décombres *m.* *pl.*, ordures *f.* *pl.*; rebuts *m.* *pl.*; débris *m.* *pl.*; blague, bêtise *f.*; fatras *m.*

rubble *n.* rocaille *f.*; blocaille *f.*

rubric *n.* rubrique *f.*

rudder *n.* gouvernail *m.*

ruddy *a.* rouge, rougeâtre; coloré

rude *a.* impoli, mal élevé; grossier; rude; violent; **–ness** *n.* impolitesse *f.*; grossièreté *f.*; rudesse *f.*

rudiment *n.* rudiment *m.*; **–s** *pl.* éléments, rudiments *m.* *pl.*; **–ary** *a.* rudimentaire

rue *vt.* regretter, se repentir de; — *n.* rue *f.*; **–ful** *a.* triste; déplorable

ruff *n.* fraise *f.*

ruffian *n.* brute *f.*; bandit, brigand *m.*

ruffle *n.* volant *m.*, ruche *f.*; (fig.) trouble *m.*; (drum) roulement *m.*; — *vt.* troubler; froisser; plisser, rucher

rug *n.* tapis *m.*; **bedside** — descente de lit *f.*

rugged *a.* rude; raboteux; solide; **–ness** *n.* rudesse *f.*; aspérité *f.*

ruin *n.* ruine *f.*; **go to** — tomber en ruine; — *vt.* ruiner; perdre; abîmer; **–ation** *n.* ruine, perte *f.*; **–ed** *a.* abîme; ruiné; en ruines

ruinous *a.* ruineux

rule *n.* règle *f.*; règlement *m.*; autorité *f.*; ordonnance *f.*; décision *f.*; **as a** — en général; en principe; **slide** — règle à calcul *f.*; — *vt.* régler (sur), régir; décider; tracer à la règle; — *vi.* régner; — **out** éliminer, écarter; **–r** *n.* souverain *m*.; roi *m*.; (measuring) règle *f*., mètre *m*.

rule of thumb *n*. approximation *f*.

ruling *a*. dirigeant; dominant; — *n*. décision, ordonnance *f*.

rum *n*. rhum *m*.; **–runner** *n*. contrebandier d'alcool *m*.

Rumania *n*. Roumanie *f*.; **–n** *a. & n*. Roumain

rumble *n*. grondement *m*.; grouillement *m*.; (coll.) bagarre *f*.; — **seat** *n*. banquette arrière *f*., — *vi*. gronder; grouiller

ruminate *vi*. ruminer; méditer

rummage *n*. choses usagées *f. pl*., objets usagés *m. pl*.; — **sale** vente d'objets usagés *f*.; — *vt*. fouiller

rumor *n*. bruit *m*., rumeur *f*.; — *vt*., **it is –ed that** le bruit court que

rump *n*. croupe *f*.; — **steak** *n*. romsteck *m*.

rumple *vt*. froisser, chiffonner

rumpus *n*. chahut, chamaillis, fracas *m*.

run *n*. course *f*.; cours *m*., marche *f*.; suite *f*.; parcours, trajet *m*.; libre accès *m*.; durée *f*.; (fish) remonte *f*.; (luck) veine *f*.; (sports) point *m*.; (stocking) échelle *f*., maille partie *f*.; **first** — *a*. (movies) en exclusivité; **in the long** — à la longue; **on the** — à courir; qui court; qui s'enfuit; — *vi*. courir; fuir, s'enfuir, se sauver; couler; marcher, fonctionner; (eyes) pleurer; (fish) remonter; (material) déteindre; durer; (pol.) être candidat, poser sa canditature; — *vt*. faire courir; courir; diriger; tenir; — **across** rencontrer, tomber sur; — **along** longer; filer, s'en aller; — **an errand** faire une course; — **a red light** brûler un feu rouge; — **a temperature** avoir de la fièvre; — **away** se sauver, s'échapper, s'enfuir; — **away with** enlever; — **down** descendre en courant; couler; délabrer; — **for it** se sauver; — **into** rencontrer; heurter; — **on** continuer; — **out** expirer; s'épuiser; cesser; prendre fin; — **over** écraser; déborder; — **through** parcourir; transpercer; (money) manger, gaspiller; — **up** monter en courant; laisser accumuler; — **up against** se heurter contre, se briser contre; avoir à lutter avec; **–ner** *n*. coureur *m*.; courrier *m*.; galet *m*.; **–ning** *a*. courant; continu, soutenu; de suite; **–ning** *n*. course *f*.; marche *f*., fonctionnement *m*.; direction *f*.; **–ning board** marchepied *m*.

run-down *a*. épuisé; déchargé; délabré; — *n*. (coll.) résumé *m*., explication *f*.

rung *n*. traverse *f*., barreau, échelon *m*.

runner-up *n*. deuxième, accessit *m*.

run-of-the-mill *a*. ordinaire, commun

runt *n*. avorton, nain *m*.

runway *n*. piste *f*.

rupture *n*. rupture *f*.; hernie *f*.; — *vt*. rompre; — *vi*. se rompre; **–d** *a*. rompu; hernié

rural *a*. rural; de la campagne; agreste; champêtre

rush *n*. ruée *f*.; bond *m*.; hâte *f*.; (bot.) jonc *m*.; — **hours** heures d'affluence *f. pl*.; — **order** commande urgente *f*.; — *vi*. se précipiter, s'élancer; se dépêcher; — *vt*. dépêcher; faire (quelque chose) d'urgence

rusk *n*. biscotte *f*.

russet *a*. roussâtre; rustique

Russia *n*. Russie *f*.; U.R.S.S. *f*.; **–n** *a. & n*. russe; Soviétique *m*.

rust *n*. rouille *f*.; — *vi. & vt*. (se) rouiller; **–y** *a*. rouillé; rouilleux; **–proof** *a*. antirouille; inoxydable

rustic *a*. agreste, rustique; — *n*. compagnard, paysan *m*.; **–ate** *vi*. vivre à la campagne, se faire campagnard

rustle *n*. froissement *m*.; — *vi*. bruire; — *vt*. froisser; faire bruire

rut *n*. ornière *f*.; routine *f*.

rutabaga *n*. rutabaga *m*.

ruthless *a*. impitoyable; brutal; **–ly** *adv*. sans pitié; **–ness** *n*. dureté, cruauté, inhumanité *f*.

rye *n*. seigle *m*.; (drink) whisky de seigle, whisky irlandais *m*.; — **bread** pain de seigle *m*.

S

Saar *n*. Sarre *f*.; **–lander** *n*. Sarrois *m*.

Sabbath *n*. sabbat *m*.; dimanche *m*.

saber, sabre *n*. sabre *m*.

sable *n*. zibeline *f*.; (heraldry) sable *m*.

sabotage *n*. sabotage *m*.; — *vt*. saboter

saccharin *n*. saccharine *f*.

sack *n*. sac *m*.; pillage *m*.; — *vt*. mettre en sac; saccager, piller

sackcloth *n*. toile à sacs *f*.; toile d'emballage *f*.; sac *m*.

sacrament *n*. sacrement *m*.; **–al** *a*. sacramental

sacred *a*. sacré; saint; consacré

sacrifice *n*. sacrifice *m*., immolation *f*.; offrande *f*.; (com.) vente à perte; — *vt*. sacrifier, immoler; renoncer à; (com.) vendre à perte

sacrificial *a*. sacrificatoire

sacrilege *n*. sacrilège *m*.

sacrilegious *a*. sacrilège

sacristan *n*. sacristan *m*.

sacristy *n*. sacristie *f*.

sacrosanct *a*. sacro-saint

sad *a*. triste; morne; **–den** *vt*. attrister; **–ly** *adv*. tristement; très, fort; **–ness**

n. tristesse *f.*

saddle *n.* selle *f.*; **-bag** *n.* sacoche, musette *f.*; **-cloth** *n.* housse de cheval *f.*; — **horse** *n.* cheval de selle *m.*; — *vt.* seller; charger; **be -d with** avoir sur le dos

safe *n.* coffre-fort *m.*; — *a.* sauf; sûr; à l'abri; sans danger; — **and sound** sain et sauf; **-ly** *adv.* sans danger; sans accident; à coup sûr; **-ness** *n.* sûreté; sécurité *f.*; **-ty** *n.* sûreté, sécurité *f.*; **-ty catch** cran de sûreté; — **pin** épingle de sûreté *f.*; **-ty valve** soupape de sûreté *f.*

safe-conduct *n.* sauf-conduit *m.*

safe-deposit box *n.* (bank) coffre-fort *m.*

safeguard *n.* sauvegarde *f.*; — *vt.* sauvegarder

safekeeping *n.* bonne garde *f.*

safety island *n.* refuge; refuge pour pietons *m.*

safety match *n.* allumette de sûreté *f.*

safety razor *n.* rasoir de sûreté *m.*

saffron *n.* safran *m.*

sag *n.* fléchissement *m.*; flèche *f.*; — *vi.* fléchir, s'affaisser; pendre; **-ging** *a.* fléchissant; (com.) creux

sagacious *a.* sage, intelligent, sagace

sagacity *n.* sagacité *f.*

sage *a.* sage, prudent; — *n.* sage *m.*; philosophe *m.*; (bot.) sauge *f.*

said *a.* ledit, susdit

sail *n.* voile *f.*; toile *f.*; voyage *m.*; promenade à la voile *f.*; — *vt.* naviguer; conduire; — *vi.* aller à la voile; naviguer; voguer; planer; **-ing** *a.*, **-ing ship** voilier *m.*; **-ing** *n.* navigation *f.*; marche *f.*; départ *m.*; **-or** *n.* marin, matelot *m.*

sailboat *n.* bateau à voiles *m.*; canot à voiles *m.*

sailcloth *n.* toile à voile *f.*

saint *n.* saint *m.*, sainte *f.*; **-ed** *a.* saint; canonisé; **-ly** *a.* saint

Saint Helena *n.* Sainte-Hélène *f.*

sake *n.*, **for the — of** pour; pour l'amour de; à cause de; dans l'intérêt de

salaam *n.* salamalec *m.*; — *vi.* faire des salamalecs

salable *a.* qui peut se vendre, qui se vend bien

salacious *a.* lubrique, lascif; **-ness** *n.* lubricité, lascivité *f.*

salad *n.* salade *f.*; **fruit —** macédoine de fruits *f.*; — **bowl** saladier *m.*; — **dressing** sauce *f.*; huile *f.* et vinaigre *m.*; assaisonnement pour salade *m.*

salaried *a.* aux appointements, salarié

salary *n.* salaire; traitement *m.*, appointements *m. pl.*

sale *n.* vente *f.*; vente de soldes *f.*; solde(s) *m.* (*pl.*); **auction —** vente aux enchères;

for — à vendre; **on —** en vente; solde(s); **-s slip** *n.* reçu *m.*

salesclerk *n.* vendeur *m.*, vendeuse *f.*

salesman *n.* vendeur *m.*; représentant *m.*; (commis) voyageur *m.*; **-ship** *n.* art de vendre *m.*

salesroom *n.* salle des ventes *f.*

sales tax *n.* impôt sur la vente *m.*

saleswoman *n.* vendeuse *f.*

salicylic *a.* salicylique

salient *a. & n.* saillant

saline *a.* salin

saliva *n.* salive *f.*; **-ry** *a.* salivaire

sallow *a.* jaunâtre, olivâtre

salmon *n.* saumon *m.*; — **trout** *n.* truite saumonée *f.*

saloon *n.* buvette *f.*; café *m.*; bar *m.*

salsify *n.* salsifis *m.*

salt *n.* sel *m.*; **coarse —** gros sel *m.*; **rock —** sel gemme *m.*; **table —** sel blanc *m.*; **-ed** *a.* salé; — **water** *n.* eau de mer *f.*; — *vt.* saler; **-y** *a.* salé; de sel

saltceller, salt shaker *n.* salière *f.*

saltine *n.* biscuit très salé *m.*

saltpetre *n.* salpêtre *m.*

salt-water *a.* salé, d'eau de mer

salubrious *a.* salubre

salutary *a.* salutaire

salutation *n.* salutation *f.*; salut *m.*

salute *n.* salut *m.*; salve *f.*; — *vt.* (guns) salver; (person) saluer

salvage *n.* sauvetage *m.*; récupération *f.*; relevage *m.*; — *vt.* sauver; récupérer; relever

salvation *n.* salut *m.*

salve *n.* onguent, baume *m.*; — *vt.* adoucir, calmer

salvo *n.* salve *f.*

Samaritan *n.* samaritain *m.*

same *a.* même; identique; **all the —** tout de même; quand même; **it's all the — to me** cela m'est égal; **at the — time** en même temps; à la fois; **the — to you** à vous de même; **-ness** *n.* identité *f.*; monotonie *f.*

sample *n.* échantillon *m.*; exemple *m.*; — *vt.* goûter, déguster; essayer; échantillonner; **-r** *n.* (person) échantillonneur *m.*; modèle *m.*

sampling *n.* choix *m.*

sanctify *vt.* consacrer; sanctifier

sanctimonious *a.* confit; béat

sanction *n.* sanction *f.*; consentement *m.*; — *vt.* sanctionner

sanctity *n.* sainteté *f.*

sanctuary *n.* sanctuaire *m.*; asile, refuge *m.*

sand *n.* sable *m.*; — *vt.* sablonner; sabler; poncer; passer au papier de verre; **-y** *a.* sablonneux, sableux, sablé; (hair) blond roux

sandal *n.* sandale *f.*

sandbag *n.* sac à terre *m.*; — *vt.* protéger par des sacs à terre

sand bar *n.* banc de sable *m.*

sandblast *n.* jet de sable *m.*; — *vt.* décaper

sandbox *n.* boîte à sable *f.*

sandpaper *n.* papier de verre *m.*; — *vt.* poncer, doucir, passer au papier de verre

sand pit *n.* sablière *f.*

sandstone *n.* grès *m.*

sandstorm *n.* tempête de sable *f.*, simoun *m.*

sandwich *n.* sandwich *m.*; — **man** homme-affiches *m.*; — *vt.* intercaler; serrer

sane *a.* sain (d'esprit); raisonnable; sensé

sanforize *vt.* rendre irrétrécissable

sanguinary *a.* sanguinaire

sanitarium *n.* sanatorium *m.*

sanitary *a.* sanitaire; hygiénique

sanitation *n.* système sanitaire *m.*; hygiène *f.*

sanity *n.* santé (d'esprit) *f.*

San Marino *n.* Saint-Marin *m.*

Sanscrit *a. & n.* sanscrit *m.*

sap *n.* sève *f.*; (mil.) sape *f.*; — *vt.* saper, miner; **-per** *n.* sapeur *m.*

sapling *n.* jeune arbre *m.*

Saracen *n. & a.* Sarrasin *m.*

sarcasm *n.* sarcasme *m.*; ironie *f.*

sarcastic *a.* sarcastique

sarcophagus *n.* sarcophage *m.*

Sardinia *n.* Sardaigne *f.*

sash *n.* ceinture *f.*; écharpe *f.*; cadre, (window) châssis *m.*

Satan *n.* Satan *m.*

satanic *a.* satanique

satchel *n.* sacoche *f.*; valise *f.*

sateen *n.* satinette *f.*

satellite *n.* satellite *m.*

satiate *vt.* rassasier (de); — *a.* rassasié

satiation, satiety *n.* satiété *f.*

satin *n.* satin *m.*; — *a.* satiné; de satin; **-y** *a.* satiné

satirical *a.* satirique

satirist *n.* auteur satirique *m.*

satirize *vt. & vi.* satiriser

satisfaction *n.* satisfaction *f.*; contentement *m.*; réparation *f.*; dédommagement *m.*

satisfactory *a.* satisfaisant; acceptable

satisfy *vt. & vi.* satisfaire, contenter; remplir; faire réparation; suffire à; convaincre

saturate *vt.* saturer; tremper; **become –d** s'imprégner

saturation *n.* saturation *f.*; imprégnation *f.*

Saturday *n.* samedi *m.*

saucedish *n.* saucière *f.*

saucepan *n.* casserole *f.*

saucer *n.* soucoupe *f.*; **flying —** soucoupe volante *f.*

saucy *a.* impertinent; insolent; effronté

Saudi Arabia *n.* Arabie Soudite *f.*

sauerkraut *n.* choucroute *f.*

saunter *vi.* flâner, aller lentement

sausage *n.* saucisse *f.*; saucisson *m.*; — **meat** *n.* chair à saucisse *f.*

savage *a.* sauvage; brutal; féroce; — *n.* sauvage *m. & f.*; **-ry** *n.* sauvagerie *f.*; brutalité *f.*; férocité *f.*

save *vt.* sauver; préserver; protéger; réserver, retenir; économiser, mettre de côté; éviter; épargner; — *prep.* sauf, excepté, à l'exception de; hormis; **-r** *n.* sauveur *m.*; sauveteur *m.*; personne économe *f.*

saving *a.* qui sauve; économe; — *n.* sauvetage *m.*; salut *m.*; épargne, économie *f.*; **-s bank** *n.* caisse d'épargne *f.*; **-s bond** *n.* bon d'épargne *m.*

Saviour *n.* Le Sauveur *m.*

savor *n.* saveur *f.*; goût *m.*; — *vt.* savourer; **-y** *a.* savoureux; piquant

saw *n.* scie *f.*; — *vt.* scier

sawdust *n.* sciure (de bois) *f.*

sawhorse *n.* chevalet *m.*

sawmill *n.* scierie *f.*

saw-toothed *a.* en dents de scie

Saxon *n. & a.* Saxon *m.*

say *n.* voix *f.*; mot *m.*, parole *f.*; **have one's —** dire son mot; — *vt.* dire; parler; faire; réciter; **to — nothing of** sans parler de; **that is to —** c'est-à-dire; **-ing** *n.* proverbe, adage, dicton *m.*; **it goes without -ing** cela va de soi

scab *n.* croûte *f.*; gale *f.*; jaune *m.*; — *vi.* former une croûte

scabbard *n.* gaine *f.*, fourreau *m.*

scads *n. pl.* (coll.) des tas *m. pl.*; — **of** beaucoup de

scaffold *n.* échafaud *m.*; **-ing** *n.* échafaudage *m.*

scalawag *n.* fripon *m.*

scald *n.* échaudure *f.*; — *vt.* échauder; blanchir; **-ing** *n.* échaudage *m.*; — *a.* bouillant, tout bouillant

scale *n.* écaille *f.*; tartre *m.*, incrustation *f.*; (weight) balance *f.*; plat de balance *m.*; (measurement) échelle, graduation, série *f.*; cadran *m.*; règle *m.*; étendue *f.*; (mus.) gamme *f.*; — **on a large — en grand**; — *a.* à l'échelle; — *vt.* écailler; escalader; dessiner à l'échelle; établir à l'échelle; — *vi.* s'écailler; peser

scaling *n.* escalade *f.*; graduation *f.*

scallion *n.* ciboule *f.*

scallop *n.* coquille (Saint-Jacques) *f.*;

pétoncle *m.*; (sewing) dentelure *f.*; feston *m.*; — *vt.* faire cuire en coquille; (sewing) découper, festonner

scalp *n.* épicrâne *m.*; scalpe *m.*; **—er** *n.* trafiqueur *m.*; — *vt.* scalper; (coll.) vendre des billets à des prix exorbitants

scalpel *n.* scalpel *m.*

scaly *a.* écailleux

scamp *n.* vaurien, garnement *m.*

scamper *vi.* courir vite; se sauver

scan *vt.* scruter; parcourir; (verse) scander; **—ner** *n.* analyseur *m.*, (radar) antenne tournante *f.*; **—ning** *a.* analyseur, explorateur

scandal *n.* scandale *m.*; médisance *f.*; **—ize** *vt.* scandaliser; **—ous** *a.* scandaleux; diffamatoire

scandalmonger *n.* médisant *m.*

Scandinavia *n.* Scandinavie *f.*; **—n** *a.* & *n.* scandinave *m.* & *f.*

scant *a.* à peine rempli; modique

scantily *adv.* à peine; insuffisamment

scanty *a.* insuffisant; étroit; sommaire

scapegoat *n.* bouc émissaire *m.*

scapular *n.* scapulaire *m.*

scar *n.* cicatrice *f.*; — *vi.* se cicatriser

scarce *a.* rare; **—ly** *adv.* à peine; ne . . . guère; presque (pas)

scarcity *n.* manque *m.*; rareté *f.*; disette *f.*

scare *vt.* épouvanter, effrayer, faire peur à, effarer

scarecrow *n.* épouvantail *m.*

scarf *n.* écharpe *f.*, fichu *m.*; cache-nez *m.*; foulard *m.*

scarlet *a.* & *n.* écarlate *f.*; — **fever** scarlatine *f.*

scathing *a.* mordant, acerbe, cinglant

scatter *vt.* disperser; éparpiller, diffuser; — *vi.* se disperser; s'éparpiller; **—ed** *a.* dispersé; épars; **—ing** *n.* petit nombre *m.*

scatterbrained *a.* évaporé, écervelé

scavenger *n.* balayeur *m.*

scenario *n.* scénario *m.*

scene *n.* scène *f.*; lieu *m.*; décor *m.*; paysage *m.*; **—ry** *n.* paysage *m.*; (theat.) décor *m.*

scenic *a.* scénique

scent *n.* odeur *f.*; parfum *m.*, senteur *f.*; piste, trace *f.*; — *vt.* parfumer; flairer; **—ed** *a.* parfumé

scepter *n.* sceptre *m.*

sceptic *n.* sceptique *m.* & *f.*; **—al** *a.* sceptique; **—ism** *n.* scepticisme *m.*

schedule *n.* horaire *m.*; liste *f.*; tarif *m.*; programme, plan *m.*; **—d** *a.* dans le programme; **be —d** devoir

scheme *n.* schéma *m.*; combinaison *f.*; projet, plan *m.*; intrigue, machination *f.*; — *vi.* projeter; intriguer, comploter;

—r *n.* intrigant *m.*

scheming *n.* machinations *f. pl.*; — *a.* intrigant

schism *n.* schisme *m.*

schizophrenia *n.* schizophrénie *f.*

scholar *n.* érudit, lettré, savant *m.*; boursier *m.*; **—ly** *a.* érudit, savant; **—ship** *n.* bourse *f.*; érudition, science *f.*; savoir *m.*

scholastic *a.* scolaire; (phil.) scolastique; **—ism** *n.* scolastique *f.*

school *n.* école *f.*; académie *f.*; faculté; classe *f.*; (fish) troupe de poissons *f.*; **elementary** — école primaire *f.*; **high** — école secondaire (supérieure) *f.*; **private** — école libre *f.*; — *vt.* instruire, former; enseigner; **—ing** *n.* instruction, éducation, enseignement *m.*; formation *f.*; — *a.* scolaire, classique

schoolbook *n.* livre de classe, livre classique *m.*

schoolboy *n.* écolier, élève *m.*

schoolgirl *n.* écolière, élève *f.*

schoolhouse *n.* école *f.*

schoolroom *n.* salle de classe *f.*

schoolteacher *n.* maître, professeur *m.*

schooner *n.* goélette *f.*, schooner *m.*; (glass) chope *f.*

sciatica *n.* sciatique *f.*

science *n.* science *f.*

scientific *a.* scientifique

scientist *n.* homme de science, savant *m.*

scimitar *n.* cimeterre *m.*

scintillate *vi.* étinceler, scintiller

scissors *n. pl.* ciseaux *m. pl.*

sclerosis *n.* sclérose *f.*

scoff *vi.* se moquer; — *vt.* tourner en dérision; **—ing** *n.* moquerie, raillerie *f.*

scold *vt.* & *vi.* gronder; — *n.* grondeuse *f.*; **—ing** *a.* grondeur; **—ing** *n.* gronderie *f.*; **—ingly** *adv.* en grondant

scoop *n.* cuiller *f.*; pelle *f.*; main *f.*; (journalism) primeur *f.*; nouvelle(s) *f.* (*pl.*); — *vt.* excaver; ramasser; écoper

scoot *vi.* filer; **—er** *n.* patinette, trottinette *f.*; **motor —er** scooter *m.*

scope *n.* portée, étendue *f.*; champ *m.*

scorch *vt.* roussir; brûler; dessécher; — *vi.* roussir; **—er** *n.* journée d'une chaleur accablante *f.*; **—ed** *a.* brûlé; **—ing** *a.* brûlant; torride

score *n.* entaille *f.*; compte *m.*; sujet *m.*; score *m.*, points *m. pl.*, marque *f.*; (mus.) partition *f.*; (number) vingtaine *f.*; — *vt.* entailler, encocher; compter, marquer; blâmer; faire; (mus.) orchestrer

scorn *n.* dédain, mépris *m.*; — *vt.* & *vi.* dédaigner, mépriser; **—ful** *a.* dédaigneux

Scot n. Écossais m.

scotch n. scotch, whisky écossais m.; — vt. faire manquer, faire avorter; mettre fin à

Scotch a. & n. écossais m.; — terrier terrier griffon m.

scot-free a. indemne; sans frais

Scotland n. Écosse f.

Scotsman n. Écossais m.

Scottish a. & n. écossais m.

scoundrel n. gredin, scélérat m.

scour vt. récurer; frotter; nettoyer; parcourir; chercher, fouiller; — the country battre la campagne; –ing n. recurage m.; nettoyage m.

scourge n. fléau m.; — vt. fouetter, châtier

scout n. éclaireur m.; boy — boy scout, éclaireur m.; girl — éclaireuse f.; — vi. aller en reconnaissance; — vt. éclairer, reconnaître

scoutmaster n. chef de troupe m.

scow n. chaland m.

scowl n. froncement de sourcils m.; air menaçant m.; — vi. froncer les sourcils, se refrogner

scraggy a. rocailleux; escarpé; maigre

scramble n. mêlée f.; (avi. mil.) alerte d'avions f.; — vi. se bousculer, se battre; — vt. brouiller; –d eggs œufs brouillés m. pl.

scrap n. fragment, petit morceau, bout m.; parcelle f.; (talk) bribes f. pl.; dispute, querelle f.; –s pl. restes m. pl.; — heap tas de ferraille m.; rebut m.; — iron ferraille f.; — vt. mettre au rebut; supprimer, desaffecter; — vi. se battre

scrapbook n. album m.

scrape n. difficulté f., mauvais pas m.; — vt. gratter, racler; érafler; frotter; — vi. gratter, grincer; –r n. grattoir, racloir m.

scratch n. égratignure f.; coup d'ongle m.; rayure f.; grattement, grincement m.; (sports) scratch m.; (coll.) argent, fric m.; — paper n. papier à brouillon m.; start from — partir de zéro; — vt. égratigner; érafler; rayer; gratter; — vi. gratter, grincer

scratch-pad n. bloc-notes m.

scrawl n. griffonnage m.; — vt. griffonner

scrawny a. maigre, décharné

scream n. cri aigu, cri perçant m.; — vt. crier, pousser un cri (perçant), hurler; –ing a. perçant, qui crie

screech n. cri perçant m.; — vi. pousser des cris perçants; — owl n. chat-huant m.

screen n. écran m.; paravent m.; — vt. cacher, masquer; (films) mettre à l'écran; (sift) passer

screw n. vis f.; (naut.) hélice f.; — vt. visser; serrer; — vi. tourner; — up pincer, grimacer; tortiller

screw driver n. tournevis m.

screw thread n. filet m.

scribble n. griffonnage m.; — vt. griffonner

scribe n. copiste m.; scribe m.; — vt. pointer, tracer; –r n. pointe à tracer f.

scrimmage n. mêlée f.

scrip n. coupons, tickets, bons m. pl.

script n. écriture f.; scénario m.

scriptural a. biblique, scriptural; de l'Ecriture Sainte

Scripture n. Ecriture Sainte f.

scriptwriter n. scénariste m.

scrofula n. scrofules f. pl.

scroll n. rouleau m.; (arch.) volute f.

scrounge vt. récupérer, glaner

scrub n. nettoyage, récurage m.; (bot.) brousse f.; — vt. nettoyer, récurer; laver; –by a. rabougri

scuff n. nuque f.

scruple n. scrupule m.; hésitation f.

scupulous a. scrupuleux; méticuleux, minutieux

scrutinize vt. scruter, examiner

scrutiny n. examen rigoureux m.

scuff vt. frotter, user

scuffle n. mêlée, bagarre f.; — vi. se battre, se bousculer

scullery n. laverie f.; — maid souillon f.

sculptor n. sculpteur m.

sculpture n. sculpture f.; — vt. sculpter

scum n. écume f.; rebut m.

scurry vi. se hâter, courir

scurvy n. scorbut m.

scuttle vt. (naut.) saborder; — vi., — away filer; — n. seau, panier m.

scythe n. faux f.; — vt. faucher

sea n. mer f.; océan m.; at — en mer; désorienté; by the — au bord de la mer; heavy — grosse mer f.; high –s le large m.; on the high –s au grand large; — a. de mer, de la mer; — breeze brise du large f.; — captain capitaine de vaisseau m.; — legs pied marin m.; — level niveau de la mer; — lion otarie f., phoque m.; — urchin oursin m.; — wall digue f.

seaboard n. côte f.; bord de la mer

seacoast n. côte f., littoral m.

seafarer n. marin, matelot m.

seafaring a. marin, de la mer

seafood n. poisson de mer m.; coquillages m.; — pl., fruits de la mer m. pl.

sea-going a. maritime; de haute mer

seal n. sceau m.; cachet m.; (zool.) phoque m.; — vt. sceller; cacheter; fer-

mer; –ing a., — **wax** cire à cacheter f.
sealskin a. & n. peau de phoque f.
seam n. couture f.; joint m.; couche, veine
f.; — vt. couturer; –less a. sans couture
seaman n. marin, matelot m.; –ship n.
art de naviguer m.
seamstress n. couturière f.
seaplane n. hydravion m.
seaport n. port de mer m.
sea power n. puissance maritime f.
sear vt. dessécher, flétrir; — a. fané, séché
search n. recherche f.; visite f.; — warrant mandat de perquisition m.; in —
of à la recherche de; — vt. chercher
(dans); fouiller; (customs) visiter; perquisitionner; sonder; — vi. chercher,
rechercher; –ing a. pénétrant; minutieux
searchlight n. projecteur, phare m.
sea shell n. coquillage m., coquille f.
seasick a. qui a le mal de mer; –ness n.
mal de mer m.
seaside n. bord de la mer m.
season n. saison f.; temps m.; in — de
saison; off — morte-saison f.; out of —
hors de saison, mal à propos; — ticket
carte d'abonnement f.; — vt. assaisonner; mûrir; conditionner; tempérer; —
vi. mûrir; sécher; –able a. de saison; à
propos; –al a. saisonnier, des saisons;
–ed a. assaisonné; mûr; sec; expérimenté; –ing n. assaisonnement m.;
condiment m.
seat n. siège m.; place f.; banquette f.;
fond m.; derrière m.; centre, foyer m.;
— cover n. housse f.; — vt. asseoir; be
–ed s'asseoir; être assis, –ing n. places
f. pl.; disposition des places f.; –ing
capacity nombre de places m.
seaward(s) adv. vers la mer
seaweed n. varech m.
seaworthy a. en état de tenir la mer
secede vi. faire scission, faire sécession
secession n. sécession f.
seclude vt. éloigner, tenir éloigné, tenir
retiré; — oneself se retirer; –d a. retiré
seclusion n. retraite, solitude f.
second n. seconde f.; instant m.; second
m.; (com.) article de deuxième qualité,
deuxième choix m.; — a. second, deuxième; autre, nouveau; — floor premier
étage m.; — hand (watch, clock) trotteuse f.; — lieutenant sous-lieutenant
m.; — nature seconde nature f.; —
sight clairvoyance f.; — vt. seconder;
(debate) appuyer; –ary a. secondaire;
–ly adv. en second lieu, deuxièmement
second-class a. (rail.) de seconde (classe);
de second ordre; de deuxième qualité
secondhand a. de seconde main; usagé;

d'occasion; — **dealer** brocanteur m.
second-rate a. de qualité inférieure; de
second ordre; médiocre
secrecy n. mystère, secret m.; discrétion
f.
secret a. secret; caché; — n. secret m.;
keep a — garder un secret; in —, –ly
adv. en secret, secrètement; –ive a.
réservé
secretary n. secrétaire m. & f.; private —
secrétaire particulier m.
secrete vt. sécréter; cacher
secretion n. sécrétion f.
sect n. secte f.; –arian a. & n. sectaire
m.; –arianism n. esprit sectaire m.
section n. section f.; coupe, tranche f.;
profil m.; division, partie f.; (city) quartier m.; (store) rayon m.; — vt. sectionner, diviser en sections; –al a. en
sections; (drawing) en coupe
sector n. secteur m.
secular a. séculier, laïque, profane, temporel; –ize vt. séculariser
secure a. assuré; en sûreté; hors de danger; à l'abri (de); ferme, fixe, solide; —
vt. obtenir; se procurer; retenir; mettre en sûreté; fixer, assujettir
security n. sécurité, sûreté f.; (com.) gage,
nantissement m., caution f.
securities n. pl. fonds, titres m. pl.,
valeurs f. pl.; actions f. pl.
sedan n. voiture à 6 places f.; (voiture à)
conduite intérieure f.; — chair n. chaise
à porteurs f.
sedate a. posé, composé; –ness n. calme
m., tranquillité f.
sedative a. & n. sédatif m.
sedentary a. sédentaire
sediment n. sédiment m.; lie f.; –ary a.
sédimentaire; –ation n. sédimentation
f.
sedition n. sédition f.
seditious a. séditieux
seduce vt. séduire, dépraver
seduction n. séduction f.; charme m.
seductive a. séduisant; –ness n. séduction f.; charmes m. pl.
see n. (eccl.) siège épiscopale m.; — vt.
voir; apercevoir; observer; regarder;
comprendre; envisager; trouver; visiter; as far as I can — à ce que je vois;
— fit trouver bon; — to it faire; — to
the door accompagner à la porte;
éconduire; — about s'occuper de; —
off dire adieu; — through pénétrer;
persévérer; –ing a. voyant; –ing that vu
que, attendu que; –ing n. vue, vision f.;
–ing is believing voir c'est croire
seed n. graine f.; semence f.; pépin m.;
(fig.) germe m.; — vt. semer, ensemen-

cer; **–ling** n. jeune plante f.; plante semée f.; **–y** a. d'aspect minable

seek vt. chercher, rechercher; demander; essayer, tâcher; **— out** rechercher

seem vi. sembler, paraître; avoir l'air; **–ing** a. apparent; **–ingly** adv. apparemment, en apparence; **–ly** a. convenable, bienséant

seep vi. suinter; fuir; s'infiltrer; **–age** n. suintement m.; fuite f.; infiltration f.

seer n. prophète m.; visionnaire m.

seesaw n. bascule f.; balançoire f.; **—** vi. basculer

seethe vi. bouillir, bouillonner; grouiller

segregate vt. séparer; mettre à part; **—** vi. se grouper à part

segregation n. ségrégation, séparation f.

segregationist n. ségrégationiste m.

seismograph n. sismographe m.

seize vt. saisir; s'emparer de; empoigner; prendre

seizure n. saisie, prise f.; accès m.; attaque f.

seldom adv. rarement

select vt. choisir; **—** a. choisi; de choix; d'élite; **–ion** n. choix m.; sélection f.; recueil m.; **–ive** a. sélectif; **–ivity** n. sélectivité f.

selectman n. conseiller municipal m.

selenium n. sélénium m.

self a. même; **—** n. moi m.

self-acting a. automatique

self-addressed a. adressé par le destinataire

self-apparent a. évident; qui va de soi

self-assurance n. confiance en soi

self-assured a. posé; maître de soi

self-centered a. égocentrique

self-confidence n. confiance en soi

self-confident a. sûr de soi

self-conscious a. embarrassé, gêné; **–ness** n. embarras m.; gêne f.

self-contained a. réservé, circonspect; (technical) incorporé

self-control n. maîtrise de soi f.; sang-froid m.; **–led** a. réservé, maître de soi; (technical) auto-entretenu

self-defense n. (law) légitime défense f.

self-denial n. renoncement m.; abnégation f.

self-discipline n. discipline f.

self-educated a. autodidacte

self-esteem n. amour-propre m.

self-evident a. évident; qui saute aux yeux

self-explanatory a. qui s'explique de soi-même, clair, concis

self-expression n. expression de l'individu f.

self-governed a. autonome

self-government n. autonomie f.

self-help n. efforts personnels m. pl.

self-induced a. inspiré par l'individu

self-indulgence n. indulgence de soi f.

self-indulgent a. qui ne se refuse rien

selfish a. égoïste, intéressé; **–ness** n. égoïsme, intérêt m.

self-liquidating a. qui s'amortit; se liquidant soi-même

self-made a. parvenu par ses propres moyens

self-possessed a. maître de soi

self-possession n. maîtrise de soi f.; sang-froid, aplomb m.

self-preservation n. conservation de soi-même f.

self-propelled a. autopropulsé

self-propelling a. automoteur

self-protection n. protection de soi f.

self-regulating a. à autorégulation

self-reliance n. indépendance f.

self-reliant a. indépendant

self-respect n. respect de soi m.; amour-propre m.

self-restraint n. retenue f.

self-righteous a. qui se croit juste, content de soi

self-sacrifice n. abnégation f.

selfsame a. identique

self-satisfied a. suffisant; content de soi

self-service n. & a. libre-service m.

self-starter n. autodémarreur m.

self-styled a. soi-disant

self-sufficient a. suffisant en soi

self-supporting a. indépendant, qui gagne sa propre vie

self-taught a. autodidacte

sell vt. vendre; **–out** vendre tout; épuiser; **–er** n. vendeur m., vendeuse f.; **–ing** n. vente f.

seltzer n. eau de seltz f.

selvage n. lisière f.

semantic a. sémantique; **–s** n. pl. sémantique f.

semaphore n. sémaphore m.

semblance n. apparence, semblant m.

semester n. semestre m.

semiannual a. semi-annuel; **–ly** adv. tous les six mois

semiautomatic a. semi-automatique

semicircle n. demi-cercle m.

semicolon n. point et virgule m.

semifinal n. demi-finale f.

semimonthly a. bimensuel

seminar n. séminaire, groupe d'études m.

seminary n. seminaire m.

semiofficial a. demi-officiel

Semitic a. sémitique

semitransparent a. demi-transparent

semitropical a. subtropical

senate *n.* sénat *m.*
senator *n.* sénateur *m.*; **–ial** *a.* sénatorial
send *vt.* envoyer; expédier; **— away, — back** renvoyer; **— for** envoyer chercher; faire venir; **— in** faire entrer; remettre; **— out** lancer; émettre; jeter; **–er** *n.* expéditeur, envoyeur *m.*; **–ing** *n.* expédition *f.*; envoi *m.*
Senegal *n.* Sénégal *m.*
senile *a.* sénile
senility *n.* sénilité *f.*
senior *a.* aîné; père; supérieur; ancien; **— n.** aîne *m.*; ancien *m.*; (Amer. college) étudiant de quatrième année *m.*; **–ity** *n.* ancienneté *f.*
sensation *n.* sensation *f.*; impression *f.*; sentiment *m.*; **–al** *a.* sensationnel
sense *n.* sens *m.*; sensation *f.*; sentiment *m.*; raison *f.*; **common —** sens commun *m.*; **make — (out) of** comprendre; **talk — parler** raison; **— of smell** odorat *m.*; **–s** *pl.* raison, tête *f.*; **— vt.** sentir, pressentir; **–less** *a.* insensé, déraisonnable; (unconscious) sans connaissance
sensibility *n.* sensibilité *f.*
sensible *a.* raisonnable, sensé; pratique; perceptible, sensible
sensitive *a.* sensible; **–ness** *n.* sensibilité *f.*
sensitivity *n.* sensibilité *f.*
sensitize *vt.* sensibiliser; **–ed** *a.* sensible
sensory *a.* sensoriel
sensual *a.* sensuel; voluptueux; **–ity** *n.* sensualité *f.*
sensuous *a.* voluptueux
sentence *n.* phrase *f.*; (law) sentence *f.*, arrêt *m.*; peine *f.*; **prison —** peine de prison; **— vt.** condamner
sentiment *n.* sentiment *m.*; opinion *f.*; **–al** *a.* sentimental; **–ality** *n.* sentimentalité *f.*
sentinel *n.* sentinelle *f.*; factionnaire *m.*
sentry *n.* factionnaire *m.*; sentinelle *f.*
separable *a.* séparable
separate *a.* séparé; distinct; détaché; particulier, individuel; **— vt.** séparer; détacher, dégager; **— vi.** se séparer; se détacher; se quitter
separation *n.* séparation *f.*
sepia *n.* sépia *f.*
September *n.* septembre *m.*
septic *a.* septique; **— tank** fosse septique *f.*
septicemia *n.* (med.) septicémie *f.*
sepulchral *a.* sépulcral
sepulchre *n.* sépulcre *m.*
sequel *n.* suite *f.*; conséquence *f.*
sequence *n.* suite, série, succession *f.*
sequin *n.* séquin *m.*; (decoration) paillette *f.*
Serbia *n.* Serbie *f.*

serenade *n.* sérénade *f.*; **— vt.** donner une sérénade à
serene *a.* serein; calme, tranquille
serenity *n.* sérénité *f.*; calme *m.*; tranquillité *f.*
serf *n.* serf *m.*; **–dom** *n.* servage *m.*
sergeant *n.* sergent *m.*; **— at arms** huissier *m.*; **first —** sergent chef, adjudant *m.*; **master —** adjudant chef *m.*
serial *a.* de série; **— number** numéro de série; **— n.** roman-feuilleton *m.*
series *n.* série, suite *f.*; (mus.) gamme *f.*; **in —** en série
serious *a.* sérieux; grave; **–ly** *adv.* sérieusement, gravement; grièvement; **take –ly** prendre au sérieux; **–ness** *n.* gravité *f.*; sérieux *m.*
sermon *n.* sermon *m.*; **–ize** *vt. & vi.* sermonner
serpent *n.* serpent *m.*; **–ine** *a.* serpentin, serpentant, sinueux
serrate *a.* en dents de scie
serried *a.* serré, compact
serum *n.* sérum *m.*
servant *n.* domestique *m. & f.*; servant *m.*, servante *f.*; serviteur *m.*; **civil —** fonctionnaire *m. & f.*
serve *vt.* servir; desservir; suffire; (time) faire des années de prison; **— vi.** servir; **— as** servir de; **–r** *n.* serveur (serveuse)
service *n.* service *m.*; emploi *m.*; administration *f.*; utilité *f.*; (auto.) entretien *m.*; dépannage *m.*; (eccl.) office *m.*; (law) délivrance *f.*; **at your —** à votre disposition; **be of —** être utile; servir; **— station** station-service *f.*, poste d'essence *m.*; **— vt.** entretenir; **–able** *a.* utilisable
serviceman *n.* soldat *m.*
servicing *n.* entretien *m.*; dépannage *m.*
servile *a.* servile; bas
servility *n.* servilité *f.*; bassesse *f.*
serving *n.* service *m.*
servitor *n.* serviteur *m.*
servitude *n.* servitude *f.*, esclavage *m.*
servomotor *n.* servo-moteur *m.*
sesame *n.* sésame *m.*
session *n.* séance *f.*; session *f.*; **be in —** siéger
set *n.* jeu *m.*; série *f.*; ensemble *m.*; collection *f.*; coterie *f.*; (dishes) service *m.*; (hair) mise *f.*; (radio) poste *m.*; (theat.) décor *m.*; scène *f.*; **— vt.** poser; placer, mettre, asseoir; donner; ajuster; régler; (bone) remettre, réduire; (date) fixer; (gem) enchâsser; (type) composer; **— vi.** se coucher; prendre; se figer; **— aside** écarter, mettre à part; **— back** remettre, retarder; **— forth** avancer, exposer; partir, se mettre en

route; — out se mettre en route; — the table mettre le couvert; — up établir; monter; — upon attaquer; — a. fixe; figé; réglé; imposé; déterminé; prêt; –ting a. couchant; –ting n. coucher m.; mise f.; réglage m.; montage m.; prise f.; (bone) réduction f.; (gem) monture f.; (theat.) décor m.; (type) composition f.; –ting up n. établissement m.; installation f.

setback n. revers m.; recul m.

setscrew n. vis de serrage f.

settee n. canapé m.

setter n. setter, chien d'arrêt m.

settle vt. arranger; résoudre, décider, déterminer; terminer; établir; coloniser; calmer; — vi. s'établir; s'installer; se calmer; déposer, se précipiter; — down se ranger; se caser; se calmer; –ment n. colonie f.; paiement m.; règlement m.; accord m.; –r n. colon m.

setup n. organisation f.; arrangement m.; montage m.

seven a. & n. sept; –teen a. & n. dix-sept; –teenth a. & n. dix-septième; –th a. & n. septième; –ty a. & n. soixante-dix

seventy-one soixante et onze

seventy-two soixante-douze

sever vt. rompre; couper; –ance n. séparation f.

several a. plusieurs; divers; différent; séparé

severance n. séparation f.

severe a. sévère; rigoureux; austère

severity n. sévérité f.; rigueur f.; austérité f.

sew vt. coudre; –ing n. couture f.; ouvrage m.; –ing machine machine à coudre f.

sewage n. eaux d'égout f. pl.

sewer n. égout m.

sex n. sexe m.; –ual a. sexuel; –uality n. sexualité f.

sextant n. sextant m.

sextet n. sextuor m.

sexton n. sacristain m.

shabby a. usé, râpé; minable; mesquin

shack n. case, cabane, hutte f.

shackle vt. enchaîner, entraver; –s n. pl. fers m. pl.

shad n. alose f.

shade n. ombre f.; nuance f.; (lamp) abat-jour m.; (window) store m.; — vt. ombrager; nuancer; ombrer; –d a. ombragé; ombré

shadiness n. ombre f.; ombrage m.

shadow n. ombre f.; — vt. ombrager; (person) filer; –y a. vague; mystérieux

shady a. ombreux; ombragé; (coll.) louche

shaft n. puits m.; (elevator) cage f.; arbre m.; souche f.; manche m.; flèche f., trait m.; (arch.) tige f.; (light) rayon m.

shaggy a. poilu; touffu; à longs poils

shake n. secousse f.; — of the head hochement de tête m.; — vt. secouer; agiter; hocher; ébranler; — vi. trembler, trembloter; chanceler; — a fist at menacer du poing; — hands with serrer la main à; — down faire tomber; extorquer; — off secouer; se défaire de; –n a. bouleversé, confus; –r n. (salt) salière f.; (cocktail) frappe-cocktail m.

shake-up n. bouleversement m.; renversement m.; remaniement m.

shaking a. tremblant; (voice) ému; — n. tremblement m.; secouement m.

shaky a. tremblant; chancelant; faible

shallot n. échalote f.

shallow a. peu profond; superficiel; plat; — water hauts-fonds m. pl.; –ness n. manque de profondeur m.

sham a. feint, simulé, faux; — n. feinte f.; imposture f.; — vt. feindre, simuler

shambles n. pl. carnage m.; désordre m.

shame n. honte f.; what a —! quel dommage!; — vt. humilier, faire honte à; –ful a. honteux; –less a. effronté; honteux; scandaleux

shamefaced a. penaud; honteux

shampoo n. shampooing m.; — vt. (se) laver les cheveux, donner un shampooing à

shamrock n. trèfle m.

shank n. (meat) manche f.; tibia m.

shanty n. hutte, cabane, case f.

shape n. forme f.; façon f.; out of — déformé; — vt. façonner, former; tailler; –less a. informe; –liness n. jolie taille f.; belle forme f.; symétrie f.; –ly a. bien fait, bien tourné

share n. part, portion f.; intérêt m.; (com.) action f., titre m., (plow) soc m.; — vt. partager; avoir part à; — vi. participer

sharecropper n. métayer m.

shareholder n. actionnaire m. & f.

shark n. requin m.

sharp a. aigu, tranchant, pointu; net, marqué; vif; fin; rusé, malin; piquant; — turn tournant brusque m.; — adv., two o'clock — deux heures précises; — n. (mus.) dièse m.; –en vt. tailler; aiguiser; affiler; aviver; –ener n. aiguisoir m.; (pencil) taille-crayons m.; –(er) n. (cards) tricheur m.; –ly adv. sévèrement; vivement; nettement; brusquement; –ness n. acuité, finesse f.; sévérité f.; netteté f.; piquant m.

sharp-edged *a.* affilé, tranchant
sharpshooter *n.* tireur d'élite *m.*
sharp-witted *a.* spirituel
shatter *vt.* fracasser, briser; — *vi.* se fracasser, se briser
shatterproof *a.* incassable; de sécurité
shave *n.* action de raser *f.*; **have a** — se raser; se faire raser; **have a close** — (fig.) l'échapper belle; — *vt.* raser, faire la barbe à; planer; **-r** *n.* barbier *m.*; **electric -r** rasoir électrique *m.*
shaving *n.* action de (se) raser *f.*; (wood) copeau *m.*; — **brush** blaireau *m.*; — **cream** savon à barbe *m.*
shawl *n.* châle, fichu *m.*
she *pron.* elle
sheaf *n.* gerbe *f.*; (papers) liasse *f.*
shear *vt.* tondre; couper; **-s** *n. pl.* ciseaux *m. pl.*; cisailles *f. pl.*; **-ing** *n.* tondaison *f.*; **-ing machine** *n.* tondeuse *f.*
sheath *n.* gaine *f.*; fourreau *m.*; enveloppe *f.*; **-e** *vt.* rengainer; revêtir
shed *n.* hangar *m.*; baraque *f.*; — *vt.* (tears) verser; (skin) jeter; — **light on** éclairer; **-ding** *n.* mue *f.*; perte *f.*
sheen *n.* luisant, lustre *m.*
sheep *n.* mouton *m.*, brebis *f.*; **black** — brebis galeuse *f.*; **-ish** *a.* penaud
sheepskin *n.* peau de mouton *f.*, parchemin *m.*; (coll.) diplôme *m.*
sheer *a.* pur, véritable; à pic
sheet *n.* drap *m.*; (paper) feuille *f.*; (glass) verre à vitres *m.*; (metal) tôle *f.*; (naut.) écoute *f.*; (mus.) feuille de musique *f.*; **-ing** *n.* drap *m.*, toile pour draps *f.*; tôlerie *f.*
shelf *n.* étagère, tablette *f.*, rayon *m.*
shell *n.* (peas, nuts) écaille, cosse *f.*; (egg) coque; (empty egg) coquille *f.*; (earth) écorce *f.*; (shellfish) coquillage *m.*; (cannon) obus *m.*; (gun) cartouche *f.*; **tortoise** —, **turtle** — écaille *f.*; — *vt.* (nuts) écaler; (peas) écosser; (oysters) ouvrir; (mil.) bombarder
shellac *n.* laque, gomme-laque *f.*; — *vt.* laquer
shellfire *n.* tir à obus *m.*
shellfish *n.* crustacé *m.*
shelter *n.* abri *m.*; asile *m.*; — *vt.* abriter, protéger
shelve *vt.* mettre sur les rayons; classer
shelving *n.* bois à faire des étagères *m.*; toile (papier) à recouvrir les étagères *f.* (m.)
shepherd *n.* berger, pâtre *m.*; pasteur *m.*; **-ess** *n.* bergère *f.*; — *vt.* garder; mener
sherbet *n.* sorbet *m.*
sheriff *n.* sheriff, chef de gendarmerie *m.*
sherry *n.* vin de Xérès *m.*
shield *n.* bouclier *m.*; (heraldry) écu *m.*;

(fig.) protection *f.*; (mech.) armature, gaine *f.*; blindage, capot, carter, écran *m.*; — *vt.* protéger; blinder
shift *n.* déplacement *m.*; changement *m.*; (industry) équipe (d'ouvriers) *f.*; (auto.) levier de changement de vitesse *m.*; (typewriter) touche à majuscules *f.*; — *vt.* déplacer; — *vi.* se déplacer; changer; (auto.) changer de vitesse; — **for oneself** se tirer d'affaire; **-less** *a.* faible; incapable; paresseux; **-y** *a.* peu digne de confiance; (eyes) fuyant
shilly-shally *vi.* être indécis; temporiser
shimmer *vi.* scintiller, reluire; — *n.* faible clarté *f.*
shimmy *n.* dandinement des roues avant *m.*; — *vi.* dandiner
shin *n.* tibia, devant de la jambe *m.*; **-ny (up)** *vi.* (coll.) grimper
shine *n.* brillant, poli *m.*; **take a** — **to** s'éprendre de; — *vt.* polir; (shoes) cirer; — *vi.* luire, reluire, briller; **-r** *n.* (coll.) œil poché *m.*
shingle *n.* bardeau *m.*; (coll.) enseigne (d'un médecin) *f.*
shining *a.* luisant; brillant, éclatant; — *n.* éclat *m.*; splendeur *f.*
ship *n.* vaisseau, navire *m.*; paquebot *m.*; — *vt.* envoyer, expédier; embarquer. (oars) rentrer; **-ment** *n.* cargaison *f.*, chargement *m.*; envoi *m.*, expédition *f.*; **-per** *n.* expéditeur *m.*; **-ping** *n.* envoi *m.*, expédition *f.*; commerce maritime *m.*; **-ping room** *n.* salle d'expédition *f.*
ship-to shore *a.*, — **telephone** liaison radio maritime *f.*
shipwreck *n.* naufrage *m.*; **-ed** *a.* naufragé; — *vi.* faire naufrage
shipyard *n.* chantier de construction *m.*
shirk *vt.* manquer à, éviter
shirr *vt.* froncer
shirt *n.* chemise *f.*; **-ing** *n.* toile à chemises *f.*
shirtmaker *n.* chemisier *m.*
shiver *n.* frisson *m.*; — *vi.* frissonner; **-ing** *a.* qui frossonne; à faire frissonner
shoal *n.* banc de sable *m.*; endroit peu profond *m.*; banc de poissons *m.*
shock *n.* choc *m.*; coup *m.*; secousse *f.*; — **absorber** amortisseur *m.*; — **treatment** électronarcose *f.*; — *vt.* choquer; offenser; **-ing** *a.* choquant; **-proof** *a.* à l'épreuve des secousses (persons) inébranlable
shoddy *a.* de mauvaise qualité, inférieur
shoe *n.* chaussure *f.*; soulier *m.*; (wooden) sabot *m.*; (horse) fer *m.*; — **polish** cirage *m.*; — **store** cordonnerie *f.*; (magasin de) chaussures *m.*; — *vt.* chausser; (horse) ferrer

shoehorn *n.* chausse-pied *m.*

shoelace *n.* lacet *m.*

shoemaker *n.* cordonnier *m.*

shoestring *n.* lacet *m.*; **on a —** (coll.) avec très peu d'argent; **— potatoes** pommes-allumettes *f. pl.*

shoe tree *n.* forme à chaussures *f.*

shoot *n.* rejeton, scion *m.*; pousse *f.*; partie de chasse *f.*; **—** *vt.* tirer, lancer; fusiller; **—** *vi.* s'élancer; se précipiter; bourgeonner, pousser; **–ing** *n.* tir *m.*; action de tirer *f.*; **–ing** *a.*, **–ing star** étoile filante *f.*

shop *n.* boutique *f.*, magasin *m.*; (industry) atelier *m.*; **–keeper** *n.* marchand *m.*; boutiquier *m.*; **–lifter** *n.* voleur à l'étalage *m.*; **talk —** parler affaires; **— window** *n.* vitrine, devanture *f.*; **–per** *n.* acheteur, client *m.*; **–ping bag** *n.* filet à provisions *m.*; **–ping plaza** *n.* place marchande *f.*; quartier commerçant *m.*; **—** *vi.* faire des emplettes; **–worn** *a.* défraîchi; **— for** chercher à acheter; **go –ping** faire des emplettes; faire des courses

shore *n.* rivage *m.*, côte *f.*; **— leave** permission (d'aller à terre) *f.*; **—** *vt.* étayer

shore line *n.* ligne de côte *f.*, littoral *m.*

short *a.* court; bref; concis; serré; **— subject** *n.* court métrage *m.*; **be — of** être à court de; manquer de; **cut — couper court (à); fall — of** rester au-dessous de; **— circuit** *n.* (elec.) court-circuit *m.*; **–age** *n.* insuffisance *f.*; **–en** *vt.* raccourcir; **–ening** *n.* matière grasse *f.*; **–ly** *adv.* bientôt; **–s** *n. pl.* short *m.*; caleçon court *m.*

shortcake *n.* gateau recouvert de fruits frais *m.*

shortchange *vt.* rendre la monnaie insuffisante

short-circuit *vt.* court-circuiter

shortcoming *n.* faiblesse, insuffisance *f.*

shorthand *n.* sténographie *f.*

shorthanded *a. & adv.* avec une insuffisance de personnel

short-lived *a.* de courte durée

shortsighted *a.* myope; peu prévoyant

short-tempered *a.* qui s'emporte facilement

short-term *a.* à courte échéance

short-wave *a.* à ondes courtes

shot *n.* coup de feu *m.*; portée *f.*; plomb *m.*; (med.) piqûre *f.*; (coll.) verre d'alcool *m.*

shotgun *n.* fusil de chasse *m.*; **— shell** cartouche chargée à plomb *f.*

shoulder *n.* épaule *f.*; **— strap** bretelle *f.*; **—** *vt.* mettre sur les épaules; se charger de

shoulder blade *n.* omoplate *f.*

shout *n.* cri *m.*; **—** *vt. & vi.* crier

shove *n.* coup *m.*, poussée *f.*; **—** *vt.* pousser; bousculer; **— off** partir; démarrer; (naut.) pousser au large

shovel *n.* pelle *f.*; **—** *vt.* pelleter

show *n.* spectacle *m.*; étalage *m.*; parade *f.*; **— window** vitrine *f.*; **—** *vt.* montrer, faire voir; démontrer; **— off** étaler, faire parade de; faire valoir; se faire voir; **— up** révéler, démasquer; (coll.) arriver; paraître; **–y** *a.* fastueux, voyant

showcase *n.* vitrine *f.*

showdown *n.* explication armée *f.*; moment décisif *m.*

shower *n.* douche *f.*; pluie, averse *f.*; **—** *vt.* accabler, combler

showman *n.* impresario *m.*; acteur *m.*; **–ship** *n.* art de présenter *m.*

showroom *n.* salle de vision, salle d'exposition *f.*

shred *n.* morceau *m.*, rognure *f.*; **—** *vt.* couper en petits morceaux

shrew *n.* mégère *f.*; (zool.) musaraigne *f.*; **–ish** *a.* acariâtre

shrewd *a.* fin; rusé; **–ness** *n.* finesse, ruse *f.*

shriek *n.* cri perçant *m.*; **—** *vi.* pousser des cris perçants

shrill *a.* perçant, aigu

shrimp *n.* crevette *f.*

shrine *n.* chapelle *f.*; reliquaire *m.*, châsse *f.*

shrink *vi.* se resserrer, se rétrécir, se raccourcir; reculer; **–age** *n.* rétrécissement *m.*

shrivel *vi.* (se) rider

shroud *n.* linceul, drap mortuaire *m.*; (naut.) hauban *m.*; **—** *vt.* défendre, protéger; couvrir d'un drap mortuaire

Shrove Tuesday *n.* mardi gras *m.*

shrub *n.* arbrisseau, arbuste *m.*; **–bery** *n.* verdure *f.*; arbrisseaux *m. pl.*

shrug *n.* haussement d'épaules *m.*; **—** *vt.* lever, hausser

shuck *vt.* écosser; éplucher; **—** *n.* cosse *f.*

shudder *n.* frissonnement *m.*; **—** *vi.* frissonner, frémir; trembler

shuffle *n.* mélange *m.*; mouvement traînant *m.*; **—** *vt.* mélanger, mêler; battre; **—** *vi.* traîner les pieds

shuffleboard *n.* jeu de palets *m.*

shuffling *a.* évasif; (gait) qui traîne les pieds; **—** *n.* battement de cartes *m.*; marche traînante *f.*

shun *vt.* éviter

shunt *vt.* changer de voie; dévier

shut *vt.* fermer, renfermer; **—** *vi.* se fermer; **— down** faire cesser; fermer; **— in** renfermer, garder à l'intérieur; **— off**

fermer, interrompre; — **out** garder à l'extérieur; — **up** renfermer; se taire; **-ter** n. volet m.; **store** m.; (phot.) obturateur m.

shutdown n. cessation f.; fermeture f.

shut-in n. malade m. & f (qui ne peut pas quitter la maison)

shuttle n. navette f.; — vi. faire la navette

shuttlecock n. volant m.

shy vi. faire un écart; se jeter de côté; — a. réservé; timide; farouche; **-ness** n. réserve, timidité f.; **to be** — **of** manquer de; **-ly** adv. timidement

shyster n. avocat malhonnête m.

Siam n. Siam m.; **-ese** a. & n. siamois m.

Siberia n. Sibérie f.; **-n** n. & a. Sibérien m.

Sicilian a. & n. sicilien m.

Sicily n. Sicile f.

sick a. malade; indisposé; dégoûté; **get** — tomber malade; **-en** vt. rendre malade, dégoûter; **-en** vi. tomber malade; **-ly** a. maladif; **-ness** n. mal m.; maladie f.

sickbed n. lit de malade m.

sickle n. faucille f.

sick leave n. congé de convalescence m.

sickroom n. chambre de malade f.

side n. côté m.; flanc m.; bord m.; parti m.; — **by** — côte à côte; **on all -s de tous côtés; on one** — d'un côté; — a. de côté; oblique; auxiliaire, supplémentaire; — **dish** entremets m.; — vi., — **with** appuyer, prendre le parti de

sideboard n. buffet m., desserte f.

side light n. détail révélateur, détail intéressant m.

side line n. distraction f.; intérêt secondaire m.

sidelong a. oblique

side show n. exhibition de fête foraine f.

side-step vt. esquiver, éviter; — vi. faire un écart

sideswipe vt. prendre en écharpe

sidetrack vt. écarter, dévier

sidewalk n. trottoir, pavé m.

sidewards, sideways, sidewise adv. de côté, latéralement

siding n. (rail.) voie de garage f.

sidle vi. approcher latéralement

siege n. siège m.; **lay** — **to** assiéger; **raise a** — lever un siège

siesta n. sieste f.

sieve n. tamis m.; — vt. tamiser; trier

sift vt. tamiser, passer au tamis; trier; examiner, juger; **-er** n. tamis m.

sigh n. soupir m.; — vi. soupirer; pousser un soupir

sight n. vue f.; vision f.; aspect m.; specta-

cle m.; (gun) mire f.; — **draft** n. (com.) effet à vue m.; **at** — à première vue; **by** — (com.) de vue; **in** — en vue; **lose** — **of** perdre de vue; **on** — à vue; **out of** — hors de vue; — **unseen** sans examiner d'avance; — vt. apercevoir, remarquer; **-less** a. aveugle

sight-see vi. visiter les curiosités; **-ing** n. tourisme m.; voyage m.; visites f. pl.; **-r** n. touriste, visiteur m.

sign n. signe m., marque f., symbole m.; enseigne f., pancarte f.; — vt. signer; — **off** cesser d'émettre; — **off** n. (radio) fin de message f.; — **up** enrôler, inscrire; — **language** n. langage par signe m.; **-post** n. poteau indicateur m., borne f.; **-er** n. signataire m. & f.

signal n. signal, signe m.; — **corps** n. transmissions f. pl.; — **light** n. (nav.) fanal m.; — **lights** n. pl. feux de route m. pl.; — vt. signaler; — a. signalé, insigne; **-ize** vt. signaler

signature n. signature f.; (end) fin de message f.

signet n. cachet m.

significance n. signification f.; importance f.

significant n. significatif, signifiant

signify vt. signifier

silage n. fourrage ensilé m.

silence n. silence m.; — vt. faire taire; **-r** n. amortisseur m.

silent a. silencieux; (movies) muet; — **partner** n. commandataire m.

silica n. silice f.; **-te** n. silicate m.

siliceous a. siliceux

silicone n. silicone m.

silk n. soie f.; — a. de soie; **-en, -y** a. soyeux

silkworm n. ver à soie m.

sill n. seuil, appui m.

silliness n. sottise f.

silly a. sot; niais, simple

silver n. argent m.; — **plate** argenterie f.; — a. d'argent, en argent; argenté; — vt. argenter

silver-plated a. plaqué d'argent

silversmith n. orfèvre m.

silverware n. argenterie f.

similar a. semblable; **-ity** n. similarité, ressemblance f.; **-ly** adv. de la même façon

simile n. comparaison f.

similitude n. similitude f.

simmer vi. mijoter; — vt. faire mijoter

simper n. minauderie f.; — vi. sourire niaisement

simple a. simple, naïf; pur; **-ness** n. simplicité f.

simple-minded a. simple, idiot

simpleton n. niais, sot m.

simplicity *n.* simplicité *f.*

simplification *n.* simplification *f.*

simplify *vt.* simplifier

simulate *vt.* feindre, simuler

simultaneous *a.* simultané; **−ness** *n.* simultanéité *f.*

sin *n.* péché *m.*; **mortal —** péché capital *m.*; **original —** péché originel; **—** *vi.* pécher; **−ful** *a.* pécheur; **−ner** *n.* pécheur *m.*

since *conj.* puisque; depuis que; comme; **—** *prep.* depuis; **—** *adv.* depuis

sincere *n.* sincère

sincerity *n.* sincérité *f.*

sine *n.* (math.) sinus *m.*

sinecure *n.* sinécure *f.*

sinew *n.* nerf *m.*; tendon *m.*; **−y** *a.* nerveux; vigoureux

sing *vt. & vi.* chanter; **−er** *n.* chanteur *m.*; cantatrice *f.*; **−ing** *n.* chant *m.*

singe *n.* roussi *m.*; **—** *vt.* brûler légèrement, flamber, roussir

single *a.* seul, particulier, singulier, simple; célibataire; **— file** *adv.* à la file indienne; **−ness** *n.* nature simple *f.*; sincérité *f.*

single-breasted *a.* droit, non croisé

singlehanded *a.* sans aide, seul

single-minded *a.* sincère; qui n'a qu'un seul but

singly *adv.* un à un

singsong *n.* chant monotone *m.*; (fig.) psalmodie *f.*; **—** *a.* monotone, traînant

singular *n. & a.* singulier *m.*; **−ity** *n.* singularité *f.*

sinister *a.* sinistre

sink *n.* évier *m.*; **—** *vi.* couler; s'enfoncer; s'abaisser, succomber; **—** *vt.* enfoncer; creuser; abaisser; perdre; plonger, précipiter; **−er** *n.* (fishline) poids, plomb *m.*; (coll.) beignet *m.*

sinking fund *n.* caisse d'amortissement *f.*

sinuosity *n.* sinuosité *f.*

sinuous *a.* sinueux

sip *n.* petit coup *m.*; gorgée *f.*; **—** *vt.* déguster, siroter

sir *n.* monsieur *m.*; (title) Sir, chevalier

sire *n.* père *m.*; Sire *m.*

siren *n.* sirène *f.*

sirloin *n.* aloyau *m.*

sirup, syrup *n.* sirop *m.*

sister *n.* sœur *f.*; (eccl.) religieuse *f.*; **−ly** *a.* de sœur, comme une sœur

sister-in-law *n.* belle-sœur *f.*

sit *vi.* s'asseoir; demeurer; siéger; être situé; **— down** s'asseoir; **— up** se dresser sur son séant; **−ter** *n.* celui qui est assis *m.*; garde des enfants *f.*; **−ting** *n.* séance *f.*; **−ting room** salon *m.*

sit-down strike *n.* grève sur le tas *f.*

site *n.* site, emplacement *m.*

situate *vt.* localiser; **−d** *a.* situé; sis; **be −d** se trouver

six *a. & n.* six *m.*; **−teen** *n. & a.* seize *m.*; **−teenth** *n. & a.* seizième *m.*; **−th** *a. & n.* sixième *m.*; **−tieth** *a. & n.* soixantième *m.*; **−ty** *a. & n.* soixante *m.*

sizable *a.* de grandeur appréciable, assez grand

size *n.* grandeur, taille *f.*; grosseur *f.*; mesure *f.*; pointure *f.*; colle *f.*; **—** *vt.* encoller; **— up** évaluer; **−d** *a.* de taille, de grandeur

sizing *n.* colle *f.*, collage, encollage *m.*

sizzle *vi.* griller en crépitant

sizzling *a.* crépitant; excessivement chaud

skate *n.* patin *m.*; (fish) raie *f.*; **roller —** patin à roulettes *m.*; **—** *vi.* patiner; **−r** *n.* patineur *m.*

skating *n.* patinage *m.*; **— rink** *n.* patinoire *f.*

skein *n.* écheveau *m.*

skeleton *n.* squelette *m.*; **— key** *n.* passepartout *m.*

skeptic *n.* sceptique *m.*; **−al** *a.* sceptique; **−ism** *n.* scepticisme *m.*

sketch *n.* esquisse *f.*; **—** *vt.* esquisser, ébaucher; **−y** *a.* esquissé, ébauché

sketchbook *n.* album *m.*

skewer *n.* brochette *f.*; **—** *vt.* embrocher

ski *n.* ski *m.*; **—** *vi.* faire du ski; **— jump** *n.* saut à ski *m.*; **— lift** *n.* remonte-pentes, télésiège *m.*

skid *n.* dérapage *m.*; **—** *vi.* déraper

skiff *n.* esquif *m.*

skilful *a.* adroit; habile

skill *n.* habileté *f.*; **−ed** *a.* adroit, habile; **−ed worker** *n.* spécialiste *m. & f.*

skillet *n.* poêle épaisse *f.*

skim *vt. & vi.* écumer, effleurer; (milk) écrémer; **— milk** *n.* lait écrémé *m.*; **−mer** *n.* écumoire *f.*; écrémeur *m.*

skimp *vi.* être frugal, économiser; **— on** lésiner sur; **−y** *a.* frugal, chiche

skin *n.* peau *f.*; pelure *f.*; écorce *f.*; **−flint** *n.* avare *m.*; **— graft** *n.* greffe épidermique *f.*; **—** *vt.* écorcher, dépouiller; dénuder; **−tight** *a.* collant

skin-deep *a.* superficiel

skin-dive *vi.* explorer au scaphandre autonome

skinny *a.* décharné, maigre

skip *n.* saut *m.*; **—** *vt.* sauter

skipper *n.* sauteur *m.*; capitaine *m.*

skipping rope *n.* corde à sauter *f.*

skirmish *n.* escarmouche *f.*; **—** *vi.* escarmoucher

skirt *n.* (dress) jupe *f.*; (forest) bord *m.*; **—** *vt.* contourner

skit *n.* saynète *f.*; scénario *m.*

skittish *a.* ombrageux; capricieux, volage

skulduggery *n.* roublardise *f.*
skulk *vi.* se cacher, rôder
skull *n.* crâne *m.*
skullcap *n.* calotte *f.*
skunk *n.* putois *m.*
sky *n.* ciel *m.*; **−light** *n.* lucarne *f.*;
−line *n.* silhouette des bâtiments
d'une ville *f.*; horizon *m.*; **−rocket** *n.*
fusée *f.*; **−rocket** *vi.* (coll.) monter
rapidement; **−scraper** *n.* gratte-ciel *m.*;
maison démesurément haute *f.*; **−writing**
n. publicité aérienne *f.*
slab *n.* plaque, dalle *f.*; tranche *f.*
slack *n.* mou *m.*; **−s** *pl.* pantalon *m.*; **—** *a.*
mou; inactif, mort; **—** *vt.* relâcher; **−en**
vt. relâcher, détendre; **−en** *vi.* se détendre; **−er** *n.* lâche, paresseux *m.*; embusqué *m.*
slag *n.* crasses *f. pl.*
slain *n. pl.* morts *m. pl.*
slake *vt.* (lime) éteindre; (thirst) apaiser
slam *vt.* fermer avec bruit; **—** *n.* claquement *m.*; insulte *f.*; (cards) schlem *m.*;
grand **—** grand schlem *m.*; small **—** petit schlem *m.*; make a **—** faire schlem
slander *n.* médisance *f.*; **—** *vt.* colomnier,
diffamer; **−er** *n.* calomniateur *m.*; **−ous**
a. calomniateur, médisant
slang *n.* jargon, argot *m.*
slant *n.* pente *f.*; (coll.) interprétation *f.*;
point de vue *m.*; **—** *vt.* interpréter, préparer, destiner; **—** *vi.* être en pente;
−ing *a.* en pente; oblique; de travers;
−wise *adv.* en biais
slap *n.* claque, tape *f.*; soufflet *m.*; **— in
the face** gifle *f.*; **—** *vt.* taper, claquer; **—
in the face** gifler
slapstick *n.* bouffonnerie *f.*; burlesque *f.*
slash *n.* taillade *f.*; baisse, réduction *f.*; **—**
vt. balafrer, taillader; réduire
slat *n.* latte *f.*; lamelle *f.*
slate *n.* ardoise *f.*; liste *f.*; (pol.) liste des
candidats *f.*; **—** *vt.* couvrir d'ardoise;
destiner
slaughter *n.* carnage, massacre *m.*; abattage *m.*; **—** *vt.* abattre; massacrer
slaughterhouse *n.* abattoir *m.*
Slav *n.* Slave *m. & f.*; **−ic** *a.* slave; **−onic**
a. slave
slave *n.* esclave *m. & f.*; **— driver** *n.* (fig.)
maître sévère et cruel *m.*; **—** *vi.* travailler comme un esclave; **−r** *n.* négrier *m.*;
−ry *n.* esclavage *m.*; white **−ry** prostitution *f.*
slavish *a.* servile; d'esclave
slaw *n.* salade de choux *f.*
slay *vt.* tuer; **−er** *n.* tueur, meurtrier *m.*;
−ing *n.* meurtre, assassinat *m.*
sled *n.* traîneau *m.*
sledge hammer *n.* marteau à frapper *m.*

sleek *vt.* lisser, polir; **—** *a.* lisse, poli
sleep *n.* sommeil *m.*; **—** *vi.* dormir; go to
— s'endormir; put to **—** endormir; **−er**
n. dormeur *m.*; voiture-lits *f.*, wagon-
lits *m.*; **−iness** *n.* somnolence *f.*; **−ing bag**
n. sac de couchage *m.*; **−ing car** *n.* wagon-lits, sleeping (-car) *m.*; **−ing room** *n.*
chambre à coucher *f.*; **−ing sickness** *n.*
maladie du sommeil *f.*; **−less** *a.* sans
sommeil, blanc; **−y** *a.* endormi; be **−y**
avoir sommeil
sleepwalking *n.* somnambulisme *m.*
sleet *n.* grésil *m.*; **—** *vi.* grésiller
sleeve *n.* manche *f.*; **−less** *a.* sans manche
sleigh *n.* traîneau *m.*; **— bell** *n.* clochette
f., grelot *m.*
sleight *n.* tour d'adresse *m.*; ruse *f.*; **— of
hand** paresseux *m.* tour de passe-passe
slender *a.* mince, svelte; chétif
sleuth *n.* détective *m.*
slice *n.* tranche *f.*; **—** *vt.* trancher
slick *a.* lisse, glissant; **—** *vt.* lisser; **—** *n.*
(oil) couche d'huile *f.*; **—** *adv.* d'emblée;
−er *n.* imperméable *m.*
slide *n.* glissade, glissoire *f.*; coulisse *f.*;
(microscope) fiche *f.*; (projection) diapositif *m.*; **— rule** règle à calcul *f.*; **—**
vt. & vi. glisser, faire glisser
sliding scale *n.* échelle mobile *f.*
slight *n.* dédain *m.*; **—** *vt.* dédaigner; manquer à; **—** *a.* mince, insignifiant; léger
slim *a.* mince, svelte; **−ness** *n.* minceur *f.*
slime *n.* limon *m.*, bourbe *f.*; bave *f.*
sliminess *n.* viscosité *f.*
slimy *a.* visqueux, vaseux; gluant
sling *n.* écharpe *f.*; lancement *m.*; (gun)
bretelle *f.*; **—** *vt.* lancer, jeter
slingshot *n.* lance-pierres *m.*; fronde *f.*
slink *vi.* s'en aller furtivement
slip *n.* glissade *f.*; erreur *f.*; barde *f.*; écoulement *m.*; (bot.) scion *m.*; (undergarment) chemise *f.*; combinaison *f.*; (pa-
per) bout *m.*; **— cover** *n.* housse *f.*; **—** *vt.*
glisser; faire une erreur; **—** *vi.* glisser;
se tromper; faire un faux-pas
slipper *n.* pantoufle *f.*; mule *f.*
slippery *a.* glissant
slipshod *a.* négligé
slit *n.* fente *f.*; **—** *vt.* fendre
sliver *n.* éclat; **—** *vi.* éclater
slobber *n.* bave *f.*; **—** *vi.* baver
sloe *n.* prunelle *f.*; **— gin** *n.* prunelline *f.*
slogan *n.* slogan *m.*
sloop *n.* chaloupe *f.*
slop *n.* rinçure *f.*; eau de vaisselle *f.*; la-
vasse *f.*; **—** *vt.* répandre; **−py** *a.* négligé;
désordonné; peu soigné; sale
slope *n.* pente, déclivité *f.*; talus *m.*; **—** *vi.*
s'incliner
slot *n.* fente, ouverture *f.*; **— machine** *n.*

machine à sous *f.*
sloth *n.* paresse *f.*; (zool.) paresseux *m.*; **–ful** *a.* paresseux
slouch *vt. & vi.* abaisser la tête; rabaisser le chapeau; se dandiner lourdement; — *n.* attitude affaissée *f.*; — **hat** *n.* chapeau mou *m.*
slough *n.* bourbier *m.*; dépouille *f.*; — *vt.* se dépouiller de
Slovakia *n* Slovaquie *f.*
slovenly *a.* malpropre; sale
slow *a.* lent; tardif; — *vt.* ralentir; — **down** ralentir; **–ly** *adv.* lentement; **–ness** *n.* lenteur *f.*; (clocks) retard
slow-motion *a.* (films) film tourné au ralenti
sludge *n.* cambouis *m.*; calamine *f.*; dépôt carboné *m.*; boues *f. pl.*
slug *n.* (zool.) limace *f.*; (print., bar) lingot *m.* (token) jeton *m.*; — *vt.* (coll.) assomer
sluggish *a.* indolent; lent; **–ness** *n.* indolence *f.*; lenteur *f.*
sluice *n.* écluse *f.*; **–gate** *n.* porte éclusière *f.*; — *vt.* vanner
slum *n.* quartier misérable *m.*; **go –ming** visiter les quartiers misérables
slumber *n.* sommeil *m.*; — *vi.* sommeiller
slump *n.* chute, baisse *f.*; affaissement *m.*; — *vi.* baisser; s'affaisser; s'enfoncer
slur *n.* tache *f.*; blâme *m.*; (mus.) coulé *m.*; — *vt.* salir; passer légèrement; (mus.) lier les notes
slush *n.* neige à moitié fondue *f.*
sly *a.* fin; rusé; **on the** — en cachette; furtivement
smack *n.* goût *m.*; claque *f.*; (fishing) bâteau de pêche *m.*; — *vt.* claquer; — *vi.* avoir le goût; rappeler
small *n.* partie la plus mince *f.*; — **of the back** reins *m. pl.*; — *a.* petit; léger; menu; — **change** *n.* menue monnaie *f.*; — **fry** enfants *m. pl.*; — **hours** heures matinales *f. pl.*; — **intestine** *n.* intestin grêle *m.*; — **talk** bavardage *m.*; **–ish** *a.* assez petit; **–ness** *n.* petitesse *f.*
smallpox *n.* petite vérole *f.*
small-town *a.* provincial
smart *n.* douleur aiguë *f.*; — *vi.* sentir une cuisante douleur; faire sentir une cuisante douleur; — *a.* intelligent, vif; élégant; **–ness** *n.* intelligence *f.* élégance *f.*
smash *vt.* briser, écraser; — *n.* fracas *m.*; collision *f.*; grande réussite *f.*
smashup *n.* collision *f.*, accident *m.*
smattering *n.* connaissance superficielle *f.*; notions *f. pl.*
smear *n.* tache *f.*; avilissement *m.*; — *vt.* tacher, barbouiller; avilir; (coll.) ca-

lomnier, diffamer
smell *n.* odeur *f.*; — *vt. & vi.* sentir
smelt *n.* éperlan *m.*
smelt *vt.* fondre; **–er** *n.* fonderie *f.*
smile *n.* sourire *m.*; — *vi.* sourire
smirk *vi.* sourire, minauder
smite *vt.* frapper; enflammer
smith *n.* forgeron *m.*; **–y** *n.* forge *f.*
smithereens *n. pl.* atomes *m. pl.*; **break to** — atomiser
smock *n.* tablier *m.*, blouse *f.*
smoke *n.* fumée *f.*; vapeur *f.*; — *vt. & vi.* fumer; — **house** *n.* fumoir *m.*; **–less** *a.* sans fumée; **–r** *n.* fumeur *m.*
smoke screen *n.* rideau de fumée *m.*
smokestack *n.* cheminée
smoking *n.* action de fumer *f.*; — **car** *n.* wagon des fumeurs *m.*; **no** — défense de fumer
smoking jacket *n.* veston d'intérieur *m.*
smoky *a.* fumeux; enfumé
smolder *vi.* brûler sans flamme
smooth *vt.* unir; lisser; apaiser; flatter; dérider; — *a.* uni; poli, lisse, doux; **–ness** *n.* douceur *f.*; poli, calme *m.*
smooth-spoken, smooth-tongued *a.* à langue dorée
smother *vt.* étouffer, suffoquer; couvrir
smudge *n.* barbouillage *m.*; dépôt de suie *m.*; tache; — *vt.* barbouiller
smug *a.* content de sol
smuggle *vt.* faire la contrebande; **–r** *n.* contrebandier *m.*
smuggling *n.* contrebande *f.*
smut *n.* tache de suie *f.*; obscénités *f. pl.*; — *vt.* noircir; **–ty** *a.* taché de suie; grossier
snack *n.* casse-croûte *m.*; goûter *m.*; collation *f.*
snag *n.* bosse *f.*, nœud *m.*; entrave, difficulté *f.*; — *vt.* accrocher
snail *n.* limaçon, escargot *m.*; **at a –'s pace** à pas de tortue
snake *n.* serpent *m.*; — *vi.* onduler
snap *n.* claquement *m.*; bruit sec *m.*; fermoir *m.*; (coll.) quelque chose de facile *m.*, — *vi.* claquer; se briser; — **at** prendre dans les dents; parler sur un ton hargneux; — *vt.* casser, briser; **–per** *n.* fermoir *m.*, fermeture *f.*
snapshot *n.* instantané *m.*
snare *n.* piège *m.*; — *vt.* prendre au piège
snarl *vi.* grogner, gronder; emmêler; — *n.* grognement *m.*; (coll.) emboutcillage *m.*
snatch *n.* prise *f.*; accès *m.*; morceau *m.*; — *vt.* saisir, arracher violemment
sneak *n.* lâche *m.*; — *vt.* voler; — *vi.* se glisser; — **thief** *n.* voleur *m.*
sneer *n.* ricanement *m.*, raillerie *f.*; — *vi.* ricaner

sneeze *vi.* éternuer; — *n.* éternuement *m.*

snicker *n.* ricanement *m.*; — *vi.* ricaner

sniff *vi.* renifler; — *n.* reniflement *m.*; respirée *f.*

sniffle *n.* reniflement *m.*; — *vi.* renifler; pleurnicher; —**s** *n. pl.* reniflement *m.*; rhume de cerveau *m.*

snip *n.* coupure *f.*; petit morceau *m.*; —*vt.* couper; rogner

snipe *n.* bécassine *f.*; — *vi.* tirer; canarder; —**r** *n.* franc-tireur *m.*

snivel *vi.* pleurnicher

snob *n.* snob; parvenu *m.*; —**bish** *a.* snob; vulgaire; —**bishness** *n.* snobisme *m.*; suffisance *f.*

snoop *n.* curieux *m.*; espion *m.*; — *vi.* épier

snooze *n.* petit somme *m.*; — *vi.* somnoler

snore *n.* ronflement *m.*; — *vi.* ronfler

snoring *n.* ronflement *m.*; — *a.* qui ronfle

snorkel *n.* schnorchel *m.*

snort *n.* ébrouement *m.*; — *vi.* s'ébrouer

snout *n.* museau *m.*; groin *m.*

snow *n.* neige *f.*; — *vi.* neiger; —**y** *a.* neigeux

snowball *n.* boule de neige *f.*

snowbound *a.* bloqué par la neige

snow-capped *a.* couronné de neige

snowdrift *n.* amas de neige *m.*

snowfall *n.* chute de neige *f.*

snowflake *n.* flocon de neige *m.*

snow line *n.* limite des neiges *f.*

snowplow *n.* chasse-neige *m.*

snow slide *n.* avalanche de neige *f.*

snow storm *n.* tempête de neige *f.*

snub *n.* affront *m.*; — **nose** nez camus *m.*; — *vt.* tourner le dos à

snuff *n.* tabac à priser *m.*; — **box** tabatière *f.*; — *vt.* éteindre; moucher

snuffle *vi.* renifler

snug *a.* serré; commode, confortable; bien

snuggle *vi.* se serrer

so *adv.* ainsi; si; tellement; tant; aussi; comme cela; de même; alors; **and** — **on** et ainsi de suite; — **as to** pour; — **much** tant; — **that** pour que, afin que; de sorte que; — **long!** au revoir, à bientôt

soak *vt. & vi.* tremper; —**ing** *a.*, —**ing wet** trempé, mouillé (jusqu'aux os); —**ing** *n.* action de tremper *f.*; arrosage *f.*

soap *n.* savon *m.*; — **bubble** bulle de savon *f.*; —**suds** mousse de savon *f.*; **toilet** — savonnette *f.*; — *vt.* savonner; —**y** *a.* savonneux

soapbox *n.* caisse à savon *f.*; plate-forme improvisé *m.*

soapstone *n.* stéatite *f.*

soar *vi.* prendre l'essor; s'élever

sob *n.* sanglot *m.*; — *vi.* sangloter

sober *a.* sobre; pas ivre; — *vt.* calmer; ramener à la raison

sobriety *n.* sobriété *f.*; modération *f.*

so-called *a.* soi-disant; ainsi nommé

sociability *n.* sociabilité *f.*

sociable *a.* sociable; amical

social *a.* social; sociable; — **security assurances** sociales *f. pl.*; — **service,** — **work** travail d'amélioration sociale *m.*; —**ism** *n.* socialisme *m.*; —**ist** *n.* socialiste *m. & f.*; —**ite** *n.* mondain *m.*, mondaine *f.*; —**ize** *vt.* socialiser

society *n.* société *f.*; monde *m.*

sociological *a.* sociologique

sociology *n.* sociologie *f.*

sock *n.* chaussette *f.*; coup de poing *m.*; — *vt.* donner un coup de poing à, frapper du poing

socket *n.* douille *f.*; soc. *m.*; (elec.) prise *f.*; (eye) orbite *f.*; (tooth) alvéole *m.*; socle *m.*; — **wrench** clé à tube *f.*

sod *n.* motte de terre *f.*; gazon *m.*

soda *n.* soude *f.*; soda *m.*; **baking** —, **bicarbonate of** — bicarbonate de soude *m.*; — **water** soda *m.*; eau de Seltz *f.*

sodium *n.* sodium *m.*; — **chloride** *n.* chlorure de soude *m.*

sofa *n.* sofa, canapé *m.*; — **bed** *n.* canapé qui se transforme en lit, lit-divan *m.*

soft *a.* mou, doux; tendre, faible, facile, délicat; efféminé; (water) non-calcaire; — **coal** charbon *m.*; — **drink** boisson rafraîchissante *f.*, boisson non-alcoolisée *f.*; —**en** *vt.* amollir, adoucir, attendrir; —**ness** *n.* douceur *f.*; mollesse *f.*

softball *n.* baseball (jouée avec une balle molle) *m.*

softhearted *a.* sensible; sentimental; compatissant

soft-pedal *vt.* étouffer, adoucir; minimiser

soft-spoken *a.* doux

soggy *a.* humide

soil *n.* souillure *f.*; terre *f.*; sol, terrain *m.*; — *vt.* souiller, salir

sojourn *n.* séjour *m.*; — *vi.* séjourner

sol *n.* (mus.) sol *m.*

solace *n.* consolation *f.*; — *vt.* consoler

solar *a.* solaire; du soleil; — **plexus** *n.* plexus solaire *m.*; —**ium** *n.* solarium *m.*

sold *a.*, — **out** épuisé; complet; tout vendu

solder *n.* soudure *f.*; — *vt.* souder; —**ing** *n.* soudure *f.*; —**ing iron** *n.* fer à souder *m.*

soldier *n.* soldat *m.*

sole *n.* (foot) plante du pied *f.*; (shoe) semelle *f.*; (fish) sole *f.*; — *vt.* ressemeler; — *a.* unique, seul

solemn *a.* solennel; —**ity** *n.* solennité *f.*; —**ize** *vt.* solenniser

solicit *vt.* solliciter; inviter; —**ation** *n.* sollicitation *f.*; —**or** *n.* solliciteur *m.*; (law) avoué *m.*; —**ous** *a.* plein de sollicitude; —**ude** *n.* sollicitude *f.*

solid *a.* solide; massif; réel; grave, profond; (color) uni; — *n.* corps solide *m.*; **–arity** *n.* solidarité *f.*; **–ify** *vt.* solidifier; **–ify** *vi.* se solidifier; **–ity** *n.* solidité *f.*; — **geometry** *n.* géométrie dans l'espace *f.*
soliloquy *n.* monologue *m.*
solitaire *n.* solitaire *m.*; (game) patience *f.*
solitary *a.* solitaire; retiré
solitude *n.* solitude *f.*
solo *n.* solo *m.*; **–ist** *n.* soliste *m. & f.*; — *a. & adv.* seul
solstice *n.* solstice *m.*
soluble *a.* dissoluble
solution *n.* solution *f.*
solve *vt.* résoudre
solvency *n.* solvabilité *f.*
solvent *n.* dissolvant *m.*; — *a.* (com.) solvable
Somalia *n.* Somalie *f.*
somber *a.* sombre
some *a.* quelque, un peu de; du, de la; — *pron.* un peu; certains; quelques-uns; les uns; les autres
somebody, someone *pron.* quelqu'un
somehow *adv.* de façon ou d'autre
somersault *n.* culbute *f.*; — *vi.* culbuter
something *pron.* quelque chose
sometime *adv.* un jour, un de ces jours; — *a.* ancien, ci-devant, honoraire
sometimes *adv.* quelquefois, de temps en temps; tantôt
somewhat *adv.* un peu; assez
somewhere *adv.* quelque part; — **else** ailleurs; autre part
somnambulist *n.* somnambule *m. & f.*
somnolent *a.* somnolent
son *n.* fils *m.*
sonata *n.* sonate *f.*
song *n.* chanson *f.*; chant *m.*; **–ster** *n.* chanteur *m.*; **–stress** *n.* chanteuse *f.*
Song of Songs Cantique des Cantiques *f.*
sonic *a.* sonique; — **boom** *n.* grondement sonique *m.*
son-in-law *n.* gendre *m.*
sonorous *a.* sonore
soon *adv.* bientôt, tôt, de bonne heure; **as** — **as** aussitôt que; **how** —? dans combien de temps?
soot *n.* suie *f.*; **–y** *a.* couvert de suie; fuligineux
soothe *vt.* flatter; apaiser
soothsayer *n.* devin *m.*
sop *n.* morceau trempé *m.*; (fig.) os à ronger; cadeau, présent *m.*; — *vt.* tremper; **–ping** *a.* trempé
sophisticated·*a.* sophistiqué, blasé
sophistication *n.* sophistication *f.*
sophomore *n.* étudiant universitaire de deuxième année *m.*
sophomoric *a.* jeune, inexpérimenté

soporific *n. & a.* soporifique *m.*
sorcerer *n.* sorcier *m.*
sorceress *n.* sorcière *f.*
sorcery *n.* sorcellerie *f.*, sortilège *m.*
sordid *a.* sordide
sore *n.* ulcère *m.*, plaie *f.*; — *a.* douloureux; écorché; violent; **–ness** *n.* mal *m.*; douleur *f.*; sensibilité *f.*
sorority *n.* société d'étudiantes˚ universitaires *f.*
sorrow *n.* chagrin *m.*, affliction, tristesse *f.*; — *vi.* être affligé; être en deuil; **–ful** *a.* triste, affligé; affligeant; **–fulness** *n.* chagrin *m.*, tristesse *f.*
sorry *a.* affligé; triste; fâché; désolé; **be** — regretter
sort *n.* sorte, espèce, classe, mantière *f.*, genve *m.*; — *vt.* séparer, classer, trier, assortir
so-so *a.* comme ci comme ça
sot *n.* sot, imbécile *m.*; ivrogne *m.*
soul *n.* âme *f.*, esprit *m.*; être *m.*; **–ful** *a.* plein d'émotion; plein d'âme
sound *n.* son, bruit *m.*; (med.) sonde *f.*; (geog.) goulet, détroit *m.*; — *a.* sain, bien portant, vigoureux; — **barrier** *n.* barrière du son *f.*; — **effect** effet sonore *m.*; — **track** piste sonore *f.*; — **truck** camion d'enregistrement *m.*; — **wave** onde sonore *f.*; — *vt. & vi.* sonner; (med.) sonder; **–ing** *n.* sondage *m.*; **–ing** *a.*, **–ing board** table d'harmonie *f.*; **–ing line** ligne de sonde *f.*; **–ness** *n.* solidité *f.*
soundproof *a.* insonore; — *vt.* insonoriser
soup *n.* soupe *f.*, potage *m.*; — **plate** assiette creuse; — **tureen** *n.* soupière *f.*
sour *a.* aigre; acide; — *vt.* rendre acide; aigrir; — *vi.* tourner; s'aigrir; **–ness** *n.* aigreur *f.*
south *n.* sud, midi *m.*; **–east** *n.* sud-est *m.*; **–ern** *a.* méridional, du sud; **–erner** *n.* méridional; **–land** *n.* midi *m.*; **–ward** *adv.* vers le sud; **–west** *n.* sud-ouest *m.*
sovereign *a.* souverain; **–ty** *n.* souveraineté *f.*
Soviet *n.* Soviet *m.*; — *a.* soviétique
sow *n.* truie *f.*; — *vt.* semer, ensemencer; **–er** *n.* semeur *m.*
soybean *n.* soya *m.*
spa *n.* ville d'eau *f.*
space *n.* espace *m.*; distance *f.* intervalle *m.*; — *vt.* espacer; — **capsule** *n.* astronef *m.*; — **fiction** *n.* fiction interplanétaire *f.*; **–r** *n.* (typewriter) barre d'espacement *f.*
spacious *a.* spacieux, vaste; **–ness** *n.* grandeur, immensité *f.*
spade *n.* bêche *f.*; (cards) pique *m.*; — *vt. & vi.* bêcher
Spain *n.* Espagne *f.*

span *n.* empan *m.*; portée, travée *f.*; durée *f.*; — *vt.* couvrir, traverser

spangle *n.* paillette *f.*

Spaniard *n.* Espagnol *m.*

Spanish *a. & n.* espagnol *m.*

spank *vt.* fesser; –**ing** *n.* fessée *f.*

spar *n.* espar *m.*; (geol.) spath *m.*; — *vi.* boxer

spare *vt. & vi.* épargner, ménager, traiter avec indulgence; — *a.* maigre; de rechange; disponible; — **parts** pièces de rechange *f. pl.*; — **time** loisir *m.*; — **tire** pneu de rechange *m.*

sparerib *n.* plat de côte *m.*

sparing *a.* rare; frugal; chiche

spark *n.* étincelle *f.*; — **plug** bougie *f.*

sparkle *n. & vt.* étinceler

sparkling *a.* étincelant; (drink) mousseux

sparse *a.* épars

Sparta *n.* Sparte *f.*; –**n** *a. & n.* spartiate *m. & f.*

spasm *n.* spasme *m.*; –**odic** *a.* spasmodique

spastic *a.* spasmodique, spastique

spat *n.* guêtre *f.*; (coll.) dispute *f.*; — *vi.* se disputer

spatial *a.* de l'espace

spatter *n.* éclaboussure *f.*; — *vt.* éclabousser

spatula *n.* spatule *f.*

spawn *n.* frai *m.*; — *vt. & vi.* frayer; engendrer

spay *vt.* châtrer

speak *vt. & vi.* parler, discourir; prononcer; — **out** lever la voix; — **up** parler plus haut; –**er** *n.* parleur, conférencier *m.*; (organization) président *m.*; (radio) haut-parleur *m.*

spear *n.* lance *f.*; harpon *m.*; épieu *m.*; — *vt.* percer à coups de lance; harponner

spearhead *n.* fer de lance *m.*; pointe *f.*; (mil.) point d'attaque *m.*

special *a.* spécial; particulier; — **delivery** par exprès; — **delivery letter** *n.* lettre exprès *f.*; –**ist** *n.* spécialiste *m. & f.*; –**ize** *vt.* spécialiser; –**ize** *vi.* se spécialiser; –**ty** *n.* spécialité *f.*

species *n.* espèce, sorte *f.*

specific *n. & a.* spécifique *m.*; — **gravity** *n.* poids spécifique *m.*; –**ation** *n.* spécification *f.*

specify *vt.* spécifier

specimen *n.* spécimen, modèle *m.*

specious *a.* spécieux

speck *n.* tache *f.*, point *m.*; — *vt.* tacher

speckle *n.* petite tache, bigarrure *f.*; — *vt.* tacheter, moucheter

spectacle *n.* spectacle *m.*; –**s** *pl.* lunettes *f. pl.*

spectacular *n.* représentation à grand spectacle; — *a.* spectaculaire

spectator *n.* spectateur *m.*

specter *n.* spectre *m.*, apparition *f.*

spectral *a.* spectral

spectroscope *n.* spectroscope *m.*

spectrum *n.* spectre *m.*

speculate *vi.* spéculer; jouer

speculation *n.* spéculation, méditation *f.*

speculator *n.* spéculateur *m.*

speech *n.* discours *m.*; langage *m.*, harangue *f.*; plaidoyer *m.*; **figure of** — *n.* figure de rhétorique *f.*; –**less** *a.* interdit; muet

speed *n.* vitesse *f.*; — **limit** vitesse maxima *f.*; — *vi.* se dépêcher; aller très vite; — *vt.* dépêcher, hâter; — **up** intensifier; presser; aller plus vite; –**y** *a.* rapide; hâtif

speedboat *n.* canot automobile *m.*; **vedette** *f.*; hors-bord *m.*

speedometer *n.* indicateur de vitesse *m.*; tachymètre *m.*

speed-up *n.* accélération *f.*

speedway *n.* piste d'autos *f.*

spell *n.* charme *m.*; sortilège *m.*; moment *m.*; attaque *f.*, accès *m.*, crise *f.*; — *vt.* épeler, orthographier; remplacer; –**er** *n.* livre d'orthographe *m.*; –**ing** *n.* orthographe *f.*; –**ing bee** concours d'orthographe *m.*

spellbound *a.* charmé, fasciné

spend *vt.* dépenser, employer; consommer; dissiper; épuiser; –**er** *n.* dépensier, dissipateur *m.*

spendthrift *n.* prodigue *m.*

spent *a.* épuisé; dépensé

sperm *n.* sperme *m.*

spermatozoa *n. pl.* spermatozoïdes *m. pl.*

sperm whale *n.* cachalot *m.*

spew *vt.* vomir

sphere *n.* sphère *f.*

spherical *a.* sphérique

spheroid *n.* sphéroïde *m.*

sphinx *n.* sphinx *m.*

spice *n.* épice *f.*; — *vt.* épicer

spick-and-span *a.* impeccable

spicy *a.* aromatique, épicé

spider *n.* araignée *f.*

spigot *n.* fausset *m.*; robinet *m.*

spike *n.* épi de blé *m.*; pointe *f.*; **long clou** *m.*, cheville *f.*; — *vt.* clouer

spill *vt.* répandre, renverser

spillway *n.* déversoir *m.*

spin *vt. & vi.* filer; faire tournoyer; — *n.* promenade en auto *f.*; –**ning** *n.* filature *f.*; –**ning jenny** jenny *f.*; –**ing mill** filature *f.*; –**ing wheel** rouet *m.*

spinach *n.* épinards *m. pl.*

spinal *a.* spinal; — **column** *n.* colonne vertébrale *f.*; — **cord** *n.* moelle épinière *f.*

spindle *n.* fuseau *m.*, broche *f.*; pivot *m.*

spine *n.* épine dorsale *f.*; (book) dos *m.*
spinet *n.* épinette *f.*
spinnaker *n.* foc de yacht *m.*
spinster *n.* vieille fille *f.*
spiny *a.* épineux
spiral *a.* spiral; en spirale; — *n.* spirale *f.*
spire *n.* aiguille, flèche (de clocher) *f.*
spirit *n.* esprit *m.*, âme *f.*; courage, feu *m.*; génie *m.*; fantôme *m.*; liqueur spiritueuse *f.*; in high —s joie *f.*, abandon *m.*; low — abattement *m.*; raise one's —s remonter le courage de quelqu'un; — lamp *n.* réchaud à alcool *m.*; — level *n.* niveau à bulle d'air *m.*; — *vt.* animer, encourager; — away enlever; —ed *a.* animé, vigoureux; —less *a.* inanimé; —ual *a.* spirituel; —ual *n.* (mus.) chant religieux populaire *m.*; —ualism *n.* spiritisme *m.*; —ualist *n.* spiritualiste *m.*
spit *n.* (rod) broche *f.*; salive *f.*; — *vt.* embrocher; cracher; —tle *n.* crachat *m.*; —toon *n.* crachoir *m.*
spite *n.* dépit *m.*, rancune *f.*; in — of en dépit de, malgré; — *vt.* contrarier; —ful *a.* malicieux, rancunier
spitfire *n.* mégère *f.*; (avi.) spitfire *m.*
splash *n.* éclaboussure *f.*; — *vt.* éclabousser
spleen *n.* rate *f.*; (fig.) spleen *m.*
splendid *a.* splendide; magnifique, brillant
splendor *n.* splendeur *f.*; éclat *m.*
splice *n.* jointure, soudure *f.*; (film) collure *f.*; — *vt.* joindre à onglet; (naut.) épisser
splint *n.* éclisse *f.*
splinter *n.* éclat (de bois) *m.*; — *vt.* briser, fendre; — *vi.* voler en éclats
split *n.* fente *f.*; querelle *f.*; division *f.*; (dance) grand écart *m.*; demi-bouteille *f.*; — *vt.* fendre, briser; — *vi.* se fendre; crever; —ting *n.* fendage *m.*; (atom) fissure *f.*; —ting *a.* écrasant
splotch *n.* tache *f.*; — *vt.* tacher
splurge *n.* faste, parade *f.*; — *vi.* faire parade; se payer une fête
splutter *vi.* bredouiller
spoil *n.* pillage *m.*; butin *m.*; dépouille *f.*; — *vt.* gâter, abîmer; — *vi.* se gâter; — for désirer; —er *n.* spoliateur *m.*; —age *n.* dégats *m. pl.*; choses gatées *f. pl.*
spoilsport *n.* trouble-fête *m.*
spoke *n.* rais, rayon *m.*
spokesman *n.* porte-parole *m.*
sponge *n.* éponge *f.*; — bath *n.* bain anglais *m.*; — cake (genre de) gâteau de Savoie *m.*; — *vt.* éponger; — *vi.* (coll.) vivre en parasite; —r *n.* pique-assiette *m.*
spongy *a.* spongieux
sponsor *n.* garant *m.*; parrain *m.*; marraine *f.*; (rad.) annonceur *m.*, commanditaire, patron; — *vt.* présenter; payer

les frais; —ship *n.* parrainage *m.*; patronage *m.*
spontaneity *n.* spontanéité *f.*
spontaneous *a.* spontané; —ly *adv.* spontanément; —ness *n.* spontanéité *f.*
spool *n.* rouleau *m.*; bobine *f.*; — *vt.* embobiner
spoon *n.* cuiller, cuillère *f.*; table— cuiller à bouche *f.*; tea— cuiller à café *f.*; — *vt.* prendre dans une cuiller; —ful *n.* cuillerée *f.*
sporadic *a.* sporadique
sport *n.* sport *m.*; divertissement, amusement, jeu *m.*; — *vt. & vi.* faire parade de; se divertir, badiner; —ing *a.* juste, équitable; —ing goods articles de sport *m. pl.*; —ive *a.* sportif; gai; — shirt *n.* chemise de sport *f.*
sportsman *n.* sportif *m.*; —ship *n.* attitude du sportif *f.*
spot *n.* tache *f.*; lieu *m.*, place *f.*; (ground) coin *m.*; (coll.) pétrin, mauvais pas *m.*; — *vt.* tacher; tacheter; (coll.) marquer; —less *a.* sans tache; —ted *a.* tacheté; —ty *a.* taché, inégal
spotlight *n.* projecteur intensif, spot *m.*
spot welding *n.* soudage par points *m.*
spouse *n.* époux *m.*, épouse *f.*
spout *n.* tuyau de décharge *m.*; jet *m.*; — *vi.* jaillir; — *vt.* faire jaillir; énoncer, dire, prononcer
sprain *n.* foulure, entorse *f.*; — *vt.* se fouler; se donner une entorse à
sprawl *vi.* s'étaler
spray *n.* écume *f.*; vapeur *f.*; rameau *m.*; — *vt. & vi.* vaporiser; couvrir d'écume; —er *n.* vaporisateur *m.*
spread *n.* étendue *f.*; rayonnement *m.*; (bed) dessus de lit, couvre-lit *m.*; collation *f.*; — *vt.* répandre, faire rayonner, vulgariser; — *vi.* se répandre, rayonner
sprig *n.* brin *m.*, brindille *f.*
sprightliness *n.* vivacité, gaieté *f.*, feu *m.*
sprightly *a.* vif, gai
spring *a. & n.* (season) printemps *m.*; (water) source *f.*; (mech.) ressort *m.*; (movement) élan, saut *m.*; — *vi.* s'élancer, bondir; — from naître de; —y *a.* élastique
springboard *n.* tremplin *m.*
springlike *a.* printanier
springtime *n.* printemps *m.*
sprinkle *vt. & vi.* asperger, arroser; (fig.) parsemer; — *n.* légère pluie *f.*; —r *n.* arroseur *m.*; arroseur automatique *m.*; pomme d'arrosage *f.*
sprinkling *n.* arrosage *m.*; petite quantité *f.*; connaissance superficielle *f.*, notions *f. pl.*
sprint *n.* course *f.*; sprint *m.*; — *vi.* cou-

rir à toute vitesse; **–er** n. coureur rapide m.

sprite n. esprit, fantôme m.

sprocket n. (mech.) dent f.; galet m.; **— wheel** roue dentée f.; pignon m.

sprout n. jet, rejeton m.; pousse f.; **Brussels –s** choux de Bruxelles m. pl.; **—** vi. germer, pousser

spruce vi., **— up** se faire beau; **—** a. pimpant; bien mis; **—** n. sapin m.

sprung a. déformé

spry a. vif, animé, actif; **–ness** n. activité, vivacité f.

spume n. écume f.; **—** vi. écumer, mousser

spun a. filé, en fil

spur n. éperon m.; aiguillon m.; ergot m.; stimulant m.; hâte f.; **on the — of the moment** à l'impromptu; **—** vt. éperonner, instiguer, inspirer

spurious a. faux, falsifié

spurn vt. mépriser, dédaigner

spurt n. jet, jaillissement; **—** vi. jaillir

sputter n. bredouillement m.; **—** vi. bredouiller, balbutier

sputum n. expectorations f. pl.

spy n. espion m., espionne f.; **—** vt. épier, espionner; **–glass** n. longue-vue f.

squab n. jeune pigeon m.

squabble n. querelle f.; bagarre f.; **—** vi. se chamailler

squad n. escouade f.; équipe f.; **rescue —** équipe de secours f.

squadron n. escadron m.; escadre f.

squalid a. sale, malpropre

squall n. cri alarmant m.; (weather) rafale f., coup de vent, grain m.; **—** vi. crier, brailler

squalor n. misère, saleté f.

squander vt. dissiper, gaspiller

square n. carré m.; équerre f.; place f.; **—** vt. & vi. carrer; régler, ajuster; **—** a. carré; convenable; conforme; balancé; juste, honnête; équitable; **— dance** quadrille américain m.; **— root** racine carrée f

squash n. courge, gourde f.; foule, presse f.; écrasement m.; (sport) jeu de paume m.; **—** vt. écraser

squat vi. s'accroupir, se tapir; **—** a. accroupi, blotti; **–ter** n. colon, squatter m.

squawk n. cri rauque m.; **—** vi. crier

squeak n. cri perçant m.; **—** vi. jeter des cris perçants; grincer; **–y** a. criard; (mech.) glapissant

squeal n. cri (du cochon) m.; **—** vi. (like a pig) crier; (coll.) manger le morceau, chanter

squeamish a. délicat; dégoûté; **–ness** n. délicatesse exagérée f.

squeegee n. essuie-glace m.; rouleau en

caoutchouc m.

squeeze n. compression f.; serrement m.; **—** vt. presser, serrer; **— out** exprimer; éliminer; **–r** n. presse f.; **lemon –r** presse-citrons m.

squelch n. réplique écrasante f.; **—** vt. écraser

squib n. (fig.) satire f.; bon mot m.

squint n. regard louche m.; **—** vi. loucher; cligner les yeux

squint-eyed a. louche

squire n. écuyer m.; propriétaire m.; cavalier m.; **—** vt. accompagner

squirm vi. se tortiller

squirt n. jet m.; **—** vt. jeter; **—** vi. jaillir

squirt gun n. seringue f.

stab n. coup de poignard m.; **make a — at** tenter, essayer; **—** vt. poignarder

stability n. stabilité, constance f.

stabilize vt. stabiliser; **—** vi. devenir stable; **–r** n. stabilisateur m.

stable n. étable, écurie f.; **—** vt. établer; **—** a. stable, fixe; constant, ferme

stack n. (hay) meule f.; (wood) pile f.; tas m.; **—** vt. entasser; mettre en meule

stadium n. stade m.

staff n. bâton m.; état-major m.; soutien m.; personnel m.; (mus.) portée f.

stag n. cerf m.; **— party** soirée pour hommes f.; **— go —** aller sans compagne

stage n. échafaudage m., estrade f.; théâtre m., scène f.; degré, état m.; relais m.; journée f.; voiture publique f.; **— box** n. avant-scène f.; **–coach** n. diligence f.; **— effect** n. effet scénique m.; **— fright** n. trac m.; **–hand** n. machiniste m. **— manager** n. régisseur m.; **— whisper** n. aparté m.; **—** vt. monter; mettre en scène

stagger vi. chanceler; hésiter, vaciller; **—** vt. ébranler, étonner; échelonner; **–ed** a. échelonné

staging n. mise en scène f.; échafaud m.; **— area** n. camp temporaire (avant l'embarquement) m.

stagnant a. stagnant; inactif

stagnate vi. être stagnant

stagy a. théâtral, artificiel

staid a. grave, posé; **–ness** n. gravité f.

stain n. tache, souillure f.; bonté f.; couleur f.; **—** vt. tacher; teindre; teinter; souiller; **–less** a. sans tache; qui ne se tache pas; **–less steel** n. acier inoxydible m.

stair n. marche d'un escalier f.; **–s** n. pl. escalier m.

staircase n. escalier m.

stairway n. cage d'escalier f.

stake n. poteau m.; enjeu m.; **—** vt. garnir de pieux; mettre en jeu; subventionner

stalactite *n.* stalactite *f.*
stalagmite *n.* stalagmite *f.*
stale *a.* vieux, usé, gâté; rassis; éventé; **–ness** *n.* vieillesse *f.*
stalk *n.* tige, queue *f.*; démarche fière *f.*; — *vi.* marcher fièrement; — *vt.* suivre à la piste
stallion *n.* étalon *m.*
stalwart *a.* vaillant, vigoureux
stamen *n.* étamine *f.*
stamina *n.* force, vigueur *f.*
stammer *vi.* bégayer, balbutier; **–er** *n.* bègue *m. & f.*
stamp *n.* poinçon, coin *m.*; empreinte, impression *f.*; cachet *m.*, estampe *f.*; trempe *f.*; **postage** — timbre (-poste) *m.*; — **pad** *n.* tampon *m.*; **revenue** — timbre fiscal *m.*; **rubber** — timbre en caoutchouc *m.*; — *vt.* frapper du pied; broyer; imprimer; timbrer; (mail) affranchir; — **out** éliminer
stampede *n.* ruée *f.*; (cattle) fuite (de bœufs) *f.*; sauve-qui-peut *m.*; — *vi.* fuir; se ruer; — *vt.* provoquer une fuite, effaroucher
stance *n.* attitude *f.*
stanch, staunch *vt.* étancher; — *a.* solide; ferme; sûr
stand *n.* station *f.*; place *f.*; délai *m.*; pause, halte *f.*; résistance *f.*; embarras *m.*; guéridon *m.*, console *f.*, étalage *m.*; stand *m.*; **–s** *pl.* tribune *f.*; — *vi.* se lever; se mettre debout; rester debout; être debout; résister; supporter; — **aside** se tenir à l'écart; — **back** reculer; — **by** se tenir à l'écart; soutenir; se tenir prêt; attendre; — **for** signifier; tolérer; supporter; — **in for** remplacer; — **off** se tenir à l'écart; repousser; — **on** insister sur; — **out** se détacher; — **still** se tenir tranquille; ne pas bouger; — **to** courir le risque de; avoir des chances de; — **up** se lever, se mettre debout; — **up against** opposer; combattre; — **up for** défendre, soutenir, appuyer; **–ing** *n.* position *f.*; durée *f.*; **–ing** *a.* debout; permanent; **–ing room** place debout *f.*; promenoir *m.*
standard *n.* étendard *m.*; pavillon *m.*; étalon *m.*; titre *m.*; modèle *m.*; type *m.*; mesure *f.*; **gold** — étalon d'or *m.*; — **of living** niveau de la vie *m.*; — *a.* normal, ordinaire; classique; — **time** heure normale *f.*; — **works** classiques *m. pl.*; **–ization** *n.* standardisation *f.*; **–ize** *vt.* standardiser
standard-bearer *n.* porte-drapeau, enseigne *m.*; porte-étendard *m.*
stand-by *n.* service de secours *m.*; suppléant *m.*; adjoint *m.*

stand-in *n.* (movies) remplaçant *m.*
standpoint *n.* point d'arrêt *m.*
standstill *n.* point mort *m.*; affaire nulle *f.*
stanza *n.* strophe *f.*
staple *n.* denrée *f.*; matière première *f.*; crampon *m.*; — *a.* établi; principal; — *vt.* fixer (avec des crampons); **–r** *n.* brocheuse *f.*
star *n.* étoile *f.*; astre *m.*; (type) astérisque *m.*; (theat.) vedette *f.*; **shooting** — étoile filante *f.*; — *vt.* étoiler; parsemer; présenter comme vedette; — *vi.* apparaître comme vedette; **–less** *a.* sans étoiles; **–let** *n.* (movies) starlette, starlet *f.*; **–ry** étoilé; brillant
starboard *n.* tribord *m.*
starch *n.* empois *m.*; amidon *m.*; — *vt.* empeser
star-chamber *a.* clandestin
stare *n.* regard fixe *m.*; — *vi.* regarder fixement
stark *a. & adv.* fort; vrai, pur; tout-à-fait
starlight *n.* lumière des étoiles *f.*
starlit *a.* étoilé
star-spangled *a.* étoilé, parsemé d'étoiles
start *n.* tressaillement *m.*; saut *m.*; élan *m.*; premier pas *m.*; commencement *m.*; début *m.*; — *vi.* tressaillir; — *vt.* commencer, débuter; se mettre à; se mettre en route; — **out** se mettre en route; **–er** *n.* (auto) démarreur *m.*; **–ing point** *n.* point de départ *m.*
starting gate, starting post *n.* barrière *f.*
startle *vt.* effrayer; faire tressaillir, étonner
startling *a.* étonnant
starvation *n.* inanition *f.*; faim *f.*
starve *vt.* faire mourir de faim, affamer; — *vi.* mourir de faim
state *n.* état *m.*, condition *f.*; rang *m.*, dignité, pompe *f.*; — *vt.* établir, régler; constater, détailler; déclarer; — **house** *n.* parlement *m.*; **–liness** *n.* grandeur *f.*; **–ment** *n.* déclaration *f.*; procès-verbal *m.*; (com.) relevé de compte *m.*
statecraft *n.* politique *f.*
stateroom *n.* cabine *f.*
statesman *n.* homme d'état *m.*; **–ship** *n.* politique *f.*, art de gouverner *m.*
static *n.* (rad.) parasites *m. pl.*; **–s** *n.* statique *f.*; — *a.* statique
station *n.* situation, position, condition *f.*; poste *m.*, place *f.*, emploi *m.*; état, rang *m.*; (rail.) gare *f.*; — **house, police** — commissariat de police *m.*; — *vt.* poster, placer
station agent *n.* chef de gare *m.*
stationary *a.* stationnaire, fixe
stationer *n.* papetier, marchand de papier *m.*; libraire *m.*; **–'s** *n.* papeterie, librairie *f.*; **–y** *n.* papeterie *f.*

Stations of the Cross n. calvaire m.

statistic n. statistique f.; **–s** pl. statistique f.; **–al** a. statistique; **–ian** n. statisticien m.

statuary n. (sculptor) statuaire m.; (statues) statuaire f.

statue n. statue f.

statuesque a. de statue; comme une statue

statuette n. statuette f.

stature n. stature, taille f.

status n. condition f.; rang m.; **— quo** n. statu quo m.

statute n. statut m., loi f.

statutory a. conforme à la loi; défini par la loi

staunch, stanch a. loyal, sûr; **–ness** n. loyauté, fidélité, force f.

stave n. douve f.; (mus.) portée f.; **— vi., — in** défoncer; **— off** écarter, différer

stay n. séjour m.; soutien m.; **–s** n. pl. corset m. pl.; **— vt.** arrêter, empêcher; **main — (fig.)** principal soutien m.; **— vi.** rester, demeurer, s'arrêter; attendre, rester immobile; **— up** rester en haut; veiller

stay-at-home n. casanier m.

stead n. place f., lieu m.

steadfast a. stable, fixe; constant; **–ness** n. fermeté, constance f.

steadily adv. fermement; régulièrement

steadiness n. fermeté f.; régularité f.

steady vt. affermir, assurer; **— a.** ferme, solide

steak n. bifteck, steak m.

steal n. vol m.; **— vt.** voler; **— vi.** s'échapper; aller doucement, se glisser, aller à la dérobée

stealth n. action clandestine f.; **by —** à la dérobée; **–ily** adv. clandestinement; **–y** a. furtif

steam n. vapeur f.; **— engine** n. machine à vapeur f., locomotive f.; **— (pressure) cooker** n. marmite à vapeur f.; **— vi.** fumer; naviguer à la vapeur; **— vt.** (cooking) cuire à la vapeur

steamboat n. vapeur, paquebot m.

steampipe n. tuyau à vapeur m.

steam roller n. rouleau à vapeur m.

steamship n. vapeur, paquebot m.

steam shovel n. excavateur à vapeur m.

steed n. coursier, cheval m.

steel n. acier m.; **— a.** d'acier; **— mill** n. aciérie f.; **— wool** n. paille de fer, paille d'acier f.; **— vt.** endurcir; **–works** n. aciérie f.; **–y** a. d'acier

steep vt. tremper, infuser; **— a.** escarpé; raide; **–ness** n. raideur, pente f., escarpement m.

steeple n. clocher m.

steeple jack n. ouvrier qui monte sur les clochers m.

steer vt. gouverner, diriger; conduire; **— n.** bœuf m.; **–age** n. (boat) dernière classe f.; **–ing** a. de direction; **–ing wheel** n. volant m.

steersman n. timonier m.

stein n. chope f.

stellar a. stellaire

stem n. tronc m.; tige, queue f.; pédoncule m.; race f.; **— vt.** opposer, arrêter

stench n. puanteur f.

stencil n. pochoir m.; (duplicating machine) stencil m.; **— vt.** marquer au pochoir

stenographer n. sténographe m. & f.

stenotype, stenotyping n. sténotypie f.

stentorian a. de stentor

step n. pas m., marche f.; échelon m.; marche pied m.; **— vi.** faire un pas, marcher; **— se** mettre à l'écart; **— in** entrer; **— out** sortir; **— up** s'approcher; monter; augmenter

stepbrother n. beau-frère m.

stepchild n. beau-fils m., belle-fille f.

stepdaughter n. belle-fille f.

stepfather n. beau-père m.

stepladder n. échelle double f.; marche-pied m.

stepmother n. belle-mère f.

steppe n. steppe m.

steppingstone n. marchepied m.; moyen de parvenir m.

stepsister n. belle-sœur f.

stepson n. beau-fils m.

stereophonic a. stéréophonique

stereoscope n. stéréoscope m.

stereotype n. cliché m.; **— vt.** stéréotyper; **— a.** stéréotype m.

sterile a. stérile

sterility n. stérilité f.

sterilization n. stérilisation f.

sterilize vt. stériliser; **–r** n. stérilisateur m.

sterling a. sterling; vrai, véritable; honnête

stern n. poupe f.; **— a.** sévère; austère; rude; **–ness** n. sévérité f.

sternum n. sternum m.

stethoscope n. stéthoscope m.

stevedore n. arrimeur m.

stew n. étuvée, estouffade f., ragoût m.; compote f.; **— vt.** cuire à l'étuvée

steward n. intendant, économe, maître d'hôtel m.; **–ess** n. (boat) femme de chambre de bord f.; (avi.) hôtesse f.

stick n. bâton m.; canne f.; **— vt.** coller, fixer; percer; **— vi.** être collé, s'attacher; **— se** mettre à l'écart; **— to** persévérer dans; **— up** (coll.) voler à main armée; **— up for** défendre; **–er** n. vignette (à coller) f.; **–y** a. collant

stickler *n.* personne meticuleuse *f.*; colle *f.*, problème difficile *m.*

stickpin *n.* épingle à cravate *f.*

stiff *a.* raide; obstiné; gêné, affecté; empesé; — **neck** *n.* torticolis *m.*; **-en** *vt.* raidir; **-en** *vi.* se raidir; **-ness** *n.* raideur *f.*

stifle *vt.* étouffer

stifling *a.* étouffant

stigma *n.* stigmate *m.*; flétrissure *f.*; **-tize** *vt.* stigmatiser

stiletto *n.* poinçon *m.*; stylet *m.*

still *n.* silence *m.*; alambic *m.*; (movies) photographie vue fixe *f.*; — *a.* tranquille, calme; — **life** nature morte *f.*; — *adv.* encore, toujours; — *vt.* calmer, apaiser; distiller

stillborn *a.* mort-né

stilted *a.* ampoulé; gauche

stilts *n.* échasses *f. pl.*

stimulant *n. & a.* stimulant *m.*

stimulate *vt.* stimuler, piquer

stimulation *n.* stimulation *f.*

stimulus *n.* stimulant *m.*; aiguillon *m.*

sting *n.* piqûre *f.*; remords *m.*; aiguillon *m.*; — **ray** raie, torpille *f.*; — *vt.* piquer; mordre; **-er** *n.* (insects) aiguillon, dard *m.*; **-ing** *a.* piquant, mordant

stinginess *n.* mesquinerie *f.*

stingy *a.* chiche, avare, mesquin

stink *n.* puanteur *f.*; — *vi.* puer; **-er** *n.* (coll.) cochon, chameau *m.*

stint *n.* limite, restreinte *f.*; tache *f.*, travail du jour *m.*; — *vt. & vi.* restreindre, être parcimonieux

stipend *n.* salaire *m.*, appointements *m. pl.*

stipple *vt.* pointiller

stipulate *vi.* stipuler

stipulation *n.* stipulation *f.*

stir *n.* tumulte *m.*, agitation *f.*; — *vt.* remuer, agiter; inciter, animer; faire naître, provoquer; — *vi.* se remuer, se révolter; apparaître; — **up** fomenter; **-ring** *a.* émouvant

stirrup *n.* étrier *m.*

stitch *n.* point *m.*; maille *f.*; (med.) agrafe *f.*; — *vt.* piquer; coudre; brocher; — **up** recoudre, faire un point à

stock *n.* tronc *m.*; bloc *m.*; famille, race *f.*; assortiment *m.*; (cattle) bétail *m.*; (com.) actions *f. pl.*; (bot.) matthiole *f.*; (punishment) pilori *m.*; (inventory) stock, matériel, inventaire *m.*; (theat.) répertoire *m.*; **laughing** — risée *f.*; **exchange** bourse *f.*; — *a.* classique, banal, d'usage; — *vt.* emmagasiner, garder, tenir; — **up on** s'approvisionner de; **-y** *a.* trapu

stockade *n.* palissade *f.*

stockbroker *n.* agent de change *m.*

stockholder *n.* actionnaire *m. & f.*

stocking *n.* bas *m.*; chaussette *f.*

stockpile *n.* dépôt *m.*; provision *f.*; réserve *f.*; — *vt.* emmagasiner

stockyard *n.* parc à bestiaux *m.*; abattoir *m.*

stodgy *a.* fade; lourd; trapu

stoic *n. & a.* stoïcien *m.*; **-al** *a.* stoïque; **-ism** *n.* stoïcisme *m.*

stoke *vt.* garnir, alimenter; chauffer; **-er** *n.* chauffeur *m.*

stole *n.* étole *f.*

stolid *a.* lourd; flegmatique; **-ness** *n.* flegme *m.*

stomach *n.* estomac *m.*; cœur *m.*; envie *f.*; **turn the** — donner mal au cœur; — *vt.* supporter

stone *n.* pierre *f.*; caillou *m.*; (seed) pépin, noyau *m.*; — *a.* de pierre; — *adv.*, — **dead** raide-mort; — **deaf** complètement sourd; — *vt.* lapider; ôter les pépins (de)

stonecutter *n.* tailleur de pierre(s) *m.*

stonemason *n.* maçon *m.*; **-ry** *n.* maçonnerie *f.*

stoneware *n.* grès *m.*

stonework *n.* ouvrage en pierre *m.*; maçonnerie *f.*

stony *a.* pierreux

stool *n.* tabouret *m.*; (med.) selle *f.*; — **pigeon** *n.* (coll.) mouchard *m.*

stoop *n.* inclination *f.*; abaissement *m.*; (arch.) perron *m.*; — *vi.* s'incliner, se baisser

stop *n.* pause *f.*; arrêt *m.*, halte *f.*; obstacle *m.*; (organ) jeu *m.*; (phot.) ouverture du diaphragme *f.*; — **signal** (street) feu rouge *m.*; (auto.) feu stop, signal de freinage *m.*; — *vt.* arrêter, faire cesser; boucher; — *vi.* s'arrêter, cesser; — **in** venir voir, faire visite; — **off**, — **over** interrompre son voyage; **-page** *n.* cessation *f.*; panne *f.*; **-per** *n.* bouchon *m.*; **-per** *vt.* boucher; **-ping** *n.* arrêt *m.*

stopgap *a.* temporaire, provisoire

stop light *n.* feu rouge *m.*; (auto.) feu stop, signal de freinage *m.*

stopover *n.* halte *f.*, séjour *m.*

stop watch *n.* chronographe, compte-secondes *m.*

storage *n.* entreposage, emmagasinage *m.*; frais d'entrepôt *m. pl.*; — **battery** *n.* accumulateur *m.*

store *n.* magasin, dépôt *m.*; quantité *f.*; provisions *f. pl.*; **department** — grand magasin *m.*; **in** —, à venir; en réserve; **set** — **by** faire grand cas de; — *vt.* emmaganiser, mettre en dépôt

storehouse *n.* dépôt, magasin *m.*

storekeeper *n.* commerçant, boutiquier *m.*

storeroom *n.* magasin *m.*, réserve *f.*
storied *a.* historié
storm *n.* orage *m.*, tempête *f.*; assaut *m.*; — **coat** *n.* pardessus d'hiver avec col de fourrure *m.*; — **troops** troupes d'assaut *f. pl.*; — **window** contre-fenêtre *f.*; fenêtre extérieure utilisée en hiver *f.*; — *vi.* tempêter; — *vt.* assaillir; **-ing** *n.* assaut *m.*; **-y** *a.* orageux, violent
story *n.* histoire *f.*; récit *m.*; conte *m.*; fable *f.*; mensonge *m.*; (arch.) étage *m.*; **short** — nouvelle *f.*, conte *m.*
storyteller *n.* conteur, raconteur *m.*
stout *a.* fort; résolu; gros; corpulent; — *n.* stout *m*, bière noire anglaise *f.*; **-ness** *n.* embonpoint *m.*
stouthearted *a.* brave, résolu
stove *n.* poêle *m.*; (range) cuisinière *f.*
stovepipe *n.* tuyau de poêle *m.*
stow *vt.* serrer, entasser; (naut.) arrimer; — **away** serrer; s'embarquer en cachette
stowaway *n.* passager clandestin *m.*
straddle *vi.* écarter les jambes; marcher les jambes écartées; être à califourchon; — *vt.* être à califourchon (sur); ne pas prendre parti (sur)
straggle *vi.* rester en arrière; **-r** *n.* traînard *m.*
straight *a.* droit; direct; franc; honnête, sincere; (beverage) sec; — *adv.* directement; droit; **-way** *adv.* tout de suite; **-en** *vt.* redresser; ranger; **-en up** ranger; se tenir droit; **-ness** droiture *f.*; rectitude *f.*; franchise *f.*
straightforward *a.* franc, honnête, sincère; loyal
straightway *adv.* tout de suite, sur-le-champ
strain *n.* effort *m.*; tension *f.*; (med.) entorse *f.*; manière *f.*; style *m.*; trace *f.*; (music) mélodie *f.*; — *vt.* tendre; filtrer; serrer, forcer; se fouler; — *vi.* s'efforcer; **-er** *n.* passoire *f.*
strait *n.* détroit *m.*; défilé *m.*; gorge *f.*; embarras *m.*; — *a.* étroit; sévère, pénible; **-en** *vt.* resserrer
strait-laced *a.* sévère; prude
strait jacket *n.* camisole de force *f.*
strand *n.* côte *f.*, rivage *m.*; grève *f.*; fil *m.*, fibre *f.*; brin *m.*; — *vt. & vi.* échouer
strange *a.* singulier; étrange; étranger; inconnu; **-ness** *n.* étrangeté, singularité *f.*; **-r** *n.* étranger *m.*; inconnu *m.*
strangle *vt.* étrangler
strangle hold *n.* prise de cou *f.*; prise inébranlable *f.*
strangulate *vt.* étrangler
strangulation *n.* étranglement *m.*
strap *n.* sangle, courroie, bretelle *f.*; — *vt.* attacher, lier, boucler; **-ping** *a.* solide,

bien découplé
stratagem *n.* strategème, artifice *m.*
strategic *a.* stratégique
strategist *n.* stratégiste *m.*
strategy *n.* stratégie *f.*
stratify *vt.* stratifier
stratosphere *n.* stratosphère *f.*
stratum *n.* couche *f.*; strate *f.*
straw *n.* paille *f.*; last — comble *m.*; — **vote** vote non-officiel qui s'informe de l'opinion publique *m.*
strawberry *n.* fraise *f.*; — **bed** *n.* fraisière *f.*
stray *n.* bête épave *f.*; bête égarée *f.*; — *a.* égaré; — *vi.* s'égarer
streak *n.* raie, bande *f.*; filet *m.*; — *vt.* rayer, bigarrer; **-y** *a.* rayé, bariolé
stream *n.* courant, torrent *m.*; ruisseau *m.*; rivière *f.*; flot *m.*; jet *m.*; — *vi.* couler, ruisseler; briller; **-er** *n.* banderole *f.*; serpentin *m.*
streamline *vt.* donner un profil aérodynamique à; caréner; moderniser; **-d** *a.* à profil aérodynamique; moderne
street *n.* rue *f.*; — **floor** rez-de-chaussée *m.*
streetcar *n.* tramway *m.*
street sweeper *n.* balayeur *m.*; (machine) balayeuse *f.*
streetwalker *n.* fille publique *f.*
strength *n.* force *f.*; résistance *f.*; forces *f. pl.*; solidité *f.*; **at full** — au complet; **-en** *vt.* fortifier; — *vi.* se fortifier
strenuous *a.* ardu; énergique; **-ness** *n.* ardeur *f.*
streptococcus *n.* streptocoque *m.*
streptomycin *n.* streptomycine *f.*
stress *n.* importance *f.*; violence *f.*; effort *m.*; accent tonique *m.*; — *vt.* souligner; accentuer; appuyer sur
stretch *n.* étendue *f.*; tension *f.*; **at a** — d'arrache-pied; — *vt.* étendre, élargir, allonger; exagérer; — *vi.* s'étendre, s'élargir, se déployer; **-er** *n.* (med.) brancard *m.*; **-ing** *n.* tension *f.*; allongement *m.* forcer
strew *vt.* parsemer, répandre çà et là; joncher
striated *a.* strié
stricken *a.* atteint; rayé
strict *a.* strict; exact; formel; sévère, rigoureux; **-ly** *adv.* rigoureusement, strictement; formellement; absolument; **-ness** *n.* sévérité, rigueur *f.*; exactitude *f.*; **-ure** *n.* contraction *f.*
stride *n.* enjambée *f.*; pas *m.*; — *vi.* marcher à grands pas
stridency *n.* stridence *f.*
strident *a.* strident
strife *n.* lutte *f.*; contestation *f.*; différend *m.*
strike *n.* grève *f.*; (geol.) découverte

(d'un gisement) *f.*; — *vt.* frapper, heurter, battre; rencontrer, tomber sur; affliger; étonner, épouvanter; lancer, jeter, pousser; choquer, imprimer, graver; marquer; faire; — **a bargain** conclure un marché; — **a match** frotter une allumette; — *vi.* se mettre en grève, (labor) faire la grève, être en grève; — **out** partir, se lancer; — **up** se faire; commencer; **-r** *n.* gréviste *m. & f.*

strikebreaker *n.* (labor) briseur de grève *m.*

striking *a.* frappant

string *n.* corde *f.*, cordon *m.*, ficelle, attache *f.*, fil *m.*; fibre *f.*, tendon, filament *m.*; suite *f.*; — **bean** haricot vert *m.*; — *vt.* mettre des cordes à; corder; bander; enfiler; — **along** (coll.) ménager; accepter (l'avis d'un autre); — **up** pendre; **-ed** *a.* à cordes; **-y** *a.* fibreux

stringency *n.* sévérité, rigueur *f.*

stringent *a.* fort, rigoureux

strip *n.* bande *f.*, ruban *m.*; — *vt.* dépouiller; déshabiller; dégarnir

stripe *n.* raie *f.*; barre *f.*; type *m.*, trempe, sorte *f.*; (mil.) chevron, galon *m.*; — *vt.* rayer; **-d** *a.* rayé, à raies

stripling *n.* jeune homme *m.*; débutant *m.*

strive *vi.* s'efforcer (de), tâcher (de); combattre; lutter

striving *n.* effort *m.*; lutte *f.*

stroke *n.* coup *m.*; trait de plume *m.*; (med.) attaque d'apoplexie *f.*; (swimming) brassée *f.*; — **of luck** coup de veine *m.*; **on the** — **of** à l'heure sonnante; — *vt.* caresser

stroll *n.* promenade *f.*; — *vi.* se promener; **-er** *n.* promeneur *m.*; voiture d'enfant *f.*; **-ing** *a.* ambulant

strong *a.* fort; vigoureux, robuste; puissant, énergique; solide, ferme; impétueux

strongbox *n.* coffre-fort *m.*

stronghold *n.* place forte *f.*

strontium *n.* strontium *m.*

strop *n.* cuir à repasser *m.*; — *vt.* repasser sur le cuir

structural *a.* de structure, structural

structure *n.* construction *f.*; édifice *m.*; structure *f.*

struggle *n.* combat *m.*, lutte *f.*; — *vi.* s'efforcer (de), se débattre, lutter (contre)

struggling *a.* pauvre; débutant

strum *vt.* gratter

strut *n.* démarche fière *f.*; (arch.) entretoise *f.*; — *vi.* se pavaner; — *vt.* entretoiser

strychnine *n.* strychnine *f.*

stub *n.* tronc, tronçon, chicot *m.*; (cigarette) mégot *m.*; (ticket) volet *m.* sou-

che *f.* — *vt.* cogner; **-by** *a.* trapu, court

stubble *n.* chaume *f.*; poils de la barbe *m. pl.*

stubbly *a.* couvert de chaume; non-rasé

stubborn *a.* obstiné; entêté, têtu; tenace; **-ness** *n.* obstination *f.*, entêtement *m.*

stucco *n.* stuc *m.*

stuck *a.* coincé, collé

stud *n.* clou *m.*; bouton de plastron *m.*; (arch.) montant *m.*; — **farm** haras *m.*; — **horse** étalon *m.*; — *vt.* clouter, couvrir de clous; couvrir; **-ded** *a.* parsemé, constellé; **-ding** *n.* lattis *m.*

student *n.* étudiant *m.*

studied *a.* étudié, savant; recherché, voulu

studio *n.* atelier, studio *m.*

studious *a.* studieux; diligent

study *n.* étude *f.*; attention *f.*; méditation *f.*; cabinet *m.*; — *vt.* étudier; faire des études de

stuff *n.* matière, étoffe *f.*; (coll.) choses *f. pl.*, machins, ettrucs, rebuts *m. pl.*, — *vt.* fourrer; empailler; (cram) bourrer; (crowd) encombrer; (cooking) farcir; **-ing** *n.* empaillage *m.*; (cooking) farce *f.*; **-y** *a.* moisi, mal aéré; lourd; fastidieux, affecté

stultify *vt.* rendre ridicule; rendre inutile

stumble *n.* faux pas *m.*; — *vi.* trébucher, faire un faux pas; — **on** trouver par accident

stumbling block *n.* pierre d'achoppement *f.*

stump *n.* tronc, tronçon, bout, chicot *m.*; moignon *m.*; (coll.) estrade *f.*; — *vi.* marcher lourdement; faire une tournée de conférences en faveur de quelque chose; — *vt.* laisser sans réponse, maîtriser, triompher de

stun *vt.* étourdir, abasourdir; **-ning** *a.* ravissant; accablant

stunt *n.* tour *m.*, acrobatie *f.*; — *vt.* empêcher de croître; rabougrir; — *vi.* faire des acrobaties

stupefaction *n.* stupéfaction *f.*; stupeur *f.*

stupefy *vt.* hébéter, stupéfier

stupendous *a.* prodigieux, étonnant

stupid *a.* stupide; bête; **-ity** *n.* stupidité *f.*; bêtise, niaiserie *f.*

stupor *n.* stupeur *f.*

sturdiness *n.* force, vigueur, hardiesse *f.*

sturdy *a.* vigoureux, fort, robuste

stutter *vi. & vt.* bégayer, bredouiller; — *n.* bégaiement *m.*; **-er** *n.* bègue *m. & f.*; **-ing** *n.* bégaiement *m.*

sty *n.* étable à cochons *f.*; (med.) orgelet *m.*

style *n.* style *m.*; goût, genre *m.*; manière, façon *f.*; modèle *m.*; chic *m.*, élégance *f.*;

— *vt.* appeler; donner le titre de; dessiner

stylish *a.* de bon ton; élégant; **—ness** *n.* chic, ton *m.*, élégance *f.*

stylist *n.* styliste *m.*; **—ic** *n.* stylistique *f.*

stylize *vt.* styliser

stylus *n.* style *m.*

styptic *a.* hémostitique

suave *a.* suave

suavity *n.* suavité, douceur *f.*

subcommittee *n.* sous-commission *f.*, sous-comité *m.*

subconscious *a. & n.* subconscient *m.*

subcontract *vt.* sous-traiter; — *n.* soustraite *m.*; **—or** *n.* sous-entrepreneur *m.*

subcutaneous *a.* sous-cutané

subdivide *vt.* subdiviser

subdivision *n.* subdivision *f.*

subdue *vt.* subjuguer; vaincre; dompter; amortir; atténuer

subhead, subheading *n.* sous-titre *m.*

subject *n.* sujet *m.*; — *vt.* subjuguer, exposer; — *a.* sujet, soumis à; **—ion** *n.* sujétion *f.*; soumission *f.*; **—ive** *a.* subjectif

subjugate *vt.* subjuguer, assujettir

subjugation *n.* subjugation *f.*, assujettissement *m.*

subjunctive *a. & n.* subjonctif *m.*

sublease, sublet *vt.* sous-louer

sublimate *n. & a.* sublimé *m.*; — *vt.* sublimer

sublimity *n.* sublimité *f.*

submarine *n. & a.* sous-marin *m.*

submerge *vt.* submerger; plonger

submersion *n.* submersion *f.*; plongée *f.*

submission *n.* soumission *f.*; résignation *f.*

submissive *a.* soumis (à); **—ness** *n.* soumission *f.*

submit *vt.* soumettre; — *vi.* se soumettre

subnormal *a.* inférieur à la normale

subordinate *vt.* subordonner, soumettre; — *n. & a.* subordonné *m.*

subpoena *n.* assignation, citation *f.*; — *vt.* citer (à comparaître en justice)

subscribe *vt.* souscrire; s'abonner; consentir; **-r** *n.* abonné *m.*

subscription *n.* souscription *f.*; abonnement *m.*; cotisation *f.*

subsequent *a.* subséquent, suivant, qui suit; ultérieur

subservience *n.* utilité *f.*; subordination *f.*; dépendance *f.*; servilité *f.*

subservient *a.* subordonné; utile

subside *vi.* baisser; se calmer, s'apaiser

subsidiary *n. & a.* auxiliaire *m.*; subsidiaire *m.*; filiale *f.*

subsidize *vt.* subventionner

subsidy *n.* subvention *f.*

subsist *vi.* subsister, exister; **-ence** *n.* subsistence, existence *f.*; allocation *f.*

subsoil *n.* sous-sol *m.*

substance *n.* substance, matière *f.*; essentiel, *m.* corps *m.*; réalité *f.*; fortune *f.*

substantial *a.* substantiel; essentiel; réel; matériel, fort; solide

substantiate *vt.* établir; prouver par des faits

substantive *n.* substantif *m.*

substation *n.* sous-station *f.*

substitute *vt.* substituer; remplacer, suppléer, — *vi.* être substitué — *n.* remplaçant, suppléant *m.*; factice *m.*

substitution *n.* substitution *f.*; remplacement *m.*

substratum *n.* couche inférieure *f.*

substructure *n.* substructure *f.*

subterfuge *n.* subterfuge, faux-fuyant *m.*

subterranean *a.* souterrain

subtitle *n.* sous-titre *m.*

subtle *a.* subtil; fin; **—ty** *n.* subtilité *f.*; finesse *f.*

subtly *adv.* subtilement; avec finesse

subtract *vt.* soustraire; **—ion** *n.* soustraction *f.*

suburb *n.* ville de la banlieue *f.*, faubourg *m.*; **—an** *a.* faubourien, banlieusard; **—anite** *n.* banlieusard, faubourien *m.*; **—ia** *n.* banlieue *f.*

subvention *n.* subvention *f.*; — *vt.* subventionner

subversion *n.* subversion *f.*, renversement *m.*

subversive *a.* subversif

subvert *vt.* subvertir

subway *n.* passage souterrain *m.*; (rail.) métro *m.*

succeed *vt.* succéder; suivre; — *vi.* réussir, parvenir, arriver

success *n.* succès *m.*; réussite *f.*; **—ful** *a.* prospère, heureux, qui a du succès; **—ion** *n.* succession *f.*; héritage *m.*; suite, série *f.*; **in** **—ion** de suite; consécutif, successif **—ive** *a.* successif; **—or** *n.* successeur *m.*

succinct *a.* concis; succinct

succor *n.* secours *m.*, aide *f.*; — *vt.* secourir, aider, assister, seconder

succumb *vi.* succomber

such *a.* tel; pareil, semblable; de la sorte; — *pron.* ceux; tel; — **as** *prep.* tel que

suck *n.* action de sucer *f.*; — *vt. & vi.* sucer; téter; **-er** *n.* (candy) sucette *f.*; (fish) rémora *m.*; (animal) suçoir; (octopus) ventouse *f.*; (bot.) drageon *m.*; (coll.) nigaud, innocent *m.*

suckle *vt.* allaiter

suckling *n.* nourrisson *m.*; — **pig** cochon de lait *m.*

sucrose *n.* saccharose *m.*

suction *n.* aspiration *f.*; — **pump** pompe

aspirante *f.*
Sudan *n.* Soudan *m.*
sudden *a.* brusque; soudain, subit; **all of a** — tout à coup; brusquement; **-ly** *adv.* soudainement, soudain; tout à coup; brusquement; **-ness** *n.* brusquerie *f.*; rapidité *f.*
suds *n.* mousse de savon *f.*
sue *vt.* poursuivre en justice; supplier, implorer; demander
suede *n.* suède *m.*
suet *n.* suif *m.*
Suez *n.*, — **Canal** Canal de Suez *m.*
suffer *vt.* souffrir; essuyer, subir; supporter; permettre; — *vi.* souffrir; **-ance** *n.* tolérance *f.*; **-ing** *a.* souffrant; **-ing** *n.* souffrance *f.*
suffice *vi.* suffire; — *vt.* suffire à
sufficiency *n.* suffisance *f.*
sufficient *a.* suffisant; **-ly** *adv.* suffisamment, assez
suffix *n.* suffixe *m.*
suffocate *vt. & vi.* suffoquer, étouffer
suffocation *n.* étouffement *m.*
suffuse *vt.* répandre, remplir
suffusion *n.* suffusion *f.*; épanchement *m.*
sugar *n.* sucre *m.*; **beet** — sucre de betterave *m.*; **brown** — sucre brut *m.*; **cane** — sucre de canne *m.*; **granulated** — sucre en poudre *m.*; **lump** — sucre en morceaux *m.*; **powdered** — sucre de confiseur *m.*; — **beet** betterave à sucre *f.*; — **bowl** sucrier *m.*; — **cane** canne à sucre *f.*; — **mill** moulin à cannes *m.*; — *vt.* sucrer; saupoudrer de sucre; **-y** *a.* sucré
suggest *vt.* suggérer, insinuer, inspirer; **-ion** *n.* suggestion *f.*; **-ive** *a.* suggestif; évocateur
suicide *n.* suicide *m.*; **commit** — se suicider
suit *n.* (men's) complet *m.*; (women's) tailleur *m.*; costume *m.*; (request) requête *f.*; (law) procès *m.*; (cards) couleur *f.*; — *vt.* convenir à; aller à; **-ability** *n.* convenance *f.*; conformité *f.*; **-able** *a.* à propos; bon; sortable; convenable; **-or** *n.* prétendant *m.*; soupirant *m.*
suitcase *n.* valise *f.*
suite *n.* suite *f.*; train *m.*; (furniture) mobilier *m.*
sulfide *n.* sulfure *m.*
sulfite *n.* sulfite *m.*
sulfur *n.* soufre *m.*; **-ic** *a.* sulfurique; **-ous** *a.* sulfureux
sulk *n.* bouderie *f.*; — *vi.* bouder; **-y** *a.* boudeur; maussade; **-iness** *n.* maussaderie *f.*
sulky *n.* voiture légère à deux roues (utilisée aux courses attelées) *f.*

sullen *a.* maussade; chagrin; sombre
sully *vt.* souiller, tacher
sultan *n.* sultan *m.*; **-a** *n.* sultane *f.*
sultry *a.* d'une chaleur étouffante; suffocant
sum *n.* somme *f.*, tout, total *m.*; **in** — total en somme, somme toute; — *vt.* additioner; — **up** résumer; **-ming** *n.*, **-ing up** résumé *m.*
summarize *vt.* résumer
summary *n.* sommaire, résumé *m.*; — *a.* sommaire
summer *n.* été *m.*; — **resort** station estivale *f.*; — **sausage** saucisson *m.*
summerhouse *n.* pavillon *m.*; villa *f.*
summertime *n.* été *m.*, saison d'été *f.*
summit *n.* sommet *m.*; cime *f.*; comble *m.*; — **conference** conférence au sommet *f.*
summon *vt.* sommer; citer, assigner; ordonner, commander; appeler; convoquer; **-s** *n.* citation, assignation *f.*; appel *m.*
sump *n.* puisard *m.*, fosse *f.*
sumptuous *a.* somptueux; **-ness** *n.* somptuosité *f.*; luxe *m.*, richesse *f.*
sun *n.* soleil *m.*; — **parlor,** — **porch** solarium *m.*; — **visor** abat-jour *m.*; — *vt.* exposer au soleil; — **oneself** prendre le soleil; **-ny** *a.* ensoleillé; **it is -ny** il fait du soleil
sun-bathe *vi.* prendre le soleil
sunbeam *n.* rayon de soleil *m.*
sunbonnet *n.* capeline *f.*
sunburn *n.* hâle *m.*; coup de soleil *m.*; **-ed** *a.* hâlé; brûlé (par le soleil); — *vt.* bruler, hâler
sundae *n.* coupe (glace, sirop et fruit) *f.*
Sunday *n.* dimanche *m.*
sunder *vt.* séparer, partager
sundial *n.* cadran solaire *m.*
sundown *n.* coucher du soleil *m.*
sundries *n. pl.* diverses choses *f. pl.* (com.) divers *m. pl.*
sundry *a.* divers
sunfast, sunproof *a.* inaltérable au soleil
sunglasses *n. pl.* lunettes contre lessoleil *f. pl.*
sunken *a.* creux; enfoncé
sunlight *n.* soleil *m.*; lumière du soleil *f.*; jour *m.*
sun parlor *n.* (house) solarium *m.*
sunrise *n.* lever du soleil *m.*
sunset *n.* coucher du soleil *m.*
sunshine *n.* soleil *m.*
sunspot *n.* tache solaire *f.*
sunstroke *n.* insolation *f.*
sun tan *n.* hâle *m.*
sup *vi.* souper
superable *a.* surmontable
superabundance *n.* surabondance *f.*

superabundant *a.* surabondant
superannuated *a.* suranné; retraité
superb *a.* superbe
supercargo *n.* subrécargue *m.*
supercharge *vt.* supercompresser; **-er** *n.* supercompresseur *m.*
supercilious *n.* hautain, arrogant; **-ness** *n.* hauteur *f.*
superficial *a.* superficiel
superfine *a.* surfin
superfluous *a.* superflu; inutile
superhighway *n.* autostrade *f.*
superhuman *a.* surhumain
superimpose *vt.* superposer, surimposer
superintend *vt.* surveiller; **-ent** *n.* surintendant *m.*; inspecteur *m.*
superior *a. & n.* supérieur *m.*; **-ity** *n.* supériorité *f.*
superlative *n.* superlatif *m.*; — *a.* superlatif, suprême
superman *n.* surhomme *m.*
supermarket *n.* supermarket, grand magasin d'alimentation *m.*
supernatural *a.* surnaturel
supernumerary *n. & a.* surnuméraire *m.*
supersaturate *vt.* sursaturer
supersede *vt.* remplacer; faire supprimer; (law) surseoir à
supersensitive *a.* hypersensible
supersonic *a.* supersonique, ultrasonore
superstition *n.* superstition *f.*
superstructure *n.* édifice *m.*; superstructure *f.*
supervene *vi.* survenir
supervise *vt.* surveiller, diriger
supervision *n.* surveillance *f.*; direction *f.*
supervisor *n.* surveillant; inspecteur *m.*; directeur *m.*
supine *a.* couché sur le dos; — *n.* (gram.) supin *m.*
supper *n.* souper *m.*; **have** — souper
Supper, The Last la Sainte Cène *f.*
suppertime *n.* heure du souper *f.*
supplant *vt.* supplanter, remplacer
supple *a.* souple, flexible; **-ness** *n.* souplesse, flexibilité *f.*
supplement *n.* supplément *m.*; — *vt.* suppléer à; ajouter à, augmenter; **-al, -ary** *a.* supplémentaire
suppliant *n. & a.* suppliant *m.*
supplicant *n.* suppliant
supplicate *vt.* supplier
supplication *n.* supplication *f.*
supplier *n.* fournisseur *m.*; pourvoyeur, approvisionneur *m.*
supply *n.* fourniture *f.*; provision *f.*; approvisionnement *m.*; (mil.) ravitaillement *m.*; — **and demand** l'offre et la demande; — *vt.* approvisionner; fournir, pourvoir; munir

support *n.* soutien, appui, support *m.*; — *vt.* soutenir; entretenir; appuyer; assister; souffrir; supporter; faire subsister; — **oneself** gagner sa vie; **-able** *a.* supportable; **-er** *n.* soutien, partisan *m.*; (sport) slip (pour sportif) *m.*; (med.) suspensoire *m.*
suppose *vt.* supposer, imaginer; penser, croire; s'imaginer; **-d** *a.* censé; supposé; présumé; soi-disant; prétendu
suppress *vt.* supprimer; empêcher; étouffer, cacher; refouler, réprimer; **-ion** *n.* répression *f.*; refoulement *m.*
suppurate *vi.* suppurer
supremacy *n.* suprématie, supériorité *f.*
supreme *a.* suprême
Supreme Court *n.* Cour Suprême *f.*; grand tribunal *m.*
surcease *n.* arrêt *m.*, interruption *f.*
surcharge *n.* surcharge *f.*; surtaxe *f.*; — *vt.* surcharger
surd *n.* (sound) sourd *m.*; (math.) irrationnel *m.*
sure *a.* sûr, certain; assuré, ferme; **to be** —! assurément! certainement!; **be** — **to** ne pas manquer de; **make** — s'assurer; —! *interj.* mais oui, bien sûr; entendu; **-ly** *adv.* sûrement; assurément
sure-footed *a.* au pied sûr
surety *n.* sûreté *f.*; caution *f.*
surf *n.* brisant, ressac *m.*
surface *n.* surface *f.*; **on the** — (fig.) en apparence; — *vt.* mettre une nouvelle surface à; — *vi.* revenir à la surface
surfacing *n.* apprêtage; (road) revêtement *m.*
surfboard *n.* aquaplane *m.*
surfeit *n.* satiété *f.*; surabondance *f.*; — *vt.* soûler, rassasier; — *vi.* se soûler; se gorger
surge *n.* vague *f.*, flot *m.*, houle *f.*; — *vi.* s'élever, s'enfler; se soulever
surgeon *n.* chirurgien *m.*
surgery *n.* chirurgie *f.*
surgical *a.* chirurgical
surging *a.* houleux
surly *a.* hargneux, maussade, bourru
surmise *n.* conjecture *f.*; — *vi.* conjecturer; — *vi.* se douter de
surmount *vt.* surmonter
surname *n.* surnom, nom de famille *m.*; — *vt.* surnommer
surpass *vt.* surpasser, dépasser; **-ing** *a.* supérieur
surplice *n.* surplis *m.*
surplus *n.* surplus *m.*; excédent *m.*
surprise *n.* surprise *f.*; étonnement *m.*; — *vt.* surprendre; étonner; **be -d** s'étonner
surprising *a.* surprenant; étonnant
surrealist *n.* surréaliste *m.*

surrender n. reddition f.; cession f.; — vi. se rendre; — vt. rendre; céder; renoncer à

surreptitious a. subreptice, clandestine

surrogate n. délégué m.; — **court** cour qui s'occupe des testaments f. — vt. subroger

surround vt. environner, entourer; **–ings** n. pl. environs m. pl.; milieu m.

surtax n. surtaxe f.; — vt. surtaxer

surveillance n. surveillance f.

survey n. coup d'œil m.; examen m.; inspection f.; référendum m.; arpentage m.; — vt. surveiller, examiner, observer; consulter; arpenter; **–ing** n. arpentage m.; **–or** n. arpenteur m.

survival n. survivance f.

survive vi. survivre; — vt. survivre à

survivor n. survivant m.

susceptibility n. susceptibilité f.

suspect n. personne suspecte f.; — vt. soupçonner, se douter de

suspend vt. suspendre; **–ers** n. pl. bretelles f. pl.

suspense n. suspens, doute m., incertitude f.; cessation f.; **in** — en suspens

suspension n. suspension f.; — **bridge** n. pont suspendu m.

suspicion n. soupçon m.; doute m.; méfiance, défiance f.

suspicious a. soupçonneux; suspect; méfiant; **–ness** n. méfiance f.; doute m.

sustain vt. soutenir, maintenir, entretenir; subir, essuyer, éprouver; **–ed** a. soutenu

sustenance n. subsistance f.; entretien m.

suture n. suture f.; — vt. suturer

swab n. faubert m.; (cotton) tampon d'ouate m.; — vt. fauberter; laver, nettoyer

swaddle vt. emmailloter

swaddling clothes n. pl. maillot m.

swagger vi. faire le fanfaron, fanfaronner; se pavaner; — **stick** (mil.) bâton d'officier m.; **–er** n. fanfaron m.; **–ing** a. important

swallow n. (bird) hirondelle f.; gorgée f.; avalement m.; coup m.; — vt. avaler, engloutir; gober; — **up** engloutir

swamp n. marécage, marais m.; — vt. embourber; engloutir; submerger; inonder; **–y** a. marécageux

swan n. cygne m.; — **dive** saut d'ange, plongeon en nage m.

sward n. gazon m., pelouse f.

swarm n. essaim m.; fourmillière f.; — vi. essaimer; fourmiller; grouiller

swarthy a. basané; noir, sombre

swashbuckler n. fanfaron m.

swastika n. croix gammée f.; svastika m.

swatch n. échantillon m.

swath n. andain m., fauchée f.

swathe n. maillot m., langes m. pl.; — vt. emmailloter

sway n. pouvoir m., domination f.; prépondérance f.; — vt. influencer; balancer; détourner; — vi. vaciller; se balancer; s'incliner

sway-backed a. ensellé

swear vi. jurer; blasphémer; — vt. jurer; — **to** certifier, attester; — **in** faire prêter serment à; **–ing** n. jurons m. pl.; **–ing in** n. assermentation f.

sweat n. sueur, transpiration f.; — vi. suer, transpirer; bûcher, travailler dur; (wall) suinter; **–shop** n. entreprise dont les ouvriers sont surmenés f.; **–ing** n. transpiration f.; (wall) suintement m.

sweater n. chandail; pull-over; maillot m.; tricot m.

Swede n. Suédois m.

Sweden n. Suède f.

Swedish a. suédois

sweep n. balayage, coup de balai m.; (chimney) ramoneur m.; (naut.) aviron m.; **at a** —, **at one** — d'un seul coup; **make a clean** — faire table rase; — vt. balayer; couvrir; (chimney) ramoner; — **away**, — **off** balayer; emporter; — **out**, — **up** balayer; nettoyer; **–er** n. balayeur m.; **carpet –er** n. balayeuse f., balai méchanique m.; **–ing** n. action de balayer f.; **–ings** n. pl. balayures f. pl.; **–ing** a. général; complet

sweepstake(s) n. (pl.) sweepstake(s) m.; poule(s) f.

sweet a. doux (douce); savoureux, odorant; sucré; mélodieux; gracieux; tendre; aimable, agréable; gentil; frais; — **potato** patate f.; — n. bonbon m., confiserie f.; sucrerie f.; **–en** vt. sucrer, **–ening** n. sucrage m.; sucre m.; **–ness** n. douceur f.

sweetbread n. ris de veau m.

sweetheart n. amoureux m., amoureuse f.; ami m., amie f.

sweetmeats n. pl. confiserie f.; sucreries f. pl.

swell n. élévation f.; (sea) houle f.; élégant m.; — vt. enfler, gonfler; augmenter; — vi. s'enfler; se gonfler; s'augmenter; accroître; — a. (coll.) formidable; épatant; excellent; élégant; **–ing** n. enflure f.; enflement m.; gonflement m.

swelter vi. étouffer de chaleur; **–ing** a. étouffant de chaleur

swerve vi. dévier; fléchir; se dérober; — n. crochet m., embardée f.

swift n. martinet m.; — a. prompt; rapide; léger; **–ly** adv. vite, rapidement; **–ness** n. vitesse, rapidité f.

swift-footed *a.* au pied léger
swill *n.* eaux grasses *f. pl.*
swim *n.* bain de mer *m.*; — *vi.* nager; — *vt.* traverser à la nage; **–mer** *n.* nageur *m.*; **–ming** *a.* (fig.) tournant; noyé; **–ming** *n.* natation *f.*; **–ming pool** piscine *f.*; **–suit** costume de bain *m.*
swindle *n.* escroquerie *f.*; — *vt. & vi.* escroquer; filouter; **–r** *n.* escroc *m.*; filou *m.*
swine *n.* cochon *m.*; porc *m.*
swineherd *n.* porcher *m.*
swing *n.* oscillation *f.*; dandinement *m.*; branle *m.*; escarpolette *f.*; balançoire *f.*; (mus.) swing *m.*; **in full** — en plein travail; en activité; — *vt.* balancer; tourner; basculer; brandir; — *vi.* se balancer; tourner; **–ing** *a.* balançant; rythmé; battant; **–ing door** porte battante *f.*
swipe *n.* coup *m.*; — *vt.* frapper; (coll.) chiper; voler
swirl *n.* tourbillon *m.*; — *vi.* tourbillonner
swish *n.* sifflement *m.*; froissement *m.*; — *vt.* faire siffler; — *vi.* bruire
Swiss *a. & n.* suisse *m.*
switch *n.* baguette *f.*; (rail.) aiguille *f.*; (elec.) interrupteur, bouton *m.*; (coll.) changement *m.*, substitution *f.*; — *vt.* (whip) cingler; agiter; échanger; (rail.) aiguiller; — **off** couper, éteindre; — **on** allumer
switchboard *n.* (phone) standard (téléphonique) *m.*; — **operator** standardiste *m. & f.*
switchman *n.* (rail.) aiguilleur *m.*
Switzerland *n.* Suisse *f.*
swivel *n.* pivot *m.*; — **chair** fauteuil tournant *m.*; — *vi.* pivoter
swollen *a.* enflé, gonflé; (river) en crue
swoon *n.* évanouissement *m.*; — *vi.* s'évanouir
swoop *n.* descente *f.*; attaque *f.*; ruée *f.*; coup *m.*; — *vi.* fondre, s'abattre
sword *n.* épée *f.*; sabre *m.*
swordsman *n.* épéiste *m.*; duelliste *m.*
syllabification *n.* division en syllabes *f.*
syllable *n.* syllabe *f.*
syllabus *n.* sommaire, programme *m.*; syllabus *m.*
sylph *n.* sylphe *m.*; sylphide *f.*
sylvan *a.* sylvestre
symbol *n.* symbole *m.*; **–ic(al)** *a.* symbolique; **–ism** *n.* symbolisme *m.*; **–ize** *vt.* symboliser
symmetrical *a.* symétrique
symmetry *n.* symétrie *f.*
sympathetic *a.* sympathique; compatissant
sympathize *vi.* sympathiser; — **with** avoir de la compassion pour; être partisan de; comprendre, se rendre compte de; **–r** *n.*

partisan *m.*
sympathy *n.* sympathie *f.*; compassion *f.*; condoléances *f. pl.*
symphonic *a.* symphonique
symphony *n.* symphonie *f.*; — **orchestra** orchestre symphonique *m.*
symposium *n.* réunion *f.*; discussion *f.*; banquet *m.*
sympton *n.* symptôme, indice *m.*; **–atic** *a.* symptomatique
synagogue *n.* synagogue *f.*
synchronize *vt.* synchroniser
syncopate *vt.* syncoper
syndicate *n.* syndicat *m.*; — *vt.* faire publier (un écrit) dans plusieurs journaux
synod *n.* synode *m.*
synonym *n.* synonyme *m.*; **–ous** *a.* synonyme
synopsis *n.* résumé *m.*, analyse *f.*
syntax *n.* syntaxe *f.*
synthesis *n.* synthèse *f.*
synthesize *vt.* synthétiser; produire synthétiquement
synthetic *a.* synthétique
syphilis *n.* syphilis *f.*
syphilitic *a.* syphilitique
Syria *n.* Syrie *f.*; **–c** *n.* syriaque *m.*; **–n** *a. & n.* syrien *m.*
syringe *n.* seringue *f.*; — *vt.* seringuer
syrup *n.* sirop *m.*; **–y** *a.* siropeux
system *n.* système, régime *m.*, méthode *f.*; réseau *m.*; **–atic** *a.* systématique; méthodique; **–atize** *vt.* systématiser

T

tab *n.* oreille, oreillette *f.*; touche *f.*; patte *f.*; (coll.) addition *f.*; **keep** — **on** surveiller, contrôler
table *n.* table *f.*; tableau *m.*; bureau *m.*; liste *f.*; tablette *f.*; tablier *m.*; **set the** — mettre la table; — **of contents** table *f.*; **turn the** **–s on** faire tourner les chances contre; — *vt.* (a proposition) ajourner; classer
tablecloth *n.* nappe *f.*
tableland *n.* plateau *m.*
tablespoon *n.* cuiller à bouche, cuiller à soupe *f.*; **–ful** *n.* cuillerée à bouche *f.*
tablet *n.* tablette *f.*; plaque *f.*; comprimé *m.*; (paper) bloc *m.*
tableware *n.* service de table *m.*
tabloid *n.* journal de petit format *m.*; journal sensationnel *m.*
taboo, tabu *n. & a.* tabou *m.*; — *vt.* interdire
tabular *a.* en forme de table; tabulaire
tabulate *vt.* disposer en forme de table; classer, cataloguer
tachometer *n.* tachymètre *m.*

tacit *a.* tacite

taciturn *a.* taciturne

tack *n.* petit clou *m.*, broquette *f.*; (naut.) amure *f.*; — *vt.* accrocher, attacher; (naut.) louvoyer; **thumb—** *n.* punaise *f.*

tackle *n.* attirail *m.*; appareil *m.*; articles *m. pl.*; (sport) action de saisir, de renverser *f.*; **block and** — moufle *m.*; — *vt.* saisir, renverser; plaquer; chercher à résoudre, aborder

tacky *a.* collant; pas encore sec

tact *n.* tact *m.*; savoir-faire *m.*; **–ful** *a.* (plein) de tact; **–less** *a.* sans tact

tactical *a.* tactique

tactics *n. pl.* tactique *f.*

taffeta *n.* taffetas *m.*

tag *n.* étiquette *f.*; — *vt.* attacher une étiquette à; — **along** *vi.* (coll.) accompagner (sans être invité)

Tahiti *n.* Taïti *m.*

tail *n.* queue *f.*; culée *f.*; (coin) pile *f.*; (shirt) pan *m.*; — **turn** — tourner les talons, se sauver, s'échapper; **–light** *n.* (auto.) feu rouge arrière *m.*; **–s** *n. pl.* habit à queue *m.*

tailor *n.* tailleur *m.*; — *vi.* exercer l'état de tailleur; — *vt.* confectionner, façonner, faire

tailor-made *a.* (fait) sur mesure

tail spin *n.* chute en vrille *f.*

taint *n.* souillure, tache *f.*; infection *f.*; — *vt.* gâter; souiller, infecter, corrompre

take *n.* prise *f.*; (coll.) profit *m.*; butin *m.*; — *vt.* prendre; saisir, s'emparer de; tenir; mener, conduire; amener; emporter; louer; accepter, recevoir, admettre; tolérer, souffrir, supporter; penser, croire, supposer; — *vi.* prendre; avoir effet; réussir; — **after** ressembler à, tenir de; — **along** emporter; amener; — **apart** démonter; — **away** enlever, emporter; emmener; — **back** reprendre; rapporter; — **down** descendre; — **in** duper, rouler, tromper; rentrer; recevoir; comprendre, comporter; — **off** enlever, ôter; partir; filer; (avi.) décoller; — **off one's clothes** se déshabiller; — **on** prendre; se charger de, s'occuper de; assumer; (industry) embaucher; — **out** enlever; sortir; accompagner dehors; — **over** prendre possession de; prendre la direction de; — **to** s'habituer à, s'accoutumer à, se faire à; s'adonner à; — **up** monter; prendre, rétrécir; occuper; étudier; absorber; — **an examination** passer un examen; — **a walk** faire une promenade; se promener; — **care of** se charger de, s'occuper de; prendre soin de; soigner; garder, surveiller; — **charge of** se charger de; pren-

dre la direction de; — **effect** entrer en vigueur; produire son effet; — **it easy** se ménager; — **place** avoir lieu; — **prisoner** faire prisonnier; **–n** *a.* pris; saisi; occupé; **be –n ill** tomber malade

takeoff *n.* (avi.) décollage *m.*; imitation, satire *f.*

taking *n.* prise *f.*

talcum *n.* talc *m.*

tale *n.* conte *m.*, histoire *f.*

talent *n.* talent *m.*; génie *m.*; flair *m.*; **–ed** *a.* de talent; doué

talk *n.* conversation *f.*; discours *m.*; causerie *f.*; propos *m. pl.*; paroles *f. pl.*; — *vi.* parler, causer, jaser; raisonner; — *vt.* parler; — **over** discuter; **–ative** *a.* bavard; loquace; **–ativeness** *n.* loquacité *f.*; **–er** *n.* bavard, causeur *m.*; **–ing** *a.* parlant; parlé; **–ing** *n.* conversation *f.*

tall *a.* grand; haut; (coll.) incroyable; **–ness** *n.* hauteur *f.*; grande taille *f.*

tallow *n.* suif *m.*

tally *n.* compte *m.*; taille *f.*; entaille, coche *f.*; — *vi.* correspondre; — *vt.* pointer, contrôler

talon *n.* serre, griffe *f.*

tambourine *n.* tambourin *m.*

tame *vt.* apprivoiser; dompter; — *a.* apprivoisé, dompté, doux, domestique; abattu, humilié; **–ness** *n.* docilité *f.*, caractère doux *m.*; **–r** *n.* apprivoiseur, dompteur *m.*

tamp *vt.* pilonner; bourrer

tamper *vt.* expérimenter (avec); — **with se** mêler de; altérer; fausser, falsifier

tan *n.* tan *m.*; (sun) hâle *m.*; (color) brun-jaune *m.*; — *vt.* tanner; hâler; (coll.) fesser; **–ner** *n.* tanneur *m.*; **–nery** *n.* tannerie *f.*; **–ing** *n.* tan *m.*

tang *n.* goût âpre *m.*; saveur *f.*

tangent *n.* tangente *f.*; — *a.* tangent, tangentiel

tangerine *n.* mandarine *f.*

tangible *n.* tangible, tactile; sensible; **matériel**

Tangiers *n.* Tanger *m.*

tangle *vt.* embarrasser, embrouiller; **emmêler**; — *n.* embrouillement *m.*; embarras *m.*

tank *n.* citerne *f.*; réservoir *m.*; (mil.) tank, char *m.*; **gas** — réservoir à essence *m.*; — **car** wagon-citerne *m.*; **–er** *n.* bateau-citerne *m.*

tankard *n.* chope *f.*

tannic *a.* tannique

tannin *n.* tanin *m.*

tantalize *vt.* tourmenter, tantaliser, taquiner

tantalizing *a.* qui tantalise; (fig.) ravissant; délicieux; séduisant; provocant

tantalum *n.* tantale *m.*

tantamount *a.* équivalent

tantrum *n.* accès de colère *m.*

tap *n.* tape *f.*, coup léger *m.*; cannelle *f.*, robinet *m.*; — **dance** danse à claquettes *f.*; — **water** eau du robinet *f.*; **on** — en vidange; — *vt.* percer; taper; frapper

tap-dance *vi.* danser à la claque

tape *n.* ruban *m.*; bande *f.*; **adhesive** — sparadrap *m.*; **recording** — ruban magnétique *m.*; **red** — paperasseries *f. pl.*; — **measure**, — **line** mètre en ruban *m.*; — **recorder** *n.* magnétophone *m.*; — *vt.* entourer d'un ruban; entourer de sparadrap; enregistrer sur ruban

taper *n.* bougie *f.*; — *vi.* se terminer en pointe; — *vt.* tailler en cône, côner; diminuer; **–ed**, **–ing** *a.* conique; en pointe; effilé

tapestry *n.* tapisserie *f.*

tapeworm *n.* ver solitaire *m.*

taproot *n.* racine principale *f.*

taps *n.* (mil.) signal d'éteindre les lumières dans les casernes *m.*

tar *n.* goudron *m.*; matelot *m.*; — *vt.* goudronner; **–ry** *a.* goudronneux

tarentella *n.* tarentelle *f.*

tardiness *n.* lenteur *f.*; manque de ponctualité *f.*

tardy *a.* tardif, lent; en retard

tare *n.* ivraie *f.*; (com.) tare *f.*

target *n.* cible *f.*; but *m.*

tariff *n.* tarif *m.*

tarnish *n.* ternissure *f.*; — *vi.* se ternir

tarpaulin *n.* bâche *f.*; prélart *m.*

tarragon *n.* estragon *m.*

tarry *vi.* tarder, attendre; demeurer

tart *n.* tarte *f.*; — *a.* aigre; acide; mordant, piquant; **–ness** *n.* aigreur, acidité *f.*

tartar *n.* tartre *m.*

Tartar *a. & n.* tartare *m.*

tartar *n.* (chem.) tartre *m.*; **cream of** — crème de tartre *f.*

task *n.* tâche, besogne *f.*; travail *m.*; (school punishment) pensum *m.*; **take to** — réprimander; — **force** (mil.) groupe chargé d'une mission spéciale *m.*

taskmaster *n.* surveillant tyrannique *m.*

Tasmania *n.* Tasmanie *f.*

tassel *n.* gland *m.*, houppe *f.*

taste *n.* goût *m.*; saveur, odeur *f.*; petit morceau, petit peu *m.*; penchant *m.*; — *vt.* goûter; déguster; sentir; — *vi.* avoir le goût; sentir; **–ful** *a.* de bon goût; **–less** *a.* sans goût; fade, insipide; **–r** *n.* dégustateur *m.*

tastiness *n.* saveur *f.*, goût *m.*

tasty *a.* délicieux; savoureux

tat *vt.* confectionner de la dentelle; faire de la frivolité; **–ting** *n.* frivolité; **tit for**

— à bon chat bon rat

tatter *n.* guenille *f.*, lambeau *m.*; **–ed** *a.* en lambeaux

tattle *vi.* cancaner; commérer; bavarder

tattletale *n.* rapporteur *m.*

tattoo *n.* tatouage *m.* (mil.) retraite *f.*; — *vt.* tatouer; **–ing** *n.* tatouage *m.*

taunt *n.* insulte *f.*; raillerie *f.*; — *vt.* insulter; tourner en ridicule

taupe *n.* gris-jaune *m.*

taut *a.* raide, tendu; **–ness** *n.* raideur *f.*

tautology *n.* tautologie *f.*

tavern *n.* cabaret *m.*, auberge *f.*; taverne *f.*; — **keeper** aubergiste *m.*

tawdry *a.* clinquant; de mauvais goût, vulgaire

tawny *a.* tanné; basané

tax *n.* taxe *f.*, impôt *m.*; contributions *f. pl.*; — **collector** percepteur *m.*; receveur *m.*; — *vt.* taxer; mettre à l'épreuve; **–able** *a.* imposable, sujet à la taxe; **–ation** *n.* taxation *f.*; impôts *m. pl.*

taxpayer *n.* contribuable *m. & f.*

taxi(cab) *n.* taxi *m.*; — *vi.* (avi.) rouler

taxidermist *n.* empailleur *m.*

taxidermy *n.* empaillage *m.*, taxidermie *f.*

taximeter *n.* taximètre *m.*

tea *n.* thé *m.*; **to come to** — venir prendre le thé; — **bag** *n.* sachet de thé *m.*; — **ball** boule à thé *f.*

teach *vt.* enseigner, apprendre; professer; **–er** *n.* professeur *m.*; instituteur *m.*, institutrice *f.*; maître d'école *m.*; maîtresse d'école *f.*; **–er's college** école normale *f.*; **–ing** *n.* enseignement *m.*; **–ing staff** *n.* corps enseignant *m.*

teacup *n.* tasse à thé *f.*

teakettle *n.* bouilloire *f.*

team *n.* équipe *f.*; (horses) attelage *m.*; — *vt.* atteler; — *vi.*, — **(up) with** collaborer avec; se joindre à

teamwork *n.* travail d'équipe *m.*, collaboration *f.*

teapot *n.* théière *f.*

tear *n.* larme *f.*; **–s** *pl.* larmes *f. pl.*, pleurs *m. pl.*; — **gas** gaz lacrymogène *m.*; **–ful** en pleurs; larmoyant; **–fully** *adv.* en pleurant

tear *n.* déchirure *f.*; — *vt.* déchirer; arracher; — *vi.* se déchirer; aller à toute vitesse; — **down** démolir; — **up** déchirer

tearoom *n.* salon de thé *m.*; pâtisserie *f.*

tease *vt.* taquiner, tourmenter; — *n.* taquin *m.*; **–r** *n.* question difficile *f.*

teasing *a.* taquin; raillant; — *n.* taquinerie *f.*; raillerie *f.*

teaspoon *n.* cuiller à café *f.*; **–ful** *n.* cuillerée à café *f.*

teat *n.* tétin *m.*; mamelon *m.*; tette *f.*

technical *a.* technique; **–ity** *n.* technicité

f.; détail (technique) *m.*
technician *n.* technicien *m.*
technique *n.* technique *f.*
technological *a.* technologique
technology *n.* technologie *f.*
tedious *a.* ennuyeux, fatigant; **–ness** *n.* ennui *m.*
tedium *n.* ennui *m.*
tee, T *n.* té *m.*; **golf** — *m.* dé; pointe de départ *m.*; — *vi.*, — **off** commencer
teem *vi.* fourmiller, foisonner, abonder, grouiller; pleuvoir à verse; **–ing** *a.* fécond, fertile
teen-age *a.* adolescent; âgé de 13 à 19 ans; **–r** *n.* adolescent *m.*
teens *n. pl.* numéros de 13 à 19 *m. pl.*; adolescence *f.*
teeth *n.* dents *f. pl.*; **–e** *vi.* faire les dents; **–ing** *n.* dentition *f.*
teeter *vi.* vaciller; se balancer; faillir tomber
teeter-totter *n.* balançoire *f.*
teetotaler *n.* buveur d'eau *m.*
telecast *n.* émission de télévision *f.*
telegram *n.* télégramme *m.*
telegraph *n.* télégraphe *m.*; — *vt.* télégraphier; **–ic** *a.* télégraphique; **–y** *n.* télégraphie *f.*
telelens *n.* téléobjectif *m.*
telemeter *n.* télémetre *m.*
telelogical *a.* téléologique
teleology *n.* téléologie *f.*
telepathic *a.* télépathique
telepathy *n.* télépathie *f.*
telephone *n.* téléphone *m.*; **dial** — téléphone automatique *m.*; — **booth** *n.* cabine téléphonique *f.*; — **directory** *n.* annuaire *m.*; — **exchange** *n.* central téléphonique *m.*; — **operator** *n.* standardiste *m. & f.*; — **receiver** *n.* recepteur *m.*; — *a.* téléphonique; — *vt. & vi.* téléphoner (à)
telephonic *a.* téléphonique
telephony *n.* téléphonie *f.*
teleprinter *n.* télétype, téléscripteur *m.*
telescope *n.* télescope *m.*; longue-vue *f.*; — *vt.* télescoper; — *vi.* se télescoper
telescopic *a.* télescopique
teletypewriter *n.* télétype *m.*
televise *vt.* téléviser
television *n.* télévision *f.*; — **set** téléviseur *m.*
tell *vt.* dire; raconter, conter; apprendre; marquer, indiquer; ordonner; distinguer; savoir; — *vi.* porter; **–er** *n.* conteur, raconteur *m.*; (bank) caissier, payeur *m.*; **fortune** — *n.* diseuse de bonne aventure *f.*; **–ing** *a.* efficace; frappant; **–ing** *n.* récit *m.*, narration *f.*
telltale *a.* révélateur

tellurium *n.* tellure *m.*
temerity *n.* témérité, audace *f.*
temper *n.* caractère *m.*; naturel *m.*; humeur *f.*; irritation *f.*; colère *f.*; (metal) trempe *f.*; **lose one's** — se mettre en colère, s'emporter; — *vt.* tempérer, modérer; adoucir; broyer; tremper; **–ed** *a.* trempé, recuit
tempera *n.* détrempe *f.*
temperament *n.* tempérament *m.*; humeur *f.*, caractère *m.*; **–al** *a.* d'humeur inégale, capricieux
temperance *n.* tempérance, modération *f.*
temperate *a.* tempéré, modéré; **–ness** *n.* modération *f.*; douceur *f.*
temperature *n.* température *f.*; fièvre *f.*
tempest *n.* tempête *f.*, orage *m.*; **–uous** *a.* orageux
temple *n.* temple *m.*; (anat.) tempe *f.*
temporal *a.* temporel; (anat.) temporal
temporary *a.* temporaire, provisoire, intérimaire; passager
temporize *vi.* temporiser; transiger (avec)
tempt *vt.* tenter; **–ation** *n.* tentation *f.*; **–er** *n.* tenteur *m.*; **–ress** *n.* tentatrice *f.*
ten *n. & a.* dix *m.*; **about** — dizaine *f.*; **–th** *n. & a.* dixième *m.*
tenable *a.* tenable
tenacious *a.* tenace
tenacity *n.* ténacité *f.*; entêtement *m.*
tenancy *n.* (law) usufruit *m.*; location *f.*
tenant *n.* tenancier, fermier *m.*; locataire *m. & f.*; — *vt.* tenir à bail; habiter; **–less** *a.* sans habitant
tend *vt.* garder, surveiller; avoir soin de; soigner; — *vi.* tendre; contribuer; **–er** *n.* offre *f.*; (rail.) tender *m.*; **legal –er** monnaie légale *f.*; **–er** *vt.* offrir
tendency *n.* tendance *f.*; disposition *f.*; penchant *m.*, inclination *f.*
tendentious *a.* tendancieux
tender *a.* tendre; affectueux; délicat; sensible; **–ness** *n.* tendresse *f.*; délicatesse *f.*; sensibilité *f.*
tenderfoot *n.* bleu, débutant *m.*
tenderhearted *a.* sensible
tenderloin *n.* filet *m.*
tendril *n.* vrille *f.*
tenement *n.* immeuble d'habitation dans un quartier misérable *m.*
tenet *n.* dogme, principe *m.*
tenor *n.* caractère *m.*; teneur *f.*; (mus.) ténor *m.*
tense *n.* temps *m.*; — *a.* tendu, raide; nerveux; **–ness** *n.* tension *f.*
tensile *a.* de traction; extensible
tension *n.* tension *f.*; traction *f.*; raideur *f.*; voltage *m.*
tent *n.* tente *f.*; — *vi.* camper
tentacle *n.* tentacule *m.*

tentative *a.* d'essai; experimental
tenuous *a.* ténu, insaisissable, mince; **–ness** *n.* ténuité *f.*
tenure *n.* possession, occupation, tenure *f.*
tepid *a.* tiède
term *n.* terme *m.*; limite *f.*; période *f.*; (com.) échéance *f.*; condition, stipulation *f.*; expression *f.*; inscription *f.*; **school —** semestre *m.*; trimestre *m.*; **be on good –s with** être bien avec; **come to –s with** s'arranger avec; **—** *vt.* appeler, nommer
terminal *a.* final, terminal; **—** *n.* terminus *m.*; gare *f.*; (elec.) borne *f.*
terminate *vt.* terminer, mettre fin à; **—** *vi.* se terminer, finir
termination *n.* fin, limite *f.*, terminaison *f.*
terminology *n.* terminologie *f.*
terminus *n.* terminus *m.*; (railroad) gare *f.*
termite *n.* termite *m.*
tern *n.* sterne *m.*
terrace *n.* terrasse *f.*; **—** *vt.* terrasser, disposer en terrasse
terra cotta *n.* terre cuite *f.*
terrestrial *a.* terrestre
terrible *a.* terrible, épouvantable; atroce
terrific *a.* terrible; (coll.) formidable; épatant; excellent; **–ally** *adv.* terriblement
terrify *vt.* effrayer, épouvanter, terrifier
territorial *a.* territorial
territory *n.* territoire *m.*
terror *n.* terreur *f.*; épouvante *f.*; effroi *m.*; **–ism** *n.* terrorisme *m.*; **–ist** *n.* terroriste *m.*; **–ize** *vt.* terroriser
terror-stricken *a.* épouvanté
terrycloth *n.* étoffe bouclée *f.*; tissu-éponge *m.*
terse *a.* net; concis; **–ness** *n.* netteté, concision *f.*
tertiary *a.* tertiaire
test *n.* épreuve *f.*; essai *m.*; examen *m.*; test *m.*; **— tube** *n.* éprouvette *f.*; **—** *vt.* éprouver; mettre à l'épreuve; essayer; examiner; vérifier, contrôler; **–er** *n.* essayeur *m.*; vérificateur *m.*
testament *n.* testament *m.*; **–ary** *a.* testamentaire
testator *n.* testateur *m.*
testicle *n.* testicule *m.*
testify *vt.* témoigner; **—** *vi.* déposer
testimonial *n.* certificat *m.*, attestation *f.*; témoignage *m.*
testimony *n.* témoignage *m.*, preuve *f.*; déposition *f.*
testiness *n.* irritabilité *f.*
testy *a.* maussade, bourru; irritable
tetanus *n.* tétanos *m.*
tether *n.* attache (des chevaux) *f.*; **—** *vt.* attacher
tetragonal *a.* tétragone, quadrilatère

tetrahedron *n.* tétraèdre *m.*
tetrameter *n.* tétramètre *m.*
text *n.* texte *m.*; **–ual** *a.* textuel, de texte
textbook *n.* texte *m.*; livre classique *m.*; manuel *m.*
Thailand *n.* Thaïland *m.*
Thames *n.* Tamise *f.*
than *adv.* que, (before numbers) de
thank *vt.* remercier; **–s** *n. pl.* grâces *f. pl.*; remerciments *m. pl.*; **–s!** merci, merci bien, merci beaucoup; je vous remercie; **–fulness** *n.* reconnaissance *f.*; **–less** *a.* ingrat
thanksgiving *n.* action de grâces *f.*
that *a.* ce, cet, cette; **—** *conj.* que, qui; afin que, pour que, de manière que; **—** *pron.* cela, ça, ce; **— one** celui-là, celle-là
thatch *n.* chaume *m.*; **—** *vt.* couvrir de chaume; **–ed** *a.* de chaume
thaw *n.* dégel *m.*; **—** *vt. & vi.* dégeler
the *art.* le, la, les
theater *n.* théâtre *m.*
theatrical *a.* théâtral, scénique; **—** *n.* spectacle *m.*
thee *pron.* toi, te
theft *n.* vol, larcin *m.*
their *a.* leur, leurs; **–s** *pron.* le leur; la leur; les leurs; à eux, à elles
theist *n. & a.* théiste *m.*
them *pron.* eux, elles; les; **–selves** *pron.* eux-mêmes, elles-mêmes, se
theme *n.* thème *m.*
then *adv.* alors; après, puis, ensuite; donc, par conséquent; **till —** jusque là, d'ici là; **now and —** de temps en temps, de temps à autre
thence *adv.* de là
thenceforth *adv.* dès lors
theocratic(al) *a.* théocratique
theologian *n.* théologien *m.*
theologic(al) *a.* théologique
theology *n.* théologie *f.*
theorem *n.* théorème *m.*
theoretic(al) *a.* théorique; **–ally** *adv.* en principe
theorist *n.* théoricien *m.*
theorize *vi.* théoriser
theory *n.* théorie *f.*
theosophy *n.* théosophie *f.*
therapeutic *a.* thérapeutique; **–s** *n.* thérapeutique *f.*
therapy *n.* traitement *m.*
there *adv.* là; y; **here and —** çà et là; **— is, — are** il y a; voilà
thereabouts *adv.* environ
thereafter *adv.* après, ensuite; dès lors
thereby *adv.* par là, ainsi
therefore *adv.* ainsi, donc; aussi
therefrom *adv.* de là, de cela
therein *adv.* là-dedans

thereon *adv.* là-dessus
thereupon *adv.* là-dessus; sur quoi
therm *n.* microthermie *f.*
thermic *a.* thermique
thermodynamics *n.* thermodynamique *f.*
thermometer *n.* thermomètre *m.*
thermos (bottle) *n.* thermos *m.*, bouteille isolante *f.*
thermostat *n.* calorifère *f.*; thermostat *m.*
these *pron. pl.* ceux-ci, celles-ci; — *a.* ces
thesis *n.* thèse *f.*
they *pron.* ils, elles; eux; on
thick *n.* épaisseur *f.*; fort *m.*; — *a.* épais, gros, grand; touffu; trouble; grossier; fréquent; –en *vt. & vi.* épaissir; –ness *n.* épaisseur *f.*; grosseur *f.*
thicket *n.* taillis, fourré *m.*
thickheaded *a.* à la tête dure; bête; idiot
thickset *a.* trapu
thick-skinned *a.* insensible
thick-witted *a.* bête, stupide
thief *n.* voleur *m.*
thieve *vt. & vi.* voler; –ry *n.* vol, larcin *m.*
thievish *a.* voleur
thigh *n.* cuisse *f.*
thimble *n.* dé à coudre; –ful *n.* dé, doigt *m.*
thin *a.* mince, maigre; léger; ténu; (hair) rare; (voice) grêle; — *vt.* amincir; délayer; — *vi.* maigrir; s'amincir; –ly *adv.* à peine; –ness *n.* maigreur, minceur *f.*; légèreté *f.*; rareté *f.*
thine *pron.* à toi; le tien, la tienne
thing *n.* chose *f.*; objet *m.*; article *m.*; affaire *f.*; effet *m.*; créature *f.*, être *m.*; latest — dernier cri *m.*
think *vt. & vi.* penser; croire; trouver; juger; réfléchir; songer; s'imaginer; I — so je pense que oui; — of penser à; — out peser, méditer; — over réfléchir; –able *a.* concevable, imaginable; –er *n.* penseur *m.*; –ing *a.* qui pense; –ing *n.* pensées *f. pl.*
thin-skinned *a.* susceptible, sensible
third *a.* troisième; — *n.* (fraction) tiers *m.*
thirst *n.* soif *f.*; altération *f.*; — *vi.* avoir soif; –y *a.* altéré; avide; be –y avoir soif
thirteen *a.* treize; –th *a.* treizième; treize
thirtieth *a.* trentième
thirty *a.* trente
this *a.* ce, cet, cette; — *pron.* ceci; cela; celui(-ci), celle(-ci)
thong *n.* courroie *f.*; lanière *f.*
thoracic *a.* thoracique
thorax *n.* thorax *m.*
thorium *n.* thorium *m.*
thorn *n.* épine *f.*; –y *a.* épineux
thorough *a.* complet; profondi; approfondi; –ly *adv.* complètement, tout à fait; parfaitement; à fond; –ness *n.* profondeur *f.*; assiduité *f.*

thoroughbred *a.* (horse) de race, pur sang; — *n.* (horse) cheval de race *m.*
thoroughfare *n.* voie, rue *f.*
thoroughgoing *a.* assidu, consciencieux
those *a.* ces; — *pron.* ceux(-là), celles(-là)
thou *pron.* tu; toi
though *conj.* bien que, quoique, encore que; — *adv.* cependant, pourtant
thought *n.* pensée *f.*; réflexion *f.*; idée *f.*; méditation *f.*; intention *f.*; –ful *a.* pensif; prévenant; –fulness *n.* prévenance *f.*; réflexion *f.*; –less *a.* irréfléchi; sans prévenance
thousand *a.* mille; — *n.* (un) millier *m.*; –th *a. & n.* millième *m.*
thrash *vt.* battre, rosser; –ing *n.* raclée, rossée *f.*
thread *n.* fil *m.*; (screw) filet, filetage *m.*; — *vt.* enfiler; fileter
threadbare *a.* râpé; usé
threat *n.* menace *f.*; –en *vt.* menacer; intimider; –ening *a.* menaçant
three *a.* trois
three-act *a.* en trois actes
three-cornered *a.* triangulaire; (hat) tricorne
threefold *a.* triple
three-legged *a.* à trois pieds
three-ply *a.* à trois épaisseurs
threesome *n.* partie de trois *f.*
three-speed *a.* à trois vitesses
three-wheeled *a.* à trois roues
thresh *vt.* battre; –er *n.* (person) batteur *m.*; (machine) batteuse *f.*; –ing *n.* battage *m.*; –ing machine *n.* batteuse *f.*
threshold *n.* seuil, pas *m.*; limite *f.*
thrice *adv.* trois fois
thrift *n.* économie, frugalité *f.*; –iness *n.* économie *f.*; –y *a.* économe, frugal
thrill *n.* frémissement, tressaillement *m.*; émotion *f.*; — *vt.* émouvoir, émotionner; faire frémir; — *vi.* frémir, tressaillir; –er *n.* (coll.) écrit mélodramatique *m.*; –ing *a.* émouvant, passionnant
thrive *vi.* réussir; bien marcher; prospérer
thriving *a.* florissant; prospère
throat *n.* gorge *f.*; gosier *m.*; clear one's — s'éclaircir la voix; have a sore — avoir mal à la gorge; cut– *a.* concurrence ruineuse
throb *vi.* palpiter, battre; — *n.* battement *m.*, pulsation *f.*; –bing *n.* pulsation *f.*, battement *m.*
throes *n. pl.* agonie *f.*; douleurs *f. pl.*
thrombosis *n.* thrombose *f.*
throne *n.* trône *m.*
throng *n.* foule *f.*; — *vi.* affluer, se presser; — *vt.* encombrer
throttle *n.* étrangleur *m.*; — *vt.* étrangler
through *prep.* à travers; par; go — traver-

ser, parcourir; fouiller; — *adv.* à travers; jusqu'au bout; — *a.* direct; (coll.) fini

throughout *prep.* partout (dans)

throw *n.* jet *m.*; coup *m.*; lancée *f.*; lancement *m.*; — *vt.* jeter, lancer; projeter; (horse) démonter; (wrestling) terrasser; — **away** jeter, rejeter; — **back** renvoyer; — **off** jeter; se défaire de; enlever; dépister; — **out** jeter, rejeter; expulser, metter à la porte; (clutch) débrayer; — **up** rejeter, vomir; (hands) lever; abandonner, renoncer à

throwback *n.* retour *m.*

thrust *n.* poussée *f.*; coup, trait *m.*; — *vt.* pousser; enfoncer; fourrer; — *vi.* porter un coup

thruway *n.* autostrade *f.*

thud *n.* bruit sourd *m.*; — *vi.* tomber avec un bruit sourd

thug *n.* bandit, gangster *m.*

thumb *n.* pouce *m.*; — **index** encoches *f. pl.*; — *vt.* manier; — **a ride** (coll.) faire de l'auto-stop; — **through** parcourir, jeter un coup d'œil à

thumbnail *n.* ongle du pouce *m.*; — *a.* petit, minuscule

thumbtack *n.* punaise *f.*

thump *n.* coup (de poing) *m.*; coup sourd *m.*; — *vt.* taper, bourrer, battre

thunder *n.* tonnerre *m.*; foudre *f.*; **clap of** — coup de foudre *m.*; — *vt. & vi.* tonner; **-ing** *a.* tonnant

thunderbolt *n.* coup de foudre *m.*

thundercloud, thunderhead *n.* cumulus à bords blancs *m.*

thunderstorm *n.* orage *m.*

thunderstruck *a.* abasourdi

Thursday *n.* jeudi *m.*

thus *adv.* ainsi; donc; aussi; de cette manière, de cette façon; — **far** jusqu'ici

thwart *n.* (naut.) banc de nage *m.*; — *vt.* faire avorter, contrecarrer

thy *a.* ton, ta, tes

thyme *n.* thym *m.*

thyroid *a.* thyroïde

tiara *n.* tiare *f.*

Tibet *n.* Thibet *m.*

tick *n.* tic-tac *m.*; trait *m.*, marque *f.*; (zool.) tique *f.*; — *vi.* faire tic-tac; marcher, fonctionner; **-er** *n.* télégraphe imprimeur *m.*; (coll.) cœur *m.*; **-ing** *n.* tic-tac *m.*; coutil à matelas *m.*

ticket *n.* billet *m.*; ticket *m.*; bulletin *m.*; **complimentary** — billet de faveur *m.*; **one-way** — billet simple *m.*; **round-trip** — billet d'aller et retour *m.*; **season** — carte d'abonnement *f.*; — **collector** contrôleur *m.*; — **window** guichet *m.*

tickle *vt.* chatouiller; amuser; — *vi.* avoir des chatouillements; **-r** *n.* question difficile *f.*

tickling *n.* chatouillement *m.*

ticklish *a.* chatouilleux; délicat; difficile

tidal *a.* de la marée; — **wave** vague de fond *f.*

tidbit *n.* friandise, bouchée *f.*

tiddlywinks *n. pl.* jeu de puce *m.*

tide *n.* marée *f.*; (fig.) fortune *f.*; **flood** — marée montante *f.*; **high** — marée haute *f.*; **low** — marée basse *f.*

tidewater *n.* eau de marée *f.*

tidily *adv.* avec soin; avec ordre

tidiness *n.* bon ordre *m.*; propreté *f.*

tidings *n. pl.* nouvelles *f. pl.*

tidy *a.* en bon ordre; ordonné; propre; bien tenu; considérable, assez grand; — *vt.* ranger, arranger; mettre de l'ordre dans

tie *n.* cravate *f.*; nœud *m.*; lien *m.*; liaison *f.*; nombre égal *m.*; égalité *f.*; (rail.) traverse *f.*; — **game** match à égalité *m.*; — **clip** pince à cravate *f.*; — *vt.* lier, attacher, nouer; — *vi.* être à égalité; — **a knot** faire un nœud; — **up** ficeler, attacher; panser; immobiliser

tier *n.* rangée *f.*; gradin, étage *m.*

tie-up *n.* suspension des affaires *f.*; arrêt de la circulation *m.*

tiff *n.* querelle *f.*

tight *a.* serré; collant; tendu; imperméable; étanche; ivre, gris, soûl; avare; — *adv.* fermement; bien; **-s** *n. pl.* maillot *m.*; **-en** *vt.* serrer, reserrer, raidir; **-ly** *adv.* étroitement; fortement; bien; **-ness** *n.* tension *f.*; étroitesse *f.*

tightfisted *a.* avare, ladre

tight-fitting *a.* collant

tight-lipped *a.* aux lèvres serrées; silencieux; impassible

tightrope *n.* corde *f.*; — **artist** funambule *m. & f.*; danseur de corde *m.*

tile *n.* tuile *f.*; carreau *m.*; — *vt.* carreler; **-d** *a.* en tuiles; carrelé

tiling *n.* carrelage *m.*

till *n.* tiroir-caisse *m.*; — *prep.* jusqu'à; à; — *conj.* jusqu'à ce que; — *vt.* labourer, cultiver; **-able** *a.* arable, labourable; **-age** *n.* labour, labourage *m.*; **-er** *n.* laboureur, cultivateur *m.*; (naut.) barre *f.*; **-ing** *n.* labour *m.*

tilt *n.* pente, inclinaison *f.*; joute *f.*; **at full** — à toute vitesse; — *vt. & vi.* pencher, incliner

timber *n.* bois (de construction) *m.*; poutre *f.*; (coll.) étoffe *f.*, calibre *m.*; trempe *f.*; — *vt.* boiser, blinder

timberland *n.* pays boisé *m.*

timbre *n.* timbre *m.*

time *n.* temps *m.*; heure *f.*; époque *f.*; moment *m.*; saison *f.*; âge m.; fois *f.*; (mus.) mesure *f.*; **a short — after** peu après; **at all —s** toujours; **at no —** jamais; **at the same —** en même temps; à la fois; d'autre part; **at –s** parfois; **for the — being** pour le moment; **from — to —** de temps en temps, de temps à autre; **in —** à temps; avec le temps; **keep —** suivre la mesure; **on —** à l'heure; **spare —** loisir *m.*; temps disponible *m.*; **what — is it?** quelle heure est-il?; **— exposure** pose *f.*; **— lag** retard *m.*; **— limit** délai *m.*; limite de temps *f.*; **— signal** signal horaire *m.*; **—** *vt.* régler, mesurer, calculer; chronométrer; **–less** *a.* éternel; **–liness** *n.* à propos *m.*; opportunité *f.*; **–ly** *a.* opportun, à-propos

time-honored *a.* consacré; vénérable

timekeeper *n.* chronométreur *m.*; controlleur

timepiece *n.* montre *f.*; pendule *f.*

timesaver *n.* économiseur de temps *m.*

timetable *n.* horaire, indicateur *m.*

timeworn *a.* vénérable; usé par le temps

timid *a.* timide; peureux; **–ity** *n.* timidité *f.*

timing *n.* réglage *m.*; chronométrage *m.*; calcul *m.*

timpani *n.* timbales *f. pl.*

tin *n.* étain *m.*; fer-blanc *m.*; (baking) plat *m.*; **— can** boîte *f.*; **— plate** ferblanterie *f.*; **—** *vt.* étamer; **–ny** *a.* d'étain; grêle

tincture *n.* teinture *f.*; **—** *vt.* teinter, teindre

tinder *n.* mèche de briquet *f.*

tine *n.* fourchon *m.*, dent *f.*

tin foil *n.* feuille d'étain *f.*; papier d'étain *m.*

tinge *n.* teinte *f.*; **—** *vt.* teindre

tingle *vi.* tinter; picoter; **—** *n.* tintement *m.*; fourmillement *m.*

tingling *n.* tintement *m.*; fourmillement, picotement *m.*

tinker *n.* chaudronnier *m.*; **—** *vi.* bricoler; **— (with)** *vt.* rafistoler

tinkle *vi.* tinter; **—** *n.* tintement *m.*

tinsel *n.* clinquant *m.*; faux brillant *m.*

tinsmith *n.* ferblantier *m.*

tinware *n.* ferblanterie *f.*

tint *n.* teinte *f.*; **—** *vt.* teinter, colorer

tiny *a.* tout petit; minuscule

tip *n.* bout *m.*, pointe, extrémité *f.*; pourboire *m.*, gratification *f.*; (coll.) tuyau, conseil *m.*; **—** *vt.* donner un pourboire à; embouter; **— over** renverser; **–ping** *n.* pourboires *m. pl.*

tipple *vi.* boire à l'excès; **–r** *n.* ivrogne *m.*

tipsiness *n.* ivresse *f.*

tipsy *a.* ivre, gris

tiptoe *n.* pointe des pieds *f.*; **on —** sur la pointe des pieds; **—** *vi.* marcher sur la pointe des pieds

tirade *n.* tirade, diatribe *f.*

tire *n.* pneu *m.*; **flat —** pneu à plat *m.*; crevaison *f.*; **spare —** pneu de rechange; **—** *vt.* fatiguer, lasser; **—** *vi.* se fatiguer, se lasser; **–d** *a.* fatigué; las (lasse); **grow –d of** se lasser de; **–dness** *n.* fatigue, lassitude *f.*; **–less** *a.* infatigable, inlassable; **–some** *a.* fatigant; ennuyeux

tissue *n.* tissu *m.*; **— paper** papier de soie *m.*

titanic *a.* titanique

tit for tat, à bon chat bon rat

tithe *n.* dîme *f.*

titillate *vi. & vt.* chatouiller, titiller

title *n.* titre *m.*; droit *m.*; **—** *vt.* intituler; **–d** *a.* titré; **—** *n.* (law) titre de propriété; acte *m.*; **— rôle** *n.* premier rôle *m.*

titlist *n.* champion *m.*

titrate *vt. & vi.* titrer

titter *n.* petit rire *m.*; **—** *vi.* pousser de petits rires

titular *a.* titulaire

to *prep* à; vers; en; chez; jusqu'à; de; pour; **—** *adv.*, **come —** reprendre connaissance; **go — and fro** aller et venir

toadstool *n.* champignon vénéneux *m.*

toast *n.* pain grillé, toast *m.*; **—** *vt.* griller; boire à la santé de; **–er** *n.* grille-pain *m.*

toastmaster *n.* celui qui annonce les toasts *m.*, celui qui préside à un banquet *m.*

tobacco *n.* tabac *m.*, **— pouch** *n.* blague à tabac *f.*

toboggan *n.* toboggan *m.*

today *adv.* aujourd'hui; **a week from —** d'aujourd'hui en huit

toddle *vi.* marcher à petits pas; **–r** *n.* enfant qui commence à marcher *m.*

toddy *n.* grog *m.*

to-do *n.* remue-ménage *m.*; bruit, tapage *m.*

toe *n.* orteil, doigt du pied *m.*; (shoe) bout *m.*, pointe *f.*; **—** *vt.*, **— the line** se conformer, s'aligner

toenail *n.* ongle d'orteil *m.*

toffee *n.* (candy) caramel au beurre *m.*

together *adv.* ensemble; avec; à la fois; de concert; **bring —** rassembler, réunir

toggle *n.* barrette *f.*; cabillot *m.*; **— switch** *n.* levier articulé *m.*

toil *n.* travail, labeur *m.*; **—** *vi.* travailler, peiner; **–er** *n.* travailleur *m.*; **–some** *a.* pénible

toilet *n.* cabinets *m. pl.*, toilette *f.*; **— paper** papier hygiénique *m.*; **— water** eau de Cologne *f.*

token *n.* jeton *m.*; témoignage, signe *m.*, marque *f.*; **by the same —** de plus; **— of love** gage d'amour *m.*

tolerance *n.* tolérance *f.*

tolerant *a.* tolérant

tolerate *vt.* supporter, tolérer

toleration *n.* tolérance *f.*

toll *n.* taxe *f.*; droit de passage *m.*; (bell) son *m.*, son de cloches; **death —** mortalité *f.*; **— bridge** pont à péage *m.*; **— call** communication interurbaine *f.*; **-gate** barrière *f.*; **— house** péage *m.*; — *vt. & vi.* sonner

tomato *n.* tomate *f.*

tomb *n.* tombe *f.*; tombeau *m.*

tomboy *n.* garçon manqué *m.*

tombstone *n.* pierre tombale *f.*

tomfoolery *n.* nigauderie *f.*

tomorrow *adv.* demain; **day after —** àpres-demain *m.*; **— morning** demain matin; **week from —** de demain en huit

ton *n.* tonne *f.*; **-nage** *n.* tonnage *m.*, jauge *f.*

tone *m.* ton, accent, son *m.*; voix *f.*; nuance *f.*; **— vt.**, **— down** atténuer, adoucir; **-less** *a.* atone; sans éclat

tongs *n. pl.* pinces, tenailles, pincettes *f. pl.*

tongue *n.* langue *f.*; (buckle) ardillon *m.*; (shoe) languette *f.*; **native —** langue maternelle *f.*

tongue-tied *a.* interdit

tonic *a.* tonique; **— n.** tonique, fortifiant *m.*

tonight *adv.* ce soir; cette nuit

tonsil *n.* amygdale, tonsile *f.*; **-litis** *n.* amygdalite *f.*; **-lectomy** *n.* amygdalotomie *f.*

tonsure *n.* tonsure *f.*; **— vt.** tonsurer

too *adv.* trop; aussi; de plus, d'ailleurs; **— much** trop, trop de

tool *n.* outil, instrument, ustensile *m.*; **-box** coffre à outils *m.*; **— vt.** travailler, usiner; équiper; dorer; **-ing** *n.* usinage *m.*; dorure *f.*

toot *n.* cornement, coup de klaxon *m.*; (naut.) coup de sirène *m.*; **— vt.** corner, donner un coup de klaxon; sonner; **— vi.** corner; sonner

tooth *n.* dent *f.*; **— powder** poudre dentifrice *f.*; **-ed** *a.* denté; dentelé; **-less** *a.* édenté, sans dents

toothache *n.* mal de dents *m.*; **have a —** avoir mal aux dents

toothbrush *n.* brosse à dents *f.*

tooth paste *n.* pâte dentifrice *f.*

toothpick *n.* cure-dents *m.*

top *n.* sommet, haut *m.*, cime *f.*; dessus *m.*; tête *f.*; (toy) toupie *f.*; **— a.** (le) plus haut, supérieur; (floor) dernier; (quality) premier; **— hat** chapeau haut de forme *m.*; **— vt.** surmonter; coiffer; surpasser, dépasser; être à la tête de

topcoat *n.* pardessus *m.*

topflight *a.* excellent, supérieur, premier

top-heavy *a.* trop lourd du haut

topic *n.* sujet *m.*, matière *f.*; **-al** *a.* actuel, d'actualité; topique

topknot *n.* chignon *m.*; (bird) huppe *f.*

topmost *n.* le plus haut, le plus élevé

topographer *n.* topographe *m.*

topography *n.* topographie *f.*

topple *vt.* faire tomber; **— vi.** tomber; branler

top-secret *a.* extrèmement secret

topsoil *n.* terre végétale *f.*

topsy-turvy *a. & adv.* sens dessus dessous

tor *n.* pic *m.*

torch *n.* torche *f.*, flambeau *m.*

torchlight *n.* lumière de flambeau *f.*; **— procession** retraite aux flambeaux *f.*

toreador *n.* toréador *m.*

torment *n.* tourment *m.*; torture *f.*, supplice *m.*; **— vt.** tourmenter, torturer; **-or** *n.* tourmenteur *m.*; bourreau *m.*

torn *a.* déchiré

tornado *n.* ouragan *m.*, tornade *f.*

torpedo *n.* torpille *f.*; **— boat** torpilleur *m.*; **— tube** lance-torpille *m.*; **— vt.** torpiller

torpid *a.* engourdi

torpor *n.* torpeur *f.*

torque *n.* couple de torsion *m.*

torrent *n.* torrent *m.*; **in -s** (rain) par torrents, à verse; **-ial** *a.* torrentiel

torrid *a.* torride, brûlant

torso *n.* torse *m.*

tort *n.* (law) dommage *m.*

tortoise-shell *n.* écaille *f.*; **— a.** d'écaille

tortuous *a.* tortueux, sinueux

torture *n.* torture *f.*; supplice, tourment *m.*; **— vt.** torturer, mettre au supplice; **-r** *n.* bourreau *m.*

toss *n.* jet, lancement *m.*; coup *m.*; **— vt.** jeter, lancer; choisir (à pile ou face); hocher; secouer, agiter; (of horse) démonter; **— vi.** (s')agiter, (se) tourner; **— off** faire rapidement; expédier; (drink) lamper; **-ing** *n.* lancement *m.*; agitation *f.*

tossup *n.* chance égale *f.*

tot *n.* petit enfant *m.*

total *a.* total; global; complet; **— n.** total, montant *m.*; **— vt. & vi.** totaliser; **-ity** *n.* totalité *f.*; **-ize** *vt.* totaliser

totalitarian *a.* totalitaire

totter *vi.* chanceler; tituber; **-ing** *a.* chancelant; titubant

touch *n.* toucher, tact *m.*; coup *m.*; touche *f.*; contact, rapport *m.*; communication *f.*; soupçon *m.*, pointe *f.*; **in — with** en rapport avec, en communication avec; **— vt.** toucher; effleurer; émouvoir, attendrir; **— vi.** se toucher; **— off** déclencher; — **up** faire des retouches; **–iness** *n.* susceptibilité *f.*; **–ing** *a.* touchant, émouvant, attendrissant; **–y** *a.* qui se pique facilement; susceptible; difficile

touchdown *n.* touché *m.*

touchstone *n.* pierre de touche *f.*

tough *a.* dur, difficile; fort; tenace; **–en** *vt.* durcir, endurcir; **–ness** *n.* dureté *f.*, difficulté *f.*; force *f.*; ténacité *f.*

tour *n.* voyage *m.*, excursion *f.*; tour *m.*, tournée *f.*; — *vi.* voyager; — *vt.* visiter; **–ist** *n.* touriste *m. & f.*

tournament *n.* tournoi *m.*; concours *m.*

tousle *vt.* ébouriffer

tout *vi.* (coll.) donner des tuyaux; — *n.* pisteur *m.*

tow *n.* remorque *f.*; filasse *f.*; — *vt.* remorquer; **–ing** *n.* remorque *f.*

toward(s) *prep.* vers; envers; pour

towel *n.* serviette *f.*; essuie-mains *m.*; — **rack** porte-serviettes *m.*; — *tt.* essuyer; frotter; **–ling** *n.* tissu-éponge *m.*

tower *n.* tour *f.*; pylône *m.*; (church) clocher *m.*; — *vi.* dominer; **–ing** *a.* très haut; énorme

town *n.* ville *f.*; — **hall** hôtel de ville *m.*

township *n.* commune *f.*

townsman *n.* habitant de la ville *m.*

townspeople *n.* habitants de la ville, citoyens *m. pl.*

toxic *a.* toxique

toxicology *n.* toxicologie *f.*

toxin *n.* toxine *f.*

toy *n.* jouet *m.*; joujou *m.*; — **dog** chien de salon *m.*; — *vi.*, — **with** s'amuser avec

trace *n.* trace *f.*; vestige *m.*; trait *m.*; — *vt.* tracer; calquer; **–able** *a.* qu'on peut suivre; attribuable; **–r** *n.* (mil.) traceuse *f.*

trachea *n.* trachée *f.*

tracheotomy *n.* trachéotomie *f.*

tracing *n.* tracé *m.*; calque *m.*; — **paper** papier à calquer *m.*

track *n.* piste, trace *f.*; chemin *m.*, voie *f.*; (rail.) voie ferrée *f.*; rail(s) *m.* (*pl.*); (sports) courses à pied *f. pl.*; (tractor) chenille *f.*; **keep** — **of** ne pas perdre de vue; surveiller; suivre; **on the right** — sur la bonne voie; **throw off the** — dépister; — *vt.* suivre, traquer; — **down** dépister

tract *n.* étendue *f.*; brochure *f.*; (anat.) appareil *m.*

tractable *a.* traitable, docile

traction *n.* traction *f.*

tractor *n.* tracteur *m.*

trade *n.* commerce *m.*; métier *m.*; — **wind** vent alizé *m.*; — *vi.* faire du commerce; — *vt.* échanger; **–r** *n.* commerçant, marchand *m.*

trade-in *n.* reprise en compte *f.*

trademark *n.* marque (de fabrique) *f.*

tradesman *n.* marchand, fournisseur *m.*

trade-union *n.* syndicat (ouvrier) *m.*; **–ism** *n.* syndicalisme *m.*

trading *n.* commerce *m.*; — *a.* commerçant, marchand; commercial

tradition *n.* tradition *f.*

traditional *a.* traditionnel

traffic *n.* circulation *f.*; trafic, commerce *m.*; mouvement *m.*; — **jam** embouteillage *m.*; — **light** feu *m.*; — **manager** chef de mouvement *m.*; — **sign** indicateur *m.*; — **ticket** procès-verbal *m.*, contravention *f.*; — *vi.* trafiquer

tragedian *n.* tragédien *m.*

tragedy *n.* tragédie *f.*

tragic *a.* tragique

tragicomedy *n.* tragicomédie *f.*

trail *n.* trace, piste *f.*; traînée *f.*; sentier *m.*; — *vt.* traquer, suivre à la piste; — *vi.* traîner; ramper; **–er** (auto.) baladeuse *f.*; caravane *f.*; roulotte *f.*; (film) film-annonce *m.*; **–ing** *a.* rampant; qui (se) traîne

train *n.* train *m.*; suite *f.*; série *f.*; (dress) queue *f.*; — *vt.* exercer; former, élever; préparer; (animal) dresser; (sports) entraîner; (cannon) pointer, orienter; — *vi.* s'exercer; s'entraîner; **–ed** *a.* exercé; dressé; **–er** *n.* entraîneur *m.*; dresseur *m.*; **–ing** *n.* formation, éducation *f.*; entraînement *m.*; dressage *m.*; **physical** **–ing** éducation physique *f.*

trait *n.* trait *m.*

traitor *n.* traître *m.*; **–ous** *a.* traître, perfide

trajectory *n.* trajectoire *f.*

trammel *n.* tramail *m.*; — *vt.* entraver

tramp *n.* pas lourd *m.*; vagabond, chemineau *m.*; — **steamer** cargo, chemineau *m.*; — *vi.* marcher à pas lourds

trample *vt.* fouler (aux pieds); piétiner; écraser

trance *n.* transe, hypnose *f.*; extase *f.*

tranquil *a.* tranquille, calme; paisible; **–ize** *vt.* tranquilliser, calmer; apaiser; **–izer** *n.* calmant *m.*; **–lity** *n.* tranquillité *f.*, calme *m.*

transact *vt.* faire; **–ion** *n.* affaire *f.*; conduite *f.*; opération *f.*

transatlantic *a.* transatlantique

transcend *vt.* aller au delà de; surpasser, dépasser; **–ence, –ency** *n.* transcendance *f.*; **–ent** *a.* transcendant; **–ental** *a.* transcendantal

transcribe *vt.* transcrire; **–r** *n.* transcripteur *m.*

transcript *n.* copie, transcription *f.*; enregistrement *m.*; **–ion** *n.* transcription *f.*; enregistrement *m.*

transfer n. transfert m.; transport m.; correspondance f., bulletin de correspondance m.; — vt. transférer; transmettre; virer; calquer; — vi. faire une correspondance; —able a. transmissible; mobilier; —ence n. transfert m.

transfigure vt. tranfigurer

transfix vt. transpercer

transform vt. transformer; convertir; métamorphoser; —ation n. transformation f.; conversion f.; métamorphose f.; —er n. transformateur m.

transfuse vt. transfuser

transgress vt. transgresser; — vi. pécher; —ion n. violation, transgression f.; péché m., faute f.; —or n. transgresseur m.; pécheur m., pécheresse f.

transient a. transitoire, passager, de passage; momentané

transistor n. transistor m.

transit n. transport m.; transit m.; passage; —ion n. transition f.; passage m.; —ive a. transitif; —ory a. transitoire, de passage

translate vt. traduire

translation n. traduction f.; version f.

translator n. traducteur m.

translucence n. translucidité f.

translucent a. translucide

transmission n. transmission f.; transport m.; émission f.

transmit vt. transmettre; transporter; (radio) émettre; —ter n. émetteur m., transmetteur m.

transmute vt. transmuer, transformer

transoceanic a. transocéanique

transom n. vasistas m., imposte f.

transparency n. transparence f.; transparent m.; (phot.) diapositive f.

transparent a. transparent; clair

transpiration n. transpiration f.

transpire vt. & vi. transpirer

transplant vt. transplanter; —ation n. transplantation f.

transport n. transport m.; — vt. transporter; —ation n. transport m.

transpose vt. transposer

transposition n. transposition f.

transverse a. transversal; en travers

trap n. piège m.; trappe f.; (sink) collecteur m.; set a — tendre un piège, dresser un piège; — door trappe f.; —shooting tir aux pigeons m.; — vt. prendre au piège; — vi. trapper; —ped a. pris (au piège); —per n. trappeur m.; —pings n. pl. apparat m., atours m. pl.

trapeze n. trapèze m.

trapezoid n. quadrilatère irrégulier m.

trash n. débris m. pl.; camelote f.; —y a. de camelote

traumatic a. traumatique

travel n. voyage(s) m. (pl.); — vi. voyager, faire un voyage; parcourir; aller, circuler, marcher; —er n. voyageur m.; —ing n. voyages m. pl.; —ing a. de voyage; —ing salesman commis voyageur m.

traveler's check n. chèque de voyage m.

travelogue n. conférence avec projections décrivant un voyage f.

traverse n. traverse f.; — vt. traverser, passer à travers de

travesty n. travestissement m.; parodie f.; — vt. travestir; parodier

trawl n. chalut m.; — vi. & vt. pêcher au chalut; —er n. chalutier m.

tray n. plateau m.; cuvette f.

treacherous a. traître, perfide

treachery n. trahison, perfidie f.

treacle n. mélasse f.

tread n. pas m.; (stair) giron m.; (tire) chape f., roulement m.; — vi. marcher; — vt. fouler; — water nager debout

treadle n. pédale f.

treadmill n. moulin de discipline m.

treason n. trahison f.; —able a. traître, perfide; de trahison

treasure n. trésor m.; — vt. priser, aimer beaucoup; —r n. trésorier m.

treasury n. trésorerie f.; trésor m.

treat n. régal m.; plaisir m.; — vt. régaler; payer; traiter; soigner; — oneself to se payer, s'offrir

treatise n. traité m.

treaty n. traité m., convention f., accord m.

treble a. triple; — clef clef de sol f.; — vt. tripler

tree n. arbre m.; family — arbre généalogique m.

trek n. voyage m.; — vi. voyager

trellis n. treillis, treillage m.

tremble n. frisson m., vibration f.; — vi. trembler, vibrer

trembling a. tremblant; — n. tremblement m.; vibration f.

tremendous a. énorme; terrible

tremolo n. trémolo m.

tremor n. tremblement, choc m., secousse f.; frémissement m.

tremulous a. tremblotant

trench n. tranchée f., fossé m.; — coat imperméable m.

trenchant a. tranchant

trencherman n. gros mangeur m.

trend n. tendance f.; — vi. tendre

trepidation n. trépidation f.

trespass n. (eccl.) péché m., offense f.; (law) violation f.; — vi. pécher; — on violer; empiéter; pénétrer sans autori-

sation dans une propriété; –er n. (eccl.)
transgresseur, pécheur m.; personne qui
commet une violation de propriété f.
tress n. tresse, boucle f.
trestle n. tréteau, chevalet m.; (rail.) pont
(sur chevalets) m.
trey n. (cards) trois m.
triad n. triade f.
trial n. procès m., cause f., jugement m.;
essai m., épreuve f.; — a. d'essai, d'é-
preuve; experimental — **balance** n. balance de vérification f.
triangular a. triangulaire
triangulation n. triangulation f.
tribal a. de tribu
tribe n. tribu f.
tribesman n. membre d'une tribu m.
tribulation n. tribulation f.
tribunal n. tribunal m.; cour (de justice) f.
tribune n. (person) tribune f., tribun m.
tributary a. tributaire; — n. affluent, tributaire m.
tribute n. tribut, hommage m.
trice n., **in a** — en un clin d'œil; tout de
suite
trick n. tour m., ruse f.; truc m.; habitude,
manie f.; (cards) levée f.; **card** — tour
de cartes m.; **play a** — on jouer un tour
à; — vt. jouer un tour à; tromper, duper; **–ery** n. tricherie f.; tromperie f.;
–iness n. nature compliquée f.; **–y** a.
compliqué, difficile; rusé
trickle vi. ruisseler, dégoutter, couler; —
n. filet m.; petit peu m.
trickling a. dégouttant
tricolor n. drapeau français, drapeau tricolore m.
tricycle n. tricycle; (com.) triporteur m.
triennial a. triennal; trisannuel
trifle n. bagatelle, vétille f.; rien m.; — vi.
jouer; vétiller; s'occuper à des choses
peu importantes
trifling a. peu important, insignifiant
trigger n. gâchette, détente f.
trigonometry n. trigonométrie f.
trill n. (mus.) trille m.; –vt. triller; rouler;
— vi. faire des trilles
trillion n. trillion m.
trilogy n. trilogie f.
trim n. ornement m., ornementation f.;
bon état, bon ordre m.; équilibrage m.;
(hair) coupe f.; **in** — en forme; — a.
soigné; élégant; propre; — vt. orner,
ornementer, parer; garnir; équilibrer;
tailler, couper; (hair) rafraîchir; **–ming**
n. ornement m., ornementation f.; garniture f., garnissage m.; parure f.; (sewing) passementerie f.; taille f.; **–mings**
n. pl. garniture f., accompagnements
m. pl.; **–ness** n. élégance f.; belle taille f.

Trinidad n. Trinité f.
trinity n. groupe de trois m.; (eccl.) Trinité f.
trinket n. babiole f.; bibelot m.
trip n. voyage m., excursion f.; trébuche-
ment, faux pas m.; **take a** — faire un
voyage; — vt. faire trébucher; donner
un croc-en-jambe à; — vi. trébucher,
faire un faux pas
tripe n. tripes f. pl.; gras-double m.; bê-
tises f. pl.; camelote f.
triphammer n. marteau à bascule m.
triple a. triple; — vt. & vi. tripler
triplet n. trijumeau m., trijumelle f.;
(mus.) triolet m.; –s n. pl. trois jumeaux
triplicate n. triple, triplicata m.; **in** — en
triple (exemplaire)
tripod n. trépied m.; pied (à trois branches) m.
triptyque n. (auto.) triptyque m.
trite a. banal; **–ness** n. banalité f.
triumph n. triomphe m.; victoire f.; succès
m.; — vi. triompher; — **over** triompher
de; l'emporter sur; –al a. de triomphe;
triomphal; –ant a. triomphant; de triomphe
triumvirate n. triumvirat m.
trivet n. trépied m., chevrette f.
trivial a. trivial; sans importance, insignifiant; léger; **–ity** n. insignifiance f.
trochaic a. trochaïque
troche n. (med.) tablette f.
Trojan a. & n. Troyen m.
troll n. (fishing) moulinet m.; — vi. pêcher à la cuiller; –ing n. pêche à la cuiller f.
trolley n. trolley m., poulie f.; (car) tramway m.; chariot m.; — **bus** trolley-auto-
bus m.
trollop n. souillon f.
troop n. troupe, bande f.; — vi. aller en
troupe; s'attrouper; — **in** entrer en
troupe; **–er** n. soldat, troupier m.
troopship n. transport militaire m.
trophy n. trophée m.
tropic n. tropique m.; **–al** a. tropical
trot n. trot m.; — vi. trotter, aller au trot;
–ter n. cheval de trot m.
troubadour n. troubadour, trouvère m.
trouble n. difficulté f.; peine f.; ennui m.;
trouble m.; **be in** — avoir des ennuis,
avoir des difficultés; **be worth the** — to
valoir la peine de; **take the** — to prendre la peine de; — vt. préoccuper, tourmenter, affliger, inquiéter; déranger, ennuyer, incommoder; donner de la peine
à; troubler; — vi. s'inquiéter; se déranger; **–d** a. inquiet; trouble; **–some** a. difficile; ennuyeux, incommode
troublemaker n. fomentateur, fauteur m.
trough n. auge f.; baquet m.; abreuvoir

m.; (wave) creux *m.*

trounce *vt.* écraser; rosser

troupe *n.* troupe *f.*; **–r** *n.* (theater) membre d'une troupe *m.*

trousers *n. pl.* pantalon *m.*

trousseau *n.* trousseau *m.*

trout *n.* truite *f.*

trowel *n.* truelle *f.*; déplantoir *m.*

troy (weight) *n.* poids troy *m.*

Troy *n.* Troie *f.*

truant *n.* élève absent sans permission *m. & f.*

truce *n.* trève *f.*; **flag of —** drapeau parlementaire *m.*

truck *n.* camion *m.*, camionnette *f.*; wagon *m.*; chariot *m.*; affaire *f.*; rapports *m. pl.*; **— driver** camionneur *m.*; **— farm** jardin maraîcher *m.*; **—** *vt.* porter en camion; camionner; **–er** *n.* camionneur *m.* **–ing** *n.* camionnage *m.*

truculent *a.* truculent; féroce

trudge *vi.* marcher lourdement

true *a.* vrai, véritable; fidèle; juste; réel; **—** *adv.* vrai; juste; **come —** se réaliser; **hold —** en être de même; **—** *n.*, **out of —** hors d'aplomb; décentré; faussé; gauchi; **—** *vt.* ajuster; défausser, dégauchir

truism *n.* axiome, truisme *m.*

truly *adv.* vraiment, véritablement; en vérité; fidèlement

trump *n.* atout *m.*; **no —** sans-atout; **—** *vt.* couper; **— up** forger, inventer

trumpet *n.* trompette *f.*; **—** *vi.* sonner de la trompette; (elephant) barrir; **—** *vt. & vi.* proclamer; **–er** *n.* trompette *m.*; trompettiste *m.*

truncate *vt.* tronquer

truncheon *n.* gros bâton *m.*

trundle *n.* roulette *f.*; **—** *vt.* faire rouler; pousser

trunk *n.* (tree) tronc *m.*; (luggage) malle *f.*; (elephant) trompe *f.*; **— line** (rail.) ligne principale *f.*; (telephone) ligne interurbaine *f.*; **–s** *pl.* caleçon; caleçon de bain; cache-sexe *m.*

truss *n.* cintre *m.*; armature *f.*; bandage (herniaire) *m.*; **—** *vt.* armer, renforcer; lier, ligoter

trust *n.* confiance *f.*; crédit *m.*; charge *f.*; garde *f.*; syndicat, trust *m.*; **in —** en dépôt; **on —** à crédit; **—** *vt.* se fier à; confier; espérer; faire crédit à; **—** *vi.* se fier; se confier; **–ed** *a.* de confiance; fidèle; **–ful** *a.* confiant; **–ing** *a.* plein de confiance

trustee *n.* dépositaire *m.*; administrateur *m.*; curateur *m.*; **–ship** *n.* administration *f.*

trustworthiness *n.* fidélité, loyauté *f.*

trustworthy *a.* digne de foi, digne de con-

fiance, fidèle

trusty *a.* fidèle, loyal, sûr

truth *n.* vérité *f.*; vrai *m.*; **in —, to tell the — à** vrai dire; **–ful** *a.* vrai; véridique; **–fulness** *n.* véracité; véridicité *f.*

try *n.* essai *m.*; **—** *vt.* essayer, tenter, tâcher; expérimenter; éprouver; mettre à l'épreuve; faire l'essai de; goûter; (law) juger; **—** *vi.* essayer, tâcher; **— on** essayer, tâcher; **— out** essayer, mettre à l'épreuve; **–ing** *a.* pénible, dur, difficile; fatigant

tryout *n.* essai *m.*, épreuve *f.*

tryst *n.* rendez-vous *m.*, assignation *f.*

tub *n.* baquet *m.*, cuve *f.*, cuvier *m.*; (bath) baignoire *f.*; bain *m.*; **–by** *a.* boulot; gros

tube *n.* tube, tuyau *m.*; canal, conduit *m.*; (radio) lampe, ampoule *f.*; **inner — chambre** à air *f.*; **test — éprouvette** *f.*; **—** *vt.* tuber

tuber *n.* tubercule *m.*; tuberacée *f.*

tubercular *a.* tuberculeux

tuberculosis *n.* tuberculose *f.*

tuberous *a.* tubéreux

tubing *n.* tube, tuyau *m.*; tuyautage *m.*

tubular *a.* tubulaire; à tubes

tuck *n.* pli, rempli *m.*; troussis *m.*; **—** *vt.* plisser; remplier; raccourcir; rentrer; **— in** (bedding) rentrer; border

Tuesday *n.* mardi *m.*; **Shrove — mardi** gras *m.*

tuft *n.* (hair) touffe *f.*; (bird) houppe *f.*; mèche *f.*; pompon *m.*; flocon *m.*; huppe *f.*; aigrette *f.*; **—** *vt.* former en touffes **–ed** *a.* en touffe, en houppe, huppé

tug *n.* traction *f.*; serrement *m.*; (naut.) remorqueur *m.*; **— of war** lutte (de traction) à la corde *f.*; **—** *vt. & vi.*; tirer; tirailler

tugboat *n.* remorqueur *m.*

tuition *n.* (frais d') instruction *f.*, enseignement *m.*

tumble *n.* chute, culbute *f.*; **—** *vi.* faire une chute, tomber; faire des culbutes; s'agiter; **— into** se jeter dans; **— out of** sauter de; **–r** *n.* acrobate *m. & f.*; verre *m.*; (elec.) culbuteur *m.*; (lock) gorge *f.*

tumble-down *a* délabré; qui tombe en ruines

tumescent *a.* tumescent

tumor *n.* tumeur *f.*

tumult *n.* tumulte, trouble *m.*; **–uous** *a.* tumultueux; turbulent

tun *n.* fût *m.*; tonne *f.*; (naut.) tonneau

tundra *n.* toundra *f.*

tune *n.* air *m.*; accord *m.*; **in —** (piano) d'accord, (engine) au point; **out of — désaccordé**; **—** *vt.* accorder, mettre d'accord; (radio) syntoniser **— in** accrocher;

accorder; — **up** s'accorder; (engine) mettre au point, régler; **–ful** *a.* harmonieux, mélodieux; **–r** *n.* accordeur *m.*

tungsten *n.* tungstène *m.*

tunic *n.* tunique *f.*

tuning *n.* accordage *m.*; mise au point *f.*, réglage *m.*; — **fork** diapason *m.*

Tunis *n.* Tunis *m.*

Tunisia *n.* Tunisie *f.*

tunnel *n.* tunnel, souterrain *m.*; — *vt. & vi.* percer (un tunnel)

turbid *a.* trouble; **–ity** *n.* turbidité *f.*

turbojet *n.* turboréacteur *m.*

turbomotor *n.* turbomoteur *m.*

turbulence *n.* turbulence, agitation *f.*

turbulent *a.* turbulent, tumultueux

tureen *n.* soupière *f.*

turf *n.* gazon *m.*; turf *m.*

turgid *a.* turgide, enflé, ampoulé; **–ity** *n.* enflure, emphase *f.*

Turk *n.* Turc *m.*, Turque *f.*; **–ey** *n.* Turquie *f.*; **–ish** *a.* turc, turque; **–ish bath(s)** hammam(s) *m.* (*pl.*); **–ish towel** serviette éponge *f.*

turkey *n.* dindon *m.*, dinde *f.*

turmoil *n.* trouble *m.*, agitation *f.*

turn *n.* tour *m.*; tournure *f.*; tournant *m.*; virage *m.*; service *m.*; **(done)** **to a —** (cuit) au point; **in —** tour à tour, à tour de rôle; **out of —** avant son tour; **— of mind** tour d'esprit *m.*; — *vt.* tourner, retourner; passer; — *vi.* tourner; se tourner, se retourner; changer, se changer; dépendre; devenir; **— around** tourner; se retourner; **— away** détourner; **— back** rebrousser chemin, retourner sur ses pas; repousser; **— down** retourner; refuser; repousser; baisser; (collar) rabattre; **— in** aller se coucher; **— off** fermer, éteindre, couper; tourner; **— on** ouvrir, allumer; se jeter sur; **— out** mettre dehors; retourner; produire, confectionner, fabriquer; éteindre, fermer, couper; tourner; arriver; paraître; se réunir, se rassembler; **— over** tourner, retourner; donner; capoter; **— up** relever; retrousser; retourner; trouver, arriver, se présenter; **–ing** *a.* tournant; **–ing** *n.* rotation *f.*; changement *m.*; virage *m.*; **–ing point** tournant *m.*; moment critique *m.*

turncoat *n.* renégat *m.*

turnip *n.* navet *m.*

turnout *n.* foule, assemblée *f.*

turnover *n.* changement *m.*; écoulement *m.*; **apple —** chausson aux pommes *m.*

turnpike *n.* grande route à péage *f.*

turnstile *n.* tourniquet *m.*

turntable *n.* plaque tournante *f.*; tourne-disques *m.*

turpentine *n.* térébenthine *f.*

turpitude *n.* turpitude *f.*

turret *n.* tourelle *f.*

turtle *n.* tortue *f.*

Tuscany *n.* Toscane *f.*

tusk *n.* défense, grosse dent *f.*

tussle *n.* lutte *f.*; mêlée *f.*; corps-à-corps *m.*; — *vi.* lutter

tutelage *n.* tutelle *f.*

tutor *n.* précepteur *m.*; — *vt.* instruire; donner des leçons particulières à; **–ial** *a.* individuel; particulier

tuxedo *n.* smoking *m.*

TV (television) *n.* télévision *f.*

twaddle *n.* balivernes *f. pl.*

twang *n.* son aigu *m.*; ton nasillard *m.*; **speak with a —** parler du nez; — *vt.* gratter, pincer; faire résonner; — *vi.* résonner, vibrer

tweak *vt.* pincer; tirer

tweed *n.* tweed *m.*, cheviote *f.*

tweet *n.* pépiement *m.*; — *vi.* pépier

tweezers *n. pl.* pinces *f. pl.*; (hair) pinces à épiler *f. pl.*

twelfth *a.* douzième

twelve *a.* douze; une douzaine de; — **o'clock (noon)** midi; (midnight) minuit

twentieth *a.* vingtième

twenty *a.* vingt

twenty-one *a.* vingt et un

twice *adv.* deux fois

twiddle *vt.* (thumbs) **tourner**

twig *n.* brindille *f.*

twilight *n.* crépuscule *m.*

twill *n.* croisé *m.*

twin *n.* jumeau *m.*, jumelle *f.*; **— beds lits** jumeaux *m. pl.*

twine *n.* ficelle *f.*; — *vt.* tordre; entrelacer; — *vi.* se tordre; s'enlacer

twin-engine (d) *a.* bimoteur

twinge *n.* élancement *m.*; — *vi.* élancer

twinkle *n.* scintillement *m.*; pétillement *m.*; lueur *f.*; — *vi.* scintiller; pétiller

twinkling *n.* scintillement *m.*; **— of an eye** clin d'œil *m.*

twirl *vt.* tortiller; (faire) tourner; faire des moulinets avec; — *vi.* tournoyer

twist *n.* torsion *f.*; tour *m.*; coude *m.*; cordon *m.*; tortillon *m.*; (tobacco) rouleau *m.*; **— of the wrist** tour de poignet *m.*; — *vt.* tordre; tortiller; — *vi.* se tordre; se tortiller; tourner; serpenter; **— one's ankle** se donner une entorse; **–ed** *a.* tordu; **–er** *n.* (coll.) tornade *f.*; **–ing** *a.* tortueux

twit *vt.* railler; taquiner

twitch *n.* tic *m.*, crispation *f.*; (pain) élancement *m.*; — *vt.* crisper, contracter; — *vi.* se crisper, se contracter; avoir un tic

twitter *n.* gazouillement *m.*; émotion *f.*; —

vi. gazouiller

two *a.* deux

two-edged *a.* à deux tranchants

two-faced *a.* hypocrite; à deux visages

two-fisted *a.* (coll.) fort, vigoureux

twofold *a.* double

two-handed *a.* à deux mains

two-legged *a.* bipède

two-piece *a.* en deux pièces

two-seater *n.* voiture à deux places *f.*

two-step *n.* pas de deux *m.*

two-way *a.* (street) à deux sens

tycoon *n.* magnat industriel *m.*

type *n.* type *m.*; genre *m.*; (print.) caractère *m.*; **set** — composer; — *vt.* écrire à la machine, dactylographier, taper

typesetter *n.* compositeur *m.*

typesetting *n.* composition *f.*

typewriter *n.* machine à écrire *f.*

typhoid *a.* typhoïde; — **fever** fièvre typhoïde *f.*

typhoon *n.* typhon *m.*

typhus *n.* typhus *m.*

typical *a.* typique, caractéristique; **–ly** *adv.* d'une manière typique

typify *vt.* être caractéristique de; représenter, symboliser

typist *n.* dactylographe, dactylo *m. & f.*

typographer *n.* typographe *m.*

typographic(al) *a.* typographique

typography *n.* typographie *f.*

tyrannical *a.* tyrannique

tyrannize *vt.* tyranniser; — *vi.* faire le tyran

tyranny *n.* tyrannie *f.*

tyrant *n.* tyran *m.*

U

ubiquitous *a.* qui se trouve partout

udder *n.* mamelle *f.*; pis *m.*

ugliness *n.* laideur *f.*

ugly *a.* laid

ulcer *n.* ulcère *m.*; **–ate** *vt.* ulcérer; **–ation** *n.* ulcération *f.*; **–ous** *a.* ulcéreux

ulna *n.* cubitus *m.*

ulterior *a.* ultérieur; — **motive** arrière-pensée *f.*, motif caché *m.*

ultimate *a.* final; dernier; décisif; **–ly** *adv.* en fin de compte

ultimatum *n.* ultimatum *m.*

ultra *a.* extrême

umbilical *a.* ombilical

umbrage *n.* ombrage *m.*; take — s'offenser

umbrella *n.* parapluie *m.*; — **stand** porte-parapluies *m.*

umpire *n.* arbitre *m.*; — *vt.* arbitrer

umpiring *n.* arbitrage *m.*

unabashed *a.* sans être décontenancé

unabated *a.* non-diminué

unabating *a.* soutenu

unable *a.* incapable; impuissant; **be** — **ne pas pouvoir**

unabridged *a.* intégral, non abrégé

unaccented *a.* sans accent; atone

unacceptable *a.* inacceptable

unaccommodating *a.* peu accommodant; désobligeant

unaccompanied *a.* seul, inaccompagné; (mus.) sans accompagnement

unaccomplished *a.* inaccompli, inachevé; qui manque de talent

unaccountable *a.* inexplicable

unaccounted *a.*, — **for** inexpliqué; disparu, perdu; qui manque

unaccredited *a.* non-accrédité

unaccustomed *a.* peu habitué; inaccoutumé

unacknowledged *a.* non-reconnu; (letter) sans réponse

unacquainted *a.*, **be** — **with** ignorer; ne pas connaître

unaddressed *a.* sans adresse

unadorned *a.* sans parure, sans ornement; pur, simple

unadulterated *a.* naturel, pur, san mélange

unadvisable *a.* peu sage; imprudent

unaffected *a.* sans affectation, sans pose; sans recherche; sincère; réfractaire; qui n'est pas changé

unaffiliated *a.* non-affilié

unaided *a.* sans aide

unalloyed *a.* sans alliage, pur

unalterable *a.* immuable

unaltered *a.* sans changement

unambitious *a.* sans ambition

unanimous *a.* unanime; **–ly** *adv.* unanimement; à l'unanimité

unannounced *a.* sans se faire annoncer

unanswerable *a.* sans réponse, sans réplique

unanticipated *a.* imprévu

unappeased *a.* inapaisé

unappetizing *a.* peu appétissant

unappreciated *a.* inapprecié; méconnu

unappreciative *a.* insensible; qui manque de discernement

unapproachable *a.* inabordable, inaccessible

unarmed *a.* sans armes

unashamed *a.* sans honte; éhonté

unasked *a.* non-demandé; sans être invité

unassailable *a.* inattaquable

unassimilated *a.* inassimilé

unassisted *a.* sans aide

unassuming *a.* sans prétention, modeste

unattached *a.* indépendant; libre; qui n'est pas attaché

unattainable *a.* impossible à atteindre; in-

accessible
unattended *a.* seul, sans être accompagné
unattractive *a.* peu attrayant; peu sympathique; laid
unauthorized *a.* sans autorisation, inautorisé
unavailing *a.* inutile
unavoidable *a.* inévitable
unavoidably *adv.* inévitablement
unavowed *a.* inavoué
unaware *adv.* ignorant; **be — of** ignorer; **—s** *adv.* à l'improviste; par inadvertance
unbalance *vt.* déséquilibrer **—d** *a.* instable, non balancé
unbearable *a.* insupportable; intolérable
unbeatable *a.* invincible
unbeaten *a.* non-battu
unbecoming *a.* peu convenable; déplacé; qui ne va pas bien
unbeknown *a.* inconnu; **—** *adv.* à l'insu (de)
unbelievable *a.* incroyable
unbeliever *n.* incrédule *m. & f.*
unbelieving *a.* incrédule
unbend *vt.* détendre; redresser; **—** *vi.* se détendre; se déraidir; **—ing** *a.* ferme, inflexible
unbiased *a.* impartial; sans prévention, sans parti pris
unbidden *a.* sans être invité
unblemished *a.* sans tache; sans défaut
unblock *vt.* désencombrer
unbolt *vt.* déverrouiller
unborn *a.* pas encore né; à venir
unbound *a.* délié; (hair) dénoué; (books) non-relié; **—ed** *a.* illimité, sans bornes; démesuré
unbreakable *a.* incassable; inébranlable
unbridled *a.* débridé; effréné
unbroken *a.* non-cassé, non-brisé; intact; indompté; non-rompu; continu
unbuckle *vt.* déboucler
unburden *vt.* soulager, alléger
unburied *a.* non-enterré; déterré
unbusinesslike *a.* irrégulier; peu organisé
unbutton *vt.* déboutonner
uncalled *a.* non-appelé; **— for** déplacé, mal à propos; immérité
uncanny *a.* mystérieux, étrange; inquiétant
uncared-for *a.* délaissé; à l'abandon
unceasing *a.* continu, incessant; soutenu; **—ly** *adv.* sans cesse
uncensored *a.* non-expurgé
unceremonious *a.* sans façon
uncertain *a.* incertain; douteux; indéterminé; mal assuré; **—ty** *n.* incertitude *f.*
uncertified *a.* non-diplômé
unchain *vt.* déchaîner
unchallenged *a.* indisputé; sans être con-

tredit
unchangeable *a.* immuable, invariable
unchanged *a.* toujours le même; inchangé
unchanging *a.* immuable, invariable
uncharitable *a.* peu charitable
uncharted *a.* qui ne se trouve pas sur la carte
unchecked *a.* sans frein; non verifié
unchivalrous *a.* peu courtois
unchristened *a.* non baptisé
unchristian *a.* peu chrétien; infidèle
uncivil *a.* incivil, impoli; **—ized** *a.* incivilisé; barbare
unclaimed *a.* non-réclamé; **— letter** lettre de rebut *f.*
unclasp *vt.* défaire, dégrafer; desserrer
uncle *n.* oncle *m.*
unclean *a.* malpropre; impur; **—liness** *n.* saleté, malpropreté *f.*
unclench *vt.* desserrer
unclothed *a.* déshabillé, nu, sans vêtements
uncock *vt.* désarmer
uncoil *vt.* dérouler
uncolored *a.* non-coloré; incolore
uncombed *a.* non-peigné, mal peigné
uncomfortable *a.* mal à l'aise, inquiet; incommode; peu confortable; gênant, désagréable
uncommon *a.* peu commun; peu ordinaire; rare
uncommunicative *n.* peu communicatif
uncomplimentary *a.* peu flatteur
uncompromising *a.* intransigeant; absolu
unconcern *n.* indifférence, insouciance *f.*; **—ed** *a.* indifférent, insouciant, dégagé
unconditional *a.* sans condition(s); catégorique; inconditionnel
unconfirmed *a.* non-confirmé
uncongenial *a.* peu sympathique
unconnected *a.* sans rapport; sans suite
unconquerable *a.* invincible; insurmontable
unconquered *a.* non-vaincu; indompté
unconscionable *a.* sans conscience
unconscious *a.* sans connaissance; inconscient; **be —** être sans connaissance; **be — of** ignorer; **—ly** *adv.* inconsciemment; **—ness** *n.* inconscience *f.*; évanouissement *m.*
unconsidered *a.* inconsidéré
unconstitutional *a.* inconstitutionnel
unconstrained *a.* spontané; désinvolte
uncontested *a.* incontesté
uncontrollable *a.* irrésistible, ingouvernable
uncontrolled *a.* sans frein; indépendant
unconventional *a.* original
unconvinced *a.* non-convaincu; sceptique
unconvincing *a.* peu convaincant

uncooked *a.* non-cuit; cru

uncork *vt.* déboucher; **–ed** *a.* sans bouchon; débouché

uncouple *vt.* découpler; débrayer

uncouth *a.* grossier, rude; malappris; **–ness** *n.* rudesse *f.*; grossièreté *f.*

uncover *vt.* découvrir

uncrowned *a.* sans couronne, non-couronné

unction *n.* onction *f.*; **extreme —** extrême-onction *f.*

unctuous *a.* onctueux; grasseux; **–ness** *n.* onctuosité *f.*

uncultivated *a.* inculte; peu cultivé

uncultured *a.* incultivé

uncurbed *a.* sans frein, débridé; libre

uncured *a.* non-guéri

uncut *a.* non-coupé, non-taillé

undamaged *a.* non-endommagé; indemne

undated *a.* sans date, non-daté

undaunted *a.* intrépide

undeceive *vt.* détromper, désabuser, non-trompé

undecided *a.* indécis; hésitant

undecipherable *a.* indéchiffrable

undefeated *a.* invaincu

undefended *a.* sans défense

undefinable *a.* indéfinissable

undefined *a.* indeterminé, indéfini; vague

undelivered *a.* non-délivré; non livré

undemonstrative *a.* réservé, peu démonstratif

undeniable *a.* incontestable, indéniable

undeniably *adv.* incontestablement

under *prep.* sous, au-dessous de; **— lock and key** sous clef; **— repair** en réparation; **— the circumstances** dans les circonstances; **—** *a.* inférieur; de dessous; **—** *adv.* dessous, au-dessous

underage *a.* mineur

underbid *vt.* offrir moins que, demander moins cher que; (cards) demander au-dessous des valeurs

underbrush *n.* broussailles *f. pl.*

undercarriage *n.* dessous, châssis *m.*

undercharge *vt.* accepter trop peu d'argent, ne pas faire payer assez

underclothes, underclothing *n.* vêtements de dessous *m. pl.*, linge *m.*, lingerie *f.*

undercover *a.* secret, clandestin

undercurrent *n.* courant (de fond) *m.*

undercut *vt.* vendre moins cher que; couper

underdeveloped *a.* insuffisamment développé

underdog *n.* opprimé *m.*; concurrent dont les chances sont peu favorables *m.*; perdant probable *m.*

underdone *a.* pas assez cuit

underestimate *vt.* sous-estimer, faire trop peu de cas de

underexposed *a.* (phot.) qui manque de pose

underexposure *n.* (phot.) manque de pose *m.*

underfed *a.* mal nourri, sous-alimenté

undergarment *n.* sous-vêtement *m.*

undergo *vt.* subir; essuyer, éprouver

undergraduate *n.* (America) étudiant de collège *n.*

underground *a.* souterrain; **—** *adv.* sous terre, sous le sol; **—** *n.* (rail.) métro *m.*, chemin de fer souterrain *m.*; (war) résistance *f.*; maquis *m.*

undergrowth *n.* sous-bois *m.*; broussailles *f. pl.*

underhand(ed) *a.* clandestin, secret; sournois; (sports) par en dessous; **—** *adv.* en secret; sous main, sournoisement; par en dessous

underlie *vt.* être au fond de, être à la base de

underline *vt.* souligner

underling *n.* subalterne, subordonné *m.*

underlying *a.* fondamental

undermanned *a.* à court de personnel; à court d'équipage

undermentioned *a.* sous-mentionné

undermost *a.* le plus bas

undermine *vt.* miner, saper; (fig.) détruire

underneath *prep.* sous, au-dessous de; **—** *a.* inférieur; de dessous; **—** *adv.* dessous, au-dessous

undernourished *a.* sous-alimenté, mal nourri

underpaid *a.* mal payé, mal rétribué

underpass *n.* passage souterrain *m.*

underpin *vt.* étayer, étançonner; **–ning** *n.* étayage, étançonnement *m.*

underprivileged *a.* nécessiteux, indigent; déshérité

underrate *vt.* sous-estimer, faire trop peu de cas de; mal juger

undersea *a.* sous-marin

undersecretary *n.* sous-secrétaire *m.*

undersell *vt.* vendre moins cher que, vendre à meilleur marché que

undershirt *n.* gilet, tricot *m.*

undersigned *a.* soussigné

undersized *a.* petit, trop petit; moins grand que les autres

underskirt *n.* jupon *m.*

understand *vt.* comprendre; se rendre compte de; savoir; connaître; s'entendre; **–able** *a.* compréhensible; **that is —able** cela se comprend; **–ing** *a.* qui comprend; sympathique; **–ing** *n.* compréhension, appréhension *f.*; entendement *m.*; intelligence *f.*, jugement *m.*; accord *m.*, entente *f.*; **have an —ing with**

être d'intelligence avec; **on the –ing that** à condition que

understate *vt.* amoindrir; **–ment** *n.* amoindrissement *m.*

understood *a.* compris; entendu, convenu; qui va sans dire

understudy *n.* doublure *f.*; — *vt.* doubler

undertake *vt.* entreprendre; se charger de; **–r** *n.* entrepreneur de pompes funèbres *m.*

undertaking *n.* entreprise *f.*; affaire *f.*

undertone *n.* ton bas *m.*; **in an** — à demi-voix

undertow *n.* contre-marée *f.*, ressac *m.*

undervalue *vt.* sous-évaluer, sous-estimer; déprécier

underwear *n.* sous-vêtements *m. pl.*, linge *m.*, lingerie *f.*

underweight *a.* qui manque de poids; trop maigre

underworld *n.* bas-fonds *m. pl.*, enfers *m. pl.*

underwrite *vt.* souscrire, garantir; **–r** *n.* assureur *m.*; **–rs** *n. pl.* syndicat de garantie *m.*

undeserved *a.* immérité; injuste; **–ly** *adv.* à tort, injustement

undeserving *a.* indigne; peu méritant, sans mérite

undesirable *a.* peu désirable, indésirable

undetected *a.* inaperçu

undetermined *a.* indécis, indéterminé

undeterred *a.* non-découragé

undeveloped *a. a.* inexploité; non-développé

undeviating *a.* constant, fidèle; droit

undigested *a.* mal digéré; indigeste

undignified *a.* peu digne, qui manque de dignité

undiluted *a.* pur; concentré; non dilué

undiminished *a.* non diminué

undiplomatic *a.* peu diplomatique; indiscret

undiscernible *a.* imperceptible

undiscerning *a.* peu pénétrant; sans discernement

undisciplined *a.* indiscipliné

undiscovered *a.* inconnu; caché; non-découvert

undiscriminating *a.* sans goût, sans discernement

undisguised *a.* non-déguisé; ouvert; **–ly** *adv.* ouvertement, franchement

undismayed *a.* non-découragé; sans perdre de courage; sans peur

undisputed *a.* incontesté, indisputé

undistinguished *a.* obscur; médiocre

undistinguishable *a.* indistinguible

undisturbed *a.* tranquille, paisible, calme; non dérangé

undivided *a.* indivisé, entier; non-partagé; unanime

undo *vt.* défaire; dénouer; réparer; **–ing** *n.* ruine, perte *f.*

undone *a.* défait; ruiné; perdu; inaccompli, inachevé

undoubtedly *adv.* sans (aucun) doute; indubitablement

undraped *a.* nu

undress *n.* déshabillé *m.*; — *vt.* déshabiller, dévêtir; — *vi.* se déshabiller, se dévêtir; **–ed** *a.* déshabillé, dévêtu; (manufacturing) brut, non-préparé; (cooking) au naturel

undrinkable *a.* impotable, inbuvable

undue *a.* indû; peu justifié; illégitime

undulate *vi.* ondoyer, onduler

unduly *adv.* indûment; trop; à l'excès

undutiful *a.* peu fidèle à ses devoirs

undying *a.* immortel

unearned *a.* non gagné; immérité

unearth *vt.* déterrer; **–ly** *a.* sinistre, surnaturel

uneasiness *n.* inquiétude *f.*; malaise *m.*

uneasy *a.* inquiet; agité; mal à l'aise

uneducated *a.* qui manque d'instruction

unemotional *a.* impassible, peu émotionnable

unemployed *a.* sans travail; désœuvré; **— person** chômeur *m.*

unemployment *n.* chômage *m.*

unencumbered *a.* non-encombré, non-embarrassé, débarrassé

unending *a.* interminable, sans fin

unendurable *a.* insupportable

unenterprising *a.* peu entreprenant

unenviable *a.* peu enviable

unequal *a.* inégal; irrégulier; au-dessous de; **–led** *a.* sans égal; inégalé

unequivocal *a.* sans équivôque; clair

unerring *a.* infaillible

unessential *a.* non-essentiel

uneven *a.* inégal; irrégulier; (number) impair; (terrain) accidenté; **–ness** *n.* inégalité *f.*

uneventful *a.* calme, sans incident(s); monotone

unexcelled *c.* que l'on n'a pas surpassé

unexciting *a.* ennuyeux; monotone; peu passionnant

unexpected *a.* inattendu; imprévu; inopiné; inespéré

unexpired *a.* non-périmé

unexplained *a.* inexpliqué

unexploded *a.* non-éclaté

unexplored *a.* inexploré

unexposed *a.* (phot.) vierge

unexpurgated *a.* intégral, non expurgé

unfading *a.* impérissable

unfailing *a.* infaillible, certain, sûr

unfair *a.* injuste; inéquitable; **—ness** *n.* injustice *f.*
unfaithful *a.* infidèle; déloyal; inexact; **—ness** *n.* infidélité *f.*; inexactitude *f.*
unfaltering *a.* assuré, ferme
unfamiliar *a.* peu familier; inconnu; **be — with** ne pas connaître; ignorer; **—ity** *f.* manque de connaissance *f.*; ignorance *f.*
unfashionable *a.* qui n'est pas à la mode; démodé
unfasten *vt.* détacher; défaire
unfathomable *a.* insondable; impénétrable
unfavorable *a.* peu favorable; défavorable; désavantageux; (wind) impropice
unfeasible *a.* impraticable
unfeeling *a.* insensible
unfeigned *a.* non-simulé; franc, sincère
unfettered *a.* libre, sans entraves
unfilled *a.* non-rempli, vide
unfinished *a.* inachevé
unfit *a.* incapable; inapte; impropre; indigne; **—ness** *n.* incapacité *f.*; inaptitude; **—ting** *a.* peu convenable; mal à propos; déplacé
unflagging *a.* infatigable
unflattering *a.* peu flatteur
unflinching *a.* qui ne bronche pas
unfold *vt.* déplier; dérouler; exposer; — *vi.* se dérouler
unforseen *a.* imprévu, inattendu
unforgettable *a.* inoubliable
unforgivable *a.* impardonnable
unforgiving *a.* implacable
unfortified *a.* sans fortifications, non-fortifié, ouvert
unfortunate *a.* infortuné, malheureux; regrettable; **—ly** *adv.* malheureusement, par malheur
unfounded *a.* sans fondement
unfrequented *a.* peu fréquenté; écarté
unfriendliness *n.* manque d'amitié *m.*; hostilité *f.*
unfriendly *a.* peu amical; hostile; mal disposé
unfrock *vt.* défroquer
unfruitful *a.* peu fructueux; inutile
unfulfilled *a.* non-satisfait; inaccompli
unfurl *vt.* déployer; (naut.) déferler
unfurnished *a.* non-meublé
ungainly *a. & adv.* maladroit, gauche
ungenerous *a.* peu généreux
ungentlemanly *a.* mal élevé; peu comme il faut
unglazed *a.* non-glacé; non-verni; mat
ungodliness *n.* impiété *f.*
ungraceful *a.* sans grâce, disgracieux; gauche
ungracious *a.* de mauvaise grâce, malgracieux, mal vu; **—ness** *n.* mauvaise grâce *f.*

ungrammatical *a.* peu grammatical
ungrateful *a.* ingrat, peu reconnaissant; **—ness** *n.* ingratitude *f.*, manque de reconnaissance *m.*
ungratified *a.* non-satisfait; inassouvi
ungrounded *a.* sans fondement
ungrudging *a.* libéral, généreux
unguarded *a.* sans défense; non-gardé; inattentif; indiscret
unguent *n.* onguent *m.*
unhallowed *a.* profane; non-béni
unhampered *a.* libre, qui n'est pas gêné
unhand *vt.* lâcher; **—y** *a.* maladroit, gauche
unhappily *adv.* tristement; malheureusement
unhappiness *n.* chagrin *m.*, tristesse *f.*; malheur *m.*
unhappy *a.* triste; malheureux, infortuné; peu content, mécontent
unharmed *a.* sain et sauf; intact
unhealthiness *n.* insalubrité *f.*
unhealthy *a.* malsain, insalubre; maladif
unheard-of *a.* inouï; inconnu
unheeded *a.* inaperçu; négligé
unheeding *a.* inattentif; insouciant
unhesitating *a.* résolu, qui n'hésite pas; **—ly** *adv.* sans hésitation, sans hésiter
unhindered *a.* sans obstacle, sans empêchement
unhook *vt.* décrocher; dégrafer
unhoped *a.*, **— for** inespéré
unhorse *vt.* démonter
unhurt *a.* sain et sauf; sans mal; intact
unidentified *a.* non-identifié; inconnu
unification *n.* unification *f.*
uniform *a.* uniforme, régulier; **—** *n.* uniforme *m.*; costume *m.*; tenue *f.*; **—ity** *n.* uniformité, régularité *f.*; unité *f.*; **—ly** *adv.* uniformément
unify *vt.* unifier
unilateral *a.* unilatéral
unimaginable *a.* inimaginable
unimaginative *a.* qui manque d'imagination
unimpaired *a.* non-altéré, non affaibli, non-diminué; intact
unimpeachable *a.* inattaquable, sûr
unimpeded *a.* sans empêchement
unimportant *a.* peu important, sans importance
unimpressed *a.* impassible, froid; peu impressionné
unimpressive *a.* peu imposant, peu impressionnant; ordinaire, médiocre
uninformed *a.* ignorant; **be — ignorer**; ne pas connaître
uninhabitable *a.* inhabitable
uninhabited *a.* inhabité
uninitiated *a.* non-initié
uninjured *a.* non-blessé; sain et sauf; sans

mal; intact

uninspired *a.* sans inspiration

uninsured *a.* non-assuré

unintelligible *a.* inintelligible

unintentional *a.* involontaire; fait par inadvertance

uninterested *a.* non-intéressé; qui ne s'intéresse pas

uninteresting *a.* peu intéressant, sans intérêt

uninterrupted *a.* ininterrompu; suivi

uninvited *a.* sans être invité; inconvivié

uninviting *a.* peu engageant; peu appétissant

union *n.* union *f.*; (labor) syndicat *m.*; **–ism** *n.* syndicalisme *m.*; **–ist** *n.* syndicaliste *m. & f.*, syndiqué *m.*; **–ize** *vt.* syndicaliser

Union of South Africa *n.* Union de l'Afrique du Sud *f.*

unison *n.* unisson *m.*; **in —** à l'unisson; de concert

unit *n.* unité *f.*; élément *m.*

Unitarian *a. & n.* unitarien *m.*

unite *vt.* unir; unifier; joindre; **—** *vi.* s'unir, se joindre; se confédérer; se combiner; **–d** *a.* uni; unique; réuni

United Arab Republic *n.* République Arabe Unie *f.*

United Nations *n.* Nations Unies *f. pl.*

United States *n.* Etats-Unis *m. pl.*

unity *n.* unité *f.*; concorde *f.*, accord *m.*

univalent *a.* monovalent, univalent

universal *a.* universel

universe *n.* univers *m.*

university *n.* université *f.*; **—** *a.* universitaire

unjust *a.* injuste

unjustifiable *a.* injustifiable

unjustified *a.* non justifié

unkempt *a.* mal peigné; dépeigné; mal tenu

unkind *a.* peu aimable; cruel; méchant; **–ly** *a.* peu aimable; peu favorable; **–ly** *adv.* cruellement, méchamment; **–ness** *n.* manque de bienveillance *m.*; méchanceté *f.*

unknowing *a.* ignorant; **–ly** *adv.* sans le savoir

unknown *a.* inconnu; ignoré; obscur; **—** to à l'insu de; **—** *n.* inconnu *m.*; (math.) inconnue *f.*

unknot *vt.* dénouer, défaire

unlace *vt.* délacer, défaire

unlawful *a.* illégal, illicite

unleash *vt.* lâcher

unleavened *a.* sans levain; azyme; **—** bread azyme *m.*

unless *conj.* à moins que; si

unlettered *a.* illettré, peu lettré

unlicensed *a.* non-autorisé; sans patente

unlike *a.* différent; peu ressemblant; dissemblable; **–lihood** *n.* improbabilité, invraisemblance *f.*; **–ly** *a.* peu probable, invraisemblable

unlimited *a.* illimité; sans bornes

unload *vt.* décharger; **–ed** *a.* déchargé; non chargé; **–ing** *n.* déchargement *m.*

unlock *vt.* ouvrir

unlooked *a.*, **— for** inattendu

unlucky *a.* malheureux, infortuné; de mauvais augure

unmanageable *a.* intraitable; indocile

unmanly *a.* indigne d'un homme; peu viril

unmannerly *a.* mal élevé, impoli, grossier

unmarked *a.* non-marqué; sans marque; sans blessure

unmarketable *a.* invendable

unmarried *a.* non-marié, célibataire

unmask *vt.* démasquer; dévoiler

unmatched *a.* sans égal, incomparable, sans pareil

unmentionable *a.* dont on ne doit pas parler

unmerciful *a.* impitoyable

unmerited *a.* non-mérité, immérité

unmindful *a.* négligent, oublieux

unmistakable *a.* clair, évident

unmistakably *adv.* clairement, évidemment

unmixed *a.* sans mélange; sans alliage; pur

unmolested *a.* sans être molesté, sans obstacle

unmoved *a.* impassible; inflexible

unnamed *a.* anonyme; sans nom

unnatural *a.* contre nature; non-naturel; (laugh) forcé

unnavigable *a.* innavigable

unnecessarily *adv.* sans nécessité, inutilement

unnecessary *a.* inutile, superflu, peu nécessaire

unneeded *a.* dont on n'a pas besoin; peu nécessaire

unneighborly *a.* de mauvais voisin

unnerve *vt.* démonter

unnoticed *a.* inaperçu, inobservé

unobservant *a.* inattentif, peu observateur

unobserved *a.* inobservé, inaperçu

unobstructed *a.* non-encombré, libre

unobtainable *a.* qui est impossible à obtenir

unobtrusive *a.* effacé; discret

unoccupied *a.* libre, disponible; inoccupé; inhabité

unofficial *a.* non-officiel; non confirmé

unopened *a.* (letter) non-décacheté

unopposed *a.* sans opposition

unorthodox *a.* peu orthodoxe; original

unostentatious *a.* sans faste; simple

unpack *vt.* défaire; dépaqueter

unpaid *a.* non-payé; sans traitement; non-acquitté

unpalatable *a.* désagréable, dégoûtant

unparalleled *a.* sans pareil; sans précédent

unpardonable *a.* impardonnable

unpatriotic *a.* peu patriotique; (person) peu patriote

unpaved *a.* non-pavé

unperceivable *a.* imperceptible

unperceived *a.* inaperçu

unperturbed *a.* peu ému; froid; impassible

unpin *vt.* défaire

unpitying *a.* impitoyable

unplaced *a.* sans place, non-placé

unplayable *a.* injouable

unpleasant *a.* désagréable; déplaisant; peu aimable; **–ness** *n.* chose désagréable *f.*; nature désagréable *f.*

unpleasing *a.* désagréable, peu agréable

unpolished *a.* non-poli; rude, grossier

unpolluted *a.* non-pollué; pur; sain

unpopular *a.* impopulaire; **–ity** *n.* impopularité *f.*

unpracticed *a.* inexpérimenté

unprecedented *a.* sans précédent, sans exemple; inouï

unprejudiced *a.* sans préjugés, sans prévention, impartial

unpremeditated *a.* non-prémédité

unprepared *a.* non-préparé; improvisé; sans préparation

unprepossessing *a.* peu engageant

unpresuming *a.* sans présomption

unpretentious *a.* modeste, sans prétention(s)

unprincipled *a.* sans principes; sans mœurs

unprocurable *a.* impossible à obtenir

unproductive *a.* improductif; stérile

unprofitable *a.* inutile; peu profitable, improfitable; peu lucratif

unpromising *a.* qui ne promet rien; qui s'annonce mal

unprompted *a.* spontané

unpropitious *a.* défavorable, impropice

unprotected *a.* sans protection, non-protégé, sans défense; exposé

unproved *a.* non-prouvé, improuvé; inéprouvé

unprovided *a.* dépourvu; **— for** *a.* sans ressources

unprovoked *a.* non-provoqué, improvoqué

unpublished *a.* non-publié; inédit

unpunished *a.* impuni

unqualified *a.* incapable; incompétent; sans réserve, catégorique

unquenchable *a.* inassouvissable

unquestionable *a.* incontestable, indubitable, indiscutable

unquestioned *a.* incontesté, indisputé

unquestioning *a.* sans question

unravel *vt.* effiler; débrouiller; **—** *vi.* s'effiler; se débrouiller

unread *a.* non-lu; illettré

unreadable *a.* illisible

unreal *a.* irréel; imaginaire

unreasonable *a.* déraisonnable, peu raisonnable

unrecognizable *a.* méconnaissable

unrecognized *a.* non-reconnu; méconnu

unreconcilable *a.* irréconciliable

unreconciled *a.* irréconcilié

unrecorded *a.* non-enregistré; qui n'est pas mentionné

unredeemed *a.* non-racheté; non dégagé

unrefined *a.* non-raffiné; grossier, peu raffiné

unregistered *a.* non-enregistré; non-inscrit

unrehearsed *a.* spontané; sans répétition(s)

unrelated *a.* sans rapport; non-apparenté

unrelenting *a.* implacable, inflexible

unreliability *n.* inexactitude *f.*; manque de fidélité *m.*

unreliable *a.* peu fidèle; sur lequel on ne peut pas compter

unremitting *a.* soutenu, ininterrompu

unremunerative *a.* peu lucratif, peu rémunérateur

unrepentant *a.* impénitent

unrequited *a.* non-partagé; non récompensé

unreserved *a.* sans réserve, franc; non réservé; complet

unresponsive *a.* peu sensible; impassible; froid

unrest *n.* agitation *f.*; inquiétude *f.*

unrestrained *a.* libre; non-restreint

unrestricted *a.* sans restriction; absolu

unrevenged *a.* non-vengé, invengé

unrewarded *a.* sans récompense

unripe *a.* vert, qui n'est pas mûr

unrivaled *a.* sans rival; sans pareil

unroll *vt.* dérouler; **—** *vi.* se dérouler

unromantic *a.* peu sentimental; peu romanesque

unruffled *a.* calme; imperturbable

unruly *a.* intraitable, insoumis

unsaddle *vt.* desseller; désarçonner

unsafe *a.* peu sûr; dangereux

unsanitary *a.* non-hygiénique

unsatisfactory *a.* peu satisfaisant

unsatisfied *a.* peu satisfait, mécontent

unsatisfying *a.* peu satisfaisant

unscathed *a.* sans blessure; sain et sauf; intact

unscientific *a.* peu scientifique

unscrew vt. dévisser

unscrupulous a. peu scrupuleux; sans scrupule

unseal vt. desceller; décacheter

unseasonable a. hors de saison; mal à propos

unseasoned a. non-assaisonné; inexpérimenté; (wood) vert

unseat vt. (horseman) démonter, désarçonner; (pol.) invalider

unsecured a. mal assujetti; non-garanti

unseeing a. aveugle

unseemliness n. inconvenance f.

unseemly a. peu convenable; malséant

unseen a. invisible; inaperçu

unselfish a. désintéressé; altruiste; **-ness** n. désintéressement m.

unserviceable a. inutilisable

unsettle vt. troubler; déranger; **-d** a. troublé, inquiet; dérangé; indécis; non colonisé; (bill) non-réglé, impayé

unshakeable a. inébranlable, ferme

unshaken a. inébranlé, ferme

unshapely a. difforme; informe; mal fait

unshaven a. non-rasé

unsheathe vt. dégainer

unsheltered a. sans abri; exposé

unsightly a. désagréable à la vue; laid; sale

unsigned a. non-signé

unsinkable a. insubmersible

unskilful a. malhabile, inhabile; maladroit

unskilled a. inexpert; inexpérimenté; — labor main-d'œuvre f.

unsociable a. insociable; peu aimable, peu amical

unsoiled a. sans tache

unsold a. invendu

unsolicited a. non-sollicité; spontané

unsolved a. non-expliqué; non-résolu

unsophisticated a. simple, ingénu; naïf

unsound a. malsain, non-sain, maladif; peu solide; mauvais, faible, peu convaincant; **-ness** n. manque de solidité m.; faiblesse f.

unsparing a. prodigue; impitoyable; infatigable

unspeakable a. inexprimable, indicible

unspecified a. non-spécifié

unspoiled a. non-gâté

unspoken a. non-prononcé; tacite

unsportsmanlike a. peu loyal, antisportif

unstable a. instable; inconstant

unstained a. sans tache; non-teint

unstamped a. non-affranchi, sans timbre

unsteadiness n. instabilité f.; irrésolution f.; irrégularité f.

unsteady a. peu solide, instable; irrésolu; irrégulier; (step) chancelant; (voice) mal assuré

unstrap vt. déboucler

unstressed a. sans accent; inaccentué

unstring vt. (fig.) détraquer

unsubdued a. insoumis; indompté

unsubsidized a. sans subvention

unsuccessful a. manqué, raté; sans succès; non réussi; refusé; **be** — échouer; **-ly** adv. sans succès

unsuitable a. qui ne convient pas; peu convenable; inopportun; peu fait, inapte; **-ness** n. inaptitude f.; inopportunité f.

unsuited a. peu fait, inapte; mal adapté

unsullied a. sans tache, sans souillure

unsupported a. sans soutien, sans appui

unsurpassed a. sans égal, sans pareil

unsuspected a. non-suspect; insoupçonné

unsuspecting, unsuspicious a. sans défiance, sans soupçons; qui ne se doute pas

unsweetened a. non-sucré

unswerving a. ferme, constant; qui ne s'écarte pas

unsymmetrical a. sans symétrie; asymétrique

unsympathetic a. peu compatissant; indifférent; peu sympathique

unsystematic a. sans méthode; sans système

untainted a. non-gâté; non-corrompu

untalented a. sans talent(s)

untamed a. non-apprivoisé; indompté

untapped a. (fig.) inutilisé

untarnished a. non-terni; (fig.) sans tache

untenable a. insoutenable; intenable

untenanted a. inhabité, inoccupé

untested a. pas encore mis à l'épreuve; inéprouvé, inessayé

unthinkable a. inconcevable, inimaginable

unthinking a. irréfléchi

untidiness n. désordre m.; malpropreté f.

untidy a. en désordre; négligé; malpropre

untie vt. délier, détacher, défaire, dénouer, déficeler

until prep. jusqu' à; — conj. jusqu'à ce que; **wait** — attendre que

untilled a. non-labouré; inculte, incultivé

untimely a. inopportun, mal à propos; hors de saison; indu; prématuré

untiring a. infatigable, inlassable

unto prep. à; vers; jusqu'à

untold a. non-compté; énorme; incalculable; inouï

untouchable n. hors-caste m.

untouched a. intact; sain et sauf; indifférent; non-discuté

untoward a. incommode; malheureux, fâcheux; malséant

untraceable a. introuvable

untrained a. inexpert, inexpérimenté, inexercé; (animal) non-dressé

untranslatable a. intraduisible

untraveled *a.* qui n'a pas beaucoup voyagé; inexploré

untried *a.* non-essayé, inessayé; pas encore mis à l'épreuve

untrimmed *a.* sans ornement, sans garniture; simple

untrodden *a.* non-frayé; inexploré

untroubled *a.* calme, tranquille

untrue *a.* faux (fausse); inexact; infidèle

untrustworthy *a.* qui n'est pas digne de confiance; infidèle; douteux

untruth *n.* mensonge *m.*; –ful *a.* menteur; mensonger; faux; –fulness *n.* fausseté *f.*

unturned *a.*, **leave no stone —** faire tout son possible

untutored *a.* illettré, sans instruction

unusable *a.* inutilisable

unused *a.* non-employé; inutilisé; peu habitué

unusual *a.* exceptionnel, rare; peu commun; peu usité; –ness *n.* rareté *f.*

unvanquished *a.* invaincu

unvaried *a.* sans variété; monotone; uniforme

unvarnished *a.* non-verni; (fig.) simple, sans fard

unvarying *a.* invariable; uniforme

unveil *vt.* dévoiler; inaugurer; –ing *n.* inauguration *f.*

unverified *a.* invérifié; non-corroboré

unversed *a.* peu versé

unvoiced *a.* sourd

unwanted *a.* non-voulu, non-désiré

unwarrantable *a.* injustifiable

unwarranted *a.* peu justifié; déplacé; sans garantie

unwary *a.* imprudent, imprévoyant

unwavering *a.* ferme, résolu, constant

unwearying *a.* infatigable

unwelcome *a.* importun, mal venu; désagréable

unwell *a.* indisposé; souffrant, malade

unwholesome *a.* malsain; insalubre

unwieldy *a.* peu maniable

unwilling *a.* inserviable; qui ne veut pas; be — ne pas vouloir, être peu disposé; –ly *adv.* à contre-cœur; –ness *n.* mauvaise volonté *f.*

unwind *vt.* dérouler; débobiner

unwise *a.* peu sage, imprudent

unwitting *a.* inconscient; –ly *adv.* inconsciemment; sans le savoir

unwonted *a.* inaccoutumé

unworkable *a.* impraticable

unworked *a.* non-travaillé; inexploité

unworldly *a.* d'un autre monde; peu mondain; peu naturel

unworthiness *n.* manque de mérite, peu de mérite *m.*

unworthy *a.* indigne; peu méritoire

unwounded *a.* sans blessure

unwrap *vt.* défaire

unwrinkled *a.* sans rides; uni; lisse

unwritten *a.* non-écrit; oral

unyielding *a.* ferme, inflexible, qui ne cède pas

up *adv.* haut; en haut; debout; relevé; (sun) levé; be — against se heurter à; get — se lever; go — monter; it's — to you (to) c'est à vous (de); speak — parler plus haut; — there là-haut; — to jusqu'à; walk — and down se promener de long en large; –s *n. pl.*, –s and downs vicissitudes *f. pl.*

upbraid *vt.* reprocher

upbringing *n.* éducation *f.*

upgrade *n.* montée *f.*; be on the — monter; reprendre

upheaval *n.* soulèvement *m.*; bouleversement *m.*

uphill *a.* montant; — *adv.* en montant; go — monter

uphold *vt.* soutenir, maintenir; confirmer

upholster *vt.* tapisser, couvrir; garnir; –er *n.* tapisseur *m.*; –ing, –y *n.* tapisserie *f.*; garniture *f.*

upkeep *n.* entretien *m.*

upland *n.* haut pays *m.*

uplift *n.* élévation *f.*; — *vt.* soulever, élever

upon *prep.* sur; à; vers; sous; de; en

upper *a.* supérieur; de dessus; (plus) haut, plus élevé; — classes hautes classes *f. pl.*; — hand dessus *m.*; — part dessus *m.*

upper-class *a.* de la haute classe

uppermost *a.* le plus haut, le plus élevé; le plus important; — *adv.* en dessus

upright *a.* droit; vertical, perpendiculaire; debout; honnête, intègre; — *n.* montant *m.*; –ness *n.* droiture, intégrité *f.*

uprising *n.* soulèvement *m.*, insurrection *f.*

uproar *n.* chahut, tumulte, vacarme, grand bruit *m.*; –ious *a.* tumultueux

uproot *vt.* déraciner; arracher, extirper

upset *n.* désordre *m.*; renversement *m.*; bouleversement *m.*; — *vt.* renverser; bouleverser; troubler, inquiéter, agiter; déranger; démonter; émouvoir; indisposer; — *vi.* se renverser; — *a.* renversé; trouble, ému; bouleversé; dérangé

upshot *n.* issue *f.*, résultat *m.*

upside-down *a.* sens dessus dessous; renversé; bouleversé

upstairs *adv.* en haut; — *n.* étage supérieur *m.*; go — monter (l'escalier) — *a.* d'en haut

upstanding *a.* honnête

upstart *n.* parvenu *m.*

upstream *adv.* en amont

up-to-date *a.* moderne

uptown *adv.* dans un quartier commercial, vers un quartier commercial (qui ne se trouve pas au centre)

upturn *n.* reprise *f.*; **–ed** *a.* relevé

upward *a.* montant, ascendant; **–(s)** *adv.* en montant; vers le haut; vers le ciel; en haut; en dessus; au-dessus

uranium *n.* uranium *m.*

urban *a.* urbain; **–ity** *n.* urbanité *f.*; **–ization** *n.* urbanisation *f.*; **–ize** *vt.* urbaniser

urbane *a.* poli

urchin *n.* marmot *m.*; gamin *m.*

urea *n.* urée *f.*

uremia *n.* urémie *f.*

ureter, urethra *n.* uretère *m.*

urge *n.* impulsion, poussée *f.*; désir *m.*, envie *f.*; — *vt.* pousser, exhorter; encourager; recommander; insister; **–ncy** *n.* urgence *f.*; importance *f.*; nécessité *f.*; **–nt** *a.* urgent, pressant

urinal *n.* urinoir *m.*

urinalysis *n.* analyse de l'urine *f.*

urinate *vi.* uriner

urine *n.* urine *f.*

urn *n.* urne *f.*; (coffee) grosse cafetière *f.*

Uruguay *n.* Uruguay *m.*

us *pron.* nous

usable *a.* utilisable

usage *n.* usage *m.*; traitement *m.*; coutume *f.*; emploi *m.*

use *n.* emploi *m.*; usage *m.*; service *m.*; utilisation *f.* utilité *f.*; **be of** — servir, être utile; **for the** — **of** à l'usage de; **make** — **of** se servir de; profiter de; **what's the** — **of?** à quoi bon?; **–d** *a.* usagé; — *vt.* employer, se servir de, utiliser, user de; — **up** user, épuiser; **be –d to** être habitué à; être accoutumé à; avoir l'habitude de; **get –d to** s'habituer à, s'accoutumer à, se faire à; **–d car** automobile d'occasion; **–ful** *a.* utile; **–fulness** *n.* utilité *f.* **–less** *a.* inutile; vain; **–lessness** *n.* inutilité *f.*; **–r** *n.* usager *m.*; consommateur *m.*; abonné *m.*

usher *n.* huissier *m.*; (theat.) ouvreuse *f.*; (wedding) garçon d'honneur *m.*; — *vt.*, — **in** introduire, faire entrer; (fig.) inaugurer

U.S.S.R.: Union of Soviet Socialist Republics *n.* U.R.S.S.: Union des Républiques Soviétiques Socialistes *f.*

usual *a.* ordinaire, habituel; usuel; d'usage; accoutumé; **as** — comme d'ordinaire, comme d'habitude; **–ly** *adv.* d'ordinaire, d'habitude

usurp *vt.* usurper; **–ation** *n.* usurpation *f.*; **–er** *n.* usurpateur *m.*

usury *n.* usure *f.*

utensil *n.* ustensile *m.*; **kitchen –s** batterie de cuisine *f.*

uterus *n.* matrice *f.*

utilitarian *a.* utilitaire; **–ism** *n.* utilitarisme *m.*

utility *n.* utilité *f.*; **public** — (entreprise de) service public *m.*

utilization *n.* mise en valeur *f.*; utilisation *f.*

utilize *vt.* utiliser, se servir de; mettre en valeur

utmost *a.* dernier, extrême; le plus grand; — *n.* le plus possible *m.*; dernier degré *m.*; **do one's** — faire tout son possible

Utopia *n.* Utopie *f.*; **–n** *a.* utopique

utter *a.* absolu, complet; — *vt.* pousser; prononcer; débiter; dire; **–ance** *n.* parole(s) *f. pl.*; expression *f.*; **–ly** *adv.* complètement, tout à fait

uvula *n.* uvule *f.*; **–r** *a.* uvulaire

V

vacancy *n.* vide *m.*; vacance *f.*; poste vacant *m.*

vacant *a.* vide; libre, inoccupé; vague

vacate *vt.* quitter; vider; évacuer

vacation *n.* vacances *f. pl.*

vaccinate *vt.* vacciner

vaccination *n.* vaccination *f.*

vaccine *n.* vaccin *m.*

vacillate *vi.* vaciller

vacillation *n.* vacillation *f.*

vacuous *a.* vide; niais

vacuum *n.* vide *m.*; — **bottle** bouteille isolante, bouteille thermos *f.*; — **cleaner** *n.* aspirateur *m.*; — **seal** *n.* joint hermétique *m.*; — **tube** *n.* lampe à vide *f.*; tube à vide *m.*; — *vt.* nettoyer à l'aspirateur

vagabond *a.* vagabond, errant; — *n.* vagabond *m.*

vagary *n.* caprice *m.*

vagina *n.* vagin *m.*; **–l** *a.* vaginal

vagrancy *n.* vagabondage *m.*

vagrant *n.* vagabond *m.*

vague *a.* vague; imprécis; **–ness** *n.* vague *m.*; imprécision *f.*

vain *a.* vain; inutile, futile; vaniteux; **in** — en vain; inutilement; **–ness** *n.* vanité *f.*

vainglorious *a.* vaniteux, orgueilleux

valance *n.* draperie, garniture *f.*

vale *n.* vallée *f.*, val, vallon *m.*

valedictorian *n.* élève reçu premier pendant sa dernière année de high-school *m. & f.*

valedictory *n.* discours d'adieu *m.*; — *a.* d'adieu

valentine *n.* carte qu'on envoie le jour de la Saint-Valentin *f.*; personne chérie *f.*

valiant *a.* vaillant, brave; **–ly** *adv.* vaillamment

valid *a.* valide, valable, bon; **–ate** *vt.* valider; **–ation** *n.* validation *f.*; **–ity** *n.* validité *f.*; justesse *f.*

valley *n.* vallée *f.*; val, vallon *m.*

valor *n.* valeur, vaillance *f.*; **–ous** *a.* valeureux, vaillant

valuable *a.* de valeur, de prix, précieux; **–s** *n. pl.* objets de valeur *m. pl.*

valuation *n.* évaluation, estimation *f.*

value *n.* valeur *f.*, prix *m.*; **face** — valeur nominale, valeur faciale *f.*; **of no** — sans valeur; — *vt.* estimer, évaluer; tenir à; **–d** *a.* précieux, estimé; **–less** *a.* sans valeur

valve *n.* soupape *f.*, clapet *m.*; vanne *f.*; valve *f.*; (anat.) valvule *f.*; **safety** — soupape de sûreté *f.*

vamp *n.* empeigne *f.*; avant-pied *m.*; (coll.) femme fatale *f.*; (mus.) accompagnement improvisé *m.*; — *vt.* raccommoder; séduire; improviser

van *n.* avant-garde *f.*; (vehicle) camion *m.*; camionnette *f.*; (rail.) fourgon *m.*

vanadium *n.* vanadium *m.*

vandal *n.* vandale *m.*; **–ism** *n.* vandalisme *m.*

vandyke *n.* barbe en pointe *f.*

vane *n.* girouette *f.*; bras *m.*; ailette *f.*

vanguard *n.* avant-garde *f.*

vanilla *n.* vanille *f.*; — **bean** *n.* gousse de vanille *f.*

vanish *vi.* disparaître; s'évanouir

vanity *n.* vanité *f.*; orgueil *m.*; (furniture) coiffeuse *f.*; table de toilette *f.*; — **case** poudrière *f.*

vanquish *vt.* vaincre; **–er** *n.* vainqueur *m.*

vantage *n.* avantage *m.*; — **point** *n.* terrain favorable *m.*

vapid *a.* insipide, fade; **–ity**, **–ness** *n.* insipidité, fadeur *f.*

vapor *n.* vapeur *f.*; — **lamp** *n.* tube à décharge *m.*; **–ize** *vt.* vaporiser, gazéifier; **–izer** *n.* vaporisateur, atomiseur *m.*; **–ous** *a.* vaporeux

variability *n.* variabilité *f.*

variable *a.* variable, inconstant, changeant; — *n.* variable *f.*

variance *n.* désaccord *m.*; **at** — en désaccord

variant *n.* variante *f.*

variation *n.* variation *f.*; changement *m.*; différence *f.*

varicose *a.* variqueux; — **vein** varice *f.*

varied *a.* varié; divers

variety *n.* variété *f.*; diversité *f.*; assortiment *m.*; — **store** *n.* prisunic *m.*

various *a.* divers; varié; différent; plusieurs

varnish *n.* vernis *m.*; vernissure *f.*; — *vt.* vernir; farder; glisser sur; **–ing** *n.* vernissage *m.*

varsity *n.* (university) classes supérieures *f. pl.*; — **team** *n.* première équipe, équipe des classes supérieures

vary *vt.* varier, diversifier; — *vi.* varier, changer; différer; **–ing** *a.* variable, changeant

vascular *a.* vasculaire

vasomotor *a.* vasomoteur

vassal *n.* vassal *m.*; **–age** *n.* vassalage *m.*, vassalité *f.*

vast *a.* vaste, immense; **–ly** *adv.* énormément, immensément; **–ness** *n.* immensité *f.*

vat *n.* cuve *f.*; cuveau *m.*

Vatican *n.* Vatican *m.*; — **City** *n.* Cité du Vatican *f.*

vaudeville *n.* attractions sur scène *f. pl.*

vault *n.* (arch.) voûte *f.*; (bank) chambre forte *f.*; (cellar) cave *f.*; (cemetery) caveau *m.*; (motion) saut *m.*; — *vt.* voûter; — *vi.* sauter

vaunt *vt.* vanter, se vanter de

veal *n.* veau *m.*; — **chop** *n.* côtelette de veau *f.*; — **cutlet** *n.* escalope de veau *f.*

vector *n.* (avi.) vecteur *m.*; — *vt.* (avi.) diriger par radio

veer *vi.* tourner, virer; (naut.) changer de bord

vegetable *a.* végétal; — *n.* légume *m.*; végétal *m.*; — **garden** *n.* jardin potager *m.*

vegetal *a.* végétal

vegetarian *a. & n.* végétarien *m.*

vegetate *vi.* végéter

vegetation *n.* végétation *f.*

vehemence *n.* véhémence, force *f.*

vehement *a.* véhément; **–ly** *adv.* avec véhémence

vehicle *n.* voiture *f.*; véhicule *m.*; moyen *m.*

vehicular *a.* véhiculaire

veil *n.* voile *m.*; voilette *f.*; — *vt.* voiler; cacher; **–ed** *a.* voilé; caché

vein *n.* veine *f.*; nervure *f.*; disposition, humeur *f.*; **–ed** *a.* veiné; nervuré; marbré; **–ing** *n.* marbrure *f.*

vellum *n.* vélin *m.*; papier vélin *m.*

velocipede *n.* vélocipède *m.*

velocity *n.* vitesse *f.*

velvet *n.* velours *m.*; — *a.* de velours; velouté; **–een** *n.* velours de coton *m.*; **–y** *a.* velouté

venal *a.* vénal; **–ity** *n.* vénalité, corruption *f.*

vend *vt. & vi.* vendre; **–or** *n.* vendeur *m.*; machine à sous *f.*

veneer *n.* placage *m.*; bois de placage *m.*;

contreplaqué *m.*; (fig.) vernis *m.*; — *vt.* plaquer
venerable *a.* vénérable
venerate *vt.* vénérer
veneration *n.* vénération *f.*
venereal *a.* vénérien
Venetian *a. & n.* vénitien *m.*; — **blind** jalousie *f.*
Venezuela *n.* Vénézuéla *m.*
vengeance *n.* vengeance *f.*; **take** — se venger
vengeful *a.* vindicatif
venial *a.* véniel, pardonnable
Venice *n.* Venise *f.*
venison *n.* venaison *f.*
venom *n.* venin *m.*; **-ous** *a.* venimeux; vénéneux
vent *n.* passage, trou *m.*; soupirail *m.*; lumière *f.*; **give** — **to** donner libre cours à; — *vt.* décharger
ventilate *vt.* ventiler, aérer
ventilation *n.* ventilation, aération *f.*, aérage *m.*
ventilator *n.* ventilateur *m.*
ventricle *n.* ventricule *m.*
ventriloquist *n.* ventriloque *m. & f.*
venture *n.* enterprise *f.*; — *vt.* hasarder, risquer; oser; **-some** *a.* aventureux; risqué, aventuré
venue *n.* (law) voisinage *m.*, juridiction *f.*
veracious *a.* véridique
veracity *n.* véracité, véridicité *f.*
veranda(h) *n.* véranda *f.*
verb *n.* verbe *m.*; **-al** *a.* verbal; oral; littéral; **-ally** *adv.* verbalement; **-ose** *a.* verbeux, prolixe; **-osity** *n.* verbosité, prolixité *f.*
verbatim *adv.* mot pour mot
verdant *a.* verdoyant, vert
verdict *n.* verdict *m.*; jugement *m.*
verdigris *n.* vert-de-gris *m.*
verge *n.* bord *m.*; bordure *f.*; verge *f.*; **on the** — **of** sur le point de; à la veille de; — *vi.*, — **on** friser, toucher à
verger *n.* bedeau, sacristain *m.*
verifiable *a.* vérifiable, contrôlable
verification *n.* vérification *f.*
verify *vt.* vérifier; contrôler; confirmer
veritable *a.* véritable
verity *n.* vérité *f.*
vermiform *a.* vermiforme; — **appendix** *n.* appendice du cæcum *m.*
vermilion *n.* vermillon *m.*; — *a.* vermeil, vermillon
vermin *n.* vermine *f.*
vernacular *a.* vernaculaire; vulgaire
versatile *a.* varié; souple; versatile
versatility *n.* souplesse *f.*; versatilité *f.*
verse *n.* vers *m.*; strophe *f.*; couplet *m.*; poésie *f.*; (eccl.) verset *m.*; **-d** *a.* versé;

expérimenté
versify *vt.* versifier, mettre en vers
version *n.* version *f.*; interprétation *f.*
versus *prep.* contre
vertebra *n.* vertèbre *f.*; **-l** *a.* vertébral; **-te** *n. & a.* vertébré *m.*
vertex *n.* sommet *m.*
vertical *a.* vertical; **-ness** *n.* verticalité *f.*
vertiginous *a.* vertigineux
vertigo *n.* vertige *m.*
very *adv.* très; bien, fort; **at the** — **latest** au plus tard; **at the** — **most** tout au plus; **not** — peu; — **much** beaucoup; — *a.* même; propre; seul; justement
vesicle *a.* vésicule *f.*
Vespers *n.* vêpres *f. pl.*
vessel *n.* vaisseau *m.*; vase *m.*; navire *m.*; instrument *m.*
vest *n.* gilet *m.*; — *vt.* revêtir, investir; **-ed** *a.* dévolu; **-ed interests** droits acquis *m. pl.*
vestal *a.* virginal; — **virgin** *n.* vestale *f.*
vestige *n.* vestige *m.*, trace *f.*
vestigial *a.* qui tient des vestiges
vestment *n.* vêtement *m.*
vest-pocket *a.* de poche; petit
vestry *n.* sacristie *f.*
veteran *n.* vétéran *m.*; ancien combattant *m.*; — *a.* expérimenté; de vétéran
veterinarian, veterinary *n.* vétérinaire *m.*
veto *n.* veto *m.*; — *vt.* mettre le veto à; interdire
vex *vt.* vexer, fâcher; **-ation** *n.* vexation *f.*; dépit *m.*, contrariété *f.*, ennui *m.*; **-atious** *a.* contrariant, fâcheux, ennuyeux; **-ed** *a.* vexé, fâché, contrarié
via *prep.* via; par; — **air mail** par avion
viability *n.* viabilité *f.*
viaduct *n.* viaduc *m.*
vial *n.* fiole *f.*
viand *n.* mets *m.*; viande *f.*
vibrate *vi.* vibrer; osciller; — *vt.* faire vibrer
vibration *n.* vibration *f.*; oscillation *f.*
vibrator *n.* vibrateur *m.*; oscillateur *m.*; (elec.) vibreur *m.*
vicar *n.* vicaire *m.*; curé *m.*; **-age** *n.* cure *f.*, presbytère *m.*; — **general** *n.* grand vicaire *m.*
vicarious *a.* substitutif; **-ly** *adv.* par substitution; à la place d'un autre
vice *n.* vice *m.*; défaut
vice-admiral *n.* vice-amiral *m.*
vice-chairman *n.* vice-président *m.*
vice-consul *n.* vice-consul *m.*
vice-president *n.* vice-président *m.*
viceroy *n.* vice-roi *m.*
vicinity *n.* voisinage *m.*; environs, alentours *m. pl.*
vicious *a.* vicieux; hargneux; — **circle** cer-

cle vicieux *m.*
vicissitude *n.* vicissitude *f.*; péripétie *f.*
victim *n.* victime *f.*; **–ize** *vt.* tromper; abuser
victor *n.* vainqueur *m.*; **–ious** *a.* victorieux; **–y** *n.* victoire *f.*
Victorian *a.* victorien
victual *vt.* aprovisionner; **–s** *n. pl.* (coll.) provisions *f. pl.*, vivres *m. pl.*
video *n.* télévision *f.*; — *a.* vidéo, visuel; — **signal** *n.* signal d'image *m.*
vie *vi.* rivaliser; disputer
Vienna *n.* Vienne *f.*
Viennese *a. & n.* viennois
Viet Nam *n.* Viet-Nam *m.*
view *n.* vue *f.*; regard *m.*; perspective *f.*; aperçu *m.*; opinion *f.*, avis *m.*; idée *f.*; **bird's-eye** — vue à vol d'oiseau *f.*; **in** — en vue; **in** — **of** vu; en considération de; **point of** — point de vue *m.*; — *vt.* regarder; voir; envisager; **–er** *n.* spectateur *m.*
viewfinder *n.* viseur *m.*
viewpoint *n.* point de vue *m.*
vigil *n.* veille *f.*; (eccl.) vigile *f.*; **keep a** — veiller; **–ance** *n.* vigilance *f.*; **–ant** *a.* éveillé, alerte, vigilant; **–antly** *adv.* avec vigilance
vigilante *n.* membre d'un comité de surveillance *m.*
vigor *n.* vigueur *f.*; énergie *f.*; **–ous** *a.* vigoureux; robuste; fort
vile *a.* vil, bas; abominable; sale; **–ness** *n.* bassesse *f.*
vilification *n.* dénigrement *m.*
vilify *vt.* diffamer, dénigrer
villa *n.* villa *f.*; maison de campagne *f.*
village *n.* village *m.*; **–r** *n.* villageois *m.*
villain *n.* scélérat *m.*; (theat.) traître *m.*; **–ous** *a.* vil; scélérat; infâme; **–y** *n.* scélératesse, infamie *f.*
vim *n.* vigueur, énergie *f.*
vindicate *vt.* justifier; défendre, soutenir; revendiquer
vindication *n.* justification, défense *f.*; revendication *f.*
vindicator *n.* défenseur *m.*
vindictive *a.* vindicatif; vengeur; **–ness** *n.* esprit de vengeance *m.*
vine *n.* vigne *f.*
vinegar *n.* vinaigre *m.*; — **cruet** *n.* vinaigrier *m.*
vineyard *n.* vigne *f.*, vignoble *m.*
vintage *n.* vendange *f.*; crû *f.*; année *f.*; — **wine** *n.* vin de crû, grand vin, vin de marque *m.*
vintner *n.* vigneron, viticulteur *m.*; marchand en vins *m.*
vinyl *n.* vinyl *m.*; — *a.* vinylique
viola *n.* (mus.) alto *m.*

violate *vt.* violer
violation *n.* violation *f.*; infraction, contravention *f.*
violator *n.* violateur; contravenant *m.*
violence *n.* violence *f.*
violent *a.* violent; fort; **–ly** *adv.* violemment, avec violence
violin *n.* violon *m.*; **–ist** *n.* violoniste *m.&f.*
violincello *n.* violoncelle *m.*
viper *n.* vipère *f.*
virago *n.* mégère *f.*
virgin *a.* vierge; virginal; — *n.* vierge *f.*; **–al** *a.* virginal; **–ity** *n.* virginité *f.*
virile *a.* viril; mâle
virility *n.* virilité *f.*
virtual *a.* vrai; de fait; virtuel; **–ly** *adv.* de fait; virtuellement; presque
virtue *n.* vertu *f.*; qualité *f.*; **by** — **of en** vertu de, en raison de
virtuosity *n.* virtuosité *f.*
virtuoso *n.* virtuose *m. & f.*
virtuous *a.* vertueux
virulence *n.* virulence *f.*
virulent *a.* virulent
virus *n.* virus *m.*
visa *n.* visa *m.*
visage *n.* visage *m.*, figure *f.*
viscid *a.* visqueux
viscosity *n.* viscosité *f.*
viscount *n.* vicomte *m.*; **–ess** *n.* vicomtesse *f.*
viscous *a.* visqueux
vise *n.* étau *m.*
visibility *n.* visibilité *f.*; vue *f.*
visible *a.* visible; visuel
vision *n.* vision *f.*, vue *f.*; apparition *f.*; imagination *f.*; **–ary** *a. & n.* visionnaire *m. & f.*
visit *n.* visite *f.*; — *vt.* rendre visite à; (place) visiter; **–ation** *n.* visite *f.*; apparition *f.*; **–ing** *a.* en visite; de visite; **–or** *n.* visiteur *m.*
visor *n.* visière *f.*; paresoleil *m.*; protège-vue *m.*
vista *n.* vue, perspective, échappée *f.*
visual *a.* visuel; optique; **–ize** *vt.* se représenter
vital *a.* vital, essentiel; — **statistics** état civil *m.*; **–ity** *n.* vitalité *f.*; vie, vigueur *f.*; **–ly** *adv.* d'une manière vitale; (coll.) très, fort, extrêmement; **–s** *n. pl.* parties vitales *f. pl.*
vitamin *n.* vitamine *f.*
vitiate *vt.* vicier, corrompre
vitreous *a.* vitreux
vitrify *vt.* vitrifier; — *vi.* se vitrifier
vitriol *n.* vitriol *m.*; acide sulfurique *m.*; **–ic** *a.* acide; mordant
vituperation *n.* injures, insultes *f. pl.*
vituperative *a.* injurieux

vivacious *a.* vif; enjoué; gai; animé; **–ness** *n.* vivacité *f.*

vivacity *n.* vivacité *f.*; animation *f.*

vivid *a.* vif; vivant; **–ly** *a.* d'une manière vivante; **–ness** *n.* vivacité *f.*; vigueur *f.*; imagination *f.*

vivify *vt.* vivifier, animer

vixen *n.* (zool.) renarde *f.*; femme querelleuse *f.*

viz: videlicet à savoir, c'est-à-dire

vocabulary *n.* vocabulaire *m.*

vocal *a.* vocal; bruyant; **— cords** cordes vocales *f. pl.*; **–ist** *n.* chanteur *m.*, chanteuse *f.*; **–ization** *n.* vocalisation *f.*; **–ize** *vt.* vocaliser

vocation *n.* vocation *f.*; profession *f.*; métier *m.*; **–al** de(s) métiers; professionnel; **–al school** école des arts et des métiers *f.*

vociferate *vi.* vociférer

vociferation *n.* vocifération *f.*

vociferous *a.* vociférant; criard; **–ly** *adv.* bruyamment

vodka *n.* vodka *m.*

vogue *n.* vogue, mode *f.* **in — en** vogue, à la mode

voice *n.* voix *f.*; **in a low — à** voix basse, à mi-voix; **—** *vt.* exprimer; voiser; **–d** *a.* exprimé; voisé; sonore; **–less** *a.* sans voix; non voisé; sourd

void *a.* vide; nul; **null and —** nul et caduc; **— of** dénué de; **—** *vt.* vider, évacuer, annuler; **—** *n.* vide *m.*

volatile *a.* volatil; (fig.) vif, léger; volage

volatility *n.* volatilité *f.*

volcanic *a.* volcanique

volcano *n.* volcan *m.*

volition *n.* volonté, volition *f.*; gré *m.*

volley *n.* volée, décharge, salve *f.*; (sports) volée *f.*

volleyball *n.* volleyball *m.*

volt *n.* volt *m.*; **–age** *n.* voltage *m.*, tension *f.*; **high –age** haute tension *f.*; **–aic** *a.* voltaïque

voltmeter *n.* voltmètre *m.*

volubility *n.* volubilité *f.*

voluble *a.* facile; qui parle avec volubilité

volume *n.* volume *m.*; livre, tome *m.*

volume control *n.* réglage de puissance *m.*

voluminous *a.* volumineux; **–ness** *n.* grosseur, étendue *f.*

voluntarily *adv.* volontairement

voluntary *a.* volontaire; spontané

volunteer *n.* volontaire *m.*; **—** *vt.* offrir volontairement, donner volontairement; **—** *vi.* s'offrir; **—** *a.* de volontaire

voluptuous *a.* voluptueux; **–ly** *adv.* voluptueusement; **–ness** *n.* sensualité *f.*; volupté *f.*

vomit *n.* vomissement *m.*; **—** *vt. & vi.* vomir; **–ing** *n.* vomissement *m.*

voracious *a.* vorace; dévorant; **–ly** *adv.* avec voracité; **–ness** *n.* voracité *f.*

voracity *n.* voracité *f.*

vortex *n.* tourbillon *m.*

votary *n.* adorateur, dévoué *m.*; sectateur *m.*; partisan *m.*

vote *n.* voix *f.*; vote, scrutin *m.*; suffrage *m.*; résolution *f.*; **put to a —** mettre aux voix; **—** *vt. & vi.* voter, donner sa voix; **–r** *n.* votant, électeur *m.*

voting *n.* vote, scrutin *m.*

votive *a.* votif

vouch *vt. & vi.* affirmer, garantir; **— for** répondre de; **–er** bon *m.*; fiche *f.*, reçu *m.*; passavant *m.*

vow *n.* vœu *m.*; serment *m.*; **—** *vt. & vi.* vouer; faire vœu; jurer

vowel *n.* voyelle *f.*

voyage *n.* voyage *m.*; **—** *vi.* voyager; **–r** *n.* voyageur *m.*

vulcanite *n.* caoutchouc vulcanisé *m.*

vulcanize *vt.* vulcaniser

vulgar *a.* vulgaire; commun; grossier, de mauvais goût; **–ism** *n.* expression vulgaire *f.*; **–ity** *n.* vulgarité *f.*; grossièreté *f.*; **–ization** vulgarisation *f.*; **–ize** *vt.* vulgariser

Vulgate *n.* Vulgate *f.*

vulnerability *n.* vulnérabilité *f.*

vulnerable *a.* vulnérable

W

wad *n.* liasse *f.*; bourre *f.*; paquet *m.*; **—** *vt.* (garment) ouater; **–ding** *n.* ouate *f.*; bourre *f.*

waddle *n.* dandinement *m.*; **—** *vi.* se dandiner

wade *vi.* marcher dans l'eau; patauger; **— across** passer à gué

wafer *n.* gaufrette *f.*; (eccl.) hostie *f.*

waffle *n.* gaufre *f.*; **— iron** *n.* gaufrier *m.*

waft *vt.* transporter; **—** *vi.* flotter

wag *n.* mouvement de la queue *m.*; (person) farceur *m.*; **—** *vt.* remuer, agiter

wage *vt.*, **— war** faire la guerre; **–(s)** *n. & n. pl.* salaire *m.*; gages *m. pl.*; paye *f.* récompense *f.*

wage earner *n.* salarié, gagne-pain *m.*

wager *n.* pari *m.*, gageure *f.*; **—** *vt.* parier, gager

wagon *n.* charrette *f.*; chariot *m.*; fourgon *m.*

waif *n.* enfant abandonné, enfant sans domicile *m.*

wail *n.* gémissement *m.*, plainte *f.*; **—** *vi.* gémir; se lamenter

wainscoting *n.* lambrissage *m.*; boiserie *f.*

waist *n.* taille, ceinture *f.*; (naut.) embelle *f.*

waistband *n.* ceinture *f.*

waistcoat *n.* gilet *m.*

waistline *n.* taille, ceinture *f.*

wait *n.* attente *f.*; **in —** en embuscade, à l'affût; **—** *vt. & vi.* attendre; **— for** attendre; **— on** servir; **— up** ne pas se coucher; attendre l'arrivée de quelqu'un (la nuit); **-er** *n.* garçon *m.*; **head -er** maître d'hôtel *m.*; **-ing** *n.* attente *f.*; service *m.*; **-ing game -ing tactics** tactique attentiste *f.*; **lady in -ing** dame d'honneur *f.*; **-ing list** *n.* liste supplémentaire *f.*; **-ing room** salle d'attente *f.*; antichambre *f.*

waitress *n.* serveuse *f.*

waive *vt.* renoncer à; ne pas exiger; ne pas insister sur; **-r** *n.* abandon *m.*; désistement *m.*

wake *n.* veillée (mortuaire) *f.*; (naut.) sillage *m.*; (fig.) traces *f. pl.*, suite *f.*; **—** *vi.* se réveiller; **—** *vt.* réveiller; éveiller; **-ful** *a.* éveillé, vigilant; **-fulness** *n.* vigilance *f.*, état de veille *m.*; **-n** *vt.* réveiller; éveiller; **— -n** *vi.* se réveiller; s'éveiller

waking *n.* veille *f.*; réveil *m.*; **—** *a.* de veille

Wales *n.* (Pays de) Galles *m.*

walk *n.* promenade *f.*; marche *f.*; démarche *f.*; avenue, allée *f.*; promenoir *m.*; métier *m.*, profession *f.*; **go for a —, take a —** faire une promenade, (aller) se promener; **—** *vi.* marcher; aller à pied; se réveiller; (horse) aller au pas; **—** *vt.* faire marcher; promener; (streets) courir; **-er** *n.* marcheur *m.*; piéton *m.*; promeneur *m.*; **-ing** *n.* marche *f.*; promenade(s) *f.* (*pl.*)

walkie-talkie *n.* radio-téléphone portatif *m.*

walkout *n.* grève *f.*

walk-up *n.* appartement sans ascenseur *m.*

wall *n.* mur *m.*, muraille *f.*; paroi *f.*; **— bracket** *n.* console murale *f.*; **— plug, — socket** *n.* prise de courant murale *f.*; **—** *vt.* murer; **-in, — up** murer; **-ed** *a.* muré

wallet *n.* portefeuille *m.*

walleyed *a.* qui à l'œil vairon

wallflower *n.* (fig.) tapisserie *f.*

wallop *n.* (gros) coup *m.*; **—** *vt.* rosser, frapper; tanner la peau à

wallow *vi.* se vautrer; se baigner

wallboard *n.* panneau de fibres de bois *m.*

wallpaper *n.* papier peint *m.*

walnut *n.* noix *f.*; (wood, tree) noyer *m.*

waltz *n.* valse *f.*; **—** *vi.* valser

wan *a.* pâle, blafard, blême; triste; **-ness** *n.* pâleur *f.*

wand *n.* baguette *f.*

wander *vi.* errer; vaguer; s'écarter; divaguer; **-er** *n.* voyageur, vagabond *m.*; **-ing** *a.* errant, vagabond; nomade; in-cohérent; **-ing** *n.* vagabondage *m.*; voyages *m. pl.*; divagation *f.*

wanderlust *n.* désir de voyager *m.*

wane *n.* décroissance *f.*, déclin *m.*; **—** *vi.* décroître; décliner

wangle *vt.* resquiller, carotter

waning *n.* déclin *m.*

want *n.* désir *m.*; besoin *m.*; défaut, manque *m.*; indigence *f.*; **for — of** faute de; **—** *vi.* manquer; **—** *vt.* vouloir, désirer; manquer; falloir; avoir besoin de; exiger; demander; **-ed** *a.* voulu, désiré; recherché par la police; **-ing** *a.* qui manque, manquant

wanton *a.* impudique; gratuit; **—** *n.* femme impudique *f.*; **-ness** *n.* libertinage *m.*; étourderie *f.*

war *n.* guerre *f.*; **cold — guerre** froide *f.*; **— of nerves** guerre des nerfs *f.*; **total —** guerre totale *f.*; **—** *vi.* faire la guerre; lutter; **-ring** *a.* en guerre

warble *n.* gazouillement *m.*; **—** *vi.* gazouiller; chanter en gazouillant; **-r** *n.* fauvette *f.*; oiseau chanteur *m.*

ward *n.* pupille *m.*; quartier, arrondissement *m.*; (hospital) salle (d'hôpital) *f.*; **—** *vt.*, **— off** prévenir; parer

warden *n.* directeur de prison *m.*; gardien *m.*; **air raid —** chef d'îlot *m.*

wardrobe *n.* garde-robe *f.*; vêtements *m. pl.*; armoire *f.*

wardroom *n.* carré des officiers *m.*

ware *n.* articles *m. pl.*; marchandise *f.*; **-s** *pl.* marchandise(s) *f.* (*pl.*)

warehouse *n.* magasin *m.*; entrepôt, dépôt *m.*; garde-meuble *m.*

warfare *n.* guerre *f.*

warehouseman *n.* magasinier *m.*; garde-magasin *m.*

warhead *n.* partie explosible *f.*

war horse *n.* cheval de bataille *m.*; vétéran *m.*

warily *adv.* prudemment

wariness *n.* prudence *f.*; défiance *f.*

warlike *a.* belliqueux; guerrier, martial

warm *a.* chaud; chaleureux; cordial; généreux; **be —** (person) avoir chaud; (weather) faire chaud; **—** *vt.* chauffer, réchauffer; **—** *vi.* se chauffer, se réchauffer; **-ing** *n.* chauffage *m.*; **-th** *n.* chaleur *f.*; cordialité *f.*

warm-blooded *a.* à sang chaud

warmhearted *a.* généreux

warmonger *n.* belliqueux *m.*

warmup *n.* temps de chauffage *m.*; répétition *f.*

warn *vt.* avertir, prévenir; **-ing** *n.* avertissement *m.*

warp *n.* chaîne *f.*; (wood) courbure, voilure *f.*; **—** *vt.* ourdir; (wood) faire voiler, déjeter; (naut.) touer; (fig.) pervertir, fausser; — *vi.* se déjeter; se déformer; se voiler; **-ed** *a.* déjeté, voilé; perverti, faussé

warrant *n.* mandat, ordre *m.*; warrant *m.*; garantie *f.*; — **of arrest** mandat d'arrêt *m.*; — **officer** *n.* adjutant *m.*; — *vt.* garantir; certifier; justifier; **-ed** *a.* garanti; justifié; **-y** *n.* garantie *f.*

warren *n.* garenne *f.*

warrior *n.* guerrier, soldat *m.*

Warsaw *n.* Varsovie *f.*

warship *n.* navire de guerre *m.*

wart *n.* verrue *f.*

wartime *n.* temps de guerre *m.*

wary *a.* prudent; attentif

wash *n.* lavage *m.*; blanchissage *m.*; lessive *f.*; (art) lavis *m.*; (naut.) sillage *m.*; — *vt.* laver; blanchir; lotionner; — **one's hands** se laver les mains; — *vi.* se laver; — **away** enlever; emporter; — **down** laver; (food) arroser; — **out** laver; rincer; enlever; **-able** *a.* lavable; **-ed** *a.* lavé; **-ed out** délavé; raté; **-er** *n.* laveur *m.*; plongeur *m.*; **-ing** *n.* lavage *m.*; blanchissage *m.*; linge *m.*; **-ing machine** laveuse méchanique *f.*; **-ing soda** soude *m.*

washbowl *n.* cuvette de lavabo *f.*

washcloth *n.* gant-éponge *m.*, lavette *f.*

washroom *n.* lavabos *m. pl.*; cabinets *m. pl.*

washstand *n.* lavabo *m.*

washtub *n.* cuvier *m.*

waste *n.* gaspillage *m.*; déchets *m. pl.*, rebut *m.*; désert *m.*; — **of time** perte de temps *f.*; **-paper** papiers *m. pl.*, papiers de rebut *m. pl.*; — **pipe** tuyau d'écoulement *m.*; — *a.* de rebut; — *vt.* gaspiller; (time) perdre; user, consumer; — *vi.* s'user; se perdre; maigrir; **-d** *a.* gaspillé; perdu; dévasté; **-ful** *a.* gaspilleur; prodigue; **-fulness** *n.* gaspillage *m.*; prodigalité *f.*

wastebasket *n.* corbeille (à papiers) *f.*

wastepaper *a.*, — **basket** corbeille (à papiers) *f.*

watch *n.* surveillance *f.*; garde *f.*; (naut.) quart *m.*; bordée *f.*; (timepiece) montre *f.*; **on the** — sur ses gardes, en observation; **be on the** — **for** guetter; — **pocket** gousset de montre *m.*; — *vt.* observer; regarder; veiller (sur); surveiller; assister à; — *vi.* veiller; — **out** être sur ses gardes; prendre attention, prendre garde; — **out!** attention!, prenez garde!; — **over** garder; surveiller; **-er** *n.* observateur *m.*; **-ful** *a.* attentif; alerte, vigilant; **-fulness** *n.* vigilance *f.*

watchdog *n.* chien de garde *m.*

watch fire *n.* feu (de bivouac) *m.*

watchmaker *n.* horloger *m.*

watchman *n.* veilleur de nuit *m.*; garde, gardien *m.*

watchtower *n.* tour d'observation *f.*

watchword *a.* mot d'ordre *m.*

water *n.* eau *f.*; **by** — en bateau; **cold** — eau fraîche *f.*; **drinking** — eau potable *f.*; **fresh** — eau douce *f.*; **running** — eau courante *f.*; **turn on the** — ouvrir l'eau; **under** — submergé; inondé; — **closet** *m.*; cabinets *m. pl.*; — **color** aquarelle *f.*; — **cure** hydrothérapie *f.*; — **faucet** robinet *m.*; — **front** quartier de la ville qui fait face à l'eau *m.*; — **gauge** hydromètre *m.*; — **glass** verre *m.*; (chem.) silicate de soude *m.*; — **level** niveau d'eau *m.*; — **line** niveau d'eau *m.*; (naut.) flottaison *f.*; — **lily** *n.* lis d'eau *m.*; — **main** conduite principale *f.*; — **polo** waterpolo *m.*; — **power** force hydraulique *f.*; — **softener** adoucisseur d'eau *m.*; — **system** canalisation d'eau *f.*; — **tower** château d'eau *m.*; — **wheel** roue hydraulique *f.*; — *vt.* arroser; diluer; couper; abreuver; — *vi.* larmoyer, pleurer; — **down** atténuer; **-ing** *n.* irrigation *f.*; arrosage *m.*; dilution *f.*; abreuvage *m.*; (eyes) larmoiement *m.*; **-ing can** arrosoir *m.*; **-y** *a.* aqueux; larmoyant; (color) déteint

watercress *n.* cresson *m.*

waterfall *n.* chute d'eau, cascade *f.*

waterlog *vt.* imprégner d'eau; **-ged** *a.* plein d'eau

watermark *n.* (paper) filigrane *m.*; **-ed** *a.* à filigrane

watermelon *n.* pastèque *f.*

waterproof *a.* imperméable; — *vt.* rendre étanche

waterspout *n.* gouttière *f.*; tuyau *m.*; trombe *f.*

watertight *a.* étanche

waterway *n.* voie d'eau (navigable) *f.*

waterworks *n. pl.* service des eaux *m.*

watt *n.* watt *m.*; **-age** *n.* wattage *m.*; consommation en watts *f.*

wave *n.* (gesture) geste, salut *m.*; vague, onde *f.*; (hair) ondulation *f.*; **permanent** — indéfrisable *f.*; **tidal** — raz de marée *m.*; — *vi.* ondoyer; flotter, se balancer; tournoyer; faire un geste, saluer; — *vt.* agiter; (hair) onduler; **-d** *a.* ondulé

wave length *n.* longueur d'onde *f.*

waver *vi.* vaciller, chanceler; **-ing** *n.* vacillation, irrésolution *f.*; **-ing** *a.* irrésolu, vacillant; — *n.* hésitation, indécision *f.*

wavy *a.* ondoyant; ondulé, onduleux

wax *n.* cire *f.*; — **paper** papier ciré *m.*; —

adv. bien; alors; as —. aussi; as — as aussi bien que; comme; **very** — très bien; — *a.* bien; bon; **be** — aller bien, se porter bien; — *interj.* eh bien
well-advised *a.* prudent, sage
well-behaved *a.* sage; bien élevé
well-being *n.* bien-être *m.*
wellborn *a.* de haute naissance
well-bred *a.* bien élevé; bien éduqué
well-chosen *a.* bien choisi
well-earned *a.* bien mérité
well-educated *a.* instruit
well-informed *a.* au courant; bien renseigné; instruit
well-kept *a.* bien tenu; (secret) bien gardé
well-known *a.* connu; célèbre; fameux
well-mannered *a.* bien élevé
well-meaning *a.* bien intentionné
well off *a.* aisé; qui a du bien
well-read *a.* instruit; savant
well-shaped *a.* bien formé
well-spent *a.* bien utilisé
well-suited *a.* **to be** — to être fait pour
well-to-do *a.* prospère, riche, aisé
Welsh *a.* gallois; **-man** *n.* Gallois *m.*
welt *n.* zébrure *f.*
welter *n.* désordre *m.*, confusion *f.*
welterweight *n.* poids mi-moyen *m.*
wen *n.* loupe *f.*, goître *m.*
wench *n.* fille *f.*; donzelle *f.*; gaillarde *f.*
wend *vi.* aller, poursuivre; — *vt.* se diriger, poursuivre son chemin
west *n.* ouest, occident *m.*; — *adv.* vers l'ouest; — *a.* de l'ouest; **-erly** *a.* de l'ouest; **-ern** *a.* occidental, de l'ouest; **-ward** *adv.* vers l'ouest
wet *n.* humidité *f.*; — *vt.* mouiller, humecter, arroser; — *a.* mouillé, humide, **get** — se mouiller; **soaking** — mouillé jusqu'aux os; — **blanket** trouble-fête, rabat-joie *m.*; — **nurse** nourrice *f.*; **-ness** *n.* humidité *f.*
whack *n.* coup *m.*; — *vt.* battre, rosser
whale *n.* baleine *f.*; **-r** *n.* baleinier *m.*; — *vi.* faire la pêche à la baleine
wharf *n.* quai *m.*; embarcadère *m.*; appontement *m.*; — *vi.* amarrer; **-age** *n.* quayage *m.*
what *pron.* que, qu'est-ce que, qu'est-ce qui; ce qui, ce que; quoi; — *a.* quel; — **is the matter?** qu'y a-t-il?; — **is the matter with him?** qu'a-t-il?; **-'s the use?** à quoi bon?; — **time is it?** quelle heure est-il?; — *interj.* quoi; comment
whatever *pron.* tout ce qui, tout ce que; n'importe quoi; quoi que ce soit; — *a.* quelconque; quel . . . . que; aucun
whatsoever *pron.* quoi que ce soit; quelconque
wheat *n.* froment, blé *m.*; **-en** *a.* de blé

wheedle *vt.* enjôler, flatter
wheel *n.* roue *f.*; **spinning** — rouet *m.*; **steering** — volant *m.*; — *vt. & vi.* rouler, faire tourner **-ed** *a.* à roues
wheelbarrow *n.* brouet *m.*
wheel base *n.* distance entre les essieux *f.*
wheel chair *n.* fauteuil roulant *m.*, voiture de malade *f.*
wheelwright *n.* charron *m.*
wheeze *vi.* respirer avec bruit; siffler
wheezing *n.* respiration sifflante *f.*
wheezy *a.* sifflant; asthmatique
whelp *n.* petit chien *m.*; — *vi.* mettre bas
when *adv.* quand; lorsque; tandis que; où; **since** — depuis quand
whenever *adv.* quand; n'importe quand; toutes les fois que
where *adv.* où
whereabouts *n.* situation *f.*; où l'on se trouve
whereas *conj.* puisque, comme; vu que; tandis que
whereby *adv.* par quoi; par lequel
wherefore *adv.* pourquoi; — *n.* les pourquoi *m. pl.*
wherein *adv.* en quoi; où; dans lequel
whereof *adv.* de quoi
whereupon *adv.* sur quoi; là-dessus
wherever *adv.* n'importe où; où que; partout où
wherewithal *n.* de quoi; ce qu'il faut
whet *vt.* aiguiser; exciter
whether *conj.* soit que; que; si
whetstone *n.* pierre à aiguiser *f.*
which *pron.* lequel, laquelle; qui, que; — *a.* quel; quoi; — **one** lequel; — **way par** où; **of** — dont; duquel
whichever *a.* quel (que); — *conj.* quoi que; — *pron.* n'importe lequel
whiff *n.* souffle *m.*, bouffée *f.*
while *n.* temps, espace de temps *m.*; **a little** — ago tout à l'heure; **in a little** — tout à l'heure; **be worth** — valoir la peine; — *vt.*, **to** — **away** tuer (le temps); — *conj.* pendant que, tandis que; tant que; à mesure que; bien que, quoique
whim *n.* caprice *m.*, fantaisie *f.*
whimper *vi.* pleurnicher; — *n.* pleurnichement *m.*; **-er** *n.* pleurnicheur *m.*; **-ing** *n.* pleurnichement *m.*
whimsical *a.* capricieux; bizarre
whine *n.* plainte *f.*; gémissement *m.*; — *vi.* se plaindre, geindre, gémir, se lamenter
whining *a.* plaintif, pleurnicheur; — *n.* plaintes *f. pl.*, pleurnichement *m.*; sifflement *m.*
whinny *n.* hennissement *m.*; — *vi.* hennir
whip *n.* fouet *m.*; **riding** — cravache *f.*; — **hand** avantage, dessus *m.*; — *vt.* fouetter; battre, vaincre; **-ped cream**

crème fouettée *f.*; –ping *n.* fouettée *f.*;
fouettement *m.*; coups de fouet *m. pl.*
whirl *n.* tourbillon *m.*; tournoiement *m.*;
— *vt.* faire tourner avec vitesse; — *vi.*
tournoyer, pirouetter
whirlpool, whirlwind *n.* tourbillon *m.*
whirr, whir *n.* ronflement *m.*; — *vi.* ronfler
whisk *n.* mouvement brusque *m.*; époussette *f.*; — broom petit balai *m.*; — *vt.*
agiter; — away enlever, chasser; enlever; — *vi.* passer rapidement
whisker *n.* poil (de la barbe) *m.*; –s *pl.*
barbe *f.*; side –s favoris *m. pl.*
whisper *n.* chuchotement *m.*; — *vt. & vi.*
chuchoter
whistle *n.* sifflet *m.*; sifflement *m.*; —
vt. & vi. siffler
whit *n.* point, iota *m.*
white *a.* blanc (blanche); pâle; pur; turn
— blanchir; pâlir; — elephant *n.* (fig.)
fardeau *m.*; chose encombrante *f.*; —
— heat *n.* incandescence *f.*; — *n.* blanc
m.; –ness *n.* blancheur *f.*
whitecap *n.* mouton *m.*
white-collar, — worker *a. & n.* employé
(dans un bureau)
whitefish *n.* merlan *m.*
white-hot *a.* chauffé à blanc, incandescent
whiten *vt.* blanchir
whitewash *n.* blanc de chaux, lait de
chaux *m.*; — *vt.* passer au chaux, blanchir à la chaux; (fig.) justifier, donner
des apparences légitimes à
whither *adv.* où
whitish *a.* blanchâtre
whittle *vt.* couper, tailler; amenuiser
whiz *n.* sifflement *n.*; (coll.) expert, génie *m.*; — *vi.* siffler; passer très vite
who *pron.* qui, qui est-ce qui; quel
whoever *pron.* qui que; quiconque, celui
qui; qui que ce soit
whole *n.* total, tout *m.*; totalité *f.*; entier *m.*; — number *n.* nombre entier *m.*;
— note *n.* (mus.) ronde *f.*; on the —
pour la plupart; dans l'ensemble; à tout
prendre, en somme — *a.* tout, entier,
complet; sain
wholehearted *a.* sincère, de tout cœur
wholesale *n.* gros *m.*; — *a. & adv.* en gros;
— *vt.* vendre en gros; –r *n.* marchand en
gros *m.*
wholesome *a.* sain, salutaire
whole-wheat *a.* de blé entier
wholly *adv.* entièrement, complètement,
tout cà fait
whom *pron.* que; qui; lequel; of — dont,
duquel
whomever *pron.* quiconque, celui que
whoop *n.* huée *f.*; houp *m.*; — *vi.* huer,
crier; –ing cough *n.* coqueluche *f.*

whore *n.* prostituée *f.*
whorl *n.* volute *f.*
whose *pron.* dont, de qui, à qui
why *adv.* pourquoi; — *interj.* mais
wick *n.* mèche *f.*
wicked *a.* méchant, scélérat; mauvais;
–ness *n.* méchanceté *f.*
wicker *n.* osier *m.*; — *a.* en osier
wicket *n.* guichet *m.*
wide *a.* large; vaste, ample; — *adv.* largement; au loin; far and — partout; —
awake *a.* tout à fait éveillé; ouvert; –ly
adv. largement; très; beaucoup; –n *vt.*
élargir; –n *vi.* s'élargir
wide-eyed *a.* abasourdi
wide-felt *a.* ressenti partout
wide-open *a.* ouvert
widespread *a.* répandu
widow *n.* veuve *f.*; — *vt.* rendre veuve;
priver; –ed *a.* veuf; –er *n.* veuf *m.*;
–hood *n.* veuvage *m.*
width *n.* largeur *f.*
wield *vt.* manier, tenir, porter
wife *n.* femme, épouse *f.*; –ly *a.* de femme,
d'épouse
wig *n.* perruque *f.*
wiggle *vt.* manier, tortiller; — *vi.* se tortiller
wigwag *vt.* agiter; signaler par l'emploi de
drapeaux
wild *a.* sauvage, farouche; agreste, inculte; irrégulier, dissolu; –s *n. pl.* désert
m.; –ness *n.* férocité *f.*; état sauvage *m.*;
fureur *f.*; extravagance *f.*
wildcat *n.* lynx *m.*; — *a.* spéculatif, risqué;
— strike grève non autorisée *f.*
wilderness *n.* désert *m.*
wildfire *n.* feu grégeois *m.*; like — extrêmement vite
wild-goose chase *n.* entreprise infruc-
tueuse *f.*; démarches inutiles *f. pl.*
wile *n.* fourberie, ruse *f.*
wilful *a.* entêté; prémédité; –ly *adv.* à dessein, exprès; avec entêtement; –ness *n.*
entêtement *m.*, obstination *f.*
wiliness *n.* astuce *f.*
will *n.* volonté *f.*; disposition *f.*; (law)
testament *m.*; at — à volonte; of one's
own free — de son plein gré; — *vt.* vouloir; laisser par testament; léguer; –ing
a. disposé, consentant; be –ing vouloir
bien; –ingness *n.* consentement *m.*;
bonne volonté *f.*
willow *n.* saule *m.*; weeping — saule pleureur *m.*; –y *a.* svelte, souple
will power *n.* volonté *f.*
willy-nilly *adv.* bon gré mal gré
wilt *vi.* se faner, se flétrir
wily *a.* rusé, fin; malin
wimple *n.* guimpe *f.*

win *vt. & vi.* gagner; acquérir; — **a prize** remporter un prix; — **over** gagner; **-ner** *n.* gagnant *m.*; **-ning** *a.* gagnant; engageant

wince *vi.* broncher; faire une grimace

winch *n.* treuil *m.*

wind *n.* vent *m.*; haleine *f.*; **get one's second** — reprendre haleine; — **instrument** instrument à vent *m.*; — *vt.* essoufler; **-ed** *a.* essoufflé, hors d'haleine; **-y** *a.* venteux; it is **-y** il fait du vent

wind *n.* tour *m.*; tournant *m.*; — *vt.* tourner, tordre; envelopper, entourer; enrouler; — *vi.* tourner, se tordre, serpenter; — **up** remonter; terminer; **-ing** *n.* détour, tournant *m.*; enroulement *m.*; bandage *m.*; **-ing** *a.* sinueux, en lacet; **-ing sheet** *n.* linceul *m.*

windfall *n.* aubaine *f.*

windjammer *n.* voilier *m.*

windlass *n.* treuil, guindeau *m.*

windmill *n.* moulin à vent *m.*

window *n.* fenêtre; croisée *f.*; (ticket) guichet *m.*; (store) vitrine, devanture *f.*; **French** — porte-fenêtre *f.*; **stained-glass** — vitrail *m.*; — **envelope** enveloppe à fenêtre *f.*

window dresser, window trimmer *n.* étalagiste *m.*

window dressing *n.* art de l'étalage *m.*; (coll.) trompe-l'œil *m.*

windowpane *n.* carreau *m.*

window-shopping *n.* lèche-vitrines *m.*

window sill *n.* appui, rebord (de fenêtre) *m.*

windpipe *n.* trachée-artère *f.*; gosier *m.*

windshield *n.* pare-brise *m.*; — **wiper** essuie-glace *m.*

wind-swept *a.* venteux

wind tunnel *n.* tunnel aérodynamique *m.*

windward *a. & adv.* vers le vent, sous le vent

wine *n.* vin *m.*; — **grower** vigneron *m.*

winecellar *n.* cave au vin *f.*

wineglass *n.* verre à vin *m.*

wing *n.* aile *f.*; **-s** *pl.* (theat.) coulisses *f. pl.*; — *vi.* voler, s'envoler; **-ed** *a.* ailé

wingspan, wingspread *n.* envergure *f.*

wink *n.* clin d'œil *m.*; clignement d'œil *m.*; — *vi.* clignoter; cligner de l'œil; fermer les yeux

winnow *vt.* vanner; éplucher

winsome *a.* séduisant

winter *n.* hiver *m.*; — *vi.* hiverner; passer l'hiver; **-ize** *vt.* équiper pour l'hiver

wintergreen *n.* wintergreen *m.*, pyrole *f.*; gaulthérie (du Canada) *f.*; palommier *m.*

wintertime *n.* hiver *m.*, saison d'hiver *f.*

wintry *a.* d'hiver; froid, glacial

wipe *n.* action d'essuyer; — *vt.* essuyer; — **one's nose** se moucher; — **out** détruire, exterminer; effacer

wire *n.* fil (de métal) *m.*; télégramme *m.*; **pull -s** (coll.) arranger les choses, user de l'influence; — *vt.* munir de fils; faire une installation électrique; — *vi.* (coll.) télégraphier; **-less** *a.* san fil; **-less** *n.* radio

wire cutter *n.* coupe-fil *m.*

wire-haired *a.* à poil dur

wire tapping *n.* captation *f.*

wiring *n.* canalisation, pose de fils *f.*

wiry *a.* de fil, de en fil (de metal); (hair) raide; (person) sec

wisdom *n.* sagesse *f.*; — **tooth** dent de sagesse *f.*

wise *n.* manière, façon *f.*; **in no** — d'aucune façon; — *a.* sage; prudent

wish *n.* souhait *m.*; désir *m.*; vœu *m.*; — *vt. & vi.* désirer, vouloir; souhaiter; **-ful** *a.* désireux

wishbone *n.* lunette *f.*

wishy-washy *a.* fade, indifférent

wisp *n.* touffe, poignée *f.*

wistful *a.* pensif; plein de regret

wit *n.* esprit *m.*; bel esprit *m.*; — *vt.* savoir; **to** — à savoir, c'est-à-dire; **-less** *a.* sans esprit; **-tingly** *adv.* à dessein; **-ty** *a.* spirituel

witch *n.* sorcière *f.*; **-craft** *n.* sorcellerie *f.*; sortilège *m.*; — **hunt** *n.* chasse aux sorcières; (pol.) persécution des adversaires *f.*

with *prep.* avec; de; par; parmi; à; malgré

withdraw *vt.* retirer; rappeler; — *vi.* se retirer, s'éloigner; **-al** *n.* retrait, rappel *m.*; retraite *f.*

wither *vt.* flétrir, faner, dessécher; — *vi.* se faner, se dessécher

withhold *vt.* retenir, détenir; empêcher; **-ing** *a.*, **-ing tax** impôt retenu à la source *m.*

within *adv.* dedans, à l'interieur; — *prep.* à l'intérieur de; dans; à portée de; à moins de; avant

without *prep.* sans; hors de; **do** — se passer de; — *adv.* dehors; au dehors, en dehors; — *conj.* sans que

withstand *vt.* résister, s'opposer à

witness *n.* témoin, témoignage *m.*; **to bear** — **to** témoigner de; — *vt.* attester, être temoin de, assister à

witticism *n.* bon mot *m.*

wizard *n.* magicien, sorcier *m.*

wobble *vi.* chanceler, vaciller, tituber; branler

wobbly *a.* vacillant, branlant

woe *n.* douleur *f.*; malheur *m.*; **-ful** *a.* triste, malheureux

woman *n.* femme *f.*; **-ly** *a.* féminin; de femme

womb *n.* matrice *f.*; sein, ventre *m.*

wonder *n.* étonnement *m.*, admiration *f.*; miracle *m.*; — *vi.* s'étonner; se demander; **-ful** *a.* merveilleux; **-ment** *n.* étonnement *m.*, admiration *f.*

wonderland *n.* pays des merveilles *m.*

wondrous *a.* merveilleux

wont *n.* coutume, habitude *f.*; **-ed** *a.* accoutumé, habituel

woo *vt.* courtiser; faire la cour à

wood *n.* bois *m.*; forêt *f.*; **-ed** *a.* boisé; **-en** *a.* de bois, en bois; **-en** (fig.) gauche **-y** *a.* ligneux; fibreux; — alcohol *n.* alcool méthylique *m.*

wood carving *n.* sculpture sur bois *f.*

woodcut *n.* gravure sur bois *f.*, bois *m.*, xylographie *f.*

woodcutter *n.* bûcheron *m.*

woodland *n.* bois *m.*

woodshed *n.* bûcher *m.*

woodsman *n.* homme des bois *m.*

wood wind *n.* bois *m.*

woodwork *n.* boiseries *f. pl.*; charpenterie *f.*; menuiserie *f.*

woof *n.* trame *f.*

woofer *n.* haut-parleur (pour les sons graves) *m.*

wool *n.* laine *f.*; **steel** — laine d'acier *f.*; **-en** *a.* de laine; **-ens** *n. pl.* étoffes de laine *f. pl.*; **-y** *a.* laineux; touffu

word *n.* mot *m.*; parole *f.*; nouvelle *f.*, renseignement *m.*; recommandation *f.*; **in a** — en un mot, bref; **send** — **to** savoir, avertir, prevenir; **-s** *pl.* dispute *f.*; **have -s with** se disputer avec; s'expliquer; — *vt.* exprimer, rédiger; **-iness** *n.* verbosité *f.*; **-ing** *n.* termes *m. pl.*; **-y** *a.* verbeux, prolixe

work *n.* travail *m.*; occupation *f.*; ouvrage *m.*; opération *f.*; œuvre *f.*; besogne, tâche *f.*; **at** — au travail; en jeu; **-s** *pl.* usine *f.*; — *vi.* travailler; (function) marcher, aller; fonctionner; agir; — *vt.* faire travailler; travailler; opérer; accomplir; exploiter; développer; élaborer; — **out** résoudre, trouver; s'arranger; — **up** susciter, causer; **-able** *a.* pratique; réalisable; **-er** *n.* ouvrier, travailleur *m.*; **-ing** *a.* qui travaille; ouvrier; **-ing class** classe ouvrière *f.*; ouvriers *m. pl.*; **-ing** *n.* travail *m.*; marche *f.* fonctionnement *m.*

workbench *n.* établi *m.*

workbook *n.* manuel *m.*

workday *n.* jour ouvrable *m.*

workhouse *n.* hôpital *m.*; maison de travail *f.*; prison municipale *f.*

workman *n.* ouvrier *m.*; **-like** *a.* bien tra-

vaillé; **-ship** *n.* fini *m.*, construction *f.*; exécution *f.*

workout *n.* exercice *m.*; essai *m.*

workroom, workshop *n.* atelier *m.*

world *n.* monde, univers *m.*, terre *f.*; milieu *m.*; **a** — **of** pas mal de; — **war** guerre mondiale *f.*; **-liness** *n.* mondanité *f.*; **-ly** *a.* du monde; mondain

world-famous *a.* très connu, célèbre

world-wide *a.* universel

worm *n.* ver *m.*; — *vt.* (coll.) tirer; **-y** *a.* vermoulu

worm-eaten *a.* vermoulu

worn *a.* usé

worry *n.* ennui, souci *m.*; inquiétude *f.*; tracasserie *f.*; chagrin, dépit *m.*, contrariété *f.*; — *vt.* harasser, tourmenter, tracasser; inquiéter; — *vi.* s'inquiéter; se tracasser; **don't** — ne vous inquiétez pas; soyez tranquille

worse *a.* pire, plus mauvais; — *adv.* plus mal, pis; **so much the** — tant pis; **-n** *vt.* aggraver, empirer; **-n** *vi.* s'aggraver, empirer

worship *n.* adoration *f.*, culte *m.*; — *vt.* adorer

worst *n.* pire, pis; **at the** — au pis; — *vt.* vaincre, défaire; l'emporter sur; — *a.* le pire, le plus mauvais; — *adv.* le pis, le plus mal

worsted *n.* laine filée, laine peignée *f.*

worth *n.* valeur *f.*, prix *m.*; mérite *m.*; — *a.* qui vaut; digne de; **be** — valoir; **be** — **the trouble, be** — **while** valoir la la peine; **-iness** *n.* mérite *m.*; **-less** *a.* sans valeur; **-y** *a.* digne; **be -y of** mériter, être digne de

worthwhile *a.* qui vaut la peine

would-be *a.* soi-disant

wound *n.* blessure *f.*; plaie *f.*; — *vt.* blesser; froisser

wraith *n.* apparition *f.*

wrangle *n.* querelle *f.*; — *vi.* se quereller; **-er** *n.* querelleur *m.*; vacher *m.*

wrap *n.* (garment) manteau *m.*; emballage *m.*; — *vt.* emballer; envelopper, entourer; **-per** *n.* emballage *m.*; couverture *f.*; chemise *f.*; robe de chambre *f.*; **-ping** *n.* emballage *m.*, couverture *f.*; **-ping paper** papier d'emballage *m.*

wrath *n.* colère *f.*, courroux *m.*; **-ful** *a.* courroucé

wreak *vt.* exécuter, infliger

wreath *n.* guirlande, couronne *f.*; **-e** *vt.* couronner, enguirlander

wreck *n.* naufrage *m.*; ruine *f.*; accident *m.*; — *vt.* causer un naufrage; causer la destruction de; ruiner; détruire; saboter; **-age** *a.* débris *m. pl.*; décombres *m. pl.*; **-ed** *a.* détruit; naufragé; **-er** *n.*

(auto.) voiture de dépannage *f.*; (house) démolisseur *m.*; **–ing** *n.* ruine, destruction *f.*

wrench *n.* torsion *f.*; (tool) clé *f.*; **monkey** — clé anglaise *f.*; — *vt.* arracher, tordre; se fouler

wrestle *vi.* lutter; — **with** lutter avec, lutter contre; s'attaquer à; **–r** *n.* lutteur *m.*

wrestling *n.* lutte *f.*, catch *m.*

wretch *n.* misérable *m.*; malheureux *m.*; **–ed** *a.* misérable; malheureux, méprisable; pitoyable; **–edness** *n.* misère *f.*; malheur *m.*

wriggle *vi.* se tortiller; frétiller; — *vt.* tortiller

wring *vt.* tordre, tortiller; arracher; **–er** *n.* essoreuse *f.*

wrinkle *n.* ride *f.*; faux pli *m.*; (fig.) nouveau tour *m.*; — *vt.* rider; froncer; — *vi.* se rider; **–d** *a.* ridé

wrist *n.* poignet *m.*

wrist watch *n.* montre-bracelet *m.*

writ *n.* assignation *f.*; mandat *m.*

write *vt.* écrire; — *vi.* écrire; être écrivain; — **down** noter; inscrire; — **off** rayer, (com.) amortir; — **out** rédiger; — **up** rédiger, faire le procès-verbal de; **–r** *n.* écrivain *m.*, auteur *m.*

writhe *vi.* se tordre

writing *n.* écrit, ouvrage *m.*; écriture *f.*; **in** — par écrit; — **paper** *n.* papier à écrire *m.*

wrong *n.* tort *m.*; dommage, détriment *m.*, injustice *f.*; **be in the** — avoir tort; — *vt.* faire tort à; — *a.* faux; injuste; impropre; mauvais; mal; **be** — avoir tort; **what's** — qu'y a-t-il; **what's** — **with you** qu'avez-vous; — *adv.* mal; à tort; **do** — faire mal; **to go** — s'égarer; se détraquer, se déranger; **–ful** *a.* injuste; **–ly** *adv.* à tort; **rightly or –ly** à tort ou à raison

wrongdoer *n.* malfaiteur *m.*

wrongdoing *n.* mal, crime *m.*

wrought *a.* travaillé, ouvragé; — **iron** fer forgé *m.*

wry *a.* tors, tordu, difforme

X

xenon *n.* xénon *m.*

xerophagy *n.* xérophagie *f.*

xerophilous *a.* xérophile

xerophyte *n.* xérophyte *m.*

X ray *n.* rayon X *m.*; — **picture** *n.* radiogramme *m.*; — **specialist** *n.* radiologiste *m. & f.*

xylophone *n.* xylophone *m.*

Y

yacht *n.* yacht *m.*; **–ing** *n.* yachting *m.*

yachtsman *n.* yachtman *m.*

yam *n.* patate *f.*

yank *n.* secousse *f.*; — *vt.* tirer brusquement

Yankee *n.* (coll.) Américain *m.*; habitant du Nord des Etats-Unis *m.*; habitant de la Nouvelle-Angleterre *m.*

yap *n.* aboiement *m.*; jappement *m.*; — *vi.* aboyer; japper

yard *n.* cour *f.*; chantier *m.*; (naut.) vergue *f.*; (rail.) dépôt *m.*; (measure) yard *m.* (= 91 cm.); — **master** *n.* maître de chantier *m.*

yardstick *n.* mètre en bois *m.*

yarn *n.* fil (pour tissage) *m.*; (coll.) histoire *f.*

yawl *n.* yole *f.*

yawn *n.* bâillement *m.*; — *vi.* bâiller; **–ing** *a.* qui bâille; (fig.) béant

ye *pron.* vous

yea *adv.* oui; vraiment

year *n.* an *m.*, année *f.*; **leap** — année bissextile *f.*; **last** — l'année passée; **school** — année scolaire *f.*; **–ly** *a.* annuel; **–ly** *adv.* annuellement

yearbook *n.* annuaire *m.*

yearling *n.* animal d'un an *m.*

yearn *vi.*, — **for** soupirer après; **–ing** *n.* désir ardent *m.*, aspiration *f.*

yeast *n.* levure *f.*, levain *m.*; levain en cubes *m.*

yell *n.* hurlement *m.*; cri *m.*; — *vi.* hurler; pousser un cri

yellow *n.* jaune *m.*; — *a.* jaune; lâche; infame; **turn** — jaunir; — **fever** fièvre jaune *f.*; — *vt. & vi.* jaunir; **–ish** *a.* jaunâtre

yelp *vi.* glapir, japper; — *n.* jappement *m.*

Yemen *n.* Yemen *m.*

yen *n.* désir *m.*

yeoman *n.* yeoman *m.*; hallebardier *m.*

yes *adv.* oui; (after negation) si; — **man** *n.* girouette *f.*

yesterday *adv.* hier; **day before** — avanthier

yet *adv.* encore; cependant, toutefois; déjà; malgré tout; **as** — jusqu'ici

yield *n.* produit, rendement *m.*; — *vt.* céder; produire, rendre, donner; accorder; procurer; — *vi.* céder; succomber; consentir; **–ing** *a.* complaisant; souple; mou (molle)

yodel *n.* tyrolienne *f.*; — *vi.* chanter une tyrolienne; iouler

yoke *n.* joug, attelage *m.*; couple *m.*; (dress) empiècement *m.*; — *vt.* mettre au joug; subjuguer; accoupler

yokel *n.* provincial, rustique *m.*

yolk *n.* jaune d'œuf *m.*

yon, yonder *a.* qui est là; — *adv.* là-bas

yore *adv.* jadis, autrefois; **in days of** — au temps jadis

you *pron.* vous; tu; toi; on

young *a.* jeune; nouveau; tendre; **-er** *a.* cadet

youngster *n.* jeune personne *f.*, jeune homme *m.*; enfant *m.*

your *a.* votre, vos; ton, ta, tes; **-s** *pron.* le vôtre, la vôtre, les vôtres; à vous; le tien, la tienne; à toi; **-self** *pron.* vous-même, vous; toi-même, toi

youth *n.* jeunesse *f.*; jeune homme *m.*; **-ful** *a.* jeune; de jeunesse; **-fulness** *n.* jeunesse *f.*

yowl *n.* hurlement, jappement *m.*; — *vi.* hurler, japper

Yule *n.* Noël *m.*; — **log** bûche de Noël *f.*

Yuletide *n.* fêtes de Noël *f. pl.*

Z

zany *n.* bouffon *m.*; — *a.* (coll.) niais; fou; capricieux

zeal *n.* zèle *m.*; ardeur *f.*; **-ous** *a.* zélé

zealot *n.* fanatique *m. & f.*

zenith *n.* zénith *m.*; comble *m.*

zero *n.* zéro *m.*; (fig.) rien; — **hour** *n.* (mil.) heure de l'attaque, heure H *f.*

zest *n.* goût *m.*; appétit *m.*; enthousiasme *m.*

zigzag *n.* zigzag *m.*; — *a.* en zigzag; — *vi* faire des zigzags

zinc *n.* zinc *m.*; — *vt.* zinguer

Zion *n.* Sion *m.*

zip code number *n.* code postale d'arrondissement *m.*

zipper *n.* fermeture éclair *f.*

zircon *n.* zircon *m.*

zither *n.* cithare *f.*

zodiac *n.* zodiaque *m.*

zone *n.* zone *f.*; — *vt.* repartir en zones

zoo *n.* jardin *n.* jardin zoologique, zoo *m.*

zoologist *n.* zoologiste *m.*

zoology *n.* zoologie *f.*

zoom *n.* bourdonnement *m.*; — *vi.* monter verticalement; bourdonner

zoonosis *n.* zoonose *f.*

Zulu *a. & n.* zoulou *m.*

TRAVELER'S CONVERSATION GUIDE
Guide de Conversation pour le Voyage

STATION (OR AIRPORT)

Where do I go through customs?
I have nothing to declare.
All I have are my personal things and a few packages of cigarettes.
I need a porter.
Where is my baggage?
This is not my suitcase. Please look for mine.
This is my baggage.
I checked two trunks.
I'll carry this suitcase.
Are meals included on that flight?

Are the cars air-conditioned?

TAXI

Will you get a taxi for me, please?

Take me to the Hotel ⸻.
How much is the fare?
Is it very far?
I am in a great hurry
Drive carefully, please.
Stop at the next corner.
Faster, please.
Not so fast.
Slower.
Stop!
Go on.
Go straight ahead.
Turn to your left. (right)
This is for you.

HOTEL

Where is the office?
I have a reservation.
I want a single room with bath.

Have you a two-bed room?
Is it a front room?

I'm going to stay two weeks. (a week)

LA GARE (OU L'AEROPORT)

Où se trouve la douane?
Je n'ai rien à déclarer.
Je n'ai que des effets personnels et quelques paquets de cigarettes.
J'ai besoin d'un porteur.
Où sont mes bagages?
Cette valise n'est pas à moi. Allez chercher la mienne, s'il vous plaît.
Voici mes bagages.
J'ai fait enregistrer deux malles.
Cette valise, je vais la porter.
Est-ce que le prix du billet comprend les repas?
Est-ce que les wagons sont climatisés?

LE TAXI

Voulez-vous bien me chercher un taxi?
L'Hôtel ⸻, s'il vous plaît.
Le tarif, c'est combien?
Est-ce que c'est très loin?
Je suis très pressé.
Conduisez avec soin, s'il vous plaît.
Arrêtez (-vous) à la prochaine rue.
Plus vite, s'il vous plaît.
Pas si vite.
Plus lentement.
Arrêtez-vous!
Continuez.
Allez tout droit.
Tournez à gauche. (droite)
Voici pour vous.

L'HÔTEL

Où est le bureau?
J'ai fait réserver une chambre.
Je voudrais une chambre à un lit avec bain.
Avez-vous une chambre à deux lits?
Est-ce que la chambre donne sur la rue?
Je vais rester quinze jours. (huit jours)

501

Can I pay by the week or by the month?	Est-ce qu'on peut payer par semaine ou par mois?
Do you have anything less expensive?	Avez-vous quelque chose de moins cher?
Are meals included in the price?	Est-ce le prix de la chambre comprend les repas? Combien de repas?
How many?	
What are your meal hours?	A quelle heure sert-on les repas?
Is there a bank near here?	Est-ce qu'il y a une banque près d'ici?
Is there a post office near here?	Est-ce qu'il y a un bureau de poste près d'ici?
Are there towels in the room?	Y a-t-il des serviettes dans la chambre?
Bring me some ice, please.	Apportez-moi de la glace, s'il vous plaît.
Is the water here drinkable?	L'eau ici est potable, n'est pas?
Don't you have any pillows?	N'avez-vous pas d'oreillers?
Please call me at eight o'clock.	Je voudrais qu'on m'appelle à huit heures.
Is there laundry service?	Puis-je faire blanchir mon linge ici?
I want this suit pressed.	Pouvez-vous donner un coup de fer à ce complet.
I want this dress cleaned.	Pouvez-vous nettoyer cette robe.
I would like an extra blanket.	Je voudrais une couverture supplémentaire.
Do you have a map of ———?	Avez-vous une carte de ———?
Do you have any stamps?	Avez-vous des timbres?
May I have the bill, please?	La note, s'il vous plaît.
Are taxes and service included?	Taxes et service compris, n'est pas?
Do you accept travelers' checks?	Acceptez-vous les chèques de voyageur?
Will you have my bags taken down, please?	Voulez-vous bien faire descendre mes bagages?

RESTAURANT

LE RESTAURANT

Do you have a table for two?	Avez-vous une table pour deux?
I would like to sit near a window. (outside) (inside)	Je préférerais une table près d'une fenêtre. (sur la terrase) (à l'intérieur)
I'll have the table d'hote dinner.	Le menu régulier (ordinaire), s'il vous plaît.
May I have a menu?	La carte, s'il vous plaît.
May I keep this as a souvenir?	Est-ce que je peux garder cela comme souvenir?
I have no napkin.	Je n'ai pas de serviette.
Bring me some butter, please.	Du beurre, s'il vous plaît.
How do you prefer the steak?	Comment préférez-vous le bifteck?
I prefer it very rare. (medium rare) (medium) (well-done)	Je le préfère saignant. (juste à point) (bien cuit) (très bien cuit)
What do you have for dessert?	Qu'avez-vous comme dessert?
Bring me some more bread please.	Apportez-moi encore du pain, s'il vous plaît.

Coffee with cream, please. (milk)

Tea with lemon. (milk)
Waiter, the check, please.
Where is the washroom?
They have fish. (meat, fowl)

Do you want pork? (beef, veal, lamb, chicken, turkey, duck)

I want my eggs fried. (poached, scrambled, soft-boiled, with ham, with bacon)
A glass of milk, please.
Orange juice and black coffee.
Rolls and butter.
Crescent rolls and coffee with milk.
Continental breakfast. (coffee, rolls, butter and jam)
Toast and jam.
Waiter, I need a glass. (fork, spoon, knife)

Un café à la crème, s'il vous plaît. (au lait)
Un thé au citron, (au lait)
Garçon, l'addition, s'il vous plaît.
Où se trouvent les cabinets?
Il y a du poisson. (de la viande, de la volaille)
Voulez-vous du porc? (du bœuf, du veau, de l'agneau, du poulet, du dindon, du canard)
Je préfère les œufs sur le plat. (pochés, brouillés, à la coque, au jambon, au lard)
Un verre de lait, s'il vous plaît.
Un jus d'orange et un café noir.
Des petits pains avec du beurre.
Des croissants et un café au lait.
Un café (déjeuner) complet.

Du pain grillé avec de la confiture.
Garçon, je n'ai pas de verre. (de fourchette, de cuillère, de couteau)

MONEY

Where can I cash a check?
What is the rate of exchange?
Here is my passport.

L'ARGENT

Où puis-je toucher un chèque?
Quel est le cours du change?
Voici mon passeport.

POST OFFICE

I want to send this letter by airmail.
How much postage is needed for foreign mail?
When will this letter reach the United States by regular mail?

How much is it by regular mail?

I'd like to register this letter.

Are there any letters for me?
Is the post office open on Saturday?

LE BUREAU DE POSTE

Je veux expédier cette lettre par avion.
Quel est l'affranchissement pour l'étranger?
Quand est-ce que cette lettre arrivera au États-Unis, si je l'expédie par courrier ordinaire?
Combien est-ce par courrier ordinaire?
Je voudrais faire recommander cette lettre.
Y a-t-il des lettres pour moi?
Le bureau de poste est-il ouvert le samedi?

RAILROAD

Where is the ticket window?
Two first-class (second) tickets to ———.
One way.
No, round trip.
Is this the train to ———?

LE CHEMIN DE FER

Où se trouvent les guichets?
Deux billets de première (seconde) classe pour ———.
Aller seulement.
Non, aller et retour.
Ce train va à ———?

Does it have Pullman cars?	Y a-t-il des wagons-lits?
I want an upper (lower) berth.	Je veux une couchette supérieure. (inférieure)
I want a one-berth compartment. (two-berth)	Je veux un compartiment individuel. (double)
When do we reach ———?	A quelle heure arrivons-nous à ———?
Are we on time?	Sommes-nous à l'heure?
How late are we?	De combien sommes-nous en retard?
Is there a dining car?	Y a-t-il un wagon-restaurant?
How late do they serve breakfast?	Jusqu'à quelle heure sert-on le petit déjeuner?
When do they start serving lunch?	À quelle heure commence-t-on à servir le déjeuner?
The first service is at noon.	Le premier service est à midi.
The second service is at one-thirty.	Le deuxième service est à une heure et demie.
I'm going to bed.	Je vais me coucher.
Is the berth made up?	Le lit est fait?
Please take down that suitcase.	Voulez-vous bien descendre cette valise?
I feel a draft.	Je sens un courant d'air.
May we turn off the fan?	Si l'on fermait le ventilateur?
May I open the window? (door)	Puis-je ouvrir la fenêtre? (porte)
Have you seen the conductor?	Avez-vous vu le contrôleur?

AUTOMOBILE — L'AUTOMOBILE

Forty liters of gas, please.	Quarante litres d'essence, s'il vous plaît.
Will you please check the oil and water?	Voulez-vous bien vérifier l'huile et l'eau?
Fill the tank.	Faites le plein.
I've run out of gas.	J'ai une panne d'essence.
I have a flat tire.	J'ai un pneu dégonflé.
Can you fix this puncture?	Pouvez-vous réparer cette crevaison?
Check the tires, including the spare.	Vérifiez les pneus, y compris le pneu de rechange.
Add some air if necessary.	Gonflez-les un peu s'il le faut.
Where is the next gas station?	Où se trouve le prochain poste d'essence?
I want to leave the car here overnight.	Je veux laisser l'auto ici jusqu'à demain matin.
Wash it and change the oil.	Lavez-la et vidangez l'huile.
What do you charge for greasing?	Combien pour le graissage?
Is the road in good condition?	Le chemin est en bon état?

PHOTOGRAPHY — LA PHOTOGRAPHIE

Is picture taking permitted?	Est-ce qu'on peut photographier?
May I take my camera into the church? (museum)	Puis-je garder mon appareil photographique dans l'église? (le musée)
What is the fee for taking pictures?	Quelle est la taxe pour photographier?

I need some 620 films. (120, color)

Where can I buy camera supplies?

My camera doesn't work. Can you fix it?
Can you have this film developed?

I want three prints of each.
Do you have movie film?

Do you have flashbulbs?
May I have these enlarged?
When will it be ready?
Does the price include developing?

Will you put in the film?

J'ai besoin de quelques pellicules six-neuf, petite bobine. (six-neuf, grosse bobine, en couleur)
Où puis-je acheter du matériel photographique?
Mon appareil ne marche pas. Pouvez-vous le réparer?
Pouvez-vous faire développer cette pellicule?
Je veux trois épreuves de chaque.
Avez-vous des films cinématographiques?
Avez-vous des lampes flash?
Puis-je faire agrandir ces clichés?
Quand est-ce que ce sera prêt?
Est-ce que le prix comprend la développement?
Voudriez-vous mettre la pellicule?

SHOPPING

I'm going shopping.
Is there a department store near here?

How much is this?
It's too expensive.
May I see something better?

May I see some shirts? (gloves, ties, handkerchiefs, socks, stockings)

Do you have it in white?
I prefer solid colors.
I'd like to try on this dress.
This suit doesn't look very well on me.

What size?
Can you have them sent to the hotel?

I'll take these postal cards.

LES EMPLETTES

Je vais faire des emplettes. (courses)
Est-ce qu'il y a un grand magasin près d'ici?
C'est combien?
C'est trop cher.
Puis-je voir quelque chose de meilleure qualité?
Je voudrais voir des chemises? (gants, cravates, mouchoirs, chaussettes, bas)
L'avez-vous en blanc?
Je préfère les couleurs unies.
Je voudrais essayer cette robe.
Ce tailleur ne me va pas très bien. (f.)
Ce complet ne me va pas très bien. (m.)
Quelle taille?
Pourrez-vous les faire envoyer à l'hôtel?
Je voudrais ces cartes postales.

KINDS OF STORES

Bookstore
Department store
Drugstore (prescriptions, patent medicines only)
Florist
General Hardware, (paint, wallpaper)

Jewelry
Leather goods

LES MAGASINS

Librairie
Grand magasin
Pharmacie

Fleuriste
Marchand de couleurs, Quincaillerie
Bijouterie
Maroquinerie

Perfumery	Parfumerie
Stationery	Papeterie
Tobacco, matches, stamps, bicycle licenses	Bureau de tabac
Watchmaker, watch repairs	Horlogerie
Variety, ten-cent stores	Prisunic, monoprix, uniprix
Bakery (bread, hard rolls)	Boulangerie
Butcher shop (beef, veal)	Boucherie
Dairy products (milk, cream, cheese, butter, margarine)	Laiterie
Delicatessen, pork (some canned goods)	Charcuterie
Fowl, rabbits	Marchand de volaille
General grocery	Grand magasin d'alimentation
Horsemeat	Boucherie chevaline
Pastries (fancy bread and rolls)	Pâtisserie
Pushcarts (usually only one item of fresh produce)	Marchand des quatre saisons
Spices, staples (sometimes fresh vegetables, fruits, and wine)	Épicerie
Vegetables	Marchand de légumes
Wines & Liqueurs (bottled, bulk)	Marchand de vin
Dressmaker, women's clothes	Couturière
Men's ready-made clothes	Vêtements de confection
Shoes	Chaussures
Tailor, men's made-to-order clothes	Tailleur
Women's hats	Modiste
Barber shop	Coiffeur pour hommes
Beauty shop	Coiffeur pour dames

GENERAL EXPRESSIONS

LES EXPRESSIONS ORDINAIRES

Good morning.	Bonjour
I don't speak French. (English)	Je ne parle pas français. (anglais)
I understand it a good deal, but I don't speak it.	Je comprends assez bien, mais je ne parle pas.
Where are you going?	Où allez-vous?
Come here, please.	Venez ici, s'il vous plaît.
I want to show you something.	Je veux vous montrer quelquechose.
Speak slowly, please.	Parlez lentement, s'il vous plaît.
Wait here.	Attendez ici.
I have no time today.	Je n'ai pas le temps aujourd'hui.
What can I do for you?	Qu'y a-t-il pour votre service?
Can you tell me. . . . ?	Pouvez-vous me dire. . . . ?
I think so. (not)	Je crois que oui. (non)
Is there a doctor near here?	Y a-t-il un médecin près ici?
What do you think?	Qu'en pensez-vous?
You know what I mean?	Vous savez ce que je veux dire?
How do you say that in French?	Comment dit-on cela en français?
What is that for?	A quoi est-ce que cela sert?
Do you understand me?	Me comprenez-vous?
I understand you when you speak slowly.	Je vous comprends quand vous parlez lentement.

Sorry, but I don't understand you.	Je regrette, je ne vous comprends pas.
Please repeat that question.	Veuillez répéter la question?
Now I understand.	Maintenant je comprends.
You are too kind.	Vous êtes trop aimable.
Thank you very much.	Merci beaucoup.
You are welcome.	De rien.
How are you?	Comment allez-vous?
Fine, thank you, and you?	Bien, merci, et vous?
Of course	Bien entendu
Right and left	À droite et à gauche
After all	Après tout
Willingly	Volontiers
By force	De force
From time to time	De temps en temps

WEATHER

LE TEMPS

What is the weather like?	Quel temps fait-il?
It is fine weather. (bad, sunny, cold, cool, hot, windy)	Il fait beau. (mauvais, du soleil, froid, frais, chaud, du vent)
It is raining.	Il pleut.
It is snowing.	Il neige.
It is cloudy.	Il y a des nuages.

DIVISIONS OF TIME

TELLING TIME

L'HEURE

What time is it?	Quelle heure est-il?
It is one o'clock. (two)	Il est une heure. (deux heures)
It is 10:15.	Il est dix heures et quart.
It is 10:30.	Il est dix heures et demie.
It is a quarter to eleven.	Il est onze heures moins le quart.
It is 11:20.	Il est onze heures vingt.
It is twenty minutes to eleven.	Il est onze heures moins vingt.
It is noon. (midnight)	Il est midi. (minuit)
It is 2 A.M.	Il est deux heures du matin.
It is 2 P.M.	Il est deux de l'après midi.
The train leaves at 2 P.M.	Le train part à quatorze heures.
It is 6 P.M.	Il est six heures du soir.

DAYS OF THE WEEK

JOURS DE LA SEMAINE

Monday	lundi
Tuesday	mardi
Wednesday	mercredi
Thursday	jeudi
Friday	vendredi
Saturday	samedi
Sunday	dimanche

MONTHS OF THE YEAR

January	janvier
February	février
March	mars
April	avril
May	mai
June	juin
July	juillet
August	août
September	septembre
October	octobre
November	novembre
December	décembre

MOIS DE L'ANNÉE

SEASONS OF THE YEAR
Spring: summer: fall: winter

SAISONS DE L'ANNÉE
printemps: été: automne: hiver

CONVERTING TEMPERATURES

FAHRENHEIT TO CENTIGRADE
Subtract 32° and multiply by 5/9.
$50°F = 10°C.$ $-4°F = -20°C.$

CENTIGRADE TO FAHRENHEIT
Multiply by 9/5 and add 32°.
$40°C = 104°F.$ $20°C = 68°F.$

CONVERTING METRIC MEASURES

AMERICAN TO FRENCH
1 gallon = 3.785 liters (3.8)
1 pound = .4536 kilos (.45)
1 inch = 2.54 centimeters (2.5)
1 yard = .9144 meters (.9)
1 mile = 1.6093 kilometers (1.6)
1 acre = .4047 hectares (.4)

FRENCH TO AMERICAN
1 liter = .2642 gallons (.26)
1 kilo = 2.2046 pounds (2.2)
1 centimeter = .3937 inches (.4)
1 meter = 1.094 yards (1.1)
1 kilometer = .6214 miles (.6)
1 hectare = 2.471 acres (2.5)

The figures in parentheses are approximate equivalents.

To convert American measurements into their approximate French equivalents, or vice versa, multiply as indicated in the examples.

Examples: To determine the approximate number of liters in ten gallons, multiply 3.8 (liters per gallon) × 10 = 38.1 liters.

To determine the approximate number of miles in 14 kilometers, multiply .6 (miles per kilometer) × 14 = 8.4 miles.

FRENCH ROAD SIGNS

French traffic signs, like those in the United States, show typical shapes but some bear symbols while others have only words. The most common are shown on the following pages. The three distinct shapes are triangular, circular, and rectangular.

△ — Triangular signs indicate danger ahead.

○ — Circular signs give explicit instructions.

□ — Rectangular signs contain specific information.

French traffic proceeds on the right-hand side of the street.

LES SIGNAUX DE LA ROUTE	ROAD SIGNS
Tournant	Curve
Virage	Turn
Virage à Droite (Gauche)	Curve to the Right (Left)
Virages sur . . . km.	Winding Road for . . . Kilometers
Priorité	Right of Way
Prudence	Caution
Pont Coupé	Bridge Out
Passage à Niveau	Level Crossing
Sortie d'École	School Exit
Chaussée Glissante	Slippery Pavement
Chaussée Rétrécie	Narrowing Pavement
Chaussée Déformée	Rough Road, Bumpy Road
Travaux	Road Under Repair
Travaux ralentir	Slow! Construction
Chute de Pierres	Rock Slide, Fallen-rock Zone
Passage à Niveau	Railroad Crossing
Intersection	Crossroads, Side Road
Sens Unique	One-way Street
Sens Obligatoire	One-way Traffic (as indicated)
Serrez à Droite	Keep to the Right
Limite de Vitesse	Speed Limit
Défense de Doubler	No Passing
Entreé Interdite	No Entry
Interdiction de Stationner, Stationne-ment Interdit	No Stopping
Interdiction de Parquer	No Parking
Parcage Autorisé	Parking Allowed
Stationnement Autorisé Jours Pairs (Impairs)	Parking on Even (Odd) Calendar Dates
Stationnement Pair—Impair	Parking on Even-numbered Side of the Street on Even Calendar Dates: Odd Side on Odd Dates
Stationnement Réglementé	Parking Restricted

Stationnement Réservé aux Cars (Autobus, Taxis, Voitures de Tourisme)	Parking Reserved for Buses (Taxis, Passenger Cars)
Circulation Interdite	No Thoroughfare
Ralentissez	Slow
Deviation	Detour
Interdit à Tous les Véhicules Automobiles	Closed to All Motor Vehicles
Interdit aux Poids Lourds	Closed to Heavy Traffic
Interdit aux Cyclistes	Closed to Cyclists
Fin d'Interdiction de Stationner	End of No Parking Zone
Fin d'Interdiction de Dépasser	End of No Passing Zone
Fin de Sens Unique	End of One-way Traffic, Two-way Traffic Begins
Signaux Sonores Interdits	Use of Horns Forbidden
Vitesse Maximum	Speed Limit
Hauteur Limitée	Low Clearance
Dispositif de Contrôle Obligatoire, Disque Obligatoire	Parking Only with Disk in Window to Indicate Time of Arrival
Zone Bleue	Zone in Which Parking Disk Must be Used
Fin de Chantier	End of Construction Area
Bac	Ferry
Pont Étroit	Narrow Bridge
Poste de Douane	Customs
Hôpital	Hospital
Secours Routier Français	French Highway Aid, Emergency Telephone
Allumez vos Lanternes	Turn on Headlights

I. DANGER SIGNS

CURVE SIGNS

Curve · Left · Right · Dangerous · S-curve

CROSSING SIGNS

Railroad Signs (guarded) · (unguarded) · Dangerous Crossroad · You Have Priority · Right Has Priority

GENERAL SIGNS

Bump or Dip

Hill

Side Road

Narrow Road

Caution

Slippery Pavement

Crosswalk

Cattle Crossing

School

Men Working

Drawbridge

Stop Ahead

Stop

Yield Ahead

Yield

II. DEFINITE INSTRUCTION SIGNS

NO ENTRY SIGNS

Closed to Traffic

No Entry

No Autos

No Motorcycles

No Vehicles

Ian Longfield

GENERAL SIGNS

**No
Left Turn**

**No
Passing**

**End No Passing
Zone**

**Bicycle
Path**

**No
Bicycles**

50 km. per hr.

**cars 50
trucks 30**

**End
Speed Limit**

No Horns

One Way

**No
Parking**

**Traffic
Circle**

Keep Right

Customs

**Stop—Police
(check-point)**

III. INFORMATIVE SIGNS

Parking

Gas Station

**Telephone
512**

Garage

Hospital

THE *NEW CENTURY* DICTIONARIES

VELAZQUEZ SPANISH/ENGLISH DICTIONARY

VEST-POCKET DICTIONARIES

French

German

Italian

Spanish

INSTANT CONVERSATION GUIDES

French

German

Spanish

vt. cirer; — *vi.* croître, s'accroître; se faire; **-en** *a.* de cire; **-y** *a.* de cire, comme de la cire

way *n.* voie *f.*; chemin *m.*, route *f.*; passage *m.*; moyen, expédient *m.*; manière, façon *f.*; **all the —** jusqu'au bout; **by the — à** propos; **by —** of par; **get out of the —** laisser passer; se ranger; **give —** céder le pas; se ranger; (floor) se casser **look the other —** ne pas regarder; détourner les yeux; **lose one's —** se perdre, s'égarer; **make —** faire place (à); **on the —** en route; **out of the —** isolé; **start on one's —** se mettre en route; **the right —** la bonne voie, la bonne route *f.*; **the wrong —** la mauvaise voie, la mauvaise route *f.*; **go the wrong —** se tromper de chemin; prendre la mauvaise route; **under —** en route; en train; **— in** entrée *f.*; **— out** sortie *f.*

wayfarer *n.* voyageur *m.*

waylay *vt.* guetter au passage

wayside *n.* bord de la route *m.*; **leave by the —** abandonner; laisser en arrière

wayward *a.* vagabond; rebelle

we *pron.* nous; on

weak *a.* faible; débile; mou (molle); pauvre; sans vigueur; **-en** *vi.* s'affaiblir; — *vt.* affaiblir; **-ening** *n.* affaiblissement *m.*; **-ling** *n.* faible *m.*; **-ness** *n.* faiblesse *f.*; faible *m.*

weakhearted *a. & adv.* qui manque de courage; sans courage

weak-kneed *a.* irrésolu; aux genoux faibles

weakling *n.* personne faible *f.*, homme faible *m.*; homme qui manque de force *m.*

weak-minded *a.* peu intelligent

wealth *n.* bien *m.*, richesses *f. pl.*; **-y** *a.* riche, opulent

wean *vt.* sevrer; priver de

weapon *n.* arme *f.*; **-ry** *n.* arsenaux d'un pays *m. pl.*; armement *m.*

wear *n.* usure *f.*; usage *m.*; — *vt.* porter; user; — *vi.* faire de l'usage; s'user; **— away** *vt.* user; ronger; effacer; **— away** *vi.* s'user; **— out** user; fatiguer, epuiser; **-able** *a.* propre à porter; **-ing** *a.* fatigant

weariness *n.* lassitude, fatigue *f.*; ennui *m.*

wearisome *a.* ennuyeux

weary *vt.* fatiguer; ennuyer; — *a.* las, fatigué, ennuyé

weather *n.* temps *m.*; **— bureau** bureau météorologique *m.*; **— forecast** prévisions météorologiques *f. pl.*; **man** météorologue *m.*; **— report** bulletin météorologique *m.*; **the — is nice** il fait beau; **the — is bad** il fait mauvais; —

vt. resister à; user, décolorer

weather-beaten *a.* battu par le vent

weatherproof *a.* à l'épreuve du temps; imperméable

weave *n.* texture *f.*; — *vt.* tisser; entrelacer; mêler, entremêler; **-r** *n.* tisserand *m.*

weaving *n.* tissage *m.*

web *n.* tissu *m.*; (spider) toile d'araignée *f.*; membrane *f.*; **-bed** *a.* palmé

web-footed *a.* aux pieds palmés

wed *vt.* épouser, se marier avec; — *vi.* se marier; **-ding** *n.* mariage *m.*, noces *f. pl.*; **-ding cake** gâteau de noces *m.*; **-ding ring** alliance *f.*

wedge *n.* coin *m.*; — *vt.* fendre; serrer, forcer; coincer; caler; **-d** *a.* en forme de coin; cunéiforme

wedlock *n.* mariage *m.*

Wednesday *n.* mercredi *m.*; **Ash —** mercredi des cendres *m.*

wee *a.* tout petit

weed *n.* mauvaise herbe *f.*; **-s** *pl.* habits de deuil *m. pl.*; — *vt.* sarcler; **— out** sarcler; éliminer; **-er** *n.* sarcleur *m.*; (tool) sarcloir *m.*; **-ing** *n.* sarclage *m.*

week *n.* semaine *f.*; huit jours *m. pl.*; **two -s** quinze jours *m. pl.*; deux semaines *f. pl.*; **a — from today** d'aujourd'hui en huit; **-ly** *a.* hebdomadaire

weekday *n.* jour de la semaine *m.*; jour ouvrable *m.*; — *a.* des jours ouvrables

weekend *n.* fin de semaine *f.*; week-end *m.*

weep *vi.* pleurer; **-er** *n.* pleureur *m.*; **-ing** *n.* pleurs *m. pl.*, larmes *f. pl.*; **-ing willow** saule pleureur *m.*; **-y** *a.* larmoyant

weigh *vt.* peser; soupeser; examiner, considérer; — *vi.* peser; **— anchor** lever l'ancre; **— down** surcharger; **— in** se faire peser; **-ing** *n.* pesée *f.*

weight *n.* poids *m.*, pesanteur *f.*; fardeau *m.*; importance *f.*; force *f.*; **gain —** prendre du poids; **lose —** perdre du poids; maigrir; — *vt.* charger; plomber; **-iness** *n.* pesanteur *f.*; importance *f.*; **-less-ness** *n.* non-pesanteur *f.*; **-y** *a.* pesant, important

weird *a.* mystérieux, surnaturel

welcome *n.* bon accueil *m.*; bienvenue *f.*; — *interj.* soyez le bienvenu; — *a.* bienvenu; agréable; **you're —** de rien; ce n'est rien; il n'y a pas de quoi; à votre service; — *vt.* accueillir, faire bon accueil à

weld *n.* soudure *f.*; — *vt.* souder (à chaud); **-er** *n.* soudeur *m.*; **-ing** *n.* soudage *m.*

welfare *n.* bien-être *m.*; **— state** état socialiste *m.*; **— work** bonnes œuvres *f. pl.*; assistance sociale *f.*

well *n.* puits *m.*; — *vi.* sourdre; jaillir —